Immigration, Refugees and Forced Migration

Immigration, Refugees and Forced Migration

Law, Policy and Practice in Australia

Mary Crock
Professor of Public Law, The University of Sydney

Laurie Berg
University of Technology, Sydney

THE FEDERATION PRESS
2011

Published in Sydney by
> The Federation Press
> PO Box 45, Annandale, NSW, 2038.
> 71 John St, Leichhardt, NSW, 2040.
> Ph (02) 9552 2200. Fax (02) 9552 1681
> E-mail: info@federationpress.com.au
> Website: http://www.federationpress.com.au

National Library of Australia Cataloguing-in-Publication entry
> Crock, Mary
> Immigration, Refugees and Forced Migration / Mary Crock and Laurie Berg
>
> Includes bibliographical references and index.
> ISBN 978 186287 797 9 (pbk)
> ISBN 978 186287 834 1 (hbk)
>
> Emigration and immigration law – Australia.
> Refugees – Legal status, laws, etc – Australia.
> Migrant labour – Australia.
> Australia – Emigration and immigration.

342.94082

© The Federation Press
This publication is copyright. Other than for the purposes of and subject to the conditions prescribed under the Copyright Act, no part of it may in any form or by any means (electronic, mechanical, microcopying, photocopying, recording or otherwise) be reproduced, stored in a retrieval system or transmitted without prior written permission. Enquiries should be addressed to the publisher.

© Commonwealth of Australia
Commonwealth legislation herein is produced by permission, but does not purport to be the official or authorised version. It is subject to Crown copyright. The *Copyright Act 1968* permits certain reproduction and publication of Commonwealth legislation. In particular, s 182A of the Act enables a complete copy to be made by or on behalf of a particular person. For reproduction or publication beyond that permitted by the Act, permission should be sought in writing from the Australian Government Publishing Services. Requests in the first instance should be addressed to the Manager, AGPS Press, Australian Government Publishing Service, GPO Box 84, Canberra, ACT, 2601.

Typeset by The Federation Press, Leichhardt, NSW.
> Printed by Ligare Pty Ltd, Riverwood, NSW.

List of Chapters

Part I
History and Context

1	Immigration Law in Context	2
2	Immigration Law and the Growth of Nationhood	17

Part II
Legal Frameworks

3	Defining Powers: Immigration Control and the Australian Constitution	52
4	The Impact of International Law	77
5	The Administration of Migration Law and Policy	111

Part III
Border Control and Common Entry Criteria

6	Border Control and Common Entry Requirements	146

Part IV
Family Migration

7	Family Reunion I – Spousal Relationships	176
8	Family Reunion II – Immediate and Other Family	207

Part V
Skilled Migration, Students and Temporary Visas

9	Building a Clever Country: Permanent Labour Migration	232
10	The Business of Temporary Labour Migration	269
11	Students, Visitors and Other Temporary Entrants	298

Part VI
Refugees and Forced Migration

12	The Refugee and Humanitarian Program	328
13	The Definition of Refugee	363
14	The Extent of Australia's Protection Obligations	406

Part VII
Unlawful Status and Enforcement

15	Unlawful Status and Visa Cancellations	438
16	The Enforcement of Decisions	473
17	The Deportation of Permanent Residents: Character, Conduct and Criminality	519

Part VIII
Appeals and Judicial Review

18	Immigration Appeals – Merits Review	560
19	Judicial Review of Migration Decisions	615

Part IX
Conclusion

20	Facing the Future: Immigration and Global Citizenship	660

Contents

Acknowledgements	xix
Abbreviations	xxii
Ministers Responsible for Immigration: 1901–Present	xxv
List of Illustrations	xxvii
Table of Cases	xxviii
Table of Statutes	xliii

Part I
History and Context

1 Immigration Law in Context   2

  1.1 The *idea* of the migrant: Lived experiences and attitudes to immigration   2
  1.2 Evolving approaches to justice in immigration   5
    1.2.1 The liberal debate between open and closed borders   5
    1.2.2 Citizenship and belonging   7
  1.3 Themes and theories: An overview of the book   8
    1.3.1 Immigration, citizenship and the constitution of a nation   10
    1.3.2 Conflicting legalities: The influence of international legal principle   11
    1.3.3 Of government, administration and control   11
    1.3.4 The place of the family   12
    1.3.5 The business of migration: Skilled migrants, tourism and the international student sector   13
    1.3.6 Refugees and forced migration   14
    1.3.7 Unlawful status: Arrest, detention and enforcement   15
    1.3.8 Having the last word: Immigration appeals and judicial review   15

2 Immigration Law and the Growth of Nationhood   17

  2.1 Becoming Australian: Of citizenship, alienage and belonging   17
  2.2 Citizenship and the Australian Constitution   21
  2.3 The evolution of Australia's early immigration laws   23
    2.3.1 The operation of the dictation test   28
    2.3.2 Common understandings: The role played by the judiciary in determining 'immigrant' status   28
    2.3.3 The dictation test as a general exclusionary device   33
  2.4 Migration law as a benchmark for the treatment of societal 'outsiders': The 'race' factor in the development of an Australian citizenship   36
  2.5 Historical legacies: Australian citizenship today   39

	2.5.1	Citizenship, British heritage and the continuing significance of migration law	39
	2.5.2	Citizenship as birthright	41
2.6		Legacies of using migration law as a benchmark for exclusion	49

Part II
Legal Frameworks

3 Defining Powers: Immigration Control and the Australian Constitution — 52

- 3.1 Constitutional frameworks — 52
- 3.2 The legislative power: The reach of the 'immigration' power and the rise of the 'aliens' power — 54
- 3.3 High Court reactions to provisions threatening usurpation of the judicial power of the Constitution — 61
  - 3.3.1 Legislation restricting or ousting judicial review — 61
  - 3.3.2 The nature and extent of the judicial power: A case study of immigration detention — 65
- 3.4 Immigration control and plenary power (reprise) — 70

4 The Impact of International Law — 77

- 4.1 The central significance of international law — 79
- 4.2 International law and the Australian judiciary: High principle and domestic pragmatism — 81
  - 4.2.1 The Teoh experiment — 83
  - 4.2.2 Al-Kateb and the resurgence of legal formalism — 86
- 4.3 Conflicting legalities: Border control, the *Tampa* Affair and the 'Pacific Strategy' – A case study — 89
  - 4.3.1 Setting the scene — 89
  - 4.3.2 International law of the sea — 91
  - 4.3.3 International refugee law — 93
  - 4.3.4 Judicial responses to the *Tampa* Affair — 95
  - 4.3.5 International refugee law and human rights law: Operation Relex and the Pacific Strategy — 98
  - 4.3.6 The interdiction program — 98
  - 4.3.7 Offshore processing under the Pacific Strategy — 101
  - 4.3.8 Refugees and asylum seekers under Labor: Continued dissonances with international law — 104
- 4.4 Complaints to the international human rights treaty bodies — 105
- 4.5 How will Australia's approach to international law be viewed in time? — 108

5 The Administration of Migration Law and Policy — 111
- 5.1 The changing face of immigration decision-making — 111
- 5.2 The first revolution: Post-war policy and administration — 112
  - 5.2.1 External scrutiny of migration decision-making — 116
  - 5.2.2 Curial review as an agent of change — 119
- 5.3 From discretion to codification — 121
  - 5.3.1 The 1989 and 1993 Regulations — 123
  - 5.3.2 The 1994 Regulations — 124
  - 5.3.3 Judicial responses to the regulatory regime — 126
- 5.4 Contracting for control: The privatisation and outsourcing of administrative functions — 128
  - 5.4.1 Health assessments — 131
  - 5.4.2 Skills assessments — 132
  - 5.4.3 Immigration detention — 132
  - 5.4.4 Removals — 133
- 5.5 System failures: New contractualism and the problem of discretion — 134
  - 5.5.1 Fault lines in the administration — 134
  - 5.5.2 Judicial responses to contracting out — 137
- 5.6 Ethics and the regulation of migration advice — 141

Part III
Border Control and Common Entry Criteria

6 Border Control and Common Entry Requirements — 146
- 6.1 Of borders and concepts of entry — 146
- 6.2 Visas, entry permits and immigration clearance — 148
- 6.3 Common entry criteria: Protecting the public interest — 155
  - 6.3.1 'Health concern non-citizens' — 156
  - 6.3.2 Character tests — 167

Part IV
Family Migration

7 Family Reunion I – Spousal Relationships — 176
- 7.1 The place of families in the migrant intake — 176
- 7.2 Immigration on grounds of partnership — 179
  - 7.2.1 Partnership migration – an overview — 179
  - 7.2.2 The legal attributes of a valid partnership — 184
  - 7.2.3 Proving a genuine and continuing partnership — 187
  - 7.2.4 'Sham' marriages and serial sponsorships — 192
- 7.3 The family violence exceptions — 195
  - 7.3.1 The evolution of the family violence exceptions — 196
  - 7.3.2 The meaning of 'family violence' — 197
  - 7.3.3 Evidence of family violence: The triumph of form over substance — 198

8 Family Reunion II – Immediate and Other Family — 207
- 8.1 Family and the regulation of compassion — 207
- 8.2 Sponsoring children — 209
  - 8.2.1 Definition of child: The family unit and notions of dependency — 209
  - 8.2.2 The child visas — 211
  - 8.2.3 Custody criteria — 216
- 8.3 The Parent visas — 218
- 8.4 'Innocent illegals' and vulnerable children — 221
- 8.5 Aged dependent relatives — 222
- 8.6 'Remaining' relatives — 223
- 8.7 'Special Need Relatives' and Carers — 226

Part V
Skilled Migration, Students and Temporary Visas

9 Building a Clever Country: Permanent Labour Migration — 232
- 9.1 Putting the 'skill' in migration — 232
- 9.2 An overview of General Skilled Migration programs — 235
  - 9.2.1 Early history and evolution of skilled migration — 236
  - 9.2.2 Controlling skilled migration: The first points tests — 237
  - 9.2.3 The 1989 reforms — 238
  - 9.2.4 The 1999 reforms — 239
  - 9.2.5 Recent trends — 240
- 9.3 The General Skilled Migration points test — 241
  - 9.3.1 The Skilled Occupations List — 243
  - 9.3.2 Front end loading: Outsourcing of qualifications assessment — 245
  - 9.3.3 Work experience in Australia and overseas — 247
  - 9.3.4 English language proficiency — 248
  - 9.3.5 Local versus overseas qualifications — 251
  - 9.3.6 Migration Occupations in Demand and other skills shortages lists — 251
  - 9.3.7 Regional migration initiatives — 252
- 9.4 Employer nomination — 254
  - 9.4.1 The employer's approval as sponsor — 254
  - 9.4.2 The nominated position — 255
  - 9.4.3 The nominated employee — 255
- 9.5 Distinguished Talent visas — 257
- 9.6 Business skills migration — 259
  - 9.6.1 The early history of business migration — 260
  - 9.6.2 The business migration regime after 2003 — 260
  - 9.6.3 Business owners and senior executives — 261
  - 9.6.4 Investment-based migration — 264

	9.6.5	Established Business in Australia	265
	9.6.6	Regional development	266
9.7	Future reform agendas		267

10 The Business of Temporary Labour Migration — 269

10.1	Introduction		269
10.2	The development of a temporary business migration scheme		270
10.3	Overview of the temporary business visa scheme		271
10.4	Short-term business visitor visas		273
10.5	Long-term temporary business visas		273
	10.5.1	Sponsorship requirements	274
	10.5.2	Nominated position	277
	10.5.3	The nominated employee	278
	10.5.4	Merits review	280
	10.5.5	Cancellation of temporary business visas	280
	10.5.6	Employer sanctions	280
	10.5.7	Controversies over the temporary business visas	281
	10.5.8	An agenda for reform of temporary labour migration	284
10.6	Working holiday makers		285
10.7	The Seasonal Migration Program		286
	10.7.1	The structure of the program	288
	10.7.2	A labour market issue	290
	10.7.3	Eschewing permanent settlement	291
	10.7.4	Migration as development	292
	10.7.5	The potential for worker exploitation	294

11 Students, Visitors and Other Temporary Entrants — 298

11.1	The international student program		299
	11.1.1	Early years: The shift from regional development to a growth industry	299
	11.1.2	The modern international student program	301
	11.1.3	Student visa requirements	303
	11.1.4	Students and visa conditions	304
	11.1.5	Student visa cancellations	307
	11.1.6	Dovetailing with general skilled migration program	313
	11.1.7	Student protections and oversight of education providers	315
11.2	The admission of visitors		318
	11.2.1	The evolution of the law governing the admission of visitors	318
	11.2.2	The genuine visitor	320
	11.2.3	Risk factor profiles	322
	11.2.4	Visitors and restrictions on work	325

Part VI
Refugees and Forced Migration

12 The Refugee and Humanitarian Program — 328
  12.1 The concept of refugee — 328
  12.2 Australia's offshore refugee and humanitarian program — 330
  12.3 Legal and policy responses to asylum seekers in Australia — 333
      12.3.1 The Determination of Refugee Status Committee (DORS) 1978-90 — 335
      12.3.2 Formal merits review authorities: The Refugee Status Review Committee (1990-93) and the RRT — 340
      12.3.3 The Coalition years: 1996-2007 — 341
      12.3.4 The treatment of refugees and asylum seekers after 2007 — 345
  12.4 Process matters: Assessing the procedures for determining refugee status — 348
      12.4.1 Onshore refugee status determinations — 350
      12.4.2 Offshore refugee status determinations — 351
      12.4.3 Administrative appeals — 352
      12.4.4 Ministerial discretion — 355
  12.5 Refugees and the courts: The development of an Australian jurisprudence on refugees — 357
  12.6 The politics of refugee protection — 360

13 The Definition of Refugee — 363
  13.1 Frameworks for protection — 363
  13.2 Countries of nationality or habitual residence — 365
  13.3 'Well-founded fear': Standard of proof and the 'real chance' test — 366
      13.3.1 The 'real chance' test and onus of proof — 370
      13.3.2 The relevance of past events — 371
      13.3.3 The use of country information and other corrobative strategies — 374
      13.3.4 Refugees *sur place* — 375
  13.4 Persecution — 378
      13.4.1 The nature of the harm — 379
      13.4.2 An 'eggshell skull' rule for refugees? — 383
      13.4.3 Policies of general application — 384
      13.4.4 State responsibility for persecution — 385
      13.4.5 Situations of generalised violence — 387
  13.5 The nexus requirement – 'for reasons of' — 388
  13.6 The Convention grounds — 390
      13.6.1 Race — 390
      13.6.2 Nationality — 392
      13.6.3 Religion — 392
      13.6.4 'Particular social group' — 395
      13.6.5 Political opinion — 403

14 The Extent of Australia's Protection Obligations — 406

- 14.1 The politics of protection elsewhere: Qualifications on the rights of refugees — 407
  - 14.1.1 The declaration of 'safe' countries of origin — 408
  - 14.1.2 Internal relocation — 409
  - 14.1.3 Safe third countries and effective nationality — 412
  - 14.1.4 Protection obligations under s 36(3) of the *Migration Act* and the 'seven-day' rule — 416
  - 14.1.5 A right to enter and reside — 416
- 14.2 Cessation of refugee status — 419
- 14.3 Refugees who are undeserving of protection: The national security exception to the *non-refoulement* rule — 423
  - 14.3.1 Article 1F(a) – Crimes again peace, war crimes and crimes against humanity — 424
  - 14.3.2 Article 1F(b) – Serious non-political crimes committed outside the country of refuge — 425
  - 14.3.3 Article 1F(c) – Acts contrary to the purposes and principles of the United Nations — 428
- 14.4 Complementary protection — 428
- 14.5 Human trafficking — 431

Part VII
Unlawful Status and Enforcement

15 Unlawful Status and Visa Cancellations — 438

- 15.1 Becoming unlawful – An overview — 438
- 15.2 Unlawful status by operation of law: Unauthorised arrivals and overstayers — 440
- 15.3 Loss of lawful status: Cancellation of visa on grounds of irregularity upon or before entry into Australia — 441
  - 15.3.1 Offshore cancellation under s 128 — 441
  - 15.3.2 The procedure for cancellation under s 109 — 442
  - 15.3.3 The meaning of 'incorrect answer' — 443
  - 15.3.4 The cancellation decision — 444
- 15.4 Loss of lawful status: Cancellation of temporary visas after entry into Australia — 448
  - 15.4.1 The general cancellation power under s 116 — 448
  - 15.4.2 The cancellation of business visas — 451
  - 15.4.3 The automatic cancellation of student visas — 452
  - 15.4.4 The cancellation of visas on character grounds — 452
- 15.5 General requirements for the regularisation of unlawful status — 453
  - 15.5.1 Time limits, Bridging visas and other 'threshold' requirements — 453
  - 15.5.2 The Schedule 3 criteria — 454

15.6	Substantive visas available to unlawful non-citizens	460
	15.6.1 Permanent visas available to unlawful non-citizens	460
	15.6.2 Temporary visas available to unlawful non-citizens	462
15.7	From compassion to control: Historical approaches to unlawful migration	462
15.8	Immigration offences	466
	15.8.1 Offences relating to entry and stay in Australia	466
	15.8.2 Offences relating to migration fraud	470
	15.8.3 Offences relating to detention	470
	15.8.4 Offences relating to decisions made under the Act	471

16 The Enforcement of Decisions 473

16.1	Introduction	473
16.2	Border applicants, immigration clearance and detention	474
	16.2.1 Control measures before entry: Interdiction of ships and aircraft	474
	16.2.2 Control measures at point of entry	476
	16.2.3 Special detention measures and *Chu Kheng Lim*	479
	16.2.4 Detention policy after *Chu Kheng Lim*	481
16.3	The arrest and detention of actual and suspected unlawful non-citizens after entry into Australia	482
	16.3.1 The legislative scheme governing arrest and detention	482
	16.3.2 The rights of detainees: Access to legal advice	487
16.4	Issues surrounding immigration detention	488
	16.4.1 The detention facilities	488
	16.4.2 International oversight of immigration detention in Australia	494
16.5	Release from detention	495
	16.5.1 Bridging visas A-E	495
	16.5.2 Security for compliance with conditions of a Bridging visa	498
	16.5.3 The trafficking visas: Bridging visa F (BVF)	499
	16.5.4 Removal Pending visas	500
	16.5.5 Seizure of assets and costs of detention	500
16.6	The removal of unlawful non-citizens	500
	16.6.1 Theories of removal and deportation	500
	16.6.2 The evolution of legislative scheme	501
	16.6.3 Removal and the courts	502
16.7	The execution of deportation orders and determinations to remove	505
	16.7.1 Stay orders and injunctive relief	505
	16.7.2 Stay orders and release from detention	508
	16.7.3 Delay in removal	510
	16.7.4 Choosing the destination of a removee and removal as disguised extradition	511
	16.7.5 Timing and methods of deportation or removal	517

17 The Deportation of Permanent Residents: Character, Conduct and Criminality — 519
- 17.1 Introduction — 519
- 17.2 A brief history of criminal deportation law — 521
  - 17.2.1 The special status of British subjects and 'absorbed persons' — 523
  - 17.2.2 Shifting constitutional powers: The move from 'immigration' to 'alien' — 524
  - 17.2.3 Migration (Offences and Undesirable Persons) Amendment Act 1992 — 525
- 17.3 Broadening the scope for removal: The Migration Legislation Amendment (Strengthening of Provisions relating to Character and Conduct) Act 1998 (Cth) — 527
  - 17.3.1 The character test — 528
  - 17.3.2 General and criminal conduct — 529
  - 17.3.3 'Substantial criminal record' — 530
  - 17.3.4 'Criminal association' — 531
  - 17.3.5 'Significant risk' of engaging in certain conduct — 533
  - 17.3.6 Constraints on the right to 'natural justice' and AAT review — 533
  - 17.3.7 Closing the last loopholes: Responding to the decisions in *Sales* and *Nystrom* — 536
- 17.4 Immigration politics, and 'bad aliens': The evolution of policies governing deportation and removal — 536
  - 17.4.1 Introduction — 536
  - 17.4.2 Protecting the Australian community — 542
  - 17.4.3 'Community expectations' versus the significance of an offender's ties with Australia — 548
  - 17.4.4 International obligations — 553
- 17.5 A free and confident nation? — 557

Part VIII
Appeals and Judicial Review

18 Immigration Appeals – Merits Review — 560
- 18.1 Introduction — 560
- 18.2 A brief history of the merits review of migration, refugee and citizenship decisions — 560
  - 18.2.1 Review of decisions by the AAT and the 'Section 203' Commissioner — 561
  - 18.2.2 The introduction of generalist review of migration decision-making — 563
  - 18.2.3 Migration Internal Review Office and the Immigration Review Tribunal — 564
  - 18.2.4 The Migration Review Tribunal — 566
  - 18.2.5 Refugee status appeals — 567

18.3	Other avenues of redress	570
	18.3.1 The Commonwealth Ombudsman	571
	18.3.2 The Australian Human Rights Commission	573
18.4	The quasi-inquisitorial experiment: The tribunals' manner of operating	575
	18.4.1 Threshold issues: The tribunals' power to review	577
	18.4.2 Notice of appeal and time limits	580
	18.4.3 The applicant's right to appear and give evidence	586
	18.4.4 The use of interpreters	589
	18.4.5 The right to be represented	591
	18.4.6 Representatives and fraud on the tribunal	592
18.5	The conduct of the hearing	593
	18.5.1 Hearing both sides	594
	18.5.2 Disclosable information	596
	18.5.3 Where a hearing is not required	597
	18.5.4 Information supplied by the applicant	598
	18.5.5 Non-disclosable information	599
18.6	The investigative and reasoning process	602
	18.6.1 Onus and standard of proof	602
	18.6.2 The duty to hear and consider all substantive issues raised	603
	18.6.3 Paradoxical functions: 'Inquisitorial' tribunals with no duty to make further inquiries	604
	18.6.4 Credibility findings and challenges to the methodology adopted by the tribunals	610
	18.6.5 Findings on material questions of fact and the duty to provide reasons for decisions	612

19 Judicial Review of Migration Decisions 615

19.1	Introduction	615
19.2	Constitutional guarantees	617
19.3	The first revolution: Immigration and the new administrative law	620
	19.3.1 Natural justice or procedural fairness	621
	19.3.2 Merits review by another name: Relevancy and reasonableness as grounds of review	629
19.4	The codification of migration decision-making and the introduction of 'non-reviewable' discretions	632
19.5	Declaration of hostilities: The first Part 8 of the Migration Act	634
19.6	Battlelines	640
	19.6.1 The privative clause	640
	19.6.2 Slippery concepts: Defining the 'jurisdictional error'	645
	19.6.3 Further attempts to constrain the judicial review of migration decisions	647
	19.6.4 The judicial review of decisions made extra-territorially	649
	19.6.5 Judicial review as dysfunction: Australian 'exceptionalism' and the burden of legal formalism	653
19.7	Towards the future	657

Part IX
Conclusion

20 Facing the Future: Immigration and Global Citizenship — 660
- 20.1 Introduction — 660
- 20.2 The impact of immigration on the development of public law in Australia — 661
- 20.3 The focus of power and the discretion question: Regulation versus leeways of choice — 664
- 20.4 The exercise of power: Responsibility and good international citizenship — 666
  - 20.4.1 The tenure of permanent residents — 667
  - 20.4.2 Human rights and asylum seekers — 667
  - 20.4.3 Mandatory detention — 670
  - 20.4.4 The human rights of temporary workers and students — 671
- 20.5 Recognising and enforcing human rights: Of Bills of Rights and judicial review — 671
- 20.6 Towards the future — 674

Index — 676

Acknowledgements

Mary Crock

This book is the successor in title to my 1998 text, *Immigration and Refugee Law in Australia* (Sydney: The Federation Press, 1998). Envisaged originally as a second edition, the work developed an autonomous identity with the passage of time and the momentous events of more than a decade. My first and heartfelt thanks go to Laurie Berg who agreed in 2008 to come in as co-author. In addition to her contribution throughout, especially in the chapters on substantive migration and refugee law, she took primary responsibility for the three chapters on skilled and student migration.

I gratefully acknowledge financial support that I have received from the Australian Research Council (ARC) for the research and writing of chapters that explore Australia's rich immigration history;[1] and issues relating to refugee children and youth.[2] The book has also been enriched by funding from the University of Sydney Research Institute for the Humanities and Social Sciences;[3] and the NSW Law Foundation.[4] As writing this book spanned more than one period of sabbatical leave, thanks are due also to Dean Gillian Triggs, Lee Burns and to the colleagues who have covered my teaching as required over the years.

The size and conceptual range of this book should be evidence in itself that a great many people have assisted us over the years with their insights and ideas. A number of our academic colleagues have read chapters in draft, sometimes on multiple occasions. Others have shared with us their research findings, both published and pending. The joy for me as a teacher is that a number of those listed here (in alphabetical order) began as my students and have blossomed as academics in their own right. For your joint and several generosity, thank you to: Edwin Ohiambo Abuya, Anna Boucher, Lenni Benson, Michel Beine, Jacqueline Bhabha, Tony Blackshield, Frank Brennan, Brian Burgoon, Jennifer Burn, Terry Carney, Stephen Castles, François Crépeau, Robin Creyke, Azadeh Dastyari, Catherine Dauvergne, Andrew Edgar, John Evans, Michelle Foster, Maryellen Fullerton, Peter Gerangelos, Sandy Gifford, Guy Goodwin-Gill, Matthew Groves, Jim Hathaway, Michael Hiscox, Jessie Hohmann, France Houle, Helen Irving, Mary-Anne Kenny, Alison Kesby,

---

1 Research for Chapters 2, 18 and 19 in particular was supported by the ARC grant held by Mary Crock and Helen Irving entitled 'The Impact of Migrants on the Development of Public Law in Australia: An Historical and Cultural Study'. For archival work related to this research, I am indebted to the late Rosemary Bell who threw herself into our project with great joy and gusto. She will be sorely missed at our book launch.
2 In this context I acknowledge the support of the MacArthur Foundation and the ARC which funded the *Seeking Asylum Alone* Project referred to throughout the book and which is funding a project on refugee children and youth that began in 2010. Thanks also to the Sidney Myer Foundation which underwrote the pilot for this work with a project entitled: 'In Need of Protection: A Case study of the treatment of Separated Afghan Children in Australia's Refugee Determination Process'.
3 Mary Crock was awarded a writing fellowship that brought some relief from teaching in 2006.
4 This organisation funded a small grant in 2003 under the Law Foundation Legal Scholarship Support Grant scheme.

Susan Kneebone, Marilyn Lake, Stephen Legomsky, Audrey Macklin, David Martin, Jane McAdam, Pat McGovern, John McMillan, Jenni Milbank, Hitoshi Nasu, Gerald Neuman, Louise Newman, Sudrishti Reich, Henry Reynolds, Kim Rubenstein, Ben Saul, Ed Santow, Tim Stephens, Savitri Taylor, Eicho Thielemann, Anne Twomey and Stephen Yale-Loehr.

Our objective in writing this book was to capture the spirit of immigration law and policy in Australia as it has operated over time and as it now governs this complex and politically fraught area of administrative law. My own grounding in the practice of migration law – in particular in the accreditation of Australia's legal specialists in immigration – means that I have a great interest in the human and real-time impact of immigration and refugee law and policy. I have been blessed by many sustaining friendships within Australia's tightly knit community of migration practitioners who include lawyers, judges, parliamentarians, journalists, tribunal members, migration agents and refugee advocates. This book has been enriched greatly by the generosity of the following people, some of whom have variously read our work in draft, drawn our attention to significant cases and legislative developments and generally shared their insights with us. They are: Andrew Bartlett, Margaret Beazley, Rosemary Bell, Michael Black, Elizabeth Biok, David Bitel, Julian Burnside, John Cameron, Michael Chaaya, Nicholas Chen, Michael Clothier, Richard Conti, Pamela Curr, Marianne Dickie, Peter Gray, Brian Harradine, Libby Hogarth, Maureen Horder, Michael Jones, Michael Kah, Brian Kelleher, Paul Kelly, Joanne Kinslor, Michael Kirby, Marion Le, Margaret McAleese, Murray McInnis, David Manne, Shane Marshall, Ron Merkel, Debbie Mortimer, Kerry Murphy, Yuko Nakushima, Tony North, Denis O'Brien, Pamela O'Neill, Margaret Piper, Nicholas Poynder, David Prince, Peter Prince, Mark Robinson, Kelly Ryan, Ronald Sackville, Stephen Scarlett, Matthew Smith, Brian Tamberlin, Graham Thom and Murray Wilcox. Special mention in this regard is due to John Gibson whose case law digest was of invaluable assistance.

Over the years, many people within the Department of Immigration (in its various incarnations) have helped us with access to policy documents, statistics and other information critical to research and writing for this book. Special thanks are due here to Robyn Bickett, Mark Cully, Anita Davis, Rebecca Irwin, Peter Speldewinde, Angus Tye and various officers in the statistics section.

I am deeply grateful to the many students who have read drafts of our chapters over the years and who will continue to be the primary consumers of the work. The book is richer for the critical feedback you have provided. Very special thanks are due to the students, past and present, who have worked as my research assistants or written essays that we cite in the text. These include: Fiona Allison, Jason Cabarus, Catherine Chang, Matthew Costa, Christine Ernst, Leah Friedman, Daniela Gavshon, Daniel Ghezelbash, Mark Gibian, Sally Gibson, Naomi Hart, Meena Krishnamoorthy, Courtney Meade, Daniel Miller, Georgina Perry, Louise Pounder, Cathy Preston-Thomas, Hannah Quadrio, Anna Samson, Deborah Siddoway – Barker and Michelle Wen.

I join with Laurie in thanking Chris Holt, Diane Young, Ann Cunningham, Kathy Fitzhenry, and the staff at The Federation Press for their patient faith in us and for their care in nurturing the book through to publication. Special thanks for indulging our more creative side with the photographs that divide the major sections of the book. Thanks also to my brother Paul Crock for his photographic work on the cover.

My greatest debt is to Ron McCallum, my husband and partner in an adventure that now spans a quarter of a century; three natural children and two more from Cambodia and Afghanistan; two grandchildren; eight books and far too much plane travel. He is my best critic, my inspiration and love of my life who has always been my 'Australian of the Year'.

Finally, I dedicate this work to Gerard, Daniel and Kate (lest they need the knowledge contained in this book); and to Leang Thai and Riz Wakil (for whom it was applied).

Laurie Berg

First I would like to thank Mary Crock for inviting me to collaborate with her in this endeavour. It has been extremely intellectually rewarding to be engaged in a work which traverses the vast scope of migration laws and policies, and has such historical breadth. But it has been an even greater privilege simply to learn from someone who has made such a significant contribution to migration law research in Australia. I have been tremendously influenced by Mary's conceptual approach to the field, as well as her passionate commitment to achieving just results, in the lives of real people just as much as in policy settings.

I join with Mary in acknowledging the numerous academic colleagues, policy-makers and practitioners who have contributed to the development of this book. I would like to especially thank Professor Jenni Millbank for inspiring me and fostering my own voice, and Professor Isabel Karpin for generously and indefatigably sharing with me her wisdom and encouragement. Many colleagues have helped me immeasurably to deepen my thinking about migration laws and policies in Australia and abroad. However, I must single out Anna Boucher, Azadeh Dastyari, Katherine Fallah, Professor Andrew Jakubowicz, Professor Audrey Macklin, Professor Jane McAdam, Melissa McAdam, Ali Mojtahedi, Anna Samson, Frances Simmons, Jenny Stanger, and Merima Trbojevic. I am particularly grateful to Associate Professor Jennifer Burn and Sudrishti Reich for sharing with me their encyclopaedic knowledge of immigration laws.

Since embarking on this book, I have taken up a position at the Faculty of Law, University of Technology, Sydney. I am indebted to my colleagues and friends at UTS for the supportive and stimulating environment I found there. In particular, Dean Jill McKeough, Professor Lesley Hitchens and Bronwyn Olliffe provided all the support I required to complete this work. At the same time, I have been undertaking a PhD at Faculty of Law, University of Sydney and would like to thank Professor Ron McCallum for his guidance and friendship, and Professors Terry Carney and Hilary Astor for their counsel.

Finally, I wish to thank my family and friends for enriching my life with their insight, humour and love.

Abbreviations

AAT	Administrative Appeals Tribunal
AATA	Administrative Appeals Tribunal of Australia
ABC	Australian Broadcasting Corporation
ABS	Australian Bureau of Statistics
ACM	Australasian Correctional Management
ACTU	Australian Council of Trade Unions
ADJR	Administrative Decisions (Judicial Review)
AEGIS	Australian Expert Group in Industry Services
AFP	Australian Federal Police
AHRC	Australian Human Rights Commission
AIM	Australian Institute of Management
ALP	Australian Labor Party
ALRC	Australian Law Reform Commission
ANAC	Australian Nursing Assessment Council
ANZSCO	Australian and New Zealand Standard Classification of Occupations
APEC	Asia-Pacific Economic Co-operation
ARC	Administrative Review Council
ART	Administrative Review Tribunal
ASCO	Australian Standard Classification of Occupations
ASIO	Australian Security and Intelligence Organisation
AusAID	Australian Agency for International Development
AWU	Australian Workers Union
BAP	Business Advisory Panel
BIA	Board of Immigration Appeals
BSC	Business Skills Category
BV	Bridging visa
CAAIP	Committee to Advise on Australia's Immigration Policies
CAT	Convention Against Torture and All forms of Cruel, Inhumane and Degrading Treatment or Punishment
CDPP	Commonwealth Director of Public Prosecutions
CEDA	Committee for Economic Development of Australia
CEDAW	Convention on the Elimination of all Forms of Discrimination against Women
CERD	International Convention on the Elimination of all forms of Racial Discrimination
CES	Commonwealth Employment Service
CFMEU	Construction, Forestry, Mining and Energy Union
CFO	Commission for Filipinos Overseas
CIPL	Centre for International and Public Law
COAG	Council of Australian Governments
CPA	Comprehensive Plan of Action
CRC	Convention on the Rights of the Child
CRICOS	Commonwealth Register of Institutions and Courses for Overseas Students
CRPD	Convention on the Rights of Persons with Disabilities
CSL	Critical Skills List
CSWAP	Canada's Seasonal Agricultural Workers' Program
Cth	Commonwealth
DEET	Department of Employment, Education and Training
DEETYA	Department of Employment, Education, Training and Youth Affairs
DEEWR	Department of Education, Employment and Workplace Relations

DEIR	Department of Employment and Industrial Relations
DEST	Department of Education, Science and Training
DFAT	Department of Foreign Affairs and Trade
DIAC	Department of Immigration and Citizenship
DIEA	Department of Immigration and Ethnic Affairs
DILGEA	Department of Immigration, Local Government and Ethnic Affairs
DIMA	Department of Immigration and Multicultural Affairs
DIMIA	Department of Immigration and Multicultural and Indigenous Affairs
DIR	Department of Industrial Relations
DORS	Determination of Refugee Status
EETEP	Extended Eligibility Temporary Entry Permit
ENS	Employer Nomination Scheme
ENSOL	Employer Nomination Skilled Occupation List
ESOS	Education Services for Overseas Students
ETA	Electronic Travel Authority
FCA	Federal Court of Australia
FCAFC	Federal Court of Australia Full Court
FMCA	Federal Magistrates Court
GATS	General Agreement on Trade in Services
HAMC	Hell's Angels Motor Cycle Club Inc
HAS	Health Assessment Service
HCA	High Court of Australia
HRA	Human Rights Act
HRC	Human Rights Commission
HREOC	Human Rights and Equal Opportunity Commission
HSA	Health Services Australia
IAAAS	Immigration Advice and Application Assistance Scheme
ICCPR	International Covenant on Civil and Political Rights
IDC	Inter-Departmental Committee
IDC	Immigration Detention Centre
IELTS	International English Language Test System
ILO	International Labour Organization
IMR	Independent Merits Review
IOM	International Organisation for Migration
IRP	Immigration Review Panel
IRPC	Immigration Reception and Processing Centre
IRT	Immigration Review Tribunal
IRTA	Immigration Review Tribunal of Australia
JCPA	Joint Committee of Public Accounts
JSCMR	Joint Standing Committee on Migration Regulations
LTTE	Liberation Tigers of Tamil Eelam
MAL	Migration Alert List
MARA	Migration Agents Registration Authority
MHS	Medibank Health Solutions (formerly HSA)
MIA	Migration Institute of Australia Ltd
MIAC	Minister for Immigration and Citizenship
MIEA	Minister for Immigration and Ethnic Affairs
MILGEA	Minister for Immigration, Local Government and Ethnic Affairs
MIMA	Minister for Immigration and Multicultural Affairs
MIMIA	Minister for Immigration and Multicultural and Indigenous Affairs
MIRO	Migration Internal Review Office
MOC	Medical Officer of the Commonwealth
MODL	Migration Occupations in Demand List
MOU	Memorandum of Understanding
MRT	Migration Review Tribunal
MRTA	Migration Review Tribunal of Australia
MSI	Migration Series Instruction

NGO	Non-Government Organisation
NOOSR	National Office of Overseas Skills Recognition
NSWCCA	New South Wales Supreme Court, Court of Criminal Appeal
NSWSC	New South Wales Supreme Court
NUMAS	Numerical Multifactor Assessment System
OECD	Organisation for Economic Co-operation and Development
OET	Occupational English Test
OMARA	Office of the Migration Agents Registration Authority
ORE	Occupations Requiring English
OSP	Overseas Student program
OSS	Occupational Shares Scheme
PAM	Procedures Advice Manual
PASA	Pre-application skills assessment
PEPAE	Permanent entry permit after entry
PES	Professional Employment Service
PIC	Public Interest Criteria
PNG	Papua New Guinea
POL	Priority Occupations List
PQS	Pre-qualified Sponsorship
PRC	People's Republic of China
QCA	Supreme Court of Queensland, Court of Appeal
RMOC	Review Medical Officer of the Commonwealth
ROSCO	Resolution of Status for Chinese and Others
RRT	Refugee Review Tribunal
RSA	Refugee Status Assessment
RSE	Recognised Seasonal Employer
RSRC	Refugee Status Review Committee
SAL	Skilled Australian-linked
SAR	International Convention on Maritime Search and Rescue
SAS	Special Air Services
SASC	South Australian Supreme Court
SBS	Standard Business Sponsorship
SIEV	Suspected Illegal Entry Vessel
SOL	Skilled Occupation List
SOLAS	International Convention for the Safety of Life at Sea
SOPF	Subsidised Postgraduate Fund Scholarships
SOSP	Subsidised Overseas Student Program
SSASSL	Sydney and Surrounding Areas Skills Shortages List
STNI	Skilled State/Territory Nominated Independent (subclass 137) visa
TAFE	Technical and Further Education
TEP	Temporary Entry Permit
TRA	Trades Recognition Australia
UKHL	United Kingdom House of Lords
UN	United Nations
UNCLOS	United Nations Convention on the Law of the Sea
UNCRC	United Nations Convention on the Rights of the Child
UNHCR	United Nations High Commissioner for Refugees
VCCL	Victorian Council for Civil Liberties
VET	Vocational Education and Training
WASCA	Supreme Court of Western Australia, Court of Appeal
WHM	Working Holiday maker
WHV	Working Holiday visa

Ministers Responsible for Immigration: 1901–Present

Name	Party	Period	Title
William Lyne	Protectionist Party	1901-1903	Minister for Home Affairs
John Forrest	Protectionist Party	1903-1904	Minister for Home Affairs
Lee Batchelor	Australian Labor Party	1904	Minister for Home Affairs
Dugald Thomas	Free Trade Party	1904-1905	Minister for Home Affairs
Littleton Groom	Protectionist Party	1905-1906	Minister for Home Affairs
Thomas Ewing	Protectionist Party	1906-1907	Minister for Home Affairs
John Keating	Protectionist Party	1907-1908	Minister for Home Affairs
Hugh Mahon	Australian Labor Party	1908-1909	Minister for Home Affairs
George Fuller	Commonwealth Liberal Party	1909-1910	Minister for Home Affairs
King O'Malley	Australian Labor Party	1910-1913	Minister for Home Affairs
Joseph Cook	Commonwealth Liberal Party	1913-1914	Minister for Home Affairs
William Archibald	Australian Labor Party	1914-1915	Minister for Home Affairs
King O'Malley	Australian Labor Party	1915-1916	Minister for Home Affairs
Fred Bamford	National Labor Party	1916-1917	Minister for Home and Territories
Patrick Glynn	Nationalist Party	1917-1920	Minister for Home and Territories
Alexander Poynton	Nationalist Party	1920-1921	Minister for Home and Territories
George Pearce	Nationalist Party	1921-1925	Minister for Home and Territories
Reginald Wilson	Nationalist Party	1925-1926	Minister for Markets and Migration
Thomas Paterson	Country Party	1926-1928	Minister for Markets and Migration
Neville Howse	Nationalist Party	1928	Minister for Home and Territories
Aubrey Abbott	Country Party	1928-1929	Minister for Home and Territories
Arthur Blakeley	Australian Labor Party	1929-1932	Minister for Home Affairs
Archdale Parkhill	United Australia Party	1932	Minister for Home Affairs/ Minister for the Interior
John Perkins	United Australia Party	1932-1934	Minister for the Interior
Eric Harrison	United Australia Party	1934	Minister for the Interior
Thomas Paterson	Country Party	1934-1937	Minister for the Interior
John McEwen	Country Party	1937-1939	Minister for the Interior
Harry Foll	United Australia Party	1939-1941	Minister for the Interior
Joseph Collings	Australian Labor Party	1941-1945	Minister for the Interior
Arthur Calwell	Australian Labor Party	1945-1949	Minister for Immigration
Harold Hold	Liberal Party of Australia	1949-1956	Minister for Immigration
Athol Townley	Liberal Party of Australia	1956-1958	Minister for Immigration
Alexander Downer, Sr	Liberal Party of Australia	1958-1963	Minister for Immigration

MINISTERS RESPONSIBLE FOR IMMIGRATION: 1901–PRESENT

Hubert Opperman	Liberal Party of Australia	1963-1966	Minister for Immigration
Billy Snedden	Liberal Party of Australia	1966-1969	Minister for Immigration
Phillip Lynch	Liberal Party of Australia	1969-1971	Minister for Immigration
Jim Forbes	Liberal Party of Australia	1971-1972	Minister for Immigration
Lance Barnard	Australian Labor Party	1972*	Minister for Immigration
Al Grassby	Australian Labor Party	1972-1974	Minister for Immigration
Clyde Cameron	Australian Labor Party	1974-1975	Minister for Labour and Immigration
James McClelland	Australian Labor Party	1975	Minister for Labour and Immigration
Tony Street	Liberal Party of Australia	1975**	Minister for Labour and Immigration
Michael McKellar	Liberal Party of Australia	1975-1979	Minister for Immigration and Ethnic Affairs
Ian MacPhee	Liberal Party of Australia	1979-1982	Minister for Immigration and Ethnic Affairs
John Hodges	Liberal Party of Australia	1982-1983	Minister for Immigration and Ethnic Affairs
Stewart West	Australian Labor Party	1983-1984	Minister for Immigration and Ethnic Affairs
Chris Hurford	Australian Labor Party	1984-1987	Minister for Immigration and Ethnic Affairs
Mick Young	Australian Labor Party	1987-1988	Minister for Immigration, Local Government and Ethnic Affairs
Clyde Holding	Australian Labor Party	1988	Minister for Immigration, Local Government and Ethnic Affairs
Robert Ray	Australian Labor Party	1988-1990	Minister for Immigration, Local Government and Ethnic Affairs
Gerry Hand	Australian Labor Party	1990-1993	Minister for Immigration and Ethnic Affairs
Nick Bolkus	Australian Labor Party	1993-1996	Minister for Immigration and Ethnic Affairs
Philip Ruddock	Liberal Party of Australia	1996-2003	Minister for Immigration and Multicultural Affairs/ Minister for Immigration and Multicultural and Indigenous Affairs
Amanda Vanstone	Liberal Party of Australia	2003-2007	Minister for Immigration and Multicultural and Indigenous Affairs/ Minister for Immigration and Multicultural Affairs
Kevin Andrews	Liberal Party of Australia	2007	Minister for Immigration and Citizenship
Chris Evans	Australian Labor Party	2007-2010	Minister for Immigration and Citizenship
Chris Bowen	Australian Labor Party	2010-	Minister for Immigration and Citizenship

*   Caretaker 5-19 December 1972
**   Caretaker 11 November –20 December 1975

Sources: DIAC, 'History: Portfolio Ministers', produced on request; National Library of Australia, 'From Calwell Onward: Immigration Ministers in the Library's Oral History Collection' (June 2005) <http://www.nla.gov.au/pub/nlanews/2005/jun05/>; National Library of Australia, 'Immigration Ministers in Manuscripts' <http://www.nla.gov.au/pub/nlanews/2005/aug05/>

List of Illustrations

Part I
1. 'Kanakas working in the cane fields in North Queensland' date unknown, from the collection of the John Oxley Library, State Library of Queensland, neg no: 171328, Copyright expired.
2. 'Chinese miner in traditional garb relaxing with a long stemmed pipe' date unknown, Richard Daintree, from the collection of John Oxley Library, State Library of Queensland, neg no 51355, Copyright expired.
3. 'Re-enactment of the landing of Governor Phillip at Farm Cove' 1938, Sam Hood, from the collection of the State Library of NSW, Call Number Home and Away – 17969, Copyright expired.

Part II
1. 'Al- Khafaji' 2004, © Andrew Taylor/Fairfax Media
2. 'Tampa standoff' 2001, © Phil Oakley

Part III
1. 'Police and two asylum seeker boys, Christmas Island' 2001 © Phil Oakley

Part IV
1. 'German couple getting married in the Snowy Mountains' 1958, from the collection of the National Archives of Australia, A12111, 1/1958/13/15.
2. 'Migration office' 1962, from the collection of the National Archives of Australia, A12111, 1/1962/14/31.

Part V
1. 'Greek Migrant Learning English, Bonegilla reception camp' 1942 © Thurston Hopkins/Hulton Archive/Getty Images.
2. 'Pineapple canning factory' 1959, Don Edwards, from the collection of the National Archives of Australia, A12111, 1/1959/16/244, Copyright expired.

Part VI
1. 'SIEV' 2001 © Phil Oakley.
2. 'Group of refugees' 2001 © Phil Oakley.

Part VII
1. 'Dock soldiers' 2001 © Phil Oakley.
2. 'At his wife's grave, Christmas Island' 2001 © Phil Oakley.

Part VIII
1. 'Jason Kioa and his legal team' 2004 © Elvina Kioa.

Part IX
1. 'The tiger 11 soccer team' 2003, © Freddie Steen.
2. 'Riz becomes an Australian' 2007 © Mary Crock.

Table of Cases

0661990 [2008] MRTA 1343: 9.91
061034333 [2008] MRTA 142: 9.56
071176030 [2008] MRTA 58: 7.53
071275442 [2007] MRTA 376: 9.71
071410355 [2008] MRTA 304: 9.68
071555387 [2008] MRTA 1347: 9.89, 9.93
071750949 [2009] MRTA 199: 9.46
071810442 [2008] MRTA 1183: 7.53
071889268 [2008] MRTA 1303: 9.91
071937828 [2008] MRTA 1360: 9.72
071945992 [2009] MRTA 23: 9.75
0800016 [2009] MRTA 1024: 9.46
0800018 [2009] MRTA 233: 9.93
0800741 [2008] MRTA 1425: 9.46
0800801 [2009] MRTA 463: 9.74
0800835 [2008] MRTA 521: 7.30
0801537 [2009] MRTA 584: 10.36
0801708 [2009] MRTA 123: 9.72
0802770 [2009] MRTA 346: 9.69, 9.72
0804279 [2008] MRTA 1327: 9.89
0804429 [2008] MRTA 1239: 11.81
0804599 [2009] MRTA 993: 8.13
0806152 [2009] MRTA 704: 10.35
0808613 [2009] MRTA 499: 9.91
0906655 [2009] MRTA 2784: 7.53
A v MIMA [1999] FCA 227: 14.38
A234/2003 v MIMIA [2003] FCA 1110: 13.107
AB v MIAC (2007) 96 ALD 53: 17.100
Abbasi v MIMIA [2002] FCA 568: 11.26
Abbott and MILGEA, Re (1991) AALD [2781-2]: 17.65
Abcjkl [2003] MRTA 5977: 16.61
Abdi v MIMA (2000) 61 ALD 101: 14.17
Abebe v Commonwealth (1999) 197 CLR 510: 3.34, 3.35, 13.21, 13.32, 19.66-19.67, 19.71-19.72, 19.82
Abedi v MIMA (2001) 114 FCR 186: 18.118
Adams v Howerton (1982) 673 F2d 1036 (9th Cir): 7.25
Adan v Secretary of State for the Home Department [1999] AC 293: 13.71-13.72
Addo v MIMA [1999] FCA 940: 18.117
Aguilar, Re [1992] IRTA 39: 11.77
Ahamed v MILGEA (1991) 30 FCR 137: 16.15
Ahmadi v MIMA [2001] FCA 1070: 13.48, 13.55
Ahmed [2002] MRTA 2520: 16.68
Ahmed v MIMA [1999] FCA 430: 16.63
Ah Sheung v Lindberg [1906] VLR 323: 2.35
Ah Yin v Christie (1907) 4 CLR 1428: 2.41
Air Caledonie International v Commonwealth (1988) 165 CLR 462: 6.01
Airservices Australia v Canadian Airlines International Ltd (1999) 202 CLR 133: 5.98
Ainsworth v Criminal Justice Commission (1992) 175 CLR 564: 19.12-19.13, 19.27
Akbar v MIAC [2009] FMCA 279: 9.56
Akbas v MIEA (1985) 7 FCR 363: 15.32

Akers v MIEA (1989) 98 ALR 261: 12.91
Akpan v MIEA (1982) 58 FLR 47: 16.86
Akpata v MIMIA [2003] FCA 514: 16.49
Akyaa v MIEA [1987] FCA 137: 13.121
Alakoc, Re [1991] IRTA 194: 6.35
Alam v MIMIA [2004] FMCA 583: 11.27
Alamdar v MIMA [2001] FCA 1698: 18.134
Al-Anezi v MIMA (1999) 92 FCR 283: 13.09
Al-Kateb v Godwin (2004) 219 CLR 562: 1.19, 3.48, 3.50, 3.51, 3.52, 4.01, 4.10, 4.14, 4.26-4.29, 4.77, 12.98, 16.28, 16.75, 16.111, 16.113, 16.116, 16.134, 17.10, 20.06-20.07, 20.10, 20.21
Al Khafaji v MIMIA [2002] FCA 1369: 14.34
Al Masri v MIMIA (2002) 192 ALR 609: 4.27, 16.111
Alsalih v Manager Baxter Immigration Detention Facility [2004] FCA 352: 16.49
Al-Zafiry v MIMA [1999] FCA 443: 14.26
Ali, Re [1992] IRTA 690: 8.08
Ali v MIEA (1992) 38 FCR 144: 15.82
Ali v MIMA [2007] FMCA 1405: 7.78, 7.86
Alin v MIMIA [2002] FCA 979: 7.72, 7.74-7.75, 7.84
Ally v MIAC [2008] FCAFC 49: 7.86
Ally v MIMA [2007] FMCA 430: 7.47
Alpaslan v MIEA (1985) 9 ALN N78: 16.86
Alshamali v MIMA [1999] FCA 279: 7.32
Ameri and MILGEA, Re (1989) 16 ALD 640: 17.66, 17.82-17.83
An v MIAC (2007) 160 FCR 480: 9.69, 9.70, 9.72
Anarwala [2002] MRTA 1875: 16.68
Ang v MIEA (1994) 48 FCR 437: 16.115
Annetts v McCann (1990) 170 CLR 596: 4.20, 19.27
Antipova v MIMIA (2006) 151 FCR 480: 7.48
Aomatsu v MIMIA (2005) 146 FCR 58: 9.56
Appellant P119/2002 v MIMIA [2003] FCAFC 230: 18.86
Applicant A v MIEA (1997) 190 CLR 225: 13.03, 13.48, 13.51, 13.63, 13.64, 13.74, 13.99, 13.101-13.105, 13.107, 13.111-13.112, 13.118-13.119, 13.124
Applicant ANBD of 2001 v MIMA (2002) 126 FCR 453: 14.56-14.57
Applicant M 117 of 2007 v MIAC [2008] FCA 1838: 16.133, 18.128
Applicant M256/2003 v MIMIA [2006] FCA 590: 13.54
Applicant NADL of 2001 v MIMA [2002] FCA 274: 18.132
Applicant S v MIMA [2001] FCA 1411: 13.109
Applicant S v MIMA (2004) 217 CLR 387: 13.58, 13.64, 13.75, 13.102, 13.109
Applicant S1174 of 2002 v RRT [2004] FCA 298: 19.75
Applicant VAAN of 2001 v MIMA (2002) 70 ALD 289: 16.70
Applicant VFAD of 2002 v MIMA (2002) 194 ALR 304: 16.108

Applicant Z v MIMA (1998) 90 FCR 51: 13.63
Aqbal v Hurford (1984) 7 ALN N79: 16.103
Arcadi, Re [1994] IRTA 4513: 6.63
Arias and DIMA, Re (1996) 44 ALD 679: 17.69
Arif v MIMA [2002] FCA 1053: 18.76, 18.81
Arkan v MIMA [2000] FCA 1134: 16.63
Armani, Re [1992] IRTA 999: 8.35
Arquita v MIMA (2000) 106 FCR 465: 14.51
Arquita and MIMA, Re [1999] AATA 410: 14.62
Arslan v Durrell (1983) 48 ALR 577: 15.32
Arslan v Durrell (1984) 4 FCR 73: 15.32
Asif v MIMA (2000) 60 ALD 145: 7.41
Associated Provincial Picture Houses v Wednesbury Corporation [1948] 1 KB 223: 4.14, 18.128, 19.42, 19.69
Ates v MIEA (1983) 67 FLR 449: 16.87
Attorney-General v Zaoui [2006] 1 NZLR 289: 14.64
Attorney-General (Canada) v Cain [1906] AC 542: 2.35
Attorney-General (Cth) v Ah Sheung (1906) 4 CLR 949: 2.58
Attorney-General (NSW) v Quin (1990) 170 CLR 1: 19.40
Attorney-General (NSW) v Ray (1989) 90 ALR 263: 16.94, 16.114, 19.11
Australian Building Construction Employees and Builders' Labourers' Federation v Commonwealth (1986) 161 CLR 88: 16.22
Australian Coarse Grain Pool Pty Ltd v Barley Marketing Board of Queensland (1982) 46 ALR 398: 16.102
Australian Coal and Shale Employees' Federation v Aberfeldi Coal Mining Co Ltd (1942) 66 CLR 161: 19.78
Australian Meat Holdings Pty Ltd v Kazi [2004] QCA 147: 15.98
Aw v MIAC [2009] FMCA 566: 9.93
Ayan v MIMIA (2003) 126 FCR 152: 3.27, 19.62
Aygun v MIEA (1983) 68 FLR 276: 16.86
AZAAD v MIAC [2010] FCAFC 156: 18.76
Azemoudeh v MIEA (1985) 8 ALD 281: 6.15, 12.84-12.85, 19.17
Babicci v MIMIA [2004] FCA 1645: 7.53
Babicci v MIMIA (2005) 141 FCR 285: 7.53, 15.60
Bagus v MILGEA (1994) 50 FCR 396: 8.49
Baidakova v MIMA [1998] FCA 1436: 15.67-15.68
Baik v MIAC (2008) 217 FLR 386: 19.99
Bainbridge v MIAC (2010) 181 FCR 569: 17.49
Baias v MILGEA, Re (1996) 43 ALD 284: 17.81
Baker v Canada [1999] 2 SCR 817: 4.28
Bakri and DIEA, Re (1987) 12 ALD 517: 17.59
Baldassara v MIMIA [2005] FCA 239: 9.99
Balineni v MIAC [2008] FMCA 888: 9.29
Ballibay and MIMA, Re [2000] AATA 1147: 14.62
Banks v Transport Regulation Board (Vic) (1968) 119 CLR 222: 5.25
Banu v Hurford (1987) 12 ALD 208: 12.85
Barbaro and MIEA, Re (1981) 3 ALN N21: 17.81
Bardek and MIEA, Re (1987) 8 ALD 382: 17.65
Barrett v MIEA (1989) 18 ALD 129: 16.101, 19.33
Barton v Commonwealth (1974) 131 CLR 477: 16.128, 16.130-16.131
Barzideh v MIEA (1996) 69 FCR 417: 14.22

Batey v MILGEA, Re [1992] FCA 494: 17.65
Batey, Re (1991) 25 ALD 369: 17.77
Beattie-Bjurhammar, Ulla Helene [2002] MRTA 5189: 8.28
Becker and MIEA, Re (1977) 1 ALD 158: 5.14, 17.54, 17.82, 18.03, 18.07
Beckner v MIEA, Re (1991) 30 FCR 49: 17.60
Bedlington v Chong (1998) 87 FCR 75: 15.51, 19.54
Beecham Group Ltd v Bristol Laboratories Pty Ltd (1968) 118 CLR 618: 16.102
Beets, Re (1979) 2 ALD 417: 17.62
Behrooz v Secretary, DIMIA (2004) 219 CLR 486: 3.48, 4.12, 4.26, 16.47, 20.06
Bel Kacem v MIMIA (2005) 196 FLR 144: 11.20
Bengescue v MIEA (1994) 35 ALD 429: 17.65, 17.98
Berenguel v MIAC (2010) 264 ALR 417: 5.58
Berman, Re [1994] IRTA 3937: 6.36, 6.38
Beyazkilinc v Manager, Baxter Immigration Reception and Processing Centre (2006) 155 FCR 465: 16.137
Birceru and MIMA, Re [1997] AATA 434: 17.69
Birch [2004] MRTA 6775: 9.101
Biswas v MIAC [2009] FMCA 95: 9.46
Black v MIAC [2007] FCA 1249: 17.55
Black, Ex parte; Re Morony (1965) 83 WN (Pt 1) (NSW) 45: 2.35
Blair v MIMA [2001] FCA 1014: 6.40
Blanco v MIMA [2005] FMCA 136: 19.97
Boakye-Danquah v MIMIA (2002) 116 FCR 557: 15.64
Bodruddaza v MIMA (2007) 228 CLR 651: 3.40, 18.56, 19.98, 20.06
Bolat v MIMA [2007] FMCA 1640: 7.65
Bolkus v Tang Jia Xin (1994) 69 ALJR 8: 16.25
Bolton, Re; Ex parte Beane (1987) 162 CLR 514: 16.109
Bong and MILGEA, Re (1990) 20 ALD 143: 17.66
Boonstoppel v Hamidi (2005) 192 FLR 327: 15.103
Boshoff v MIMA [2006] FMCA 1919: 9.99
Boughey v R (1986) 161 CLR 10: 13.15
Bouianov v MIMA [1998] FCA 1348: 18.120
Bozanich v MIMA [2002] FCA 81: 15.63
Braun v MILGEA (1991) 33 FCR 152: 11.24, 15.97
Bray v F Hoffman-La Roche Ltd (2003) 130 FCR 317: 19.88
Bretag v IRT and MILGEA [1991] FCA 582: 7.47
Bridle v Gomravi [2005] SASC 295: 15.103
Bromley London Borough Council v Greater London Council [1983] 1 AC 768 at 821: 19.42
Broussard v MIEA (1989) 21 FCR 472: 15.32, 18.117, 19.33
Brown v MIAC [2010] FCA 52: 17.97
Brunswick Corporation v Stewart (1941) 65 CLR 88: 5.54
Budiyal v MIMA (1998) 82 FCR 166: 18.72
Bui v MIMA (1999) 85 FCR 134: 6.40, 6.49, 6.52, 6.53
Buksh v MILGEA (1991) 102 ALR 647: 5.44, 5.59
Bullock v Federated Furnishing Trades Society of Australasia (No 1) (1985) 5 FCR 464: 16.102
Bunnag v MIAC [2008] FCA 357: 7.46, 18.129
C v MIEA (1999) 94 FCR 366: 13.118
Cabal v MIMA [2001] FCA 546: 18.118

Cain and MILGEA, Re (1990) 20 ALD 418: 17.59
Cakmak v MIMIA (2003) 135 FCR 183: 7.61, 7.67, 7.74
Calado v MIMA (1997) 81 FCR 450: 13.82, 13.86
Calvin's Case (1608) 7 Co Rep 1a [77 ER 377]: 2.63, 2.72, 2.78
Campbell and DILGEA, Re [1993] AATA 344: 17.65
Cam v MIMA (1998) 84 FCR 14: 18.114
Cao v MIMA [2007] FMCA 1239: 7.76
Canada (Attorney General) v Ward (1993) 103 DLR (4th) 1; [1993] 2 SCR 689: 13.20, 13.98, 13.100, 13.103, 13.111, 14.10
Canangga, Re [1990] IRTA 34: 11.84
Capello v MIEA (1980) 2 ALD 1014: 16.104
Cardenas v MIMA [2001] FCA 17: 10.28
Cardile v LED Builders Pty Ltd (1999) 198 CLR 380: 16.107
Carlos v MIMA [2001] FCA 301: 8.15
Carter v Repatriation Commission (2001) 113 FCR 314: 11.89
Chakera v MIMA (1993) 42 FCR 525: 8.45
Chalmers v Commonwealth (1946) 73 CLR 19: 11.89
Chan and MIEA, Re (1977) 17 ALR 432: 17.5, 17.64
Chan Yee Kin v MIEA (1989) 169 CLR 379: 4.14, 12.20, 12.92-12.95, 13.10-13.12, 13.14-13.17, 13.19, 13.25-13.27, 13.29, 13.45, 13.49, 13.51, 13.57, 13.69, 13.121, 16.89, 19.42, 19.50, 19.52, 20.08
Chand v MILGEA (1993) 30 ALD 777: 15.53
Chand v MILGEA (1996) 44 ALD 583: 7.42
Chand, Re [1990] IRTA 10: 11.77

Cheaib v MIMA (1997) 75 FCR 308: 15.11
Chee v MIMA [1997] FCA 46: 15.74
Chemaly v MIMA [1998] FCA 1403: 18.132
Chen v MIMA [2001] FCA 285: 16.63
Chen v MILGEA (1992) 37 FCR 501: 8.62
Chen v MILGEA (1994) 48 FCR 591: 18.25
Chen (No 2) v MIEA (1994) 51 FCR 322: 8.62
Chen Shi Hai v MIMA (2000) 201 CLR 293: 13.13, 13.52, 13.58, 13.63-13.64, 13.66, 13.75, 13.90, 13.106
Cheng v MIMIA [2007] FCAFC 71: 11.45
Cheuk Por Leung, Re [1993] IRTA 2238: 8.60
Chey v MIAC [2007] FCA 871: 19.74
Chhun v MIMIA [2006] FMCA 203: 19.97
Chia Gee v Martin (1905) 3 CLR 649: 2.32, 2.35, 3.09
Chin Yow v United States of America 208 US 8 (1908): 3.62
Chiorny v MIMA (1997) 44 ALD 605: 6.16
Chishti, Re [1997] IRTA 8671: 15.87
Chai v MIMIA [2005] FCA 1460: 17.96
Christie v Ah Foo (1904) 29 VLR 533: 2.36
Chu Kheng Lim v MILGEA (1992) 176 CLR 1: 1.19, 2.5, 2.35, 3.42, 3.43, 3.44, 3.46, 4.07, 4.12, 4.21, 4.47, 4.71, 16.15, 16.21-16.25, 16.30, 16.57, 16.109, 17.10, 20.06-20.07
Chu Sing Wun v MILGEA (1993) 118 ALR 345: 6.64
Chu Sing Wun v MILGEA (1997) 47 ALD 538: 6.64

Chua v MIEA (1986) 13 FCR 158: 16.118, 16.120
Chumbairux v MIEA (1986) 74 ALR 480: 7.22
Chun Wang v MIMA (1997) 71 FCR 386: 18.61
Clarkson v R [1986] VR 464: 4.44
Cockrell v MIAC (2007) 100 ALD 52: 17.88, 17.100
Coco v The Queen (1994) 179 CLR 427: 16.109
Collins (No 2) v MIEA (1982) 5 ALD 32: 16.101, 16.103
Commissioner for ACT Revenue v Alphaone Pty Ltd (1994) 49 FCR 576: 18.76, 18.93
Commissioner for Superannuation v Scott (1987) 71 ALR 408: 8.45
Commonwealth v Colonial Combing, Spinning and Weaving Co Ltd (1922) 31 CLR 421 (Wooltops case): 3.55
Commonwealth v Tasmania (1983) 158 CLR 1: 4.08, 13.81
Conyngham v MIEA (1986) 68 ALR 423: 5.27, 5.29
Copland v MIMA [2006] FMCA 39: 15.64
Council of Civil Service Unions v Minister for Civil Service [1985] 1 AC 374: 19.03
Council of the Shire of Sutherland v Heyman (1985) 157 CLR 424: 16.49
CSR Ltd v Maddalena [2006] HCA 1: 9.14
Craig v South Australia (1995) 184 CLR 163: 18.101, 19.11, 19.91-19.92
Cruz, Re [1992] IRTA 1411: 6.35
Cujba v MIMA (2001) 111 FCR 110: 11.84
Cunliffe v Commonwealth (1994) 182 CLR 272: 3.45, 5.100
Dage v Baptist Union of Victoria [1985] VR 270: 16.102
Daguio v MIEA (1986) 71 ALR 173: 12.89, 15.32, 16.118
Dahlan v MILGEA [1989] FCA 507: 8.05, 12.77, 12.89-12.91, 19.48
Dai v MIAC (2007) 165 FCR 458: 11.46, 15.70
Djalic v MIMIA (2004) 139 FCR 292: 17.79
Dallikavak v MIEA (1985) 9 FCR 98: 16.112
Damanik v MIMA [2000] FCA 771: 17.54
Damouni v MILGEA (1989) 87 ALR 97: 8.06, 12.77, 12.89-12.91, 19.48
Danian v Secretary of State for the Home Department [1999] EWCA Civ 3000; [2000] Imm AR 96: 13.39
Darko v MIMIA [2003] FCA 304: 11.77
Davis v Commonwealth (1988) 166 CLR 79: 3.55, 3.58
Davis v MIMIA [2004] FCA 686: 7.40
Deputy Commissioner of Taxation v Richard Walter Pty Ltd (1995) 183 CLR 168: 19.78
de Braic, Ex parte (1971) 124 CLR 162: 3.09
De Ronde v MIMIA (2004) 188 FLR 266: 9.47
Dertli v MIMA (1999) 56 ALD 409: 18.119
De Silva v MIMA (2000) 98 FCR 364: 18.76, 18.79-18.80
De Silva v MIMA (2001) 113 FCR 350: 16.66
De Souza v MIMIA [2003] FCA 1636: 8.35
Dean v Woodward (1984) 6 ALN N288: 16.103
Delatabua v MIMIA [2004] FCA 884: 16.67
Dhanoa v MIAC (2009) 229 FLR 317: 9.29
Dhayakpa v MIEA (1995) 62 FCR 556: 14.56-14.57, 17.98
Dhillon v MILGEA (1989) 86 ALR 651: 7.37, 7.38

Dhingra v R [1999] NSWCCA 359: 15.101
Dib v MIMA (1998) 82 FCR 489: 11.25, 11.89
Dietrich v R (1992) 177 CLR 292: 4.07
Din v MIEA (1997) 147 ALR 673: 5.58, 15.86, 15.90
Dissanayake v MIMA [2001] FCA 491: 18.139
Doan v MIMA [2000] FCA 909: 7.67, 7.73
Donohoe v Wong Sau (1925) 36 CLR 404: 2.35, 2.42, 2.50, 2.63, 2.78
Doukmak v MIMA (2001) 114 FCR 432: 15.11
Dowlat v MIAC [2009] FMCA 171: 8.22
Drake v MIEA (1979) 24 ALR 577: 18.01, 18.06, 19.02
Drake and MIEA, Re (No 2) (1979) 2 ALD 634: 17.56, 18.03, 18.07
Dranichnikov v MIMA (2003) 214 CLR 496: 13.97
Dred Scott v Sandford, 60 US 393 (1856): 2.76, 4.77
Driscoll v R (1977) 137 CLR 517: 6.63
Du v MIMA [2000] FCA 1115: 7.71, 7.74-7.75
Dusa, Re [1991] IRTA 285: 6.34
Durrani v MIMIA [2005] FCA 629: 18.66
Ebrahimi v MIEA (1988) 15 ALD 360: 5.28, 5.29
Ebner v Official Trustee (2000) 205 CLR 337: 19.36
EC v MIMA (2004) 138 FCR 438: 8.23
Elliott v MIMIA [2006] FCA 67: 8.49
El Mohamad v MIMA [2007] FMCA 345: 7.47
Ejueyitsi v MIAC [2006] FMCA 1900: 7.66
Emiantor v MIMA (1997) 48 ALD 635: 13.13, 18.132
Emiantor v MIMA [1998] FCA 1186: 13.13, 18.120
Epiha and MILGEA, Re (1988) 18 ALD 114: 17.65
Eremin v MILGEA (1990) 21 ALD 69: 5.52, 5.55-5.57
Eremin v MILGEA, Re [1990] FCA 266: 5.55-5.56, 5.59
Ertan v Hurford (1986) 11 FCR 382: 16.86-16.87
Eschersheim, The [1976] 1 WLR 430: 4.28
Epitoma Pty Ltd v Australasian Meat Industry Employees Union (No 2) (1984) 3 FCR 55: 16.102
Evans v MIMIA (2003) 135 FCR 306: 17.45
Ex Christmas Islanders Association Inc v Attorney-General (Cth) (No 2) (2006) 91 ALD 313: 19.99
F W, Re [1996] IRTA 6790: 15.53
FAI Insurances Ltd v Winneke (1982) 151 CLR 342: 19.20
Fan v MIAC (2010) 240 FLR 318: 9.47
Fanchon and MIAC, Re [2008] AATA 20: 17.31
Farajvand v MIMA [2001] FCA 795: 13.94
Fazal Din v MIMA [1998] FCA 961: 19.75, 19.106
Felizarta, Re [1991] IRTA 263: 6.63
Feng Guan Lin, Re [1995] IRTA 6107: 16.59
Ferati v MIMA [1998] FCA 1709: 19.38
Ferrando v Pearce (1918) 25 CLR 241: 16.128
Ferreras, Re [1991] IRTA 299: 11.76
Foley v Padley (1984) 154 CLR 349: 5.54
Foo v MIMIA [2003] FCA 1277: 16.67
Forster v Jododex Aust Pty Ltd (1972) 127 CLR 421: 19.13
Foster v Neilson 2 Pet 253 at 324, 7 LEd 415 (1829): 4.07
Francis and DIEA, Re (1996) 42 ALD 555: 17.98
Fuduche v MILGEA (1993) 117 ALR 418: 8.61, 8.64

Fung, Re [1991] IRTA 150: 8.57
Gaffar v MIMA (2000) 59 ALD 421: 9.75
Gaillard v MIEA (1983) 5 ALN N25: 16.103
Gallo and MIEA, Re (1980) 3 ALN N12: 17.64
Gamaethige v MIMA (2001) 109 FCR 424: 19.38
Ganzon v MIMIA [2002] FCA 1628: 8.58
Garath v MIAC (2006) 91 ALD 790: 8.63
Garland v Brit Rail Engineering [1983] 2 All ER 402: 4.28
Gauthiez v MIEA (1994) 53 FCR 512: 8.49, 8.53
General Newspapers Pty v Telstra Corporation (1993) 45 FCR 164: 19.102
Gersten v MIMA [2000] FCA 855: 13.51
Gherga v MIMIA [2004] FCA 351: 7.42-7.43
Gido-Christian v MIAC [2007] FMCA 825: 15.21
Gilbert v MIAC [2008] FCA 16: 15.75
Gilbert and MILGEA, Re [1993] AATA 510: 17.65
Glusheski v MIMA, Re [2000] AATA 717: 17.88-17.89
Godley v MIMIA (2004) 83 ALD 411: 17.29
Goldie v Commonwealth [2002] FCAFC 10: 16.39
Goldie v MIMA (1999) 56 ALD 321: 17.27
Gogebakan and MIEA, Re (1987) 6 AAR 544: 17.65, 17.83
Gogebakan v MILGEA, Re (1988) 92 ALR 167: 17.83
Gonzales and MIMIA, Re [2002] AATA 895: 17.85
Graham v MIMIA [2003] FCA 1287: 7.35
Grech v Heffey (1991) 34 FCR 93: 16.29-16.30
Griffith University v Tang (2005) 221 CLR 99: 19.102
Griffiths v MIMA (2003) 176 FLR 272: 17.97
Gry, Re [1996] IRTA 8209: 15.85
Gui v MIMA S219/1999 [2000] HCATrans 280: 13.30
Gui v MIMA [1998] FCA 1592: 13.31
Guo Heng Li v MIMA [1999] FCA 1147: 18.62
Guo v MIMA [2000] FCA 146: 9.91
Guo Bin v MIMA (1999) 58 ALD 153: 8.15
Gunaleela v MIEA (1987) 15 FCR 543: 12.88, 16.15
Gunaseelan v MIMA [1997] FCA 434: 13.85
Gungor v MIEA (1982) 42 ALR 209: 17.59
Gungor and MIEA, Re (1980) 3 ALD 225: 17.64
Gunner v MIMA (1997) 50 ALD 507: 17.24
Guven v MIMA [2006] FMCA 311: 7.83
Haidari v MIAC [2009] FMCA 1178: 8.22
Halmi v MIMA [2000] FCA 113: 17.54
Hamdi v Rumsfeld 124 S Ct 2633 (2004): 19.101
Hampshire County Council v Beer (t/as Hammer Trout Farm) [2003] EWCA Civ 1056: 5.98
Han, Latif [2004] MRTA 817: 11.81
Hand v Hell's Angels Motor Cycle Club Inc (1991) 25 ALD 667: 6.65-6.67, 11.78, 17.19, 17.26, 17.34
Haneef v MIAC (2007) 161 FCR 40: 17.39
Hanna v MARA [1999] FCA 1657: 5.104
Hao Jiang v MIAC [2007] FCA 907: 19.14
Haoucher v MIEA (1990) 169 CLR 648: 4.23
Haoucher, Re (1987) 12 ALD 217: 17.14, 17.81, 17.83
Hapugoda and MIMA, Re [1997] AATA 108: 14.62
Hartnett v MARA [2004] FCAFC 269: 5.104
Hasan v MIAC [2007] FCA 697: 15.70

Hasan v MIAC (2010) 184 FCR 523: 18.68
Hayes, Audrey Joan [2003] MRTA 4607: 15.57
Hehar v MIMA (1997) 48 ALD 620: 14.17
Helvaci v MIMA [2007] FMCA 1306: 7.65, 7.78
Helvaci v MIAC [2009] HCATrans 96: 7.78
Henry, Re [1995] IRTA 4935: 6.37
Herft v MIAC [2007] FMCA 756: 7.84, 19.74
Herijanto v RRT (2000) 170 ALR 379: 19.75, 19.106
Hernandez-Montiel v INS, 225 F 3d 1084 (9th Cir 2000): 13.101
Heshmati v MILGEA [1990] FCA 460: 13.38
Heshmati v MILGEA (1991) 31 FCR 123: 13.38, 19.34
Hilton and MIEA, Re (1980) 2 ALD 1035: 17.64
Hindi v MIEA (1988) 20 FCR 1: 18.117
Ho v MIMIA [2005] FMCA 1104: 15.61
Ho, Re (1975) 10 SASR 250: 2.18
Hollis v MIMA (2003) 202 ALR 483: 17.89
Hordila and MIMA, Re [1997] AATA 82: 17.65
Horta v Commonwealth (1994) 181 CLR 183: 4.08
Hossain v MIAC [2009] FMCA 405: 9.53
Hossain v MIAC (2010) 183 FCR 157: 11.43, 15.43
Hossain v MIAC (No 2) (2010) 114 ALD 523: 18.67
Hossain v MILGEA (1991) 23 ALD 771: 5.29
Howells v MIMIA (2004) 139 FCR 580: 17.55, 17.57-17.58
Hreinsson, Re [1994] IRTA 4037: 6.63
Hsiao v MILGEA (1992) 36 FCR 330: 15.25
Htun v MIMA (2001) 194 ALR 244: 13.122
Huang v MIAC [2007] FMCA 720: 8.47
Huang v MIEA [1996] FCA 1040: 8.62-8.63
Huang v MIMA [2001] FCA 284: 16.63
Huang v MIMA [2001] FCA 901: 18.114, 18.139
Huang v Owen (1989) 17 ALD 695: 16.105
Hudson and MARA [2004] AATA 1007: 5.104
Hughes Aircraft Systems International v Airservices Australia (1997) 76 FCR 151: 5.98
Human Rights and Equal Opportunity Commission v Secretary (1996) 67 FCR 83: 16.42
Humayun v MIMIA (2006) 149 FCR 558: 11.43
Hunter Valley Developments Pty Ltd v Cohen (1984) 3 FCR 344: 16.101
Husein Ali Haris v MIMA [1998] FCA 78: 13.87
Huynh v MIMIA (2006) 152 FCR 576: 8.10, 8.15, 8.46
Ibrahim v MIAC (2009) 229 FLR 350: 9.94
Ibrahim v MIMA (2000) 63 ALD 37: 18.132
Ibrahim v MIMIA [2002] FCA 1279: 7.74
Ibrahim v MIMIA [2005] FMCA 1239: 8.14
Imad v MIMA [2001] FCA 1011: 6.40, 6.43, 6.44
Immigration and Naturalization Service v Cardoza-Fonseca 480 US 421 (1987): 13.15
Inguanti v MIMA [2001] FCA 1046: 5.70, 6.40, 6.43, 6.44
Irving v MILGEA (1993) 44 FCR 540: 6.71, 6.72
Irving v MILGEA (1995) 59 FCR 423: 6.71
Irving v MILGEA (1996) 68 FCR 422: 17.27
Islam v MIMIA (2006) 202 FLR 281: 11.27
Islam v Secretary of State for the Home Department [1999] 2 AC 629: 13.66, 13.77, 13.111-13.113
Ismail, Re [1995] IRTA 6272: 7.29
Issa v MIMIA [2002] FCA 933: 8.59, 8.66
Isse v MIMA [2006] FMCA 253: 7.73, 7.76
Ivusic v R (1973) 127 CLR 348: 2.35
Jafar Heshmati v MILGEA [1990] FCA 460: 12.42
Jaffari v MIMA (2001) 113 FCR 10: 18.64, 18.66
James v MIMA [2002] FCAFC 91: 8.43
Jankovic v MIEA (1995) 56 FCR 474: 8.08, 8.51
Januzi v Secretary of State for the Home Department [2006] 2 AC 426: 14.14
Jason Kiat Chung Lo, Re [1996] IRTA 7986: 15.27
Jayasekara v MIMIA (2006) 156 FCR 199: 11.44, 15.70
Jayasekara v MIMA [2007] HCATrans 163: 11.44
Jayasinghe v MIMA [2006] FCA 1700: 7.47
Jerger v Pearce (No 1) (1920) 28 CLR 526: 17.08
Jerger v Pearce (No 2) (1920) 28 CLR 588: 17.08, 19.15
Jeong v MIMIA [2005] FMCA 804: 15.60
Jia v MIMA (1999) 93 FCR 556: 19.39, 19.93
Jia Le Geng v MIMA [1998] FCA 768: 17.24
Jia Le Geng and MIMA, Re (1996) 42 ALD 700: 17.98
Jian Xin Liu v MIMA [2001] FCA 1437: 7.44
Jiang v MIAC [2007] FCA 907: 15.70
Johnson v MIMIA (2003) 130 FCR 394: 15.98
Jovcevski v MILGEA, Re [1989] FCA 422: 15.25
Jong Kim Koe v MIMA (1997) 74 FCR 508: 13.19, 14.20
Jumbunna Coal Mine NL v Victorian Coalminers' Association (1908) 6 CLR 309: 4.12, 4.27
Jupp and MIMIA, Re [2002] AATA 458: 17.85
Jushi v MIAC [2005] FMCA 1116: 9.43
Kable v Lord (1812-1814) NSW Sel Cas (Kercher) 475: 2.21
Kailey v MIMIA [2005] FMCA 1044: 7.72
Kandiah v MIMA [1998] FCA 1145: 18.140
Kartinyeri v Commonwealth (1998) 195 CLR 337: 2.81, 4.12, 4.27, 20.07
Kashayev v MIEA (1994) 50 FCR 226: 13.97
Kaufman, Re (1997) 44 ALD 701: 15.86
Kayikci v MIAC (2009) 107 ALD 112: 7.41
Kenny v MILGEA (1993) 42 FCR 330: 3.14
K-Generation Pty Limited v Liquor Licensing Court (2009) 237 CLR 501: 18.55
Khan v MIEA (1987) 14 ALD 291: 18.117
Khan v MIMA (1997) 47 ALD 19: 13.38
Khan v MIMA [2005] FMCA 1970: 15.61
Khanfer v MIMIA [2003] FMCA 238: 15.59, 15.61
Khant v MIAC (2009) 112 ALD 241: 18.130
Kharroubi v MIMA [1998] FCA 178: 18.132
Khawar v MIMA (1999) 168 ALR 190: 13.77
Khergamwala v MIAC [2007] FMCA 690: 18.105
Kiloul v MIMIA [2006] FMCA 650: 11.20
Kim v MIAC [2007] FMCA 166: 10.37
Kim v MIAC [2007] FMCA 798: 8.35
Kim v MIMIA [2005] FMCA 1699: 9.68
Kim v Witton (1995) 59 FCR 258: 11.24
Kioa v West (1984) 6 ALN N21: 16.103
Kioa v West (1985) 159 CLR 550: 2.66, 3.62, 4.14-4.16, 4.21, 12.18, 12.86, 15.32, 16.86, 18.92, 18.96, 18.101, 19.16, 19.20, 19.23-19.24, 19.26, 19.29, 19.31, 19.35, 19.103, 20.08
Kirk v Industrial Relations Commission (2010) 239 CLR 531: 19.90
Koe v MIEA (1997) 78 FCR 289: 13.07, 13.09

Koe v MIMA (1997) 74 FCR 508: 13.08
Koh Ah Soo v MIEA (1986) 10 ALN N46: 19.30
Kokcinar v MIAC [2008] FMCA 1307: 18.55
Kola v MIMIA (2002) 120 FCR 170: 14.21, 14.32
Kolotau v MIMIA [2002] FCA 1145: 19.55
Koon Wing Lau v Calwell (1949) 80 CLR 533: 2.35, 2.45, 2.46, 3.10, 17.09, 19.15, 20.07
Koowarta v Bjelke-Petersen (1982) 153 CLR 168: 4.08
Koncz, Re [1995] IRTA 5934: 8.60
Kopalapillai v MIMA (1998) 86 FCR 547: 18.132
Koroitamana v Commonwealth (2006) 227 ALR 406: 2.79
Kord v MIMA [2001] FCA 1163: 13.48
Kovac v Immigration and Naturalization Service 407 F 2d 102 at 107 (9th Circuit) (1969): 13.45
Kozel v MIMA (2004) 138 FCR 181: 7.75
Kruger v Commonwealth (1997) 190 CLR 1: 4.07
Krummrey v MIMIA (2005) 147 FCR 557: 15.39-15.40
Kruse v Johnson [1898] 2 QB 91: 5.53
Kumar v MIEA [1989] FCA 293: 7.14
Kyi v MIMA [2001] FCA 580: 18.139
Lace Holdings Pty Ltd v MIMA (2002) 117 FCR 79: 10.26
Lachmaiya and MIEA, Re (1994) 19 AAR 148: 6.68, 15.27
Lafu v MIAC (2009) 112 ALD 1: 17.80
Lam v MIMA [2001] FCA 1866: 15.68-15.69
Latu v MIEA (1985) 8 ALN N293a: 16.89
Lay Kon Tji v MIEA (1998) 158 ALR 681: 14.22
Leaupepe and MILGEA, Re (1990) 21 ALD 382: 17.66
Lee v MIAC (2008) 221 FLR 416: 9.93
Leha v MIMA, Re [2000] AATA 1054: 17.85
Leng v MIAC [2007] FMCA 1961: 10.27
Li v MIAC [2007] FCA 1098; 96 ALD 361: 7.42, 18.127
Li v MIAC [2010] FMCA 583: 9.69
Li v MILGEA (1992) 33 FCR 568.
Li v MIMA (No 2) [2007] FMCA 22: 6.18, 15.36
Li Shi Ping v MILGEA (1994) 35 ALD 395: 18.25
Li Shi Ping v MILGEA (1994) 35 ALD 557: 13.38 on appeal (1994) 35 ALD 225: 13.38
Li Tian v MIAC (2008) 220 FLR 139: 9.70
Liang v MIAC (2009) 175 FCR 184: 8.65
Liang v MIAC (2007) 220 FLR 1: 9.60
Liechtenstein v Guatemala (the Nottebohm Case) [1955] ICJ Reports 4: 2.77
Limbu v MIMA [2001] FCA 436: 11.26
Lin v MIMIA (2004) 136 FCR 556: 8.66
Liu v MIMA [2001] FCA 257: 13.91
Liu v MIMA (2001) 113 FCR 541, 18.71, 18.80
Liu v MIAC [2008] FMCA 725: 15.53
Lloyd v Wallach (1915) 20 CLR 299: 17.08, 19.15
Lobo v MIMA [2006] FCA 1562: 9.91
Lobo v MIMIA (2003) 132 FCR 93: 9.91
Lobo v MIMIA [2005] FMCA 1024: 9.91
Local Government Board v Arlidge [1915] AC 120: 18.94
Loh and MILGEA, Re (1990) 52 AALB [1869]: 17.66
Long v MIMIA (2002) 122 FCR 159: 16.96
Long v MIMIA [2002] FCAFC 438: 16.96
Long v MIMIA (2003) 76 ALD 610: 17.96
Long v MIMIA [2003] FCAFC 218: 19.62
LSLS v MIMA [2000] FCA 211: 13.115
Lu, Re [1991] IRTA 207: 6.42
Lu v MIMIA (2004) 141 FCR 346: 17.74
Luc, Re [1994] IRTA 3817: 8.57
Lumanovska v MIMIA [2003] FCA 1321: 7.42
Luu v Renevier (1989) 91 ALR 39: 12.91
Ly v MIMA [2000] FCA 15: 11.81
Ly and MIMA, Re [2000] AATA 339: 17.97
M175 of 2002 v MIAC [2007] FCA 1212: 18.81
M238 of 2002 v MIMIA [2003] FCAFC 260: 17.86
M238/2002 v MIMIA [2003] FCA 936: 17.43
M38/2002 v MIMIA (2003) 131 FCR 146: 16.137
M93 of 2004 v MIMIA [2006] FMCA 252: 13.70
Macabenta v MIMA (1998) 154 ALR 591: 15.90
Macabenta v MIMA (1998) 90 FCR 202: 15.90
Macabenta v MIMA S5/1999 [1999] HCATrans 191: 15.90
Maddalena v CSR Ltd [2004] WASCA 231: 9.14
Magyari v MIMA (1997) 50 ALD 341: 13.21, 13.65
Majeed, Re [2002] MRTA 6429: 11.34
Mahboob v MIEA [1996] FCA 1319: 19.58
Maitan v MIEA (1988) 78 ALR 419: 12.89
Mai Xin Lu v MIEA (unreported, FCA, French J, 19 July 1996): 13.79
Malik v MIMA (2000) 98 FCR 291: 7.67, 7.73, 18.101
Malincevski and MILGEA, Re (1991) 24 ALD 331: 17.82
Mandavi v MIMA [2002] FCA 70: 13.91
Manoher v MILGEA (1991) 24 ALD 405: 16.101, 16.105
Mann v Ah On (1905) 7 WALR 182: 2.35, 2.36
Manokian v MIMA (1997) 48 ALD 632: 5.70
Mardini v MIMIA [2005] FMCA 1409: 7.76
Mardini v MIMA [2006] FCA 488: 7.76
Mardnali, Re [1993] IRTA 2186: 8.08
Markwald v Attorney General [1920] 1 Ch 348: 2.19
Marshall, Re [1996] IRTA 6397: 15.58
Martinez v MIAC (2009) 177 FCR 337: 17.49
Maroun v MIAC (2009) 112 ALD 424: 18.67-18.68
Mashood v Commonwealth (2003) 133 FCR 50: 8.41
Masila v MIMA [2001] FCA 1611: 16.63
Masuoka v IRT (1996) 67 FCR 492: 9.65
Mataka v MIEA [1996] FCA 1503: 13.16
Mayer v MIEA (1984) 4 FCR 312: 4.14, 12.18
Mayer v MIEA (1985) 157 CLR 290: 4.14, 12.18, 16.124
Mazhar v MIMA (2000) 183 ALR 188: 7.82, 18.76, 18.79, 18.81
Mcbeth, John [2003] MRTA 3546: 15.57
McCarthy, Kevin [2002] MRTA 339: 15.53
McDonald v Director General of Social Security (1984) 1 FCR 354: 13.19, 18.114
McIvor and DIMA, Re (1997) 45 ALD 731: 17.69
McPhee v MILGEA (1988) 16 ALD 77: 19.47
McNamara v MIMIA [2004] FCA 1096: 15.60
McQuade, Re [1996] IRTA 7840: 15.27
Meadows v MIMA [1998] FCA 1706: 18.131, 18.133

Meera Mohideen Seyed Ahamed v MILGEA, Re [1991] FCA 287: 11.69
Meggs v MIEA (1986) 11 ALN N127: 7.22, 7.29
Mendoza v MILGEA (1991) 31 FCR 405: 5.59
Mercado v MIAC [2007] FMCA 1216: 9.60
Meroka v MIMA [2002] FCA 482: 7.67, 7.74-7.75
MGC, Re [1996] IRTA 6788: 15.53
MIAC v Ejueyitsi (2007) 159 FCR 94: 7.75
MIAC v Haneef (2007) 163 FCR 414: 17.35-17.40
MIAC v Hart (2009) 179 FCR 212: 9.99
MIAC v Kamruzzaman (2009) 112 ALD 550: 9.46
MIAC v Kumar (2009) 238 CLR 448: 7.40, 18.55, 18.106-18.107, 18.109-18.110
MIAC v Le (2007) 164 FCR 151: 10.26, 18.129, 19.93
MIAC v MZYCE (2010) 116 ALD 156: 18.140
MIAC v Ryerson (No 2) [2008] FMCA 1400: 8.10
MIAC v Sok (2008) 165 FCR 586: 7.80
MIAC v SZCWF (2007) 161 FCR 441: 13.119
MIAC v SZGUR [2011] HCA 1: 18.130
MIAC v SZJGV; MIAC v SZJXO (2009) 238 CLR 642: 13.41-13.43
MIAC v SZKKA [2008] HCATrans 86: 18.66
MIAC v SZKKC (2007) 159 FCR 565: 18.66, 19.98
MIAC v SZKTI (2009) 238 CLR 489: 18.45, 18.100
MIAC v SZLSP (2010) 187 FCR 362: 19.41
MIAC v SZGUR [2011] HCA 1: 18.130
MIAC v SZJSS [2010] HCA 48: 19.37
MIAC v SZIAI (2009) 259 ALR 429: 18.45, 18.130
MIAC v SZIZO (2009) 238 CLR 627: 18.70
MIAC v SZNVW (2010) 183 FCR 575: 18.130
MIEA v Baker (1997) 73 FCR 187: 17.27-17.29
MIEA v Conyngham (1986) 11 FCR 528: 5.27, 11.78
MIEA v Daniele (1981) 39 ALR 649: 17.59
MIEA v Gaillard (1983) 49 ALR 277: 15.32
MIEA v Gungor (1982) 39 ALR 649: 17.61
MIEA v Gungor (1982) 42 ALR 209: 17.61
MIEA v Guo Wei Rong (1997) 191 CLR 559: 13.03-13.04, 13.18, 13.21, 13.28, 13.121, 13.123, 18.115, 18.137
MIEA v Pochi (1980) 4 ALD 139: 7.85, 19.40
MIEA v Ran Rak Mayer (1985) 157 CLR 290: 5.67, 12.18-12.19, 12.30, 12.85-12.86
MIEA v Tang Jia Xin (No 1) (1993) 116 ALR 329: 16.25
MIEA v Tang Jia Xin (No 2) (1993) 116 ALR 349: 16.25
MIEA v Teoh (1995) 183 CLR 273: 1.19, 4.05, 4.07, 4.14-4.21, 4.23-4.27, 4.29, 17.95, 17.98, 20.07, 20.10
MIEA v Wu Shan Liang (1996) 185 CLR 259: 13.17, 18.114-18.115, 18.139, 19.52
MILGEA v Batey, Re (1993) 40 FCR 493: 17.77
MILGEA v Dela Cruz, Re (1992) 34 FCR 348: 15.18, 15.25
MILGEA v Dhillon [1990] FCA 144: 7.36, 7.37
MILGEA v Mok (No 2) (1994) 55 FCR 375: 13.16
MILGEA v Msilanga (1992) 34 FCR 169: 16.105
MIMA v Abdi (1999) 87 FCR 280: 13.72
MIMA v Al-Sallal (1999) 94 FCR 549: 14.22
MIMA v Al Shamry (2001) 110 FCR 27: 18.97, 18.104
MIMA v Ali (2000) 106 FCR 313: 17.61

MIMA v Applicant C (2001) 116 FCR 154: 14.32
MIMA v Bhardwaj (2002) 209 CLR 597: 18.49-18.50, 18.52-18.53, 18.55, 18.124
MIMA v Capitly (1999) 55 ALD 365: 18.72, 18.75
MIMA v Chan (2001) 34 AAR 94: 17.39
MIMA v Darboy (1998) 52 ALD 44: 13.91
MIMA v Dunne (1999) 94 FCR 72: 15.64
MIMA v Eshetu (1999) 197 CLR 611: 13.27, 19.67, 19.69-19.72, 19.82, 19.110
MIMA v Epeabaka (1999) 84 FCR 411: 18.114, 18.116
MIMA v Farahanipour (2001) 105 FCR 277: 13.39
MIMA v Gui [1999] FCA 1496: 13.30
MIMA v Graovac [1999] FCA 1690: 8.45
MIMA v Gnanapiragasam (1998) 88 FCR 1: 14.26
MIMA v Gunner (1998) 84 FCR 400: 17.24
MIMA v Hildalgo (2005) 145 FCR 564: 8.50
MIMA v Hou [2002] FCA 574: 11.33
MIMA v Hu (1997) 79 FCR 309: 9.42
MIMA v Hughes (1999) 86 FCR 567: 18.113
MIMA v Ibrahim (2000) 204 CLR 1: 4.40, 12.18, 13.51, 13.53, 13.56-13.58, 13.73
MIMA v Jang (2000) 175 ALR 752: 14.17
MIMA v Jia (2001) 205 CLR 507: 17.24, 19.39, 19.93
MIMA v Khawar (2002) 210 CLR 1: 13.68-13.69, 13.75, 13.78, 13.111, 14.13, 14.15, 19.83-19.84
MIMA v Kheirollahpoor [2001] FCA 1306: 13.39
MIMA v Kord (2002) 67 ALD 28: 13.51
MIMA v Li (2000) 103 FCR 486: 18.53
MIMA v Ozmanian (1996) 141 ALR 322: 155.51, 19.53
MIMA v Pires (1998) 90 FCR 214; 160 ALR 97: 8.10, 8.15
MIMA v Mohammed (2000) 98 FCR 405: 13.39
MIMA v Thiyagarajah (1997) 80 FCR 543: 14.23
MIMA v Thiyagarajah (2000) 199 CLR 343: 14.25, 14.27-14.28, 14.32-14.33
MIMA v Respondents S152/2003 (2004) 222 CLR 1: 13.70
MIMA v Saravanan [2002] FCAFC 81: 11.75, 11.77
MIMA v Savvin (2000) 98 FCR 168: 13.10
MIMA v Sarrazola (No 2) (2001) 107 FCR 184: 13.77, 13.118
MIMA v SBAA [2002] FCAFC 195: 18.134
MIMA v SBAN [2002] FCAFC 431; 18.140
MIMA v Seligman (1999) 85 FCR 115: 5.58, 5.70, 6.38-6.40, 6.49
MIMA v Shen (2002) 70 ALD 636: 19.99
MIMA v Singh (2000) 98 FCR 469: 18.137
MIMA v Singh (2002) 209 CLR 533: 14.49, 14.56, 14.59-14.60
MIMA v SRT (1999) 91 FCR 234: 17.61
MIMA v SZIAI (2009) 259 ALR 429: 13.24
MIMA v SZGMF [2006] FCAFC: 18.100
MIMA v W157/00A (2002) 125 FCR 433: 17.96
MIMA v Y [1998] FCA 515: 13.119
MIMA v Yusuf (2001) 206 CLR 323: 7.40, 13.62, 18.119, 18.136-18.138, 18.140, 19.11, 19.88, 19.92-19.93
MIMA v Zamora (1998) 85 FCR 458: 13.108-13.109
MIMA v Zheng [2000] FCA 50: 13.89-13.90
MIMA, Re; Ex parte Applicants S134/2002 (2003) 211 CLR 441: 18.121-18.122, 18.124, 19.82, 19.84, 19.87

MIMA, Re; Ex parte Applicant S20/2002 (2003) 198 ALR 59: 19.11, 19.71, 19.93, 19.110-19.112, 20.09
MIMA, Re; Ex parte Durairajasingham (2000) 168 ALR 407: 18.132, 18.140, 19.40
MIMA, Re; Ex parte Cassim (2000) 175 ALR 209: 19.94
MIMA, Re; Ex parte Cohen, Re (2001) 177 ALR 473: 19.94
MIMA, Re; Ex parte Epeabaka (2001) 206 CLR 128: 19.38
MIMA, Re; Ex parte Ervin, B29/1997 [1997] HCATrans 213 and [1997] HCATrans 214: 6.74
MIMA, Re; Ex parte Holland [2001] HCA 76: 7.31
MIMA, Re; Ex parte Lam (2003) 214 CLR 1: 4.13, 4.23, 19.40
MIMA, Re; Ex parte Miah (2001) 206 CLR 57: 13.27, 18.96, 19.14, 19.58, 19.75, 19.90, 19.108
MIMA, Re; Ex parte Majeed M77/2000 [2001] HCATrans 403: 11.34
MIMA, Re; Ex parte SE (1998) 158 ALR 735: 5.79, 5.80
MIMA, Re; Ex parte Te (2002) 212 CLR 162: 2.75
MIMA, Re; Ex parte Te; Re MIMA; Ex parte Dang (2002) 212 CLR 162: 2.57, 3.17, 3.24-3.27
MIMIA v Ahmed (2005) 143 FCR 314: 11.36, 15.39-15.40, 18.53
MIMIA v Al Khafaji (2004) 219 CLR 664: 3.48, 3.50, 4.10, 4.14, 4.26, 4.27, 14.31, 14.34, 16.111, 16.113, 16.116, 16.134, 20.06, 20.21
MIMIA v Al Masri (2003) 126 FCR 54: 4.27, 16.111, 16.113, 16.116
MIMIA v Alam (2005) 145 FCR 345: 11.27, 11.35
MIMIA v Awan (2003) 131 FCR 1: 11.19, 11.33
MIMIA v B (2004) 219 CLR 365: 4.12
MIMIA v Ball (2004) 138 FCR 450: 17.33
MIMIA v Godley (2005) 141 FCR 552: 17.26, 17.29
MIMIA v Griffiths [2004] FCAFC 22: 17.97
MIMIA v Hamdan [2005] FCAFC 113: 5.108
MIMIA v Hicks (2004) 138 FCR 475: 17.33
MIMIA v Huynh (2004) 211 ALR 126: 17.43
MIMIA v Lat (2006) 151 FCR 214: 9.93
MIMIA v Nystrom (2006) 228 CLR 566: 1.19, 3.29, 15.75, 17.11, 17.48, 19.93
MIMIA v QAAH of 2004 (2006) 231 CLR 1: 12.20, 14.40-14.43, 14.45-14.48
MIMIA v S152/2003 (2004) 222 CLR 1: 13.03
MIMIA v SCAR (2003) 128 FCR 553: 18.130
MIMIA v SGLB (2004) 207 ALR 12: 18.125-18.127, 19.71, 19.93, 19.110, 20.09
MIMIA v VBAO (2004) 139 FCR 405: 13.54
MIMIA v VFAD of 2002 (2002) 125 FCR 249: 16.107-16.108, 16.110
MIMIA v Walsh (2002) 189 ALR 694: 2.67, 3.28
MIMIA v X (2005) 146 FCR 408: 6.48
MIMIA v Yu (2004) 141 FCR 448: 11.43, 11.45
MIMIA v Zhou (2006) 152 FCR 115: 11.43
MIMIA, Re; Ex parte Ame (2005) 222 CLR 439: 2.68, 2.69, 2.70, 3.28
MIMIA, Re; Ex parte Palme (2003) 216 CLR 212: 19.62
Minh Son Do v MIMA [2002] FCA 1081: 9.75

Minister for Aboriginal Affairs v Peko-Wallsend (1985) 162 CLR 24: 19.16, 19.43
Mitrevski v MIMA [2001] FCA 221: 16.70
MM International (Australia) Pty Ltd v MIMIA [2004] FCAFC 323: 9.65
Mo v MIAC [2010] FCA 162: 11.43, 15.43
Mo, Yeuk Wing [2004] MRTA 947: 11.77
Mocan v RRT (1996) 42 ALD 241: 18.117
Modi v MIMA [2001] FCA 529: 15.67-15.68
Mohamed v MIMA (2007) 161 FCR 408: 7.76
Mohammed v MIMIA [2004] FCA 970: 11.28
Mohankumar v MIEA (unreported, FCA, Morling J, 30 March 1988): 12.88
Mok v MILGEA (1992) 47 FCR 1: 13.16
Mok Gek Bouy v MILGEA and Paterson (1993) 47 FCR 1: 19.37
Monakova v MIMA [2006] FMCA 849: 15.63
Montes-Granados v MIMA [2000] FCA 60: 14.17
Moore v MIAC [2007] FCA 626: 15.75
Morais v MILGEA (1995) 54 FCR 498: 9.42
Morales v MILGEA (1995) 60 FCR 550: 6.68
Morales and MILGEA, Re (1995) 38 ALD 727: 6.68
Moran v MIMIA (2006) 151 FCR 1: 15.75
Morato v MILGEA (1992) 39 FCR 401: 13.97, 13.103, 19.53
Morgan v MIMA [1999] FCA 1059: 7.76
Morrison v Behrooz (2005) 155 A Crim R 110: 15.103
Morrison v MIAC [2008] FCA 54: 17.86
Morsed v MIMIA (2005) 88 ALD 90: 11.42, 15.43, 18.67
Mosfequr Rahman, Re [2005] MRTA 118: 15.64
Mouradian v MRT [2001] FCA 1413: 16.67
Mr B, Re [1996] IRTA 6394: 15.58
Mujedenovski v MIAC (2009) 112 ALD 10: 7.50, 17.30
Muin v RRT; Lie v RRT (2002) 190 ALR 601: 18.66, 19.75, 19.106
Muliyana v MIAC [2009] FMCA 691: 7.84
Muliyana v MIAC [2010] FCAFC 24: 7.47, 7.85
Mulugeta and MILGEA, Re (1989) 19 ALD 639: 17.66
Mulwala Golden Inn Restaurant Pty Ltd and Zhu v MIAC [2010] FMCA 228: 9.69
Murphyores Inc Pty Ltd v Commonwealth (1976) 136 CLR 1: 16.127
Musgrove v Toy [1891] AC 272: 2.35, 19.15
Myeong Il Kim v Witton (1995) 59 FCR 258: 15.66
MZWMQ v MIMIA [2005] FCA 1263: 18.100
MZUAZ v MIMIA [2003] FCA 1390: 16.49
MZXLT v MIAC (2007) 211 FLR 428: 14.33
MZXOT v MIAC (2008) 233 CLR 601: 3.39, 18.56, 19.09
MZXQS v MIAC (2009) 107 ALD 33: 13.122
N05/04771 [2006] MRTA 309: 9.71
N05/50659 [2005] RRTA 207: 13.37
N1045/00A v MIMA [2001] FCA 1546: 14.32
N93/00732 [1994] RRTA 1363: 13.62, 13.93
N93/01995 [1994] RRTA 1702: 14.21
NAAA v MIMA (2002) 117 FCR 287: 19.93
NABE v MIMIA (No 2) (2004) 144 FCR 1: 19.103
NABD/2002 v MIMA (2005) 216 ALR 1: 13.95
NABD v MIMIA (2005) 216 ALR 1: 13.33
NABL v MIMA [2002] FCA 102: 16.63

NABM of 2001 v MIMIA (2002) 124 FCR 375: 14.17
NACM of 2002 v MIMIA (2003) 134 FCR 550: 13.121
NADH v MIMA (2004) 214 ALR 264: 19.93
NAEN v MIMIA (2004) 135 FCR 410: 14.33
NAFG v MIMIA (2003) 131 FCR 57: 14.26
Nagalingam v MILGEA (1992) 38 FCR 191: 13.19, 14.22
Nagaratnam v MIMA (1999) 84 FCR 569: 13.64
NAGV and NAGW v MIMIA (2005) 222 CLR 161: 14.27-14.29, 14.33
NAGV of 2002 v MIMIA [2002] FCA 1456: 14.27
NAHF v MIMA (2003) 128 FCR 359: 18.94
Naidu v MIMIA (2004) 140 FCR 284: 8.66
Naidu and MIEA, Re (1996) 42 ALD 137: 15.27
NAIS v MIMIA (2005) 228 CLR 470: 19.63, 19.93
NAIZ v MIMIA [2005] FCAFC 37: 14.17
NALZ v MIMIA (2004) 140 FCR 270: 14.16
NAMJ v MIMIA (2003) 76 ALD 56: 18.130
Nance, Re [1995] IRTA 5065: 6.37
NAPI v MIMIA [2004] FCA 57: 14.33
NAPS v MIMIA [2003] FCA 1091: 18.83
NAPS v MIMIA [2004] FCA 159: 18.83
NAPU v MIMIA [2004] FCAFC 193: 13.97
NAQJ v MIMIA [2004] FCA 946: 13.92
Naresh, Ram [2004] MRTA 1409: 8.13
Nassif v MIMIA (2003) 129 FCR 448: 9.88
Nassouh v MIMA [2000] FCA 788: 7.40
Naumovska v MIEA (1982) 60 FLR 267: 15.23-15.24
Naumovska v MIEA (1983) 88 ALR 589: 15.23
NAUV v MIMIA (2003) 79 ALD 149: 18.77
NAUV v MIMIA (2004) 82 ALD 784: 18.77
NBCY v MIMIA (2004) 83 ALD 518: 13.54, 14.35
NBDY v MIMA [2006] FCAFC 145: 15.20
NBKE v MIAC [2007] FCA 126: 13.06
NBKS v MIMIA (2006) 156 FCR 205: 18.101
NBKT v MIMA (2006) 156 FCR 419: 13.41, 18.04
NBLC v MIMIA (2005) 149 FCR 151: 14.35
NBGM v MIMA (2006) 231 CLR 52: 14.40, 14.43, 19.93
NBGM v MIMIA (2004) 84 ALD 40: 14.41
Ndegwa v MIMIA [2005] FMCA 74: 7.45
Nelson, Re [1990] IRTA 28: 6.34
NEAT Domestic Trading Pty Ltd v AWB Ltd (2003) 216 CLR 277: 5.95-5.98, 19.102
Ng v MIMA [2002] FCA 1146: 9.99
Nguet Huong Phung v MIEA [1997] FCA 373: 8.26
Nguyen v MIMA (2000) 101 FCR 20: 18.84
Nguyen v MIAC [2007] FCAFC 38: 7.50
Nguyen v MIMA [2007] FMCA 1315: 7.47
Nguyen v MIMA (1998) 88 FCR 206: 8.22
Nguyen, Re [1995] IRTA 5667: 6.37
Nguyen Thanh Trong v MILGEA (1996) 68 FCR 463: 18.55
Nguyen Van Chuong v MIEA [1996] FCA 653: 16.58
NBKT v MIMA (2006) 156 FCR 419: 18.104, 18.127
Nice Shoes Aust Pty Ltd v MIMIA [2004] FCA 252: 9.65, 10.23
Nolan v MIEA (1988) 165 CLR 178: 2.05, 2.35, 2.70, 3.10, 3.14-3.17, 3.20, 17.13

Nolan v MIEA (1992) 27 ALD 755: 15.18, 15.26
Nolan, Re (1986) 9 ALD 407: 17.81
Nonferral (NSW) Pty Ltd v Taufia (1998) 43 NSWLR 312: 15.98
Nong v MIMA (2000) 106 FCR 257: 11.32, 11.36
Norris, Re, [1995] IRTA 6352: 15.65
Nottinghamshire County Council v Secretary of State for the Environment [1986] 2 WLR: 5.54
Nystrom v MIMIA (2005) 143 FCR 420: 3.12, 3.29, 17.01, 17.03, 17.48, 17.87, 17.89, 20.04
Obele and MIAC [2010] AATA 58: 17.30
Octet Nominees Pty Ltd v Minister for Community Services (1986) 68 ALR 571: 5.54
O'Driscoll, Re [1994] IRTA 3532: 6.63
Officer in Charge of Cells, ACT Supreme Court, Re; Ex parte Eastman (1994) 123 ALR 478: 3.61
O'Keefe v Calwell (1949) 77 CLR 261: 2.35, 3.09
Okere v MIMA (1998) 87 FCR 112: 13.77
Omar v MIMA (2000) 104 FCR 187: 13.32
On v Commonwealth (1952) 86 CLR 1255: 2.18
Ovcharuk v MIMA (1998) 88 FCR 173: 14.49, 14.51-14.52, 14.57-14.58
Ovcharuk and MIMA, Re [1997] AATA 329: 14.62
Ozmanian v MILGEA (1996) 137 ALR 103: 19.53
Paduano v MIMIA (2005) 143 FCR 204: 15.62
Pak Siu Ling v MILGEA [1991] FCA 29: 5.59
Paki-Titi and MILGEA, Re (1990) 21 ALD 359: 17.66
Palko v MIEA (1987) 16 FCR 276: 7.22, 7.29
Pandey v MIMIA [2005] FMCA 1081: 7.74
Pandari v MIEA [1998] FCA 1698: 18.132
Panta v MIMA (2006) 203 FLR 376: 11.89
Papaioannou, Re [1991] IRTA 113: 6.34, 6.35
Pape v Federal Commissioner of Taxation (2009) 238 CLR 1: 19.13
Paramananthan v MIMA (1998) 94 FCR 28: 13.58, 13.64, 13.85, 18.120
Parisi v MIMIA [2005] FMCA 218: 10.23
Park Oh Ho v MIEA (1988) 20 FCR 104: 7.55, 16.15
Park Oh Ho v MIEA (1989) 167 CLR 637: 7.55, 16.15, 16.30, 16.94, 16.113-16.114
Parkes Rural Distributions Pty Ltd v Glasson (1984) 155 CLR 234: 5.95
Parkin v O'Sullivan (2006) 162 FCR 444: 6.75
Paramananthan v MIMA (1998) 94 FCR 28
Parekh v MIAC [2007] FMCA 633: 9.42
Parramatta City Council v Pestell (1972) 128 CLR 305: 5.54
Patel v MIMIA [2003] FCA 115: 15.59, 15.61
Patrick Stevedores Operations No 2 Pty Ltd v Maritime Union of Australia (No 3) (1998) 195 CLR 1: 16.107
Patterson, In re; Ex parte Taylor (2001) 207 CLR 391: 2.57, 2.63, 2.82, 3.10, 3.14-3.15, 3.17-3.21, 3.26, 3.30, 16.40
Patto v MIMA (2000) 106 FCR 119: 14.22
Paul v MIMA (2001) 113 FCR 396: 18.101, 18.96-7
Pearlman v Keepers and Governors of Harrow School [1979] QB 56: 19.89
Perera v MIMIA [2005] FCA 1120: 8.66
Perera v MIMA (1999) 92 FCR 6: 18.77
Perampalam v MIMA (1999) 84 FCR 274: 13.58, 13.76, 14.17, 18.20

Percerep and MILGEA, Re (1990) 20 ALD 669: 17.66, 17.76, 17.82
Percerep and MIMA, Re [1997] AATA 527: 17.66, 17.69, 17.76
Periannan (Murugasu) v MIEA (unreported, FCA, Wilcox J, 28 July 1987): 12.88, 13.71
Perkins v Cuthill (1981) 34 ALR 669: 16.104
Perkit v MIAC (2009) 109 ALD 361: 9.29
Pesava v MILGEA (1989) 18 ALD 95: 12.90, 19.30
Phan v MIAC [2007] FMCA 88: 15.64
Phan v MIMA (2000) 171 ALR 323: 18.77, 18.81, 18.139
Phillips v MIAC [2007] FMCA 572: 10.37
Plaintiff M168/2010 By His Litigation Guardian Sister Brigid (Marie) Arthur v Commonwealth [2011] HCATrans 4: 3.52
Plaintiff M61/2010E v Commonwealth and Plaintiff M69 of 2010 v Commonwealth (2010) 272 ALR 14: 3.64-3.66, 5.63, 5.67, 6.05, 12.13, 12.75, 12.82, 13.02, 18.29, 18.55, 19.13, 19.55, 19.93, 19.102-19.103, 19.116, 20.24
Plaintiff M90/2009 v MIAC [2009] HCATrans 279: 18.86
Plaintiff P1/2003 v MIMIA [2003] HCATrans 787: 19.102
P1/2003 v MIMIA [2003] FCA 1029: 19.102
Plaintiff S157 v Commonwealth (2003) 211 CLR 426: 1.19, 3.31, 3.37, 3.38-3.40, 4.12, 18.94, 18.96, 19.82-19.88, 19.93, 19.95, 20.06
Pochi v McPhee (1981) 149 CLR 139: 17.20
Pochi v McPhee (1982) 151 CLR 101: 2.75, 3.13, 17.10, 17.13, 17.81, 20.07
Pochi and MIEA, Re (1979) 2 ALD 33: 17.62, 17.64, 17.81, 18.111, 19.40
Police v Kakar [2005] SASC 222: 15.103
Polites v Commonwealth (1945) 70 CLR 60: 4.27
Polyukhovich v Commonwealth (1991) 172 CLR 501: 4.08
Pomenti v MIMA [1998] FCA 1400: 18.102
Poskus v MIMIA [2005] FCA 118: 11.88
Post Office v Estuary Radio [1968] 2 QB 740: 4.28
Potter v Minahan (1908) 7 CLR 277: 2.35, 2.37-2.42, 2.50, 2.63, 2.78, 3.09
Prashar v MIMA [2001] FCA 57: 13.92, 19.33
Prahastono v MIMA (1997) 77 FCR 260: 13.59
Prahastono v MIMA [1997] FCA 586: 13.56
Prasad v MIEA (1985) 6 FCR 155: 7.38, 18.128, 19.33
Prasad and MIEA, Re (1994) 35 ALD 780: 6.68, 15.27
Preston, Re [1991] IRTA 56: 8.57
Preston v MIMIA (No 2) [2004] FCA 107: 17.86
Prestoza, Re [2002] MRTA 6067: 15.65
Puafisi and MIAC [2009] AATA 689: 17.30
Public Service Board (NSW) v Osmond (1986) 159 CLR 656: 19.16, 19.62
Pull v MIMIA [2007] FCA 20: 15.75, 17.86
Pushpanathan v Canada [1998] 1 SCR 982: 14.63
Q05/05585 [2005] MRTA 1154: 9.56
QAAA of 2004 v MIMIA (2007) 98 ALD 695: 19.93
QAAB v MIMIA [2004] FCAFC 309: 15.51
QAAE v MIMIA [2003] FCAFC 46: 13.09
Qalo, Re [1991] IRTA 596: 8.08
Qalovi v MIEA (1994) 50 FCR 301: 15.53

Qi v MIMA [2002] FCA 326: 10.21
Qiao v MIAC [2008] FMCA 380: 8.10
Qiu v MIMA (1994) 55 FCR 439: 15.86
Qu v MIMA [2001] FCA 1299: 11.18-11.19
Queensland v Commonwealth (1989) 167 CLR 232: 4.08
R v Australian Broadcasting Tribunal; Ex parte 2HD Pty Ltd (1979) 144 CLR 45: 16.127
R v Carter; Ex parte Kisch (1934) 52 CLR 221: 2.35
R v Coldham; Ex parte Australian Workers Union (1983) 153 CLR 415 at 418: 19.81
R v Collins; Ex parte ACTU-Solo Enterprises Pty Ltd (1976) 8 ALR 691 : 12.75
R v Commonwealth Industrial Court Judges; Ex parte Cocks (1968) 121 CLR 313: 19.08
R v Davey; Ex parte Freer (1936) 56 CLR 381: 2.44
R v Director-General of Social Welfare (Vic); Ex parte Henry (1975) 133 CLR 369: 3.10
R v Forbes; Ex parte Kwok Kwan Lee (1971) 124 CLR 168: 2.35, 3.09, 15.74
R v Governor of Brixton Prison; Ex parte Soblen [1963] 2 QB 243: 16.128-16.130
R v Governor of Metropolitan Gaol; Ex parte Di Nardo (1962) 3 FLR 271: 15.25, 19.11
R v Governor of Metropolitan Gaol; Ex parte Molinari [1962] VR 156: 2.35
R v Governor of Metropolitan Gaol; Ex parte Tripodi (1961) 3 FLR 134: 19.09
R v Gray; Ex parte Marsh (1985) 157 CLR 351: 19.08
R v Green; Ex parte Cheung Cheuk To (1965) 113 CLR 506: 2.35, 3.09
R v Hardy [1996] NSWSC 524: 15.101
R v Hickman; Ex parte Fox and Clinton (1945) 70 CLR 598: 3.37, 19.78-19.79, 19.81-19.82
R v Home Department State Secretary; Ex parte Sivakumaran [1988] AC 958 at 992-4: 13.15
R v Home Secretary; Ex parte Khawaja [1984] AC 74: 3.62
R v Immigration Officer at Prague Airport; Ex parte European Roma Rights Centre [2004] UKHL 55: 6.07
R v Immigration Appeal Tribunal; Ex parte Jonah [1985] Imm AR 7: 14.16
R v Judges of Commonwealth Industrial Relations Court (1968) 121 CLR 313: 3.31
R v Kidman (1915) 20 CLR 425: 2.35
R v Kovacs [2009] 2 Qd R 51: 7.56-7.57
R v Liveris; Ex parte Da Costa (1962) 3 FLR 249: 2.35, 19.11
R v Macfarlane; Ex parte O'Flanagan and O'Kelly (1923) 32 CLR 518: 2.02, 2.35, 2.58, 3.09, 3.10
R v McLean (2001) 121 A Crim R 484: 7.50, 15.101
R v Panel on Take Overs and Mergers; Ex parte Datafin [1987] 1 QB 815: 5.96
R v Secretary of State for Foreign Affairs; Ex parte Greenberg [1947] 2 All ER 550: 16.121
R v Secretary of State for Home Affairs; Ex parte Duke of Château Thierry [1917] 1 KB 922: 16.128
R v Secretary of State for the Home Office; Ex parte Gunes [1991] Imm AR 278: 14.10
R v Superintendent of Chiswick Police Station; Ex parte Sacksteder [1918] 1 KB 578: 16.128

R v Troutman (unreported, NSWCCA, 23 April 1997): 15.101
R v Wilson; Ex parte Kisch (1934) 52 CLR 234: 2.43, 2.45, 6.72
R (on the application of Anufrijeva) v Secretary of State for the Home Dept [2004] 1 AC 604: 18.57
Rafiq v MIMIA [2004] FCA 564: 8.66
Rajaratnam v MIMA (2000) 62 ALD 73: 13.76
Rajanayake v MIMA [2001] FCA 352: 13.120
Rajendran v MIMA (1998) 86 FCR 526: 14.26
Rahman v MIMA [1999] FCA 846: 18.72
Rahman v MIMA [2001] FCA 1236: 11.85
Ramani, Re [1991] IRTA 147: 5.44
Ram v MIEA (1995) 57 FCR 565: 13.74, 13.101
Ramirez v MIMA (2000) 176 ALR 514: 13.120
Ramos [2002] MRTA 5201: 15.56
Rana-Vajracharya, Supriya [2003] MRTA 6884: 8.28
Randhawa v MILGEA (1994) 52 FCR 437: 14.12, 14.16
Rasul v Bush 123 S Ct 2686 (2004): 19.101
Ratley, Re [1992] IRTA 924: 6.35
Ratnam v MIEA [1997] FCA 330: 13.20
Reggie [2001] MRTA 4453: 7.86
Ren and MIAC, Re [2007] AATA 1805: 17.31
Ren v MIAC (2008) 100 ALD 567: 17.31
Renata v MIEA [1986] FCA 361: 17.60
Reyes-Reyes v Ashcroft, 284 F.3d 782 (9th Cir. 2004): 13.101
Refugee Appeal No 71427/99 (unreported, New Zealand Refugee Status Appeals Authority, 16 August 2000): 13.111
Rezaei v MIMA [2001] FCA 1294: 14.38
Richardson v Forestry Commission (1988) 164 CLR 261: 4.08
Ridge v Baldwin [1964] AC 40: 5.25
Rifki v MIEA (1983) 5 ALD 117: 16.103
Rizki v MILGEA (1989) 18 ALD 643: 12.90-12.91, 16.105
Roach v Electoral Commission (2007) 233 CLR 162: 3.02
Robel v MIMIA [2005] FMCA 1154: 9.42
Robertson, Re [1993] IRTA 2311: 8.60
Robinson v MIMIA (2005) 148 FCR 182: 6.41-6.43, 6.46
Robtelmes v Brenan (1906) 4 CLR 395: 2.23, 2.35, 9.12, 16.128,
Roguinski v MIMA [2001] FCA 1327: 13.57
Rokobatini v MIMA [1999] FCA 492: 11.74
Rokobatini v MIMA (1999) 57 ALD 257: 11.74
Romero and MIAC [2010] AATA 196: 17.97
Rooney v MIMA [1996] FCA 656: 15.74
Rose and DIMA, Re [1997] AATA 567: 17.69
Rosenauer, Re [1992] IRTA 945: 6.35
RRT, Re; Ex parte Aala (2000) 204 CLR 82: 19.14, 19.72-19.74
RRT, Re; Ex parte H (2001) 179 ALR 425: 19.38, 19.93
Rubrico v MIEA, Re (1989) 23 FCR 208: 15.25
Ruddock v Taylor (2005) 222 CLR 612: 16.40
Ruddock v Vadarlis (2001) 110 FCR 49: 1.19, 3.54, 3.57, 3.62, 3.63, 4.36, 4.44, 4.47, 4.48, 6.03, 20.05

Ruhl v MIMA (2001) 184 ALR 401: 17.54
S v Secretary, DIMIA (2005) 143 FCR 217: 16.47
S14/2002 v MIMIA [2003] FCA 1153 affirmed in S14/2002 v RRT [2004] FCAFC 171: 18.118
S273 of 2003 v MIMIA [2005] FMCA 983: 13.13
S395/2002 v MIMA (2003) 216 CLR 473: 13.33, 13.115-13.117, 14.16-14.17, 19.93
Saadi v United Kingdom 13229/03 [2008] ECHR 80: 4.28
SAAP v MIMIA [2002] FCA 577: 18.97-18.98
SAAP v MIMIA (2005) 215 ALR 162: 18.97-18.98, 18.100, 19.35, 19.93, 19.96
Sacharowitz v MILGEA (1992) 33 FCR 480: 8.06
Sadiqi v Commonwealth (No 2) (2009) 260 ALR 294: 19.102
Saeed v MIAC (2010) 267 ALR 204: 5.29, 18.55, 18.94, 19.35, 19.93, 19.116, 19.103
Sajatovic and MIEA, Re (1979) 2 ALN 549: 17.64
Sale v Haitian Centers Council Inc 113 S Ct 2549 (1993): 19.101
Salazar-Arbelaez and MIEA, Re (1977) 18 ALR 36: 17.64
Saleem v MRT [2004] FCA 234: 15.21
Salemi v MacKellar (No 2) (1977) 137 CLR 396: 15.32, 16.86, 19.15, 19.22-19.25, 19.29
Salerno v National Crime Authority (1997) 75 FCR 133: 5.95
Sales v MIAC (2008) 171 FCR 56: 17.48-17.49
Saliba v MIMA (1998) 89 FCR 38: 18.120
Sam v MIAC [2007] FMCA 1217: 10.33
Sanchez-Trujillo v INS 801 F 2d 1571 (1986): 13.98
Sanders v Snell (1998) 196 CLR 329: 4.23
Sandoval v MIMA (2001) 194 ALR 71: 6.19, 11.77, 15.14-15.16
Saravanan v MIMA [2001] FCA 938: 15.15
Saulog, Re [1990] IRTA 29: 11.74, 11.84
Savvin v MIMA (1999) 166 ALR 348: 13.09
Say v MIMA (2006) 91 ALD 212: 17.03
SBAQ v MIMIA [2002] FCA 985: 18.134
SBBR v MIMIA [2002] FCA 842: 13.35
SCAL v MIMIA [2003] FCA 548: 13.118
SCAL v MIMIA [2003] FCAFC 301: 13.118-13.119
SCAM v MIMIA (1997) 191 CLR 559: 13.29
SCAS v MIMA [2002] FCA 598: 18.134
Scargill v MIMIA (2003) 129 FCR 259: 8.49, 8.54
Schlieske v MIEA (1987) 79 ALR 554: 16.126
Schlieske v MIEA (1988) 84 ALR 719: 16.126-16.128, 16.131-16.132
Schmidt v Secretary of State for Home Affairs [1969] 2 Ch 149: 2.35
Sciascia v MILGEA (1991) 31 FCR 364: 6.63
SDAV v MIMIA [2002] FCA 1022: 13.29
SDAV v MIMIA (2003) 199 ALR 43: 19.109
Secretary, DIMIA v Mastipour (2003) 207 ALR 83: 16.48
Seiler v MIEA (1994) 48 FCR 83: 16.115
Sellamuthu v MIMA (1999) 90 FCR 287: 18.120, 18.133
Seneca-Pinchon v MIEA, Re [1996] IRTA 6473: 15.58
Sergi and MIEA, Re (1979) 2 ALD 224: 17.62, 17.64
Sevim v MIMA (2001) 114 FCR 126: 7.45
Seyfarth v MIMIA (2005) 142 FCR 508: 17.33
Sezdirmezoglu v MIEA (1983) 51 ALR 561: 15.32

SFGB v MIMIA [2002] FCA 1389: 13.32
SGBB v MIMIA (2003) 199 ALR 364: 13.97
Shadali v MIMA [2007] FMCA 1230: 7.47
Shahid v MIMIA [2004] FCA 1412: 9.46
Shahidul and MIMA, Re [1998] AATA 331: 14.62
Shao v MIMIA [2005] FCA 478: 9.65
Shao v MIMIA (2007) 157 FCR 300: 18.67
Sharpe and MILGEA, Re [1994] AATA 87: 17.65
Shaw v MIMA (2003) 218 CLR 28: 1.19, 2.57, 2.70, 3.14, 3.19-3.22, 17.89, 20.07
Shaw v MIMIA (2005) 142 FCR 402: 17.57, 17.89
Shead v MIMA [2001] FCA 933: 10.22
Shek v MIMIA [2006] FCA 522: 11.43
Sheng v MIEA [1986] FCA 27: 16.118, 16.121
Sherzad v MIAC [2008] FCAFC 145: 8.49
Shi v Migration Agents Registration Authority (2008) 235 CLR 286: 15.40, 18.01, 19.02
Shillabeer v Hussain (2005) 220 ALR 239: 15.102
SHKB v MIMIA [2004] FCA 545: 13.76
Shrestha v MIMA (2001) 64 ALD 669: 11.33
Shrestha v MIMA [2001] FCA 1578: 15.67
Shrestha v MIAC [2008] FMCA 842: 11.20
Shrimpton v Commonwealth (1945) 69 CLR 613: 16.127
Shumilov v MIMA (2001) 65 ALD 487: 18.139
Sidhu v MRT [2004] FCAFC 341: 11.18
Silva v MILGEA, Re [1989] FCA 212: 15.25
Silveira v Australian Institute of Management (2001) 113 FCR 218: 5.73, 5.93-5.95, 5.98, 9.44
Simsek v Macphee (1982) 148 CLR 636: 4.14, 4.23, 12.18, 12.30
Sim v MILGEA [1989] FCA 8: 12.91
Simonsz v MIEA (1995) 56 FCR 492: 15.77
Singh v Commonwealth (2004) 222 CLR 322: 2.71-2.80
Singh v MIAC [2008] FMCA 587: 8.22
Singh v MIEA (1985) 9 ALN N13: 16.86
Singh v MIEA (1994) 127 ALR 383: 15.20
Singh v MIMA [1999] FCA 416: 18.127
Singh v MIMA [2000] FCA 1858: 14.17
Singh v MIMA [2006] FMCA 1163: 6.07, 15.17-15.18
Singh-Dhillon v Mahoney [1986] FCA 334: 16.87
Singh-Dhillon v MIEA (1987) 14 FCR 351: 16.87, 16.112, 16.114
Singthong v MIEA (1988) 18 FCR 486: 6.16, 19.30
Sinnathamby v MIEA (1986) 66 ALR 502: 12.88, 19.30
Sivakumar v Canada (Minister for Employment and Immigration) (CA) [1994] I FC 433: 14.63
Sivalingam v MIMA [1998] FCA 1167: 18.132
Slayman, Re [1996] IRTA 7927: 15.27
Smith v Leech Brain & Co [1962] 2 QB 405: 13.59
Smith v MIMIA [2002] FCA 306: 16.63
Smits v Roach (2006) 227 CLR 423: 18.87
SNMX v MIAC [2009] AATA 539: 2.80
Soltanyzand v MIMA [2001] FCA 1168: 18.81
Soegianto v MIMA [2001] FCA 1612: 15.67
Somaghi v MILGEA (1991) 31 FCR 100: 12.42, 13.38-13.39, 19.34
Somaghi v MILGEA [1990] FCA 463: 13.38
Sok v MIAC [2007] FMCA 1525: 7.80, 7.84
Sok v MIAC (2008) 238 CLR 251: 7.78, 7.80
Sok v MIMIA [2004] FCA 1235: 7.67

Sok v MIMIA (2005) 144 FCR 170: 7.65, 7.61, 7.67-7.68
Song Mao Li, Re [1995] IRTA 5785: 15.54
Sook Rye Son v MIMA (1999) 161 ALR 612: 18.72, 18.77-18.78
Soysa, Re [2003] MRTA 1549: 10.32
SRCCCC and MIMIA, Re [2004] AATA 315: 14.57
SRLLL and MIMIA, Re (2002) 35 AAR 523: 14.62-14.63
SRIII and MIMA, Re [2001] AATA 945: 14.62
Srokowski v MIEA (1988) 15 ALD 775: 16.113, 16.116, 16.134
Srour v MIMA (2006) 155 FCR 441: 7.20
SRYYY v MIMIA (2005) 147 FCR 1: 14.51-14.52, 14.54
STCB v MIMIA (2006) 231 ALR 556: 13.119
Strangio, Re (1994) 35 ALD 676: 6.68
STYB v MIMIA [2004] FCA 705: 13.118
STXB v MIMIA (2004) 139 FCR 1: 13.119
Su v MIAC [2007] FMCA 318: 15.57
Su v MIMIA (2005) 64 ALD 77: 8.52
Su Wen Jian v MIEA [1996] FCA 1422: 13.87
Sun v MIEA (1997) 151 ALR 505: 19.38
Sun Zhan Qui v MIEA (1997) 81 FCR 71: 18.72, 19.69
Suntharajah v MIMA [2001] FCA 1391: 14.32
Surinakova v MILGEA (1991) 33 FCR 87: 9.53, 18.117
Surya Cahyana v MIMIA [1998] FCA 390: 7.34
Susaki v MIMA [1999] FCA 196: 15.57
Susiatin v MIMA [1998] FCA 825: 18.61
SXCB v MIMIA [2005] FCA 102: 13.97
SYLB v MIMIA (2005) 87 ALD 498: 14.17
SYSB v MIMIA [2005] FCA 1259: 18.86
SZAJB v MIAC (2008) 168 FCR 410: 14.15
SZALZ v MIMIA [2004] FMCA 275: 13.59
SZAOG v MIMIA (2004) 86 ALD 15: 18.20
SZAPC v MIMIA [2005] FCA 995: 19.40
SZATV v MIAC (2007) 233 CLR 18: 14.12, 14.14-14.16, 19.93
SZAYW v MIMIA (2006) 230 CLR 486: 18.26, 18.47, 19.93
SZBEL v MIMIA (2006) 228 CLR 152: 18.45, 18.73, 18.76
SZBQJ v MIMIA [2005] FCA 143: 13.60, 13.106
SZBPQ v MIMIA [2005] FCA 568: 13.106
SZBXV v MIMA [2007] FCA 1286: 13.106
SZBYR v MIAC (2007) 235 ALR 609: 18.97, 18.100-18.101, 18.104, 19.93
SZCIJ v MIMA [2006] FCAFC 62: 18.96
SZCRP v MIMA (2005) 149 FCR 36: 18.94
SZDFZ v MIAC (2008) 168 FCR 1: 18.76
SZDPY v MIMA [2006] FCA 627: 18.104
SZDTM v MIAC [2008] FCA 1258: 13.92, 18.76
SZEAM v MIMIA [2005] FMCA 1367: 13.07
SZEEU v MIMA (2006) 150 FCR 214: 18.97, 18.100, 19.96, 19.108
SZEGA v MIMIA [2006] FCA 1286: 13.85
SZEJF v MIMIA [2006] FCA 724: 18.76
SZEWL v MIMIA [2006] FCA 968: 19.108
SZFDE v MIAC (2007) 232 CLR 189: 5.105, 15.57, 18.87-18.88
SZFDZ v MIMA (2006) 155 FCR 482: 19.99
SZFEH v MIMIA [2005] FMCA 963: 18.120

SZFJQ v MIMIA [2006] FMCA 671: 13.06
SZEPZ v MIMA (2006) 159 FCR 291: 18.82
SZFIG v MIMIA [2006] FCA 1218: 14.35
SZFWB v MIAC [2007] FCA 167: 19.40
SZFZN v MIAC [2006] FMCA 1153: 13.76
SZGKB v MIMIA [2005] FMCA 1544: 14.35
SZGGT v MIMIA [2006] FCA 435: 18.104
SZGSI v MIAC (2007) 160 FCR 506: 18.100, 18.103
SZGYT v MIAC [2007] FMCA 883: 13.44
SZHWY v MIAC (2007) 159 FCR 1: 5.109
SZIAI v MIAC (2008) 104 ALD 22: 13.24, 18.127-18.129
SZIBW v MIAC [2008] FCA 160: 18.82
SZIBW v MIAC [2009] HCATrans 73: 18.82
SZIBW v MIAC and RRT [2007] FMCA 1660: 18.82
SZILQ v MIAC (2007) 163 FCR 304: 18.76
SZIIF v MIAC (2008) 102 ALD 366: 19.63
SZIOZ v MIAC [2007] FCA 1870: 18.76
SZITH v MIAC (2008) 105 ALD 541: 18.76
SZITR v MIMA (2006) 44 AAR 382: 14.51
SZJBA v MIAC (2007) 164 FCR 14: 18.127, 18.129
SZJBD v MIAC (2009) 179 FCR 109: 18.81, 18.83
SZJLE v MIMA [2007] FMCA 970: 19.74
SZJQP v MIAC (2007) 98 ALD 575: 19.98
SZJSP v MIAC [2007] FCA 1925: 19.14
SZJTQ v MIAC (2008) 172 FCR 563: 13.106
SZJZE v MIAC [2007] FCA 1653: 18.77
SZJZN v MIAC (2008) 169 FCR 1: 13.44
SZJYA v MIAC (No 2) (2008) 102 ALD 598: 18.76
SZKKC v MIAC [2009] FCA 362: 18.66
SZKCQ v MIAC (2008) 170 FCR 236: 18.100
SZKJU v MIAC [2008] FCA 802: 18.132
SZKLX v MIAC [2007] FCA 1414: 18.81
SZKHD v MIAC [2008] FCA 112: 13.41
SZKOZ v MIAC [2007] FCA 1798: 13.41, 13.44
SZKSU v MIAC [2008] FCA 610: 18.132
SZKTI v MIAC (2008) 168 FCR 256: 18.100
SZKTQ v MIAC [2008] FMCA 91: 5.110
SZKUV v MIAC [2008] FMCA 326: 13.54
SZLGS v MIAC [2008] FMCA 253: 13.119
SZLIQ v MIAC [2008] FCA 1405: 18.105
SZMCD v MIAC (2009) 174 FCR 415: 14.16
SZMKY v MIAC (2008) 105 ALD 493: 13.106
SZMNF v MIAC [2008] FMCA 983: 8.11
SZNKV v MIAC [2010] FCA 56: 19.41
SZNIM v MIAC [2009] FMCA 790: 14.16
SZOFE v MIAC (2010) 185 FCR 129: 18.68
SZOBI v MIAC (No 2) [2010] FCAFC 151: 18.68-18.69
SZJRU v MIAC (2009) 108 ALD 515: 13.106
Tabet v MIMA [1997] FCA 547: 18.61
Tagle v MIEA (1983) 67 FLR 164: 16.86
Tamani and DILGEA, Re [1993] AATA 60: 17.65
Tan v MIAC [2007] FCA 1427: 15.53
Tan v MIAC (2007) 211 FLR 118: 16.41
Tang and Director-General of Social Services, Re [1981] AATA 42: 7.39
Tang Jia Xin v Bolkus [1996] FCA 1379: 16.25
Tang Jia Xin v MIEA (1993) 47 FCR 176: 16.25
Tang v MIEA (1986) 67 ALR 177: 7.14
Tang v MIMA [2006] FMCA 60: 7.47, 7.74, 7.83
Taiem v MIMA (2002) 186 ALR 361: 13.09
Tapel v MIAC [2008] FCA 857: 17.79

Tarasovski v MILGEA (1993) 45 FCR 570: 15.20, 15.27
Tat v MILGEA [1990] FCA 228: 12.91
Taubale v MIMA [2006] FMCA 387: 11.77
Taveli v MIEA (1990) 23 FCR 162: 15.32
Tcherchian and MIEA, Re (1978) 1 ALN N20: 17.64
Tennakoon v MIMA [2001] FCA 615: 16.69
Tenenboim and MIEA, Re (1980) 2 ALN 1036: 17.64
Teo v MIEA (1995) 57 FCR 194: 15.82
Thain and MILGEA, Re (1989) 21 ALD 215: 17.66, 17.76
Thain Re (unreported, AAT, DP Forgie, 1988): 17.76
Thalary v MIEA [1997] FCA 201: 13.55, 13.93
Tharmalingam v MIMA [1999] FCA 1180: 14.26
Thompson v MIAC [2009] FMCA 1043: 8.11
Thomson, Re [1995] IRTA 5348: 7.63
Thevendram v MIMA [1999] FCA 182: 18.132, 18.140
Theunissen v MIMIA (2005) 88 ALD 97: 7.61
Tian v MIAC (2008) 174 FCR 1: 9.70
Tian v MIMIA [2004] FCAFC 238: 11.45
Tickner v Bropho (1993) 40 FCR 183: 18.128
Tide Sequence Industries Pty Ltd v MIMIA (2005) 145 FCR 155: 10.26
Tikoisuva v MIMA [2001] FCA 1347: 11.89
Tin v MIMA [2000] FCA 1109: 18.101
Tirtabudi v MIAC (2008) 101 ALD 103: 17.78
Tjandra v MIMA (1996) 67 FCR 577: 15.74
Tuncok v MIMIA [2004] FCAFC 172: 17.79
Tobasi v MIMA (2002) 122 FCR 322: 18.76-18.77, 18.80-18.81
Todea, Re (1994) 2 AAR 470: 17.98
Toia v MIAC (2009) 177 FCR 125: 15.75
Tolibao-Cortes [2001] FCA 1193: 7.51
Tooheys Ltd v Minister for Business and Consumer Affairs (1981) 36 ALR 64: 19.61
Total Eye Care Australia v MIMA [2007] FMCA 281: 10.22-10.23
Toy v Musgrove (1888) 14 VLR 349: 2.24, 2.25, 4.33
Tran v MIMA [2003] FCA 44: 7.46
Tran v MIMA [2002] FCA 1522: 18.101
Tran, Van Hiep, Re [2001] MRTA 932: 8.10
Tran Viet Cuong, Re [1995] IRTA 4968: 8.08
Trobridge v Hardy (1955) 94 CLR 147: 16.109
Trujillo v MIMA [2001] FCA 1452: 13.57
Truth About Motorways Pty Ltd v Macquarie Infrastructure Investment Management Limited (2000) 200 CLR 591: 4.44
Turner v MIEA (1981) 55 FLR 180: 16.86
Tutugri v MIMA (1999) 95 FCR 592: 16.67
Uddin v MIMIA [2005] FMCA 841: 11.43, 18.67
Uma Chand v MIEA [1997] FCA 1198: 13.84
United States v Wong Kim Ark, 169 US 649 (1898): 2.77
Usman v MIMA [2005] FMCA 966: 8.35
Utter v Cameron [1974] 2 NSWLR 50: 16.128, 16.130
Uyanik and MILGEA, Re (1989) 10 AAR 38: 17.66
V v MIMA (1999) 92 FCR 355: 13.120
V05/01163 [2005] MRTA 750: 11.18

TABLE OF CASES

V05/05518 [2007] MRTA 499: 8.13
V95/03527 [1996] RRTA 246: 13.115
V97/06531 [1997] RRTA 2775: 13.122
V97/06042 [1997] RRTA 2528: 13.122
V346 of 2000 v MIMA (2001) 111 FCR 536: 18.101
Vabaza v MIMA [1997] FCA 148: 17.98
Vadarlis v MIMA M93/2001 [2001] HCATrans 563: 3.54
VAF v MIMIA (2004) 206 ALR 471: 18.101
Vaitaiki v MIEA (1998) 150 ALR 608: 17.96
Van Son v MIMIA [2003] FCA 875: 17.96
VAS v MIMA [2002] FCAFC 350: 19.40
VAZ v MIMA [2001] FCA 1805: 16.70
Vazquez v MIEA (unreported, FCA, Davies J, 18 December 1990): 16.113, 16.116, 16.134
Vazquez and MILGEA, Re (1989) 20 ALD 33: 17.65
VBAS v MIMIA (2005) 141 FCR 435: 13.48
VBOA v MIMIA (2006) 233 CLR 1: 13.48, 13.54
VCAD v MIMIA [2004] FCA 1005: 13.92
VCCL v MIMIA (2001) 110 FCR 452: 4.39
VEAL v MIMA (2005) 225 CLR 88: 18.107-18.109, 19.93
Velasco and MIMA, Re (1997) 44 ALD 655: 17.69
Videto v MIEA (1985) 8 FCR 167: 16.89, 19.33
Victoria v Commonwealth and Hayden (1975) 134 CLR 338: 3.58
Victorian Council for Civil Liberties v MIMA (2001) 110 FCR 452: 3.57, 4.36-4.37, 4.39-4.40, 4.44-4.45, 19.09
Voitenko v MIMA (1998) 92 FCR 355: 13.119
von Kraft v MIAC [2007] FCA 917: 15.20
VQAD v MIMIA [2003] FMCA 481: 13.58
VSAI v MIMIA [2004] FCA 1602: 13.58
VTAO v MIMIA (2004) 81 ALD 332: 13.106
Vu v MIMIA [2005] FCA 1836: 7.40, 7.42
VWEX v MIMIA [2004] FCA 460: 16.70
VWYJ v MIMIA [2006] FCAFC 1: 14.51
W, Re [1995] IRTA 6159: 15.87
W04/01311 [2005] MRTA 547: 7.30
W04/07318 [2006] MRTA 82: 9.74
W148/00A v MIMA (2001) 185 ALR 703: 13.23
W244/01A v MIMA [2002] FCA 52: 13.91
W250/01A v MIMA [2002] FCA 400: 13.58
W284 v MIMA [2001] FCA 1788: 18.76, 18.79-18.80
W352 v MIMA [2002] FCA 398: 13.32
W97/164 and MIMA, Re (1998) 51 ALD 432: 14.51
WABR v MIMA (2002) 121 FCR 196: 13.115
WABZ v MIMIA (2004) 134 FCR 271: 18.86
WACB v MIMIA (2004) 210 ALR 190: 18.63
WACB v MIMIA (2002) 122 FCR 469: 18.65
WACO v MIMIA (2003) 131 FCR 511: 18.81
WAEF v MIMIA [2002] FCA 1121: 13.35
WAFV v RRT (2003) 125 FCR 351: 13.35
'WAG' and MIMA, Re (1996) 44 ALD 663: 17.98
WAGH v MIMIA (2003) 131 FCR 269: 14.31
WAGJ v MIMIA [2002] FCAFC 277: 18.127
WAHK v MIMIA (2004) 81 ALD 322: 14.44
WAKN v MIMIA (2004) 138 FCR 579: 14.50-14.52
WAJS v MIMA [2004] FCAFC 139: 19.40
Walton v Ruddock (2001) 115 FCR 342: 6.20, 11.77, 15.35-15.36
Walsh v MIMA (2001) 116 FCR 524: 2.67-2.68, 2.70

Walsh, Ex parte; In re Yates (1925) 37 CLR 36: 2.35, 3.10, 4.77, 6.72
Walsh and MIMA [2001] AATA 378: 2.67
Wang v MIMA (2001) 105 FCR 548: 13.63, 13.90
Wang v MIMA (2005) 145 FCR 340: 9.43
Wang v MIMA [2002] FCA 167: 18.53
Waniewska v MIEA (1986) 70 ALR 284: 15.32
WAR and MIMA, Re [2001] AATA 475: 14.62
Warnakulasuriya v R [2009] WASC 257: 15.102
WAT and MIMIA, Re [2002] AATA 1150: 14.62
Water Conservation and Irrigation Commission (NSW) v Browning (1947) 74 CLR 492: 16.127
Waters v Commonwealth (1951) 82 CLR 188: 4.44
Waterside Workers' Federation of Australia v Gilchrist, Watt and Sanderson Ltd (1924) 34 CLR 482: 19.78
Watsana Singthong v MIEA, Re [1988] FCA 115: 11.69
WBA and MIMIA, Re [2003] AATA 1250: 14.62
Weerasinghe v MIMIA [2004] FCA 261: 11.45, 15.70
Weheliye v MIMA [2001] FCA 1222: 13.63
Weir v MIAC (2008) 104 ALD 67: 15.08
Weir and MIEA, Re (1988) 33 AALB [1226]: 17.65
Wen Zhou Xie [2005] MRTA 140: 9.71
White v Repatriation Commission (2001) 114 FCR 494: 11.89
Wiggan and MIEA, Re (1987) 12 ALD 226: 17.59, 17.65, 17.81, 17.83
Williams and MIMA, Re [2007] AATA 1012: 17.31
Williamson v Ah On (1926) 39 CLR 95: 2.45, 2.55
Wing-Yuen Sui v MIEA (1996) 47 ALD 528: 17.60
Wolseley v MIMA [2006] FMCA 1149: 9.76
Woo v MIMIA [2002] FCA 1596: 7.42
Woods v MARA [2004] FCA 1622: 5.104
Woolley, re; Ex parte Applicants M276/2003 (2004) 225 CLR 1: 3.48, 3.52, 4.14, 4.26, 16.111, 16.113, 20.06
WorkCover Corporation (San Remo Macaroni Co Pty Ltd) v Da Ping (1994) 175 LSJS 469: 15.98
Woudneh v MILGEA [1988] FCA 318: 13.94
Wu Shan Liang v MIEA (1996) 185 CLR 259: 12.20
X v MIMIA [2005] FCA 429: 6.48
X v MIMA (2002) 67 ALD 355: 18.118
Xia and MIAC, Re [2007] AATA 1803: 17.31
Xiang v MIMIA (2004) 81 ALD 301: 8.65
Xie v MIMA (2000) 61 ALD 641: 8.10-8.11
Xin v MIMA [2006] FMCA 1925: 9.99
Xu v MIAC [2007] FMCA 285: 11.89
Yao-Jing Li v MIMA (1997) 74 FCR 275: 13.19
Yap, Re [1993] IRTA 1863: 8.57
Yong v MIMA (2000) 62 ALD 687: 11.18
Yong Khim Teoh v MIMA [1996] FCA 572: 15.74
Youssef v MIEA (1987) 14 ALD 550: 15.32
Yu v MIAC (2007) 209 FLR 470: 9.101
Yu v MIMIA [2002] FCA 912: 18.62-18.63
Yuen v MILGEA (1991) 24 ALD 713: 6.63
Z v MIMA (1998) 90 FCR 51: 18.120
Zadvydas v Davis 533 US 678 (2001): 4.28
Zaouk v MIMA (2007) 159 FCR 152: 7.75
Zan v MIMA [2001] FCA 473: 18.139
Zeng v MIMIA [2005] FMCA 546: 8.46
Zeng v MIAC [2007] FMCA 169: 8.45
Zhan v MIMIA (2003) 128 FCR 469: 18.67, 18.68

Zhang v MIMIA [2005] FCAFC 30: 7.40
Zhang v MIMA [2007] FMCA 664: 9.75
Zhang v MIAC (2007) 161 FCR 419: 18.67, 19.97
Zhang v MIAC [2008] HCATrans 79: 18.67
Zhang de Yong v MILGEA (1993) 45 FCR 384; on appeal (1994) 121 ALR 83: 18.25, 18.94
Zhang Jia Qing v MIMA [1997] FCA 1177: 15.38
Zhaou v MIMIA [2002] FCA 748: 15.37-15.38
Zhong v MIAC (2008) 171 FCR 444: 15.20
Znaty v MIEA (1972) 126 CLR 1: 2.35, 16.128, 16.130-16.131
Zubair v MIMIA (2004) 139 FCR 344: 10.38, 15.39-15.40, 18.53

UN Human Rights Committee
A v Australia, Communication No 560/1993: Australia, CCPR/C/59/D/560/1993 (30 April 1997): 3.46, 4.47, 4.70, 4.71, 4.72, 16.57
A K v Australia, Communication No 148/1999: Australia, CAT/C/32/D/148/1999 (11 May 2004): 4.70
Ali Aqsar Bakhtiyari and Roqaiha Bakhtiyari v Australia, Communication No 1069/2002: Australia, CCPR/C/79/D/1069/2002 (6 November 2003): 4.70, 4.74
Applicants D and E v Australia, Communication No 1050/2002: Australia CCPR/C/87/D/1050/2002 (9 August 2006): 4.70
Baban v Australia, Communication No 1014/2001: Australia, CCPR/C/78/D/1014/2001 (18 September 2003): 4.70
C v Australia, Communication No 900/1999: Australia, CCPR/C/76/D/900/1999 (13 November 2002): 4.70
Danyal Shafiq v Australia, Communication No 1324/2004: Australia, CCPR/C/88/D/1324/2004 (13 November 2006): 4.70
Madafferi v Australia, Communication No 1011/2001: Australia, CCPR/C/81/D/1011/2001 (26 August 2004): 4.70
Sadiq Shek Elmi v Australia, Communication No 120/1998: Australia. CAT/C/22/D/120/1998 (25 May 1999): 4.70, 4.74, 14.68
Winata v Australia, Communication No 930/2000: Australia, CCPR/C/72/D/930/2000 (16 August 2001): 4.70
Y v Australia, Communication No 772/1997: Australia, CCPR/C/69/D/772/1997 (8 August 2000): 4.70

International Court of Justice
Nationality Decrees Issued in Tunis and Morocco (Advisory Opinion) (1923) Permanent Court of International Justice 6, Series B, No 4, 24: 2.77

Table of Statutes

Constitution: 17.01
　s 42: 2.51
　s 44: 2.04
　s 51: 2.26, 3.02-3.03, 3.30, 20.07
　s 51(6): 2.26, 2.46, 3.08
　s 51(9): 2.26
　s 51(16): 2.81
　s 51(19): 1.21, 2.04, 2.26, 2.35, 2.46, 2.67, 2.71, 2.73, 2.75, 2.82, 3.08, 3.12-3.13, 3.19, 3.42, 16.23, 17.13
　s 51(20): 20.07
　s 51(26): 2.26, 20.07
　s 51(27): 1.21, 2.04, 2.26, 2.35, 2.45-2.46, 2.75, 3.09-3.10, 3.19, 17.13
　s 51(29): 2.04, 2.26, 3.08, 3.19, 4.08, 20.07
　s 51(30): 2.26
　s 61: 3.03, 3.55-3.57, 3.64, 3.66, 4.23, 6.03
　s 71: 3.03, 3.31, 3.42
　s 73: 3.03, 19.80
　s 75: 3.03, 3.31, 3.34
　s 75(i): 3.31
　s 75(ii): 3.31
　s 75(iii): 3.31, 19.102
　s 75(iv): 3.31
　s 75(v): 3.31, 3.34, 3.64, 3.66, 4.67, 18.137, 19.01, 19.08, 19.11, 19.57, 19.66, 19.71, 19.73, 19.80, 19.102
　s 76: 3.31, 3.34
　s 77: 3.31, 3.34
　s 116: 3.02
　s 117: 2.04, 3.18
　Ch III: 3.03, 3.06, 3.30, 3.40, 16.21, 17.79, 19.66

Commonwealth
Acts Interpretation Acts 1901: 2.60, 6.68, 20.33
　s 15AB: 4.12
Administrative Appeals Tribunal Act 1975: 18.03, 19.97
　s 28: 17.42, 18.07
　s 37: 17.42, 18.07
　s 43(1)(c)(ii): 17.20
　s 44: 17.81, 18.03, 19.97
　s 66E: 17.20
　Sch cl 2: 17.20
Administrative Decisions (Effect on International Instruments) Bill 1995: 4.25
　s 4: 4.22
Administrative Decisions (Judicial Review) Act 1977: 3.32, 5.19, 5.25, 5.49, 5.73, 5.93, 5.96, 5.103, 9.44, 12.85, 16.86, 19.01, 19.16-19.17, 19.24, 19.57, 19.63-19.64, 20.08, 20.33
　s 3(3): 5.93
　s 3(4): 19.60
　s 5: 5.25
　s 5(1)(e): 13.10
　s 5(2)(g): 13.10
　s 5(3): 19.59
　s 6: 5.25
　s 6(1)(c): 13.10
　s 6(2)(g): 13.10
　s 7: 5.25
　s 13: 12.30, 12.85, 19.62, 18.106
　s 13A: 18.106
　s 14: 18.106
　s 15: 16.101-16.102, 16.104
　s 18: 5.25
　Sch 2: 19.62
Aliens Deportation Act 1948: 17.09, 17.11
Anti-People Smuggling and Other Measures Act 2010: 15.94, 15.96
Australian Citizenship Act 1948: 2.56-2.57, 2.59-2.60, 2.65-2.66, 2.70-2.71, 3.16, 15.28
　ss 5-9: 17.10, 17.13
　s 7: 2.59
　ss 10-15: 6.02
　s 10C(4)(c)(i): 2.67, 2.79
　s 12: 2.66
　ss 14-14A: 3.11
　s 14A: 3.12
　s 21: 15.28
　s 25: 2.65
　Pt III: 6.02
Australian Citizenship Act 2007: 2.65, 2.70, 2.80, 8.41
　s 10(2)(b): 2.79
　s 12(1)(a)-(b): 2.66
　s 15: 2.65
　s 21(5): 2.80
　s 21(7): 2.70
　s 34: 15.28, 15.100
　s 36(2)(b): 2.66
　Div 2, Pt 2C: 2.65
Australian Citizenship Amendment Act 1984: 2.59, 2.65, 17.13
　s 7: 3.11
　s 12: 3.11
Australian Citizenship Amendment (Citizenship Test Review and Other Measures) Act 2009: 2.80
Australian Federal Police Act 1979: 18.31
Australian Human Rights Commission Act 1986 (*formerly* Human Rights and Equal Opportunities Commission Act 1986): 18.42
　s 5: 18.31
　s 11(1)(f): 18.41
　s 20(1): 18.41
　s 20(5): 18.41
　s 20(6)(b): 16.42, 18.42
　ss 21-23: 18.41
　s 47: 4.09, 4.16
　s 51(1)(f): 18.41

Border Protection Act 1999 (Cth): 6.02
Border Protection Legislation Amendment Act 1999
   s 3: 14.19, 16.42
   Sch 1, item 65: 14.19
   Sch 1, Pt 3: 16.42
Border Protection Legislation Amendment Bill 1999: 14.29
Border Protection (Validation and Enforcement Powers) Act 2001: 6.03, 12.06, 12.48, 16.04, 15.94
Commonwealth Franchise Act 1902: 2.51
Complaints (Australian Federal Police) Act 1981: 18.31
Contract Immigrants Act 1905: 2.23, 2.36, 9.12-9.13
Crimes Act 1914: 18.09
   s 19B: 15.95
   s 23C: 17.36
   s 29: 15.104
   s 86: 15.101
Criminal Code: 14.73
   Div 73: 15.95
   Div 270: 16.74
   Div 271: 16.74
   s 5.4: 15.96
   s 5.6(2): 15.96
   s 6.2: 15.93
   s 73.3A: 15.96
   s 147.1(1): 15.104
Criminal Code Amendment (Trafficking in Persons Offences) Act 2005: 16.74
Education Services for Overseas Students Act 2000: 11.57-11.59, 11.63
   s 20: 11.37, 15.43
   s 28: 11.58
   Div 2: 11.59
   Pt 4: 11.58
   Pt 6, Div 2, ss 97-103: 11.57
Education Services for Overseas Students Amendment (Re-registration of Providers and Other Measures) Act 2010: 11.66
Education Services for Overseas Students (Registration of Providers and Financial Regulation) Act 1991: 11.11, 11.56
   s 20: 11.37-11.39, 11.41, 11.43, 11.47, 11.49
Extradition Act 1988: 14.61
Family Law Act 1975: 7.66, 8.27
   s 70B: 8.28
   s 114: 7.68
Federal Court of Australia Act 1976: 16.97, 19.01, 19.16
   s 20: 16.98
   s 23: 16.98, 16.100-16.101, 16.107-16.109, 19.63
   s 25(1AA): 19.97
Freedom of Information Act 1982: 5.19
   s 9: 5.19
   s 11: 5.19
   s 18: 5.19
High Court Rules 2004
   r 25.14: 19.09
Human Rights Commission Act 1981: 4.16
Human Rights (Parliamentary Scrutiny) Bill 2010: 20.35

Immigration Act 1901: 2.27-2.29, 2.36, 2.38-2.39, 2.41, 17.10
   s 3: 2.42, 2.50
   s 3(a): 2.27, 2.31, 2.43
   s 3(b): 2.27
   s 3(c): 2.27
   s 3(d): 2.27
   s 3(f): 2.27
   s 3(g): 2.27
   s 3A: 2.45
   s 4: 2.35
   s 5(1): 2.31
   s 5(2): 2.31
   s 5(3): 2.45
   s 7: 2.31
   s 8: 2.31
   s 8A: 2.35
   s 8AA: 2.35
Immigration Legislation Amendment (Procedural Fairness) Act 2002: 18.96
Immigration Restriction Act 1901: 2.26-2.27, 5.30
   s 3: 17.01
   s 8: 17.01, 17.05
Judiciary Act 1903: 3.31, 19.01, 19.57
   s 39B: 16.110
   s 44(4): 19.99
Jurisdiction of the Federal Magistrates Service Legislation Amendment Act 2001
   s 3: 16.97
   Sch 3: 16.97
Marriage Act 1961: 7.29
   s 11: 7.29
   s 12: 7.29
   s 88E: 7.29
   Pt VA: 7.29
Migration Act 1958 – 1973
   s 5(1): 17.10
Migration Act 1958 – 1 May 1987
   ss 14-14A: 3.11
   s 16: 15.23
Migration Act 1958 – 19 December 1989
   s 6A(1)(b): 7.21, 8.01
   s 6A(1)(c): 12.19, 12.23, 12.85, 12.87
   s 6A(1)(e): 7.21, 8.01, 8.05, 12.23, 12.32, 12.77, 12.89-12.92, 14.67, 19.46-19.48
   s 6(2): 5.30-5.31
   s 6B: 5.31
   s 7: 5.31
   s 7(4): 15.74, 16.81, 17.10
   s 8: 2.23, 6.06, 9.12
   s 12. 2.35, 3.11, 7.29, 16.81, 17.10, 17.14,
   ss 12-13: 17.14, 17.56, 17.62
   ss 12-14: 5.31
   s 12(c): 17.14
   s 12(b)(ii): 17.14
   s 13: 2.35, 3.11, 15.03, 16.81, 16.106, 17.10
   ss 13-14: 2.35
   s 14: 5.37, 6.08, 15.03, 17.11, 17.14
   s 14A: 17.14, 17.83
   s 15: 15.03, 15.05, 17.16
   s 18: 2.35, 4.16, 4.31, 5.108, 16.32, 16.82-16.83, 16.86, 16.88, 16.94
   s 22: 16.120

TABLE OF STATUTES

Migration Act 1958 – 1 September 1994
  s 13: 15.77, 16.92
  s 20: 15.18, 15.25-15.26, 15.74
  s 20(10): 15.24
  s 20(11): 15.24
  s 20(12): 15.24
  s 20(15): 15.24
  s 21A: 16.76
  s 21B: 16.76
  s 21C: 16.76
  s 22A: 16.32
  s 35(1): 15.29, 15.32
  s 47(1)(f): 12.78
  s 47(1)(g): 12.78
  s 54R: 3.41, 3.43, 16.23, 16.57
  s 54RA: 16.24
  s 59: 16.83, 16.92
  s 60: 16.83
  s 70: 16.122
  s 77: 15.03
  s 88: 16.28
  s 89: 3.41, 16.29
  ss 88-89A: 16.15
  s 63: 16.112
  s 92: 16.30
  s 93: 16.30
  s 115: 12.39, 18.23
  s 117A: 12.78
  s 118: 18.16
  s 120: 5.36
  s 208: 16.76
  s 209: 16.76

Migration Act 1958 (current)
  s 4AA: 16.17, 20.21
  s 5: 12.13, 15.12, 16.07, 18.106
  s 5(9): 12.74
  s 5CB: 7.35, 7.50, 7.87
  s 5CB(1): 7.33
  s 5CB(2)(b): 7.38
  s 5CB(2)(d): 7.33, 7.35
  s 5D: 5.30
  s 5F: 7.50, 7.87
  s 5F(2): 7.36, 7.38
  s 7A: 3.59, 6.03, 16.04, 20.05
  s 10: 17.14
  s 11: 6.19
  s 11A: 6.19
  ss 29-43: 5.33
  ss 31-38: 5.36
  s 31: 5.41
  ss 32-37: 5.48
  ss 32-34: 6.07
  s 32: 5.35
  s 33: 15.02, 19.96
  s 33(2): 14.49-14.50
  s 34: 5.44, 15.02, 15.74-15.75
  s 36: 4.44, 12.24, 13.02, 14.19, 14.22, 14.29
  s 36(2): 12.19, 14.28, 14.45, 19.70
  s 36(2)(a): 14.19, 14.40
  s 36(2)(aa): 14.64
  s 36(3)-(5): 14.19, 14.30
  s 363(3): 14.31-14.35
  s 36(4): 14.19
  s 36(5): 14.19

  s 36A: 3.41, 12.24
  s 36A(8): 12.24
  s 39: 8.03, 9.27
  s 46: 5.41
  s 46A: 3.64, 3.66, 5.41, 12.13, 12.67, 16.06-16.07, 19.102
  s 46A(1): 12.67, 16.06
  s 46A(2): 3.64-3.65, 12.67
  s 46B: 5.41, 16.07
  s 47(3): 5.33
  s 48: 5.36, 5.41, 8.03, 8.40, 12.40, 15.50
  s 48A: 5.36, 12.40, 15.08
  s 48B: 12.40, 15.08, 15.51, 19.54, 19.54
  s 48B(6): 19.54
  s 49: 15.50
  s 51A: 19.96
  s 53(3): 18.60-18.61
  ss 54A-54H: 18.23
  ss 55: 17.14
  s 55A: 17.14
  s 57: 18.95, 18.106
  s 60: 6.24
  s 65: 5.41, 19.70
  s 65(1): 18.113
  s 66: 18.59, 18.61
  s 66(2): 18.59, 18.61
  s 66(3): 18.59, 18.61
  s 66(4): 18.61
  s 72: 16.18
  s 73: 6.19
  s 82(7): 15.03, 15.05
  ss 84-91: 8.03
  ss 85-91: 7.05
  s 87(1)-(2): 8.03
  s 89: 18.23
  ss 91A-91W: 15.08
  s 91E: 5.41
  ss 91F-91G: 14.08
  s 91K: 5.41
  ss 91M-91Q: 13.08
  ss 91N-91Q: 14.31
  s 91N: 13.08, 14.36
  s 91N(3): 14.31, 14.36
  s 91P: 14.36
  s 91R: 13.48-13.49, 13.56, 13.58, 13.76
  s 91R(1)(c): 13.58
  s 91R(2): 13.48
  s 91R(3): 13.40-13.43
  s 91S: 13.119
  s 91T: 14.61
  s 91V(4): 12.64
  s 91V(5): 12.64
  s 91V(6): 12.64
  ss 92-96: 5.47, 9.28
  s 93: 9.28
  s 96: 9.20
  s 97: 15.05
  s 97A: 15.19
  ss 97-104: 15.12
  ss 99-100: 15.13
  ss 101-105: 15.13
  s 101: 6.09
  s 101(b): 6.19, 15.14-15.15
  s 102: 6.09, 15.24

Migration Act 1958 (Cth) (cont)
　s 104: 15.26
　s 105: 15.24
　ss 107-109: 15.14
　s 107: 15.13, 15.19, 15.21
　s 109: 6.09, 6.24, 15.05, 15.12, 15.18-15.20, 15.22, 15.25, 15.30, 15.34, 17.31
　s 111: 6.09, 15.13
　s 114: 6.10
　ss 116-118: 10.38
　s 116: 6.12, 6.17, 6.20, 6.24, 6.75, 11.42-11.44, 15.05, 15.11, 15.30, 15.34-15.35, 18.16
　s 116(1): 6.19
　s 116(1)(b): 11.39, 15.97
　s 116(1)(d): 6.19, 15.14, 15.16
　s 116(1)(fa): 11.31, 11.33
　s 116(1)(fa)(i): 11.33
　s 116(g): 15.35
　s 116(3): 11.34, 15.11
　s 117: 15.10, 15.30
　s 118A: 15.34
　ss 118A-127: 15.34
　ss 119-127: 15.30
　s 119: 15.37, 15.39-15.40, 18.106
　s 119(1)(a): 6.16
　s 119(1)(b): 15.37
　s 120: 6.16, 6.21, 15.35-15.35, 18.106
　s 121: 6.21, 15.35-15.37
　s 121(3)(b): 15.37
　s 123(2): 18.16
　s 127: 18.62
　s 128: 15.05, 15.11
　s 129: 18.16, 18.106
　s 134: 15.22, 18.54
　ss 134-137: 15.41
　s 134(3): 15.42
　s 134(10): 9.88
　ss 137J-137P: 15.43
　s 137J: 11.37, 11.43
　s 137J(2): 11.38
　s 137K: 11.37
　s 137P: 11.37
　s 140: 6.31, 15.05
　ss 140A-140ZH: 10.25
　s 140H: 10.25
　s 140L: 9.64, 10.39
　s 140Q: 10.40
　s 142: 16.76
　s 147: 17.37
　ss 147-148: 16.94
　s 153: 16.94
　s 161: 5.41
　s 164D: 5.41
　s 166: 6.01
　s 172(4): 15.05
　s 173: 15.05
　s 177: 16.21
　ss 177-178: 4.72
　s 180: 17.20
　s 180A: 17.18-17.19, 17.21, 17.23, 17.25, 17.51
　s 182: 16.21
　s 183: 3.41, 3.43, 4.72, 16.21, 16.57
　s 184: 16.24
　ss 189-199: 16.01

s 189: 3.50, 4.44, 15.03, 16.01, 16.10, 16.36, 16.58, 17.23, 19.103
s 189(1): 16.09, 16.33
s 189(2): 16.09, 16.33
ss 189-190: 6.08
s 192: 16.11
s 192(7): 16.11
ss 193-196: 16.14
ss 193-195: 16.41
s 193(3): 16.42, 18.42
s 194A: 16.37
s 195: 5.41, 15.47, 15.52-15.53
s 195A: 3.66, 12.13, 12.67, 12.79, 16.75
s 195A(2): 3.64
s 196: 3.50, 16.109
s 196(3): 16.107, 16.109
s 197A: 15.102-15.103
ss 197AA-197AG: 16.17
s 197B: 15.104
s 198: 3.51, 5.37, 15.03, 16.84, 16.96, 17.23
s 198(6): 16.137
s 198(3): 16.84
s 198(2A): 16.84
s 198A: 12.55, 12.67, 16.06
s 198B: 12.55
s 198C: 12.55
s 198D(3)(c): 4.59
s 200: 17.01, 17.14-17.15, 17.20, 17.23-17.24, 17.47-17.48, 17.50-17.51, 17.54, 17.61, 17.63, 17.66, 17.79, 18.05, 18.07, 18.09, 18.53
ss 200-204: 3.11
ss 200-205: 6.77
s 201: 17.14-17.15, 17.48, 17.52, 17.88
s 201(b)(i): 17.14
s 202: 17.15, 18.09
s 203: 17.13, 17.15, 18.09
s 203(6): 18.09
s 203(8): 18.09
s 204: 17.83
s 206: 16.112
s 217: 16.22
s 218: 16.122-16.124
s 221: 16.76
s 229: 15.93
s 230: 15.93
s 232A: 14.57, 15.95
s 233: 15.95
s 233A: 15.95
s 233B: 15.95
s 233C: 15.95
s 233D: 15.96
s 233E: 15.95
s 234: 15.03, 15.95, 15.100, 15.105
s 234A: 15.95
s 235: 15.03, 15.97-15.98, 15.100, 15.105
s 235(3): 15.97
s 236: 15.100
s 236A: 15.95
s 236B: 15.95
ss 240-241: 7.50, 15.101
s 243: 7.51, 15.101
s 245: 15.101
s 245A: 16.05

s 245AB: 15.99
s 245AC: 15.99
ss 245F-245FA: 16.04
s 245F: 4.44, 16.05
s 245F(1): 16.04
s 245F(4): 16.05
s 245F(9): 16.10, 16.33
s 245F(12)-(15): 16.05
s 245FA: 16.05
ss 249-252A: 16.31
ss 252A-252E: 16.31
s 250: 16.09
s 251(6): 16.31
s 252: 6.09, 16.05, 16.12
ss 252A-252B: 16.05
s 253: 16.30, 16.41
s 253(1)-(3): 16.29
s 253(4)-(7): 16.29
s 256: 6.14, 6.17, 12.63, 16.14, 16.41-16.42, 18.42
ss 257-258: 16.32
ss 261A-261K: 16.31
Pt 3: 5.102
s 276: 5.99, 5.103
s 277: 5.102-5.103
s 280: 5.102
s 281: 5.102
s 290: 5.102
s 314: 5.103
s 316: 5.100
s 334: 6.09, 15.105
s 335: 15.105
s 337: 6.17, 18.13
s 338: 18.13, 18.54, 18.54
s 338(2)(d): 10.37
s 338(3): 15.22, 15.30
s 339: 18.55, 19.58
s 346: 18.15
s 347: 18.19, 19.58
s 348: 18.19
s 349: 18.15-18.16
s 349(2): 15.39
s 349(4): 5.36
s 351: 5.36, 5.86, 6.45, 8.04, 15.54
s 353: 18.50, 18.89
s 353(1): 18.19
s 353(2): 18.19
s 357A: 19.96
s 359: 18.112
s 359A: 18.97, 19.96
s 359A(4)(c): 18.106
s 359AA: 18.112
s 360: 7.81, 18.44, 18.50, 18.71
s 360(1)(a): 18.71
s 366A: 18.44
s 366A(3): 18.85
s 366B: 18.44
s 366C: 18.44
s 367: 16.59
s 368: 18.95
s 368(1): 18.135
ss 370-372: 15.105
s 375: 18.55, 18.95, 18.106
s 375A: 18.55, 18.90, 18.95, 18.106
s 376: 18.55, 18.95, 18.106

ss 377-378: 15.105
s 391: 5.36
s 395: 18.95
s 395A: 18.95, 18.101, 18.103, 18.106
s 395A(1)(b): 18.95
s 395A(1)(c): 18.95
s 395A(3): 18.95
s 395A(4): 18.110
s 395A(4)(b): 18.95
s 395A(4)(ba): 18.105
s 395A(4)(ca): 18.95
s 395A(4)(c): 18.95
s 395AA: 18.95, 18.100
s 412: 18.45
s 414: 18.45
s 415(2): 18.26
s 415(4): 5.36
s 416: 12.69
s 417: 5.36, 5.86, 8.04, 12.69, 12.79, 12.81-12.82,
   14.65-14.66, 14.68, 19.53-19.54
s 417(1): 19.53-19.54
s 417(3): 19.54
s 417(7): 19.53-19.54
s 420: 19.68-19.69, 18.89
s 420(1): 12.69
s 422B: 18.90, 18.96, 19.96
s 424: 18.95
s 424A: 18.76, 18.95, 18.98-18.99, 18.101,
   18.105-18.106, 19.96, 19.108
s 424A(1)(b): 18.95
s 424A(1)(c): 18.95
s 424A(2)(a): 18.98
s 424A(2A): 18.95
s 424A(3)(a): 18.95
s 424A(3)(b): 18.95, 18.105
s 424A(3)(ba): 18.105
s 424A(3)(c): 18.95, 18.106
s 424AA: 18.95, 18.100, 18.112
s 424B: 18.112, 18.118
s 425: 18.26, 18.44, 18.71, 18.74, 18.76, 18.86
s 425(1)(a): 18.71-18.72, 18.74-18.77, 18.79
s 426(2): 18.72
s 427: 18.44
s 427(6): 18.26
s 427(6)(a): 18.84
s 427(7): 18.26, 18.44, 18.86
s 429: 18.26, 18.47
s 430: 18.95, 18.138
s 430(1): 18.40
s 430(1)(b): 18.140
s 430(1)(c): 18.136-18.138
ss 430-430B: 18.65
s 431: 18.26
ss 432-434: 15.105
s 437: 18.95, 18.106
s 438: 18.95, 18.106
ss 439-440: 15.105
s 441A: 18.80
s 441G: 18.70
s 454: 8.04
Pt 8: 3.34-3.36, 3.39, 5.33, 5.49-5.50, 16.01, 16.13,
   16.97, 18.60, 19.01, 19.37, 19.42, 19.56, 19.59,
   19.64-19.66, 19.69, 19.71, 19.76-19.77, 19.82,
   19.105

Migration Act 1958 (Cth) (cont)
  s 474: 3.38, 19.77-19.79, 19.82, 19.85
  s 474(2): 3.37-3.38, 19.78, 19.85
  s 474(3): 3.37
  s 475: 16.96, 16.125, 19.58
  s 475(2): 19.58
  s 475(2)(e): 19.58
  s 475(4): 19.59
  s 475A: 16.110
  s 476: 3.34, 6.39, 19.59, 19.82
  s 476(1): 18.137, 19.59
  s 476(1)(a): 19.68
  s 476(1)(d): 19.59
  s 476(1)(g): 19.59
  s 476(2): 19.60
  s 476(3)(d)-(g): 19.60
  s 476(2)(b): 3.39
  s 476A: 19.97
  s 477: 19.59, 19.98
  s 477A: 18.60, 19.98
  s 478: 18.65
  s 478(1)(b): 18.61
  s 478(2): 19.58
  s 479: 19.60
  s 481: 16.97, 19.63
  s 481(2): 19.63
  s 482: 16.97, 19.65
  s 482(2): 16.100
  s 482(3): 19.65
  s 483A: 19.97
  s 485: 3.34, 19.57
  s 486: 3.34
  s 486(a): 19.82
  s 486A(1A): 19.98
  s 486B: 19.76
  s 486D: 19.99
  s 486I: 19.99
  Pt 8C: 5.92, 16.34, 16.37, 18.39
  ss 486L-486M: 18.39
  ss 486L-486Q: 16.34
  s 486N: 5.92
  s 486O: 18.39
  s 488: 15.106
  s 489: 6.08
  s 494B(4): 18.69
  s 494C(4): 18.69
  s 494C(4)(a): 18.69
  s 495D: 16.66
  s 496: 6.24, 17.26, 19.54
  s 499: 11.49, 11.74, 17.53-17.55, 17.57, 17.88
  s 499(1): 17.25
  s 499(1A): 17.25
  s 499(2): 17.55
  s 499(2A): 17.25
  s 500: 6.77, 14.53, 17.20, 17.42, 18.09, 18.54
  s 500(6A): 17.42
  s 500(6B): 17.42
  s 500(6F): 17.42, 18.106
  s 500(6I)-(6L): 17.42
  ss 500A-501J: 15.05, 15.12
  s 501: 3.15, 3.19, 6.58, 6.60, 6.62, 6.68, 6.77, 16.84, 15.22, 15.51, 15.75, 15.98, 15.103, 17.01-17.03, 17.23-17.24, 17.29, 17.31, 17.34, 17.37, 17.42, 17.45-17.46, 17.48-17.54, 17.56-17.58, 17.63, 17.70, 17.73, 17.78-17.79, 17.84, 17.88, 17.90, 17.92-17.94, 17.98-17.100, 19.39
  ss 501-503: 6.24
  ss 501-506: 17.04
  s 501(1): 17.26, 17.43, 17.57
  s 501(2): 17.43, 17.48, 17.59, 17.79
  s 501(2)(c): 17.28
  s 501(3): 17.43-17.44
  s 501(4): 17.43
  s 501(6): 17.26, 17.40
  s 501(6)(b): 17.26, 17.34, 17.37
  s 501(6)(c): 17.26, 17.28, 17.30
  s 501(7): 17.33
  s 501(7)-(10): 17.26
  s 501(8): 17.32
  s 501(11): 17.41
  s 501A: 6.58, 16.84, 15.51
  s 501A(3): 17.44
  s 501B: 6.58, 16.84, 15.51, 17.44
  s 501B(5): 17.44
  s 501C: 6.58, 17.44, 18.60, 18.106
  s 501D: 17.44
  s 501E: 5.41, 6.59, 17.47
  s 501G: 18.60, 18.106
  s 501HA: 17.49
  s 502; 6.77, 17.21, 17.77
  s 503: 17.34
  s 503A: 17.42, 17.45
  ss 503A-503D: 18.55
  ss 504-506: 5.33
  s 505: 6.24, 6.39
  Pt 2
    Div 3: 6.07
    Subdiv 3AB: 17.43
    Subdiv 3C: 17.15
    Subdiv 3F: 15.11
    Subdiv 12B: 15.101
    Div 4: 15.03, 16.10
    Div 6: 16.20
    Div 7(2): 16.17
    Div 10: 15.03,
    Div 12A: 16.04
  Pt 4A: 17.14
  Pt 4B: 3.41,16.20-16.25, 16.27, 16.57
  Pt 5
    Div 5: 18.44, 18.94
    Div 6: 18.60
    Div 7: 18.44
    Div 8A: 18.60
  Pt 7
    Div 4: 18.44, 18.70
    Div 5: 18.60, 18.94
    Div 6: 18.44
  Div 7A: 18.60, 18.70
  Pt 9: 15.91
Migration Act 1958 (date unspecified): 2.27, 2.47, 3.11, 3.15, 3.29, 3.39, 3.41, 3.57, 4.27, 4.29, 4.33, 4.45, 5.02, 5.07, 5.30, 5.58, 5.79-5.80, 5.104, 6.02, 6.04, 7.13, 8.01, 12.19, 12.24, 12.37-12.38, 12.76, 13.04, 16.02, 16.48, 16.49, 17.09, 17.13
Migration Agents Regulations 1998
  Sch 2: 5.103

Migration Amendment (Abolishing Detention Debt) Act 2009: 16.76
Migration Amendment Act 1979: 12.24
Migration Amendment Act 1992: 3.41, 16.01
Migration Amendment Act (No 1) 1999: 15.94
Migration Amendment (Complementary Protection) Bill 2009: 14.64, 20.14
Migration Amendment (Designated Unauthorised Arrivals) Bill 2006: 4.35, 4.57, 4.64, 6.04
Migration Amendment (Detention Arrangement) Act 2005
   s 3: 16.17
   Sch 1: 16.17
Migration Amendment (Excision from Migration Zone) Act 2001: 6.04, 12.06, 12.48
Migration Amendment (Excision from Migration Zone) (Consequential Provisions) Act 2001: 12.06, 14.30
Migration Amendment (Judicial Review) Bill 2004: 3.38-3.39
   cl 2: 3.38
Migration Amendment (Immigration Detention Reform) Bill 2009: 16.35
Migration Amendment Regulations (No 1) 2001: 12.06
Migration Amendment Regulations (No 2) 2000: 8.27
Migration Amendment Regulations (No 3) 2003: 8.41
Migration Amendment Regulations (No 11) 2003
   Sch 8: 14.74
Migration Amendment Regulations (No 3) 2004: 10.26
Migration Amendment Regulations (No 5) 2009: 8.41
Migration Amendment Regulations (No 5) 2001: 12.06
Migration Amendment Regulations (No 6) 2001: 12.06
Migration Amendment Regulations 2005 (No 1): 9.67
Migration Amendment Regulations 2005 (No 8): 11.42
Migration Amendment Regulations 2006 (No 2): 9.102
Migration Amendment Regulations 2008 (No 5): 16.06
   reg 3: 16.134
   Sch 1: 16.134
Migration Amendment Regulations (No 6) 2009: 1.17
Migration Amendment (Review Provisions) Act 2007: 18.105, 19.96
Migration Amendment (Sponsorship Obligations) Bill 2007: 10.13, 10.40
Migration Amendment (Visa Capping) Act 2010: 9.27
Migration (Iraq and Kuwait) (United Nations Security Council Resolution No 661) Regulations 1991: 12.83
Migration Legislation Amendment Act 1989: 6.19
   s 35: 17.14

Migration Legislation Amendment Act (Electronic Transactions and Methods of Notification) Act 2001: 18.66
Migration Legislation Amendment Act (No 1) 2008: 17.49, 18.66
Migration Legislation Amendment Act (No 2) 1994: 16.24, 17.14
Migration Legislation Amendment Act (No 4) 1997: 17.43
Migration Legislation Amendment Act (No 5) 1995: 5.24
Migration Legislation Amendment Act (No 6) 1995: 12.40
   s 6: 16.24
   s 9: 16.24
Migration Legislation Amendment (No 1) Act 1998: 15.11
Migration Legislation Amendment (No 1) Act 2001: 19.76
Migration Legislation Amendment (No 6) Act 2001: 13.49, 14.61
   Sch 1, Pt 1, cl 15: 13.48
Migration Legislation Amendment Bill (No 4) 1997: 19.76
Migration Legislation Amendment (Immigration Detainees) Act 2001: 15.104
Migration Legislation Amendment (Judicial Review) Bill 1998: 19.76
Migration Legislation Amendment (Judicial Review) Act 2001: 12.06, 19.76, 19.79
Migration Legislation Amendment (Migration Agents) Act 1997: 5.100
Migration Legislation Amendment (Overseas Student) Act 2000: 11.57
Migration Legislation Amendment (Procedural Fairness) Act 2002: 15.19, 18.106, 19.96
Migration Legislation Amendment (Sponsorship Measures) Act 2003: 10.13, 10.37
Migration Legislation Amendment (Strengthening of Provisions relating to Character and Conduct) Act 1998: 6.56-6.57, 6.69, 17.23, 17.26
Migration Legislation Amendment (Strengthening of Provisions relating to Character and Conduct) Bill 1997: 6.56, 17.22
Migration Legislation Amendment (Transitional Movement) Act 2002: 4.59
Migration Legislation Amendment (Transitional Movement) Bill 2002: 4.59
Migration Legislation Amendment (Worker Protection) Act 2008: 10.13, 10.40
Migration Litigation Reform Act 2005: 3.39, 19.97, 19.99
   s 3: 16.97
   Sch 1: 16.97
Migration (Offences and Undesirable Persons) Amendment Act 1992: 17.17-17.18, 17.20-17.21, 17.77
Migration Reform Act 1992: 3.34, 12.42, 16.01, 16.28, 19.37, 19.56
Migration Reform (Transitional) Regulations 1994: 5.48

Migration Regulations 1989 (Cth): 5.39, 19.51
  reg 2: 6.63, 6.67, 6.70
  reg 2(1): 8.08, 8.13
  reg 2A: 8.13
  reg 3A: 5.45, 7.23, 7.50
  reg 3B: 6.68
  reg 4: 5.45, 6.63
  reg 8E: 18.23
  reg 9A: 5.45
  reg 27: 15.29, 15.32
  reg 35AA: 15.78-15.81
  reg 42(1A): 15.78-15.79
  reg 42(1B): 15.78
  reg 42(1C): 15.79
  reg 42(1D): 15.79
  reg 117A: 18.22, 15.79
  reg 117B: 18.22
  reg 118: 15.79
  reg 118I: 18.22
  regs 119F-119H: 15.79
  reg 119I: 18.22
  reg 142A: 18.22
  regs 126-130: 5.36
  reg 126: 7.18
  reg 127: 8.01
  reg 129: 5.56-5.57, 15.79
  reg 131A: 15.82
  reg 131A(i)(v): 15.82
  reg 134: 15.79
  reg 143: 6.70
  reg 144: 5.45
  reg 173A: 15.81
  reg 178: 16.83
  Sch 1: 5.45
  Sch 1, cl 4: 6.63
Migration Regulations 1993: 5.40, 5.44, 6.17
  Sch 2: 5.40
  Sch 3: 5.40
  reg 2.46: 6.17
  reg 2.46(b)(i): 16.13
Migration Regulations 1994: 5.32-5.37, 5.40-5.45, 5.74, 5.104, 7.13, 9.94
  reg 1.03: 6.24, 6.32, 6.49, 7.13, 8.07-8.09, 8.09, 8.11, 8.21, 8.29, 8.36, 8.43, 9.102, 11.24, 11.73 11.88, 18.26
  reg 1.04: 8.13, 8.16
  reg 1.05: 8.35
  reg 1.05(1)(b): 8.35
  reg 1.05(2): 15.76
  reg 1.05A: 8.07, 8.09, 8.43-8.44, 8.47
  reg 1.07(2): 5.43
  reg 1.08(a)-(c): 16.61
  reg 1.09A: 7.24
  reg 1.09A(3): 7.39, 7.50
  reg 1.11: 9.88
  reg 1.12: 8.07
  reg 1.14: 8.21, 8.25
  reg 1.15: 8.48, 8.50
  reg 1.15A: 7.39, 7.46, 7.50
  reg 1.15A(1A)(a): 7.29
  reg 1.15A(3): 7.39-7.41, 7.51
  reg 1.15AA: 8.56
  reg 1.15AA(1): 8.58-8.59
  reg 1.15AA(1)(e)(i): 8.66
  reg 1.15B: 9.52
  reg 1.15B(5): 9.53
  reg 1.15C: 9.52
  reg 1.15D: 9.52
  reg 1.15E: 9.52
  reg 1.15I: 9.28
  reg 1.16AA: 6.32
  reg 1.19: 9.48
  reg 1.20B: 10.30-10.31
  reg 1.20J: 7.52
  reg 1.20J(1): 7.53
  reg 1.20J(2): 7.52
  reg 1.20G(2): 10.30-10.31
  reg 1.20GA(1)(a)(i): 10.31
  Div 1.4B: 7.52
  regs 1.21-1.27: 7.63
  reg 1.21: 7.63
  reg 1.21(1): 7.65-7.66
  reg 1.21(1)(a)(v): 7.66
  reg 1.23: 7.61, 7.72, 7.85
  reg 1.23(2): 7.66
  reg 1.23(2)(b): 7.74-7.75,
  reg 1.23(4): 7.65
  reg 1.23(4)(b): 7.63
  reg 1.23(9)(c): 7.70
  reg 1.23(10)(c)(iii): 7.65
  regs 1.24-1.26: 7.66
  reg 1.24: 7.63
  reg 1.26: 7.70, 7.72
  reg 1.26(c): 7.75
  Div 1.5: 7.80, 7.83
  reg 1.3: 7.34
  reg 2.02: 5.43
  reg 2.03: 5.43
  reg 2.03A(2): 7.33
  reg 2.03A(3): 7.35, 7.48
  reg 2.03A(5): 7.35
  reg 2.07: 5.41
  reg 2.07AJ: 14.74, 14.78
  reg 2.07AK: 14.74
  regs 2.07A-20.07K: 5.41
  reg 2.07AJ: 16.06
  reg 2.08AB: 5.41
  reg 2.08AC: 5.41
  reg 2.12: 5.36, 5.41, 8.03, 8.40 15.50
  Pt 1, Div 2.2A: 6.23
  reg 2.12A: 14.36
  reg 2.12A-2.12B: 14.08
  reg 2.20: 16.18
  reg 2.20(7)-(11): 16.64
  reg 2.25A: 6.24, 6.39
  reg 2.25A(1): 6.28
  reg 2.25A(3): 6.39
  reg 2.25B: 6.39
  reg 2.26A(5): 9.53
  reg 2.26A(7): 9.47
  reg 2.26B: 9.28
  Div 2.7: 6.23
  reg 2.39: 6.23
  reg 2.41: 15.20
  reg 2.43: 11.39
  reg 2.43(1)(k): 15.35
  reg 2.43(2): 11.34, 11.46
  reg 2.43(2)(a): 15.31

TABLE OF STATUTES

li

reg 2.50: 15.41
reg 2.52: 6.24
reg 2.53: 6.24
reg 2.55(3)(c): 18.67
reg 2.59: 10.20
reg 2.59(h): 10.20
reg 2.59(d): 10.23
reg 2.72(10)(c): 10.11
reg 2.72(1)(cc): 10.11
reg 2.72(10): 10.30
reg 2.72(10AB): 10.30
reg 2.72(10)(aa): 10.30
regs 2.77-2.94B: 10.25
regs 2.78-2.87: 10.28
reg 3.02: 6.08, 15.24
reg 3.03: 6.08
reg 3.04: 6.08
reg 4.02(4)(f)(i): 16.68
reg 4.09: 18.15
reg 4.10: 18.15, 18.19
reg 4.13: 18.18
reg 4.23: 18.15, 18.19
reg 4.24: 18.15, 18.19
reg 4.25: 18.15, 18.19
reg 4.26: 18.15
reg 4.27: 16.59
reg 4.31B: 18.26
reg 4.39: 18.60
reg 4.40: 18.60
reg 5.02: 18.60
reg 5.03: 18.61, 18.72
reg 5.17: 9.52
reg 5.19(2): 9.66
reg 5.19A: 9.95
reg 5.41: 6.24
Sch 1: 5.36, 5.42-5.44, 15.49
  cl 1219: 5.35
  cl 1225: 10.52
Sch 2: 5.36, 5.42-5.45, 7.13, 7.15, 7.29, 8.27, 15.49, 15.52
  subclass 010: 16.60
  subclass 020: 16.60
  subclass 030: 16.61
  subclass 040: 16.62
  subclass 041: 16.62
  subclass 050: 16.63
    cl 050.223: 16.69
    cl 050.224: 16.69
  subclass 051: 16.63
  subclass 060: 14.74
  subclass 100: 6.23, 6.51, 7.13-7.14, 7.19, 7.28, 7.32, 7.64
    cl 100.223: 6.23
  subclass 101: 6.51, 8.16, 12.78
  subclass 102: 6.51, 8.18, 8.26
  subclass 103: 8.36, 8.38
    cl 103.211: 8.37
  subclass 110: 7.64
  subclass 114: 8.43
  subclass 115: 8.48
  subclass 116: 8.38, 8.56
    cl 116.212: 8.38
  subclass 117: 8.21, 8.23
    cl 117.211(b): 8.23, 8.26

    cl 121.211(b)(i)(A): 9.66
    cl 121.211(b)(ii): 9.66
    cl 124.211(2)(c): 9.76
    cl 131.214: 9.93
  subclass 132: 9.86, 15.41
    cl 132.215: 9.103
  subclass 134: 9.20, 9.61
  subclass 136: 9.43
  subclass 137: 9.62
  subclass 139: 9.61
  subclass 143: 8.34
    cl 143.213: 8.35
  subclass 151: 6.40, 6.51
  subclass 155: 17.16
  subclasses 160-165: 9.85
    cl 160.212(a): 9.89
    cl 160.213: 9.89-9.90
    cl 160.214: 9.89
    cl 160.219A: 9.88
    cl 161.213: 9.90
  subclass 173: 8.34
  subclass 200: 6.51, 12.10
    cl 200.212: 14.30
  subclass 201: 6.51, 12.10
  subclass 202: 6.51, 6.55, 12.10
  subclass 203: 6.51, 12.10
  subclass 204: 6.51, 12.10
  subclass 208: 12.11
  subclass 209: 12.11
  subclass 210: 12.11
  subclass 211: 12.11
  subclass 212: 12.11
  subclass 213: 12.11
  subclass 214: 12.11, 16.26
  subclass 300: 6.51, 7.13-7.14, 7.19, 7.87
    cl 300.214: 7.29
  subclass 305: 12.78
  subclass 309: 6.51, 7.13, 7.28, 7.87, 8.17
  subclass 310: 7.24
  subclass 417: 10.51
  subclass 418: 6.30
  subclass 435: 12.83, 15.85
  subclass 443: 12.83, 15.85
  subclass 437: 12.83
  subclass 444: 5.35
  subclass 445: 6.51, 7.64, 8.17
  subclass 447: 12.13, 16.06
  subclass 451: 12.13, 16.06
  subclass 456: 10.03, 10.07, 10.10, 10.14, 10.17-10.18
  subclass 457: 6.30, 9.67, 9.86, 10.03, 10.07, 10.10-10.12, 10.17-10.18, 10.24, 10.30-10.37, 10.39-10.49, 10.66, 10.71, 10.81, 10.87, 17.35, 20.30
    cl 457.111: 10.11
    cl 457.111(2): 10.21
    cl 457.223(4): 10.32
    cl 457.611: 10.33
  subclass 461: 6.51
  subclass 462: 10.51
  subclass 475: 9.52, 9.60
  subclass 485: 9.47, 9.50, 11.52
  subclass 487: 9.45, 9.50, 9.52, 9.60, 11.55

Migration Regulations 1994 (Cth) (*cont*)
Sch 2 (*cont*)
subclass 676: 6.16, 11.71
cl 676.211: 11.73
cl 676.211(2): 11.76
cl 676.214: 11.82
cl 676.221(2)(d): 11.82
subclass 679: 11.87
subclass 658: 16.134
subclass 771: 15.73
subclass 773: 2.79, 6.13, 15.05, 15.08, 16.13
subclass 784: 12.78
subclass 787: 14.74
subclass 801: 6.51, 7.13-7.14, 7.19, 7.28, 7.64, 7.72, 15.56
subclass 802: 6.51, 8.16, 8.42
cl 802.213: 8.16
cl 802.215: 8.42
cl 802.216: 8.42
cl 802.226A: 8.42
subclass 804: 8.36, 12.78
subclass 812: 12.78
subclass 814: 7.24, 7.64
cl 836.213: 8.38
subclass 815: 15.83-15.85
subclass 816: 15.83, 15.85-15.86
subclass 818: 15.83, 15.87
subclass 820: 6.51, 7.14, 7.19, 7.28, 7.64, 7.87, 8.17, 15.54, 15.56
cl 820.111(a): 15.72
cl 820.211: 15.77
cl 820.211(2): 15.77
cl 820.211(2)(d)(ii): 15.72
cl 820.211(2)(d)(i): 15.76
cl 820.211(2A): 15.76
cl 820.2111(8): 7.87
cl 820.2111(9): 7.87
subclass 826: 7.24
cl 826.212(2)(e): 15.77
subclass 832: 15.73
cl 832.21: 15.75
subclass 835: 8.48
subclass 836: 8.38, 8.56, 15.76
cl 836.213: 8.38
subclass 837: 8.21, 15.76
subclass 838: 8.43, 15.76
subclass 840: 8.32
subclass 844: 7.64
subclass 845: 7.64, 9.86
cl 845.216: 9.91
cl 845.222: 9.84
subclass 846: 9.86
cl 846.222: 9.84
subclass 850: 14.39
subclass 851: 12.13
subclass 852: 6.51, 14.74
subclass 855: 6.41
subclass 856: 7.64
cl 856.213(b)(i)(A): 9.66
cl 856.213(b)(ii): 9.66
subclass 857: 7.64
subclass 858: 7.64
subclass 864: 8.34
subclass 866: 12.67, 14.39, 15.08, 15.71
cl 866.215: 14.30
subclass 880: 11.51
subclass 881: 11.51
subclass 882: 9.61, 11.51
subclass 884: 8.34
subclass 885: 9.45, 9.86, 11.51, 11.55
subclass 886: 9.45, 11.51
subclass 890-893: 9.86
subclass 890: 6.51
subclass 891: 6.51
subclass 892: 6.51
cl 892.213: 9.102
subclass 893: 6.51
subclass 976: 11.71
Sch 3: 5.43, 5.46, 7.06, 15.52-15.53, 15.56, 15.59, 15.63-15.65, 15.72, 15.77
cll 3001-3002: 15.52
cl 3002: 15.76
cl 3003: 15.58
cl 3004: 15.77
Sch 4: 5.42, 7.05, 10.14, 15.12
cl 4001: 6.24
cl 4005: 6.24, 6.30-6.31, 6.39, 6.43-6.44
cl 4006: 6.31
cl 4006A: 6.24, 6.28, 6.30
cl 4007: 6.24, 6.30, 6.51-6.52
cl 4008: 6.31
cl 4011: 11.76, 11.81, 11.85
cl 4011(2): 11.81, 11.87
cl 4011(2A): 11.80
cl 4011(3): 11.80
cll 4005-4008: 5.45
cll 4015-4018: 8.25, 8.27-8.28
cl 4015: 8.28
cl 4016: 8.30
cl 4017: 8.28
cl 4018: 8.30
Sch 5: 5.36, 5.42, 5.46, 7.05, 7.13, 15.49
cl 5001: 17.47
Sch 5A: 5.42. 11.18
Sch 5B: 5.42, 11.18
Sch 6: 5.42, 5.47
cl 6311: 9.52
Sch 6, Part 3: 9.48
Sch 6A: 5.42, 5.47
Sch 6B: 5.42, 9.28
Sch 7: 5.42, 5.47, 9.84
Sch 8: 5.42, 5.45, 11.21
Condition 8101: 11.23
Condition 8102: 11.22
Condition 8104: 11.34
Condition 8105: 11.26, 11.28, 11.34-11.35
Condition 8105(2): 11.28
Condition 8105(3): 11.27
Condition 8202: 11.36-11.37, 11.41-11.42, 11.44-11.46, 11.48-11.49, 15.70
Condition 8202(3): 11.49
Condition 8206: 11.29
Condition 8208: 11.46
Sch 9: 5.42
Sch 10: 5.42
Sch 11: 5.42
Sch 12: 5.42
Migration Regulations (Amendment) 1995: 9.100

Migration Review Regulations 1989
  reg 8E: 12.39
  reg 21: 5.36
  reg 119K: 12.83
  reg 140: 12.78
  Sch 1: 5.45
  Pt 2A: 12.39
Migration (Visa Application) Charge Act 1997: 6.23
Nationality Act 1920: 2.53
Nationality and Citizenship Act 1948: 2.05, 2.54
  ss 7-9: 3.11
  Pt II: 3.11
Naturalization Act 1903: 2.52
Ombudsman Act 1976: 18.31, 18.42
  s 3(3A): 18.32
  s 5: 18.30
  s 5(2)-(3): 18.32
  s 6(2): 18.35
  s 7(3)(b): 16.42, 18.42
  s 8(2): 18.33
  s 9: 18.33
  s 13: 18.33
  ss 15-17: 18.33
Pacific Island Labourers Act 1901: 2.23, 2.36, 9.12, 10.70, 17.01
  s 8: 2.35
Papua New Guinea Independence Act 1975
  s 4: 2.67
Passports Act 1902
  s 3: 2.50
PNG Independence (Australian Citizenship) Regulations 1975
  reg 4: 2.67
Public Service Act 1922
  s 15: 5.17
Racial Discrimination Act 1975: 15.90
  s 9: 15.86
Sex Discrimination Act 1984: 18.41
Social Security Act 1991: 8.36
  s 94: 6.50
  Pt 2.11-2.15: 6.23
Social Security Legislation Amendment (Newly Arrived Resident's Waiting Periods and Other Measures) Act 1997: 1.17
Statute Law Revision Act 1950: 2.23, 9.12
Statutory Rules
  SR 1 1990
    reg 6: 15.79
  SR75 1996: 15.77
    reg 13.2: 15.77
  SR 60 1991: 7.23-7.24
  SR 285 1991: 8.01, 8.08
    reg 26: 18.22
  SR 117 1995: 7.63
  SR 211 1996: 7.19, 7.52, 15.77
    reg 130: 15.77
  SR 354 1997: 7.63
War Precautions Act 1914: 2.36
WarTime Refugees Removal Act 1948: 2.36, 2.46, 17.09
  s 4: 2.46
  s 5: 2.46
  s 7: 2.46

Wheat Marketing Act 1989: 5.96
  s 57(3B): 5.95
Workplace Relations Act 2006: 10.44
Workplace Relations Amendment (Work Choices) Act 2005: 10.44
  s 26: 10.44

New South Wales
Coloured Races Restriction Bill 1896: 2.26
Interpretation Act 1987
  s 16: 2.60
Parliamentary Electorates and Elections Act 1912
  s 20: 2.60

Queensland
WorkCover Queensland Act 1996
  s 12(1): 15.98

South Australia
Coloured Races Restriction Bill 1896: 2.26

Tasmania
Coloured Races Restriction Bill 1896: 2.26

Victoria
Chinese Act 1881: 2.22
An Act to Regulate the Residence of Chinese Population in Victoria 1857, 21 Vict c 41: 2.22
Chinese Immigrants Act 1865, 30 Vict c 8: 2.22
Interpretation of Legislation Act 1984
  s 55: 2.60

Canada
Immigration and Refugee Protection Act 2001: 14.64

Fiji
Constitution of the Fijian Islands
  s 12: 2.79

Germany
Act to Control and Restrict Immigration and to Regulate the Residence and Integration of EU Citizens and Foreigners, 30 July 2004, BGB1.I at 1950 (FRG): 9.17

Nauru
Constitution
  Pt II, Art 3: 4.63

New Zealand
Asiatic Restriction Bill 1861: 2.26

Papua New Guinea
Constitution
  Preamble: 4.63
  Art 42: 4.63

United Kingdom
Asylum and Immigration Act 1996: 15.99
Terrorism Act 2000: 17.35
Habeas Corpus Act 1679: 19.101

United States of America
Constitution
  Article VI, Section 2: 4.07
  14th Amendment: 2.66

Immigration and Nationality Act (US)
§204.11(c)(6): 8.42
Immigration Reform and Control Act: 15.99

Europe
European Convention on Human Rights: 1.05
Art 8: 17.100

International
Convention on Protection of Children and Cooperation in Respect of Intercountry Adoption 1993: 8.17
Art 1: 8.17, 8.20w
Art 4: 8.20
Convention on the Elimination of all Forms of Discrimination against Women 1979 (CEDAW): 4.09
Convention on the Rights of Persons with Disabilities 2006 (CRPD): 4.69, 18.41
Arts 10-23: 17.101
Art 29: 17.101
Optional Protocol to: 4.69
Declaration on the Rights of Mentally Retarded Persons: 18.41
International Convention for the Safety of Life at Sea 1979 (SOLAS): 4.52
International Covenant on Civil and Political Rights 1966 (ICCPR): 4.09, 4.27, 4.54, 4.69-4.70, 14.69, 18.41, 20.20, 20.32
Art 2: 4.58, 4.72
Art 2(3): 16.109
Art 6: 4.53, 17.99-17.100
Art 7: 4.53, 4.58, 17.99-17.100
Art 9: 4.58, 4.72-4.73
Art 9(1): 16.57, 16.109
Art 9(4): 16.57, 16.109
Art 10: 4.58
Art 14: 4.66
Art 14(7): 17.100
Art 17: 17.100, 20.20
Art 23: 4.09, 7.10, 17.100, 20.20
Art 41: 4.09
First Optional Protocol to: 4.69
Second Optional Protocol: 17.99
International Convention on Maritime Search and Rescue 1974 (SAR): 4.52
International Convention on the Elimination of all forms of Racial Discrimination 1966 (CERD): 4.09, 4.69, 18.41
Art 14: 4.69
UN Convention Against Torture and All forms of Cruel, Inhumane and Degrading Treatment or Punishment 1984: 4.54, 4.69-4.70, 12.81, 14.68, 14.69, 20.32
Art 3: 4.53, 4.58, 14.68, 17.99
UN Convention Against Transnational Organized Crime: 7.56, 14.73; 15.94
Protocol Against the Smuggling of Migrants by Land, Sea and Air
Preamble: 15.94
Art 3: 15.94
Art 6: 15.94, 15.95

Protocol to Prevent, Suppress and Punish Trafficking in Persons, Especially Women and Children (Palermo Protocol): 7.56, 14.73, 16.72, 15.94
Art 2(b): 14.73
Art 3(a): 14.73
Art 7(1): 14.74
UN Convention on Economic, Cultural and Social Rights: 20.32
UN Convention on the Law of the Sea (UNCLOS): 4.37, 13.48
Art 98: 4.37, 4.52
UN Convention on the Rights of the Child 1989: 4.09, 4.27, 4.62, 4.69, 8.63, 14.69, 17.94, 17.97, 20.20, 20.32
Art 3: 4.16, 17.95
Art 9: 8.28, 17.100
Art 21: 8.20-8.20, 20.20
Art 24: 4.09
Art 37: 4.58
UN Convention relating to the Status of Refugees 1951: 1.34-1.35, 4.10, 4.41, 4.45, 4.54, 4.57, 12.01-12.02, 12.04, 12.08, 12.15, 12.18-12.20, 12.26, 12.49, 12.57-12.59, 12.67, 12.77, 12.85, 12.88, 12.92, 13.01-13.04, 13.06, 13.25, 13.30-13.32, 13.45, 13.47, 13.55, 13.57, 13.66-13.68, 13.71-13.72, 13.74, 13.76, 13.78, 13.80, 13.84, 13.86, 13.97, 13.106-13.107, 13.109-13.112, 13.114, 13.118-13.119, 13.121, 13.123, 14.01-14.07, 14.10-14.12, 14.18, 14.64, 17.98, 20.32
Protocol to: 1.34, 12.02, 12.18-12.20, 13.02, 14.03, 20.32
Art IV: 12.18
Art 1: 4.55, 12.02, 13.02, 13.06, 14.63
Art 1(2): 14.10
Art 1A: 4.14, 12.02, 13.01, 13.40, 13.77, 13.91, 13.106, 14.18, 14.40-14.41, 14.45-14.48
Art 1C: 14.37-14.46
Art 1E: 14.18, 14.22-14.25, 14.29
Art 1F: 14.49-14.57, 14.58-14.59, 14.61-14.6
Art 1F(a): 14.54-14.55
Art 1F(b): 14.56, 14.58-14.59
Art 1F(c): 14.63
Art 2: 14.63
Art 16: 4.66
Art 17: 4.63
Art 21: 4.63
Art 22: 4.63
Art 26: 4.63
Art 31: 4.55, 4.57, 4.63, 4.73, 14.05-14.06-14.07
Art 31(1): 4.56
Art 31(2): 4.57
Art 32: 4.63, 19.104
Art 33: 12.03, 12.25, 14.01, 14.37, 19.104
Art 33(1): 14.25-14.26
Art 33(2): 14.53
Art 34: 4.63
Art 38: 12.18
Vienna Convention on the Law of Treaties 1969: 4.56, 12.58
Art 3: 4.56
Art 26: 4.56
Art 31: 4.56

PART I History and Context

1

Immigration Law in Context

1.1 The *idea* of the migrant: Lived experiences and attitudes to immigration

[1.01] The transnational movement of human beings has shaped the nations of the globe in ways that are both obvious and more subtle. Australia shares with other 'New World' countries like New Zealand, the United States of America and Canada the experience of beginning as a series of colonies founded by Britain (and by Diaspora Irish and Scottish nationals). These first migrations transfigured the demographic face of the Australian continent, at the expense of the country's Indigenous peoples. Like elsewhere in the fledgling British Commonwealth, this country's founders showed an acute consciousness of the role that immigration would play in the formation of Australia as an Anglo-Saxon polity.[1]

[1.02] However, the distinctive manner in which Australia was settled seems to have generated some unique responses to immigration. The *lived experience* of immigration has influenced not only substantive laws in Australia but also the very way Australians think about the cross-border movement of people. It bears recalling that Anglo Australia did not just begin as a colony of Great Britain. It began as a penal colony established to take the overflow from the prisons of Great Britain. A sizeable number of the first Australian settlers came in chains as convicts. To say that the first immigration intakes were 'planned' is something of an understatement. Because of the physical challenges facing those attempting to reach Australia – difficulties that endure to this day – immigration in all forms continued to be a highly managed affair. Australia's vastness, its fragile environment and the cultural isolation of the settlers encouraged equal control in the manner of its population. Settlements have always been clustered together on the perimeters of the continent; bigger cities have been favoured over smaller communities. It is a lived experience that has engendered what some have called a 'culture of control'.[2]

[1.03] Public engagement with migration law and policy in modern Australia presents many paradoxes. On the one hand, Australians seem to have an innate

---

[1] See Chapter 2 and Mary Crock, 'Defining Strangers: Human Rights, Immigrants and the Foundations of a Just Society' (2008) 31 *Melbourne University Law Review* 1053.

[2] See Kathryn Cronin, 'A Culture of Control: An Overview of Immigration Policy-making' in James Jupp and Marie Kabala (eds), *The Politics of Australian Immigration* (Canberra: AGPS, 1993).

appreciation of the role that immigration has played in forming and growing their nation. With just over one in four Australians born overseas,[3] this may not be surprising. The Australian self-image suggests an open-minded, egalitarian and fair society that celebrates cultural diversity and individual endeavour. Yet in matters pertaining to immigration control and border protection, in more recent years, many Australians seem to have become 'fervent believers in queues'.[4] At the levels of both rational debate and emotive rhetoric, concerns about who comes to this country and on what terms have long been tied closely to broader issues of national identity, economic prosperity and social justice, especially in the local labour market. The phenomenon of unauthorised boat arrivals has seen national security, international relations and Australia's humanitarian obligations to refugees and asylum seekers added to these themes. These experiences are not unique to Australia. Neither is the moral panic engendered by irregular migration. What sets Australia and Australians apart, however, is the depth of the expectation that the government can and should control immigration in all of its incidents.

[1.04] Although passionate views about irregular migration rate highly in the political discourse of Western and non-Western countries alike, one does not see the same convictions about government regulation in nations whose land borders are particularly porous to human movement. The liberal immigration policy of the United States, for example, is archetypical in this regard. Like Australia, it is a nation truly built of and by immigrants. Many have come from within the region across land borders that are notoriously difficult to police; others from the old worlds of England and Europe. The US is also a country defined by what might be called entrepreneurial migration. Its early history is one dominated by free settlement where individuals were able to accrete wealth and power such that they often came to assume sole responsibility for the provision of basic public infrastructure and amenities. The American experience in this regard departs quite markedly from that of Australia where the population has traditionally looked to government rather than private enterprise for the delivery of public services.[5]

[1.05] The experiences at the centre of colonial Empire in Great Britain, Spain and France also offer interesting counterpoints. Recent decades have seen each confront the reality of significant immigration of people from their foreign territories (both the return of the former colonising population and a labour migration by the formerly colonised): the periphery of the Empire returning to the centre. Although France toyed briefly with closed border – zero immigration – policies in the 1960s, it quickly came to the realisation that banning the admission into French society of all foreign

---

3   In 2009, 27 per cent of Australians met this description: see Australian Bureau of Statistics, '3412.0 - Migration, Australia, 2008-9' (2010), available at <http://www.abs.gov.au/ausstats/abs@.nsf/Latestproducts/3412.0Main%20Features12008-09?opendocument&tabname=Summary&prodno=3412.0&issue=2008&num&view=>.
4   John Button, 'What Future for Labor?' (2002) 6 *Quarterly Essay* 1 at 18.
5   For an excellent account of aspects of America's immigration history, see Hiroshi Motomura, *Americans in Waiting: The Lost History of Immigration and Citizenship in the United States* (New York: Oxford University Press, 2006).

nationals was neither practicable nor desirable.⁶ In spite of its small geographical size, Britain has traditionally maintained surprisingly generous migration policies in a range of areas, not the least in relation to the admission of 'patrials'.⁷ In the case of Spain there is the added historical dimension that (Moorish) parts of Spanish territory were acquired from African neighbours by conquest (these same neighbours from where people are seeking to emigrate).⁸ The impact that such historical territorial conquests have on modern day migration patterns is evident also in the complicated relationship between the US and Mexico.⁹ While public concerns in Western Europe about unauthorised entry and cultural integration may remain intense, in none is there the same expectation that the relevant government should be able to control such commerce.¹⁰ Instead, there is a fundamental tenor in mainstream European attitudes that immigration from former colonies is an inevitable consequence of history. And like the United States' Bill of Rights (and constitutional and statutory human rights instruments in Canada and New Zealand), the European Union legal apparatus has generated a human rights consciousness which, overall, tends to soften tendencies toward hard-line immigration control.¹¹

[1.06] In acknowledging the significance of Australia's history and lived experiences of immigration, we do not suggest that the country's laws and policies are in some way pre-determined or inevitable. On the contrary, the controversies that arose during the incumbency of the Conservative Coalition government between 1996 and 2007 suggest that political leadership can have a tremendous impact on the way the public sees and responds to the idea of immigration. That decade of Coalition rule began with public statements of anxiety by government and minor party leadership alike that the culture and practices of ethnic minorities presented challenges to 'Australian values'.¹² Several years later the focus of government and of the public discourse was on loss of 'border control' at the hands of asylum seekers.¹³ Ironically, this period saw simultaneously both huge increases in the levels of skilled migration to Australia and a surge in hostility towards irregular migrants – in particular towards asylum seekers and refugees.

---

6   Richard Alba and Roxane Silberman, 'Decolonization Immigrations and the Social Origins of the Second Generation: The Case of North Africans in France' (2002) 36(4) *International Migration Review* 1169 at 1171.
7   Christian Joppke, 'Multiculturalism and Immigration: A Comparison of the United States, Germany and Great Britain' (1996) 25 *Theory and Society* 449; Salman Rushdie, 'The New Empire Within Britain' *New Society* (9 December 1982) 421.
8   Gary P Freeman, 'Modes of Immigration Politics in Liberal Democratic States' (1995) 29(4) *International Migration Review* 881.
9   Douglas S Massey and Kristin E Espinosa, 'What's Driving Mexico-US Migration? A Theoretical, Empirical, and Policy Analysis' (1997) 102(4) *American Journal of Sociology* 939.
10 Wayne Cornelius, Philip Martin and James Hollifield (eds), *Controlling Immigration* (Stanford, Calif: Stanford University Press, 1994).
11 See, for example, discussion of the treatment of irregular migration in the European Convention of Human Rights in Laurie Berg, 'At the Border and Between the Cracks: The Precarious Position of Irregular Migrant Workers in International Law' (2007) 8 *Melbourne Journal of International Law* 1.
12 Ghassan Hage, *Against Paranoid Nationalism: Searching for Hope in a Shrinking Society* (Melbourne: Pluto Press, 2003).
13 For an account of this period, see David Marr and Marianne Wilkinson, *Dark Victory* (Sydney: Allen & Unwin, 2003).

1.2 Evolving approaches to justice in immigration

[1.07] This book explores the political, social and cultural forces that have shaped and are shaping immigration law in Australia. We attempt to capture and explain some of the momentous changes that have occurred in law and policy since the first attempts, in December 1989, to 'codify' decision-making through detailed regulations. It is a study of revolution and counter-revolution: of the impact that the courts and tribunals have had on law and policy through the review of migration decisions; and of the increasingly extreme steps taken by government to assert control over every aspect of its immigration program. In spite of the many policy shifts and the concomitant legal reforms over the past decade, many would argue that we have yet to achieve migration laws and procedures that are just, clearly expressed and readily comprehensible. Some question their efficiency; others their rationality.

[1.08] In this book we have sought to distil some of the patterns, trends, ethical and philosophical issues thrown up by immigration law in Australia in recent times. While attentive to the distinctive characteristics of the Australian context, we remain aware also of the more enduring features of (Western) immigration policy wherever it is found. This is almost universally an area of law that operates – literally as well as figuratively – to define a state as a nation. Further, and in spite of its strongly domestic focus, immigration is patently the most international and internationalising area of public administration: migrants bring the world inside national borders and force a community to consider events occurring in other parts of the globe. Migration policies are regularly made in response to foreign events, and these policies themselves can shape conditions in distant countries. In every Western country, the contours of immigration policy have other idiosyncratic elements. For example, unlikely alliances have been struck between anti-immigration environmentalists and extreme right-wing nationalists, both seeking a more restrictive immigration program. At the same time, 'open borders' advocates for fairer global wealth distribution often side with laissez-faire industrialists who are keen to augment their local workforces through the importation of foreign labour.

[1.09] Australian approaches to immigration policy have both unique and universal dimensions and are illuminated through an awareness of significant theoretical perspectives that have developed in the field of immigration scholarship around the world. In this section, we examine some of the major contributions in this field and sketch the relevance of these insights for the study of Australian immigration laws. The themes in this overview will return as motifs in our more detailed examination of the different doctrinal areas of immigration law throughout the text.

1.2.1 The liberal debate between open and closed borders

[1.10] The hallmark debate for Anglo-American scholars concerned with just immigration policies in modern liberal democracies relates to the liberal principles for permitting or restricting movement of people across national borders. Proponents of the ethical imperative for open borders and those favouring closed borders differ in the sources on which they draw within the diverse liberal philosophical tradition.

On one hand, the most basic tenet of liberalism – the equal moral worth of all individuals – requires the coexistence of all with equal rights, including the equal right to move between countries. At the same time, a strong community-focused strain in liberalism (known as 'communitarianism') insists on closed borders as a necessity if one is to cultivate or create a robust liberal society.[14]

[1.11] Frederick Whelan expresses the logic of open borders theorists in this way:

> It seems clear from the outset that a moral theory that set out to attend to the claims of all human beings as such, on an equal basis, is going to have some difficulty in justifying borders that set off groups of people from each other and act as barriers to the free movement of individuals.[15]

Joseph Carens, a vigorous advocate of open borders in his early career, provides detailed and far-ranging arguments for this position. These include the utilitarian perspective that the greatest good of the greatest number must involve paying attention to those outside of the nation who have the most to gain from entry, as well as the libertarian perspective that the human entitlement to freedom requires the admission of those whose liberty is not protected in their current situations.[16]

[1.12] In contrast, communitarians emphasise the intrinsic moral value of human community. Within this tradition, the (liberal) community is seen as a system that allows individuals to achieve the highest form of self-actualisation. One of the most prominent liberal political philosophers, John Rawls, takes as his premise an imagined society which he sees as a necessarily 'closed system isolated from other societies'.[17] Rawls' celebrated liberal theory of justice as a balance of individuals' interests in freedom and equality seems to be predicated on the assumption that national borders are fixed: he does not really grapple with issues relating to international movement. Michael Walzer presents a more explicit defence of closed borders as a necessary condition for the just liberal community.[18] For him, fair distribution of wealth and protection of individual rights are possible only within 'a group of people committed to dividing, exchanging and sharing social goods, first of all among themselves'.[19] Closed borders are required, in the first instance, to create an established group and a fixed population within which decisions about justice can be made. Generally, justice viewed in this way does not require the community admit anyone at all, or anyone in particular.

[1.13] However distinct, these two extreme positions do tend towards a certain convergence. Walzer, for instance, would acknowledge that adjustments must be made for mutual aid. A community that is faced with needier outsiders has obligations to admit them, but may choose from among them on the basis of their connection

---

14 Mark Gibney in Mark Gibney (ed), *Open Borders? Closed Societies? The Ethical and Political Issues* (New York: Greenwood Press, 1988) xi at xiii-iv.
15 Federick G Whelan, 'Citizenship and Freedom of Movement: An Open Admission Policy?' in Gibney, ibid, at 7.
16 Joseph Carens, 'Aliens and Citizens: The Case for Open Borders' (1987) 49 *The Review of Politics* 251
17 John Rawls, *Theory of Justice* (Cambridge, Mass: Belnap Press, 1971) at 8.
18 Michael Walzer, *Spheres of Justice: A Defence of Pluralism and Equality* (Princeton: Basic Books, 1983) Ch 3 'Membership'.
19 Ibid at 31.

with the community. He concludes that we have a higher obligation to those for whose plight we are responsible or who are persecuted because they are like us in some way.[20] Equally, Carens would allow for the limiting of open admissions in order to protect the integrity of the liberal state itself. Borders could be closed, it seems, in the face of a threat to basic liberal democratic values, presumably including social institutions and freedom from violence (most relevantly the threat of terrorism).[21]

[1.14] Strains from this decades long debate hold obvious resonances in the Australian public discourse. The present constitutional framework in Australia, which assigns to the Commonwealth Parliament virtually unfettered power to make laws about alienage and immigration admissions, is almost archetypal Walzer. This expansive power was invoked by former Prime Minister Howard's mantra for the 2001 federal election: 'We will decide who comes to this country and the circumstances in which they come'.[22] These rhetorical devices serve to insulate discussions about the admission of non-citizens from domestic discourse on human rights. They also work to sustain the Australian self-image as a beneficent shelter to those in need while reserving the nation's right, à la Walzer, to dole out this humanitarian consideration in a limited and purely discretionary manner.[23] In spite of the language of rights that has existed in the legislation since 1989, immigration remains preeminently a privilege bestowed on the migrant.

1.2.2 Citizenship and belonging

[1.15] More recently, political theorists in the Western world have renewed their preoccupation with theories of 'equal citizenship' as a framework for considering questions of justice.[24] In response, migration scholars like Linda Bosniak have examined the utility of the citizenship rubric to resolve debates about the inclusion of migrants in liberal democratic states.[25] Bosniak parses the varying dimensions of citizenship, dividing understandings of the term into four categories: legal status, rights, political activity and collective identity. She argues that, while at first glance citizenship appears to function as a unitary package, on closer inspection it is clear that these aspects of citizenship often operate independently of each other. A group holding legal citizenship may nonetheless be denied the exercise of political participation rights or equal access to social benefits. The experience of Indigenous Australians is instructive on this point. Equally, a non-citizen may achieve some amount of inclusion at some times, for certain purposes.

---

20 Ibid at 48.
21 Carens, above n 16, at 259.
22 John Howard, address delivered at the Federal Liberal Party Campaign Launch, Sydney, Australia, 28 October 2001.
23 Catherine Dauvergne, *Humanitarianism, Identity, and Nation: Migration Laws in Canada and Australia* (Vancouver: UBC Press, 2005).
24 See, for example, Will Kymlicka and Wayne Norman, 'Return of the Citizen: A Survey of Recent Work on Citizenship Theory' (1994) 104 *Ethics* 352.
25 Linda Bosniak, *The Citizen and the Alien: Dilemmas of Contemporary Membership* (Princeton: Princeton University Press, 2006).

[1.16] Bosniak demonstrates that these qualities of citizenship discourse can have dangerous consequences. Because of the aspirational content of the term 'citizen', its use has proliferated as a call for justice, embracing as it does inclusion, equality and belonging. She describes this as 'soft' citizenship. Yet this call is often made with the unconscious limitation that such inclusions should take place only within the pre-existing confines of the nation state, erecting therefore a 'hard' external boundary that excludes outsiders from its emancipatory potential. The malleability of the term conceals this exclusive tendency. The slippery nature of this popular discourse is complicated further within modern societies where it is frequently difficult to characterise people as obvious insiders or outsiders.

[1.17] The ambiguities which lie at the heart of evocations of 'equal citizenship' are borne out in Australia which shares with all Western democracies a fundamentally schizophrenic approach to the treatment of non-citizens living within its borders. The extent to which the legal status of alienage 'matters' in the context of other legal entitlements is a subject of great contestation. An early reform of the Rudd Labor government in 2009 was the removal of the so-called '45-day rule' which since 1997 had denied permission to work to asylum seekers who had applied for refugee status more than 45 days after arriving in Australia.[26] This change tied community support and labour market participation to migrants' particular situation at the time of applying for asylum (the substantive visa they held, their ability to show a compelling need to work and a reason for delaying their asylum claim). But, at the same time, other disabilities for migrants that were introduced by the conservative Howard government were not disturbed. For instance, permanent residents were made ineligible in 1997 for most social security benefits for the first two years after their arrival in Australia.[27] This stand is in addition to a scattered constellation of other disabilities attaching to non-citizenship status ranging from denial of the right to vote in federal elections to denial of the right to work in the public sector. In most other respects though, permanent residents in Australia are accorded rights equal to others in the workplaces, families or communities in which they live.[28] We shall see the fundamental ambivalence about the significance to be accorded to immigration status, in its many forms, played out in the focus areas of this book.

1.3   Themes and theories: An overview of the book

[1.18] Few today would dispute that migration in the modern world is inevitable. The concept that any modern democracy could close its borders to any movement of people is now unthinkable. Leaving to one side the practical porosity of many land borders, the demands of international commerce are such that exclusionary policies can spell economic disaster. Furthermore, the pressures of large-scale (involuntary) population movements vary in response to wars and environmental

---

26   *Migration Amendment Regulations (No 6) 2009* (Cth).
27   *Social Security Legislation Amendment (Newly Arrived Resident's Waiting Periods and Other Measures) Act 1997* (Cth).
28   For a survey of the legislative consequences of citizenship, see Kim Rubenstein, *Australian Citizenship Law in Context* (Sydney: LawBook, 2002).

and other catastrophes. This literally compulsive crossing of boundaries is reflected, at a figurative level, by the migration of rules and social policies. Jacqueline Bhabha argues that immigration has lead to 'rights spillovers', enriching domestic human rights discourses.[29] She points out that migrants compel a society to think beyond itself by literally bringing home events that are occurring in different parts of the globe. The 'globalisation' of the law, and legal consciousness, is promoted by the presence of non-citizens in so far as foreign happenings must be considered when deciding to deport or remove. Finally, Bhabha echoes Bosniak in highlighting the difficulties in determining membership in communities of polyglot cultural heritage. Cultural indeterminacy forces the re-evaluation of substantive notions of citizenship and increases pressure for the 'universalisation' of rights and entitlements.

[1.19]   Immigration is a quintessential example of social policy that requires consideration of polycentric factors. The fascination and complexity for those charged with controlling immigration are in the number of legal and political considerations that must be taken into account. It is a jurisdiction that stands at the intersection of the three main strands of public law: constitutional, administrative and international. Constitutional issues have arisen over the nature and extent of the executive's power to act in protection of Australia's borders. Immigration cases have tested the ability of parliament and the executive to make laws governing the admission, exclusion and expulsion of persons found not to be 'Australian'.[30] They have shaped jurisprudence on the power of the courts and the exercise of 'judicial' power.[31] Throughout history, but more particularly in recent years, migration cases have tested the significance of international law in its intersection with Australian domestic laws and practices.[32] In many instances the landmark cases cannot be understood properly outside of their (often complex) political contexts.

[1.20]   In this book we examine the ways that historical, social and political forces have shaped the treatment of migrants in Australia and the ongoing national discourse. Our focus, however, is on legal developments and their significance. In the midst of what some have labelled an 'immigration revolution',[33] we seek to identify anomalies in the law and the unresolved policy tensions which underlie legal regulation of this field and, to some extent, Australian laws more broadly. If immigration does indeed bring the world to Australia, the trans-border movement of people touches virtually every aspect of the laws and policies that together define the identity and character of community in Australia.

---

29 See Jacqueline Bhabha, 'Rights Spillovers: The Impact of Migration on the Legal System of Western States' in Elspeth Guild and Joanne van Selm (eds), *International Migration and Security: Opportunities and Challenges* (New York: Routledge, 2005) at 28.

30 See, eg, *MIMIA v Nystrom* (2006) 228 CLR 566; *Shaw v MIMA* (2003) 218 CLR 28; *Ruddock v Vadarlis* (2001) 110 FCR 491.

31 See Chapter 3 below. See, eg, *Plaintiff S157/2002 v Cth* (2003) 211 CLR 476; *Chu Kheng Lim v MILGEA* (1992) 176 CLR 1.

32 See Chapter 4 below. See, eg, *MIEA v Teoh* (1995) 183 CLR 273; *Al Kateb v Godwin* (2004) 219 CLR 562

33 Andrew Markus, James Jupp and Peter McDonald, *Australia's Immigration Revolution* (Sydney: Allen & Unwin, 2009).

1.3.1 Immigration, citizenship and the constitution of a nation

[1.21] In Chapters 2 and 3, we trace the evolution of concepts of citizenship in Australia and the particular role that immigration law played in the constitution of the nation. When the Australian colonies came together as a federation in 1901, the decision was made not to include the concept of Australian citizenship in the Australian Constitution.[34] Instead, the new Commonwealth Parliament was given the power to legislate for the peace, order and good government of Australia with respect to immigration and emigration, as well as naturalisation and aliens.[35] The lack of constitutional entrenchment of an Australian citizenship has had enduring implications for the evolution of constitutional law in this country. As well as creating great uncertainty about the status of its inhabitants, the omission altered at a very fundamental level the focus of the Constitution. With no entrenched citizenship, it follows (or at least it is not surprising) that the Constitution says little about the relationships (rights or duties) between Australian citizens and their federal government.

[1.22] Not only did immigration law in this area regulate physical movement and the legal status of people crossing Australian borders: it also served as a benchmark for determining the civil rights and entitlements of individuals across Australian society. In 2004-05 the High Court heard a series of cases involving children born in immigration detention and individuals born as Australian citizens who lost that status when Australia relinquished the colonial territory on which they were born.[36] In each instance, the court rejected arguments that citizenship in Australia is an inherent birthright. It confirmed that the parliament has almost untrammelled power to determine both membership of the Australian community and the rights and entitlements attaching to non-citizen or 'alien' status. Again, immigration law has been central to this. As well as providing a legal basis (legitimacy) for exclusionary policies, Australia's immigration laws have been the legal vehicles used to delineate the relationship between citizens, aliens and government.

[1.23] An issue of enduring importance that emerges as a recurrent theme throughout the book is the role played by the courts through the migration cases in shaping the ethical character as well as demographical identity of Australia as a nation. The textual voids in the Constitution have been a central feature of this caselaw. In the absence of articulated principles on issues of membership and belonging in the Constitution, the courts have been forced to rely on 'mere inferences' and on the common law heritance of the Anglo-Australian legal system. Wedged between popular anti-migrant opinion and the traditional imperative that they defend the legal entitlements of the outsider in the name of the rule of law, the judiciary has been criticised as 'activist' and contrarian. Conflict between the various arms of government over immigration is not unique to Australia. However, the depth of the controversies in this country has been exceptional as we explore in a series of case studies.

34　Official Report of the National Australasian Convention Debates, Melbourne, 2 March 1898, 1750-68 (John Quick).
35　See Australian Constitution s 51(27), (19) respectively.
36　See Chapter 2.5.2.

1.3.2 Conflicting legalities: The influence of international legal principle

[1.24] Although one of the only Western countries to lack a Bill or Charter of Rights, Australia has been far from immune from the influence of the human rights regimes enshrined in international law. The evolving international framework has been a major source of progressive reform in refugee law, for instance, as demonstrated by advocacy for the need for a form of 'complementary protection' in Australian law.

[1.25] Still, as we explore in Chapter 4, Australian courts have refused to countenance the application of core international human rights principles to modify contentious immigration and border control laws. We examine in separate case studies attempts to challenge the indefinite detention of failed asylum seekers (in 2004) and the government's refusal to permit the Norwegian tanker, the *Tampa*, to land on Australian shores with its cargo of 433 asylum seekers in 2001. The 'Pacific Solution' then adopted by Australia created a precedent that other refugee receiving countries have used to justify their own diversionary strategies when presented with a flow of asylum seekers.[37] It may also have given legal or moral succour to the Labor government, in more recent efforts to interdict and deflect asylum seekers at sea. Although the Labor government dismantled detention centres on Nauru and Papua New Guinea, the imperative of border control continues to drive our regional engagement (especially now with Indonesia and East Timor). The 'excision' of outlying Australian island territories from Australia's migration zone continues, in the face of international human rights obligations to the contrary.

[1.26] In Chapter 4 we note that at least some of the disappointments in Australian practice in this area can be explained by limitations and uncertainties in international law itself. These – and the absence of any real accountability mechanisms beyond the court of world opinion – have allowed Australia to deny that its actions have constituted breaches of its international legal obligations. Nowhere is the 'wriggle room' in international law more apparent than in the arguments made by Australia in defence of action taken to interdict and deflect asylum seekers wishing to claim protection as refugees on its territory. Indeed, international law provides surprisingly little in the way of a rights regime for asylum seekers who take to the seas in their quest for safe haven.

1.3.3 Of government, administration and control

[1.27] Australia's exceptional ability to control immigration has been matched by a long historical preoccupation with the selection of 'appropriate' migrants. Paradoxically, in spite of their sociological significance, the laws regulating the admission and exclusion of non-citizens have attracted until recently surprisingly little interest amongst lawyers and legal academics in Australia. The reasons for the neglect appear to have lain in the traditionally closed and highly politicised nature of the migration decision-making process. If there is a theory of state behind every

---

37 See the special issue devoted to offshore processing in (2006) 18(2) *International Journal of Refugee Law*.

system of administrative law, immigration regulation raises some of the weightiest questions that exercise scholars of public law and policy. Regulating the admission of non-citizens into the Australian community (for a week as a tourist or a lifetime as a skilled permanent resident) involves the consideration of macro-economics, labour market theories and the social effects of modifying our demography. At a mechanistic level, questions arise about the appropriate procedures that should be adopted to select migrants; what should be the proper role of review in the overall administrative scheme; and what should be the relationship between parliament, the executive and the courts.

[1.28] In Chapter 5 we examine historical trends in the administration of immigration in Australia, tracing the movement from discretionary decision-making, through 'codification' to the segmenting effects of outsourcing aspects of the decision-making function. Chapter 6 surveys the laws governing physical admission into the country, as well as the common entry criteria designed to either limit the negative impact of migration on society or to protect the Australian community from harmful influences. Here we discuss the considerable simplification which continues to occur, both at the level of available visas granting entry and the procedures for assessing eligibility for a visa grant which have been articulated with progressively greater clarity.

1.3.4 The place of the family

[1.29] There are pragmatic reasons why Australia's elected representatives continue to favour immigration to some extent. With a high proportion of the population born overseas, there has been a natural tendency over the years for migrants to seek the admission of close and extended family members. The self-perpetuating phenomenon of 'chain migration' means that family migration will always feature strongly in Australia's immigration program. Nevertheless, there have been quite remarkable changes in the family intake programs over the years. In light of the prominence that has been given to skilled migration since the 1960s, family migration has been seen increasingly as undesirable, both because of its long-term networking effect and its medium-term impact on the labour market and social welfare.

[1.30] The most obvious manifestation of the sharper economic focus of the program is the declining prominence given to families in the annual migrant intake. Other, more enduring, changes to family migration are explored in Chapter 7, dealing with partner entry, and Chapter 8, focusing on migration of other family members. It will be seen that the recent history of the law in this area has been one of shrinking entitlement. Efforts to reduce the economic costs associated with family migration have been reflected in moves to upgrade the responsibilities of sponsors, to adopt more of a user-pays approach to visa costs, and to limit the access of newly arrived migrants to social security support. At the same time, the overweening concern in this area appears to have been the prevention of program abuse through fraudulent applications claiming sham relationships or non-genuine relationships of convenience. Interestingly, as we will see in later chapters, devices introduced in the context of family migration have been adopted later across much of the skilled and business migration program to shape migration laws and policies in Australia more broadly.

1.3.5 The business of migration: Skilled migrants, tourism and the international student sector

[1.31] The influence of labour market regulation on Australian immigration policy has been something of a constant throughout history. However, the past decade has seen a surge in the intake of skilled migrants accompanied by dramatic changes in thinking about labour migration. In the early years, attention was paid to the macro-economic impact of labour migration and to how migrant workers might affect the working conditions of Australian workers. The focus was on the physical constitution of the labour market by local workers and permanent migrant workers whose terms and conditions of work were regulated in an integrated manner. In contrast, the modern rules seem to be fixed more closely on the micro-management of the labour market in terms of who is available to perform specific tasks. Much less attention is paid now to the broader impacts of foreign workers and businesses on the local workforce. Increasing emphasis has been placed on the engagement of 'fully formed' migrants, preferencing those most likely to move directly into a given position in the market. In Chapter 9 we analyse the operation of skilled and business migration programs facilitating the entry of permanent migrants chosen mainly for the economic or labour market contribution they are expected to make.

[1.32] Chapter 10 explores the highly divisive area of temporary skilled migration. The source of the controversy is not, on the whole, the broad policy issues raised by temporary skilled migration. In as much as these are concerned with reconciling the immediate labour needs of employers and protecting local labour interests, they do not differ significantly from permanent migration. Rather, the contention stems from the radical growth in numbers of temporary migrant workers across a short period. For the first time in Australian history, the mid 1990s saw the number of temporary migrants (staying in Australia for at least one year) exceed the number of people arriving for permanent settlement. By June 2008 there were around half a million temporary migrants with work rights in Australia – almost 5 per cent of the total labour force, although these numbers fell later with the onset of the global financial crisis later that year. Temporary labour migration stands apart in terms of the potential for exploitation of workers involved in the scheme, especially at the low end of the wage scale. The early years of the new Millennium saw an unprecedented rise in concerns about employer exploitation of migrants in Australia on temporary work visas. Tales of abuse and even worker deaths prompted novel public debates in Australia. These centred on the rights of temporary migrants; the appropriate balance between easy deployment of labour to meet skills shortages; what constitutes effective government oversight; and the relationship between temporary migration to Australia and Australia's regional development efforts. All are issues that have long occupied civil society agitators and government policy-makers from Germany to the United States. The role of union advocacy in this area over others within skilled migration policy also marks it as unique. Numerous parliamentary reviews of the temporary skilled migration scheme and legislative amendments introduced by successive governments have not yet achieved an easy reconciliation of the competing pressures of economic policy and industrial fairness.

[1.33] Chapter 11 deals with the short-term migration of international students and tourists, areas of the migration program designed foremost to serve the highly lucrative tourism and foreign education industries. The linking of the foreign student visa program with the general skilled migration program in the latter years of conservative rule caused all manner of problems in this area, as we explore in this chapter. Accessibility of visas and simplicity of administration directly influence how well Australia is able to position itself as an attractive holiday destination and as a provider of quality education within competitive international markets. At the same time, compliance dominates government attention in these areas as the government attempts to control the admission of temporary migrants; to ensure their timely departure and in some cases to streamline their ultimate reception as permanent migrants through the skilled or family programs.

1.3.6   Refugees and forced migration

[1.34] An aspect of immigration policy that traditionally assumes disproportionate significance is the admission of non-citizens as refugees or on humanitarian grounds. Within the overseas program, a certain number of places are reserved for the admission from overseas of refugees and other hardship cases. This has been a feature of the program for many years and is generally the subject of little controversy. In addition to this planned intake, however, Australia receives a number of requests for asylum each year from non-citizens within the country. The volume and provenance of such on-shore claims cannot be determined in advance. As a signatory to the UN Convention relating to the Status of Refugees[38] and its attendant Protocol,[39] Australia has assumed certain obligations towards refugees, as defined at international law. It is this unplanned portion of the annual program that is considered most threatening to the integrity of the government's control of immigration and, indeed, at times Australia's borders themselves.

[1.35] As we explore in Chapters 12-14, Australia's on-shore refugee determination processes are a fertile ground for students of law, politics and international relations. The system now in place is the product of a variety of institutional forces. On the one hand, the courts' protection of judicial review and broader developments in the administrative law have forced more open or transparent procedures. Most refugee applicants whose claims are rejected at first instance have access to tribunal review. The role played by international law through the Refugee Convention, as the ultimate source of Australia's obligation not to 'refoule' a refugee to a place where they have a well-founded fear of persecution, provides certain core rights or principles which might otherwise have been legislated away in the absence of a Charter of Rights.

[1.36] On the other hand, the furore that seems always to surround the arrival of boats carrying asylum seekers provides a focal point for people disaffected with

---

[38]   *Convention Relating to the Status of Refugees* (adopted 28 July 1951, entered into force 22 April 1954) 189 UNTS 137. Australia's accession took place on 22 April 1954. See Aust TS 1954 No 5.

[39]   Protocol Relating to the Status of Refugees (adopted 31 January 1966, entered into force 4 October 1967) 606 UNTS 267.

the immigration program. The depth of community concern allows the government to implement punitive policies that would not be tolerated were they applied more widely. The assertion by successive governments that they need to 'send a clear message' of deterrence to aspiring refugee claimants manifests not only in the perpetuation of detention in remote outposts like Christmas Island. We also see enduring evidence of the 'battle royal' between courts and parliament, as the inevitable jurisprudential evolution of refugee law is met by legislative curtailments of its scope.

1.3.7 Unlawful status: Arrest, detention and enforcement

[1.37] Australia's experience of unlawful or irregular migration has been relatively limited in world terms, thanks in large measure to its geography and isolation. Ironically, the limited lived experience of irregular migration seems to have generated an abnormal preoccupation with border control. In Chapters 15-17 we consider the evolution of the law in this area. We document both the progressive toughening of the government's approach to immigration outlaws and Australia's concern with controlling the quality and quantity of migrants entering the country. The legal methods used to restrict unlawful entry and stay have been consistently refined. The grounds on which non-citizens lose their right to remain in Australia have never been clearer. In Chapter 16, we examine in turn the mechanics of immigration enforcement at and before the point of entry; arrest; detention; and removal orders. We explore the recent extent to which approaches to detention represent a departure from the mandatory detention model introduced in 1992 under the Labor government, fortified by the Howard Coalition government.

[1.38] In Chapter 17 we examine in detail the real losers in the populist battle to 'clean up' the immigration program. These are the 'deportees': permanent residents convicted of serious crimes. We recount here the gradual development of a zero tolerance policy that has seen individuals who have spent most of their lives in Australia – in some cases all bar a few days – deported on the ground that they are of 'bad character'. It is a trend that seems to transcend party lines. The change of government in 2007 brought no appreciable changes to either policy or practice in this contentious area. It is yet another area in which Australian immigration law has parted company with the laws and policies of comparator states.

1.3.8 Having the last word: Immigration appeals and judicial review

[1.39] Despite successive efforts to circumscribe the role of the courts, the High Court has safeguarded its role as the ultimate arbiter of the legality of migration decisions. The book concludes in Chapters 18 and 19 with an account of the law governing the review of migration decisions – first at an administrative level in what is known as merits review, and then in judicial review. In this respect we return full circle to the role that immigration has played in the development of public (administrative) law in this country. It is not always a happy or a pretty story. In fact we tend to agree with commentators who suggest that the immigration cases have had a distorting effect on basic principles of administrative law.[40] As Australia moves into a new Millennium, our final plea is that we turn away from the 'exceptionalist' tendencies evident in the immigration jurisprudence. It is time indeed to take this area of public law back into the mainstream.

---

40 See, for example, Michael Taggart, '"Australian Exceptionalism" in Judicial Review' (2008) 36 *Federal Law Review* 1; and Anthony North and Peace Decle, 'The Courts and Immigration Detention: Once a Jolly Swagman Camped by a Billabong' (2003) 10 *Australian Journal of Administrative Law* 5.

2

Immigration Law and the Growth of Nationhood

2.1 Becoming Australian: Of citizenship, alienage and belonging

[2.01] The law governing immigration and citizenship in Australia cannot be understood fully without some appreciation of Australian history and of how attitudes to what might loosely be termed 'citizenship' and 'alienage' have – and have not – changed over the years. Quite apart from the high proportion of Australians either born overseas or who have a foreign-born parent,[1] Australia is a country that was self-consciously 'created' out of a *selected* population. Migration laws have been vehicles for controlling both entry to territory and, just as importantly, participation in the community. In this respect, it will be argued that immigration law in this country has played a significant role in determining what it means to be 'Australian'.

[2.02] In the period following Federation in 1901, the fixation was on the racial composition of the migration intake and on the social and cultural identity of the developing society. More recently, the focus has been on border protection and measures to maximise the economic worth of the migration program. A unifying thread running through from the earliest days, however, is the expectation that immigration to Australia should be a controlled affair – and the preserve of the executive arm of government as defender of Australian sovereignty. The only state in the world that lays claim to an entire continent, Australia is also one of very few nations where, by accident of geography, population and history, there has been an ability to regulate closely who enters and leaves the country. As Isaacs J commented in *R v Macfarlane; Ex parte O'Flanagan and O'Kelly*:

> The history of this country and its development has been, and must inevitably be, largely the story of its policy with respect to population from abroad. That

---

1   At Federation in 1901, 23 per cent of Australia's population consisted of persons born overseas. By 1947 this percentage had decreased to 10 per cent. The major migration flows from Europe for several decades after the Second World War, and in recent decades from an increasingly wide range of countries (in Asia and Africa), saw an increase of the proportion of Australians born overseas to 27 per cent by 2009. See Australian Bureau of Statistics, '3412.0 – Migration, Australia, 2008-9' (2010), available at <http://www.abs.gov.au/ausstats/abs@.nsf/Latestproducts/3412.0Main%20Features12008-09?opendocument&tabname=Summary&prodno=3412.0&issue=2008&num&view=>.

naturally involves the perfect control of the subject of immigration, both as to encouragement and restriction with all their incidents.[2]

[2.03] The notion of immigration control as *natural* and its obverse – unauthorised entry – as anathema resonates in the recent history of refugee law in Australia, as we shall see later in the book.

[2.04] If immigration control is part of Australia's 'deep' culture, the process of articulating who is and is not 'Australian' has been less straightforward. From 1 January 1901, all natural born and naturalised British subjects resident in Australia became members of a new political entity and thereafter might be called 'Australians'. But at Federation no new nationality was created. The sole reference to the term 'citizen' in the Australian Constitution is in s 44 which makes citizens or subjects of a foreign power ineligible for election to the Commonwealth Parliament. The Constitution makes no reference to Australian citizenship, nor does it furnish the Commonwealth with an express power to make laws with respect to citizenship. The terms 'subject of the Queen', 'resident' or 'people of the Commonwealth' are used to refer to membership of the Australian community.[3] On the other hand, the list of enumerated powers conferred on the federal legislature include powers to legislate with respect to 'immigration and emigration' (s 51(27)); 'naturalization and aliens' (s 51(19)); and 'external affairs' (s 51(29)). In the words of John Quick,[4] citizenship in Australia was a mere 'legal inference' derived from both the text of the Constitution and the act of federating the Australian colonies in 1901.

[2.05] At Federation, Australia did not acquire the status of independent nation and a subject of the Queen born or resident in Australia was legally indistinguishable from a British subject.[5] Australian citizenship as a legal term of art only emerged with the passage of the *Nationality and Citizenship Act 1948* (Cth) which commenced operation on Australia Day 1949 (this was later renamed the *Australian Citizenship Act 1948*). As will be explored in this chapter, the omission forces consideration of what citizenship has meant in Australia as both a normative and practical concept.[6]

[2.06] The concrete attributes of citizenship are described by some theorists as bestowing 'status' in the sense that rights and privileges denote full membership of a given community.[7] In this context, Australian history provides a vivid illustration of the gulf that can separate legal form and content, and of the very different meanings that can be ascribed to the word 'citizenship'. All persons physically present in the country at Federation were formally brought together as members

---

2   (1923) 32 CLR 518 at 557.
3   See, for example, s 117 of the Constitution.
4   'Again, I ask are we to have a Commonwealth citizenship? If we are, why is it not to be implanted in the *Constitution*? Why is it to be merely a legal inference?' See *Record of the Debates of the Constitution*, Vol V, 1767, cited in Kim Rubenstein, *Australian Citizenship Law in Context* (Melbourne: Law Book Co, 2002) at 24.
5   *Nolan v MIEA* (1988) 165 CLR 178 at 183.
6   See Kim Rubenstein, 'Citizenship and the Centenary: Inclusion and Exclusion in 20th Century Australia' (2000) 24 *Melbourne University Law Review* 576 and Part 2.4 below.
7   See TH Marshall, *Citizenship and Social Class, and Other Essays* (Cambridge: Cambridge University Press, 1950) and TH Marshall, *Sociology at the Crossroads and Other Essays* (London: Heinemann, 1963).

of the Commonwealth of Australia, as British subjects bearing a common allegiance to the British Monarch. If the act of federating created a notional common citizenship, however, the new country's laws and policies conferred differential rights and privileges on the people living within its polity. The newly created 'Australians' were not created equal.

[2.07] It is beyond the scope of this book to engage in any detail with the many and varied theoretical understandings of citizenship – as legal, formal membership,[8] as participation in civic life,[9] as entitlement to benefits,[10] as a constraining mechanism aimed at social control,[11] as a compact requiring mutual consent,[12] or as a device for exclusion and group definition.[13] At the same time, the legislative silences in early Australia mean that it is only through an examination of laws and policies affecting membership, participation and entitlement that a true appreciation can be had of what it meant to be an Australian citizen. What emerges most starkly in this analysis is the role that migration law has played in the development of an Australian identity. Not only did the law in this area regulate physical movement and the legal status of people crossing Australian borders, it also served as a benchmark for determining the civil rights and entitlements of individuals across Australian society.

[2.08] As explored in Part 2.4 of this chapter, notions of Australian citizenship developed as social rather than as purely territorial concepts. Australia's indigenous peoples were grouped together with migrants and people of colour in their shared experience of exclusion and deprivation. This was a double irony for Australia's first peoples: because Australian citizenship should have been a quintessential birthright (*jus soli*) as the original and true native Australians and because connection with land and place is so essential to aboriginal culture and law.[14]

---

8   The literature on the various meanings of citizenship is voluminous and extends across many disciplines. See Kim Rubenstein and Daniel Adler, 'International Citizenship: The Future of Nationality in a Globalized World' (2000) 7 *Indiana Journal of Global Legal Studies* 519; Rubenstein, above n 4, Ch 1.2; Linda Bosniak, 'Citizenship Denationalized' (2000) *Indiana Journal of Global Legal Studies* 447.

9   See, for example, Roberto Alejandro, *Hermeneutics, Citizenship and the Public Sphere* (Albany: State University of New York Press, 1993); Bosniak, above n 8; Linda Bosniak, 'Universal Citizenship and the Problem of Alienage' (2000) 94 *Northwestern University Law Review* 963; Carole Pateman, *The Disorder of Women: Democracy, Feminism and Political Theory* (Cambridge: Polity Press, 1989); and Will Kymlicka and Wayne Norman, 'The Return of the Citizen: A Survey of Recent Work on Citizenship Theory' (1994) 104 *Ethics* 352.

10 Marshall, *Citizenship and Social Class*, above n 7; Rubenstein, above n 4; Joseph Carens, 'Aliens and Citizens: The Case for Open Borders' (1987) 49 *Review of Politics* 251.

11 Baron de Charles de Secondat Montesquieu, *The Spirit of the Laws*, Franz Neumann (ed), Thomas Nugent (trans) (New York: Hafner Publishing Company, 1949).

12 See Peter Schuck and Rogers Smith, *Citizenship without Consent* (New Haven: Yale University Press, 1985); David Wishart, 'Allegiance and Citizenship as Concepts in Constitutional Law' (1986) 15 *Melbourne University Law Review* 662.

13 See, for example, Rubenstein, above n 6; Catherine Dauvergne, 'Citizenship, Migration Laws and Women: Gendering Permanent Residency Statistics' (2000) 24 *Melbourne University Law Review* 280; Sandra Berns, 'Law, Citizenship and the Politics of Identity: Sketching the Limits of Citizenship' (1998) 7 *Griffith Law Review* 1.

14 John Chesterman and Brian Galligan, *Citizens Without Rights* (Melbourne: Cambridge University Press, 1997).

[2.09] Rubenstein[15] argues that the notion of citizenship in Australia has been complicated considerably by the failure to insert provisions in the Australian Constitution that address either the legal status of Australian citizen, or the consequences of citizenship in this country. In this chapter, it will be argued that the omission was no accident, but a reflection of the complex forces at work when the colonies founded by Britain came together at Federation. The control of immigration was crucial to this process because it quite literally determined who was to be considered a constituent member of the new polity. Indeed, in some respects citizenship in Australia seems to have developed in the space left unregulated by the (exclusionary) migration law – a bit like Dworkin's hole in the doughnut.[16]

[2.10] The chapter begins with a short discussion of the constitutional debates over the articulation of an Australian citizenship. The role played by the Australian Constitution in shaping the nation – and the control of immigration – is indeed complex and for this reason will be re-visited in Chapter 3. For present purposes, this brief introduction to the constitutional issues provides a base from which to explore the evolution of the country's first immigration laws and the way these were used to determine membership of, and exclusion from, a distinctly Australian polity.[17] The centrality of racial identity as the discrimen between 'subject', 'citizen' and 'alien' is examined in two contexts. The first relates to the operation of the 'dictation test' which was administered selectively to 'immigrants' of colour: see Part 2.3. A coda to this part acknowledges that the exclusionary device was also used cynically to exclude other 'undesirable' individuals. Second, a particular study is made in Part 2.4 of the parallels between Australia's early treatment of migrants and its handling of its indigenous peoples. The discussion underscores the role played by 'race' in the development of notions of Australian citizenship but demonstrates also the nexus between exclusionary measures devised for migrants and those applied to 'created' outsiders within the Australian polity.

[2.11] The legacy of Australia's immigration history is explored in the last part of the chapter with an examination of a series of cases in which the constitutional status of 'alien' has been considered. In this section a case study is presented on the status of children born in Australia to non-citizen parents. As explored further in Chapter 3, one legacy of the failure to entrench an Australian citizenship in the Constitution is the High Court's acceptance that Federal Parliament has extraordinary power to determine both membership of the Australian community and the rights and entitlements attaching to non-citizen or 'alien' status. Again, immigration *law* has been central to this. As well as providing a legal basis (legitimacy) for exclusionary policies, Australia's immigration laws have been the legal vehicles used to explore the relationship between citizens, aliens and government within the limits of constitutional law.[18]

---

15 See Rubenstein, above n 4.
16 See Ronald Dworkin, *Taking Rights Seriously* (Cambridge: Harvard University Press, 1977) at 31.
17 The arguments made are not novel. See, for example, Rubenstein, above n 4; Catherine Dauvergne, *Humanitarianism, Identity, and Nation: Migration Laws of Australia and Canada* (Vancouver: UBC Press, 2005).
18 For a discussion of the significance of law as a mechanism for legitimising behaviour in a very different context, see David Fraser, *Law After Auschwitz: Towards a Jurisprudence of the Holocaust* (Durham: Carolina Academic Press, 2005).

2.2 Citizenship and the Australian Constitution

[2.12] The eventual silence in the Constitution on matters of citizenship certainly does not reflect an absence of interest in the concept by the delegates to the Federal Constitutional Conventions. As Rubenstein has chronicled, the decision not to include a notion of citizenship in the Australian Constitution was made after careful deliberation, with delegates advancing a variety of reasons for the omission.[19]

[2.13] Federation marked the establishment of a new democratic and representative political entity and debates about the creation of the Commonwealth demanded terminology that could be employed to describe those who were to be part of the new body politic. With the republican United States Constitution as a source of inspiration and practical help, the term 'citizen' was used liberally in the Convention debates as a synonym for subject, elector, resident or simply person. It was applied to members of the existing political communities, the British colonies, and the new community to be created by the federal compact. Often only a close examination of the context reveals the meaning in which the term was used, and failure to do so often leads to greater significance being attributed to delegates' remarks on citizenship than they might otherwise deserve.

[2.14] Delegate from Victoria and later author of the authoritative annotation of the Constitution, John Quick,[20] was responsible for a motion extolling the 'apparently logical contention' that the Commonwealth have power to make laws with respect to citizenship and that the Constitution include a definition of the term.[21] Despite its frequent use in the Convention Debates, when attempts were made to define the term 'citizenship' to include a head of power over the topic, and to enshrine a prohibition on discrimination between citizens of the States, irreconcilable difficulties arose that were only resolved by omitting the term altogether.

[2.15] Some saw no need to define the term 'citizenship', using the logic of 'we know who we are'.[22] Sir Isaac Isaacs saw the task of definition as fraught with 'innumerable difficulties'. There were problems in finding agreement between those who saw citizenship as a way of recognising rights and entitlements and those who saw the status as a way of conferring rights on people. The pervading difficulty facing the framers of the Constitution was the presence in Australia of a range of individuals who were literally and figuratively outsiders to the youthful Anglo-Saxon communities of settlers. These were Australia's indigenous inhabitants, the Asians and other people of colour who had made their way into the various colonies since the arrival of the first fleet from England. Rubenstein argues that the desire to carve out an Australian polity with certain racial characteristics is probably the chief reason why

---

19 See Rubenstein, above n 4, at 30-3. See also Helen Irving, *To Constitute a Nation: A Cultural History of Australia's Constitution* (1997) Ch 9, 'Citizens'.
20 John Quick and Robert Garran, *The Annotated Constitution of the Australian Commonwealth* (1901).
21 See *Official Records of the Debates of the Australasian Federal Convention*, 3rd Session, Melbourne 1898, at 1752.
22 See the account of South Australian delegate to the Constitutional Convention in Melbourne in 1898, Josiah Symon, in Rubenstein, above n 4, at 29.

the Australian Constitution did finally go to the vote without a clause creating an Australian citizenship.[23]

[2.16] In their annotated Constitution, Quick and Garran lament that despite the 'apparently logical' contentions in the 1889 Convention that there should be a national citizenship 'above, beyond and immeasurably superior to State citizenship' these contentions were not accepted, and consequently legal membership of the Commonwealth must be deduced from the Constitution rather than flowing from explicit provision.[24] Nonetheless they acknowledge that 'there might have been an impropriety' in preferring citizen over subject.[25] The nearest concept in the Constitution equivalent to citizenship of the Commonwealth is 'people of the Commonwealth' but that is a subsidiary status to subjects of the Queen common to the individual units of the Empire. Quick and Garran regarded the new status as at least an embryonic Australian nationality. They suggest that people of the Commonwealth who 'territorially' may be termed Australians, although 'constitutionally' remaining British subjects or subjects of the Queen, nonetheless acquired the 'character' of a member of the people of the Commonwealth. This, they state, is a national character not lost either when travelling between the States of the Federation, between parts of the Empire or outside it.[26]

[2.17] In their study of how Australia's early laws impacted on the citizenship of the country's indigenous inhabitants, Chesterman and Galligan point out that the absence of citizenship provisions in the Constitution cannot be 'blamed' for all the discriminatory practices that became entrenched after Federation.[27] The real disenfranchisement of the 'unwanted' inhabitants of Australia occurred through a web of state and federal enactments. What these authors might have noted, however, is that these enactments were facilitated by the silences in the Constitution in both the legal form and practical meaning of the concept of citizen. The most striking irony for the immigration scholar is the correlation between the measures taken by the newly federated colonialists – nearly all migrants themselves – to exclude from the 'Australian' polity indigenous people and non-white migrants.

[2.18] The peculiar evolution of Australian citizenship laws reflects the fact that the colonialists began first as British subjects. This status pertained to all persons born on British territory, colonial or otherwise, and could not be renounced.[28] A person might also involuntarily become a British subject should the territory in which they were born be conquered, occupied and annexed.[29] Until Australia Day 1949 the

---

23 See ibid. Irving, above n 19, highlights the difficulty that constitutional entrenchment of the term 'citizen' would have created at a time when the legally appropriate term for membership of the polity was 'subject'. This problem, she suggests, must be distinguished from the proposal, also debated at the Convention, to include a provision, styled on the Fourteenth Amendment of the United States Constitution, governing the acquisition of 'citizenship' by birth and protecting the rights of 'citizens'. It was the latter proposal that attracted opposition on racial grounds.
24 See Quick and Garran, above n 20, at 955.
25 Ibid at 957.
26 Ibid at 957-8.
27 See Chesterman and Galligan, above n 14, Ch 3.
28 See *Re Ho* (1975) 10 SASR 250 at 253.
29 *On v Commonwealth* (1952) 86 CLR 1255.

only formal nationality possessed by Australians was that of British subject. One concomitant of a single sovereign reigning over the Empire and Commonwealth was a shared nationality. However, it was not a universal nationality because distinctions were drawn between the British subjects of various polities. Colonial naturalisation was of limited effect as a naturalised British subject in one part of the British Empire would not generally be recognised as such in another. The colonies that eventually formed the Australian Commonwealth were no exception to this rule.

[2.19] While the Australian colonies were legislating to enable the 'naturalisation' of newcomers to their communities from as early as 1828,[30] there were only limited attempts before Federation to address the issue of mutual recognition between the colonies of such naturalisation processes. Rubenstein notes that, as a precursor to Federation, the Federal Council of Australasia did pass an *Australian Naturalisation Act* in 1897.[31] However, as New South Wales was not a member of this Council, the measure could not be said to apply across Australia. In other respects, the portability of status between Britain and colonies in Australia was uncertain.[32]

[2.20] As explored in the following sections, after Federation, membership of the Australian community was defined as much by who was excluded as by who was included in various enactments addressing the status of persons already in the country. While some concessions were made for 'Asiatics' born in Australia, in most respects persons of colour born overseas were treated in the same way as the country's first peoples. Both groups were denied both participation in and protection by the new Australian polity. To understand how this point was reached, however, it is useful to go back a little further in time to examine the formative role played by immigration law in the colonies. It is beyond the scope of this work to examine comparative experiences throughout other British colonies and in other parts of the 'New World'. Having said this, emergent historical research suggests that the development of the White Australia Policy was far from unique. It was part of a much broader international trend that saw the creation of racial hierarchies characterised by a bi-polarisation of the world's populations into (superior) 'white' and (inferior) 'coloured'.[33]

2.3 The evolution of Australia's early immigration laws

[2.21] For a country built on immigration, Australia is unusual in that it was colonised in a deliberate and almost systematic fashion. The process began with the transportation of convicts and continued with the importation of free settlers given

---

30   See Clive Parry, *Nationality and Citizenship Laws of the Commonwealth and of the Republic of Ireland* (London: Stevens and Sons, 1957); Rubenstein, above n 4, at 50-1.
31   See Rubenstein, above n 4, at 51.
32   Note that an individual naturalised in Australia under the 1903 Act was not recognised as a British subject in the United Kingdom. See *Markwald v Attorney General* [1920] 1 Ch 348.
33   See Marilyn Lake and Henry Reynolds, *Drawing the Global Colour Line: White Men's Countries and the Question of Racial Equality* (Melbourne: Melbourne University Press, 2008). On the role that immigration laws have played around the world in doing the 'dirty work' of excluding people from membership of communities, see Catherine Dauvergne, *Making People Illegal: What Globalisation Means for Migration and Law* (Vancouver: Cambridge University Press, 2008) at 123.

assisted passage. The measured nature of the first program of white immigration to Australia was a reflection of Britain's contemporary dominance as a colonial power. The homogeneous background of the first settlers and their geographic isolation from the Anglo-European culture with which they were familiar appear to have encouraged a precocious interest in controlling the character and composition of the early colonial societies. Asian or 'coloured' people were excluded from entry into the country, while the aboriginal people were denied participation in the community: see below. The colonies' concern to control immigration was unusual given that foreigners in contemporary Britain were given unrestricted rights of entry and residence.[34] So too was the care taken to enact *laws* to achieve the outcomes sought. As Bruce Kershaw notes,[35] Australia's very first settlers showed a very early preoccupation with establishing a rule of law in Australia that was appropriate to prevailing needs and conditions. The adoption of British law without modification was not an option.[36] If the law was needed to control the transplanted population, in part by giving legitimacy to the governors, it was also needed to define the population.

[2.22] Fear of being overrun by an alien culture ensured that immigration control was placed high on the colonies' law-making agenda. Victoria was the first to legislate against the admission of non-Europeans in 1855, when concerns grew about the number of Chinese people coming into the colony in search of gold. The Victorian 'Act to Make Provision For Certain Immigrants' limited the number of Chinese passengers who could be brought in any one vessel to one for every 10 tonnes of registered tonnage.[37] Marilyn Lake suggests that this legislation was not only the first race-based immigration restriction in the world, it actually defined the notion of 'immigrant' in racial terms – as any adult male of Chinese descent.[38] The measure proved ineffective in the heat of the gold rush: Chinese migrants simply disembarked in South Australia and travelled overland to the goldfields.[39] However, anti-Asian rioting in the Victorian gold fields in 1857 spurred the colonial governments in Victoria and in adjoining colonies to introduce further restrictive measures. These included the introduction of a residence tax for Asian immigrants[40] which had such a dramatic impact on the population of resident Chinese nationals that the Act of 1855 was repealed as unnecessary in 1865.[41] Similar legislation was re-introduced in 1881 with the *Chinese Act 1881* (Vic). The ensuing years saw the introduction of

---

34 See Kathryn Cronin, 'A Culture of Control: An Overview of Immigration Policy-Making' in James Jupp and Marie Kabala (eds), *The Politics of Australian Immigration* (Canberra: AGPS, 1993) at 84.
35 Bruce Kercher, *An Unruly Child: A History of Law in Australia* (Sydney: Allen and Unwin, 1995).
36 A significant number of the first settlers were convicts transported to Australia for life. Considered dead under British law, it was plain from the start that the new colony would be ungovernable if the convicts were considered to be outside of the law. For an example of how the law in the colonies was adapted from the start, see *Kable v Lord* (1812-1814) NSW Sel Cas (Kercher) 475.
37 See Myra Willard, *History of the White Australia Policy* (Melbourne: Melbourne University Press, 1923) at 21.
38 Private correspondence with Mary Crock, 18 June 2008. Note that California introduced a landing tax payable by a ship's master for each alien passenger in 1852. However, the measure was a tax rather than a measure to restrict arrivals. See Lake and Reynolds, above n 33, at 17-18.
39 Ibid at 20-1.
40 See *An Act to Regulate the Residence of Chinese Population in Victoria 1857*, 21 Vict c 41.
41 See *Chinese Immigrants Act 1865*, 30 Vict c 8, discussed in Willard, above n 37, at 35.

measures by all the colonies to limit first Asian, and then any 'coloured', migration.[42] The measures were not without controversy; in many respects they ran counter to contemporary trends favouring freedom of movement (for trade and people) within the British dominions.[43]

[2.23] The moves to restrict coloured migration were part of a broader vision of Australia as an emerging nation. Immigration control was linked inextricably with labour policies designed to foster local industries and protect the wages and conditions of workers. It is a defining aspect of the Federation of the Australian States and Territories that the early politicians were determined that the nation would not be built on the backs of indentured 'coloured' labourers brought in from overseas.[44] In this, and in other respects, the founders of Australia's Constitution looked quite explicitly at the experience of the Americans, for whom the slavery battles of the great Civil War were still a recent memory. As Lake and Reynolds document, there was considerable cross fertilisation between the two countries in what the respective politicians were both reading and doing as legislators.[45] The earliest federal laws reflected these policies in measures that both restricted the admission of non-white migrants and ensured the removal of Pacific Island labourers brought out to work the Queensland sugar cane fields before December 1906.[46]

[2.24] The status of the colonies as satellites of Britain made the task of restricting entry more complex than it might otherwise have been. On the most basic level, it was uncertain as to when and under what auspice power passed from Britain to the Australian colonies allowing unilateral decisions to be made about who should or should not be admitted into their communities. The matter came to a head in 1888 when a ship named the 'Afghan' arrived in Victoria bearing a number of Chinese nationals. The Collector of Customs – and the unions – refused to allow the ship to dock when it was discovered that some of the passengers had fraudulent travel documents. The ship was forced to sail on to New South Wales, whereupon one passenger disembarked and returned to Melbourne. Chung Teong Toy brought an action in the Victorian Supreme Court claiming that the refusal to allow him entry was unlawful.[47] The claim was upheld by a majority of the Full Bench of the Victorian Supreme Court on the ground that the prerogative power to exclude aliens did not extend to the colonial governments in Australia. The case was taken on appeal to the Privy Council which found not so much that the Collector of Customs

---

42 See Willard, above n 37, at 17ff, 201-2; Quick and Garran, above n 20, at 624-7; Anthony Palfreeman, *The Administration of the White Australia Policy* (1967) Ch 1; and Charles Howarth, '"White Australia" and Victoria' (1972) *Twentieth Century* 5.
43 See, for the 1860 Peking Convention, discussed in Lake and Reynolds, above n 33, at 143ff.
44 See Mary Crock, 'Migration Law and the Labour Market: Targeting the Nation's Skills Needs' in Paul Ronfeldt and Ron McCallum (eds), *Labour Law Outlook* (Sydney: ACIIRT, 1997); Lenore Layman, 'To Keep Up the Australian Standard: Regulating Contract Migration 1901-1950' (1996) 70 *Labour History* 25; and Chapter 9 below.
45 See Lake and Reynolds, above n 33, Part 3: Transnational solidarities, in particular at 138ff.
46 See *Pacific Island Labourers Act 1901* (Cth) (repealed by *Migration Act 1958* (Cth)), s 8. The legislation was upheld by the High Court in *Robtelmes v Brenan* (1906) 4 CLR 395. See also the *Contract Immigrants Act 1905* (Cth) (repealed by *Statute Law Revision Act 1950* (Cth)), discussed at Chapter 9.2.1.
47 See *Toy v Musgrove* (1888) 14 VLR 349.

had acted within power, but rather that it could not countenance an action brought by an alien asserting a right to enter British territory. The Council ruled that Mr Toy had no standing to press his claim because of his 'outsider' status. The case stands as one of the earliest of the Australian precedents confirming that the right to exclude aliens is a basic incident of governmental power within a self-governing colony.[48] It is also an early example of a tendency to view immigration law as a weapon of government: attempts by aliens to turn the weapon *on* government were not welcomed.

[2.25] The ruling in *Toy v Musgrove*[49] suggests that the power to regulate immigration had been transferred from London in the second half of the 19th century, probably when the various colonies were granted autonomy.[50]

[2.26] The desire to achieve uniformity in immigration laws is said to have been one of the more pressing reasons favouring the Federation of the colonies and the establishment of a Commonwealth in 1901.[51] The *Immigration Restriction Act 1901* (Cth) was one of the first pieces of legislation passed by Federal Parliament when it sat for the first time in May 1901. This Act borrowed from legislation used successfully in the South African province of Natal and adopted by New South Wales, Western Australia and Tasmania before Federation as a means of restricting non-European migration. Similar legislation had been introduced in Victoria but failed to be passed. The federal legislation received broad-based support. Although its method of controlling immigration attracted a deal of debate,[52] the Act's avoidance of overtly racist language was seen as positive. As Willard notes,[53] the British imperial government was alive to the offence caused by such enactments within its dominions. The Coloured Races Restriction Bills passed during 1896 in New South Wales, South Australia and Tasmania and the Asiatic Restriction Bill 1861 of New Zealand were all refused the Royal assent.[54]

---

48 For discussion of parallel developments in the US, see Stephen Legomsky and Cristina Rodriguez, *Immigration and Refugee Law and Policy* (New York: Foundation Press, 5th ed, 2009) Ch 2; and Donald Galloway, *Essentials of Canadian Law: Immigration Law* (Concord, Ont: Irwin Law, 1997).
49 (1888) 14 VLR 349.
50 See *Musgrove v Toy* [1891] AC 272 and the commentaries of Thomas Haycraft, 'Alien Legislation and the Prerogative of the Crown' (1987) 13 *Law Quarterly Review* 165 at 173; John Waugh, '*Chung Teong Toy v Musgrove* and the Commonwealth Executive' (1991) 2 *Public Law Review* 160; David Wood, 'Responsible Government in the Australian Colonies: *Toy v Musgrove* Reconsidered' (1988) 16 *Melbourne University Law Review* 760; Charles A Price, *The Great White Walls are Built: Restrictive Immigration to North America and Australasia 1836-1888* (Canberra: Australian Institute of International Affairs, Australian National University Press, 1974).
51 See AT Yarwood, *Asian Migration to Australia: The Background to Exclusion 1896-1923* (New York: Cambridge University Press, 1964) at 21. Two critical heads of power were conferred on the federal legislature by s 51 of the Constitution: those permitting the making of laws with respect to immigration and emigration (s 51(27)) and naturalisation and aliens: s 51(19). It was on the first of these placita that the new Federal Parliament relied as the basis for its migration legislation. See also: s 51(6) (defence); s 51(9) (quarantine); s 51(26) (the people of any race); s 51(29) (external affairs); and s 51(30) (relations with Islands of the Pacific) and the discussion below, Chapter 3.
52 See Willard, above n 37, at 120; Yarwood, above n 51, at 22ff; Commonwealth Parliamentary Debates *Hansard* House of Representatives, Vol 4, 6 September 1901 at 4625-66.
53 Willard, above n 37, at 110-13.
54 See also Yarwood, above n 51.

[2.27] In comparison with these acts, the *Immigration Restriction Act 1901*[55] was discreet. It did not openly veto the admission of non-European aliens, but defined six classes of 'prohibited immigrants'. The first of these consisted of persons who 'when asked to do so by an officer, [fail] to write out at dictation and sign in the presence of the officer a passage of fifty words in length in an European language directed by the officer'.[56] The provision was amended in 1905 to read 'in any prescribed language'. The other classes of prohibited immigrants were paupers; idiots or insane persons; persons suffering from a 'loathsome or contagious disease'; certain criminals; and prostitutes or persons living on the prostitution of others.[57]

[2.28] The key to the restrictive function of this legislation was the term 'immigrant', defined implicitly as a person 'entering' Australia. Immigrants were the only persons who were incontestably susceptible to control at point of entry. An attempt was made on at least one occasion to restrict the movement of undesirable persons *between* the states when a 'demented female stowaway' and her infant child were found on the RMS *Medina*, a vessel that arrived in Sydney from Hobart in 1915. However, then Prime Minister WM Hughes ruled that there was no proper legal basis for either preventing the landing or imposing a bond on the woman and her child because she could not be described as an immigrant from overseas.[58]

[2.29] For immigrants from abroad, the most significant exclusionary device was the dictation test, described originally as the 'Education Test'. The test is another example of Australian borrowings from the New World and British colonial experience. Literacy tests were used in Mississippi in 1860 to disenfranchise black Americans and in Natal as a measure to restrict coloured migration.[59] The parliamentary debates preceding the passage of the *Immigration Act 1901* leave little doubt that the objective of the drafters was to create a regime that would discriminate on grounds of race and colour, rather than on any educational proficiency. As Yarwood documents:

> By the time the Bill passed the Senate, the following points had emerged:
> 1. The dictation test would not be applied to 'qualified European immigrants';
> 2. The Customs Officer would select a language with which the intending immigrant was unfamiliar.
>
> If any further assurance were needed on the second point, it was given when the Senate rejected (by 23:3) a motion that the test should be in a language known to the immigrant.[60]

[2.30] The device is interesting in its awkwardness and self-consciousness. While the resolve to exclude 'outsiders' is clear, the drafting demonstrates that the

---

55 Renamed the *Immigration Act 1901* in 1912, and repealed by the *Migration Act 1958*.
56 See *Immigration Act 1901*, s 3(a).
57 See *Immigration Act 1901*, s 3(b), (c), (d) and (f). Note that s 3(g) also prevented the admission of contract workers who had not been given special clearance by the government on the basis of their special skills.
58 Because the woman was not an 'immigrant', the *Immigration Act 1901* did not apply. See National Archive Collection A2, 1915/267.
59 See Lake and Reynolds, above n 33, at 145-6.
60 Yarwood, above n 51, at 24 (footnotes omitted).

Australian Parliament recognised the need to give their policies the legitimacy of legal enactment if their objectives were to be achieved.[61]

2.3.1 The operation of the dictation test

[2.31] The administration of the 'dictation test' was as simple as it was draconian. Any immigrant found in the country within first one and, later, three years of entry could be asked to sit the test.[62] Immigrants who evaded an officer or entered the country at a place where no officer was stationed could be asked to comply with the requirements of s 3(a) 'at any time' after their entry.[63] Those who failed were liable to deportation, a fine and imprisonment.[64] Under s 8, non-British subjects convicted of any crime of violence were liable to undergo a dictation test on their release from prison. Those who failed were deemed to be prohibited immigrants and were subject to mandatory deportation.

[2.32] The dictation test was a thinly disguised device to exclude uneducated non-white migrants. The test could be changed as often as desirable to ensure that individuals who did not fit an officer's ideal of white Australia would be excluded. The immigration official chose the language in which the test was administered.[65] The standard test was difficult enough to ensure that only those most proficient in the English language would pass. Willard provides the following example of a dictation test administered in Western Australia on 1 May 1908:

> Very many considerations lead to the conclusion that life began on sea, first as single cells, then as groups of cells held together by a secretion of mucilage, then as filament and tissues. For a very long time low-grade marine organisms were simply hollow cylinders, through which salt water streams.[66]

[2.33] Of the 153 applicants subjected to a test in 1903, only 13 passed. As the entry requirement became more widely known, the number of Asians seeking admission declined. The 1914 Commonwealth Immigration Return records that only 19 'Asiatics' were refused entry in that year; none passed the dictation test; and more than twice the number of Asian people left Australia than arrived in the country.[67]

2.3.2 Common understandings: The role played by the judiciary in determining 'immigrant' status

[2.34] The reliance on 'mere legal inferences' in Australia's early days as a nation was not restricted to the terms of the Constitution. Faced with the task of creating a legal framework for the control of immigration, the first Federal Parliament opted for legislation that did not codify who was or was not an immigrant. Instead, it chose a

---

61　See generally Lake and Reynolds, above n 33, at 147-50.
62　*Immigration Act 1901*, s 5(2).
63　Ibid, s 5(1).
64　Ibid, s 7.
65　See *Chia Gee v Martin* (1905) 3 CLR 649.
66　Willard, above n 37, at 126.
67　See Willard, above n 37, at 126; Yarwood, above n 51, at 49. Both sources provide similar statistics.

statutory style characterised by broad discretions and decisional mechanisms that, on their face, revealed little of the real criteria applied in making decisions. The result was to throw much of the onus onto the courts to explain and interpret the scope and effect of the legislation. The degree of trust shown by the government in the courts in this arrangement reveals an extraordinarily close relationship between the two: the judiciary appears to have been both philosophically and juridically in tune with the policy initiatives of the government. Given that many of the first judges on the High Court of Australia were former politicians who had participated in the crafting and passage of the legislation on which they were asked to rule, this symbiosis is perhaps not surprising.[68]

[2.35] Although academic opinion on the subject was divided,[69] the judiciary accepted the notion that the power to admit, exclude or expel aliens was one of the prerogative powers of government, and an inherent part of state sovereignty.[70] The Commonwealth Parliament's power to make laws about immigration and aliens, made express in s 51(19) and (27) of the Constitution, was given a wide interpretation. In *Ah Sheung v Lindberg*, the word immigration was held to extend beyond its common meaning of:

> Leaving an old home in one country to settle in a new home in another country, with a more or less defined intention of staying there permanently, or for a considerable time.[71]

Cussen J held that the term covered persons seeking entry to Australia whether they intended to reside permanently or not.[72] The term was interpreted so as to allow the Federal Parliament to control both entry into the country and a person's 'absorption' into the Australian community.[73] The courts upheld Parliament's power under the

---

68 For example, the first Chief Justice, Sir Samuel Griffith, was formerly Premier and former Chief Justice of Queensland. Justice Sir Edmund Barton was the first Prime Minister of Australia and Leader of the Constitutional Conventions which led to Australia becoming a Federation in 1901. Justice Richard Edward O'Connor was a former Minister of Justice and Solicitor-General of New South Wales and the first Leader of the Government in the Senate. The next justices appointed to the bench in 1906 were Sir Isaac Isaacs, formerly Solicitor-General and attorney, and prominent in the Constitutional Convention debates; and Henry Bournes Higgins, a lawyer who also took part in the Convention debates and served in Parliament before his appointment. See Tony Blackshield, Michael Coper and George Williams, *The Oxford Companion to the High Court of Australia* (Melbourne: Oxford University Press, 2001) at 309ff, 53ff, 509ff, 359ff, 321ff.
69 Compare *Chitty on the Law of the Prerogatives of the Crown* (London: Butterworth and Son, 1820); Haycraft, above n 50; William Searle Holdsworth, *A History of English Law* (1938) at 393-400 (deportation is a prerogative power); WF Craies, 'The Right of Aliens to Enter British Territory' (1890) 6 *Law Quarterly Review* 27; John M Evans, *De Smith's Judicial Review of Administrative Action* (London: Stevens and Sons, 4th ed, 1980) at 157ff (contra).
70 See, for example, *Musgrove v Toy* [1891] AC 272; *Robtelmes v Brenan* (1906) 4 CLR 395 at 415; *Attorney-General (Canada) v Cain* [1906] AC 542 at 547; *R v Carter; Ex parte Kisch* (1934) 52 CLR 221 at 223; *Schmidt v Secretary of State for Home Affairs* [1969] 2 Ch 149 at 168, 172; *R v Liveris; Ex parte Da Costa* (1962) 3 FLR 249. See also, below, Part 2.4.
71 [1906] VLR 323 at 332.
72 See also *Mann v Ah On* (1905) 7 WALR 182 at 184-5; *Chia Gee v Martin* (1905) 3 CLR 649; *R v Macfarlane; Ex parte O'Flanagan and O'Kelly* (1923) 32 CLR 518 at 557 and 580; and *Koon Wing Lau v Calwell* (1949) 80 CLR 533 at 558 and 589.
73 *Ah Sheung v Lindberg* [1906] VLR 323 at 332. See also *Potter v Minahan* (1908) 7 CLR 277 at 286-7 and 303; *R v Macfarlane; Ex parte O'Flanagan and O'Kelly* (1923) 32 CLR 518 at 555, 575 and 582; *Koon Wing Lau v Calwell* (1949) 80 CLR 533 at 560.

Constitution to authorise the Minister to impose conditions on the admission of persons for a period of temporary residence as well as on those seeking entry on a permanent basis.[74] While some debate surrounded the significance of an immigrant becoming assimilated or absorbed into the Australian community,[75] the High Court accepted the ability of Parliament to pass laws preventing such absorption.[76] It also upheld legislation aimed at revoking a non-citizen's permission to remain where this had been granted formerly.[77] From the outset, the High Court has also taken an expansive view of statutes empowering the Minister to exclude,[78] detain[79] and deport aliens.[80]

[2.36] Where the courts appear to have been more prepared to engage with decisions made by the early migration officials was in the review of decisions involving the admission of individuals. While the courts upheld some challenges to the way the dictation test was administered,[81] the case law as a whole suggests a judiciary that was highly supportive of government policies. Examples of the High Court's

---

74   See, for example, *Robtelmes v Brenan* (1906) 4 CLR 395 at 415; *R v Macfarlane; Ex parte O'Flanagan and O'Kelly* (1923) 32 CLR 518 at 533, 554-5, 574, 581 and 583; *Ex parte Walsh; In re Yates* (1925) 37 CLR 36 at 64, 81-3, 107 and 137; *O'Keefe v Calwell* (1949) 77 CLR 261 at 277, 287 and 294; *R v Governor of Metropolitan Gaol; Ex parte Molinari* [1962] VR 156; and *R v Green; Ex parte Cheung Cheuk To* (1965) 113 CLR 506.

75   For a synthesis of the 'wide' and 'narrow' views of the immigration power, see generally W Anstey Wynes, *Legislative, Executive and Judicial Powers in Australia* (Sydney: Law Book Co, 5th ed, 1976) at 304-11; Jean Malor, 'Deportation Under the Immigration Power' (1950) 24 *Australian Law Journal* 302; Patrick H Lane, 'Immigration Power' (1966) 39 *Australian Law Journal* 302; Michael Coper, 'The Reach of the Commonwealth's Immigration Power: Judicial Exegesis Unbridled' (1976) 50 *Australian Law Journal* 351; David Wood, 'Deportation, the Immigration Power and Absorption into the Australian Community' (1986) 16 *Federal Law Review* 288.

76   See *O'Keefe v Calwell* (1949) 77 CLR 261 at 288; and *R v Forbes; Ex parte Kwok Kwan Lee* (1971) 124 CLR 168 at 172.

77   See *Ex parte Walsh; In re Yates* (1925) 37 CLR 36 at 85, 127; *R v Kidman* (1915) 20 CLR 425; and *Koon Wing Lau v Calwell* (1949) 80 CLR 533.

78   See *Chia Gee v Martin* (1905) 3 CLR 649; *Mann v Ah On* (1905) 7 WALR 182; *Potter v Minahan* (1908) 7 CLR 277; *Donohoe v Wong Sau* (1925) 36 CLR 404; and *Koon Wing Lau v Calwell* (1949) 80 CLR 533 at 558-9, 589.

79   See *Ex parte Walsh; In re Yates* (1925) 37 CLR 36 at 96; *Koon Wing Lau v Calwell* (1949) 80 CLR 533 at 555-6; *Znaty v Minister for Immigration* (1972) 126 CLR 1 at 9-10; and *Chu Kheng Lim v MILGEA* (1992) 176 CLR 1.

80   The following cases involve challenges to the most important deportation provisions enacted between 1901 and 1988:
    Pacific Island Labourers Act 1901, s 8: *Robtelmes v Brenan* (1906) 4 CLR 395.
    Immigration Act 1901:
       s 4: *O'Keefe v Calwell* (1949) 77 CLR 261; *Koon Wing Lau v Calwell* (1949) 80 CLR 533.
       s 8A: *R v Carter; Ex parte Kisch* (1934) 52 CLR 221.
       s 8AA: *Ex parte Walsh; In re Yates* (1925) 37 CLR 36.
    Migration Act 1958:
       s 13: *R v Governor of Metropolitan Gaol; Ex parte Molinari* [1962] VR 156; *Ivusic v R* (1973) 127 CLR 348.
       ss 13 and 14: *R v Governor of Metropolitan Gaol; Ex parte Molinari* [1962] VR 156; *Ex parte Black; Re Morony* (1965) 83 WN (Pt 1) (NSW) 45.
       s 18: *R v Forbes; Ex parte Kwok Kwan Lee* (1971) 124 CLR 168.
       s 12: *Nolan v MIEA* (1988) 165 CLR 178.
    Wartime Refugees Removal Act 1949: *Koon Wing Lau v Calwell* (1949) 80 CLR 533.

81   See, for example, *Christie v Ah Foo* (1904) 29 VLR 533; *Mann v Ah On* (1905) 7 WALR 182 discussed in Yarwood, above n 51, at 50.

acceptance of the philosophy underlying the early restrictive legislation are found when one compares the different ways in which the judges applied tests devised to determine who was an 'immigrant' for the purposes of the migration legislation.[82] It is difficult to reconcile some of the early decisions of the court except by reference to the basic notions of white superiority and the desire to minimise 'coloured' migration.

[2.37] In *Potter v Minahan*,[83] for example, Isaacs J seems to have placed considerable importance on an applicant's conformity with the norms of Australian society at the turn of the century. He said:

> The ultimate fact to be reached as a test whether a given person is an immigrant or not is whether he is or is not at that time a constituent party of the community known as the Australian people. Nationality and domicile are not the tests; they are evidentiary facts of more or less weight in the circumstances, but they are not the ultimate or decisive considerations.[84]

[2.38] In that case the respondent, James Francis Kitchen Minahan was born to a white woman in Victoria and taken to China by his Chinese father at the age of five. He attempted to re-enter Australia aged about 29. Speaking no English, he was identified as an 'immigrant' for the purposes of the *Immigration Act 1901* and was subjected to a dictation test. Court documents relating to the man's prosecution as a prohibited immigrant before a Melbourne Magistrate tell a rather sad story of loss and double alienation. Minahan's father died when Minahan was 19 and still a student in China. He left the young man with Minahan's carefully preserved birth certificate (issued in Victoria) and instructions relating to his return to Australia. The father appears to have had a half share in a business in Australia and had maintained friendships with individuals who were prepared to come forward to offer financial and evidential support for the young Eurasian man when he tried to re-enter the country. These friends gave evidence of the relationship between Minahan's parents and of the young man's early days in Melbourne before his departure to China. The testimony of one Dern Hoy made particular mention of Minahan's Anglo-Saxon features:

> When he was young man he had a pointed face ...When I went home [to China] everybody called him the foreign devil boy. The accused has half caste features. I recognize him by his half caste features ...

Under examination, Minahan confirmed that his school mates had called him a foreign devil: 'I swore at them'. He also asserted that he and his father had always intended to return to Australia and that he had acted on his intention after failing his school examinations in China on three successive occasions.[85]

[2.39] When Minahan failed to pass the dictation test, he sought a declaration that he should not be submitted to the test because he was not an 'immigrant' for

---

82 The early Commonwealth legislation (now repealed) included: *Pacific Island Labourers Act 1901*; *Immigration Act 1901*; *Contract Immigrants Act 1905*; *War Precautions Act 1914*; *Wartime Refugees Removal Act 1949*.
83 (1908) 7 CLR 277.
84 Ibid at 308.
85 Affidavit filed in the High Court on 22 April 1908, NAA Barcode 3148842.

the purposes of the *Immigration Act 1901*. The magistrate's finding in his favour was appealed ultimately to the High Court. Minahan cross-claimed that he had never properly 'failed' the test in question because the administering officer had abandoned the dictation when Minahan confirmed that he could not speak or write English.

[2.40] As there was no possibility that the applicant's parents were legally married, the High Court accepted that the applicant was deemed to have acquired both his mother's (British) nationality and her domicile in Victoria. The court held that this domicile of origin had not been displaced by a domicile of choice in China. On this basis the majority ruled that Minahan was not an 'immigrant', but a member of the Australian community who was returning home when he sought to re-enter the country.[86] Higgins J disagreed with Isaacs J on the question of the applicant's immigration status but ruled that the administration of the dictation test had involved a fatal error of law.[87] In the result, the 'half-caste' Minahan gained admission. The historical record does not reveal how he fared thereafter.

[2.41] If Mr Minahan was held to be 'coming home', the same logic was not applied to the applicant in *Ah Yin v Christie*.[88] Ah Yin was the foreign born infant child of a Chinese man who had settled in Australia and acquired domicile here. The man sought to obtain entry for his child when his wife died in China. Even though the child had acquired the domicile of his (Asian) father in Australia, the court held that the applicant was an immigrant and so could be subjected to a dictation test and to deportation. In so doing, the court relied heavily on the repeal in 1905 of certain provisions in the *Immigration Act 1901* that had ensured favourable treatment for returning residents and for certain close family members of residents. The legislation was identical to that applicable in *Potter v Minahan* – a case decided one year later, in 1908. One is left to wonder whether the court would have found it easier to hold Ah Yin's 'home' to be with his father in Australia if, like Mr Minahan, one of his parents had been of Anglo-Saxon descent.

[2.42] A later case that is even more difficult to reconcile with *Potter v Minahan* is that of *Donohoe v Wong Sau*.[89] The respondent was born in Australia of naturalised Chinese parents and, like Mr Minahan, was raised in China. When Miss Wong Sau sought to return to Australia as the wife of a Chinese market gardener from New South Wales, she was excluded on the basis that Australia was not her 'home', and charged with being a 'prohibited immigrant' on her failure to pass the dictation test. Not only was the applicant in that case a British subject, she was also legally

---

86 *Potter v Minahan* (1908) 7 CLR 277 at 289, 295-8, 302-3.
87 Ibid at 313-15 (Isaacs J) and 321-2 (Higgins J). Notes for the Guidance of Officers issued in 1906 after this case provide careful instructions on the proper administration of the dictation test before stating: 'The necessity of carrying out these instructions cannot be too strongly impressed, as in the past convictions have been quashed in cases in which the officer did not read the full passage required by law, and make it clear to the immigrant what the law required him to do ... It is intended that the dictation test shall be an absolute bar to admission. Officers will therefore take means to ascertain whether, in their opinion, the immigrant can write English. If it is thought that he can, the test must be administered in some other European language, one with which the immigrant is not acquainted'. NAA Barcode 5112 at p 1.
88 (1907) 4 CLR 1428.
89 (1925) 36 CLR 404.

domiciled in Australia as the spouse of a New South Wales resident. The High Court in this instance agreed with the analysis of Isaacs J, and rejected the applicant on the basis that she was not 'a constituent part of the Australian community'.[90] The case came to the High Court by way of appeal from a decision of the New South Wales' Court of Quarter Sessions which had quashed the respondent's conviction as a prohibited immigrant under s 3 of the *Immigration Act 1901*. The restoration of the conviction brought with it a six-month gaol term and deportation.

2.3.3 The dictation test as a general exclusionary device

[2.43] The fact that the dictation test was designed as a device to exclude unwanted immigrants generally is demonstrated by other cases brought before the courts. These include some of the more notorious instances of misuse of power. For example, shortly before the outbreak of the Second World War the test was applied in an attempt to exclude one Egon Kisch who sought entry to Australia as part of a campaign to foster world-wide opposition to Adolf Hitler. Mr Kisch was fluent in so many European languages that the immigration officer was reduced to administering a test in Scottish Gaelic, a language with which the officer had little familiarity. The High Court pronounced the decision to deport the applicant unlawful on the basis that Scottish Gaelic was not 'an European language' for the purposes of the legislation, but at best a rarely used dialect.[91] On this basis, the High Court issued a writ of prohibition against the magistrate who had convicted Mr Kisch of the offence of being a prohibited immigrant.[92] The case was one of high drama. Kisch was a seasoned campaigner and communist organiser of some international standing. He was well represented before the High Court – by Albert B Piddington no less.[93] Heidi Zogbaum describes the presentation of evidence in the High Court as follows:[94]

> To the amusement of the court and many newspaper readers, Piddington demonstrated that the officer in charge of the Gaelic test himself had only the haziest notion of the language. He translated the set text as, 'As well as we could benefit and if we let her scatter free to the bad', but Piddington explained to the nonplussed listeners that the correct translation was, 'Lead us not into temptation but deliver us from evil'. The language test never quite recovered from the ridicule.

For its part, the Scottish community in Australia was incensed at the downgrading of their language, 'declar[ing] war in the pages of the *Sydney Morning Herald*'.[95]

[2.44] Even as late as 1936, the dictation test was used to exclude immigrant women who defied the sexual mores of their times. Mabel Freer was a (white) daughter of the British empire, born in Bombay to an English Army family. At the age of 26, with two children and recently divorced, she fell in love with an Australian army officer who

---

90   Ibid at 408 (Isaacs J).
91   *Immigration Act 1901*, s 3(a), read together with s 5 of the 1934 legislation.
92   See *R v Wilson; Ex parte Kisch* (1934) 52 CLR 234; Yarwood, above n 51, at 51.
93   Piddington was himself appointed to the High Court but resigned before taking his seat when his independence was questioned. See Graham Fricke, *Judges of the High Court* (Melbourne: Hutchinson of Australia, 1986) at 80.
94   Heidi Zogbaum, *Kisch in Australia: The Untold Story* (Melbourne: Scribe, 2004) at 97 and note 12.
95   Ibid at 98.

was unhappily married and separated from his wife. The pair planned to migrate to Australia and to marry upon the lieutenant obtaining his own divorce. According to historian Raelene Frances,[96] the young man's father-in-law was concerned at this turn of events. He lobbied army acquaintances who in turn persuaded the immigration authorities that Mrs Freer was an undesirable immigrant. Without any explanation as to why she was being singled out, Mrs Freer was detained and required to submit to a dictation test in Italian. Although she attempted to avoid the operation of the test by blocking her ears when the officer read the passage chosen, Evatt J declined to rule either the administration of the test or its application to Mrs Freer unlawful.[97] Frances records the protest when the young woman was eventually admitted to Australia after the matter went to the Federal Cabinet. No apology or compensation was offered for the sullying of Mrs Freer's reputation:

> Her solicitor protested to the attorney-general, 'It seems hard to believe that any government would, in light of the circumstances ... go so far as to exclude a British citizen from its territory.' In his opinion, the way in which the dictation test was used constituted a breach of the basic principles of British justice: a denial of the 'primary right to which every British subject is entitled – open accusation and open opportunity to reply.[98]

[2.45] The courts' support of government initiatives in the immigration field was manifest at different levels. While there were notable dissentients,[99] the language used in the early cases suggests that many judges shared the popular fear that an open immigration program would bring ruin to the country. In *Williamson v Ah On*,[100] the High Court was concerned with the validity of s 5(3) and (3A) of the *Immigration Act 1901*, which cast on immigrants the burden of proving legitimate entry into Australia. The provisions were challenged on the basis that they were not incidental to the immigration power contained in s 51(27) of the Constitution, but were a usurpation of the judicial power of the Commonwealth. With Powers, Rich and Starke JJ in the majority,[101] Isaacs J found the reverse onus of proof to be both within power and totally justified. He said:[102]

> [It] seems to me only elementary self-protection and to be inseparable from any self-governing constitution. I must confess to some surprise that it is necessary to justify [the provisions]. For, otherwise, persons who are criminals, anarchists, public enemies, or loathsome hotbeds of disease, may, by secret or fraudulent entry into the country and being sheltered for a time by their associates, defy and

---

96 Raelene Frances, '"White Slaves" and White Australia: Prostitution and Australian Society' (2004) 19 *Australian Journal of Feminist Studies* 185 at 196ff.
97 See *R v Davey; Ex parte Freer* (1936) 56 CLR 381.
98 See Frances, above n 96, at 197. For a more detailed account of Mrs Freer's troubles, see Kel Robertson, Jessie Hohmann and Iain Stewart, 'Dictating to One of Us: The Migration of Mrs Freer' (2005) 5 *Macquarie Law Journal* 241.
99 See comments by Knox CJ and Gavan Duffy J in *Williamson v Ah On* (1926) 39 CLR 95 at 100-3; Rich and Williams JJ in *Koon Wing Lau v Calwell* (1949) 80 CLR 533 at 569-70, 584-93; *R v Wilson; Ex parte Kisch* (1934) 52 CLR 234.
100 (1926) 39 CLR 95.
101 Knox CJ and Gavan Duffy J dissented and Higgins J did not decide the issue as he held that there was sufficient factual evidence of the respondent's entry in 1911 as an immigrant. See (1926) 39 CLR 95 at 101-2, 108ff, 122-3, 126 and 128-9.
102 Ibid at 104.

injure the entire people of a continent. There is nothing in the Constitution, and nothing in natural justice, which requires this court to sanction such an absurd and almost fatal situation.

[2.46] A later example of judicial concern about the social impact of non-white immigration is found in the judgment of Webb J in *Koon Wing Lau v Calwell*.[103] That case concerned the constitutional validity of the *Wartime Refugees Removal Act 1949* (Cth) as part of a campaign to rid Australia of the Asian and other non-white migrants who had sought refuge in the country during the Second World War. Section 4 purported to apply to all alien refugees who entered Australia during the War who were not domiciled in the country at time of entry. Sections 5 and 7 allowed the Minister to make an order to deport these people and to keep them in custody pending such deportation. The Act was upheld by a majority of the High Court as a valid exercise of the aliens and defence powers conferred by s 51(19) and (6) of the Constitution.[104] Latham CJ and McTiernan J also upheld the Act as a valid exercise of the immigration power in s 51(27) of the Constitution. As one of the majority, Webb J spoke in the following terms about the persons for whom the legislation was intended:

> Their presence here is wholly the result of the operations of war, and is as visible and tangible, and in the opinion of Parliament, may be as undesirable, as the unrepaired damage done by enemy bombing to an Australian city, and may be as validly dealt with under the defence power.[105]

[2.47] Many years were to pass before community and governmental attitudes to non-white, non-Anglo-Saxon migration became more relaxed.[106] Pressure for change in the immigration system seems to have mounted with the advent of large-scale migration to Australia after the Second World War.[107] The increased human traffic into the country brought with it demands for a clearer statement of ministerial and departmental powers to admit and expel non-resident aliens. The government responded in 1958 by introducing a new legislative scheme. The *Migration Act 1958* (Cth), which was subject to few significant amendments until 1989, abolished the dictation test and conferred on the Minister broad and apparently unfettered discretions to deal with the admission, exclusion and deportation of non-citizens.

[2.48] The following chapters contain a more detailed examination of this legislation – and of the domestic and international laws that continue to give it shape. Before turning to these matters, however, it is well to reflect further on the relationship between Australia's first immigration laws and the development of notions of Australian citizenship. The picture that emerges from an exploration of this aspect of Australia's legal history is one of a migrant community setting out to establish and build a new nation in a certain image. That image was self-consciously white, Anglo-Saxon and astute to the pitfalls experienced by other 'created' nations: what

---

103   (1949) 80 CLR 533.
104   Ibid at 563-9, 583, 593-5.
105   Ibid at 594-5.
106   On Australia's attitudes towards and treatment of Jewish migrants, see Paul Bartrop, *Australia and the Holocaust 1933-45* (Melbourne: Australian Scholarly Publishing, 1994).
107   See Ken Rivett, *Australia and the Non-white Migrant* (Melbourne: Melbourne University Press, 1975); M Armit, *Australia and Immigration 1788-1988* (Canberra: AGPS, 1988); and Layman, above n 44.

'old' Europe termed the New Worlds of Canada and North America. Migration law was used to reinforce this.

2.4 Migration law as a benchmark for the treatment of societal 'outsiders': The 'race' factor in the development of an Australian citizenship

> 'I do not think that the doctrine of the equality of man was really ever intended to include racial equality. There is no racial equality. There is that basic inequality. These races are, in comparison with white races ... unequal and inferior'. Edmund Barton[108]

> 'The unity of Australia is nothing, if that does not imply a united race. A united race not only means that its members can intermix, intermarry and associate without degradation on either side, but implies one inspired by the same ideas ...' Alfred Deakin[109]

[2.49] One obvious by-product of the decision not to make Australian citizenship explicit at time of Federation was a bifurcation in what might be termed the form and the content of citizenship in Australia. At a time when the law recognised no formal status of Australian citizenship, the meaning of citizenship as a normative construct was to be found in how different groups in the society were treated – in their rights, entitlements and in their ability to participate in important decision-making processes. Migration law was deeply implicated in this in so far as the term 'immigrant' came to be an indicium of non-citizenship in both formal and practical senses. Even after legislative provision was finally made for Australian citizenship in 1948, the creation of that legal status did not bring an end to discrimination or differential access to *substantial* citizenship on grounds of race and colour. It is here that the treatment of certain immigrants came to parallel quite expressly the treatment of others who were not regarded as societal equals.

[2.50] In the area of immigration, there were many aspects of law and policy that were sharply at odds with today's more racially neutral laws and policies. Cases such as *Potter v Minahan* and *Donohoe v Wong Sau* demonstrate that birth on Australian territory never guaranteed full membership of the Australian community, at least in the case of individuals born in Australia who subsequently left the territory.[110] Even if they had been born in Australia, individuals of colour were required to possess 'Certificates of Exemption' if they wished to avoid being subjected to a dictation test on their return to Australia. While indigenous persons of colour were exempt from the regulatory regime that required Australians to hold passports and in some cases possess permits before they could leave the country, the ease of egress was not matched by the same freedom to return.[111] Chesterman and Galligan suggest that the arrangements were a deliberate attempt to encourage non-white residents to leave the country. Although these laws did not apply to Australia's 'Aboriginal natives',

---

108   Commonwealth Parliamentary Debates, 26 September 1901 at 5233.
109   Commonwealth Parliamentary Debates, 12 September 1901 at 4807.
110   On this point, see also the status of Papua New Guineans born while Papua New Guinea was subject to Australian control. See further below Part 2.5.2.
111   See *Passports Act 1902* (Cth), s 3; Chesterman and Galligan, above n 14 at 99.

the restrictions placed on the freedom of movement of Australia's first peoples left little room to doubt that these people were effectively aliens in their own land.[112] The early migration laws also had little in the way of family reunion programs: the acceptance of one family member held no guarantee that others would be allowed to follow. Indeed, s 3 of the *Immigration Act 1901* was amended in 1905 to make it more difficult for immigrants of colour to have their immediate family join them in Australia.

[2.51] Chesterman and Galligan note[113] that the *Commonwealth Franchise Act 1902* excluded from the vote any 'aboriginal native of Australia, Asia, Africa or the islands of the Pacific except New Zealand'. The legislation made an exception for persons who had accrued the right to vote at State elections (by virtue of s 41 of the Constitution), thereby tying the franchise to State electoral laws. For most purposes, however, the effect of the legislation was to deny the vote to both aboriginal Australians and permanent residents of colour other than New Zealand Maoris.[114]

[2.52] Provision for the naturalisation of immigrants to Australia was next on the agenda, with the *Naturalization Act 1903* (Cth). Here, there was no need to include Australia's indigenous peoples as they were already deemed to be British subjects by birth. This Act operated to exclude from naturalization any 'aboriginal native of Asia, Africa, or the islands of the Pacific except New Zealand'. Exclusion from the Australian polity was reinforced by denying access to social security, in the form of invalid and old age pensions as well as to family allowances. As Chesterman and Galligan recount,[115] the denial of income security was further reflected in racially discriminatory employment and even tariff laws. Virtually the only benefit for the non-white Australian was the prohibition placed on involvement in military training and active combat during times of war – a concession that, of course, would have constituted an insult to Australian-born persons of colour. The authors comment at some length on the pressures placed on Australia by Britain to deal more equitably with its non-white population, in particular with Indian-born British subjects.

[2.53] Although the *Nationality Act 1920* (Cth) saw Australia's naturalisation laws align formally with those of Britain and most of its Empire,[116] the power to confer nationality remained a discretionary one.[117] In practice, effective change in the approach to non-white Australians was slow. By 1925, concessions were being made for Turks and other near-East (near-European) peoples, and legislation was passed giving Indians voting and pension entitlements. 'Asiatics' were given the right to vote, but had no access to social security. As Chesterman et al recount, problems persisted because of the failure of the States to mirror developments at the federal level, and

---

112 See Chesterman and Galligan, above n 14, at 145.
113 Ibid at 85.
114 See Patricia Grimshaw, 'Colonising Motherhood: Evangelical Social Reformers and Koorie Women in Victoria, Australia, 1880s to the Early 1900s' (1999) 8(2) *History Review* 329 (describing the history of black women suffrage in Australia).
115 See Chesterman and Galligan, above n 14, at 86-7, 98-100.
116 See David Dutton, *One of Us? A Century of Australian Citizenship* (Sydney: UNSW Press, 2002).
117 Ann Mari Jordens, *Redefining Australians: Immigration, Citizenship, and National Identity* (Sydney: Hale and Iremonger, 1995).

because of the continuing denial of social security benefits to non-white residents of Asian origin. It was not until 1947 that these restrictions were lifted.[118] Tragically, the enlightenment on matters of racial equality and equity remained incomplete. Chesterman and Galligan write:[119]

> By 1947, the racial exclusion in the field of social services had been narrowed to Australian Aborigines. While no doubt this would have been welcomed by those other 'aboriginal natives' previously excluded, the Commonwealth excluded its own Aboriginal population from the enhanced welfare state benefits.

[2.54] The exclusion of Australia's indigenous peoples continued, even after the *Nationality and Citizenship Act 1948* formally declared these people to be Australian citizens. The exclusion went to the very heart of the qualities making up the 'Australian citizen':

> These qualities were negative. That is, the Australian citizen was thought to be simply a 'natural-born or naturalized' person *who was not an 'aboriginal native'*. It was the 'aboriginal native', in other words, who was the key boundary marker to Australian citizenship.[120]

Had these authors been reflecting on the period closer to Federation, this comment would have been equally apposite, save that non-white migrants would have to be added to the class of excluded persons. Put another way, the earliest Australian citizens were 'natural-born or naturalised' persons in Australia who were not 'aboriginal natives' or other persons of colour.

[2.55] Chesterman and Galligan argue that Australia's failure to acknowledge and deal with the racism of early laws excluding aboriginal people helps to explain the difficulties that continue in achieving true reconciliation and racial equity in this country between indigenous and non-indigenous Australians. The early treatment of non-white members of the Australian community, born of some incipient inability to recognise in people of colour the commonalities of the human condition, may also explain the extraordinary angst that continues to characterise the discourse on asylum seekers and illegal migration. We may no longer indulge in the colourful language that described unwanted immigrants as 'loathsome hotbeds of disease',[121] and aboriginal Australians as 'horrible, degraded, dirty creatures'.[122] However, illegal migrants and asylum seekers are still characterised in terms of the 'other'; people who are 'not like us'; people with whom we would not like to live.[123]

[2.56] If Australia's racist past has created problems in the way we see outsiders seeking admission into Australia, it has also made the country susceptible to internal divisions and destructive behaviour over immigration and ethnic difference at a more general level. There has been a tendency to sensationalise crimes associated

---

118   See Chesterman and Galligan, above n 14, at 105-7, 115-17.
119   See ibid at 117.
120   Ibid at 120.
121   See Isaacs J in *Williamson v Ah On* (1926) 39 CLR 95 at 104.
122   See the speech by WA Senator Matheson, quoted in Chesterman and Galligan, above n 14, at 89.
123   In this context, see, for example, the language used by Prime Minister Howard in the course of the 'children overboard' controversy in October 2001. See Mary Crock and Ben Saul, *Future Seekers: Refugees and the Law in Australia* (Sydney: Federation Press, 2002) at 42.

with particular racial groups.[124] In 2006, the decision to comprehensively revise the *Australian Citizenship Act 1948* saw the institution of a citizenship test requiring both proficiency in English and knowledge of fundamental aspects of Australian history and culture.[125]

[2.57] In the context of long-term permanent residents convicted of serious crimes, Australia's historical ambivalence in its treatment of citizenship has also created on-going problems. Interestingly, in the latter instance, the High Court of Australia has turned around to face Australia's history. As explored in the following chapter, in at least one case it gave constitutional recognition to a broader notion of citizenship than that conveyed in the *Australian Citizenship Act 1948*. Whilst acknowledging that some long-term residents of Australia who are British nationals may gain immunity from removal,[126] the court has declined to extend the same protections to any other foreign nationals.[127]

2.5 Historical legacies: Australian citizenship today

> 'Citizenship … is a concept which is and can be pressed into service for a number of constitutional purposes … But it is not a concept which is constitutionally necessary, which is immutable or which has some immutable core element ensuring its lasting relevance for constitutional purposes.'[128]

2.5.1 Citizenship, British heritage and the continuing significance of migration law

[2.58] If anything emerges from the foregoing discussion, it is that from Federation onwards there has always been both legal and normative notions of Australian citizenship. The fact that these have been shaped in large measure by *migration* law and by Australia's colonial origins is born out in the continuing ambiguity surrounding the rights in Australia of British nationals. Before 1949, and indeed up until at least 1987, there was an unresolved tension between the practicality of membership in the Australian community and the legal reality of a common nationality shared with subjects in other parts of the British Empire. Hence, while the High Court in *Ah Sheung* was 'not disposed to give any countenance to the novel doctrine that there is an Australian nationality as distinguished from a British nationality', it held that the immigration power does not extend to 'Australians…who are merely absent from Australia on a visit *animo revertendi*'.[129] The tension is highlighted by the breadth of the

---

124 See, for example, the controversy in Sydney surrounding the conviction and sentencing of ethnic Lebanese rapists in mid-2002. See, for example, Mark Findlay, 'Law-and-order bandwagon leaves justice bleeding', *The Australian*, 9 August 2002, 11 <http://www.theaustralian.news.com.au/common/story_page/>.
125 See Andrew Robb, *Australian Migrant Integration – Past Successes, Future Challenges* (2006) Andrew Robb AO MP <http://www.andrewrobb.com.au/news/default.asp?action=article&ID=140>.
126 See the discussion of *In re Patterson; Ex parte Taylor* (2001) 207 CLR 391; and *Shaw v MIMA* (2003) 218 CLR 28 in Chapter 3, below.
127 See *Re MIMA; Ex parte Te; Re MIMA; Ex parte Dang* (2002) 212 CLR 162, discussed in Chapter 3, below.
128 Gaudron J in *Chu Kheng Lim v MILGEA* (1992) 176 CLR 1 at 54.
129 *Attorney-General (Cth) v Ah Sheung* (1906) 4 CLR 949 at 951.

immigration power, which from early times was held to be sufficient to support legislation restricting the entry of British subjects not born or naturalised in Australia.[130]

[2.59] An apparent contradiction remained for some time after the commencement of the *Australian Citizenship Act 1948*. While this Act established a new Australian nationality, the country's British origins were not forgotten. Until 1 May 1987[131] Australian citizens were also defined as British subjects by the Act,[132] although the prefatory words 'the status of' were added to the definition in 1969.[133] Indeed, even though the British subject status referred to was derivative, in the sense that it depended on Australian citizenship, allegiance remained to the Queen of the United Kingdom. It was therefore not a neutral status until relatively recently.

[2.60] The *Australian Citizenship Act 1948* and consequential amendments to other legislation saw the replacement of 'British subject' with the term 'citizen'. Similar alterations to terminology were made at State and Territory levels, particularly in relation to statutes imposing qualifications for entitlements.[134] However, the changes are not comprehensive, so the various *Acts Interpretation Acts* incorporate provisions to resolve any confusion that may arise from the use of both terms.[135]

[2.61] Notwithstanding its lack of constitutional treatment or definition,[136] the term 'citizen' has been used frequently by members of the High Court in a variety of contexts, both as a generic term for person or resident and in more substantive contexts. This jurisprudence is well analysed by Rubenstein.[137] It is beyond the scope of this book to consider the extent to which race or other factors continue to be relevant to citizenship in the normative or practical sense of the word.[138] What is of enduring interest is the link between citizenship and migration law. If an individual's race is no longer relevant to citizenship status, identification as an *immigrant* continues to be highly significant. Just as migrants continue to be quintessential *outsiders*, so immigration law continues to define who are the *insiders* (and citizens). The ability to fit into one of the categories prescribed for migration to Australia remains the most important precondition to full acceptance as a member of the Australian polity.

[2.62] As explored in the following case studies, there are particular resonances of Australia's past in the modern day refusal to see the conferral of citizenship as anything other than the preserve of the Australian Parliament. The Australian courts have been reluctant to acknowledge any fundamental legal principle *outside of statute*

---

130 See *R v Macfarlane; Ex parte O'Flanagan and O'Kelly* (1923) 32 CLR 518 at 557-65 (Isaacs J) and below, Chapter 4.
131 The commencement date for the *Australian Citizenship Amendment Act 1984*.
132 *Australian Citizenship Act 1948*, s 7 (repealed).
133 See Sir Ninian Stephens, 'The First Half Century of Australian Citizenship' in Kim Rubenstein (ed), *Individual, Community, Nation: Fifty Years of Australian Citizenship* (Melbourne: Australian Scholarly Publishing, 2000) at 4.
134 Such as, for example, *Parliamentary Electorates and Elections Act 1912* (NSW), s 20.
135 See for example, *Interpretation Act 1987* (NSW), s 16; *Interpretation of Legislation Act 1984* (Vic), s 55.
136 See Helen Irving, 'Still Call Australia Home: The Constitution and the Citizen's Right of Abode' (2008) 30(1) *Sydney Law Review* 133, for a discussion of the concept of 'constitutional citizenship' in Australia.
137 See Rubenstein, above n 4, Ch 6.
138 Again, that task is ably performed by Rubenstein, above n 4, Ch 5.

conferring citizenship on persons physically present in Australia – even if they were born here.

2.5.2 Citizenship as birthright

[2.63] Early cases such as *Potter v Minahan*[139] and *Donohoe v Wong Sau*[140] demonstrate that the early Australian courts did not recognise the concept of *jus soli* as a unique criterion for the attribution of citizenship in the sense of membership of the Australian community. *Jus soli* is the legal notion of citizenship by birth within a physical territory.[141] If the early Australian case law says anything about the legal rights attaching to birth within Australian territory, it is that persons born in Australia could acquire a form of tenure permitting them to remain in the country. Depending ultimately on the question of an individual's 'membership of the Australian community' as defined by the white Anglo-Saxon judges, this tenure either allowed freedom of movement into and out of Australia or it was extinguished when the person left the country. Hence, James Minahan was permitted to re-enter Australia on the basis that he was 'coming home', while Miss Wong Sau was excluded on the assumption that she was 'alien' to the country.[142] In the following chapter it will be seen that the principle of legal tenure linked to physical presence on Australian territory re-emerged briefly in more recent years in the context of the High Court's consideration of limits on the constitutional power to expel certain long-term permanent residents in Australia.[143]

[2.64] The debates about the legal status of individuals born on Australian territory are one obvious by-product of the decision to omit any reference to an Australian citizenship in the Constitution. In practical terms, the issue for the High Court has been to determine the nature and scope of Parliament's power to legislate so as to confer or deny citizenship on these individuals. The case law favours a very expansive reading of parliamentary power in this area. The High Court has upheld legislation both declaring former citizens to be 'aliens' and denying citizenship to children born within Australia to non-citizen parents.

[2.65] In 1948, transitional provisions in the *Australian Citizenship Act 1948* automatically conferred Australian citizenship on certain British subjects born before to 26 January 1949 in Australia or Australian territory, or to an Australian.[144] Under the *Australian Citizenship Act 2007* (Cth) (which replaced the 1948 Act), Australian citizenship can be acquired automatically (by birth and in other circumstances as defined) or by application (by descent, adoption by grant or in circumstances involving the resumption of citizenship).[145] Australian citizenship may also be resumed after loss

---

139 (1908) 7 CLR 277.
140 (1925) 36 CLR 404.
141 See *Calvin's Case* (1608) 7 Co Rep 1a [77 ER 377]. *Jus soli* is to be compared with the concept of *jus sanguinis*, or citizenship by descent, which can entitle children born of citizens to the same status as their parents.
142 This was so notwithstanding the fact that Minahan was born in Australia before Federation, while Wong Sau was born in the country to a non-alien after Federation.
143 See *Re Patterson; Ex parte Taylor* (2001) 207 CLR 391 and the discussion in Chapter 3.2ff.
144 *Australian Citizenship Act 1948*, s 25 (now repealed).
145 *Australian Citizenship Act 2007*.

in certain circumstances[146] and, should Australia incorporate additional territory, the Minister may by legislative instrument declare that persons connected with that territory are Australian citizens.[147]

[2.66] Traditionally, rules for the acquisition of a nationality at birth have been based on the place of birth (*jus soli*), descent (*jus sanguinis* or 'blood' ties), or a combination of both. Unlike the United States of America,[148] Australian citizenship is no longer acquired simply by birth within the territory of the nation. The *Australian Citizenship Act 1948* was amended on 20 August 1986 to impose added requirements of descent *or* residence. Even after the re-organisation of this Act in 2007, there continue to be requirements that an applicant have one parent who is an Australian citizen or permanent resident[149] *or* that the applicant be 'ordinarily resident' in Australia for 10 years after birth in the country: s 12(1)(b). Interestingly, the alterations in 1986 were made in response to a migration case – *Kioa v West*[150] – in which a visa-less Tongan couple had used the citizenship of their Australian-born child as leverage so as to gain discretionary leave to remain in the country. The net effect of the changes is that individuals born on Australian territory at different times have acquired different rights to citizenship.

[2.67] In the case of Susan Walsh, the acquisition of Australian citizenship at birth was not enough to ensure that she would keep that legal status forever. Ms Walsh was born in Papua in July 1970 to an Australian citizen father and an indigenous Papuan mother. She was an Australian citizen at birth on the basis of place of birth – in 1970 Papua was Australian territory.[151] When Papua gained its independence on 16 September 1975,[152] regulations were made that purported to strip most Papuans of their Australian citizenship.[153] Then Ms Walsh sought to regain her citizenship by applying to be registered as the child of an Australian citizen under what was s 10C(4)(c)(i). As Rubenstein notes:[154]

> This provision, like all provisions regarding citizenship by descent, refers to people who are 'born outside of Australia'. Those words are there because, normally, a person born inside Australia is and remains an Australian citizen by birth and does not need to think about an entitlement to citizenship by descent. Ms Walsh

---

146   Ibid Div 2, Pt 2C.
147   Ibid s 15.
148   United States Constitution, 14th Amendment (ratified 1868). Paragraph 1 provides that '[a]ll persons born or naturalized in the United States, and subject to the jurisdiction thereof, are citizens of the United States and of the State wherein they reside'. On the effect of this amendment, see Schuck and Smith, above n 12, Ch 3.
149   *Australian Citizenship Act 2007*, s 12(1)(a). Should a parent have died before the person is born, the status of the parent at the time of the person's birth is deemed to be the status of the parent at the time of death: see s 36(2)(b).
150   (1985) 159 CLR 550.
151   Note that she could not claim citizenship by descent to her Australian citizen father because she was not born outside Australia. Although exceptions were made for children born to diplomats and 'enemy aliens', neither applied in this case. See further Rubenstein, above n 4, at 90; Kim Rubenstein, 'The Lottery of Citizenship: The Changing Significance of Birthplace, Territory and Residence to the Australian Membership Prize' (2005) 22(2) *Law in Context* 45.
152   *Papua New Guinea Independence Act 1975* (Cth), s 4.
153   *PNG Independence (Australian Citizenship) Regulations 1975* (Cth), reg 4.
154   Rubenstein, 'The Lottery of Citizenship', above n 151.

according to the delegate was not born outside Australia, because, at the time of her birth she was born in Australia. The consequence of this was Ms Walsh was not entitled to her citizenship by birth, because that Territory had changed, nor was she entitled to her citizenship by descent, because she was born within Australian territory. If we think back to the two types of citizenship which all countries provide for in different ways – *jus soli* (by birth in territory) and *jus-sanguinis* (through descent). Ms Walsh was being denied both.

As Rubenstein documents, Ms Walsh's attempts to regain her status as an Australian citizen failed at every level. Her appeal on the merits of the decision to refuse her status to the Administrative Appeals Tribunal failed, although Deputy President Breen complained that the case revealed a 'serious anomaly in the legislation'.[155] Neither the Full Federal Court nor the High Court were prepared to find a legal error in the tribunal's narrow reading of the legislative text in question.[156] In essence, the power to make legislation with respect to 'naturalisation and aliens'[157] seems to have been accepted as a basis for both making and un-making citizenship.

[2.68] The issues in the *Susan Walsh* matter were considered further in the challenge mounted on behalf of Amos Ame, a case that came before the High Court in its original jurisdiction.[158] Mr Ame was born in Papua New Guinea in 1967 as an Australian citizen. He was stripped of that status in 1975 with the introduction of the Papua New Guinea Constitution. For the High Court, much seems to have turned on the fact that Ame never visited mainland Australia as a child. The statutory framework of the time provided that Australian citizenship would not be taken from Papua New Guinea nationals who held entry permits allowing them to live and work in Australia. Counsel for Mr Ame argued that the Australian Constitution did not permit legislation revoking the most fundamental of citizenship rights: the right to entry and residence in mainland Australia.

[2.69] The court drew back from addressing the issue of whether it is permissible generally to legislate so as to limit the ability of citizens to enter and reside in Australia. Rather, the majority focused on the rights that had attached to Australian citizens who were resident in Papua New Guinea before 1975, ruling that this group were citizens in name only because they never had a right to enter or remain in Australia without the issue of an Australian entry permit. Their Honours held:[159]

> Although indigenous Papuans were Australian citizens before Independence Day, they were treated by Australian law, and regarded by the framers of the Papua New

---

155 See *Walsh and MIMA* [2001] AATA 378.
156 See *MIMIA v Walsh* (2002) 189 ALR 694 (*Susan Walsh*); *Walsh v MIMIA* B41/2002 (25 June 2003) (failed special leave application), available at <http://www.austlii.edu.au/au/other/hca/transcripts/2002/B41/1.html>. Note, however, that she was successful at first instance in the Federal Court. See *Walsh v MIMIA* (2001) 116 FCR 524.
157 Constitution, s 51(19).
158 See *Re MIMIA; Ex parte Ame* (2005) 222 CLR 439. This meant that the issues could be fully argued before the court, rather than being dealt with under the summary 'special leave' regime to which the Susan Walsh case was subject. This case is discussed by Kim Rubenstein, who was also counsel for Mr Ame, in Kim Rubenstein, 'Advancing Citizenship: The Legal Armory and Its Limits' (2007) 8 *Theoretical Inquiries in Law* 509, available at <http://www.bepress.com/til/default/vol8/iss2/art7>.
159 See *Re MIMIA; Ex parte Ame* (2005) 222 CLR 439 at [23].

Guinea Constitution as not having, on that account alone, a right to permanent residence in Australia. The right to permanent residence referred to in s 65(4)(a) is ... the right which a small number of Papuans had received by grant, not a right which all Papuans had by virtue of birth in the Territory of Papua at a time when it was an external Territory of Australia. The construction which the applicant seeks to place on s 65 must be rejected. On Independence Day, the applicant became a citizen of Papua New Guinea by virtue of the Papua New Guinea Constitution. That Constitution was antagonistic to dual citizenship. In recognition of that policy of the new Independent State, Australia, by reg 4, withdrew the applicant's Australian citizenship. That withdrawal was not arbitrary. It was consistent with the maintenance of proper relations with the new Independent State, and with the change that occurred in Australia's relationship with the inhabitants of that State.

The court went on to uphold the constitutionality of the regulations that had stripped Mr Ame of both Australian citizenship and any right he might otherwise have had to enter or remain in Australia. Although the situation of the Papua New Guineans was arguably different from that of Australian citizens within Australia proper, a strong implication from the majority judgment is that the Australian Constitution confers on Australia's Parliament extensive powers to make laws with respect to both the form and content of citizenship in this country.

[2.70] Kirby J agreed with the majority in substance but was at pains nevertheless to stress the special status of Papua New Guineans and other 'Protected Persons'. His Honour agreed that these people had never been 'real' Australian citizens and cautioned against assumptions that 'genuine' citizenship could be subject to the same easy legislative interference:[160]

> The change in the applicant's status as a citizen, as an incident to the achievement of the independence and national sovereignty of a former territory of the Commonwealth, affords no precedent for any deprivation of constitutional nationality of other Australian citizens whose claim on such nationality is stronger in law and fact than that of the applicant. The acceptance of the validity of constitutional powers propounded by the respondent in this case does not therefore present any risk that later laws might purport to divest Australian nationals of their status as such, based on the decision in this case.
>
> It follows that, having regard to the particular historical circumstances of this case and the fragile and strictly limited character of the 'citizenship' of Australia which the applicant previously enjoyed, no requirement was implicit in the Australian Constitution that afforded the applicant rights of due process that might arise in another case in other circumstances of local nationality having firmer foundations. Nor is it necessary, in light of these conclusions, to consider further the fundamental constitutional questions that would arise were the Federal Parliament ever to attempt to extend the deprivation of Australian nationality (including statutory citizenship) beyond the strictly limited categories of cases provided by the present law. The laws which the applicant challenged in these proceedings replace shadows with substance; appearances and mere titles with a new enforceable reality. There is no constitutional infirmity in the Australian laws that have facilitated that outcome.

---

160   Ibid at [117]-[119].

As it has been defined by this Court up to *Nolan* and since *Shaw*, the 'aliens' power applied to the applicant. Indeed, it did so from his birth. It did so notwithstanding the provision to him of a nominal statutory status of 'citizen' which, when examined, fell far short of constitutional nationality. No question therefore arises of depriving the applicant of a supposed status of 'non-alien' for Australian constitutional purposes. The territories and aliens powers reinforce and supplement each other. They afford an ample constitutional foundation for the validity of the Australian laws impugned by the applicant.

As in many cases fought to establish the nature and extent of governmental power, the obvious injustice of the *Walsh* and *Ame* decisions was addressed in 2007 when the *Australian Citizenship Act 2007* was enacted to replace the 1948 legislation.[161]

[2.71] A broad reading of the Australian Parliament's powers to legislate citizenship was confirmed in 2004 in a case involving a child born in Australia to non-citizen parents who had sought asylum in the country.[162] Tania Singh was born in Victoria in 1998, and had lived in Australia continuously thereafter. Her parents and a brother born in India were Indian citizens. Her case came to the High Court on the basis that her birth in Australia operated at law to deem her to have something akin to Australian citizen status. Notwithstanding the amendments made to the *Australian Citizenship Act 1948* in August 1986, Tania Singh argued she could not be described at law as an 'alien' for the purposes of s 51(19) of the Constitution.

[2.72] The case for Tania Singh turned largely on the contention that the silences in the Constitution with respect to Australian citizenship have to be read in conjunction with common law understandings of alienage enshrined in old English cases such as *Calvin's Case*.[163] Tania Singh was presented as a 'natural born' Australian by virtue of her birth on Australian soil.[164] Without going to the issue of her status as an Indian national, it was argued that Tania's birth in Australia meant that the child's primary allegiance was to the Queen of Australia (Elizabeth II). In something of a bootstrap argument, it was submitted that as notions of nationality in the Constitution imply allegiance to the Crown, Tania's birth in Australia and her 'continuing fidelity' to the Australian Queen must mean that she had acquired the status of either 'citizen' or 'non-alien' for constitutional purposes.[165] It was submitted for Ms Singh that alienage in Australia had a 'fixed connotation' for constitutional purposes that could not be altered by Parliament.[166]

[2.73] Although two members of the High Court accepted these arguments, the majority ruled against Tania Singh, confirming that the term 'alien' had no fixed

---

161   *Australian Citizenship Act 2007*, s 21(7). This amendment has not stopped a broader range of individuals from West Papua from attempting to claim citizenship in Australia. See Anthony Gough, 'Immigration Starts Deporting Papua New Guineans Claiming Aust-ralian Citizenship as Another Boatload Arrives', *Courier Mail*, 24 December 2010, available at <http://www.couriermail.com.au/news/queensland/immigration-starts-deporting-papua-new-guineans-claiming-australian-citizenship-as-another-boatload-arrives/story-e6freoof-1225975957261>.
162   *Singh v Commonwealth* (2004) 222 CLR 322.
163   (1608) 7 Co Rep 1a [77 ER 377]. The case is referred to by Kirby J, ibid at [222]-[223].
164   (2004) 222 CLR 322 at [219].
165   Ibid at [225].
166   Ibid at [229].

meaning or legal import at the time of Federation in 1901. The majority approached the case by relying heavily on historical materials in the approach to the interpretation of s 51(19) of the Constitution. It may be surmised from the earlier parts of this chapter that reliance on historical practices and interpretations is unlikely to produce a generous reading of either immigration or citizenship law in Australia. So it was in *Singh*.[167]

[2.74] Leading the majority, Gleeson CJ found that at the time the Australian Constitution was drafted the notion of alienage was a constantly shifting concept, as revealed in the very different arguments made for and against the inclusion of an Australian citizenship in the Convention debates leading to the drafting of the final document. According to his Honour, the only uniform principle emerging from these debates was a shared intention that the power to legislate with respect to membership of the new Australian community be as broad and unfettered as possible. The Chief Justice found accordingly that the Constitution provided no impediment to Parliament legislating so as to prevent or restrict the ability of persons born in Australia to acquire Australian citizenship.[168]

[2.75] Like the other members of the court (both majority and dissenting judges), the Chief Justice was at pains nevertheless to emphasise that Parliament's power to legislate with respect to aliens was not without constitutional limit. He found that s 51(19) and (27) empowered Parliament to legislate with respect to matters of nationality and immigration; to create and define the concept of Australian citizenship; to prescribe the conditions on which citizenship may be lost or acquired; and to link citizenship with the right of abode.[169] However, Parliament could not create its own definition of the term 'alien' so as to capture people who could not possibly answer the description of 'aliens' in the Constitution.[170] Gleeson CJ did not go further so as to articulate a constitutional definition of a 'non-alien'.

[2.76] On this point, the other members of the majority – Gummow, Hayne and Heydon JJ – were prepared to identify one attribute of alienage: the existence of allegiance to a foreign state or sovereign.[171] Tania Singh, their Honours ruled, appeared to owe allegiance to India and for this reason could readily be described as an alien, in spite of her birth on Australian soil. The judges otherwise agreed with the Chief Justice's finding that the term 'alien' has no fixed meaning under the Constitution. They pointed out that the English approach to the *jus soli* principle – unlike that of the United States[172] – has varied over time. If there was no fixed and immutable concept of citizenship by birthright under British law, then neither could it be said that this principle pertained in Australian law.

---

167 For a close analysis and critique of the approach taken by the majority in this case, see Michelle Foster, 'Membership in the Australian Community: *Singh v The Commonwealth* and its Consequences for Australian Citizenship Law' (2006) 34 *Federal Law Review* 161.
168 (2004) 222 CLR 322 at [31].
169 Ibid at [4]. See also *Re MIMA; Ex parte Te* (2002) 212 CLR 162 at [31].
170 See Gibbs J in *Pochi v McPhee* (1982) 151 CLR 101 at 109.
171 (2004) 222 CLR 322 at [154]ff.
172 Where the courts had consistently applied (but for two exceptions) the territorial birthright citizenship theory. The exceptions included the *Dred Scott v Sandford*, 60 US 393 (1856).

[2.77] The final member of the majority, Kirby J, arrived at the same conclusion using a typically different route. His Honour favoured a broader examination of the concept of nationality at international law.[173] Kirby J noted that the most striking attribute of international jurisprudence was the variety in approaches taken to the conferral of citizenship. The fact that the laws of some countries recognise the concept of citizenship by birthright alone cannot lead one to conclude that the notion of *jus soli* has the standing of customary international law. The conferral of citizenship is a quintessential province of domestic law.[174]

[2.78] In *Singh*, two of the judges – McHugh and Callinan JJ – offered spirited dissents to the reasoning of the majority. Both ruled that Ms Singh should be considered a 'natural born' member of the Australian people, relying heavily on the child's acquired allegiance to the monarch of Australia and the strength of the old common law notions of *jus soli* embodied in cases such as *Calvin's Case*.[175] McHugh J placed special reliance on the reasoning and result in *Potter v Minahan*,[176] emphasising the significance of the Australian-born child of a Chinese alien father having been recognised as a returning member of the community. Having said this, his Honour did not offer a very insightful explanation for the conflicting finding in *Donohoe v Wong Sau*.[177] He said:[178]

> In *Donohoe v Wong Sau* (1925) 36 CLR 404, this Court ... held that, in some circumstances, a natural born British subject could enter Australia as an immigrant and therefore be subject to federal laws made under the immigration power. Isaacs J (at 408) said that, when Ms Lucy Wong Sau entered the Commonwealth, she was not 'a member of this community. She was not Australian in point of language, bringing-up, education, sentiment, marriage, or of any of those indicia which go to establish Australian nationality.' The decision in *Donohoe* was treated as one of fact and that decision does not affect the *dicta* in *Potter* concerning the acquisition of British nationality. Nor does it affect the statements in *Potter* that upon birth in Australia Minahan owed permanent allegiance to the sovereign of Australia.

His Honour did not address the point at which birth in Australia gives rise to rights that are portable once an individual leaves Australia. Both Mr Minahan and Ms Wong Sau were born in Australia – the latter *after* Federation – and both had parents who were regarded as members of the Australian community. In truth, as the majority bring out, the historical jurisprudence relevant to citizenship in Australia does not support the notion that membership of the early Australian community was ever simple from a legal perspective.

---

173 See *Singh* (2004) 222 CLR 322 at [219]ff.
174 See ibid at [257]; Ian Brownlie, *Principles of Public International Law* (Oxford: Oxford University Press, 6th ed, 2003) at 373. See also *United States v Wong Kim Ark*, 169 US 649 at 667-8 (1898) (Gray J for the court); *Nationality Decrees Issued in Tunis and Morocco (Advisory Opinion)* (1923) Permanent Court of International Justice 6, Series B, No 4, 24; and *Liechtenstein v Guatemala (the Nottebohm Case)* [1955] ICJ Reports 4.
175 (1608) 7 Co Rep 1a at 18a [77 ER 377 at 399].
176 (1908) 7 CLR 277.
177 (1925) 36 CLR 404.
178 *Singh* (2004) 222 CLR 322 at [114].

[2.79] As Foster notes,[179] the majority's rulings in *Singh* left open some possibilities for children born in Australia to immigrant parents because of the emphasis placed on the link between a person's status as an alien and allegiance to a foreign power. These were pursued in *Koroitamana v Commonwealth*,[180] a case involving two children born in Australia to Fijian parents who were unlawful non-citizens. The children had three siblings who were all Australian citizens.[181] Although Fijian law recognised as citizens children born abroad to Fijian nationals on registration of the subjects' birth,[182] the parents had not registered the children with the Fijian government. Accordingly, the children were effectively stateless unless (as it was argued) Australian law operated to deem the children to be constitutional non-aliens by virtue of their birth in Australia. On this occasion the High Court was unanimous in rejecting claims that the children were not aliens for the purpose of the Constitution. Gleeson CJ and Heydon J expressed concern that the power of the Australian Parliament to decide the citizenship of the children could depend on the 'choice of the parents of the applicants whether to register them as Fijian citizens'.[183] While Kirby J found that the alien status of the applicants lay in their entitlement to Fijian citizenship,[184] five members of the bench made it clear that it will always be open to the Australian Parliament to treat a stateless person as an alien.[185]

[2.80] A common feature of many of the cases in which attempts have been made to secure citizenship for children born in Australia is that the children's parents were (failed) asylum seekers. Although not emphasised by the courts, this fact helps to explain the persistence of crusading advocates like Professor Kim Rubenstein. In *SNMX v MIAC*[186] Professor Rubenstein succeeded in persuading the AAT that s 21(5) of the *Australian Citizenship Act 2007* conferred on the Minister broad discretion to grant citizenship to migrant children in Australia. The applicant in that case was the five-year-old child of an asylum seeker. It was claimed that the child would suffer significant hardship or disadvantage unless granted citizenship status. The tribunal accepted that the simple reference to eligibility in s 21(5) rendered *ultra vires* the requirement in the Minister's policy that only permanent resident children should be considered for citizenship under that provision. Even before the tribunal delivered its ruling – awarding the child citizenship – the government responded with a Bill to amend the *Australian Citizenship Act 2007* so as to limit the operation of s 21(5) to permanent resident children.[187]

---

179   See Foster, above n 167, at 166-7.
180   (2006) 227 ALR 406.
181   Presumably the other children had either been born in Australia and 'ordinarily resident' in the country for over 10 years (*Australian Citizenship Act 1948*, s 10C; replaced by s 10(2)(b) of the 2007 Act); or they had benefitted from 'innocent illegals' provisions in *Migration Regulations 1994* (Cth), Sch 2, subclass 832 (now repealed). See further Chapter 15 at [15.73].
182   See s 12(1) of the Constitution of the Fijian Islands.
183   See (2006) 227 ALR 406 at [13].
184   Such that the children could not be truly characterised as stateless. See ibid at [82].
185   Ibid at [15] (Gleeson CJ and Heydon J); and [45]-[49] (Gummow, Hayne and Crennan JJ). Callinan J concurred with the majority grudgingly, on the basis that the ruling in *Singh* was a binding precedent: see at [86].
186   [2009] AATA 539.
187   The new s 21(5) reads: '(5) A person is eligible to become an Australian citizen if the Minister is satisfied that the person: (a) is aged under 18 at the time the person made the application; and (b)

2.6 Legacies of using migration law as a benchmark for exclusion

[2.81] In practical terms, the issue of race has faded from the jurisprudence governing the 'black letter' of citizenship law in Australia. In *Kartinyeri v Commonwealth*, Gaudron J said:[188]

> Section 51(xxvi) (the Constitution's conferral of power to legislate with respect to 'race') does not authorise special laws affecting rights and obligations in areas in which there is no relevant difference between the people of the race to whom the law is directed and the people of other races. A simple example will suffice. Rights deriving from citizenship inhere in the individual by reason of his or her membership of the Australian body politic and not by reason of any other consideration, including race. To put the matter in terms which reflect the jurisprudence that has developed with respect to anti-discrimination law, race is simply irrelevant to the existence or exercise of rights associated with citizenship. So, too, it is irrelevant to the question of continued membership of the Australian body politic. Consequently, s 51(xxvi) will not support a law depriving people of a particular racial group of their citizenship or their rights as citizens. And race is equally irrelevant to the enjoyment of those rights which are generally described as human rights and which are taken to inhere in each and every person by reason of his or her membership of the human race.

[2.82] The same may not be as true of the broader discourse on migration law and citizenship as membership of an Australian polity when viewed through the lens of constitutional law and international law. The early constructions of citizenship in Australia continue to shape many aspects of the modern discourse on what it is to be 'Australian'. On the one hand, High Court rulings on the power to legislate with respect to naturalisation and aliens (s 51(19)) have given continued relevance to Australia's origins as a British colony.[189] On the other, indigenous Australians have yet to gain full legal recognition of their original ownership of the country.

[2.83] There is another respect in which, it would seem, that Australia has either come full circle, or perhaps failed to move on from the imaginings of its founding men and women. In 2001, the federal government placed the three portfolios of immigration, multicultural affairs and indigenous affairs under the care and control of a single minister. Grouping aspiring migrants together with immigrant Australians and indigenous Australians, the unfortunate implication was that the federal government somehow saw migrants and indigenous Australians collectively as 'outsiders' to the Australian polity. This characterisation (intentional or otherwise) did not sit easily with the reality of the country's polyglot urban communities. It is difficult to see that aboriginal Australians would have seen the grouping as anything other than offensive. Happily, the portfolio of Indigenous Affairs was taken away from the Minister for Immigration in January 2006. For present purposes, however, the preceding five years stand testament to the significance that migration law continues to have in defining many aspects of citizenship in Australia.

---

is a permanent resident …'. See *Australian Citizenship Amendment (Citizenship Test Review and Other Measures) Act 2009* (Cth).
188   (1998) 195 CLR 337 at 366.
189   See *In re Patterson; Ex parte Taylor* (2001) 207 CLR 391, discussed in Chapter 3, below.

PART II Legal Frameworks

'Al- Khafaji' 2004, © *Andrew Taylor/Fairfax Media*

3

Defining Powers: Immigration Control and the Australian Constitution

3.1 Constitutional frameworks

[3.01] In Chapter 2 it was argued that immigration law has played a central role in defining what it is to be an Australian citizen. The regulation of immigration became significant because of the decision not to provide expressly for an Australian citizenship in the Australian Constitution. The omission meant that right of entry and tenure in the country came to be regarded as a benefit attaching to the obverse of the status of *immigrant*.

[3.02] This chapter explores in greater detail the cases in which notions of citizenship and alienage have been developed. The central contention again is that the failure to provide for an Australian citizenship in the Constitution has had a profound impact on the evolution of constitutional law in this country. As well as creating great uncertainty about the status of Australia's inhabitants, the omission altered at a very fundamental level the focus of the Constitution. With no entrenched citizenship, it follows (or at least it is not surprising) that the Constitution says little about the relationships (rights or duties) between Australian citizens and their federal government.[1] Instead, the central concern of this document is to set out the relative powers of the machinery of state. Australia's Constitution is built on the separation of powers between the executive, the legislature and the judiciary, with each to operate in balance with the others so as to avoid the tyranny of untrammelled or dictatorial power. In practice, however, the articulation of powers for the legislature in s 51 of the Constitution seems to have encouraged the judiciary to concede pre-eminent authority to parliament and the executive.[2]

[3.03] The executive power of government is conferred by s 61 of the Constitution which provides:

> The executive power of the Commonwealth is vested in the Queen and is exercisable by the Governor-General as the Queen's representative, and extends to the execution and maintenance of this Constitution, and of the laws of the Commonwealth.

---

1   The only express reference to anything approximating a right in this regard is in s 116 of the Constitution which enshrines freedom of religion.
2   See the opening comments of Gleeson CJ in *Roach v Electoral Commission* (2007) 233 CLR 162.

IMMIGRATION CONTROL AND THE AUSTRALIAN CONSTITUTION

As Winterton notes,[3] this power has always been something of a mystery, sometimes defined as a 'residue' of governmental powers after legislative and judicial powers are excluded. The Constitution provides in much greater detail for the legislative powers of the federal legislature, with s 51 enumerating the range of matters in respect of which parliament may make laws for the 'peace, order and good government' of Australia. Finally, s 71 provides that the 'judicial' power of the government is to be vested in a supreme court, to be called the High Court of Australia. The powers and original jurisdiction of this court (and by extension superior federal courts of record) are set out in Chapter III of the Constitution.[4]

[3.04]   The failure to provide for either an Australian citizenship or for a Bill of Rights has placed migrants in a very vulnerable situation for two reasons. First, the Constitution vests very express powers in the Australian Parliament to make laws that are either directed at migrants or that are relevant to issues of status or entitlement. Migrants have no text on which they can rely to countermand these powers. Bills of Rights at least provide a structure within which to assert entitlements in the face of punitive legislation. The absence of this normative framework highlights the second problem for migrants – and for the federal judiciary. The textual voids in the Constitution mean that courts are forced to rely heavily on the common law and the legal principles that have evolved therein. The necessity to invoke matters of principle – at best implied from the structures of the Constitution or from particular clauses – inevitably has left the courts open to charges of judicial creativity and even activism.

[3.05]   In practice, it is the judges who stand between the individual and the tyranny of the state. They are inevitably called in aid by individuals who are profoundly unpopular and/or profoundly lacking in status or power: the people who count for nothing before the imperatives of simple majoritarian democracy. In this context, it is not surprising that immigration cases have become a significant point of conflict between the courts and the two other branches of government in Australia. While this phenomenon is in no way unique in global terms,[5] the depth of the controversy in Australia is without precedent in this country. It is our view that the conflict owes much to the silences in the Australian Constitution.

[3.06]   This chapter is divided into three main parts. It begins in Part 3.2 with an historical review of cases that have seen parliament and the courts exploring the reach of the powers to legislate with respect to immigration and non-citizens generally. In this section, particular study is made of a line of cases involving the deportation or removal from Australia of long-term permanent residents. As the matter is considered in Chapter 2, the issue of the extent of the legislative power to create or deny

---

3   See George Winterton, 'The Relationship between Commonwealth Legislative and Executive Power' (2004) 25 *Adelaide Law Review* 21.
4   See ss 73 and 75 in particular, discussed further below Part 3.3.
5   See, for example, William R Bishin, 'Judicial Review in Democratic Theory' (1977) 50 *Southern California Law Review* 1099; Patrick J Monahan, 'Judicial Review and Democracy: A Theory of Judicial Review' (1987) 21 *UBC Law Review* 87; and David Feldman, 'Democracy, the Rule of Law and Judicial Review' (1990) 19 *Federal Law Review* 1.

citizenship is not canvassed here.[6] There follows in Part 3.3 an introduction to the battle royal that has raged between parliament and the High Court over the exercise of the judicial power conferred by Chapter III of the Constitution. The account of the constitutional power over judicial review is a brief one that is resumed in Chapter 19 where issues relating to curial review are given more detailed treatment. This section is dominated rather by a study of various cases in which challenges have been made to the government policy of mandatory detention for non-citizens who enter or remain in Australia without a visa. The chapter concludes by exploring whether the power of the executive to control immigration to Australia can ever be called a 'plenary' or unfettered power.

3.2 The legislative power: The reach of the 'immigration' power and the rise of the 'aliens' power

[3.07] The historical and juridical origins of Australian nationhood tell the story of a country self-consciously absorbed in the role that immigration would play in shaping its identity. With a judiciary drawn from the ranks of the men who drafted the Australian Constitution, it is hardly remarkable that the early rulings by the High Court favoured a broad reading of the powers conferred on the new legislature relevant to immigration control.[7] In fact, the instances where the High Court has found unconstitutional any enactment dealing with immigration remain few and far between, even to this day. What *is* extraordinary is the focus thrown on the judicial function in the curial review of both legislative and administrative action in the field of migration law. Cases involving migrants and refugees have quite frequently represented the cutting edge of constitutional and administrative law in Australia.

[3.08] In the early days, constitutional debates over the reach of the powers of the legislature (and of the executive/ administration) focused on the express power to legislate with respect to immigration and emigration.[8] Later years saw attention turned to other powers of obvious relevance such as the 'naturalisation and aliens' power in s 51(19), the 'external affairs' power in s 51(29) and the 'defence' power in s 51(6).

[3.09] Some issues relating to the extent of the power to legislate with respect to immigration and emigration in s 51(27) were well settled by the mid 1970s.[9] It was accepted, for example, that the power covered all acts of entry into Australia by non-citizens, whether for permanent or temporary residence;[10] that it covered the process of absorption into the community;[11] and that it facilitated the imposition of

---

6 See Chapter 2.5.2.
7 See above Chapter 2, [2.34]-[2.36].
8 Australian Constitution, s 51(27).
9 See Michael Coper, 'The Reach of the Commonwealth's Immigration Power: Judicial Exegesis Unbridled' (1976) 50 *Australian Law Journal* 351.
10 See, for example, *Chia Gee v Martin* (1905) 3 CLR 649; *Potter v Minahan* (1908) 7 CLR 277; *R v Macfarlane; Ex parte O'Flanagan and O'Kelly* (1923) 32 CLR 518; *Ex parte de Braic* (1971) 124 CLR 162.
11 See, for example, *R v Macfarlane; Ex parte O'Flanagan and O'Kelly* (1923) 32 CLR 518; *O'Keefe v Calwell* (1949) 77 CLR 261; and *R v Forbes; Ex parte Kwok Kwan Lee* (1971) 124 CLR 168.

conditions preventing such absorption.[12] What was not so clear was the extent to which the power extended to laws affecting persons who had become absorbed into the community.

[3.10] One line of authority favoured an expansive interpretation of s 51(27) on the ground that an immigrant can never lose that status, but will always remain susceptible to government control.[13] The opposing view was that s 51(27) could not be used to justify laws affecting persons who had become part of the Australian community.[14] Although the 'narrow' view of the immigration power has proved most popular,[15] the High Court found other heads of power to justify legislation affecting the most 'absorbed' of immigrants. With the narrow exception of the ruling in *Re Patterson; Ex parte Taylor*,[16] the result has been to render notions of absorption all but irrelevant in the context of determining the constitutionality of immigration laws. This was so, even in cases involving British subjects who once enjoyed quasi-citizen status here.

[3.11] Special concessions were made for the nationals of Britain and Ireland residing in Australia until as late as 1 May 1987, when Part II of the *Nationality and Citizenship Act 1948* (Cth) was repealed.[17] Before 1987, the *Migration Act 1958* (Cth) also gave more favourable treatment to immigrants who were British subjects and Irish citizens than it did to other non-citizens in its regime for deporting permanent residents convicted of serious crimes. Under s 12 of this Act, criminal 'aliens' were always susceptible to deportation, while s 13 provided that 'immigrants' could not be deported if they had been resident in the country for five years. Aliens were defined as any persons who were not British subjects, Irish citizens or 'protected persons'. After May 1987, all non-citizens became equally liable to deportation if convicted of serious crimes within 10 years of gaining permanent residence. Provisions were added to discount as a period of residence any time spent as the inmate of a prison or other corrective institution.[18]

[3.12] The most contentious deportation and admission cases have involved people who have or had lived in Australia for lengthy periods as permanent residents. The arguments in the more recent cases concerning such persons have all centred on the reach of parliament's power to legislate with respect to aliens under s 51(19) of the Constitution. As we explore further in Chapter 17, all have involved permanent

---

12 See, for example, *R v Green; Ex parte Cheung Cheuk To* (1965) 113 CLR 506; and *R v Forbes; Ex parte Kwok Kwan Lee* (1971) 124 CLR 168.
13 See, for example, *R v Macfarlane; Ex parte O'Flanagan and O'Kelly* (1923) 32 CLR 518 at 555; and *Ex parte Walsh; In re Yates* (1925) 37 CLR 36 at 81-2.
14 For example, *Ex parte Walsh; In re Yates* (1925) 37 CLR 36 at 62-5, 109-10, 137; *Koon Wing Lau v Calwell* (1949) 80 CLR 533 at 576-7 and 587-8; and *R v Director-General of Social Welfare (Vic); Ex parte Henry* (1975) 133 CLR 369 at 373 and 383.
15 See the comments of Gaudron J in *Nolan v MIEA* (1988) 165 CLR 178 at 194-5. Note, however, that the other judges in *Nolan* did not address this issue.
16 (2001) 207 CLR 391 (*Taylor*).
17 See *Australian Citizenship Amendment Act 1984*, s 7, which took effect on 1 May 1987. Such residents were given access to Australian citizenship pursuant to *Nationality and Citizenship Act 1948*, ss 7-9.
18 See former ss 14 and 14A (now ss 200-204) and Chapter 17.

residents convicted of serious crimes: the most recent ones aliens 'by the barest of threads'.[19]

[3.13] The starting point in the modern jurisprudence is *Pochi v Macphee*,[20] a case involving an Italian national who fitted exactly the prevailing (statutory) definition of 'alien'. Even though he had been accepted at one stage as a citizen, Mr Pochi had never taken the oath of allegiance required to gain the formal status of citizen. He argued that the legislation affecting him was wholly invalid because it could have applied to persons who were not 'aliens' for the purposes of the common law. The traditional notion of 'alien' was described by Blackstone in 1858 in the following terms:[21]

> Natural-born subjects are such as are born within the dominions of the Crown of England; that is, within the ligeance, or as it is generally called, the allegiance of the king; and aliens, such as are born out of it.

Pochi asserted that the reference to 'aliens' in s 51(19) of the Constitution should be read down in accordance with this definition of the term 'alien'. When the case came before the High Court, however, his arguments met with little sympathy. The constitutional definition of alien, the court held, had to be determined according to Australian, and not British, law. Gibbs CJ commented[22] that 'Parliament can ... treat as an alien any person who was born outside Australia, whose parents were not Australians, and who has not been naturalized as an Australian'. However, he added that the issue of alienage had to conform to a certain extent to the ordinary meaning of the word: parliament cannot simply create its own, arbitrary, definition of the word 'alien'.

[3.14] Gibbs J's equation of the term 'alien' with 'non-citizen' found majority support by the High Court in *Nolan v MIEA*[23] and in *Kenny v MILGEA*,[24] the latter case involving a returning resident seeking readmission into Australia. Under this characterisation, citizenship brought with it immunity from deportation and a guarantee of readmission into Australia, while the absence of this status implied vulnerability to both expulsion and exclusion. For a brief period between 2001 and 2003, the High Court was less inclined to take such a binomial approach, at least in the case of British permanent residents in Australia under threat of deportation or removal.[25] The (brief) change in thinking becomes apparent when the two cases of *Nolan* and *Taylor* are considered.

[3.15] Both Nolan and Taylor were British nationals who had lived in Australia continuously from a very early age. Nolan had never accrued 10 years 'lawful

---

19 See *Nystrom v MIMIA* (2005) 143 FCR 420 at [1] (Moore and Giles JJ).
20 (1982) 151 CLR 101 (*Pochi*).
21 Cited by Gibbs CJ in *Pochi* (1982) 151 CLR 101 at 108. See Blackstone, *Commentaries on the Laws of England* (Vol 1, 1857) at 367 and John Quick and Robert Garran, *The Annotated Constitution of the Australian Commonwealth* (1901) at 599.
22 *Pochi* (1982) 151 CLR 101 at 109.
23 (1988) 165 CLR 178 (*Nolan*).
24 (1993) 42 FCR 330 (*Kenny*).
25 See *Re Patterson; Ex parte Taylor* (2001) 207 CLR 391 (*Taylor*). (Compare *Shaw v MIMA* (2003) 218 CLR 28.)

permanent residence' in the country – and immunity from deportation – because of the amount of time he spent in correctional institutions.[26] His deportation was ordered following conviction on a drug-related offence. Taylor, on the other hand, had acquired immunity from deportation, but was subjected to the cancellation of his permanent visa on grounds that he was of bad character.[27] Unlike the regime for the deportation of criminal permanent residents, the 'character and conduct' provisions in the *Migration Act* are not subject to temporal limitations.[28]

[3.16] Nolan argued that he could not be labelled an 'alien' because, at the time his deportation order was signed, the concessions made for British subjects in the *Australian Citizenship Act 1948* were still in force. A majority of the court rejected his argument, holding that the constitutional power to legislate with respect to aliens was not limited by any statutory definition of the term alien. It was enough that Nolan had never acquired the status of Australian citizen.[29] Gaudron J dissented, preferring to define alienage by reference to 'membership of the community which constitutes the body politic of the nation state'.[30] For her Honour, this approach yielded a different outcome from that reached by her colleagues as it required an examination of matters beyond the formal (non-Australian) citizenship of Mr Nolan.

[3.17] As Rubenstein notes, Gaudron J's dissent became part of the majority in *Taylor*.[31] Rather than following *Nolan*, the High Court acknowledged for the first time that notions of alienage in this country are complicated by Australia's origins as a colony of Britain and by its slow and meandering move towards full independence as a sovereign nation. In *Taylor*, the majority[32] recognised the significance of the colonial ties in the special status conferred on British subjects. For a range of reasons, the majority ruled that Taylor could not be considered to be an alien, and so could not be removed from the country.

[3.18] Gaudron J held that Taylor would only acquire the status of 'alien' if some change had occurred to alter the relationship that pertained between himself and the 'body politic constituting the Australian community'. She rejected the argument that the passage of citizenship legislation in 1948 had constituted such a change. McHugh, Kirby and Callinan JJ agreed on this point, stressing the significance of Taylor's allegiance to the Queen of the United Kingdom (and of Australia) as well as the length and continuity of his residence in Australia. As McHugh J points out,[33] s 117 of the Constitution entrenches certain rights in a 'subject of the Queen, resident in any state', not to be subjected to any 'disability or discrimination'. Kirby J, with

---

26   See former ss 12 and 14A of the Act, discussed in *Nolan* (1988) 165 CLR 178 at 178-9.
27   See *Migration Act 1958*, s 501 and the discussion in Chapter 17 below.
28   See further Chapter 17.3.3 below.
29   *Nolan* (1988) 165 CLR 178 at 186.
30   Ibid at 189.
31   (2001) 207 CLR 391. See Kim Rubenstein, *Australian Citizenship Law in Context* (Melbourne: Law Book Co, 2002) at 68.
32   Finding the ratio of the majority of Gaudron, McHugh, Kirby and Callinan JJ in that case is not an easy task, as McHugh J acknowledged in the later case of *Re MIMA; Ex parte Te; Ex parte Dang* (2002) 212 CLR 162 at [87] (*Te and Dang*). The minority (Gleeson CJ, Gummow and Hayne JJ) upheld the reasoning in *Nolan's* case. See the discussion in Rubenstein, above n 31, at 70.
33   *Taylor* (2001) 207 CLR 391 at [121].

whom Callinan J agreed, drew attention to the fact that British subjects in Australia continued to enjoy many of the privileges of citizenship after 1948, even though they never sought to take out Australian citizenship.[34] His Honour went further[35] to imply into the Constitution an obligation to consult with the Australian people before effecting any legislative change that might operate to exclude from the Australian polity persons who were previously members of it.

[3.19] Changes in the constitution of the High Court meant that the authority established in *Taylor* did not survive for long. The status and entitlements of British subjects in Australia were considered again in *Shaw v MIMA*.[36] Shaw was born in the United Kingdom in 1972, migrating to Australia with his family in 1974 at the age of two. He had remained in Australia since that time, but never applied for, nor was granted, Australian citizenship. After being convicted of a series of criminal offences, Shaw's visa was cancelled in 2001 on grounds that he was of bad character.[37] By a narrow majority of 4:3 the High Court upheld the legislative provisions in question as a valid exercise of legislative power. Although the Minister invoked the immigration power (s 51(27)), the external affairs power (s 51(29)) and notions of implied power, the case was ultimately decided on the basis of the aliens power (s 51(19)) – resurrecting the notion that parliament's power to make laws with respect to 'aliens' extends to all non-citizens, without exception.

[3.20] The joint judgment of Gleeson CJ, Gummow and Hayne JJ (with whom Heydon J agreed) returned to the reasoning in *Nolan*. Noting that the court in *Re Patterson; Ex parte Taylor* did not overrule *Nolan*, their Honours suggested that the case represents an anomaly on its facts[38] and/or was not based on the aliens power for its holding in any event.[39] The judges confirmed that Australian law now views citizenship and alienage in strictly binomial terms: all persons who are not citizens are aliens.[40]

[3.21] The three minority judgments dissent strongly from the majority's retreat from *Taylor*. McHugh J,[41] Kirby J[42] and Callinan J[43] affirm that decision as a binding precedent illustrating the court's return to a 'more complex notion of Australian nationality in keeping with the constitutional text and Australia's history'.[44]

[3.22] In many respects, the driving force behind the reasoning of the minority judges in *Shaw* appears to be a fear that untrammelled power to legislate with respect to citizenship would undermine fundamental historical understandings about who

---

34 Ibid at [302].
35 Ibid at [309].
36 (2003) 218 CLR 28 (*Shaw*).
37 See *Migration Act 1958*, s 501. See further Chapter 17 below.
38 *Shaw* (2003) 218 CLR 28 at [36].
39 Ibid at [39].
40 Ibid at [2].
41 Ibid at [48].
42 Ibid at [73].
43 Ibid at [166].
44 Ibid at [73] (Kirby J).

is and is not a member of the Australian polity. This is put most forcefully by Kirby J:[45]

> [T]he notion that, retrospectively, by legislation, [non-alien British subjects] status could be changed to 'alien' within the Constitution would put in peril to such a unilateral alteration the constitutional status of a very large number of people in a category that dates back to the beginnings of European settlement of Australia and the original notion of nationality in the Australian Constitution. The present case is thus not concerned merely with the constitutional position of persons such as Messrs Nolan, Taylor and Shaw, with their discouraging criminal records.

The majority, however, shared no such fears, stating emphatically that a power of parliament is 'not given any meaning narrowed by an apprehension of extreme examples and distorting possibilities of its application to some future law'.[46]

[3.23] The reasoning in the foregoing cases was based largely on the applicants' special status as British subjects. It may come as no surprise that attempts to extend the line of argument to include applicants who did not enter Australia as British subjects have been unsuccessful, even as the facts of the cases have become more and more extreme. The High Court has confirmed that non-citizens convicted of any sort of crime are now liable to be removed on character grounds irrespective of their age on arrival.

[3.24] Te and Dang were such applicants.[47] Both had entered Australia at young ages as refugees from the conflict in Vietnam. Although they had formed strong attachments within the Australian community, both had lengthy criminal records, and the Minister had moved to deport them on these grounds.

[3.25] In six separate judgments,[48] the High Court held that the applicants of both *Ex parte Te* and *Ex parte Dang* remained aliens. Two strands of reasoning emerged. The first, advanced by Gaudron, Gummow, McHugh and Hayne JJ, centred on the view that the characterisation of an 'alien' is wholly within the legislative function of the government. As Gaudron J stated:[49]

> The process whereby an alien born individual attains the status and entitlements that attach to a non-alien is called 'naturalisation'. The argument for the prosecutor is predicated on the proposition that the common law permits and the Constitution recognises that that process can occur other than in the circumstances and by the procedures designed by Parliament. That proposition is without foundation.

This approach defers strongly to parliament to define and characterise who is or is not an alien.

[3.26] Gleeson CJ and Kirby JJ adopted a second line of reasoning, which McHugh J also addressed. In their Honours' opinion, the key factor was whether or not absorption into the Australian community would suffice to bring the applicants outside the

---

45 Ibid at [98].
46 Ibid at [32].
47 *Re MIMA; Ex parte Te; Ex parte Dang* (2002) 212 CLR 162 (*Te* and *Dang*).
48 Callinan J did not submit a separate judgment but agreed with the order of the court. See ibid at [215].
49 Ibid at [56].

purview of the aliens power. Both Gleeson CJ and McHugh J held that absorption into the community does not necessarily mean a person is not an alien.[50] Kirby J, who advanced a strong view in *Taylor* that absorption *may* lead to the loss of alienage, held that even if further categories of non-citizen non-aliens existed, the plaintiffs did not fall within them. He noted that arguments as to absorption would not assist Te and Dang:[51]

> Far from showing allegiance or being absorbed into the Australian body politic, the repeated conduct of the applicants constitutes a public renunciation of the norms of the community.

[3.27] The judges who adopted the 'absorption' line of argument also indicated less willingness to defer to the parliament's definition of alien. Gleeson CJ was careful to stress that 'Parliament cannot, simply by giving its own definition of alien expand the power … to include persons who could not possibly answer the description of "aliens" in the ordinary meaning of the word'. His Honour thereby signalled that the courts do retain some oversight of the aliens power. Kirby J also cautioned that 'because the word "alien" involves a constitutional concept, it is ultimately for this Court to define its outer boundaries in accordance with the Constitution'.[52] *Te* and *Dang's* cases illustrate that, while the High Court has accepted the 'absorption' doctrine in relation to the immigration power, it has categorically rejected it in relation to the aliens power.[53]

[3.28] As noted earlier, the more recent cases involving Papua New Guinean nationals stripped of their status as Australian citizens in 1975[54] represent an interesting extension to this jurisprudence. In these cases the High Court suggested that the Australian citizenship conferred by legislation is not necessarily inconsistent with a concurrent constitutional status as alien. The example in those cases was individuals who had no absolute entitlement to enter or remain in Australia in spite of their nominal status as Australian citizens.[55]

[3.29] While these cases stand as recent judicial rulings on the reach of the aliens power, it is worth noting that the government's persistent attempts to deport permanent residents of very long standing have not gone without reproach from the courts. In cases such as *Nystrom v MIMIA*,[56] the courts' attention has been turned away from

---

50 Ibid at [41] and [91] respectively.
51 Ibid at [203].
52 Ibid at [161].
53 *Ayan v MIMIA* (2003) 126 FCR 152 illustrates the Federal Court's approach to the issues raised in cases such as *Te and Dang*. In that case, Sackville J stated that 'whatever view one takes of the appellant's criminal conduct, it might be thought difficult to resist the proposition that in every respect, except citizenship, he is an Australian': at [1]. Nonetheless, the court followed *Te* in stating: 'The appellant remains an alien, within the reach of the Act … despite circumstances which would lead to the conclusion that, since his arrival as an infant, he had been absorbed into the community (so as to satisfy, for instance, the notion of absorption as it affects the immigration power …) and despite the fact that, from a social and human point of view, the appellant could be described as an Australian': at [37] (Allsop J).
54 See *MIMIA v Walsh* (2002) 189 ALR 694; *Walsh v MIMIA* B41/2002 (25 June 2003) (failed special leave application); and *Re MIMIA; Ex parte Ame* (2005) 222 CLR 439.
55 See the discussion in Chapter 2.5.2.
56 (2005) 143 FCR 420.

constitutional issues and towards other provisions in the *Migration Act* that suggest a tenure of sorts for long-term permanent residents who have become absorbed into the Australian community. In spite of such rulings, the High Court has held ultimately that the Australian Parliament generally does have power to order the removal of non-citizens, no matter how extensive the length of their tenure in the country.[57]

3.3 High Court reactions to provisions threatening usurpation of the judicial power of the Constitution

[3.30] *Taylor's* case notwithstanding, the High Court's rulings on the aliens power have made it very difficult to challenge the constitutionality of migration legislation on the grounds that the relevant empowering placita in s 51 are not sufficiently broad in their scope. It has taken very exceptional circumstances for a constitutional challenge to meet with any success. Even in these cases, plaintiffs have gained no relief from arguments going to the scope of the parliament's power to legislate with respect to immigrants or aliens. The plaintiffs' (generally) partial success has centred rather on the extent to which legislation could operate to allow the executive to usurp powers reserved to the courts under Chapter III of the Constitution. In this section, two groups of cases are considered in turn. The first involves cases in which attempts have been made to reduce or exclude altogether the curial review of immigration cases. The second (overlapping) group of cases are those in which other arguments have been raised about the nature and extent of the judicial power. Both types of challenges have been made in cases centring on Australia's mandatory immigration detention laws.

3.3.1 Legislation restricting or ousting judicial review

[3.31] The Rule of Law in Australia is predicated on the notion that the judicial power can only be exercised by a court of law. This power is vested in the High Court of Australia – the only court provided for expressly by the Constitution[58] – and thus by implication in all federal courts of law. As we explore further in Chapter 19, ss 75 and 76 of the Constitution detail the original jurisdiction of the High Court. The first of these provisions specifies five matters, two of which are of particular significance in the present context.[59] Section 75(iii) gives the High Court original jurisdiction in cases

---

57 *MIMIA v Nystrom* (2006) 228 CLR 566, discussed in Chapter 17 below.
58 Section 71 of the Constitution provides that the judicial power of the Commonwealth shall be vested in a federal supreme court to be known as the High Court of Australia. The actual creation of the court, however, is stated to be a matter for parliament, which 'may establish' the court, comprised of a Chief Justice and at least two other justices. The High Court was created by the *Judiciary Act 1903* (Cth). It reached its present size of seven justices (inclusive of the Chief Justice) in 1912. See JM Bennett, *Keystone of the Federal Arch: A Historical Memoir of the High Court of Australia to 1980* (Canberra: AGPS, 1980) at 12-20; and James Crawford, *Australian Courts of Law* (Melbourne: Oxford University Press, 3rd ed, 1993) at 178-98.
59 Section 75(i) and (ii) relate to matters arising under any treaty or affecting consuls or other foreign representatives. Neither jurisdiction has been used in the High Court, in part because no treaty has force in Australia until its terms are enacted by the Federal Parliament. Section 75(iv) gives the High

in which the Commonwealth or one of its officers is a party. Section 75(v) provides that the court has original jurisdiction in all matters in which writs of mandamus or prohibition or an injunction are sought against an officer of the Commonwealth.[60] The provisions operate to create a constitutionally guaranteed right to seek judicial review in the High Court of most federal administrative action.[61]

[3.32] The entrenching of a constitutional entitlement to judicial review raised few concerns in government until the 1980s. It was in those years that reforms in administrative law (which included the creation of the Federal Court and the passage of the *Administrative Decisions (Judicial Review) Act 1977* (Cth)) opened the way for administrative challenges that would have been inconceivable in earlier times.[62] The exposure of the courts to the humanity of migration cases led in turn to a propensity for intervention that politicians found confronting to their understanding of immigration control as the province of the executive. It was the arrival of 'boat people' in November 1989 that led to the first attempt by the Australian Parliament to reign in the ability of the courts to review executive action relevant to immigration control. The incident set in train a sequence of executive action, litigation and legislative reaction that has continued into the new millennium.

[3.33] Many and varied devices have been assayed over the years in attempts to curtail the judicial review of migration decisions. The most significant of these are discussed in greater detail in Chapter 19. For present purposes it suffices to consider three instances where parliament has tried to limit the role played by the courts in the oversight of migration decision-making.

[3.34] The first was the government's initial response to the controversy engendered by the Cambodian asylum seekers who arrived in 1989 and related specifically to curial oversight of immigration detention and is discussed in the case study that follows. The second was the legislation passed in the wake of these events which

---

Court power to hear disputes between two or more States and between residents or two or more States. It is referred to as the High Court's diversity jurisdiction: Leslie Zines, *Cowen and Zines's Federal Jurisdiction in Australia* (Melbourne: Federation Press, 3rd ed, 2002) ch 1.

60 The phrase 'officer of the Commonwealth' has been read broadly to include everyone from Ministers of the Crown (and their delegates) to judges of lower federal courts: see, for example, *R v Judges of Commonwealth Industrial Relations Court* (1968) 121 CLR 313. Although no mention is made of the 'quashing' writ – certiorari – the High Court has found ways of getting around this omission where this writ can be issued in conjunction with the other named remedies: see LJW Aitken, 'The High Court's Power to Grant Certiorari – the Unresolved Question' (1986) 16 *Federal Law Review* 370. Compare comments by Callinan J in *Plaintiff S157 v Commonwealth* (2003) 211 CLR 426 at [131] (*Plaintiff S157*). The interpretation of the phrase 'officer of the Commonwealth' is considered further below, at [3.64]-[3.65].

61 See Margaret Allars, *Introduction to Australian Administrative Law* (Sydney: Butterworths, 1990) at 99-100. As the s 75 jurisdiction is specified in the Constitution, it cannot be abrogated by the parliament. On the other hand, the legislature can confer further jurisdiction on the High Court. Section 76 enables parliament to confer original jurisdiction on the High Court. This is referred to as the court's 'vested' jurisdiction: see James Crawford, *The Creation of States in International Law* (New York: Oxford University Press, 1979) at 181-2. It can also confer on other federal courts jurisdiction commensurate with that of the High Court under ss 75 and 76: see s 77.

62 Perusal of the Commonwealth Law Reports between 1901 and 1970 reveals little more than 50 cases involving migrants and refugees. The dearth of cases reflects the expense and complexity of the old prerogative writ system that served as the unique source of access to curial review. See further Chapter 19 below.

introduced the first Part 8 of the *Migration Act 1958*.⁶³ These amendments truncated the judicial review powers of the Federal Court by removing the court's ability to review migration decisions on the broad grounds of natural justice, relevancy, reasonableness and apprehended bias.⁶⁴ They were controversial because the provisions represented the first occasion in which the Federal Court's powers to rule on the legality of administrative action were not co-extensive with those of the High Court. Upheld in a very close (4:3) ruling by the High Court,⁶⁵ the amendments had a disastrous impact because their effect was to force all disgruntled applicants to lodge in the High Court. The practical implication of that finding was that in some instances the Federal Court could be asked to 'affirm a decision that was in fact unlawful'. All members of the court recognised that the only avenue available to applicants in these circumstances was the High Court. The Chief Justice and McHugh J remarked:⁶⁶

> In the present case, the Parliament has chosen to restrict severely the jurisdiction of the Federal Court to review the legality of decisions of the Refugee Review Tribunal. That restriction may have significant consequences for this Court because it must inevitably force or at all events invite applicants for refugee status to invoke the constitutionally entrenched s 75(v) jurisdiction of this Court. The effect on the business of this Court is certain to be serious. Nevertheless, we can see nothing in ss 75, 76 and 77 of the Constitution which prevents the Parliament from enacting ss 476, 485 and 486 of the Act.

[3.35] The other members of the court made similar comments, with some calling directly on the government to reconsider the wisdom of Part 8 of the *Migration Act* (as it then stood).⁶⁷ By 2001, that court had a backlog of many thousands of migration cases which meant in turn that applicants were facing a wait of many years in Australia before having their cases determined.

[3.36] The third, more radical, assault on judicial power occurred in the immediate aftermath of the *Tampa* Affair in 2001 with the replacement of this regime with the 'second' Part 8 which includes a fully fledged privative clause.⁶⁸ Again, the measure was upheld as within the judicial power. On this occasion, however, the High Court severely undermined the government's victory under constitutional law. It did this by ruling that, while a privative clause can operate to prevent judicial oversight of decisions that are made lawfully, it cannot prevent the courts from intervening to correct a ruling affected by 'jurisdictional error'.

---

63 See *Migration Reform Act 1992* (Cth), inserting Part 8 of the *Migration Act 1958*. The relevant provisions came into force on 1 September 1994.
64 See *Migration Act 1958*, ss 476ff (as at 1 September 1994); and the discussion in Chapter 19.5 below.
65 See *Abebe v Commonwealth* (1999) 197 CLR 510, discussed in Chapter 19 at [19.66] below.
66 Ibid at [50].
67 Kirby J commented: 'The prospect of this Court having to hear and determine, in its original jurisdiction, applications of this kind, in default of the availability of equivalent redress in the Federal Court (or of effective remitter to the Federal Court), is extremely inconvenient. It is also expensive and time-consuming. These considerations suggest the need for further attention to legislation which has such an outcome'. See ibid at [207].
68 A 'privative clause' operates to prevent or restrict court review of administrative decisions. See generally Mary Crock and Ed Santow, 'Privative Clauses and the Limits of the Law' in Matthew Groves and HP Lee (eds), *Australian Administrative Law* (Melbourne: Cambridge University Press, 2007) at 345. For fuller explanation of this term, see below at [3.37]-[3.39] and Chapter 19.6.1.

[3.37] In *Plaintiff S157 v Commonwealth*[69] the High Court responded to the attempt to restrict judicial review with a curious mix of deference and assertion. Privative clauses having been used frequently in Australian legislation over many years, it may not be surprising that the measure was upheld as constitutional. What the court did was to confirm that privative clauses cannot be read literally: they have a constitutional meaning that qualifies their practical effect. The High Court ruled that a privative clause neither confines the judicial power of a court nor expands the powers of the bureaucracy whose decisions may be under challenge.[70] Rather, it reinforces the fact that the role of the court is to review the basic *legality* of an administrative decision. Hence, the High Court made it clear that any tribunal decision evidencing 'jurisdictional error' would fall outside the privative clause scheme and therefore be open to review by either the Federal or High Courts.[71] The court stated:

> [A] failure to exercise jurisdiction [or] an excess of the jurisdiction conferred by the Act ... is 'regarded, in law, as no decision at all.' Thus, if the question cannot properly be described in the terms used in s 474(2) as 'a decision made under this Act' ... [it] is, thus, not a 'privative clause decision' as defined in ss 474(2) and (3) of the Act.[72]

The effect of this pronouncement was to underscore the significance of a court identifying a jurisdictional error, making it clear that such an error vitiates a decision.[73]

[3.38] In spite of the clear terms of the Constitution, the Australian government did not abandon altogether its attempts to reign in the power of the courts in the immigration area. Following the ruling by the High Court in *Plaintiff S157*, a Bill was introduced into the Federal Parliament, proposing an amendment to the privative clause in s 474 of the *Migration Act*.[74] The Bill aimed to expand the definition of 'privative clause' to include:

> (b) a purported decision that would be a privative clause decision within the meaning of subsection 474(2) if there had not been:
> (i) a failure to exercise jurisdiction; or

---

69   (2003) 211 CLR 476.
70   See, for example *R v Hickman; Ex parte Fox and Clinton* (1945) 70 CLR 598 at 617 (Dixon J). His Honour there stated, in obiter, that administrative decisions are not considered 'invalid' provided that they meet certain requirements: that 'they do not upon their face exceed the ... authority [conferred by the legislation in question]; that they ... amount to a bona fide attempt to exercise powers [conferred]; and [that they] relate to the subject matter of the legislation'. This case is discussed below at Chapter 19 at [19.78]-[19.83].
71   Further, the High Court took pains to make clear that the construction of s 474 has implications for remitter of actions by it to both the Federal Court and the Federal Magistrates Court. In short, '[t]he limitation, ... of the jurisdiction otherwise enjoyed by the Federal Court and the Federal Magistrates Court ... will be controlled by the construction given to s 474. Decisions which are not protected by s 474 such as that in this case ... will not be within the terms of the jurisdictional limitations just described; jurisdiction otherwise conferred upon federal courts ... will remain, to be given full effect in accordance with the terms of that conferral': *Plaintiff S157* (2003) 211 CLR 426 at [96]-[97].
72   Ibid at [77].
73   The practical impact of this ruling is explored below in Chapter 19.
74   Migration Amendment (Judicial Review) Bill 2004 (Cth).

(ii) an excess of jurisdiction;
in the making of the purported decision.[75]

[3.39] The Explanatory Memorandum stated: 'A "purported decision" is a decision that would be a privative clause decision, had it not been affected by jurisdictional error'.[76] If accepted, this would clearly have expanded the ambit of administrative action falling within the scope of the privative clause. The accompanying explanatory material made it clear that this amendment was aimed at closing the 'loop-hole' identified in *Plaintiff S157*,[77] by bringing jurisdictional errors within the scope of the privative clause.[78] The Bill was never fully debated, nor was it put to a vote. However, some aspects were included in the *Migration Litigation Reform Act 2005* (Cth) which came into force on 1 December 2005. The references to *purported* decisions remain in the *Migration Act* in the context of denying jurisdiction to the inferior federal courts: a change that in effect restores a regime that existed under the first Part 8 of the *Migration Act*.[79]

[3.40] Attempts to constrain the power of the courts have continued over time. However, the decision of the High Court in *Plaintiff S157* represented something of a judicial line in the sand. So, for example, the court has since ruled unconstitutional an attempt to place enforceable time limits on applications for judicial review.[80] As we explore in the following case study, curial review of administrative action is probably the only area where the High Court has held firm in its interpretation of the 'judicial power' conferred by Chapter III of the Constitution. The court has been less concerned to insist on control of actions associated traditionally with the exercise of judicial power: arrest and detention. As in so many of these points of high drama and controversy in immigration, the modern jurisprudential story involves 'boat people'. On this occasion the starting point was the arrival of boats from Cambodia in and after November 1989. The boats carried mostly ethnic Chinese fugitives from unrest in that country following the expulsion of the Vietnamese forces which had in turn subdued the genocidal Khmer Rouge regime.[81]

3.3.2 The nature and extent of the judicial power: A case study of immigration detention

[3.41] Chu Kheng Lim was one of this group of Cambodian nationals who came to Australia by boat in November 1989 without authorisation and sought protection

---

75 Migration Amendment (Judicial Review) Bill 2004 (Cth), cl 2.
76 Explanatory Memorandum, Migration Amendment (Judicial Review) Bill 2004, [7].
77 Commonwealth of Australia, 'Migration Amendment (Judicial Review) Bill 2004' in *Bills Digest*, Parl Paper No 118 (2003-4) at 8.
78 Explanatory Memorandum, Migration Amendment (Judicial Review) Bill 2004, [8].
79 See *Migration Act 1958*, s 476(2)(b). Note that the constitutionality of the regime was upheld in *MZXOT v MIAC* (2008) 233 CLR 601. See Lisa Burton, '*MZXOT v MIAC*: Last Stop on Route 75(v)?' (2009) 16 *Australian Journal of Administrative Law* 115.
80 See *Bodruddaza v MIMA* (2007) 228 CLR 651; *Plaintiff M61/2010E v Commonwealth and Plaintiff M69 of 2010 v Commonwealth* (2010) 272 ALR 14; and the discussion in Chapter 19 below.
81 See, for example, Ben Kiernan, *The Pol Pot Regime: Race Power and Genocide in Cambodia under the Khmer Rouge* (New Haven: Yale Nota Bene, 3rd ed, 2008).

as refugees.[82] Under the law and policies then prevailing,[83] he was deemed not to have entered the country and was taken into custody pending the determination of his claim. After a series of administrative errors and other delays engendered by raw politics surrounding the Cambodian cases, he was still in detention without a final determination of his claims two years later. He and his colleagues applied to the Federal Court for release on the ground that their continued detention was unlawful. Two days before the case was to be heard, the government rushed through parliament special amendments to the *Migration Act 1958*.[84] These had the effect of mandating the detention of the boat people – referred to as 'designated persons' – for 273 days or until they either left the country or were granted an entry permit. The amending legislation included a provision that purported to direct that no court could order the release of a designated person.[85] This was the first of many legislative indications that the Federal Parliament did not want the federal courts to intervene in or review migration rulings. Lim sought declaratory and injunctive relief in the High Court on the basis that the amendments were unconstitutional.

[3.42] In *Chu Kheng Lim v MILGEA*,[86] the plaintiffs argued that parliament's power to legislate with respect to aliens was tempered by both implied and explicit restrictions placed on the legislature by the Constitution. According to the plaintiffs, the requirement that all 'designated persons' be kept in detention, and the specification that no court order their release, amounted to a usurpation by the legislature of the judicial power vested in the courts by s 71 of the Constitution. The plaintiffs contended that the power conferred on the migration officials to detain aliens for an extended period, without trial, was one that could only be exercised validly by a court. The argument was that detention amounts to punishment and that penalties were the preserve of the judiciary who alone are vested with the judicial power. In such circumstances, they argued, the constitutionality of the amending Act could not be supported merely by reference to the aliens power in s 51(19) of the Constitution.

[3.43] A majority of the High Court agreed with the plaintiffs' submissions regarding s 54R of the Act (now s 183).[87] The judges took exception to the attempt to oust curial review of the plaintiffs' detention and, to the extent that it did exclude such review, declared the provision invalid.[88] However, in all other respects the court rejected the plaintiffs' arguments. The court held that the power to detain aliens was

---

82 Andrew Hamilton, 'Three Years Hard' (1993) 3 *Eureka Street* No 1 at 24-30 and No 2 at 22-8; Mary Crock, 'Climbing Jacob's Ladder: The High Court and the Administrative Detention of Asylum Seekers in Australia' (2003) 15 *Sydney Law Review* 338; and Mary Crock, *Protection or Punishment: The Detention of Asylum Seekers in Australia* (Sydney: The Federation Press, 1993).
83 See *Migration Act 1958*, s 36A, later s 89.
84 See *Migration Amendment Act 1992* (Cth), which introduced Part 4B into the Act.
85 See *Migration Act 1958*, former s 54R, now s 183.
86 *Chu Kheng Lim v MILGEA* (1992) 176 CLR 1 (*Chu Kheng Lim*).
87 The provision remains in the Act because the High Court ruling meant that it was capable of being read down. It must be read now so as to prohibit any court from ordering the release of a designated person being held in *lawful* custody.
88 *Chu Kheng Lim* (1992) 176 CLR 1 at 35-7.

not necessarily punitive, thereby sanctioning the concept of administrative detention. Brennan, Deane and Dawson JJ found that giving the executive the authority to detain does not infringe the Constitution's exclusive vesting of the judicial power of the Commonwealth in the courts, as it takes its character from the executive powers to exclude, admit and deport of which it is an incident.[89] They acknowledged that Australian citizens enjoy a 'constitutional immunity from being imprisoned by Commonwealth authority except pursuant to an order by a court in the exercise of the judicial power of the Commonwealth'.[90] The court found that this immunity did not extend to immigration detainees because these people were not being subjected to incarceration by way of criminal sanction. Rather, they were being locked up so as to protect the national interest. Brennan, Deane and Dawson JJ rejected the suggestion that the detention provisions were unnecessarily harsh on the basis that the detainees were to some extent voluntary prisoners who were free to return to their country of origin at any time they wished.[91]

[3.44] In *Chu Kheng Lim* the High Court drew back from striking down a legislative regime aimed at deterring unlawful migration. Given the normative impact that such a ruling would have had on the government's border control measures, it is perhaps not surprising that the court decided on a relatively conservative approach to the legislation under challenge. The vehemence of the government's feeling on the issue may have contributed to the pressure on the court to defer to parliament and to the doctrine of separation of powers.[92] As noted earlier, the High Court made it plain that it would not have been prepared to uphold the constitutionality of the detention provisions in question if the legislation had affected the rights of Australian citizens. Imprisonment is presumptively an act of punishment and it is well established that punishment is a key aspect of the judicial power. During the hearing of the case, the bench expressed its concern that the definition of 'designated person' could be interpreted to render liable to mandatory detention persons with quasi-citizenship status in Australia. The example given was New Zealand citizens who happened to be on a boat in Australian territorial waters between the dates specified in the legislation.[93] In the result, the High Court upheld the detention provisions precisely because they did not affect Australian citizens. In effect, the High Court found that the alien status of the applicants transformed the nature of the measures being taken so that their detention did not constitute punishment such as would constitute a

---

89 Ibid at 32.
90 Ibid at 29.
91 Ibid at 31-2. As explored further below, the fiction of the three walled prison was picked up a decade later in the context of another *cause célèbre*. The federal government moved to prevent a Norwegian cargo vessel named *MV Tampa* from disembarking 433 asylum seekers rescued at sea from a sinking Indonesian ferry. In the Full Federal Court, French J ruled that the actions taken by the government did not amount to 'detention' because the 'rescuees' in question were merely being restrained from entering Australia. They were free to travel to any other part of the world.
92 See Senate Commonwealth Parliamentary Debates *Hansard* Senate, Vol 20, December 1992, 4286ff; Nicholas Poynder, 'An Opportunity for Justice Goes Begging: Chu Kheng Lim v Minister for Immigration, Local Government and Ethnic Affairs' (1994) 1 *Australian Journal of Human Rights* 414; and Margo Kingston, 'Politics and Public Opinion' in Crock (ed), *Protection or Punishment*, above n 82.
93 See *Chu Kheng Lim* (1992) 176 CLR 1 at 22-3 and 53-8.

usurpation of the judicial power. In the final analysis, the court upheld the legislation on the basis of the power to legislate with respect to aliens.[94]

[3.45] The sharp distinction drawn between the rights of citizens and of non-citizens has been confirmed by the High Court in many other cases.[95] For example, a majority of the bench in *Cunliffe v Commonwealth*[96] rejected the notion that rights implied into the Constitution extend to non-citizens, with Mason CJ a partial dissentient.[97] The case involved a challenge to the constitutionality of provisions in the Act that restricted the giving of 'immigration assistance' by any persons save those registered by the government as migration agents. The plaintiff solicitor challenged the new scheme on bases which included arguments that the provisions constituted an infringement of the implied right to freedom of speech. The question then arose as to whether such a freedom could be claimed when the right was being claimed in respect of a non-citizen. As Rubenstein points out,[98] Brennan and Deane JJ distinguished between the non-citizen's right to the protection of the law and the right to invoke constitutional guarantees such as that protecting freedom of speech. Both judges found that aliens have no right to such protections because they 'have no constitutional right to participate in or to be consulted on matters of government' and stand 'outside the people of the Commonwealth'.[99]

[3.46] In *Chu Kheng Lim* the High Court conceded that the detention provisions in question would not have been tolerated had they been directed at Australian citizens or permanent residents. In the absence of a Bill of Rights, however, the Constitution afforded the plaintiffs little protection.[100] In 2004 a series of cases were decided in the High Court that placed this central finding beyond question.

[3.47] By 2004, Australia's policy of mandatory detention was well entrenched. This was in spite of a litany of protests – particularly against the persistent policy of detaining children and at-risk adults – and violent unrest in the centres that rendered living conditions very difficult.[101] In a series of cases that raise real questions about the political influences at play on the most powerful judges in the land, Australia's Constitution once again emerged as a document that can be interpreted so as to afford few protections to the vulnerable non-citizen. Whether it need be interpreted in this fashion, however, is an open question.

[3.48] The cases involved, respectively, failed asylum seekers who could not be removed to their countries of origin and who therefore faced indefinite detention

---

94 Crock, 'Climbing Jacob's Ladder', above n 82, at 346-56.
95 See in this context, see above Part 3.2 and Chapter 19 below.
96 (1994) 182 CLR 272.
97 Ibid at 299.
98 Kim Rubenstein, 'Citizenship in Australia: Unscrambling its Meaning' (1995) 20 *Melbourne University Law Review* 503 at 515-16.
99 *Cunliffe v Commonwealth* (1994) 182 CLR 272 at 328 and 336.
100 As explored in the following chapter, an attempt by the Cambodian asylum seekers to use international complaints mechanisms also failed to translate into practical outcomes. See *A v Australia*, Communication No 560/1993: Australia, CCPR/C/59/D/560/1993 (30 April 1997), discussed below at Chapter 4.4.
101 See, for example, Tom Mann, *Desert Sorrow: Asylum Seekers at Woomera* (Adelaide: Seaview Press, 2003); and Julian Burnside (ed), *From Nothing to Zero: Letters from Refugees in Australia's Detention Centres* (Melbourne: Lonely Planet Publications, 2003).

in Australia;[102] non-citizens detained in intolerable conditions;[103] and non-citizen children detained by reason of their unlawful status.[104] In each instance, arguments were made to the effect that the *circumstances* of the plaintiffs' detention were such that the custody could not be described as 'administrative' or even protective of the state of Australia. Accordingly, it was argued that the detention had become punitive. Under the Constitution, this transformation would require the involvement of judicial sanction – a factor that was missing in each instance. So, for example, in *Al-Kateb* and *Al Khafaji* it was argued that the inability to remove the plaintiffs from Australia meant that their continued detention had become punitive. In *Behrooz*, it was the poor conditions in detention that had this effect. As for the children, in *Re Woolley* it was argued that the detention of children is never administrative because the incarceration can serve no purpose that is not punitive.

[3.49] In all of the cases, a central issue for the High Court was whether the constitutionality of a statute should be determined on the face of the document or by its practical impact. A majority of the court opted for a strictly textual approach in each instance, ruling that the substantive impact of a legislative measure is irrelevant to its constitutionality. This meant that the court rejected contentions that the judicial power in the Constitution qualifies the operational impact of legislation that on its face may have a legitimate purpose.

[3.50] In *Al-Kateb* and *Al Khafaji* a bare majority of the High Court (4:3) ruled that the effect of the *Migration Act* was unambiguous: under ss 189 and 196 unlawful non-citizens must be detained until they are either granted a visa or removed from the country. McHugh, Hayne, Callinan and Heydon JJ ruled that that the legislation could not be read 'subject to a purposive limitation or an intention not to affect fundamental rights'.[105] Again, their Honours were swayed by the fact that the detainees were aliens in constitutional terms. They confirmed that the power to make laws with respect to aliens was a subject power which gave the Federal Parliament virtually untrammelled authority to legislate with respect to non-citizens. The incarceration of the plaintiffs was within constitutional power as long as the authorising legislation on its face met the requirements of the Constitution. For the majority, the *constitutionality* of the provisions could not be called in question by allegations that the legislation was in breach of *international* legal obligations Australia might have assumed.[106]

[3.51] McHugh J described his ruling as 'tragic', laying all of the blame in the mandatory terms of the legislation and the failure to provide for a Bill of Rights in the Constitution. The minority judges disagreed. Gleeson CJ[107] avoided the controversy over the Constitution by arguing that basic tenets of statutory interpretation operated to render unlawful the continued detention of any person who could not be

---

102 See *Al-Kateb v Godwin* (2004) 219 CLR 562 (*Al-Kateb*); and *MIMIA v Al Khafaji* (2004) 219 CLR 664 (*Al Khafaji*).
103 See *Behrooz v Secretary, DIMIA* (2004) 219 CLR 486 (*Behrooz*).
104 See *Re Woolley; Ex parte Applicants M276/2003* (2004) 225 CLR 1 (*Re Woolley*).
105 See *Al-Kateb* (2004) 219 CLR 562 at [33] (McHugh J), agreeing with Hayne J (with whom Callinan and Heydon JJ concurred).
106 Ibid at [63] (McHugh J). On this point, see further Chapter 4.
107 Ibid at [22] (Gleeson CJ).

removed from Australia as envisaged by s 198 of the *Migration Act*. In other words, his Honour held that detention under this Act was expressed by parliament to serve a purpose, namely so as to determine eligibility for the grant of a visa or to prepare a person for removal. Where the stated purpose could not be fulfilled (because the detainee was neither eligible for a visa nor capable of being removed from Australia) the detention ceased to be lawful. The minority judges all ruled that the aliens power in the Constitution is not plenary, but must be read subject to the limitations imposed by other parts of the Constitution and (wherever possible) so as to remain compliant with fundamental principles enshrined in the common law and in international law. The minority dissented on the question of whether changes in circumstance can transform administrative detention into a punitive regime. Kirby J underscored his analysis of the law by stressing the importance of adopting an interpretative approach that is consistent with Australia's obligations under international law.[108]

[3.52] The ruling in *Al-Kateb* appears to have been a watershed of sorts. In the subsequent decisions, Kirby J was the only judge to rule that poor conditions in detention could render administrative detention punitive in contravention of Chapter III of the Constitution.[109] In *Re Woolley*,[110] all seven judges agreed that legislation mandating the detention of unlawful non-citizens could not be partitioned so as to have the effect of legitimating the detention of some unlawful non-citizens and not others. Mandatory detention means that personal characteristics such as age and state of health are irrelevant to determining the lawfulness of the provisions in question. In *Re Woolley*, the High Court confirmed that there is nothing in Australian constitutional law that prevents the Federal Parliament from legislating to detain non-citizen children, however powerless the children may be to control the circumstances of either their entry into Australia or their departure from the country.[111] This principle was reinforced in 2011 in a failed attempt to have the High Court declare unlawful the detention of children under the law then in force.[112]

3.4 Immigration control and plenary power (reprise)

[3.53] The question left hanging at this point of Australia's constitutional story is the extent to which the government's power over non-citizens (and immigration generally) is constrained at all by the Constitution. It has been seen that the High Court has been careful not to write itself out of the equation altogether: the various attempts to exclude the judicial review of executive and legislative action have been politely but firmly rebuffed by the court. However, the High Court has not shown the

---

108 Ibid at [167]-[168], [175], [190].
109 Ibid at [153], [159].
110 (2004) 225 CLR 1.
111 Ibid at [97]ff (McHugh J), at [162] (Gummow J), at [212] (Kirby J), at [226] (Hayne J), at [263] (Callinan J).
112 See *Plaintiff M168/2010 By His Litigation Guardian Sister Brigid (Marie) Arthur v Commonwealth* [2011] HCATrans 4; and Judith Bessant, 'Soul Searching Needed on Child Detention', *The Age*, 25 January 2011, available at <http://www.theage.com.au/opinion/politics/soul-searching-is-needed-on-child-detention20110124-1a2y5.html>.

[3.54] Indeed, in one case in 2001 that the High Court declined to hear in full,[113] suggestions were made that in some instances the power of the executive government is *plenary* in the sense that it is *not* subject to constraint by the federal legislature. In the litigation that arose in the course of the *Tampa* Affair, which is the subject of special study in Chapter 4, French J ruled that the government's actions were not rendered unlawful by the fact that there was no (or may have been no) legislative basis for what occurred. His Honour suggested that the nature of the executive power conferred on the government under the Australian Constitution may be such that legislation is not needed to render lawful any actions taken to protect Australia's borders.[114]

[3.55] The point was explored by Professor George Winterton in 2004 in an article that examines in detail the nature of the executive power of the Commonwealth.[115] He began by acknowledging that s 61 of the Constitution describes but does not define the power of executive government.[116] As to the central question of whether any legislative sanction was necessary for the action taken in the *Tampa* Affair, Winterton dissected the meaning of the words in s 61 that extend the executive power to the 'execution and maintenance of this Constitution and of the laws of the Commonwealth'. As Australia was 'born into a common law environment', Winterton noted that the High Court has accepted that the executive power includes the Crown's prerogative powers. He described these as the common law and the non-statutory powers of the Crown,[117] and identified as the central issue:

> whether the Commonwealth government is limited to powers derived from the prerogative, or whether it can undertake (without legislative authority other than the appropriation of the necessary funds) any activity which is considered appropriate for a national government.[118]

[3.56] Winterton argued that s 61 should be read as having two components. The first relates to the breadth of the executive power, which he said should extend to any matters on which it can legislate, including matters appropriate to a national government. The second relates to the activities the government can undertake in regard to those subjects (the depth of the power).[119] Here, the debate has been between those who propose that the scope of government activity should be limited to the execution of either legislation made by parliament or the exercise of prerogative power; and those who propose that government activity can extent to 'anything appropriate to a national government'.

---

113   See *Vadarlis v MIMA* M93/2001 [2001] HCATrans 563.
114   *Ruddock v Vadarlis* (2001) 110 FCR 491 at 543-4.
115   Winterton, above n 3.
116   See the comments of Isaacs J in *Commonwealth v Colonial Combing, Spinning and Weaving Co Ltd* (1922) 31 CLR 421 at 440 (known as the *Wooltops* case). This much is implicit in the use of the words 'the executive power ... extends to' in s 61. See also *Davis v Commonwealth* (1988) 166 CLR 79 at 92 (Mason CJ, Deane and Gaudron JJ).
117   Winterton, above n 3, at 26.
118   Ibid at 29.
119   Ibid at 29.

[3.57] The *Tampa* litigation did indeed bring out both approaches. At first instance, North J took the view that no issues arose about the exercise of prerogative power in matters relating to immigration control because the *Migration Act 1958* had effectively covered the field. His Honour therefore ruled that the failure to comply with the terms of this legislation rendered unlawful the actions taken by the executive in blockading the *MV Tampa* and preventing the disembarkation of the 'rescuees'.[120] On appeal, Black CJ devoted considerable attention to the nature of the prerogative powers and whether these extended to a general right in nations to expel or exclude 'aliens'. Winterton quotes the Chief Justice who remarked:

> It would be a very strange circumstance if the at best doubtful and historically long unused power to exclude or expel should emerge in a strong modern form from s 61 of the Constitution by virtue of general conceptions of 'the national interest'. This is all the more so when according to English constitutional theory new prerogative powers cannot be created.[121]

In contrast, French J, with whom Beaumont J agreed in substance and outcome, drew a sharp line between the prerogative power and the executive power of the government. The latter, according to his Honour, should be 'measured by reference to Australia's status as a sovereign nation and by reference to the terms of the Constitution itself'.[122] Within this construct, it was sufficient for French J that the subjects of the action taken were non-citizens.

[3.58] Winterton noted that some support for the approach taken by French J is to be found in High Court jurisprudence in which various judges have coupled discussion of the prerogative with allusion to power derived from 'the necessities of modern national government'.[123] He nevertheless proceeded to critique the approach adopted by the Federal Court judges, expressing serious concerns about the effect of abandoning the notion that prerogative power should operate as a yardstick against which to measure the executive power of the Australian government. He pointed out that the notion that the prerogative should have such a guiding role is implicit in the long established principle that the common law should be used to interpret both statutes and constitutions. In spite of its uncertainty, the prerogative 'constitutes a substantial body of principles, rules and precedents, established over hundreds of years'. Such principles provide surer guidance than vague notions of sovereignty and what is 'appropriate' for national governments. Finally, Winterton noted that untrammelled executive power that is not subject to the oversight of parliament, is essentially undemocratic and antithetic to the rule of law.[124]

[3.59] Amidst the flurry of legislative change on 26 September 2001, French J's comments did not go unnoticed by government drafters who clearly did not share Professor Winterton's concerns about untrammelled executive power. Amendments

---

120 *Victorian Council for Civil Liberties v MIMA* (2001) 110 FCR 452 at 478-82 [110]-[122].
121 See *Ruddock v Vadarlis* (2001) 110 FCR 491 at 501 [30]; Winterton, above n 3, at 30-1.
122 Ibid at 542 [191]; Winterton, ibid.
123 See Winterton, ibid at 33-4, discussing *Davis v Commonwealth* (1988) 166 CLR 79; and Mason and Jacobs JJ in *Victoria v Commonwealth and Hayden* (1975) 134 CLR 338.
124 Winterton, ibid at 35-6.

IMMIGRATION CONTROL AND THE AUSTRALIAN CONSTITUTION

made to the *Migration Act* included a new s 7A which confirms the power of the executive to act outside of any legislative authority. The new section reads:

> The existence of a statutory power under this Act does not prevent the exercise of any executive power of the Commonwealth to protect Australia's borders, including, where necessary, by ejecting persons who have crossed those borders.

In referring to 'persons', the Act makes no distinction between citizens and foreigners.

[3.60] Whether the High Court would agree to this interpretation of the executive power in another case of lesser political intensity remains an open question. In terms of the outcome in the *Tampa* litigation, the remarks made by French J were backed by findings that indicated other bases in which the majority grounded their acceptance that the Australian government had acted within the law. Some of these may not have found ready support had the case been accepted for full hearing in the High Court.

[3.61] For example, in his judgment, Beaumont J held that the action had to fail because there was no 'relevant substantive cause of action (that is, a legal right) recognised by law and enforceable by [the] court'. He held that the Federal Court had no inherent jurisdiction to issue a writ of *habeas corpus*[125] and that, in any event, a writ to force release from detention could not be used to compel the government to admit an individual onto Australian territory. His Honour held that the executive alone has power to authorise such an entry.[126]

[3.62] Taken to its logical conclusion, this last aspect of Beaumont J's ruling sits curiously with the long tradition of judicial review of immigration applications in Australia. Before the introduction of the current regulatory scheme in immigration, no applicant for a visa or entry permit could lay claim to a 'right' to enter the country. However, this fact did not prevent the Australian courts from entertaining any number of challenges to visa refusals, from persons both outside Australia and within the country. This point is made forcefully by Black CJ in his dissent. His Honour said:[127]

> As in *Chin Yow*, so too here, the fact that the rescued people did not have any 'right' to enter Australian waters does not answer the question whether they have been detained. Nor does it deprive them of the ability to seek redress from this Court by way of habeas corpus. As Brennan, Deane and Dawson JJ said in *Lim* at 19, citing, amongst other cases, *Lo Pak* and *Kioa v West* (1985) 159 CLR 550 at 631:
>> Under the common law of Australia ... an alien who is within this country, *whether lawfully or unlawfully*, is not an outlaw. Neither public official nor private

---

125 His Honour cited *Re Officer in Charge of Cells, ACT Supreme Court; Ex parte Eastman* (1994) 123 ALR 478 where the High Court held that *habeas corpus* could not be used as a means of collaterally impeaching the correctness of orders made by a court of competent jurisdiction that had not been shown to be a nullity. In that case the High Court also held that the High Court's jurisdiction to entertain this writ could only arise as an incident of an action brought within the court's original jurisdiction. See Beaumont J (2001) 110 FCR 491 at [102]-[103].

126 For a critique of this plainly erroneous aspect of the ruling, see David Clark, 'Jurisdiction and Power: Habeas Corpus and the Federal Court' (2006) 32 *Monash Law Review* 275.

127 *Ruddock v Vadarlis* (2001) 110 FCR 491 at 511, referring to *Chin Yow v United States of America* 208 US 8 (1908).

person can lawfully detain him or her or deal with his or her property except under and in accordance with some positive authority conferred by the law.' (Emphasis added, citations omitted)

See also per McHugh J at 63.

The House of Lords similarly held that illegal entrants were entitled to seek redress by means of habeas corpus in *R v Home Secretary; Ex parte Khawaja* [1984] AC 74, with Lord Scarman stating (at 111) that:

'There is no distinction between British nationals and others. He who is subject to English law is entitled to its protection. This principle has been in the law at least since Lord Mansfield freed 'the black' in *Sommersett's case*'

It is, therefore, important to focus not on the lack of any right of the rescued people to enter Australia, but on whether the rescued people were, in a real and practical sense, detained by the Commonwealth. (emphasis added)

[3.63] In spite of the rulings of the majority in *Ruddock v Vadarlis*, the preponderance of jurisprudence from both the Federal Court and, more importantly, the High Court, probably does not support the view that the power of the Australian government in the immigration field can be described as *plenary* in the sense of being without fetter of any kind. To begin with, the very fact that the *Tampa* litigation was entertained by the Federal Court is itself indicative of the central role played by the courts and judicial review within the construct of Australian democracy. Beaumont J was on his own in ruling that, if a person has no *right* to be in Australia, any dispute relating to their entry or presence in the country is not justiciable by the courts.[128] While French J agreed with Beaumont J in the result, he made it plain that he regarded the applicant Vadarlis as acting with the highest public interest motives and that the matter was very properly one that should be scrutinised closely by the courts. The only reason that the High Court declined to entertain an appeal was that the 'rescuees' by that stage had been conveyed to Nauru and New Zealand, where their refugee claims were being assessed by various government and non-governmental authorities. Access to Christmas Island was no longer an issue.

[3.64] The decision by the Rudd and then Gillard Labor governments to maintain a regime for processing the asylum claims of unauthorised boat arrivals offshore on the 'excised offshore place' of Christmas Island[129] kept alive issues relating to the reach of the executive power in the management of immigration to Australia. Asylum seekers interdicted at sea are detained offshore pending a decision by the Minister to exercise the non-delegable, non-compellable discretion under s 46A(2) of the *Migration Act* to allow an application for a Protection visa. Although not permitted to apply for a visa without this permission, extra-statutory procedures have been established to allow asylum seekers to undergo 'Refugee Status Assessment' (RSA) and indeed for the 'Independent Merits Review' (IMR) of negative rulings.

[3.65] In 2010, actions were brought by two Tamil asylum seekers whose refugee claims were denied on Christmas Island under the offshore regime.[130] Each plaintiff

---

128 Note, however, that one academic did take this view: John McMillan, 'The Justiciability of the Government's Tampa Actions' (2002) 13 *Public Law Review* 89.
129 For an explanation of these terms, see Chapter 4.3.7 and Chapter 12.4.2.
130 See *Plaintiff M61/2010E v Commonwealth and Plaintiff M69 of 2010 v Commonwealth* (2010) 272 ALR 14 (*Plaintiffs M61/M69*). For a fuller discussion of this case, see Mary Crock and Daniel Ghezelbash,

instituted proceedings in the original jurisdiction of the High Court,[131] alleging that they were not afforded procedural fairness and that the processes were affected by other errors of law. Plaintiff M69 alleged that s 46A of the *Migration Act* is invalid if the provision has the effect of precluding judicial oversight of the RSA at the centre of the plaintiff's claim.

[3.66] The High Court delivered a unanimous decision that was carefully crafted to avoid determination of a range of potentially controversial issues. The first of these was embodied in the defence mounted by the Minster and his Department that the offshore RSA and IMR regimes were founded in an exercise of a non-statutory executive power under s 61 of the Constitution which is not susceptible to judicial review. Avoiding altogether the issue of the executive power, the court accepted the plaintiffs' submission that the power to inquire being exercised was *statutory*, because it is linked to the Minister's consideration of whether to exercise his power under s 46A(2) or s 195A(2) of the Act.[132] The court dealt with the challenge to s 46A in a similar fashion. The court rejected the contention that s 46A is invalid because its effect is to confer on the Minister a power 'free from any judicially enforceable limitation'.[133] The court ruled that it is not unconstitutional to confer on a Minister a discretion that the Minister is under no legal obligation to consider exercising. Such a power precluded the enforcement of *consideration* of the power, but did not mean the power had no enforceable limits. This is because where the Minister makes a decision to exercise the power, s 75(v) can be engaged to enforce limits on the power – as was done in the plaintiffs' cases.[134]

***

[3.67] The Australian courts may have guarded jealously their constitutional right to review government action. Putting to one side attempts to curtail such review, however, the jurisprudence suggests that the constitutional power of the federal government to control immigration is very close to plenary in nature. This is particularly true of powers expressed through parliament in the language of legislation. The shift of focus in the 1980s and 1990s away from the 'immigration' power in favour of the 'aliens' power reflects the strengthening discourse in Australia on citizenship. Unhappily for the non-citizen, however, the move has also heightened the increasing vulnerability of the constitutional alien. The High Court has been faced with the interpretation of increasingly punitive legislation permitting mandatory immigration detention and even the summary removal from Australia of non-citizens who

---

'Due Process and Rule of Law as Human Rights: The High Court and the "Offshore" Processing of Asylum Seekers' (2010) 18(2) *Australian Journal of Administrative Law* 101.

131   M61 named the Commonwealth, the Minister and the person who conducted the review as defendants. M69 jointed the Secretary of the Department as a fourth defendant.

132   The court found that the Minister's practice and the published policies governing the RSA and IMR processes indicate that the Minister had made a decision to tie the non-reviewable, non-compellable discretions conferred by ss 46A and 195A to the assessment and review outcomes. For a fuller discussion of this case, see Crock and Ghezelbash, above n 130.

133   Submissions of Plaintiff M69 in the matter of *Plaintiff M61 v Commonwealth of Australia & Ors; Plaintiff M69 v Commonwealth of Australia & Ors*, at [18].

134   The implications of this case for the judicial review of offshore processing decisions are discussed further in Chapter 19.6.4.

may have been permanent residents of long standing. A majority of current justices have paid little heed to traditions of freedom and justice in Australia's common law heritage. Just as importantly, the same jurists have paid scant regard to obligations Australia has assumed in signing and ratifying a range of international treaties and conventions. It is to these matters that we now turn.

4

The Impact of International Law

[4.01] If cases involving migrants and refugees have become focal points for discussion and debate about fundamental issues of constitutional law in Australia, they have also forced consideration of law in the broader context of Australia's international obligations. The issue of the relationship between domestic and international law in this country has been claimed to provoke 'deep anxieties' for the government.[1] While cases such as *Al-Kateb*[2] provide few bases for dissent from this assessment, the root causes of this anxiety – and of Australia's failure to embrace norms of international human rights law – are many and complex.

[4.02] Australia has signed, ratified and/or acceded to virtually all the relevant international human rights instruments. Indeed, Australia (proudly) played a significant role in developing the framework for the international protection of human rights after the Second World War. For example, it was Australia's accession to the UN Convention relating to the Status of Refugees that brought that instrument into operation.[3]

[4.03] At the same time, a variety of factors seem to have made Australians especially resistant to giving primacy to the norms of international law. Australia's geographical and cultural isolation seems to have created a predisposition to national insecurity or at best defensiveness. Australians as island people have had a long standing, almost primordial, fear of invasion.[4] More importantly, the country's geography has allowed it to achieve control of immigration to a degree that countries with shared land borders could not imagine possible. This is turn seems to have fuelled public expectations that governments will control immigration and governmental resistance to legal norms that might impinge on the (sovereign) right to deliver the outcomes expected. For a country 'girt by sea', the arrival of *boats* carrying unauthorised would-be migrants has been and continues to be pure anathema. Although

---

1 See Hilary Charlesworth, Madelaine Chiam, Devika Hovell and George Williams, 'Deep Anxieties: Australia and the International Legal Order' (2003) 25 *Sydney Law Review* 423. See also Hilary Charlesworth, Madelaine Chiam, Devika Hovell and George Williams, *No Country is an Island: Australia and International Law* (Sydney: UNSW Press, 2006) (*No Country is an Island*).
2 *Al-Kateb v Godwin* (2004) 219 CLR 562 (*Al-Kateb*).
3 See generally Charlesworth et al, *No Country is an Island*, above n 1, at 68-70.
4 For a good collection of old newsreel images from the days of the White Australia Policy, see ABC Documentary, Alec Morgan, *Admission Impossible* (Sydney: Film Australia, 2006), first broadcast in 1992.

most irregular migration to Australia now occurs by air, there is something about boat people that invokes the deepest fears in Australians.[5]

[4.04] If the physical arrival of these erstwhile seafarers evokes an emotional response, the concept of international law creating rights in these people that override the restrictive measures of Australia's domestic law has been equally hard to accept. The failure to either enact specific international legal obligations into Australia's domestic law or to provide for an entrenched system for the protection of fundamental human rights reflects the ambivalence of Australian attitudes. Sadly, it also creates a ready environment for legal conflict and controversy. The only Western secular democracy without a Bill of Rights, there is growing evidence that Australia is becoming increasingly isolated in its legal culture. It is not the only country to institute naval blockades and interdiction programs to stop the arrival of boat people.[6] Nor is it the only country to have incarcerated non-citizens without charge or trial for years on end.[7] However, in 2004 it became the only Western country in which the prevailing jurisprudence from the nation's highest court sanctioned the constitutionality of *all* such measures on the basis of domestic laws acknowledged by some to be in contravention of international law.[8]

[4.05] This chapter begins with an examination of the role that international law has played and continues to play in shaping immigration and refugee law in this country. Part 4.2 provides a brief overview of how judicial attitudes to international law have changed over the years, paying particular attention to the seismic shift in attitude that occurred between 1995, when the case of *MIEA v Teoh*[9] was decided, and the series of High Court rulings in the immigration detention cases in 2004. This is followed by a case study of international legal issues raised by one of the most contentious areas of migration law and policy: border control measures involving interdiction and offshore processing (where prolonged detention has once again been in issue). The chapter concludes with a brief explanation of various

---

5   See Mary Crock, Ben Saul and Azadeh Dastyari, *Future Seekers II: Refugees and Irregular Migration in Australia* (Sydney: The Federation Press, 2006) Ch 3. Australians are far from unique in this regard. The arrival of unauthorised migrants by boat seems to engender responses in most countries of asylum that are disproportionate to the threats posed. See, for example, Irving Abella and Harold Troper, *None is Too Many* (Toronto: Lester & Orpen Dennys, 1986).

6   In many respects, Australia modelled its blockade in the interdiction program instituted by the United States of America to halt the arrival of boat people from Haiti and Cuba. Numerous accounts of this program have been written. The following are a sample only: Janice D Villiers, 'Closed Borders, Closed Ports: The Plight of Haitians Seeking Political Asylum in the United States' (1994) 60(3) *Brooklyn Law Review* 841; Bill Frelick, 'Haitian Boat Interdiction: First Asylum and First Principles of Refugee Protection' (1993) 26 *Georgetown Immigration Law Journal* 675; Hiroshi Motomura, 'Haitian Asylum Seekers: Interdiction and Immigrants' Rights' (1993) 26 *Georgetown Immigration Law Journal* 695; Thomas David Jones, 'A Human Rights Tragedy: The Cuban and Haitian Refugee Crises Revisited' (1995) 29 *Georgetown Immigration Law Journal* 479; Thomas David Jones and Judith Hippler Bello, 'Cuban American Bar Association, Inc v Christopher 43 F 3d 1412. Haitian Refugee Center, Inc v Christopher. 43 F 3d 1431' (1996) 90 *American Journal of International Law* 477.

7   Again, Australia has looked to America as an example, with Guantanamo Bay in Cuba being the precedent.

8   See Crock, Saul and Dastyari, *Future Seekers II*, above n 5, Ch 12.

9   (1995) 183 CLR 273.

complaints mechanisms established under the auspices of the United Nations to which Australia has subscribed by ratifying optional protocols to various human rights instruments.

[4.06] Australia's obligations under international law are drawn from the 'hard' (binding) law of international treaties and conventions, and from the 'soft' (non-binding) law of international guidelines and the recommendations and general comments of international organisations such as the UN Human Rights Committee, the UN Committee Against Torture, the UN Committee on the Rights of the Child and the Committee on the Rights of Persons with Disabilities.[10] The country is bound also by less choate norms or rules represented by customary international law, which in turn is evidenced by State practice and the writings of eminent publicists.[11] As explored in later parts of this chapter, the pervading problem is that international law is alternatively difficult to define with precision and/or relatively easy to manipulate in the hands of governments uncomfortable with its norms. Absent the persuasive pressure of international politics, the mechanisms for the enforcement of international law are often ineffectual. It is a regime in which notions of fundamental human rights are often vulnerable to the superior claims of state sovereignty and national security. This is a particular problem for migrants and refugees. Without the backing of a national government to intercede on their behalf, legal principles and the soft law of guidelines and recommendations by non-government organisations can offer scant protection.

4.1   The central significance of international law

[4.07] According to the traditional (dualist) view of the Westminster system of government that pertains in Australia, international law operates in a sphere that is independent of the municipal or domestic laws of a country. Treaties and Conventions are binding on states parties at an international level, but are not binding at the local level unless enacted into law by the domestic parliament of the country involved.[12] This conceptualisation of the international and domestic systems of law as separate entities has been eroded steadily in Australia,[13] although it still serves to bolster the findings of judges facing uncomfortable conflicts between federal enactments and norms of international human rights law.

---

10   See the discussion of these bodies at Part 4.4 below.
11   For an explanation of these concepts, see Gillian Triggs, *International Law: Contemporary Principles and Practices* (Sydney: LexisNexis Butterworths, 2006) at 43-77.
12   See *MIEA v Teoh* (1995) 183 CLR 273 (*Teoh*) at 287, affirming *Chu Kheng Lim v MILGEA* (1992) 176 CLR 1 (*Chu Kheng Lim*) at 74; and *Dietrich v R* (1992) 177 CLR 292 at [24]. See also *Kruger v Commonwealth* (1997) 190 CLR 1 at 161; and Triggs, ibid, Ch 3.43-3.44. Compare the situation in America under the Constitution of the United States 1787, Article VI, Section 2. This has been interpreted so that the international obligations are assumed if the Treaty is 'self-executing': see *Foster v Neilson* 2 Pet 253 at 324, 7 LEd 415 (1829).
13   For example, administrative decision-makers may need to take account of the legitimate expectations generated by treaties that Australia has entered into, but not incorporated into domestic law. See *Teoh* (1995) 183 CLR 273 at 316 and the discussion below.

[4.08] The plain truth is that Australian governments are probably more cognisant of international law – and are doing more in reliance on its norms and principles than at any other time in the country's history. For example, the High Court's expansive interpretation of the external affairs power in s 51(29) of the Constitution has enabled the federal government to use the signing and ratification of international instruments to support legislation in a wide range of areas traditionally viewed as the domain of the States.[14]

[4.09] Putting aside for one moment the controversial cases, there is hardly an aspect of Australia's immigration program that does not reflect international law at one level or another. The abandonment of an intake policy based on nationality and race reflects acceptance of basic principles of non-discrimination that became binding on Australia upon signing and ratifying the International Convention on the Elimination of all forms of Racial Discrimination (CERD)[15] and the Convention on the Elimination of all Forms of Discrimination against Women (CEDAW).[16] The family migration program demonstrates deference to both of these conventions as well as to a variety of principles enshrined in the International Covenant on Civil and Political Rights (ICCPR)[17] and the UN Convention on the Rights of the Child (CRC).[18] These include the right to marry and found a family[19] and the rights of children to the special protection of a state.[20] The program for the importation of skilled migrants to Australia is also underpinned by a variety of international instruments and agreements that reflect Australia's commitment to ensure respect for the basic human rights of workers. These include undertakings assumed by Australia pursuant to the General Agreement on Trade in Services (GATS).[21]

---

14   See, for example, *Koowarta v Bjelke-Petersen* (1982) 153 CLR 168; *Commonwealth v Tasmania* (1983) 158 CLR 1; *Richardson v Forestry Commission* (1988) 164 CLR 261; *Queensland v Commonwealth* (1989) 167 CLR 232; *Polyukhovich v Commonwealth* (1991) 172 CLR 501; and *Horta v Commonwealth* (1994) 181 CLR 183. For commentary on the external affairs power, see Leslie Zines, *The High Court and the Constitution* (Sydney: The Federation Press, 5th ed, 2008) Ch 13; Mary Crock, 'Federalism and the External Affairs Power' (1983) 14 *Melbourne University Law Review* 238; Donald R Rothwell, 'The High Court and the External Affairs Power' (1993) 15 *Adelaide Law Review* 209; and HP Lee and George Winterton (eds), *Australian Constitutional Perspectives* (Sydney: Law Book Co, 1992) at 60.
15   *International Convention on the Elimination of all forms of Racial Discrimination* (adopted 7 March 1966, entered into force 4 January 1969) 660 UNTS 195.
16   *Convention on the Elimination of All Forms of Discrimination against Women* (adopted 18 December 1979, entered into force 3 September 1981) 1249 UNTS 13.
17   *International Covenant on Civil and Political Rights* (adopted 16 December 1966, entered into force 23 March 1976 except Art 41 which came into force 28 March 1979) 999 UNTS 171; ratified by Australia 13 August 1980 except Art 41 which was ratified by Australia 28 January 1993.
18   *Convention on the Rights of the Child* (adopted 20 November 1989, entered into force 2 September 1990) 1577 UNTS 3; ratified by Australia 17 December 1990; declared an international instrument for the purposes of s 47(1) of the *Human Rights and Equal Opportunity Commission Act 1986* (Cth) on 22 December 1992; gazetted 3 January 1993) See now *Australian Human Rights Commission Act 1986* (Cth).
19   See ICCPR, Art 23.
20   See ICCPR, Art 24, and CRC.
21   *General Agreement on Trade in Services* (adopted 15 April 1994, entered into force 1 January 1995) Marrakesh Agreement Establishing the World Trade Organisation, Annex 1A, 1867 UNTS 187. See Laurie Berg, 'At the Border and Between the Cracks: The Precarious Position of Irregular Migrant Workers Under International Human Rights Law' (2007) 8(1) *Melbourne Journal of International Law* 1.

[4.10] Even in the areas where Australia's human rights record has been called into question, the available evidence does not support a finding that Australia is either unaware or completely uncaring about the obligations it has assumed under international law. The programs for the recognition of refugees within the care, control and immediate jurisdiction of Australia are prime examples in point. Australia attends the annual meetings of the United Nations High Commission for Refugees' (UNHCR's) Executive Committee and plays an active role in promoting and/or debating conclusions made by that committee.[22] At a practical level, the country has spent and continues to spend enormous amounts of money on non-citizens whose right to enter and remain in Australia is in contention. Absent a respect for obligations assumed under international law, these people would be returned without ceremony to their countries of origin and/or nationality. Although practical obstacles to effecting such returns can and have prevented such actions,[23] politics and practicalities are not the only factors at play in even the most contested of cases. As we explore in greater detail below, the *Tampa* Affair and the related 'Pacific Strategy'[24] are illustrative of the lengths to which Australia was prepared to go to comply (or at least appear to comply) with its basic obligations under the UN Convention relating to the Status of Refugees not to *refoule* or send back refugees to whom protection obligations are owed.[25]

4.2 International law and the Australian judiciary: High principle and domestic pragmatism

[4.11] As the Federal Parliament became more familiar with using the law of nations to expand the range of matters on which to legislate, it was perhaps inevitable that Australian judges would also be affected by the move towards internationalisation of the law.[26] Two long-accepted principles are immediately relevant. The first is the rule that statutes should be construed so as to accord with Australia's international obligations. The second is that a presumption exists against a legislative intention to abrogate fundamental rights and liberties in the absence of clear words of statutory intendment.

[4.12] The first principle assumes that where a statute is ambiguous or 'silent' on a particular matter, it will be given a construction that accords with Australia's

---

22   See, for example, DIAC, *Refugee and Humanitarian Issues: Australia's Response*, June 2009. In 2010 Australia chaired the Executive Committee to UNHCR, shepherding through a Conclusion on Refugees with Disabilities. See ExCom Conclusion on refugees with disabilities and other persons with disabilities protected and assisted by UNHCR No 110 (LXI), 12 October 2010.
23   The cases of *Al-Kateb* (2004) 219 CLR 562 and *MIMIA v Al Khafaji* (2004) 219 CLR 664 (*Al Khafaji*) are examples in point. See the discussion above, Chapter 3.3.2.
24   The policies introduced following the *Tampa* Affair were initially known as the 'Pacific Solution'. The unfortunate (genocidal) connotations of the latter term led to the adoption of the more neutral 'Pacific Strategy'. See Part 4.3 below.
25   The law and practice governing the treatment of asylum seekers and refugees are discussed in Chapters 12-14 below.
26   See Ninian Stephen, 'The Expansion of International Law: Sovereignty and External Affairs' (1995) 29 *Quadrant* 20; and Mary Crock, 'Judging Refugees: The Clash of Power and Institutions in the Development of Australian Refugee Law' (2004) 26 *Sydney Law Review* 51.

obligations under international law.²⁷ The main difficulty with this principle – and indeed the area in which most subjective judicial discretion turns – is in the identification of ambiguity. While it is accepted that international law may fill legislative 'gaps', profound disagreement prevails in relation to the level of uncertainty required before recourse may be had to international law for this purpose. It is in this space, sadly, that politics and the law are most likely to collide. Political pressure and overwhelming public support for harsh or regressive policies play out inevitably in judicial decision-making.

[4.13] Successive federal governments have been happy for their various Ministers to play an active role on the world stage. They have been less pleased with curial attempts to use international standards in the assessment of Australia's domestic legislation and policies. The resort to international law in this context can be perceived as an affront to the sovereignty of Parliament if the legal norms relied on have not been incorporated into the municipal law through legislation.²⁸ The cases engendering most conflict between the government and the courts have been those involving migrants and refugees.

[4.14] Judicial attitudes to international law in Australia have followed the trajectory of a rollercoaster. A gradual change appears to have occurred throughout the 1980s in the courts' attitude towards and use of international standards in the review of migration decisions. In the early years of that decade there was a marked reluctance to explore, much less sanction, points of divergence between actions of the Australian executive and binding norms of international law.²⁹ Attempts to rely on international instruments that had been signed and ratified by Australia, but not 'legislated', met with a simple re-statement of the duality and mutual independence of the international and domestic spheres of law.³⁰ By 1989, however, the High Court showed no hesitation in scrutinising and correcting the bureaucracy's interpretation of Art 1A(2) of the Refugee Convention. In *Chan Yee Kin v MIEA*³¹ the High Court linked the misinterpretation of the international definition of refugee with the legal concept of 'unreasonableness'.³² The internationalisation of Australian administrative law seems to have reached its zenith in 1995 with the decision of the High Court

---

27 This is a common law principle that allows for consideration of both hard and soft international law – the latter in the form of unincorporated treaties to which Australia is a signatory. Note that s 15AB of the *Acts Interpretation Act 1901* (Cth) allows only for consideration of treaties referred to in the statute. See Dennis Pearce and Robert Geddes, *Statutory Interpretation in Australia* (Sydney: Butterworths, 1996) at 64-6. See, for instance, *Jumbunna Coal Mine NL v Victorian Coalminers' Association* (1908) 6 CLR 309 (*Jumbunna*); *Chu Kheng Lim v MILGEA* (1992) 176 CLR 1 at 153, 166; *Kartinyeri v Commonwealth* (1998) 195 CLR 337 (*Kartinyeri*); *Behrooz v Secretary, DIMIA* (2004) 219 CLR 486 (*Behrooz*); *MIMIA v B* (2004) 219 CLR 365; and *Plaintiff S157 v Commonwealth* (2003) 211 CLR 426 at [29] (Gleeson CJ). See further discussion below at 4.2.2.
28 On this point, see Michael Kirby, 'The Australian Use of International Human Rights Norms: Bangalore to Balliol' (1993) 16 *UNSW Law Journal* 363 at 368-72. See also *Re MIMA; Ex parte Lam* (2003) 214 CLR 1 at [98] (McHugh and Gummow JJ).
29 See, for example, *Simsek v Macphee* (1982) 148 CLR 636 at 641-2.
30 See, for example, *Mayer v MIEA* (1984) 4 FCR 312 at 314; (1985) 7 FCR 254 (FFC); and (1985) 157 CLR 290 (HC); and *Kioa v West* (1985) 159 CLR 550 (*Kioa*) at 570-1.
31 (1989) 169 CLR 379.
32 See *Associated Provincial Picture Houses v Wednesbury Corporation* [1948] 1 KB 223.

in *MIEA v Teoh*.³³ Thereafter Australia's most senior judges sounded a retreat from international law, reaffirming the pre-eminence of domestic law. The undoubted low-point in the years that followed was the series of rulings in 2004 in *Al-Kateb; Al Khafaji* and *Re Woolley*.³⁴

4.2.1   The Teoh experiment

[4.15]   For administrative lawyers, *Teoh*'s case represents a particularly interesting contrast to the landmark ruling of the High Court in *Kioa v West*³⁵ decided one decade earlier in 1985. Both cases involved applicants seeking residence in Australia who had Australian citizen children. Jason Kioa and his wife were Tongan students who had overstayed their visas and who faced deportation because of their unlawful status. Ah Hin Teoh, on the other hand, was an applicant for residence on spouse grounds who had been convicted of criminal offences relating to the importation and possession of heroin. He sought leniency on the basis that his offences had been committed to support his wife's drug addiction. His request was rejected on the grounds of his character and criminal record. Teoh and Ms Lim had a total of seven Australian citizen children between them, all of whom were in state care when the father's case came before the High Court. Like Jason Kioa, Teoh claimed that he had been denied procedural fairness.

[4.16]   In *Kioa* and *Teoh*, arguments were raised about the failure of the respective decision-makers to adequately consider the interests of the Australian-born children. Both applicants sought to rely on international legal standards. In *Kioa v West* reliance was placed on the UN Declaration relating to the Rights of the Child which was referred to in the Preamble of the *Human Rights Commission Act 1981* (Cth) (repealed). In view of the precatory nature of this preamble and the general terms of the declaration, the High Court found little difficulty dismissing this aspect of Kioa's case.³⁶ Teoh, on the other hand, invoked the more forceful obligations created by Art 3(1) of the CRC. This requires states parties to make the best interests of the child a primary consideration in all actions concerning children 'whether undertaken by public or private social welfare institutions, courts of law and administrative authorities or legislative bodies'.³⁷ *Kioa v West* broke new ground with its holding that unlawful non-citizens could have a right to be heard before deportation under what was s 18 of the *Migration Act 1958* (Cth). In its own way, the High Court's ruling in *Teoh* was just as radical a departure.

[4.17]   In *Teoh*, the High Court confirmed the basic principle that Australia's obligations at international law are not binding on decision-makers until those obligations

---

33   (1995) 183 CLR 273.
34   See *Al-Kateb* (2004) 219 CLR 562; *Al Khafaji* (2004) 219 CLR 664; and *Re Woolley; Ex parte Applicants M276/2003* (2004) 225 CLR 1 (*Re Woolley*). These cases are discussed above, Chapter 3.3.2 and below.
35   (1985) 159 CLR 550.
36   (1985) 159 CLR 550 at 570-1.
37   Australia ratified this Convention on 17 December 1991 and one year later the Attorney General declared it an international legal instrument relating to human rights and freedoms pursuant to s 47 of the *Human Rights and Equal Opportunity Commission Act 1986*.

are translated into domestic law by statute.[38] All parties to the case accepted that the CRC had not been so incorporated. Nevertheless, a majority of the High Court found that the fact that Australia had signed and ratified the Convention created in Mr Teoh a legitimate expectation that he would be granted a hearing if his case was not to be decided in accordance with the Convention, with the best interests of his children a primary consideration. The High Court was at pains to stress that Teoh's expectation created special procedural entitlements, but did not mean that the decision-maker could be compelled to rule on the case in a particular way. In other words, the court held that Teoh had a right to be heard before any decision was made that did *not* treat the interests of his children as being of paramount importance.

[4.18] The basis for the expectation identified by the majority is articulated by Mason CJ and Deane J in their joint judgment:

> [R]atification of a convention is a positive statement by the executive government of this country to the world and to the Australian people that the executive government and its agencies will act in accordance with the Convention.[39]

Their Honours concluded that such a positive statement 'is an adequate foundation for a legitimate expectation, *absent statutory or executive indications to the contrary*, that administrative decision-makers will act in conformity with the Convention' (emphasis added). Like Toohey J,[40] Mason CJ and Deane J found that their formulation of legitimate expectation had an objective quality and was not dependent on the state of mind or the actual knowledge of either the applicant or the decision-maker.

[4.19] In some respects, the decision of Gaudron J was more radical than that of her colleagues. She held that quite apart from any question of international legal obligations in the Minister, the very fact that Mr Teoh had Australian-born children created an expectation that their best interests would be given paramount consideration. Similar arguments had been raised unsuccessfully by Kioa in 1985.[41]

[4.20] The dissentient in *Teoh* was McHugh J who rejected the notion that the doctrine of legitimate expectation should be extended in the manner envisaged by the majority. He questioned the usefulness of the expression in any event but disagreed most particularly with the majority's 'objective' formulation of the doctrine. His Honour found it implausible to isolate the notion of expectation from the state of mind of the person affected by a decision and could not see how Mr Teoh could lose an expectation that he had never held.[42] He considered also the practical implications for the executive of the majority ruling. He pointed to the large number of treaties entered into by Australia and the 'years of effort, education and expenditure of resources' that would have to go into schooling the bureaucracy in the obligations imposed by each instrument. He rejected the idea that the signature and ratification of an international instrument is a statement to the Australian public as well as to

---

38   (1995) 183 CLR 273 at 286-7 and 298.
39   Ibid at 291.
40   Ibid at 301.
41   Ibid at 304.
42   Ibid at 314. McHugh J pointed to the difficulty of identifying any 'legitimate expectation' in cases like *Kioa* (1985) 159 CLR 550 and *Annetts v McCann* (1990) 170 CLR 596.

the world. Instead, McHugh J emphasised the contractual nature of treaties and conventions with the parties involved being the nation states and not the individual members of those states.[43]

[4.21] The High Court's decision in *Teoh* presents something of a contrast to the generally conservative ruling in *Chu Kheng Lim* discussed earlier.[44] The majority's re-definition of the notion of legitimate expectation was a quite radical departure from the traditional reluctance of the courts to acknowledge any intercept between norms of international law and the domestic laws governing administrative decision-making.

[4.22] For its part, the Australian government reacted swiftly to the majority decision, taking advantage of the proviso expressed that the signature and ratification of an international instrument gave rise to a legitimate expectation *in the absence of statutory or executive indications to the contrary*. On 10 May 1995, then Foreign Minister Evans and Attorney General Lavarch issued a joint ministerial statement that Australia's assumption of obligations at international law should not be taken to give rise to any legitimate expectation that the terms of the instruments would be observed by domestic decision-makers. The statement was followed in due course by legislation to similar effect.[45] The Bill lapsed with the prorogation of parliament in 1996, was resurrected by the Coalition government but ultimately was not pursued.

[4.23] The reason that subsequent governments did not pursue legislation to overrule the High Court's decision in *Teoh* is that the High Court to some extent did the work instead. Changes in the composition of the High Court saw a questioning of whether that decision 'laid down any universal requirement as to what is necessary to support a legitimate expectation'.[46] In the later case of *Re MIMA; Ex parte Lam*[47] McHugh, Gummow and Hayne JJ all cast doubt on the precedential value of the ruling.[48] They noted that the ruling was at odds with both the 'dualist' approach to international law – whereby international agreements are said to affect domestic law only when their terms are enacted by domestic parliaments – and to earlier decisions of the High Court.[49] McHugh J described the majority's ruling as an 'erratic application of the "invocation" principle [that] remains for analysis and decision'. His Honour continued:[50]

> Basic questions of the interaction between the three branches of government are involved. One consideration is that, under the Constitution (s 61), the task of the Executive is to execute and maintain statute law which confers discretionary powers upon the Executive. It is not for the judicial branch to add to or vary the

---

43 See *Teoh* (1995) 183 CLR 273 at 316-17.
44 *Chu Kheng Lim* (1992) 176 CLR 1. See Penelope Mathew, 'International Law and the Protection of Human Rights in Australia: Recent Trends' (1995) 17 *Sydney Law Review* 177 at 202.
45 See Administrative Decisions (Effect of International Instruments) Bill 1995 (Cth), s 5.
46 See Callinan J in *Sanders v Snell* (1998) 196 CLR 329 at 351 [53]. Compare Michael Taggart, 'Legitimate Expectation and Treaties in the High Court of Australia' (1996) 112 *Law Quarterly Review* 50 at 54.
47 (2003) 214 CLR 1 at [102].
48 For a commentary on this case, see Wendy Lacey, 'A Prelude to the Demise of *Teoh*: The High Court Decision in *Re MIMA; Ex parte Lam*' (2004) 26 *Sydney Law Review* 131.
49 Their Honours drew attention to the ruling in *Haoucher v MIEA* (1990) 169 CLR 648.
50 *Re MIMA; Ex parte Lam* (2003) 214 CLR 1 at [102].

content of those powers by taking a particular view of the conduct by the Executive of external affairs.[51] Rather, it is for the judicial branch to declare and enforce the limits of the power conferred by statute upon administrative decision-makers, but not, by reference to the conduct of external affairs, to supplement the criteria for the exercise of that power.

[4.24] There are only a small number of international instruments that are likely to give rise to the type of legitimate expectation identified in *Teoh*'s case. Many of these would involve issues of human rights. Margaret Allars[52] presents a series of reasons as to why the federal government should have welcomed the High Court's ruling as an opportunity to improve the integrity of administrative decision-making in Australia. She argues that the court's extension of the notion of legitimate expectation creates a useful new role for the courts in assuring the accountability of the administration who perform the very tasks that involve the observance or otherwise of the government's international obligations. The role is appropriate, Allars posits, given the broad and largely unchecked powers given to the executive to enter into treaties. While the treaties that are entered into by the government must be tabled in both Houses, Parliament does not decide in advance which instruments are to signed and ratified. Neither is the matter justiciable by the courts.

[4.25] The decision in *Teoh* seems to have raised the profile of these procedures. Coincidental to the presentation of the Administrative Decisions (Effect of International Instruments) Bill 1995, then Attorney General Lavarch announced a review to ensure Australia's treaty commitments are adequately recognised in Commonwealth administrative decision-making.[53] The results of this review are substantial improvements in the accountability mechanisms attaching to the making of treaties.

4.2.2   Al-Kateb and the resurgence of legal formalism[54]

[4.26] While it may not be so surprising that the precedential value of the *Teoh* decision has been called in question in subsequent cases, a gulf has opened since 1995 between the reasoning of the majority in that case and the way in which the High Court has approached issues involving international law in more recent times. In the series of challenges made to Australia's mandatory immigration detention regime in 2004, the High Court made it patently clear that norms of international human rights law cannot be invoked to temper the legal effect of domestic laws expressed in clear terms of statutory intendment. The cases involved failed asylum seekers who could not be removed to their countries of origin;[55] asylum seekers detained in very poor conditions;[56] and asylum seeker children arriving without visas.[57]

---

51   Compare *Simsek v Macphee* (1982) 148 CLR 636 at 641-2.
52   Margaret Allars, 'One Small Step for Legal Doctrine, One Giant Leap Towards Integrity in Government' (1995) 17 *Sydney Law Review* 204.
53   See Senate Legal and Constitutional References Committee, *Trick or Treaty* (Canberra: AGPS, 1995).
54   Juliet Curtin, '"Never Say Never": Al-Kateb v Godwin' (2005) 27 *Sydney Law Review* 355.
55   *Al-Kateb* (2004) 219 CLR 562; and *Al Khafaji* (2004) 219 CLR 664.
56   See *Behrooz* (2004) 219 CLR 486.
57   See *Re Woolley* (2004) 225 CLR 1.

[4.27] The most extreme of these cases were those of *Al-Kateb* and *Al Khafaji*, discussed in the previous chapter. The whole High Court acknowledged either expressly or by implication that the detention laws challenged in those cases are in breach of obligations Australia has assumed as a signatory to the ICCPR and the CRC. However, the majority was not prepared either to read down the terms of the domestic legislation (for example, so as to give the laws a purposive effect) or to overrule them outright. The majority's ruling in *Al-Kateb* is of particular interest in the way in which the different judges dealt with the issue of the interface between domestic and international law. As intervener in the proceedings, the Human Rights and Equal Opportunity Commission (HREOC)[58] drew attention to the common law rule that a statute should be interpreted in conformity with international law 'as far as its language permits'.[59] In *Jumbunna*, the statute in question was unambiguous in its terms and yet O'Connor J proceeded to read the legislation down so as to both comply with international law and preserve its validity. He did so in reliance on the presumption that parliament does not intend to exceed its jurisdiction. In *Al-Kateb*, Callinan and Hayne JJ (with whom Heydon J agreed) preferred later authorities that adopted but slightly modified the *Jumbunna* principle. These cases suggest that recourse should only be had to principles of international law if there is scope for reading down the statutory provisions in question – either because the words used are unclear or their meaning is ambiguous.[60] For all four judges in the *Al-Kateb* majority, the words of the *Migration Act* were clear and unambiguous. Their combined effect was to mandate the detention of unlawful non-citizens until they were either granted a visa or removed from the country – even if indefinite detention resulted because removal was not possible in the foreseeable future.[61]

[4.28] The majority's assertion that the legislation at the heart of the *Al-Kateb* case was capable of only one interpretation was contested vigorously by the three minority judges who each offered separate criticisms of their brethren's reasoning. Given the eminence of the dissenters, the majority's protestations of interpretative clarity and assertions about the legal irrelevance of international law have a particularly hollow ring. At the very least, the majority's reluctance to consider the human rights implications of the detention laws places the Australian jurisprudence on a markedly

---

58   Now Australian Human Rights Commission.
59   *Jumbunna* (1908) 6 CLR 309 at 363. See HREOC Submission, available at <http://www.hreoc.gov.au/legal/intervention/khafaji.htm>.
60   The cases discussed here were *Polites v Commonwealth* (1945) 70 CLR 60 at 68, 77, 81; and *Teoh* (1995) 183 CLR 273; and *Kartinyeri* (1998) 195 CLR 337 at 384-6. See *Al-Kateb* (2004) 219 CLR 562 at [298] (Callinan J) and [238] (Hayne J).
61   Hayne J commented by way of aside that you can never say that a person could 'never' be returned: see *Al-Kateb* (2004) 219 CLR 562 at [229]. His Honour appears to have been mindful of the fact that the stateless Palestinian, Akram Al-Masri, was removed from Australia shortly after the Full Federal Court ordered his release in a decision which the High Court appeal in *Al-Kateb* took as its point of departure. See *Al Masri v MIMIA* (2002) 192 ALR 609; and *MIMIA v Al Masri* (2003) 126 FCR 54. Although Akram Al Masri gave up his fight for protection as a refugee, it is arguable that he should have received protection. In 2008 he was shot and killed outside a courthouse near the Khan Younis refugee camp, allegedly by Fatah militia who wrongly believed that he was an Israeli collaborator. See Paul Bibby, Jason Koutsoukis, Mark Metherell and Jordan Baker 'Deported Refugee Shot Dead', *Sydney Morning Herald*, 2-3 August 2008, at 1 and 6.

different trajectory from that of the United Kingdom,[62] the United States of America[63] and Canada.[64] Just as importantly, it sits uneasily with what Gleeson CJ identified as a basic canon of common law statutory construction. The Chief Justice avoided the controversy over the application of international human rights law by invoking instead the presumption that a statute should be interpreted if at all possible so as to respect the fundamental rights and freedoms of the individual. His Honour described this presumption as a 'principle of legality', and 'expression of legal value [that is] not a factual prediction, capable of being verified or falsified by a survey of public opinion'.[65] Unlike the majority, his Honour could not find in the migration legislation any legislative intention to overrule this presumption.

[4.29] By 2004, the issue of immigration detention had become acutely political. Mandatory detention – in particular the detention of children – was becoming increasingly controversial.[66] In taking the approach that it did, the majority in *Al-Kateb* implicitly drew back from the public debate insofar as its ruling confirmed the primacy of the Australian parliament even where the decrees of that body place the country in breach of obligations it has assumed under international law. This and the other cases are also a powerful manifestation of high judicial deference to the law-makers. The message delivered by the majority is that in the absence of an overriding Bill of Rights or other form of supreme law, it is not the role of the courts to countermand unjust and offensive laws. The politics of the issue seemed to have weighed particularly heavily on McHugh J who comes close to denouncing unincorporated international law as a threat to Australian sovereignty and to the autonomy of the Australian Constitution. In an echo of his dissent in *Teoh*, McHugh J railed against the presumption of compliance with international law, stating that the concept 'bears no relationship with the reality of the modern legislative process'. Given the explosion in the nature and sources of international law, his Honour questions whether parliament 'has in mind or is even aware' of all the rules that might apply.[67] For Kirby J such views are pure anathema: his judgment in *Al-Kateb* is in large measure a systematic refutation of McHugh J's reasoning.

[4.30] To understand how the High Court of Australia could have changed its attitude to international law so dramatically in the space of less than a decade, it is necessary to look more closely at what was happening in immigration law over the period in question. As the following case study demonstrates, the laws and poli-

---

62 See, for example, *Saadi v United Kingdom* 13229/03 [2008] ECHR 80; EU Procedural Directive; *Garland v Brit Rail Engineering* [1983] 2 All ER 402; *Post Office v Estuary Radio* [1968] 2 QB 740; and *The Eschersheim* [1976] 1 WLR 430. See generally Murray Hunt, *Using Human Rights Law in English Courts* (Oxford: Hart Publishing, 1997); and The Right Hon Lady Justice Mary Arden, 'Meeting the Challenge of Terrorism: The Experience of English and Other Courts' (2006) 80 *Australian Law Journal* 818.
63 See *Zadvydas v Davis* 533 US 678 (2001); Margaret Taylor 'Behind the Scenes of St Cyr and Zadvydas: Making Policy in the Midst of Litigation' (2002) 16 *Georgetown Immigration Law Journal* 271; and other articles in this symposium issue.
64 See *Baker v Canada* [1999] 2 SCR 817 at 861.
65 *Al-Kateb* (2004) 219 CLR 562 at [20].
66 Pressure from government backbenchers led to softening of the detention policy and changes to the *Migration Act 1958* in June 2005. See below Chapter 16 at [16.17].
67 *Al-Kateb* (2004) 219 CLR 562 at [65].

cies relating to border control represent a heightened point of conflict between the country's domestic laws and its international legal obligations. They have also been a source of exquisite tension between the executive and the judiciary.

4.3 Conflicting legalities: Border control, the *Tampa* Affair and the 'Pacific Strategy' – A case study[68]

[4.31] In the previous chapter we considered how the framework of Australia's Constitution might have contributed to the poor regime for the protection of human rights in this country. Before returning to the important issue of international law and the interpretation of domestic statutes, it is well to note that at least some of the disappointments in state practice around the world can be explained by limitations and uncertainties in international law itself. This – and the absence of any real accountability mechanisms beyond the court of world opinion – has allowed Australia to contest assertions that its actions have constituted breaches of its international legal obligations. Nowhere is the 'wriggle room' in international law more apparent than in the arguments made by Australia in defence of action taken to interdict and deflect asylum seekers wishing to claim protection as refugees on its territory. What the discussion reveals is that international law provides surprisingly little in the way of a rights regime for asylum seekers who take to the seas in their quest for safe haven. The ambiguity of the law creates a fertile field for jurisprudential and sociological debate. At the same time, the *Tampa* incident represents a fascinating example of how formalistic characterisations of the rule of law can be manipulated for political ends.

[4.32] The case study begins with an overview of the events at the centre of the *Tampa* Affair which are de-constructed from the legal perspectives of international law of the sea and then international refugee law. There follows a discussion of the role that international law did (and did not) play in the Australian judiciary's determination of the legal challenges brought on behalf of the asylum seekers at the centre of the controversy. The case study concludes with analyses of the issues arising under both refugee law and international human rights law in subsequent interdiction and deflection programs.

4.3.1 Setting the scene

[4.33] The most contentious recent[69] incident surrounding the control of Australia's borders began on 26 August 2001 when the Australian Search and Rescue

---

68 Portions of the material that follows draw from articles and chapters published previously on the *Tampa* Affair. See Mary Crock, 'In the Wake of the Tampa: Conflicting Visions of International Refugee Law in the Management of Refugee Flows' (2002) 12 *Pacific Rim Law and Policy Journal* 49; and 'Durable Solutions or Politics of Misery? Refugee Protection in Australia after *Tampa*' in Natalie Bolzan, Michael Darcy and Jan Mason (eds), *Fenced Out, Fenced in: Border Protection, Asylum and Detention in Australia* (Sydney: Common Ground, 2006) Ch 3 (pp 23-52).

69 In fact it is difficult to find another such incident in Australian history that has raised as many complex legal questions and attracted similar public notoriety. Before Federation, a case that raised similar questions and attracted a deal of media interest was that of *Toy v Musgrove* (1888) 14 VLR 349. This was a case involving a Chinese-born national of New South Wales who sought to challenge his exclusion from the colony when a passenger vessel named the *Afghan* was denied permission

organisation coordinated the rescue of an overcrowded Indonesian ferry, the *Palapa I*, that was foundering in the Indian Ocean. The call for assistance was answered by a Norwegian flagged container ship, *MV Tampa*, which took on board no less than 433 mainly Afghan asylum seekers. The vessel initially set a northerly course for Merak, in Indonesia. In response to threats and protests from the rescuees, it changed its course and headed south to the Australian territory of Christmas Island. The Australian government responded to the *Tampa's* request to offload its human cargo on the Island by threatening the master, Captain Rinnan, with prosecution under the *Migration Act* for people smuggling. When the *Tampa* persevered in its quest – citing *force majeure* and medical emergency – Australia closed the port at Christmas Island and sent Special Air Services (SAS) troops out to take command of the ship by force.[70]

[4.34] The Australian government not only refused the *Tampa* the right to offload its human cargo on Australian soil. The incident also became the basis for blocking the admission of all further boat people; for the 'excision' from Australia's 'migration zone' of external territories such as Christmas Island; and for the establishment of an elaborate and expensive program for the deflection of asylum seekers to the Pacific Islands of Nauru, Papua New Guinea and New Zealand.[71]

[4.35] In this case study, two phases of the *Tampa* Affair and its aftermath are examined. The first relates to the events surrounding and following the rescue of the 433 individuals plucked from the sinking Indonesian ferry. The second concerns the interdiction program that followed and the establishment of detention facilities on Nauru and Papua New Guinea's Manus Island. The latter initiative formed the basis for attempts in 2006 to normalise the arrangements for all unauthorised boat people either intercepted en route to Australia or at point of arrival on the Australian mainland.[72]

[4.36] The standoff that developed between Captain Rinnan of the *Tampa* and the Australian government in late August 2001 raised questions of law in at least three broad areas: international law of the sea, international refugee law and Australian law.[73] Overlaying these legal contexts, the situation becomes complicated further

---

to unload its passengers. See above, Chapter 2 at 2.24ff. In the period between the two World Wars, another case that received enormous media attention was that of Egon Kisch, an anti-fascist campaigner who was invited to undertake a speaking tour of the country to warn Australians about the dangers of fascism. Mr Kisch enjoyed more success in his bid to enter the country than did the hapless Mr Toy. See Heidi Zogbaum, *Kisch in Australia: The Untold Story* (Melbourne: Scribe, 2004) and above, Chapter 2.3.3.

70 For a more complete account of these events, see Don Rothwell, 'The Law of the Sea and the MV *Tampa* Incident: Reconciling Maritime Principles with Coastal State Sovereignty' (2002) 13 *Public Law Review* 118 at 118 and 123-4. See also James C Hathaway, 'Immigration Law is Not Refugee Law' in US Committee for Refugees, *World Refugee Survey 2001* at 39.
71 See discussion in Chapter 6.1 below.
72 See Migration Amendment (Designated Unauthorised Arrivals) Bill 2006 (Cth), discussed below at [4.64].
73 Note that the issues of constitutional law raised by this case are discussed in Chapter 3.3.4 above. To these other areas of law could be added. The affair also raised issues of mercantile law, as the *Tampa* was a commercial cargo vessel. For a discussion of the incident within the context of constitutional and human rights law, see the special issue devoted to the affair in (2002) 13 *Public Law Review*.

when sited within the context of the events of September 2001.[74] The decision of the Federal Court in the litigation induced by the *Tampa* standoff[75] was handed down only hours before the terrorist attacks in America on September 11. The momentous events of that day were to hang over the aftermath of the litigation and the *Tampa* Affair. They help to explain why public opinion in Australia firmed so quickly and completely against the boat people and why Prime Minister Howard was able to use the fear factor as such a potent weapon: his government's tough line on asylum seekers helped to win a federal election that everyone had thought the conservatives would lose.[76] The political play at home was replicated at an international level. The Australian government backed the UNHCR into an uncomfortable corner and with it the International Organisation for Migration (IOM). The two agencies agreed to take responsibility for processing half of the refugee claims of the asylum seekers from the *Tampa* and from the *Acheng*, a second vessel intercepted while en route from Christmas Island. Deals were brokered with Nauru and New Zealand, then with Papua New Guinea, to set up detention facilities in those countries. Throughout, the Australian government argued strongly that it was acting in compliance with its obligations under international law. It was able to do this in part because of the pervasive sense of moral panic that engulfed the nation and the world at that time, silencing bodies like UNHCR. The other factor was that the structures of international law provided no mechanism for the definitive resolution of the relevant legal issues.

4.3.2   International law of the sea

[4.37]   The international law of the sea is the primary legal framework governing the treatment of persons rescued at sea. One of the most significant and fundamental of all the obligations enshrined in the UN Convention on the Law of the Sea (UNCLOS) relates to maritime search and rescue. As Rothwell notes, Art 98 of the UNCLOS 'imposes a duty upon the Masters of all ships to render assistance to persons found at sea in danger of being lost and to proceed "with all possible speed to the rescue of persons in distress"'.[77] The decorations received by Captain Rinnan following the *Tampa* Affair[78] underscore his model behaviour when he first

---

74   September 11 2001 was the day on which a series of coordinated attacks were made on the iconic World Trade Center Buildings in New York and on the Pentagon in Washington DC.

75   See *Victorian Council for Civil Liberties v MIMA* (2001) 110 FCR 452 (*VCCL v MIMIA*). The case was taken on appeal to the Full Federal Court. See *Ruddock v Vadarlis* (2001) 110 FCR 491. Leave to appeal to the High Court was refused.

76   The best account of this period in Australian history is found in David Marr and Marianne Wilkinson, *Dark Victory: The Campaign to Re-elect the Prime Minister* (Sydney: Allen and Unwin, 2003). For an example of government ministers linking the *Tampa* events with the terrorist attacks in the US, see interview of Peter Reith (Defence Minister), *Sunrise*, Network 7, 13 September 2001; and discussion 'Are asylum seekers terrorists?' with Phillip Adams, Late Night Live, 18 September 2001, transcript available at <http://www.abc.net.au/rn/talks/lnl/s369701.htm>. On the turn in the conservative government's fortunes, see Fran Kelly, 'Howard's electoral fortunes turn around', The 7.30 Report, 20 September 2001, transcript available at <http://www.abc.net.au/7.30/content/2001/s371736.htm>.

77   See Rothwell, above n 70, at 119.

78   The Captain was knighted by the King of Norway and named Shipmaster of the Year by Lloyds List and the Nautical Institute. See Maritime Union of Australia, 'Tampa Captain knighted', News Release, 15 February 2002, available at <http://labor.net.au/news/1736.html>.

encountered the sinking *Palapa I*. He took all 433 'rescuees'[79] on board the MV *Tampa*, even though the vessel was licensed to carry only 50 people and equipped to cater for fewer still.[80] The Australian government agreed that the Captain acted nobly in saving the asylum seekers from drowning. However, it argued that Rinnan should have continued on the *Tampa's* planned (commercial) trajectory, which was towards Singapore. It also asserted that the ship should have made for Indonesia as the nearest point of disembarkation.[81] (In fact Captain Rinnan initially attempted to do just this: the *Tampa* travelled northwards for some four hours towards Indonesia before backtracking and making its way to Christmas Island.[82]) As Rothwell explains, however, there were no strict legal bases for these assertions. Despite amendments to the 1979 International Convention on Maritime Search and Rescue in 1998,[83] the law and state practice on precisely what should happen once people are rescued at sea remain somewhat unclear.[84]

[4.38] The acute politics of the affair is apparent in the fact that Prime Minister Howard became intimately involved in the standoff that followed Rinnan's request to land the asylum seekers on Australian territory at Christmas Island.[85] The complexity of the situation from a legal perspective was this. Rinnan believed with some reason that the law entitled him to bring the rescuees to Christmas Island. This was the closest geographical landfall to the point of rescue.[86] The legal principles of necessity and *force majeure* also justified his insistence on pursuing landfall at this point (although the Australian government contested the assertion that anyone was at risk of death or further injury). On the other side of the ledger, the use of SAS servicemen to board the *Tampa* and take control of the vessel under armed guard, and the closure of Flying Fish Cove, were difficult to justify. These are measures that should have been reserved to vessels representing a threat to Australia – not applied to a merchant vessel that had rescued asylum seekers at risk of drowning.[87] While the Norwegian

---

79 This is the term coined by North J in the Federal Court in the litigation brought by public interest advocates in the *Tampa* Affair. His Honour explained his choice of word as an attempt to find a neutral (and non-emotive) term to describe the people at the heart of the incident. See *VCCL v MIMA* (2001) 110 FCR 452 at 457.

80 Rothwell notes that the Captain acted therefore in excess of what he was strictly required to do under the law of the sea, above n 70, at 120-1. See also Jessica Tauman, 'Rescued at Sea but Nowhere to Go: The Cloudy Legal Waters of the *Tampa* Crisis' (2002) 11(2) *Pacific Rim Law and Policy Journal* 461 at 477-8; and Jean-Pierre Fonteyne, 'All Adrift in a Sea of Illegitimacy: An International Law Perspective on the Tampa Affair' (2001) 12 *Public Law Review* 249.

81 Flying Fish Cove on Christmas Island is not rated to dock a vessel with the dimensions of the *Tampa*. The Immigration Department's Mr Robert Illingsworth asserted that the *Tampa* Captain was obliged to keep the ship under power during the standoff with the Australian authorities.

82 The Captain changed course at the urging of the asylum seekers and because of the poor state these people were in. Rinnan reportedly feared that he would have deaths on board if medical assistance was not obtained as a matter of urgency. See Marr and Wilkinson, above n 76, at 20ff.

83 See [1986] ATS No 29, in force on 22 June 1985; and (1998) Select Documents on International Affairs No 46, London 18 May 1998.

84 See Ivan Shearer (ed), *O'Connell's The International Law of the Sea*, Vol II (Oxford: Clarendon Press, 1984) at 855-7; and Rothwell, above n 70, at 120-1.

85 See Marr and Wilkinson, above n 76, at 25.

86 Christmas Island was 75 nautical miles south from the site of the initial rescue, while the Indonesian Port of Merak was some 246 miles to the north. See Rothwell, above n 70, at 118.

87 See the analysis by Rothwell, above n 70, of these actions at 121-5.

Captain was threatened with fines as a people smuggler, he clearly did not fit this description. In our view, the principles of international law of the sea did not support the action taken by the Australian government. In the absence of any international court or other authority to support Captain Rinnan, however, it was the superior physical force of Australia's SAS officers that prevailed.[88]

4.3.3 International refugee law

[4.39] The other area of law that was of obvious relevance throughout this incident was that of international refugee law. It was apparent from very early in the piece that the *Tampa* rescuees wished to seek asylum in Australia on the basis that they were refugees: some had tried earlier to reach Australia for this purpose and had failed.[89] The doomed Palapa I had been the latest in a string of boats bringing larger and larger groups of asylum seekers to Australia – inducing near hysteria in the Australian media.[90]

[4.40] Throughout the initial crisis period, the *Tampa* rescuees' status as refugees had not been determined: they remained 'asylum seekers' only. As a matter of law, this should not have been an issue. Most of the rescuees were from Afghanistan – and the vast majority of earlier arrivals from that country were gaining recognition as Convention refugees.[91] The disingenuous nature of the government's behaviour was that everyone *knew* the group included Convention refugees. As the UNHCR Handbook makes clear, the refugee status determination procedure does not *create* refugees, it merely declares a status that either exists or does not.[92] Still, in the absence of any status determinations having been made, the government relied on the fact that the Refugee Convention does not provide a right to claim asylum.[93] It then asserted that Australia had no legal obligation to accept the rescuees, on the basis that either Norway or Indonesia had primary responsibility for their care and protection as a matter of law.

---

88   The shortcomings of the international legal regime governing persons rescued at sea is discussed by RP Schaeffer, 'The Singular Plight of Seaborne Refugees' (1978-80) 8 *Australian Yearbook of International Law* 213; and James Z Pugash, 'The Dilemma of the Sea Refugee: Rescue Without Refuge' (1977) 18 *Harvard International Law Journal* 577. Both articles chronicle the arrangements made following outflow of boat people from Vietnam following the fall of Saigon to the North Vietnamese. See also the comments by Tauman, above n 80.

89   The Afghanis on board the *Tampa* made their intentions clear to the Norwegian ambassador who visited the ship at its Christmas Island mooring. See Hathaway, above n 70, at 39; and the letter from the rescuees cited by North J at *VCCL v MIMA* (2001) 110 FCR 452 at [28].

90   For an analysis of the saturation media coverage of this event, see Kieran O'Doherty and Martha Augoustinos, 'Protecting the Nation: Nationalist Rhetoric on Asylum Seekers and the Tampa' (2008) 18 *Journal of Community and Applied Psychology* 576.

91   Before the US intervention in Afghanistan led to the defeat of the ruling Taliban in late 2001, over 80 per cent of Afghan asylum seekers in Australia were gaining recognition as refugees. Of the 130 *Tampa* asylum seekers accepted by New Zealand, all but one were recognised at first instance as refugees and offered permanent resettlement. This point was made forcefully by North J. See *VCCL v MIMA* (2001) 110 FCR 452 at 471. A decade after the *Tampa* incident, a very high percentage of asylum seekers from Afghanistan continued to gain recognition as refugees.

92   See UNHCR *Handbook on Procedures and Criteria for Determining Refugee Status Under the 1951 Convention and the 1967 Protocol relating to the Status of Refugees* UCR/IP/4/Eng/REV.1 (1979) at [28].

93   See *MIMA v Ibrahim* (2000) 204 CLR 1 at [137] (Gummow J).

[4.41] As the country of embarkation, Indonesia was urged to take the rescuees back. Even though Indonesia was not a signatory to the Refugee Convention, Australia argued that the rescuees would not face persecution in that country because Indonesia has long offered de facto protection to the predominantly Muslim asylum seekers from Afghanistan and the Middle East. The problem with this argument was that the rescuees had never been lawfully present in Indonesia, even if their presence had been tolerated. This made it very difficult to invoke a legal basis for their return. In the period following the *Tampa* Affair, Australia was able to broker an agreement with Indonesia to take in asylum seekers interdicted en route to Australia who had passed through that country before undertaking their sea journey. However, this was a diplomatic achievement (based on the exchange of large amounts of money and other concessions). The fact that it was not based on any legal obligation on the part of Indonesia became obvious in 2009 when the Rudd Labor government attempted to secure the same arrangements in respect of asylum seekers intercepted at sea by the Australian vessel, the *Oceanic Viking*.[94]

[4.42] A fallback argument was that Norway had responsibility for the *Tampa* rescuees because the *Tampa* was flying a Norwegian flag at the time of the rescue. As Hathaway points out,[95] the problem with laying responsibility at the feet of Norway in this fashion was that the *Tampa* is a commercial ship. Under international law of the sea, such vessels do not carry with them the full range of state responsibilities: this rule applies only to military or other state-owned and operated ships.[96] Goodwin-Gill acknowledges that difficulties in attaching legal responsibility to vessels rescuing refugees at sea have led to a general tendency to focus on the coastal states receiving the refugees.[97] The situation is one of inherent legal uncertainty, however, with the result that state practice has varied greatly at the height of crises involving fugitives taking to boats in any numbers.[98] If any precedents exist for flagship states taking responsibility for refugees rescued at sea, the countries involved have generally been geographically proximate to the scene of the rescue, and have been willing to participate in a management program.[99]

[4.43] Although Australia argued that it should not be liable for the *Tampa* rescuees, in fact it did assume responsibility for ensuring that the group were treated in accordance with the basic premises of international refugee law. As we

---

94 See Tom Allard and Karuni Rompies, 'Share Asylum Burden, Indonesians Plead', *Sydney Morning Herald*, 21 November 2009, available at <http://www.smh.com.au/world/share-asylum-burden-indonesians-plead-20091120-iqwq.html>.
95 See Hathaway, above n 70, at 41, note 11.
96 See the discussion of the nationality of ships in RR Churchill and AV Lowe, *The Law of the Sea* (Manchester: Juris Publishing, 3rd ed, 1999) at 257-63.
97 On this point, see the discussion of Guy Goodwin-Gill and Jane McAdam, *The Refugee in International Law* (Oxford: OUP, 3rd ed, 2006) at 277-84. The authors stress the responsibility of the state of 'first port of call', rather than asserting obligations in the flag states of rescue vessels.
98 Tauman provides examples of some of the more egregious instances of humanitarian neglect, amongst them the tragedies of the *St Louis* – which resulted in the ultimate death of 907 refugees from Nazi Germany; of the *Struma* – where 769 Romanian Jews were left to drown; and of the Vietnamese boat people who were left by a United States naval vessel to die of starvation in the South China Seas. See Tauman, above n 80, at 461-2, 492-3.
99 See Schaeffer, above n 88, and Pugash, above n 88.

explain in greater length later in the book,¹⁰⁰ Australia's primary responsibility was to ensure that the asylum seekers were not *refouled* or returned to a place of persecution. Hathaway criticises Australia's behaviour on the basis that it adopted 'mechanistic' strategies to avoid the assumption of responsibility. The Professor groups together in this respect both the physical expulsion of the *Tampa* and its human cargo and the legislative measures taken to nominally remove Australian jurisdiction.¹⁰¹ Whether Australia did this in reality is open to question. Australia bankrolled the major actors (Nauru, Papua New Guinea, IOM and UNHCR), and assumed some responsibility itself for determining the refugee claims of the rescuees. Until the last refugees were resettled, Australia maintained tight control of the centres established in Nauru and in Papua New Guinea. This extended to exercising a veto over applications for visas for outsiders to visit those places. It is difficult to see how else to characterise Australia's behaviour other than as constituting de facto assumption of jurisdiction.¹⁰²

4.3.4 Judicial responses to the *Tampa* Affair

[4.44] If the *Tampa* standoff attracted a good deal of attention internationally (at least until the terrorist attacks on September 11), it induced some extraordinary reactions inside Australia. Not the least of these was the decision by a Melbourne lawyer with no prior background in immigration law to bring an action in his own name in an attempt to force the Australian government to land the rescuees on Christmas Island and to process their refugee claims. Eric Vadarlis assembled a legal team that included the Victorian Council for Civil Liberties and Julian Burnside QC. Vadarlis succeeded at first instance before North J in the Federal Court, who held that the asylum seekers were being detained by the Australian authorities in circumstances where there was no basis under Australian law for the action being taken.¹⁰³ However, the victory was both narrow and short-lived. A basic problem was that the government refused to allow Vadarlis access to anyone on board the *Tampa* apart from the Norwegian Consul. Although he was handed a letter from the rescuees, Vadarlis was unable to gain direct instructions from the rescuees for the purpose of mounting a legal challenge under the *Migration Act*.¹⁰⁴ As a result, the applicants were acknowledged as having standing only to bring an action for orders

---

100 See Chapter 14 at [14.01].
101 See Hathaway, above n 70, at 41. For a discussion of the legislative changes 'excising' certain offshore territories from Australia's migration zone, see Chapter 6.1 below; and Mary Crock, 'Echoes of the Old Countries or Brave New Worlds? Legal Responses to Refugees and Asylum Seekers in Australia and New Zealand' (2001) 14 *Revue Québécoise de Droit International* 55 at 80.
102 This underscores the assertions made by the Australian government about the lawfulness of its actions. See generally DIMIA, *Interpreting the Refugees Convention* (Canberra: DIMIA, 2002). On this point, see also Théodor Meron, 'Extraterritoriality of Human Rights Treaties' (1995) 89 *American Journal of International Law* 78 at 80-1. See Crock, above n 68, at 61.
103 See *VCCL v MIMA* (2001) 110 FCR 452.
104 On the behaviour of the government on this issue, see Marr and Wilkinson, above n 76, at 112-13. Vadarlis argued that the refusal to allow him access to the rescuees constituted a breach of his implied constitutional freedom of communication. He sought an injunction and mandamus to allow him to give legal advice to the rescuees. See *VCCL v MIMIA* (2001) 110 FCR 452 at 489-90; and *Ruddock v Vadarlis* (2001) 110 FCR 491.

in the nature of *habeas corpus* so as to seek the release of the *Tampa* rescuees.[105] They were held to have no right to mount any other kind of legal challenge. In particular, both North J and the Full Federal Court held that the applicants had no standing to seek a writ of mandamus to compel the Minister to act in accordance with the law.[106]

[4.45] The ruling by North J shows a deep awareness of the overriding principles of refugee law raised by the predicament in which the rescuees found themselves – that judge was not afraid to say outright that at least some of those being detained had to be Convention refugees:

> It is notorious that a significant proportion of asylum seekers from Afghanistan processed through asylum status systems qualify as refugees under the *Convention relating to the Status of Refugees* (1951) (the Refugees Convention). Once assessed as refugees, this means that they are recognised as persons fleeing from persecution in Afghanistan. While such people no doubt make decisions about their lives, those decisions should be seen against the background of the pressures generated by flight from persecution.[107]

[4.46] Having said this, throughout this judgment and those of the Full Federal Court delivered after a speedily determined appeal, the presiding judges seem to have made a special effort to avoid adverting to rules of international law. The acutely political nature of the affair seems to have drawn the focus of the litigants deliberately inwards. The very fact that North J felt compelled to speak of those rescued by the *Tampa* as 'rescuees', rather than as 'asylum seekers', is an example in point.

[4.47] The one area where the courts were prepared to hear argument related to the question of the detention of the rescuees. The Full Federal Court agreed with North J that any person has a right to apply for the release of another individual if that person is being held without lawful excuse. Even though the applicants had standing to question the detention of the rescuees, however, it did not follow automatically that the writ of *habeas corpus* would run. The remedy was dependent on the applicants demonstrating that the rescuees were being detained and that their custody was unlawful. In the Full Federal Court, the majority held against the applicants on both these counts. French J, with whom Beaumont J agreed, looked back to that other great controversy concerning the detention of unauthorised boat

---

105 The Federal Court, both at first instance, and on appeal, acknowledged that the liberty of the person is a human right of such fundamental importance that any person has the right under the common law to challenge the legality of another's detention. See *VCCL v MIMIA* (2001) 110 FCR 452 at 469; and *Ruddock v Vadarlis* (2001) 110 FCR 49 at 509 (Black CJ) and at 518 (Beaumont J). See also *Waters v Commonwealth* (1951) 82 CLR 188 at 190; *Truth About Motorways Pty Ltd v Macquarie Infrastructure Investment Management Limited* (2000) 200 CLR 591 at 600 (Gleeson CJ and McHugh J), at 627 (Gummow J) and at 652-3 (Kirby J); and *Clarkson v R* [1986] VR 464 at 465-6.
106 The applicants argued that the *Migration Act 1958* operated to require the landing of the rescuees because the status of the rescuees as unlawful non-citizens meant that they had to be taken into immigration detention within Australia pursuant to s 189 of that Act. In the alternative, Vadarlis argued that s 245F required the government to bring the rescuees to the mainland of Australia, where they would then be entitled to lodge formal claims for refugee status pursuant to s 36 of the Act. See the description of the s 245F provisions by Black CJ: *Ruddock v Vadarlis* (2001) 110 FCR 491 at 506-7.
107 *VCCL v MIMA* (2001) 110 FCR 452 at 471.

arrivals: *Chu Kheng Lim*.[108] Invoking the so-called 'three walled prison' argument, he ruled (counter-intuitively) that the rescuees were not being 'detained' at law because they were free to travel anywhere they wished (except to Australia).[109] The judge studiously ignored the fact that this characterisation of immigration detention in *Lim* had been repeated and roundly rejected by the UN Human Rights Committee[110] and by the European Court of Human Rights – a point made by Black CJ in his powerful dissent.[111]

[4.48] Beaumont J agreed with French J, but delivered a judgment that in more than one respect was less than fully rational. Crock offers the following reflections:

> Leaving aside the correctness or otherwise of his reasoning, Beaumont J's judgment in the *Tampa* case is interesting in the wider context of the affair, coinciding as it did with the September 11 terrorist attacks. The judgment is replete with a sense of urgency, if not moral panic. The judge underscores passages and words. His conclusion – that an alien has no **right** to enter Australia – is placed quite literally in bold print. The effect is to emphasize and re-emphasize the *outsider* status of the rescuees. The word 'alien' appears no less than 27 times in the 30 paragraphs of his judgment.
>
> None of the judges in the appeal court mentions the tumultuous events that occurred in America on the day North J handed down his ruling – September 11 2001. As the world came to learn about Osama Bin Laden, Al Qaeda and the Taliban in Afghanistan, it was no time at all before Australia's politicians were warning a frightened public that the Afghan and Middle Eastern boat people 'could be terrorists'.[112] One is left to wonder whether Beaumont J would have been quite as vehement absent '9-11'.
>
> The tonal change between the primary judgment and the appeal rulings could not be more marked. Of the four Federal Court judges, North J at first instance is the only one to spend much time describing the rescuees, identifying them as fugitives from Afghanistan who 'it is probable … are people genuinely fearing persecution'. Dissenting in the Full Court, Black CJ agreed with the substance of North J's rulings. However, his carefully reasoned judgment sticks closely to legal principle, assiduously avoiding any emotive descriptions of the people behind the action. Beaumont J's postscript does acknowledge the potential that the rescuees could be refugees, but his addendum underscores (again, quite literally), the international nature of the legal obligation not to *refoule* refugees. His Honour draws attention to the fact that what became known as the 'Pacific solution' did not involve the *refoulement* of the rescuees: they all would have their asylum claims assessed outside of Australia.[113]

---

108   See *Chu Kheng Lim v MILGEA* (1992) 176 CLR 1, discussed above at Chapter 3.3.2.
109   *Ruddock v Vadarlis* (2001) 110 FCR 491 at 548.
110   See A v Australia, Communication No 560/1993: Australia, CCPR/C/59/D/560/1993 (30 April 1997) and the other cases discussed below, Part 4.4.
111   *Ruddock v Vadarlis* (2001) 110 FCR 491 at 510.
112   See, for example, comments attributed to the former Minister for Defence as reported in Robert Manne, 'Australia's New Course', *The Age*, 12 November 2002.
113   See *Ruddock v Vadarlis* (2001)110 FCR 491 at 521; and Crock, above n 68, at 68.

4.3.5 International refugee law and human rights law: Operation Relex and the Pacific Strategy

[4.49] It is beyond the scope of this chapter to explore all of the international legal issues by the *Tampa* Affair and its aftermath. With the passage of time, detailed analyses have been produced of Australia's conduct and of similar initiatives taken by other countries as the phenomenon of 'refugee boats' (as they were described in the 1970s[114]) has spread around the world.[115] For present purposes it suffices to outline the relevant principles called into question by Australian laws and practices in two key areas. The first involves the program for stopping the boats carrying asylum seekers towards Australia. The second concerns the establishment of detention facilities both outside Australia and on territory 'excised' from the 'migration zone' for the purpose of processing the refugee claims of asylum seekers interdicted before coming to Australia.

4.3.6 The interdiction program

[4.50] The *Tampa* incident marked the institution and/or tightening of a range of measures designed to deter boat people and to impose physical impediments to the arrival of boats carrying asylum seekers to Australia.[116] The program for intercepting 'suspected illegal entry vessels' (SIEVs) was codenamed 'Operation Relex'. Persons apprehended on the boats interdicted during the course of the *Tampa* standoff were sent to Nauru and to Manus Island for the processing of their refugee claims. In accordance with a Memorandum of Understanding reached with Indonesia,[117] later boats were towed or escorted back into Indonesian waters. The intercepted vessels included the 'SIEV 4', which took water and sank when under tow by Australia, necessitating the recovery from the sea of the asylum seekers. Photographs of the rescue were misused by the government in October 2001 to promote the fiction that the asylum seekers had thrown their children overboard to 'blackmail' Australia into accepting them. A Senate inquiry[118] into this affair and the work of investigative journalists[119] drew suggestions of Australian involvement in incidents at sea resulting in two confirmed deaths by drowning, and three other suspected drownings. The worst of these incidents was the sinking on 19 October 2001 of a supposedly unidentified

---

114 See the Cabinet papers from 1979 discussed below at Chapter 12 at [12.27].
115 See, for example, Andreas Fischer-Lescano, Tillmann Lohr and Timo Tohidipur, 'Border Controls at Sea: Requirements Under International Human Rights and Refugee Law' (2009) 21 *International Journal of Refugee Law* 256 ('Border Controls at Sea'); Angus Francis, 'Bringing Protection Home: Healing the Schism Between International Obligations and National Safeguards Created by Extraterritorial Processing' (2008) 20 *International Journal of Refugee Law* 273; and the articles collected in (2006) 18(4) *International Journal of Refugee Law*. The Border Controls at Sea article includes in turn a review of the collected literature on this subject.
116 Most of these are discussed in Chapter 6.1 below.
117 Francis, above n 115, sets out the details of these documents at 273-4, note 1.
118 Senate Select Committee Inquiry into A Certain Maritime Incident, 23 October 2002. The report can be found at <http://www.aph.gov.au/Senate/Committee/maritime_incident_ctte/report/index.htm>. See also Patrick Weller, *Don't Tell the Prime Minister* (Melbourne: Scribe Short Books, 2002).
119 See, for example, Four Corners, 'To Deter and Deny' ABC TV, screened 15 April 2002, transcript available at <http://www.abc.net.au/4corners/stories/s531993.htm> ('To Deter and Deny').

vessel (later dubbed 'SIEV X') which went down in the High Seas beyond Indonesia's Sunda Strait with the loss of 353 lives. Allegations emerged of Indonesian officials forcing asylum seekers at gunpoint onto a vessel of dubious structural integrity and which was severely overloaded. Australian surveillance operations appear to have been aware that the vessel had left, but allegedly did nothing to track its passage. Certainly no one came to the assistance of the asylum seekers in a timely fashion when the ship went down.[120]

[4.51] The Coalition government resisted strongly suggestions that Australia was in any way responsible for these 'adverse' events, arguing that such tragic occurrences simply underscore the hazards of using people smugglers to circumvent regular immigration procedures. Leaving aside the SIEV X disaster which may be forever shrouded in dark mysteries, Operation Relex placed Australia in potential breach of a range of international laws.

[4.52] The first and most obvious problem related to obligations imposed under the UNCLOS. Taking unseaworthy boats under tow or forcing them back to sea placed the lives of the asylum seekers at obvious risk, contrary to the fundamental obligation to protect life at sea. In addition to Art 98 of UNCLOS, the International Convention for the Safety of Life at Sea (SOLAS)[121] and the International Convention on Maritime Search and Rescue (SAR)[122] oblige ships' masters to render assistance when aware of an emergency at sea, regardless of the nationality or status of the persons on board the vessel in distress. Documentary footage obtained by Australian journalists suggests that the interdiction operation exacerbated rather than relieved the distress experienced on board at least some of the boats interdicted and towed back to Indonesia. This is especially so in those instances where lives were lost at sea or at the point where boats were left to ground themselves on the Indonesian shoreline.[123]

[4.53] These incidents during the course of the interdiction program arguably placed Australia in breach of Art 3 of the UN Convention Against Torture and All forms of Cruel, Inhumane and Degrading Treatment or Punishment 1984 (CAT)[124] and Arts 6 and 7 of the ICCPR.[125] These are the articles that enshrine the right to life and the obligation not to commit acts that constitute torture or cruel, inhuman and degrading treatment.

---

120   The best account of this disaster is contained in Tony Kevin and Anthony Charles Kevin, *A Certain Maritime Incident: The Sinking of SIEV X* (Melbourne: Scribe Publications, 2004). See also <www.sievx.com>.
121   *International Convention for the Safety of Life at Sea* (adopted 1 November 1974, entered into force 30 June 1980) 1184 UNTS 2, Chapter V, regulation 33(1).
122   *International Convention on Maritime Search and Rescue* (adopted 27 April 1979, entered into force 22 June 1985) 1405 UNTS 97, Annexe §2.1.10.
123   See 'To Deter and To Deny', above n 119.
124   Adopted 10 December 1984, entered into force 26 June 1987, 1465 UNTS 85.
125   See UN Human Rights Committee, General Comment No 20: Art 7 (prohibition of torture, or other cruel, inhuman or degrading treatment or punishment), HRI/GEN/1/Rev 7, 10 March 1992 at [9]; and Francis, above n 115, at 277 note 18.

[4.54] As others have explored at great length,[126] Operation Relex – like other interdiction programs before and after it[127] – also placed Australia in breach of non-refoulement and other provisions enshrined in the Refugee Convention, CAT and the ICCPR. To begin with, the country to which interdicted persons were returned – Indonesia – was not (and in 2011 still was not) a signatory to the Refugee Convention. Indeed, the SIEV X incident provides a basis for doubting whether the protection offered to Muslim asylum seekers in Indonesia was 'effective' in the sense of providing some form of tenure or sanctuary to these people. The obligation not to *refoule* refugees to a place where they face persecution extends to *indirect* as well as direct return.[128]

[4.55] The program has been criticised further as one that penalises asylum seekers on the basis of the allegedly illegal mode of their entry. Article 31(1) of the Refugee Convention prohibits states parties from imposing penalties on account of their illegal entry or presence, on refugees 'coming directly from a territory where their life or freedom was threatened in the sense of Article 1'. The Australian government's argument was that the boat people intercepted by Australia were not covered by Art 31 because they were not coming directly from a country in which their lives or freedoms were threatened. They were said rather to be 'secondary movement' refugees seeking not 'protection', but a preferred migration outcome.[129] Then Minister Ruddock stated that the primary goal of the government in taking its tough stance against asylum seekers was to prevent refugees from 'forum shopping'. The Minister's view was that UN processes are undermined if refugees are allowed take matters into their own hands, jumping the 'queue' of persons recognised by the UN as refugees and ear-marked for resettlement in third countries.[130]

[4.56] Once again, the overwhelming impression conveyed by this 'official' version is one of formalist and mechanistic interpretation of the relevant international law – arguably putting Australia in contravention of the basic principles of good faith compliance with its treaty obligations.[131] At the very least, it was an approach that runs counter to the interpretation of Art 31(1) that UNHCR would like to see countries adopt.[132]

---

126   See, for example, Francis, above n 115; Hathaway, above n 70; Goodwin-Gill and McAdam, above n 97, at 244-53.
127   See for example, Stephen Legomsky, 'The USA and the Caribbean Interdiction Program' (2006) 18(4) *International Journal of Refugee Law* 677 (and other articles in this symposium issue on offshore processing); and Gregor Noll, 'Visions of the Exceptional: Legal and Theoretical Issues Raised by Transit Processing Centres and Processing Zones' (2003) 5 *European Journal of Migration and Law* 303.
128   See Goodwin-Gill and McAdam, above n 97, at 252-3, 389 and 400.
129   See 'Article 31: Refugees Unlawfully in the Country of Refuge', in DIMIA, above n 102, at 123ff.
130   This characterisation of the refugees is underscored by the government by removing one place in Australia's overseas 'humanitarian' intake for every asylum seeker recognised as a refugee in Australia.
131   See the *Vienna Convention on the Law of Treaties* (adopted 23 May 1969, entered into force 27 January 1980) 1155 UNTS 331 at Arts 3, 26 and 31. See Francis, above n 115, at 275ff; and Fischer-Lescano et al, 'Border Controls at Sea', above n 115, at 259-60.
132   On this point, see Guy Goodwin-Gill, 'Article 31 of the 1951 Convention relating to the Status of Refugees: Non Penalisation, Detention and Protection', paper prepared for UNHCR Global Consultations, October 2001, available at <http://www.unhcr.org/419c778d4.html >.

4.3.7 Offshore processing under the Pacific Strategy

[4.57] The second aspect of Australia's response to illegal boat arrivals in 2001 involved the establishment of offshore processing centres – first on Nauru and Manus Island in Papua New Guinea and later on the 'excised offshore territory' of Christmas Island. The legality of these measures under international law was brought back before the public eye in 2006 with the proposal to extend the program for the deflection of asylum seekers to those arriving by boat who manage to make landfall on the Australian mainland. Abandoned to some extent with the change in government in November 2007,[133] there are aspects of the so-called Pacific Strategy that are ripe for criticism – not the least in the apparent disregard for local human rights standards in those two countries and in the inferior protection outcomes for asylum seekers processed offshore. First, the creation of two different systems to process refugee claims from people differentiated only by their mode of arrival again raises questions about Australia's compliance *in good faith* with its treaty obligations to effectively implement the Refugee Convention and other human rights instruments. These obligations include a duty to ensure that fair and effective status determination procedures are established.[134] Allegations have been made that the regime contravenes Art 31 of the Refugee Convention because it (again) amounts to a penalisation of unauthorised boat arrivals who seek refugee protection. This point was acute in relation to the proposal in 2006 to extend offshore processing to all unauthorised arrivals (including those arriving on Australia's mainland),[135] which many said was being made in response to Indonesian concerns over the grant of asylum to 43 refugees from West Papua. These refugees had travelled to Australia directly from the country of alleged persecution. For this reason, justifications based on characterisations of the fugitives as 'secondary movement' refugees did not apply.[136]

[4.58] Within the broader framework of human rights law, the program was also vulnerable to criticism. Of particular relevance in this regard are the prohibitions on arbitrary detention[137] and on cruel, inhuman or degrading treatment in the ICCPR,[138] the CAT[139] and the CRC.[140]

---

133 See Senator Chris Evans, MIAC Media Release, 'Last Refugees Leave Nauru', 8 February 2008; and 'Labor Unveils New Risk-Based Detention Policy', 29 July 2008. Note that the Labor government has committed to maintaining offshore processing on Christmas Island. See Mary Crock, 'First Term Blues: Labor, Refugees and Immigration Reform' (2010) 17 *Australian Journal of Administrative Law* 205.
134 See Francis, above n 115, at 275 and 278-9; and the discussion below at Chapter 12.4.
135 See Migration Amendment (Designated Unauthorised Arrivals) Bill 2006 (Cth).
136 See discussion below at [12.60]. It will be recalled that Art 31(2) precludes states from penalising refugees who enter their territory illegally when coming directly from a country in which they face persecution.
137 See ICCPR, Art 9, including Art 9(4) which speaks of entitlement to judicial review of any measures involving the deprivation of liberty.
138 See ICCPR, Arts 7 and 10. Note that the terms of this instrument apply to individuals both within the territory of a signatory state and *subject to its jurisdiction*. See ICCPR, Art 2.
139 See CAT, Art 3 (which also has extraterritorial operation).
140 Article 37(b) of the CRC requires states parties to ensure that 'no child shall be deprived of his or her liberty unlawfully or arbitrarily. The arrest, detention or imprisonment of a child shall be in conformity with the law and shall be used as a measure of last resort and for the shortest appropriate period of time'.

[4.59] One of the more tendentious arguments made in defence of Australia's Pacific Strategy was that the individuals taken to Nauru and Manus Island were not 'detained' at all. Rather, they were subjected by the host countries of Nauru and Papua New Guinea to geographic restrictions on their freedom of movement as conditions on the visas granted on arrival in the country. Father Frank Brennan SJ provides an excoriating critique of the word games that were played by Australia's Minister for Immigration:

> The Minister's first defence is to claim that the facilities in those places (Nauru and Manus Island) are not detention centres despite the *Migration Legislation Amendment (Transitional Movement) Act 2002* speaking of 'the detention of the person in a country in respect of which a declaration is in force (s 198D(3)(c)). And the bills digest for the Migration Legislation Amendment (Transitional Movement) Bill 2002 speaks of the removal of persons 'to a place such as a "Pacific Solution" detention facility on Nauru or Papua New Guinea'. Even Senator George Brandis and Mr John Hodges in the Senate Select Committee on a Certain Maritime Incident have referred to the 'detention centres' in those places and the 'detainees' kept therein. In his evidence on 1 May 2002, Mr Hodges said, 'Nauru is by far the worst of the detention centres.'[141]

[4.60] Rhetoric aside, a conscious effort appears to have been made to ensure that processing on Nauru and Manus Island conformed with (no more and no less than) the minimum procedures established by the United Nations in its front-line relief operations in cases of large-scale refugee flows. The rationale seems to be that refugees should not be able to gain a procedural advantage by forum shopping.[142] As well as being unfair to those 'screened out' by UNHCR, the elaborate systems of countries like Australia are decried as magnets that encourage asylum seekers to by-pass the 'regular' refugee management processes. The involvement of UNHCR and of IOM in Australia's Pacific Strategy gave credence to what was again a rather formalistic vision of the world's refugee problem and what should be done to resolve it.

[4.61] While the *Tampa* rescuees taken in by New Zealand fared well,[143] the arrangements on Nauru and Manus Island raise a variety of issues about compliance with international human rights law. The conditions in the holding centres on Nauru, in particular, were deplorable. Quite apart from the poor processing systems which resulted in legally uncertain outcomes (see further below), the detainees were left to languish in the tropical heat for years with poor food and living conditions, poor medical care and little or no access to education or useful occupations. By the time

---

141 See Frank Brennan SJ AO, 'Developing Just Refugee Policies in Australia: Local, National and International Concerns', University of Sydney, 7 August 2002, unpublished paper on file with authors, at 13.

142 Then Minister Ruddock drew attention to the inequity implicit in the fact that asylum seekers who access Australia's refugee determination processes are many times more likely to gain recognition as refugees than are those processed by UNHCR in its front-line field operations. See, for example, 'Refugees plight a "lifestyle choice"', *The Australian*, 8 January 2002.

143 New Zealand had its quota of 131 asylum seekers processed within weeks of arrival. In January 2002, all but one had gained recognition as refugees and were granted permanent residence in New Zealand. See Oxfam and Community Aid Abroad, 'Adrift in the Pacific: The Implications of Australia's Pacific Refugee Solution' (Oxfam, March 2002), Appendix One.

they were resettled in Australia or elsewhere, many were suffering from psychoses induced by their lengthy detention.[144]

[4.62] In this context two further points can be made about Australia's compliance with its obligations under the Refugee Convention. The fact that asylum seekers on Nauru faced rejection as refugees in circumstances where they would have had their claims recognised in Australia raises questions about compliance with the foundational obligation not to *refoule* Convention refugees. Statistics supplied by IOM in January 2006[145] showed that of 55 unaccompanied and separated children processed on Nauru, 32 were returned to Afghanistan in 2002-03.[146] In comparison, no such children processed on mainland Australia were returned over the same period. These statistics underscore the obvious fact that particularly vulnerable asylum seekers do not fare well in systems that deny any form of assistance or representation.

[4.63] It is worth noting in this context that Nauru is not a party to the Refugee Convention, while Papua New Guinea has ratified but made a number of reservations.[147] From the perspective of the domestic laws of both Nauru and Papua New Guinea, the establishment of the detention facilities and the indefinite incarceration of the asylum seekers without judicial oversight are questionable. Both Nauru and Papua New Guinea are countries with Bills of Rights that prohibit arbitrary detention.[148] The financial inducements of the Australian government resulted in both instances in the establishment of facilities that, at the very least, sat uneasily with the human rights regimes of the host governments.

[4.64] Within the Australian Parliament, appreciation seems to have grown by August 2006 that the processing arrangements and protection outcomes on Nauru were extremely punitive. Facing apparent defeat in the Senate, Prime Minister Howard withdrew the contentious Migration Amendment (Designated Unauthorised Arrivals) Bill 2006 (Cth) after its passage through the House of Representatives.[149] In the final analysis, the regime was described by the in-coming Labor Minister for

---

144 See Michael Gordon, *Freeing Ali: The Human Face of the Pacific Solution* (Sydney: UNSW Press, 2005).
145 See Mary Crock, *Seeking Asylum Alone: A Study of Australian Law, Policy and Practice Regarding Unaccompanied and Separated Children* (Sydney: Themis Press, 2006) Ch 2.2.3, Table 5.
146 Edmund Rice Centre, *Deported to Danger* available at <http://www.erc.org.au/research/pdf/1096416029.pdf>.
147 Papua New Guinea does not accept the following Convention obligations: paid employment (Art 17); housing (Art 21); public education (Art 22); freedom of movement (Art 26); non-discrimination against refugees who enter illegally (Art 31); expulsion (Art 32); and naturalisation (Art 34).
148 For the Nauruan Constitution, see Part II, Protection of Fundamental Rights and Freedoms, Art 3: <http://www.naurugov.nr/parliament/constitution.html>; and for the Constitution of Papua New Guinea, see the Preamble and Art 42 (Liberty of the Person): <http://www.nefc.gov.pg/Constitution%20of%20PNG%20FINAL.pdf>.
149 See 'PM "to blame" for Migration Bill Failure', *The Age*, 15 August 2006, <http://www.theage.com.au/news/National/PM-to-blame-for-migration-bill-failure/2006/08/15/1155407783579.html>. Earlier in the year, the Senate Legal and Constitutional Affairs Committee took the radical step of recommending against the passage of the Bill. See Senate Legal and Constitutional References Committee, *Inquiry into the provisions of the Migration Amendment (Designated Unauthorised Arrivals) Bill 2006*, tabled 13 June 2006.. Although it was passed in the Lower House, five Coalition members of parliament either crossed the floor to vote with the Opposition or abstained from the vote. See ABC News, *Migration Bill Passes Lower House*, 10 August 2006, available at <http://www.abc.net.au/news/newsitems/200608/s1711636.htm>.

Immigration, Senator Evans, as little short of an embarrassment, so blatant were the abuses of international law. He said in July 2008:

> At my first meeting with Department officials as Minister for Immigration, I asked who was detained at the immigration detention centre on Nauru and at what stage were their claims for asylum.
>
> I was told there were eight Burmese and 81 Sri Lankans there. Virtually all of this group had already been assessed as refugees but had been left languishing on Nauru.
>
> When I asked why the eight Burmese had not been settled in Australia in accordance with international law there was an embarrassed silence.
>
> Eventually the answer emerged. The Howard government had ordered they stay put. They had been left rotting on Nauru because the Howard government wanted to maintain the myth that third-country settlement was possible.
>
> Sadly, Australia's treatment of asylum seekers had sunk this low.[150]

4.3.8 Refugees and asylum seekers under Labor: Continued dissonances with international law

[4.65] In our view, the great disappointment of the first term of the Labor government elected in 2007 was that it did not move to make Australian law and practice more obviously compliant with obligations Australia has assumed under international law. It did not dismantle completely the Pacific Strategy. The regime for the excision of Australia's offshore territories was not altered, in spite of the universal condemnation it has attracted.[151] Nor did the policy changes relating to immigration detention mark an end to immigration detention centres.[152]

[4.66] Although refugee advocates initially fell very quiet after the election of the Rudd Labor government, there are many features of the Labor government's policies and practices that continue to place Australia in breach of international law. Many of the objections made about the regime in place on Nauru and Manus Island continue to be apposite to the Christmas Island arrangements and would apply equally to the 'regional' processing solution mooted for East Timor or elsewhere after the 2010 election. As Francis notes,[153] UNHCR has identified certain core processing requirements for status determinations to be regarded as offering a fair and effective determination of refugee status. These include fair decision-making, including rights to: representation; an impartial and qualified interpreter; and a personal interview providing an opportunity for a claimant to present evidence of personal circumstances and country of origin information. It also includes a right to review by an independent review body. The right to effective remedies, including access to national courts, is enshrined in both Art 16 of the Refugee Convention and Art 14 of the ICCPR.

---

150   Senator Chris Evans, 'New Directions in Detention – Restoring Integrity to Australia's Immigration System', Australian National University, Canberra, Tuesday 29 July 2008, available at <http://www.minister.immi.gov.au/media/speeches/2008/ce080729.htm>.
151   'Border Controls at Sea', above n 115, at 263 catalogue's criticisms by academics, UNHCR, EXComm and NGOs.
152   See further the discussion in Chapter 12 below.
153   See above n 115, at 296-309. Note that Francis is a little too hasty in his assumption at 309 that Australia's offshore processing scheme had been disbanded.

[4.67] The regime for processing claims on Christmas Island acknowledges most of these rights, but it remains a system that is different from and inferior to that pertaining on mainland Australia. There is no automatic right to the review of primary decisions. Although curial review is available by virtue of the constitutional guarantees set out in s 75(v) of the Constitution,[154] access to the courts is restricted by the often insuperable difficulties in obtaining legal counsel. In brief, a great many of the criticisms levelled at processing on Nauru still apply to the Christmas Island regime.[155]

[4.68] Once in opposition, the conservative Coalition parties in Australia had no compunction in 2009 in offering vocal *ex post facto* criticisms of the Rudd government's 'softening' of policies towards asylum seekers and refugees.[156] Scant regard was paid to the effect this rhetoric might have in encouraging people smugglers to try their hand, given the international coverage given to the criticisms.[157] The issue was used quite pointedly as a device to reignite the xenophobia and fearful introspection that delivered such electoral dividends for the Conservatives in the wake of the *Tampa* Affair. The complaints were not immediately successful in restoring the political fortunes of parties still rent with internal divisions. However, the game playing provided an effective check on any government plans to wind back further its border control strategies.

4.4 Complaints to the international human rights treaty bodies

[4.69] Australia's migration laws have felt the impact of international law in one other respect that is worthy of mention. In 1992 the then Labor government acceded to the First Optional Protocol to the ICCPR.[158] This action opened the way for complaints to be made to the UN Human Rights Committee by individuals alleging a breach of any of the rights protected by the ICCPR. In due course, accession to the optional protocol to the CAT allowed for complaints to be made to the Committee Against Torture.[159]

---

154 See also *Plaintiff M61/2010E v Commonwealth and Plaintiff M69 of 2010 v Commonwealth* (2010) 272 ALR 14, discussed in Chapter 3 at [3.65]-[3.66] and Chapter 19 at [19.102]-[19.104].
155 See further Chapter 12, below; and Crock, above n 145, Ch 13.
156 See, for example, The ABC News (Australia), 'Asylum Seeker Situation "An Absolute Mess"', 9 January 2010, available at <http://www.abc.net.au/news/stories/2010/01/09/2788842.htm?section=justin>. On this point, see Mary Crock and Daniel Ghezelbash, 'Do Loose Lips Bring Ships? The Role of Policy, Politics and Human Rights in Managing Unauthorised Boat Arrivals' (2010) 19 *Griffith Law Review* 238.
157 See, for example, Xinhua (Chinese National News Service), 'Australia Abandons Offshore Refugee Processing: Opposition', 23 December 2009, available at <http://news.xinhuanet.com/english/2009-12/23/content_12694229.htm>.
158 *First Optional Protocol to the ICCPR* (adopted 16 December 1966, entered into force 23 March 1976) 999 UNTS 302. Australia has acceded to a similar mechanism under CAT. See *Optional Protocol to the Convention against Torture and Other Cruel, Inhuman or Degrading Treatment or Punishment* (adopted 18 December 2002, entered into force 22 June 2006) GA Resolution A/RES/57/199 of 9 January 2003. Article 14 of CERD also establishes an individual complaints mechanism.
159 See Nicholas Poynder, 'Human Rights: A v Australia: Views of the UN Human Rights Committee dated 30 April 1997' (1997) 22(3) *Alternative Law Journal* 149; and Nicholas Poynder, 'A (name deleted) v Australia: A Milestone for Asylum Seekers' (1997) 4(1) *Australian Journal of Human Rights* 155.

Australia is party to a range of other human rights treaties that involve supervising committees to which individuals can lodge complaints alleging breaches of human rights protected by the various treaties.[160] These include Committees established under CERD, the CRC, as well as the newest of the Conventions, the Convention on the Rights of Persons with Disabilities (CRPD).[161] Australia's ratification of the Optional Protocol[162] to this most recent Convention may well result in the lodging of complaints against Australia – most notably in the context of the laws and policies restricting the grant of visas to disabled persons who (typically) fail to meet the 'health' requirements for migrant visas.[163] For the most part, however, complaints involving challenges to Australia's immigration laws, policies and practices have been made under the first two of these treaties: the ICCPR and the CAT.

[4.70] As of July 2007 the Human Rights Committee and the Committee Against Torture had made decisions (or issued 'opinions') in 51 complaints made against Australia (out of a total of 64).[164] Fourteen of the complaints were upheld, with a number of the recommendations made including suggestions that Australia pay compensation to the offended parties. Of 19 concerning migrants, eight involved claims made under the CAT (two being upheld[165]), while the balance alleged breaches of the ICCPR. Of these, six involved complaints alleging arbitrary detention and/or cruel and inhuman treatment of both adults and children held in immigration detention. All were upheld.[166] Other areas of contention have related to the deportation of very long-term permanent residents convicted of serious crimes and the denial of family life that this involves[167] – particularly in instan-

---

160   For an account of the operation of these committees, see Triggs, above n 11, at 946ff.
161   *Convention on the Rights of Persons with Disabilities* (adopted 13 December 2006, entered into force 3 May 2008) A/61/611. On the operation of the CRPD, see Marianne Schulze, *Understanding the UN Convention on the Rights of Persons with Disabilities: A Handbook on the Human Rights of Persons with Disabilities* (2009) available at <http://www.makingitwork-crpd.org/resource-library/crpd>.
162   Australia signed the CRPD on 30 March 2007, ratifying the Convention on 17 July 2008 and the Protocol on 21 August 2008.
163   The likelihood of such future complaints led to the establishment of a Senate inquiry into the health rules in immigration in late 2009. See Joint Standing Committee on Migration, 'Inquiry into the Migration Treatment of Disability' at <http://www.aph.gov.au/house/committee/mig/disability/index.htm>. See also Ben Saul, 'Migrating to Australia with Disabilities: Non-discrimination and the Convention on the Rights of Persons with Disabilities' (2010) 16 *Australian Journal of Human Rights* 63.
164   The jurisprudence of the Committees is available at <http://tb.ohchr.org/default.aspx>.
165   See A K v Australia, Communication No 148/1999: Australia, CAT/C/32/D/148/1999 (11 May 2004); and Sadiq Shek Elmi v Australia, Communication No 120/1998: Australia, CAT/C/22/D/120/1998 (25 May 1999).
166   Danyal Shafiq v Australia, Communication No 1324/2004: Australia, CCPR/C/88/D/1324/2004 (13 November 2006); Applicants D and E v Australia, Communication No 1050/2002: Australia CCPR/C/87/D/1050/2002 (9 August 2006); Ali Aqsar Bakhtiyari and Roqaiha Bakhtiyari v Australia, Communication No 1069/2002: Australia, CCPR/C/79/D/1069/2002 (6 November 2003); Baban v Australia, Communication No 1014/2001: Australia, CCPR/C/78/D/1014/2001 (18 September 2003); C v Australia, Communication No 900/1999: Australia, CCPR/C/76/D/900/1999 (13 November 2002); and A v Australia, Communication No 560/1993: Australia, CCPR/C/59/D/560/1993 (30 April 1997).
167   See, for example, Madafferi v Australia, Communication No 1011/2001: Australia, CCPR/C/81/D/1011/2001 (26 August 2004).

ces where children are involved who have been raised in Australia.[168] Australia's policy of excluding persons on grounds of health has also been the subject of complaint.[169]

[4.71] In the context of the preceding discussion, one of the most significant of the cases decided by the Human Rights Committee was that of A v Australia.[170] This was the second complaint involving Australia processed through to final decision. It was brought by one of the Cambodians detained under the same legislative regime challenged in *Chu Kheng Lim*.[171] The failure of this litigation opened the way for a complaint to be lodged with the Human Rights Committee.[172] In A v Australia, the complainant's claims were upheld by the 18-member Human Rights Committee.

[4.72] Mr A, one of 26 Cambodians who arrived in Australia by boat in November 1989, was placed in detention in Broome, Sydney, Darwin and finally Port Hedland. He was not released until January 1994 when his wife was granted refugee status in Australia. Mr A claimed that the provisions requiring the detention upon arrival in Australia of all 'designated persons'[173] were contrary to Australia's obligations under Arts 9(1), 9(4) and 2(3) of the ICCPR. In simple terms, he alleged that the legislative regime allowed no scope for considering whether his detention for over four years was necessary or reasonable in the circumstances and that as a result his detention was 'arbitrary'. The restrictions placed on the judicial review of his detention[174] meant that he was denied his right to bring legal proceedings in a court to challenge his detention.[175]

[4.73] The Committee rejected Australia's argument that the law under challenge could not be considered 'arbitrary' because it was made in accordance with the parliamentary processes of a democratically elected government. The Committee held that, in considering whether a legislative regime is arbitrary, it will consider whether it includes elements of 'inappropriateness, injustice and lack of predictability'.[176] The Committee accepted that Art 9(1) of the ICCPR extended to people in immigration

---

168   See Winata v Australia, Communication No 930/2000: Australia, CCPR/C/72/D/930/2000 (16 August 2001).
169   See, for example, Y v Australia, Communication No 772/1997: Australia, CCPR/C/69/D/772/1997 (8 August 2000).
170   Communication No 560/1993: Australia, CCPR/C/59/D/560/1993 (30 April 1997).
171   (1992) 176 CLR 1.
172   It is a precondition of a communication that the author have exhausted all local remedies in her or his attempt to seek redress for a breach of the ICCPR. See Torkel Opsahl, 'The Human Rights Committee' in Philip Alston (ed), *The United Nations and Human Rights: A Critical Appraisal* (Oxford: Clarendon Press, New York: OUP, 1992); and Centre for Human Rights, *Civil and Political Rights: The Human Rights Committee*, Fact Sheet No 15 (Geneva: Centre for Human Rights, 1991). On the workings of the Committee and its history, see Dominic McGoldrick, *The Human Rights Committee* (Oxford: Clarendon Press, New York: OUP, 1991).
173   See then ss 177-178 of the *Migration Act 1958*.
174   See *Migration Act 1958*, s 183.
175   Mr A also sought a ruling that he was entitled to compensation under Art 9(5) of the ICCPR. Although this aspect of the complaint was ruled inadmissible by the Human Rights Committee in the preliminary stages of the complaint, the Committee nevertheless made a ruling on this point in its final ruling: see para 11 of the Committee's Assessment of the merits.
176   See Van Alphen v The Netherlands, Communication 305/1988: Netherlands.

detention.¹⁷⁷ It held that the Article should be read in conjunction with Art 31 of the Convention relating to the Status of Refugees and with conclusion 44 of the Executive Committee of the UNHCR. The effect of these provisions is to require states to detain asylum seekers only where such measures are necessary in order to determine a person's identity; or where a person represents a risk to national security.

[4.74] The Human Rights Committee does not have the power to enforce its decisions in any direct way. Rather, its efficacy is reliant on the state parties to the Convention respecting the decisions it makes or, at a more pragmatic level, paying heed to the opprobrium of other members of the international community if its rulings are ignored. The Australian government responded to the criticism levelled at it by passing laws to enable the release of specified groups from immigration detention.¹⁷⁸ However, the practice of mandatory detention did not change in any real sense. Subsequent complaints made about the detention regime have all been considered by the Human Rights Committee to confirm the original finding that Australia's regime involves 'arbitrary' detention. Interestingly the Coalition government appears to have stopped caring about adverse findings by either the Human Rights Committee or the Committee Against Torture. An adverse ruling by the Human Rights Committee¹⁷⁹ did not prevent the removal to Pakistan of the Bakhtiyari family in January 2005.¹⁸⁰ Nor did the ruling of the Committee Against Torture in the case of Sadiq Elmi¹⁸¹ prevent the eventual removal of that individual. As Charlesworth et al note, the Australian government appeared in 2006 to have adopted a no response, no publicity attitude to adverse UN Committee findings. It is a strategy that appears to have been more successful in burying the international criticisms than the former tactic of issuing strident rebuffs of the UN treaty bodies (including at one time threats to renounce accession to the Optional Protocols that allow for individual complaints to be made).¹⁸² For its part, the Labor government moved quickly to distance itself from its predecessor when elected in 2007.

4.5 How will Australia's approach to international law be viewed in time?

[4.75] The forces of globalisation in law as in everything else are inexorable. Just as the pressure has mounted for the United States to modify actions it has taken in

---

177 See Human Rights Committee, General Comment 8, Article 9 (Sixteenth session, 1982), HRI/GEN/1/Rev 1 at 8 (1994).

178 These included the elderly and children in whose best interests it was to order their release from detention. See further Chapter 16.2.4 below.

179 See Ali Aqsar Bakhtiyari and Roqaiha Bakhtiyari v Australia, Communication No 1069/2002: Australia, CCPR/C/79/D/1069/2002 (6 November 2003).

180 See 'Bakhtiyari Family has Left Australia', *The Age*, 30 December 2004, available at <http://www.theage.com.au/news/National/Bakhtiyaris-removal-underway/2004/12/30/1104344891430.html>.

181 See Sadiq Shek Elmi v Australia, Communication No 120/1998: Australia, CAT/C/22/D/120/1998 (25 May 1999). This case was the subject of a major Senate inquiry in 2000. See Senate Legal and Constitutional References Committee, *A Sanctuary Under Review: An Examination of Australia's Refugee and Humanitarian Determination Processes* (Canberra: 2000).

182 See Charlesworth et al, *No Country is an Island*, above n 1, at 85-91.

defiance of international law, so it became almost inevitable that Australia would be forced eventually to modify its harsh laws. In July 2008 Labor Minister Chris Evans outlined fundamental changes in the premises underlying immigration detention. He announced that thereafter detention would be based on seven key 'immigration values':

1. Mandatory detention is an essential component of strong border control.
2. To support the integrity of Australia's immigration program, three groups will be subject to mandatory detention:
   a. all unauthorised arrivals, for management of health, identity and security risks to the community
   b. unlawful non-citizens who present unacceptable risks to the community and
   c. unlawful non-citizens who have repeatedly refused to comply with their visa conditions.
3. Children, including juvenile foreign fishers and, where possible, their families, will not be detained in an immigration detention centre (IDC).
4. Detention that is indefinite or otherwise arbitrary is not acceptable and the length and conditions of detention, including the appropriateness of both the accommodation and the services provided, would be subject to regular review.
5. Detention in immigration detention centres is only to be used as a last resort and for the shortest practicable time.
6. People in detention will be treated fairly and reasonably within the law.
7. Conditions of detention will ensure the inherent dignity of the human person.[183]

[4.76] If this encouraged the hope that the egregious human rights abuses of Australia's immigration detention regime would indeed become things of the past, the continuing use and expansion of the detention centre on Christmas Island have served to dampen expectations of deep reform. Reports of abuses within the detention centres may have diminished. However, there are many aspects of the law that have not changed either fast enough or at all – as we explore further in the course of this book.

[4.77] As for the courts, it remains to be seen also whether the approach taken by the majority in cases such as *Al-Kateb* will stand the test of time. The High Court's great dissenter, Justice Michael Kirby, certainly did not think so. His Honour concluded his judgment in *Al-Kateb* with these words which convey a potent message for Australia as a nation:

> With every respect to those of a contrary view, opinions that seek to cut off contemporary Australian law (including constitutional law) from the persuasive force of international law are doomed to fail. They will be seen in the future much as the reasoning of Taney CJ in *Dred Scott v Sandford*, Black J in *Korematsu* and Starke J in *Ex parte Walsh* are now viewed: with a mixture of curiosity and embarrassment. The dissents of McLean J and Curtis J in *Dred Scott* strongly invoked international law to support the proposition that the appellant was not a slave but a free man. Had the interpretive principle prevailed at that time, the United States Supreme Court might have been saved a serious error of constitutional reasoning; and much injustice, indifference to human indignity and later suffering might have

---

183   See Senator Evans, above n 150.

been avoided. The fact is that it is often helpful for national judges to check their own constitutional thinking against principles expressing the rules of a 'wider civilization'.[184]

---

[184] *Al-Kateb* (2004) 219 CLR 562 at 629.

5

The Administration of Migration Law and Policy

5.1 The changing face of immigration decision-making

[5.01] The story of the administration of immigration to Australia is one that has always been linked closely to the big questions of national identity and the distribution of powers between the various arms of government: executive, legislative and judicial. In 2001, this was illustrated vividly in then Prime Minister Howard's vehement rejection of assertions that asylum seekers might have a *right* to enter Australia in order to seek protection as refugees. When the Prime Minister stated that '*We* will determine who enters this country and on what terms', it was plain that his use of the collective noun *we* was a reference to himself and to the Ministers of his (executive arm of) government – and not the Australian courts. Indeed, one of the enduring fascinations of immigration as an area of law has been the struggle that has occurred within the branches of government over who should have the final say in the definition and administration of government policy.[1]

[5.02] In this chapter, three distinct phases are identified in the recent administrative history of immigration to Australia. The first occurred after the Second World War with the break down and eventual abandonment of the White Australia Policy. These were also years of great change in the general relationship between citizen and state in Australia, with a marked push for more accountability within the administration. The post-war era has been described as the 'sunrise' years for administrative law in Australia.[2] The beginning of the second phase was marked by the move in 1989 to replace broad administrative discretions with a rigid regulatory regime. This period saw the transformation of the once modest *Migration Act 1958* (Cth) into a

---

1   In this respect immigration has represented in microcosm broader debates over whether the federal government should be subject to a Bill of Rights. See Michael McHugh speaking at a NSW Bar Association forum, 'Does Australia Need a Bill of Rights?', available at <http://www.nswbar.asn.au/docs/resources/lectures/bill_rights.pdf>. See also Julian Burnside QC speaking at the 2004 Australian Lawyers Alliance national conference, reported in Ian Munro, 'Bill of Rights Needed Now, Says QC' *The Age*, 22 October 2004, available at <http://www.theage.com.au/articles/2004/10/21/1098316788936.html>.
2   See Australian Institute of Administrative Law (National Administrative Law Forums) publication: Lindsay Curtis, 'The Vision Splendid: A Time for Re-Appraisal' in Robin Creyke and John McMillan (eds), *The Kerr Vision: At the Twenty-Five Year Mark* (Canberra: Centre for International and Public Law (CIPL), ANU,1998) 36.

much more substantial document. This Act, together with its attendant Regulations, grew subsequently to a point where it rivalled the nation's taxation and social security laws. In more recent years, this 'codified' system has been altered again by a tendency to privatise and outsource many of the administrative functions that used to be performed by public servants employed within the immigration bureaucracy. The trend has been described as the era of the new 'contractualism'.[3]

[5.03] Throughout the three phases, a major impetus for change has been the emergence of the judiciary as a (sometimes dissenting) force in the interpretation and enforcement of legal principle. Indeed, it will be argued that moves to outsource decision-making owe much to a desire in the executive government to re-assert absolute control over immigration decision-making – with commercial contracts used to achieve outcomes that could not be achieved through the public service bureaucracy. Whether these trends have actually delivered better portfolio administration, however, is debatable. As we explore in Part 5.5, the immigration administration in recent years has been plagued by what can only be described as a series of disastrous system failures, intermixed with allegations of misuse of public office and poor 'culture' within the administration itself. The chapter concludes by considering the professionals who stand beside aspiring migrants in their interactions with the immigration bureaucracy. Examining the ethical rules binding lawyers and migration agents, we provide a brief account of the regulation of the migration advice industry in Australia.

5.2   The first revolution: Post-war policy and administration

[5.04] The Second World War and the influx of post-war migrants with their rich and diverse cultural heritage wrought changes in the social fabric and outlook of the Australian society that were reflected inevitably in the country's migration program. Although the White Australia Policy was not formally abolished until 1973, the 1960s saw a gradual relaxation of the restrictions placed on non-European migration.[4] The changes had begun with non-European citizens who had been working in Australia for many years as businessmen and women. The desire by ex-servicemen to bring home their Asian wives led to further concessions allowing the admission of non-European spouses and immediate family members. By 1966, a limited number of people of 'mixed descent' was being accepted also on the basis of special skills or special circumstances. In that year, Minister Opperman estimated that some 15,000 people meeting this description had been settled in Australia in the previous 20 years.[5] The ensuing years saw a slow but steady rise in the intake of non-European people. Campbell and Whitmore note that 39,672 people of non-European origin were admitted as migrants between 1966 and 1971. Of the

---

3   Jonathan Boston, *The State Under Contract* (Wellington: Bridget Willams Books, 1995).
4   See SBS, *Immigration Nation: The Secret History of Us* (Renegade Films, 2011).
5   See Henry P Opperman, *Australia's Immigration Policy* (Canberra: AGPS, 1966) at 12; and Anthony C Palfreeman, 'The White Australia Policy' in Frank S Stevens (ed), *Racism: The Australian Experience*, Volume 1: *Prejudice and Xenophobia* (Sydney: Australian and New Zealand Book Co, 1971) at 141-2.

170,011 people admitted in 1970-71, 9066 were of non-European or mixed descent.[6] Over this period, public debate about the merits of the White Australia Policy also increased.[7]

[5.05] The move to a non-racial immigration policy was probably inevitable. However, this fact does not diminish the act of leadership shown by Prime Minister Whitlam when he announced in parliament:[8]

> [W]e have an obligation to remove methodically from Australia's laws and practices all racially discriminatory provisions and from international activities any hint or suggestion that we favour policies, decrees or resolutions that seek to differentiate on the basis of the colour of their skin. As an island nation of predominantly European inhabitants situated on the edge of Asia, we cannot afford the stigma of racialism.

[5.06] The decision to abolish the White Australia Policy came 11 years after Canada had abandoned its racially based immigration policies, and seven years after the United States had moved to ensure non-racial selection procedures in its immigration program.[9]

[5.07] The push for a more ordered style of public administration in the field of migration also gained momentum in the late 1960s and early 1970s. The passage of the *Migration Act* had seen the abolition of the dictation test used since Federation as a device to exclude unwanted immigrants.[10] The legislation had gone some way towards codifying decision-making by setting out the Minister's powers. However, it still gave no indication of how discretions would be exercised in individual cases. The day-to-day administration of the Act was governed by circulars produced within the Department that were not generally available to the public. Anecdotal accounts of migration in the 1960s[11] suggest that procedures were well-articulated in some areas and virtually non-existent in others.

[5.08] In choosing between applicants, more attention seems to have been given to a person's physical appearance than to factors such as qualifications, relationship to Australian parties or hardship. There can be little dispute that the unwritten selection

---

6   See Enid Campbell and Harry Whitmore, *Freedom In Australia* (Sydney: Sydney University Press, 1973) at 185; Department of Immigration (1966-1972), *Australian Immigration: Quarterly Statistical Summary* (Canberra: AGPS) Vols 1-26; and P Pyne and Charles A Price, 'Selected Tables on Australian Immigration 1947-78, with Commentary' in *Australian Immigration: A Bibliography and Digest* No 4, 1979 and Supplement, 1981 (Canberra: Department of Demography, Institute of Advanced studies, Australian National University).
7   See, for example, Herbert I London, *Non-White Immigration and the White Australia Policy* (Sydney: Sydney University Press, 1970); and Ken Rivett (ed), *Immigration: Control or Colour Bar?* (Melbourne: Melbourne University Press, 1962).
8   Commonwealth Parliamentary Debates, *Hansard*, House of Representatives, Vol 84, 24 May 1973 at 2649.
9   See Freda Hawkins, *Critical Years in Immigration: Australia and Canada Compared* (Kingston: McGill-Queens University Press, 1988) at 94.
10 See above, Chapter 2.3.1.
11 See David A Martin (ed),*The New Asylum Seekers: Refugee Law in the 1980s* (Dordrecht: Martinus Nijhoff Publishers, 1988) at 91-5. The authors are indebted also to Mr Norman Hoffman who was employed continuously with the Department for over 30 years from January 1960. Interview with Mary Crock, 11 December 1989.

criteria were directed at screening out coloured people and were anti-Semitic.[12] There was no real system of internal review by senior departmental members. The work of individual officers appears to have been based on highly subjective considerations with little official direction or supervision.

[5.09] The Department began the 1970s with an unenviable reputation for arbitrary and, at times, overtly political, decision-making. When he took office in 1972, Prime Minister Whitlam described the Department as 'racist, sexist, narrow and hidebound'.[13] While that reputation persisted to some extent, the 1970s saw the introduction of successive measures designed to improve internal procedures and the public image of the agency.

[5.10] The first changes within the Department occurred in the early 1970s after the election of the Whitlam government. Minister Al Grassby oversaw the initial changes brought about by the abolition of the White Australia Policy. After Grassby's failure to be re-elected in 1974 (and the threats made against him[14]), Whitlam's ministers were reputedly less than keen to assume responsibility for the immigration portfolio. In the result, the Prime Minister ordered that the Department be dismantled. As Hawkins notes,[15] it was reconstituted as the Department of Labour and Immigration and the settlement, ethnic affairs, English language and passports contingents were hived off to other bureaucracies.

[5.11] This reorganisation was accompanied by the setting up of a departmental taskforce to review internal procedures. The result was the development of more complex forms and procedures and the institution of a rudimentary objective test which provided more guidance as to the qualities sought in prospective migrants.

[5.12] The new system was known as the Structured Selection Assessment System. Hawkins describes it as a 'half-way house', giving officers some objective standards to apply, but requiring them also to make a subjective assessment of an applicant's worth. Officers had to complete a two-part interview report in which grades were given for 'economic' factors and for 'personal and social' factors. The 'personal and social' factors included attitude to migration, expectations, responsiveness, initiative, self-reliance and independence; presentation (appearance, personal hygiene, speech and behaviour); family unity; community, sport and cultural interests; and past convictions, if any. Applicants were assessed on a scale that ranged from 'very good', through 'good', 'adequate', 'barely adequate' to 'not favourable'.[16]

---

12 See Paul Bartrop, *Australia and the Holocaust 1933-45* (Melbourne: Scholarly Publishing, 1994); Al Grassby, *The Tyranny of Prejudice* (Melbourne: AE Press, 1984) at 48-9; John Pilger, *A Secret Country* (London: Cape Publishing, 1992) at 104-8; and Department of Immigration (1970), 'Australia's Immigration Policies' *Immigration Reference Paper* (Canberra: AGPS, July 1970) at 6.
13 See Hawkins, above n 9, at 101; and Mr Clyde Holding MP Commonwealth Parliamentary Debates, *Hansard*, House of Representatives, 1 June 1989 at 3447-8.
14 See Grassby, above n 12, at 45.
15 Hawkins, above n 9, at 108-10.
16 See ibid at 106. Hawkins's comments correspond with those made by Mr Norman Hoffman at his interview with the author on 11 December 1989.

[5.13] After the defeat of the Whitlam government in 1975, the old structure of the Department was restored, but the movement towards reform continued. In August 1977, a new permanent head was appointed to the Department in the person of LWB Engledow. Hawkins describes the initiatives put in place by the new Secretary to 'weld the Department together into an effective organisation' and to 'revitalise it'.[17] These included the establishment in November 1977 of a Joint Management Review to examine most aspects of the Department's functions and management except for Australia's basic immigration and refugee policies. The committee was chaired by an external consultant engaged by the Public Service Board and included a senior official from the Department, a staff member from the Public Service Board and a Canadian immigration official on a two-year exchange visit. The appointment of this task force may have been the first example of the 'new administrative law' beginning to bite.

[5.14] The fact that the Department had been operating somewhat as a 'law unto itself' was born out in the general absence of published policies and guidelines setting out how decisions were to be made. This was a source of immediate difficulty when external review bodies were established with the brief of reviewing departmental rulings. In one of the first immigration cases to be considered by the Administrative Appeals Tribunal (AAT),[18] counsel for the Minister was asked to provide written evidence of the Minister's policy concerning the deportation of permanent residents convicted of serious criminal offences. The only published material that counsel was able to produce for the tribunal were two press statements dated 21 December 1960 and 19 January 1961 respectively. AAT President Brennan J made it clear that tribunal members were willing and, indeed, anxious, to give effect to government policy. However, he pointed out that they could only do so if the Minister made his policy public. His Honour held that a letter from the Minister's solicitor setting out the 'real' policy allegedly used by the Minister was insufficient in this regard.[19] The direct response of the Minister to *Re Becker* was the policy on criminal deportation dated 28 March 1978. Given the embarrassment this case must have caused the administration, it is not unreasonable to surmise that the incident encouraged the new Secretary to pursue his reforms with more zeal than might otherwise have been the case.

[5.15] The Joint Management Review presented its report, *Immigration Functions Related to Control and Entry*, in July 1978. The report criticised the Act for its 'excessive discretionary features' and noted the absence of a formal base for policy, or any policy at all except in relation to the most simple issues. It also identified the departmental officers' failure to adhere to policy as a major problem. The results, it found, were confusion in the community and uncertainty within the Department concerning the objectives, roles and priorities of the government's immigration policies and the extent to which provisions of the legislation were to be enforced.

[5.16] Mr Engledow's efforts to reform the administration of the Department led to the creation of a review section within the Department so as to improve the quality of primary decision-making. The review branch was established at the end of 1977

---

17 Hawkins, above n 9, at 120-4.
18 See *Re Becker and MIEA* (1977) 1 ALD 158.
19 Ibid at 163-5.

to deal with appeals to the AAT. It began operations in January 1979 and grew from there as the external review of migration decisions increased.[20] The drive to have policies made more explicit saw the first statement on the determination of refugee status for applicants in Australia in 1977.[21] By 1979, the old Structured Selection Assessment System had been replaced by a 'points' test for the selection of migrants that closely resembled a model developed in Canada. The 'Numerical Multifactor Assessment System', or NUMAS as it was known, increased the objectivity of decision-making. It made public both the criteria to be used in selecting migrants and the priority to be given to certain characteristics such as family relationship, age, skills and qualifications. As Hawkins notes,[22] NUMAS itself was examined in 1981 by the Committee of Review of Migration Assessment and replaced with a test that was gentler on family reunion applicants. The procedural improvements accompanying the articulation of selection criteria included the drafting of clearer forms and precedents for both public and departmental use.[23]

5.2.1 External scrutiny of migration decision-making

[5.17] The 1970s and 1980s saw other moves that contributed equally to the opening-up of migration decision-making. Public awareness of the Department's aims and functions was fostered by the publication of annual reports in accordance with the requirements of the *Public Service Act 1922* (Cth), s 15. In 1977 and 1982 respectively, two non-statutory bodies were established to review particular migration decisions and to make recommendations to the Minister. One was the Determination of Refugee Status (DORS) Committee. The other was the system of Immigration Review Panels. The DORS Committee was set up to both advise the Minister on the grant of refugee status and to reconsider cases where refugee status had been refused. The Immigration Review Panels were created to review (generally on paper) limited classes of migration decisions.

[5.18] The reforms within the Department during the 1970s and 1980s were part of a more general movement favouring change in the system of public administration and review. The Commonwealth Administrative Review Committee (the Kerr Committee) was established on 29 October 1968 and reported in August 1971. The recommendations of this committee and of other committees on prerogative writ procedures (the Ellicott committee) and on administrative discretions (the Bland committee) provided a framework for a legislative package that changed the whole culture within the public service.

[5.19] Outside the Department, the Ombudsman and the Human Rights Commission were given authority to investigate complaints of maladministration and breaches of human rights respectively. Freedom of information legislation was introduced in 1982, ensuring within the bureaucracy a new accountability to the public. The *Freedom of Information Act 1982* (Cth) enabled applicants for the first time

---

20 See the Department's *Review '78*, at 39; *Review '79*, at 67; and *Review '82*, at 74-6.
21 See the Department's *Review '78*, at 28.
22 Hawkins, above n 9, at 142-6.
23 See the Department's *Review '78*, at 13.

to access their personal file within the Department.[24] As importantly, the Department was required under s 9 to make available to the public the 'internal law' contained in its manuals and policy circulars.[25] The package of administrative law reforms was completed by the establishment of the Federal Court and by the passage of the *Administrative Decisions (Judicial Review) Act 1977* (Cth) *(ADJR Act)* which simplified the law and procedures governing judicial review. For the first time, the review of migration decisions became a real and viable option for disgruntled applicants. The result was a sharp increase in the number of migration cases brought before the courts. In all the circumstances, it was probably inevitable that the courts would eventually adopt a more interventionist approach to the decisions under review.

[5.20] The changes within the Department during the 1980s did not satisfy the demands for reform from outside of the government and its bureaucracy. In 1985, two major reports on the operation of the Act were released.[26]

Together, the two reports offered a comprehensive critique of migration decision-making and review in the mid-1980s. In spite of the amendments made to the Act in 1979 and 1980, the reports found many of the same shortcomings in the migration system as were apparent to the Joint Management Review in 1978. For example, the reports complained of the breadth of the discretions conferred by the Act, and of the absence of binding criteria for making decisions. They noted the potential this created for arbitrary decision-making and influence peddling with the Minister.[27] Again, the reports recommended that immediate moves be made to replace the Act with legislation providing clear criteria for departmental officers.[28] Both stressed the need to institute a proper system for reviewing cases on their merits.[29] On the specific issue of the form the review system should take, the Administrative Review Council (ARC) recommended the abolition of the Immigration Review Panels and the Commissioners appointed under s 14 (now s 203) of the Act.[30] In their place it suggested a two-tier system comprising immigration adjudicators at first instance, followed by the AAT.

[5.21] No immediate attempt was made to implement the recommendations made by the ARC. Instead, after the federal election in 1987, the government established the Committee to Advise on Australia's Immigration Policies (CAAIP).[31] The CAAIP

---

24   See *Freedom of Information Act 1982*, ss 11 and 18.
25   See generally Peter Bayne, *Freedom of Information* (Sydney: Law Book Co, 1984).
26   See Administrative Review Council (ARC), *Report No 25: Review of Migration Decisions* (Canberra: AGPS, 1985); Human Rights Commission, *Report No 13: Human Rights and the Migration Act* (Canberra: AGPS, 1985); Commonwealth Parliamentary Debates *Hansard*, House of Representatives, Vol 109, 7 June 1978 at 3159; and Sean Cooney, *The Transformation of Migration Law* (Melbourne: BIPR, 1995) at 18-21.
27   See Human Rights Commission, above n 26, at [197] and [316]; and ARC, above n 26, at [81]-[82], [120]-[121].
28   See Human Rights Commission, above n 26, at [294]-[305] and ARC, above n 26, at [138]-[157], respectively.
29   See Human Rights Commission, above n 26, at [306]-[318] and ARC, above n 26, at [92], [122]-[133] and [173]-[180] respectively.
30   See Human Rights Commission, above n 26, at [173]-[180], [191]-[199] and [200]-[210].
31   See Committee to Advise on Australia's Immigration Policies, *Report: Immigration A Commitment to Australia* 3 Vols (Canberra: AGPS, 1988) (CAAIP Report).

Report (1988) contained many recommendations similar to those made by the ARC, including those relating to the review of migration decisions. CAAIP recommended a two-tiered appeals system constituted by an internal departmental review unit and the AAT at second instance.[32] It also proposed a Model Bill to replace the Act.[33]

[5.22] One of the more interesting features of the Model Bill was the attempt to build a mechanism for rule-based decision-making that would allow some flexibility to deal with the hard cases. This was to be achieved by creating rules which specified three kinds of criteria: essential, or mandatory, criteria; procedural criteria detailing how decisions should be approached; and what were described as the 'objectives' of a set of criteria. This was intended to permit decision-makers some latitude to deal with cases that did not meet all of the mandatory criteria for a decision, and yet came within the stated objectives of a regulation.[34] This rather novel blueprint for flexible rule-making was rejected in favour of a much tighter regulatory system. The concept of new legislation was abandoned in favour of amending the existing Act.

[5.23] In addition to these systemic reviews and overhauls, the immigration portfolio has been subjected since that time to scrutiny from a variety of sources outside the Department. The creation of a Joint Standing Committee on Migration Regulations on 17 May 1990 (later the Joint Standing Committee on Migration) allowed parliament and politicians from the major political parties to make a formal contribution to the formulation and assessment of policies. This committee's terms of reference are to inquire into and report on changes made or proposed to be made to migration legislation or any other matter referred by the Minister. It has prepared many reports on subjects as varied as illegal migration;[35] refugees and humanitarian migration;[36] the health rules affecting migrants;[37] skilled migration;[38] the appointments process for membership of the Immigration Review Tribunal;[39] the Migration Agents Registration Scheme;[40] the migration treatment of disability;[41] and the management of immigration detention centres (various).[42] In most instances, the reports have resulted in changes being made to the legislative provisions (if any) under inquiry. From time to time other parliamentary committees have been convened to inquire into particular matters. Examples include the committee convened to inquire into the so-called 'children overboard affair' and the sinking of the un-named suspected illegal entry vessel known as 'SIEV X': the Select Committee for an inquiry into a

---

32   See ibid, Vol 1, at 115.
33   See ibid, Vol 3.
34   See cll 17 and 84.
35   *Illegal Entrants in Australia: Balancing Control and Compassion* (Canberra: AGPS, September 1990).
36   *Australia's Refugee and Humanitarian System: Achieving a Balance Between Refuge and Control* (Canberra: AGPS, August 1992).
37   *Conditional Migrant Entry: The Health Rules* (Canberra: AGPS, December 1992).
38   *Review of Skilled Migration* (Canberra: AGPS, March 2004).
39   *The Immigration Review Tribunal Appointments Process* (Canberra: AGPS, December 1994).
40   *Protecting the Vulnerable? The Migration Agents Registration Scheme* (Canberra: AGPS, May 1995). On this point, see further Part 5.6 below.
41   *Inquiry into Migration Treatment of Disability* (Canberra: AGPS, June 2010).
42   For a full list of the committee's inquiries and reports, see <http://www.aph.gov.au/house/committee/mig/reports.htm>.

certain maritime incident;[43] and the Senate Select Committee on Ministerial Discretion in Migration Matters.[44]

[5.24] The administration of the immigration portfolio in Australia seems to attract an almost constant stream of inquiries. Barely a year has passed without reports from committees established both within the parliamentary system and outside. Reports have been prepared on the operation of the system for review of migration decisions[45] and on Australia's treatment of refugees and asylum seekers.[46] Endless inquiries have been conducted into the economic impact of immigration and on what Australia should be doing to attract more business people and skilled migrants.[47] The content of relevant reports is discussed where appropriate throughout the book.

5.2.2 Curial review as an agent of change

[5.25] In spite of the proliferation of formal inquiries, it is arguable that the most influential of the 'external' agents for change have been the courts in the judicial review of migration decisions. By the early 1970s, the courts' attitudes to executive power were changing. Old distinctions between 'judicial' and 'executive' power,[48] and between 'rights' and 'privileges' in people affected by an exercise of power, had begun to be broken down.[49] In many ways, the *ADJR Act* improved access to the law by simplifying procedures and codifying the remedies.[50] With the judiciary becoming more attuned to the idea of accountability in administrative decision-making, the impact of the legislation was great, nonetheless. Easy access to the Federal Court encouraged litigation. More importantly, judicial review proved to be a very effective weapon for disgruntled migrant applicants. Unlike the other avenues of appeal or review available which were universally recommendatory in their function, the Federal Court had the power to intervene directly in the decision-making process.

---

43   See <http://www.aph.gov.au/senate/committee/maritime_incident_ctte/index.htm>, discussed above, Chapter 4 at [4.50]ff.

44   See <http://www.aph.gov.au/Senate/committee/minmig_ctte/index.htm>; and the discussion below Part 5.5.

45   See Committee for the Review of the System for Review of Migration Decisions, *Report* (Canberra: AGPS, 1992) and *Migration Legislation Amendment Act (No 5) 1995* (Cth).

46   See National Population Council, *The National Population Council's Refugee Review* (Canberra: AGPS, July 1991); *Inquiry into the Circumstances of the Immigration Detention of Cornelia Rau* (July 2005) available at <www.minister.immi.gov.au/media_releases/media05/palmer-report.pdf> (the Palmer Report); Commonwealth Ombudsman, *Inquiry into the Circumstances of the Vivian Alvarez Matter* (Report 03-2005) available at <www.immi.gov.au/media/publications/pdf/alvarez_report03.pdf> (Comrie Report). Both reports are discussed in Part 5.5 below.

47   See the Joint Committee of Public Accounts investigation (Canberra: AGPS, 1991) and Business Skills Panel reports on the business migration program; and reports following inquiries into temporary and permanent skilled migration: see Committee of Inquiry into the Temporary Entry of Business People and Highly Skilled Specialists (1995) (the Roach Report); and Committee of Review of the Employer Nomination Scheme and Labour Agreements (1997) (the Lin Report).

48   See *Ridge v Baldwin* [1964] AC 40, accepted by the Australian High Court in *Banks v Transport Regulation Board (Vic)* (1968) 119 CLR 222.

49   See *Banks v Transport Regulation Board (Vic)* (1968) 119 CLR 222 and Mark Aronson, Bruce Dyer and Matthew Groves, *Judicial Review of Administrative Action* (Sydney: Law Book Co, 4th ed, 2009) at [12.150].

50   See *ADJR Act*, ss 5, 6, 7 and 16; and David Bennett, 'The Assimilation of Judicial Review to Review on the Merits' (1989) 58 *Canberra Bulletin of Public Administration* 94 at 94-7.

It could order a stay of deportation and decisions that were found to be ultra vires could be remitted to the decision-maker to be decided in accordance with the law.

[5.26] Traditionally, the courts had read broad legislative discretions as a parliamentary directive to hold back from reviewing decisions made in the exercise of such powers. Throughout the 1970s and 1980s judicial attitudes to apparently unfettered powers turned the notion of ministerial accountability on its head. Instead of seeing such provisions as a way of empowering the Minister, the courts began to see such legislation as an indication of the breadth of the Minister's responsibility to decide cases in accordance with all relevant considerations. The change in approach increased greatly the scope for judicial intervention. Almost any fault of omission or commission in the decision-making process became a ground for arguing that an error of law had been made. In some instances, the rulings of the Federal Court made it virtually impossible to distinguish between the judges' purported application of the rule of law from a simple review of cases on their merits.

[5.27] The problems caused by the old discretionary system are illustrated by two cases from the 1980s in which the Federal Court struck down decisions made in exercise of the supposedly unfettered statutory power to grant an entry permit. The first involved a group of American singers called 'the Platters' who sought temporary entry for the purpose of conducting a concert tour. In *Conyngham v MIEA*,[51] the Platters brought an action in the Federal Court in conjunction with their sponsor, when their applications for temporary visas were refused. They claimed that the Minister had breached the rules of natural justice by accepting the recommendations of a special committee without giving the group and their sponsor an opportunity to counter adverse statements made about them. The Committee was the National Disputes Committee for Australian Actors and Artists, set up to arbitrate complaints by Actors Equity which protects the interests of local actors and artists. Wilcox J found that the refusal to grant the visas was rendered unlawful by the Minister's failure to consider relevant policy guidelines.[52]

[5.28] An example of (perceived) judicial insensitivity to the plight of the administrator is the ruling of Einfeld J in *Ebrahimi v MIEA*.[53] That case concerned a family of Afghan refugees who were denied visas on the basis that they failed to meet the criteria for entry on humanitarian or on other grounds. Einfeld J found the decision flawed because proper consideration had not been given to the applicant's case. He held that the breadth of the legislative discretion to admit people from overseas demanded that full and proper consideration be given to every matter relevant to the grant of a visa. What his Honour did not consider – indeed, he found that he was bound not to consider – were the conditions under which the primary decision-maker had been operating when making the ruling in question. Evidence before the judge suggested that the pressures on the official had been great.[54]

---

51 (1986) 68 ALR 423 (*Conyngham*).
52 See also *MIEA v Conyngham* (1986) 11 FCR 528 (FFC).
53 (1988) 15 ALD 360 (*Ebrahimi*).
54 Unreported, FCA, Einfeld J, 23 May 1988, at 15-16.

[5.29] The rulings in *Ebrahimi* and *Conyngham* caused consternation in bureaucratic circles because of the impossible standards the judges seem to have been setting for decision-makers. In this context, it is noteworthy that the standards of decision-making required of the harassed consular official in *Ebrahimi* were not adopted by the courts in other cases involving similar applications for review. If anything, later decisions confirmed the primacy of ministerial control of migration from overseas.[55] Having said this, there can be little doubt that some of the more interventionist of the Federal Court decisions in the late 1980s encouraged the government towards a system of more rigid legislative control.[56]

5.3 From discretion to codification

[5.30] In many respects, the legislative regime governing migration decision-making before December 1989 was defensive. Like the early *Immigration Restriction Act 1901* (Cth), the *Migration Act*[57] as it existed until 1989 was concerned more with limiting than facilitating entry into Australia. The legislation was dominated by provisions pertaining to the removal, deportation, arrest and detention of immigration outlaws. For example, it set out the consequences of entering Australia without an entry permit or visa before any mention was made of the Minister's power to grant either an entry permit or a visa: compare ss 5D and 6(2).

[5.31] The Act was also old-fashioned in so far as it operated as 'machinery' legislation: on its face it revealed little about how the government's immigration portfolio was administered. The statute merely conferred power on the Minister and/or the Department's 'officers' to grant entry permits (ss 6(2), 6B); grant, cancel or revoke temporary entry permits (s 7); or deport unlawful non-citizens (s 18) and other undesirables (ss 12-14). The policies governing the exercise of these (and other) powers were set out in 14 or so departmental manuals that were altered whenever the government so directed. There was no obligation to table the manuals in parliament or otherwise to submit the documents to parliamentary scrutiny.

[5.32] The Act as amended in 1989 retained (and indeed still retains) some of the features of machinery legislation in that the operation of the system can be gauged only by reading the Regulations accompanying the Act. However, the legislative package no longer merely facilitated the making of decisions: it governed every aspect of decision-making. The Act now sets out both general and highly specific regulation-making powers, ensuring that the Minister has close to absolute control of most aspects of the migration process.[58]

---

55   See, for example, *Hossain v MILGEA* (1991) 23 ALD 771. For a more recent case in which the High Court ruled that visa applicants overseas are entitled to procedural fairness, see *Saeed v MIAC* (2010) 267 ALR 204.
56   The academic who has argued this point most forcefully is Professor John McMillan. See John McMillan, 'The Courts vs The People: Have the Judges Gone Too Far?' Paper delivered to the Judicial Conference of Australia, Launceston Colloquium, 22 April 2002; and John McMillan, 'Judicial Constraint and Activism in Administrative Law' (2002) 30 *Federal Law Review* 335.
57   Unless noted otherwise, all references to section numbers are to the *Migration Act* (as amended).
58   See *Migration Act*, ss 29-43, 504-506.

[5.33] The most striking feature of the post-1989 system when compared with the earlier regime is the extent to which discretions are confined. The government's policy is no longer exclusively in the form of guidelines, but has been reduced into law through the medium of subordinate legislation. The Act, together with the Regulations, sets out exhaustively the steps that must be followed and the criteria that must be applied in order to make lawful migration decisions. Even the Minister's power to decide a case outside the rules set by the legislation is strictly confined. For example, the Act stipulates that applications for a visa must be made on the correct form, in accordance with the Regulations and accompanied by the correct fee. If the applicant meets the criteria set out in the Regulations, the legislation requires the grant of a visa. Should the applicant fall short of all the requirements, the visa cannot be granted. The Minister must not consider an invalid visa application: s 47(3). Strict time limits apply for the lodging of both applications for visas and requests to have adverse decisions reviewed. The tribunals are given no discretion to allow appeals to be heard out of time.[59]

[5.34] The policies regarding the interpretation of the Act and the Regulations are set out in the Procedures Advice Manuals (PAMs) and the Migration Series Instructions (MSIs) as well as in various Gazette Notices and Press Releases. Although the quality of the PAMs has varied over the years, these manuals are of critical importance to practitioners as they are relied on heavily by primary decision-makers and contain many useful shortcuts and cross-references.[60]

[5.35] Another feature that distinguishes the post-1989 regime from earlier models is the simplicity of the basic legal concepts governing entry and stay in Australia. In place of the old dual system of visas issued to persons overseas and entry permits granted within the country non-citizens now receive only one documentary authority to enter or remain: the visa. The legal status of non-citizens has also been simplified into a binomial system of lawful (visaed) non-citizens and unlawful non-citizens (or those without visas).[61] New Zealand citizens have lost their exempt status and are now granted temporary visas that operate nevertheless as authorities for New Zealand citizens to remain in Australia permanently.[62]

[5.36] The Act and the Regulations provide for many different classes of visas.[63] As well as setting out the criteria for the grant of each type of document, the legislation stipulates the grounds on which a person may move between categories of visa-holders or make successive applications.[64] Both primary decision-makers and the review authorities are bound by the Regulations and the reviewers must not purport to make a decision that is not authorised by the Act or Regulations.[65] The only residual discretion is the power given to the Minister to override a decision by the review bodies and to substitute a decision that is more favourable to the applicant.

---

59 See *Migration Act*, Part 8; and Chapters 18 and 19 of this book.
60 The documents are available electronically through the LEGEND.com product.
61 See Chapter 16.
62 See *Migration Act*, s 32; and *Migration Regulations 1994* (Cth), Sch 1, cl 1219; Sch 2, subclass 444.
63 See *Migration Act*, ss 31-38 of the Act; and *Migration Regulations*, Schs 1 and 2.
64 See *Migration Act*, ss 48 and 48A; and *Migration Regulations*, Sch 5 and reg 2.12.
65 See ss 349(4) (MRT) and 415(4) (RRT).

Before 1 September 1994, this discretion was limited severely by the fact that not all applicants had access to review,[66] and some applicants were precluded from making any application at all.[67] The Minister had no power to intervene in such cases. The procedural and other requirements attached to the exercise of the residual discretions ensured that the powers were used sparingly. The Minister could only intervene if satisfied that it was in the public interest. The decision and a statement of reasons had to be tabled in both houses of parliament within 15 sitting days.[68]

[5.37] The curtailment of discretion was seen most markedly in the regime for the enforcement of decisions. The Act and Regulations separated the assessment of applications for entry from the removal process. Removal was (and still is) mandatory for those who had exhausted their right to appeal an adverse decision.[69] Provision was (and still is) made for the seizure of assets to facilitate the recovery of the cost of deportation and detention: Div 10 of the Act.

5.3.1   The 1989 and 1993 Regulations

[5.38] Since the Act was amended in 1989, the government has experimented with different types of regulatory formats, generating a deal of confusion in the process. The transitional provisions ensure that superseded Regulations continue to apply to any decisions made during the currency of the repealed Regulations. The complexity engendered by the changes is illustrated by the move on one occasion to amend retrospectively Regulations that had already been repealed.[70]

[5.39] Of the three regulatory schemes, the greatest difference is between the 1989 model and that introduced in February 1993. The *Migration Regulations 1989* (Cth) (*1989 Regulations*) were organised around schedules containing key codes with alphanumeric symbols representing the criteria for each visa and entry permit. The schedules listed the major criteria for each permit, using the key codes and referring to additional criteria set out in the body of the Regulations. The system was complicated by the fact that the *1989 Regulations* also contained decisional criteria not referred to in the schedules.[71]

[5.40] In 1993, this regime was abandoned in favour of transferring the bulk of the information required for decision-making into the schedules. The *Migration Regulations 1993* (Cth) (*1993 Regulations*) left less material in the Regulations themselves. Instead, schedules to the Regulations dealt with each type of decision in turn, repeating the prerequisites in each case either directly or by reference to other schedules. The criteria for the grant of visas to 'primary persons' – the principal applicants – were set out in Sch 2. The criteria concerning visas for the applicant's dependants were set

---

66 See, for example, former s 120 of the *Migration Act*; and *Migration Review Regulations 1989* (Cth) (*Review Regulations 1989*), reg 21.
67 See, for example, *Migration Regulations 1989* (Cth) (*1989 Regulations*), regs 126-130.
68 See, for example, *Migration Act*; ss 351, 391 and 417.
69 See ibid, ss 14, 198; and Chapters 13 and 14 of this book.
70 See Statutory Rules No 88 of 1993 regarding 'prescribed non-citizens'.
71 See Michael Clothier and Mary Crock, 'Immigration Law' in Adrian Evans (ed), *Lawyers Practice Manual, Victoria* (Sydney: Law Book Co, 1994) Ch 14.4.

out in Sch 3. With some modifications, this model was maintained in the *Migration Regulations 1994* (Cth) (*Migration Regulations*) and has remained largely unchanged since that time.

5.3.2 The 1994 Regulations

[5.41] Under the present regulatory scheme, the Minister's power to grant a visa is predicated on the making of a 'valid' application for a visa,[72] as well as on the Minister being satisfied that all the criteria for the grant of the visa have been met under s 65. Section 31 of the Act provides that the *Migration Regulations* may both prescribe classes of visas and the criteria for the grant of visas in these classes. The Act provides also that the Regulations can prescribe the way in which an application for a visa is to be made. While the Act remains the source of power, the Regulations provide the mechanism of how that power is to be administered.

[5.42] The *Migration Regulations* consist of five parts dealing with the general administration and regulation of the migration system. This is followed by schedules, the most important of which deal with:

1.	Classes of visas and the requirements for making a valid visa application.
2.	Provisions with respect to the grant of *subclasses* of visas.
3.	Additional criteria applicable to unlawful non-citizens.
4.	Public interest criteria.
5.	Special return criteria.
5A. and 5B.	Evidentiary requirements for student visas (primary and secondary applicants)
6., 6A. and 6B.	General points test – Qualifications and points (old and new tests).
7.	Business skills points test – Attributes and points.
8.	Visa conditions.
9.	Special entry and clearance arrangements.
10.	Certain prescribed forms.
11. and 12.	Memoranda of Understanding between Australia and the Peoples' Republic of China regarding the resettlement in Australia of Sino-Vietnamese refugees who have been resident in China.

[5.43] The most important of these schedules are Schs 1 and 2. The first sets out the generic visa classes and is divided into three parts dealing in turn with permanent visas; temporary visas; and bridging visas. Schedule 1 also sets out the approved form to be used, the applicable fee, and where the application is to be made (outside or inside Australia; in immigration clearance). The Schedule also lists the particular subclasses that fall within a particular class of visa: reg 1.07(2).

---

72   The requirements for making a valid application have become increasingly precise (and complicated) over the years. In the *Migration Act*, see ss 46 (valid visa application); 46A (applications by 'offshore entry persons'); 46B (applications by 'transitory persons'); 48 (applications after cancellation of a visa); 91E (applicants who have access to a 'safe third country'); 91K (applications by holders of 'temporary safe haven' visas); 161 (applications by holders of criminal justice visas); 164D (applying for other visas); 195 (detainees); and 501E (effect of cancellation of visa on character grounds). See *Migration Regulations*, regs 2.07, 2.07A-2.07AK (valid applications, various visas); 2.08AB (application for visa- prescribed circumstances); 2.08AC (personal identifiers); and 2.12 (certain non-citizens whose visas are cancelled in Australia).

[5.44] The criteria prescribed for the grant of visas (referred to as 'subclasses' of visas) are contained in Sch 2: regs 2.02 and 2.03. The class/subclass arrangement means that a non-citizen can apply for a visa in a Sch 1 class, but must meet the criteria prescribed for one of the Sch 2 subclasses within the class. Where there is more than one subclass in a class, it is possible for an applicant to be considered for the grant of a visa against the criteria specified in each of the subclasses. This has the effect of moderating the otherwise strict requirement that applicants seek the correct visa using the correct application forms or lose their right to apply.[73] The class/subclass device is not as generous as the system that operated under the *1993 Regulations*. This had allowed applicants for family reunion to be considered against the criteria for preferential as well as concessional entry.[74]

[5.45] Each subclass in Sch 2 deals exhaustively with the circumstances in which a visa of that type can be granted either before or after entry into Australia. Common criteria such as those pertaining to health, public interest or illegal status are referred to through the device of key paragraph numbers. These link Sch 2 to separate schedules where the common criteria are spelt out. In this respect the *Migration Regulations 1994* are simpler to use than the 1989 version which split the common criteria between many different provisions.[75] Schedule 2 also sets out the conditions subject to which each visa subclass is granted. It does this by numerical cross-referencing to the conditions listed in Sch 8.

[5.46] Schedule 3 specifies extra criteria that certain unlawful non-citizens must meet in particular visas. Schedule 4 contains the public interest element of the visa criteria. It contains the health, character and security requirements that non-citizens must meet in order to be granted the visa. Schedule 5 contains criteria that are applicable only to visa applications lodged overseas by people who have previously been in Australia and who breached immigration law in some way. The effect of this Schedule is to effectively impose an exclusion period on people who have been removed from Australia.

[5.47] Schedules 6, 6A and 7 need to be examined in conjunction with ss 92-96 of the Act. The Act enables the Minister to assess a visa applicant by reference to a system of 'points' tests. These Schedules list certain qualifications and give a point value to them, allowing the applicant to achieve a certain score.

[5.48] The system is complicated slightly by the fact that the criteria governing the grant of some types of visas are set out in the Act rather than the Regulations. These are the transitional (permanent) and (temporary) visas created by the *Migration Reform (Transitional) Regulations 1994* (Cth); and the special visas set out in ss 32-37 of the Act which cover New Zealand citizens; ex-Australian citizens; long-term illegal migrants or 'absorbed persons'; refugees; bridging visas; and criminal justice visas.

---

73   See *Re Ramani* [1991] IRTA 147.
74   See *Migration Act*, former s 34; and *Buksh v MILGEA* (1991) 102 ALR 647 at 655.
75   For example, the health criteria are set out in *Migration Regulations*, Sch 4, cll 4005-4008. In the *1989 Regulations*, reference had to be made to Sch 1, H and H^1, reg 144. Public interest criteria are found now in Sch 4, cll 4001-4011. Previously they were split between Sch 1, D and E, regs 3A, 4, 9A and 143.

The criteria for the grant of the different visas and the more detailed operation of the regulatory regime provide the focus for much of the balance of this book.

[5.49] The final and, in some respects, most significant change that was made to the Act in 1994 was the creation of a special regime governing the judicial review of migration decisions. Part 8 of the Act set out when and on what grounds 'judicially reviewable' migration decisions could be scrutinised by the Federal Court. As well as limiting the range of applications that could be brought by disgruntled migrants in the Federal Court, the legislation excluded many of the more open-ended heads of review that had been so popular in cases brought under the *ADJR Act*. Provided a decision was one to which Part 8 of the Act applied, it was no longer possible to argue before the Federal Court that a migration decision is unlawful on grounds of unreasonableness, relevancy or denial of procedural fairness.

[5.50] Amendments to the Act in 2001 saw the repeal of the first Part 8 of the Act and its replacement with a comprehensive 'privative' clause regime that seems on its face to strip all courts of the power to review migration decisions. As explored below, the 2001 changes have since been interpreted by the Australian courts so as to preserve the power of the judiciary to review migration cases.

5.3.3 Judicial responses to the regulatory regime

[5.51] The codification of entry criteria in the Regulations changed the role played by the courts in reviewing migration decisions. In some respects, there was less room for judicial creativity in ruling on how a decision should be made. The fact that migration policy, as expressed in the Regulations, had undergone the scrutiny of parliament further reduced the legitimacy of wholesale judicial activism. At the same time, judges at all levels reacted to the harsh operation of the legislation. On the one hand, the courts have demonstrated a reluctance to uphold direct challenges to the regulatory regime as a whole. On the other, they have not shied away from holding the government to account when there has been a systemic failure to comply with the dictates of the legislative regime.

[5.52] The judiciary's reluctance to intervene after 1989 is well illustrated by an early case in which the validity of the *1989 Regulations* was brought into question. In *Eremin v MILGEA*,[76] a challenge was mounted to the entire regulatory regime, but in particular as it operated in compassionate cases.

[5.53] The difficulties inherent in challenging the validity of Regulations on the grounds of unreasonableness or inconsistency lie in the nature of the instruments involved. It is one thing to persuade a court that a decision-maker has acted unreasonably in exercising a discretion conferred by statute. It is quite another to show that the Governor-General and parliament were acting unreasonably in making or allowing a regulation. This is particularly so where there is no question of bad faith on the part of the legislators. The standard test for showing that delegated legislation is unreasonable is couched in language similar to that used when discussing

---

76 [1990] 21 ALD 69 (*Eremin*).

the reasonableness of an exercise of discretionary powers. In *Kruse v Johnson*, Lord Russell of Killowen CJ spoke of:[77]

> [Delegated laws that were] unequal in their operation ... manifestly unjust; ... disclos[ing] bad faith; ... [and involving] such oppressive or gratuitous interference with the rights of those subject to them as could find no justification in the minds of reasonable men.

[5.54] The courts' application of these principles, however, appears to be much more conservative in cases involving a challenge to delegated legislation than in cases where it is only the exercise of a statutory power that is in question. It is rare indeed to find cases in which the courts have been prepared to find Statutory Rules or Regulations unreasonable.[78] In the absence of some special circumstance, most judges appear to consider it inappropriate to intervene in relation to Regulations that have been a matter for the political judgment of a Minister and of the parliament.[79] The same reasoning seems to underlie the courts' reluctance to find delegated legislation invalid on the ground of inconsistency with a primary enactment. The assumption appears to be that, if there was no move to disallow a regulation, the regulation should be upheld as a proper expression of parliament's will.

[5.55] Eremin was a marine electrician on a Soviet merchant ship who sought refugee status when the ship docked in Sydney. He applied for various entry permits, including a permit under what was then reg 129 of the *1989 Regulations*. Such permits were available only to non-resident non-citizens who could demonstrate that they would suffer 'serious and lasting consequences' from an event occurring after their arrival in Australia, that had been 'gazetted' by the Minister. Eremin was refused refugee status. He failed to gain entry on humanitarian grounds because the event affecting him, namely the break-up of the Soviet Union and the resultant turmoil in his home State, was never gazetted by the Minister.[80]

[5.56] Eremin challenged the validity of reg 129 on grounds that included the allegation that internal inconsistencies in reg 129 rendered the provision an unreasonable exercise of the regulation-making power. At both first instance and on appeal, the courts held that the gazettal requirements were a valid part of the Minister's prerogative to control the grant of permits on humanitarian grounds. As the system was designed to promote consistent and speedy decision-making, the courts found it antithetical to require the Minister to 'hear' individual applicants before making a decision about gazettal.[81] The Full Federal Court stated:[82]

---

77 [1898] 2 QB 91 at 99-100.
78 See for example the cases discussed by Margaret Allars, *Introduction to Australian Administrative Law* (Sydney: Butterworths, 1990) at 186-8.
79 See, for example, the comments of the English House of Lords in *Nottinghamshire County Council v Secretary of State for the Environment* [1986] 2 WLR 1 at 5, 8 and 23. See also *Parramatta City Council v Pestell* (1972) 128 CLR 305; *Foley v Padley* (1984) 154 CLR 349; *Octet Nominees Pty Ltd v Minister for Community Services* (1986) 68 ALR 571 at 582-3; affirmed on appeal (1987) 15 FCR 199; and *Brunswick Corporation v Stewart* (1941) 65 CLR 88 at 97.
80 See *Re Eremin v MILGEA* [1990] FCA 266; and *Eremin v MILGEA* (1990) 21 ALD 69 (FFC).
81 See *Re Eremin v MILGEA* [1990] FCA 266 at [28]; and *Eremin v MILGEA* (1990) 21 ALD 69 at 74.
82 [1990] 21 ALD 69 at 75.

Regulation 129 is an integer in a scheme evidently designed to promote the making of speedy decisions by those charged with day-to-day administration of it ... [This task] ... would be impeded rather than assisted if the questions of specification by the minister had to be considered by reference to each individual applicant.

[5.57] A critical issue in *Eremin's* case was the broader operation, or non-operation, of reg 129. During its lifetime the regulation was never made operable, for the simple reason that the Minister never gazetted any event or situation. Neither at first instance nor on appeal did the Federal Court address the question of whether it is lawful for the Minister to frustrate the operation of a regulation by refusing to activate the provision when given the power to do so. The Full Federal Court was not prepared to enter into this controversy. Instead, the court commented simply that the scheme 'reflects a policy, the formulation or criticism of which is not for the judicial branch of government'.[83]

[5.58] In contrast to this reluctance to overrule the Regulations as a whole, the Federal Court on other occasions has taken a literalist approach to legislative requirements, with quite spectacular consequences for the migration bureaucracy. For example, in *Din v MIEA*[84] it ruled unlawful an entire series of English language tests because the authority to conduct the examinations had not been given by the Minister. The practical impact of the decision was to require the re-processing of literally thousands of visa applications.[85] In *MIMA v Seligman*,[86] it was also prepared to rule unlawful one aspect of the Regulations (relating to health requirements) on the basis that certain aspects were beyond the scope of the regulation-making powers conferred by the *Migration Act*.

[5.59] The refusal to sustain challenges to the legislation has not prevented various judges from criticising the Regulations for their complexity and at times draconian effect. In *Buksh v MILGEA*, Einfeld J described the Act and the Regulations as 'a minefield of complexity ... incomprehensible for normal people'.[87]

[5.60] If the government has heard the judiciary's criticism of its regulatory scheme, its response has been focused less on the problems generated by the drafters of the Regulations than on the curial messengers themselves. The pressure on the courts to refrain from intervening in the review of migration cases remains as great today as it has ever been.

5.4 Contracting for control: The privatisation and outsourcing of administrative functions

[5.61] The third and most recent change within the immigration portfolio is one that reflects a quite marked shift in thinking about the whole administrative process

---

83 Ibid at 77.
84 (1997) 147 ALR 673.
85 The High Court made a ruling to similar effect in *Berenguel v MIAC* (2010) 264 ALR 417, a case which also involved a challenge to an IELTS test.
86 (1999) 85 FCR 115.
87 (1991) 102 ALR 647 at 655 (*Buksh*). See also *Pak Siu Ling v MILGEA* [1991] FCA 29 at [25]; *Re Eremin v MILGEA* [1990] FCA 266 at [5]-[6]; and *Mendoza v MILGEA* (1991) 31 FCR 405.

in Australia. The 1990s saw an increasing amount of government activity being privatised in one form or another, a trend that has affected quite profoundly the government's approach to the administration of migration in Australia. Privatisation has occurred in both traditional areas of contracting out, such as information technology contracts, as well as in 'core' areas of the immigration portfolio.[88] In the result, immigration officers under the direct control of the Minister for Immigration now perform very different tasks from those contained in the job descriptions of officers some 10 or so years ago. Departmental officers once handled virtually every aspect of the migration process – from the assessment of basic skills in aspiring migrants through the medical fitness of applicants to the process of resettling refugees. Most of these bureaucratic functions are now performed by private organisations. Even the management of immigration detention facilities has not been immune.

[5.62] Underpinning the trend is the old preoccupation with controlling immigration. Indeed, it could be said that the new strategies are designed at least in part to improve the ability of government to ensure control of both the formulation of policy and its implementation to the letter.

[5.63] The list of functions performed by private companies, or undergoing the tender process, is long. By the time of the 1999-2000 Portfolio Budget Statements, the Department had tendered, or was in the process of tendering, the following aspects of its operations to private companies: the Electronic Travel Authority (for electronic visa issue); health assessment services (under independent medical practitioners); generalist skills assessment for prospective independent and skilled-Australian-linked migration applicants (determinations by a commercial service provider); the control and management of immigration detention centres (first by Australasian Correctional Management, later by Group 4 Falck, then to Serco); Information Technology services; the Immigration Advice and Application Assistance Scheme;[89] departmental research contracts; and various others such as postal and travel services arrangements.[90] By 2010, the list had been expanded to include the provision of resettlement services for migrants arriving under the offshore humanitarian scheme and even the review of refugee status determinations made on the 'excised' offshore territory of Christmas Island.[91] These trends do not appear to have been party political as the arrangements have continued under both Coalition and Labor governments.

[5.64] Privatisation is defined as the transfer of state-owned assets (by sale or lease) to private ownership or control.[92] However, in common usage, the term applies

---

88 See David Hayward and Ron Aspin, 'Contracting Out: Time for a Policy Rethink', Australian Political Science Association Annual Conference, Brisbane, 24-26 September 2001, available at <http://www.sisr.net/publications/0109hayward.pdf>.
89 Interestingly, this is one area that was returned to government control in 2009 with the creation of the Office of Migration Agents Registration Authority. See further Part 5.6 below.
90 Portfolio Budget Statement 1999-2000, Immigration and Multicultural Affairs Portfolio, available at <http://www.immi.gov.au/budget/pbs.99.pdf> at 31-3.
91 See *Plaintiff M61/2010E v Commonwealth and Plaintiff M69 of 2010 v Commonwealth* (2010) 272 ALR 14, discussed above, Chapter 3 at [3.65] and Chapter 19 at [19.102]-[19.104].
92 See Stephen P King, 'Why Privatisation? A Review of the Australian Experience' in Margaret Mead and Glen Withers (eds), *Privatisation: A Review of the Australian Experience* (Sydney: CEDA, 2002) at 14.

to a range of government initiatives to sell off, corporatise, or contract out various assets and services that were traditionally owned by or performed by government. Of these forms of privatisation, contracting out, or 'outsourcing', is perhaps the most important.

[5.65] The high profile contracting out of detention centres has generated some discussion in the media,[93] as has the more recent privatisation of settlement services for refugees and offshore humanitarian entrants.[94] However, most of the contracts tendered by the Department have passed largely unnoticed.

[5.66] There are a variety of reasons as to why governments might elect to have private parties perform public bureaucratic functions. A powerful impetus behind many of the early moves to outsource and privatise was the 'managerialist' desire to reduce the cost and improve the efficiency of government in the provision or delivery of basic services. Beyond this, however, the new 'contractualism' has other rationales. The traditional vision of the public service was of public servants paid and controlled by the government responsible for every aspect of running a bureaucracy. The more modern approach is to focus more carefully on the functions of government so as to identify those aspects of administrative decision-making that should remain the preserve of public servants. The change in approach has forced a re-thinking about expertise generally or, more particularly, who should be consulted so as to determine attributes or criteria that are central to making a decision.

[5.67] In as early as 1978, for example, it was recognised that the determination of refugee status was a process that would benefit from the advice of specialists with experience in the fields of law, international relations, human rights and government policy. Hence, one of the earliest examples of quasi-outsourcing was the establishment of the first advisory committee on refugees: the DORS Committee. This committee was comprised of representatives from key government departments who had both portfolio responsibilities relevant to refugees and relevant expertise. The government officials were joined by a representative from the UN High Commission for Refugees attending as observer.[95] It is well to remember, however, that these arrangements did not alter the ultimate power of the Immigration Minister: the Committee had an advisory function only.[96] In more recent times private individuals have been brought back into refugee status determination processes in the context of the processing of 'offshore' claims on Christmas Island. In considering challenges brought by two unsuccessful refugee

---

93   See 'Private Detention Centres Reap Mammoth Profits' PM Archive, Thursday, 23 November 2000 ABC Online, available at <http://www.abc.ned.au/pm/s215963.htm>.
94   In January 2006 controversy arose following the death of a two-year-old boy whose refugee father was unable to use a telephone to call for help on the evening following the family's arrival in Australia. Responsibility for the resettlement of the family was vested in a private company, Australian Language Services. See Greg Ray, 'Toddler Dies on First Day Here', *The Age*, 29 December 2005, available at <http://www.theage.com.au/articles/2005/12/28/1135732644354.html>.
95   See further Chapter 12 below.
96   Some have suggested that it was for this reason that the High Court found in 1985 that the deliberations of the DORS Committee could be considered in the context of an application for the judicial review of a refugee decision made by the Minister. See *MIEA v Ran Rak Mayer* (1985) 157 CLR 290; and below, Chapter 13.

claimants, the High Court declined to engage with the many complex legal issues raised by reliance on non-government decision-makers in this area. In a unanimous and sparsely written judgment, the court focused narrowly on the statutory basis for the inquiry process established.[97]

[5.68] Some aspects of the current outsourcing program make eminent good sense. The Department's contracting out of vehicle fleet arrangements, postal services, national travel contracts and photocopying are examples in point.[98] The extent of the cultural change, however, is apparent in the assertion in 2001 that all corporate service functions would proceed to market testing 'unless, in respect of particular functions, there were clear reasons for not doing so'.[99] By 2002-03 the Department was able to assert that a 'substantial proportion of departmental activity is delivered under contract'.[100] What this means for the notion of 'public service' in immigration is an open question.

[5.69] It has been the privatisation of the 'core' activities of the portfolio – those that relate to the actual substantive business of determining who does or does not have the right to enter Australia – that has had the most impact on the scheme for prospective migrants and asylum seekers. Four of these areas are examined here: health; skills assessments; immigration detention; and the removal or enforcement process. In each instance, attempts to challenge the new arrangements using the judicial process have failed.

5.4.1   Health assessments

[5.70] The 'health criteria' determination process was one of the first areas of 'core' decision-making to be outsourced.[101] As explored in Chapter 6, the *Migration Act* requires visa applicants to be in good health, as determined by a Medical Officer of the Commonwealth (MOC). The MOC's opinion on whether an applicant meets the health criteria is binding on the Department, although in some instances there is the possibility for the Minister to waive certain criteria. MOCs are private doctors appointed by the Minister – they are not public servants. It is possible to seek internal review of the MOC's health ruling by petitioning Health Services Australia, the authority contracted by the government to make health assessments. However, the Migration Review Tribunal (MRT) may not 'go behind', or question, the expressed opinions of MOCs. In *Manokian v MIMA*,[102] Davies J held that the opinions of MOCs are not decisions refusing to grant a visa and accordingly are not reviewable by the MRT. This line of reasoning follows on from several cases in which courts have

---

97   See *Plaintiff M61/2010E v Commonwealth and Plaintiff M69 of 2010 v Commonwealth* (2010) 272 ALR 14; Mary Crock and Daniel Ghezelbash, 'Due Process and Rule of Law as Human Rights: The High Court and the "Offshore" Processing of Asylum Seekers' (2010) 18(2) *Australian Journal of Administrative Law* 101.
98   See Portfolio Budget Statement 1999-2000, at 31-2.
99   See Portfolio Budget Statement 2000-2001, at 22.
100 Portfolio Budget Statement 2002-03, at 15.
101 See Portfolio Budget Statement 1999-2000.
102 (1997) 48 ALD 632.

upheld the non-reviewability of MOC decisions,[103] while nonetheless finding alternate grounds of relief for the applicants.[104]

5.4.2 Skills assessments

[5.71] A second area in which there has been most dramatic change is in the assessment of qualifications and experience for the purpose of selecting skilled migrants.[105] This function is no longer undertaken by officers of the Department, but by trade or professional associations nominated or 'gazetted' in the Commonwealth Government Gazette. In practice these bodies are usually either the generic bodies established to determine standards and qualifications for workers in Australia, or the peak representative bodies for particular professions or industries.

[5.72] Each of the assessing bodies has its own requirements, procedures and fees.[106] These dictate whether internal review of the assessor's decision is available: the same body that made the original decision will normally be responsible for reviewing it. Although appeals to the specialist immigration tribunal – the MRT – are available on matters related to the grant or refusal of visas, the assessment of skills and qualifications is no longer part of such appeals. In fact, as explored further in Chapters 9 and 10, the assessment of skills now precedes and is strictly separated from the process of applying for a visa. A valid application for a skilled visa cannot be made without the applicant first obtaining an evaluation of her or his qualifications and experience.

[5.73] In *Silveira*,[107] the applicant applied to the Federal Court for judicial review of her skills assessment. The court declined to entertain the application on the basis that the ruling had been made by a private company rather than by a government authority. The court ruled that the decision was one that had been made under a contract with the government rather than by a government official acting 'under an enactment' as required for the decision to be justiciable under the *ADJR Act*. The court noted that, however, the applicant might be able to found an action in damages for breach of contract.[108]

5.4.3 Immigration detention

[5.74] The management and operation of Australia's immigration detention centres were put out to competitive tender during the Howard government's first term of office in 1997-98. This resulted in the letting of contracts for the provision

---

103 *Inguanti v MIMA* [2001] FCA 1046.
104 See, for example, *MIMA v Seligman* (1999) 85 FCR 115, where the court held that the decision of the MOC was not valid as the Regulations did not allow the MOC to determine for him or herself the criteria of a 'condition'. The court did not decide if the decision of the MOC was a 'judicially reviewable decision'. See further the discussion of the justiciability of outsourced decision-making, below.
105 See Portfolio Budget Statement 1999-2000, at 32.
106 Kim Rubenstein, *Australian Citizenship in Context* (Sydney: Law Book Co, 2000) at 143.
107 *Silveira v Australian Institute of Management* (2001) 113 FCR 218 (*Silveira*).
108 Ibid. See further Chapter 19 below.

of detention services by Australasian Correctional Services, operating in facilities constructed by the federal government. The services included accommodation, food, health care and medical treatment, education, recreational equipment and services and, in addition, welfare and counselling services.[109]

[5.75] Under the terms of contract, immigration detention centres throughout Australia were run by Australasian Correctional Management (ACM) until 2002, when the results of a fresh tender process lead to Group 4 Falck Global Solutions (Group 4) (GSL) taking over management contracts. The change of government in 2007 saw the tender for the centres go to Serco.

[5.76] The problems with the privatised management of the detention centres have been many. Riots broke out at several of the centres between 2000-02, prompting significant public scrutiny and questions about the operation of the centres. Numerous government and independent reports have been prepared, canvassing the problems in the management of the centres both by ACM and its successor, GSL.[110] These concerns included problems with ACM and GSL staff; abuse of detainees (both by staff and by other detainees); inappropriate use of force; alleged harassment; understaffing; as well as breaches of basic security.[111] It will be recalled that virtually all significant court challenges to the operation of Australia's detention centres have failed.[112]

5.4.4 Removals

[5.77] Private correctional companies have been contracted to deal with the removal from Australia of overstayers, asylum seekers who have exhausted all avenues in seeking a visa, and criminal deportees.[113] Off-duty police officers are also sometimes hired in this capacity. The responsibilities of a private contractor include guarding of individuals in transit, as well as obtaining documentation and other functions.[114] The contractors are required to be trained in restraint methods, though

---

109 Portfolio Budget Statements 1999-2000, at 32.
110 The reports are too numerous to list here. Various reports are collected at the websites of the following investigative bodies: Senate Legal and Constitutional References Committee, Joint Standing Committee on Migration and Foreign Affairs, Defence and Trade References Committee (accessed through <www.aph.gov.au>); Human Rights Commission (accessed through <www.humanrights.gov.au>); and the Commonwealth Ombudsman (accessed through <www.comb.gov.au>). See also the Palmer Report, above n 46, prepared by former police commissioner Mick Palmer into the wrongful detention of Cornelia Rau. These reports and cases are discussed further in Chapter 16 below.
111 See, for example, Elizabeth Wynhausen, 'At the Mercy of Private Guards', *The Weekend Australian*, 18 September, Inquirer Section, at 22; and Commonwealth Ombudsman, *Report of an Own Motion Investigation into DIMA's Immigration Detention Centres*, March 2001, at 26 and 38-42 respectively. See also Knowledge Consulting (Keith Hamburger AM investigating officer), *Report on behalf of DIMIA Concerning Allegations of Inappropriate Treatment of Five Detainees During Transfer from Maribyrnong Detention Centre to Baxter Detention Centre* (17 and 18 December 2004).
112 See above Chapter 3.3.2 and below Chapter 16.4.
113 In addition, airlines that allow a non-documented or fraudulently documented person to reach Australia are responsible both physically and financially for the removal of that person, see Senate Legal and Constitutional References Committee, *A Sanctuary Under Review: An Examination of Australia's Refugee and Humanitarian Determination Processes* (Canberra: AGPS, 2000) at 302.
114 Ibid at 305.

the Department alleges that only a low percentage of removees have been subject to restraint (either chemical or physical).[115]

[5.78] In 2000, the Senate Legal and Constitutional References Committee noted that the Department only keeps individual files on removals. It does not collect and collate information on removals. DIMIA's 'capacity to be aware of systematic problems and trends' is therefore limited.[116] The pervading problem, however, is that the devolution of the removal function to a private organisation makes it virtually impossible to hold the government to account for either the methods used to effect removal or for what happens to the people when they reach the destination nominated for their removal.[117]

[5.79] The case of SE, decided by a single judge of the High Court in 1998, highlights the difficulties facing a removee wishing to challenge the legality of the government's outsourced removal process. In *Re MIMA; Ex parte SE*,[118] DIMIA was attempting to remove SE, a failed asylum seeker from Somalia. Because he had come by airplane, SE was treated as a 'turn around', which meant that it was the legal responsibility of British Airways to remove him from Australia. SE claimed, in part, that:

> The proposed removal … is unlawful in that (a) it involves the detention in custody of a non-citizen by a private contractor, where the detention is for the purpose of removing the non-citizen from Australia and delivering him or her to his or her country of nationality, and such detention is not authorised by the *Migration Act*, nor by any other law of the Commonwealth.[119]

[5.80] The question was whether the removal would be lawful if it involved SE being restrained or held in custody during the removal process, either in or outside Australia, other than by an officer of the Commonwealth authorised under the *Migration Act*. Hayne J did not address the substance of this argument. He held that the removal of the applicant, although at the behest of the Australian government, was effected by the private airline carrier.[120] Accordingly, there was no evidence that any restraint would be imposed by, on behalf of, or at the direction of the Australian government. In this way, the government was able to disavow any responsibility for actions taken by the contractor during removal.

5.5 System failures: New contractualism and the problem of discretion

5.5.1 Fault lines in the administration

[5.81] By the time the Coalition government was elected for a fourth consecutive term of office in 2004, the trend towards the contracting out of all manner of

---

115 Ibid at 303.
116 Ibid at 314.
117 For two accounts of shortcomings in these arrangements, see Edmund Rice Centre, *Deported to Danger* (September 2004), available at <http://www.erc.org.au/research/pdf/1096416029.pdf>; and David Corlett, *Following Them Home: The Fate of the Returned Asylum Seekers* (Melbourne: Black Inc, 2005).
118 (1998) 158 ALR 735 (Hayne J).
119 Ibid at [5].
120 Ibid at [12].

public services and functions was well entrenched. Within the immigration portfolio, however, any promised gains in efficiency and productivity had been lost in a litany of system failures. As the preceding section suggests, most were focused in the contentious areas of immigration enforcement in the arrest, detention and removal of persons supposed to be immigration outlaws. Following the inquiries surrounding the wrongful arrest and detention of permanent resident Cornelia Rau[121] and the removal of a citizen of 20 years' standing, Vivian Solon-Alvarez, no less than 202 cases were referred to the Federal Ombudsman for investigation. The scandals followed close on the heels of a major parliamentary inquiry into the exercise of the Immigration Minister's overriding discretion to intervene in migration cases. Although superficially very different controversies, it will be argued in this Part that all are products of the structural changes that have occurred in the administration of immigration in Australia. Put another way, the controversies reveal fault lines in the system that will continue to generate administrative problems until the root causes are acknowledged and addressed.

[5.82] In his analysis of the failures that lead to both the prolonged incarceration of Cornelia Rau, and the detention and removal of Vivian Solon-Alvarez, Palmer writes at some length about what he describes as the 'silo-ing' of functions within the administration of the immigration portfolio. Palmer uses this term to describe the division and quarantining of administrative functions, with different people and bodies given responsibility for each function. Palmer found that this compartmentalisation was both inefficient and dangerous because inadequate provision was made for communication and responsibility sharing between the functionaries. No individual appears to have had oversight of the entirety of the processes being followed so as to be able to exercise judgment over the propriety of the treatment being accorded to the two women.

[5.83] In the time immediately following the breaking of these two scandals, there was a tendency to lay the blame for these administrative failures at the feet of the immigration bureaucracy. The Department was upbraided for being imbued with a culture of secrecy, denial and lack of sensibility. Whether or not these criticisms were well-founded, it is interesting that much less attention was paid to the structural factors that might have contributed to the 'outcomes' observed.

[5.84] The contracting out of administrative functions inevitably involves the definition and isolation of specific tasks. What is less obvious is that the contracting out of functions inevitably spreads across the administrative process so that officials within the bureaucracy become more conscious of the particular tasks allotted to them. They may also become more circumspect about intruding into the domains defined as the territories of other officials. Indeed, for a government determined to take a very hard line on the enforcement of immigration laws, the 'silo-ing' of functions is done deliberately so as to ensure that human sensibilities do not subvert the policy outcomes articulated by the politicians. This, of course, is what is wrong with the system. In an area as fraught with human complexity as immigration, the compartmentalisation of decision-making is highly inappropriate because it removes

---

121 See the Palmer Report, above n 46.

the ability to respond flexibly to a situation that demands humane or compassionate responses.

[5.85] In the detention of unlawful non-citizens, the process of compartmentalisation is physical as well as conceptual. The detention facilities are located in increasingly remote geographical locations. Private management of the centres means that the people charged with restricting the physical movement of the detainees have no connection with the grant or refusal of visas. Nor do they have power to release those in custody. The guards stand outside the immigration process: they also operate outside of the accountability structures created to oversee the operation of the public service. Contractual obligations notwithstanding, the physical and legal isolation of the detention centre workers has inevitably led some to respond to the difficult environment of the centres with abuse and violations of the human rights of the detainees.[122] It would be a mistake to view the abuses as accidents or aberrations. They are an almost inevitable product of the way the system is constructed.

[5.86] The final point of controversy during the Coalition government's third term in office was the exercise of discretionary powers permitting the override of adverse administrative decisions. These are powers that permit the Minister, acting personally, to make a decision more favourable to an applicant. The Minister cannot be compelled to consider a petition and the process is one that is not amenable to judicial oversight of any kind.[123] Although dismissed by the government as a political exercise, the inquiry instituted by the Senate in late 2003 served to highlight concerns that have arisen about the way in which ministerial discretions conferred by the Act have been exercised. The inquiry was sparked by allegations that the former Minister, Phillip Ruddock, had been in effect selling his power to grant visas on humanitarian or compassionate grounds. No proof of misbehaviour was forthcoming at the Senate hearings. However, the opposition-dominated committee found that the number of people seeking ministerial intercession and the procedures in place to handle the many requests were far from ideal. The Committee found that a removal of the discretions was undesirable because of the complexity and human impact of immigration decisions. It concluded:[124]

> [O]n balance it seems appropriate to maintain the ministerial discretion in some form as a final safety net in cases where the system appears to have produced an unduly harsh or unreasonable outcome. Having said that, immediate steps need to be taken to improve accountability and transparency to prevent the risk of corruption endemic to such an unfettered ministerial power.

As Jessie Hohmann notes,[125] '[t]he flaws inherent in a non-compellable, non-reviewable, non-delegable discretion are a lack of accountability and transparency, and a susceptibility to allegations of bias and politicization'.

---

122   See above, Part 5.4.3.
123   See further Chapter 19.4 below. Examples of such powers are found in ss 351 and 417 of the *Migration Act*.
124   See Senate Select Committee on Ministerial Discretion in Migration Matters, *Inquiry into Ministerial Discretion in Migration Matters* (Canberra: March 2004).
125   Jessie Hohmann, 'Report on the Senate Select Committee on Ministerial Discretion in Migration Matters: Inconclusive Witch Hunt or Valuable Contribution to the Australian Migration Debate?' (2004) 19 *Immigration Review* 5 at 10.

[5.87] Again, the tendency throughout this affair was to focus on allegations about how various Immigration Ministers had used or were using the power conferred on them. What was almost completely absent was reflection on how these powers related to those conferred on lesser administrators and bureaucrats. In reality, the powers conferred on the Minister take their significance from the fact that other players have little or no discretion. It is a system that has been designed over many years by governments of varied political persuasions to progressively reduce and remove altogether the ability of ordinary bureaucrats to intervene and respond with compassion and/or good sense to the hard cases.

[5.88] With the remove of time, it is not difficult to see the connections between the dramatic system failures in the Rau and Solon-Alvarez cases and the regime criticised by the Senate in 2004. If anything emerged from the Senate's rather political inquiry, it was that no single person could be expected to deal with the volume of petitions that have been funnelled onto the desk of the Immigration Minister in recent years. Consideration of cases and access to ministerial intervention has had to be selective. It is hardly surmising that success is often dependent on an individual's ability to have their case drawn to the attention of the Minister personally. By the same token, it is clearly unreasonable to expect such arrangements to operate as an effective safety net within a bureaucracy as large, complex and geographically diverse as immigration.

[5.89] In 2004 the Senate Select Committee recommended[126] that the migration legislation be amended so as to allow for the grant of a new class of visas allowing for the grant of 'complementary protection' for individuals with strong compassionate or humanitarian grounds for wanting to remain in Australia. While such a gesture could go some way towards relieving pressure on the Immigration Minister, it would not redress the principal shortcomings in the administration of this area of law and policy.

[5.90] The system that both produced the abusive outcomes suffered by Cornelia Rau and Vivian Solon-Alvarez and causes Ministers to be flooded with individual petitions suffers from two major deficiencies. It is too inflexible and it lacks effective oversight mechanisms. The problem is not that the Minister has too much discretion. It is that the Minister's administrators have *too little* discretion. Their tasks are too closely defined and confined; their ability to respond appropriately to the complexity of the human situations has been stripped back too far. While the bureaucrats' powers have been contained, mechanisms for the review of decisions have also been reduced or removed altogether.

5.5.2 Judicial responses to contracting out

> The avenues of redress that the administrative law system provides ... ensure that individual members of the community are treated fairly, lawfully, rationally, openly and efficiently by agencies, ... [and] enhance and complement other

---

126 Inquiry into Ministerial Discretion in Migration Matters, above n 124, at 148.

mechanisms of government accountability' such as ministerial responsibility and public service accountability.[127]

[5.91] The immediate effect of contracting out all or part of a service provided traditionally by government is that the avenues for the review of government action are reduced or closed off. Because traditional administrative law remedies do not apply to private bodies or individuals, the careful system of accountability that is created by this legal regime is not necessarily available when government contracts out its services. In its *Competitive Contracting Out Report*, the ARC provides a useful summary of the difficulties in obtaining meaningful recourse when a government contracts out a service. These include a lack of ability to seek judicial review under the *ADJR Act*, possible lack of external review (whether on a question of law or on the merits of a decision); the inability to use freedom of information legislation permitting discovery of documents; and a lesser ability by the Ombudsman to conduct a review of a private agency.[128]

[5.92] It would be difficult to lay the entire blame for the troubles experienced within Australia's detention centres at the feet of the private contractors managing the facilities. Nevertheless, the privatisation of the centres did coincide with a marked decline in the conditions within the centres. In the context of various reviews, it is interesting that the Immigration Department has accepted that it owes the ultimate duty of care to detainees, regardless of who is placed in charge of the detention centres under contract.[129] The Ombudsman has expressed the view that this duty is non-delegable in character, and has suggested that the agency relationship between the Department and the contractor means that actions in negligence could be brought against the Department.[130]

[5.93] It is the contracting out of decision-making in areas related directly to the grant of visas that the greatest reduction in review rights has occurred. There is a certain irony in this, as the changes in this area have been much less contentious within the public discourse and yet are likely to affect a very broad range of people at quite a profound level. The case of *Silveira*,[131] discussed earlier, encapsulates the issues at stake. Ms Silveira applied for a skilled visa but was determined by the (non-government) assessor, the Australian Institute of Management (AIM), not to have the required qualifications and experience. An application for *ADJR Act* review

---

127　Administrative Review Council, *The Contracting Out of Government Services* (Report No 42, 1998) at 3.7 and 2.4-2.11.
128　Ibid at 3.18, Table.
129　See Commonwealth Ombudsman, *Report of an Own Motion Investigation into Immigration Detainees Held in State Correctional Facilities* (March 2001) at 30-4, available at <http://www.ombudsman.gov.au/commonwealth/publish.nsf/attachmentsbytitle/reports_2001_dima_statecorrectional.pdf/$file/correctional+facilities.pdf>. See also Joint Standing Committee on Migration, *Report of inspections of detention centres throughout Australia* (Canberra: August 1998) at 5.
130　Commonwealth Ombudsman, above n 129, at 30-4. The fact that the government recognises its ultimate responsibility for the welfare of those in the Immigration Detention Centres is borne out in the decision in 2005 to allow the Ombudsman to review the cases of all persons detained for more than two years. See *Migration Act* Part 8C (Reports on persons in detention for more than two years) and specifically the Secretary of the Department's obligation to report to Commonwealth Ombudsman under **s** 486N of the *Migration Act*.
131　(2001) 113 FCR 218.

of the visa refusal that included AIM would have permitted her to challenge the AIM ruling on bases such as the failure to take into account all relevant considerations; the denial of natural justice or procedural fairness; and even unreasonableness. In ruling that AIM was a private body and not amenable to judicial review, Emmett J found that its powers came entirely from its memorandum and articles of association – and not from the migration legislation. Indeed, his Honour pointed out that organisations gazetted as relevant assessing authorities under the *Migration Act* acquired no special powers or functions by virtue of their gazettal. Visa applicants could apply like anyone else to have their qualifications assessed. In making an assessment, AIM was not performing any public duty the performance of which could be compelled by mandamus. Nor could the assessment produced on payment of the applicant's fee be regarded as a 'report' within the meaning of s 3(3) of the *ADJR Act* because (again) the assessment process stood apart from the process of applying for a visa.

[5.94] Emmett J's ruling confirmed that the 'front-end loading' of the skilled visa process (requiring applicants to have their skills and qualifications assessed before applying for a visa) has indeed confined the grounds on which adverse visa decisions can be challenged.

[5.95] The fact that the Australian courts generally are conceding their powers to review public administration in private hands is borne out in a series of other cases involving the contracting out of various public functions.[132] The most extreme example is undoubtedly the High Court case of *NEAT Domestic Trading Pty Ltd v AWB Ltd*,[133] a case that might have proved 'an isolated authority, quickly forgotten',[134] but for the controversy surrounding the private company at the heart of this case.[135] The statutory scheme in this case involved a private company set up for the express purpose of overseeing and brokering deals for a government enterprise – the Wheat Export Authority – charged with the bulk export of Australian wheat.[136] This arrangement was unusual. In *Silveira*, as in other cases where government has devolved specific functions to private agencies, the relevant assessment process was referred

---

132 See, for example, *Salerno v National Crime Authority* (1997) 75 FCR 133; and *Parkes Rural Distributions Pty Ltd v Glasson* (1984) 155 CLR 234.
133 (2003) 216 CLR 277 (*NEAT Domestic Trading*). For analyses of this decision, see Christos Mantziaris, 'A 'Wrong Turn' on the Public/Private Distinction Case Note; Neat Domestic Trading Pty Ltd v AWB Ltd' (2003) 14 *Public Law Review* 197; Margaret Allars, 'Public Administration In Private Hands' (2005)12 *Australian Journal of Administrative Law* 126; and Graeme Hill, 'The Administrative Decisions (Judicial Review) Act and "Under an Enactment": Can NEAT Domestic be Reconciled with Glasson?' (2004) 11 *Australian Journal of Administrative Law* 135.
134 See Allars, above n 133, at 145.
135 As explained below, the private entity tasked to advise the Wheat Board was the Australian Wheat Board Incorporated or AWBI. AWBI was investigated in 2006 over allegations that it paid kickbacks or bribes to Saddam Hussein to secure lucrative contracts selling Australian wheat to Iraq. See Inquiry into certain Australian companies in relation to the UN Oil-For-Food Programme (the Cole Enquiry). The report is available at <http://www.ag.gov.au/agd/WWW/unoilforfoodinquiry.nsf/Page/Report>.
136 The AWBI was established to operate outside the statutory scheme regulating trade in wheat. The company was given the power to veto grain exports. See s 57(3B) of the *Wheat Marketing Act 1989* (Cth) which provides that the Wheat Export Authority cannot consent to the bulk export of wheat grown in Australia without the prior approval in writing of AWBI. The arrangements give AWBI an effective monopoly over the export of Australian wheat under what has been known as the 'single desk' policy for wheat exports. It is this scheme that NEAT Domestic Trading sought to challenge.

to bodies or authorities that were already performing the processes in question. In other words, the entities asked to perform the 'public' functions devolved on them had a 'life' apart from the contracts received from government. In *NEAT Domestic Trading*, the divide between the public authority and the private corporation was not nearly as marked. Indeed, one might say that the arrangements looked like a colourable device to place decisions that were really being made by a government authority beyond the reach of public administrative law remedies.

[5.96] In the High Court, only two of the five justices were prepared to find AWBI amenable to judicial review under the *ADJR Act*. The majority (McHugh, Hayne and Callinan JJ) focused on the private character of the corporation, ruling that its power to grant export approvals derived from its corporate identity and not from the *Wheat Marketing Act 1989* (Cth). Their Honours found that '[i]t is not possible to impose public law obligations on AWBI while at the same time accommodating pursuit of its private interests'.[137] Gleeson CJ agreed with the majority in the result,[138] but joined Kirby J in finding that the incorporation of AWBI could not assume that incorporation as a private company would make it immune from judicial review. The Chief Justice noted that AWBI did not represent private interests, but effectively the interests of all the grain growers in Australia. Kirby J held that the AWBI was exercising powers of 'an administrative character' and that it was making decisions 'under an enactment' such that its decisions were justiciable under the *ADJR Act*. His Honour also found that AWBI was exercising 'public power', drawing on a line of English cases.[139]

[5.97] As Margaret Allars notes in her analysis of the case, there is much in the majority's ruling in *NEAT Domestic Trading* that is out of step with the development of the test of justiciability at general law. She goes so far as to say that the assumptions made by the majority are flawed, 'in light of the increasing interpenetration of the norms of public and private law'. She writes:[140]

> It cannot be assumed that administration changes its character when placed in private hands. There is in any event no ready identifier for an institutional arrangement which is private rather than public. Nor is it easy to determine what makes a function or power public or private.

[5.98] In this context, as in the contracting out of many aspects of migration decision-making, the unspoken issue is the extent to which contracting out is undertaken in whole or in part so as to avoid the inconvenience of administrative law review. The saga in 2006 of AWBI's misadventures in Iraq may well demonstrate that it is not in the public interest to quarantine from judicial scrutiny public administration placed in private hands. For the moment, rulings such as *NEAT Domestic Trading* and *Silveira* suggest that the Australian courts have yet to face up to – let alone begin to fill – one

---

137 *NEAT Domestic Trading* (2003) 216 CLR 277 at [51].
138 His Honour held that the plaintiff had not made out the ground of review pleaded, namely that AWBI had made decisions that were unlawful by reason of inflexible application of policy: (2003) 216 CLR 277 at [27].
139 See *R v Panel on Take Overs and Mergers; Ex parte Datafin* [1987] 1 QB 815.
140 See Allars, above n 133, at 146.

of the 'significant fissures in Australian jurisprudence',[141] namely the relationship between public and private power.

5.6 Ethics and the regulation of migration advice

[5.99] The decision in 1989 to transform immigration decision-making from a discretionary to a regulated model (linking decisional criteria to rights) had a profound impact on the immigration advice industry. Until that time, few lawyers had made immigration a specialty. The task of securing visas and entry permits had been the preserve of migration agents – a special breed of paralegal professionals who made it their business to establish and maintain contacts with key politicians with access to the Minister. Interestingly, the depth of political involvement in immigration seems to have heightened the politicians' sensitivity to the abuse of migrant applicants. In 1992, the regulatory regime was extended to cover agents and all persons engaging in the provision of 'immigration assistance'.[142]

[5.100] The structures for the regulation of agents were strengthened and formalised in 1998 with the outsourcing of the regulatory function to the Migration Agents Registration Authority (MARA). The role of this body (and of its successor in title) included the investigation of complaints about services provided by registered migration agents. It was also vested with power to take disciplinary action against migration agents, including the issue of cautions, suspension or cancellation of registration or barring a former agent from registration.[143] The agency had no power to regulate persons giving immigration assistance in foreign countries. Controversially, the statutory scheme drew no distinction between lawyers and migration agents with no legal training.[144]

[5.101] When MARA was established by the Coalition government in the late 1990s, it came to be run by the Migration Institute of Australia Ltd (MIA), a voluntary professional organisation of migration agents. Concerns arose in due course about a perceived conflict of interest in the professional representative and advocacy body for migration agents also acting as a regulator of the profession. Following an investiga-

---

141 See Allars, above n 133, at 145, citing Finn J in *Hughes Aircraft Systems International v Airservices Australia* (1997) 76 FCR 151 at 179-80; and Gummow J in *Airservices Australia v Canadian Airlines International Ltd* (1999) 202 CLR 133. Allars points out that the Australian jurisprudence stands in quite marked contrast to that of the English Court of Appeal. See *Hampshire County Council v Beer (t/as Hammer Trout Farm)* [2003] EWCA Civ 1056. As noted earlier, the High Court attempted to re-open this controversy in the context of the offshore (and privatised) processing of refugee claimants on Christmas Island. See above, [5.63].
142 This phrase is defined in *Migration Act*, s 276.
143 Its functions are set out in s 316.
144 The High Court confirmed the validity of the scheme in *Cunliffe v Commonwealth* (1994) 182 CLR 272. In this case two solicitors challenged the *Migration Legislation Amendment (Migration Agents) Act 1997* (Cth) on the basis, inter alia, that the Code of Conduct infringed their implied constitutional right to freedom of political communication. A narrow majority of the High Court (Brennan, Dawson, Dawson and McHugh JJ, with Mason CJ, Deane and Gaudron JJ in dissent) held that the statutory scheme did not breach any implied freedoms, in part because the scheme involved non-citizens and so could be supported by the power to legislate with respect to aliens. In the result the legislation was upheld as valid.

tion by the Commonwealth Ombudsman,[145] and a government-appointed External Reference Group,[146] MARA moved to appoint two advisers who were independent from the MIA to the committee that considers serious complaints against migration agents. In July 2009, the Labor government assumed control of the regulatory function, abolishing MARA and creating the Office of the Migration Agents Registration Authority (OMARA). Although nominally independent, this body answers to and is controlled by the Department (DIAC).

[5.102] Part 3 of the *Migration Act* regulates who can provide immigration assistance and establishes an oversight regime for registered migration agents. Providing immigration advice or assistance without being registered as an agent is a strict liability offence punishable by 60 penalty points. Exceptions are made for lawyers providing advice about court proceedings only,[147] as well as for close family members of a visa applicant; certain employers or sponsors of visa applicants; and others such as electorate workers who are frequently approached by constituents with immigration problems.[148] Charging a fee or soliciting a benefit without being registered as an agent attracts a penalty of 10 years' imprisonment.[149] An applicant must not be registered if not a person of integrity or not fit and proper.[150]

[5.103] The ethical obligations of migration agents are set out in the Code of Conduct contained in Sch 2 to the *Migration Agents Regulations 1998* (Cth).[151] These ethical rules are binding on lawyers who give 'immigration legal assistance' in addition to their legal professional obligations.[152] The Code requires agents and lawyers who give immigration advice to be of good character; to be honest; and to have sound knowledge of migration law, practice and procedure and of business procedure in order to conduct business as a migration agent and to properly manage client records. A breach of the Code attracts disciplinary action by the OMARA. Decisions to cancel, refusal and suspend migration agents' registration are reviewable by the AAT and are subject in turn to judicial review both on appeal from the AAT and under the *ADJR Act* as decisions made 'under an enactment'.

[5.104] Agents will be regarded as lacking personal integrity or otherwise not being a fit and proper person to give immigration assistance where they have failed to advise a client of a conflict of interest.[153] Gross failures to comply with the Code of Conduct have included destroying clients' documents and failing to notify a client as to the refusal of her visa;[154] failure to act in a timely manner where the client has

---

145 Commonwealth Ombudsman, *Migration Agents Registration Authority: Complaint-Handling Process*, June 2007.
146 External Reference Group, *2007-2008 Review of Statutory Self-Regulation of the Migration Advice Profession*, Final Report (Canberra: DIAC, May 2008).
147 *Migration Act*, s 277, defined as 'immigration legal assistance'.
148 Ibid, s 280.
149 Ibid, s 281.
150 Ibid, s 290.
151 Ibid, s 314.
152 Complex definitions explain when a 'lawyer gives immigration legal assistance' in s 277 and when a 'person gives immigration assistance' in s 276.
153 *Woods v MARA* [2004] FCA 1622.
154 *Hudson and MARA* [2004] AATA 1007.

provided all the necessary information and documentation to meet the statutory deadlines;[155] and knowingly making a misleading or inaccurate statement in support of an application under the *Migration Act* or Regulations.[156]

[5.105] Unlawful conduct by a migration agent or lawyer can have ramifications beyond disqualification of the adviser. Advice that is bad enough to constitute fraud can affect the validity of a decision made by the Department or a tribunal. In *SZFDE v MIAC*,[157] the High Court found that fraud can infect an administrative decision so as to constitute a constructive failure to exercise jurisdiction. In this matter, the appellants had not attended their hearing before the Refugee Review Tribunal (RRT) on the advice given by their adviser who had fraudulently held himself out to be a solicitor and licensed migration agent. In fact, the man's practising certificate, and registration as a migration agent, had been cancelled. The High Court held that the process followed by the tribunal was compromised by 'third party fraud', with the result that its decision was infected by jurisdictional error. The court emphasised that fraud had been perpetrated on the tribunal, and did not conclusively determine whether the decision would have been rendered invalid by a fraud which had 'merely' been perpetrated on the review applicants rather than on the tribunal itself.

[5.106] For lawyers, providing immigration assistance means being subject to dual regulation. Ethical obligations arise under both the professional conduct rules for legal practitioners and the Migration Agents' Code of Conduct. Lawyer Michael Clothier[158] notes that, in general, the criteria to be satisfied in the agents' Code of Conduct involve far more detail than the lawyers' rules, but the qualitative standards are not nearly as high. For example, while lawyers must ordinarily act honestly and fairly in their clients' best interests, the Code of Conduct includes no such general principle. Rather, these rules proscribe accepting a client in circumstances that involve a conflict of interest as defined in cl 2.1A of the Code.

[5.107] Unlike migration agents, lawyers are bound by legal professional privilege in relation to their communications with clients. The Full Federal Court has considered these requirements as they affect lawyers in immigration matters in two contexts. The first involved a claim of privilege against the Minister; the second a claim against the RRT.

[5.108] In *Hamdan*, a lawyer acting for an unlawful non-citizen was served with a notice under s 18 of the *Migration Act*. The notice stated that the Minister had reason to believe that the lawyer had information relevant to ascertaining the client's whereabouts and specifically demanded that the lawyer provide the client's mobile telephone number.[159] The lawyer resisted the demand, citing legal professional privilege. Upholding the lawyer's defence, the Full Federal Court reasoned that the

---

155 *Hanna v MARA* [1999] FCA 1657.
156 *Hartnett v MARA* [2004] FCAFC 269.
157 (2007) 232 CLR 189.
158 Michael Clothier, 'The Law of Layering – Professional Ethics for Immigration Lawyers', paper presented at the Law Council of Australia, RILC and Immigration Lawyers Association of Australia, Annual CPD Migration Law Conference, Melbourne, 20 and 21 March 2009.
159 *MIMIA v Hamdan* [2005] FCAFC 113.

giving of the telephone number to the lawyer was a communication between client and lawyer for the dominant purpose of obtaining legal advice or the provision of legal services. As the communication was prima facie privileged, the Minister bore the onus of proving that maintaining the client's confidentiality was incompatible with the lawyer's basic ethical responsibilities. The court ruled that, because the client had engaged in no unlawful action to evade detention, the privilege remained intact.

[5.109] In *SZHWY*,[160] an applicant for a Protection visa was asked by the RRT Member about his conversations with a previous solicitor. The Full Federal Court held that legal professional privilege applies before the RRT, and the RRT had committed a jurisdictional error by asking a question that intruded on the privilege without advising the asylum seeker of his right not to answer.

[5.110] In contrast, conversations between migration agents and their clients attract no similar protections. In *SZKTQ*, the Federal Magistrates Court upheld a tribunal decision where the presiding member had asked the applicant to disclose communications with his agent.[161] The court noted that the Code of Conduct provides that migration agents must preserve the confidentiality of their clients and must not disclose confidential information about their clients without the clients' written consent. However, it ruled that the Code's obligations do not amount to legal professional privilege because the duty is not enforceable against third parties (such as the Minister or tribunal). The duty does not extend beyond the relationship between agent and client.

[5.111] As Michael Clothier points out, these judgments illustrate the gulf between the ethical obligations of immigration lawyers and migration agents. The protections available to clients of lawyers are withheld from the clients of migration agents. This is information that should be widely available to all in need of immigration advice so that they can make an informed decision in choosing an adviser or advocate.

---

160   *SZHWY v MIAC* (2007) 159 FCR 1.
161   *SZKTQ v MIAC* [2008] FMCA 91.

PART III Border Control and Common Entry Criteria

6

Border Control and Common Entry Requirements

6.1 Of borders and concepts of entry

[6.01] The only persons who have an unqualified right to enter, live and work in Australia are people who are able to demonstrate Australian citizenship.[1] Australian citizenship can be acquired by birth, descent, adoption or by grant, although children born in Australia will only acquire Australian citizenship at birth if one parent is a citizen or permanent resident.[2] All non-citizens are subject to some form of control. This chapter examines the law governing physical admission into the country, as well as the common entry criteria that apply to most categories of non-citizens who seek permanent or temporary stay.

[6.02] As the events surrounding the *Tampa* Affair and Operation Relex attest, the protection of Australia's geographical borders became a matter of acute political sensitivity at the turn of the new millennium. Well before the hapless *Palapa I* began to founder in the high seas near Australia's Christmas Island,[3] the Australian Parliament had begun to respond to the growth in the number of unauthorised boat arrivals to the north of Australia. The *Migration Act 1958* (Cth) was amended in 1999 to permit Australian officials to board ships and aircraft in Australia's territorial sea, the 'contiguous' and 'exclusive economic' zones and even on the high seas. The *Border Protection Act 1999* (Cth) permits the 'hot pursuit' of ships which fail to comply with requests to board and the pursuit of 'motherships' that are reasonably suspected of being used for illegal activities. It empowers customs officials to carry firearms and use other defence equipment; and provides for the forfeiture, seizure and disposal of ships and aircraft used in contravention of immigration laws.

[6.03] The legislation passed in 1999 also enabled officials to bring non-citizens to Australia, for example, for the processing of refugee claims or as the result of rescue at sea. As became plain during the course of the *Tampa* Affair, however, the laws made no provision for interdiction or other measures designed to *stop* non-citizens

---

1 See *Air Caledonie International v Commonwealth* (1988) 165 CLR 462 at 469; and s 166 of the *Migration Act 1958* (Cth).
2 *Australian Citizenship Act 1948* (Cth), Part III, ss 10-15. See the discussion in Chapter 2.5.2 above.
3 See above, Chapter 3.4 and Chapter 4.3.

rescued at sea from being landed on continental Australia. At the height of the furore that surrounded both the stand off with the *Tampa* and the aftermath of the terrorist attacks in America of 11 September 2001, the Australian Parliament passed a raft of enactments designed to strengthen the government's power to control the entry into Australia of non-citizens. The *Border Protection (Validation and Enforcement Powers) Act 2001* (Cth) validated in retrospect all actions taken by the government to prevent the landing of the asylum seekers rescued by the *Tampa*. It also expanded exponentially the powers of immigration and customs officers to search, detain and move persons aboard ships intercepted at sea.[4] What is more extraordinary is the insertion into the *Migration Act* of s 7A, which asserts that the executive power of the Commonwealth extends independently of any legislation to the protection of Australia's borders, including, where necessary, by ejecting persons who have crossed those borders.[5] In referring to 'persons', the Act makes no distinction between citizens and foreigners. The Act also imposes mandatory sentences for people convicted of people smuggling offences. Adult offenders are liable for five years' gaol, and eight years for repeat offences.

[6.04] The centrepiece of Australia's 'Pacific Strategy' is to be found in the companion legislation to these border protection provisions. To discourage the use of the Australian territory of Christmas Island and nearby reefs as delivery points for asylum seekers travelling from Indonesia,[6] parliament empowered the Minister to declare parts of Australia's territory to be outside Australia's 'migration zone'. Under the *Migration Amendment (Excision from Migration Zone) Act 2001* (Cth), people coming ashore at Ashmore Reef, on the Keeling or Cocos Islands or on Christmas Island were deemed *not* to have entered Australia's migration zone. This legislation introduced the concepts of 'excised offshore places' and 'offshore entry persons' and operates to prevent people on these territories from having the right to access Australia's refugee protection regime – or indeed to make any application for a visa to enter Australia. Although a subject of contention until the government gained control of the Senate in July 2006, subsequently Regulations have extended the reach of these provisions to cover most of Australia's offshore territories.[7] However, in 2006

---

4   As we have argued in another context, the changes made exceed the type of initiative envisaged by the United Nations in the Protocol against the Smuggling of Migrants by Land, Air and Sea, made pursuant to the UN Convention Against Transnational Organised Crime. See Mary Crock, Ben Saul and Azadeh Dastyari, *Future Seeker II: Refugees and Irregular Migration in Australia* (Sydney: Federation Press, 2006) at 116-17.
5   This provision appears to have been enacted in response to the suggestion by French J that the executive power of government enshrined in s 61 of the Constitution includes an inherent power to control the movement of non-citizens across Australia's borders, with or without the authorisation of the legislature. See *Ruddock v Vadarlis* (2001) 110 FCR 491 at 543-4; and above Chapter 3.1 and 3.4.
6   Australia has experienced the arrival of boats carrying asylum seekers on a number of occasions over the past 30 years. While earlier episodes saw boats coming down from Vietnam, Cambodia and the Peoples' Republic of China, in the late 1990s people smugglers operating through Indonesia made that country an important point of transit for asylum seekers wishing to come on to Australia. The other major change in the pattern of arrivals in recent years relates to the countries of origin of the asylum seekers. The most recent arrivals have been nationals of Iraq, Iran, Afghanistan and the Middle East, with a sprinkling from other refugee-producing countries. See Andreas Schloenhardt, 'Australia and the Boat People: 25 Years of Unauthorised Arrivals' (2000) 23 *University of New South Wales Law Journal* 33.
7   See Crock, Saul and Dastyari, above n 4, at 118-19.

a successful campaign was mounted to defeat attempts to extend the legislation so as to prevent all asylum seekers reaching Australia's mainland by boat from seeking refugee protection under the *Migration Act*.[8]

[6.05] As explored further in throughout the book, these measures are designed primarily to prevent asylum seekers from entering Australia for the purpose of accessing the country's refugee status determination processes. They do not mean that Australia has abdicated altogether obligations it has assumed as a party to the UN Convention relating to the Status of Refugees and other human rights instruments.[9] It is a regime that is unusual if not unique in terms of state practice: the closest approximation is the program in the United States to interdict boat arrivals from Haiti and Cuba.[10] In both instances the objective has been to deny asylum seekers access to the full domestic asylum adjudication processes and to the protections of administrative law.[11] Other precedents are to be found in laws and policies in Australia's recent past[12] that used to 'deem' certain non-citizens not to have 'entered' the country until they have passed through a clearance process at point of entry. It is to these processes that we now turn.

6.2 Visas, entry permits and immigration clearance

[6.06] In order to streamline procedures at point of entry, there has long been an administrative practice of physically assessing people before they come to Australia. Notification of a person's acceptability for permanent or short-term stay was (and is) given in the form of a 'visa'. Until 1 September 1994, most visas did no more than provide evidence that a person had been approved for travel to Australia. A right to enter the country followed upon the issue at point of disembarkation of an *entry permit*. In addition, there were classes of non-citizens who were exempt from the requirement of holding either a visa or an entry permit.[13] The largest group exemption was that given to New Zealand citizens.

---

8   See Migration Amendment (Designated Unauthorised Arrivals) Bill 2006 (Cth) and Michelle Grattan, 'Can Howard find refuge?' (opinion piece) *The Age*, 14 May 2006, available at <http://www.theage.com.au/news/opinion/can-howard-find-refuge/2006/05/13/1146940772267.html>; and 'PM dumps asylum laws' *The Age*, 14 August 2006, available at <http://www.theage.com.au/news/national/pm-dumps-controversial-asylum-laws/2006/08/14/1155407711432.html>; and Senate Legal and Constitutional Affairs Committee, Legislation Committee, Inquiry into the provisions of the Migration Amendment (Designated Unauthorised Arrivals) Bill 2006 (13 June 2006), available at <http://www.aph.gov.au/SENATE/committee/legcon_ctte/completed_inquiries/2004-07/migration_unauthorised_arrivals/index.htm>.
9   On this point, see Guy Goodwin-Gill and Jane McAdam, *The Refugee in International Law* (London: OUP, 3rd ed, 2007) Ch 5.
10 For a recent collection of articles on various interdiction and deflection programs around the world, see (2006) 18 *International Journal of Refugee Law* 487.
11 The effectiveness of this strategy was undermined severely by the decision of the High Court in *Plaintiff M61/2010E v Commonwealth and Plaintiff M69 of 2010 v Commonwealth* (2010) 272 ALR 14. See Mary Crock and Daniel Ghezelbash, 'Due Process and Rule of Law as Human Rights: The High Court and the "Offshore" Processing of Asylum Seekers' (2010) 18(2) *Australian Journal of Administrative Law* 101 and the discussion in Chapter 19 at [19.102]-[19.104].
12 See Mary Crock, *Administrative Law and Immigration Control in Australia: Actions and Reactions* (unpublished PhD Thesis, University of Melbourne, 1994) at 67-71.
13 See former s 8 of the *Migration Act*.

[6.07] In 1994, the old system of visas, entry permits and exempt entrants was abandoned altogether. Under Part 2, Div 3 of the *Migration Act*, all non-citizens entering Australia are required to hold a *visa* of one kind or another. Possession of a valid visa is now the sole criterion for determining the lawful status of a non-citizen within Australia. The fact that the visa connotes a legal entitlement to enter Australia is borne out by special provisions which deem some individuals to be the holders of visas even though they hold no formal documentation to evidence their status.[14] Valid visas confer a right to enter the country, providing the holder has passed through *immigration clearance* either overseas or at point of arrival in the country. The present regime simplifies the paperwork involved in gaining entry to Australia, but retains the two-step procedure that ensures that entry documentation is double-checked at or before admission. As Kesby notes,[15] the institution of visa screening has in some respects redefined the concept of border. Like many other countries,[16] Australia sometimes uses 'pre-screening' procedures whereby visa documentation is checked at point of disembarkation and would-be migrants are prevented from boarding the plane to come to Australia.[17]

[6.08] Immigration clearance involves the production to an immigration official at a port of entry of a valid passport or other travel documentation together with the person's visa, a passenger card (setting out personal details and travel arrangements) and customs declaration. The evidence required to be shown to clearance officers is set out in s 166 of the Act and regs 3.02 and 3.03 of the *Migration Regulations 1994* (Cth). If a non-citizen does not provide evidence within two working days of entry that he or she holds a valid visa,[18] he or she risks becoming an 'unlawful non-citizen'.[19] The official examines the documentation offered, and checks the departmental computer database to determine whether the passenger features on any immigration alert list.[20] Provision is made in the Act for persons in immigration clearance to provide information regarding their identity and any other matters required by the Act or the Regulations.[21] Failure to comply with a request for such information renders a non-citizen liable to detention on grounds of 'reasonable suspicion' that she or he is an unlawful non-citizen.[22] The procedures followed in taking a non-citizen through immigration clearance are set out in Part 3 of the Regulations and in Migration Series Instruction (MSI) 99.[23]

---

14 See, for example, ss 32-34 of the *Migration Act*.
15 See Alison Kesby, 'The Shifting and Multiple Border and International Law' (2007) 27(1) *Oxford Journal of Legal Studies* 101.
16 See, for example, *R v Immigration Officer at Prague Airport; Ex parte European Roma Rights Centre* [2004] UKHL 55.
17 For a case in which this appears to have been done, see *Singh v MIMA* [2006] FMCA 1163. In this instance the applicants were twin sisters who had been granted permanent residence after a six-year struggle to prove their dependency on their parents. Their visas were cancelled when they returned to Fiji from Australia.
18 *Migration Regulations 1994* (Cth), reg 3.04.
19 *Migration Act*, s 14.
20 Ibid, s 489.
21 Ibid, s 166.
22 Ibid, ss 189-190.
23 See also MSI-109 (passenger cards) and MSI-093 (travel documents). MSIs operate as policy instructions that are incorporated in due course into the formal Procedural Advice Manual (PAM).

[6.09] The Act makes it obligatory for non-citizens to answer all questions in their visa applications and passenger cards, and to ensure that only 'correct' answers are provided in both instances.[24] The penalty for providing false or misleading information is cancellation of the visa issued[25] and prosecution for an offence,[26] even if an error was made through inadvertence.[27] It is worth noting that the power to cancel on the ground of false and misleading information extends to all visas – both permanent and temporary.[28] The Act gives the departmental officials power to supplement their examination of a passenger's travel documents with searches of the person, and of the person's clothing and other belongings, to determine whether there is or may be evidence for grounds for cancelling the person's visa.[29]

[6.10] The present regime governing immigration clearance has the attraction of being both simple and highly explicit in its directions to immigration officials. The problem for the users of the system is its inflexibility and its heavy bias in favour of the immigration authorities at the expense of the non-citizens seeking entry into Australia. While non-citizens face heavy sanctions for inadvertently providing false or misleading information at any stage in the immigration process, aberrant officials face no equivalent penalties. In the event that a non-citizen successfully challenges a decision to cancel a visa and to take the person into custody, he or she cannot claim damages for wrongful detention.[30]

[6.11] Under the system in force before 1994, the admission of non-citizens was much more discretionary than is now the case. The absence of a visa did not preclude the grant of an entry permit. For example, of the 3064 'undocumented arrivals' who landed in Australia in 1990-91, only 528 were refused admission.[31] Conversely, those who arrived with a visa had no 'right' to an entry permit. Persons adjudged to lack *bona fides* could find themselves in the same position as persons who came to the country without entry documentation.

[6.12] The present regime greatly simplifies the law regarding admission to Australia. Gone are the legal fictions whereby unauthorised arrivals were deemed not to have 'entered' Australia and were subjected to differential detention arrangements and harsh turn-around provisions.[32] Where a non-citizen arrives with a visa and some form of irregularity is detected, a decision must be made to cancel the visa.[33] The procedures for questioning detention are also articulated with greater clarity, as is the law governing the grant of visas to unauthorised arrivals.

---

24 See *Migration Act*, ss 101 and 102.
25 Ibid, s 109.
26 Ibid, s 334.
27 Ibid, s 111.
28 See further Chapter 15.3.2; and [6.28] and [6.60] below.
29 See *Migration Act*, s 252.
30 Ibid, s 114.
31 See Joint Standing Committee on Migration, *Asylum, Border Control and Detention* (Canberra: AGPS, 1994) at 15; and Crock, above n 12, at 68.
32 See Crock, above n 12.
33 See *Migration Act*, s 116; and below, Chapter 15.4.

[6.13] There are now very few options available to non-citizens who arrive in Australia with no visa or who have their visa cancelled as the result of an anomaly. Only four classes of visa can be granted to persons in immigration clearance: the Norfolk Island Permanent Resident (Residence) (Class AW) visa; the Protection (Class AZ) visa; the Border (Temporary) (Class TA) visa; and the visa created for New Zealand nationals – Special Category (Temporary) (Class TY). Of these, the most significant is the Border visa, as it covers the largest group of non-citizens who arrive with inadequate documentation as a result of innocent oversight.[34] Those covered include certain returning residents; non-citizens who were in Australia on temporary permits who can show a good reason why they left the country without obtaining a visa to re-enter; non-citizens who obtain visas for themselves but fail to seek appropriate visas for their children; and persons seeking temporary stay in Australia as tourists or short-term visitors. Eligibility for a Protection visa is dependent on an applicant gaining recognition as a refugee.

[6.14] In spite of the quite dramatic alterations to the law, the process of presenting for immigration clearance remains much the same in experiential terms. Non-citizens are required still to present their documentation at point of entry. The checking process remains a traumatic one for persons who either arrive without a visa, or who arrive with a visa that is found to be invalid. In spite of various calls that have been made to make the process more transparent, applicants are not afforded any kind of assistance until they have been through the initial screening interview. This is so even if the individual affected is an unaccompanied child or is otherwise in a vulnerable situation. Unaccompanied children are no longer placed automatically in immigration detention, as was the case until 2005. However, they do not have a guardian appointed until they have been assessed as having some entitlement to apply for a visa to remain in Australia.[35] The standard practice is that all new arrivals are questioned by immigration officials before being allowed access to advisers of any kind. There is no statutory obligation on such officials to either inform interviewees of their rights or to provide forms so that interviewees can apply for a visa: applicants are expected to make a request for these things.[36] For asylum seekers, this means in practice that they must articulate a fear of being returned home by using trigger words such as 'refugee' and 'persecution'. Because the initial interviews are conducted behind closed doors – and in the case of boat people, in remote locations like Darwin, Port Hedland or Christmas Island – it can be extremely difficult for new arrivals to make contact with people who can assist them. Often it is only the practical impossibility of removal to a country of origin that prevents immediate turn-arounds.[37]

---

34 See *Migration Regulations*, Sch 2, subclass 773.

35 For a discussion of the procedures for 'screening' asylum seeker children in Australia, see Mary Crock, *Seeking Asylum Alone: Unaccompanied and Separated Children and Refugee Protection in Australia* (Sydney: Themis Press, 2006) at 119-31. For a discussion of the guardianship arrangements for such children, see Chapter 2.2.1 and Chapter 7.2 of this report.

36 See *Migration Act*, s 256.

37 In the course of the research for the *Seeking Asylum Alone* Report, a young Afghan woman was identified who was 15 years of age when she arrived in Australia with an 11-year-old presumed to be her brother. The pair were 'screened out' on the basis that the girl had failed to articulate a 'protection claim'. They spent eight months detained at Woomera Detention Centre with a group of adults whose refugee claims had been rejected before they were discovered by refugee advocates who arranged for their refugee claims to be heard. See Crock, above n 35, at 121.

[6.15] Although an old case, the treatment afforded the applicant in the case of *Azemoudeh v MIEA* is illustrative of the problems inherent in the 'screening' regime for new arrivals.[38] In that instance, Wilcox J went so far as to order the return from Hong Kong of an Iranian who was removed before he could lodge an application for refugee status. The man's solicitor had attended Sydney airport with a partially completed refugee status application form but had been denied access to his client. Wilcox J held that the failure to consider Mr Azemoudeh's claim for refugee status rendered the decision to remove him unlawful.

[6.16] Putting the asylum seekers to one side, the cases that have continued to cause most angst are those in which non-citizens have been adjudged as lacking *bona fides* during the immigration clearance process. The typical scenario is that of tourists who are discovered with documentation suggesting that they will be seeking employment or engaging in business activities in Australia. Non-citizens may disembark with a valid visa, only to find themselves delivered into immigration detention with a visa cancelled on the grounds that they are not a *bona fide* visitor and/or that they present a risk of overstaying their visa. The reported cases include some of the more egregious instances of heavy-handed official behaviour. Burchett J's ruling in *Singthong v MIEA*[39] is an example in point. There, a Thai woman was granted a temporary entry permit upon arrival, only to have her permit revoked when a customs officer discovered correspondence in her luggage suggesting that she intended to seek work in Australia. Ms Singthong was strip searched and taken shoeless to Villawood detention centre in Sydney's West while her belongings were flown out of the country. Burchett J expressed his outrage at the treatment afforded to the applicant and held that the cancellation decision was vitiated by the failure to accord the applicant procedural fairness. The enforcement powers in the Act no longer permit strip searching, except in the context of searches conducted within detention centres. However, visitors who are found with work-related documents can still encounter difficulties. In *Chiorny v MIMA*,[40] Olney J granted relief to a tourist who found herself in the same predicament as Ms Singthong. She was found to have an Australian boyfriend whom the interviewing officer took as being a de facto spouse. On this basis she was judged to lack bona fides as a visitor. In setting aside the decision to cancel the applicant's subclass 676 visa, his Honour criticised the primary decision-maker for failing to explain adequately the line of questioning that was put to the applicant. While he did not make a finding on the factual determinations made, he expressed concern about the inferences drawn from the interviews conducted and criticised the interviewer for failing to keep a proper record of what was said by the parties. Olney J ruled that the cancellation decision was unlawful because the applicant had not been given the particulars required under ss 119(1)(a) and 120 of the Act.

[6.17] The present legislation governing immigration clearance acknowledges that border applicants do have some rights to a hearing, albeit in a strictly limited sense. The specification that persons in immigration detention must be given access

---
38   (1985) 8 ALD 281.
39   (1988) 18 FCR 486.
40   (1997) 44 ALD 605.

to legal advice on request[41] creates the framework for a rudimentary hearing. The limited nature of these hearing rights is underscored by the fact that no right of appeal lies from a decision to cancel a visa while a person is in immigration clearance.[42] In the *Migration Regulations 1993* (Cth) (*1993 Regulations*), non-citizens in immigration clearance at one stage were given a right of appeal, provided that the intention to appeal was notified within five minutes of the person's visa being cancelled.[43] The only avenue for seeking redress of a visa cancellation under s 116 is a legal challenge in the Federal Court. The range of people eligible for the 'bridging visa' is limited. Such visas facilitate release from custody while an application for a visa is being processed.[44]

[6.18] The dilemma posed by these border cases is that, while non-citizens are required to conform to the terms of their visa, there is nothing inherently unlawful about a tourist seeking future employment opportunities while in Australia. Nor is it illegal for a tourist to form a relationship with an Australian party. At the same time, migration officials at point of entry are asked to assess visa holders to ensure that they meet the criteria prescribed for the class of visa held. In these circumstances, it is not surprising that the courts should scrutinise with care decisions made at point of entry to cancel visas that would appear to be valid on their face.[45]

[6.19] In *Sandoval v MIMA*,[46] a Venezuelan citizen's Tourist (Short Stay) visa was cancelled at the airport on the basis that he had given an incorrect answer in his application form, within the meaning of s 101(b) of the *Migration Act*. In answer to the question 'Why do you want to visit Australia?', Mr Sandoval had written that his Australian friends (a Ms Fenner and Dr Fenck) were offering him a great opportunity to improve his English and that he was going to help them translate their books (in return for food and accommodation at their home). On his arrival at the Australian airport, Mr Sandoval was interviewed about the genuineness of his visit and a search of his luggage was conducted. Correspondence was found revealing the existence of an intimate relationship between and Mr Sandoval and Ms Fenner, with mention of marriage and starting a new life in Australia. After further questioning, the immigration inspector cancelled the visa under s 116(1) of the Act, stating that Mr Sandoval had made misleading statements. On appeal to the Federal Court, Gray J observed that a person may have various purposes for visiting a country, but that the 'purpose' with which the relevant visa application form was concerned was 'what the visa applicant proposes to do during the period for which the visa is to be granted'. His Honour also recalled the legislative history of the Act, noting that earlier provisions referred to the making of 'a statement which is false or misleading in a material particular', in contrast to the current provisions, which simply refer to 'incorrect answers'.[47] His Honour concluded:[48]

---

41 *Migration Act* s 256.
42 See the definition of 'Part 5 reviewable decision' in s 337 of the Act.
43 See *1993 Regulations*, reg 2.46.
44 See s 73 of the Act; and Chapter 16.4.
45 For another example of a tourist whose visa was cancelled as a result of employment related documentation found in his luggage, see *Li v MIMA (No 2)* [2007] FMCA 22.
46 (2001) 194 ALR 71 (*Sandoval*).
47 See s 11A of the *Migration Act* inserted by the *Migration Legislation Amendment Act 1989* (Cth) as it stood before amendment by s 11 of the *Migration Reform Act 1992* (Cth).
48 *Sandoval* (2001) 194 ALR 71 at [50].

> I am of the view that the question 'Why do you want to visit Australia?' requires an applicant to give a reason, disclosing a purpose, genuinely held by the applicant, falling within the criteria for the visa concerned. It does not require an applicant to set out all of the reasons that he or she may have for wishing to come to Australia. As long as the reason specified in the answer is a genuine one, the answer cannot be said to be incorrect for the purposes of s 101(b) of the Migration Act.

Gray J held therefore that it was not open to the immigration officer (Mr Vella), as a matter of law, to be satisfied that Mr Sandoval had given an incorrect answer on the basis Mr Sandoval had omitted information he considered relevant:

> Unless he was satisfied that the answer itself, or the material supplied with it, contained incorrect information he could not lawfully have found that the ground specified in s 116(1)(d) was made out. In purporting so to find, Mr Vella made an error of law, being an error involving an incorrect interpretation of the applicable law. Such an error is a ground for judicial review …[49]

[6.20] With the successive changes to the regime governing the judicial review of migration decisions, it has become increasingly difficult to challenge adverse credibility findings made at point of entry into Australia. In *Walton v Ruddock*,[50] the applicant had his Electronic Travel Authority (visa) cancelled at the airport under s 116 of the Act. This visa allows the holder to travel to, and enter, Australia on multiple occasions for a period of 12 months and, on each occasion, to remain in Australia for a period not exceeding three months. One of the primary criteria that must be satisfied is that the applicant has 'an intention to visit Australia only for tourism purposes'. The applicant arrived in Australia on the 21 November and had a return ticket to the United States for 12 December following. However, on arrival, an immigration official was not satisfied the applicant met this criteria. The reasons and evidence cited in support of this decision were the applicant's shipment of personal effects and a letter found in his luggage stating that he was moving to Australia and intended to lodge an application for permanent residency. An interview had also been conducted separately with the applicant's partner (Ms Hart), an Australian citizen, in which she stated that, if the applicant could not obtain permanent residency in Australia, his return air ticket would be a safeguard, and that she would like this to be the applicant's first Christmas in Australia.

[6.21] On appeal to the Federal Court, the applicant contended that by failing to disclose these statements to the applicant, the delegate had not given him particulars of information that 'would be the reason, or part of the reason, for cancelling [the] visa', or an opportunity to comment on that information (as required by ss 120 and 121 of the Act). However, Merkel J dismissed this ground of appeal on the basis that the record of the cancellation decision did not state or imply that Ms Hart's statements were a reason, or part of the reason, for the delegate's decision to cancel the visa. Merkel J also rejected the applicant's contention that the delegate had breached the rules of natural justice by failing to give him an opportunity to respond to Ms Hart's statements, which were adverse matters taken into account in the delegate's decision to cancel the visa. His Honour first found that Ms Hart's statements were

---

49   See *Sandoval* (2001) 194 ALR 71 at 88 [51].
50   (2001) 115 FCR 342.

not necessarily inconsistent with the genuineness of the applicant's visit. His Honour went on to note that, even if an adverse interpretation of the statements were taken, he was satisfied that the 'gravamen or substance of the issue' raised by the statement was put to the applicant, and he was on notice as to its 'essential features'.[51]

6.3 Common entry criteria: Protecting the public interest

[6.22]   Before turning to specific aspects of the migration program, it is worth considering briefly some of the common criteria that must be met by all but a small minority of entrants. These prerequisites to entry are designed to either limit the negative impact of migration on society or to protect the Australian community from harmful influences. They include devices to ensure the support of new arrivals who might otherwise place demands on the social security system and public interest tests to prevent the admission of persons who present a risk to the community by virtue of their health or criminal propensities.

[6.23]   Over the years successive governments have firmed in their resolve to enforce the notion of 'user-pays' in the migration process. Where requirements that applicants for permanent entry obtain sponsors and assurances of support used to be 'honour' arrangements, such matters are now legally enforceable obligations dealt with in the Act and the Regulations. In some cases an assurance is mandatory; in others it is discretionary.[52] An assurance of support may be 'requested' by the Minister.[53] Where the assurance of support is mandatory the criteria specify that 'an assurance of support ... has been given'. In both cases the assurance of support must have been 'accepted by the Minister' at the time of the decision. To ensure that at least some of the cost of the initial settlement process is covered by the sponsor, the assurance of support now involves the lodgment of bonds,[54] and the up-front payment of a visa application charge.[55] The bond covers payments made to the assured person under specified government assistance programs.[56]

[6.24]   Public interest criteria include matters concerning a person's health[57] and good character, as well as questions of national security and public order.[58] Australia's immigration laws have always sought to limit the admission of non-citizens who could pose a threat to the Australian community. The Minister's mandate to protect the public interest reinforced the virtual inviolability of the discretionary power to admit or exclude aliens. Once the Minister's powers were codified, however, the general criteria for judging the suitability for migrants had to be particularised. As

---

51   Ibid at [69].
52   See *Migration Regulations*, Div 2.7.
53   See, for example, *Migration Regulations*, Sch 2, cl 100.223 (regarding the subclass 100 Partner visa).
54   *Migration Regulations*, reg 2.39.
55   Ibid, Part 1, Div 2.2A; and the *Migration (Visa Application) Charge Act 1997* (Cth).
56   See *Social Security Act 1991* (Cth), Part 2.11-2.15; and *Migration Regulations,* reg 2.39.
57   See *Migration Act*, ss 60, 496 and 505; and *Migration Regulations*, regs 1.03 (interpretation of 'community services'); 2.25A (referral to Medical Officer of the Commonwealth); 5.41 (fees); and Sch 4, cll 4005, 4006A and 4007.
58   See *Migration Act*, ss 501-503; and *Migration Regulations*, regs 1.03 (interpretation of 'public interest criterion'), 2.52 and 2.53, and Sch 4, cl 4001.

well as spelling out the tests to be met by applicants, the Regulations had to articulate also the circumstances in which health and character tests could be waived.

[6.25] The codification of public interest criteria has brought its own problems, with challenges made to the interpretation or application of the statutory criteria. Cases that have caused particular difficulty are those involving the assessment of risk to the Australian community in the areas of health and public order/character. In efforts to have the final say, the government has been torn between spelling out its public interest criteria exhaustively and attempting to build back into the legislative scheme a form of ministerial discretion that is 'non-compellable and non-reviewable'.[59] As noted in Chapter 5, health assessment was one of the first matters to be 'outsourced' by the Immigration Department to a specialised non-government organisation. The desire to avoid litigation in this area is underscored by legislation that has made it increasingly difficult for anyone to 'go behind' or challenge assessments made in this context. It is a measure of the human impact of the health rules that the tribunals and courts have continued to find ways around these constraints.

6.3.1 'Health concern non-citizens'

[6.26] Screening the health of non-citizens coming into the country has always been a matter of high priority for federal governments. On the one hand, health testing is seen as essential to safeguard the wellbeing of the Australian population. Poor control of 'health concern non-citizens' is seen rightly as a potential public relations disaster and a threat to community confidence in the immigration program. From other points of view, however, the processes put in place have been criticised as overly complicated, demanding and time consuming, particularly for shorter term visitors and business entrants.[60] Questions have been raised also about the restrictive views taken of people with disabilities. As explained below, no distinction is drawn between disability and disease for the purposes of the health rules. In many situations, if an applicant would be eligible to receive a Commonwealth government disability pension, this will operate as a bar to the grant of a visa. Although a special inquiry into the health rules was made in 1992, it was not until late in 1995 that significant changes were made to the criteria and procedures used in screening the health of non-citizens coming to Australia.[61] In the intervening years the trend has been towards increasing rigidity in the operation of the rules.

[6.27] The present Regulations require applicants in all visa classes except diplomatic or short-term medical treatment categories to meet specified health criteria. The tests imposed on applicants vary according to the class of visa sought and the nature and length of the non-citizen's proposed stay in Australia. Some applicants are required to do no more than furnish a statutory declaration that he or she is free of certain diseases and conditions. Other non-citizens can be required to submit to a

---

59   See Joint Standing Committee on Migration Regulations (JSCMR), *Conditional Migrant Entry: The Health Rules* (Canberra: AGPS, December 1992) at rec 3.
60   See Committee of Inquiry into the Temporary Entry of Business People and Highly Skilled Specialists (1995) (the Roach Report) at [4.50]-[4.58].
61   See JSCMR, above n 59.

chest x-ray; or a full medical examination carried out by medical practitioners under the auspices of relevant health authorities.

[6.28] Traditionally, the immigration authorities have taken quite a relaxed approach to the health processing of temporary residents and short-term visitors. There is now a presumption – for some a requirement[62] – that these people will take out private health insurance or meet any health care costs incurred during their stay in the country. Temporary residents are no longer eligible for Medicare or other health-related benefits. Provided that they do not propose to work in health sensitive industries; do not fall into classes of individuals known to present health risks; and are in general good health, most applicants for temporary visas are not required to undergo a full health assessment.[63] The safeguard, for the government, is that where an applicant fails to disclose matters relevant to the assessment of health (or character), the visa issued may be liable to be cancelled as a result of the false or misleading information provided.[64]

[6.29] In practice, applicants for temporary visas permitting a stay of three months or less are usually not subjected to health testing unless they meet the policy descriptor of being of 'special significance'. Persons targeted for health testing irrespective of length of stay are persons deemed to be of high risk because of their exposure to 'blood-borne contact' (such as medical workers, tattooists, sex workers and intravenous drug users) or because of the vulnerability of the people and places they are likely to visit (such as child care centres and preschools). Older persons and parents seeking to visit for more than six months also fall into this category, as do pregnant women and persons with known or suspected health conditions.[65]

[6.30] In spite of the provision in the Regulations for fast track screening, in practice all applicants for permanent residence continue to have their health monitored very closely before being granted a visa. The health criteria that apply to migrants to Australia fall into three broad groupings. The first is the general test set out in Sch 4, cl 4005 of the Regulations which applies to all applicants for permanent or provisional visas[66] with the exception of partner, child, interdependent and certain humanitarian visas. The second test (in Sch 4, cl 4006A) is applied to temporary visa

---

62 For example, non-citizens entering Australia under an employer nomination may have some of the health requirements waived if the employer gives the Minister a written undertaking to meet all of the costs associated with a disease or condition that would otherwise cause the applicant to fail to meet the health requirements: see Sch 4, cl 4006A, of the Regulations.

63 Under reg 2.25A(1), the Minister may proceed without seeking a medical opinion in respect of an applicant for a temporary visa where there is no information known to immigration authorities from the application *or otherwise* that suggests that the applicant may not meet the health criteria. The inclusion of the words 'or otherwise' expands the ambit of the Department's health inquiry mandate that was formerly limited to the information contained on an application form. As well as allowing officials to take into account information supplied by members of the public, the change could allow the use of statistical data on matters of health and the spread of disease from different parts of the world. The fact that the government may be moving towards the use of more epidemiological data in health assessments is supported by the provision in reg 2.25A(1) for the fast tracking of applicants for permanent visas who come from 'gazetted' countries and who present no 'known' health risk.

64 See *Migration Act*, ss 109 and 116.

65 See generally DIAC *Form 1163i – Health requirement for temporary entry to Australia*.

66 A provisional visa is a temporary visa that is a precondition for the eventual grant of a permanent residence visa.

applicants such as (subclass 457 (Business (Long Stay)) and creates limited exceptions in cases where health insurers and sponsoring employers guarantee to cover the health costs of temporary visa holders who would otherwise fail to meet the health criteria. The third test (in Sch 4, cl 4007) allows for the waiver of the health rules in limited circumstances for certain close family, business and humanitarian visa applicants.[67]

[6.31] A common feature of all of the health rules is the requirement that visa applicants are required to be free from tuberculosis or from a disease or condition that represents a threat to public health in Australia. Persons who have suffered from tuberculosis can be required to sign an undertaking that they will present for regular health testing after their admission into Australia. The tests also operate on their face to exclude people with a 'disease or condition' that 'would be likely to': (a) require health care or community services or meet the *medical* requirements for the provision of a community service; and (b) prejudice the access of Australians to health care or community services or result in a 'significant cost' to the Australian community in the area of health care or community services (irrespective of whether an applicant would access such services in practice).[68] There is no discretion in the Minister (or the Migration Review Tribunal (MRT)) to waive the requirements of the cl 4005 test. The concession made in cl 4007 for close family, business and humanitarian visa applicants is that the issues of 'significant cost' and 'prejudice to the Australian community' can be overlooked as long as the potential costs or use of community services and prejudice are not *'undue'*. Where one member of a family group fails the assessment, the whole group will be denied visas.[69]

[6.32] The outsourcing of medical assessments has led to a rather complex and fractured system from the perspective of the migrant. The Immigration Department has maintained a section charged with the formulation and implementation of health policy (in conjunction with other relevant federal and State departments). The process of assessing a person's health status is carried out by the 'Health Assessment Service' (HAS) for persons outside of Australia and by 'Health Services Australia' (HSA) for persons in the country. Medical practitioners appointed by HAS are referred to as 'Approved Medical Practitioners' while general medical staff are referred to as 'Medical Advisors'. In addition, reg 1.03 of the *Migration Regulations* provides that 'Medical Officers of the Commonwealth' (MOCs) are doctors appointed by the Minister under reg 1.16AA to give their opinion on whether individual applicants meet the health requirement. MOCs also appear to be referred to as 'Panel Doctors'. The operation of the HAS and HSA are supervised by what appear to be a roving team known as 'Global Medical Directors' who are responsible for auditing and supervising the panel doctors. In addition, both the HAS and HSA operate an internal

---

67   The health waiver applies to partner visas; all child visas; refugee and humanitarian visas; temporary humanitarian visas; and close ties, business skills (permanent) and New Zealand Citizen family relationships visas.
68   Until 1 November 1995, a further restriction was placed on the admission of people suffering from a disease or condition of an hereditary nature that might affect the health status of children born to them in Australia: see former cll 4006 and 4008 of Sch 4 to the *Migration Regulations*.
69   See *Migration Act*, s 140.

appeal system whereby 'Review Medical Officers of the Commonwealth' (RMOCs) undertake a medical review of adverse assessments made by MOCs.[70]

[6.33] The issues that have generated most litigation are those relating to the characterisation of a disease or condition; the determination of what will constitute a significant cost; and when an applicant will be considered to 'access' community services so as to prejudice Australian users of those services. There is also case law on the question of what will constitute 'undue' cost or prejudice for the purpose of the health waiver. Each of these matters will be considered in turn.

[6.34] The tribunal – formerly the Immigration Review Tribunal (IRT) and now the MRT – is given power to review visa refusals, but no authority to question the health assessments carried out by the government's medical officers. The officers' opinion constitutes a separate decision by a person not acting as a delegate of the Minister.[71] These officers are required to assess the health status of the applicants, but they also proffer advice on the likely cost burden the applicant would place on the Australian community.

Identifying a disease or condition

[6.35] In early cases where fresh evidence became available to the tribunal suggesting improvements in the applicant's health after the initial assessment, some IRT members would attempt to negotiate a reassessment of the applicant by the medical officer, with varied degrees of success.[72] Other devices were used by the IRT to avoid negative medical assessments in cases where the tribunal took the view that justice favoured the grant of a visa. While it could not question the opinion formed by the medical officer, the tribunal took the view that it could determine the factual question of whether or not an applicant suffered from a 'disease or condition' for the purposes of the Act.

[6.36] In *Re Berman*,[73] the tribunal dissected the medical opinion furnished and concluded that the relevant officer had left scope for a finding that the applicant no longer suffered from a disease or condition. The IRT considered the time that had elapsed since the first assessment; opinions of other doctors; and the continuing good health of the applicant. It concluded that the risk of re-occurrence of Mrs Berman's disease was not real or serious or substantial. This finding, taken together with the fact that she did not presently suffer from the disease, meant that she was free from that disease. In reaching this conclusion, the tribunal adopted a two-stage inquiry. The first required the making of an immediate diagnosis of the applicant's situation, with a finding that the disease or condition existed being conclusive of the inquiry. If no disease or condition could be detected, a second stage of inquiry ensued to establish the likelihood of the disease or condition occurring or re-occurring within a

---

70   See DIAC, *PAM3*, Ch 6.
71   See, for example, *Re Nelson* [1990] IRTA 28; *Re Papaioannou* [1991] IRTA 113; and *Re Dusa* [1991] IRTA 285.
72   See, for example, *Re Papaioannou* [1991] IRTA 113; *Re Cruz* [1992] IRTA 1411; *Re Ratley* [1992] IRTA 924; *Re Rosenauer* [1992] IRTA 945; and *Re Alakoc* [1991] IRTA 194.
73   [1994] IRTA 3937.

reasonable time frame. The tribunal noted that this approach was necessary because some diseases or conditions are incipient or inchoate, so that an applicant may not show obvious or demonstrable symptoms at a given date. If the second stage inquiry established that the applicant was not at risk, it followed that she or he was 'free from' the disease or condition specified.

[6.37] In *Re Nguyen*[74] the tribunal examined the medical officer's assessment of a young Vietnamese woman who, as the result of her premature birth, had lower than average intelligence. The tribunal once again intervened on the ground that the applicant did not have a 'disease or condition' that could activate the health concern provisions. On the basis of literature submitted to it, the IRT drew a distinction between what the medical officer assessed as 'borderline intellectual functioning' and 'mental retardation'. It held that while the latter state could be considered a 'condition', the former could not. Similar reasoning was used in *Re Henry*[75] to admit a woman whose legs were paralysed as a result of childhood poliomyelitis, who was wrongly assessed as a person suffering from systemic paraplegia.[76]

[6.38] Interestingly, in the decade or more that has passed since cases like *Re Berman*[77] were decided, the Federal Court in rare cases has continued to find some wriggle room in the straight jacket of the health assessment system. As in earlier cases, dispute has arisen over the characterisation of an individual suffering from a condition that manifests in a wide variety of forms, with varying impacts on the individual's need for assistance. A number of the cases have involved families with a child suffering from a form of mental disability such as Downs Syndrome. In cases such as *MIMA v Seligman*[78] it is evident that the child (or young person) in question is both a cherished member of the family and unlikely to be a burden on the community because of both the talents of the child and the degree of family support.

[6.39] In *Seligman*[79] the Federal Court held that the focus of the consideration will be whether the medical officer's opinion is 'of a kind authorised by the regulations'. If an opinion 'travels beyond the limits of what is authorised, then to act upon it as though it is binding is to act upon a wrong view of the law and to err in the interpretation of the law or its application, a ground of review for which s 476 of the Act provides'.[80] The

---

74 [1995] IRTA 5667.
75 [1995] IRTA 4935.
76 See also *Re Nance* [1995] IRTA 5065 where a Romanian orphan was wrongly assessed as intellectually as well as physically disabled.
77 [1994] IRTA 3937.
78 (1999) 85 FCR 115 (*Seligman*) at [66].
79 Ibid.
80 Note that the challenge in *Seligman* went to the substantive validity of the regulation in question rather than to the exercise of the discretion in that case. In that case what was then reg 2.25B of the *Migration Regulations* was held to be ultra vires and invalid (but severable). It was purportedly made pursuant to s 505 of the *Migration Act*, which authorises the making of Regulations providing that the Minister is to get a specified person to give an opinion on a specified matter. However, the court noted ((1999) 85 FCR 115 at [54]) that reg 2.25A directed the medical officer to consider some things and not others in the formation of his or her opinion as to whether the disease or condition would be likely to result in a significant cost to the Australian community in the areas of health or community services. Namely, it required the medical officer to disregard the applicant's prospective use of such services – an assessment which the court held was required by cl 4005(c). At the time

court observed[81] that reg 2.25A(3) requires the Minister to take the relevant opinion to be 'correct' where:

(1) what is provided is an opinion;
(2) the opinion is that of the medical officer of the Commonwealth who provides it;
(3) the opinion is the opinion of the medical officer 'on a matter referred to in sub-reg (1) or (2)'; and
(4) the opinion addresses satisfaction of the requirements at the time of the Minister's decision.

[6.40] Later cases adopting the approach outlined in *Seligman* suggest that the opinion of a medical officer will be difficult to challenge. In *Blair v MIMA*,[82] for example, Carr J acknowledged that the court was entitled to consider the medical officer's opinion. However, he rejected the applicant's claims that the medical officer had failed to exercise his jurisdiction, or that the opinion was vitiated by legal error. In that instance the MOC had formed an opinion that a secondary applicant for a subclass 151 Former Resident visa with Downs Syndrome and a mild intellectual disability would require ongoing assisted schooling and speech therapy, and would be eligible for long-term income support in the future at significant cost to the Australian community. This opinion was then relied on by the MRT, which affirmed the decision to refuse the visa. Dismissing the appeal, Carr J held that the applicant had not proved on balance that the officer had ignored additional material; purported to make adverse findings on that material; or formed his opinion in an arbitrary and capricious manner so as to amount to an actual or constructive failure to form an opinion. These issues were dealt with 'assuming but without so deciding that the Opinion is subject to judicial review'. Carr J also added that, in his view, the MOC was not under any obligation to provide reasons as to why he rejected (if he did so) any expert medical evidence proffered. The other grounds of appeal based on legal error on the part of the tribunal were also unsuccessful.[83]

---

of the decision, Sch 4, cl 4005, provided that the health criterion will be satisfied if the applicant or person concerned:
  (c) is not a person who has a disease or condition that, during the applicant's proposed period of stay in Australia would be likely to:
    (i) result in a significant cost to the Australian community in the areas of health care or community services; or
    (ii) prejudice the access of an Australian citizen or permanent resident to health care or community services.

Therefore the regulation was held to be both 'internally inconsistent because what it requires the Medical Officer to do is inconsistent with the language of the criterion which it imports', and 'beyond the power conferred by s 505 because the limitation it imposes upon that opinion means it does not address the relevant criterion': ibid at [58]. Following the decision in *Seligman*, reg 2.25B was repealed: SR 199 No 81. However, cl 4005 was also amended, to incorporate the wording and effect of this former regulation. Challenges to the validity of this re-worded clause have been unsuccessful.

81 See *Seligman* (1999) 85 FCR 115 at [48] and [49].
82 [2001] FCA 1014.
83 *Bui v MIMA* (1999) 85 FCR 134; *Imad v MIMA* [2001] FCA 1011; and *Inguanti v MIMA* [2001] FCA 1046, discussed below at [6.43]ff.

[6.41] The later case of *Robinson v MIMIA*[84] involved a young boy presenting as the son of a subclass 855 (Labour Agreement) visa applicant. The boy suffered from a mild form of Downs Syndrome but was assessed nonetheless by the MOC and RMOC as an individual who would be likely to require special education and other assistance during his lifetime. This meant that he was assessed as a person whose admission would result in significant cost to the Australian community. Siopis J ruled that the MRT had committed a jurisdictional error by relying on the determination by an RMOC. His Honour held that the medical assessments were unlawful because the officers had failed to determine the exact form or level of the boy's impairment, relying instead on a blanket determination that anyone with Downs Syndrome would fail to meet the health test.

[6.42] *Robinson* is a reminder of past controversies in what was then the IRT over when an individual could be considered 'likely to prejudice access to health care' of any Australian citizen or permanent resident. Two approaches emerged. One view was that all the circumstances of an individual should be considered in determining the impact that person would have on scarce community resources, but taking into account also the benefits that person might bring to the country. The alternative approach was to focus less on the subjective circumstances of the applicant than on the general burden posed by an individual with the disease or condition of the applicant, weighed against the demands made by other individuals in Australia in the same diagnostic category as the applicant. In the early days the IRT appears to have favoured the view that any burden on the community should be balanced against the benefits that might accrue through the admission of an applicant and of his or her family unit as a whole. This approach was echoed in the recommendations of the Health Rules Report (at para 4.41) but does not seem to have been followed by some medical officers. For example, in *Re Lu*,[85] a negative assessment was made of an adopted child rendered blind by her premature birth on the basis of the cost to the Australian community. On the basis of evidence provided of the technological aids that are now available to enable blind persons to participate fully in social and professional life in Australia, the IRT rejected the assessment made and invoked the Minister's power to waive the health criteria. In spite of the contrary recommendations made in the Health Rules report, the changes made in November 1995 and maintained ever since did not adopt anything like a balancing approach in the area of health assessments. As noted earlier, the *Migration Regulations* in Sch 4, cl 4005, now require a medical officer to assess the potential cost and other burdens that would flow from admitting an applicant *without regard to whether that person will use the services* involved. The officer is required to focus not on the actual burden that is likely to be imposed by a person (given his or her private resources), but the burden that would be posed by a person in the applicant's diagnostic category.

---

84 (2005) 148 FCR 182 (*Robinson*).
85 [1991] IRTA 207.

[6.43] In *Imad v MIMA*,[86] Heerey J dismissed the applicant's claim that cl 4005 was invalid because it was 'incapable of meaning or application'. His Honour articulated the test set out in cl 4005(c) as follows:[87]

> The criterion in cl 4005(c) requires the applicant to be not a person who has a disease or condition of a kind described in paragraphs (i) and (ii). The 'person' referred to in (i) is not the applicant but a hypothetical person who suffers from the disease or condition which the applicant has. The criterion requires assessment as to whether or not a disease or condition is such that it would be likely to require health care or community services and that provision of health care or community services would result in a significant cost to the Australian community. The assessment of the likelihood of health care or community services is a qualification or characterisation of the kind of disease or condition in question, just like saying 'this is a surgical procedure which usually requires general anaesthetic'. It is not a prediction of whether the particular applicant will, in fact, require health care or community services at significant cost to the Australian community.

Heerey J commented that this converse task (inquiring into the financial circumstances of a particular applicant or any family members of friends or other sources of financial assistance) would be an inappropriate task for a medical officer. He therefore held that the MRT had not erred in failing to take into account the capacity of the applicant's family to pay for her medical expenses; this 'objective' test was specifically mandated by cl 4005. This approach was also followed in *Inguanti v MIMA*[88] although it has clearly been modified by the ruling in *Robinson*, discussed at [6.41].

[6.44] Certainly, the application of this test in the manner suggested by the court in *Imad* has delivered some very unsatisfactory outcomes. In *Inguanti*, the visa applicant (Mr Urso) was an Italian-born American citizen whose application for a preferential family visa was denied on the basis that he failed to meet the health criteria set out in cl 4005. The medical officer found that the Mr Urso's intellectual disability was sufficiently severe to prevent him from living independently (he needed regular supervision and assistance with daily activities); that Mr Urso would meet the eligibility criteria for government-supported accommodation and special programs for people with disabilities, and was likely to require nursing home care in the foreseeable future. He therefore concluded the applicant was 'a person who has a disease or condition that during the applicant's proposed period of stay in Australia, would be likely to result in a significant cost to the Australian community in the area of community services and prejudice access to services in short supply'. Schedule 4, cl 4005, rendered it irrelevant that Mr Urso and his sister had each inherited A$414,500 from their mother's estate; that Mr Urso held A$420,000 in a trust account; that he received pension and union payments each month; and that his sister had a large family in Australia who would always keep house and care for him.

[6.45] Paradoxically, the decision was set aside by Heerey J on the grounds that the medical officer had treated the question as being 'whether Mr Urso's condition, as distinct from a condition of that nature suffered by a hypothetical person, would

---

86 [2001] FCA 1011.
87 Ibid at [13]-[14].
88 [2001] FCA 1046.

be likely to result in a significant cost to the Australian community' (by assessing his personal eligibility for government-supported accommodation and special programs). However, perhaps realising the unsatisfactory results of this approach, Heerey J concluded by stating that '[w]hatever the outcome of any further proceedings, I must say that this is a very strong case for compassionate consideration under s 351'.

[6.46] The ameliorative ruling by Siopis J in *Robinson* notwithstanding, there is little doubt that these provisions do continue to make it difficult for both medical officers and the MRT to make positive recommendations in the cases where applicants suffer from a disease or condition that would see Australians in a similar state of health receiving some form of government assistance or using community resources.

Significant cost and health care

[6.47] The recent history of the health rules in Australia suggests that the process has indeed become increasingly mechanistic. The relevant policy guidelines state that the MOC's cost assessment must cover either the visa period (for temporary visas) or a period of five years for permanent resident applicants (three years for those aged 70, phased in from 68).[89] The guidelines no longer provide a monetary estimate.[90] However, practitioners have been advised that the unofficial rule of thumb is that 'significant cost' will be shown where it can be estimated with reasonable certainty that a person will require treatment costing more than $20,000 over five years (or a pro rata equivalent for elderly applicants).[91]

[6.48] Because the rules operate on theoretical costs rather than on what a person will actually consume, it has become virtually impossible for individuals with serious diseases and conditions such as HIV-AIDS to obtain visas permitting long-term stay in Australia. Although Finkelstein J found in one case that a self-funded visitor who was HIV positive would not be a burden on the Australian community,[92] the judge was overruled on appeal. The Full Federal Court in *MIMIA v X*[93] ruled that the RMOC had committed no error in law by simply adding together the cost of antiretroviral treatments and the monthly monitoring costs. The court found that the law required consideration of the cost of the drug regimen even though the treatments were both paid for by the applicant and self-administered. The judges ruled that Finkelstein J was in error in supposing that because health care 'imports an element of personal attention or activity by a provider of health care', self-administered treatment cannot be considered as health care.

---

89   PAM3, Sch 4/4005-4007 – The health requirement, section 56.2.
90   Until 1 July 2001 'significant cost' was defined in PAM3 as 50 per cent above the average per capita health care and community services costs for Australians. See Migration Practice Essentials Pty Ltd, *Health Criteria*, June 2006, 23.
91   See Migration Practice Essentials, ibid.
92   See *X v MIMIA* [2005] FCA 429.
93   *MIMIA v X* (2005) 146 FCR 408.

Access to community services

[6.49] The rigidity of the health rules is perhaps most apparent in the reference made to an applicant meeting the medical criteria for the provision of a 'community service'. The phrase 'community service' has been interpreted broadly to include supported accommodation, home and community care and the payment of income support. In *Seligman*,[94] the Federal Court emphasised the words 'in the areas of', and was guided by dictionary definitions of the word 'service'. On this basis, it was held that 'community services' could encompass the provision of a disability-related government pension. This was reiterated in *Bui v MIMA*,[95] where the Federal Court stated that the activities covered 'do not exclude the provision of financial benefit or other support involving a cost', but could extend to 'special training and financial support' referred to by the medical officer in his assessment. To avoid doubt, a definition of 'community services' has since been inserted in reg 1.03 of the Regulations, stating that the term includes the provision of an Australian social security benefit, allowance or pension.

[6.50] More importantly, the phrase 'community service' links the health rules to s 94 of the *Social Security Act 1991* (Cth) which sets out the criteria for the grant of a disability support pension. It should be noted in this context that only the *medical criteria* for the grant of such pensions are relevant. To be eligible for a disability support pension an individual must suffer from a physical, intellectual or psychiatric impairment that rates at least 20 points on what are known as the 'Impairment Tables'. In addition he or she must have a continuing inability to work. The Impairment Tables are scheduled to the *Social Security Act* and operate to grade the levels of impairments for different diseases and conditions. As a matter of practicality, most people who achieve an impairment rating of 20 or more would probably find it difficult to convince anyone that they would be able to sustain full time work (at least 30 hours per week) at award wages or above for a period of at least two years – without requiring excessive leave or work absences. However, these are matters of fact that can be the subject of submissions. The Impairment Tables provide a link between immigration and social security that makes it easier to designate monetary values to particular illnesses or disabilities in so far as eligibility for a pension of some kind imputes a federal government payment of designated amounts (in addition to any other expenditure on medicines or community services).

Undue cost and undue prejudice

[6.51] In practical terms, the MRT's power to question the assessment of medical officers in matters concerning cost and burdens on the community appears to be limited to those visa classes in which it is possible to waive the health requirements. In addition to the immediate family and humanitarian visas, waiver is available in respect of certain employment-related visas.[96] In these cases, the Regulations require

---

94 See *MIMA v Seligman* (1999) 85 FCR 115.
95 (1999) 85 FCR 134 at [35].
96 Schedule 4, cl 4007, applies to the following subclasses: 100 Partner; 101 Child; 102 Adoption; 151 Former Resident; 200 Refugee; 201 In-country Special Humanitarian; 202 Global Special

the applicant's employer to sign an undertaking in respect of an applicant's potential health costs for the duration of his or her stay in Australia. Pursuant to cl 4007(2), the requirements of par 4007(1)(c) may be waived if the Minister is satisfied that the granting of the visa would be unlikely to result in:

> (i) undue cost to the Australian community; or
> (ii) undue prejudice to the access to health care or community services of an Australian citizen or permanent resident.

[6.52] The interpretation of these provisions was considered by the Federal Court in *Bui v MIMA*.[97] In that case, the applicant had received a letter which stated that the Minister had 'the power to waive the criterion where the Minister is satisfied that compassionate or compelling circumstances justify waiver of the criteria', and invited him to provide reasons for waiver on these grounds. While both the trial judge and the Full Court on appeal noted that these terms were not explicit in cl 4007(2), it was held that they were broad considerations which 'may properly have a part to play' in the exercise of the discretion. The Full Court added that there was nothing in the exchange of correspondence or the record of the ministerial decision to indicate that the delegate took any unduly restrictive approach to the exercise of the waiver.

[6.53] The ground of appeal based on the medical officer's opinion was also unsuccessful. The medical officer had presented a document entitled 'Waiver Opinion', in which he stated: 'In my opinion, the likely cost to the Australian community of health care or community services is $420,000 (in financial support)'. No basis for this estimate was offered. While the court accepted that the officer went beyond his statutory function in doing so (the document was said to have 'no more legal status than any other piece of gratuitous advice that might be proffered to the decision-maker'), there was nothing in the materials to indicate that the Minister's delegate regarded himself as bound by that opinion. With respect to the 'questionable estimate of the cost which the applicant would impose on the community', the court raised concerns about the quality of the decision-making process.[98] However it held that these matters in themselves did not indicate error of law or procedure infecting the decision of the delegate in such a way that it would be reviewable.

[6.54] The government's policy documents detail what might constitute 'extensive' or 'substantial' prejudice in access to services, focusing on situations where facilities or procedures are in high demand and where Australians are required to wait for considerable periods of time before gaining access to the service. Compelling circumstances and the factors that should be taken into account are also addressed in Procedures Advice Manual 3 (PAM3). These underscore the fact that the public interest criteria are designed to assess the likely financial and social impact that an

---

Humanitarian; 203 Emergency Rescue; 204 Woman at Risk; 300 Prospective Marriage; 309 Partner (Provisional); 445 Dependent Child; 461 New Zealand Citizen Family Relationship (Temporary); 801 Partner (Permanent); 802 Child; 820 Partner (Temporary); 852 Witness Protection (Trafficking) (Permanent); and 890 Business Owner; 891 Investor; 892 State/Territory Sponsored Business Owner; 893 State/Territory Sponsored Investor.

97 (1999) 85 FCR 134.
98 Ibid at [43].

individual might have on the community. The guidelines discount the strength of emotional ties:

> For example, the genuineness of the relationship between the applicant and the sponsor is not sufficient reason to waive the health requirements for a Partner case.[99]

'Reasonable weight' must be given to humanitarian circumstances, as well as to 'the immigration history of the sponsor, including compliance to date with immigration requirements and any undertakings'. How such matters relate to the health status of an applicant is not explained.

[6.55] The toughness in the approach taken emerged forcefully in 2001 with the self-immolation of one Shahraz Kiane outside Parliament House in Canberra. Mr Kiane was an asylum seeker who had been granted a Protection visa as a refugee in 1997. He tried for four and a half years to sponsor his family to join him in Australia under the 'split family' provisions of a 202 Global Special Humanitarian visa. He was denied on the basis that his youngest daughter had cerebral palsy and so would be eligible for a disability pension, thus representing an undue cost for the Australian community. The man's relatives in Australia offered to tender to the government the amount of the costs assessed by the medical officer: all to no avail. Notwithstanding a scathing report by the Ombudsman following the man's death,[100] the government maintained its position and the family were not granted visas to come to Australia from Pakistan.

6.3.2 Character tests

[6.56] The other area involving common entry criteria that has been controversial for the government is in the exclusion of non-citizens on grounds of public order or bad character. After the federal election in late 1998, one of the first initiatives of the re-elected Coalition government was to (re-) introduce and to push through the *Migration Legislation Amendment (Strengthening of Character and Conduct Provisions) Act 1998* (Cth) (the *Character and Conduct Act*).[101] The legislation both reflects the prevailing animosity towards so-called 'bad aliens' and speaks of the changes that have occurred in governmental attitudes towards our review authorities. As we explore in Chapter 17.3, the legislation alters the role and powers of the one generalist tribunal operating in the area of immigration law: the Administrative Appeals Tribunal (AAT).

[6.57] The *Character and Conduct Act* had as its primary aim the strengthening of powers vested in the Minister for Immigration to cancel or refuse visas and to

---

99   See PAM3, Ch 90, [90.3]: 'Compelling Circumstances'.
100 See Commonwealth Ombudsman, *Report on the Investigation into a Complaint about the Processing and Refusal of a Subclass 202 (Split Family) Humanitarian Visa Application*, August 2001, available at <www.comb.gov.au/commonwealth/publish.nsf/AttachmentsByTitle/reports_2001_dima_visa.pdf/$FILE/DIMA-Kiane-aug01.pdf>.
101 This legislation was put to the previous parliament as the Migration Legislation Amendment (Strengthening of Character and Conduct Provisions) Bill 1997 (Cth). The Bill had not been passed when Parliament was prorogued for the election.

remove non-citizens on grounds of criminality or bad conduct. This was not the first time that a Minister demonstrated a commitment to keeping the migration program 'clean' by moving to change the law governing the exclusion or expulsion of 'bad aliens'. Another occasion was in the late 1980s and early 1990s when the regime for deporting criminal permanent residents was given shape. In that instance a decision was made in government to de-politicise this area of migration decision-making by giving the AAT determinative power over criminal deportation appeals.[102] The decision appears to have been made on the understanding that the change would produce decisions that were fairer to all those affected and more consistent over all. In contrast, the prime effect of the *Character and Conduct Act* was to restore to the Minister the power to have the final say in controversial cases. However, the Act did not signal a return to the regime in place before 1992. Rather, it altered dramatically the ability of individuals to access the independent review of the merits of a decision and reduced the role of the AAT where it retained jurisdiction to hear a case. By creating a system where the ultimate power to admit or expel lies with the Minister, the legislation resulted in the re-politicisation of character and conduct cases.

[6.58] In summary, where either the Minister's delegate or the AAT make a non-adverse (ie favourable) decision on character or conduct, the Act empowers the Minister, acting personally, to intervene so as to refuse or cancel a visa. The Minister must 'reasonably suspect' that a person does not pass the character test. Where the Minister forms this view, she or he may choose between two powers – powers to which the rules of natural justice do or do not apply. These powers are expressed (as in other parts of the Act) to be non-compellable and non-reviewable.[103] The Minister's power extends to cases where an original decision remains subject to an application for review by the AAT.[104]

[6.59] If a visa is refused or cancelled on character grounds a person cannot make an application for another visa unless permitted by regulation (s 501E). In practical terms, this will mean that cancellation means permanent exile in most cases.

[6.60] It is worth noting at this point that the Act also allows for the cancellation of visas issued to persons who have failed to disclose their criminal records or who have provided other false or misleading information or material: s 109. This provision

---

102 Before 1992, the AAT had a recommendatory function only, with the ultimate fate of criminal permanent residents determined by the Minister. For a discussion of the earlier legislation, see Mary Crock, *Immigration and Refugee Law in Australia* (Sydney: Federation Press, 1998) at 233-4.
103 See s 501B of the Act.
104 See s 501B(5) of the Act. According to s 501C(3), where the Minister chooses to exercise the powers conferred by either s 501(3) or s 501A(3) (as soon as practicable after the making of the original decision), the Minister must:
 (a) give the person (in the way the Minister considers appropriate in the circumstances) written notice of the decision and particulars of 'relevant information'. This is defined as information that is personal to the applicant and not just about a class of persons of which the applicant is a member.
 (b) except in cases where the applicant is not entitled to make representations, the Minister must invite the person to make representations. Regulations set out who is not entitled to make representations and the period that will be allowed for the making of submissions (if any). (s 501C)
 Decisions revoking an original decision must be notified to parliament in writing.

replaces former provisions that deemed unlawful those non-citizens who entered Australia on the basis of false or misleading information or otherwise in contravention of the legislation.[105] Cancellation or refusal decisions made under s 501 on character grounds are reviewable by the AAT: s 501. In relation to primary decisions made before 24 December 1992, character issues were examined by the IRT as part of its broader mandate to review visa and entry permit decisions within its jurisdiction. The MRT does not have equivalent powers.

[6.61] The present arrangements for the making and review of character rulings at point of entry reflect the resolve of successive governments to exclude undesirable elements from Australia using mechanisms that maximise the Minister's control over the decisions made. Moving the review function from the IRT to the AAT concentrates in one tribunal the function of hearing criminal deportation appeals and challenges to character assessments. Subject to the limitations placed on the AAT, it also provides applicants with high quality determinative review, presumably in the hope of discouraging recourse to the courts.

[6.62] Interestingly, the more recent jurisprudence in this area relates to cases where non-citizens have been admitted to Australia and s 501 is invoked to effect their removal, most usually because of something that has occurred after their entry. The battles involving exclusion from Australia of undesirable persons were fought (and won by the government) in the 1990s.

[6.63] Many of the character cases that have come before the tribunals and courts have involved family reunion applications. Typically, it is the Australian citizen or resident partner who is seeking to sponsor for permanent residence a male non-citizen who has committed an offence or other breach of the law. The emotive nature of the cases seems to have encouraged some reviewers to err in favour of the parties involved where the Minister would have preferred the public's interest to be given priority.[106] The push for closer articulation of government policies and laws also

---

105   See Chapter 15.3,2 below.
106   One example of the type of case against which the then Labor government reacted was the ruling of the IRT in *Re Felizarta* [1991] IRTA 263. In considering the definition of 'good character' in the *Migration Regulations 1989* (Cth) (*1989 Regulations*), the tribunal postulated that the conjunctive 'and' between two paragraphs meant that only persons falling foul of both limbs of the definition could be legally of 'bad character': See *1989 Regulations*, Sch 1, cl 4, and regs 2(1) and 4(1) 'good character'. This interpretation had the effect of excluding only those who had been convicted of a serious offence *and* who showed habitual disregard for the law or for human rights: compare *Re Hreinsson* [1994] IRTA 4037; and *Re Arcadi* [1994] IRTA 4513. Of even greater concern was the IRT's ruling in *Re O'Driscoll* [1994] IRTA 3532. In that case the applicant had spent a number of years in Australia between 1968 and his deportation in 1979, during which period he was charged and eventually acquitted of murder, and convicted of three less serious charges: *Driscoll v R* (1977) 137 CLR 517. He had been deported not on the basis of his criminal convictions – which would have led to a life-time ban on his readmission – but on the basis of deemed unlawful status flowing from his failure to declare his criminal record on first arriving in the country. O'Driscoll sought (and was refused) re-entry into Australia in September 1990 on the basis of his marriage to an Australian citizen. On appeal to the IRT, the tribunal accepted the applicant's expressions of contrition, as well as evidence from O'Driscoll's family and associates to the effect that he was a reformed character. The tribunal then took the unusual step of overriding the Department's decision and issuing the visa sought, rather than referring the matter back for consideration in accordance with the ruling made.

owed something to the evolving Federal Court jurisprudence which ran against the intention of the government. For example, in *Sciascia v MILGEA*,[107] the Full Federal Court held that the obligation to reveal serious criminal convictions upon arrival in Australia (see former s 20 of the Act) did not apply to a petty criminal who had spent numerous short periods in prison.[108]

[6.64] In *Chu Sing Wun v MILGEA*,[109] Beaumont J found that the Minister had erred in law by balancing doubts about the applicant's good character against the interests of the Australian community. His Honour held that the regulatory regime did not call for the exercise of discretion, but for the formulation of a particular belief. Upon the decision being remitted for reconsideration, the Minister's delegate confirmed the original assessment of the applicant's bad character, relying (again) on allegations of the businessman's connections with triads in Hong Kong. Mr Wun again challenged the ruling in the Federal Court. Nicholson J ruled that the second decision, like the first, was vitiated by errors of law. The matter was remitted again for reconsideration![110]

[6.65] A case that caused great consternation about the reviewers' interpretation of the public interest criteria was *Hand v Hell's Angels Motor Cycle Club Inc*.[111] The action arose out of the refusal or failure by the Minister to grant tourist visas to 23 foreign members of the Hell's Angels Motor Cycle Club Inc (HAMC) who wanted to attend an international gathering in Adelaide. The Minister's reluctance to grant visas to the applicants was based on information gathered by the Department about criminal activities entered into by different HAMC members around the world. The Department asserted that the proposed gathering was no more than an event designed to bring together club members for the purpose of discussing and planning HAMC's international criminal activities.

[6.66] The Full Federal Court held[112] that general information concerning the criminal activities of HAMC members could be relevant in determining the 'good character' of the applicants and for this reason was a proper matter to put to them. However, the court said that it was another thing to use such material as the basis for concluding that the applicants would themselves engage in activities 'threatening harm to the Australian community' as defined in the Regulations. It held that the test set out in the definition was one of likelihood: a mere chance or possibility that the applicants would engage in harmful activities was not sufficient.

[6.67] Although the applicant Hell's Angels eventually lost the case, the Minister did not wait for the Full Court's ruling before moving to remedy the perceived deficiencies of the regulatory criteria. The government expanded the definition of 'public interest criteria' by placing a reverse onus on members of 'declared bodies'

---

107 (1991) 31 FCR 364.
108 In *Yuen v MILGEA* (1991) 24 ALD 713 the court held it unreasonable to refuse entry to a man who had led a blameless life with the exception of a 30-year-old (questionable) conviction for being a member of a triad.
109 (1993) 118 ALR 345.
110 See *Chu Sing Wun v MILGEA* (1997) 47 ALD 538.
111 (1991) 25 ALD 667.
112 Ibid at 675.

to demonstrate their innocence of criminal intent or involvement in disruptive activities.[113]

[6.68] Eventually, the government took the issues of public interest and good character out of the Regulations and dealt with them in the Act. The transition back to ministerial discretion truly controlled by the Minister was completed by the provision for the issue of ministerial certificates precluding administrative review of an exclusion decision in serious cases. Decisions under s 501 are normally reviewable by the AAT. Where a ministerial certificate is issued, the Minister must notify both Houses of Parliament within 15 sitting days. The certificate can be disallowed under the *Acts Interpretation Act 1901* (Cth). In spite of these contentious cases, it would be a mistake to think that either the AAT or the Federal Court has customarily taken an irresponsible approach to the issue of good character in immigration cases. There was, however, quite a marked change when the Coalition government came to power in 1996. Before that date, the AAT tended to interpret the words 'good character' according to ordinary usage of the phrase and ordinary community standards. It looked at 'the aggregate of the subject's distinguishing qualities objectively to determine whether the person is held in good repute'.[114] This approach saw the AAT take a lenient view in a case where a past failure to declare details of past criminal acts could be excused by the various circumstances affecting the applicant.[115] On the other hand, it found against applicants whose past misdemeanours pointed to a fundamental dishonesty or other intent to breach Australia's immigration laws.[116] The tribunal also took a firm line against applicants whose past conduct in countries with a poor human rights record is likely to make the applicants a source of discord amongst certain ethnic groups within the Australian community.[117]

Public interest and civil liberties: Border control or thought control?

[6.69] As Maher argued in as early as 1994,[118] even before the changes wrought by the *Character and Conduct Act*, the character regime was not one designed to please civil libertarians and exponents of free speech. Great powers were and are vested in the Minister to determine which controversial individuals or groups can or cannot enter Australia.

[6.70] The interplay between freedom of speech and the Minister's role as protector of the public interest arose as an issue when the Minister decided to rule against the grant of a visitor's visa to the historian and apologist for Adolf Hitler, David Irving. Irving was refused a visitor's visa in early December 1992 on the grounds that he was not of good character and that he was 'likely to become involved in activities

---

113 See *1989 Regulations*, para (c) of the definition of 'public interest' in reg 2(1), and reg 3B. The amending rules were notified one day after Olney J's judgment in the *Hell's Angels* case.
114 See *Re Lachmaiya and MIEA* (1994) 19 AAR 148 at 155-6; and *Re Strangio* (1994) 35 ALD 676 at 681.
115 See *Re Strangio* (1994) 35 ALD 676.
116 See *Re Lachmaiya and MIEA* (1994) 19 AAR 148; and *Re Prasad and MIEA* (1994) 35 ALD 780.
117 See *Re Morales and MILGEA* (1995) 38 ALD 727. Note, however, that the decision of the AAT was set aside in *Morales v MILGEA* (1995) 60 FCR 550.
118 See Laurence W Maher, 'Migration Act Visitor Entry Controls and Free Speech: The Case of David Irving' (1994) 16(3) *Sydney Law Review* 358.

disruptive to, or violence threatening harm to the Australian community'.[119] The Minister had a discretion to waive the public interest criteria (*Migration Regulations 1989* (Cth), reg 143) but declined to do so in Irving's case after receiving submissions from concerned community groups. The Minister's decision was made in spite of the fact that Irving had visited Australia on two previous occasions to conduct public lectures, without significant incident.

[6.71] Although the Minister's decision was upheld at first instance by French J, the Full Federal Court took a more critical approach.[120] The judges acknowledged that the clear intention of the Regulations was to create a 'heckler's veto' on the admission of persons holding unpopular opinions, placing a higher value on order and calm within the community than on democratic ideals of free speech. All three members of the court opined that the evidence before the Minister should not have been sufficient to convince the Minister that Irving's visit would have the effects alleged. However, they declined to find any error in law. Subsequent attempts by Irving's supporters to have him visit the country have met with no greater success.[121]

[6.72] In a sense, the *Irving* case brought the issue of immigration control and the public interest full circle. As Maher comments, the legislation governing the admission of controversial individuals has a number of precedents in Australian history. Efforts were made to exclude members of the Communist Party at various stages between 1920 and 1960.[122] Trade unionists have also been targeted.[123] Ironically, in view of the *Irving* case, a decision was made during the 1930s to exclude the Czech-born Egon Kisch who sought entry to Australia for the avowed purpose of warning Australia about the dangers of fascism.[124]

[6.73] Few would dispute the unsavoury nature of Mr Irving's reconstruction of history and the emotions his opinions generate. One of the problems with cases such as these is that the publicity given to the applicant as a result of refusing a visa acts to ferment and polarise public opinion. One might ask how many people in Australia would now know anything of Mr Irving had he been allowed to enter the country and deliver his lectures when he first applied for a visa. In a sense, refusal of entry can act as a publicity opportunity for the applicant such that it becomes a self-fulfilling prophecy that the (later) grant of a visa would result in the incitement of discord. Although it is not easy to see a solution to this problem, the earlier public interest cases serve as a reminder of the dangers of allowing immigration control to become a form of thought control.

[6.74] The conflict between freedom of speech and determining the public interest in the admission of controversial visitors has continued to be a live issue. In July 1997, then Acting Minister, Senator Vanstone, caused a storm by cancelling the visitor visa of one Lorenzo Ervin, a Black American brought to Australia to give a series

---

119 See *1989 Regulations*, reg 2.
120 *Irving v MILGEA* (1993) 44 FCR 540.
121 See *Irving v MILGEA* (1995) 59 FCR 423.
122 See Maher, above n 118, at 8.
123 See *Ex parte Walsh; In re Yates* (1925) 37 CLR 36.
124 *R v Wilson; Ex parte Kisch* (1934) 52 CLR 234; and above, Chapter 2.2.

of lectures on the dangers of racism. The cancellation followed complaints made by certain right-wing political groups and by the independent Member for Oxley, Ms Pauline Hanson, who pointed to Mr Ervin's past criminal convictions in America. The case became a cause célèbre when Mr Ervin was placed in prison for three days. He was released after the cancellation decision was challenged in the High Court, with the Minister finally conceding that Mr Ervin had been denied procedural fairness and that the ruling was otherwise flawed at law.[125]

[6.75] Almost a decade later, a similar controversy arose when a US political activist by the name of Scott Parkin was targeted by the Australian Security and Intelligence Organisation (ASIO) for engaging in protests against the War in Iraq. Mr Parkin had been admitted into Australia and a decision was made to cancel his visa under s 116 of the *Migration Act*. Reliance was placed on what was alleged to be an adverse ASIO report. Attempts to use discovery procedures to find the basis for both the assessment and the decision to cancel the visa failed[126] and the activist was removed from Australia.

[6.76] With the new provisions governing the judicial review of migration decisions, the Minister's power to regulate entry on public interest grounds is probably as absolute now as it is ever likely to be. As Maher argues, the real risk to Australian society may be posed less by the people sought to be excluded than by a legislative regime that threatens to stifle free speech.[127]

[6.77] As we explore further in Chapter 17, the removal of persons on grounds of criminal conduct after they have entered Australia is dealt with in a complex array of provisions. A non-citizen who commits a criminal offence may be subject to either criminal deportation (ss 200-205) *or* the cancellation of their visa on grounds of bad character (s 501) based on the same facts. Both decisions are reviewable by the AAT (s 500), but the situation is complicated by the fact that, under s 502, the Minister may issue a conclusive certificate preventing review of a decision to deport or cancel a visa on character grounds. The power of the Minister to cancel a visa on character grounds may conflict with the ability of the AAT to determine criminal deportation rulings.

[6.78] The issue of the proper limits on government control over who enters or remains in Australia recurs throughout the following chapters. These examine the principal visa categories within the migration program: family reunion, skills-based migration, refugee and special humanitarian migration and temporary entrants. In each area, the government has adopted different control mechanisms in response to the variety of issues affecting the groups involved.

---

125 See *Re MIMA; Ex parte Ervin* [1997] HCATrans 213 and [1997] HCATrans 214. For a sample of the press comments, on the case, see, for example, Megan Saunders, 'No Justice for Panther: Brennan', *The Australian*, 11 July 1997, at 3.
126 See *Parkin v O'Sullivan* (2006) 162 FCR 444.
127 See Maher, above n 118.

PART IV Family Migration

7

Family Reunion I – Spousal Relationships

7.1   The place of families in the migrant intake

[7.01]   The vigour of the discourse on state sovereignty and border control can mask the fact that there are practical considerations limiting the ability of any government to be overly exclusionary in approach. Family migration features, and will always feature, strongly in Australia's immigration program. The ability to create and maintain basic family relationships is a defining aspect of a free, democratic society. Family is also demonstrably important to the success of an immigration program in so far as personal relationships foster stability, happiness and economic wellbeing. Furthermore, family-friendly migration policies provide a competitive advantage for countries seeking to attract highly skilled migrants in an increasingly globalised labour market. As the Swiss writer, Max Frisch, wrote in 1990: 'We asked for workers, but people came'.[1] Motomura explains that there is inevitably a gap between the 'imagined lives [of] guestworkers and the rich texture of their real lives as immigrants':

> [M]igration is in large part a social process of network building, so it shouldn't surprise us that immigrants are husbands and wives, and sons and daughters, and brothers and sisters – or that they form these relationships over time.[2]

[7.02]   While it is inconceivable that a country like Australia would restrict all family migration, there have been quite remarkable changes in the family intake programs over the years. The variations underscore how laws and policies in this sensitive area have dramatically shaped the culture, character and even appearance of this country.

[7.03]   The history of family migration to Australia up until the 1970s was one of quite extraordinary generosity, with the striking exception of the White Australia Policy. Providing family members did not fall foul of the colour bar, few restrictions were placed on sponsoring all manner of relatives. The emphasis was on permanent migration of Europeans and on building family and community. In the mass migration programs conducted after the Second World War whole villages were encouraged

---

1   Max Frisch, *Überfremdung I, In Schweiz Als Heimat?* (1990), cited in Hiroshi Motomura, 'We Asked for Workers, But Families Came: Time, Law and the Family in Immigration and Citizenship' (2006) 14 *Virginia Journal of Social Policy and the Law* 103 at 103.
2   See Motomura, ibid.

to make the move to Australia. As explored in Chapters 9 and 10, the selection of migrants on the basis of specific skills was not given prominent consideration until well into the 1960s.[3] Since that turning point, the story has been one of increasing focus on the economics of migration, with the long-term networking effect of family migration being seen by some as detrimental to the economic interests of Australian society. In the words of the social demographer, Bob Birrell, sequential family sponsorships became 'the chains that bind' the country (from moving forward).[4] The most obvious manifestation of the changed attitude to family is in the balance that is struck between family migration and skilled and business migration in the annual intake program.

[7.04] Until March 1996, over half of the migrants admitted to Australia each year comprised family members of Australian citizens or permanent residents. In 1995-96, for example, 56,720 places were allotted to 'family' migrants in the migration (non-humanitarian) intake of 82,560 places. The ratio between family and skilled migrants shifted steadily after the conservative Coalition government came to power in March 1996. The 1997-98 planning levels allowed 32,000 of the 68,000 places in the non-humanitarian program for family migrants.[5] By 2002-03 planning levels allocated 43,200 of the 100,000 to 110,000 places in the non-humanitarian program to family migrants. By 2007-08, 50,000 visas were allocated to family, representing a mere 31 per cent of the total migration program of 159,000 places.[6] These changes mean that family migrants no longer constitute the largest single component in the immigration program. Interestingly, the 2009-10 figures foreshadow a slight reversal of this trend, with the first decrease (by over 6000) in visa grants for skilled migrants in over a decade and an increase (by about 4000) in the family quota. This shift appears to signal an ideological change of sorts under the Labor government,[7] accompanied as it was in March 2010 by a relaxation in the rules governing long-term partner relations.[8]

[7.05] While the intake of family migrants has altered dramatically, the broad groupings within the family stream have remained fairly constant. The composition of the family reunion categories reflects the values the government (and Australian society) places on the various degrees of family relationship. Within the offshore program, spousal or de facto partners, dependent children, some parents and others in defined relationships with Australians are given special treatment. These groups, formerly referred to as *preferential* family cases, are given the right to be granted a visa on the basis of criteria that turn on their relationships with Australian parties,

---

3   For an interesting first hand account of those years, see Harry Martin, *Angels and Arrogant Gods: Migration Officers and Migrants Reminisce 1945-85* (Canberra: AGPS, 1988).
4   Bob Birrell, *The Chains that Bind: The Australian Experience of Chain Migration* (Canberra: DIEA, 1989).
5   DIMA, *Fact Sheet 2: 1997-98 Migration Program planning levels.* Note that the 1995-96 family intake figures included the 'concessional family places' which later became known as 'skilled Australian-Linked'. After 1997-08 the latter group was counted as part of the skilled migration intake.
6   DIAC, *Report on Migration Program 2007-08* (Canberra).
7   See <http://www.immi.gov.au/media/statistics/statistical-info/visa-grants/migrant.htm>.
8   From 27 March 2010 foreign partners became eligible for immediate permanent residence if they could show that they had lived as a couple for three years. Previously, a partnership of five years was required. Labor has also abolished all distinctions between married, de facto and 'interdependent' partnerships. See below, [7.27].

providing that public interest and re-entry criteria are met.[9] Partners and dependent children also receive special treatment in another respect. The issue of visas in these classes is demand driven and cannot be capped.[10] In contrast, parents who do not meet the 'balance of family' test, siblings, nephews and nieces are subject to a points test and are treated as part of the skilled intake – unless they are a carer or, in the case of a sibling, a remaining relative. Traditionally, the skilled migration points test has given credit for familial relationship along with factors such as skilled occupation, age, employment and educational qualifications. However, since 1 September 2007, family members have enjoyed significantly fewer advantages in the skilled categories.[11]

[7.06] Where permanent residence is sought after entry into the country, family members, again, are granted concessions.[12] In these cases, however, the policy favouring the reunification of relatives is tempered by a countermanding concern to discourage onshore applications (a trend begun in the 1980s). The fear in these as in all onshore cases is that such applications involve 'queue jumping' and threaten the integrity of Australia's program which is seen primarily as the selection of migrants from *overseas*.

[7.07] This chapter is the first of two that focus on family migration. It begins with the issue of partner migration, with the consideration of other family members following in Chapter 8. Overall, the recent history of the law in this area has been one of shrinking entitlement. Distinctions have been drawn in some of the visa categories between onshore and offshore applications.[13] Concerns about the economic costs associated with family migration have been reflected in moves to upgrade the responsibilities of sponsors; to adopt more of a user-pay approach to visa costs; and to limit the access of newly arrived migrants to social security support.[14]

[7.08] While the laws governing spousal migration remain generous, the overweening concern in this area appears to have been the prevention of program abuse by individuals entering into sham marriages or relationships of convenience. The antidote to fraud in this area was to introduce a system of two-year provisional visas before the grant of permanent residence: see Part 7.2.1 below. Interestingly, as we will see in later chapters, this device has since been adopted across much of the skilled and business migration program in changes that demonstrate how devices used first to control family migration now shape migration laws and policies in Australia more broadly.

---

9   See *Migration Regulations 1994* (Cth), Schs 4 and 5.
10 See *Migration Act 1958* (Cth), ss 85-91.
11 See further Chapters 8 and 9 below.
12 For example, family applicants are usually subject to more lenient Sch 3 requirements compared to other visa categories.
13 Nearly all family visas have an onshore counterpart (the Adoption visa being an exception). Most have identical criteria to the offshore visa with a couple of exceptions. Examples include the visa criteria of aged parents, and, in the case of partner visas, who can be included as a secondary applicant.
14 Terry Carney and Anna Boucher, 'Social Security and Immigration: An Agenda for Future Research?' (2009) 23(1) *Zeitschrift für Ausländisches und Internationales Arbeits- und Sozialrecht* (ZIAS) 36.

[7.09] This chapter begins with an overview of the law and policy governing immigration on grounds of partnership. After an overview of the system as it now operates we examine in Part 7.2.2 the legal attributes of a valid partnership, looking at both the requirements of a legal marriage and the rules attaching to de facto unions between both same-sex and heterosexual couples. In Part 7.2.3 we explore the requirements for proving a genuine relationship and in Part 7.2.4 the problems of sham marriages and serial sponsorships. Part 7.3 of the chapter then examines in detail the concessions made for non-citizen partners who are victims of 'family violence'. However well intentioned, the rules in these cases have been described as the triumph of form over substance. As ever, the evolution of the law and policy suggests a cat-and-mouse game between migrant applicants, the legislature and the federal judiciary. Too frequently, vulnerable migrant partners have continued to fall through cracks in the system intended to protect them.

7.2 Immigration on grounds of partnership

7.2.1 Partnership migration – an overview

[7.10] The right to marry and/or found a family is a fundamental human right. While many may oppose immigration in abstract terms, community acceptance is overwhelming of the notion that Australian nationals and permanent residents should be permitted to live in Australia with the partner of their choice. The domestic politics involved, together with Australia's obligations under Art 23 of the *International Covenant on Civil and Political Rights*, have made the government reluctant to place too many restrictions on partner reunions from abroad.[15]

[7.11] Australian migration policy in this area has typically been socially progressive, giving long-standing recognition to parties in a de facto relationship as well as those in a legal marriage. While some in Australia continue to oppose the recognition of same-sex marriage, Australia has long been at the forefront of countries accepting same-sex relationships as the basis of migration. Since 1 July 2009, same-sex partners have been treated in the same way as heterosexual de facto spouses. All partners, whether married or de facto, and whether gay or heterosexual, are now eligible for the partner visa class. We sketch the evolution of these policy reforms below.

[7.12] Having said this, the deference shown to Australians' right to live in Australia with the partner of their choice has diminished somewhat in the face of evidence of Australian parties engaging in abusive behaviour involving the sponsorship of successive foreign partners. Moves to protect the migrant parties in such situations are discussed in Part 7.3 below.

---

15   Compare Hiroshi Motomura, 'The Family and Immigration: A Roadmap for the Ruritanian Lawmaker' (1995) 43 *American Journal of Comparative Law* 511; and John Guendelsberger, 'The Right to Family Reunification in French and US Immigration Law' (1988) 21 *Cornell International Law Journal* 1.

Offshore and onshore applications

[7.13] The *Migration Act 1958* (Cth) and *Migration Regulations 1994* (Cth) provide two mechanisms for the sponsored migration of offshore non-citizens on partnership grounds. Where the parties are in a pre-existing marriage or de facto relationship or are fiancé(e)s planning to marry before the visa grant, an application can be made for a provisional subclass 309 (Partner (Provisional)) visa. After the end of the provisional period (see below), the 309 visa-holder may be eligible for a permanent subclass 100 (Partner) visa. The alternative is for the Australian party to sponsor the non-citizen for entry to Australia with a view to marriage after the non-citizen's arrival. Persons granted a subclass 300 (Prospective Marriage) visa are required generally to marry their Australian sponsor within the nine-month visa period. After marriage they can apply in Australia for the onshore partner visas (provisional and permanent). Normally, they will become eligible for the permanent subclass 801 (Partner) visa at the expiration of a two-year period: see the exceptions below. The only additional obstacles for offshore applicants are the re-entry bans and exclusion periods affecting applicants who have been in Australia previously and who have either been deported or removed from Australia or have had a visa cancelled because of their criminal conduct.[16]

[7.14] It is in the cases of persons wishing to gain residence on partner grounds after entry into the country that greater restrictions have been introduced. Onshore applicants who are married and persons in a de facto relationship may apply for a temporary subclass 820 (Partner) visa, and be eligible later for a permanent subclass 801 (Partner) visa. In the context of broad departmental discretion governing the granting of residency to partners, the courts came to question government attempts to improve control of spousal migration through the promulgation of policy guidelines. For example, in the 1980s, the courts held unlawful decisions to deny in-country applications for change of status on marriage grounds that had been made solely on the basis of the applicant's illegal status.[17] As we explore further below, the curial defeat of many of the initiatives forced the translation of policy into increasingly explicit legislation.

[7.15] Under the present system, change of status on partner grounds is much more restricted for applicants who are unlawful non-citizens or who entered Australia with visa conditions that preclude the grant of further visas.[18] Most foreign spouses or partners are required still to serve a two-year provisional period as temporary residents before they are given permanent residence, although permanent status is granted immediately to persons who have been living together for at least three years.[19] To obtain permanent residence after the two years, the partner relationship, generally, must be ongoing. However, concessions are made where the Australian sponsor dies or has committed family violence against their partner or a child in the

---

16　See *Migration Regulations*, Sch 2, subclass 309, read with Sch 5.
17　See *Tang v MIEA* (1986) 67 ALR 177 and *Kumar v MIEA* [1989] FCA 293.
18　See Chapter 15 at Parts 15.5 and 15.6.
19　See Sch 2, subclasses 801 and 820, and the definition of 'long-term partner relationship' in reg 1.03 of the *Migration Regulations 1994*. Note that before 27 March 2010 the relationship had to be of five years' duration.

family (see Part 7.3 below); and/or where a child is involved and both partners have formal family law or maintenance obligations. As with applications made overseas, the chief concerns in the processing of onshore partner cases relate to the validity, genuineness and continuity of relationships.

Proving the partnership

[7.16] For applications lodged both within and outside Australia, the major requirements for the partner visas relate to the validity, genuineness and continuity of the relationship. As explored in more detail below, the key criteria of a partner visa are that the applicant and sponsor are in a de facto or married relationship, with a mutual commitment to a shared life together, to the exclusion of all others. The relationship must be genuine and continuing and the parties must live together or not live separately and apart on a permanent basis. De facto couples must have been in the relationship for at least 12 months before lodging their application.

[7.17] In spite of the significant litigation which has arisen about the application of these criteria (and earlier versions of them), heavy departmental scrutiny of applicants' relationships is a relatively recent phenomenon – the product of a policy change after the election of the conservative Coalition government in 1996. The fact that relatively few overseas marriages were questioned before that time is reflected in the small number of such cases brought to the review tribunals.

The shift from permanency to provisional status

[7.18] Efforts to curb perceived abuse of the generous entitlements to permanent residency for migrant spouses in Australia date back to December 1989. It was at this time that the idea of a provisional period for spouse applicants was first introduced.[20] For those applying within Australia, permanent residence was granted only after a delay of one year and on condition that the relationship in question remained current.

[7.19] Until 1996, the benefit of applying offshore was that permanent residence would flow automatically: for subclass 100 visa holders on entry into Australia; and for subclass 300 visa holders upon entry into the promised marriage. In that year, concerns about the incidence of 'sham marriages' entered into to secure permanent residence in Australia led to the extension of provisional periods to foreign spouses sponsored from abroad.[21] In 2002, specialist units, known as 'bona fides units' (BFUs), were established to increase the scrutiny of spouse applications being processed at overseas posts and within Australia.[22]

[7.20] At present, the general rule, applicable to both onshore and offshore applicants, is that the foreign spouse is required to wait out a provisional period of two years before permanent residency is granted. At the end of the two years the permanent residence visa will be granted so long as the partner relationship is still genuine

---

20 See *Migration Regulations 1989* (Cth) (*1989 Regulations*), reg 126.
21 See SR 211 of 1996.
22 These changes also saw the institution of programs to interview applicants both overseas and in onshore applications.

and ongoing, although there are some exceptions where permanent residency will be granted even though the relationship has ended. These exceptions are where the sponsoring partner has died; where the sponsor has committed family violence (see Part 7.3 below); and where there is a child involved in respect of whom both the visa applicant and the sponsor each has certain family law or child maintenance order responsibilities. In this context the reference to children of a relationship is not limited to the adopted or biological children of the parties: the exception applies whenever there is a child to whom parenting arrangements apply.[23] The two year period runs from the date of applying for the visas – the temporary and permanent visas being applied for at the same time and on the same form. The two-year waiting period does not apply in cases where, at the time of applying for the visas, the partners have been together for at least five years, or for at least two years and have a dependent child.

The move towards an inclusive framing of 'partnerships'

[7.21] Before 19 December 1989, eligibility for residence was available to a foreign spouse of an Australian resident regardless of the applicant's immigration status and of the nature or duration of the marriage. Indeed, s 6A(1)(b) of the 1958 Act (as it existed until 1989) did not even state that applicants had to be sponsored by their Australian partner: it merely empowered the Minister to grant residence to the foreign spouse of an Australian citizen or permanent resident. De facto spouses were considered under the catch-all provisions of s 6A(1)(e) which allowed the Minister to grant residence in cases involving strong humanitarian or compassionate grounds. In 1985 Australia became one of the first countries in the world to accept same-sex relationships as the basis for migration, assessing same-sex applications through ministerial discretion under the compassionate and humanitarian visa category.[24]

[7.22] In the early context of such broad ministerial discretion, courts regularly challenged the government's attempts to control spousal migration through narrow policy directives. For example, in reviewing a policy that specified that a marriage be 'genuine and on-going', the courts held that the breadth of the Minister's discretion required the consideration of all facets of an application for entry on spouse grounds. This included the plight of non-Australian parties in either abusive relationships or in genuine, but short-lived, unions. In *Chumbairux v MIEA*,[25] Burchett J held that the only prerequisite for residency on marriage grounds was the existence of a legally valid marriage between the applicant and an Australian party. His Honour held that

---

23   In *Srour v MIMA* (2006) 155 FCR 441 the Federal Court held that, where children are part of a relationship, there will be a presumption that both partners have parental responsibilities unless there is evidence (such as a court order) to the contrary.

24   Audrey Yue, 'Same-Sex Migration in Australia: From Interdependency to Intimacy' (2008) 14(2-3) *Gay and Lesbian Quarterly* 239 at 239; Joseph Chetcuti, 'Relationships of Interdependency: Immigration for Same-Sex Partners' in Robert Aldrich and Gary Wotherspoon (eds), *Gay Perspectives: Essays in Gay Culture* (Sydney: Department of Economic History, University of Sydney, 1992). Peter de Waal documents the first known case of same-sex family reunion. A British citizen, John Cummaskey, was granted permanent residency in 1985 to be with his Australian partner Aubrey Koelmeyer on the basis of 'strong compassionate circumstances': Peter de Waal, *Lesbians and Gays Changed Australian Immigration: History and Herstory* (Sydney: Gay and Lesbian Immigration Task Force NSW, 2002) at 26-7.

25   (1986) 74 ALR 480.

the decision-maker had erred in law by treating the breakdown of the applicant's marriage as an absolute bar to the consideration of his case on its merits.[26]

[7.23] As in sponsorships of married spouses, the major issue in de facto visa applications has been the 'genuineness' of unions. Concerns about abuse of the system (see Part 7.2.4) led in 1991 to the introduction of a requirement that eligibility to apply for residence be limited generally to persons cohabiting as de facto spouses for at least six months before the application was made.[27] This requirement was extended in 1997 to cohabitation for 12 months preceding the visa application.

[7.24] When the spouse visa was codified in 1989, politicians refused initially to incorporate same-sex couples in the family category, bringing to an end the ability of same-sex partners to gain permanent residence in Australia other than through the exercise of the Minister's residual discretion. Two years later, the interdependency category was introduced, a mechanism which formally recognised same-sex and 'non familial' relationships of emotional interdependency.[28] As Minister Ray acknowledged to the Senate in 1991, the visa was directed primarily at 'giving homosexuals rights'[29] but the regulatory criteria were left deliberately vague for reasons of political pragmatism.[30] To be eligible for an interdependency visa, the applicant had to have a genuine and continuing relationship of at least six months (except in exceptional circumstances) with the Australian sponsor (who was not a family member), which involved residing together, being closely interdependent, and having a continuing commitment to mutual emotional and financial support.[31] The prior residence requirement later increased to 12 months.

[7.25] This move was a watershed in providing lesbians and gay men for the first time with a positive basis for sponsoring their partner to settle in Australia. Indeed, the interdependency provisions may well have been the first Australian legislative provisions drafted with the aim of giving legal recognition to lesbian and gay relationships.[32] They meant that, for the first time, lesbians and gay men could sponsor their partner to immigrate from outside Australia, rather than gaining a temporary entry permit and requesting change of status after arrival. However coy Australia's treatment of the issue, it recognised the immigration-related rights of gay couples well before some other Western countries. Indeed, at the time of writing, homosexual partners of United States citizens still had no right to residence in that country on the basis of their relationship, even where they were married under American state or foreign law.[33]

---

26   Ibid at 494. See also *Meggs v MIEA* (1986) 11 ALN 127 and *Palko v MIEA* (1987) 16 FCR 276.
27   See reg 3A of the *1989 Regulations*, as amended by SR 60 of 1991. Cohabitation in this context was (and is) defined as living together or 'not living apart'.
28   See SR 60 of 1991 creating former subclasses 310 and 826 (temporary) and subclass 814 (permanent).
29   Commonwealth Parliamentary Debates, *Hansard*, Senate, 5 June 1991 at 4342-4.
30   Stephen Warne, 'Moving in the Right Direction: Migration for Same-Sex Couples' (1994) 19(5) *Alternative Law Journal* 218 at 219.
31   As originally expressed in reg 1.09A of the *1989 Regulations* (as amended).
32   Warne, above n 30, at 222.
33   See generally Lena Ayoub and Shin-Ming Wong, 'Separated and Unequal' (2006) 32 *William Mitchell Law Review* 559. US immigration law does not include gay or lesbian partners within its statutory definition of 'spouse', so bi-national same-sex couples may not legally seek residency on the basis

[7.26] However, the provisions also served to entrench the inequality of same-sex couples under Australian law on a number of levels. First, the criteria of eligibility (recognising unusually close non-sexual relationships as well as same-sex partnerships) formalised the differences between heterosexual de facto spouses and heterosexual couples. Second, the interdependency visa initially stipulated a two-year provisional period, applying overseas or within Australia, whereas heterosexual couples were initially granted immediate permanent residence (although these provisional periods subsequently converged to one and then two years). Just as significantly, an application on the basis of a de facto or marital relationship was available even if the relationship had ceased as a result of family violence (see Part 7.3 below). The family violence protections were not available to interdependent couples. Finally, while the independent visa category mirrored the de facto spouse category, there was no equivalent of the prospective spouse class for lesbians and gay men (which required neither cohabitation nor financial interdependency).

[7.27] In July 2009, along with a raft of other changes recognising same-sex couples under federal law, same-sex partners of Australian citizens and permanent residents became eligible to apply for the same partner visa as heterosexual de facto partners: the meaning of 'de facto partner' was re-defined to include the words 'whether of the same sex or a different sex'. All married and de facto couples (whether opposite- or same-sex) are now eligible for the Partner visa. Same-sex de facto partners and their children are also considered 'members of the family unit' for visa purposes. This removed all discrimination against same-sex couples other than their continued ineligibility for the Prospective Marriage visa, given that (domestic and overseas) same-sex marriages are not recognised under Australian law. We now explore the legal requirements of the Partner visa.

7.2.2 The legal attributes of a valid partnership

[7.28] Since July 2009, foreign married or de facto partners of Australian citizens or permanent residents have been eligible for a temporary subclass 820 (Partner) visa (and later for a permanent subclass 801 (Partner) visa) if applying onshore. If applying overseas, these people are eligible for a temporary subclass 309 (Partner (Provisional)) visa (and later for a permanent subclass 100 (Partner) visa). Parties to a married or de facto relationship (whether same- or opposite-sex) must have a mutual commitment to a shared life together, to the exclusion of all other persons. The relationship must be genuine and continuing and the parties must live together or not live separately and apart on a permanent basis.

---

of their relationship. The Ninth Circuit in *Adams v Howerton* (1982) 673 F2d 1036 (9th Cir) ruled that, while the *Immigration and Nationality Act* (US) did not define the term 'spouse', the policy direction to limit its reach to heterosexual relationships was constitutional. American consulates abroad seem to permit non-marital partners (gay or straight) the ability to visit the US as tourists when their partners apply for temporary work visas: see Michael Scaperlanda, 'Kulturkampf in the Backwaters: Homosexuality and Immigration Law' (2002) 11 *Widener Journal of Public Law* 475 at 493. This does not, however, entitle a gay couple to reside permanently in the US.

Additional requirements for married couples

[7.29] Where the parties to a relationship are married in Australia, the union will generally be recognised as legal for immigration purposes as long as the requirements of the *Marriage Act 1961* (Cth) have been observed.[34] The recognition of marriages entered into abroad is governed by Part VA of this Act, omitting s 88E.[35] The effect is that foreign marriages are recognised if the ceremony was considered valid under the local law, with the exception of same-sex, polygamous, under-age, incestuous and non-consensual marriages. Recognition of valid foreign marriages includes arranged marriages and marriages conducted by proxy, provided that the requisite consent and intention to be bound are present. However, for the purposes of applying for a prospective marriage visa there is now an obligation that the parties have met and that they be 'known personally' to each other.[36]

[7.30] Before 1 August 1991, different ages were prescribed for male and female parties to a marriage. Where either party was domiciled (ie, normally resident) in Australia, the age was 18 for males and 16 for females. For parties domiciled abroad, the age limit was 16 for males and 14 for females. The age limits now apply to both males and females: if either party is domiciled in Australia, 18 years, or 16 years at the discretion of a State or Territory judge or magistrate who finds that the 'circumstances of the case are so exceptional and unusual as to justify' the marriage. If neither party is domiciled in Australia at the time of the marriage, the age requirement is 16 years.[37] The effect of these provisions has been to create in some cases 'limping' marriages, or marriages that are considered valid abroad but not in Australia. For applicants caught in this situation, policy suggests that once both parties reach marriageable age they may be considered as de facto partners or they may apply for a Prospective Marriage visa to re-marry in Australia.[38]

[7.31] A polygamous marriage conducted in Australia under foreign (in this case, Islamic) law was considered in *Re MIMA; Ex parte Holland*.[39] An Australian man sought to sponsor the applicant as his second wife under Islamic law and argued that she be accepted as his de facto spouse for immigration purposes. In the High Court, Kirby J ruled that the MRT had committed no error in law in both ruling that the second Islamic marriage had no status under Australian law and that the couple failed to meet the requirements of exclusivity in their de facto relationship demanded by the migration legislation.

[7.32] The non-recognition of polygamous marriages under Australian law had been considered previously in *Alshamali v MIMA*.[40] There the applicant's subclass 100 Spouse visa was cancelled after the Department discovered that the applicant had

---

34 *Migration Regulations*, reg 1.15A(1A)(a).
35 *Migration Act*, s 12.
36 See *Migration Regulations*, Sch 2, cl 300.214. See *Meggs v MIEA* (1986) 11 ALN N127; *Palko v MIEA* (1987) 16 FCR 276; and *Re Ismail* [1995] IRTA 6272.
37 See *Marriage Act 1961*, ss 11 and 12.
38 PAM 3 at 20.2. See *0800835* [2008] MRTA 521 and *W04/01311* [2005] MRTA 547.
39 [2001] HCA 76.
40 [1999] FCA 279.

failed to disclose a second wife and three children living overseas. He had also not informed his Australian wife of his other marriage. In addition, there was conflicting evidence about the relationship, with the applicant's Australian wife claiming that it had never been a genuine marriage. The tribunal held that, regardless of this latter claim, the applicant's failure to disclose the existence of his other marriage was 'deliberate and contrived ... to further his own interests in remaining in Australia', and in such circumstances the man was not eligible for the grant of a spouse visa.[41] This decision was upheld by the Federal Court.

De facto couples

[7.33] The *Migration Act* provides that a person is in a de facto relationship with another person if they are not married to each other, but have a mutual commitment to a shared life to the exclusion of all others. The relationship between them must be genuine and continuing and they must live together or not live separately and apart on a permanent basis. The detail spelt out in the Regulations reflects the jurisprudence that has emerged from the relevant court and tribunal decisions, as we explore further below (in Part 7.2.3). In other respects, the government treats alike couples who are legally married and those in genuine spousal relationships outside of a lawful marriage. Like married couples, de facto couples must not be related by family;[42] however, both applicant and sponsor must be at least 18 years of age[43] and, unlike spouses, the definition of de facto partner has included same-sex couples since 2009.[44]

[7.34] As noted, the couple must be committed to each other to the exclusion of all others. Care is taken to ensure that, where one partner is legally married to someone else, that partner can only be party to a de facto relationship if it can be shown that the 'legal' marriage is at an end and (for example) there are reasons why divorce is not possible. In *Surya Cahyana v MIMIA*,[45] the couple had married in Indonesia in December 1993 and one month later made an application for a spouse visa. The application was refused on the grounds that the visa applicant did not meet the definition of 'spouse' in reg 1.3. First, the couple did not cohabit before getting married, and therefore did not satisfy the requirement that as at the date of the visa application they had been together as husband and wife for six months. The applicant could not demonstrate any exceptional circumstances or compelling reasons for waiving the six-month cohabitation requirement. Second, and more importantly, at the time of the marriage ceremony the applicant was still legally married to his first wife: the divorce was not finalised until later.[46]

[7.35] Importantly, the visa applicant and sponsor must have been in the de facto relationship (which includes living together, or at least not living apart on a

---

41 Ibid at [8].
42 *Migration Act*, s 5CB(2)(d).
43 *Migration Regulations*, reg 2.03A(2).
44 *Migration Act*, s 5CB(1).
45 [1998] FCA 390.
46 Ibid at [3].

permanent basis) for the 12 months immediately before making the application for the visa.⁴⁷ This 12-month pre-existing relationship rule will not apply if the applicant can establish that there are 'compelling and compassionate circumstances' for the grant of the visa. Instances under policy of what might amount to 'compelling and compassionate circumstances' include where there is a child of the partnership, and where the relationship or cohabitation was illegal or fraught with danger in the country where the couple was residing (for instance, same-sex relationships in countries which criminalise homosexual behaviour). However, it is not sufficient for the decision-maker to consider only whether there is a child of the partnership. He or she must consider whether there are other 'compelling and compassionate circumstances' arising out of the relationship more broadly.⁴⁸ The 12-month rule also does not apply if, at the time of the application, the relationship was registered under Victorian, Tasmanian or ACT law.⁴⁹

7.2.3 Proving a genuine and continuing partnership

Married and de facto couples

[7.36] Part of the definitions of both 'married' and 'de facto' relationships are requirements that the couple have a mutual commitment to a shared life to the exclusion of all others, have a genuine and continuing relationship and live together, or not separately and apart, on a permanent basis.⁵⁰

These characteristics draw heavily on the jurisprudence. In as far back as 1990, the Full Federal Court ruled:

> It is not necessarily inconsistent with a genuine marriage relationship that it was entered into by one or both parties with a view to material benefit or advancement, as for example with the hope of becoming eligible to reside in a particular country. *The true test, we would say the only test, is whether at the time at which the matter has to be decided it can be said that the parties have a mutual commitment to a shared life as husband and wife to the exclusion of others.* (Emphasis added)⁵¹

While the mutual commitment test now forms part of the definition of 'spouse' and 'de facto partner', the government did not respond as favourably to the further findings of the court on the significance of the breakdown in a marriage relationship.

[7.37] In the first instance ruling in *Dhillon*,⁵² the evidence before the decision-maker suggested that the relationship between the applicant and his Australian wife had been somewhat ambivalent, virtually from its outset. The applicant's private correspondence revealed a romantic attachment (albeit unfulfilled) to another woman overseas, and that his wife had fallen pregnant to another man before the applicant's arrival in Australia. The wife attested to having married the applicant 'to help him

---

47   *Migration Regulations*, regs 2.03A(3) and *Migration Act*, s 5CB.
48   *Graham v MIMIA* [2003] FCA 1287 at [8].
49   *Migration Regulations*, reg 2.03A(5).
50   *Migration Act*, ss 5F(2) and 5CB(2).
51   *MILGEA v Dhillon* [1990] FCA 144 at [11] (*Dhillon*).
52   *Dhillon v MILGEA* (1989) 86 ALR 651 at 655-7.

out and have a better future in Australia'.[53] Nevertheless, both at first instance and on appeal, the Federal Court held that the material presented was not sufficient to support the conclusion that the couple's marriage was fraudulent.[54] The trial judge noted that the fact that it was all downhill after cohabitation, and that the wife was acutely unhappy and disappointed by the applicant's attitude and behaviour, spoke against a contrived marriage. The acrimonious nature of the breakup, the Full Federal Court held, may have meant that the marriage was not ongoing; it did not mean that it was not genuine. On balance, their Honours found that the decision-maker had taken too limited a view of the matters that were relevant to the determination of the case.

[7.38] The courts did not go so far as to say that the breakdown of an applicant's marriage was irrelevant to the grant of residency. The final episode in the *Dhillon* saga saw the applicant divorce his Australian wife and marry his Indian fiancée. French J ultimately upheld the Minister's (second) decision that the marriage was not genuine because Dhillon never intended to remain permanently with his Australian wife.[55] The courts did, however, criticise the manner in which the immigration authorities went about their inquiries into the genuineness of relationships.[56] The government resolved the ambiguities surrounding the effect of marriage failures by spelling out in ss 5F(2)(c) and 5CB(2)(b) that unions must be 'genuine and continuing', with a mutual commitment to a shared life as husband and wife.[57]

[7.39] In considering whether the applicant meets the definition of de facto partner or spouse, the Minister is now directed by regs 1.09A(3) and 1.15A(3) to consider all the circumstances of the relationship, including:[58]

(a) the financial aspects of the relationship, including:
  (i) any joint ownership of real estate or other major assets;
  (ii) any joint liabilities;
  (iii) the extent of any pooling of financial resources, especially in relation to major financial commitments;
  (iv) whether one person in the relationship owes any legal obligation in respect of the other; and
  (v) the basis of any sharing of day-to-day household expenses; and

(b) the nature of the household, including:
  (i) any joint responsibility for the care and support of children;
  (ii) the living arrangements of the persons; and
  (iii) any sharing of the responsibility for housework; and

(c) the social aspects of the relationship, including:

---

53   Ibid at 662.
54   See *Dhillon* [1990] FCA 144.
55   See *Dhillon v MILGEA* (1994) 48 FCR 107.
56   See *Prasad v MIEA* (1985) 6 FCR 155.
57   And earlier in reg 1.15A.
58   These build on the 10 factors that may indicate the existence of such a relationship for the purposes of social security entitlements listed by the AAT in *Re Tang and Director-General of Social Services* [1981] AATA 42.

(i) whether the persons represent themselves to other people as being married to each other;
(ii) the opinion of the persons' friends and acquaintances about the nature of the relationship; and
(iii) any basis on which the persons plan and undertake joint social activities; and

(d) the nature of the persons' commitment to each other, including:
(i) the duration of the relationship;
(ii) the length of time during which the persons have lived together;
(iii) the degree of companionship and emotional support that the persons draw from each other; and
(iv) whether the persons see the relationship as a long-term one.

[7.40] In *Nassouh v MIMA*,[59] the Federal Court held that these considerations are mandatory, and must be taken into account in forming an opinion as to whether a married or de facto relationship is genuine and continuing. The Full Court has confirmed this approach. The tribunal's reasons must disclose that the tribunal has in fact had regard to these matters and routine citation of statutory provisions will not necessarily demonstrate that regard.[60] At the same time, the Full Court has cautioned that the tribunal need not laboriously evaluate each of the considerations in reg 1.15A(3). Rather, it must consider evidence adduced by the applicant which appears to fall under the headings: financial aspects, nature of the household, social aspects and nature of the commitment.[61] The tribunal is not required to make specific findings concerning these matters to which it refers.[62] The weight accorded to the evidence in relation to these elements is a matter for the tribunal.[63]

[7.41] The Federal Court has noted that the specific considerations are objective in the sense that they are not simply matters of impression or subjective opinion. They can be verified by documents, facts and evidence.[64] Decision-makers have been cautioned against placing too much emphasis on an applicant's demeanour and overall credibility. In *Asif v MIMA*,[65] the Full Federal Court considered a refusal of a spouse visa on the ground that the marriage was not genuine. In coming to this decision, reference was made to Mr Asif's history of lying to the Department, damaging his credibility. The Full Federal Court held that the credibility of a visa applicant, while important, is not necessarily decisive. In deciding whether a marriage is genuine it is proper to take into account evidence from sources other than the visa applicant. The tribunal was found to have closed its mind to the evidence of Mr Asif's wife – thereby conflicting with reg 1.15A(3). Similarly, in *Kayikci v MIAC*, the Federal Court ruled that the tribunal should not have dismissed strong evidence of a genuine and ongoing relationship on the basis of the applicant's general lack

---

59   [2000] FCA 788 at [10].
60   *Zhang v MIMIA* [2005] FCAFC 30 at [14]-[15]. See also *MIAC v Kumar* (2009) 238 CLR 448.
61   *Zhang v MIMIA* [2005] FCAFC 30 at [20]. See also *MIMA v Yusuf* (2001) 206 CLR 323 at [75].
62   *Davis v MIMIA* [2004] FCA 686 at [35].
63   *Vu v MIMIA* [2005] FCA 1836 at [51].
64   *Kayikci v MIAC* (2009) 107 ALD 112 at [21].
65   (2000) 60 ALD 145.

of credibility. The fact that he made two visa applications in which he said he was 'married' before he in fact married the sponsor should not have been determinative of his case.[66]

[7.42] As noted earlier, four indicia of a genuine relationship have been articulated in the migration legislation. Each has been considered by the courts. First, it is clear that regular communication and financial interdependence[67] are important. Examining the nature of the household, the decision-maker must explore not only whether the applicant and sponsor have used the same address, but whether they have actually resided at that address.[68] It is not sufficient that a couple has cohabited; they must have lived together as partners.[69] Difficulties have arisen where couples have lived apart for almost the whole relationship. This presents a difficulty due to the absence of the visual relationship and day-to-day opportunity for the performance of obligations and courtesies to one another that characterise most partnerships.[70] In this situation the tribunal has looked to the totality of the evidence presented before it to ascertain whether it can be satisfied that there was a genuine, ongoing relationship. However, at the same time, the tribunal is alert to the fact that positive evidence of continuous close contact can be consistent equally with a sham marriage. In *Chand*, Wilcox J acknowledged that it is possible for people who wish to present the facade of marriage to ensure that there is contact between them by way of telephone calls and postcards, letters, and even financial payments, which will give the appearance of a genuine marriage when there is not one, in fact.[71]

[7.43] On the social aspects of the relationship, the Federal Court has noted that there may be some tension between the particular requirement in subpara (ii) to consider the opinions of friends and acquaintances as to the nature of the relationship, and the tribunal's discretion not to hear a witness.[72]

[7.44] Typically, most attention has been given to the nature of the persons' commitment to each other. In *Jian Xin Liu v MIMA*,[73] Conti J stated:

> In determining the propriety of one person's commitment to a marriage, the very nature of the task requires an evaluation, based on human experience, understanding and perception of the available spectrum of potentially relevant circumstances of each particular case.

In that case the court upheld the tribunal's decision that the marriage was not genuine, finding instead that the marriage was contrived for the purpose of the applicant obtaining an Australian visa. The court held that the tribunal had not erred in taking into account the applicant's former wife's motivations and adverse intentions.

---

66 *Kayikci v MIAC* (2009) 107 ALD 112 at [21].
67 See, for example, *Li v MIAC* [2007] FCA 1098; 96 ALD 361.
68 *Woo v MIMIA* [2002] FCA 1596; *Vu v MIMIA* [2005] FCA 1836.
69 *Gherga v MIMIA* [2004] FCA 351; *Lumanovska v MIMIA* [2003] FCA 1321.
70 See *Chand v MILGEA* (1996) 44 ALD 583.
71 Ibid at 586.
72 *Gherga v MIMIA* [2004] FCA 351 at [24].
73 [2001] FCA 1437 at [23].

[7.45] In *Sevim v MIMA*,[74] the tribunal had considered that a genuine marriage required some parity of commitment between the parties. The Federal Court rejected this approach, and required instead a simple commitment by each to the other, as husband and wife (in this case), to the exclusion of others. Gray J concluded that there must be many marriages where parties have different levels or degrees of commitment, or where the commitment of the parties to each other is of a different quality. Such differences do not matter in the application of the test.[75]

[7.46] The courts have been careful to direct the tribunal to consider the particular circumstances and characteristics of the parties to the relationship in question. In *Tran v MIMA*,[76] Finkelstein J overruled the MRT's refusal of a spouse visa on the basis of lack of commitment to a mutual relationship. His Honour found that the tribunal should have taken into account the impaired cognitive ability of the applicant who suffered from schizophrenia. His Honour found that:[77]

> In deciding whether two parties are in a married relationship (as defined), the decision-maker is required to have regard to the particular circumstances of the relationship.

However, where a particular quality of one of the parties is relevant to the couple's ability to satisfy the criteria in reg 1.15A, it is also clear that the applicant bears the onus of satisfying the court as to that quality. An example is where the impaired mental capacity of the sponsor was important in explaining a couple's failure to live together.[78]

[7.47] There has been an increasing tendency in both the tribunal and in the courts to conflate issues relating to the breakdown of marriage on grounds of family violence (see below Part 7.3.2) with issues relating to the genuineness of the original relationship. The jurisprudence marks a sharp departure from earlier decisions where the Federal Court took the view that events surrounding a marriage breakdown should not influence findings of fact required to be made as at the date of an initial application for a visa.[79] Although there have been some exceptions,[80] there has been a series of cases where findings that marriages were abusive have lead to the conclusion that the marriage or relationship in question was never 'genuine' for immigration purposes. As explored in Part 7.3 below, in many instances it is the woman in the relationship who stands to lose most.[81] It is also an approach that makes a mockery

---

74 (2001) 114 FCR 126.
75 Ibid at [71]. See also *Ndegwa v MIMIA* [2005] FMCA 74 at [6].
76 [2003] FCA 44.
77 Ibid at [14].
78 *Bunnag v MIAC* [2008] FCA 357 at [38].
79 See, for example, *Bretag v IRT and MILGEA* [1991] FCA 582.
80 In *Jayasinghe v MIMA* [2006] FCA 1700 the court found error in the tribunal's reliance on evidence relating to conduct engaged in after the date of the initial application.
81 See, for example, *El Mohamad v MIMA* [2007] FMCA 345; *Tang v MIMA* [2006] FMCA 60; *Nguyen v MIMA* [2007] FMCA 1315; and *Shadali v MIMA* [2007] FMCA 1230. While the facts in these cases are quite different, there is a common feature that the female applicants entered their marriages in good faith, and were deceived by their sponsoring husbands. See the discussion of *Ally v MIMA* [2007] FMCA 430, below Part 7.3. Compare, however, the ruling in *Muliyana v MIAC* [2010] FCAFC 24.

of the legislative intention behind provisions introduced to provide protection to victims of family violence.

Additional requirements for de facto couples

[7.48] As noted above, in the case of de facto couples, the decision-maker must determine that the couple satisfied the legislative elements of a genuine and continuing relationship not only at the time of application and at the time of decision but throughout a 12-month period before the date of application.[82] This 12-month rule does not apply where the applicant establishes that there are 'compelling and compassionate circumstances' for the grant of the visa. Consideration of whether compelling and compassionate circumstances have been established was previously at the time of application only, but is now assessed at any time of the visa application process.[83]

7.2.4 'Sham' marriages and serial sponsorships

[7.49] As the grounds for migrating to Australia became more restrictive throughout the 1980s, statistical evidence suggested that more and more people were seeking entry on spouse grounds. From 11,600 spouse, de facto and fiancé arrivals in 1983-84,[84] the annual figures surged to 27,790 in 1995-96.[85] These numbers have continued to rise incrementally, with partner arrivals totalling 42,100 in 2008-09.[86]

[7.50] This rise in applications for residence on spouse grounds has fed anxieties about fraudulent sponsorships, or 'immigration' marriages, although the increase needs to be considered in proportion given corresponding increases in the overall migrant intake.[87] In a 2005 report, the Department reported several incidents of contrived marriages and relationships. Of the 3999 allegations of fraud received by the department, 48 per cent were incidents of contrived or 'sham' relationships.[88] As discussed earlier, in the case of both overseas and onshore sponsorships, the issue of sham marriages was first addressed by defining more strictly the eligibility of spouses.[89] In addition, stringent penalties were introduced in 1991 for persons

---

82 *Migration Regulations*, reg 2.03A(3).
83 *Antipova v MIMIA* (2006) 151 FCR 480 at [104]. Note that this case pre-dated the redrafting of the definition of 'de facto' partner, which transferred the 12-month rule into separate visa criteria – reg 2.03A.
84 Joint Standing Committee on Migration Regulations (JSCMR), *Second Report: Change of Status on Grounds of Spouse/De Facto Relationships* (Canberra: AGPS, 1991) at 13-14.
85 Siew-Ean Khoo, 'The Context of Spouse Migration to Australia' (2001) 39(1) *International Migration* 111 at 115-16.
86 DIAC, *Report on Migration Program 2008-09* (Canberra) at 12.
87 The subject became one of the first terms of reference for JSCMR when that committee was formed in 1990: see JSCMR, above n 84. For comparative treatment of this phenomenon, see special issue 'The Marriage of Convenience in European Immigration Law' (2006) 8 (3-4) *European Journal of Migration and Law* and Maria Isabel Medina, 'The Criminalization of Immigration Law: Employer Sanctions and Marriage Fraud' (1997) 18 *Immigration and Nationality Law Review* 643.
88 See DIMIA, *Managing the Border: Immigration Compliance – 2004-05* (Canberra: 2005) at 89.
89 See *1989 Regulations*, reg 3A (now *Migration Regulations*, regs 1.09A and 1.15A, and *Migration Act*, ss 5CB and 5F).

either arranging sham marriages or de facto relationships, or applying for a visa (or sponsoring an applicant) on the basis of a sham marriage or relationship. For the first group, ss 240-241 of the Act now create offences attracting a $100,000 fine, 10 years in prison or both.[90] For the second, s 243 creates an offence punishable by two years' imprisonment and provides that a non-citizen convicted of such an offence becomes unlawful.[91]

[7.51] The Federal Court has taken the view that the rejection of a visa application on the ground that the marriage in question is a sham must be reached on clearly articulated grounds. In *Tolibao-Cortes*,[92] Heerey J held that the terms of reg 1.15A(3) do not relieve the decision-maker of the obligation to make relevant findings of fact. In that case, the decision-maker, although hinting that the relationship in question was contrived, did not make any firm *findings* to this effect and made no attempt to discount evidence that contradicted such a conclusion.

[7.52] It is often assumed that the clearest indication of 'marriage fraud' is evidence of repeated attempts of the Australian party to sponsor a spouse from overseas. In the past, the only barrier to serial sponsorships was the requirement that proof be adduced as to the genuineness of the relationship. Sponsors, however, were under no obligation to advise either their partner or the immigration authorities about previous sponsorships (or, indeed, about previous criminal convictions related to family violence which has often been linked to serial sponsorship). In such cases, it was only the criminal record of the person sponsored from abroad that was considered relevant as a public interest issue. In 1996, the Regulations were amended to address the problem of spousal abuse associated with serial sponsorship.[93] Under reg 1.20J, the Minister must not approve the sponsorship of an applicant for a partner or prospective marriage visa unless the Minister is satisfied that no more than one other person has been successfully sponsored previously by the potential sponsor. A further limitation is that, if another person has been granted a visa as a result of a previous sponsorship, more than five years must have passed since the date of the application for that visa before a new sponsorship will be approved. Under reg 1.20J(2), the Minister retains a discretion to grant the visa if there are compelling circumstances affecting the Australian sponsor.

[7.53] In *Babicci v MIMIA*[94] the Full Federal Court adopted a dictionary interpretation of the phrase 'compelling circumstances', interpreting 'compelling' to mean 'to force or drive, especially to a course of action'. Mr Babicci had previously sponsored two former spouses for visas and, in order to sponsor his most recent wife, he had to demonstrate the existence of compelling circumstances affecting him as sponsor. The matters relied on by Mr Babicci included the fact that he was sick, had psychological and emotional problems and that he was not at fault in the dissolution of his earlier

---

90   For an example of conviction, see *R v McLean* (2001) 121 A Crim R 484.
91   For examples of convictions, see *Nguyen v MIAC* [2007] FCAFC 38 and *Mujedenovski v MIAC* (2009) 112 ALD 10.
92   [2001] FCA 1193.
93   See *Migration Regulations*, Div 1.4B, inserted by SR 211 of 1996.
94   (2005) 141 FCR 285 at [8].

marriages.[95] Whilst the tribunal expressed sympathy and compassion for the applicant, it did not accept that Mr Babicci's circumstances were 'compelling'. The Full Federal Court found no error in the way the tribunal construed the phrase, ruling that the circumstances must be so powerful that they lead the decision-maker to conclude that the prohibition in reg 1.20J(1) should be waived.[96] The Federal Court judgment at first instance had concluded that compelling circumstances were such that evoke interest or attention in a powerful or irresistible way.[97] Among the circumstances that decision-makers seem to find compelling so as to permit a third sponsorship for partner migration is where the relationship involves a dependent child.[98]

Because of these legislative measures, sponsors are now required to provide information about previous sponsorships. Where such sponsorships are revealed, the visa applicant will be asked in an interview about his or her knowledge of these sponsorships.

[7.54] Once in Australia, the family violence provisions provide some protection for foreign spouses who hold provisional visas that lead to permanent residence. The operation of the family violence provisions is considered below in Part 7.3.

[7.55] Immigration marriage scams can, in extreme cases, amount to labour or sexual exploitation of the foreign party or a form of human trafficking.[99] As Iredale and others have documented, before the introduction of the limit on serial sponsorships, there were a disturbing number of cases of Australian sponsors (almost invariably male) nominating one partner after another for entry on spouse grounds.[100] There is also caselaw which documents the importation of women to work in brothels.[101]

[7.56] Where there is evidence of coercion or exploitation, such immigration fraud can become a matter of criminal law.[102] Australia's ratification of the Trafficking Protocol and Rome Statute of the International Criminal Court[103] saw the introduction of new criminal offences to combat human trafficking and slavery. In *R v Kovacs*,[104] Kovacs and his wife were convicted of arranging a fraudulent marriage, and of further offences relating to slavery and rape. They had brought a foreign domestic worker to Australia by organising a sham marriage between the woman and an Australian citizen friend of theirs. In order to obtain a spouse visa, the woman and the

---

95 Ibid at [9].
96 Ibid at [24] and [25]. See also *071176030* [2008] MRTA 58; *0906655* [2009] MRTA 2784.
97 *Babicci v MIMIA* [2004] FCA 1645.
98 See, for example, *071810442* [2008] MRTA 1183.
99 Andreas Schloenhardt, *Trafficking in Persons and Sham Marriages in Australia* (Brisbane: University of Queensland Human Trafficking Working Group, May 2009).
100 See Robyn Iredale, 'Serial Sponsorship: Immigration Policy and Human Rights' (1995) 3 *Just Policy* 37.
101 See *Park Oh Ho v MIEA* (1988) 20 FCR 104 (and on appeal to the High Court *Park Oh Ho v MIEA* (1989) 167 CLR 637).
102 See *United Nations Convention against Transnational Organized Crime*, GA Res 55/25, UN GAOR, 55th sess, 62nd plen mtg, Annex II (*Protocol to Prevent, Suppress and Punish Trafficking in Persons, Especially Women and Children*), Agenda Item 105, preamble, UN Doc A/RES/55/25 (8 January 2001) (*Trafficking Protocol*).
103 2187 UNTS 90. See generally MC Bassiouni, 'Enslavement as an International Crime' (1991) 23 *New York Journal of International Law and Politics* 445.
104 [2009] 2 Qd R 51.

Australian were married in the Philippines. The woman was clearly aware that the marriage was fraudulent but she did not expect to live and work in the conditions she met in Australia. After her arrival in the country, she was forced to work extremely long hours in the Kovacs' business and home, without receiving a regular salary. She was also repeatedly raped by Mr Kovacs, and threatened with deportation and prison if she contacted the police.

[7.57] The most concerning aspect of the scenario enacted in *Kovacs* is the vulnerability of the migrant. In addition to being a victim of serious criminal activity and a foreigner in an unfamiliar country (with scant knowledge of the local language and legal system), the Filipina woman at the centre of the case risked removal by making her story public. Her irregular immigration status increased her dependency on her captors. As explored further in Chapter 14.5, Australia has sought to redress this abuse and power imbalance by introducing visa concessions that give victims of trafficking security of immigration status.

7.3 The family violence exceptions

[7.58] Special concessions have been made for migrants who suffer violence at the hands of their sponsoring partners since 1991, following shortly after the introduction of a codified immigration system in December 1989.[105] The obvious policy rationale for the measure was that the introduction of strict requirements of continuity in relationships can place sponsored parties in a position of acute disadvantage. If the intention was to redress potential abuse, it is difficult to fault the concept of allowing victims of 'family violence' to remain as permanent residents in spite of the breakdown of their relationships. The phenomenon is sadly a feature of partner migration all around the world.[106] The countervailing policy consideration has been how to deal with the inevitable misuse of the provisions by persons whose relationship has failed but who cannot be described as victims of 'violence'.

[7.59] Various devices have been used to strike a balance between compassion and the minimisation of abuse of the system, with numerous attempts made to refine the criteria activating the family violence concessions. On the one hand, the task of assessing claims has been placed in the hands of putative family violence experts. At the same time discretions vested in decision-makers at primary and review levels have been systematically reduced. In fact the rules represent another interesting case study of both outsourcing and privatisation in immigration decision-making. Whether the resulting regime always results in fair and rational decisions, however, is open to question.

---

105 On the operation of the early laws, see Edwin Odhiambo-Abuya, 'The Pain of Love: Spousal Immigration and Family Violence in Australia – A Regime in Chaos?' (2003) 12(3) *Pacific Rim Law & Policy Journal* 673.

106 See, for example, Uma Narayan, '"Mail-Order" Brides: Immigrant Women, Family Violence and Immigration Law' (1995) 10(1) *Hypatia* 104 (on the United States); Sundari Anitha, 'Neither Safety nor Justice: The UK Government Response to Family Violence Against Immigrant Women' (2008) 30(3) *Journal of Social Welfare and Family Law* 189; Lucy Williams and Yu Mei-Kuei, 'Family Violence in Cross-Border Marriage – A Case Study from Taiwan' (2006) 2(3-4) *International Journal of Migration, Health and Social Care* 58.

[7.60] After outlining the development of the relevant laws and policies, we consider four areas within the now considerable body of case law on this subject. These concern the question of defining 'family violence'; the evidence required to be submitted (and by whom); issues relating to the referral of cases to expert assessors; and the relationship between family violence and the ab initio requirement of a genuine, ongoing relationship. This section concludes with some comments on continuing gaps in the coverage of the family violence provisions.

7.3.1 The evolution of the family violence exceptions

[7.61] The family violence provisions allow the applicant to be granted permanent residence where otherwise ineligible because the partner relationship with the Australian sponsor has ceased. The family violence provisions apply where acceptable evidence shows that the visa applicant and/or a relevant child[107] or family member has been subjected to violence inflicted by the sponsoring partner, or by a third party at the instigation of the sponsoring partner.[108]

[7.62] In 1993 concerns were raised by the Family Violence Monitoring Committee that the 'acceptable evidence' requirements were difficult for people to satisfy, particularly those from non-English speaking backgrounds. Accordingly, in July 1995 new provisions articulated in much greater detail the evidence required to enliven the concession, and at the same time broadening the range of matters that could be used to prove that violence had occurred.[109]

[7.63] Acceptable evidence now includes: court-recognised undertakings where there has been an allegation of family violence; and a statutory declaration from the applicant, and from two 'competent persons' stating their opinion that the applicant has suffered from family violence.[110] 'Competent person' is defined to include doctors, psychologists, nurses, social workers, Family Court counsellors, and managers and coordinators of women's refuges, and family violence crisis and counselling services.[111] A police record of an assault on the victim allegedly committed by the perpetrator is acceptable as a substitute for one statutory declaration from a 'competent person'.[112] Interim apprehended violence orders will not be accepted, however, unless it can be shown that the alleged perpetrator of the family violence has been granted a hearing.[113] The problem of concocted allegations has been dealt with by specifying, for example, that expert opinions cannot be sought from two people holding the same qualifications.[114]

---

107 The person affected must be the child of either the applicant or the sponsor (or of them both); and/or, in the case of an offshore visa, a family unit member.
108 *Migration Regulations*, reg 1.23. See *Cakmak v MIMIA* (2003) 135 FCR 183; *Sok v MIMIA* (2005) 144 FCR 170 and *Theunissen v MIMIA* (2005) 88 ALD 97.
109 See Odhiambo-Abuya, above n 105; and Carina Hickling, 'Standing up for Basic Rights: A Case Study of Illawarra Filipino Women's Group' (Paper Presented at the 1st International Conference Women and Politics in Asia, Halmstad, Sweden, 6-7 June 2003).
110 *Migration Regulations*, reg 1.24.
111 Ibid, reg 1.21.
112 For an example of how the former provisions operated against an applicant who alleged family violence where there was a police record alleging family violence, see *Re Thomson* [1995] IRTA 5348.
113 *Migration Regulations*, reg 1.23(4)(b), original regulation inserted by SR 354 of 1997.
114 See regs 1.21-1.27, introduced by SR 117 of 1995.

[7.64] A further concern with the original provisions was that they did not extend beyond the partner visa class, even though family violence is obviously not restricted to applicants within that visa class. The provisions are available now to most visa classes that involve the grant of residence on grounds of married or de facto relationships, as well as key business and skills visas.[115]

[7.65] By 2005, concerns had arisen over the number of men in failed relationships who were invoking the family violence exceptions. In July of that year the *Migration Regulations* were amended to provide for decision-makers and review authorities to be able to refer cases for assessment by an 'independent expert' where the evidence submitted is 'non-judicial'[116] and where reasonable doubts emerge about the claims being made. The 'experts' gazetted for this purpose include officers within the federal government agency, Centrelink, who are required to furnish an opinion as to whether family violence has occurred.[117] An opinion once sought must be taken as correct.[118]

7.3.2 The meaning of 'family violence'[119]

[7.66] Many of the issues that have arisen in the family violence cases derive from claims brought by men alleging violence on the part of female sponsors. These cases have sparked debate over the nature of the harms that must be suffered by a victim. Faced with male claimants who do not exhibit serious physical injury at the hands of a sponsoring partner, the question has been whether psychological violence satisfies the criteria for family violence. The Federal Court has been divided in its approach, which may reflect an anxiety about encouraging unmeritorious claims or the social currency of gender stereotyping in the context of family violence claims. Nevertheless, the general trend seems to favour reading the term so as to include both psychological violence and physical violence to property.[120]

[7.67] The debate over defining 'violence' began in *Malik v MIMA*,[121] where Wilcox J ruled that this legislative reference encompasses non-physical damage suffered by an applicant. His Honour defined such violence as 'conduct against the victim,

---

115 Family violence provisions apply to the following visa subclasses: Partner: 100, 801 and, 820; (formerly) interdependency: 110 and 814; dependent child: 445; business and related visas: 845, 846, 855, 856, 857, 858.
116 Orders made by a court or magistrate must be taken as conclusive: reg 1.23(4).
117 See reg 1.21(1), read with Gazette Notice IMMI 05/064, F2005L01620, 30 June 2005. The Procedures Advice Manual 3 (PAM3) advises decision-makers to send claims made by male applicants to an independent expert. See, for example, *Bolat v MIMA* [2007] FMCA 1640; *Sok v MIMIA* (2005) 144 FCR 170; *Helvaci v MIMA* [2007] FMCA 1306.
118 See reg 1.23(10)(c)(ii).
119 The term 'family violence' was introduced to replace former references to 'domestic violence' in October 2007. These changes align the migration legislation with relevant provisions of the *Family Law Act 1975* (Cth). See reg 1.23(2) and evidence requirements in regs 1.24-1.26. See also the replacement of the phrase 'court counsellor' with 'family consultant' in reg 1.21(1)(a)(v) in the definition of 'competent person'.
120 See *Ejueyitsi v MIAC* [2006] FMCA 1900. Violence to property alone is specifically included in the definition of 'relevant family violence' in reg 1.21(1): 'conduct towards the property of the alleged victim ... that causes them to reasonably fear for or be reasonably apprehensive about their ... wellbeing'. The definition of 'violence' also includes 'threats of violence'.
121 (2000) 98 FCR 291.

usually a course of conduct, that causes the victim to have fear or apprehension about his or her personal well-being or safety'.[122] This interpretation has been adopted in subsequent cases.[123] Lindgren J took a different view in *Doan v MIMA*,[124] preferring to confine the term to actual physical violence. His Honour acknowledged that the words 'family violence' appeared in the applicant's lawyer's letters to the MRT, but noted that the applicant's statement 'did not refer to any physical violence'. Rather, the material presented to the tribunal referred to 'torture and humiliation' and 'agony'.[125] He therefore concluded that the MRT was entitled to reject Mr Doan's claims of family violence. This was also the view taken by the Full Federal Court in *Cakmak v MIMIA*.[126] That court ruled expressly that the definition of family violence clearly included physical violence but did not include 'mere' emotional violence or psychological violence:[127]

> However, belittling, lowering self esteem, 'emotional violence' or 'psychological violence' and such behaviour as surrogates or synonyms for violence is, we think, to broaden the scope of the regulations beyond their words. There must be 'violence', or the 'threat of violence', involving the application, or threat of application, of force such that the alleged victim is caused to fear for, or be apprehensive about, his or her well-being or personal safety.

In that instance the claimant was a man who adduced evidence of a single incidence of physical violence involving scratching and the throwing of water.[128]

[7.68] Ultimately, this definition was overturned by the Full Federal Court on appeal in *Sok v MIMIA*.[129] There, the court adopted a wider definition of violence to include psychological and emotional abuse and even economic deprivation. Explaining the departure from earlier reasoning, Marshall J noted that a more expansive interpretation brings the reference to family violence in immigration into line with behaviour that can breach an injunction granted pursuant to the *Family Law Act 1975*.[130] While it seems now to be settled that violence can extend to psychological violence, questions remain about the level of violence and, especially, the degree of evidence that is required to substantiate a claim.

7.3.3 Evidence of family violence: The triumph of form over substance

[7.69] As noted earlier, the government's response to the spike in the number of men claiming concessional treatment on the basis of family violence has been to make the evidentiary requirements increasingly explicit. Ironically, this has probably done more to assist than deter disingenuous claimants, provided they are able to find compliant professionals prepared to supply statutory declarations using the

---

122 Ibid at [4].
123 See *Sok v MIMIA* (2005) 144 FCR 170; and *Meroka v MIMA* (2002) 117 FCR 251.
124 [2000] FCA 909.
125 Ibid at [42].
126 (2003) 135 FCR 183.
127 Ibid at [62].
128 This was affirmed by Heerey J in *Sok v MIMIA* [2004] FCA 1235.
129 (2005) 144 FCR 170.
130 See s 114(1)(a), (b) and (c) of the *Family Law Act 1975*.

correct phrasing. For its part, the Federal Court has confirmed that strict compliance with the Regulations is necessary in order to obtain the benefit of the family violence provisions.

[7.70] A person who claims to have been the victim of family violence will be 'taken to have suffered family violence' if, inter alia, the alleged victim presents evidence of a competent person in the prescribed form.[131] The Regulations require that the statutory declaration made by a competent person must set out their qualifications, state that in the deposer's opinion the applicant has suffered family violence, name the person who committed the violence and detail the evidence on which the opinion is based.[132]

[7.71] In *Du v MIMA*,[133] Mathews J stressed the 'specific and peremptory' terms of the Regulations. Her Honour said:

> It is not sufficient compliance, in my view, for a competent person simply to note the consistency between a person's presentation and their account of family violence, or even the occurrence of family violence. The Regulations require that the competent person express an opinion in very specific terms, namely, as to whether relevant family violence as defined in reg 1.23 has been suffered by a person.
>
> This involves not only an opinion that past acts of violence have occurred but also an assessment of the state of mind of the alleged victim.

[7.72] This passage has been cited with approval in many subsequent cases,[134] including by Sundberg J in *Alin v MIMIA*.[135] Mr Alin's appeal against the refusal of a subclass 801 (Spouse) visa was dismissed primarily on the basis that his claims invited a review of the merits of the tribunal's decision. However, Sundberg J added that, even if he had found a discernible ground of review, the appeal would have failed on the basis that the statutory declarations from the two 'competent persons' (a doctor and psychologist) did not satisfy reg 1.26. He stated that neither revealed an awareness of the definition of family violence in reg 1.23, nor made reference to the applicant's state of mind (namely that the violence caused the applicant to fear for or be apprehensive about his personal wellbeing or safety).[136]

[7.73] The relevant statutory declaration submitted by Dr Munir stated that Mr Alin had later consulted him and complained of 'lack of sleep, irritability, lack of enjoyment of life, anxiety symptoms and feeling stressed for several months', relating the symptoms to the dissolution of his marriage. The doctor diagnosed reactive anxiety/depression secondary to divorce. Similar symptoms were recounted in the statutory declaration from Mr Garcia, a psychologist, who stated the applicant 'was subjected to a series of actions that may indicate that he suffered family violence'. The MRT had rejected Mr Alin's claims on the basis that the incidents relied on were

---

131 *Migration Regulations*, reg 1.23(9)(c).
132 Ibid, reg 1.26.
133 [2000] FCA 1115 at [18]-[19].
134 See, for example, *Kailey v MIMIA* [2005] FMCA 1044 at [15] and the cases discussed below.
135 [2002] FCA 979.
136 Ibid at [12].

not sufficiently serious for the applicant to have the benefit of the family violence exception to the general requirement that there be a genuine and continuing marriage relationship at the time of decision (paraphrasing Lindgren J in *Doan*), and that he was not suffering the fear or apprehension referred to by Wilcox J in *Malik*.

[7.74] In response to the statements made in *Du* and *Alin*, subsequent statutory declarations submitted to the MRT have attempted to conform to the specific requirements articulated by Mathews J. This has led some judges to describe the regime as a triumph of form over substance.[137] However, Ryan J in *Meroka v MIMA*[138] took a slightly more relaxed approach. After examining the standard departmental form to be completed by competent persons, his Honour observed:[139]

> I do not consider that the competent person need state expressly that in his or her opinion relevant family violence has been suffered. The requisite statement of opinion may be conveyed by implication having regard to the way in which the standard form directs the attention of the competent person to the definition of 'family violence' in Reg 1.23(2)(b).

[7.75] Although this position was affirmed in *Kozel v MIMA*,[140] the Full Federal Court has drawn together the judgments in *Du*, *Alin* and *Meroka* to hold that:[141]

> It is not sufficient for the competent person to state that the victim's presentation is consistent with the claim of family violence. Nor is it sufficient to state that the alleged victim may have, or appears to have, suffered family violence. Similarly it is not sufficient for the competent person merely to recite the possession of an opinion that the alleged victim has suffered family violence. Ultimately the regulation requires that the competent person must state that in his or her opinion, 'relevant family violence ... has been suffered'. It must be apparent from the declaration that the competent person attributes the same meaning to 'family violence' as reg 1.23(2)(b) although, in our view, it is not necessary for the declarant to refer to that definition.

[7.76] In many other cases relatively small departures from the regulatory requirements have led to the rejection of the statutory declarations supplied. For example, statutory declarations sworn under State laws have been ruled out as non-compliant (they must be sworn under federal laws).[142] So too have statutory declarations that have been sworn before 'competent persons' who do not meet the description or diversity requirements in the Regulations.[143] The fact that these approaches can lead to rather extreme results is borne out in cases like *Cao v MIMA*[144] where evidence

---

137 See *Ibrahim v MIMIA* [2002] FCA 1279; *Cakmak v MIMIA* (2003) 135 FCR 183 at [14]-[15]; *Pandey v MIMIA* [2005] FMCA 1081; *Tang v MIMA* [2006] FMCA 60; and *Isse v MIMA* [2006] FMCA 253.
138 [2002] FCA 482.
139 Ibid at [11].
140 (2004) 138 FCR 181. See also *Zaouk v MIMA* (2007) 159 FCR 152 where the Full Court confirmed that reg 1.26(c) does not require the recitation by a competent person of the reg 1.23(2)(b) definition.
141 *MIAC v Ejueyitsi* (2007) 159 FCR 94 at [34].
142 See *Mohamed v MIMA* (2007) 161 FCR 408; *Isse v MIMA* [2006] FMCA 253; and *Morgan v MIMA* [1999] FCA 1059.
143 See, for example, *Mardini v MIMIA* [2005] FMCA 1409 where the declarations were by two medical practitioners; and, on appeal, *Mardini v MIMA* [2006] FCA 488 at [41].
144 [2007] FMCA 1239.

was rejected (at first instance – although not on appeal) from the coordinator of an organisation that provided crisis accommodation. The assertion was that the statutory declaration did not specify that the testator was the coordinator of a *women's* refuge.

Referral of cases to an independent expert

[7.77] The fact that the family violence provisions have been tightened to counter the disproportionate number of claims being made by male applicants (relative to the incidence of spousal violence against males reported in the community) is borne out most forcefully in the discretion to refer cases for assessment by independent experts. In practice, referrals are made to expert officers within the social security agency, Centrelink, whose opinion must then be accepted by the decision-maker. If the case law is any indication, most referrals are of male applicants and most result in a negative outcome for the person claiming to have been a victim of family violence. In this context, the Department's policy guidelines (directing that claims made by male applicants be referred to an independent expert) do appear to be biased against male victims of family violence, either on their face or in the way they are being interpreted.

[7.78] In the result, applicants have found it virtually impossible to challenge decisions once individual cases have been referred to Centrelink. Successful challenges to the referrals themselves have occurred only on procedural grounds, notably where tribunals have referred cases without first affording the applicant the opportunity for a hearing. As the High Court confirmed in *Sok v MIAC*,[145] referrals can only be made where the decision-maker is unable to make a finding after having invited the applicant to give evidence both by way of written declarations and oral argument at a hearing.

[7.79] Mr Sie Sok, a citizen of Cambodia, married an Australian citizen who sponsored his Partner visa application in 2002. In 2005, after an interview and a visit to two addresses where it was thought that Sok and his wife were living, a delegate of the Minister refused to grant his permanent visa on the basis that the delegate was not satisfied that Sok was the spouse of the sponsor. It was only when review of this decision was pending at the MRT that Sok claimed that he had been the victim of family violence at the hands of his wife. In response to the written evidence supporting Sok's claim, the tribunal recorded a finding that it was not satisfied that the applicant had suffered relevant family violence. Sok was not invited to appear to give evidence or make submissions. The tribunal then sought and followed the opinion of an independent expert that Sok had not suffered relevant family violence. Sok made written submissions in response. The tribunal scheduled a hearing and then cancelled it, and told Sok that it would seek a further opinion from an independent expert. The second independent expert again opined that Sok had not suffered relevant family violence. The tribunal finally held a hearing at which Sok presented evidence and

---

145 (2008) 238 CLR 251 at [5]. Note that, while the High Court was considering an earlier version of the Regulations, the wording of the regulation before it was relevantly the same as the current version. See also *Ali v MIMA* [2007] FMCA 1405 and *Helvaci v MIMA* [2007] FMCA 1306 (note that, although the High Court confirmed this ruling, the Federal Magistrate's decision was overturned by consent in the High Court at *Helvaci v MIAC* [2009] HCATrans 96).

arguments to support his claim. In October 2006, the tribunal affirmed the delegate's decision to refuse to grant the permanent visa, ruling that it was required to take as correct the independent expert's opinion that the applicant had not suffered family violence.

[7.80]   On appeal, the Federal Magistrates Court declared the tribunal's decision to be 'unlawful, void and of no force and effect' on the basis that the tribunal had failed to discharge its legal obligation to invite the applicant to a hearing before seeking the opinion of an independent expert.[146] The Full Federal Court then allowed the Minister's appeal on the basis that the regulations relating to family violence in Div 1.5 only applied to the original decision-maker and not to the tribunal in the exercise of its review function.[147] The Full Court concluded that the tribunal had erred in considering the family violence issue after not having raised the issue before the Minister's delegate.[148] This view was held by the Full Court notwithstanding that the Minister had argued that nothing in the *Migration Regulations* or *Migration Act* as a whole precluded the tribunal from dealing with a claim of family violence when this claim was first made before the tribunal.[149]

[7.81]   In 2008, the High Court ruled in favour of Sok, holding that the Regulations in relation to family violence are not confined in their application to cases where the visa applicant has claimed family violence before the initial consideration of the visa application.[150] The High Court ruled that the tribunal may not refer a family violence claim to an independent expert before inviting the applicant to give evidence and present arguments. This interpretation was adopted for two key reasons. First, the Regulations require an evaluation of the claim made by the visa applicant before the decision-maker can come to a view that the alleged victim has not suffered such violence. Only then can he or she opt to seek the opinion of an independent expert. Secondly, obtaining the opinion of an independent expert is dispositive of the issue of family violence: it must be accepted by the decision-maker. Because the independent expert is not required to grant the applicant a hearing, the opinion cannot be described as evidence or submissions. Thus, seeking such an opinion without first offering the applicant a hearing would impermissibly neutralise the requirement of the tribunal to provide a hearing under s 360 of the Act.[151]

[7.82]   Consistent with this approach, the Federal Court in *Mazhar v MIMA*[152] ruled that the invitation to attend a hearing before a tribunal cannot be a 'charade' or empty gesture. This requirement lends weight to the view that referrals must take place only after a hearing is conducted for the purpose of collecting all relevant information.

---

146   *Sok v MIAC* [2007] FMCA 1525 at [20], [27].
147   *MIAC v Sok* (2008) 165 FCR 586 at [61].
148   Ibid at [67].
149   *Sok v MIAC* (2008) 238 CLR 251 at [21].
150   Ibid at [28].
151   Ibid at [40].
152   (2000) 183 ALR 188 at [31].

Family violence and the ab initio requirements of a genuine relationship[153]

[7.83] If the jurisprudence on family violence suggests a distrust of claims made by male applicants, there is one line of cases where the reasoning adopted has had a disproportionately adverse impact on women claimants. These are the cases where adjudicators have accepted that the applicants have been the victims of sometimes egregious family violence. However, their claims for concessional treatment have been denied on the basis that the violence suffered was evidence that the applicants did not meet the requirements for a genuine, ongoing spousal relationship. The courts have made it clear that the existence of a partnership is a necessary pre-condition to the consideration of the family violence exceptions. Before a family violence allegation can be considered, the decision-maker must be satisfied that the applicant and her or his sponsor were in a spousal or de facto relationship in the first place.

[7.84] In cases where a claimant raises issues of family violence that have occurred only after sponsorship is withdrawn, this approach may be (prima facie) understandable.[154] However, consideration needs to be given to the possibility that the withdrawal of sponsorship is itself part of a pattern of spousal abuse that does not really come to a head until the withdrawal occurs. The experience of the applicant in *Muliyana v MIAC*[155] is illustrative. Mrs Muliyana married her husband in an arranged marriage in India in 2005. Her husband had acquired permanent residence in Australia and he returned to work in Australia while Mrs Muliyana completed her studies and began work in India while waiting for permission to join him. According to her, at the end of that year, her husband's family demanded that she leave her job and live with them. They were very controlling toward her and reported all her activities to her husband in Australia which caused problems between him and her. She travelled to be with her husband in November 2006 and in December they returned to India, where Mr Muliyana left his wife at her parents' house, promising to return in a couple of days. In fact he returned to Australia without her and refused to maintain contact with her. The husband's parents refused to allow Mrs Muliyana to stay in India, sending her back to Australia. When she appeared at her Australian home, her husband refused to let her in, assaulted and threatened to kill her. She called the police and Mr Muliyana gave an undertaking to the Federal Magistrates Court not to assault, harass or intimidate her. The tribunal accepted her evidence but found that the sponsor had informed the Department that the relationship was over before the physical assault. It ruled that the man's behaviour indicated that he did not consider himself to be in a relationship with her at that time. The tribunal concluded that the family violence had not occurred during the currency of the relationship, as required by the Regulations as interpreted by the courts.[156] On appeal, Smith FM found that the Regulations did not require any causal connection, or particular chronological relationship, between the family violence and a subsequent separation.[157] The Federal Magistrate favoured

---

153 Note that Div 1.5 of the Regulations was amended on 9 November 2009 to require that the family violence must have occurred when the married or de facto relationship was in existence.
154 See, for example, *Guven v MIMA* [2006] FMCA 311 at [22]; *Tang v MIMA* [2006] FMCA 60.
155 [2009] FMCA 691.
156 *Sok v MIAC* [2007] FMCA 1525 at [37]-[39].
157 *Muliyana v MIAC* [2009] FMCA 691 at [29], following *Herft v MIAC* [2007] FMCA 756 at [9]-[13].

interpreting the Regulations to require the decision-maker be satisfied of two matters only: namely, that the partnership has ceased, and that the applicant was a victim of family violence at the hands of the sponsor. However, Smith FM felt bound to follow previous judicial authority interpreting the family violence exception as applicable only where the relationship has come to an end as a result of the violence.[158] On 9 November 2009, reg 1.23 of the *Migration Regulations* was amended to specify that, to be granted a visa on the basis of family violence, the violence must have occurred while the married or de facto relationship was in existence. The amendment seemed on its face to confirm the more conservative approaches taken by the courts in earlier years. Whether the reform did dramatically alter the law, however, is debatable. On appeal, the Full Federal Court in *Muliyana v MIAC*[159] disagreed with the ruling of Smith FM. In spite of the legislative changes, the court held that the regulatory provision should be read broadly so as to capture violence at the hands of an abusive (former) spouse, even if this occurred technically after the relationship had broken down.

[7.85] Further problems have arisen in determining the relevance (if any) of events occurring after the initial application for a visa was made. In *Jayasinghe v MIMA*,[160] Middleton J ruled that the critical point in time is the date at which the application for a spouse visa was first made. However, his Honour noted:[161]

> This does not mean that evidence subsequent to the visa application did not need to be considered at all. Evidence of events subsequent to the visa application is relevant if it 'tends logically to show the existence or non-existence of facts relevant to the issue to be determined'.[162] The Tribunal must consider all relevant evidence which may include evidence of events subsequent to the date of application insofar as it assists in the task of determining whether the applicant and the sponsor were in a marriage relationship at the time of application. The question of whether particular evidence is relevant and the weight it is to be given is clearly a matter for the Tribunal.

In that case the applicant and his sponsor had more than a few difficulties in meeting the requirement of a valid marriage. The sponsor had been married twice before and was in fact still legally married to a third man when she purported to marry the applicant. The applicant was also found to have been in a relationship with someone other than his sponsor at the time of the claimed union.

[7.86] A more problematic case is that of *Ally v MIMA*,[163] a matter involving a Tanzanian woman sponsored by an Australian citizen born in the Democratic Republic of Congo. Although the tribunal did make a finding of fact that the couple had never cohabitated as husband and wife, the assessment of their initial relationship relied heavily on ex post facto suppositions. Particular reliance was placed on

---

158 *Alin v MIMA* [2002] FCA 979 at [14]. Note that at time of writing PAM 3 still directs decision-makers that 'there is *no requirement* that there be a cause-and-effect link between the family violence and the relationship ending'. See para 20.5 of PAM3, Sch 2 – 820 visa.
159 [2010] FCAFC 24.
160 [2006] FCA 1700.
161 Ibid at [35].
162 See *MIEA v Pochi* (1980) 4 ALD 139 at 160 (Deane J).
163 See *Ally v MIAC* [2007] FMCA 430; and *Ally v MIAC* [2008] FCAFC 49.

the fact that the sponsoring husband had not told his wife that he was HIV positive. The applicant wife only became aware of this when her husband was charged with deliberately infecting two women. His actions became the basis for the applicant's claim of family violence.[164] The tribunal declined to even consider the claim. Instead, it reasoned that the man's failure to inform his wife of his illness was evidence that he was never committed to the marriage in the first place. Although this was not the only piece of evidence considered by the tribunal, it is noteworthy that neither Smith FM nor the Full Federal Court found fault with the tribunal's reasoning.

Continuing gaps in protection for migrant partners

[7.87] For people who come to Australia on a Prospective Marriage visa (subclass 300), access to the family violence provisions is more limited. The provisions are only available to holders (and former holders) of the prospective marriage visa if they have actually married their Australian fiancé(e) sponsor. Where the person has married their Australian sponsor and the spouse relationship has ended and there has been family violence committed by the Australian partner, holders and former holders of the prospective marriage visa can still proceed to apply for the temporary partner visa.[165] As with others seeking to rely on the family violence exception, they will need to show that at least some of the violence occurred during the period of the married or de facto relationship. Those who satisfy the criteria for the temporary partner visa do not have to wait the usual two-year period for grant of the permanent partner visa. In order to benefit from the family violence concessions, the applicant must have applied for a subclass 820 Partner or 309 Partner (Provisional) visa on the basis of her or his marriage or de facto relationship where nominated by their partner for the visa. The catch 22 is that, where an applicant tries to invoke the family violence exceptions, arguments might well be raised that the relationship founding the application was not genuine and ongoing at the time of *applying* as required by s 5CB or 5F. This threshold requirement cannot be avoided.

[7.88] The Australian Law Reform Commission considered these issues in the context of its Equality Before the Law Reference in as early as 1994. The Commission's recommendations included the suggestion that overseas posts keep a central database on serial sponsors; and that applicants be informed where their sponsor has brought other spouses to Australia and/or has prior convictions for offences involving family violence.[166] As noted above, applicants are now given information about any previous sponsorships. The difficulty is that whether or not the applicant is given this information in fact often depends on the sponsor providing the information in the first place. has often been solely dependent on the information that is provided by the sponsor. Having said this, the Department has made changes to its computer systems which assist migration officers to identify serial sponsors.

---

164 Note that a similar claim was accepted in the earlier case of *Reggie* [2001] MRTA 4453.
165 See *Migration Regulations*, cl 820.211(8) and (9).
166 See Australian Law Reform Commission, *Report No 69, Part I: Equality Before the Law: Justice for Women* (Canberra: ALRC, 1994) Ch 10.5-10.7.

[7.89] The Department also has programs of long standing that are designed to educate potential partner migrants. In May 1995, the Department launched a video that was developed specifically for Filipina women. Entitled *Marrying and migrating to Australia: The Filipino-Australian experience*, the video explores the cultural differences that can arise in a marriage, and what help there is available if there are problems in the marriage. The Commission for Filipinos Overseas (CFO), established by the government of the Philippines, provides counselling services for women intending to migrate to Australia as a spouse. The Department only accepts migration applications from women who have attended a CFO counselling session. As part of the counselling session, the video has become mandatory viewing for prospective Filipino migrants.

[7.90] Following the success of the first video, the Department developed a further video, intended for a more general audience. *Marrying and migrating – you have to work at it* is aimed at migrants from countries where there is a large percentage of spousal migration. Then Minister Ruddock, when launching this video, stated that 'spouse migration is the biggest single category of the immigration program to Australia and that Government is concerned that it contribute effectively to the social fabric of our community'.[167]

---

167 MPS 36/97 14 April 1997, 'Video to help spouse and fiancé applicants'.

8

Family Reunion II – Immediate and Other Family

8.1 Family and the regulation of compassion

[8.01] Changes in the regime governing spousal migration have been matched with successive restrictions on the other categories of family reunion migration. Once again, restrictions were placed first on the ability of families to sponsor members from within Australia. In place of a general discretion to deal humanely with family and other compassionate cases,[1] the *Migration Act 1958* (Cth) and Regulations were altered in 1989 so as to require applicants to fit within narrow criteria established for defined circumstances. In most cases onshore applications were only permitted where circumstances had altered after the person's arrival in Australia.[2] Since 1989, preferential, immediate or 'other' family migration has been restricted to five broad categories, each of which is discussed in this chapter. They are: child, parent, aged dependent relatives, 'remaining' relatives and a category designed to allow the sponsorship of a relative on the basis of an Australian party's need for special assistance. The latter has been described variously as the special need relative and more recently the carer visa classes.

[8.02] In addition to the standard family classes in the offshore program, provision is or has been made for a range of other relatives to gain access to permanent residence. These included 'innocent illegals', such as long-term unlawful non-citizens who spent their formative years in Australia.[3] Until December 1993, concessions were

---

1   See *Migration Act 1958* (Cth), s 6A(1)(b) and (e).
2   When the *Migration Act 1958* was amended in 1989, change of status became a two-step process, with applicants being required to obtain an 'extended eligibility temporary entry permit' (EETEP) before they could seek permanency. The family EETEP in reg 127 of the *Migration Regulations 1989* (Cth) (*1989 Regulations*) required people to show that the events on which their applications were based had occurred after their arrival in Australia. So, for example, a dependent relative had to have reached retirement age after their arrival. Orphan, remaining or special need relatives had to show that their status had occurred as a result of a death or permanent incapacitation after their arrival in Australia. In recognition of the harshness of these measures, the temporal requirement was removed in August 1990; and the reference to need based on 'death or permanent incapacitation' was replaced with a less stringent test in September 1991: see SR 285 of 1991. The family EETEP was replaced in February 1993 with a one-step process for change of status on family grounds.
3   See further Part 8.4 below.

made also for unlawful non-citizens who could show a compelling case for the grant of residence.[4]

[8.03] The categories for 'other' family reunion were given preference until 1996 in so far as no limit was placed on the number of eligible cases each year, and the Minister had no power to suspend the processing of applications. In more recent times, the Minister's ability to 'cap' or limit the number of visas issued each year has been extended. The only classes that are not subject to such controls are those relating to partners and dependent children.[5] Even here, however, the Minister has discretion to set an annual quota for the grant of Fiancé (Prospective Marriage) visas: see Chapter 7. The visas granted to parents are subject to capping and there is discretion to impose a quota on Aged Dependent Relative, Remaining Relative and Carer visa grants.[6] Constraints have also been placed on family reunions by limiting the ability of family members to apply for change of status within Australia; by restricting movement between visa classes; and by constraining sequential applications made after a visa is refused or cancelled.[7]

[8.04] The need for a general discretion to deal with the hard cases has been recognised also in the provision made for the Minister to override adverse decisions of the review bodies. The Minister has the power to substitute a more favourable decision under s 351 for the Migration Review Tribunal (MRT); s 417 for the Refugee Review Tribunal (RRT); and s 454 for the Administrative Appeals Tribunal (AAT).[8] This non-compellable, non-reviewable discretion has been used most frequently to overcome the inflexibility of the Regulations in family cases.

[8.05] The current specificity of the criteria prescribed for each of the (onshore) family visa classes is the result of successive governments' responses to the Federal Court, when it struck down departmental policies during the 1980s which sought to restrict the number of persons granted permits on compassionate grounds. The problems for the government caused by the breadth of the old s 6A(1)(e) were well illustrated by the interpretation given to the phrase 'strong humanitarian or compassionate grounds' by Hill J in *Dahlan v MILGEA* where his Honour said:[9]

> The courts have not sought to create an all-embracing test of what constitutes strong compassionate or humanitarian grounds; nor would such an exercise be either possible or desirable. The words are very broad. Compassion is an emotion akin to pity; it is felt when the circumstances of others excite our sympathy so that we suffer with them. Hence compassionate grounds will exist when the circumstances of an applicant are such as to enliven in the reasonable man his compassion. By humanitarian grounds are meant no doubt grounds the denial of which would be inhumane having regard to the ordinary views of mankind.

---

4   See former subclass 812.
5   See *Migration Act*, s 87(1) and (2).
6   Ibid, ss 39 and 84-91.
7   Ibid, s 48 of the Act, read with *Migration Regulations 1994* (Cth), reg 2.12.
8   See further Chapter 14.4 and Chapter 19.4 below.
9   See *Dahlan v MILGEA* [1989] FCA 507 at [24].

[8.06] In line with this reasoning, the Federal Court consistently rejected government attempts to distinguish between 'compassionate' and 'humanitarian' grounds for the grant of residence. It held that the two concepts overlapped to such an extent that any distinction would be meaningless and therefore legally invalid.[10] Dr Evan Arthur, then director of the Department's Asylum Policy Branch, wrote frankly of what the government perceived as the impact of the courts' rulings:[11]

> [The] Department had virtually only one criterion left to it. This was the requirement that to establish the existence of compassionate or humanitarian grounds, applicants had to show that if they were forced to leave Australia, they would face a situation that would evoke strong feelings of pity or compassion in an ordinary member of the Australian public.

Whether the current regime strikes a fair balance between compassion and control is a matter that continues to be debated.

8.2 Sponsoring children

8.2.1 Definition of child: The family unit and notions of dependency

[8.07] Although Australia has a long history of (independent) child migration,[12] most child migrants today arrive in the company of family members. The law is generous in so far as such children can include natural children and adopted children as well as step-children and, in the orphan relative visa category, grandchildren, nieces, nephews and step-grandchildren, step-nieces and step-nephews. As explored in greater detail elsewhere,[13] Australian immigration law and policy exhibit a disturbing tendency to treat children as appendages to, or, worse, as the possessions of, adults. In some areas, Australian migration law and policy either fail adequately to acknowledge children as rights bearers or fail to 'see' the children at all.[14] This is reflected to some extent in the way children are defined: children are included in visa applications as members of a family unit if they are 'dependent' on the (adult) primary applicant for a visa (and they are located in the same country as the applicant).[15] Dependency is presumed if a child is under the age of 18 and not married or engaged to be married.[16]

---

10   See *Damouni v MILGEA* (1989) 87 ALR 97; and *Sacharowitz v MILGEA* (1992) 33 FCR 480.
11   See Evan Arthur, 'The Impact of Administrative Law on Humanitarian Decision-Making' (1989) 66 *Canberra Bulletin of Public Administration* 90 at 95.
12   For an account of child migration to Australia, see Senate Community Affairs References Committee, *Lost Innocents: Righting the Record – Report on Child Migration*, 30 August 2001; and Mary Crock, *Seeking Asylum Alone: Unaccompanied and Separated Children and Refugee Protection in Australia* (Sydney: Themis Press, 2006) Ch 2, at 34-7.
13   See Mary Crock, Mary-Anne Kenny and Fiona Allison, 'Children and Immigration and Citizenship Law' in G Monaghan and L Young (eds), *Children and the Law in Australia* (Sydney: LexisNexis, 2008), 238-255.
14   Two areas that pose particular problems in this regard are refugee status determinations and removal decisions made on grounds of bad character. See Ibid and Mary Crock, 'Re-thinking the Paradigms of Protection: Children as Convention Refugees in Australia' in Jane McAdam (ed), *Moving On: Forced Migration and Human Rights* (Oxford: Hart Publishing, 2008), 155-180.
15   See definition of 'member of the family unit' in the Regulations, reg 1.12; definition of 'relative' in reg 1.03; definition of 'close relative' in reg 1.03.
16   See reg 1.03 'dependent child' and reg 1.05A. See also Department of Immigration and Citizenship, *Policy and Procedures Manual 3: Migration Regulations, Div 1.2 – Interpretation, Reg 1.03 – Dependent child*, [2.2].

[8.08] The definition of dependent child has been amended over the years to increase the range of children in a family who are eligible for migration. The provision in reg 1.03 as in force between 1991 and 1999 allowed for the sponsorship of children under the age of 18 who were 'wholly or substantially in the daily care and control' of the sponsor, as well as children over 18[17] who were 'dependent' on the sponsor or who were unable to work because of a disability. Although an improvement on even earlier definitions,[18] parents still faced problems sponsoring children left in the care of relatives overseas while they established themselves as migrants in Australia.[19]

[8.09] Since 1 November 1999 the phrase 'dependent child' has been defined in regs 1.03 and 1.05A as single, not engaged to be married, and either under 18; *or* over 18 but financially dependent on their parent; *or* physically/mentally incapacitated for work. The significance of this change is two-fold. First, for children who are under 18, there is no requirement to demonstrate specific details of dependency or control. Secondly, for children aged over 18, the child must be both financially dependent and in full-time education.[20] For children sought to be included in an application for refugee or humanitarian visas, the definition of dependence is a little more expansive, including where the child is dependent on the other person for financial, psychological *or* physical support.[21]

[8.10] The relaxation of the criteria seems to have been made in recognition of the fact that adult children can continue to depend heavily on their parents while they undertake tertiary study or vocational training. Although the review authorities have taken a generous view of the Regulations throughout,[22] some controversy has arisen over the latitude given for adult children who chose to remain dependent on their parents by enrolling in a course of study.[23] The underlying concern seems to have been that adult children were falsely gaining admission as dependents so as to circumvent the stringent requirements for skilled migration that would other-

---

17 See, for example, *Re Qalo* [1991] IRTA 596; *Re Ali* [1992] IRTA 690; *Re Mardnali* [1993] IRTA 2186; and *Re Tran Viet Cuong* [1995] IRTA 4968.

18 The original definition in 1989 allowed only for the sponsorship of children under 18 who were wholly or substantially in the daily care and control of the sponsor: see *1989 Regulations*, reg 2(1), amended on 17 September 1991 by SR 285 of 1991.

19 In *Jankovic v MIEA* (1995) 56 FCR 474 the Full Federal Court held that, although not decisive, legal custody is an important element when determining if a child is wholly and substantially in the daily care and control of a particular person.

20 Note that no upper age limit is set upon whether a child can be considered to be 'dependent'. Adult children who have a mental or physical disability such that they cannot work may also be considered a 'dependent child': reg 1.03. However, as is noted in DIAC Policy, such adult children are unlikely to pass the health criteria and as such the entire family unit eligibility will be affected ('one fails all fail'): *PAM3 Migration Regulations, Div 1.2 – Interpretation, Reg 1.03 – Dependent Child*, [10.20].

21 *Migration Regulations*, reg 1.05A. In respect of psychological dependence, DIAC policy states that this must be something more than the 'normal emotional ties' of family – rather, 'a mental or emotional impairment or a medical condition preventing the person from living independently' *PAM3, Migration Regulations, Div 1.2 – Interpretation, Reg 1.05a – Dependent*, [13].

22 The tribunal has stressed the need to be sensitive to how different cultures approach the task of child-rearing: see eg *Re Tran, Van Hiep* [2001] MRTA 932 and *MIAC v Ryerson (No 2)* [2008] FMCA 1400.

23 See, for example, *Qiao v MIAC* [2008] FMCA 380; *MIMA v Pires* (1998) 160 ALR 97; *Xie v MIMA* (2000) 61 ALD 641.

wise apply. In other words, it was thought that adult children should only be regarded as dependants if their reliance on their parents was not the result of choices made by themselves or their parents, rather than some subjective need to remain reliant. In *Huynh v MIMIA*[24] the Full Federal Court ruled that as a matter of statutory construction there was nothing in the legislation to suggest the disqualification of children who chose to remain dependent on their parents. The court held at [33]:

> There is no apparent reason why an implication of the existence of a need, as opposed to an objective state of affairs, that the child be reliant on the parent should be made when the legislation remains silent on the point … If, as a matter of choice, families or parents choose to deploy their resources in providing for their children so that the children remain dependent or reliant on them, even though they are fit to go to work, there does not seem to be any reason in policy discernible in the Act or Regulations why they cannot choose to do so.

[8.11] The court pointed out that the acts of seeking work or pursuing studies inevitably involve choices such that the super-imposition of a requirement of the absence of choice in many cases becomes meaningless.[25] While noting earlier jurisprudence to the contrary, the court held that the current legislation does not require consideration of anything other than the objective facts of dependency: the choices made by the various parties are not relevant.

8.2.2 The child visas

[8.12] Three categories of minor children are given preference[26] as sponsored migrants under the present system: dependent children, adopted children and orphaned relatives. In each instance the characteristics of those eligible for a visa are defined closely, although the review authorities appear to have worked hard to give a generous interpretation of the Regulations wherever possible. For its part, the government has been attentive to developments in the jurisprudence. It has amended the Regulations where provisions have been disproportionately harsh in their operation or in some other respect have run counter to the Minister's intentions.

[8.13] For example, the Regulations defining 'adopted' children were broadened on 31 August 1990 so as to permit the inclusion of children adopted in a customary manner, where the local laws do not provide for formal adoption.[27] Changes to the definitions of dependency discussed earlier are further examples in point.

---

24 (2006) 152 FCR 576.
25 On this point, see the comments of Weinberg J in *Xie v MIMA* (2000) 61 ALD 641 at [42] who said: 'The distinction between a person who is still working towards a first major qualification and a person who considers it necessary or desirable to pursue a further course of studies is, of course, one grounded in policy, and not in logic. There is nothing in the language of reg 1.03 which provides any direct warrant for such a distinction'. See also *Thompson v MIAC* [2009] FMCA 1043; *SZMNF v MIAC* [2008] FMCA 983 at [9].
26 Note that in addition to being one of the few migration categories that is not subject to any form of quota or capping, children are given priority in processing.
27 Compare the original reg 2(1) with reg 2A of the *1989 Regulations*, now *Migration Regulations 1994*, reg 1.04. Tribunal rulings on the recognition of customary adoption include *0804599* [2009] MRTA 993; *V05/05518* [2007] MRTA 499; *Naresh, Ram* [2004] MRTA 1409.

[8.14] In the case of children sponsored from overseas, the courts have taken a broad view of the circumstances that might lead to a child being or becoming dependent. For example, in *Ibrahim v MIMIA*[28] the Federal Magistrates Court held that consideration had to be given to the circumstances of adult children, and not to their age, education and putative ability to support themselves and to lead an independent life. In that case the adult child in question was a young woman who had been living independently, but who had been raped and virtually taken hostage by a Sheik in Lebanon who wanted the young woman as his wife. The court ruled that the MRT committed a jurisdictional error in failing to acknowledge that the young woman in these circumstances was indeed financially dependent on her parents as required for the grant of a Dependent Child visa. The court reasoned that the woman's circumstances prevented her from providing for herself as she would otherwise have done.

[8.15] In *Guo Bin v MIMA*[29] von Doussa J added that a child may be dependent on either their mother or their father – that is, it is not necessary to show that a sponsored child is dependent on both parents. In *MIMA v Pires*,[30] Mansfield J held that the expression 'wholly or substantially dependent' in an earlier iteration of the definition of dependent child was 'intended to convey that the visa applicant has a need to rely upon another person for financial support, rather than simply describing the fact that another person is providing that financial support'. This case was not followed in the later decision of *Huyhn v MIMIA*[31] in which the Federal Court rejected an argument by the Minister that children who choose to remain dependent on their parents should not be eligible for a visa. In this context it is noteworthy that the courts have held that it is possible for children to resume dependency after a period of being independent and that, '[d]epending on context, a family unit can include parents and children, whether living together or not'.[32]

Subclasses 101 and 802 Child visas

[8.16] A 'dependent child' located overseas or in Australia may be sponsored by their Australian citizen/permanent resident parent or step-parent. The central criteria that must be met are that the child must be aged less than 25, unless incapacitated for work and, if over the age of 18, must be unmarried, not in full-time work and engaged in full-time studies of some kind. Most controversy in relation to this type of visa surrounds the question of adopted children. Such children are only eligible for a child visa if adopted overseas before turning 18 years of age by parents who were either not Australian citizens or permanent residents at the time or who meet certain other requirements. The general rules are that the adopting parents must have lived in the country of adoption for at least one year before applying for the visa for their child and the adoption must be lawful under the law of the country of adoption.[33] If

---

28   [2005] FMCA 1239.
29   (1999) 58 ALD 153.
30   (1998) 90 FCR 214 at 220.
31   (2006) 152 FCR 576.
32   See *Carlos v MIMA* [2001] FCA 301.
33   See *Migration Regulations*, reg 1.04.

a child is overseas, and has been adopted by parents who were located in Australia at time of adoption, application must be made for an Adoption visa (102) (see below). If onshore, children adopted overseas *may* be eligible for the Child visa (802). However, they must have been adopted before turning 18, and fulfil the same requirements as adopted children applying from abroad.[34]

Subclass 445 Dependent Child visa

[8.17] While dependent children can be included in a visa application as secondary applicants, there will be occasions where this is not possible – for example, when the dependent child is abroad and the primary immigration application is made by a parent in Australia. In these cases a separate application must be made to bring the child to Australia. Persons holding a Partner (Provisional) visa (subclass 309), a Partner visa (subclass 820) or Dependent Child visa (subclass 445), may bring their dependent children to Australia from overseas, with the original sponsor of the child's parent acting as sponsor. Once in Australia, the child can be included in their parent's application for the permanent partner visa.

Subclass 102 Adoption visa

[8.18] Adopted children are subject to quite different rules, depending on the physical location of the parents at time of adoption. Children who are adopted overseas, while the parent or parents were resident overseas, may be treated in the same way as natural children.

[8.19] The adoption visa applies to children under the age of 18 years living *outside* Australia, who have been or will be adopted by an Australian citizen or resident who is living in Australia. Adoption must be done either with the involvement of Australian authorities, under the Adoption Convention,[35] or under a bilateral agreement with the People's Republic of China or another adoption agreement. The visa is available also to children being adopted by expatriate Australians who have resided overseas in the country of adoption for at least 12 months.

[8.20] The adoption of foreign children inevitably raises issues about the welfare of children and of their 'commodification' by adults. The Adoption Convention provides for various safeguards to ensure that intercountry adoptions are in the best interests of the children and that the child's fundamental human rights are respected.[36] This Convention calls upon states parties to ensure that adequate safeguards are adopted to prevent child abduction, and the sale or trafficking of children.[37] The Convention on the Rights of the Child states that in relation to adoption, the best

---

34 See *Migration Regulations*, Sch 2, cl 802.213.
35 *Convention on Protection of Children and Cooperation in Respect of Intercountry Adoption*, signed at The Hague on 29 May 1993. Australia ratified the Convention in 1998.
36 The Adoption Convention, Art 1(a), para 4 of the Adoption Convention's Preamble, and Art 21 of the *Convention on the Rights of the Child* (CRC) (adopted 20 November 1989, entered into force 2 September 1990) 1577 UNTS 3; ratified by Australia 17 December 1990.
37 Adoption Convention, Art 1(b). Article 4 states that a child must be 'adoptable', that due consideration ought to be given to whether the adoption is in the child's best interests, that relevant consent has been obtained, and that, depending on the age and maturity of a child, the child has been

interests of a child are to be paramount, given the potential difficulties associated with the process.[38]

Subclass 117 and 837 Orphan Relative visas

[8.21] 'Orphan relatives' are unmarried minors who are a 'relative' of an Australian sponsor and whose parents or guardians are unable to care for them because they have either died, disappeared or are permanently incapacitated.[39] Settlement in Australia must be in the child's best interests. Their sponsoring relative must be over 18, a citizen/resident, living in Australia and must have been lawfully resident in Australia for a reasonable period (usually two years).[40]

[8.22] Since the requirement that the applicant's parents have died, disappeared or are permanently incapacitated is a question of fact, the applicant's credibility becomes relevant and the decision-maker must consider relevant evidence that may corroborate the applicant's claims.[41] Further, the permanent incapacitation of a parent may be self-induced, as the Federal Court noted in the case of *Nguyen v MIMA*.[42] Here, the father of the child in question had disappeared and the mother had re-married. When the child visited his mother, he was made to feel unwelcome by the mother and step-father. Evidence was also given that entrusting the upbringing of the child to the paternal grandparents following the death of the father accorded with Vietnamese custom. Merkel J held that 'a refusal to care, abandonment of care or an unwillingness to care, do not necessarily amount to 'permanent incapacity'. However, in finding in favour of the sponsoring parties, Merkel J held that in the case of orphaned children the definition of 'permanently incapacitated' is not limited to physical or mental impairment, but may be influenced by a range of social and cultural circumstances. 'The issue involves consideration of *why* a parent cannot care for his or her child'.[43] Nevertheless, it is open to a decision-maker to find that the child *can* be cared for by the parent if the situation was of the parent's choosing, for example, voluntarily relinquishing custody to the Australian relative, and the situation has arisen primarily for reasons other than inability to care for the child (for example, to better the child's future).[44] In this respect the law operates with the interests of the child in mind in so far as it excludes children who are abandoned opportunistically by parents who reason that the child in question may thereby become eligible for migration. At the same time, since incapacitation relates to

---

counselled with respect to the adoption, and consideration has been given to the child's wishes and opinions.
38 CRC, Art 21.
39 *Migration Regulations*, reg 1.14. 'Relative' is defined in reg 1.03 as either a 'close relative' (partner, child, adopted child, parent, brother, sister or step-child, step-parent, step-brother/sister) or a grandparent, grandchild, aunt, uncle, niece, nephew, (or step-grandparent, step-grandchild, step-aunt/uncle, step-niece/nephew).
40 If sponsored by a relative who is under 21 years of age, the Minister is guardian of the orphan relative until the child reaches 18 years.
41 *Haidari v MIAC* [2009] FMCA 1178; *Dowlat v MIAC* [2009] FMCA 171.
42 (1998) 88 FCR 206.
43 Ibid at 212.
44 PAM3 Div 1.2, para 6.4.

impairment of a parent's ability to care for his or her child, the applicant's age can become relevant to whether the parent was capable of such care. Thus, an applicant who was almost 18 years old was considered by the tribunal (and by the Federal Magistrate) to be reasonably self-reliant and not requiring intensive attention from an ailing mother.[45]

[8.23] Applicants may be eligible even though, strictly speaking, they are no longer 'orphaned' because they have been adopted subsequently by an Australian relative. Such persons still need to be assessed to see if they *would have been* orphan relatives, but for the adoption.[46] In *EC v MIMA*,[47] an Australian citizen couple had formally adopted a child (with whom they had no other former connection) in Vanuatu. The child was not eligible for a Child 101 visa as the parents were Australian citizens at the time of the adoption. The child was ineligible for an Adoption 102 visa because the parents had not complied with the 12-month residence requirement, the adoption had not been approved by relevant authorities in Australia, and it was not an Adoption Convention adoption. The child was also ineligible for an Orphan Relative subclass 117 visa because there was no relationship between the parents and child other than through adoption. The Federal Court noted that subclass 117.211(b) extends eligibility to an applicant who is not an orphan relative only because the applicant has been adopted by the Australian relative. However, it held that this criterion was not intended to include as an orphan relative a child whose very adoption allows her to satisfy the definition of relative. Rather it was intended to deal with a situation where an adoption prevents a person satisfying the definition of 'orphan relative'. Kenny J concluded:

> If it were possible for a person to become a 'relative' or 'Australian relative' merely by obtaining an adoption order in a foreign jurisdiction … the visa provisions which are designed to assist in the regulation of inter-country adoptions could be readily circumvented.

[8.24] Australia's stringent requirements in relation to inter-country adoptions reflect the Commonwealth's recognition of the need 'to protect the interests of children who may be affected by such adoptions', 'to ensure that the adoption is in the best interests of the child'.[48]

[8.25] Officers are directed to consider the best interests of the child, other than simply in relation to custody.[49] They must be satisfied that there is no 'compelling reason' to believe that it is not in the 'best interests' of the child to be granted the visa: reg 1.14(c). Policy dictates that 'compelling reason' is intended to include 'strong, obvious information that leads officers to believe that granting the visa would clearly not be of benefit to the child to settle in Australia with the Australian relative'. The officer should ask whether the child is capable of understanding and in

---

45 *Singh v MIAC* [2008] FMCA 587 at [44]-[48].
46 *Migration Regulations*, Sch 2, cl 117.211(b).
47 (2004) 138 FCR 438.
48 Ibid at 448.
49 See *Migration Regulations*, Sch 4, cll 4015-4018, discussed below at Part 8.2.3.

fact understands the consequences of the application. Officers should also consider whether, in their opinion, the proposed arrangements for the child's accommodation, maintenance and care in Australia are appropriate.[50]

[8.26] Cases like *Nguet Huong Phung v MIEA*[51] illustrate some of the difficulties surrounding the child visas. In that case a couple attempted to bring their nephew to Australia under an Adoption 102 visa. They had looked after the child from the age of one month, supporting him in Vietnam financially when they moved to Australia. They adopted the child in Vietnam without the approval of the relevant authority. The child was not eligible for a subclass 102 visa because the parents had not resided overseas within the 12-month period immediately preceding the application. It was irrelevant that the parents had resided in Vietnam 'at some earlier time'. Further, the child was not eligible for a Child 101 visa as the adoption had taken place after the parents became Australian citizens. However, the Federal Court held that the child *was* eligible for an Orphan Relative visa because his natural parents were unable to care for him. The fact that the child had been 'adopted' at the time of the application by the aunt and uncle became superfluous. The court ruled that the word 'orphan' should be defined 'by reference to the circumstances of the natural parents of the child'.[52]

8.2.3 Custody criteria

[8.27] What are known as the 'custody criteria'[53] in the Regulations are examples of legislative acknowledgement that children have rights that need to be respected. Custody issues arise where one parent seeks to travel with a child without the other parent. Before 1 July 2000, the grant of visas was subject to the Minister's satisfaction that 'the grant of the visa would not prejudice the right and interests of any person who has custody or guardianship of, or access to' the child.[54] The provision was criticised because of the potential that a child could be refused entry to Australia even though a court in a foreign country had authorised the removal of the child from the jurisdiction to travel to Australia.[55] The Australian Law Reform Commission was also critical of the underlying language and presumptions which were inconsistent with provisions of the *Family Law Act 1975* (Cth) 'that give parents responsibilities for children rather than rights in them'.[56]

---

50 PAM3, Div 1.2, para 11.
51 [1997] FCA 373.
52 See now *Migration Regulations*, Sch 2, cl 117.211(b), introduced in 2002.
53 See *Migration Regulations*, Sch 4, cll 4015-4018. These provisions were inserted into the Regulations by *Migration Amendment Regulations (No 2) 2000* (Cth).
54 These criteria were included in issues to be considered at the time of determination of the visa, set out in Sch 2 to the Regulations.
55 See Kathryn Cronin, 'A Primary Consideration: Children's Rights in Australian Immigration Law' (1996) 2(2) *Australian Journal of Human Rights* 195 at 198-9; and Australian Law Reform Commission (ALRC), *Seen and Heard: Priority for Children in the Legal Process*, Report 84 (1997) at [9.77]–[9.79].
56 ALRC ibid at [9.79].

[8.28] Since 1 July 2000 in respect of almost all permanent and temporary visas[57] issued to minor children[58] the Department of Immigration must be satisfied that:[59]

(a) the law of the child's home country permits the removal of the child; or
(b) each person who can lawfully determine where the child is to live consents to the grant of the visa;[60] or
(c) the grant of the visa would be consistent with any Australian child order[61] in force in relation to the child.

[8.29] In relation to the first of these matters, it is now sufficient that one parent have a court order allowing them to bring the child to Australia – the other parent's lack of consent is irrelevant. It is assumed that such an order would have considered the best interests of the child.[62] In relation to the second matter, if the adult supporting the application has sole responsibility for the child in question, this criterion is satisfied. In other cases a decision-maker may have to seek a statutory declaration or otherwise be satisfied that there is consent.[63]

[8.30] Even if there are no unresolved custody issues in relation to a child, the Department must also be satisfied that there are no compelling reasons to believe that granting the visa would not be in the child's best interests.[64] Failure to satisfy this threshold, having satisfied the other custody criteria, would only occur exceptionally: for instance, where there is strong evidence of abuse or the overseas law simply vests custody with one parent, usually the father (with no consideration of 'best interests'). Officers are directed not to solicit evidence to establish best interests. It will only need

---

57 There are some visas where this is not a requirement, including temporary Protection visas and Protection visas: see PAM3, Sch 4, at [9].
58 Public interest criteria in cll 4015-4018 of Sch 4 to the Regulations refer to persons 'under the age of 18' and thus apply to *all* children included in the visa application, not just the dependent child of the main applicant. It follows that the same custody issues arise in relation to any relative under the age of 18 (for example, a niece or nephew) if they are included in the application and meet the definition of member of a family unit.
59 *Migration Regulations*, Sch 4, cll 4015 and 4017. See, for example, *Rana-Vajracharya, Supriya* [2003] MRTA 6884. There is no provision to 'waive' the custody requirement, even in circumstances that appear to be compelling. These criteria relate to Australia's obligations under the Hague Convention on the Civil Aspects of International Child Abduction. The objectives are to secure the prompt return of children wrongfully removed to, or retained in, any signatory state and to ensure that the rights of 'custody' and 'access' under the law of the signatory state are effectively respected in other such states. Decision-makers must take into account the effect of a visa grant in relation to these objectives, and ensure that it would not conflict with parental responsibilities and rights that a person may have for the child. The provisions also reflect Art 9 of the CRC concerning avoiding separation of children from parents, unless it is in their 'best interests'. The provisions leave the decision-making in relation to 'best interests' to the parents, or legal authorities, where there might be some continuing dispute in relation to the child's interests. See PAM3, Sch 4.4015-4018, at [3.1].
60 See, for example, *Beattie-Bjurhammar, Ulla Helene* [2002] MRTA 5189.
61 An 'Australian child order' is defined in reg 1.03 of the Regulations as a residence order, a contact order or care order or a State child order within the meaning of s 70B of the *Family Law Act 1975* (Cth).
62 PAM3 Sch 4.4015-4018, at [3.2]. The law in a particular country might state that, if a child is born out of wedlock, the father has no right to make decisions regarding the child's future. Further, if the home country of the child permits, in law, a child (of a certain age) to decide where they ought to live, then this criterion is met on the relevant child's application.
63 PAM3 Sch 4.4015-4018, at [17].
64 *Migration Regulations*, Sch 4, cll 4016 and 4018.

to be assessed if the application itself contains clear evidence, in the form of 'strong, obvious information'.[65]

[8.31] Officers are not directed, in practice, to engage in any real assessment of a child's 'best interests'. This assessment is made by parents and/or evidenced by court determinations or legal principle more generally. This would appear to be appropriate, in the circumstances, but it is evident how little opportunity there is for a child to be heard in this process. The best that can be said is that these provisions are an improvement on the earlier version of the 'custody criteria'.

8.3 The Parent visas

[8.32] The intake of parents is extremely restrictive compared to skilled or partner visas. In the 2009-10 Migration Program, only 2000 places were made available for the parent category.[66] While this represents a four-fold increase on places that had been made available to parents under the latter years of the Coalition government of 1996-2007,[67] it is clear that government priority in the family stream remains to provide for family reunion of migrants entering as the partner or child of Australians. As a result of the cap on parents visas, the backlog of parent visa applications remains large, sitting above 13,000 for the standard parent visas, with the practical result that applicants are forced to wait in a virtual queue for up to 10 years.[68]

[8.33] The frustration of migrants in Australia wishing to sponsor their parents to join them has been felt in the older, more established migrant communities as much as in the communities of newer arrivals. In the early years of the Coalition government, attempts were made to impose special levies on parents to amortise the cost to the Australian community of health care and other benefits. These failed when the Opposition and minor parties combined to disallow relevant amending Regulations that would have resulted in parents paying premiums of over $60,000 per couple. In 2003, the deadlock was broken after extensive consultations and lobbying from the migrant communities.

[8.34] The result was the introduction of a new parent visa category, the key features of which were the imposition of a one-off health charge of $25,000 per adult for a permanent visa; an extended assurance of support period of 10 years instead of the typical two years; and an increased assurance of support bond of $10,000 for the

---

65 See PAM3, 4.4015-4018, at [20]. Note that, where there is a court order granting a parent relevant rights in relation to residence, the other parent's permission is not required, but in rare cases officers may decline the visa grant based on the 'best interests' criterion in such cases: PAM3, Sch 4.4015-4018, at [12.2].
66 See DIMIA, *Australian Immigration Fact Sheet 21: Managing the Migration Program'*.
67 Settler arrivals of parents have steadily increased with the change in federal government, both in numerical terms and as a percentage of the entire migration program: from 3657 (2.6%) in 2006-07 to 6477 (4.1%) in 2008-09: DIAC, *Immigration Update 2008-09* (Cth of Australia, 2009) at 18.
68 The need to let people follow their progress in the queue is reflected in the establishment of an on-line 'parent visa queue calculator'. This can be accessed at <https://www.ecom.immi.gov.au/qcalc/QDateAnswer.do>. The 'queue date' is the date at which an application is assessed as meeting initial criteria for a parent visa. In December 2009 the queue for a subclass 103 Parent visa was 15,380 applications. By contrast, the queue for the Contributory Parent visa subclass 143 was just over 200.

main applicant and $4000 for other adult dependants: see subclass 143 (Contributory Parent), and subclass 864 (Contributory Aged Parent). The sweetener in the compromise was the introduction of a temporary visa originally attracting a payment of $15,000 per adult applicant (now over $20,000), allowing the applicant to seek permanent residence two years later upon payment of the remaining $10,000 health charge (now over $13,000), plus the assurance of support bond. The grant of a subclass 173 (Contributory Parent (Temporary)) visa or a subclass 884 (Contributory Aged Parent (Temporary)) visa allows the relevant parents to work and access Medicare. The package permitted applicants to transfer to the new scheme without incurring further application costs. In addition, pre-existing parent visa classes remain intact to cater for migrants who cannot afford the new scheme, and the number of places allocated to parents was increased. While some might contest the justice of creating two parent streams using wealth as a discrimen, the relief within the community brought by this compromise package was marked, with an immediate increase in the number of visas available at the beginning of 2003. The change of government in 2007 did not herald a dramatic change in approach in this area – in spite of the fact that the Labor Party opposed initial moves to create the contributory parent visa scheme.

[8.35] A further constraint on eligibility is that applicant parents must pass a 'balance of family test' which requires that parent visa applicants have at least half of their children living in Australia, or more of their children live in Australia than in any other single country.[69] This is a simple numerical test that does not allow consideration of particular ties between the parent and sponsoring child. In calculating the make-up of a family for the purposes of the balance of family test, reg 1.05 includes children born of previous marriages of either parent, as long as custody of the children has not been taken away from the parent being sponsored. Children who have been removed by court order, adoption or operation of law are not included for the purposes of the test.[70] Neither are children who live in a refugee camp or in a country where the child suffers persecution or abuse of human rights and it is not possible to reunite the child and the parent in another country. In cases where the whereabouts of children are unknown, the Regulations deem the children to be resident in the parent's usual country of residence.[71] However, this has not precluded the tribunals in some cases from presuming the death of children with whom the parent has lost all contact over a long period of time.[72] Having said this, it has been difficult to fault tribunal members who have refused to apply the common law presumption of death.[73] The equation is complicated further by the fact that the children in Australia are counted only if they are 'lawfully and permanently resident' here.[74]

[8.36] The range of visas open to minor children wishing to sponsor a parent or other responsible relative is much more limited than is the case for sponsoring

---

69 Note that this does not apply to applicants for a permanent contributory class of parent visa who hold a temporary contributory visa at the time of application. See Sch 2, cl 143.213 of the Regulations.
70 See *Usman v MIMA* [2005] FMCA 966.
71 See reg 1.05(1)(b). Compare *Usman v MIMA* [2005] FMCA 966.
72 See *Re Armani* [1992] IRTA 999.
73 See *Kim v MIAC* [2007] FMCA 798.
74 *De Souza v MIMIA* [2003] FCA 1636.

adults, and the criteria for the grant of visas are far more circumscribed. An infant child, applying through a next friend, cannot sponsor a working age parent while the parent remains in Australia: the visa is only available 'offshore'. In fact, the only parent visa available to onshore applicants is the Aged Parent visa (subclass 804), where a parent must be at least 65 years of age for male parents and at least 60-65 years of age for female parents.[75] Whilst other parents may apply for the (offshore) Parent visa subclass 103 from within Australia, they must be offshore for the grant of the visa. They will not be eligible for a bridging visa to remain in Australia during processing. The same procedure occurs in relation to onshore lodging of applications for Contributory Parent visas. This creates obvious difficulties for children who are under 18, who are sponsoring their parents to migrate here.

[8.37] The children must also meet sponsorship requirements, which means that the child must either be aged 18 or over, or arrange alternative sponsorship (through a community organisation, or other relative or guardian)[76] and arrange for an assurance of support (the sponsor need not be the assurer). Again, the assurer needs to be over 18 years of age, and is disqualified if he or she has been in receipt of social security benefits within the 12 months preceding the application. A significant security bond is also required. These requirements create obvious hurdles for minor child sponsors.

[8.38] Attempts have been made to use other visa classes in order to facilitate the residence of a parent for an Australian citizen child. The typical situation is where a child is born to parents, only one of whom is a resident or citizen, and the child needs to sponsor the non-resident parent to remain in Australia. This may occur where the relationship between the child's parents breaks down, or is not capable in itself of resulting in a partner visa, for example because the Australian party is married to a third person and is ineligible to sponsor the non-citizen co-parent of the child. As we explore in Part 8.7, infant children once sponsored their working age parents to migrate to Australia using what was known as the Special Need Relative visa. The Carer (subclasses 116/836) visa category, which replaced the Special Need Relative visa in 1998, now precludes children under 18 from sponsoring a relative to care for them.[77]

[8.39] Mention should be made here of the Minister's discretionary powers which are often the final resort in these cases. Where the child's parent has applied for some sort of visa and gone through the merits review process, the Minister has, on occasion, granted a 'substituted 676 visa' and allowed the parent to apply for the Aged Parent visa in Australia without being 'aged' and without having to satisfy the balance of family test. The parent must be sponsored by their minor child (using substituted sponsorship).

---

75   Regulation 1.03 defines an 'aged parent' as a parent who is old enough to be granted an age pension under the *Social Security Act 1991* (Cth). For women, the age for such pension is gradually being raised to 65, from 30 June 2005 to 1 January 2014.
76   See, for example, *Migration Regulations*, Sch 2, cl 103.211. The sponsorship requirements were amended on 27 March 2010 to enable 'relatives', rather than 'close relatives', to act as sponsors.
77   See *Migration Regulations*, Sch 2, cll 116.212 and 836.213.

8.4 'Innocent illegals' and vulnerable children

[8.40] Until 2005, a visa category existed that allowed a non-citizen to obtain permanent residence after turning 18, if they had become unlawful as a child and had spent their 'formative years' in Australia. The Close Ties (subclass 832) visa,[78] known as the 'innocent illegal' visa, made important concessions for young people who had became unlawful through no fault of their own as children, and who had formed close ties with Australia. The visa recognised that Australia was now regarded as home for these young people and it would be inappropriate to uproot them to be returned to countries of origin with which they no longer had a substantial connection. In such cases, the Close Ties visa enabled a workable and just solution to address significant humanitarian considerations.

[8.41] There was a series of amendments to the visa category which continually narrowed access to this visa. Allegations that the visa was being abused by young people who had entered Australia on student visas led to attempted amendments in 2002 (which were disallowed).[79] The visa criteria were amended in the following year to render ineligible children who arrived on student visas.[80] The visa was abolished altogether in November 2005.[81] These changes adversely affect the most vulnerable children, including those who arrived as unaccompanied minors, asylum seekers and those who may have been brought here against their will. Although attempts have been made to seek citizenship for some of these children,[82] the government has met these cases with amendments to the *Australian Citizenship Act 2007* (Cth).[83]

[8.42] The Close Ties visa was the closest equivalent to the special visas that have been created in the United States to grant residence to young non-citizens who are deemed to be at risk by virtue of their inability to access family support of any kind. In that country, Special Immigrant Juvenile Status is granted to foreign-born children who are determined to be abused, abandoned or neglected and in need of long-term foster care. The eligibility requirements include a finding by a juvenile court (not an immigration court) 'that it would not be in the alien's best interest to be returned to

---

78 Family (Residence) (Class AO). Section 48 of the *Migration Act 1958* and reg 2.12 of the Regulations prescribed various visa subclasses available to applicants who had a visa cancelled or a visa application refused since arriving in Australia. One of the visas that could be obtained was a Special Eligibility (Residence) (Class AO). The subclass also applied to former permanent residents and some people who entered Australia before 1975.
79 See *Migration Amendment Regulations 2002 (No 10)* (Cth).
80 *Migration Amendment Regulations 2003 (No 3)* (Cth).
81 *Migration Amendment Regulations 2005 (No 9)* (Cth). The media reported that the Department and Minister felt the subclass was subject to 'abuse' by young people purportedly leaving their family temporarily in order to qualify for the visa only to return to live with them once they received a permanent visa: see ABC Television, 'Rule Changes Leaves Some Facing Deportation', *The 7.30 Report*, 29 June 2005, available at <http://www.abc.net.au/7.30/content/2005/s1403524.htm>; ABC Radio, 'Close Ties Visa to be abolished', *The World Today*, 29 June 2005, available at <http://www.abc.net.au/worldtoday/content/2005/s1394601.htm>. According to the statistics provided in the DIAC's Annual Reports the number of close ties visas granted were: 172 (2005-06); 200 (2004-05); 400 (2003-04) and 562 visas (2002-03). These figures indicate that only a small number of visas were granted under this category every year and the numbers halved after the introduction of the amendments.
82 See, for example, *Mashood v Commonwealth* (2003) 133 FCR 50.
83 See the discussion in Chapter 2.5.2 above, in particular [2.72]ff.

the country of nationality or last habitual residence of the beneficiary or his or her parent or parents ...'.[84] Following the international consensus that was reached in 2007 to address the plight of vulnerable refugee children,[85] the newly elected Labor government moved swiftly to bridge this gap in Australia's laws and policies. The subclass 802 visa was amended on 26 April 2008 to include vulnerable non-citizen children who have a letter of support from a child welfare agency. These children do not need to have an Australian parent or to be sponsored.[86]

8.5 Aged dependent relatives

[8.43] The concept of dependence is one that arises also in the context of aged dependent relatives, a group described rather tortuously by reference to several definitions in regs 1.03 and 1.05A. Those eligible for an Aged Dependent Relative visa (subclasses 114 and 838) are 'relatives' who are old enough to be granted an aged pension, who do not have a spouse or de facto partner and who are dependent on their Australian relative (and have been dependent for a reasonable period).[87] A relative is further defined as a partner, child, parent, brother, sister, grandparent, grandchild, aunt, uncle, niece, nephew or step-relative within the same degree of relationship to an Australian citizen or permanent resident.

[8.44] The reg 1.05A definition of 'dependent' requires that aged dependent relatives be wholly or substantially dependent on their Australian sponsors for financial support to meet their basic needs for food, clothing and shelter and that such reliance has existed for a substantial period of time before applying. In addition, their dependence on the Australian relative must be greater than their reliance on anyone else. Alternatively, the aged dependent relatives must be wholly or substantially reliant on their Australian relative for financial support because they are incapacitated for work due to the full or partial loss of bodily or mental functions. The visa is a useful alternative for the sponsorship of aged parents who may not be able to meet the balance of family test.

[8.45] Judicial commentary on the Aged Dependent Relative visas has focused on the extent of financial dependency which is required. In *Chakera v MIMA*,[88] Heerey J analysed the requirement that the applicant be 'wholly or substantially' dependent on the sponsor. His Honour adopted the interpretation given by the Federal Court in *Commissioner for Superannuation v Scott*[89] which spoke in terms of a person being 'primarily, essentially or in the main' dependent on another. His Honour took the

---

84 See *Immigration and Nationality Act* (US) §204.11(c)(6). For a discussion of these visas, see Jacqueline Bhabha and Susan Schmidt, *Seeking Asylum Alone: Unaccompanied and Separated Children and Refugee Protection in the United States* (2006), Ch 4.1.
85 In September 2007 the Executive Committee of the UN High Commission for Refugees drafted a special conclusion on vulnerable refugee children. See UNHCR EXCOM, Conclusion on Children at Risk No 107 (LVIII) – 2007, available at <http://www.unhcr.org>.
86 See *Migration Regulations*, Sch 2, cll 802.215, 802.216 and 802.226A.
87 See *James v MIMA* [2002] FCAFC 91; [2002] FCA 383, considering the evidence which the tribunal can lawfully require in order to be satisfied that an applicant is 'formally separated' from their spouse.
88 (1993) 42 FCR 525.
89 (1987) 71 ALR 408.

view that this interpretation did not require absolute exclusivity in the dependent relationship, as long as the applicant is dependent foremost on her or his sponsor for the requisite support.[90] However, in *Scott*, Fisher and Spender JJ considered that a person may be dependent on another because they have a need for support even when that need is not being satisfied by the other.[91] The Full Federal Court held, in *Huynh*, that the test does not carry any implication of there being a necessity to provide the relevant support. Instead, the Regulations require consideration of whether, as a matter of fact, the first person is relying for support on the other person.[92]

[8.46] These cases raise issues that resonate with some of the other family visa classes. One is the question of eligibility where a sponsored person is being offered support from a variety of sources. Another is where the sponsored person has relatives in their country of origin who could but who are not in fact offering support. In *Zeng v MIMIA*[93] the visa applicant was a 70-year-old woman from China who was described as eking out a fairly meagre existence on a government pension and on periodic but irregular lump sums from her son resident in Australia. The woman's application was denied on the grounds that the payments from Australia were too irregular to establish a relationship of dependence; and because the tribunal reasoned that the woman should have sought support from her children living in China. In overturning the tribunal's decision, the Federal Magistrate ruled that substantial dependence requires the consideration of at least four factors:

- the nature of the person's needs;
- the extent to which those needs are being met from the applicant's own resources;
- the extent to which the needs are being met by the nominator; and
- whether the nominator has an obligation to meet those needs.

[8.47] The court ruled that intermittent lump sum payments can be considered as support. It also held that the existence of other individuals who might be able to render assistance is not relevant to the regulatory scheme: the only question is whether those relatives are willing and able to support the applicant as required. In *Huang v MIAC*,[94] the Federal Magistrate further considered the significance of cultural obligations of the nominator to the parent applicant. While noting that reg 1.05A does not on its face require the tribunal to consider such cultural obligations, the Federal Magistrate concluded that the relationship of dependence must be considered in light of all relevant circumstances and the tribunal's failure to consider the cultural dynamic surrounding the filial relationship in the case led it into jurisdictional error.

8.6 'Remaining' relatives

[8.48] One further class of relatives is selected on the basis of their perceived needs, as opposed to those of their sponsor: 'remaining' relatives (see subclasses

---

90   See also *Zeng v MIAC* [2007] FMCA 169.
91   See dicta of Branson and Hely JJ in *MIMA v Graovac* [1999] FCA 1690 at [13].
92   *Huynh v MIMA* (2006) 152 FCR 576 at [44].
93   [2005] FMCA 546.
94   [2007] FMCA 720.

115 and 835). Together with orphaned relatives (see [8.21]-[8.26] above) this group is singled out because they are bereft of family and other support in their country of origin, when they have people willing to support them in Australia. Remaining relatives are defined as brothers, sisters and non-dependent children who can show that neither they nor their spouse have any parent, sibling or non-dependent child resident outside Australia.[95]

[8.49] Until 1 November 2005 a further concession was made for persons who had no more than three near relatives in an overseas country other than the person's country of usual residence with whom they had had no contact. Jurisprudence developed around the concept of 'contact' to the effect that casual contact with an estranged sibling – for example, at a family wedding or similar event – should not operate to disqualify an applicant.[96] Another enduring issue emerged in the question of identifying and locating relatives, so as to show that the applicant 'usually resided' in a different country from an overseas near relative.[97] There is, however, no longer any scope for discretion to disregard relatives with whom the applicant has no social relationship, or relatives who ordinarily reside in a country other than where the applicant usually resides.

[8.50] Now, it is clear that 'near relatives' include estranged relatives. This is vividly illustrated by the case of *MIMA v Hildalgo*,[98] which was decided in accordance with the pre-2006 Regulations. Ms Hildalgo, a national of Chile, lodged an application for a remaining relative visa nominated by her father who resided in Australia, with his wife, Ms Hildalgo's step-mother. Ms Hildalgo claimed she did not know the country of residence of her mother and that her three siblings all resided in Australia. She said that her father had left when she was a few months old. While living with her mother, Ms Hildalgo claimed to have been abused by her step-father. She moved in with her grandmother when her mother became pregnant to the step-father. She said she had cut all contact with her mother and step-father and never saw them again. She lived with her grandmother until her death and was then taken in by a friend. She then established contact with her father and travelled to Australia on a business visa to see him. The tribunal found that Ms Hildalgo's natural mother and her step-sibling were 'overseas near relatives' within the meaning of reg 1.15. However, Ms Hildalgo was eligible for a remaining relative visa, under the pre-2005 criteria, because she was found to be residing in Australia, and her mother and step-sibling were taken to be usually resident in Chile, where the applicant had seen them last. The Federal Court, and Full Court, upheld this interpretation of the visa criteria. Under the current version of the Regulations, however, Ms Hildalgo would not qualify for this visa.

[8.51] Conversely, certain close relationships may fall outside of the ambit of 'near relatives'. In *Jankovic v MIEA*,[99] the court considered an application of a divorced man who claimed to be a remaining relative notwithstanding the fact that he lived in the

---

95   See the definition of 'near relative' in reg 1.15 of the Regulations.
96   *Bagus v MILGEA* (1994) 50 FCR 396; *Elliott v MIMIA* [2006] FCA 67. See also *Sherzad v MIAC* [2008] FCAFC 145.
97   *Gauthiez v MIEA* (1994) 53 FCR 512; *Scargill v MIMIA* (2003) 129 FCR 259.
98   (2005) 145 FCR 564.
99   (1995) 56 FCR 474.

same country as his former wife and their children. The court found ultimately that the children were not dependent on their father and so disqualified the applicant as a remaining relative. It commented, however, that, had the offspring emerged as dependants, the applicant would have been eligible for the visa sought because the children could have been included in his application.

[8.52] The fact that a spouse's relations are included in any computation of overseas near relatives has led some applicants to seek a legal divorce from their partner. In *Su v MIMIA*[100] the Federal Magistrates Court found no legal error in a tribunal finding that the divorce alleged was a sham and that the applicant continued in fact to live with her (former) husband in a spousal relationship.

[8.53] The final issue that can arise in these cases surrounds the meaning of the phrase, 'usually resident'. Under current visa criteria, the applicant and any partner must have no 'near relative' other than those who are 'usually resident' in Australia. If the applicant has a near relative who is an Australian citizen but is usually resident overseas, the application will fail. The meaning of 'usually resident' has been considered in a number of cases decided before the change in Regulations. In *Gauthiez v MIEA*,[101] the Minister's delegate and the IRT had found that the applicant was disqualified on the basis that he was deemed to be resident in the same country as his brother. At the time of applying the applicant had lived for some time in Australia as an unlawful non-citizen, while his brother was living in Belgium. The two brothers were deemed to reside in France on the basis of their French nationality. As Gummow J pointed out, this assumption involved an error in failing to observe the legal distinction between nationality and residence. His Honour found that the brother's 'usual residence' was in Belgium and that, if the applicant was not entitled to cite Australia as his usual country of residence, then it was probable that he had *no* country of usual residence.

[8.54] The complexity of locating the residence of family members who have been estranged from kith and kin for many years is well illustrated in the case of *Scargill v MIMIA*.[102] The appellant in that case had lived in the United States and (after the failure of his marriage to a US citizen) had come to Australia on a temporary visa. Scargill sought permanent residence on the basis that he was a 'remaining relative' of his permanent resident mother. The problem was that his long estranged father was last known to have resided in the applicant's country of nationality (the United Kingdom). No evidence could be adduced that the father had either died or left the UK. The MRT found that the applicant's country of usual residence was the UK, and so denied his application. The Full Federal Court disagreed, ruling that consideration should have been given to the distinction between nationality and residence. The court held that the phrase 'usually resides' requires consideration of the physical location of the applicant in the period leading up to the application. It found that the applicant's long absence from the UK meant that he did not 'usually reside' in that country. Rather, he should have been assessed as being a resident of Australia.

---

100 (2005) 64 ALD 77.
101 (1994) 53 FCR 512.
102 (2003) 129 FCR 259.

[8.55] While the underlying criteria for grant of visa have changed, these cases clearly illustrate that the actual physical location of an applicant's 'near relatives' will be paramount, rather than their citizenship. Again, the applicant's 'near relatives' must be usually resident in Australia for an application for a Remaining Relative visa to be successful.

8.7 'Special Need Relatives' and Carers

[8.56] The final category of 'compassionate' family visas is unusual in that it focuses on the needs of Australian citizens or residents rather than on the attributes of the relative overseas. The Carer visa (subclasses 116 and 836) replaced the Special Need Relative visa in December 1998. The criteria for the former Special Need Relative visa required the Australian party to have a 'permanent or long-term need for assistance because of death, disability, prolonged illness of other serious circumstances affecting them personally, or a member of their family unit'. Now, the term 'carer' is described in reg 1.15AA as a relative (as defined) who is willing and able to give substantial and continuing assistance to a citizen or permanent resident suffering from a defined medical condition. The Australian party must have a 'medical condition … causing physical, intellectual or sensory impairment of the ability of that person to attend to the practical aspects of daily life' which will be ongoing for at least two years. The assistance cannot be reasonably provided by any other relative, or welfare, hospital, nursing or community service in Australia.

[8.57] Although a significant concession, this definition ensures that only those Australians faced with very serious or unusual problems are able to succeed with their sponsorship. Generally, the visa will be beyond the reach of Australian parties who merely require financial or emotional support and who are at all self-sufficient.[103]

[8.58] The Carer visa requires the Australian relative to obtain a certificate from Medibank Health Solutions (MHS) (formerly known as Health Services Australia (HSA)), rating their level of impairment.[104] This means that the 'need' of the Australian party is restricted to specified medical conditions. Moreover, the impairment ratings on the certificates are binding on the decision-maker, and the MRT has no discretion to overrule a certificate.[105]

[8.59] Even where the Australian sponsor has the requisite impairment, the grant or refusal of a visa will often turn on whether the Australian party can reasonably obtain the assistance they need from any other relative, or welfare, hospital, nursing or community service in Australia. For example, in *Issa v MIMIA*,[106] a Syrian national's application for a Carer visa failed on the ground that she was not needed

---

103 See, for example, *Re Preston* [1991] IRTA 56; *Re Fung* [1991] IRTA 150; *Re Yap* [1993] IRTA 1863; and *Re Luc* [1994] IRTA 3817.
104 See *Migration Regulations*, reg 1.15AA(1).
105 Gabriel Fleming, 'Questions About the Independence of Administrative Tribunals' (1999) 7 *Australian Journal of Administrative Law* 33 at 52. The lack of the requisite HSA certificate was central to the tribunal's adverse decision in *Ganzon v MIMIA* [2002] FCA 1628 (although the applicant had also failed to respond to the tribunal's invitation to submit information and to appear at the hearing).
106 [2002] FCA 933.

to care for her mother. A certificate had been submitted to the MRT indicating that the mother met the requirements of reg 1.15AA(1). However, the tribunal was not satisfied that the direct assistance required by the mother in attending to the practical needs of daily life could not reasonably be obtained from any other relative resident in Australia or from welfare, hospital, nursing or community services. The tribunal found that the mother lived with her husband and that, while he had health problems, he was able to drive her to appointments, to the doctor and to do the shopping, including obtaining medication from a pharmacy. The tribunal noted the mother's desire to have her daughter reunited with her family, and that she had some related depression which impaired her ability to attend to the practical aspects of life. However, overall, it was not satisfied that the direct assistance she required could not be obtained from her husband and sons.

[8.60] While tribunal decisions are based on findings of fact and have no normative or precedential value, there is some evidence that the MRT today is taking a tougher line on Carer visa applications than its predecessor tribunal, the IRT, in its consideration of 'special need relative' applications. The IRT on occasion took a broad view of requirements that services offered by the foreign relative could not be provided by others in the country. The tribunal considered the cultural appropriateness, accessibility, availability and continuity of relevant services and programs available to ethnocultural minorities in the community. In a number of cases, it ruled in favour of foreign relatives in recognition that they were able to cater to the specific needs of the Australian parties in ways that were not possible through existing community care schemes.[107]

[8.61] For its part, the Federal Court also took a rather liberal approach to interpreting the law relating to special need relatives. In *Fuduche v MILGEA*,[108] Burchett J criticised vigorously a decision refusing a permit to a man sponsored as a special need relative by his Australian sister. The woman had been rejected by her family because of her illegitimate status and had been subjected to horrific deprivations throughout her life. Her brother also suffered neglect, but had remained a consistent source of moral and material support for his sister. His Honour found the decision refusing to grant the brother a permit patently unreasonable. The Australian sponsor, he held, clearly remained reliant on her brother for support and for stability in her fight against recurrent bouts of clinical depression.

[8.62] In *Chen (No 2) v MIEA*,[109] the Federal Court upheld the use of the special need relative provisions in the sponsorship of a mother by her infant Australian children. The woman had tried previously to gain residence as the de facto wife of an Australian citizen who was the father of her children. She failed because of the man's refusal to bring to an end his marriage to another woman.[110] The woman's quest for a

---

107 See, for example, *Re Cheuk Por Leung* [1993] IRTA 2238; and *Re Koncz* [1995] IRTA 5934. In *Re Robertson* [1993] IRTA 2311, the applicant was successful on the special need relative criteria, even though other relatives already resident in Australia were assisting in the care, growth and development of two 'problem children'.
108 (1993) 117 ALR 418.
109 (1994) 51 FCR 322.
110 See *Chen v MILGEA* (1992) 37 FCR 501.

family entry permit (the 'EETEP') was frustrated by the requirement that the children show that their need for her arose out of 'permanent' incapacitation. Davies J chose to construe the definition of 'special need relative' widely, rather than restrictively. In doing so, his Honour took into consideration the principles of the Declaration on the Rights of the Child, and recognised that the relationship between a child and his or her mother is a weighty or important matter. His Honour stated that the relationship between children and their parents, particularly the relationship between a child of tender years and the mother is a special one, as is universally recognised. Despite this finding, in a later decision with similar facts,[111] the Full Federal Court retreated from the wide construction that Davies J had given to 'special need relative'. The Full Court determined that the definition of 'special need relative' should not be construed so as to involve every case involving a child of tender years unable to care for himself or herself. The court then examined the phrase 'serious circumstances', and opined that it was hardly conceivable that the expression should reflect merely the tender age of a person.

[8.63] In *Huang v MIEA*,[112] Hill J expressed no opinion as to whether the decision in *Chen* was correctly decided. His Honour contented himself with agreeing with Davies J as to the need to consider the context in which the words of the regulation appear. Hill J, in *Huang*, found that the new additional requirement of sponsorship would preclude a successful application where a child under 18 seeks to sponsor their parent. While his Honour found the policy behind the legislation difficult to discern, he merely suggested that the matter should be given attention when the regulations are due for amendment. His Honour did not consider the UN Convention on the Rights of the Child.[113]

[8.64] The press release introducing the 1998 amendments to this class of visa noted that the Minister had been concerned that the 'special need relative' provisions were subject to abuse:[114]

> There has been a significant broadening of criteria for the existing category through the decisions of review tribunals and the Federal Court. We have seen ailments such as 'homesickness' and the need for child care become an acceptable special need.

Whether the Federal Court judges in *Fuduche* and *Chen* would agree with this implicit criticism of their rulings is a moot point.

[8.65] In the years that have passed since the introduction of the carer visas, the Federal Court has continued to demand a generous interpretation of the law whenever possible. In these cases, issues have again arisen about the willingness and capacity of both the sponsored overseas relative and any Australian relatives to care for the relative whose needs provide the basis for the visa application. For example, in *Xiang v MIMIA*[115] the Full Federal Court held that the MRT fell into

---

111 *Huang v MIEA* [1996] FCA 1040.
112 Ibid.
113 For a Federal Court decision where the opposite conclusion was reached on the facts and the law, see *Garath v MIAC* (2006) 91 ALD 790.
114 See MPS 151/98 Tuesday, 24 November 1998.
115 (2004) 81 ALD 301. See also *Liang v MIAC* (2009) 175 FCR 184.

error by assuming that the applicant should be required to provide assistance to an Australian party on a constant basis from the date that a visa application is lodged. In that case the applicant asserted that she was 'willing and able to provide substantial and continuing assistance' to her Australian aunt. Her application was rejected because the aunt had travelled overseas for nine months and the applicant had been working from home on a full-time basis for three years. By the time the matter came before the Federal Court, the aunt's various conditions had deteriorated to the point where she did require full-time care from the applicant. Accordingly, the court held that the MRT had fallen into error by looking beyond the question of whether the applicant was a special need relative at the time of the application and at the time of decision. The key issues for the court were the need of the Australian party at the relevant dates and the willingness and capacity of the sponsored relative to provide the needed assistance.

[8.66] Jurisprudence has been more varied on the availability of support for an Australian party from family members in Australia. In *Perera v MIMIA*[116] the court found no legal error in a ruling to the effect that the nominator's depression and anxiety could be adequately addressed by the support of family already in Australia. The fact that the mother expressed particular longing for her absent daughter (the applicant) was not enough to move the decision-makers. On the other hand, in a series of cases in 2004, the Federal Court overruled tribunal decisions denying Carer visas to family members in circumstances where other family members were available but apparently unwilling to assist the Australian sponsor. In *Lin v MIMIA*,[117] *Rafiq v MIMIA*,[118] and *Naidu v MIMIA*[119] the Federal Court ruled that the regulatory scheme for Carer visas involves two distinct conceptual steps. The first is to ascertain whether the Australian relatives can reasonably provide assistance or make assistance available to the sponsor. The second is to judge whether they would do so, so that the sponsor can reasonably obtain the assistance needed. In *Rafiq* Finn J commented that the object of reg 1.15AA(1)(e)(i) of the Regulations was

> not to effect a form of civil conscription of available relatives. Nor does it require a relative to act selflessly and contrary to that person's own wishes, even if absent any alternative means of assistance that relative might continue to provide assistance for reasons of love, duty etc.[120]

---

116 [2005] FCA 1120.
117 (2004) 136 FCR 556. See also the earlier case of *Issa v MIMIA* [2002] FCA 933.
118 [2004] FCA 564.
119 (2004) 140 FCR 284.
120 [2004] FCA 564 at [11].

PART V Skilled Migration, Students and Temporary Visas

'Greek Migrant Learning English, Bonegilla reception camp' 1942
© Thurston Hopkins/Hulton Archive/Getty Images

9

Building a Clever Country: Permanent Labour Migration

9.1   Putting the 'skill' in migration

[9.01]   The changes made to Australia's permanent labour migration program after the turn of the new Millennium have been as dramatic as at any time in the country's history. Skilled and business migration came to dominate the general immigration program, reversing the ratios that used to favour family reunification over skilled and business intakes. The total Skill Stream outcome for 2008-09 at 114,777 was the largest on record,[1] constituting 67 per cent of the total migration program for that year. The outcomes for the following year declined in response to the global financial crisis.[2]

[9.02]   The surge in the intake of skilled migrants was accompanied by revolutionary changes in thinking about labour migration. In earlier years, more attention had been paid to the macro-economic impact of labour migration and to how migrants might affect the working conditions of Australian workers. The focus was on the physical constitution of the labour market by local workers and permanent migrant workers whose terms and conditions of employment were regulated in an integrated manner. In contrast, modern rules have been fixed more closely on the micro-management of the labour market in terms of who is available to perform specific tasks. The broad impact of foreign workers and businesses on local labour has received less attention than the contributions that can be made by migrants moving directly into specific jobs. The conservative Coalition government, from the late 1990s, pioneered the use of labour market research to 'gazette' occupations in demand as the vehicle for determining eligibility for independent skilled migration. The Labor government which followed favoured migrants sponsored by employers over independent migrants, in what was described by the then Minister for Immigration as a shift from 'supply' to 'demand' driven selection.[3] In reality, however, the migration program has never really been dictated by migrant 'supply' in the sense of the qualities or desires of visa

---

1   DIAC, *Report on Migration Program 2008-2009*, at Attachment A.
2   DIAC, *Report on Migration Program 2009-2010*, at 3.
3   Senator Chris Evans, 'Changes to Australia's Skilled Migration Program', speech given at Australian National University, Canberra, 8 February 2010, available at <http://www.minister.immi.gov.au/media/speeches/2010/ce100208.htm>.

applicants. The fundamental changes that have occurred have seen employers rather than government assume greater roles as arbiter of who gains permanent residency on the basis of skills.

[9.03] These new priorities have radically transfigured the structure of the skilled migration program in several ways. First, it is no longer possible to glean the full story of immigration to Australia solely from permanent arrival data. As explored in Chapter 10, the grant of skilled visas to temporary workers has mushroomed, transforming skilled migration into a two-stage (try before you buy) process. Permanent visas granted to skilled people present in Australia more than doubled during the decade of conservative governance, moving from 16,535 in 1996-97 to 43,363 in 2005-06.[4] The pathways from temporary skills visas to permanent residence have been fostered by deliberate policies, especially by the decision in 1999 to allow foreign students graduating from Australian institutions to apply for Skill Stream visas. In 2000-01 there were no onshore grants of skill-based visas to students graduating in Australia. By 2006-07, over 21,000 such visas were being issued each year, although this fell to 15,000 in the following year and has been decreasing since 'due to processing priorities'.[5]

[9.04] Productivity and other goals have been achieved through changes in the regulatory methods used to control skilled migration. In the past, selection methods have swung wildly between the extremes of sweeping administrative discretion to rigid codification. As we explore in Chapter 5, modern trends have favoured micro management of the immigration program, achieved by the segmentation and outsourcing of decision-making to private bodies. Understanding where workers are needed has been enhanced by increasingly sophisticated labour market research. The fortunes of skilled settlers and temporary entrants have been charted against standards of productivity, fiscal impact and employment experiences.[6] Further, incentives have been built into the program to encourage skilled and business migrants to settle in regions where skill shortages are acute.

[9.05] Finally, the highly targeted approach to skilled migration has changed the demography of the program. The racial profile of applicants has altered as it has become necessary to look beyond traditional source countries to locate appropriate skilled personnel. Where traditionally the largest source region for skilled migrants was the United Kingdom/Ireland, in 2009 it was South Asia.[7] The quest for migrants who would make a life-long contribution to the Australian economy – and the relaxa-

---

4 DIAC, *Population Flows: Immigration Aspects 2005-06*, January 2007, at 6.
5 DIAC, *Population Flows: Immigration Aspects 2008-2009*, May 2010, at 127.
6 See, for example, Parliament of the Commonwealth of Australia, Joint Standing Committee on Migration, *To Make a Contribution: Review of Skilled Labour Migration Programs* (Canberra: AGPS, 2004); Bob Birrell, Leslie-Anne Hawthorne and Sue Richardson, *Evaluation of the General Skilled Migration Categories* (Canberra: AGPS, 2006); Productivity Commission, *Economic Impacts of Migration and Population Growth* (Melbourne: Productivity Commission, 2006); Access Economics, *Migrants Fiscal Impacts Model: 2008 Update* (Canberra: DIAC, 2008).
7 Data extrapolated from DIAC, 'Permanent Additions to the Resident Population by Region of Birth and Eligibility Category, 2008-09', *Immigration Update 2008-09*, January 2010, at 13.

tion in the change of status rules for foreign students – in turn reduced the average age of skilled migrants.[8]

[9.06] Australia is one of many Western countries actively competing to attract the 'best and the brightest': a trend that Ayelet Shachar describes as the global 'race for talent'.[9] Immigration policy-makers around the world have been trying to emulate each others' recruitment tactics to gain a relative advantage in the knowledge-based transnational economy. National policy-makers are no longer shaping their immigration policy solely on the basis of domestic factors.[10] A convergence of policy approaches to skilled migration can be seen in the 'points-based' system of selecting skilled migrants, which was devised by Canada and adopted by Australia in the 1970s, and which has now been embraced by a number of countries in the European Union and elsewhere. Over the past 20 years, policy changes by most Organisation for Economic Co-operation and Development (OECD) countries have led to the establishment of specific and often fast-tracked entry streams designed to encourage the recruitment of knowledge migrants.[11] It may seem extraordinary that countries are willing to reconfigure the boundaries of political membership in order to gain the net positive effects associated with skilled migration. What is clear is that admission policies, objectives and outcomes cannot be explained with reference to a single theoretical approach. Rather, they represent hybrid responses reflecting somewhat entrenched notions of culture and history.

[9.07] In this chapter we examine in turn the operation of the skilled migration program in its various manifestations, and the programs for business migration. These have fallen always into three broad groupings that reflect concepts of supply and demand and/or the exigencies of domestic politics. On the 'supply' side are the independent migrants who come to Australia with little or no prior connections with the country. At the other extreme are migrants sponsored by particular employers under what has been known for many years as the 'Employer Nomination Scheme' (ENS). Caught somewhere between these two are the quasi-independent migrants who are sponsored by relatives already in Australia and who are given preferential treatment because of these family ties.[12] The first and third of these groupings are subject to points testing. In Part 9.2 we describe the historical evolution of the general skilled migration program. In Part 9.3 we explore the selection mechanisms of the points test which governs independent and sponsored skilled applications. Although

---

8   In 2009-10, general skilled migrants were on average seven years younger than their employer-nominated counterparts. See DIAC, *Settler Arrivals 2008-2009*, December 2009, at 12.
9   Ayelet Shachar, 'The Race for Talent: Highly Skilled Migrants and Competitive Immigration Regimes' (2006) 81 *New York University Law Review* 148. See also Stephen Yale-Loehr and Christoph Hoashi-Erhardt, 'A Comparative Look at Immigration and Human Capital Assessment' (2001) 16 *Georgetown Immigration Law Journal* 99.
10 Deborah A Cobb-Clark and Marie D Connolly, 'The Worldwide Market for Skilled Migrants: Can Australia Compete?' (1997) 31 *International Migration Review* 670.
11 See OECD, *The Global Competition for Talent: Mobility of the Highly Skilled* (Paris: 2008); Frédéric Docquier and Maurice Schiff, *Measuring Skilled Migration Rates: The Case of Small States* (World Bank Policy Research Working Paper WPS 4827, 2009).
12 The Skilled – Sponsored (Migrant) visa was known previously as 'Skilled – Australian Sponsored' (to 31 August 2007), as 'Skilled Australian Linked' (to 30 June 1999) and as 'Concessional Family' (to 30 June 1997).

it can be criticised for its rigidity, the current system contains some clever features that have solved or reduced problems that used to be endemic within the permanent migration program. Here we examine in turn the effectiveness of 'front end loading' visa applications; the outsourcing of skills assessments; language proficiency requirements; and the gazetted list of skilled occupations. Part 9.4 examines the ENS and Part 9.5 the small boutique program of Distinguished Talent visas. The various regimes for those admitted on the basis of 'business skills' are considered in Part 9.6. The chapter concludes with some reflections on the relationships between policy, selection methods and outcomes, raising questions about the impact that recent policy trends might be having on race and gender equity within the program.

9.2 An overview of General Skilled Migration programs

[9.08] Australian immigration programs have always been linked intimately to labour market outcomes. At the heart of government policy in this area has been the uneasy relationship between the importation of migrant workers and the preservation and nurturing of the local workforce. The regulatory synergies between immigration control and the development of Australia as a working nation were most obvious in the country's early days when immigration served as a necessary tool for basic nation building. However, they remain a defining aspect of the modern Australian polity.

[9.09] The other imperative for Australia as an evolving society has been to foster – through protection where necessary – a local workforce. The recruitment of workers from overseas to suit specific domestic labour market rationales continues to have ramifications for local workers. It seems almost universally accepted that policy choices ought to favour education, training and skills development in local populations. What is more controversial is how the entry of foreign-born workers may either impede or foster this objective.

[9.10] In the early years of nationhood, emphasis was given to ensuring that immigration served the ideological purpose of creating an Australian workforce that was white and free. Control occurred at a macro level: little attention was paid to strictly defined categories of labour within the immigration 'program'. Regulation of immigration was used simply to restrict the pool of labour from which employers could legitimately draw. In more recent times the focus has shifted to regulation of the terms and conditions on which Australian firms may engage labour, with attention turning to the use of immigration to fill identified gaps in the skills needs of the Australian marketplace. Debates continue about the appropriate roles for government and the market in the selection of skilled migrants.[13] According to one view, migrants should be chosen to meet specific medium – or long – term needs in the labour market, bearing in mind the requirements of employers, the rights and interests of local workers and the demands of industry policy. On this view, individual Australian employers should only be entitled to sponsor foreign workers where they are able

---

13 Khalid Koser, *The Global Financial Crisis and International Migration: Policy Implications for Australia* (Sydney: Lowy Institute for International Policy, 2009); Gary Freeman and Bob Birrell, 'Divergent Paths of Immigration Politics in the United States and Australia' (2001) 27(3) *Population and Development Review* 525.

to demonstrate that suitable recruits cannot be located in the domestic workforce. The alternative approach is to focus on the age, skills and qualifications of applicants in the selection of migrants, leaving it to the market place, the mobility and the ingenuity of well-qualified migrants to sort out issues of job placement.

[9.11] Although regulatory policy has swung – sometimes wildly – between these two approaches, the prevailing tendency has now become overwhelmingly to envisage skilled migration as a tool for meeting present needs rather than predominantly as a resource for potential future growth and development. In the past three decades, policy approaches to skilled migration have been largely bipartisan. The trend toward codification began under the Labor government, intensified under the conservative Coalition government and has continued to be refined under the Labor government from 2007. Broad agreement has been reached that migrants should come to Australia able to move immediately into the working community. As well as being politically palatable to the broader electorate, this approach has enabled successive Australia governments to remain responsive to the demands of particular interest groups, including the union movement, the corporate sector and industry.

9.2.1   Early history and evolution of skilled migration

[9.12] Although agreement could not be reached on the constitutional entrenchment of Australian citizenship, the nation's founders were united in their vision that Australia should not be built on the back of indentured, 'coloured' labourers brought in from overseas.[14] The Australian workforce was to be white, free and permanent. The very first Act passed after the appropriation Bills in 1901 operated to expel from the country Pacific Island workers – 'Kanakas', as they were called – who had been brought to the country to work the cane fields of Queensland.[15] Four years later, the *Contract Immigrants Act 1905* (Cth)[16] was passed to require employers to justify the temporary employment of foreign workers by demonstrating that they were unable to recruit suitable locals. Employers also had to show that the importation of contract workers was done without a view to affecting any present or future industrial disputes; and that the remuneration and conditions offered were as advantageous as those available to the local, unionised workforce. As Layman points out, these constraints were not just aimed at the coloured workers brought in originally from the Pacific Islands.[17] They were enforced equally in respect of 'white' labour from Britain and Europe.[18]

---

14 Anthony O'Donnell and Richard Mitchell, 'Immigrant Labour in Australia: The Regulatory Framework' (2001) 14 *Australian Journal of Labour Law* 269 at 273.
15 See *Pacific Island Labourers Act 1901* (Cth), repealed by *Migration Act 1958* (Cth), s 8. The validity of the legislation was upheld by the High Court in *Robtelmes v Brenan* (1906) 4 CLR 395, discussed in Chapter 2.2.3.
16 Repealed by *Statute Law Revision Act 1950* (Cth).
17 Lenore Layman, 'To Keep Up the Australian Standard: Regulating Contract Migration 1901-1950' (1996) 70 *Labour History* 25.
18 See further Mary Crock, 'Immigration and Labour Law: Targeting the Nations Skills Needs' in Andrew Frazer, Ron McCallum and Paul Ronfeldt (eds), *Individual Contracts and Workplace Relations* (ACIRRT: Working Paper No 50, 1997) at 123.

[9.13] For the best part of a half century, it was as difficult for employers to bring in temporary workers as it was to bring in persons of colour. The *Contract Immigrants Act* remained in force until after the Second World War, when acute labour shortages led to great increases in the migration intake. Rhetorically, the needs of the community were used to justify massive increases in the immigration intake from non-traditional source countries. With the catch-cry of 'populate or perish', the language of economic interest was used to legitimise the inclusion of migrants who might otherwise have fomented considerable public discontent.

[9.14] What transpired was a bifurcation of regulatory methods between highly skilled British migrants on the one hand and low-waged non-British migrants on the other. Permanent migration remained very much the norm, and Australia's doors were opened to skilled British migrants: so much so that concerns were raised in Britain about Australia becoming something of a 'brain drain' for professionals trained at Britain's expense.[19] At the other end of the spectrum, non-British migrants were admitted as indentured workers, on two-year contracts that tied them to specific employers for the duration of their initial entry permits. Contracted migrants worked under the threat of removal, forcing many to work in appalling conditions in jobs that could not be filled from within Australia's own unionised workforce. Layman offers by way of example the use of Italian migrants to work the asbestos mines at Wittenoom which continued until Italian government health authorities intervened to stop the practice.[20]

[9.15] With the decline of the White Australia Policy the range of people eligible to migrate to Australia increased exponentially. The dramatic increase after the abolition of the policy in December 1972 was responsible, in part, for forcing the shift from macro to micro management of the immigration intake.[21] With the refinement and articulation of selection criteria for migrants, the regulation of migrant labour emphasised the terms on which firms could engage labour, through the introduction of labour market testing requirements.

9.2.2 Controlling skilled migration: The first points tests

[9.16] The early 1970s saw a new selection system for skilled migrants, '[d]esigned to make selection more objective and less open to the discretion of officials'.[22] The traditional 'demand' based programs continued, allowing employers to sponsor or nominate workers as permanent migrants. At the same time, more attention came

---

19   See Michael J Salter (ed), *Studies in the Immigration of the Highly Skilled* (Canberra: ANU Press, 1978).
20   See, for example, Lenore Layman, 'Migrant Labour Under Contract: The First Years of Post-War Migration: 1947-1952' in Richard Bosworth and Romano Ugolini (eds), *War, Internment and Mass Migration: The Italo-Australian Experience, 1940-1990* (Rome: Gruppo Editoriale Internationale, 1992) at 186-9. See also *Maddalena v CSR Ltd* [2004] WASCA 231, reversed *CSR Ltd v Maddalena* [2006] HCA 1.
21   See Freda Hawkins, *Critical Years in Immigration: Canada and Australia Compared* (Montreal: McGill/Queens' University Press, 1989) at 32ff.
22   Patrick Ongley and David Pearson, 'Post-1945 International Migration: New Zealand, Australia and Canada Compared' (1995) 29 *International Immigration Review* 765 at 772.

to be paid to the mechanisms for selecting skilled migrants either as independent or so-called concessional migrants (where a relative could act as a sponsor).

[9.17] In 1979, these new selection principles were formalised into a 'points test' whereby prospective skilled migrants were chosen according to professional skills and education. This innovative device for selecting skilled migrants had been adopted first by Canada in 1967.[23] The points test formed a relatively objective tool for selecting among a pool of potential entrants, by treating all those assessed under its guidelines in a similar fashion. It allowed for the weighting of applicants' attributes across a range of factors that could be modified as required.[24] At the same time, the Department established a longitudinal study of permanent migrants which has continued to provide data on migrants' employment outcomes, English language proficiency and use of settlement services.[25] The findings of such research studies, as well as input from a greater range of stakeholders, were fed into the process of setting immigration targets and articulating selection criteria. The significance of this re-orientation cannot be overstated. The 'points' test adopted by Canada and Australia in the 1960s and 1970s has been embraced by Germany and the United Kingdom. Western countries now compete not only for the economic benefits of skilled migration but also for the benefits of efficient policy tools to administer a skilled migration program.[26]

[9.18] True to the laissez faire character of the 1980s, it was during these years that a market-oriented approach to economic migration reached its ascendancy. A 1985 report by the Committee for Economic Development praised the use of skilled migration as a vehicle for boosting economic growth. In response, the then Labor government introduced skilled entry visas for applicants with relatives in Australia. Applicants were selected from overseas on the basis of their employability, skills, age and education (with additional credit given for family relationships). Independent migrants were assessed against the same criteria as well as for their proficiency in English.[27]

9.2.3 The 1989 reforms

[9.19] One of the most striking features of the regulatory regime introduced in 1989 was the attention paid to the articulation of decisional criteria. Designed first to improve control over the decision-making process as a whole, the new rules also

---

23 Ninette Kelley and Michael Trebilcock, *The Making of the Mosaic: A History of Canadian Immigration Policy* (Toronto: University of Toronto Press, 1998) at 358.
24 The scheme was known as the Numerical Multifactor Assessment Scheme or NUMAS. See Crock, above n 18.
25 See Susie Van der Heuvel, *The Longitudinal Survey of Immigrants to Australia* (2005), available at <http://www.immi.gov.au/media/research/lsia/index.htm>.
26 See *Act to Control and Restrict Immigration and to Regulate the Residence and Integration of EU Citizens and Foreigners*, 30 July 2004, BGBl.I at 1950 (FRG); UK Home Office, *Secure Borders, Safe Haven: Integration with Diversity in Modern Britain* (London: 2001).
27 For an account of selection policies over this period, see Wayne Parcell, Lois Sparkes and Lynne Williams, *A Brief Historical Outline of Skill Migration in Australia 1980-93* (Canberra: BIPR, 1994) at 8-9; and Bob Birrell, 'The Scale and Consequences of Professional Migration Movement to Australia Since 1983' in Martin Bell and PW Newton, *Population Shift* (Canberra: AGPS, 1996).

revealed a much more sophisticated approach to the relationship between skilled migration and labour market outcomes. Immigration control after 1989 was reconceptualised from a field of administration to a science.

[9.20] The 1989 version of the points test contained an important innovation over earlier iterations of the test which had relied on the simple application of points against enumerated factors. Visa grants were controlled more closely by placing applications in a 'pool', which allowed for their consideration over initially one year, and later two years. During each quarter, the Department determined the optimum number of visas that should be granted given the job opportunities in the labour market. Visas were then granted to the highest scoring applicants, in light of the date of applications. In other words, successful candidates were skimmed off the top of the pool of applicants. The cut-off score or 'pass mark' was set at the score achieved by the lowest scoring applicant within this cohort. Unsuccessful applicants were kept in the 'pool' for the specified period, during which time their applications would remain current.[28] Numerical limits were also achieved with the introduction of statutory powers to suspend processing and even to 'cap and kill' applications, requiring people to submit fresh applications when quotas were filled. The pooling system in more recent times enabled the government to create a bank of potential applicants whose points scores were not sufficient to meet the criteria for independent migrants. Until September 2007 (when the scheme was abolished), applicants placed in the 'pool' could be sponsored by employers, or States or Territories, to fill positions in regional areas.[29] The requirements for entry through this regional sponsorship arrangement were deliberately far less onerous.

9.2.4 The 1999 reforms

[9.21] When the Coalition came into office in 1996, the number of people arriving as family reunion migrants outnumbered those arriving as skilled migrants by more than two to one. Immigration Minister Philip Ruddock spoke of the need for a more 'balanced' migration program in order to 'restore public confidence that [the] Migration Program contributes to Australia's social and economic growth'.[30] As Siew-Ean Khoo suggests, this move away from family migration may well have been influenced by the anti-immigration sentiment spawned by the rise of the One Nation Party at that time.

[9.22] With revisions to the points test in 1999, the independent and family-sponsored categories were separated (with family ties becoming ever more marginal).[31] The points test was increasingly selective and 'targeted' in terms of required skills and qualifications, driven by the immediate needs of the marketplace as suggested by

---

28 See Crock, above n 18, at 128. The pass and pool marks are set by ministerial gazettal pursuant to s 96 of the *Migration Act*.
29 See former subclass 134 and the discussion below at Part 9.4.3.
30 Quoted in Siew-Ean Khoo, 'Immigration Issues in Australia' (2002) 19 (special ed) *Journal of Population Research* 67 at 71.
31 In 2007 family sponsored skilled migration was effectively limited to applicants with a relative resident in a designated 'regional' area. See below Part 9.4.3.

available statistical data on performance.[32] In 1999, the independent and sponsored visa classes were expanded to include visas specifically for overseas students, aimed at encouraging recently graduated students to remain in Australia. 1999 also saw the introduction of the gazetted 'Skilled Occupation List' (SOL). As we explain in Part 9.3.1 below, this was used first as the centrepiece for selecting independent (points tested) migrants. Similar lists were created later for nominated employees and for temporary skilled migrants.

[9.23] A review instituted in 2005 led to a major overhaul of the skilled migration program in 2007.[33] Skilled visa classes were reduced from 15 to 9 and changes were made to strengthen the economic returns of the program.

9.2.5 Recent trends

[9.24] The Labor government in 2007 wound back skilled migrant numbers in response to the global economic downturn.[34] If the relative proportion of skilled to family migration did not alter, there was a shift in emphasis within the skills categories. Labor has favoured workers sponsored by employers where the Coalition gave priority to independent migrants. Employer and government-sponsored (ENS) skill streams were expanded after 2008 to almost 40 per cent of the total program, with commensurate falls in the proportion of independent skilled migrants.[35] The initiative presaged what may yet become one of the biggest shake-ups of the skilled migration program since the points test was first introduced.

[9.25] In 2010, the Labor government launched the most comprehensive review of the GSM program since the inception of points testing in 1979. The move was in response to a number of criticisms made of the scheme as it had evolved. First, the points tests had led to distortions in the international education market in Australia. Aspiring migrants were seen to be pursuing qualifications for the purpose of securing eligibility for permanent residence rather than for purely vocational motives. The qualifications emanating from educational 'visa factories' were perceived to be lacking in substance, as were the English language skills of the applicants. Data from the Longitudinal Survey of Skilled Migrants in 2005 suggested that former overseas students had the lowest earnings profile of all skilled migrants. These figures indicated that skilled migrants who had studied in Australia were contributing less to the Australian economy than other skilled migrants.[36] The government reappraised the occupations that enabled an applicant to gain admission into the program, and removed incentives which had encouraged international students to seek residence.

[9.26] Second, the points tests had come to operate in a way that favoured a narrow range of qualities. While in theory points could be accrued against multiple

---

32 See, for instance, DIMA, *Review of the Independent and Skilled Australian Linked Categories* (Canberra: 1999) and Birrell et al, above n 6.
33 See Birrell et al, above n 6.
34 Senator Chris Evans, *Press Release: Budget 2009–10 – Migration Program: The Size of the Skilled and Family Programs*, 12 May 2009.
35 DIAC, *Report on Migration Program 2009-2010*, at 3.
36 Birrell et al, above n 6, at 84.

criteria, in fact it had become almost impossible to meet the pass mark without an occupation in demand and Australian qualifications or work experience. Finally, the absolute threshold age of 45 years was seen to be excessively restrictive in the context of the aging workforces of most Western countries. The points test effective from July 2011 was promised to 'deliver the best and brightest skilled migrants by emphasising high level qualifications, better English language levels and extensive skilled work experience'.[37]

[9.27] The government also moved to address the backlog which had developed as potential migrants adjusted their lives and career choices to meet the advertised criteria for permanent resident visas. Processing arrangements were adjusted to advantage applicants with a sponsoring employer. In February 2010, the Minister took the dramatic step of annulling approximately 20,000 visa applications lodged overseas before September 2007.[38] Applicants affected by this measure had their application charges refunded, although no provision was made for the refund of any other fees paid (for instance for professional advice). In May 2010, the government introduced the Migration Amendment (Visa Capping) Bill 2010 which sought to broaden exponentially the powers of the Minister to 'cap and cull' applications using a variety of criteria including category of occupation. The objective was to create a system that could easily avoid application backlogs, thought to hinder the government's ability to pick the best and brightest in any given year. The Bill was not passed when the parliament was prorogued for the election and lapsed in July 2010. It is to the more detailed operation of the system that we now turn.

9.3 The General Skilled Migration points test

[9.28] Over many years the points tests have allowed points to be awarded on the basis of employment skills and work experience; English language skills; age; and other factors that vary across the visa subclasses.[39] It is a scheme that values youthful English-speaking applicants: threshold requirements include that applicants are under 50 years of age, hold minimum English language skills, have skills required for an occupation listed on the gazetted Skilled Occupation List (SOL) (as assessed by the relevant assessment authority) and demonstrate sufficient work experience. In applying for any of the points tested skilled visas an applicant must:

1. nominate a 'skilled occupation' gazetted on the SOL.[40]
2. demonstrate the qualifications or experience required to work in the nominated occupation, as assessed by the relevant assessing authority;[41] and
3. provide evidence of English language ability, for example by completing an International English Language Test System (IELTS) test.

---

37   DIAC Factsheet, 'Introduction of a New Points Test', 11 November 2010.
38   *Migration Act*, s 39.
39   Sections 92-96 of the *Migration Act* provide for the operation of the 'points' system. Applicants' points scores are assessed under s 93 by reference to Sch 6B to the *Migration Regulations 1994* (Cth).
40   Regulation 1.15I of the *Migration Regulations* defines 'skilled occupation' as an occupation specified by the Minister through legislative instrument, which is the 'Skilled Occupation List'.
41   See *Migration Regulations*, reg 2.26B.

Points Test effective July 2011

Factor	Description	Points
Age	18-24	25
	25-32	30
	33-39	25
	40-44	15
	45-49	0
English language	Competent English – IELTS 6	0
	Proficient English – IELTS 7	10
	Superior English – IELTS 8	20
Australian work experience in nominated occupation or a closely related occupation	One year Australian (of past two years)	5
	Three years Australian (of past five years)	10
	Five years Australian (of past seven years)	15
Overseas work experience in nominated occupation or a closely related occupation	Three years overseas (of past five years)	5
	Five years overseas (of past seven years)	10
	Eight years overseas (of past 10 years)	15
Qualifications (Australian or recognised overseas)	Offshore recognised apprenticeship AQFIII/IV completed in Australia \Diploma completed in Australia	10
	Bachelor degree (including a Bachelor degree with Honours or Masters)	15
	PhD	20
Recognition of Australian Study	Minimum two years' full time (Australian study requirement)	5
Designated language		5
Partner skills		5
Professional Year		5
Sponsorship by State or Territory government		5
Sponsorship by family or State or Territory government to regional Australia		10
Study in a regional area		5

[9.29] Additional points are allocated for attributes considered to be good indicators of the applicant's 'capacity to settle in Australia and find skilled work in their nominated occupation'.[42] Hence, bonus points are awarded for additional work experience in the applicant's nominated occupation; English language ability above the minimum threshold; qualifications in Australian or recognised overseas institutions and having a partner who also meets the threshold requirements for a skilled visa. Until 2007, an applicant could attract additional (bonus) points by lodging a deposit of AUD$100,000 in a designated security for at least 12 months.[43] Until 2010, significant credit was given also to persons nominating an occupation on the gazetted lists of occupations in particular demand (the Migration Occupations in Demand List (MODL) and the Critical Skills List (CSL)). These devices were used to identify occupations considered in short supply by the Department of Education, Employment and Workplace Relations (DEEWR). Applicants with occupations

---

42   Peter Speldewinde, DIAC, 'Practical Application of General Skilled Migration Law', paper presented at the LexisNexis Immigration Law Forum, 4 June 2007.
43   See *Balineni v MIAC* [2008] FMCA 888; *Perkit v MIAC* (2009) 109 ALD 361; *Dhanoa v MIAC* (2009) 229 FLR 317.

included on these lists used to be awarded extra points under the points test and given priority processing. Earlier versions of the test favoured applicants who were young graduates with Australian qualifications and Australian work experience. In contrast, the 2011 version favours applicants who are slightly older, who are more fluent in English, who hold higher level qualifications and who have significant work experience either in Australia or overseas. The 2011 points test no longer grants points based on whether an applicant's occupation has been identified as being in acute demand.

[9.30] The General Skilled Migration program contains specific visa classes for skilled migrants with family in Australia who plan to settle in under-populated or regional areas. Public policy objectives additional to simple employability are therefore addressed. The concessions made for these applicants previously took the form of additional points and lower pass marks. For example, while the Skilled – Independent categories tended to attract a pass mark of 120 points, the Skilled – Australian sponsored categories attracted a pass mark of 110 or 100. In 2011, the pass mark for both independent and Australian-sponsored skilled visas was set at 65 points, with no distinction in the pass mark between independent and sponsored visas. We now address the elements of the points test in more detail, turning first to the threshold criteria.

9.3.1 The Skilled Occupations List

[9.31] Across most of the skilled visa classes applicants must nominate an eligible occupation. Requiring skills and experience in select occupations makes admission contingent on the need for workers in the nominated occupation.[44] It ensures that skilled migrants will 'quickly make a contribution to the Australian economy',[45] by joining the labour force without delay.

[9.32] Where skilled migration levels were once determined having regard to broad data on employment levels, intake levels are now set having regard to need in particular sectors and even in particular jobs. This has been achieved through the publication in the federal Government Gazette of occupations deemed to be in demand. The SOL was a significant innovation introduced during the years of Coalition government. Over the years the system has been expanded to include independent, skilled family-sponsored and ENS applications. Persons who are unable to identify an occupation on one of the lists are ineligible to apply as skilled migrants to Australia. This one device has served to rationalise and synchronise the regulation of skilled migration, creating a common base on which to construct pathways from temporary to permanent visas.

[9.33] The gazettal of occupations has increased the transparency and predictability of the skilled migration scheme. At the same time, the system provides almost no scope for selecting people on the basis of their potential. It has virtually removed

---

44 Joint Standing Committee on Migration, above n 6, Ch 6 at 72.
45 DIAC, *Booklet 6, General Skilled Migration*, available at <http://www.immi.gov.au/allforms/booklets/books6.htm>.

the ability of immigration officials to work outside the rules to as to 'take a punt' on applicants.[46] At the same time, the listing of 'migration' occupations is designed ostensibly to create flexibility in the system. In cases of oversupply, occupations may simply be removed from the list. However, in fact, few changes to the list were made between its introduction in 1999 and March 2010 (when the 400 occupations on the list were slashed to 161).

[9.34] The occupations on the SOL reflect classifications devised by the Australian Bureau of Statistics and Statistics New Zealand in conjunction with Australian and New Zealand employment agencies in the publication of the *Australian and New Zealand Standard Classification of Occupations* (ANZSCO).[47] The ANZSCO Dictionary divides the 'standard' occupations in Australia into eight categories that range from managers and administrators through to labourers. Each group specifies the skill levels, university and other qualifications (from degrees through diplomas and certificates) that are prescribed for the occupation. Only occupations in the first four major groupings are regarded as skilled for migration purposes. These cover:

1. Managers;
2. Professionals;
3. Technicians and trades workers; and
4. Community and personal service workers.

Those excluded from skilled migration are persons involved in clerical activities of any kind, production, sales, transport and labouring jobs.

[9.35] The original SOL played two roles within the selection criteria. It specified occupations which were a threshold for admission as a skilled migrant, and also allocated points against occupations to be assessed in the points test. Occupations were classified into 40, 50 and 60 point categories. The top tier, designated as '60 point' occupations, required qualifications where the training was specific to that occupation. Generalist professional occupations which required degree-level qualifications but did not necessarily require training for a particular occupation were awarded 50 points. Finally, 40 points were available for generalist occupations which required diploma qualifications. Until 2010, this scheme created a hierarchy that valued professional and technical work requiring vocationally specific training above occupations relying on more general academic qualifications.

[9.36] In this form, the SOL came to attract criticism. Its basic structure was seen to produce undesirable outcomes. The Department of Employment pointed to 'considerable inconsistencies or anomalies' in the list, arguing that the high scores allocated to personnel managers, sales and marketing managers and distribution managers, and the low scores allocated to research and development managers were

---

46   Mary Crock, 'Contract or Compact: Skilled Migration and the Dictates of Politics and Ideology' in Mary Crock and Kerry Lyon (eds), *NationSkilling: Migration, Labour and the Law*, APMRN, Working Paper No 11, 2002, at 59.

47   This publication is referred to as the ANZSCO Dictionary. The predecessor dictionary covered Australian occupations only and was known as the *Australian Standard Classification of Occupations* (ASCO) (Canberra: Australian Bureau of Statistics, 2nd ed, 1997). This publication was used until 1 July 2010.

difficult to justify on 'skills or labour market grounds'.[48] This criticism was more acute in light of pass marks set at a level that largely eliminated persons without 60 point qualifications. In 2010, the Minister commented:

> I am not confident that the current test is selecting the best. For example, a Rhodes scholar would not pass the points test if he or she took a degree in chemistry or mathematics or economics. On the other hand there are several occupations – cooks and hairdressers come to mind – where international students can study in Australia, acquire qualifications in the space of 92 weeks and be on the road to permanent residence shortly thereafter.[49]

[9.37] Following a government review of the SOL in the context of the transition from ASCO to ANZSCO in 2010,[50] the Labor government introduced a dramatically remodelled SOL.[51] After seeking recommendations from an independent body, Skills Australia, the new list featured less than half the number of occupations. More significantly, the SOL no longer allocated different points depending on the classification of the occupation or the qualifications required. Instead, working in an occupation on the SOL became a threshold criterion only. The emphasis changed dramatically from one that preferenced some occupations over others, to one that treats all the occupations equally. Applicants are ranked more on the basis of their educational history, English language proficiency and work experience.

[9.38] The revised SOL from 2010 was designed to be more targeted to immediate skills shortages. It sought to complement other mechanisms introduced by the Labor government to separate the international student program from (permanent) skilled migration to Australia. The lists which service other areas of skilled migration, such as the ENS, State and Territory-sponsored and temporary skilled visa classes, were left unchanged.

9.3.2 Front end loading: Outsourcing of qualifications assessment

[9.39] The 'job-ready' status of skilled migrants is achieved by requiring anyone wishing to nominate an occupation on the SOL to demonstrate eligibility to work in the occupation *before* applying for a visa.[52] The SOL provides in tabular form both the occupations and the authorities responsible for accreditation or recognition of the relevant qualifications and experience. The pre-application skills assessment (PASA) has reduced problems with admitting migrants whose skills and qualifications are not recognised in Australia.[53]

---

48 DEWR, Submission to Standing Committee on Migration, *Review of Skilled Migration* (Canberra: November 2002) at 22.
49 Evans, above n 3.
50 DIAC, *Review of the General Skilled Migration Points Test: Discussion Paper* (Canberra: 15 February 2010).
51 Specified in the Gazette: IMMI 10/079, 5 December 2010.
52 Pre-application skills assessment (PASA) is a Sch 1 requirement for all general skilled visas.
53 See, for example, Stephen Castles et al, *The Recognition of Overseas Trade Qualifications*, (Canberra: AGPS, 1989); Bruce Chapman and Robyn Iredale, 'Immigrant Qualifications: Recognition and Relative Wage Outcomes' (1993) 27 *International Migration Review* 359; Richard Jackman, 'Employment Problems For Non-English Speaking Background Professionals' (1995) 3(4) *People and Place* 40.

[9.40] The regime outsources to private organisations the assessment of an applicant's qualifications and experience. While immigration authorities retain the power to issue or refuse skilled visas, the contentious part of the determination – the assessment of qualifications and experience – is now the province of private organisations. Their task is to determine three matters: whether a person has the qualifications required for the occupation; whether their qualifications are recognised in Australia; and whether the person's qualifications meet any registration or licensing requirements operating as prerequisites to practise the nominated occupation in Australia. The bodies regulating the trades and professions in Australia have therefore acquired great power. If an accreditation agency is not prepared to confirm that the applicant meets professional (or trade) practice criteria, the applicant is not eligible for consideration as a skilled migrant.

[9.41] The vast bulk of the assessment process is carried out by three agencies: Department of Education, Science and Training (DEST), Trades Recognition Australia (TRA) and Vocational Education and Training Assessment Services (VETASSESS). Particular occupations and professions have their own assessing bodies, however. For example, all managers are assessed through the Australian Institute of Management (AIM); legal practitioners through State or Territory legal admission boards; engineers through Engineers Australia and medical practitioners through the Australian Medical Council.

[9.42] In order to assess whether an applicant can nominate a SOL occupation, the relevant Australian assessment authority must determine which skills are appropriate for that occupation. As noted earlier, the point of reference for identifying occupations is the ANZSCO Dictionary. This provides decision-makers with a ready source of definitional rules and descriptions for classifying occupations.[54] The courts have examined the meaning of the term 'occupation' within the regulatory scheme. On the one hand, it is clear that this term refers to the employment, trade or business in which a person is habitually engaged and by which a person earns a livelihood.[55] On the other, the Full Federal Court has ruled that the word 'occupation' is not synonymous with the terms 'job' or 'position'. The inquiry is broader than one that simply focuses on the 'catalogue of duties performed for a particular employer … a comparison then being made between that catalogue and a description of duties for a particular occupation specified in [ANZSCO]'.[56] Accordingly, an applicant may have more than one 'usual occupation' arising from their qualifications and employment situations.[57]

[9.43] In *Wang v MIMA*[58] the applicant faced the problem that she had been employed in China as a University lecturer and associate professor in architecture, but sought a subclass 136 skilled visa on the basis of an occupation as 'architect'. Although she met (what was then) the ASCO Dictionary qualifications to practise as

---

54   *Parekh v MIAC* [2007] FMCA 633. Note that before 1 July 2010 the relevant reference work was the ASCO Dictionary (2nd ed). See above n 47.
55   *Morais v MILGEA* (1995) 54 FCR 498; referred to with approval in *MIMA v Hu* (1997) 79 FCR 309.
56   *MIMA v Hu* (1997) 79 FCR 309 at 322.
57   *Robel v MIMIA* [2005] FMCA 1154.
58   (2005) 145 FCR 340.

an architect, she was assessed as working in the occupation of 'university lecturer', an occupation that was not on the SOL. The Federal Court could find no error in the approach taken by the decision-maker, ruling that there was no scope for going outside the ASCO definition of architect. Madgwick J noted that:

> The entire structure of the relevant criteria appears to be to minimise qualitative arguments ... The avoidance of difficult and imprecise qualitative judgments in the assessment of immigrant applications must be regarded as being in the interests of the Australian community.[59]

[9.44] In large measure, the PASA scheme has been designed to increase government control over the administrative process, by closing off avenues of judicial review in relation to key aspects of the decision under consideration. Because the reviewing bodies are mostly private corporations, decisions made by them are excluded from the framework of administrative law review. In *Silveira v Australian Institute of Management*,[60] the Federal Court held that a decision made by an assessment body such as the Australian Institute of Management was not a 'decision under an enactment' for the purposes of the *Administrative Decisions (Judicial Review) Act 1977* (Cth). As a result the court had no jurisdiction to review the decision on grounds such as relevancy, reasonableness or denial of procedural fairness. Ms Silveira's remedy might reside in a contractual claim, but administrative law could provide no relief.[61]

[9.45] Since January 2010, skilled applicants relying on their Australian trade qualifications must undertake an additional four-step skills assessment, known as the Job Ready Program, administered by TRA.[62] Applicants must complete 12 months' full-time employment in their nominated trade with an Australian employer, who must log the applicant's competencies or 'job readiness'. Along with other reforms announced in 2010, this scheme was designed to prevent international students from using the acquisition of paper qualifications to access permanent residence, and to prevent shady educational bodies marketing their services accordingly. Peter Mares notes:

> There is a great irony here. Australia has marketed itself to the world as the purveyor of high-quality education and training, yet it now has so little faith in the quality of the vocational sector of this industry that international graduates must go through a rigorous and expensive new assessment system – one that does not apply to domestic graduates of the very same courses.[63]

9.3.3 Work experience in Australia and overseas

[9.46] Work experience operates as a minimum threshold and may also attract additional points according to length of previous work and/or work experience

---

59   Ibid at [15] and [20]. See also *Jushi v MIAC* [2005] FMCA 1116.
60   (2001) 113 FCR 218.
61   See further Chapter 5.4.2.
62   A requirement for Skilled – Independent visa (subclass 885), Skilled – Sponsored visa (subclass 886) and Skilled – Regional Sponsored (Provisional) visa (subclass 487).
63   Peter Mares, 'From Queue to Pool: Skilled Migration Gets a Makeover' *Inside Story*, 10 February 2010, available at <http://inside.org.au/skilled-migration-gets-a-makeover>.

in Australia. Since November 2007, all offshore skilled visa applicants have had to be employed for 12 out of the previous 24 months in an occupation on the SOL.[64] Extra points have been available for work experience both overseas and in Australia. The 2011 points test significantly increased recognition given to extensive work experience either in Australia or overseas. Work experience undertaken must be 'legitimate' or 'genuine' and may be subject to verification by Department integrity officers.[65] Applicants must have been employed at a 'post qualification' skill level and must show they were actually employed in the capacity of their nominated skilled occupation rather than merely using skills relevant to the occupation or undertaking relevant tasks.[66] What is relevant is whether the applicant has been employed in the occupation that the applicant submitted for this purpose – not whether the applicant has been employed in any other occupation.[67]

[9.47] The word 'employed' is defined as 'engaged in an occupation for remuneration for at least 20 hours weekly'.[68] This means that limited work experience on student visas (which typically contain a condition of a maximum 20 hours work per week during semester) may not assist an applicant for a skilled visa. Students cannot circumvent this requirement by claiming that work done in excess of 20 hours per week was performed for a foreign employer through remote communications.[69] Before 2007, overseas students applying for permanent residence within six months of completing their course were exempt from the work experience threshold. When this exemption was abolished, the concept of 'a professional year' was introduced.[70] This sought to alleviate some hardship experienced by international students facing a tightening of the English language and work experience requirements when they came to apply for permanent residency on the basis of their newly minted Australian qualifications. It was also designed to address the broader perception that migrant students were not sufficiently 'job ready' at the time of their applications for residency.

9.3.4 English language proficiency

[9.48] The correlation shown between English language proficiency and labour market participation has led to an increased emphasis over the years on language

---

64 This represents a significant streamlining of the minimum requirements pertaining to skilled visas since previously the points available for work experience were tiered according to whether the nominated skilled occupation was gazetted as accruing 60 points or less.
65 See *071750949* [2009] MRTA 199.
66 See *Shahid v MIMIA* [2004] FCA 1412, where the applicant attempted unsuccessfully to argue that the performance of duties relevant to an occupation could be counted in an assessment. As well as failing to demonstrate employment (at all) for the requisite period, the applicant fell short because he had been acting in a trainee position only. See also *0800741* [2008] MRTA 1425 for discussion of the distinction between work as an employee as opposed to work as an independent contractor; and *MIAC v Kamruzzaman* (2009) 112 ALD 550.
67 *Biswas v MIAC* [2009] FMCA 95, dealing with the spouse skills qualification in the points test. See also *0800016* [2009] MRTA 1024.
68 *Migration Regulations*, reg 2.26A(7).
69 *De Ronde v MIMIA* (2004) 188 FLR 266. See also *Fan v MIAC* (2010) 240 FLR 318.
70 The Skilled – Graduate (Temporary) visa (subclass 485) allows overseas students who do not meet the criteria for a permanent skilled visa to remain in Australia for 18 months with no restrictions on work or study.

fluency as a precondition for the grant of skilled visas.[71] Mandatory pre-migration language testing has been required in a range of professions since the 1980s. Testing was expanded by the Labor government in 1993, following the peak in unemployment of migrants of non-English speaking backgrounds during the 1991-93 recession.[72] The Coalition government extended language testing to virtually all professions in 1999.[73]

[9.49] Having said this, until July 2004, English language testing was waived for onshore applicants with Australian qualifications. These people were deemed to be 'competent' in English without sitting a test. Evidence that many of these applicants were not in fact sufficiently fluent in English precipitated a policy change. One of the reasons many students were unable to demonstrate strong English language skills was that a large number of overseas students were coming to Australia on packages that included preliminary Foundation Year or high school level courses. These did not require the students to achieve the minimum competent English standard required for persons seeking a student visa for direct entry into a university course.[74]

[9.50] Successive governments have moved to reduce non-English speaking migrants' access to the Australian labour market, in what has been described as 'a shift from altruism to pragmatism'.[75] Ability in the English language is now a threshold criterion across virtually all of the skilled migration and ENS programs, as well as a source of additional points under the skilled points test. From 1 September 2007, English language proficiency was required for the PASA in all but two visa categories.[76] English language requirements have been steadily increased across the spectrum of skilled visas.

[9.51] Skilled migrants are required to undertake one of two types of tests. In most health occupations (such as nursing), applicants are required to undertake an 'Occupational English Test' (OET) as part of the assessment of formal qualifications and experience.[77] The most common tests, however, are conducted under the International English Language Test System (IELTS). Tests have four components: reading, listening, writing and speaking.

---

71   Data from the Longitudinal Survey shows a correlation between skilled migrants' self-assessed proficiency in English and the extent to which they are employed and the frequency with which they use their qualifications in their employment. See Birrell et al, above n 6, at 83, 89-90. This is the most recent among over a decade of research findings as to the differentiated experiences of immigrant workers from English and non-English speaking backgrounds. See, for example, Clive Brooks and Lynne Williams, *Immigrants and the Labour Market: The 1990-1994 Recession and Recovery in Perspective* (Canberra: AGPS, 1995).
72   Lesleyanne Hawthorne, 'English Language Testing and Immigration Policy' in Geoff Brindley and Gillian Wigglesworth (eds), *Access: Issues in Language Test Design and Delivery* (Sydney: National Centre for English Language Teaching and Research, Macquarie University, 1997).
73   With the revised points test, 'vocational' scores in English had to be demonstrated pre-arrival in all four English language skills – a major departure from the pre-1999 selection policy. See *Migration Regulations*, reg 1.19, Sch 6, Part 3.
74   Birrell et al, above n 6, at 34-5.
75   Lesleyanne Hawthorne, '"Picking Winners": The Recent Transformation of Australia's Skilled Migration Policy' (2005) 39(3) *International Migration Review* 663.
76   In the 485 Skilled – Graduate and 487 Skilled – Regional Sponsored visa subclasses, language proficiency needs to be demonstrated at the time of decision only, which means that applicants can undertake the relevant language tests after they lodge their application for a visa.
77   See generally <http://oet.com.au/>.

[9.52] The *Migration Regulations 1994* (Cth) set six levels of English proficiency, each based on IELTS or OET tests undertaken not more than two years before the date of a visa application. At the top end, a new standard of 'Superior English' was introduced with the 2011 points test announced in November 2010, requiring a score of at least 8 in each of the four components of the IELTS test. With its heightened emphasis on English language ability, the new points test awarded 20 points for Superior English language ability. 'Proficient English' is defined in reg 1.15D as a score of at least 7 in each of the four IELTS test components. 'Competent English' is defined in reg 1.15C as a score of 6 in the IELTS test and is a prerequisite for most of the skilled visa subclasses. Exceptions were previously made for the trades (ANZSCO Band 4 occupations) where the requirement used to be 'vocational English', defined in reg 1.15B as an average IELTS score of 5 across the four IELTS components. The exemption for trades occupations was removed in January 2010. 'Concessional competent English', defined in reg 1.15E as an average IELTS score of 5.5, was previously the minimum required for Skilled – Regional Sponsored (Provisional) applicants (other than those nominating a trade as their occupation).[78] However, these visa subclasses are now also required to attain at minimum an average score of 6.[79] Finally, 'functional English' is defined in reg 5.17 and Sch 6, cl 6311, as an average band score of 4.5. This category is used in relation to secondary visa applicants to determine liability to pay a 'second instalment visa application charge' (which is effectively an English language training levy).

[9.53] Until 1 September 2007 there had been provision in some cases to waive English language testing on the basis that the testing is 'not necessary' or 'not reasonably practicable'. Decision-makers could make their own assessment of the applicant's English proficiency.[80] Relevant factors for consideration included the fact that the applicant had been awarded an Australian degree in respect of which the language of instruction was English.[81] The Federal Magistrates Court ruled in 2009 that a decision to refuse a skilled visa would be infected by legal error if the decision-maker did not consider exercising this discretion where relevant.[82] It was presumably in anticipation of this approach that the discretion to waive testing was removed in 2007.

[9.54] The present system marks a significant prioritisation of English language ability. Applicants with passports from certain predominantly English speaking countries are exempt from sitting an English language test in order to meet the threshold standard but must submit to language testing to prove linguistic proficiency qualifying for additional points.[83] It remains to be seen whether the insistence on high levels of English competency as both a threshold and advantage for points

---

78 See subclasses 475 and 487.
79 This change was introduced for applicants for the offshore Skilled – Regional Sponsored (subclass 475) visa from 1 July 2009 and for the onshore Skilled – Regional Sponsored (subclass 487) visa from 1 January 2010.
80 *Migration Regulations*, reg 2.26A(5) and, for Vocational English, reg 1.15B.
81 *Hossain v MIAC* [2009] FMCA 405.
82 Ibid. See also *Surinakova v MILGEA* (1991) 33 FCR 87.
83 Persons holding passports issued by the United Kingdom, USA, Canada, Ireland and New Zealand are deemed to have 'competent English'.

tested applicants will reinstate the privilege historically accorded to British and New Zealand migrants.

9.3.5 Local versus overseas qualifications

[9.55] Allocating additional points for people trained in Australia was a major feature of the 1999 scheme. The initiative reflected concerns on the part of employers at the time of the 'knowledge economy' boom in the late 1990s that Australia was suffering from severe skills shortages (particularly in accounting and computing). As many of the overseas students in Australia were being trained in these fields, it was argued that they should be given priority in the selection of skilled migrants.[84] The students were given further incentives to seek permanent residence within six months of completing their courses. Visa subclasses were created in 2001 allowing students to apply for permanent residence without having to leave Australia at the conclusion of their studies. By 2004-05, the Skilled – Independent category was dominated by young, onshore applicants, many of whom were former students. The points test was altered again in 2007 to reward more highly those applicants who had completed advanced degrees in Australia. By the time the Labor government came to power in 2007, the benefits of transitioning international students into skilled migrants were outweighed by negative factors. These included perceived abuses of the system and poor labour market outcomes. The 2011 points test takes a significantly different approach to the points awarded for local qualifications. Previously, points were awarded for Australian qualifications only. The 2011 version awards significantly more points for more advanced qualifications whether gained in Australia or overseas. Some recognition remains for two years of full-time Australian study, but the points granted are marginal.

9.3.6 Migration Occupations in Demand and other skills shortages lists

[9.56] Between 1999 and 2010, preference was given to individuals with experience who were eligible to work in an occupation deemed to be 'in demand'. The gazetted MODL (introduced in 1999) and the CSL (introduced in 2009) itemised occupations which were considered by the Department of Employment (in its various incarnations) to be experiencing skill shortages across Australia. For a brief period, these lists were supplemented by a list specific to the Sydney region, known as the Sydney and Surrounding Areas Skills Shortages List (SSASSL). In each instance, the lists were compiled using information provided by industry groups and employers, considered in conjunction with statistical information on demand and supply trends in the Australian workplace.[85] An applicant whose occupation was included on one of these lists could qualify for 'bonus' points of up to 16 per cent of the total points necessary to satisfy the points test. Nomination of an occupation in demand had to have been done at the time of application. If the occupation was not listed at that time,

---

84 Birrell et al, above n 6.
85 DEEWR, *Skill Shortage Methodology*, available at <http://www.deewr.gov.au/Employment/LMI/SkillShortages/Documents/MethodologyPaper.pdf>.

or was deleted from the list by the time the application was assessed, the applicant was not entitled to the bonus points.[86] Nor did the addition of an occupation to one of the lists after lodgement of an application entitle the applicant to bonus points.[87]

[9.57] The plunge in labour demand that attended the global economic crisis of 2008 prompted the Labor government to reconsider its priorities. A review of the MODL, jointly conducted by DEEWR and DIAC,[88] resulted in the complete abolition of that list in February 2010, and of the CSL shortly thereafter. This signalled an attempt to re-shape the SOL as a prospective rather than retrospective articulation of occupations likely to needed in Australia in the medium term, using a 3-5 year time frame.[89] For the first time, government policy was that labour shortages should be met by employer sponsorship rather than through government regulation of entry criteria. Many holding student visas, who had planned to apply for permanent residence, found their expectations thwarted. The fortunes of many educational institutions that had catered to the student market also declined.

9.3.7 Regional migration initiatives

[9.58] The total number of Skilled visa grants for 2008-09 was 114,777. Of these, 33,474 places were allocated to State-specific and regional migration programs, an increase of 28 per cent on the previous year of 26,162. This outcome represented 29.2 per cent of the total Skill Stream in 2008-09.[90] The theory behind promoting migration to regional Australia and to low population growth metropolitan areas is to 'reduce regional inequality and enhance all-round prosperity' so that those areas can be competitive and continue to grow.[91] The revised scheme reflects concerns on the part of some States that Australia's migration settlement has been favouring the larger metropolitan centres, particularly Sydney.[92] In spite of these initiatives to encourage regional migration, perceptions have persisted that migrants who gain residence on the basis of regional concessions show poor labour market outcomes. The desirability of promoting regional growth seems to stand in constant conflict with the challenge to ensure the immediate employability of migrants.

[9.59] A variety of mechanisms have been adopted to address local labour market needs and tailor the skilled migration program to regional development. The first is the awarding of additional points under the general points tests for skilled visas to applicants who have lived and studied full time for at least two years in a regional or

---

86   *Aomatsu v MIMIA* (2005) 146 FCR 58; and *Akbar v MIAC* [2009] FMCA 279. See also, for example, *Q05/05585* [2005] MRTA 1154.
87   See *061034333* [2008] MRTA 142.
88   DEEWR and DIAC, *Select Skills: Principles for a New Migration Occupation in Demand List; Review of the Migration Occupations in Demand List*, Issues Paper No 1, August 2009; DEEWR and DIAC, *Future Skills: Targeting High Value Skills Through the General Skilled Migration Program; Review of the Migration Occupations in Demand List*, Issues Paper No 2, September 2009.
89   DEEWR and DIAC, Issues Paper No 2, ibid, at 9.
90   See DIAC, *Report on Migration Program 2008-2009*, at 11.
91   Glen Withers and Marion Powall, *Immigration and the Regions: Taking Regional Australia Seriously* (Canberra: The Chifley Institute, 2003) at 3.
92   Joint Standing Committee on Migration, *New Faces, New Places, Review of State Specific Migration Mechanisms* (Canberra: Commonwealth of Australia, 2001) at 4.

low growth metropolitan part of Australia and obtained an Australian qualification from certain educational institutions with regional campuses. The provision for these additional points was inserted into the Regulations on 1 July 2003. The revised points test of 2011 retained this concession.

[9.60] A further initiative to promote migration to regional areas is the Skilled – Regional Sponsored visa (subclasses 487 and 475). These visas are open to applicants who are sponsored by a State or Territory government under a State Migration Plan or by a relative who lives in certain regions of Australia. Designated by Gazette Notice, these cover rural and regional areas as well as some low population growth metropolitan areas. The various familial relationships which give rise to the sponsorship have been given a broad reading, including relationships by biology, adoption and marriage.[93] The development of State Migration Plans was announced in February 2010. These Memoranda of Understanding between individual States and Territories and the Minister for Immigration allow States and Territories to nominate skilled applicants under occupations required to fill skill shortages within their local labour markets. The Plans specify the eligible occupations and the number of visas that are available under this scheme. While State and Territory governments have had the capacity to nominate applicants for Skilled – Sponsored and Skilled – Regional Sponsored visas for some time, the Migration Plan scheme aims to streamline this process and give it transparency. The intention is that States and Territories may nominate only applicants whose occupation is on the Plan, with some very limited exceptions.[94]

[9.61] Another source of State-wide concessions were the 'Skills Matching' visas that were available between 1997 and 2007.[95] The subclass 134 visa was not points tested. It was offered to applicants who consented to having their details included on the Department's Skills Matching Database when they applied for a (points tested) skilled visa. If the applicant fell short of the pass mark under the points test but was assessed as meeting the (lower) pool entry mark, the application was retained ('in the pool') for two years. A visa could be granted at any time during this period if an employer or State or Territory government nominated the applicant on the basis of their skills. In spite of English language concessions and the waiving of work experience requirements, the visa subclass attracted very few migrants and was cut in September 2007.

[9.62] In addition, the Skilled State/Territory Nominated Independent (subclass 137) visa (STNI) allowed approved State/Territory government agencies to nominate applicants who had met the pool mark on the general points test and expressed interest (through the respective State websites) in being considered for nomination by the State. While more popular than the Skills Matching visa, the STNI was not tied to a job offer and succeeded only in recruiting migrants to the sponsoring State

---

93 *Liang v MIAC* (2007) 220 FLR 1; and *Mercado v MIAC* [2007] FMCA 1216. See also Hodges Report, *Review of the Independent and Skilled-Australian Linked Categories* (Canberra: AGPS, 1999).
94 DIAC, *Fact Sheet: State Migration Plans*, 3 November 2010.
95 Other non-points tested regional skilled visas included Skilled Designated Area Sponsored (subclasses 139 and 882) visas which have also been phased out.

rather than a specific regional area.[96] This was also abolished with the rationalisation of skilled visas in 2007.

9.4 Employer nomination

[9.63] The Employer Nomination Scheme (ENS) allows employers to nominate skilled employees for permanent residence in Australia. As noted earlier, this program was given increased priority after the election of the Labor government in 2007.[97] Employer sponsored migration is favoured because it ensures that migrants obtain immediate employment where their skills are most required. The Department, here, defers to employers who are thought to be in the best position to identify 'the skills they need'. The ENS process has three stages. First, the employer must be approved as a sponsor; second, the employer must have the nominated position approved. Only then can the nominee proceed with an application for an ENS visa.

9.4.1 The employer's approval as sponsor

[9.64] The conditions placed on employers are not as onerous as they once were; employers are no longer required to prove that they cannot find a local employee to work in a nominated position. The introduction of gazetted lists in this area of skilled migration in 2005 replaced the earlier requirements that employers undertake labour market testing through the placement of job advertisements.[98] However, the nominating employer must show that he or she has provided training to existing employees in the business, and that the nominated employee will enjoy pay and working conditions no less favourable than those provided under relevant Australian legislation and awards. The nominating employer must also demonstrate a satisfactory record of compliance with immigration and workplace relations laws. In particular, the employer must not have an adverse business or employment record or be subject to a bar on sponsorship imposed pursuant to s 140L of the Act.

[9.65] The local employee training commitment is designed to demonstrate that a nominating employer is not overly reliant on importing skilled labour from overseas. A flexible approach has been taken to the training requirement, with evidence accepted of different types of training schemes. In *Masuoka v IRT*,[99] the Full Federal Court ruled that the adequacy of the training depends on the characteristics of the employer's business, in particular, the nature, number and type of employees. In that case, the employer was a highly specialised small Japanese restaurant. Evidence was given from other Japanese restaurateurs and the staff that continuous on-the-job training and supervision were the norm for enterprises of this nature.

---

96   Birrell et al, above n 6, at 62.
97   One in five of the 171,318 migrants in 2008-09 was sponsored by an employer: 'Employer-backed migration is surging', *The Australian*, 31 August 2009.
98   So-called 'labour market testing' was removed as a requirement for ENS visas on 1 July 2005.
99   (1996) 67 FCR 492 at 496. See also *Nice Shoes Aust Pty Ltd v MIMIA* [2004] FCA 252; *MM International (Australia) Pty Ltd v MIMIA* [2004] FCAFC 323; and *Shao v MIMIA* [2005] FCA 478.

9.4.2 The nominated position

[9.66] The nominated position must be full time, available for three years and correspond to an occupation on the ENS Skilled Occupation List (ENSOL).[100] The tasks of any position nominated by an employer must correspond to a gazetted occupation. The ENSOL includes some occupations that are not on the general skilled migration SOL such as religious workers, academic and some occupations in the arts. A minimum salary level is applicable and in most instances employees are required to undergo a skills assessment.[101] In respect of employers seeking migrants to work in occupations other than those on the ENSOL, labour agreements may be negotiated between an employer or an industry association, relevant unions, and the Commonwealth, represented by DIAC and the DEEWR. The labour agreement is a negotiated agreement where all parties agree that a certain number of employees with specific skills should be recruited to fill a defined set of vacancies.

[9.67] A series of legislative reforms, culminating in April 2005, served to align the requirements for ENS visas more closely with the requirements for the 457 visa (see Chapter 10).[102] The gazetted occupations and employer obligations in each of these schemes are now substantially similar. In 2008-09, 30,656 ENS applications were lodged, an increase of 60 per cent over the previous year. The growth in demand reflects the increasing tendency to use the 457 visa category as a pathway to permanent residence.[103]

9.4.3 The nominated employee

[9.68] The employee visa applicant must satisfy separate criteria for the grant of an ENS visa. The applicant must be nominated by the employer for the appointment.[104] Unless exceptional circumstances apply, he or she must be under 45 years of age at the time of application and have vocational English[105] skills. In addition, applicants must undergo formal skills assessment by the relevant assessing body in Australia and have three years' post-training experience in the gazetted skilled occupation. Exceptions are made in circumstances where the visa applicant can demonstrate:

(1) work in the nominated occupation full time for the previous two years while holding a temporary visa in Australia; and
(2) work in the nominated position for the nominating employer for at least the previous one year; and

---

100 Specified in the Gazette IMMI 10/089, 5 December 2010.
101 See *Migration Regulations*, reg 5.19(2); and Sch 2, cll 121.211(b)(ii) and 121.211(b)(i)(A); and 856.213(b)(ii) and 856.213(b)(i)(A). Gazette IMMI 10/089, 5 December 2010, specifies salaries of $47,480 for all of the occupations listed in that notice.
102 Changes were introduced by the *Migration Amendment Regulations 2005 (No 1)* (Cth).
103 See DIAC, *Report on Migration Program 2008-2009*, at 9.
104 It is imperative that the employer's nomination has been approved before consideration of the visa application: *Kim v MIMIA* [2005] FMCA 1699.
105 See above Part 9.3.4.

(3) nomination for a highly paid position with a base salary specified in the ENSOL (currently $250,000 per year);[106] or
(4) the nominated position is so 'exceptional' that a waiver of usual requirements relating to age, English language proficiency and work experience is warranted.

[9.69] The term 'exceptional' is not defined in the legislation, and has been interpreted to mean 'unusual' or 'out of the ordinary'.[107] Departmental policy stipulates that the work experience requirement may be waived if the applicant or employer has shown that the position is so unusual or highly specialised that it is unlikely that a suitable person in Australia or overseas with three years' work experience could be found to fill the vacancy. Exceptional circumstances may be considered on age grounds where the applicant is under 50 years old; the position is essential to the operation of the business; and it is established that it is not possible to find a suitably qualified younger person. Where the applicant is between 50 and 55 years old, the nominated occupation must be in ANZSCO group 1, 2 or 3 and the position must be so unusual or highly specialised that it is not possible to find a suitably qualified younger person. Where the applicant is between 55 and 59 years old, the position must be in ANZSCO group 1 or 2. The occupation must normally require a person with skills and experience acquired over many years and be so unusual or highly specialised that it is not possible to find a suitably qualified younger person. Departmental policy does not generally accept that 'exceptional circumstances' exist for applicants over 59 years.

[9.70] The English language requirement may also be waived in exceptional circumstances. These may be shown where the position is such that it is not essential for the applicant to have vocational English in order to transfer their skills to the Australian workforce or train other workers. Indicia relevant to this determination include the nature of the work to be performed; how the applicant will transfer their skills to Australian employees; how the applicant will comply with occupational health and safety standards; and whether efforts have been made to recruit a suitably qualified person who has the requisite English skills.[108] Courts have ruled that the 'exceptional appointment' criteria concern the *position* that the employer needs to fill, not the characteristics of the person who is proposing to fill that position.[109] The determination of whether an approved appointment is exceptional should be made independently of the decision on an application for a visa, during the course of determining the employer's application for approval of an appointment.[110]

[9.71] The English language requirements are supposed to ensure that ENS applicants are not only highly skilled but that they are also able to transfer their skills to the Australians with whom they work. Concerns about occupational health

---

106 IMMI 10/089, 5 December 2010. Note that an employer's indication of its 'willingness' to pay the higher base salary is not sufficient. See *071410355* [2008] MRTA 304.
107 *An v MIAC* (2007) 160 FCR 480, applied in *0802770* [2009] MRTA 346. See also *Li v MIAC* [2010] FMCA 583 and *Mulwala Golden Inn Restaurant Pty Ltd and Zhu v MIAC* [2010] FMCA 228.
108 See PAM3, cl 28.4.
109 *Li Tian v MIAC* (2008) 220 FLR 139.
110 *Tian v MIAC* (2008) 174 FCR 1, citing *An v MIAC* (2007) 160 FCR 480.

and safety compliance also drives the English language requirements.[111] The MRT has considered the scope of such 'exceptional' appointments. In one matter, exemption from the vocational English standard was sought in an application for an ENS for a chef in a residence for people with psychiatric and intellectual disabilities.[112] The tribunal found the circumstances exceptional, considering the nature of the employment duties, the fact that the applicant had already transferred his skills to the Australians with whom he worked (on a temporary visa), and the great difficulty faced by the employer in finding and retaining an Australian chef for the job. In two other cases, the tribunal ruled appointments exceptional for the purposes of the English requirement, finding that all of the responsibilities and duties of a tiler did not require functional English. In both cases the applicants played a pivotal role in the company business through their own contributions and the skills they passed on to subordinate staff. The tribunal also took account of the difficulties the employers had experienced in recruiting qualified tilers in Australia.[113]

[9.72] Whether these cases represent good authority, however, is doubtful in light of a Full Federal Court decision regarding a South Korean toy designer. With minimal if any English language skills, the applicant sought an ENS visa based on his position in a manufacturing workplace wholly staffed by other South Koreans. By majority, the Full Court upheld a decision to reject his application. The court endorsed departmental policy that an appointment is not rendered exceptional by the circumstance that other persons in the workplace speak the applicant's language. According to Lindgren J, '[s]uch a view would tend to facilitate the perpetuation of foreign language workplaces, contrary to the policy underlying the [English language] requirement'.[114] In dissent, Finkelstein J considered that a position may be unusual where 'the ability to speak English is, for all practical purposes, useless both at the present time and in the foreseeable future'.[115] More recent tribunal decisions have found against the existence of 'exceptional circumstances', citing the majority view of the Full Court.[116]

9.5 Distinguished Talent visas

[9.73] In addition to the General Skilled Migration Program for importing skills into Australia, there is a highly selective scheme for admitting people each year who can demonstrate that they possess 'distinguished talents'. In 2009-10, only 208 people (including family members) entered under this category.[117]

---

111 Note that these exemptions have been criticised on the basis that poor English language skills are making these migrants disproportionately liable to workplace injuries. See Joanna Howe, 'The Migration Legislation Amendment (Worker Protection) Act 2008: Long Overdue Reform, But Have Migrant Workers Been Sold Short?' (2010) 23 *Australian Journal of Labour Law* 251.
112 *Wen Zhou Xie* [2005] MRTA 140.
113 *071275442* [2007] MRTA 376 and *N05/04771* [2006] MRTA 309.
114 *An v MIAC* (2007) 160 FCR 480 at [30] (Lindgren J, with whom Emmett J agreed).
115 Ibid at [118].
116 For example, *0802770* [2009] MRTA 346; *0801708* [2009] MRTA 123; *071937828* [2008] MRTA 1360.
117 DIAC, 'Permanent Additions to the Resident Population', *Immigration Update 2009-2010*, December 2010, at 8.

[9.74] The Distinguished Talent visa category is for people who have a recognised record of exceptional achievement in their profession, the arts or a sport, or in academia and research. On 1 November 2003, the Regulations were amended to require that the applicant must have an *internationally recognised* record of exceptional *and outstanding* achievement. Policy guidelines interpret this re-formulation to require that the applicant's achievements have or would be acclaimed as exceptional and outstanding in any country where the relevant field is practised.[118] Applicants must demonstrate that they are still prominent in the area, would be an asset to the Australian community and would have no difficulty obtaining employment or becoming established independently in Australia in their field. Before 2003, applications could be made with or without the support of an Australian who is also prominent in the applicant's field of endeavour. Since that time, however, nomination by an Australian person or organisation is mandatory. The nominator must still have a national reputation in the visa applicant's occupation, profession or field.

[9.75] There was some judicial consideration of the requirements for the Distinguished Talent visa before the 2003 changes. The standard required was set as (at least) 'achievement which significantly surpasses that of the general run of those engaged in the relevant professional occupational pursuit'.[119] In *Gaffar v MIMA*,[120] French J held:

> The requirement of an exceptional standard of achievement in an occupation, profession or activity is to be applied across a variety of occupations, professions and activities. Some will require far greater levels of knowledge and skill than others in order to rise above the ordinary and merely competent. And while the applicant for such a visa is required to be an 'asset to the Australian community' it is not required that he or she be a 'national living treasure' ... The criterion requires a demonstrated excellence in the relevant occupation which is out of the ordinary.

At the same time, judicial dicta indicate that the 'record' of achievement need not be quantifiable as large or lengthy or sustained over a period of time.[121] On the other hand, the applicant must have a record to sustain the application: outstanding *potential* is not sufficient.[122]

[9.76] If the applicant is under 18 or over 54 years of age at the time of application, she or he must show that she would be of exceptional benefit to the Australian community. Departmental policy has indicated that the reference to the Australian community 'is to be interpreted in terms of Australia as a whole and not just local community in geographic terms or a particular social, cultural or business community in Australia'.[123] This policy has been criticised for impermissibly importing the words 'as a whole'. It would appear to suffice that the person is of exceptional benefit within the person's area of particular expertise in Australia.[124]

---

118   PAM3, 6.2, as applied in *W04/07318* [2006] MRTA 82 and *0800801* [2009] MRTA 463.
119   *Minh Son Do v MIMA* [2002] FCA 1081.
120   (2000) 59 ALD 421 at [20].
121   *Zhang v MIMA* [2007] FMCA 664.
122   *071945992* [2009] MRTA 23.
123   PAM3 cl 6.1, on *Migration Regulations*, Sch 2, cl 124.211(2)(c).
124   *Wolseley v MIMA* [2006] FMCA 1149.

9.6 Business skills migration

[9.77] Business migrants have made valuable contributions to the Australian economy over many years and for this reason have traditionally been promoted by the Department as 'model' migrants. In 2002, government figures showed that in the decade following the introduction of the business skills category in 1992, 86 per cent of business migrants had become engaged in business within three years of arrival; 77 per cent of these in new businesses enterprises. Each such business employed an average staff of five; and 64 per cent were involved in exports. The average sum invested in each business was $600,000.[125] However, by 2008 it had become clear that the fiscal benefits of business migrants over time were significantly less than those represented by independent and sponsored skilled migrants. The net operating surplus per 1000 migrants entering in 2006-07 forecast for business skills migrants was $6 million in Year 1 and $5.1 million in Year 20. For Skilled – Independent migrants the figures were $5.8 million in Year 1 and $12.3 million in Year 20.[126] The fact that business skills migrants represent a less lucrative option than independent skilled migrants reflects the fact that these migrants tend to be older, with more dependants and inferior English language ability. These realities have seen increasing safeguards introduced to ensure the 'quality' of applicants under the business migration scheme.

[9.78] The business migration visa categories were among the first to road test a two-stage visa process whereby applicants must enter first as temporary migrants before seeking permanent status. The policy initiative reflected a more sophisticated understanding of business enterprises; the times frames that are needed to establish a business and the indicators that will often determine success or failure. The probationary visa scheme sought to prepare temporary migrants for permanent reception into the Australian labour force. Versions of this two-stage process have since emerged across Australia's migration program. In 2007, an 18-month Skilled Graduate visa provided overseas students with further work or study rights in Australia to enhance their prospects of gaining permanent residence. Indeed, Partner visas in the family migration program are granted in provisional form before permanent residence is afforded two years later (see Chapter 7.2.1).

[9.79] The number of visas issued in the business skills scheme has been small relative to the overall skilled migration intake. In 2008-09 the net outcome for the business skills program was 7397. Although just below planning levels, this represented a 13 per cent increase on the 2007-08 outcome of 6565.[127] Of this total intake, over 96 per cent were visas issued to State or Territory sponsored migrants.[128] While the business skills category remains a small feature in Australia's overall economic migration program, it is clear that the importation of foreign expertise and capital will play an increasingly important role in the overall strategy for bolstering Australia's economic performance. Whether this will occur through the business skills program,

---

125 Philip Ruddock, 'Australian Immigration: Grasping the New Reality' in Crock and Lyon, above n 46, at 13.
126 Access Economics, above n 6, at 26.
127 DIAC, *Report on Migration Program: 2008-09*, at 11.
128 DIAC, *Population Flows: Immigration Aspects 2008-2009*, May 2010, at 39.

the General Skilled Migration program or through employer nomination remains to be seen.

9.6.1 The early history of business migration

[9.80] In attempts to attract wealth to the country, the government has experimented over time with some very atypical selection mechanisms, at one point coming close to deliberately *relinquishing* control of selection. In 1987-88, a scheme was designed to facilitate business migration through the offices of 'Accredited Business Migration Agents'. These agents were authorised to assess, counsel and process applicants in the business migration program. The agents acted as a conduit through which applications were channelled to the Department for fast-track processing. The system was designed to take advantage of expertise in the private sector to both attract and assess potential migrants. However, in 1991, the Commonwealth Parliament's Joint Committee of Public Accounts recorded a number of crucial faults in the scheme. It recommended that the Department reassert control over admissions. As a result, the scheme was replaced in February 1992 by a new business skills category which was subject to its own points test. The Business Skills Assessment Panel was created with two functions: assessing applications and reporting to the government on how well the scheme was operating.

[9.81] One of the main problems with the early business skills schemes was the stringency of the criteria applied to business applicants. This was evidenced by the small number of business visas granted between 17 February 1992 (when the business skills scheme began) and 31 January 1994: only 1148 people were approved for entry.[129] In 1994, the Business Skills Assessment Panel recommended that a longer view be taken in assessing the merits of business migration. It emphasised the contribution that business migrants made in internationalising Australian business and the need to build bridges into the Asia-Pacific region to enhance Australia's long-term investment prospects.

[9.82] The Panel's recommendations, and the resulting changes to the program, signalled a return to a more flexible set of selection criteria. Three sets of points tests allowed for business skills attributes to be assessed according to broader criteria. Instead of looking just at the nature and size of the business, the points tests looked at the financial turnover of the business, its labour costs and its total assets. Another major innovation was the introduction of categories permitting investment-based migration and change of status for onshore business people.

9.6.2 The business migration regime after 2003

[9.83] The business skills visa classes were significantly overhauled again on 1 March 2003. The changes to the business program were motivated by the desire to achieve 'a better dispersal of business migrants', to 'increase [the number of

---

[129] See Business Skills Assessment Panel, *Migration of Business People to Australia: Directions for Change* (Canberra: DIEA, 1994) at 65.

business migrants] who successfully engage in business' and to 'address integrity concerns'.[130]

[9.84] Business migration is now subject mostly to a two-stage process, where a majority of business skills applicants must first obtain a temporary (provisional) visa. Only after a minimum of two years, and often up to four years, can an applicant apply for a permanent business visa. At this point satisfactory evidence must be provided of a specified level of business or investment activity in Australia. Exceptions are made only for certain high calibre business people and migrants in Australia on temporary visas who own or part-own an Australian business. Points tests for business skills visas have been abolished, with the exception of the State/Territory-sponsored and unsponsored Established Business in Australia classes.[131]

[9.85] Provisional Business Skills visa subclasses confer up to four years' temporary residence on prospective business migrants. After two years, provisional visa holders are eligible to apply for permanent residence, if they have operated a business, or conducted investment activity in Australia and achieved certain minimum business activity targets. Within each category of the provisional visa (Business Owner, Senior Executive and Investor) there are subclasses for people who apply independently and subclasses for people who are sponsored by Australian State or Territory government regional authorities.[132]

[9.86] Permanent visas are available to correspond with certain subclasses of provisional visa (Business Owner and Investor), and are again available to both independent and sponsored applicants.[133] In addition, the Business Skills – Established Business visas provide permanent residence to a range of temporary migrants who are already in Australia and who are owners or part-owners of a business in Australia.[134] These are also available in independent and sponsored forms. Persons holding a temporary Business (Long Stay) subclass 457 visa as independent executives may apply for the Sponsored Business Owner visa. Only business high fliers who are sponsored by a State or Territory government can apply for the permanent Business Talent visa without first holding a provisional visa.[135]

9.6.3 Business owners and senior executives

[9.87] The business skills visas are designed to attract successful business people who own or part-own a business. Also eligible are senior executives employed by major businesses who will use their business skills to obtain a substantial ownership interest in a new or existing business in Australia and actively participate in that business at a senior management level.

---

130 Ron Kessells and Jane Goddard, 'Business Visa Overhaul' [2003] *Immigration Review* 145.
131 *Migration Regulations*, Sch 2, cll 845.222 and 846.222. The points test covers factors such as the visa applicant's age, English language proficiency, net assets, business and investment experience. The business skills points test is set out in Sch 7 to the Regulations.
132 Subclasses 160-165.
133 Subclasses 890-893.
134 Subclasses 845 and 846.
135 Subclass 132.

[9.88] Business owners seeking a provisional business visa must demonstrate a genuine and realistic commitment to establish a qualifying business, or participate in an existing qualifying business in Australia. They must maintain a substantial ownership interest in that business (sufficient to give the applicant a degree of control over the operations of the business).[136] Consideration is given to research the applicant has done into the Australian business environment; the timetable for their involvement; support from proposed business partners; and pre-existing business relationships in Australia. The word 'business' is not defined for the purpose of the Regulations and may involve a legal entity operating more than one business.[137] In addition, business migrants are required to own a percentage interest in a business. In April 2010, this was increased to 51 per cent (where the business turnover is less than $400,000); 30 per cent (where the business turnover is $400,000 or more); or 10 per cent of a publicly listed company.[138]

[9.89] Applicants must also demonstrate that they have significant business and personal assets. Independent visa applicants require net assets in a qualifying business of $200,000 in two of the last four fiscal years, an annual business turnover of at least $500,000 in two of the last four fiscal years and combined business and personal assets of at least $800,000 available for transfer to Australia within two years of visa grant. Sponsored visa applicants must meet lower asset thresholds.[139] Goodwill may be considered as part of an applicant's net assets in a business but only if the goodwill has been purchased or has been built up over time and realised with the sale of the business.[140]

[9.90] Senior executives must meet similar requirements, with the exception of established business assets. Instead of prior business ownership, senior executives must demonstrate that, in at least two of the four years before applying, they occupied a position in the three highest levels of the management structure of a major business and were responsible for strategic policy development. Senior executives need not meet any business asset thresholds but must satisfy the combined business and personal assets requirement.[141]

[9.91] In addition, the business applicant for a provisional visa must demonstrate a realistic commitment to maintain 'a direct and continuous involvement in the management of that business in a manner that benefits the Australian economy'. In *Lobo v MIMIA*,[142] the Full Federal Court examined the phrase 'direct and continuous involvement' in managing a business. Mrs Lobo applied for a business visa on the basis that she was managing director of an IT consultancy

---

136 See *Migration Regulations*, Sch 2, cl 160.219A, and *Migration Act*, s 134(10).
137 *Nassif v MIMIA* (2003) 129 FCR 448.
138 *Migration Regulations*, reg 1.11.
139 See, for example, *Migration Regulations*, Sch 2, cll 160.212(a), 160.213 and 160.214.
140 See, for example, *0804279* [2008] MRTA 1327; *071555387* [2008] MRTA 1347.
141 *Migration Regulations*, Sch 2, cl 161.213 (currently at least $800,000 available for transfer to Australia within two years of visa grants – again, a concessional amount is available to sponsored visa applicants.)
142 (2003) 132 FCR 93. The case considered the identical requirements in cl 845.216 for the Established Business in Australia visa – see below Part 9.6.5.

that was run by her and her husband. The couple also had business interests in a German company which generated the lion's share of their business revenue and Mrs Lobo spent considerable time abroad handling the sale of the German company. The Department rejected her visa application, concluding that Mrs Lobo had not shown direct and continuous involvement in the running of the Australian company in the 12 months before her application. This decision was affirmed by the MRT. The case turned on Department policy guidelines which suggested that the applicant had to demonstrate that she had exercised responsibility for the day-to-day running of the whole of the business. At first instance, Gyles J found that the departmental policy contained a more stringent test than the general 'direct and continuous involvement' requirement. The Full Court agreed, finding that the term 'involvement' merely required responsibility for some aspects of the business' day-to-day affairs. The applicant need not demonstrate decision-making authority, responsibility for employees or expenditure.[143] A person can maintain a direct and continuous involvement in the daily management of a business even while she or he is outside Australia.[144] Sufficient tasks of management oversight may include knowing how to engage expert advice.[145] Still, on reconsideration, the tribunal again found that Mrs Lobo failed the 'direct and continuous involvement' test on the basis that her role in the business comprised assisting in the office and acting under supervision without being 'fully cognisant of the overall direction and performance of that business'. This decision was affirmed by the Federal Magistrates Court and Federal Court on appeal.[146]

[9.92] Further criteria relate to the professional background of the applicant for the provisional visa. The applicant must have had an overall successful business career. If for at least two of the four fiscal years before making the application the applicant was engaged in a business providing professional or technical services, the applicant must have spent no more than half of that time directly providing such services (as distinct from operating the business).

[9.93] In addition, neither the applicant nor spouse can have a history of involvement in business or investment activities that are not generally acceptable in Australia. Although this criterion is stated in the negative, it is clear that the decision-maker must be affirmatively satisfied that no history of questionable business activities exists.[147] 'Business activities' can include the manner in which a business is conducted for profit, as well as the profit-making activities themselves. The criterion has been interpreted to allow a decision-maker to consider an applicant's compliance with laws, standards, ethics and community expectations in the course of conducting a legitimate business in Australia.[148] For its part the MRT has found, and the Federal Magistrates Court has affirmed, that the employment of unlawful non-citizens in the 12 months before an application will constitute involvement in business activities

---

143   Ibid at [63] applied in *0808613* [2009] MRTA 499; *071889268* [2008] MRTA 1303.
144   *060861990* [2008] MRTA 1343.
145   *Guo v MIMA* [2000] FCA 146 at [11].
146   *Lobo v MIMA* [2006] FCA 1562; *Lobo v MIMIA* [2005] FMCA 1024.
147   *MIMIA v Lat* (2006) 151 FCR 214 at [74], considering the identical provision in Sch 2, cl 131.214.
148   *Lee v MIAC* (2008) 221 FLR 416.

of a nature that is not generally acceptable in Australia.[149] Conversely, the tribunal has considered that an applicant's spouse's criminal conviction for fraud did not adversely affect the visa application. The man was convicted under the Companies Act in Singapore and received an 18-month jail sentence for deceitful conduct that resulted in a total of US$28 million being advanced by banks to his business. Because the suspect conduct was engaged in over a short period of time the tribunal found that this did not constitute a 'history' of involvement in unacceptable business activities.[150]

[9.94] After two years, the provisional visa holder may apply for a permanent business owner visa. The grant of this visa is conditional on the applicant showing that they had and continue to have an ownership interest in one or more actively operating main businesses in Australia for at least the last two years.[151] The applicant must also demonstrate requisite levels of business assets, business turnover and combined personal and business assets in the last 12 months. In the last 12 months, as well, the business must have employed at least the equivalent of two full-time employees who were Australian citizens, permanent residents or New Zealand passport holders and who were not members of the applicant's family.

9.6.4 Investment-based migration

[9.95] Also courted under the business skills migration program are major investors who invest in 'designated investments' in Australia. The investment-linked visa was originally introduced in 1995 following the recommendations of the Business Skills Assessment Panel. To be eligible for the provisional Investor visa applicants must invest: $1.5 million in either a 'designated investment'; or securities issued by State or Territory government authorities approved by the Minister through Gazette Notice;[152] or $750,000, in the case of State/Territory sponsored investors. Further threshold criteria relate to the applicant's established expertise in business or in the management of an investment portfolio; age; and language ability. The successful fulfilment of these criteria only leads to a grant of a provisional visa. Depositing substantial sums of money in government securities is no longer viewed as sufficiently beneficial to Australia to justify immediate permanent residence.

[9.96] Since the investment-based visa category was first introduced, the amount required for investment has doubled and the time period of the investment has been extended by one year. In the absence of sponsorship, the requirement that the applicant for a provisional investor visa be less than 45 years old has also become an absolute threshold. Before 1 March 2003 the age requirement was simply one aspect of a points test and being older than 45 was not fatal to satisfying the eligibility criteria for the investment visa class.

---

149   *Aw v MIAC* [2009] FMCA 566; *071555387* [2008] MRTA 1347.
150   *0800018* [2009] MRTA 233. This is not a ruling on which we would counsel reliance.
151   The 'ownership interest' to be assessed under the Regulations, at the time of the decision, is the business identified in the application, not another business if the business described in the application has been liquidated in the interim: *Ibrahim v MIAC* (2009) 229 FLR 350.
152   See *Migration Regulations*, reg 5.19A.

[9.97] After at least two years in Australia as a holder of a provisional Investor visa, an applicant may apply for a permanent Investor visa. Applicants must show a genuine and realistic commitment to continue to maintain a business or investment activity in Australia. The designated investments must have been held continuously for at least four years and the applicant must continue to satisfy the business attributes criteria related to the grant of the provisional visa.

9.6.5 Established Business in Australia

[9.98] The Established Business in Australia permanent visa is for people on a range of temporary visas who have set up and actively managed a business in Australia. In the 12 months before the application, the applicant must have been actively involved in, and directly responsible for, the day-to-day management and overall performance of the business. The applicant must demonstrate an overall successful business career and must not have had a history of involvement in business activities that are not generally acceptable in Australia.

[9.99] The applicant must also demonstrate an ownership interest in business in Australia totalling at least: 51 per cent of a business with an annual turnover below $400,000; 30 per cent of a business with an annual turnover of $400,000 or more; or 10 per cent of a publicly listed company. In addition, the applicant must show net business assets of at least $100,000 and total business and personal assets of at least $250,000 in the 12 months before making the visa application. The 12-month period has been construed as a calendar year.[153] In *Baldassara v MIMIA*,[154] the Federal Court took a strict view of these ownership requirements. In that case, the MRT refused to grant the applicant permanent residence under this visa class when the applicant sold his business in the two years between the date he lodged his review application with the MRT and the time the MRT finally denied his application. French J considered that, in spite of the extraordinary delay in the tribunal proceedings, the Established Business in Australia visa could be granted only where the applicant had an ownership interest in an established business *at the time of decision*. Because the applicant had not acquired any other business after the sale of the business which was the basis of his application, he was not eligible for the visa. In other cases the courts have confirmed that 'ownership interest' means interest in a business as the sole proprietor; a partner in a partnership; or a shareholder in the company which carries on the relevant business (which may be held as the beneficiary of a trust).[155]

[9.100] This visa subclass is the only business visa which is subject to a points test. In this scheme, most points are awarded for the attributes of the applicant's business. Applicants for an independent Established Business in Australia visa gain 60 points if, throughout the year before the application, their business(es) employed at least three full-time employees who were not a member of the applicant's family and who were Australians or New Zealanders; and had a turnover of at least $200,000; or

---

153 *Xin v MIMA* [2006] FMCA 1925.
154 [2005] FCA 239.
155 *Ng v MIMA* [2002] FCA 1146; *MIAC v Hart* (2009) 179 FCR 212; *Boshoff v MIMA* [2006] FMCA 1919.

exported goods and services worth $100,000.[156] Applicants for a regional Established Business in Australia visa accrue 60 points for demonstrating that a business in the regional area has employed at least three full-time staff (who were Australians or New Zealanders and not family members) throughout the two years before the application. Forty points are available for applicants for the sponsored visa whose business employed two full-time staff throughout the last two years. Points for both independent and sponsored visa applicants are then given for age (between 20 and 54); language ability (including bilingual ability); and net personal assets (between $500,000 and $2,500,000). Regional applicants gain additional points for sponsorship by the appropriate regional authority. The current pass mark for both sponsored and independent applicants is 105.

[9.101] As with the skilled visa points tests, discussed earlier (at Part 9.4), the administration of the points test in the context of business visas can be extremely stringent. For example, the Federal Magistrates' Court upheld an MRT ruling that an applicant accrued no points for business attributes because the company's three full-time employees ceased work two weeks before the visa application was lodged.[157] Employees' periods of work and overtime cannot be aggregated and averaged over a relevant 12-month period. This is despite the MRT's observation that:

> [T]aking a merely arithmetical approach to the issue does not appear ... to reflect the underlying purpose of this particular visa subclass, that is that the visa is granted on the basis of an established business.[158]

9.6.6 Regional development

[9.102] The business skills program has also been tailored increasingly to foster regional development. Within each visa category (business owner, senior executive and investor) there are subclasses for applicants sponsored by an Australian State or Territory authority (located generally in a government department).[159] Significant concessions are made for these sponsored visas. For example, applicants for the sponsored business owner visa need not have owned a business themselves as long as they have a background as a senior manager with requisite qualifications and employment record.[160] The lower business asset thresholds mentioned earlier may be waived altogether for applicants who reside and operate a business in a specific regional or low population growth area. In these cases an appropriate regional authority must determine that exceptional circumstances exist.[161] These subclasses of sponsored visas are geared towards maximising the economic benefits of business

---

156 The phrasing of this provision was amended by the *Migration Regulations (Amendment) 1995* (Cth) which inserted the word 'throughout' in place of 'during'. The regulation intended to clarify that the employment of the required number of employees must have been at all times throughout the period of 12 months before the application.
157 *Yu v MIAC* (2007) 209 FLR 470.
158 *Birch* [2004] MRTA 6775 at [38].
159 As defined in *Migration Regulations*, reg 1.03, and listed in GN 8, 26 February 2003 – 'Specification of State and Territory departments and authorities for the purposes of the definition of "appropriate regional authority" in regulation 1.03 of the Migration Regulations 1994'.
160 Inserted by *Migration Amendment Regulations 2006 (No 2)* (Cth), commencing on 1 July 2006.
161 *Migration Regulations*, Sch 2, cl 892.213.

migration to the relevant State or Territory.[162] Deferring to local knowledge, sponsorship decisions are made by the relevant State authority rather than the Immigration Department. These decisions are insulated from review under administrative law (see further Chapter 5.5).

[9.103] The Business Talent visa allows for the immediate grant of permanent residence and is designed to attract people with highly successful business careers and significant personal or business assets. Sponsorship by a State or Territory authority is required. The maximum age of 55 years is waivable if the principal applicant's business has been assessed as of exceptional economic benefit to a State or Territory.[163]

9.7 Future reform agendas

[9.104] In spite of the role played by highly skilled migrants over many years in improving Australia's economic performance, it is interesting that this aspect of the migration program has not rated highly in the popular discourse. As we will see in the chapters that follow, major changes in two areas of the program – temporary skilled migration and the foreign student program – have shaken the sense of complacency and simple acceptance that skilled migration represents a Pareto improvement for the Australian labour market. The suite of reforms of the general skilled migration in 2009-10 indicate an anxiety about the impact skilled migrants have had on the Australian labour market.

[9.105] It is presumed that efforts to prioritise employer sponsorship over independent migration and the separation of the skilled migration intake from the student migration program will enhance the immediate employability of skilled migrants. Policies that eliminate barriers to migrants entering the labour market make eminent good sense. Ensuring that foreign doctors are not working in Australia as medical orderlies is obviously a worthy objective. On the other hand, over-reliance on employer sponsorship risks significant hazards for both the local labour market and new residents. Undue emphasis on the immediate employability of migrants can do little to address longer term skills shortages. Nor is it clear that employer sponsorship operates always in the interest of the migrants themselves. The risk is that the ENS could foster dependency on employers, exacerbating power differentials which already exist in the relationship of employment. As we discuss further in Chapter 10, the danger of exploitation is most pronounced where visas are dependent on the ongoing support of a sponsor.

[9.106] While research into labour migration has traditionally been confined to the disciplines of economics and political economy, scholarship is emerging with a broader focus on the workplace experience of economic stream migrants that deserves greater attention. Challenging the 'success story', these researchers argue that systemic discrimination against economic migrants continues to exist on the

---

162 PAM3 Generic Guidelines – Business Skills Visas 'State/Territory Government Appropriate Regional Authorities' section 6.1.
163 *Migration Regulations*, Sch 2, cl 132.215.

basis of gender, race and birthplace.[164] They draw attention to institutional factors that appear to be skewing program outcomes in ways that may ultimately work against Australia's national interests. As Australia positions itself to establish truly world class mechanisms for the selection of skilled migrants, this area will continue to represent fertile ground for researchers across many disciplines.

---

164 See, for example, Christina Ho and Caroline Alcorso, 'Migrants and Employment: Challenging the Success Story' (2004) 40(3) *Journal of Sociology* 237; Anna Boucher, 'Skill, Migration and Gender in Australia and Canada: The Case of Gender-based Analysis' (2007) 42 *Australian Journal of Political Science* 383; and Mary Crock, 'Women and Immigration Law' in Patricia Easteal (ed), *Women and the Law in Australia* (Sydney: LexisNexis, 2010).

10

The Business of Temporary Labour Migration

10.1 Introduction

[10.01] For most of its history as a nation, Australia has eschewed acceptance of temporary migrant workers in favour of permanent settlers. Although the rules on 'temporary skills transfers' were relaxed substantially after the Second World War, it was not until the end of the century that the balance shifted comprehensively. Since the mid-1990s, the number of overseas migrants entering Australia on temporary work visas (staying for at least one year) has exceeded the number of people arriving for permanent settlement. Since 1998-99, net long-term arrivals of overseas visitors has exceeded net permanent migration to Australia.[1] In June 2009 there were around half a million temporary migrants with work rights in Australia – almost 5 per cent of the total labour force.[2]

[10.02] In general policy terms, temporary skilled migration does not differ significantly from permanent migration in so far as governments have attempted to balance the immediate labour needs of employers against the protection of local labour interests. Nevertheless, temporary labour migration stands apart in terms of the potential for exploitation of foreign workers, especially at the lower end of the labour market. In recent years, media coverage of alleged abuses – some involving the death of workers – has led to extensive policy debates. These have questioned the balance that is being struck between easy deployment of labour (to meet skills shortages) and effective government oversight; and the relationship between temporary migration to Australia and regional development efforts in Asia and the Pacific. The role of union advocacy in this area compared with other aspects of skilled migration is also unique.[3]

[10.03] This chapter considers some of the visa categories involving temporary migrant workers: the temporary business (subclasses 456 and 457); the Working

---

1 Peter McDonald, Siew Ean Khoo and Rebecca Kippen, 'Alternative Net Migration Estimates for Australia: Exploding the Myth of a Rapid Increase in Numbers' (2003) 11(3) *People and Place* 23.
2 Peter Mares, 'The Permanent Shift to Temporary Migration' *Inside Story*, 16 June 2009.
3 See Construction, Forestry, Mining and Energy Union, *Submission to Joint Standing Committee on Migration*, Inquiry into Skilled Migration, April 2003, available at <http://www.aph.gov.au/house/committee/mig/skillmig/subs/sub45.pdf>.

Holiday visas and the Pacific seasonal migration scheme. In relation to the subclass 457 visas, government inquiries, departmental reviews and legislative amendments have gone a long way towards resetting the balance in favour of protecting the local labour market from the use of foreign labour to drive down working conditions. However, the vulnerability of low-waged migrant workers has yet to be addressed as effectively. Concerns about the marginalisation and potential for abuse of workers also shadow the Pacific seasonal migration scheme.

10.2 The development of a temporary business migration scheme

[10.04] The drive towards liberalisation of temporary labour in Australia can be traced to the Uruguay Round of trade liberalisation talks and the entry into force, in 1995, of the General Agreement in Trade of Services (GATS). This multilateral legal platform for the international trade in services included a Decision on Negotiations on Movement of Natural Persons which led to the establishment of a Negotiating Group on the Movement of Natural Persons within the World Trade Organization. Australia was one of six countries to submit a schedule of commitments that included amending its laws and policies to more readily facilitate the admission of temporary workers.[4] At a practical level, the desire to encourage large corporations to establish regional headquarters in Australia also created an impetus to make the immigration laws governing the transfer of key personnel more flexible. If Australia were to remain competitive, it had to conform to the general trend towards liberalising at least some of its policies governing temporary entry.[5]

[10.05] The temporary worker scheme at that time was cumbersome, time consuming and in most respects antithetical to good business practice, containing no less than 17 visa subclasses. Where a business wished to bring in groups of workers or a series of workers, labour agreements had to be negotiated in consultation with government departments, unions and employer groups.[6]

[10.06] The Keating Labor government established the Committee of Inquiry into the Temporary Entry of Business People and Highly Skilled Specialists (the Roach Committee) in 1994, which reported in 1995.[7] The Roach Committee recommenda-

---

4   GATS/SC/6/Suppl.1AUSTRALIA – Schedule of Specific Commitments.
5   Charles W Stahl, 'Trade in Labour Services and Migrant Worker Protection with Special Reference to East Asia' (1999) 37 *International Migration* 545; Paul Garnier, 'International Trade in Services: A Growing Trend Among Highly Skilled Migrants with a Special Reference to Asia' (1996) 5 *Asian and Pacific Migration Journal* 367.
6   Originally referred to as 'Tripartite Negotiated Agreements', the arrangements required employers to demonstrate their need for employees; their inability to satisfy their need through the hiring of workers already in Australia; and their commitment to the training of appropriate local staff. Although the Regulations made no mention of union involvement, unions originally played a strong de facto role in this process. Even before the Labor Party left office in March 1996, moves had been made to bypass these cumbersome mechanisms through the institution of Regional Headquarters Agreements. These allowed approved employers to sponsor either groups of workers or a succession of workers where they showed a need for the importation of special expertise from overseas.
7   See Commission of Inquiry into the Temporary Entry of Business People and High Skilled Specialists, *Report: Business Temporary Entry: Future Directions* (Canberra: DEET, 1995).

tions were the basis of the scheme put into effect by the Coalition government in 1996.

[10.07] The reforms simplified procedures to facilitate business travel to Australia. Key features included a general emphasis on entrepreneurs, investors and highly skilled employees, and flexibility in targeting occupations with a shortage of skilled workers. Counterbalancing this were requirements for both employers and entrants to comply with Australian labour laws and working conditions. The many different categories of visa were reduced to two new visa subclasses: the 456 (Business Short Stay) visa, for stays of three months or less, and 457 (Business Long Stay) visa of between three months and four years.[8]

[10.08] The main innovations of this regime included the removal of previous restrictions governing the sponsoring of business persons and specialists; and the abolition of labour market testing and training requirements to benefit Australian workers. The framework also included a pre-visa application arrangement whereby employers could register as sponsors if they met minimal requirements, permitting them to sponsor any number of people on temporary business entry visas.

[10.09] In announcing the reforms, then Minister Ruddock affirmed the government's commitment to working closely with business to ensure that the Australian economy maintained a competitive edge internationally. Nevertheless, the Minister asserted that the reforms represented a balance between giving businesses more flexibility to build up international competitive links, while safeguarding employment opportunities for Australian workers.[9] The scheme stayed in operation for the best part of eight years, when moves were made to integrate the regulation of temporary skilled migration with the permanent program.

10.3   Overview of the temporary business visa scheme

[10.10] The temporary business visas (subclasses 456 and 457) are designed now to both respond to immediate skills shortages and (as noted in the last chapter) to provide pathways to permanent skilled visas. The visa structure emphasises the labour priorities and skill needs of employers, usually requiring a sponsoring employer and a pre-arranged job in Australia at time of application.

[10.11] In spite of the emphasis on employer preferences, the regulatory regime continues the familiar rhetoric of national economic interest, with a number of constraints attaching to the sponsorship of foreign workers. The 457 scheme was linked into the Employer Nomination Skilled Occupations List (ENSOL) – the list of skilled occupations which are prerequisites for the grant of Employer Nomination Scheme (ENS) visas – in 2004.[10] In addition, employers must formally demonstrate

---

8   Division 1.4A, inserted by SR 76 of 1996.
9   Minister Philip Ruddock, Media Release MPS 21/96: 'Streamlined Temporary Business Entry Approved', 5 June 1996.
10 A unique list is now specified for 457 visa positions. The current list is set out in IMMI 10/085 effective 15 February 2011, authorised by the *Migration Regulations 1994* (Cth), reg 2.72(10)(aa).

that foreign workers will contribute to the creation and maintenance of local employment; expand Australian trade in goods and services; improve business links with international markets; or enhance competitiveness within sectors of the Australian economy.[11] The sponsor must show that the applicant will introduce, utilise or create in Australia, innovative technology or business skills. The sponsor must also possess a satisfactory record in (or demonstrate a commitment to) training local workers. The nominated position must meet prescribed minimum salary levels (which now include the requirement to pay market wages – see below at [10.30] ff).[12] These checks on the demand side of the application process were introduced to offset the removal in 2005 of the requirement that sponsors conduct labour market testing, designed previously to ensure that no Australian resident was available for the job.

[10.12] The deregulation of temporary skilled migration has drawn strong criticisms. The recruitment of overseas skilled workers in preference to local employees has been a matter of particular concern following the abolition of labour market testing. Employers' failure to comply with salary and other workplace obligations has threatened to undercut local wages and conditions.[13] Further concerns are that the increased importation of temporary workers may undermine local employment and training,[14] or erode the standards of Australian skills due to the lack of provision for technology, knowledge and skills transfers.[15] It has also been suggested that employers may be attracted to the temporary skilled workers as a malleable workforce precisely because the visa ties temporary skilled workers to the employer sponsoring them.[16]

[10.13] These criticisms and concerns have prompted legislative and institutional reforms. Following media accounts of employer abuse of the 457 visa scheme, the Coalition government introduced a Bill that would have strengthened sanctions on employers who failed to comply with their obligations, including the cancellation of sponsorships and the barring of further sponsorships.[17] Publicity surrounding continued abuses and ineffectual departmental oversight led the Rudd Labor government to pass similar legislation which also included monetary penalties for employer non-compliance with statutory requirements.[18] The extent to which these new sanctions have been enforced is discussed later in this chapter (see [10.47]ff).

---

11   *Migration Regulations*, Sch 2, cl 457.111.
12   Ibid, reg 2.72(10)(c) and (cc).
13   Bob Kinnaird, 'Australia's Migration Policy and Skilled ICT Professionals: The Case for an Overhaul' (2002) 10(2) *People and Place* 55.
14   Bob Birrell and Ernest Healy, 'Globalisation and Temporary Entry' (1997) 5(4) *People and Place* 43; DEWR, *Submission to the Joint Standing Committee on Migration*, Skilled Migration Enquiry, 2002.
15   Bob Kinnaird, 'Temporary-Entry Migration: Balancing Corporate Rights and Australian Work Opportunities' (1996) 4(1) *People and Place* 55 at 60.
16   Graeme Hugo, 'Migration Policies Designed to Facilitate the Recruitment of Skilled Workers in Australia' in Organisation for Economic Co-operation and Development (OECD), *International Mobility of the Highly Skilled* (Paris: OECD Publications, 2002) at 315.
17   Migration Amendment (Sponsorship Obligations) Bill 2007 (Cth). See also *Migration Legislation Amendment (Sponsorship Measures) Act 2003* (Cth).
18   *Migration Legislation Amendment (Worker Protection) Act 2008* (Cth).

10.4 Short-term business visitor visas

[10.14] The subclass 456 visa allows persons coming to Australia on short-term business assignments to enter and remain for up to three months at a time with a minimum of inconvenience and expense.[19] The visit must be for a bona fide business purpose. It must be consistent with the applicant's personal attributes and business background, and relate generally to existing business activities (whether in or outside of Australia). Applicants must have adequate funds to cover their stay. They must undertake not to engage in a work activity 'which would have an adverse impact on Australia'; and they must not be 'adversely known' to the Department.

[10.15] Departmental officers consider the applicant's age, qualifications, current employment and business activities and how they relate to the nature of the applicant's proposed business in Australia.[20] In practice, they do not investigate these matters further unless there is reason to doubt the applicant's bona fides. The object is to assess whether the applicant has a genuine intention to stay in Australia temporarily and to undertake legitimate business activities here. Like certain applicants for tourist visas (see Chapter 11.2.3), special rules apply to prospective business visitors who fit the 'risk factor' profile of persons who fail habitually to comply with visa conditions. These visitors must show that there is 'very little likelihood' of their overstaying the time limits on their visas.[21]

[10.16] All business visitor visas are subject to condition 8112 which prohibits the visa holder from engaging in work that could otherwise be done by an Australian. This condition requires that the visitor undertake only work that is finite and highly specialised in nature; required in an emergency; or otherwise in Australia's interest as assessed on a case-by-case basis. Departmental policy places a significant constraint on the work-related activities that may be undertaken where these extend beyond emergency assistance, exploring business opportunities, undertaking training or promotional work.

10.5 Long-term temporary business visas

[10.17] The subclass 457 visa provides for the streamlined admission of long-term temporary entrants. These include: personnel recruited by Australian-based companies; employees of offshore companies seeking to establish an Australian branch of their company; independent executives seeking to establish new businesses or joining

---

19   Like certain tourist visitors (see Chapter 11 at [11.71]), certain short-term business entrants are eligible for an Electronic Travel Authority (ETA), an electronically issued multiple entry visa for short-term visits. ETAs must be granted overseas or in immigration clearance to an applicant with an ETA-eligible passport. Unlike other business visitors, ETA applicants may rely on a statement alone of their intention to visit Australia temporarily, rather than being required to provide documentary evidence in support. See Public Interest Criteria (PIC) 4011, *Migration Regulations*, Sch 4; *Ministerial Direction 36, Visitors*, Schedule 1, 1208A Electronic Travel Authority (Class UD), Specification of ETA-eligible passports, GN5, 4 February 2004.

20   Consideration will be given to documentation such as: the applicant's qualifications; correspondence from the overseas employer or Australian contacts; and evidence of the applicant's material, professional and personal ties to their country of residence.

21   PIC 4011; *Ministerial Direction 36, Visitors*, above n 19.

existing businesses in Australia; personnel under labour agreements; and certain service sellers.

[10.18] The grant of a long-term business visa involves a three-stage process. The sponsoring company must apply for acceptance as a sponsor. It must then lodge a business nomination setting out the activities to be undertaken by the nominated migrant. Finally, the applicant (nominee) applies for the visa on the basis of the sponsorship. In subclass 457, the 'sponsorship' criteria focus on the sponsoring organisation and its relationship to the applicant, while 'nomination' is concerned with the proposed activities to be carried out by the applicant.

10.5.1 Sponsorship requirements

[10.19] Australian businesses may seek approval to sponsor a single person or a specified number of foreign employees within a two-year period. The facilitation of multiple nominations accomplishes the twin goals of capping the number of entries under one approved sponsorship whilst benefitting employers who need not re-establish their sponsorship credentials each time they sponsor personnel from overseas.[22]

[10.20] Australian-based business sponsors must demonstrate that they have a viable business, operating lawfully and which can fulfil its obligations as a sponsor.[23] Here, the Department will consider the nature of the sponsoring employer's business and whether any adverse information is known. The business must be solvent and either have sufficient capital or be making a level of profit that would enable it to fulfil its obligations as a sponsor. In *MM International (Australia) Pty Ltd v MIMIA*,[24] the Full Federal Court upheld an MRT decision denying a business's application for sponsorship on the basis of poor financial records and evidence of negligible profit.

Benefit to Australia test

[10.21] Sponsors must show that they will provide some benefit to Australia through the employment of temporary foreign workers.[25] This involves a showing that the recruitment of a foreign worker will either create or maintain employment for local Australians; that it will expand Australian trade in goods and services; improve business links with international markets; or contribute to competitiveness within parts of the Australian economy. The Federal Court has noted that:[26]

> The question of what amounts to a contribution within the meaning of the regulation is one of fact and degree. It is a matter for the Tribunal and is not one on which it is appropriate for this Court to differ on an application for judicial review.

---

22   Philip Ruddock, Media Release MPS 43/96 'Streamlined Temporary Business Entry Sponsorship Starts', 1 August 1996.
23   *Migration Regulations*, reg 2.59, sets out the criteria that must be met by the Australian-based business sponsor. Additional considerations apply to overseas business sponsors: reg 2.59(h).
24   [2004] FCAFC 323.
25   See *Migration Regulations*, Sch 2, cl 457.111(2).
26   *Qi v MIMA* [2002] FCA 326 at [24].

[10.22] Neither the recruitment of the nominated employee nor the work undertaken need be the sole and direct cause of any of these benefits. Rather, the nominated employment may be one contributing factor among others to the employment of locals.[27] The Regulations do not require that the nominated position actually creates additional jobs or actually prevents a loss of jobs.[28] Instead, it requires a 'contribution' to employment.

Commitment to training local workers

[10.23] Sponsors must meet benchmarks for training Australians in their business operations.[29] This must involve the introduction, use or creation in Australia of new or improved technology or business skills. In previous versions of this sponsorship requirement, the sponsor must demonstrate a 'satisfactory record of training' involving the introduction, use or creation in Australia of new or improved technology or business skills.[30] In relation to the introduction of new technology, the Federal Magistrates Court rejected as *ultra vires* departmental policy requiring that the technology be 'not widely established or readily available in Australia'.[31] In *Nice Shoes Aust Pty Ltd v MIMIA*,[32] the Federal Court ruled that satisfactory training means training of 'a degree reasonably commensurate with the nature and extent of [a company's] business operations in Australia'. The sponsor need not prove that its training of Australian citizens and permanent residents would necessarily reduce its own, or the Australian economy's, reliance on foreign labour.[33] Due to the vagueness of this requirement, in 2009 the Labor government developed 'training benchmarks' to more objectively gauge the eligibility of sponsors.

Meaning of 'direct employer'

[10.24] The sponsor must be the direct employer of any overseas recruit. This can be a problematic requirement when the visa applicant's employment will involve working on a number of projects for different employers. This situation most commonly arises with recruitment (or 'labour hire') companies that contract out the employee's labour. In most instances, recruitment companies pay the employee's salary, taxation and superannuation with the cost of the employee's labour being billed to the recipient of the employee's services.[34] After integrity issues arose in the context of the on-hire industry, from October 2007 labour hire firms seeking to recruit overseas workers were excluded from sponsorship under the 457 visa scheme, except through a negotiated labour agreement.

27　*Shead v MIMA* [2001] FCA 933 at [15].
28　*Total Eye Care Australia v MIMA* [2007] FMCA 281 at [25].
29　*Migration Regulations*, reg 2.59(d).
30　Ibid, reg 1.20D(2)(c).
31　*Total Eye Care Australia v MIMA* [2007] FMCA 281 at [41].
32　[2004] FCA 252 at [16].
33　*Parisi v MIMIA* [2005] FMCA 218.
34　Biao Xiang, 'Structuration of Indian Information Technology Professionals' Migration to Australia: An Ethnographic Study' (2001) 39(5) *International Migration* 73.

Employer obligations

[10.25] Finally, sponsorship involves a range of obligations or undertakings that were first introduced in 2004, together with sanctions for employers found to be in breach.[35] The Minister has a broad range of powers set out in ss 140A-140ZH of the *Migration Act 1958* (Cth). However, most of the detail is contained in the Regulations which provide a great deal of flexibility in prescribing eligibility criteria and sponsorship undertakings.[36] For example, the sponsor must demonstrate a record of compliance with immigration requirements. Most importantly, the sponsoring employer must undertake to comply with industrial relations laws, and provide remuneration at Australian levels. Since September 2009, employers have been required to pay foreign workers 'market rates' in addition to a (gazetted) minimum salary level. See further below at [10.30]. Certain responsibilities are imposed to ensure coverage of health care and repatriation costs for the overseas recruit. The employer must notify the Department of any change in circumstances relevant to the sponsorship and must cooperate with the Department's monitoring of the sponsor and the foreign worker.

[10.26] In *Tide Sequence Industries Pty Ltd v MIMIA*,[37] the company's application for sponsorship was denied on the basis of poor financial performance and declining profits. The Federal Court ruled that the company would clearly not be able to meet its sponsor's undertakings, specifically those relating to payment of the mandated salary. There was no inquiry into the precise details of work actually undertaken or of the salary that had been paid. In the earlier case of *Lace Holdings Pty Ltd v MIMA*,[38] the Federal Court held that a decision-maker can take into account a business's failure to comply with past undertakings, as well as its current financial circumstances and competence as an applicant for re-sponsorship. In that case, the applicant sponsor had admitted that business had slowed down. She stated that she had given the nominated employee all the work that was available but conceded that she could not afford to pay the minimum gazetted salary. No training or skills transfer had occurred.

[10.27] In contrast, in *Leng v MIAC*,[39] a case in which a business was applying as a first time sponsor, the Federal Magistrates Court ruled that past profits or activities should not be the sole determinant of whether a sponsor will meet its undertakings. The court held that the critical factors were the likely future profitability of the business and the sponsor's ability to cover the salary for the nominated position. In other words, the central question was whether the sponsor was able to fulfil its undertakings from the date of the visa grant until the end of the sponsorship undertaking.

[10.28] Having said this, the end of an employment relationship between the sponsor and visa holder does not necessarily signal the end of the employer's sponsorship

---

35 *Migration Amendment Regulations 2004 (No 3)* (Cth).
36 See *Migration Act*, s 140H, and *Migration Regulations*, regs 2.77-2.94B.
37 (2005) 145 FCR 155 at [36]-[37]. See also *MIAC v Le* (2007) 164 FCR 151.
38 (2002) 117 FCR 79.
39 [2007] FMCA 1961.

obligations.[40] These only cease when the employer ceases to be a sponsor, or five days after this event; or when the visa holder leaves Australia, or five days after this event; or when the visa holder has been granted another substantive visa, depending on the relevant sponsorship obligation.[41]

10.5.2 Nominated position

[10.29] Employer nominations relate to the positions to be filled.[42] Each position requires a nomination, which must specify the nature of the position and remuneration details.[43]

[10.30] As noted earlier, nominations were formerly restricted to occupations listed on the ENSOL, introduced in part as a trade-off when labour market testing was first restricted and later abolished altogether.[44] The number of occupations included on this list, together with the exceptions made for regional sponsorships, did not make this much of a limitation. Along with the significant Labor government reforms in 2009 the Minister specified a unique list for 457 visa positions which somewhat reduced eligible occupations.[45] More significantly perhaps, nominations must correspond at least with a gazetted minimum salary level[46] – now benchmarked in accordance with Australian industry standards (or with Australian awards, if these are higher) for the position involved. In 2009, this was supplemented with a new requirement to pay the visa holder a salary at the prevailing market rate. Specifically, employers must ensure that the terms and conditions of employment provided to 457 visa holders are no less favourable than the terms and conditions governing the treatment of a local worker in an equivalent position in the sponsor's workplace. This is ascertained by reference to the enterprise agreement or award governing the pay and conditions of Australian workers in the sponsor's workplace. If the sponsor employs no Australian workers, the onus is on the sponsor to ensure they are providing equivalent wages and conditions through looking at the relevant industrial instruments for their industry.[47] There is no requirement to prove the payment of market salary rates for nominated positions of salaries at or higher than $180,000.[48] There remains, however, a minimum salary level below which no position could be nominated, now called the Temporary Skilled Migration Income Threshold.[49]

---

40   *Cardenas v MIMA* [2001] FCA 17 at [55]-[57].
41   *Migration Regulations,* regs 2.78-2.87.
42   The requirements for nominations under Labour Agreements may differ slightly. Labour Agreements allow employers to recruit overseas workers outside of the standard sponsorship regime where, for instance, the occupation is not approved for this scheme, or where the employer is a labour hire firm or an abattoir (these were excluded from standard business sponsorship in 2007).
43   Nominations are made under *Migration Regulations,* reg 2.72.
44   Ibid, reg 1.20G(2). See above Chapter 9 at 9.4.1.
45   The current list is IMMI 10/085 effective 15 February 2011. See also *Migration Regulations,* reg 2.72(10)(aa).
46   *Migration Regulations,* reg 1.20B.
47   Ibid, reg 2.72(10).
48   Ibid, reg 2.72(10AB).
49   In July 2010, this was fixed at $47,480 per annum.

[10.31] Previously, regional nominations had less stringent occupational skills levels and salary levels than standard nominations.[50] Before May 2009, employers in regional areas were given a special dispensation to nominate positions at a lower salary level and for occupations in (what was then) Australian Standard Classification of Occupations (ASCO) groups 5 to 7.[51] This exemption from the general requirements of a standard business sponsorship was removed by the Labor government along with other reforms to the 457 visa, apparently to promote the integrity of the temporary skilled migration program and to ensure it does not undermine local training and employment opportunities.[52] Regional employers seeking to hire temporary migrant workers in occupations excluded from the standard sponsorship arrangements will now have to enter into a Labour Agreement.

10.5.3 The nominated employee

[10.32] After the approval of the employer's sponsorship and nominations, the employee can make a visa application. The applicant must be the person nominated for the position. He or she must have the skills and experience for the position and must be remunerated at at least the Temporary Skilled Migration Income Threshold and in accordance with the (market-rated) salary specified in the nomination.[53] Importantly, the applicant must demonstrate the skills necessary for the sponsored position at the time of lodgement of the visa application. Subsequent acquisition of skills will not remedy a failure to comply with these visa requirements.[54] Applicants for a 457 visa must also fulfil health and character requirements.

Non-portability in the labour market

[10.33] Almost all subclass 457 visa holders are precluded from changing employers or working in a position or occupation inconsistent with the position or occupation for which the employer sponsorship was granted.[55] The prohibition on working in a position inconsistent with the nominated position includes self employment after hours, and voluntary unpaid work for community organisations or charities is permitted only with the employer's consent. Before September 2009, visa holders wishing to either change position within an organisation, or change employers, had to lodge a fresh application. The 'new' employer also had to lodge a fresh application for sponsorship and nomination relating to the position to be filled.[56] This situation was simplified in September 2009, with visa holders no longer required to apply for

---

50   See, for example, 'Minimum Salary Levels and Occupations for the Temporary Business Long Stay Visa', IMMI 08/021, June 2008, under *Migration Regulations*, regs 1.20B, 1.20G(2) and 1.20GA(1)(a)(i).
51   Note that from 1 July 2010 the governing standards are those set out in the ANZCO Dictionary. See above Chapter 9.3.1.
52   DIAC, *Frequently Asked Questions about Changes to Subclass 457 program – Change to Pathways for ASCO 5-7 Occupations*, available at <http://www.immi.gov.au/skilled/skilled-workers/asco5-7-faq.htm>.
53   *Migration Regulations*, Sch 2, cl 457.223(4).
54   *Re Soysa* [2003] MRTA 1549.
55   The Sch 8 condition 8107 is attached to the issued visa: see Sch 2, cl 457.611. The one exception to this conditionality is Independent Executives.
56   *Sam v MIAC* [2007] FMCA 1217.

a new subclass 457 visa. However, it remains a requirement that the visa holder be nominated and have that nomination approved before they can start working for the new employer (who must also be an approved sponsor).

English language requirements

[10.34] In 2007, English language capacity was introduced as a pre-requisite for the visa. (Previously, applicants were only required to demonstrate proficiency in English where required for licensing or registration in their profession. Otherwise, functional English was not required if the applicant could demonstrate that English language competence was not necessary to the position.) The new English language requirement (at least International English Language Testing Scheme (IELTS) Level 4.5) applied only to 457 visa applicants nominating a trade occupation. As of April 2009, this requirement increased to an average IELTS score of Level 5. And in September 2009, this increased further to an IELTS test core of 5 in each of speaking, reading, writing and listening. Exemptions are available, for instance, if the applicant has qualifications from an English-language institution or (at present) a salary above $85,090.[57]

[10.35] Tailored to the trades occupations and the lower end of the salary scale, this English language requirement was introduced with a suite of changes explicitly directed at reducing the vulnerability of temporary migrant workers. A higher English language competency is thought to assist 457 visa holders by ensuring a strong knowledge of occupational health and safety requirements and an ability to seek assistance from public authorities for any employer non-compliance with labour or migration laws. Still, if this was the overarching rationale for the requirement, there are clearly contrary policy considerations at play. For instance, departmental guidelines indicate that Australia's economic situation will always be a relevant factor in the exercise of discretion to waive the language requirement. In one case the MRT waived the requirement on the basis that the applicant's employment in the field of stonemasonry would assist the continued business operations of the employer in what was then a period of economic downturn.[58] The fact that language skills can be traded off against broader economic concerns might suggest that, in fact, the language requirement is targeted at reducing foreign competition for local jobs. In other words, it may not be aimed solely at empowering foreign workers in Australian employment.

Skills assessments

[10.36] Although 457 visa applicants have always been required to meet certain skills requirements as a precondition for grant of their visa, skills assessments have traditionally not been mandatory. They are typically required where some doubt arises as to whether an applicant has the qualifications or skills to fill the nominated position. For its part, the MRT has determined that skills assessments are not

---

57 'Level of Salary and Exemptions to the English Language Requirements for Subclass 457 (Business (Long Stay)) Visas', IMMI 10/086, effective 15 February 2011.
58 *0806152* [2009] MRTA 704.

intended as a substitute for the requirement that the applicant satisfy the employment background requirement.[59] Along with other changes to address integrity issues in this visa category, in July 2009 the government introduced pilot skills assessment processes to provide for formal skills testing of some trade occupations.

10.5.4 Merits review

[10.37] Merits review is available for decisions to refuse approval of sponsorships, to cancel sponsorships and to refuse visa applications made pursuant to an approved sponsorship. Under the legislation in force before 1 November 2003, a visa applicant had merits review rights even without an approved sponsor and even if the review application was bound to fail as a result. At that time, 40 per cent of MRT review applications concerning refusals of 457 visas involved applicants without approved sponsors. Although these applications were bound to fail, the time taken to hear the cases meant that applicants could benefit from gaining up to two more years of work in Australia. This regime was changed to limit merits review to situations where the visa applicant is sponsored by an approved sponsor or where an application for review of a decision not to approve the sponsor is not finally determined at the time of the application for review of the refusal to grant the visa.[60]

10.5.5 Cancellation of temporary business visas

[10.38] Like other visa classes, the temporary business visa is subject to the general powers of cancellation.[61] For this visa, grounds include that the visa holder's current business sponsor has not complied with its undertaking or does not continue to satisfy the requirements for approval as a business sponsor, or that the visa holder has breached a condition of the visa.[62] A decision to cancel the visa on these grounds is discretionary and the decision-maker must have regard to all relevant circumstances including matters identified in policy guidelines. These are: the purpose of a visa holder's travel to and stay in Australia; the extent of non-compliance with any conditions; the degree of hardship that may be caused to the visa holder and any family members; the circumstances in which the ground for cancellation arose; the person's behaviour in relation to the Department; any other matters the visa holder raises; and any other relevant considerations. For a fuller account of the powers of cancellation, see Chapter 16 below.

10.5.6 Employer sanctions

[10.39] One of the key objects of reform of the 457 program has been the introduction of sanctions for breaches of employer undertakings. When employer undertakings were first introduced, breaches were punishable only by the sponsor

---

59   0801537 [2009] MRTA 584.
60   *Migration Act*, s 338(2)(d), inserted by the *Migration Legislation Amendment (Sponsorship Measures) Act 2003* (Cth). See *Phillips v MIAC* [2007] FMCA 572; *Kim v MIAC* [2007] FMCA 166.
61   *Migration Act*, ss 116-118.
62   See *Zubair v MIMIA* (2004) 139 FCR 344.

having their approval as a business sponsor cancelled or being barred from making further sponsorship applications for three years (unless the sponsor has previously been sanctioned or has exploited several sponsored persons in which case the bar was longer).[63] The Minister can decide to waive a bar on a sponsor's approval on the basis of the following considerations: whether the interests of Australia would be significantly affected if the bar were not waived; whether a substantial trade opportunity would be lost if the bar were not waived; whether there would be a significant detriment to the Australian community if the bar were not waived; whether the person's inability to sponsor a person would significantly damage Australia's relations with the government of another country; and whether significant new evidence or information has come to light which was not available at the time the decision to place the bar was made.[64]

[10.40] After a string of allegations of workplace abuses by sponsors, the Rudd government introduced monetary penalties for breach of employer undertakings of up to $6600 for an individual and $33,000 for a company.[65] These were modelled on proposals introduced into parliament by the Coalition government.[66] After the introduction of the *Migration Legislation Amendment (Worker Protection) Act 2008* (Cth) on 14 September 2009, the initial monitoring network focused on educating sponsors of the new requirements rather than on imposing penalties.[67] In 2009-10, 164 sponsors had been sanctioned, which was 14 per cent lower than the same period of the previous program year.

10.5.7 Controversies over the temporary business visas

[10.41] The dramatic increase in the number of 457 visas granted after 2001 increased the visibility of temporary skilled workers in Australia, raising consciousness of the policy issues surrounding this aspect of the migration program.[68] In spite of attempts to improve the protection of foreign workers, concerns remained about the extent to which the visas should be available to blue collar workers. Traditionally, 457 visa holders have been either young highly skilled professionals from English-speaking countries such as the United Kingdom, the United States, Canada, Ireland and South Africa, or older people with management skills from countries such as Japan and the US.[69] This professional, 'North-North' migration pattern is the result of policy-makers' efforts to balance the desire to maintain Australia's competitiveness in a global market with the need to protect local working conditions.

---

63   See *Migration Act*, s 140L.
64   *Migration Regulations*, reg 2.100.
65   *Migration Act*, s 140Q.
66   Migration Amendment (Sponsorship Obligations) Bill 2007 (Cth).
67   DIAC, *Subclass 457 Business (Long Stay): State/Territory Summary Report 2009-10*, 30 June, at vi.
68   Around 70,000 people (about 40,000 primary visa holders and 30,000 dependants) came to Australia on the temporary skilled migrant visa in 2005-06, an increase of 43 per cent on the previous year. As mentioned earlier, numbers plateaued with the global economic downturn. By June 2009, primary 457 visa grants were 39 per cent lower than June 2008: DIAC, *Subclass 457 Business (Long Stay) State/Territory Summary Report 2008-09*, June 2009, at iii.
69   Siew-Ean Khoo, Carmen Voigt-Graf, Graeme Hugo and Peter McDonald, 'Temporary Skilled Migration to Australia: The 457 Visa Subclass' (2003) 11(4) *People and Place* 27 at 38.

[10.42] In more recent times 457 visas have been issued increasingly to blue collar workers from developing countries. This raises concerns that these lower waged temporary workers are vulnerable to exploitative working conditions and that the visa program operates to degrade working conditions for Australian workers. Media outlets and unions reported many stories of worker abuse under the scheme operating in the mid 2000s. Abuse of migrant workers was most serious in the construction, health and hospitality industries, with workers enduring non-payment of wages, compulsory overtime, variation of employment duties and non-payment of superannuation or private health insurance contributions.[70] In one instance a chef was paid less than $10,000 for 18 months' work in a Melbourne Malaysian restaurant.[71] In another, Indian construction workers paid their employer (who was also their landlord) inflated rent for extremely poor living conditions in the Sydney suburb of Villawood.[72] Filipino nurses were reported as incurring debts of thousands of dollars to a Philippines-based migration agent (who was an associate of their employer), supposedly to cover travel and visa costs. On arrival, the nurses faced not only repayments deducted from their salary (undercutting the minimum statutory level) but also work as aged care assistants, under-utilising their nursing qualifications.[73] Other workers were dismissed after sustaining a workplace injury; pressured to sign individual work agreements with substantially reduced conditions; or verbally assaulted by employers. Many were paid the statutory minimum salary level but were placed in positions where the nominated salary was well below the market rate.

[10.43] The problems were due to deficiencies in the original structure of the 457 visa and with departmental procedures which either actually authorised this mistreatment or failed to prevent it. For example, while minimum wage requirements for sponsors might have appeared to prevent employers undercutting prevailing Australian standards, exemptions operated for regional employers and for 'overseas' businesses.[74] According to departmental data tabled in the Senate in June 2006, between November 2003 and June 2005 30 per cent of all onshore 457 visa grants were approved at salaries below the gazetted minimum.[75] By 2006, the gazetted minimum wage was substantially below the Australian average in every industry other than communication services. The ability of overseas businesses to sponsor workers on 457 visas without complying with Australian labour laws encouraged employers to contract migrant labour through an offshore labour hire agency that was exempt from Australian labour laws.

---

70   See, for example, Australian Manufacturing Workers' Union, *Temporary Skilled Migration: A New Form of Indentured Servitude*, Australian Expert Group in Industry Services (AEGIS) University of Western Sydney and the Australian Manufacturing Workers' Union, July 2006; NSW Nurses' Association, 'Dark Side of Guest Labour – 457 Visas are Loose and Open to Abuse', union news release, 4 October 2006.
71   Mares, above n 2.
72   CFMEU, 'Win for Indian Workers' (2007) 38 *Unity* 11.
73   Press release, 'ANF Responds to Workplace Ombudsman Decision on Filipino Nursing Assistants Employed under 457 Visa Scheme', 15 August 2008, available at <http://www.nswnurses.asn.au/news/14936.html>.
74   Employers in regional areas who had a certification from a Regional Certificating Body that the position could not be reasonably filled locally could gain exemptions from the minimum skill and salary levels.
75   Minister for Immigration, Senator Vanstone, Press Release, 7 April 2006.

[10.44] In the later years of the Howard Coalition government, public debate framed this issue in terms of changes in the industrial relationships landscape brought by the introduction of the *Workplace Relations Amendment (Work Choices) Act 2005* (Cth) (*Work Choices Act*), which commenced operation on 27 March 2006.[76] While federal awards continued to operate under Work Choices, the matters that they were allowed to cover were reduced to 15 and there was an expanded list of explicitly non-allowable federal award matters.[77] Awards could be displaced once an employee entered into any form of statutory workplace agreement. These agreements no longer had to conform to a global 'no disadvantage test' which had previously linked agreements to awards. These mechanisms reflected the Coalition government's desire to enhance employer flexibility and, in the context of the 457 scheme, facilitated employer nominations. They also undercut the salary levels for 457 visa holders because the standards in relevant awards no longer provided a stable benchmark. The minimum salary threshold did nothing to guard against the undercutting of prevailing wages and conditions for 457 visa holders who worked long hours or in highly paid professions.

[10.45] There are other structural aspects of the 457 visa program which make workers especially susceptible to employer abuse. First, visa holders are in a relationship of greater dependency on employers than are Australian workers. The termination of an employment contract could result in the cancellation of the 457 visa after 28 days. The threat of termination of employment discouraged migrant workers from seeking redress for abusive employer behaviour while the working relationship was on foot. Before 2007, the only sanction faced by sponsors who failed to comply with statutory requirements was the possibility that they would be precluded from sponsoring in the future. Before 1 July 2004, no sanctions applied at all for sponsors' failure to comply with statutory undertakings.

[10.46] In August 2007, the Joint Standing Committee on Migration (JSCM) reported on its inquiry into 456, 457 and occupational trainee visas, addressing eligibility requirements and the monitoring, enforcement and reporting arrangements for temporary business visas.[78] Coinciding as it did with the federal election in 2007, this report failed to gain traction. What followed rather was a series of inquiries and reports commissioned by the incoming Labor government. In May 2008, an External Reference Group made recommendations in six areas: long-term planning, streamlining application and approval processes, eliminating duplication and unnecessary administration, remaining competitive and branding.[79] Industrial relations commissioner Barbara Deegan reported on the integrity of the 457 scheme, focusing on the salary levels, English language requirements, occupational health and safety considerations, and migrant worker abuse. The report concluded that 'concerns about exploitation are well-founded, particularly in relation to visa holders

---

76   The *Work Choices Act* substantially amended the *Workplace Relations Act 1996* (Cth).
77   Section 27 of the *Workplace Relations Act*, as amended.
78   JSCM, *Temporary Visas ... Permanent Benefits: Ensuring the Effectiveness, Fairness and Integrity of the Temporary Business Visa Program*, tabled 12 September 2007.
79   Visa Subclass 457 External Reference Group, *Final Report to the Minister for Immigration and Citizenship*, April 2008.

at the lower end of the salary scale'.⁸⁰ As we have discussed throughout Part 10.5, the Rudd government responded to these reports with a variety of amendments to the scheme, especially in 2009.

10.5.8 An agenda for reform of temporary labour migration

[10.47] Still, by December 2010, key recommendations from the various reviews, parliamentary inquiries and submissions of unions and community groups had yet to be implemented, or to receive a formal response from the government. The political turmoil surrounding the replacement of Prime Minister Kevin Rudd with Prime Minister Julia Gillard in that year may have slowed the reform agenda. What remained clear is that the need for greater transparency and public accountability about the 457 visa program had yet to be met. Disaggregated data about the jobs for which 457 nominations have been approved and visa grants was still not readily available. Even if the Department is reluctant to name employers, published information should include the location of the position, detail about the industry and occupation, and base salary and other remuneration. Information should also be posted about the number and type of compliance complaints received, and the number of employers who have faced penalties under the employer sanctions provisions.

[10.48] There also remain structural features of the temporary employment scheme that impede the ability of temporary migrant workers to pursue their lawful entitlements in Australia. Temporary migrant workers should have the same workplace rights as their Australian counterparts. The fact that a 457 visa may be cancelled 28 days after the termination of employment remains a key source of vulnerability for visa holders in the workplace. Foreign workers experience much more limited labour mobility than Australian workers because they are dependent on their employer to maintain their ongoing lawful presence in the country. In our view, the government should implement a recommendation of the Deegan report that visa holders be given up to 90 days to find a new sponsor so as to retain the right to remain lawfully present in Australia.⁸¹ We also believe that the government should implement a recommendation from the 2007 parliamentary inquiry that a comprehensive, confidential complaints mechanism be introduced allowing workers to report abuses without provoking retaliatory action.⁸²

[10.49] Information about existing safeguards also needs to be communicated to visa holders. While the government has improved the information available on its website,⁸³ information should be provided at the time of the conferral of the visa and before the migrant leaves their country of origin. Foreign workers should be given information about workplace rights and obligations, including health and safety requirements in their particular industry. They should be educated about the

---

80   Visa Subclass 457 Integrity Review, *Final Report*, October 2008.
81   Ibid at 68.
82   JSCM, above n 78, recommendation 19.
83   An information booklet entitled 'Your Rights and Obligations – Immigration Facts for Workers' was released by DIAC on 8 October 2010, available at <http://www.immi.gov.au/skilled/rights-obligations-workers.htm>. It provides basic information in English, Tagalog, Indonesian, Chinese, Korean, Malay and Hindi.

industrial complaint process in Australia; their employers' obligations under the 457 scheme; and the availability of government, community, legal and union assistance.

[10.50] While it is commendable that the government has committed resources to enhancing employer monitoring to further the scheme's integrity, it is not clear that this monitoring has been focused on the migrants' conditions of work. To best protect the interests of migrant workers and safeguard Australian working standards, a monitoring system should be built around enforcing key employer obligations, including payment at market rates, occupational health and safety requirements, freedom of association and the lawfulness of dismissals.

10.6 Working holiday makers

[10.51] Through a series of bilateral agreements with countries regarded as 'low risk', Australia has for many years allowed young people aged between 18 and 30 to undertake limited work to support themselves during a holiday in Australia. The Work and Holiday visa and the Working Holiday visa (WHV)[84] are 12-month multiple entry visas available only to applicants who are nationals of countries with reciprocal working holiday agreements with Australia, or select other countries.[85] The applicants must be genuine visitors whose main purpose is to holiday in Australia. They must demonstrate that they have sufficient funds for the duration of their stay; a return airfare; and reasonable prospects of obtaining employment in Australia. Work must be incidental to the holiday. Visa holders can work for a single employer for no more than six months.[86] The typical working holiday maker (WHM) is a young person from an English-speaking country who is better educated than the average Australian worker but who is prepared to undertake low skilled jobs.[87]

[10.52] The perceived economic benefits of this program (over and above its 'cultural exchange' aspirations) include that WHMs spend more on average than they earn. They are also perceived to be useful in addressing regional labour shortages.[88]

---

84   Working Holiday visas (subclass 417) and Work and Holiday visas (subclass 462).
85   Working Holiday visas are currently available to passport holders from Belgium, Canada, Cyprus, Denmark, Estonia, Finland, France, Germany, Hong Kong, Ireland, Italy, Japan, Republic of Korea, Malta, the Netherlands, Norway, Sweden, Taiwan and the United Kingdom: *Specification under subparagraph 1225(3)(b)(i) – Class of Persons*, IMMI 09/008, April 2009. Work and Holiday visas are available to nationals from the USA, Indonesia, Malaysia, Thailand, Turkey, Bangladesh and Chile. See *Arrangements for Work and Holiday Visa Applicants from Thailand, Iran, Chile, Turkey, United States of America, Malaysia, Indonesia and Bangladesh (Item 1224A and Paragraph 462.211)*, IMMI 10/050, December 2010.
86   Condition 8547.
87   Glenys Harding and Elizabeth Webster, *The Working Holiday Maker Scheme and the Australian Labour Market* (Melbourne: Melbourne Institute of Applied Economic and Social Research, University of Melbourne, 2001) at 5-6. This 'middle class' demographic appears to be in line with working tourists elsewhere in the world: Natan Uriely, '"Travelling Workers" and "Working Tourists": Variations Across the Interaction Between Work and Tourism' (2001) 3 *International Journal of Tourism Research* 1 at 7.
88   Yan Tan, Sue Richardson, Laurence Lester, Tracy Bai and Lulu Sun, *Evaluation of Australia's Working Holiday Maker (WHM) Program* (Adelaide: National Institute of Labour Studies, Flinders University, 27 February 2009) at I and V; JSCM, *Working Holiday Makers: More than Just Tourists* (Canberra: August 1997) at 8-9.

During the years of conservative governance, the conditions attaching to this visa were progressively relaxed. In July 2006, the duration of employment permitted with any one employer was increased from three to six months. In 2005, WHMs became eligible for a second 12-month visa if they completed three months of specified work undertaken as a direct employee in regional Australia in the agricultural or mining industries. With farmers lobbying the government to create a regional seasonal migration scheme to address labour shortages in the agricultural sector, WHMs were encouraged to take on this role.[89] The requirement that work be undertaken as a direct employee was abandoned: volunteer work and work undertaken as a labour contractor are now permitted.

[10.53] The popularity of the WHM program is demonstrated by the exponential increase in visa grants: from 55,000 in 1997-98 to 194,103 in 2008-09.[90] Figures for 2009-10 appeared to be unaffected by the global economic downturn.[91] In latter years, over 20,000 visas represented a second WHV grant.[92] In terms of source nationalities, nationals from both United Kingdom and Korea dominated in 2008-09 with around 40,000 WHVs granted.[93]

10.7 The Seasonal Migration Program

[10.54] While Australia has traditionally favoured the highly skilled as temporary workers, a niche migration scheme has been developed to address labour shortages in the agricultural sector. This component of the migration program follows an international trend.[94] New Zealand admits blue collar Pacific Islander workers on temporary visas and Canada and the United States have temporary work schemes employing Mexican and Caribbean workers.[95] Every year, half a million seasonal workers from non-EU countries are employed in EU agriculture, especially in Germany.[96] Thai workers labour in Israel, Moroccans pick tomatoes in Spain and Chinese labourers pick apples in Japan.[97] In 2005, it was remarked that Australia

---

89   By mid-2008 the second working holiday visa became available after three months of work in expanded fields including plant and animal cultivation, fishing and pearling, tree farming and felling, mining and construction: *Working Holiday Visa – Definitions of 'Seasonal Work' and 'Regional Australia'*, IMMI 08/046, May 2008, under reg 1225(5).

90   Bob Kinnaird, '*Working Holiday Makers: More than Tourists* – Implications of the Report of the Joint Standing Committee on Migration' (1999) 7(1) *People and Place* 39 at 39; DIAC, *Annual Report 2008-09*, Outcome 1.1.3.

91   DIAC, *Working Holiday and Work & Holiday Visa Grants 2005-06 to 2009-10*, available at <http://www.immi.gov.au/media/statistics/pdf/visitor/2005-06-to-2009-10-whm-wah-visa-grants.pdf>.

92   DIAC, *Fact Sheet 49 – Working Holiday Program*, 20 August 2010.

93   Ibid.

94   Philip L Martin, *Managing Labour Migration: Temporary Worker Programs for the 21st Century* (Geneva: International Institute for Labour Studies, 2003).

95   Bryan Paul Christian, *Comparative Study: Policies for Facilitating High Skilled Migration to Industrial Countries* (Washington: Institute for the Study of International Migration, Georgetown University, March 2000).

96   United Nations Department of Economic and Social Affairs, *World Economic and Social Survey*, 2004, Part II, International Migration.

97   World Bank, *At Home and Away, Expanding Job Opportunities for Pacific Islanders Through Labour Mobility* (Washington: 2006) Ch 4.

and New Zealand could have been the only developed nations that did not import seasonal labour for agriculture.[98] Both countries are no longer international exceptions in this regard.

[10.55] The New Zealand Recognised Seasonal Employer (RSE) scheme was introduced in April 2007 with the key aim of encouraging earnings via remittances into rural communities and villages to fund development programs and education, housing and small business.[99] It allows employers to recruit overseas workers from Vanuatu, Tonga, Tuvalu, Kiribati and Samoa for seasonal horticulture work. To achieve registration in the scheme, employers must pledge to pay the 'relevant market rate', ensure workers are 'suitably accommodated', provide workers with food, shelter and clothing and ensure that any recruitment agents do not charge commissions. Employer approvals last for two years, with subsequent renewals for three-year periods. An RSE employer then seeks an 'Agreement to Recruit' overseas workers that allows employers to seek a certain number of workers from a designated country. Employers must guarantee to pay half the workers' travel costs, provide pay for at least an average of 30 hours per week and pay costs of removing workers from New Zealand if they overstay.[100]

[10.56] The New Zealand scheme, in turn, was strongly influenced by Canada's Seasonal Agricultural Workers' Program (CSWAP) which has brought temporary workers from the Caribbean since 1966 and Mexico since 1974. The scheme operates through bilateral agreements that provide for annual review and a formal mechanism for workers to raise grievances through their diplomatic mission. Canadian farmers need approval from local employment centres to certify that no Canadian workers are available to fill the jobs and must provide migrant workers with free housing and guarantee them a minimum of 240 hours' work over six weeks at or above the minimum wage rates. Employers must hold workers' compensation insurance to cover the migrant workers in case of industrial accidents and pay the cost of the migrants' international airfare, of which half may later be recouped from the worker. The migrants pay Canadian taxes and are covered by Canada's public health care.[101] The scheme provides continuity whereby growers can request the same workers each year which means that workers and employers develop a familiarity, workers gain some stability in a local community and employers do not need to invest constantly in retraining. Initially, the scheme was designed to

---

98 Sue Pickering and Helen Barnes, 'Towards a Sustainable Workforce Across Horticulture' [2005] *The Orchardist* 30.
99 Nic Maclellan, *Workers for All Seasons? Issues from New Zealand's Recognised Seasonal Employer (RSE) Program* (Melbourne: Institute for Social Research, Swinburne University of Technology, 2008).
100 Since commencement 100 companies have been accredited as 'Approved Employers' and over 4000 workers from the Pacific and South East Asia have had visa applications approved. Recruitment of workers is done by national labour Ministries and private recruiters. The New Zealand scheme requires recruitment agencies operating in the Pacific country to obtain a licence from the Commissioner of Labour, to recruit in consultation with community leaders, to not charge a commission and to issue all RSE workers with a labour contract. Workers must be at least 18, have a return air ticket and meet health and character requirements. See Ibid.
101 David Griffith, *The Canadian and United States Migrant Agricultural Workers Programs: Parallels and Divergence between two North American Seasonal Migrant Agricultural Labour Markets with respect to 'Best Practices'* (Ottawa: North South Institute, 2006).

deter overstaying by selecting male workers who left their wives and children at home.[102]

10.7.1 The structure of the program

[10.57] The Australian seasonal workers program was introduced as a pilot in August 2008 to recruit Pacific Islanders for temporary harvest work in the horticulture and viticulture industries. Based on models developed in Canada and New Zealand, the three-year program was planned to allow up to 2500 seasonal workers from Kiribati, Papua New Guinea, Tonga and Vanuatu to work in the horticultural industry in regional Australia for up to seven months a year in areas of labour shortage. The arrival of the first workers was delayed by several months, with 50 workers from Tonga arriving in mid February 2009. This delay has been regarded to reflect 'the complexity of the process and the poor preparedness of Australian and labour sending country government agencies for coping with these complexities in terms of developing new policy, bureaucratic processes and procedures'.[103] Indeed, as of October 2009, only 56 people had been recruited through the program.[104]

[10.58] Unlike the New Zealand and Canadian programs, the Australian scheme relies on the employment of the seasonal workers being done through labour hire companies. Initially, two such companies were approved by the government to employ and place Pacific seasonal workers for the first phase of the pilot.

[10.59] The structure of the program is geared towards supporting the rights of the seasonal workers in a number of ways. Each labour hire company is the direct employer of the workers and must guarantee seasonal workers a minimum average of 30 hours of work per week for six months, employing workers in accordance with Australian work standards, including awards and training requirements. The labour hire firm must pay the full upfront cost of workers' airfares (although it is permitted to recoup half from the worker over the period of the visa grant). Non-compliance with the terms of the undertakings may result in the labour hire companies' commission being terminated.

[10.60] These obligations are designed to ensure that wages do not fall below the mandated minimum and also provide an additional incentive to prevent growers from hiring migrant labour where local workers are available. Some, however, warn that these costs will make the scheme prohibitive for small growers and advantage large industrial growers.[105]

---

102 Tanya Basok, 'He Came, He Saw, He … Stayed. Guest Worker Programs and the Issue of Non-Return' (2000) 38(2) *International Migration* 215.
103 Rochelle Ball, 'Australia's Pacific Seasonal Worker Pilot Scheme and its Interface With the Australian Horticultural Labour Market: Is it Time to Refine the Policy?' (2010) 25(1) *Pacific Economic Bulletin* 114 at 120.
104 Nic Maclellan, 'What's Happened to all the Pacific Seasonal Workers?', Crikey.com, 26 October 2009.
105 See Nic Maclellan and Peter Mares, 'Labour Mobility in the Pacific: Creating Seasonal Work Programs in Australia' in Stewart Firth (ed), *Globalisation and Governance in the Pacific Islands* (Canberra: ANU E Press, 2006) Ch 8.

[10.61] In addition, the labour hire company is vested under the scheme with responsibility for certain aspects of the workers' welfare and pastoral care. It must:
- arrange transport to and from the Australian port of arrival and departure (at no charge to the worker);
- contribute to pre-departure briefing in the sending country conducted by the relevant Pacific Island government;
- provide an on-arrival briefing in Australia at no charge to the worker;
- ensure that Pacific seasonal workers can access suitable accommodation at 'fair and reasonable cost';
- arrange transport to and from the worksite at a 'reasonable cost' to the worker;
- arrange for workers' access to personal banking;
- provide personal protective equipment in accordance with occupational health and safety requirements;
- ensure growers provide on-site facilities (such as toilets, first aid, shelter, fresh drinking water) for workers;
- ensure growers provide on-farm induction including occupational health and safety briefings;
- ensure growers provide necessary language translations of work notices and guidelines;
- assist workers to participate in government-funded literacy or skills training; and
- assist workers to access opportunities for recreation and religious observance.[106]

Labour hire companies are required to demonstrate to the government that they have appropriate arrangements in place, in order to gain government approval.

[10.62] Australian horticulture growers with demonstrated unmet demand for labour can apply for access to Pacific seasonal workers. Participating Australian growers must demonstrate 'reasonable efforts' to employ Australians, and be willing to participate in training programs for Australians who are not 'job ready'. Growers are required to provide evidence that they have engaged in labour market testing by having lodged vacancies with local employment services for the same number of positions as are proposed to be filled by migrant workers at least two weeks before seeking seasonal migrant workers or having undertaken other recruitment through local channels.

[10.63] Some opposition to the scheme is based on concerns about the attendant risk of workers overstaying their temporary permit. The Centre for Independent Studies, for instance, has argued that the admission of agricultural workers could yield a 'camouflage to a substantial flow of undocumented labour'.[107] A number of disincentives have been built into the program to discourage workers from overstaying their temporary visas: workers are not allowed to bring their dependants. They are barred from applying for visas while in Australia (except for Protection visas). They are only able to reclaim their superannuation contributions on departure from

---

106 AusAID, *Pacific Economic Survey: Engaging with the World* (Canberra: Australian Agency for International Development, 2009).
107 Helen Hughes and Gaurav Sodhi, *Should Australia and New Zealand Open their Doors to Guest Workers from the Pacific? Costs and Benefits* (Sydney: Centre for Independent Studies, 2006) at 16.

Australia and will be permitted to return for work in future seasons only if they have fully complied with all visa requirements. These draw from mechanisms deployed in the Canadian and New Zealand schemes to enhance those programs' integrity.[108] In addition, the approved labour hire company that employs the workers is required to accept liability for the cost of removal and repatriation of workers who have breached the conditions of their visa.

10.7.2 A labour market issue

[10.64] For some time, substantial pressure has been brought to bear by industry leaders to admit Pacific workers to respond to sectoral and seasonal labour shortages in Australian agricultural sectors.[109] Generally, primary producers rely on both documented and undocumented workers to meet seasonal labour market needs. The documented workforce includes itinerant farm labourers, family members, local casual workers, students, retirees travelling around Australia and backpackers on the WHM scheme (which allows tourists aged 18-30 from certain countries to work in Australia for periods of up to three months with any one employer – discussed at Part 10.6 above).[110] The undocumented workforce is thought to consist of unauthorised residents (primarily from Pacific Island, South East Asian and Chinese backgrounds), overseas students working in excess of permitted hours, Australians working while in receipt of benefits and foreign travellers working without authorisation.[111]

[10.65] One response to labour shortages has been the development of a 'harvest trail'.[112] This has encouraged more WHMs into the rural labour market. As mentioned above, in 2005 additional incentives were introduced for travellers to take up agricultural work by allowing WHMs who do three months of 'seasonal harvest work in regional Australia' to apply for a second 12-month WHV. However, primary producers say backpackers are not sufficiently committed to the arduous work over the entire season and inevitably each season brings a crop of novice workers, who are less productive, require higher levels of supervision and are more accident prone.

[10.66] While the 457 visa program no longer requires employers to undertake labour market testing, Australian growers hoping to employ Pacific workers under this scheme have to demonstrate 'reasonable efforts' to employ Australians through

---

108   In 2004, less than 1.5 per cent of the 15,123 workers who entered Ontario under the Canadian program were listed as absent from their jobs without leave. See Nic Maclellan and Peter Mares, *Remittances and Labour Mobility in the Pacific: A Working Paper on Seasonal Work Programs in Australia for Pacific Islanders* (Melbourne: Swinburne University of Technology Institute for Social Research, 2006) at 30. In addition, the Canadian scheme withholds a proportion of the wages from Jamaican workers until their return home: Peter Mares, 'Seasonal Migrant Labour: A Boon for Australian Country Towns?' in Maureen F Rogers and David R Jones (eds), *The Changing Nature of Australia's Country Towns* (Bendigo: La Trobe University, 2006) at 139; see also Satish Chand, 'Risks and Rewards of Allowing Seasonal Workers From the Pacific into Australia' (2008) 23(2) *Pacific Economic Bulletin* 226.
109   Senate Standing Committee on Employment, Workplace Relations and Education, *Perspectives on the Future of the Harvest Labour Force* (Canberra: Cth of Australia, 2006) at [3.37].
110   Harding and Webster, above n 87.
111   Mares, above n 108, at 139.
112   National Harvest Trail Working Group, *Harvesting Australia: Report of the National Harvest Trail Working Group* (Canberra: Cth of Australia, 2000).

labour market testing and investment in broader local training initiatives. Still, some commentators observe that, worldwide, labour market tests have proven difficult to implement in practice, since employers may find bureaucratic loopholes or disingenuous means of ensuring that no local workers are found to fill vacancies.[113]

[10.67] While some unions continue to oppose the seasonal workers scheme, the Australian Workers Union (AWU), which covers many farm workers, has given it conditional support. AWU Secretary Paul Howes commented: 'We've had massive issues with illegal labour in these industries for several decades now. And what we've seen overseas that the only way to fix it up is to have a regulated system'.[114]

10.7.3 Eschewing permanent settlement

[10.68] The emergence of the scheme, under the Labor government, marks a stark move away from entrenched opposition to the facilitation of temporary labour migration of low-waged workers in our region. Even while temporary skilled migration soared under the Coalition government, the prevailing approach to seasonal migration was captured in the remark by the then Treasurer Peter Costello: 'I don't think it is a part of the Australian ethos, I don't think it is consistent with our culture and I don't think it would be acceptable'.[115]

[10.69] As early as 2003, a Senate inquiry recommended that the Australian government develop a pilot program for seasonal workers to come to Australia from the Pacific.[116] At the October 2005 meeting of the Pacific Islands Forum, held in Papua New Guinea, the issue of labour mobility was the key theme promoted by several government representatives to serve regional integration. Even after the then Prime Minister, John Howard, reiterated his opposition to temporary work schemes in Australia, a further Senate Committee recommended in October 2006 that contingency plans be made for introducing contract harvest labour in the near future.[117]

[10.70] The reasons for the longstanding government resistance to the scheme are complex. Most obviously they illustrate historical opposition to recruiting foreign labour on a temporary basis as a means of undercutting local labour standards.[118] This reflects a general bias towards permanent rather than temporary migration. Anxieties about temporary labour migration source back to the turn of the 20th century when the *Pacific Island Labourers Act 1901* (Cth) provided for the deportation of so-called 'kanakas' from sugar cane fields in Queensland. Politicians in the new Australian

---

113 Martin Ruhs, 'The Potential of Temporary Migration Programmes in Future International Migration Policy' (2006) 145(1-2) *International Labour Review* 7.
114 'Pacific Island guest worker scheme sparks union backlash' *7.30 Report*, ABC, 14 August 2008.
115 Former Treasurer Peter Costello, quoted in S Lewis and E Coleman, 'Migrants to Kickstart Economy' *The Australian*, 3 March 2005.
116 Senate Foreign Affairs, Defence and Trade References Committee, *A Pacific Engaged – Australia's Relations with Papua New Guinea and the Islands of the South West Pacific* (Canberra, 2003).
117 Senate Standing Committee on Employment, Workplace Relations and Education, above n 109, at x.
118 Lenore Layman, 'To Keep Up the Australian Standard: Regulating Contract Migration 1901-1950' (1996) 70 *Labour History* 25.

federation were determined to prevent the nation being built on the backs of bonded Pacific labourers.

[10.71] In fact, Coalition government policies saw the number of temporary entrants exceed permanent arrivals for the first time. It seems that its rhetorical opposition to short-term migrant labour was reserved for the relatively unskilled and uneducated migrants from Pacific Islands. Others have identified 'an entrenched orthodoxy within government that sees only highly skilled or capital-rich migrants as being of value to Australia'.[119] This bifurcated approach might suggest that Australia has experienced labour shortages only within highly paid industry sectors or jobs. But such a picture is belied by the reports of parliamentary committees and industry representatives.[120] It is suggested that restrictions on blue collar labour migration are based on factors other than whether the admission of a foreign worker addresses a gap in the local employment market. The emphasis on skilled, as opposed to unskilled, migration was likely deployed to enhance the palatability of the 457 program for the Australian electorate.[121]

[10.72] The election of the Labor government in November 2007 signalled a change in Australia's response to the region. While in opposition, in 2005, Labor had issued a policy paper that supported increased labour mobility in the region in return for economic and administrative reform in Pacific countries.[122] However, the current rigidities of the seasonal workers program, which may have discouraged involvement from growers and labour hire firms,[123] could well limit the potential expansion of this pilot.

10.7.4 Migration as development

[10.73] A growing literature suggests that seasonal work programs can be a 'win-win' for both developed and developing countries.[124] These schemes are said to offer many of the benefits of migration – such as relieving labour shortages in developed countries and aiding development in developing countries – with few of the perceived costs – such as permanent loss of talent in developing countries and social and fiscal costs in developing countries.

[10.74] Many Pacific Island countries are facing a decline in export earnings, population growth and high unemployment rates, lack of effective governance and poor economic development.[125] As a result of the skilled migration intake

---

119 Maclellan and Mares, above n 105, at 154.
120 Senate Standing Committee on Employment, Workplace Relations and Education, above n 109.
121 Patrick Chan, 'WorkChoices for Migration? Assessing the New Era of Skilled Migration' (2005) 28 *Immigration Review* 5 at 6.
122 Bob Sercombe, *Towards a Pacific Community*, ALP Pacific Policy Discussion Paper, 2005.
123 Ball, above n 103, at 125.
124 Global Commission on International Migration, *Migration in an Interconnected World: New Directions for Action* (Geneva: 2005); Lant Pritchett, *Let Their People Come: Breaking the Gridlock on Global Labour Mobility* (Washington DC: Center for Global Development, 2006).
125 Charles Stahl and Reginald Appleyard, *Migration and Development in the Pacific Islands: Lessons from the New Zealand Experience* (Canberra: AusAid, April 2007).

policies of most developed countries, Pacific Island nations are robbed of the skilled workers who are most needed while low-skilled workers who most need jobs are left behind and remain unemployed. Youth bulge in island nations means that employment generation will become increasingly urgent and there is growing discussion about the potential to address it through greater international labour mobility.[126] This picture is further complicated by regional security and climate change issues.

[10.75] Responding to these challenges, the World Bank has promoted the utility of the remittances generated by seasonal migration schemes to enhance regional development.[127] Remittances are widely seen to play a key role in boosting economic growth, creating savings and investment capital, and reducing poverty, as well as allowing particular households to increase consumption, especially on housing and education. Indeed, there is evidence that remittances by short-terms migrants are likely to be spent in ways that may be more immediately productive and employment-creating than remittances sent back by permanent and long-term emigrants.[128] For instance, apparently, the New Zealand scheme has seen communities in Tonga and Vanuatu coordinating their efforts to contribute some portion of remittances towards community projects such as micro-credit schemes for women.[129]

[10.76] However, the merits of remittances in long-term development strategies are the subject of heated debate among economists. Some point to the propensity of remittances to distort local markets, create dependencies and boost spending on consumable goods thereby increasing inflation.[130] Helen Hughes and Gaurav Sodhi argue that the numbers involved in any Australian scheme would be insufficient to address unemployment problems in the Pacific and would merely provide a safety-valve or reprieve for under-performing governments.[131]

[10.77] Even so, beyond the income flows to home countries, seasonal migration may have other effects in terms of enhancing regional development.[132] Returning migrants bring not only cash, but also insights about how the world works, and skills such as financial competence.[133] Indeed, as part of the Australian pilot scheme, the government has committed to ensure seasonal workers receive pre-departure and on-arrival training in financial literacy and money management skills briefing sessions, which will teach them about budgeting, managing a bank account and

---

126   See Maclellan and Mares, above n 105, at 138.
127   World Bank, above n 97. See also John Connell and Richard Brown, *Remittances in the Pacific – An Overview* (Manila: Asian Development Bank, 2005).
128   Helen Ware, 'Melanesian Seasonal Migration as a Potential Contribution to Security' (2007) 19(3) *Global Change, Peace and Security* 221 at 229.
129   Edmund Rice Centre, *Pacific Labour Mobility: Seasonal Guest Worker Schemes* (Sydney: 2009) at 1.
130   Adrienne Millbank, *A Seasonal Guest-Worker Program for Australia?*, Research Brief, Australian Parliamentary Library, No 16, 5 May 2006, at 10.
131   Hughes and Sodhi, above n 107.
132   Nicola Piper, 'Guest Editorial: The Complex Interconnections of the Migration – Development Nexus: A Social Perspective' (2009) 15 *Population, Space and Place* 93.
133   Jonathan Sibley, 'Financial Competence as a Tool for Poverty Reduction: Financial Literacy and Rural Banking the Pacific' (2007) 72 *Development Bulletin* 23.

reading a payslip. Beyond entrepreneurial skills, research indicates that returning migrants also bring back skills to build up civil society and broaden political debate.[134]

[10.78] The ultimate development impact of Australia's scheme is going to depend on the way in which it is implemented. It remains to be seen whether temporary emigrants going for seasonal harvesting work in Australia will be drawn from the pool of the unemployed or will come from those already in employment in the Pacific. Studies on Vanuatuan workers in New Zealand's RSE program show that these workers are mostly subsistence farmers who have not completed more than 10 years of schooling and would be unlikely to be accepted under existing channels, although those who participate in the program tend to have higher levels of English literacy, health and incomes than those who are not applying for the program.[135] On the other hand, other research indicates that Tongan workers coming through the RSE are poorer, more rural and less skilled or educated than Tongans not participating and that the household income resulting from their participation is thus likely to be 'pro-poor'.[136]

[10.79] Even so, the financial and social benefits of increased remittances should not overshadow the significant social costs of temporary migration for work. Seasonal workers will be separated from family for up to seven months in each year, which can impact on children's welfare and education and put an extra burden on the elderly left in the village.[137]

10.7.5 The potential for worker exploitation

[10.80] The pilot is primarily administered through the Department of Education, Employment and Workplace Relations (DEEWR) rather than the Department of Immigration, which is an important signal in terms of the significance attached to regulating working conditions. This serves to highlight the practices and corporate social responsibilities of labour recruitment and labour hire companies, growers and producers, and financial institutions.[138]

[10.81] Experience with the 457 visa program suggests that problems emerge with migrant workers who are tied to a specific employer. Arguably, there is even more scope for abuse in a seasonal migration scheme since the seasonal workers are

---

134   Ware, above n 128, at 230.
135   David McKenzie, Pilar Garcia Martinez and L Alan Winters, 'Who is Coming From Vanuatu to New Zealand under the New Recognised Seasonal Employer Program?' (2008) 23(3) *Pacific Economic Bulletin* 205.
136   John Gibson and David McKenzie, *Preliminary Impacts of a New Seasonal Work Program on Rural Household Incomes in the Pacific* (Hamilton: University of Waikato Working Paper in Economics 18/08, 2008); John Gibson, David McKenzie and Halahingano Rohurua, '*How Pro-Poor is the Selection of Seasonal Migrant Workers from Tonga under New Zealand's Recognised Seasonal Employer Program?*' (World Bank Policy Research Working Paper 4698, 2008).
137   J Dennis, *Pacific Island Seafarers – A Study of the Social and Economic Implications of Seafaring on Dependants and Communities* (Suva: Pacific Seafarers Training Program, Regional Maritime Program, Secretariat of the Pacific Community, 2003); Maclellan and Mares, above n 105.
138   OECD Watch and Brotherhood of St Laurence, *Seasonal Labour Mobility: Responsible Business Conduct, Decent Work and Regional Engagement* (Paris: OECD: 2008).

confined to a specific industry, indeed a specific labour hire firm, so do not have even the limited ability of 457 visa holders to seek to change their employer sponsor and live where they choose. Additionally, the 457 visa scheme is designed as a potential path towards permanent settlement whereas the seasonal migration scheme is a true temporary 'guestworker' program with no future prospect of surer immigration status. This enhances the dependence of the seasonal work on the labour hire firm or grower and strongly discourages workers from registering complaints.

[10.82] While overseas schemes claim broad success, both Canadian and New Zealand workers have been subject to mistreatment in some cases. Canada has seen documented cases of protests by migrant workers, cases of abuse and exploitation, substandard accommodation and industrial accidents due to insufficient training, inadequate safety equipment or overlong working hours.[139] The Canadian oversight mechanisms have been found to be lacking, with consular liaison staff seen to be too remote from workers and suffering from a conflict of interest in maintaining good relations with Canada so that they do not vigorously pursue the claims of individual workers.

[10.83] The New Zealand RSE program has yielded reports of poor housing (a claim that over 20 workers from Kiribati were accommodated in one house), contracts being paid piece rate at minimum wage rather than the 'market rate', wage deductions being made without workers being fully informed and workers' claims that they had been given inaccurate information on housing and other conditions.[140] In New Zealand, there have been reports of workers being sent home for drinking off-orchard or other offences, which raises serious concerns since the workers' lawful leisure time activities should not be subject to the oversight of employers or immigration authorities.[141]

[10.84] Indeed, in Australia, allegations of improper practices by employers arose within one week of the first seasonal workers arriving. The labour hire firm involved announced that the Tongan workers would work on casual employment contracts and would not be paid if there was no work.[142] In the result, a compromise was reached between the firms involved and the ACTU whereby the workers were employed on a casual contract with a guaranteed average employment of 30 hours a week, and with higher total wages than would have been available under a fixed employment contract.[143] Subsequently, workers under the scheme have been employed under fixed-term and casual work contracts.

---

139 Tanya Basok, *Tortillas and Tomatoes: Transmigrant Mexican Harvesters in Canada* (McGill: Queens University Press, 2003).
140 Maclellan, above n 99; Adrienne Millbank, 'Guest-Workers for Australia: Win-Win, Token Gesture or Moral Hazard?' (2008) 16(3) *People and Place* 58 at 60.
141 Nic Maclellan, 'Seasonal Workers for Australia – Lessons from New Zealand' (2008) 5(3) *Farm Policy Journal* 43 at 49.
142 'ACTU says Pacific Workers not being Paid their Full Entitlements', ABC Radio National, 2 June 2009, available at <www.radioaustralia.net.au/asiapac/stories/200906/s2587586.htm>; 'Seasonal Workers' Scheme Hits Hurdle over Employment Status', ABC News, 23 February 2009, available at <http://www.abc.net.au/news/stories/2009/02/23/2499319.htm>.
143 Ball, above n 103, at 125.

[10.85] Some have recommended the creation of 'a mechanism of independent dispute resolution to manage conflicts when these arise'.[144] In theory, seasonal workers in Australia would have access to the Fair Work Ombudsman but, in practice, workers are likely to face major hurdles in making any claims on their return, and are likely to feel that such a claim, however legitimate the grievance, will prejudice their future involvement in the program. Clear information must be provided to workers and employers as to the employment rights of migrants.

[10.86] Further, there has been almost no information available about the procedures for recruitment and pre-departure briefings for workers. The regulation and licensing of recruitment agents must be a central feature of the ongoing monitoring of workers' rights, to ensure workers are fully apprised of the implications of the scheme, understand their rights on entry to Australia and are not subject to corrupt or exploitative practices in their home country before or after their seasonal contract in Australia.

[10.87] Even before the commencement of the program, researcher Nic Maclellan warned that 'the New Zealand experience suggests that any seasonal workers scheme must involve more than monitoring of conditions for temporary workers by employers and industry groups – the scheme must be regulated by government, and there must be a system of sanctions for breaches of those regulations'.[145] The Australian pilot already seems to fail to meet these standards in numerous ways. First, while aspects of the program, like the labour market testing requirement, indicate tight regulation, the structure of the program as a whole is based on a model of outsourcing all responsibility to a private intermediary between government, workers and employers: the labour hire firm. It may be that this will prejudice the ongoing transparency of arrangements as well as the accountability of the scheme to the Australian community and the seasonal workers. In addition, there is no evidence of broad engagement with the community sector in the regional areas where the migrants are working (including community groups, trade unions, churches and academics), which has been identified as crucial in reducing the vulnerability of workers in Canada.[146] Finally, unlike new sanctions introduced for immigration law breaches by sponsors of 457 visa holders, the only penalty provided for in this pilot scheme is that the labour hire sponsor, or grower, may not be permitted to participate in the scheme in the future.

[10.88] Although seasonal labourers have already commenced work in regional Australia, much is still unknown about the conditions in which they are working and the efficacy of safeguards designed to protect them and Australian workers. At the same time, there is evidence that the dense web of government regulation designed to ensure that the scheme does not fail politically has hampered the development of

---

144 Maclellan and Mares, above n 105, at 156.
145 Maclellan, above n 141, at 43.
146 United Food and Commercial Workers Canada, 'The Status of Migrant Farm Workers in Canada' (Toronto: 2004); R Russell, 'Jamaican Workers' Participation in CSAWP and Development Consequences in the Workers' Rural Home Communities' (Ottawa: North South Institute, 2004); Basok, above n 139.

the scheme.[147] To date, the scheme has clearly provided very limited opportunities for Pacific workers. Significant questions remain about its long-term viability in its present form.

---

147   Therese MacDermott and Brian Opeskin, 'Regulating Pacific Seasonal Labour in Australia' (2010) 83(2) *Pacific Affairs* 283.

11

Students, Visitors and Other Temporary Entrants

[11.01]   The vast majority of non-citizens who enter Australia each year come for temporary purposes, as tourists, foreign students or family visitors. The fact that tourism and the foreign education industries have come to play an ever greater role in the Australian economy is reflected in immigration policies that seek to maximise the financial and other benefits that flow from foreign visitors. Whereas the focus in earlier years was on fostering the tourism industry, in more recent times the business of educating foreign students has become one of the country's biggest export earners.

[11.02]   Despite the integral part they play in high schools, university campuses and part-time employment around the country, until recently remarkably little scholarly or policy-based research has focused on foreign students in Australia. The primary focus of social research in this area during the latter years of the Howard Coalition government was directed to the capabilities of foreign students who entered the labour market on skilled visas as well as their impact on the education of local students.[1] Policy reviews such as these have led to substantial reorientation of the interplays between the temporary student and permanent skilled visa regimes. But the promotion of the interests of Australian residents in this regard has not been matched by attention to the welfare and opportunities of temporary entrants.

[11.03]   This focus shifted dramatically after a series of assaults and murders of international students in Melbourne, Sydney and Hobart in 2008 and 2009. Accusations by a leading academic that Australian providers had been derelict in ensuring adequate levels of student safety[2] were accompanied by allegations that the attacks (and a slow government response) were indicative of endemic racism in Australia.[3] In response to the attacks on Indian students, high level Australian government delegations travelled to India in an effort to counter local press reports that Australia was no

---

1   See, for example, Bob Birrell and Ernest Healy, 'How are Skilled Migrants Doing?' (2008) 16(1) *People and Place* 1; Scott Bayley, Rob Fearnside, John Arnol, John Misiano and Rocco Rottura, 'International Students in Victorian Universities' (2002) 10(2) *People and Place* 45.
2   Chris Nyland, 'Australia Now Playing it Safe on Safety: Nyland' (2009) 19(2) *Campus Review* 4.
3   Federation of Indian Students of Australia, Submission to the Senate Education, Employment and Workplace Relations References Committee, *Inquiry into the Welfare of International Students*, 16 August 2009.

longer a safe destination for overseas students. Several inquiries into the welfare of international students and regulation of the international student industry followed.[4] In turn, these prompted sharper scrutiny of the broader structure of the student visa program and its intersection with permanent migration flows.

[11.04] A defining feature of changes made during the years of Coalition rule is that the overseas student program was integrated into the country's skilled migration program. Where most foreign students used to be required to return to their countries of origin and apply for migration from abroad, more recent trends have been to actively promote education in Australia as a pathway to permanent residence. In this respect, Australia is but one of a number of developed countries that compete with each other to attract the 'best and the brightest', a trend which Ayelet Shachar coins 'the race for talent'.[5] Policy-makers try to emulate the skilled stream recruitment efforts of their international counterparts in order to gain a relative advantage in the knowledge-based global economy. Immigration policy-making has thus become a multiplayer and multilevel game. By 2007, the perception arose that linking nominated occupations, education and rights to permanent residence was a mistake. The system was not seen to be striking the right balance between meeting the expectations of foreign students on the one hand and Australia's interests and needs as a nation on the other.

[11.05] In this chapter we examine in turn the law governing the most important of the temporary entrant categories that are not immediately related to employment: students and visitors. The significance of these aspects of the migration program has been seen primarily in terms of their fiscal worth as lucrative industries. At the same time, this benefit has for a long time been seen as compromised by the compliance risks that attend temporary visa holders in Australia.

11.1 The international student program

11.1.1 Early years: The shift from regional development to a growth industry

[11.06] The education of foreign students in Australia began in the 1950s under the auspices of the foreign aid program known as the Colombo Plan. The original goals of the international education sector included promoting development in the region through the provision of full or partial stipends to promising foreign students and the fostering of bilateral relationships, in effect a cultural exchange. At the commencement of this ambitious scheme in 1952, then foreign Minister, Richard Casey MP, said that the aim was to give Asian students:

---

4   Senate Education, Employment and Workplace Relations References Committee, *Welfare of International Students* (Canberra: November 2009); Council of Australian Governments, *International Students Strategy for Australia* (Canberra: October 2010); Bruce Baird, *Stronger, Simpler, Smarter ESOS: Supporting International Students. Final Report on the Review of the Education Services for Overseas Students (ESOS) Act 2000* (Canberra: DEEWR, February 2010).

5   Ayelet Shachar, 'The Race for Talent: Highly Skilled Migrants and Competitive Immigration Regimes' (2006) 81 *New York University Law Review* 148.

[a sense of] Australia at an impressionable stage of their lives and to exchange views at our universities and with our officials [which] should do a great deal to break down prejudices and misunderstandings on both sides.[6]

[11.07] Historian Daniel Oakman has pointed to the paradoxes inherent in this scheme. It was intended to combat communism in Asia but instead had the effect of breaking down the stereotypical views Australians held of Asian values. It was devised as a mechanism to ameliorate Asian criticism of the White Australia policy but instead had the effect of wearing down popular support in Australia for racial restrictions to immigration.[7] In the 35 years after its establishment, Australia enrolled around 40,000 foreign students in domestic educational institutions.[8] Over time, many of these were privately funded students who had heard positive reports of Australian education from those who benefited from the Colombo Plan.

[11.08] In the late 1980s, Australia made full-fee paying places available in its educational institutions to overseas students. This saw immediate expansion of the numbers of international students seeking places in Australian schools and universities (aided especially by the relaxation of restrictions on overseas study within the People's Republic of China (PRC)). The move can be seen now as a precursor to broader pressures placed on educational institutions in the 1990s to lessen their dependence on government funding.

[11.09] The turmoil of the crackdowns on pro-democracy demonstrators in PRC in June 1989 raised concerns for the first time about risks associated with the overseas student program. Many Chinese students in Australia sought asylum here, highlighting the overstay potential attending the admission of students of particular nationalities. This early preoccupation has come to present as a more general concern with creating effective compliance safeguards to ensure students meet all the conditions of their temporary visas. These include satisfying course requirements, restrictions on work outside the classroom as well as departure or change of status before the expiry of the visa.

Early compliance measures

[11.10] In 1991, following the recommendations of an inter-departmental committee review, mechanisms were introduced to streamline student entry; build compliance safeguards into the selection of overseas students; and to regulate the educational institutions selling their product to overseas students. For the first time certain students (those taking courses in English language or skills-based training) were required to undergo a screening process to determine their bona fides. It was in this context that the government introduced the use of statistical data on overstay rates as an aid to selecting students. Nationalities deemed to be 'low risk' were gazetted by

---

6   Quoted in Daniel Oakman, '"Young Asians in Our Homes": Colombo Students and White Australia' (2002) 26 *Journal of Australian Studies* 89 at 89.

7   See Daniel Oakman, *Facing Asia: A History of the Colombo Plan* (Honolulu: University of Hawaii Press, 2006).

8   The Hon Alexander Downer, MP, 'Launch of "Australia and the Colombo Plan 1949-1957"', speech given in Canberra, 23 May 2005.

name and students of such nationalities benefited from more generous visa conditions, including automatic work rights, and more straightforward application processes. As we explain in more detail below (see Part 11.1.3), this gazettal of distinctions between nationalities has remained a core component of entry requirements to this day, now termed 'Assessment Levels'.

[11.11] Complementing the rationalisation of entry requirements in 1991, arrangements were made to register and accredit educational institutions. The *Education Services for Overseas Students (Registration of Providers and Financial Regulation) Act 1991* (Cth) created a Commonwealth register of institutions and courses for overseas students (CRICOS). Registration was a prerequisite for any educational institution to offer courses to international students. This sought to address concerns that had been raised about course quality, and transactions between institutions and students (including the need for protection of student funds held by providers).[9] The Act was passed following the collapse of several private educational facilities that had offered courses to overseas students, principally from the PRC. The institutions had accepted an up-front payment of full fees and closed before the courses were completed. Funds paid by students were generally not held in separate accounts and many were lost on the collapse of the businesses.

11.1.2 The modern international student program

[11.12] The 2000s saw foreign student programs emerge as pathways for the permanent migration of qualified workers. The idea was that the students' familiarity with Australian society, and facility with English, would make them efficient workers and readily absorbed as permanent residents. The attraction of permanent residence in Australia as an outcome from study in an Australian institution arguably consolidated the expansion of the international education industry in Australia. Between 1990 and 2003, Australia's share of the global population of international students rose from 1 to 9 per cent, at which point Australia became the third largest exporter of transnational education services after the United States and United Kingdom.[10] In 2003, 154,578 foreign students were studying in Australia, while 55,819 accessed branch campuses of Australian universities abroad.[11] At that time, foreign students comprised 19 per cent of all tertiary enrolments in Australia, the highest level recorded for any country.[12] By 2008, the number of overseas students in Australia had jumped to over 275,000.[13] Education had become the third largest export industry behind coal and iron ore, contributing more than 120,000 full-time

---

9   Senate Standing Committee on Education, Employment and Training, *Operation of the Education Services for Overseas Students (Registration of Providers and Financial Regulation) Act 1991* (tabled 1 December 1992).
10 Organisation for Economic Co-operation and Development (OECD), *Education at a Glance* (Paris: OECD, 2005) at 253.
11 Ana Deumert, Simon Marginson, Chris Nyland, Gaby Ramia and Erlenawati Sawir, 'Global Migration and Social Protection Rights: The Social and Economic Security of Cross-Border Students in Australia' (2005) 5 *Global Social Policy* 329 at 335.
12 OECD, above n 10, at 267.
13 DIAC, *Population Flows – 2007-2008 Edition*, March 2009, at 55.

equivalent employees to the economy.[14] Australia had clearly capitalised on its place in the Asia-Pacific region: between 2005 and 2010 the top three source countries for overseas students were India, China and South Korea.[15]

[11.13] The foreign education market in Australia has obviously become extremely lucrative for Australian universities: while the government controls student visa grants, universities can determine tuition charges and, to a large degree, international student numbers.[16] Indeed, income from international students has moved from being marginal relative to government financial support, to an essential component of funding for Australian universities. All foreign students are classified as full fee-paying students except for the 0.9 per cent with foreign aid scholarships.[17] Several Australian universities derive more than 20 per cent of income from the market, which Professor Simon Marginson describes as a 'high level of dependence'.[18] This dependency has been produced by both changes to immigration policies regarding overseas students in Australia and public funding commitments. The question for the future is how universities and other educational institutions survive a series of policy and other events that saw foreign student enrolments tumble in and after 2008-09. The general economic downturn and stock market turmoil reduced the value of individuals' savings in some of the key source countries, making students more likely to choose educational institutions closer to home. The reduction of pathways to permanent residence has also reduced the attractiveness of Australian programs.[19]

[11.14] In this section we set out in broad terms the operation of the international student visa program. We begin by laying out some of the basic mechanical requirements for student visas, the conditions placed on students and issues specific to the cancellation of student visas. We then take a more historical view of the area, exploring the Coalition government's move to position the international student program as a pathway to skilled permanent migration, with dispensations given to applicants for permanent residence who had studied and worked in Australia. It has been suggested these incentives created distortions in the skilled migration program whereby students modified their choice of professional or vocational studies based on the attractiveness of their skills to assessors of their permanent visa application.

[11.15] The controversy over the appropriate shape and role of the international student program has overtaken the earlier focus of policy-makers on compliance concerns regarding students temporarily resident in the country. We examine the Labor government's moves to de-couple the international student and skilled migration programs. We conclude by considering in more detail other regulatory attempts to regulate the education industry in its dealings with overseas students. We examine

---

14   Ibid.
15   DIAC, *Fact Sheet 50: Overseas Students in Australia*, September 2010.
16   Deumert et al, above n 11, at 335.
17   Department of Employment, Education and Training, *Higher Education: Report for the 2004 to 2006 Triennium*, available at <www.dest.gov.au/sectors/higher_education/publications_resources/profiles/higher_education_report_2004_2006_triennium.htm>.
18   Simon Marginson, 'Global Position and Position Taking: The Case of Australia' (2007) 11 *Journal of Studies in International Education* 5 at 17.
19   Khalid Khoser, *The Global Financial Crisis and International Migration: Policy Implications for Australia* (Sydney: Lowy Institute for International Policy, July 2009) at 9.

the avenues for redress available to students who have been aggrieved by education providers and the implications of the apparent vulnerability of international students to criminal attacks and workplace abuse.

11.1.3 Student visa requirements

[11.16] The linchpin of the student visa application continues to be that the applicant has been accepted to study in a course registered on the CRICOS, which is maintained by the Commonwealth Department of Education, Employment and Workplace Relations (DEEWR). Relevant courses include a range of full-fee award and non-award courses offered by primary, secondary and tertiary institutions. Of the eight available subclasses of student visas, six cover the various educational sectors and represent the range of courses that can be studied by overseas students in Australia. The seventh applies to students sponsored by AusAID or the Department of Defence. The eighth allows parents or relatives to stay in Australia as a guardian of a student visa holder.

[11.17] In addition to being accepted to study in a registered course, student visa applicants must demonstrate that they intend to be genuine students. Here applicants must demonstrate their English language proficiency; their financial capacity to undertake the study in Australia; and other matters such as age and academic record. The policy focus on the entry and evidentiary requirements for student visas has been credited with a marked reduction in the overstay rates of international students. In 2006-07 one in 75 students became unlawful whereas by 2008-09 the figure was one in 200.[20] As in earlier versions of the Regulations, differentiated evidentiary requirements reflect the statistical 'immigration risk' factors for applicants from different countries. This risk is captured in gazetted Assessment Levels which vary according to the passport held by an applicant and subclass of student visa being sought.[21] The designation of Assessment Levels is based on statistical evidence of visa compliance by students from different countries and within different educational sectors. The higher an applicant's Assessment Level (1 being the lowest and 5 the highest), the more evidence they need to prove they are a genuine student.

[11.18] All student visa applicants must show that they are genuinely seeking to enter Australia for the purpose of study and that they will abide by their visa conditions.[22] The evidentiary requirements are set out in Sch 5A to the *Migration*

---

20   Senate, Estimates, 20 October 2009, at 47.
21   Regulation 1.41 of the *Migration Regulations 1994* (Cth) requires Assessment Levels to be specified by the Minister, set out in 'Student Visa Assessment Levels', IMMI 10/003, commenced 27 March 2010.
22   Previously, certain visa subclasses were subject to the additional regulatory requirement that the Minister be satisfied that the applicant was a genuine applicant for entry and stay as a student. In those cases, Regulations required applicants to show that the proposed course would enhance the development of their careers or assist them to obtain employment. This requirement was deleted from the Regulations in response to the ruling in *Sidhu v MRT* [2004] FCAFC 341. There, the court held that the decision-maker must merely assess whether there is evidence that the applicant would be assisted by the studies in obtaining employment of any nature in the field of their studies. The issue arose where the applicant was enrolling in a course which seemed to be at odds with the student's prior professional experience. The court held that an applicant's principal intention to utilise the benefits derived from the course by seeking permanent residence and employment in Australia was no barrier to being a 'genuine' student. See also *V05/01163* [2005] MRTA 750.

Regulations 1994 (Cth) and involve English language proficiency, financial capacity (including tuition costs, living costs for the duration of the applicant's stay and travel costs) and 'other requirements'. Again, the specific requirements vary according to the applicant's Assessment Level. At one extreme an applicant for Assessment Level 4 must prove that he or she has held funds for six months before application that would be sufficient to meet all course and living expenses for the first three years of study. For Assessment Level 1, it suffices to assert that the applicant has funds sufficient to meet these expenses. In December 2010 none of the visa subclasses had any nationalities specified at Assessment Level 5. As for the 'other requirements' consideration set out in Sch 5A, courts have construed this as not constituting a clear criterion which a visa applicant must satisfy in order to obtain the visa.[23] Instead, the provision grants the decision-maker wide discretion to 'determine if there were other matters relevant to whether the applicant was a genuine applicant for entry and stay as a student'.[24]

[11.19] The various decisional factors (English language proficiency, financial capacity and other indicators of genuineness of intention) are considered in what is in essence a balancing exercise. The single question the decision-maker is required to determine is whether the applicant satisfies the criterion of genuineness for entry and stay as a student. The Full Federal Court has ruled that an application should not stand or fall on the assessment of one of these indicators alone.[25] Rather, each factor should be balanced against an assessment of all the other factors, leading to a conclusion about satisfaction of the overriding criterion.[26]

[11.20] Jurisprudence from the lower courts has supported decision-makers who have taken a strict and literal approach to the regulatory requirements, even where the effect is harsh.[27] The Federal Magistrates Court has upheld the refusal of a visa to an applicant on the basis that funding provided by his father-in-law was not an 'acceptable source of funding' under the legislative scheme.[28] Other examples of funding from unacceptable sources are a short-term loan from a friend and a shareholding in an overseas company.[29] The requirement that funds have to be held for a requisite time period has also been enforced strictly.[30]

11.1.4 Students and visa conditions

[11.21] Of the many conditions that can be imposed on the grant of a student visa some are mandatory and others discretionary.[31] The condition that is imposed may depend on the visa that is sought and the Assessment Level of the applicant.

---

23 *Yong v MIMA* (2000) 62 ALD 687 at [18].
24 *Qu v MIMA* [2001] FCA 1299 at [11]-[13].
25 *MIMIA v Awan* (2003) 131 FCR 1.
26 *Qu v MIMA* [2001] FCA 1299 at [20].
27 *Shrestha v MIAC* [2008] FMCA 842.
28 Ibid.
29 *Bel Kacem v MIMIA* (2005) 196 FLR 144.
30 *Kiloul v MIMIA* [2006] FMCA 650.
31 *Migration Regulations*, Sch 8.

[11.22] All student visas have a mandatory condition (8202) that relates to the requirement that overseas students must remain enrolled in a registered course and meet attendance requirements. Under the National Code of Practice for Registration Authorities and Providers of Education and Training to Overseas Students (the National Code) (introduced in 2007) this requires a minimum of 80 per cent of the scheduled course contact hours. Students must also make satisfactory progress in their course. Breach of this visa condition is a ground for cancellation of the visa.[32]

[11.23] In the past, all student visas were granted initially with a 'no work' condition (condition 8101). Only once the student had arrived in Australia and commenced their course could they apply for a new student visa with permission to restrictively engage in work. This was changed in April 2008 so that students are no longer required to apply separately to work. Visas are now granted with a condition 8105 allowing not more than 20 hours of work per week any week when the student's course of study or training is in session. This legislative reform simplified students' interactions with the Department especially just after arrival and served to make university students more readily available to work.

[11.24] The definition of 'work' in reg 1.03 encompasses 'an activity that normally attracts remuneration'.[33] There remains some ambiguity around the interpretation of this concept. One line of Federal Court authority recognises that, where individuals engage in activities of a domestic or social character, these should not be regarded as work. The question of whether an activity should be regarded as work is a 'matter of evaluation and degree'.[34] However, according to another view:[35]

> The test is not whether the individual performing the activity receives remuneration for it, nor whether he or she performs the activity for commercial purposes or for some other reason. The test to be applied is an objective one, namely, whether the 'activity' performed by the individual normally attracts remuneration in Australia.

[11.25] Overall, it seems that the test requires analysis that extends beyond the nature of the activity in question to the particular context of the service provided. Commercial, social, domestic or altruistic motivations may assist in determining whether a particular activity undertaken voluntarily is one that normally attracts remuneration.[36]

[11.26] There is now a body of case law on the evidence which may legally support a decision-maker's finding that an applicant has failed to comply with a 'no-work' condition. In *Abbasi v MIMIA*,[37] financial records showed that the applicant had obtained funds from an undisclosed source. The Migration Review Tribunal (MRT) concluded that it could not be satisfied that the visa applicant had not been

---

32 We discuss in more detail the extensive judicial consideration of the consequences of breach of this condition, when we consider cancellation of student visas at Part 11.1.5 below.
33 *Braun v MILGEA* (1991) 33 FCR 152 considered the definition in a previous version of the regulations, in which work was also defined as 'an activity that, in Australia, normally attracts remuneration' (for the interpretation of this definition in the context of tourist visas, see Part 11.2.4 below).
34 Ibid at 156.
35 *Kim v Witton* (1995) 59 FCR 258 at 268.
36 *Dib v MIMA* (1998) 82 FCR 489 at 495-6.
37 [2002] FCA 568.

working in excess of the hours permitted by condition 8105. On review, the Federal Magistrate acknowledged that there was no direct evidence that the applicant had breached condition 8105. It ruled that a finding of this kind would impermissibly place the burden on an applicant of establishing a negative, namely that he had not worked more than 20 hours per week.[38] The Federal Court, however, affirmed the tribunal decision. The court ruled that the MRT had not elevated the material before it to a positive finding that the applicant had been working in excess of the permitted hours. Rather, the MRT found that it could not be satisfied that the applicant had not been working excess hours. The tribunal then took that finding of fact into account in ruling that it could not be satisfied that the applicant would not breach condition 8105 if he undertook further study.[39] Similarly, the Federal Court in *Limbu v MIMA*[40] left undisturbed an MRT determination that the applicant had breached condition 8105 on the combined bases of unexplained bank deposits and the applicant's failure to furnish the tribunal with evidence of payslips.

[11.27] Questions have also arisen over whether the work condition permits the averaging of work performed by the visa holder over an extended period or whether the condition proscribes strictly the undertaking of more than 20 hours of work in any one week. Schedule 8, condition 8105(3), provides that 'week means the period of 7 days commencing on a Monday'. The provision reflects a Full Federal Court decision rejecting the view that 'a week' could refer to any period of seven consecutive days.[41] In that case, objectivity and clarity for the visa holder were said to militate that the week should be determined by reference to the starting date for a week of study.

[11.28] Finally, the condition does not apply to work undertaken as a requirement of the course.[42] The registration in the CRICOS identifies the course and course provider but not whether work experience is a course requirement. Accordingly, it falls to the applicant to provide evidence showing that work undertaken was specified as a requirement of the course.[43] Unfortunately, the informality of this process has left students open to unscrupulous course providers who have used student labour for other than educational purposes. Some have required significant unpaid work for completion of qualifications or have exploited students' willingness to accept poorly paid work which is not factored into their 20-hour work limit in condition 8105.

[11.29] In relation to transferring between education providers, previously all student visas were granted with a 'must not change education provider' condition (condition 8206). This was effective for the first year of study unless exceptional circumstances justified the change. This condition was abolished in July 2007 with the stated rationale that changing education provider is essentially an educational, rather than an immigration, matter. The change was an effort to provide more 'consumer protection' for students who may not have been provided with sufficient

---

38 Ibid.
39 Ibid.
40 [2001] FCA 436.
41 *MIMIA v Alam* (2005) 145 FCR 345; *Alam v MIMIA* [2004] FMCA 583. See also *Islam v MIMIA* (2006) 202 FLR 281 (which considered identical wording in condition 8104).
42 Condition 8105(2).
43 *Mohammed v MIMIA* [2004] FCA 970.

information about the course or educational provider before commencement of studies. Restrictions may still exist, however, if a student seeks to change education provider in the first six months of study. The 2007 reform coincided with the introduction of a suite of new regulations of the international education industry, discussed in more detail in Part 11.1.7 below.

11.1.5 Student visa cancellations

[11.30] One of the stated main goals of the student visa program is 'to support the growth of Australia's international education sector, while minimising the number of students not complying with their visa conditions'.[44] The legal provisions around student visa cancellations are many and complex. As we have seen, numerous conditions are attached to student visas. Some must be imposed when the visa is granted while others are imposed at the discretion of the Immigration Department. A student's breach of these conditions can result in either discretionary or mandatory cancellation of the visa.

Discretionary cancellations

[11.31] The Department may use the general cancellation power under s 116(1)(fa) to cancel a student's visa. Grounds for such an action include where the Department forms the view that the visa holder is no longer a genuine student (see Part 11.1.3), or has engaged in conduct not contemplated by the visa. This provision may also be used to cancel a student's visa on arrival in immigration clearance, if the visa holder is found with evidence suggesting an intention to work full time or engage in other activities outside the scope of the visa.

[11.32] The Supplementary Explanatory Memorandum to the Migration Legislation Amendment (Overseas Students) Bill 2000, which introduced this section, explained that this discretionary cancellation power was inserted in response to the decision of the Federal Court in *Nong v MIMA*.[45] This judgment held that non-compliance with condition 8202 (requiring satisfactory course enrolment, progress and attendance) could only be used as a basis for the cancellation of a student visa after the completion of the student's course, not while the course is still on foot.[46] Examples of the circumstances in which this new cancellation power might be used included:

- where there has not been an actual breach of a student visa condition but the decision-maker is nevertheless satisfied that the student is not genuine; or
- where the first academic year of the course in which the student is enrolled has not yet commenced, but the decision-maker is satisfied that the visa holder is not a genuine student; or
- where a semester for the course has not yet finished but the decision-maker is satisfied that the student is not attending the scheduled contact hours for the course in which he or she is enrolled.

---

44   DIAC, *Population Flows – 2006-2007 Edition*, March 2008, at 54.
45   (2000) 106 FCR 257.
46   Supplementary Explanatory Memorandum to the Migration Legislation Amendment (Overseas Students) Bill 2000, 6 November 2000.

[11.33] The Federal Court has observed that in introducing s 116(1)(fa) Parliament's intention was clearly not to penalise a genuine student who had failed in attendance and/or academic performance through 'innocent temporary mishap' or 'transient misadventure'.[47] The 'genuine student' concept in s 116(1)(fa)(i) is 'directed to circumstances where a student visa holder has been in literal compliance with visa conditions, for instance as to course attendances, yet has not conducted himself or herself as a genuine student for instance in relation to behaviour at lecturers [sic]'.[48] This cancellation power may be employed if a student has repeatedly deferred their studies or repeatedly enrols in numerous courses apparently to extend their stay in Australia rather than as a 'genuine student'.[49]

Mandatory cancellation for breach of work restrictions

[11.34] Section 116(3) of the *Migration Act 1958* (Cth), read with reg 2.43(2), provides for mandatory cancellation of a student visa if the Department is satisfied that the visa holder has breached conditions 8104 or 8105 (restricting students to 20 hours of work per week: see Part 11.1.4). The apparent harshness of this cancellation power is mitigated somewhat by the ability of the visa holder to appeal the cancellation. In one case, compliance officers searching a student's room found a diary with notes about times, dates and payments appearing to correlate to work done. The student, Mr Majeed, claimed that the diary notes were for another matter entirely, and that he was an exemplary student. He gave evidence that he worked in a restaurant and was physically unable to have worked the notarised hours given his work and class schedule. While the Department cancelled his visa, the ruling was eventually overturned by consent after a case that went all the way to the High Court.[50] On rehearing, the MRT overturned the initial cancellation, finding that the inconsistencies between Majeed's study timetable, work hours and diary entries suggested that condition 8105 had not been breached.[51]

[11.35] The Federal Court has reacted strongly to improper compliance conduct by Department staff. In one case, Mr Alam's student visa was cancelled after he had worked 22.25 hours during one week to help his employer who was short-staffed on one occasion. The Department officers discovered the breach of condition 8105 during a raid of Alam's house when they were looking for his friend. Without a warrant, they searched Alam's room and found the payslip attesting to more than 20 hours of work in one week. He was then taken to the Department offices, where his visa was cancelled at 11.00pm, was refused a phone call to his sister to arrange for bond money and was detained at Villawood detention centre from that evening for three weeks over the Christmas-New Year holiday period. The Full Court conceded the mandatory nature of the condition and cancellation power, but at the same time stridently criticised the misconduct of the Department officers. The cancellation was

---

47 *Shrestha v MIMA* (2001) 64 ALD 669.
48 *MIMA v Hou* [2002] FCA 574 at [32].
49 *MIMIA v Awan* (2003) 131 FCR 1.
50 *Re MIMA; Ex parte Majeed M77/2000* [2001] HCATrans 403.
51 *Re Majeed* [2002] MRTA 6429.

set aside on the basis that the information leading to the cancellation was obtained improperly.[52]

Mandatory and automatic cancellations for failure to meet course requirements

[11.36] Breaches of condition 8202 (relating to enrolment, course attendance and satisfactory academic results) raise separate issues that have attracted a great deal of judicial attention. Indeed, the condition has been described as 'difficult to construe and apply'.[53] It was amended in 2000 to overcome a Federal Court judgment which held that a visa could be cancelled for breach of condition 8202 only upon the completion of the student's course.[54] The Full Federal Court has subsequently clarified that the breach must be assessed at the completion of each semester, so that anticipatory failure to comply is not contemplated by the condition.[55]

[11.37] When a student breaches condition 8202 (by failing to meet the attendance requirement or to achieve satisfactory academic progress), the education provider has a legal obligation to send the student a written notice, known as a 'Section 20 Notice'.[56] This notice must set out the details of the breach and inform the student that they are required to visit a DIAC office at a specified place within 28 days after the date of the notice to explain the reason for the breach. The notice must also explain the effect of the automatic cancellation provisions under ss 137J and 137K of the *Migration Act*. At the same time the course provider must electronically notify the Department that the notice has been sent. This monitoring obligation has legal effect through ss 137J to 137P. This mechanism, therefore, constitutes another instance of the outsourcing of immigration compliance functions to private bodies (discussed in more detail in [11.44]ff and Chapter 5.4).

[11.38] If the student fails to comply with the Section 20 Notice – in other words does not attend the Department offices within 28 days – the student visa is automatically cancelled by operation of law under s 137J(2). In this case, the student becomes an unlawful non-citizen and liable for removal. The fact that the visa holder did not receive the notice does not vitiate the automatic cancellation. If the student's visa is automatically cancelled, the student can apply to the Minister for revocation of the cancellation (and a Bridging Visa pending a final decision on revocation). There are strictly prescribed and limited circumstances under which the Minister can revoke the cancellation, most notably if non-compliance with the condition was due to exceptional circumstances beyond the student's control.

[11.39] If the student complies with the Section 20 Notice, and attends the Department office within 28 days, the visa is not cancelled under the automatic cancellation provisions. However, DIAC is likely to consider cancelling the visa under the general cancellation power contained in s 116(1)(b) of the Act.[57]

---

52 *MIMIA v Alam* (2005) 145 FCR 345.
53 *MIMIA v Ahmed* (2005) 143 FCR 314.
54 *Nong v MIMA* (2000) 106 FCR 257.
55 *MIMIA v Ahmed* (2005) 143 FCR 314.
56 *Education Services for Overseas Students Act 2000* (Cth), s 20.
57 See also *Migration Regulations*, reg 2.43.

[11.40] This complex series of parallel processes, initiated by breach of condition 8202, has remained in place since first introduced in June 2001 alongside more stringent regulation of education providers. However, in recent years, reforms have been made in response to strong judicial criticism of the complexity of the procedures and in order to correct anomalies which have emerged. As cases continue to proceed through the courts, we can expect further exploration and amendment of these provisions in coming years.

[11.41] The first such anomaly surrounded the relative advantages of compliance and non-compliance with the Section 20 Notice. Under the regulatory framework established in 2001, a student who attended the Department office in accordance with the Section 20 Notice would be subject to mandatory visa cancellation if the decision-maker was satisfied that condition 8202 was breached. The decision-maker had no discretion in deciding to cancel the visa and there was no avenue open to the applicant to avoid that result, by showing exceptional circumstances or otherwise. On the other hand, if the student did not comply with the Section 20 Notice, and did not attend the Department office, their student visa would be automatically cancelled after 28 days. In this event, however, the student was entitled to apply for revocation of the cancellation on the ground that the Minster was satisfied that the breach was due to exceptional circumstances beyond the student's control. As a result, the student who had not originally complied with the Section 20 Notice had the opportunity to show exceptional reasons for the breach whereas the student who had complied was given no such opportunity.

[11.42] For this reason, in 2005 the Full Federal Court in *Morsed* described the Section 20 cancellation notice scheme as a 'trap'. The notice seemed to promise students the opportunity to explain their breach of condition 8202 when in fact attending the Department offices would effectively preclude them from the opportunity to provide any explanation of circumstances surrounding the breach.[58] Barely a month after judgment in *Morsed* was delivered, the scheme was amended to create an exception to the mandatory cancellation provision in s 116. Since October 2005, mandatory cancellation will occur only if the Minister is satisfied that non-compliance with condition 8202 was not due to exceptional circumstances beyond the visa holder's control.[59] One might well conclude that the cancellation under s 116 is no longer truly mandatory.

[11.43] Another series of cases construed the legislative provisions extremely strictly, in some cases striking down various versions of the Section 20 Notices. An invalid Section 20 Notice renders cancellation under s 137J (for non-attendance at the Department interview) invalid but has no effect on a cancellation under s 116 (for failure to meet course requirements). In 2005, citing the 'draconian effect of the notice under s 20', Scarlett FM revoked the automatic cancellation of a student's visa under s 137J because the notice was defective.[60] In a similar vein, the Federal Court, in two

---

58 *Morsed v MIMIA* (2005) 88 ALD 90.
59 Introduced by *Migration Amendment Regulations 2005 (No 8)* (Cth).
60 *Uddin v MIMIA* [2005] FMCA 841. Instead of informing the visa holder that he could report to any departmental 'officer' for the purpose of explaining his breach of condition 8202, the defective Section 20 Notice had required him to report to a 'compliance officer' within a specified office.

cases decided together in 2010, ruled that a Section 20 Notice form used between July 2007 and December 2009 was invalid because, throughout that time, condition 8202 had not been prescribed for s 20 purposes.[61] This meant that all s 137J cancellations made between those dates using this form were ineffective. On the other hand, the Full Court has held that, even if the Section 20 Notice is defective for the purpose of engaging s 137J, this does not affect the decision-maker's power to cancel the visa under s 116.[62]

[11.44] Another difficulty with the s 116 cancellation provision relates to the requirement in an earlier version of condition 8202 of satisfactory academic performance: the visa holder must achieve 'an academic result that is certified by the education provider to be at least satisfactory'. In other words, satisfactory progress seems to be exclusively determined by the education provider. The Full Court has observed that:[63]

> There is an obvious policy behind the way the condition is framed. Questions of academic progress should be left to the judgment of the education provider rather than a Departmental decision-maker or the Tribunal, who are less well fitted to make such judgments.

[11.45] This can work to the benefit of the student in that the course provider may exercise some discretion as to what it considers to be satisfactory, including taking the student's circumstances into account.[64] However, the Full Federal Court has held that, once a course provider has certified unsatisfactory progress, a decision-maker, whether a departmental officer, tribunal member or judge, cannot look behind the certification and deem academic performance to be satisfactory.[65] This strict approach has led the Full Court to conclude that 'there is nothing in the language of condition 8202 that invites a consideration of the internal process of the education provider which has led to a certificate or refusal to certify for a satisfactory result'.[66] As a result, it seems that the power to provide the certificate is vested in the course provider alone such that, 'if there is no certificate, compliance with condition 8202 has not been achieved'.[67]

[11.46] In *Dai v MIAC*,[68] the Full Federal Court considered the conundrum caused by the fact that vesting certification power in the education provider leaves the visa holder with no role to play in complying with condition 8208. The incongruity is caused by the words of the cancellation power which specify that the Minister must cancel a visa if satisfied 'that the visa holder has not complied with condition 8202'.[69]

---

61 *Hossain v MIAC* (2010) 183 FCR 157; *Mo v MIAC* [2010] FCA 162.
62 *Humayun v MIMIA* (2006) 149 FCR 558. See also *Shek v MIMIA* [2006] FCA 522; *MIMIA v Zhou* (2006) 152 FCR 115; *MIMIA v Yu* (2004) 141 FCR 448.
63 *Jayasekara v MIMIA* (2006) 156 FCR 199 at [16] (Heerey and Sundberg JJ). The High Court refused special leave to appeal this matter in 2007: *Jayasekara v MIMA* [2007] HCATrans 163.
64 *Weerasinghe v MIMIA* [2004] FCA 261.
65 *MIMIA v Yu* (2004) 141 FCR 448.
66 *Cheng v MIMIA* [2007] FCAFC 71 at [35].
67 *Tian v MIMIA* [2004] FCAFC 238 at [56].
68 (2007) 165 FCR 458.
69 *Migration Regulations*, reg 2.43(2).

In that case a majority of the Full Court held that the visa cancellation in question should be set aside, although for different reasons. According to North J, the fact that compliance with the condition depends solely on certification by the course provider and involves no act whatsoever of the visa holder means, effectively, that the visa holder is not capable of complying with the condition. The visa holder may achieve a certain academic result but this would not satisfy the condition since 'the academic result was irrelevant unless certified'.[70] Further, the visa holder has no statutory right to compel the education provider to provide the certification. There was no way in which the visa holder could or could not comply with the condition. Consequently, it was simply not possible for the Minister to be satisfied that the visa holder had not complied with condition 8202, and the cancellation power was not engaged.

[11.47] Taking a different approach, Gyles J considered that the root of the problem here was the failure to legislate the education provider's obligation to certify. While the course provider must keep records under the *Education Services for Overseas Students Act 2000* (Cth) (*ESOS Act*), there is no specific requirement to provide the certification. Indeed, his Honour found a great deal of uncertainty surrounding the certification mechanism. Not only is the student powerless to compel the issuing of a certificate, but there is no time frame in which the certification might be issued. As a result, his Honour reasoned, it seems impossible to determine at what point the visa holder fails to comply with the condition. Thus, his Honour found the form of the condition *ultra vires* the legislation with respect to the certification requirement, since it compelled compliance by the visa holder with requirements that were not practicable or certain.

[11.48] In dissent, Edmonds J considered that compliance with the condition was not in the hands of the education provider. Instead, the achievement of the academic result is within the power of the visa holder and this exists independently of certification. For his Honour, it was not fatal to the visa cancellation that there was no prescribed form as to how the education provider should certify the student's satisfactory academic progress. The course provider is statutorily bound to record students' results and this is sufficient to constitute certification for the purposes of condition 8202.

[11.49] In response to this decision, condition 8202 was amended on 1 July 2007, so that the education provider, rather than the Minister, is now explicitly required to assess whether a student has achieved satisfactory course progress and attendance.[71] If an education provider certifies that this has not occurred and reports the student to the Department, this constitutes non-compliance with the condition and makes the visa liable to mandatory cancellation by the Minister, unless exceptional circumstances can be demonstrated as to why the visa should not be cancelled.[72] The amendment reflects parallel changes to the *ESOS Act* and the National Code (see further below Part 11.1.7). Education providers are now required expressly to monitor and assess a student's course progress and attendance in accordance

---

70 (2007) 165 FCR 458 at [20].
71 New condition 8202(3) of *Migration Regulations*, Sch 8.
72 These exceptional circumstances are outlined in a s 499 direction.

with standards in the National Code, which was also introduced in 2007. Education providers are also required to implement intervention strategies to assist students at risk of failing the attendance and course progress requirements, and to offer internal appeals processes if considering reporting a student for failure to comply. The Minister's directions on what may amount to exceptional circumstances beyond the control of the student include where the education provider has failed to follow the monitoring, intervention and appeals processes before certifying the breach. These legislative reforms remain to be considered by the courts.

11.1.6 Dovetailing with general skilled migration program

[11.50] A defining feature of changes made in this area during the years of Coalition government was the integration of the overseas student program into the country's skilled migration program. Where most foreign students were required previously to return to their countries of origin and apply for migration from abroad, the Howard government decided in 2001 to provide a direct pathway for international students to permanent residency. Naturally, the policy sought to promote education in Australia as a destination competitive with the United Kingdom and United States. The prospect of permanent residence offered a relative advantage in the knowledge-based global economy. Additionally, no doubt, at a time of skills shortages, providing easy transition to permanent residence meant that a proportion of the burgeoning skilled migrant cohort would already be familiar with the Australian lifestyle, professional culture and English language.

[11.51] July 2001 saw the introduction of two new permanent onshore visa classes and one temporary visa class, allowing for the transition from overseas student to permanent resident without the necessity to leave Australia.[73] These points-tested skilled visas catered to students who wished to apply for residence under an occupation eligible for the skilled points test (see above Chapter 9.3.5). Students who had completed tertiary study in Australia were granted concessions for permanent residency through the skilled migration program. Those who had undertaken at least two years of study in Australia and had completed their course within six months before application had the work experience requirement for the skilled visa waived. This naturally triggered an immediate surge in student numbers. In 2007 the visa classes were rationalised, with extra points available for study in Australia (especially in a regional location) and local work experience.[74] By 2008-09, almost 20,000 migrants who arrived on a student visa were being granted permanent residence visas.[75]

[11.52] Increasingly, though, the linkages between nominated occupations, education and rights to permanent residence were seen as not striking the right balance between meeting the expectations of foreign students on the one hand and Australia's

---

73 Subclass 880 Skilled – Independent Overseas Student visa; Subclass 881 Skilled – Australian-Sponsored Overseas Student visa and Subclass 882 Skilled – Designated Area-sponsored Overseas Student visa.
74 Subclass 885 Skilled – Independent visa replaced the Skilled Independent Overseas Student (subclass 880) visa and Subclass 886 Skilled – Sponsored visa replaced Skilled Australian – Sponsored Overseas Student (subclass 881) visa.
75 Senate, Estimates, 20 October 2009, at 48.

interests and needs as a nation on the other. The concessions were thought to be too generous. Reports emerged of new permanent residents who had insufficient English language skills and work experience to succeed in the Australian labour market.[76] In 2005, to achieve sufficient points to be eligible for permanent residency, most student visa holders found they needed to study in occupations that were on the more select Migration Occupations in Demand List (MODL) (which has since been removed, see Chapter 9.3.6). September 2007 saw a new requirement that students demonstrate one year of work experience in their field before qualifying for those MODL points. Along with this reform came a dispensation, whereby students who found themselves no longer eligible for a permanent skilled visa because of lack of work experience could apply for a temporary 485 visa, known as the Skilled – Graduate visa, allowing them to work in Australia for 18 months, ostensibly to gain the work experience they were lacking.

[11.53] In 2010, under the auspices of a comprehensive review of the general skilled migration program, the Labor government re-envisioned the relationship between the overseas student program and the skilled migration program. The linkages between the overseas student program and the skilled migration program had blown out the numbers of applicants successfully gaining residence under the points test, in a time of economic downturn. They had also led to distortions among the skilled migrant population, which was now skewed towards those occupations on the MODL for which qualifications were more easily attainable such as chefs and hairdressers.[77] Further, aspiring migrants were perceived to be pursuing qualifications for the purpose of securing eligibility for permanent residence rather than for true vocational motives. In many cases the students had no intention of establishing a career in their field of study. And the qualifications emanating from educational 'visa factories' were seen to be of poor quality.

[11.54] In January 2009, priority had already been given to skilled visa applicants with skills on a Critical Skills List (CSL), which meant that applicants with qualifications on the MODL, and related work experience, were no longer assured of permanent residency. By 2010, the Minster moved to more thoroughly separate the international student program from skilled migration. As discussed in more detail in Chapter 9, this was achieved through a revision of the points test and abolition of the MODL. No longer did qualifications in select occupations or Australian education and work experience offer an almost certain road to permanent residence. Instead, the Labor government entrenched the trend of giving priority to those applicants (including students) who had the support of an employer-sponsor, whether in applying for a temporary 457 work visa, or for a permanent visa through the Employer Nomination Scheme.

[11.55] In January 2010, the government introduced a major new hurdle for students who were relying on their Australian trade qualifications to gain residence.

---

76 See, for instance, Bob Birrell, Leslie-Anne Hawthorne and Sue Richardson, *Evaluation of the General Skilled Migration Categories* (Canberra: AGPS, 2006).
77 See the speech given by Minister Chris Evans, 'Changes to Australia's Skilled Migration Program', 9 February 2010, available at <http://www.minister.immi.gov.au/media/speeches/2010/ce100208.htm>. See Chapter 9 at [9.36].

Foreign graduates of Australian vocational colleges, unlike their local counterparts, must now complete a four-step skills assessment, known as the Job Ready Program, administered by Trades Recognition Australia.[78] This speaks to concerns not only about the extent to which students with trades occupations have taken up places in the skilled migration program but also about the quality of educational facilities geared towards the international student market, especially those offering skills-based courses in trade qualifications.

11.1.7 Student protections and oversight of education providers

[11.56] According to Deumert et al, the growth of the international student market in Australia occurred through a scrambling for student numbers as revenue sources without any comprehensive pastoral care to students in return for their dollar. Their interview-based research shows that international students in Australia have been affected by a wide range of social and economic security problems, including isolation and difficulty navigating grievance systems within and outside their educational facilities.[79] Such issues are not new. In the late 1980s large numbers of international students were left without degrees or reimbursement of fees when a number of revenue-reliant English language colleges collapsed. In response, the government introduced new arrangements for the accreditation and registration of education institutions.[80]

[11.57] The *Education Services for Overseas Students Act 2000* (Cth) (*ESOS Act*) was enacted in 2000, requiring institutions to secure registration and contribute to an Assurance Fund that guarantees student fees. In addition to requiring education providers to register on the CRICOS before being eligible to enrol overseas students, registration can now be suspended under the *ESOS Act* if the Minister is satisfied that too many students from one provider are entering or remaining in Australia for 'purposes not contemplated by their visas'.[81] Importantly, at the same time, new governmental powers were introduced to collect information and issue sanctions against non-compliant education providers.[82]

[11.58] After another string of high profile collapses of colleges catering to international students, efforts were renewed in mid-2007 to ensure the financial accountability of education providers. For the first time, the education provider was required to enter into a written agreement with the student setting out the services to be provided, fees and information relating to refunds.[83] Part 4 of the *ESOS Act* established the National Code of Practice for Registration Authorities and Providers

---

78   A requirement for Skilled Independent visa (subclass 885), Skilled – Sponsored visa (subclass 886) and Skilled – Regional Sponsored visa (subclass 487).
79   Deumert et al, above n 11, at 344. See also Simon Marginson, Christopher Nyland, Erlenawati Sawir and Helen Forbes-Mewett, *International Student Security* (Melbourne: Cambridge University Press, 2010).
80   *Education Services for Overseas Students (Registration of Providers and Financial Regulation) Act 1991* (Cth) (since repealed).
81   *ESOS Act*, Part 6, Div 2, ss 97-103.
82   Introduced by the *Migration Legislation Amendment (Overseas Student) Act 2000* (Cth).
83   *ESOS Act*, s 28.

of Education and Training to Overseas Students 2007 (the National Code). This is a legislative instrument stipulating 15 standards which education providers must meet in relation to overseas students in areas such as fair advertising, educational quality control and properly informing students before binding contracts are signed. Breaches of the Code by educational facilities can result in enforcement action being taken under the *ESOS Act*.

[11.59] A key function of the regulation of the education industry is tuition protection. The *ESOS Act* and National Code include provisions regarding the refund of course fees to students if an education provider fails to deliver the course agreed. These instruments establish an assurance fund to which registered education providers must contribute. Where an educational facility fails to deliver contracted services and cannot provide a refund, the *ESOS Act* stipulates that eligible students must be placed in a comparable course by that facility's Tuition Assurance Scheme. Failing that, the ESOS Assurance Fund must endeavour to place or refund the student.[84]

[11.60] As noted earlier, great powers have been vested in educational institutions to oversee students' immigration compliance through the monitoring of students' academic performance and attendance. Where education providers have failed to fulfil their obligations under the new legislation, the problems appear to lie with either a lack of resources or the absence of rigorous data collection processes and reporting systems. Critics suggest that these reforms have concentrated on risk management both for the institutions themselves and for the government.

[11.61] There remain serious questions about whether the National Code has articulated appropriate quality standards for the industry. Problems arise at a number of levels. First, the National Code is directed primarily at the educational facilities themselves and so has failed to address malpractice by other players. A government review reported cases of false and misleading information and deceptive conduct on the part of education agents engaged by educational institutions to attract potential students.[85] No provision is made for agents to be directly regulated through the scheme. Secondly, in some instances, the standards prescribed by the National Code are so vague as to be ineffective in either providing guidance to education providers or redress for students. For instance, Standard 14.2 requires that register providers 'must have adequate education resources'.

[11.62] A second focus of concern has arisen off the back of several highly publicised closures of educational facilities: the public cost of tuition assurance and the complexities faced by students seeking to transfer and claim refunds. A small move towards addressing the needs of students in this difficult situation was the removal in November 2009 of any further visa application charge for students whose education provider closed and who needed to apply for a further student visa to continue their studies in Australia.

---

84 *ESOS Act*, Div 2.
85 Bruce Baird, *Review of the Education Services for Overseas Students (ESOS) Act 2000: Interim Report* (Canberra: DEEWR, November 2009) at 3.

[11.63] Finally, serious practical and legal barriers continue to exist to the lodging of complaints by students against their education provider. The National Code requires that education providers have internal complaints processes, and make arrangements with an external body to hear complaints at little or no cost to the student.[86] However, in practice, many students fear that initiating such a complaint may put their student visa at risk. In escalating a complaint, the scheme operates under a 'Shared Responsibility Framework' whereby its administration lies with multiple agencies including DIAC, DEEWR and State-based registration authorities.[87] Thus, student complaints may be properly directed to a State authority or DEEWR depending on the nature of the complaint. This is a confusing and cumbersome mechanism, especially for international students who may be unfamiliar with Australian agencies and customs. Moreover, the *ESOS Act* does not provide for advocacy or conciliation to assist students to resolve their complaints with their provider, whether through DEEWR or other agencies.

[11.64] Overall, the overseas student scheme, as currently devised, contains some serious institutional barriers to the provision of pastoral care by these colleges to students. First, as noted earlier, foreign education is a profit-making business which means that providers have a vested interest in cost minimisation. Second, vesting educational facilities with compliance oversight of students for immigration-related purposes[88] creates disincentives for students to seek out support from within the student's institution. The tying of student visas to the nominated educational facility means that students may be loathe to complain for fear of jeopardising their visa status and any longer term prospects of permanent residency. This may force students into a position of collusion with unprofessional, substandard or exploitative educational facilities for the pursuit of mutual benefit. Finally, the complexity of this regulatory oversight mechanism, as well as the complexity of the student visa structure, means that students are left in a position of vulnerability.

[11.65] It was not until the deaths of two Indian students in 2009 that the vulnerabilities of international students truly hit the national agenda. Attention was focused by protests in Melbourne of thousands of Indian students. Claims were made that the attacks were motivated by racism and that the concerns of international students living in Australia were not being taken seriously by public authorities. The protests prompted inquiries, diplomatic overtures to India and COAG deliberations on a national International Student Strategy. The Hon Bruce Baird completed a review of the regulation of the international education industry in Australia in February 2010.[89] His report included recommendations that standards be clarified, an independent external complaints body be created, and that a more flexible approach be taken to cancellation of student visas. The report argued that providers should be more accountable for their agents' conduct, and recommended that provision be made for an agency where students can access information, legal advice and community

---

86   Standard 8 of the National Code.
87   Items 4.9 and 4.10 of the Shared Responsibility Framework.
88   Standard 11 of the National Code.
89   Baird, above n 4.

services. The report urged the government to commission further research to understand the causes and frequency of violence against international students. Also in 2010, the Australian Institute of Criminology embarked upon a research project on the safety of international students in Australia. The project compares the rates of crime against international students with the rates of crime against the broader Australian population. Because police agencies do not collect statistics on a victim of crime's citizenship or visa status, the research uses data-matching between DIAC and police agencies.[90]

[11.66] The government has moved to loosen the link between the international student program and permanent residence on the basis of skilled migration. The aim has been to deprive substandard education providers of the ability to hold out permanent residence as an attraction to vulnerable foreign students. In February 2010, parliament passed legislation requiring the re-registration of all providers currently registered on the CRICOS by the end of 2010 – in effect, a quality audit of the industry with more stringent assessment processes for those facilities considered to be representing higher levels of risk.[91]

11.2 The admission of visitors

11.2.1 The evolution of the law governing the admission of visitors

[11.67] The introduction of a (pre-entry) visa requirement for tourists in the 1970s was driven largely by the need to prevent the entry of persons likely to use their lawful temporary presence in Australia as a mechanism for subverting immigration controls. The function of the visa, then as now, was to screen people before they entered the country so as to exclude those who were likely to breach the conditions of their entry. The earliest 'visas', however, merely conferred a right to travel to Australia: entry into the country was achieved upon the grant of a separate entry permit. What has changed over the years is the scrutiny exercised over visa applicants and the legal obstacles put in the way of those identified as potential overstayers.

[11.68] Until 1989, assessment of applicants for tourist or other visitors' visas depended very much on the judgment of departmental officers stationed at Australian embassies and consulates overseas. The legislation conferred the broadest of discretions on the Minister to grant visas (overseas) and entry permits (upon arrival): see above Chapter 6.2. The early guidelines governing the issue of visas to temporary entrants were rudimentary in nature and not generally available to the public. Those who were refused a tourist visa overseas had no right to appeal against the decision. The Minister's power to cancel a visa before the visa holder entered the country was expressed as being 'absolute'.

---

90   DIAC, 'Safety of International Students Research Project', May 2010, available at <http://www.immi.gov.au/students/_pdf/sis-research.pdf>.
91   *Education Services for Overseas Students Amendment (Re-registration of Providers and Other Measures) Act 2010* (Cth).

[11.69] Because the first visa holders had no right to enter the country, a further vetting process occurred on arrival in Australia. People holding a temporary visa and seeking a temporary entry permit could have their belongings searched. On the discovery of items suggesting an intention to work without permission or a long-term relationship with an Australian that had not been disclosed to the authorities, they could have their request for a permit denied and they could find themselves placed on the next flight (or boat) out of the country.[92]

[11.70] The present regime governing the admission of tourists and other temporary entrants is simpler but more tightly controlled than its antecedent. The double handling of applications has been reduced somewhat by merging the concepts of visas and entry permits into a single document (the visa) that confers on its holder a right to enter and remain in the country. However, on arrival, visa holders must still pass through immigration clearance where persons suspected of lacking bona fides can be subjected to the cancellation of their visa: see Chapter 6.2. In order to streamline this processing and to focus scrutiny on those perceived to be at risk of visa non-compliance, airlines are now required to provide the Immigration Department with advance information on all passengers and crew travelling to Australia. Some advanced processing of tourists may occur at point of embarkation, known as 'pre-planing'.

[11.71] Most visitors to Australia must either have an Electronic Travel Authority (Visitor) (subclass 976) (ETA visa) or a Tourist visa (subclass 676). The current version represents a significant refinement and simplification of tourist visas from times past. The primary difference between the ETAs and other tourist visas, other than the length of permitted stays and frequency of entry, is the ease of application. The ETA is an electronically issued authority for travel to Australia for multiple short-term visits within 12 months from date of grant. As with short-stay business ETAs (see Chapter 10.4), the ETA visa is available only for certain eligible passport holders from certain countries (currently 34).[93] The majority of ETAs are issued through travel agents and airlines or directly over the internet. Other visitor visa subclasses relate to short-stay business visitors, medical treatment visitors, social and cultural visitors and family-sponsored visitors. The periods of stay for these visitors vary from three to 12 months.

[11.72] The key focus of government policy in relation to the visas in these classes is the specificity of the criteria used for determining the bona fides of applicants. In addition to the regulations, policy guidelines set out the criteria used to determine whether or not an applicant is a genuine visitor. As in other areas of migration law, these provisions reflect developments both in the judiciary's interpretation of the law governing temporary entry, and in the approach taken by the MRT in its review of decisions involving visitors.

---

92 See, for example, *Re Meera Mohideen Seyed Ahamed v MILGEA* [1991] FCA 287; and *Re Watsana Singthong v MIEA* [1988] FCA 115.
93 See Gazette Notice 5, 4 February 2004 – 'Specification of ETA-eligible passports and countries listed in Reg 1.11B'.

11.2.2 The genuine visitor

[11.73] The central criterion for grant of a tourist visa is that the applicant is a genuine visitor who intends to stay in Australia temporarily and who will be economically self-sufficient for the duration of the visit.[94] On the face of the Regulations, the purpose of the applicant's visit must be other than for a purpose 'related to business or medical treatment'. For the ETA (Visitor) 976 a criterion is that '[t]he applicant states an intention only to visit Australia temporarily for tourism purposes'. Tourism is defined as participation in activities of a recreational nature including amateur sporting activities, informal study courses, relaxation, sightseeing and travel, or for visiting an Australian relative.[95]

[11.74] The straightforward appearance of the regulations mask a complex body of rules that have grown up in the course of assessing whether the applicant is a 'genuine visitor' with the sole purpose of tourism in mind. In assessing the genuineness of an intended visit, decision-makers must apply a 'balance of probabilities' test.[96] Different Ministerial directives have provided guidance on the considerations relevant to this assessment.[97] Such directions are binding on the decision-maker except where inconsistent with the Act or Regulations.[98] The Federal Court has found the Directions oblige a person performing a function or exercising a power to take specified matters into account, unlike policy which is more precatory.[99] These matters have included:[100]

- personal circumstances that may encourage the applicant to return to his or her home country, including employment, family members or property at home;
- personal circumstances at home that may encourage the applicant to remain in Australia, including a poor economic situation, few family members, military service commitments, civil or political disruption or natural disasters;
- the applicant's immigration history, including whether the applicant has travelled before, the applicant's history of immigration compliance abroad and previously in Australia – in particular, decision-makers are directed that, if an applicant previously failed to comply with the conditions of their visa, it is reasonable, in the absence of any new information, to suspect that they may not comply again and this may be a ground upon which to consider refusing to grant the visa;
- the applicant's credibility in terms of character and conduct – if false or misleading information is presented in relation to the visa application, it may be a basis on which to refuse to grant the visa;
- whether the applicant's proposed trip is consistent with business, tourism and/ or visiting friends and relatives within a short period of stay;

---

94 *Migration Regulations*, Sch 2, cl 676.211.
95 Ibid, reg 1.03.
96 *Re Saulog* [1990] IRTA 29.
97 See former Ministerial Direction No 36 of 2005. This direction was revoked on 15 May 2009 at the same time that the risk factor list was revoked.
98 *Migration Act*, s 499.
99 *Rokobatini v MIMA* [1999] FCA 492, affirmed on appeal by a majority of the Full Federal Court in *Rokobatini v MIMA* (1999) 57 ALD 257.
100 Former Ministerial Direction No 36 of 2005, at [8].

- statistical information on the immigration activities in Australia of other nationals from the applicant's home country, especially rates of overstay, breach of visa conditions and applications for Protection visas;
- intelligence and analysis reports on illegal immigration and malpractice locally developed at overseas posts, focusing on people smuggling activities, visa non-compliance and document fraud.

[11.75] The determination of the *bona fides* or genuineness of a proposed visit is based on an assessment of the likelihood that an applicant will overstay or otherwise breach visa conditions. The Full Federal Court has framed the statutory analysis in the following terms:[101]

> First, it is necessary to ascertain the precise purpose for which the visa applicant wishes to remain in Australia on a tourist visa. The next step is to see whether that purpose is in any way related to 'business' (or presumably other non-recreational activities). Finally, there is the need to decide whether that relationship, if there is one, is sufficiently close to satisfy the objects of the criterion.

[11.76] At a more general level, Marshall J stated that cl 676.221(2)(c) in Sch 2 to the Regulations is satisfied if a visa applicant's intention not to overstay a visa is genuine.[102] Finkelstein J stated that this clause requires no more than that the visa applicant means what he says when he explains why he wishes to remain in Australia as a visitor for a short period.[103] Although it is difficult to distinguish between intent and desire on the part of an applicant, if the tribunal is not persuaded that an applicant satisfies the prescribed criteria for the visa sought, then the application must fail.[104]

[11.77] An examination of the case law indicates further anomalies in the way that these policy factors play out in individual determinations. For instance, courts have found that intentions to enter Australia other than as a genuine visitor can permissibly be deduced from a receipt for shipment of personal effects from abroad to Australia, along with personal correspondence stating an intention to live in Australia and apply for a permanent partner visa.[105] Evidence that an applicant has no incentive to return home and a preference to remain in Australia with his sister has also been accepted.[106] So too has evidence that the applicant sought time away from her home because of long-standing harassment on a Refugee Convention ground.[107] The cases suggest a more restrictive approach to applicants who may aspire to permanent residency than was evident in the early 1990s when an expressed desire to remain in Australia was not considered to indicate a lack of bona fides to enter as a visitor.[108] On the other hand, courts have also found that an intention to enter as a genuine visitor should not be refuted by previously undisclosed evidence that the applicant is in love

---

101 *MIMA v Saravanan* [2002] FCAFC 81 at [50].
102 Ibid at [45]. This is the requirement for the applicant to satisfy the Public Interest Criteria (PIC) 4011.
103 Ibid at [55].
104 See, for example, *Re Ferreras* [1991] IRTA 299.
105 *Walton v Ruddock* (2001) 115 FCR 342.
106 *Taubale v MIMA* [2006] FMCA 387.
107 *Darko v MIMIA* [2003] FCA 304.
108 *Re Chand* [1990] IRTA 10. Indeed, the IRT also considered a prior or even concurrent application for a permanent entry visa not necessarily to preclude a genuine visit: see *Re Aguilar* [1992] IRTA 39.

with an Australian citizen.[109] In another case, the visa applicant admitted an intention to apply for a student visa to enable her to pursue tertiary study. Although not in Australia exclusively for 'tourism' as defined, this was not sufficient to conclude that the intention only to visit (or remain in) Australia is not genuine.[110]

[11.78] The recent judicial consideration of the refusal or cancellation of visitor visas follows a steady flow of such legal challenges throughout Australian history. The early cases typically involved some element of controversy and were brought only rarely by individuals with a special financial or other incentive to come to Australia. In the late 1980s, the African-American music group 'The Platters' was refused entry because of an adverse recommendation by the National Disputes Committee for Australian Actors and Artists, a body set up to arbitrate complaints by the watch-dog for Australian artists, Actors Equity.[111] Later, Hell's Angels motor-cyclists were thought to pose a security threat.[112] In the 1990s, controversy arose around the proposed visits of 'Holocaust denier' David Irving and African-American activist Lorenzo Ervin: see further Chapter 6 at [6.70]ff.

[11.79] The courts in these cases have always taken seriously their role in exercising oversight over the nature and extent of the government's control of the admission and expulsion of visitors and other temporary entrants. Throughout, these rulings have affected the way applications were processed and influenced the interpretation of the guidelines for deciding applications. While these decisions have generally supported the approaches taken by the Minister, they have reinforced the need to articulate clearly – in a legally binding form – the grounds on which decisions affecting temporary entrants are to be made. Controversy has continued to surround decisions concerning the admission of visitors regarded by the government as being of bad character or otherwise a threat to the public interest. After the abortive attempt to cancel the visitor's visa of the African American activist, Lorenzo Ervin, in July 1997, the Minister foreshadowed moves to reverse the onus of proof placed on the public interest criteria applicable to visitors. The changes made in response to this and other cases create a situation where visitors now bear the burden of proving that they are of good character and that their visit to Australia would not be a source of controversy: see below, Chapter 17.3.1.

11.2.3 Risk factor profiles

[11.80] The fashion for tight regulation is seen most forcefully in the use of 'risk factor' profiles in schemes governing tourist visa grants. The collection of proper statistics on overstayers began during the 1980s. The data quickly came to be used as prima facie evidence that individuals from certain countries were likely to breach the conditions of their temporary visa by overstaying or by seeking change of status (for example, by claiming refugee status). In 1989 this (somewhat sceptical) approach to individuals of certain backgrounds and descriptions was codified in the Regulations.

---

109 *Sandoval v MIMA* (2001) 194 ALR 71.
110 *MIMA v Saravanan* [2002] FCAFC 81; *Mo, Yeuk Wing* [2004] MRTA 947.
111 *MIEA v Conyngham* (1986) 11 FCR 528.
112 *Hand v Hell's Angels Motor Cycle Club Inc* (1991) 25 ALD 667.

As a result, consideration of such factors was merged seamlessly into the credibility assessment of each individual. The profiles were drawn from statistics compiled on the basis of nationality, sex and age, although the Regulations allow the Department to screen people on the additional grounds of marital status, occupation, the class of visa applied for and the place of lodgement of an application.[113] There were 39 countries whose nationals were found to present a risk of overstaying their temporary visas.[114] The gazetted risk factors were quietly abandoned by the Rudd Labor government in May 2009.

[11.81] Under the current Regulations, the only reference to risk factors is in PIC 4011 which states that applicants exhibiting specified risk factors must show that there is 'very little likelihood' that they will overstay their visa given the specific circumstances in the country of origin.[115] The two risk factors stipulated in PIC 4011(2) are evidence that the applicant has applied to migrate to Australia within the previous five years; or that the applicant fits the profiles for overstayers prepared by the Department on the basis of its statistical record. Although an applicant must not be refused solely because they match the risk factor characteristics, these provisions have the effect of throwing the onus back on to the applicant to show that he or she would not overstay.[116] The ultimate question for consideration by the decision-maker remains whether the applicant intends a genuine visit to Australia, rather than whether he or she is likely to breach the conditions of the visa.[117]

[11.82] In 2007 the average non-return rate amongst all visitors to Australia was 1.3 per cent.[118] This shows a significant improvement in the compliance rate among visitors compared with the statistics from 1994. Indeed, as of 2003, Australia had a lower average number of overstayers (across all visa classes) than the United States, New Zealand or Europe. Japan's was slightly lower (0.31 per cent compared with 0.21 per cent respectively).[119] As to the breakdown of nationalities of overstayers, among the overstaying population in Australia (of all temporary visa holders including tourists, students and working holiday makers), as of June 2008, United States and Chinese nationals had the equal highest rate (at 10 per cent), followed by United Kingdom, Malaysia and the Philippines (6 per cent).[120] Interestingly, among Chinese tourists, the rate of non-return dropped from 1.17 per cent in 2003 to 0.6 per cent in 2008, falling to the fifth lowest rate for tourist visa holders.[121]

---

113   *Migration Regulations*, Sch 4, cl 4011(2A) and (3).
114   Gazette Notice, 'Class of Persons – Public Interest Criteria Risk Factor', IMMI 08/033, dated 12 May 2008, which had effect from 14 June 2008.
115   *Migration Regulations*, Sch 4, cl 4011.
116   As noted by the tribunal in *0804429* [2008] MRTA 1239; *Han, Latif* [2004] MRTA 817.
117   *Ly v MIMA* [2000] FCA 15.
118   Non-return rate is a calculation of the visitors who arrived in Australia on a visa that has now ceased but who did not depart within the validity of that initial visa either because they remained in Australia unlawfully or applied for another type of visa while in Australia. DIAC, above n 13, at 50.
119   DIMIA, *Annual Report 2002-2003* (Canberra: Commonwealth of Australia, 2003).
120   DIAC, above n 13, at 66.
121   Ibid at 50. These rates may have been affected by the special extra criteria that apply to some PRC tourists who must come on approved tours. See *Migration Regulations*, Sch 2, cll 676.214 and 676.221(2)(d).

[11.83] Thus, the extent to which the risk factor criteria worked to confine the overall number of overstayers is unclear. Three of the top four nationalities of overstayers did not engage a risk factor profile at all and, indeed, were eligible for streamlined entry processing through the ETA scheme. Review of the raw numbers behind these statistics adds to the complexity. The top four citizenships of visitor visaed arrivals were, in order, the United Kingdom, Japan, the United States and China, in 2007-08, each with over 260,000.[122] Within the group of 39 'risk' countries in 2006-07, this compared with 296,000 visaed arrivals from Korea; and almost 60,000 from the Philippines. Conversely, in terms of raw numbers of overstayers, in June 2008, the United States and China topped the list at 4900 each, followed by the United Kingdom with 4200.[123] Of the estimated 48,500 overstayers in the community on 30 June 2008, around 40,800 came as visitors.[124] Visitor entry rates clearly correlate to overstay rates, but not necessarily from the group of 'risk' countries.

[11.84] In light of this rather conflicted data, it is not surprising that courts and tribunals have expressed concern about the Department's use of statistical material on overstay rates as a legally relevant indicator for assessing the bona fides of an applicant for a visitor's visa.[125] The Federal Court ruled in 2001 that mere reliance on the fact that a visa applicant fits a profile of applicants who have tended to breach their visa conditions is not sufficiently probative to support a finding that an individual lacks a genuine intention to enter Australia as a visitor.[126] Conti J condemned as 'guilt by association' the cancellation of the visitor visas of two Moldovan professionals. The cancellation was based on the fact that they paid an overseas agent for their visas (for which no charge is payable) and that they were sponsored by the head of the Moldovan National Olympic Committee. These actions gave the pair similar features to the profile of a group of recent overstayers. His Honour considered that such statistical information could not of itself have a rational bearing on the question of whether these applicants intended to flout their visa conditions. The absence of viable and reasonable grounds to deny the visa was held to constitute a jurisdictional error.

[11.85] Even so, the Federal Court rejected a direct challenge to cl 4011 and the Gazettal Notice as *ultra vires* the *Migration Act*.[127] PIC cl 4011 made it practically impossible for the woman applicant who was living overseas, and married to an Australian citizen living in Australia, to obtain a temporary visa. The court held nonetheless that the subordinate legislation was reasonably proportionate to the object of the Act.

[11.86] In early 2010, the Minister announced the introduction of biometric data checks for certain visa applications. Citing the global terrorism threat, the new scheme requires all visa applicants from designated countries to submit fingerprints and facial images with their visa applications. The 10 pilot locations for the scheme

---

122 DIAC, above n 13, at 48.
123 Ibid at 66.
124 Ibid.
125 See, for example, *Re Saulog* [1990] IRTA 29 and *Re Canangga* [1990] IRTA 34.
126 *Cujba v MIMA* (2001) 111 FCR 110.
127 *Rahman v MIMA* [2001] FCA 1236.

were selected on the basis of national security and fraud risks, cooperative arrangements with British biometric collection and broad geographic coverage of the scheme. Whether this biometric data scheme is intended as a permanent replacement for the risk factor profiles remains to be seen. It is also unclear whether 'risk' countries will be made public together with the risk statistics, or whether this is a move away from the relatively more transparent, albeit flawed, gazetted risk factor list.

[11.87] One further visa category of note in this context is the Sponsored Family Visitor visa, subclass 679. This visa was introduced in response to the high rejection rates of visitor visas, in part due to the impact of applying the now repealed risk factor list. By offering the option of having a relative (or other sponsor) post a monetary bond or surety, this visa permitted those who would otherwise be refused on 'genuineness' to side-step the fatal effect of PIC 4011(2). In the budget statements in May 2010, the quota for family visas was reduced, but the Minister stated it would be possible for family members to access temporary visas to come and visit. Whether this will result in further legislative changes to the visitor/tourist visa system and/or changes to visitor policy remains to be seen.

11.2.4 Visitors and restrictions on work

[11.88] Tourist visas ordinarily have a mandatory 'no work' condition, covering any 'activity' that 'in Australia normally attracts remuneration'.[128] Exceptions can be made where the visa applicant is suffering financial hardship and has a compelling need to work or if the anticipated work is voluntary and of benefit to the community, for a non-profit organisation or would not ordinarily be done for payment. Nevertheless, neither the fact that the visa holder has suffered severe financial difficulty nor the fact that the employer urgently requires the person's services will excuse a breach of a 'no work' condition.[129]

[11.89] The concept of 'remuneration' remains undefined, but other statutory contexts indicate that it encompasses not only monetary reward for services rendered, but also the provision of goods or services as a quid pro quo for services rendered.[130] The characterisation of the 'activity' of the visa holder requires consideration of the actual surrounding circumstances. These include the motivations and agreements that have resulted in the performance of the activity, and the personal and economic context in which the activity is performed, including evidence of any remuneration actually received.[131] Commercial, social, domestic or altruistic motivations may assist in determining whether a particular activity undertaken voluntarily is one that ordinarily attracts remuneration.[132] For instance, in light of all the circumstances (including the absence of remuneration), one tourist's involvement in the management

---

128 *Migration Regulations*, reg 1.03.
129 *Poskus v MIMIA* [2005] FCA 118.
130 *Xu v MIAC* [2007] FMCA 285, citing *Chalmers v Commonwealth* (1946) 73 CLR 19 at 37; *White v Repatriation Commission* (2001) 114 FCR 494 at [28]; and *Carter v Repatriation Commission* (2001) 113 FCR 314 at [28].
131 *Dib v MIMA* (1998) 82 FCR 489.
132 *Tikoisuva v MIMA* [2001] FCA 1347.

and oversight of a business in which he was a shareholder was ruled not to breach the 'no work' condition.[133] On the other hand, engaging in electronic communications with clients abroad with a view to receiving a commission paid into a foreign bank account has been found to contravene the 'no work' condition.[134]

---

[133] *Xu v MIAC* [2007] FMCA 285.
[134] *Panta v MIMA* (2006) 203 FLR 376.

PART VI Refugees and Forced Migration

12

The Refugee and Humanitarian Program

12.1　The concept of refugee

[12.01]　In spite of its relative inexperience with direct refugee movements, Australia has played a significant role in shaping the international conventions and institutions that dominate modern refugee law. Australia's involvement with the resettlement of refugees dates back to the 1920s. After the Second World War Australia was represented on the committee that established the UN High Commissioner for Refugees (UNHCR) and was an active member of the drafting committee of the Convention on the Status of Refugees done in Geneva in 1951 (the Refugee Convention).[1] It was Australia's accession to that instrument that brought the Convention into force.[2]

[12.02]　For the purposes of Australia's *domestic* migration laws, the word 'refugee' is a term of art that is defined primarily by the Refugee Convention and its subsequent Protocol.[3] The combined effect of these two instruments is to define a refugee as any person who:[4]

> owing to a well-founded fear of being persecuted for reasons of race, religion, nationality or membership of a particular social group or political opinion, is outside the country of his nationality and is unable or, owing to such fear, is unwilling to avail himself of the protection of that country.

[12.03]　In becoming party to these international instruments Australia assumed certain obligations towards people who meet this definition of refugee. The most

---

1　*Convention Relating to the Status of Refugees* (adopted 28 July 1951, entered into force 22 April 1954) 189 UNTS 137. For an account of the legal history of the protection of refugees, see Guy Goodwin-Gill and Jane McAdam, *The Refugee in International Law* (New York: 3rd ed, Oxford University Press, 2007) Ch 2 at 15-41; James C Hathaway, *The Law of Refugee Status* (Toronto: Butterworths, 1996) Ch 1 at 1-28; James C Hathaway, *The Rights of Refugees under International Law* (Cambridge: Cambridge University Press, 2005) Ch 2 at 75-96; UNHCR, *An Introduction to International Protection: Protecting Persons of Concern to the UNHCR* (Geneva: 2005) at 25-35; and Gill Loescher, 'The Origins of the International Refugee Regime' in *Beyond Charity: International Cooperation and the Global Refugee Crisis* (New York: Oxford University Press, 1996).

2　Australia's accession took place on 22 April 1954. See Aust TS 1954 No 5.

3　Refugee Convention, Art 1; Protocol Relating to the Status of Refugees (adopted 31 January 1966, entered into force 4 October 1967) 606 UNTS 267 (Protocol), Art I(2). The terms 'refugee claimant' and 'asylum seeker' are used interchangeably.

4　The Refugee Convention, Art 1A(2), and the Protocol, Art I(2). The Convention covers events causing a refugee problem before 1 January 1951, while the Protocol extends the definition to events occurring after that date.

[12.04] The duties imposed by the Refugee Convention are of less consequence in the context of Australia's selection of people overseas for inclusion in its 'offshore' refugee and special humanitarian program (see Part 12.2 below). As a sovereign nation, Australia is free to offer protection to whomsoever it chooses, irrespective of a person's international legal status as refugee. Where people come to Australia and seek asylum on or after their arrival, however, it is a different story. Claims for refugee status must be determined, and recognised refugees must be afforded some kind of protection.

[12.05] For governments concerned to control every facet of their immigration program, onshore refugee claimants inevitably present problems. There are limits in international law on the government's freedom to 'select' onshore refugees for residence and practical difficulties in attempting to restrict the admission of potential asylum seekers. Some argue the protection obligations attaching to refugees mean that the examination of asylum seekers should be carried out in isolation from the migration program.[5] In practice, the refugee determination process is run as a separate unit but is very much a part of the migration portfolio. This is borne out most forcefully in the government's decision to reduce the intake of humanitarian cases from overseas by the number of persons granted residence in Australia as refugees.[6]

[12.06] Refugee claimants within Australia – their detention, the processing of their cases and the role played by the courts in reviewing decisions – have been the single largest source of conflict in the migration field in recent years. Indeed, it is in response to onshore refugee claimants that many restrictive legislative measures have been introduced since 1992. Nowhere was this more apparent than after the *Tampa* Affair in 2001 when the Coalition government introduced no fewer than seven separate Bills that restricted everything from the rights of asylum seekers to access status processing on mainland Australia to the rights of all migrants to seek judicial review of adverse decisions.[7]

[12.07] Refugees and the law of refugee status are the subject of a vast body of literature both in Australia and internationally.[8] It is neither possible nor is it our

---

5   See, for example, Chris Sidoti, 'Retreating from the Refugee Convention: Keynote Address' *Retreating from the Refugee Convention*, Northern Territory University, 7-10 February 1997 (Conference Proceedings).
6   See below, [12.15].
7   See *Border Protection (Validation and Enforcement Powers) Act 2001* (Cth); *Migration Amendment (Excision from Migration Zone) Act 2001* (Cth); *Migration Amendment (Excision from Migration Zone) (Consequential Provisions) Act 2001* (Cth); *Migration Legislation Amendment Act (No 1) 2001* (Cth); *Migration Legislation Amendment Act (No 5) 2001* (Cth); *Migration Legislation Amendment Act (No 6) 2001* (Cth); and *Migration Legislation Amendment (Judicial Review) Act 2001* (Cth). These measures were opposed only by the Democrats, the Greens and independent Senator Brian Harradine. See above Chapter 6.1.
8   The most significant recent publications include: Goodwin-Gill and McAdam, above n 1; and Hathaway, *The Rights of Refugees*, above n 1. For an account of Australian refugee law, see Roz Germov and Francesco Motta, *Refugee Law in Australia* (Melbourne: Oxford University Press, 2003);

intention to duplicate this work. The short series of chapters in this book cannot hope to cover all the jurisprudence emerging from international fora, the Refugee Review Tribunal (RRT) and the Australian courts. Rather, the aim is to provide an overview of the history and structures of refugee determinations in Australia, and to outline some key jurisprudential trends.

[12.08] This chapter begins by examining the operation of the offshore refugee/humanitarian program. The balance of the chapter is devoted to refugees who come to Australia not through organised programs, but as asylum seekers. Part 12.3 of the chapter deals sequentially with legislative and policy responses to the successive waves of refugees who have sought protection in Australia, and Australia's evolving relationship with the UNHCR.[9] There follows in Part 12.4 an examination of legal issues thrown up by Australia's choice of status determination processes for refugee claimants. The chapter concludes with some reflections on changes in the judiciary's approach to international refugee law. Chapter 13 is concerned with the evolving law on refugees, focusing on the interpretation of the definition of refugee. Chapter 14 then examines various aspects of the law governing the reach of Australia's protection obligations both under the Refugee Convention and under other international laws.

12.2 Australia's offshore refugee and humanitarian program

[12.09] The vast majority of people granted residence in Australia on refugee or humanitarian grounds are brought in from overseas. For many years Australia has had a substantial overseas program for the admission of refugees and humanitarian migrants. According to the Department's published statistics, of the 6.8 million migrants who have come to Australia since the end of the Second World War, more than 700,000 people arrived under humanitarian programs, initially as displaced persons and more recently as refugees.[10] While the exodus of refugees after the war in Vietnam saw a spike in the intake figures in the late 1970s and early 1980s, more recently Australia has admitted around 13,000 people each year on humanitarian visas.[11]

[12.10] Leaving to one side those granted refugee status within the country, traditionally this part of the immigration program has been divided into three main categories: refugee, special humanitarian and special assistance. The first of these is designed for persons overseas who are outside their countries of origin and who

---

and Mary Crock, Ben Saul and Azadeh Dastyari, *Future Seekers II: Refugees and Irregular Migration in Australia* (Sydney: Federation Press, 2006) (*Future Seekers II*).

9   The office of the UNHCR was established in the same year as the Refugee Convention was made. Its two main functions are the protection of refugees and the search for a durable solution to refugee problems. See Goodwin-Gill & McAdam, above n 1, at 421-61; Volker Türk and Frances Nicholson, 'Refugee Protection in International Law: An Overall Perspective' in Erika Feller et al (eds), *Refugee Protection in International Law* (Cambridge: Cambridge University Press, 2003); Statute of the Office of the United Nations High Commissioner for Refugees, UNGA, A/RES/428, 14 Dec 1950; and UNHCR, 'Agenda for Protection', UN doc A/AC.96/965/Add.1, 26 June 2002.

10 DIAC, *Fact Sheet 60 – Australia's Refugee and Humanitarian Program*, 31 January 2011.

11 DIAC, *Population Flows: Immigration Aspects 2007-08* (Canberra: 2009) Ch 4 at 71-6.

would suffer persecution if returned. The relevant visa classes include the subclass 200 (Refugee), the subclass 202 (Global Special Humanitarian), the subclass 203 (Emergency Rescue) and the subclass 204 (Women at Risk). These visa classes cater for people who either meet the definition of refugee or who are perceived to be in situations of particular need. The second (or 'special humanitarian') category includes people who remain in the country in which they are at risk and who have fled situations of war or general civil strife, suffering gross abuse of human rights. Again, these people may or may not meet the Convention definition of refugee.[12]

[12.11] The third category was introduced in 1991-92 and includes sub-programs designed to offer assistance to groups of people in particularly vulnerable situations overseas who have strong familiar or other connections with Australia. For example, special assistance is (or has been) given to East Timorese from Portugal (former subclass 208); citizens of the former Yugoslavia (subclass 209); members of certain minority groups within the former Soviet empire (subclass 210); certain Burmese (subclass 211 and 213) and Sudanese (subclass 212); and certain Cambodian nationals (former subclass 214).

[12.12] Two further categories of humanitarian entrants were added during the 11 years of the Coalition government: Temporary Safe Haven and Temporary Humanitarian Concern. Although neither involves the grant of permanent visas, each has been counted nevertheless against the humanitarian intake. Temporary Safe Haven visas are curious legal devices that are bestowed on foreign nationals chosen by Australian officials on the basis of need for temporary asylum in Australia. The visas cannot be the subject of formal application by the person in need and are strictly limited to six months. Visa holders are not generally eligible for change of status to any other visa.[13] The visas were created first for persons displaced by the conflict in Kosovo and were used later for fugitives from the violence in East Timor that followed the elections there in 1999.

[12.13] Another category of temporary humanitarian visas was abolished in August 2008. This included the 'Temporary Protection visas' which had been created during the course of the arrangements known as the 'Pacific Strategy',[14] and other special visas created in 2001 for asylum seekers intercepted either in Indonesia (and referred to UNHCR for processing) or en route to Australia.[15] As explained in Chapter 6, a key element of the policy drive to deter asylum seekers is the so-called 'excision' of Australia's offshore territories from its 'migration zone'.[16] This is done by declaring that non-citizens arriving in these territories are barred from lodging a valid visa application. Asylum seekers caught in this situation are permitted to claim protection

---

12 See subclass 201 (In-country Special Humanitarian visa).
13 Change of status is allowed only where the Minister intervenes in the exercise of a non-compellable, non-reviewable discretion. For a discussion of these visa classes, see *Future Seekers II*, above n 8 at 135-6; and Germov and Motta, above n 8, at 850-1.
14 See Chapters 4 and 6 above.
15 The former subclass 451 visa was granted to persons processed by UNHCR in Indonesia who were found to be refugees and slated by UNHCR for resettlement. This visa offered five years' temporary protection only.
16 'Excised offshore place' is defined in *Migration Act 1958* (Cth), s 5, and gazettal notices.

as refugees in a modified non-statutory status determination process. Those people found to be refugees are then referred to the Minister to consider exercising a non-compellable, non-reviewable discretion to 'lift the bar' and permit them to apply for a visa.[17] Previously the only visa available to refugees on such excised zones was a temporary visa permitting entry to mainland Australia for three years only.[18] Since 2008, all 'offshore entry' persons assessed as refugees may be permitted by the Minister to apply for a permanent Protection visa.[19]

[12.14] The prevailing feature of the different categories of refugee and humanitarian visas is the extent of the government's control over the selection and admission of offshore applicants. The Minister can stop the issue of visas when the program is fully subscribed. The criteria for entry can be changed to adjust to immediate needs; and the options available to unsuccessful applicants to challenge an adverse ruling are few. Judicial review is not excluded, but applicants cannot obtain reasons for a decision and in practice require someone in Australia with sufficient resources to bring an action.[20]

[12.15] Under the Coalition government, the character of the offshore program was altered significantly around the turn of the new Millennium – in large measure in response to the political controversy surrounding the spike in the number of asylum seekers arriving by boat. The first profound change was that the humanitarian intake was merged with the onshore program so that asylum seekers recognised as refugees within Australia came to take the place quite literally of refugee and humanitarian migrants chosen abroad.[21] By counting onshore refugees as part of the intake program, the government blurred the distinction between refugees and migrants. As noted earlier, international refugee law operates so as to create obligations in states parties to the Refugee Convention to grant protection to refugees claiming asylum within their territory. Persons entering the country through organised programs come as invitees, not as individuals asserting rights. The change reinforced contemporary rhetoric about 'good' refugees being those who entered the country through regular channels, waiting patiently in designated camps for resettlement.

[12.16] The second major change instituted after the *Tampa* Affair in 2001 was manifest in legislation purporting to restrict the grant of any kind of refugee or humanitarian visa to displaced individuals who had spent seven days or more in a country in which they could have sought protection. Although an impractical measure to enforce, this 'rule' signalled a marked increase in the role played by UNHCR in the selection of refugees and humanitarian migrants. Government policies of the day advised that intake programs were to be set in consultation with

---

17 See *Migration Act*, ss 46A and 195A. See *Plaintiff M61/2010E v Commonwealth and Plaintiff M69 of 2010 v Commonwealth* (2010) 272 ALR 14 (*Plaintiffs M61/ M69*).
18 The former subclass 447 'secondary movement offshore entry' visa.
19 The subclass 851 Resolution of Status visa.
20 For a rare example of such review by the Full Court of the Federal Court of Australia, see *Rashid v MIAC* [2007] FCAFC 25.
21 These policy changes were introduced in July 1996: DIMA, *Population Flows: Immigration Aspects* (Canberra: 2000) at 24.

stakeholders in Australia but thereafter in accordance with the priorities nominated by UNHCR.[22]

[12.17] The rhetoric about 'good' refugees from UNHCR-sponsored camps was embodied in a radical increase in the number of African refugees brought into the country after 2001. A commensurate decline is apparent in refugees and humanitarian migrants from more traditional (European and Asian) source countries.[23] By 2007, the percentage of African refugees being admitted under the offshore programs had reached over 70 per cent.[24] In light of the many thousands of refugees from other countries who have relatives in Australia, it was not surprising that in the last days of the Coalition government announcements were made that the 2008 program would see a reduction in number of African refugees in favour of a more balanced intake. During the 2007 federal election campaign, refugee politics again came to the fore with the then Minister announcing that the offshore refugee intake was being diversified because of the failure of African refugees to settle well in Australia.[25] Given the high visibility of these refugees within Australia's predominantly pale-skinned society, these statements had the potential to impact cruelly on Australia's newest and most vulnerable migrants.

12.3 Legal and policy responses to asylum seekers in Australia[26]

[12.18] The status of a refugee at international law is determined for the most part by the two major international instruments concerning refugees: the Refugee Convention and Protocol. The final arbiter of whether a person is a refugee is the International Court of Justice.[27] In the absence of a ruling from this court, the determination of refugee status in individual cases is a matter for the contracting states.[28] As Stephen J pointed out in *Simsek v Macphee*,[29] the provisions of the Refugee Convention do not confer on refugees, as individuals, any general right to invoke international law to ensure their protection. For this to occur, the relevant articles of the instruments would have to be embodied in the domestic law by statute or by

---

22   In practice, UNHCR seems to have come to play an increasing role in Australia's selection processes overseas. Persons granted a subclass 200 Refugee visa are generally (although not always) persons who have submitted to UNHCR status determination procedures, thereby gaining the moniker of 'Convention Refugees'. From within this group of refugees, UNHCR then nominates those for whom resettlement in third countries is preferred over 'local' integration. Australia selects persons within this sub-group for the grant of visas according to priorities set by the government here.
23   See *Future Seekers II*, above n 8, at 16.
24   See DIAC, *Fact Sheet 60*, above n 10.
25   See, for example, Editorial, 'More Dogwhistling: Kevin Andrews is Undermining Australia's Good Name', *The Australian*, 4 October 2007, available at <http://www.theaustralian.news.com.au/story/0,25197,22526972-16382,00.html>.
26   For a most precise and meticulous account of this development, see Germov and Motta, above n 8, at 38-64.
27   See Refugee Convention, Art 38; Protocol, Art IV.
28   See UNHCR, *Handbook on Procedures and Criteria for Determining Refugee Status* (Geneva: 1979, reedited 1992) at [V].
29   (1982) 148 CLR 636 at 641-2. See also *MIMA v Ibrahim* (2000) 204 CLR 1 at [137] (Gummow J).

operation of the common law.[30] As noted in earlier chapters, the Australian courts have confirmed this principle in many cases in recent years, asserting the primacy of Australian domestic law over any international legal obligations that may have been assumed by the executive government in signing treaties or conventions.[31]

[12.19] From the outset, Australia has chosen not to enact comprehensive legislation to translate its obligations into municipal law.[32] While the Refugee Convention and its Protocol have long been accepted as the standard for determining refugee status in Australia, the Act has been amended on various occasions to put a certain distance between the UN definition of refugee and decisions made by Australian authorities. Under the conservative Coalition government, this was done with amendments to the *Migration Act 1958* (Cth) stating that entitlement to a visa is limited to non-citizens to whom Australia owes 'protection obligations'.[33] This phrase has come to be defined in a manner that has the potential to place Australian domestic law at odds with duties assumed under international law.

[12.20] The importance of the politicians' perspective in determining these obligations is seen in the fact that 'protection' visas are granted where the Minister 'is satisfied' that an applicant meets the Convention definition of refugee. According to the High Court in *Wu Shan Liang v MIEA*[34] the use of the words 'is satisfied' means that the judicial review of a refugee decision can no longer involve a simple examination of whether an applicant meets the definition of refugee as a question of objective fact.[35] Rather, the court must determine whether there was *any* evidence on which the Minister could *be satisfied* that an applicant did or did not meet the definition of refugee. Other examples can be cited of the Convention definition being interpolated in some way in domestic law.[36] In cases where apparent discrepancies have been identified between Australia's domestic legislation and obligations assumed under the Convention and Protocol, the courts have made it clear that the statute law prevails.[37]

[12.21] As explored in the following section, refugee law in Australia appears to have developed as much in response to the historical or political context as in recognition of the country's international legal obligations. The key markers in the evolution

---

30   See *Kioa v West* (1985) 159 CLR 550 at 570-1, 603 and 630; *Mayer v MIEA* (1984) 4 FCR 312 at 314-15 (affirmed in *MIEA v Mayer* (1985) 157 CLR 290).
31   See above Chapter 4.
32   The introduction of s 6A(1)(c) into the *Migration Act* in 1980 did not enact into Australian law all of the terms of the Refugee Convention and Protocol, although it clearly did incorporate the definition of refugee contained in those instruments. No Australian court has held the other parts of the instruments to have become part of the common law: see *MIEA v Mayer* (1985) 157 CLR 290 at 293, 301 and 305.
33   See *Migration Act*, s 36(2).
34   (1996) 185 CLR 259.
35   Compare the legislation in force at the time that the leading case of *Chan Yee Kin v MIEA* (1989) 169 CLR 379 was decided in 1989. At that time there was no interposition of a requirement that the Minister 'be satisfied. Rather, the definition of refugee applied as an 'objective' test of entitlement to refugee status. See further below, Chapter 13.3.
36   See, for example, the definitions of 'persecution', 'particular social group' and 'particularly serious crimes', discussed below Chapter 13.4 and 13.6.4, and Chapter 14.3 respectively.
37   See, for example, *MIMIA v QAAH of 2004* (2006) 231 CLR 1, discussed in Chapter 14.2 below.

of refugee *law* in Australia – in the sense of a body of rules governing the treatment of asylum seekers – have been the periodic arrival of boat people to the north of the country.

12.3.1 The Determination of Refugee Status Committee (DORS) 1978-90

[12.22] The juridification of refugee policy began seriously with the arrival of the first boat people from Vietnam following the fall of Saigon in 1975. Before then, Australia had no formal system for determining refugee status in onshore applicants. The few requests for asylum made within Australia were dealt with on an ad hoc basis, with reliance placed on the Minister's broad discretion to grant an entry permit.[38] In 1977 the government set up an interdepartmental advisory committee, the Determination of Refugee Status (DORS) Committee, to assist the Minister in the exercise of this discretion. The development coincided with Australia's first experience of anything approximating a large-scale influx of asylum seekers. Between 27 April 1976 and April 1981, 2087 Vietnamese nationals arrived in boats on the north coast of Australia. Given the huge numbers of people fleeing the country, however, the potential for really large flows to Australia was considerable.[39]

[12.23] The Vietnamese boat people were among the first cases handled by the DORS Committee. Those who failed to meet the definition of refugee were allowed in under the amnesty for illegal immigrants called in 1980.[40] The DORS Committee was composed of representatives from the departments of Immigration, Foreign Affairs and Trade, Prime Minister and Cabinet, and the Attorney General.[41] In addition, the legal adviser to the UNHCR attended as an observer. The function of this Committee was to consider on paper all applications for refugee status and to make a recommendation to the Minister. The Minister usually based his decision on this recommendation. In this way the Committee performed for the Minister part of the fact-finding task. Although established according to guidelines laid down by a UNHCR Executive Committee in 1977, neither the DORS Committee nor the procedures it followed had any statutory basis in Australian law. The grant of refugee status and/or protection on humanitarian grounds continued to be a matter of ministerial discretion.[42]

[12.24] The establishment of the first (non-statutory) refugee status determination regime was matched in 1979 with amendments to the *Migration Act* that provided

---

38 For an account of the history, see Klaus Neumann, *Refuge Australia* (Sydney: UNSW Press, 2005).
39 See the estimates given in 'Memorandum 380' in *1979 Cabinet Records – Selected Documents*, available at <http://www.naa.gov.au/Images/6-Refugees%20and%20migration_tcm2-27151.pdf> at 180.
40 See Des Storer and Arthur Faulkner, *Out of the Shadows: A Review of the 1980 Regularisation of Status Programme in Australia* (Geneva: ILO, 1982).
41 See Commonwealth, *Parliamentary Debates*, House of Representatives, vol 105, 24 May 1977, at 1713-19, and vol 109, 3 May 1978, at 1754. See also Christopher Avery, 'Refugee Status Decision-making: The Systems of Ten Countries' (1983) 19 *Stanford Journal of International Law* 235 at 246; Patricia Hyndman, 'Australian Immigration Law and Procedures Pertaining to the Admission of Refugees' (1988) 33 *McGill Law Journal* 716 at 727-8.
42 See *Migration Act*, s 6A(1)(c) and (e) as amended in 1980.

for the apprehension and detention of persons arriving at the border without authorisation. Section 36A gave legislative force to the notion that a person arriving without authority could be deemed not to have entered the country.[43] Section 36A(8) read:

> A person shall not, for the purposes of this Act, be deemed to have entered Australia by reason only of his having been taken from a proclaimed airport for the purpose of being kept in custody at a place outside a proclaimed airport in pursuance of sub-section (1), (2) or (3).

[12.25] The provisions echoed a popular view that the obligations imposed by the Refugee Convention can be controlled to some extent by a receiving state – in the sense that they might not apply until an individual had 'entered' Australia as a matter of law. In as late as 1987, background papers on Australia's asylum policy (although not 'official policy') were stating:

> The obligation not to 'refoule' (Article 33 of the Convention) does not apply to a person claiming refugee status who arrives in Australia without authority and who is aboard an aircraft/vessel which is *neither* a flag carrier/ national airline of the alleged persecuting state, *nor* bound to the alleged persecuting state.[44]

[12.26] Writing in 1989, Crawford and Hyndman identified as 'heretical' both this view and the notion that Australia was not obliged to entertain an asylum claim where the claim 'might more appropriately and with equal moral force be the responsibility of another signatory to the 1951 Convention'.[45] These attitudes certainly characterised the approach taken to asylum seekers during the 1980s. They help to explain also why the public discourse in more recent years has been so persistently negative in respect of unauthorised arrivals seeking protection as refugees.

[12.27] The release of Cabinet Papers from 1979 demonstrate the emergent awareness of international legal standards in Australia's response to the Vietnamese refugees – and the relationship between the law and basic notions of humanity and decency. Many of the restrictive measures introduced under the conservative Coalition government during and after the *Tampa* Affair were considered by the conservative government led by Prime Minister Malcolm Fraser in 1979. These included imposing carrier sanctions on illegal boat arrivals;[46] the use of temporary visas; and the use of remote detention facilities for the processing of refugee claims. All but the first of these were rejected, together with some more extreme suggestions that would have been blatantly in breach of basic refugee and human rights laws. These included an offer to process 'refugees' in Saigon; 'buying off' Vietnam; deterring the refugees by welcoming the hardened approach of Thailand, Malaysia and

---

43   See *Migration Amendment Act 1979* (Cth), which amended s 36 and inserted s 36A into the *Migration Act*.
44   See Department of Immigration and Ethnic Affairs (DIEA), *Refugee Policies and Refugee Status Determination Procedures: Background Paper* (Mimeo, 1987) at 22. The policy is reproduced in James Crawford and Patricia Hyndman, 'Three Heresies in the Application of the Refugee Convention' (1989) 1 *International Journal of Refugee Law* 155 at 167. The authors note that the paper is not official policy, but indicative merely of attitudes adopted by some decision-makers on some occasions.
45   See DIEA, ibid at 28; Crawford and Hyndman, ibid.
46   Introduced in 1979, see Chapter 6.1.

Indonesia (which were pushing boats back out to sea, so occasioning horrendous loss of life); and 'repatriation' of refugees to Vietnam.[47]

[12.28] The most noteworthy aspect of the Fraser government's response to this genuine crisis was the realisation that a coordinated effort would be required to both deal with the outflows and to bring pressure to bear on the Vietnamese government which ultimately had the ability to stem the outflow. In the result, Australia played an important role in formulating and implementing a policy regime that came to be known as the 'Comprehensive Plan of Action' (CPA). This was a complex multilateral agreement that saw refugee camps established throughout the Asia-Pacific region to house thousands of fugitives; as well as agreements with Vietnam allowing for the orderly departure of persons wishing to be resettled elsewhere.[48] It was through the 'Orderly Departure Program' instituted in 1982 that Australia accepted for admission over 90,000 Vietnamese refugees.[49]

[12.29] The second (post-Vietnam) group of boat arrivals did not feature so prominently on the public radar, but had quite a profound influence on evolving law and administration because of their international political significance. At the centre of the problem was Indonesia's assertion of sovereignty over West Papua, the state contingent to the former Australian colony of Papua New Guinea (PNG) to the immediate north of the country.[50] The arrest of a prominent independence activist in 1984 led to an uprising in West Papua that was put down violently by Indonesian troops. Approximately 11,000 West Papuans fled into neighbouring PNG, while a small group of political activists made their way by boat to Australia. These arrivals induced intense political concern about the impact any humanitarian gesture might have on Australia's relations with Indonesia. It is not clear whether Australia's response was born of fear of Indonesia's military might or of the domestic political fallout that would follow if there were to be a wholesale influx of refugees from West Papua. As Elizabeth Biok chronicles, Australia refused to provide specific aid to deal with the refugees who had fled to PNG.[51] It also refused to grant refugee status to

---

47 Memorandum 380, above n 39. The fact that these proposals remained for 30 years as no more than suggestions (made and dismissed) stands testament to the fortitude of then Prime Minister Malcolm Fraser, whose record as a defender of human rights has not always had the recognition it deserves. See Mike Steketee, 'Fraser Rejected Detention for Boat People', *The Australian*, 30 December 2009, available at <http://www.theaustralian.com.au/in-depth/cabinet-papers/fraser-no-to-detention/story-e6frgd9o-1111118449731>; 'Howard in War Refugee Snub: Fraser', *The Australian*, 1 January 2008, available at <http://www.theaustralian.com.au/in-depth/cabinet-papers/howard-in-war-refugee-snub-fraser/story-e6frgd9x-1111115225044>.

48 See W Courtland Robinson, 'The Comprehensive Plan of Action for Indochinese Refugees, 1989-1997: Sharing the Burden and Passing the Buck' (2004) 17 *Journal of Refugee Studies* 319; Arthur Helton, 'Refugee Determination Under the Comprehensive Plan of Action: Overview and Assessment' (1993) 5 *International Journal of Refugee Law* 544. See also Martin Tsamenyi, *The Vietnamese Boat People and International Law* (Brisbane: Griffith University, 1981).

49 The program was modelled on the program begun in 1980 for the United States. See Judith Kumin, 'Orderly Departure from Vietnam: Cold War Anomaly or Humanitarian Innovation?' (2008) 27 *Refugee Survey Quarterly* 104; Nancy Vivani, *The Long Journey: Vietnamese Migration and Settlement in Australia* (Melbourne: Melbourne University Press, 1984).

50 For an account of the history of the West Papuan region, see Elizabeth Biok, 'The Regional Perspective: Exporting Deterrence and Negating Human Rights Standards' in *Offshore Processing of Asylum Seekers: The Search for Legitimate Parameters* (2000) 9 *UTS Law Review* 69.

51 Ibid at 71-4.

the first of the activists to arrive in Australia, one Ran Rak Mayer. The case became something of a cause célèbre when a representative on the DORS Committee turned whistleblower, encouraging lawyers to lodge a request for reasons for the refusal. When these were denied, an application was made for judicial review of the decision, with the matter eventually making its way to the High Court in 1985.

[12.30] The case of *MIEA v Mayer* became an important milestone in the development of refugee law because the High Court ruled that the DORS process was an inherent part of the Minister's decision made 'under an enactment' to grant or refuse refugee status.[52] Accordingly, it held that the reasoning of that committee could properly be sought under s 13 of the *Administrative Decisions (Judicial Review Act) 1977* (Cth) (*ADJR Act*). Following this victory in the High Court, Mayer was immediately granted residence on humanitarian grounds. No reasons were ever given as to the earlier process. The broader significance of the case was that it opened the door to judicial scrutiny of the refugee status determination process. Without the ability to obtain the reasoning of the DORS Committee, it had been virtually impossible before that time to mount a serious challenge to status determinations.[53]

[12.31] The treatment of the Papuan asylum seekers who followed Mayer in 1985 presaged other aspects of Australia's response to refugees in its region. Australia refused to grant anything other than temporary visas, and appears to have gone to some lengths not to publicise the arrivals.[54] It also consolidated the practice of referring boat arrivals from West Papua to PNG. Interestingly, in view of the role this place would play in and after 2001, Manus Island was chosen as the place for processing the asylum claims of these people. In hindsight, the arrangements look very much like the deflection and offshore processing that was later to be institutionalised in the Pacific Strategy (see below at Part 12.3.3).

[12.32] Throughout the 1980s, the number of people applying for refugee status at or after entry into Australia rarely exceeded 400 per annum. Over the same period, a greater number sought residence on humanitarian or compassionate grounds under the liberal provisions of the then s 6A(1)(e) of the Act. In 1989, a congruence of events in the region caused a sudden rise in onshore refugee claimants. These events brought what might be characterised collectively as the third wave of onshore refugees – of whom boat people were once again the most politically charged.

[12.33] The most significant event in numerical terms was the violent repression on 4 June 1989 of pro-democracy demonstrators in the People's Republic of China (PRC). Thousands of Chinese students living in Australia suddenly found themselves unable to return home in safety because of their alliance with dissident movements. The PRC crackdown encouraged thousands more to come to Australia in search of protection.

---

52 (1985) 157 CLR 290.
53 See also *Simsek v Macphee* (1982) 148 CLR 636 in which Stephen J in the High Court ruled that asylum seekers had no hearing rights of any kind under Australian law.
54 Biok asserts that the refugees remained on Temporary Entry Permits (TEPs) until 2006. See Elizabeth Biok, 'Australia and Refugees in the Asia Pacific' (unpublished SJD thesis, University of Sydney, 2009) at 131.

[12.34] Over the same period, civil strife erupted in Cambodia with the withdrawal of Vietnamese troops from that country, the organisation of elections and the repatriation of thousands of refugees from neighbouring countries. Although the number of fugitives from Cambodia who arrived in and after 30 November 1989 was small, this group was to have a defining impact on immigration and refugee law in Australia. The Cambodian boat people saga is synonymous for many with the development of mandatory immigration detention. As documented by Hamilton and others, the Labor government of the day refused to countenance the possibility that the fugitives from Cambodia could be Convention refugees.[55] As well as creating obstacles to their lodging of asylum claims, a cat and mouse game developed between the government and refugee advocates that saw both the introduction of laws mandating the detention of unauthorised boat arrivals and increasing physical distance interposed between the boat people and their legal advisers.[56]

[12.35] A third defining event was the resolution of the CPA. The closure of the CPA camps saw small groups of boat people take to the seas once more in search of protection. Mixed in with these asylum seekers were Sino-Vietnamese from the PRC who had been resettled in that country after the Vietnam War and who had gravitated to the coastal regions in China's Bei-Hai Province. Dislocated in the course of slum-clearing measures, these fugitives were also characterised as persons covered by the CPA.

[12.36] A total of 652 people arrived in Australia by boat between November 1989 and November 1992. With the exception of 113 Chinese who were returned to China from Christmas Island on 7 November 1992, all claimed refugee status.[57]

[12.37] Although the boat arrivals during this period caused considerable consternation within Australia, one noteworthy feature of the political response is that the then Labor government appears to have been acutely aware of both the sources and causes of the boat arrivals. This is because the government was deeply involved both in attempts to solve the ongoing crisis in Cambodia and in the resolution of the CPA. The arrival of boats was stopped almost overnight by two initiatives. The first was a Memorandum of Understanding with the PRC to police the activities of people smugglers (or 'snake heads') in the region. The second was amendments to the *Migration Act* barring access to Australia's refugee protection regime to persons covered by the CPA.

---

55   Andrew Hamilton, 'Three Years Hard' (1993) 3(1) *Eureka Street* 24; Andrew Hamilton, 'Three Years Hard' (1993) 3(2) *Eureka Street* 22; Andrew Hamilton, 'The Cambodian Boat People: Are They Victims of Discrimination?' (1994) 69 *Law Institute Journal* 552. See also Nicholas Poynder, 'Recent Implementation of the Refugee Convention in Australia and the Law of Accommodations to International Human Rights, Have We Gone Too Far?' (1995) 2(1) *Australian Journal of Human Rights* 75; and Mary Crock, 'The Peril of the Boat People' in Hugh Selby (ed), *Tomorrow's Law* (Sydney: Federation Press, 1995).

56   See, for example, Nicholas Poynder, 'Marooned in Port Hedland: The Case of the Boat People, The UN Human Rights Committee in Practice' (1993) 18(6) *Alternative Law Journal* 272.

57   See also Janet Phillips and Harriet Spinks, 'Boat Arrivals since 1976' Background note, Parliamentary Library, available at <http://www.aph.gov.au/library/pubs/bn/sp/BoatArrivals.pdf>.

[12.38] One other factor contributed to the rise in refugee claims during this period. Amendments to the *Migration Act* in 1989 removed the avenues that had existed for the grant of visas on general compassionate or humanitarian grounds. This change encouraged anyone seeking temporary or permanent protection to apply for refugee status to safeguard their immediate position. By the end of 1991, onshore applications had peaked at 16,740 for the year, of which 77 per cent involved PRC nationals.[58]

12.3.2 Formal merits review authorities: The Refugee Status Review Committee (1990-93) and the RRT

[12.39] The government's first response to this rise in onshore refugee claims occurred in June 1990. Instead of sending all cases to the DORS Committee, the Minister increased the staff of what was the DORS secretariat, and gave it its own authority as a recommendatory body.[59] The DORS Committee was then reconstituted with some changes[60] and re-named the Refugee Status Review Committee (RSRC). The new committee was given the function of reviewing cases rejected by the first tier advisers. Procedures were streamlined in so far as departmental officers no longer supplied transcripts of initial client interviews. Instead, reports were prepared and, where a negative assessment was made, the report was put to the applicant for comment. Both the new DORS officers and the RSRC had power to recommend to the Minister that he or she grant a permit on humanitarian grounds – provided that the applicant had 'entered' Australia and was not an illegal migrant after 1 July 1991.[61]

[12.40] As Germov and Motta document, the congruence of the new boat arrivals and the move to codify migration decision-making in 1989 resulted in a much more complicated regime for the grant of entry permits (as they were then called), with no less than four categories of permits created.[62] It was at this time that the concept of temporary, rather than permanent, protection for onshore refugees was first trialled. In the first instance, provision was made for the grant of temporary permits to persons for whom permanent resettlement in Australia was either not a suitable 'durable solution' for the refugee or not in the national interest. In 1990, this regime was replaced with a more punitive scheme that envisaged the grant of four-year temporary permits to all persons recognised as refugees in Australia. Designed as a measure to discourage asylum seekers, the change was a direct response to the large number of claims being lodged by PRC nationals who had come to Australia originally on student or temporary work visas. By 1993, the government recognised the futility of the restrictive measures (which by then had gone through several iterations). As well as abandoning the temporary permit system, thus reverting to permanent residence as the norm for onshore refugees, the government introduced a range of visa options that allowed many refugee claimants to gain permanent residence on employment

---

58   See Germov and Motta, above n 8, at 34-6.
59   See *Migration Review Regulations 1989* (Cth) (*Review Regulations 1989*), Part 2A; MILGEA, *Media Release*, MPS 43/90, 27 June 1990; and MILGEA, *Media Release*, MPS 15/91, 15 March 1991.
60   The representative from the Department of Prime Minister and Cabinet was replaced by a nominee of the Refugee Council of Australia.
61   See reg 8E of the *Review Regulations 1989* and former s 115 of the *Migration Act*.
62   See Germov and Motta, above n 8, at 38-43.

or other concessional grounds.[63] Another significant change to this aspect of refugee law during Labor's term in office was the move in 1995 to restrict the ability to lodge sequential or repeat applications for either a general visa or a Protection visa after a visa had been either cancelled or refused.[64]

[12.41] For its part, the refugee processing regime was altered significantly by the establishment of a new detention facility at a disused mining camp in Port Hedland in 1991. This move began a trend that led to more radical initiatives to deter asylum seekers under the Howard Coalition government. Port Hedland was the start of concerted endeavours to place (increasingly extreme) physical distance between asylum seekers and their lawyers and advocates. This in turn dictated a new approach to status determinations because of the logistics required in having both departmental officials and legal advisers commute to the places where asylum seekers were being held (see further Part 12.4 below). For a period, informal time limits were introduced in an attempt to ensure that applications for refugee status were lodged as soon as possible after arrival.[65] While lacking the force of law, these requirements held more than a little irony for detained asylum seekers because of the lack of any commensurate obligation to process applications once they were made. These years saw the beginning of a distressingly common trend whereby asylum seekers in Australia were held for years at a time, with many months passing between the lodging of asylum claims and anything resembling a ruling being made by the immigration authorities.

[12.42] By mid 1992 it was clear that the heavy reliance placed on written submissions, both at first instance and in appeals, was unworkable. A ruling by the Federal Court in the asylum claims of two fugitives from Iran probably drove the last nail into the coffin of the DORS regime. In *Somaghi* and *Heshmati* the court ruled that the Minister committed an error of law where he or she drew adverse inferences from evidence submitted by the applicants without giving the applicants an opportunity to comment on those inferences.[66] The rulings added another step to the paper trail, requiring decision-makers to provide applicants with a statement of a proposed ruling and to then give them the opportunity to make further submissions. Legislation was passed setting up a specialist tribunal for the hearing of refugee claims in September 1992.[67] The proclamation on 1 September 1994 of the remaining parts of the *Migration Reform Act 1992* (Cth) worked to streamline migration procedures at first instance. The amendments codified the procedures to be followed by both decision-makers and applicants.

12.3.3 The Coalition years: 1996-2007

[12.43] If the boats arriving in and after November 1989 brought a significant political response, the surge in unauthorised arrivals in the late 1990s induced

---

63   See Chapter 15.6.1.
64   See *Migration Act*, ss 48, 48A and 48B, inserted by the *Migration Amendment Act (No 6) 1995* (Cth).
65   See MILGEA, *Media Release*, MPS 50/91, 13 August 1991.
66   *Somaghi v MILGEA* (1991) 31 FCR 100; *Jafar Heshmati v MILGEA* [1990] FCA 460.
67   See *Migration Reform Act 1992*, Part 4A.

near hysteria in the media and government. In some respects Australia's experiences reflect those of refugee-receiving countries all around the world at this time. The establishment of new people-smuggling routes saw an unprecedented rise in the number of truly international arrivals, with refugees from places as diverse as Sri Lanka, Somalia, Kenya, the Middle East (including Iran and Iraq) and Afghanistan.[68]

[12.44] In view of earlier events in the region, however, it is interesting to note the role that Indonesia played in the protracted drama that unfolded. Australia's relations with its much larger (predominantly Muslim) neighbour reached new lows with the successful push for East Timor to become an independent country: Indonesia was more than a little chagrined by Australia's influence on this process.[69] Unhappily, the turmoil in East Timor coincided with Indonesia becoming a significant transit country for out of region refugees and asylum seekers. Indonesia was a country of particular significance because of its geographic proximity to two Australian territories used by the people smugglers as dropping off points for their human cargo: Christmas Island (approximately 340 kilometres from the Indonesian Island of Java) and Ashmore Reef (approximately 150 kilometres from the Indonesian Island of Roti). In the result, Australia appears to have been caught off-guard. Its lack of meaningful engagement with Indonesia until well into 2000 meant that bi-lateral attempts to stop the flow of unauthorised boat arrivals were late and clumsy in their execution. Many bear an uncanny resemblance to some of the suggestions made to Cabinet at the height of the Vietnamese refugee crisis.[70]

[12.45] The first response of the Coalition government to the sudden rise in the number of unauthorised boat arrivals was to reinstitute the concept of Temporary Protection visas – this time of three, rather than four, years' duration. The human impact on this occasion, however, seems to have been greater than in the early 1990s when many of the refugees were young students who did not have immediate family responsibilities. In 1999, asylum seekers granted temporary protection were typically adult males who had come in search of asylum for themselves with the intention of having their families follow using conventional (sponsored) family reunification provisions. The institution of the temporary protection regime put an end to family reunion through regular migration. It was no coincidence that the number of children appearing on boats transiting through Indonesia jumped from around 5 per cent to 30 per cent and higher within weeks of the legislative change.[71]

[12.46] Although geographically distant from the events of 11 September 2001 in the United States, Australia became one of the first countries to manifest its alarm through legislative changes targeted specifically at refugee claimants. The changes

---

68   See *Future Seekers II*, above n 8, at 37ff.
69   See Nancy Vivani, 'The Sharp Deterioration in Relations Between Indonesia and Australia: An Australian Perspective' in Chris Manning and Peter Van Dierman (eds), *Indonesia in Transition* (Singapore: Institute of Southeast Asian Studies, 2000) at 125-6.
70   See above [12.27].
71   These figures are estimates based on a manual count of the persons recorded as boat arrivals by the Department. See DIMIA, *Fact Sheet 74a*, 31 July 2004, available at <http://sievx.com/articles/psdp/DIMIA74a_boatarrivals.pdf>.

made – together with a harsh new policy of intercepting and repelling asylum seekers seeking to enter Australia by boat – were part of a complex political strategy used by the incumbent Coalition government facing an imminent federal election. Tragically, the persons most affected by the new measures were themselves fugitives from terrorist regimes.

[12.47] Australia had entered into a 'regional cooperation arrangement' with Indonesia in 2000 whereby Indonesia was paid to intercept asylum seekers on their arrival in that country and to otherwise act to prevent the asylum seekers from travelling on to Australia.[72] The agreement with Indonesia formed the basis of the interception and deflection operations that followed in 2001-01 after the *Tampa* Affair whereby boats intercepted by Australia have been forcibly returned to Indonesia.[73] Australia has funded all of the operations associated with the asylum seekers in Indonesia. These include the expense of any voluntary repatriation; costs incurred by UNHCR in assessing refugee claims; and the cost of detaining asylum seekers in Indonesia. Asylum seekers who are recognised as refugees by UNHCR must wait in Indonesia until a signatory country to the Refugee Convention accepts them for resettlement.

[12.48] As detailed in Chapter 6, the *Border Protection (Validation and Enforcement Powers) Act 2001* (Cth) retrospectively validated any action taken by the Commonwealth in the course of the *Tampa* Affair and its aftermath. Special powers were conferred on 'officers' to search, detain and move passengers on ships which had been pursued, boarded and detained by Australian authorities.[74] Perhaps the most unusual amendments, however, were those passed to prevent the use of Christmas Island and of the nearby reefs as delivery points for asylum seekers. Parliament empowered the Minister to declare parts of Australia's offshore island territories to be outside the 'migration zone'. The *Migration Amendment (Excision from Migration Zone) Act 2001* (Cth) provides that non-citizens coming ashore at Ashmore Reef, on the Keeling or Cocos Islands or on Christmas Island are deemed *not* to have entered Australia's migration zone. The legislation operates as a bar to those people lodging asylum claims, or indeed applications of any kind for an Australian visa. The exclusionary provisions were extended later so as to encompass most of Australia's island territories.

[12.49] Central to this regime was the establishment on Nauru and on Manus Island in Papua New Guinea of holding centres for the processing of refugee claims by persons intercepted en route to Australia during the *Tampa* Affair and its immediate

---

72   The International Organisation for Migration (IOM) was then funded to interview the people taken into custody and inform them of their options. See 'Unauthorised Boat Arrivals – A Growing International Problem' in DIMA, *Annual Report 1999-2000*, available at <http://www.immi.gov.au/about/reports/annual/1999-2000/intro3.htm>; Jessica Howard, 'To Deter and Deny: Australia and the Interdiction of Asylum Seekers' (2003) 21(4) *Refuge* 35 at 41-2.
73   Described in detail above at Chapter 4.3.
74   See Chapter 6.1 above. The legislation is not limited to actions taken within Australia's territorial sea, nor is any deference made to the constraints on extraterritorial operations imposed by the UN *Convention on the Law of the Sea* (adopted 10 December 1982, entered into force 16 November 1994) 1833 UNTS 3 (UNCLOS). See generally Daniel O'Connell, *The International Law of the Sea* (2 vols) (Oxford: Clarendon Press, 1984).

aftermath. As detailed elsewhere,[75] these centres were run by the International Organisation for Migration. Refugee status processing was carried out by UNHCR and by Australian officials under arrangements that had no direct statutory basis in Australian or any other law. The asylum seekers were kept initially in what was effectively incommunicado detention: neither lawyers nor media were allowed access to the camps. Detainees were provided with no legal advice or other assistance in relation to their asylum claims. Australia asserted that the arrangements complied with its international legal obligations under the Refugee Convention because they were modelled on procedures used by UNHCR itself in field operations in African camps and elsewhere. This was a contestable assertion – UNHCR does not generally prohibit asylum seekers from obtaining legal assistance in presenting their claims. However, the involvement of UNHCR in the processing of the asylum seekers on Nauru and Manus Island effectively silenced criticism by that most influential of agencies. Popular support for the Pacific Strategy within Australia allowed the Howard government to ride out the complaints of human rights advocates in this country.

[12.50] If Australia could claim that it did not engage in any practice of refouling the *Tampa* (and *Acheng*) refugees, it cannot be said that all of its actions under what is known as 'Operation Relex' were beyond reproach. The crudity of the arrangements with Indonesia is apparent in evidence that emerged of Indonesian initiatives to sabotage boats carrying asylum seekers so as to prevent them reaching Australia.[76] Although not proven, some have claimed that 'disruption' activities may have either caused or contributed to the SIEV X tragedy in which 353 asylum seekers drowned in the seas off the southern coast of Indonesia.[77] Allegations were made of Indonesian officials forcing asylum seekers at gunpoint onto the doomed and overloaded vessel; of the Australian surveillance operations being aware that the vessel had left, but doing nothing to track its passage or to come to the assistance of the asylum seekers in a timely fashion.[78] The victims were all asylum seekers bound for Australia – many were close family members of refugees already in the country.

[12.51] Not much is known of the practical application by Australian authorities of the laws and policy adopted following the *Tampa* incident. However, accounts have emerged of Australia interdicting vessels carrying asylum seekers outside of its territorial waters as well as in the immediate proximity of its newly 'excised' territories, and of those vessels being towed or escorted back to Indonesia and West Timor. The intercepted vessels – referred to as 'Suspected Illegal Entry Vessels' (or SIEVs) – included the now infamous SIEV 4, photographs of which were misused by the government to promote the fiction of asylum seekers throwing their children

---

75   See *Future Seekers II*, above n 8, at 123ff; Michael Gordon, *Freeing Ali: The Human Face of the Pacific Solution* (Sydney: UNSW Press, 2005) and David Marr and Marianne Wilkinson, *Dark Victory* (Sydney: Allen & Unwin, 2003).
76   For a discussion of the issue of possible sabotage of refugee boats, see Marr and Wilkinson, ibid at 41-3.
77   See above Chapter 4.3.6; and Tony Kevin, *A Certain Maritime Incident: The Sinking of SIEV X* (Melbourne: Scribe Publications, 2004) at 131 and Ch 7 generally.
78   The most comprehensive collection of information on this affair is available at <http://www.sievx.com>. The site is largely the work of Marg Hutton.

overboard to 'blackmail' Australia into accepting them. With a Senate inquiry[79] into this affair and through the work of investigative journalists,[80] evidence emerged of Australian involvement in 'push back' incidents at sea resulting in two confirmed deaths by drowning, and three other suspected drownings.[81]

12.3.4 The treatment of refugees and asylum seekers after 2007

[12.52] The election of a Labor government in 2007 brought an end to the worst excesses of the policies introduced during the decade of Coalition governance. In accordance with promises made during the election campaign in 2007, the regime of Temporary Protection visas was dismantled, with the (relatively few) remaining visa holders granted permanent residence.[82] The new Minister (Senator Chris Evans) announced new guidelines for the detention of unlawful non-citizens. These favour the release on reconnaissance of children and families in all but 'last resort' cases and the use of detention only in cases where non-citizens pose a security or flight risk, and then only for the shortest possible time.[83] Renewed efforts were made to improve the 'culture' within the immigration bureaucracy'.[84] While many aspects of the Pacific strategy were abandoned, fundamental parts of the program were retained. In the result, the advances made were sadly short-lived and ultimately somewhat illusory. Children continued to be detained. In January 2011 over 1065 were being held in various facilities around Australia. Ironically, the decision not to place children and families in the detention centres left them with fewer freedoms and with worse amenities than many 'regular' detainees.[85]

[12.53] Leaving to one side its prohibitive cost,[86] the Pacific Strategy was not a sustainable policy. The idea that third countries could be persuaded to take refugees interdicted by Australia in the long term was unfounded. Most of those found to be refugees on Nauru and Manus Island were resettled ultimately in Australia – as indeed were the failed refugee claimants who could not be returned to their countries

---

79 See Senate Select Committee for an inquiry into a certain maritime incident, 23 October 2002, available at <http://www.aph.gov.au/senate/committee/maritime_incident_ctte/index.htm>.
80 See, for example, ABC Four Corners, 'To Deter and To Deny' (ABC TV: 15 April 2002), transcript available at <http://www.abc.net.au/4corners/stories/s531993.htm>.
81 See generally DIMA's Answers to Questions on Notice, 2001 Joint Committee of Public Accounts and Audit – Inquiry into Coastwatch, available at <http://sievx.com/articles/psdp/200103xxDIMA-ToCoastwatchInquiry.pdf>. Newspaper reports between December 1998 and December 2001 suggest that the death toll amongst those trying to reach Australia by boat could have been as high as 891. See Mary Crock and Daniel Ghezelbash, 'Do Loose Lips Bring Ships? The Role of Policy, Politics and Human Rights in Managing Unauthorised Boat Arrivals' (2010) 19 *Griffith Law Review* 238 at 246-7.
82 *Migration Amendment Regulations 2008 (No 5)* (Cth).
83 See Chris Evans, 'Last Refugees Leave Nauru', *Media Release*, 8 February 2008; Chris Evans, 'Labor Unveils New Risk-Based Detention Policy', *Media Release*, 29 July 2008.
84 See Andrew Metcalfe, Secretary, DIAC, speech 'New Directions in Detention – Restoring Integrity to Australia's Immigration System', Australian National University, Canberra, 29 July 2008.
85 See Mary Crock, 'First Term Blues: Labor, Refugees and Immigration Reform' (2010) 17 *Australian Journal of Administrative Law* 205.
86 Marr and Wilkinson, above n 75, at 287-8, estimated that the program to detain 2390 boat people on Nauru and Manus Island and the interception and return on 670 people to Indonesia cost 'about $500 million'.

of origin.[87] When the Labor government finally closed the camps on Nauru in 2008, there were no murmurs of protest from the Opposition benches. In spite of an almost unanimous campaign by refugee advocates urging Labor to repeal the 'excision' laws and to abolish offshore processing altogether, this did not occur. The Howard Coalition government left office in 2007 having spent close to $400 million building a super high security detention facility on Christmas Island.[88] In spite of the commitment not to detain children and to move to a regime where people were detained only where they posed a threat and for the shortest possible period of time,[89] the new facility was commissioned under the Labor government in 2008 and was expanded in 2009.[90] In January 2010 the facility was already at capacity. By the end of that year the island was so full that at least some status processing was transferred to the mainland. By 14 January 2011 there were 6730 people in immigration detention, with 3895 detained on the mainland and 2835 on Christmas Island. Of these, 1065 were children – most in 'alternative temporary detention in the Community'.[91]

[12.54] As was always going to be the case, the refugee boats started coming again: indeed patterns began establishing themselves before the change of government in 2007.[92] In 2008 and 2009, pressures were generated by the Sri Lankan government's defeat of Tamil separatists which lead to the corralling of many thousands of Tamils in refugee camps. The resurgence of the Taliban in Afghanistan and in Pakistan led to fresh flows of asylum seekers all around the world, some of whom resorted to established routes through South East Asia.[93]

[12.55] The interdiction program continued, although attempts to repel asylum seekers to Indonesia in 2009 were singularly unsuccessful.[94] In 2009, there were at

---

87 See Senator Chris Evans, 'Last Refugees Leave Nauru', above n 83.
88 See Sophie Black, 'Christmas Island — Building Our Own Private Guantanamo', *Crikey*, 28 March 2007, available at <http://www.crikey.com.au/2007/03/28/christmas-island-building-our-own-private-guantanamo/>. This article includes diagrams of the layout of the centre.
89 See Senator Chris Evans, 'Labor Unveils New Risk-Based Detention Policy', above n 83.
90 See Yuko Narushima, 'Crammed Christmas Island Centre to Cost Extra $45m', *Sydney Morning Herald*, 3 December 2009, available at <http://www.smh.com.au/national/crammed-christmas-island-centre-to-cost-extra-45m-20091202-k6f8.html>.
91 See <http://www.immi.gov.au/managing-australias-borders/detention/_pdf/immigration-detention-statistics-20110114.pdf>.
92 See Phillips and Spinks, above n 57.
93 See UNHCR, *Asylum Levels and Trends in Industrialized Countries: 2008*, 24 March 2009, available at <http://www.unhcr.org.au/pdfs/AsylumReport2008_Final_notembargoed.pdf>; UNHCR, *Asylum Levels and Trends in Industrialized Countries: First Half 2009*, 21 October 2009, available at <http://www.unhcr.org/4adebca49.html>.
94 See, in this context, the standoff that developed when a customs vessel, the *Oceanic Viking*, intercepted a boatload of mainly Tamil asylum seekers and sought to return the group to Indonesia. In spite of its denials, the government does appear to have resorted to a special deal in order to persuade the asylum seekers to leave the boat for processing in Indonesia. See Stephen Fitzpatrick, 'PM's "Special Deal" Leaves Kids in Lock-Up', *The Australian*, 20 November 2009, available at <http://www.theaustralian.com.au/news/nation/pms-special-deal-leaves-kids-in-lock-up/story-e6frg6nf-1225799951673>; Ben Doherty, 'Mothers and Infants behind Detention Centre Bars', *Sydney Morning Herald*, 20 November 2009, available at <http://www.smh.com.au/world/mothers-and-infants-behind-detention-centre-bars-20091119-ioys.html>; ABC News (Australia), 'Rudd Attacked over Indonesia Detention "Chaos",' 20 November 2009, available at <http://www.abc.net.au/news/stories/2009/11/20/2748169.htm?section=justin>; Matthew Franklin, 'Rudd

least two incidents associated with the interdiction program that resulted in multiple loss of life. On 16 April 2009 a boat carrying mainly Afghan asylum seekers exploded after being stopped by Australian coastguard forces. Five people were killed (the bodies of two were never recovered) and many of the 44 remaining were severely injured.[95] In November 2009 three Tamil asylum seekers drowned when their boat capsized at sea.[96] The April incident highlighted the senseless inequities of the excision laws which essentially strip asylum seekers of their right to access the appeal systems available to onshore refugee claimants. The entire cohort was brought to mainland Australia for medical treatment and for the assessment of their refugee claims. Although all were recognised as refugees in relatively short measure, there was some irony in the fact that the most serious of the burns victims fell technically into the category of 'transitory persons'. This was because they were taken to a sea installation from whence they were flown by helicopter to the mainland.[97] The other asylum seekers by-passed the excision laws because their first landfall was mainland Australia.

[12.56] Spooked by Opposition taunts about loss of border control, the Labor government made a number of attempts to deter irregular boat arrivals in 2010. Measures adopted included the suspension of refugee status determinations for asylum seekers from Afghanistan and Sri Lanka;[98] and the re-opening of Curtin Detention Centre in remote north Western Australia (WA).[99] Families were placed in community detention in Leonora township in WA. The boats kept coming. The change of leadership in the Labor party if anything marked a toughening of attitude. Prime Minister Gillard went to the federal election in 2010 committed to establishing an offshore processing centre in East Timor.[100] Whether this proceeds after the High Court's ruling in *Plaintiff M61/2010E v Commonwealth and Plaintiff M69 of 2010 v Commonwealth*[101] remains to be seen.

Again Denies Boat Deal', *The Australian*, 19 November 2009, available at <http://www.theaustralian.com.au/politics/rudd-again-denies-boat-deal/story-e6frgczf-1225799510650>; Paul Maley, 'PM Refuses to Say Who Prepared Refugee Plan', *The Australian*, 19 November 2009, available at <http://www.theaustralian.com.au/politics/pm-refuses-to-say-who-prepared-refugee-plan/story-e6frgczf-1225799510577>.

95   See Paul Maley, 'Three Boatpeople Die in Explosion', *The Australian*, 16 April 2009, available at <http://www.theaustralian.com.au/news/three-boatpeople-die-in-explosion/story-e6frg6n6-1225699338834>; Phillip Corey, 'Boatpeople Fight for Their Lives as Rudd Slams People Smugglers', *Sydney Morning Herald*, 17 April 2009, available at <http://www.smh.com.au/national/boat-people-fight-for-their-lives-as-rudd-slams-people-smugglers-20090417-a9l3.html>.

96   See United Press International, 'At Least 3 Die When Boat Capsized', 3 November 2009, available at <http://www.upi.com/Top_News/International/2009/11/03/At-least-3-die-when-boat-capsized/UPI-77501257262883/>.

97   See *Migration Act*, ss 198A, 198B and 198C.

98   Chris Evans, Brendan O'Conner and Stephen Smith, 'Suspension on Processing of All New Applications from Asylum Seekers from Sri Lanka and Afghanistan', Speech given at Parliament House, 9 April 2010.

99   Chris Evans, 'Curtin to Hold Suspended Asylum Seekers', *Media Release*, 18 April 2010.

100 See Crock and Ghezelbash, above n 81, at 277.

101 (2010) 272 ALR 14 (*Plaintiffs M61/ M69*), discussed above, Chapter 3 at [3.65] and Chapter 19 at [19.102]-[19.104].

12.4 Process matters: Assessing the procedures for determining refugee status

[12.57] In theory, refugees become entitled to the protection of the Refugee Convention from the moment they meet the definition of refugee, which means that any procedures adopted by a state have a declarative, rather than a constitutive, function.[102] Having said that, the idea that people either meet the definition of refugee, or they do not, is something of a legal fiction. As the following discussion demonstrates, refugee status determination processes do matter. Sadly, there are a great many instances around the world where Convention refugees fail to gain protection because of the inadequate consideration that is given to their claim.

[12.58] States that have signed the Refugee Convention and Protocol are constrained in the procedures they adopt for refugee determination by the general international obligation to perform their treaty obligations in good faith.[103] The instruments themselves, however, are silent about what such procedures should entail.

[12.59] The frequent reluctance to look seriously at the impact of process on the recognition of refugee claims has its roots in the paucity of rigorous procedures adopted by the very body established to set standards for the treatment of refugees – the UNHCR. Placed under intolerable stresses in countries of first asylum that are often lacking in every imaginable amenity, UNHCR's field operations often involve status determination processes that are crude in the extreme. Although it was envisioned initially that all states parties to the Refugee Convention would develop their own status determination procedures, in practice this has not occurred.[104] UNHCR has found itself conducting status determinations both in countries that are not parties to the Convention[105] and in others that are. Recent years have seen a number of studies criticising the shortcomings in UNHCR's processes.[106] As Michael Kagan notes, UNHCR has frequently sought to justify its actions on the basis of lack of resources. There is also the assumption that status determinations in the field in countries of first asylum often have less drastic implications for claimants than do the procedures carried out by government authorities which have the ability to return asylum seekers to the countries from which they have fled.[107]

[12.60] In countries like Australia, the problems engendered by the deficiencies in UNHCR practices are twofold. First, there has been a tendency to assume that a rigorous procedure is not important. Second, and more troublingly, it has been asserted

---

102 See Goodwin-Gill and McAdam, above n 1, at 51; UNHCR, above n 28, at para 28.
103 See the *Vienna Convention on the Law of Treaties* (adopted 22 May 1969, entered into force 27 January 1980) 1155 UNTS 331 at Arts 3, 26 and 31. See Chapter 4 at [4.59].
104 On this point, see UNHCR, 'Determination of Refugee Status', *Executive Conclusion No 8 (XXVIII)* (1977) at para (b) (encouraging states to establish indigenous status determination procedures).
105 Note that many countries in the Asian region are not signatories to the Convention. See generally Vitit Muntarbhorn, *The Status of Refugees in Asia* (New York: Clarendon, 1992).
106 On shortcomings in UNHCR procedures in Africa, see Edwin Odhiambo Abuya, 'Assessing Refugee Claims in Africa: Missing or Meeting Standards' (2006) 53 *Netherlands International Law Review* 171; and Michael Kagan, 'The Beleaguered Gatekeeper: Protection Challenges Posed by UNHCR Refugee Status Determination' (2006) 18 *International Journal of Refugee Law* 1.
107 See Kagan, ibid at 19 (note 73).

that the only equitable system is one that uses UNHCR practice as a benchmark. Both arguments are tied to the notion that refugees should not be permitted to engage in 'forum shopping' in their search for protection.[108] They represent a primary justification for the establishment of offshore processing centres with procedures that are modelled loosely on those pertaining in UNHCR field operations.[109]

[12.61] Even as an ideal, there are inherent problems in assessing asylum claims in an equitable manner. In 1990, David Martin described the dilemma of formulating a just process for resolving asylum claims as 'both tragic and surpassingly difficult'.[110] In practice it is probably impossible to devise a status determination system that is completely fair (and consistent) in its operation. Putting to one side the important issues of resource constraints, there is a multiplicity of factors that will lead decision-makers to decide cases differently when presented with essentially the same set of facts.[111] Having said this, there is clear evidence that process *does* matter. A refugee must be given the opportunity to tell her or his story. If a process does not facilitate this, then one cannot be confident that the outcome is a reliable indication of how a person should be characterised as a matter of law.

[12.62] In the *Seeking Asylum Alone* study published in 2006, significant discrepancies were observed in the outcome of refugee claims adjudicated under the mainland status determination scheme in comparison with the regime on Nauru and Manus Island. Of 55 children sent 'offshore' for processing, 32 were repatriated to Afghanistan after their refugee claims were refused.[112] In comparison, some 290 unaccompanied children claimed asylum on mainland Australia between 1999 and 2003 and not a single one was returned to the country from which they had fled.[113] Within the cohort of 'onshore' asylum seekers, it was noted that 100 per cent of children who contested adverse decisions without assistance failed in their appeals.[114] The same study found that an overwhelming majority of unaccompanied children who challenged adverse status decisions made within Australia in the RRT failed in their appeals.[115] It is to the 'mainstream' status determination processes that we now turn.

---

108   The term devised to describe the phenomenon is that of 'secondary movement refugees'. See Erica Feller, 'Asylum, Migration and Refugee Protection: Realities, Myths and the Promise of Things to Come' (2006) 18 *International Journal of Refugee Law* 509; and Stephen Legomsky, 'Secondary Refugee Movements and the Return of Asylum Seekers to Third Countries: The Meaning of Effective Protection' (2003) 15 *International Journal of Refugee Law* 567.

109   An excellent collection of articles on this phenomenon is to be found at (2006) 18(3/4) *International Journal of Refugee Law*.

110   David A Martin, 'Reforming Asylum Adjudication: On Navigating the Coast of Bohemia' (1990) 138 *University of Pennsylvania Law Review* 1247 at 1275.

111   The most important study in recent years in this context was conducted by researchers at Georgetown University's asylum clinic: Jaya Ramji-Nogales, Andrew Schoenholtz and Philip Schrag, *Refugee Roulette: Disparities in Asylum Adjudication and Proposals for Reform* (New York: NYU Press, 2009). For a comment on this study, see Stephen Legomsky, 'Learning to Live with Unequal Justice: Asylum and the Limits of Consistency' (2007) 60 *Stanford Law Review* 413.

112   Mary Crock, *Seeking Asylum Alone: A Study of Australian Law, Policy and Practice Regarding Unaccompanied and Separated Children* (Sydney: Themis Press, 2006) at 41-2 (*Seeking Asylum Alone*).

113   Note that under an arrangement brokered by Jesuit priests in Australia two young asylum seekers were sent to Pakistan and then sponsored back into Australia on tourist visas. See ibid at 125.

114   Ibid at 39-40.

115   Ibid at 125-6.

12.4.1 Onshore refugee status determinations

[12.63] When a non-citizen first presents in Australia without a visa, or without what the authorities assess to be a valid visa, the standard practice is to take the person into immigration detention where she or he is subjected to a 'screening in' interview. The objective is to obtain the person's story so as to assess whether the person engages Australia's 'protection obligations' in any way. As noted by a Senate Committee,[116] the Australian Human Rights Commission[117] and by researchers in the *Seeking Asylum Alone* Project,[118] this all important first contact with immigration places a positive onus on asylum seekers to articulate their need for protection. This is of particular concern in the case of unaccompanied and separated children or other vulnerable claimants who may not know to use the language or 'trigger' words that officers are looking for. Being 'screened in' is a precondition to the allocation of government funded advisers to assist in the preparation of asylum claims.[119] In fact, officials have no statutory obligation to provide 'visa assistance': the Act stipulates that non-citizens have no right to an application form or to a lawyer unless they request it.[120] Being screened out means that a non-citizen without a visa can be slated for immediate removal from the country.

[12.64] The *Seeking Asylum Alone* report notes:[121]

> The legislative scheme poses special challenges for children because of the emphasis that it places on applicants telling the truth; and the association it makes between lying and lack of credibility. The 'screening' interview is recorded and any later changes in an applicant's story can be used to question an applicant's credibility. Section 91V(4) of the *Migration Act* empowers interviewing officers to require detainees to make an oath or declaration to the effect that everything they said was true. The legislation provides further that where a detainee refuses to make such an oath or declaration or where the Minister 'has reason to believe' that the detainee was being 'insincere' because of the detainee's 'manner' or 'demeanour', 'then, in making a decision about the non-citizen … the Minister may draw any reasonable inference unfavourable to the non-citizen's credibility'.

[12.65] In the case of the young woman whose story is used to open the Australian report, the then 13-year-old national of Afghanistan was deemed at her first interview

---

116 Senate Legal and Constitutional References Committee, *A Sanctuary Under Review: An Examination of Australia's Refugee and Humanitarian Determination Processes* (Canberra: AGPS, 2000) (*Sanctuary Under Review*) at 85 (recommendation 3.1) and 139 (recommendation 4.8). For a commentary on this report, see Mary Crock, 'A Sanctuary Under Review: Where to From Here for Australia's Refugee and Humanitarian Program?' (2000) 23 *University of New South Wales Law Journal* 246.
117 Human Rights and Equal Opportunity Commission, *A Last Resort? The National Inquiry into Children in Immigration Detention* (Sydney: AGS, 2004) at 239.
118 See *Seeking Asylum Alone*, above n 112, at 84-5 and 119-22.
119 The scheme is known as the Immigration Advice and Application Scheme (IAAAS). Advisers are appointed through a tendering process which sees the successful tenderer paid on a per case completion basis. There is no requirement that advisers have legal qualifications or training.
120 Section 256 of the *Migration Act* states: 'Where a person is in immigration detention under this Act, the person responsible for his or her immigration detention shall, at the request of the person in immigration detention, give to him or her application forms for a visa or afford to him or her all reasonable facilities for making a statutory declaration for the purposes of this Act or for obtaining legal advice or taking legal proceedings in relation to his or her immigration detention'.
121 See *Seeking Asylum Alone*, above n 112, at 85. See also *Migration Act*, s 91V(5) and (6).

not to engage Australia's protection obligations. She and a 10-year-old boy identified as her brother were marked for removal. They spent over six months in detention until they were allocated a lawyer and allowed to lodge a full refugee claim. Both were then recognised almost immediately as refugees.

[12.66] Although unaccompanied children are no longer taken into the immigration detention centres as a matter of course, children have continued to be confined in accommodation that is highly restrictive. In fact, of the 1065 children detained in mid January 2011,[122] few had access to adequate welfare and educational facilities, although arrangements were being made to change this situation. The migration legislation still makes no provision for the automatic appointment of legal advisers to any asylum seeker. Nor is there any obligation placed on officials to advise people about the right they might have to lodge a claim for asylum.[123] As the Senate inquiry in 2000 revealed, it is not just children and vulnerable claimants who are at risk under this system. Although the Rudd Labor government acted to change some features of Australia's refugee determination regime, there are a number of key areas where Australia's initial asylum processes raise particular problems for asylum seekers. There remained in January 2011 an unhealthy reliance on keeping asylum seekers arriving by boat in detention for the duration of any assessment process. As noted below, there are real shortcomings in the processes that have been adopted to process asylum claims where people are detained in remote locations.

12.4.2 Offshore refugee status determinations

[12.67] As we have seen, the Rudd and Gillard Labor governments did not disturb the legislative framework underpinning the 'Pacific Strategy': changes were made at a policy and operational level only. However, Labor did adopt a policy of not exercising the s 198A power to transfer 'offshore entry persons' to third countries (Nauru and PNG). The practice since 2007 has been to send asylum seekers interdicted at sea to Christmas Island pending a decision by the Minister to exercise the non-delegable, non-compellable discretion under s 46A(2) to allow an application for a (regular) Protection visa.[124] As in the past, the arrangements allow asylum seekers taken to Christmas Island to immediately lodge refugee claims. Procedures have been established outside of the *Migration Act* to allow for 'Refugee Status Assessment' (RSA) and for the 'Independent Merits Review' (IMR) of negative rulings. Unlike the situation that pertained at the height of the Pacific strategy,[125] the procedures under Labor have mimicked closely those followed by decision-makers on mainland Australia. The 'offshore entry persons' on Christmas Island are subjected to an initial screening interview and are then allocated agents or advisers funded by the Australian government (and chosen under a tendering process for the offshore work). The agents interview the asylum seekers and then assist in the completion of

---

122 See <http://www.immi.gov.au/managing-australias-borders/detention/_pdf/immigration-detention-statistics-20110114.pdf>.
123 See *Sanctuary Under Review*, above n 116.
124 See *Migration Regulations 1994* (Cth), Sch 2, subclass 866.
125 When offshore asylum seekers had virtually no procedural entitlements. See *Seeking Asylum Alone*, above n 112, at Ch 13.3.

the application form. Upon completion of a written application, the asylum seekers are assessed to determine whether they are a person with respect to whom Australia has protection obligations under the Refugee Convention. The RSA is carried out by DIAC officers and involves an oral hearing which the applicant's agent is permitted to attend. The IMR is conducted by reviewers employed by a private company, 'Wizard People Pty Ltd'. Where an asylum seeker is assessed by either of these to be a refugee, a submission is made to the Minister recommending that the Minister *consider exercising* the power conferred by s 46A(2) of the Act. The Minister at this point has a non-reviewable, non-compellable discretion to determine that s 46A(1) of the Act should not apply to an application for a Protection visa. He or she can also exercise the related non-compellable discretion under s 195A to grant a Protection visa to an offshore entry person held in detention. The process is referred to as 'lifting the s 46A bar'. In practice, a positive recommendation has always been followed by a decision to both exercise the discretion contained in s 46A(2) and to grant a Protection visa in accordance with s 195A of the Act.

[12.68] It is arguable that the greatest problem with maintaining an offshore processing regime is the logistical constraints it entails. The most serious shortcomings of the former processing regimes on Nauru and those that operate still on Christmas Island and in detention centres within Australia related to the physical difficulties that arose in getting both advisers and decision-makers to the places where the asylum seekers were being held. On Christmas Island, cases continue to be processed as they were on Nauru, using a 'task force' approach that inevitably constrains the time both advisers and decision-makers have to spend with claimants and on the preparation and assessment of their cases. This means that advisers and officials are flown or shipped in for relatively short time periods during which asylum seekers are processed intensively, with all parties to the procedures being placed under tight deadlines to prepare case histories and interview the asylum seekers. The frenetic schedules make it almost impossible for advisers to gain the trust of their clients for the purposes of soliciting accurate information. In the *Seeking Asylum Alone* research, this was borne out in the regularity in which the young people saw meetings with their legal representative as indistinguishable from their interviews with (government) assessing authorities.[126] The remote location of the centre and the dispersal of clients between the detention centre and the so-called 'community' living encampments for unaccompanied minors and families further complicate the processing. Put simply, intensive RSD processing is not conducive to reliable decision-making.

12.4.3 Administrative appeals

[12.69] The greatest change in the refugee determination process during the 1990s was the institution in July 1993 of a tribunal before which refugee claimants had a right to an oral hearing on appeal from an adverse decision. The RRT has jurisdiction to review refugee decisions made both before and after 1 July 1993. Members are not required to be – and often are not – lawyers. However, the tribunal does have a

---

126   See ibid, at 123.

research section staffed with lawyers and others who have developed expertise in refugee law.[127]

[12.70] Many asylum seekers who lodge claims while in detention are afforded assistance in making their application to the RRT through the Immigration Advice and Application Assistance Scheme (IAAAS). However, funding does not cover the actual tribunal hearings: advisers who attend hearings may only address the tribunal on behalf of their clients in exceptional circumstances and at the invitation of the tribunal member. In practice this usually occurs after the member has finished examining the applicant and any witnesses.[128] The remoteness of many detention centres means that interviews are often conducted by video conferencing, a situation that is hugely challenging for applicants in the best of circumstances. The children studied in the *Seeking Asylum Alone* research encountered a process that was markedly flawed. In these situations, applicants had to cope with the double remove of the RRT member and interpreter in one State and an adviser in another, sometimes with no one in the room with the applicant except for the telephone.[129]

[12.71] In terms of the findings of the RRT, complaints have been made that tribunal members have been susceptible to pressure from government to an extent that their independence has been impugned.[130] In 2000, in the *Sanctuary under Review* Inquiry, the Senate Committee expressed concern about the practice of appointing RRT members from the ranks of senior public servants.[131] It also recommended that the practice of single member hearings be modified so as to allow members to sit in panels of three in appropriate cases.

[12.72] A central problem with the mechanism for the review of refugee decisions is the closed nature of the process and the lack of any balance in the powers given to tribunal members. Members continue to sit alone in sessions that are not open to external scrutiny of any kind. Claimants have no right to be represented or to nominate, examine or cross-examine witnesses. The tribunal does have discretion to call on a legal representative to make submissions on the law: this is usually done at the conclusion of a hearing. Although UNHCR is able to send in observers, this rarely happens in practice.

[12.73] While the Senate Committee recommended improved training of RRT members in inquisitorial techniques,[132] it is our view that there are fundamental flaws

---

127   The aim of the RRT is to provide 'a mechanism of review that is fair, just, economic, informal and quick': *Migration Act,* s 420(1). An application for review must be made within seven days of notification of the primary decision for people in detention. The Act discourages the making of serial applications for refugee status by providing that the RRT is bound to consider only fresh material submitted in support of any application made after an appeal for refugee status has been rejected once: s 416. As is the case with MRT review, the Minister retains discretion to overrule the RRT so as to make a decision more favourable to an applicant: s 417.

128   In practice, advisers are invited to speak towards the end of hearings. It is at this point that discussions take place, for example, on issues of law relevant to a case.

129   See *Seeking Asylum Alone,* above n 112, at 148-9.

130   See Chapter 18 at [18.47] and Chapter 19 at [19.37].

131   See *Sanctuary Under Review,* above n 116, at 173 (recommendation 5.6).

132   Ibid at 151 (recommendation 5.2).

in a system that gives claimants no right to be represented and no power to influence the direction a hearing might take. There is a fundamental power imbalance in the system in so far as tribunal members are placed under no obligation to inform asylum seekers of their rights at law. Claimants can be, and often are, asked questions in circumstances where they have no understanding of why a question is being asked and of the likely consequences of giving certain responses.[133]

[12.74] The RRT decision is technically the end of the RSD process.[134] In spite of the provisions in the Act that purport to exclude judicial review, failed asylum seekers do have a limited right to challenge adverse rulings in a court. They can also make an application for the Minister to exercise his or her residual discretion to grant a visa on humanitarian grounds.

[12.75] In relation to asylum seekers arriving without authorisation by boat, as noted above at [12.67], the Labor government introduced a formal appellate mechanism in the form of IMR. The conferral of an appellate function on private contractors appears to have been done in an attempt to reduce judicial oversight of offshore RSD processing. In *Plaintiffs M61/M69*, the government argued that the offshore RSA and IMR regimes were undertaken in exercise of a non-statutory executive power. Because the exercise of the power did not in itself directly determine rights,[135] there could be no obligation to afford procedural fairness in conducting the RSA and IMR processes. Nor did it matter if those who undertook the inquiry had misunderstood or misapplied the law.[136] The High Court's emphatic rejection of these arguments in November 2010 threw into disarray the rationale for offshore processing. The court ruled that, as long as the offshore RSA and IMR process is tied to the process of granting an Australian visa, individuals making decisions offshore will be required to act in accordance with both the common law rules of procedural fairness and with domestic refugee law. In a judgment that can only be described as sparse, leaving unanswered a great many questions, the ruling in *Plaintiffs M61/M69* contains no guarantees that the court would necessarily regard RSA and IMR decisions made in a regional processing centre (outside Australian territory) as immune from judicial oversight.[137]

[12.76] The decision of the High Court turned on three matters. First was the question of whether the plaintiffs were entitled to procedural fairness at the hands of the various actors in the status determination and visa process. The second concerned an examination of various aspects of the *ultra vires* doctrine in the context of the decision-makers' obligations to act in accordance with the *Migration Act* and associated case law. The third, which will not be explored here, involved a challenge to the

---

133 See further Chapter 18 below. For a longer critique, see Susan Kneebone, 'The Refugee Review Tribunal and the Assessment of Credibility: An Inquisitorial Role?' (1997) 5 *Australian Journal of Administrative Law* 78.
134 See s 5(9) of the *Migration Act* which defines the 'final' determination of an application as the end of the administrative appeal process.
135 *R v Collins; Ex p ACTU-Solo Enterprises Pty Ltd* (1976) 8 ALR 691 at 695. See Submissions of the First and Second Defendant, at [33].
136 See Crock and Ghezelbash, above n 81, at 4.1.
137 For a fuller discussion of this case, see ibid.

12.4.4 Ministerial discretion

[12.77] The last issue addressed here is the Minister's discretion to allow a failed asylum seeker to remain in Australia on humanitarian grounds. The narrow scope of the Refugee Convention has always created problems for persons in Australia who are not refugees but are unable or unwilling to return to their country of origin for serious reasons. Before 19 December 1989, the Minister's power to grant a permit to such 'humanitarian' cases was expressed in the broadest terms.[139] Permanent residence could be granted to any non-citizen legally in Australia who could demonstrate 'strong compassionate or humanitarian' grounds for the grant of a permit. There were no definite rules about the circumstances that could qualify as either 'compassionate' or 'humanitarian'. This absence of legislative guidance caused much concern about abuse of the system. In spite of the requirement that applicants hold a valid temporary entry permit, the paragraph was relied on heavily by unlawful non-citizens who made simultaneous applications for temporary and permanent permits. The government's attempts to tighten its policies in this area met with little success in the courts.[140] By 1989, applications had begun to increase markedly.[141] The combined impact of judicial trends and the rise in applications drew a sharp response from the government.

[12.78] After December 1989, the two concepts of compassion and humanitarianism were dealt with separately in the Act and Regulations,[142] each undergoing substantial change. 'Compassionate' grounds were defined to include either specified family situations or compassionate grounds involving extreme hardship or irreparable prejudice to an Australian citizen or permanent resident. For quasi-refugees, the regime for granting permanent residence on humanitarian grounds was subsumed briefly within the refugee status determination procedures. In more recent times the use of the generic terms 'compassionate' and 'humanitarian' have been abandoned altogether.

[12.79] Instead, in more recent times, humanitarian and other public interest factors are channelled through the mechanism that empowers the Minister to grant permanent visa as a matter of personal, non-compellable discretion under s 417 of the Act. This provision allows the Minister to change a decision made by a tribunal

---

138 See the discussion of the case in Chapter 19 at [19.37].
139 Former s 6A(1)(e) of the *Migration Act*.
140 See, for example, cases such as *Dahlan v MILGEA* [1989] FCA 507 and *Damouni v MILGEA* (1989) 87 ALR 97.
141 See Joint Standing Committee on Migration Regulations (JSCMR), *First Report: Illegal Entrants in Australia – Balancing Control and Compassion* (Canberra: AGPS, 1990) at 12ff, 37-8.
142 See former s 47(1)(f) and (g) of the *Migration Act*. Compassionate cases were covered later by a variety of provisions. See, for example, *Migration Regulations 1994*, Sch 2, subclasses 804, 812, 101 and 305; *Review Regulations 1989*, reg 140. The nearest equivalent for a humanitarian entry permit was the domestic protection permit in subclass 784 (previously reg 117A): see Chapter 5 and Chapter 9.7.

(whether in relation to a Protection visa or other visa class) and 'substitute a decision which is more favourable to the applicant'. The Minister may grant a visa which she or he thinks is appropriate in the public interest, even where the applicant does not meet the legal requirements for the grant. The power is entirely discretionary and non-reviewable. A similar power in the Minister to intervene personally to grant a visa may also be exercised in relation to a person in detention, under s 195A, regardless of whether they have received a tribunal decision.

[12.80] The Rudd Labor government moved quickly to distance itself from the ministerial intervention mechanism. On 9 July 2008, the Minister for Immigration stated:[143]

> Ministerial intervention powers were originally intended to provide an outcome for unique and exceptional cases but there is now an industry in people appealing to the minister.

In so doing, the Minister referenced the Senate Select Committee inquiry into Ministerial Discretion in Migration Matters, which was established (during the Coalition government) in June 2003 in the wake of allegations that the 'ministerial discretion appears to have been granted to people who had made donations to the Liberal party or their associates'.[144]

[12.81] The controversy surrounding the use of s 417 stems from two competing factors. On the one hand, the lack of transparency inherent in the exercise of ministerial discretion raises serious questions about the factors that may influence the success of applications to the Minister to intervene. On the other hand, the existence of ministerial discretion seems critical as an antidote to the otherwise highly prescriptive, codified decision-making processes under the Act. In addition, in the absence of a complementary protection regime,[145] the ministerial intervention system addresses Australia's failure to implement explicitly its non-refoulement obligations under the Torture Convention or other human rights instruments, as numerous parliamentary reviews have recognised.[146]

[12.82] The Labor government's distaste for the ministerial intervention option is borne out in the statistical data on s 417 requests since 2006. Although there has been a decline in requests for intervention after an initial increase following the change of government in late 2007, the overall trend in actual interventions has been markedly in decline. With the change of Minister in 2010, it remained to be seen in December of that year whether this trend would be permanent. The decision of the High Court in *Plaintiffs M61/M69*[147] is of interest in this context. While affirming the non-compellability of the Minister's discretions, the court showed a new willingness

---

143   Chris Evans, 'Ministerial Intervention Powers Under Review', *Media Release*, 9 July 2008.
144   Senate Select Committee on Ministerial Discretion in Migration Matters, *Report* (Canberra: Commonwealth of Australia, 2004) at xxix.
145   See the discussion of this proposal in Chapter 14.4.
146   See further Chapter 14 at [14.66]. See Elizabeth Proust, *Report to the Minister for Immigration and Citizenship on the Appropriate Use of Ministerial Powers under the Migration and Citizenship Acts and Migration Regulations* (Canberra: Commonwealth, 2008); *Sanctuary Under Review*, above n 116, at 237, [8.2].
147   (2010) 272 ALR 14.

to review the recommendations made by persons advising the Minister in processes established apart from the statutory regime. It may well be that the High Court will go on to confirm that applicants are entitled to procedural fairness during the process engaged in to advise the Minster in these cases.[148]

Ministerial intervention rates under s 417

Activity	2006-07	2007-08	2008-09	2009-10
Requests received	3303	3510	2816	2446
Requests finalised	4013	3491	2436	3037
Requests finalised by the Minister	2741	2100	1502	1937
Visas granted	847	754	606	558

Source: DIAC, Annual Report 2008-09, table 37; DIAC, Annual Report 2009-10, table 45

[12.83] In recognition that some events overseas do require a more sustained humanitarian response in the treatment of classes of foreign nationals caught in Australia, another trend has been to use the regulatory system to deal with these problems as they arise. To this end, the Regulations are amended to deal with groups of foreign nationals in situations of special need. The Chinese students in Australia at the time of the Tiananmen Square massacre, and the nationals of various states affected by the conflicts in the Persian Gulf and in the former Yugoslavia are examples in point.[149] For the most part, the recipients of these special permits receive temporary residence only, and are expected to return home on the expiry of their permits.

12.5 Refugees and the courts: The development of an Australian jurisprudence on refugees

[12.84] If structured decision-making in relation to onshore refugee claimants is a recent phenomenon in Australia, so too is the wholesale involvement of the courts in the refugee determination process. Between 1980 and 1989, few refugee cases were reviewed by the Federal Court. In spite of the growing body of foreign case law and learned articles available, little attention was given to the legal issues involved in the determination of refugee status.[150] Some judges did begin to take a greater interest in the treatment of asylum-seekers. In *Azemoudeh v MIEA*,[151] Wilcox J took the Department to task for its high-handed treatment of an Iranian asylum seeker who

---

148 See Crock and Ghezelbash, above n 81, and the discussion in Chapter 19 at Part 19.4.
149 See, for example, former Sch 2, subclasses 435 (Sri Lanka), 443 (citizens of the former Yugoslavia); and 437 (the People's Republic of China) of the *Migration Regulations*. See also the Gulf conflict (temporary) entry permit in *Review Regulations 1989*, reg 119K, and the *Migration (Iraq and Kuwait) (United Nations Security Council Resolution No 661) Regulations 1991* (Cth).
150 For a discussion of the Australian jurisprudence before 1989, see Crawford and Hyndman above n 44; Hyndman, above n 41; Dianne Ayling and Sam KN Blay, 'Australia and International Refugee Law: An Appraisal' (1989) 9 *University of Tasmania Law Review* 245. See generally, Mary Crock, 'Judging Refugees: The Clash of Power and Institutions in the Development of Australian Refugee Law' (2004) 26 *Sydney Law Review* 51.
151 (1985) 8 ALD 281.

was denied the opportunity of making a claim for refugee status. The judge could not prevent the applicant's removal, but his ruling appears to have had an impact on subsequent practice regarding border refugee claimants.[152]

[12.85] The breakthrough for refugee claimants, however, was two rulings by the High Court in 1985. These opened the way for a greater involvement of the judiciary in the review of refugee decisions. In *Mayer v MIEA*,[153] noted earlier as the key decision involving fugitives from West Papua (Irian Jaya), the court recognised what was then s 6A(1)(c) of the *Migration Act* as the source of the Minister's power to grant refugee status. It held that refugee status decisions were judicially reviewable under the *ADJR Act* and that reasons for such decisions could be sought under s 13 of that Act.[154] The case was significant because it confirmed the Minister's obligation to consider claims for refugee status made under s 6A(1)(c) of the *Migration Act*. By implication, it also established the standard governing the determination of refugee status as that set down in the Refugee Convention.[155]

[12.86] *Mayer's* case was followed closely by the High Court's decision in *Kioa v West*,[156] which put beyond doubt the fact that onshore asylum seekers were entitled to be heard before being removed. The response of the judiciary to these landmark rulings, however, was not immediate.

[12.87] Among the applications for review that were made during the late 1980s, many involved border claimants whose status as non-entrants put them outside s 6A(1)(c) of the Act. In general, the Federal Court appears to have been prepared to accept a lesser standard of treatment for these people.[157]

[12.88] Even where the Federal Court did purport to consider the Refugee Convention, it appears to have been loath to question any aspect of the Minister's interpretation of Australia's international legal obligations with respect to refugees. Crawford and Hyndman identify three 'heresies' in the government's onshore refugee policy and practice during this period. These involved the misinterpretation of the Convention definition of the term 'refugee', and the beliefs that obligations to assist refugees vary according to whether they can be sent on to a third country, and whether or not the refugee claimants had 'entered' Australia.[158] In no instance were any of the three heresies addressed with any seriousness by the Federal Court.

[12.89] To some extent, the courts' disregard for the specifics of international refugee law over this earlier period may reflect the ready availability of other protective provisions. As the 1980s drew to a close, the catch-all provisions in s 6A(1)(e) of the

---

152 See JSCMR, *Australia's Refugee and Humanitarian System: Achieving a Balance Between Refuge and Control* (Canberra: AGPS, 1992) at 147.
153 (1985) 157 CLR 290.
154 Ibid at 302.
155 See also *Banu v Hurford* (1987) 12 ALD 208.
156 (1985) 169 CLR 550. This case is discussed in detail in Chapter 19.3.1.
157 See Crawford and Hyndman, above n 44; and Hyndman, above n 41, at 736.
158 The authors provide as evidence of the government's practice cases such as *Azemoudeh v MIEA* (1985) 8 ALD 281; *Sinnathamby v MIEA* (1986) 66 ALR 502; *Gunaleela v MIEA* (1987) 15 FCR 543; *Periannan (Murugasu) v MIEA* (unreported, FCA, Wilcox J, 28 July 1987); and *Mohankumar v MIEA* (unreported, FCA, Morling J, 30 March 1988).

Act were being interpreted by the courts in a manner that ensured that most failed refugee claimants would ultimately gain residence. In doing this, the jurisprudence ran counter to many of the policies devised to restrict the grant of residence on compassionate or humanitarian grounds. The courts opened the section to unlawful non-citizens where such people had previously been regarded as ineligible for permanent residence.[159] As noted earlier in the context of the family migration cases,[160] judges began to interpret s 6A(1)(e) in a very literal fashion, looking critically at any attempts to restrict through policy the ordinary meaning of the terms 'compassionate' and 'humanitarian'.[161] In *Dahlan v MILGEA*,[162] Hill J came close to saying that s 6A(1)(e) should be available to any person whose situation would excite pity in the average Australian.

[12.90] In both *Damouni* and *Dahlan*, French and Hill JJ took the view that it was improper to require applicants under s 6A(1)(e) to meet the same or greater standards of hardship as were demanded of refugees. In these and other cases, the court ruled unlawful policy guidelines suggesting that residence under s 6A(1)(e) should be available only to persons who could demonstrate an 'individualised' fear of persecution.[163] Stressing the flexibility of the provision, French J noted that s 6A(1)(e) did not even demand that hardship be suffered by the applicant for a permit. Hardship suffered by relatives or associates of the applicant could also be relevant.[164]

[12.91] On occasion, the courts' concentration on the ordinary meaning of the words compassion and humanity, and their concern about slavish adherence to policy, brought them very close to reviewing the merits of some decisions. This was particularly so in the cases where arguments were raised as to whether the matters taken into account in reaching a decision were factually correct.[165] Section 6A(1)(e) was designed to limit eligibility for permanent residence. However, rulings by the courts in the late 1980s made it increasingly difficult to deny a permit in cases where compassionate or humanitarian grounds were found to exist. In *Damouni*, French J held that the words used in s 6A(1)(e) were 'no mere matter of form, for where grounds are found to exist, the intention of Parliament as indicated by [these] provisions ... would seem to lie in the direction of sympathetic treatment of these people'. Decision-makers who found against the grant of a permit in such cases were at risk of being found to have made a decision that was legally unreasonable,[166] or legally impermissible because of the matters taken or not taken into account.[167]

---

159   See, for example, *Daguio v MIEA* (1986) 71 ALR 173; and *Maitan v MIEA* (1988) 78 ALR 419.
160   See Chapter 8 at [8.05].
161   See, for example, *Damouni v MILGEA* (1989) 87 ALR 97 and *Dahlan v MILGEA* [1989] FCA 507.
162   [1989] FCA 507 at [54].
163   See *Rizki v MILGEA* (1989) 18 ALD 643 at 645; *Damouni v MILGEA* (1989) 87 ALR 97 at 102-3; *Dahlan v MILGEA* [1989] FCA 507 at [53]; and *Pesava v MILGEA* (1989) 18 ALD 95 at 100.
164   *Damouni v MILGEA* (1989) 87 ALR 97 at 103.
165   See, for example, *Akers v MIEA* (1989) 98 ALR 261; *Rizki v MILGEA* (1989) 18 ALD 643 at 645; and *Luu v Renevier* (1989) 91 ALR 39 at 47ff. See further Chapter 19.3.2.
166   See *Dahlan v MILGEA* [1989] FCA 507; *Rizki v MILGEA* (1989) 18 ALD 643; and *Luu v Renevier* (1989) 91 ALR 39.
167   See *Damouni v MILGEA* (1989) 87 ALR 97; *Dahlan v MILGEA* [1989] FCA 507; *Sim v MILGEA* [1989] FCA 8; *Tat v MILGEA* [1990] FCA 228.

[12.92] The touchstone for Australian refugee lawyers is the High Court's ruling in *Chan Yee Kin v MIEA*,[168] considered in the following chapter. This was the first case in which the High Court considered in detail the definition of refugee and, for the government, represented the height of what it came to consider as 'judicial activism'.[169] The problems caused by s 6A(1)(e) could be eliminated by the specification in subordinate legislation of the compassionate and humanitarian circumstances in which protection is available. The courts' use of the rules of procedural fairness could be addressed by codifying the procedures to be followed in reaching decisions. However, the judiciary's perceived generosity towards refugees presented more difficulties because the Refugee Convention restricts the government's ability to regulate the standard used to determine refugee status.

[12.93] *Chan* prompted extraordinary furore within bureaucratic and political spheres. Frequent reference was made in parliament during 1992 to the unhelpful nature of the High Court's ruling and to the need to counter its effects. The Labor government was accused of having created a rod for its own back.[170]

[12.94] Refugee law in Australia has grown exponentially as the mechanisms for hearing claims have become increasingly sophisticated and as judicial exposure to refugee claims has increased following the decision in *Chan*. It is a matter of chagrin for the government that the creation of the RRT and other measures designed to stifle judicial review have not brought about a decline in the number of applications being made for judicial review of refugee decisions. On the contrary, the number of court actions has continued to rise. Refugees have represented over many years the largest source of migration applications to the federal courts.[171] This has remained the case in the face of multiple attempts to stifle judicial review. As we explore in the following chapter, the result has been a veritable explosion in the jurisprudence on refugee law in Australia. Whether refugees have benefited from this development, however, is a moot point. While the number of people whose claims are recognised has increased over the years, the law itself in Australia seems to have become increasingly restrictive.

12.6 The politics of refugee protection

[12.95] While the focus of the chapters that follow is on the law governing the protection of refugees and other forced migrants, it is well to acknowledge the significant role played by policy and by politics in the regime that ultimately shapes the treatment of the non-citizens who come to Australia in search of protection. The

---

168 (1989) 169 CLR 379.
169 See Crock, above n 150.
170 See, for example, Commonwealth, *Parliamentary Debates*, House of Representatives, 5 May 1992 at 2372-84; 4 November 1992 at 2620-3; and 16 December 1992 at 3935.
171 See Mary Crock, 'Judicial Review and Part 8 of the *Migration Act*: Necessary Reform or Overkill?' (1996) 18 *Sydney Law Review* 267; Mary Crock, 'Reviewing the Merits of Refugee Decisions: An Evaluation of the Refugee Review Tribunal' in P McNab (ed), *Retreating from The Refugee Convention*, Northern Territory University, Darwin, Conference Proceedings, February 1997; see further, below, Chapter 19.

available statistical data on refugee claims made since 1994 shows a wide fluctuation in acceptance rates that cannot be explained solely by changes in the composition of the population of refugee claimants. Interestingly, the rises and falls extend across decision-making at both first instance (Departmental) level and at the RRT.

[12.96] Under Labor, the most significant policy change in the early to mid 1990s was the signing of a Memorandum of Understanding with the PRC which operated to bar the grant of asylum to a large section of refugee claimants from that country in and after 1994.[172] By the time government changed hands in 1996, acceptance rates had risen again at the departmental level, while RRT review stayed relatively stable at around 16-17 per cent. It was in the following year that a surge in applications – the figures almost doubled – brought a vigorous political response from then Minister Phillip Ruddock. This was the year in which reappointments to the RRT were to be made. Minister Ruddock issued a thinly veiled warning to members that they should not expect reappointment if they favoured 'reinventing' the definition of refugee (by recognising the protection claims of women victims of domestic violence).[173] In the months following these remarks, acceptance rates were cut by a third at first instance and almost halved on appeal.

[12.97] The surge in approval rates between 1998 and 2001 reflected the composition of the asylum seeker population in those years, with a large proportion of claims being made by nationals of the deeply troubled countries of Afghanistan and Iraq. The cathartic events of August and September 2001 are reflected in the data for 2003 and 2004: the tough border control policies that halted the arrival of refugee boats to Australia flowed through at every level of the administrative process. Acceptances plummeted at both departmental and RRT levels, raising real questions about the 'independence' of the review authorities.[174]

[12.98] The significance of policy is born out also in the more recent statistics. By 2005, few in government had the stomach to continue policies that saw children and vulnerable people kept in detention in remote facilities for indeterminate periods that in some instances extended for up to seven years.[175] The decision to release the children in July of that year seems to have marked a turning point in attitudes to asylum seekers generally. While the trend since the change of government in 2007 has been towards an increase in acceptances at departmental and review levels, the upwards trend began in 2005.

[12.99] The ebb and flow of protection rulings is clearly affected by the asylum seeker populations at any given time – driven in turn by world events. Even so, the statistical record in Australia suggests that in this country (as in the United States), decision-makers are influenced by their political masters.

---

172 *Migration Regulations (Amendment) 1995 (No 3)*, regs 2-3.
173 See below Chapter 13 at [13.69].
174 For a study of this phenomenon in the American context, see Ramji-Nogales, Schrag and Schoenholtz, above n 111.
175 See the discussion of these laws in Chapter 16; and the analysis of *Al Kateb v Godwin* (2004) 219 CLR 562 in Chapter 3 above.

Acceptance rates under the Coalition and Labor Governments

Year	Number recognised as refugees 1st instance	Acceptance rate at DIAC level	Acceptance rate at RRT	Total recognised as refugees
1994	1,031	13.3%	16.2%	1,480
1995	681	9.1%	17.8%	1,197
1996	1,380	18.1%	16.7%	2,002
1997	1,009	6.6%	10.2%	1,533
1998	2,492	23.8%	9.0%	3,090
1999	1,211	15.5%	10.1%	1,812
2000	4,050	32.6%	10.1%	4,607
2001	3,364	30.4%	13.5%	4,092
2002	1,234	13.7%	8.4%	1,718
2003	261	5.2%	5.8%	615
2004	346	11.2%	27.6%	1,461
2005	577	17.0%	37.9%	1,771
2006	697	21.0%	21.6%	1,296
2007	1,212	33.1%	21.7%	1,702
2008	1,397	32.8%	21.7%	1,845
2009	2,924	50.8%	23.3%	3,441

Sources: UNHCR, 2009 Global Trends: Refugees, Asylum-seekers, Returnees, Internally Displaced and Stateless Persons (15 June 2010); UNHCR, 2008 Global Trends: Refugees, Asylum-seekers, Returnees, Internally Displaced and Stateless Persons (16 June 2009); UNHCR, 2007 Global Trends: Refugees, Asylum-seekers, Returnees, Internally Displaced and Stateless Persons (17 June 2008); UNHCR, 2006 Global Trends: Refugees, Asylum-seekers, Returnees, Internally Displaced and Stateless Persons (16 July 2007); UNHCR, 2005 Global Refugee Trends: statistical overview of populations of refugees, asylum-seekers, internally displaced persons, stateless persons, and other persons of concern to the UNHCR (9 June 2006); UNHCR, Statistical Yearbook 2004 (21 August 2005); UNHCR, Statistical Yearbook 2003 (15 June 2005).

13

The Definition of Refugee

A refugee is any person who:
> ... owing to a well-founded fear of being persecuted for reasons of race, religion, nationality or membership of a particular social group or political opinion, is outside the country of his nationality and is unable or, owing to such fear, is unwilling to avail himself of the protection of that country.[1]

13.1 Frameworks for protection

[13.01] Most modern texts on refugee law begin by making the fairly obvious point that the UN Convention relating to the Status of Refugees was conceived originally as a compromise document. It was never the intention of the drafters to create entitlements to protection to all persons displaced by conflict or hardship. In the words of James Hathaway:[2]

> In sum, the first main feature of modern international refugee law is its rejection of comprehensive humanitarian or human rights based assistance in favour of a more narrowly conceived focus.

[13.02] At its inception, the Convention definition of refugee had temporal and geographical limitations in addition to the requirement that specific harms be shown. The Protocol done in New York in 1967 removed the limitations on place and time but did not alter the definition's focus on civil and political rights or the requirement that an individual face persecution.[3] While Australia has signed, ratified and even re-affirmed its commitment to the Refugee Convention and Protocol,[4] it has chosen not to enact anything but the Convention definition of refugee. The grant of a Protection visa in accordance with s 36 of the Act thereby becomes the vehicle for the grant of protection to persons who meet that definition. The policy choices reflected in the law have narrowed considerably the range of choices given to Australian

---

1 Article 1A(2) of the *Convention Relating to the Status of Refugees* (adopted 28 July 1951, entered into force 22 April 1954) 189 UNTS 137.
2 James C Hathaway, 'A Reconsideration of the Underlying Premise of Refugee Law' (1990) 31 *Harvard International Law Journal* 129 at 150.
3 Protocol Relating to the Status of Refugees (adopted 31 January 1966, entered into force 4 October 1967) 606 UNTS 267.
4 See Declaration of States Parties to the 1951 Convention and or its 1967 Protocol relating to the Status of Refugees (13 December 2001) HCR/MMSP/2001/09 (16 January 2002).

decision-makers. The regime has meant also that the jurisprudence in Australia is focused very heavily on Art 1(2) of the Refugee Convention (as amended).[5]

[13.03] For its part, the Convention definition of refugee explicitly constrains the range of people who will be deemed eligible for protection under international law. First is the requirement that the refugee be exiled from her or his country of nationality or habitual residence: protection does not extend to internally displaced persons. Second, refugees must be unable or unwilling to avail themselves of the protections that usually flow from the government of their 'home' state.[6] Then there are the qualifications placed on the required reasons for the person's flight. The refugee must demonstrate a *well-founded* fear; she or he must fear *persecution*; and that persecution must be for one or more of five stated reasons: race, religion, nationality, membership of a particular social group or political opinion.[7] The definition operates, however, in an holistic manner: the various requirements should not be disaggregated by decision-makers.[8]

[13.04] If there has been a tendency in the Australian courts over the years to acknowledge and even emphasise the limitations in the Convention definition of refugee,[9] the judiciary's approach to the international instrument has not been uniform. As will be explored in the course of this chapter, there has been something of a split between judges who read the Convention first and foremost as an instrument designed to protect human rights and those who favour a restrictive (textual) interpretation. In the political realm, it has sometimes been difficult to see much difference between the attitudes to refugees in the leading political parties. Most changes to the legislative regime governing refugees in Australia have occurred with bi-partisan support. These include a raft of changes in 2001 that inserted into the *Migration Act 1958* (Cth) domestic definitions of key concepts in the Convention definition such as 'persecution' and what will constitute a 'particular social group'.

[13.05] This chapter dissects some of the key elements of the definition of refugee, beginning in Part 13.2 with the requirement that a refugee demonstrate a 'well-founded fear'. There follows in Part 13.3 an introduction to the various issues associated with the concept of 'persecution'. These include a discussion of the harms that will constitute persecution, the requirement (if any) that an individual be targeted or singled out, and the issue of state responsibility for the harm caused to a person. Part 13.4 examines what is referred to as the 'nexus' requirement implicit in the requirement that persecution be feared 'by reason of' specified grounds. The chapter concludes with a discussion of the five grounds on which persecution must be feared.

---

5   For a recent affirmation by the High Court that the Australian jurisprudence is binding on all decision-makers involved in the grant of Protection visas, see *Plaintiff M61/2010E v Commonwealth* and *Plaintiff M69 of 2010 v Commonwealth* (2010) 272 ALR 14 (*Plaintiffs M61/ M69*).
6   See *MIMIA v S152/2003* (2004) 222 CLR 1.
7   See also *MIEA v Guo* (1997) 191 CLR 559 (*Guo*).
8   See *Applicant A v MIEA* (1997) 190 CLR 225 (*Applicant A*) at 256 (McHugh J).
9   See, for example, the comments by the High Court in *Guo* (1997) 191 CLR 559.

13.2 Countries of nationality or habitual residence

[13.06] The starting point for both the Refugee Convention and Australian law is that refugee protection is owed only to non-citizens who are outside of and cannot return to a country of which they are either nationals or where they have been resident. In most instances, this requirement is not contentious: the asylum seeker's nationality or ethnicity will be apparent, as will be the country from which they have fled. Having said that, decision-makers have been warned against blind acceptance of an applicant's assertions about nationality and country of origin.[10]

[13.07] The definition in Art 1(2) actually makes reference to 'countries' in two different contexts. A person can be a refugee if they fear return to a country 'of nationality' or to a country of 'habitual residence'. This dual reference has been interpreted so as to broaden the range of countries or territories that can be considered as a basis for granting protection. The reference to 'nationality' has been read to imply countries with an internationally recognised status capable of conferring citizenship on a person.[11] On the other hand, no such requirement attaches to a 'country of habitual residence'. Although included in recognition of the plight of stateless persons, this clause has also helped persons fleeing from territories that do not have full international recognition as states. In these cases it will suffice if the territory has the attributes of a state, such as defined borders, systems of law and a permanent identifiable community.[12] Cases involving children born in Australia can involve a real Catch 22 situation. Such children may have neither the nationality of a country in which they might be persecuted, nor will they have a country of former habitual residence. These cases underscore the need for a complementary protection scheme.[13]

[13.08] The leading case on nationality and refugee law illustrates one of the main contexts in which a person's citizenship will be in issue. The applicant, Jong Kim Koe, sought protection in Australia after fleeing violence and persecution in Timor Leste.[14] Although it was accepted that he had a good refugee claim with respect of his country of origin, it was alleged that he was or could be a national of Portugal, a country where he would not face persecution. The issue of protection elsewhere is considered in Chapter 14.1, below. For present purposes it suffices to note that persons with more than one nationality must demonstrate that they are refugees in all relevant countries.[15] In *Koe's* case, however, the central question was not just whether he was a national of Portugal, but whether his rights in that country amounted to

---

10   See *SZFJQ v MIMIA* [2006] FMCA 671, a case involving a child born in Australia to Bangladeshi parents who was wrongly assumed to be a citizen of Bangladesh. Compare also the cases involving fake passports: see *NBKE v MIAC* [2007] FCA 126.
11   See *Koe v MIEA* (1997) 78 FCR 289 (*Koe*).
12   See *Koe* (1997) 78 FCR 289 at 298-9; Legal Services, Refugee Review Tribunal (RRT), A Guide to Refugee Law in Australia (RRT, 2010) (*RRT Refugee Law Guide*), available at <http://www.mrt-rrt.gov.au/Conduct-of-reviews/ Guide-to-Refugee-Law-in-Australia/default.aspx>, Ch 2 at 2-3.
13   See *RRT Refugee Law Guide*, ibid Ch 2, at 14 16, discussing *SZEAM v MIMIA* [2005] FMCA 1367. See further Chapter 14.4.
14   See *Koe v MIMA* (1997) 74 FCR 508.
15   See *Migration Act 1958* (Cth), ss 91M-91Q. Note that these provisions apply only to applications lodged after 16 December 1999.

'effective' nationality sufficient to safeguard him against return to a country where he would face persecution.[16]

[13.09] As this case demonstrated, the determination of a person's nationality or entitlement to citizenship in a certain country raises complex issues of comparative law in respect of which it is often necessary to obtain the advice of expert witnesses.[17] In contrast, persons claiming refugee status with respect to a country of 'habitual residence' need to focus less on formal legal entitlements than on practical connections with a state or territory.[18] Where opinion has differed is in what this means in terms of a person's 'portable' entitlements. Hathaway has taken the view that a person cannot be a refugee in respect of a country unless the person has a legal right of some kind to return to that country.[19] This view has not been supported by other academics or by the judiciary in Canada or Australia.[20] What has been accepted is that it is not enough that a person is stateless, with no country to call home. To be a refugee, one must have an existing[21] fear of persecution within a specified country.[22] It is to these matters that we now turn.

13.3 'Well-founded fear': Standard of proof and the 'real chance' test

[13.10] The first case in which the Australian High Court considered the Convention definition of refugee in detail focused in large measure on the nature of the fear required to be shown by an individual claiming to be a refugee. *Chan Yee Kin v MIEA*[23] was the first case in which the court was prepared to find a decision to refuse refugee status legally unreasonable. The case was to mark a turning point in both the interpretation of the UN definition of refugee and the courts' involvement in asylum cases.[24]

---

16   Note that under s 91N the 'effectiveness' of a person's nationality is no longer an issue.
17   Under international law, nationality is regarded as the preserve of individual states. See *Hague Convention on Certain Questions relating to the Conflict of Nationality Laws* (adopted 12 April 1930, entered into force 1 July 1937) 179 UNTS 89; and the discussion in *RRT Refugee Law Guide*, above n 12, Ch 2 at 4.
18   For an example, see *Koe* (1997) 78 FCR 289. See also James C Hathaway, *The Law of Refugee Status* (Toronto: Butterworths, 1991) at 61, where reference is made to the requirement that a stateless person 'stand in a relationship which is broadly comparable to the relationship between a citizen and her country of nationality'. Note that a person may have more than one country of former habitual residence. See *Al-Anezi v MIMA* (1999) 92 FCR 283; and *Taiem v MIMA* (2002) 186 ALR 361.
19   See Hathaway, ibid, at 59-63.
20   See Guy Goodwin-Gill and Jane McAdam, *The Refugee in International Law* (New York: Oxford University Press, 3rd ed, 2007) at 68, n 89; and the cases discussed in *RRT Refugee Law Guide*, above n 12, Ch 2 at 10-11.
21   A past fear is insufficient. See *Savvin v MIMA* (1999) 166 ALR 348 at [61]-[62].
22   See *MIMA v Savvin* (2000) 98 FCR 168; and *QAAE v MIMIA* [2003] FCAFC 46.
23   (1989) 169 CLR 379 (*Chan*). See *Administrative Decisions (Judicial Review) Act 1977* (Cth), ss 5(1)(e), 5(2)(g), 6(1)(c) and 6(2)(g).
24   The reliance on unreasonableness as the primary ground for judicial review meant that the ruling had a normative impact on both the interpretation and application of principle in refugee cases. This brought the courts very close to reviewing the merits as well as the legality of refugee cases and represented a direct affront to those responsible for formulating government policy.

[13.11] Chan was a citizen of the People's Republic of China (PRC) who had been imprisoned by the Chinese authorities on a number of occasions and then exiled within the country on the ground that he was an 'anti-revolutionary'. He escaped in 1977 and entered Australia without a visa in 1980. In 1982 he applied for refugee status. His claim was rejected on the basis that the treatment to which he was subjected did not amount to persecution within the meaning of the Convention. The Minister's delegate also refused to accept that the attention Chan would receive as a result of his escape from the area to which he was assigned was sufficient to ground a 'well-founded fear of persecution' for the purposes of the Convention. Although not noted in the law reports, the case became something of a cause célèbre because it coincided with the Chinese government's brutal repression of the pro-democracy movement in the PRC.[25] In this regard, the case stands as an interesting example of how contemporary events can serve to focus the attention of the judiciary. It is impossible to prove that the cataclysmic events in Tiananmen Square on 4 June 1989 determined the outcome of the case. However, the High Court did rule (somewhat disingenuously) that the Full Federal Court below had fallen into legal error by assuming that dissidents in the PRC no longer had real reason to fear persecution in that country.[26]

[13.12] McHugh J, with whom the rest of the court agreed in substance, examined the phrase 'well-founded fear' in the context of various interpretations advanced by the UN High Commissioner for Refugees (UNHCR), by foreign courts and by learned writers.[27] His Honour chose not to dwell on the merits of the different theories advanced. Instead he noted the general consensus that the phrase 'well-founded fear' implies a bi-fold requirement that the refugee be in a subjective state of fear *and* that the fear have a rational or objective basis.

[13.13] This focus is significant for two reasons. First, the definition implies that status determination must be a case-by-case affair, in so far as it demands an assessment of a person's state of mind. This is sometimes a barrier to claims for refugee protection by children because young (or traumatised) children sometimes do not have the cognitive maturity or ability to express 'fear'.[28] In fact, the difficulties inherent in determining a subjective state of mind have led some judges to downplay this element.[29] Second, the qualifier on the fear – that the fear be 'well-founded' – means that a fear of persecution must have an objective basis such that an independent observer can see why an individual might be afraid. In status determination processes all around the world, it is this second aspect of the refugee's fear that is regarded as

---

25   The facts of the case are set out in the judgment of McHugh J: (1989) 169 CLR 379 at 417-22. The High Court's decision in *Chan* was delivered in September 1989, not long after the momentous events in the PRC in June of that year. For a discussion of the role of public opinion in the court's decision, see Mary Crock, 'Apart from Us or a Part of Us? Immigrants' Rights, Public Opinion and the Rule of Law' (1998) 10 *International Journal of Refugee Law* 49.
26   See (1989) 169 CLR 379 at 391 (Mason CJ), 399 (Dawson J) and 406 (Toohey J).
27   Ibid at 423-9.
28   The general rule in such cases is that the subjective fear will be implied. See *Chen Shi Hai v MIMA* (2000) 201 CLR 293 (*Chen Shi Hai*) at 297 and 318-19.
29   See *Emiantor v MIMA* (1997) 48 ALD 635; on appeal [1998] FCA 1186; and *S273 of 2003 v MIMA* [2005] FMCA 983.

the critical determinant. Accordingly, most attention has been paid to the standards that are required to show that a refugee *objectively* has reason to fear for her or his safety.

[13.14] While McHugh J noted the debate over the separate requirements for subjective fear and objective justification for that fear, he played down the difference in standards laid down by the English and American courts.[30] In *Chan*, he confirmed that the phrase 'well-founded fear' requires an objective examination of all the facts capable of inducing, or allaying, fear. In other words, refugee status cannot depend only on the applicant's perceptions of the circumstances giving rise to her or his fear of persecution. However, he qualified this statement by agreeing with the American Supreme Court's view that the objective justification of fear experienced by the applicant does not require proof that persecution would, in fact, occur upon the applicant's return.[31]

[13.15] Although McHugh J opted to construe the Convention definition for himself, his preferred interpretation arguably comes closest to the approach taken in the American Supreme Court's decision in *Immigration and Naturalization Service v Cardoza-Fonseca*.[32] Like the other members of the court,[33] McHugh J held that the standard for assessing an applicant's fear lay in asking whether there was a 'real chance' that the person would be persecuted on Convention grounds. His Honour indicated that fear could be justified in cases where it was unlikely that persecution would occur on the person's return. A 'real chance' of persecution could be as little as a 10 per cent chance. This language stands in contrast to the view taken by the English House of Lords in *R v Home Department State Secretary; Ex parte Sivakumaran*[34] where their Lordships spoke of 'a reasonable degree of likelihood' of persecution. McHugh J doubted whether there was any real distinction to be made between phrases such as 'real possibility', 'reasonable likelihood' and 'good reason (for fearing)'. In so doing, he chose not to examine the substantive difference, if any, in the results produced when applying the various interpretations of the Convention definition. Had he done so, McHugh J may have provided a clearer picture of the extent to which the lower Courts' view of the requirement of 'well-founded fear' may have been at odds with his own interpretation of the phrase. The House of Lords in *Sivakumaran* clearly saw a difference between the standard adopted by them and the ruling of the American Supreme Court in *Cardoza-Fonseca*.[35]

---

30 See *R v Home Department State Secretary; Ex parte Sivakumaran* [1988] AC 958 (*Sivakumaran*) and *Immigration and Naturalization Service v Cardoza-Fonseca* 480 US 421 (1987) (*Cardoza-Fonseca*).
31 (1989) 169 CLR 379 at 429-30.
32 *Cardoza-Fonseca* 480 US 421 (1987).
33 See (1989) 169 CLR 379 at 389, 398 and 406-7. Gaudron J did not express an opinion directly on this point, but see her discussion at 412-13. See also the High Court's discussion of what will constitute a justified fear in *Boughey v R* (1986) 161 CLR 10 at 21.
34 *Sivakumaran* [1988] AC 958 at 992-4, 996-7 and 1000.
35 Ibid at 993-4. McHugh J's approach finds some support, however, in the view taken by some American academics that the Supreme Court's ruling did not appear to liberalise the practice of the primary decision-makers in that country: see, for example, Deborah Anker, 'Determining Asylum Claims in the United States: Summary Report of an Empirical Study of the Adjudication of Asylum Claims Before the Immigration Court' (1990) 2 *International Journal of Refugee Law* 252; and Deborah

[13.16] In the early days of the Refugee Review Tribunal (RRT), members appear to have been content to recite passages from the High Court's ruling in *Chan* without further analysis. The problems for the tribunal began when the Federal Court delved deeper into the 'real chance' test by looking at the process that must be engaged in to determine the likelihood of future persecution. The turning point was the test case, *Mok v MILGEA*,[36] brought by three Cambodian women detained in Sydney whose refugee claims were denied. The Full Federal Court held that the real chance test did not allow the RRT to engage in a process of weighing up evidence with a view to determining the likelihood of future persecution. It found that the use of expressions such as 'I give greater weight to' suggested that the tribunal was assessing claims on the 'balance of possibilities'. The court held that assessing likelihood of persecution in this fashion ran counter to statements in *Chan* that a 'chance' of harm could be 'real' even where the likelihood of the occurrence was less than 50 per cent.[37] For the RRT, the simplicity of the test in *Chan* evaporated in the face of these court rulings. As Lindgren J noted in *Mataka v MIEA*,[38] the emphasis placed by the Federal Court on the tribunal's language did little to improve the substance of the decisions made. His Honour could well have been speaking for the tribunal when he described the task of the decision-maker following *Mok* as 'tiptoeing through a minefield'.

[13.17] In *MIEA v Wu Shan Liang*,[39] the High Court roundly criticised the Federal Court's approach on the basis that the lower courts were scrutinising too closely the written reasons of the RRT. The High Court endorsed the test as formulated by it in *Chan* in 1989 and emphasised that, in assessing whether the applicant's fear of Convention-related persecution is well-founded, percentages of likelihood of events are irrelevant. For the RRT, the result was to remove the tension and confusion surrounding the determination of a 'well-founded' fear of persecution. In *MIEA v Guo*,[40] Brennan CJ and Dawson, Toohey, Gaudron, McHugh and Gummow JJ set out their interpretation of 'well-founded fear' as follows:

> Conjecture or surmise has no part to play in determining whether a fear is well-founded. A fear is 'well-founded' when there is a real substantial basis for it. As *Chan* shows, a substantial basis for a fear may exist even though there is far less than a 50 per cent chance that the object of the fear will eventuate. But no fear can be well-founded for the purpose of the Convention unless the evidence indicates a real ground for believing that the applicant for refugee status is at risk of persecution.

[13.18] The decision in *Guo* established that terms such as 'a real chance', 'based in substance', 'not far-fetched' or 'not remote' may be used to explain or clarify the meaning of 'well-founded', but should not be used as a substitute or replacement for it.

Anker and CP Blum, 'New Trends in Asylum Jurisprudence: The Aftermath of the US Supreme Court Decision in *INS v Cardoza Fonseca*' (1989) 1 *International Journal of Refugee Law* 67.
36 (1992) 47 FCR 1.
37 *MILGEA v Mok (No 2)* (1994) 55 FCR 375.
38 [1996] FCA 1503.
39 (1996) 185 CLR 259.
40 *Guo* (1997) 191 CLR 559 at 572.

13.3.1 The 'real chance' test and onus of proof

[13.19] In spite of the reaffirmation of the tests espoused in *Chan*, questions have persisted about where the onus of proof lies in the initial assessment of whether or not an applicant faces a well-founded fear of persecution. It is clearly established that the concept of onus of proof is not appropriate in administrative inquiries and decision-making.[41] The notion of onus is particularly inappropriate in non-adversarial fora such as the RRT where the Minister is not usually a party to the hearing at all.[42]

[13.20] Nevertheless, some Federal Court judges have favoured the approach taken in *Canada (Attorney General) v Ward*,[43] holding that the starting point of the real chance test is a presumption that states will look after their nationals. Using this approach the refugee claimant does bear an onus – albeit slight – to show that her or his state will not or cannot offer protection against persecution. For example, in *Ratnam v MIEA*,[44] the court ruled that applicants must demonstrate a real chance that their country of nationality will fail in its obligation to protect against persecution as defined. There must be some material from which these conclusions can be drawn. Emmett J emphasised that it is for the RRT to determine the conclusions that can be drawn from the evidence before it.

[13.21] By way of contrast, in *Magyari v MIMA*,[45] O'Loughlin J agreed that in refugee claims no one bears a conventional onus of proof. However, his Honour held that in appropriate circumstances, there may be a duty on the Minister's delegate or the RRT to investigate the existence of evidence in support of an application. In this context, the dicta of Gleeson CJ and McHugh J in *Abebe v Commonwealth*[46] are also instructive. Their Honours commented that the fact that an applicant

> might fail to make out an affirmative case in respect of one or more of the ... steps [required to demonstrate a well-founded fear of persecution] did not necessarily mean that her claim for refugee status must fail. As *Guo* [1997] HCA 22; (1997) 191 CLR 559 at 575-576 makes clear, even if the Tribunal is not affirmatively satisfied that the events deposed to by an applicant have occurred, the degree of probability of their occurrence or non-occurrence is a relevant matter in determining whether an applicant has a well-founded fear of persecution. The Tribunal 'must take into account the chance that the applicant was so [persecuted] when determining whether there is a well-founded fear of future persecution' *Guo* [1997] HCA 22; (1997) 191 CLR 559 at 576.[47]

[13.22] Whether this approach has been accepted by decision-makers in practice is open to question. In the study made of refugee claims by unaccompanied children between 1999 and 2003, evidence emerged of decision-makers looking for asylum

---

41 See, for example, *McDonald v Director General of Social Security* (1984) 1 FCR 354 at 358-9 and 368-9; *Nagalingam v MILGEA* (1992) 38 FCR 191 at 200; and *Yao-Jing Li v MIMA* (1997) 74 FCR 275.
42 See *Jong Kim Koe v MIMA* (1997) 74 FCR 508.
43 (1993) 103 DLR (4th) 1 (*Ward*).
44 [1997] FCA 330.
45 (1997) 50 ALD 341 at 342.
46 (1999) 197 CLR 510.
47 Ibid at [83].

seekers to use 'trigger' words to express a fear of persecution.[48] In at least one instance involving a 13-year-old girl from Afghanistan, the failure to articulate a claim led to the girl and her 11-year-old brother being 'screened out' of the asylum process. In other words the pair was deemed 'not to engage Australia's protection obligations'. This finding was made in spite of the fact that the children were travelling with a group of adults, most of whom were accepted from the start as genuine asylum seekers. These cases suggest that adjudicators in Australia have implicitly regarded asylum seekers as bearing an onus of proof of sorts for the purpose of articulating a protection claim.

[13.23] This fact is borne out in the emphasis that is placed on the asylum seeker's credibility when presenting their claims. As a matter of practicality, refugees in most instances will be expected to articulate not only a claim, but a claim that is believable in all the circumstances. Although various judges have noted that the telling of falsehoods may not be a sure determinant that an individual is not a refugee,[49] in practice it is difficult to challenge a negative ruling that is premised on a finding that a claimant lacks credibility.[50]

[13.24] The most recent jurisprudence on the tribunal's duty to make its own inquiries is not helpful to applicants in this context. As we explore further in Chapter 18, it is only in exceptional circumstances that a failure to inquire will amount to a jurisdictional error of law.[51]

13.3.2 The relevance of past events

[13.25] When *Chan's* case came before the High Court, the applicant had been in Australia (unlawfully) for nine years. For this reason, one of the more important issues before the court was whether the applicant was obliged to show that his fear of persecution was still well-founded, given his long absence from his homeland and the changes that had occurred there. The High Court was unanimous in holding that the applicant's fear of persecution must be justified at the time when a claim for refugee status is considered. The court found that to rule otherwise would be to deny the primary purpose of the Refugee Convention which is to provide refugees with protection as and when this is needed.[52] However, the court mitigated the harshness of this requirement by ruling that the applicant's circumstances at the time he left China were critical to his claim for refugee status. The court held that once a well-founded fear has been established, the onus is on the government to show that events subsequent to the applicant's departure are sufficient to remove

---

48 See Mary Crock, *Seeking Asylum Alone: Unaccompanied and Separated Children and Refugee Protection in Australia* (Sydney: Themis Press, 2006) at 8.2. See discussion throughout the report of 'Halimi's' case.
49 See Steve Norman, 'Assessing the Credibility of Refugee Applicants: A Judicial Perspective' (2007) 19 *International Journal of Refugee Law* 273.
50 See, for example, *W148/00A v MIMA* (2001) 185 ALR 703.
51 See *SZIAI v MIAC* (2008) 104 ALD 22; and *MIMA v SZIAI* (2009) 259 ALR 429. See further Chapter 18.6.3.
52 (1989) 169 CLR 379 at 390, 398-9, 408, 413-15 and 432-3.

any plausible basis for the applicant's concern.[53] All five Justices held that there had been no material change in the circumstances that gave rise to the applicant's original fear of persecution. Their Honours were unanimous in finding it unreasonable to regard the applicant's experiences as anything less than persecution on Convention grounds.[54]

[13.26] The comments of Gaudron J in *Chan* about the relevance of past persecution and changes in the applicant's country of nationality provoked considerable debate in the lower courts. Her Honour stated:[55]

> The definition of 'refugee' looks to the mental and emotional state of the applicant as well as to the objective facts. It is a commonplace, encapsulated in the expression 'once bitten, twice shy', that circumstances which are insufficient to engender fear may also be insufficient to allay a fear grounded in past experience. Although the definition requires that there be 'well-founded fear' at the time of determination it would be to ignore the nature of fear and to ignore ordinary human experience to evaluate a fear as well-founded or otherwise without due regard being had to the applicant's own past experiences.
>
> If an applicant relies on his past experience it is, in my view, incumbent on a decision-maker to evaluate whether those experiences produced a well-founded fear of being persecuted. If they did, then a continuing fear ought to be accepted as well-founded unless it is at least possible to say that the fear of a reasonable person in the position of the claimant would be allayed by knowledge of subsequent changes in the country of nationality. To require more of an applicant for refugee status, would, I think, be at odds with the humanitarian purpose of the Convention and at odds with generally accepted views as to its application to persons who have suffered persecution.

[13.27] In *MIMA v Eshetu*,[56] Gummow J suggested that these statements did not represent the views of the majority in *Chan*. Gaudron J acknowledged as much in *MIMA; Ex parte Miah*,[57] but defended her views on the basis that 'nothing that was said in *Chan* or that has been said in subsequent cases suggests that what I said was wrong'.

[13.28] In *Guo*,[58] the High Court acknowledged that:

> [P]ast events are not a certain guide to the future, but in many areas of life proof that events have occurred often provides a reliable basis for determining the probability – high or low – of their recurrence. The extent to which past events are a guide to the future depends on the degree of probability that they have occurred, the regularity with which and the conditions under which they have or probably have occurred and the likelihood that the introduction of new or other events may distort the cycle of regularity. In many cases, when the past has been evaluated, the probability that an event will occur may border on certainty.

---

53 Ibid at 390, 399, 408, 415 and 432-3.
54 Ibid at 391, 399-400, 408, 415-16 and 431-5.
55 Ibid at 415.
56 (1999) 197 CLR 611 at 658.
57 (2001) 206 CLR 57 at [69].
58 (1997) 191 CLR 559 at 574-5.

[13.29] When faced with cases in which there has been an alleged change in circumstances since the applicant's departure, Federal Court judges have declined to follow Gaudron J's approach. In *SCAM v MIMIA*,[59] von Doussa J agreed with Gummow J that Gaudron J's views were not representative of the High Court majority in *Chan*. Von Doussa J emphasised that the 'real chance of persecution' necessary to meet the objective element of the definition of refugee must be present at the time when the claim for refugee status is determined. His Honour stated:[60]

> [W]here the threat of persecution that caused an asylum seeker to hold a well-founded fear at the time of departure from the country of nationality has in the meantime evaporated, and the circumstances pertaining in the country have so changed that there is no longer a real chance that the asylum seeker would risk persecution for a Convention reason if he or she were to return, any persisting fear of persecution held by that asylum seeker does not have the objective quality of being *well-founded*.

[13.30] The Federal Court has also rejected the submission that, in cases where circumstances have changed in the applicant's country of nationality, the decision-maker should embark on a two-staged analysis (by first determining whether the applicant had a well-founded fear of persecution, and then deciding whether any such fear had been displaced by a change of circumstances). In *MIMA v Gui*,[61] a gay man from Shanghai had claimed a well-founded fear of persecution by reason of his membership of a particular social group. Mr Gui's claim was that he was arrested for embracing and kissing his male partner in a public place in 1993, detained and assaulted by police. In its decision, the RRT accepted the evidence of Mr Gui's arrest, and also the more general proposition that gay men are subject to police harassment in Shanghai. However, on the basis of Mr Gui's accounts of his social life since 1993, and Country Information Reports, it concluded that Mr Gui had been able to express his sexuality over a number of years. The past harassment was assessed not as persecution on a Convention ground (in other words homophobic violence), but as Mr Gui being subjected to a general law relating to public order (that is, prohibiting sexual conduct in a public place).[62] Accordingly, Mr Gui was found not to have a well-founded fear of persecution.

[13.31] This decision was set aside at first instance in the Federal Court. Hely J held that the RRT had made findings which 'unless negated or qualified by other

---

59 [2002] FCA 964.
60 Ibid at [26]. Von Doussa J reiterated these views in *SDAV v MIMIA* [2002] FCA 1022 at [23].
61 [1999] FCA 1496.
62 As McHugh J noted in the unsuccessful attempt to gain leave to appeal to the High Court in this matter: 'The Tribunal had before it evidence that the applicant took part in managing a gay bar immediately prior to his departure from China, that an active homosexual community exists in Shanghai and did so at the time of the applicant's departure, and that homosexual acts as such are not crimes in Shanghai. Even if the applicant might have had a well founded fear of persecution in 1993 when he was arrested and interrogated, on the evidence it was open to the Tribunal to find that the objective basis needed to make that fear well founded was not present when the applicant left China or, for that matter, at the time of its decision'. See *Gui v MIMA* S219/1999 [2000] HCATrans 280. See Jenni Millbank, 'Imagining Otherness: Refugee Claims on the Basis of Sexuality in Canada and Australia' (2002) 26 *Melbourne University Law Review* 144 at 145-6 and Jenni Millbank, 'Gender, Sex and Visibility in Refugee Claims on the Basis of Sexual Orientation' (2003) 18 *Georgetown Immigration Law Journal* 71 at 88.

findings, would result in a conclusion that the applicant has a well-founded fear of persecution for a convention reason'. These findings were that the applicant had a subjective fear, and that it was grounded in past persecutory conduct engaged in for a Convention reason.⁶³ On appeal, the Full Federal Court held that the primary judge had erred in treating the events of late 1993 and early 1994 as 'creating some kind of presumption which, unless negated or qualified, must produce a finding of objectively based fear at the time of the RRT's decision'.⁶⁴ Their Honours stated that the importance or weight to be given these events was essentially a matter of fact and degree for the tribunal – and not for a court on judicial review. Their Honours ruled that the RRT was not required to engage in a staged process, making intermediate findings as to whether Mr Gui was being persecuted for a Convention reason in 1993. Rather, it should only 'address the question whether the applicant was a refugee as at the date of its decision having regard to all the circumstances placed before it up to that date'.⁶⁵

[13.32] These comments were reiterated by Tamberlin J in *SFGB v MIMIA*.⁶⁶ In that case, the RRT had made no specific findings as to whether the applicant had a well-founded fear of persecution when he left Afghanistan, but rejected his application on the basis that the Taliban was no longer a force in the country. Tamberlin J held that the task of the decision-maker is 'to examine all the material up to the date of the decision and to make a single determination at that point in time'.⁶⁷ Indeed, possible future conduct, including a so-called 'spontaneous voluntary expression of political opinion', can also provide an acceptable basis for a presently existing and well-founded fear of persecution for a Convention reason.⁶⁸ Just as past experience of persecution is not a prerequisite to recognition as a refugee,⁶⁹ others have noted that it is also wrong to examine only one aspect of a person's life story. The assessment of refugee status must be approached holistically, looking at the cumulative effect of everything that has occurred or that might occur in the future.⁷⁰

13.3.3 The use of country information and other corrobative strategies

[13.33] From the perspective of the refugee claimant, one of the most frustrating and incomprehensible aspects of status determination processes is the emphasis placed on evidence about conditions in the claimant's country of origin. Although it is common for genuine refugees to present with little in the way of hard evidence to corroborate their claims, decision-makers in Australia have access to a wealth of data on the world's trouble spots. Often, this 'country information' will be used as a yardstick against which to test the credibility of the applicant's claims. In a number

---

63 See *Gui v MIMA* [1998] FCA 1592.
64 *MIMA v Gui* [1999] FCA 1496 at [30].
65 Ibid at [35].
66 [2002] FCA 1389.
67 Ibid at [25]. For a discussion of other cases in which these matters have been considered, see Roz Germov and Francesco Motta, *Refugee Law in Australia* (Melbourne: Oxford University Press, 2003) at 170-86.
68 *Omar v MIMA* (2000) 104 FCR 187 at [38].
69 See *Abebe v MIEA* (1999) 197 CLR 510 at [192].
70 See, for example, *W352 v MIMA* [2002] FCA 398 at [21].

of instances, the High Court has cautioned decision-makers against making facile comparisons between the experiences of the applicant and the treatment afforded people seen to be in a similar situation.[71] Practitioners have complained of decision-makers relying on anodyne assessments of conditions in troubled countries made by government officials with little exposure to what is happening on the ground (views 'from the cocktail bar of the Teheran Hilton'.[72]) The availability of reports by organisations such as the US State Department, Amnesty International, Human Rights Watch as well as regular news reports seems to have altered the expectations and behaviour of decision-makers. Where a claimant can allude to events that have attracted media attention of any kind, access to this information can be advantageous. Where an event does not attract such coverage, however, the reality can be that the media silence weighs heavily on the asylum seeker.

[13.34] In fact, the sophistication of the available technology – with instant communications around the globe – has changed the face of refugee law and practice all around the world in more ways than one. Refugees (and, more importantly, people smugglers) communicate using the internet, email, text messaging and telephone when making critical decisions to travel. Decision-makers, increasingly, use similar technologies to try and test the claims made by asylum seekers.

[13.35] During the harshest days of the Coalition's policies in this area the practice developed of recording the voices of young Afghan asylum seekers. The recordings would be wired to a language laboratory in Sweden for analysis which would then send back reports on the likely national and geographic origins of the children and young persons.[73] A report contradicting the claims of a young person could be devastating – most particularly in cases where the claimant was trapped in a remote detention centre with little or no legal or other support available to contest the adverse assessment. Although criticised by some judges moved by the obvious anguish experienced by the young claimants, in most instances challenges to the use of such evidence have been dismissed.[74] In *SBBR v MIMIA*, the applicant argued that the decision-maker's reliance on the 'untested, unreliable' linguistic reports over his direct evidence about his national origins led to a result that was biased and perverse. The court held that the allegations were not made out on the facts. While the decision made may have been 'contrary to the evidence', any factual errors made were not serious enough to amount to errors of law.[75]

13.3.4 Refugees *sur place*

[13.36] The events in PRC in 1989 gave Australia its first major taste of the phenomenon of asylum seekers who become refugees by virtue of events that occur in their

---

71   See the comments in *S395/2002 v MIMA* (2003) 216 CLR 473; and *NABD v MIMIA* (2005) 216 ALR 1.
72   Law Council of Australia, quoted in Senate Legal and Constitutional Affairs Committee, *A Sanctuary Under Review: An Examination of Australia's Refugee and Humanitarian Determination Processes* (Canberra: AGPS, 2000) at 132.
73   See Crock, *Seeking Asylum Alone*, above n 48, Ch 11.2.
74   In *WAEF v MIMIA* [2002] FCA 1121, French J held that the unreliability of the Swedish language tests was not a ground for the review of decisions. See also *WAFV v RRT* (2003) 125 FCR 351.
75   *SBBR v MIMIA* [2002] FCA 842 at [9]-[11].

countries of origin while they are in Australia. Prime Minister Hawke was quick to recognise that many of the Chinese students studying in Australia at the time of the Tiananmen Square massacre were deeply involved in the pro-democracy movement in China. The effect of the PRC government's crackdown was to render these people refugees *sur place*.

[**13.37**] A *sur place* refugee[76] claim can become especially contentious where the claimant commits an act after arriving in Australia which is perceived to have the purpose of manufacturing or enhancing the grounds for refugee status. The RRT has shown a tendency to construe such acts as self-serving, and therefore undermining the applicant's credibility.[77]

[**13.38**] In the early cases of *Somaghi v MILGEA*[78] and *Heshmati v MILGEA*,[79] Lockhart J ruled against two Iranian asylum seekers who had sent inflammatory letters to the Iranian consulate in Canberra after their arrival in Australia. The judge was overturned on appeal, but only on the basis that it was not absolutely clear that the men's communications were self-serving, engaged in solely for the purpose of enhancing their refugee claim.[80] Subsequent cases supported the notion that self-serving actions should not be taken into account when determining the question of a claimant's 'well-founded fear'.[81]

[**13.39**] In recent years, however, the courts have taken a more nuanced approach, focusing more on the applicant's vulnerability to persecution than on the conduct creating that vulnerability. In *MIMA v Mohammed*,[82] a majority of the Full Federal Court held that there was no requirement of 'good faith' on the part of refugee applicants. It emphasised that the central question for determination is whether the applicant had a well-founded fear of persecution, *not* whether the claimant had acted 'solely out of a desire to put himself in a position where he could claim to be endangered'.[83] The issue arose again before the Full Court in *MIMA v Farahanipour*.[84] In that case, the RRT had rejected the applicant's claim that he had a well-founded fear if returned to Iran because there was a real chance that he would be persecuted because of his previous activities as a political dissident. The RRT did accept that the delegate's refusal of the applicant's claim coincided with the publication of an

---

76 On the meaning of this phrase, see UNHCR, *Handbook on Procedures and Criteria for Determining Refugee Status* (Geneva: 1979, reedited 1992) at [94]-[96]; Goodwin-Gill and McAdam, above n 20, at 65; Hathaway, above n 18, at 33-9 and 53.
77 See, for example, *N05/50659* [2005] RRTA 207.
78 [1990] FCA 463.
79 [1990] FCA 460.
80 See *Somaghi v MILGEA* (1991) 31 FCR 100 and *Heshmati v MILGEA* (1991) 31 FCR 123.
81 See *Li Shi Ping v MILGEA* (1994) 35 ALD 557 at 580 and on appeal (1994) 35 ALD 225; and *Khan v MIMA* (1997) 47 ALD 19.
82 (2000) 98 FCR 405, following the English Court of Appeal judgment in *Danian v Secretary of State for the Home Department* [1999] EWCA Civ 3000; [2000] Imm AR 96. In so doing, the court departed from precedent in *Somaghi v MILGEA* (1991) 31 FCR 100 at 118, which had suggested that 'actions taken outside the country of nationality ... for the sole purpose of creating a pretext of invoking a claim to well-founded fear of persecution, should not be considered as supporting an application for refugee status'.
83 See *MIMA v Mohammed* (2000) 98 FCR 405 at 408-9 (Spender J) and 419-22 (French J).
84 (2001) 105 FCR 277. See also *MIMA v Kheirollahpoor* [2001] FCA 1306.

Australian newspaper article referencing the applicant's criticisms. The tribunal found that the applicant deliberately arranged for the publication of the article for the sole purpose of making 'more plausible, or colourable, a pretended claim to a well-founded fear of persecution'. It concluded nevertheless that the applicant now had a well-founded fear of persecution and had become a refugee *sur place*.[85] The Minister unsuccessfully sought review of this decision before the Federal Court, and again at the Full Court. As part of the majority dismissing the Minister's appeal, Ryan J commented that '[s]uch a fear may be no less genuine despite the artifice by which the circumstances which gave rise to it have been engineered'.[86]

[13.40] These decisions were met with a legislative response in 2001. Section 91R(3) of the *Migration Act* now directs decision-makers to disregard any conduct engaged in by the applicant in Australia, unless the applicant satisfies the Minister that the person engaged in the conduct for a purpose otherwise than for the purpose of strengthening their refugee claim. Germov and Motta conclude that s 91R(3) puts Australian law at odds with Art 1A(2) of the Refugee Convention which contains no 'good faith' requirement.[87]

[13.41] The High Court has since ruled that s 91R(3) requires decision-makers to disregard evidence of conduct in Australia that is contrived to strengthen a refugee claim, even where the conduct does actually enhance that claim.[88] The applicant bears the onus of proving that conduct was not undertaken for the purpose of strengthening a refugee claim.[89]

[13.42] The leading High Court decision involved two appeals heard together[90] by Chinese asylum seekers who claimed to be Falun Gong practitioners. In both cases, the RRT had rejected the claims for protection, finding that neither applicant had practised Falun Gong in China and applying s 91R(3) to disregard accepted evidence of Falun Gong activities in Australia. The tribunal found that their interest in Falun Gong was 'a recent invention' designed to strengthen their claims. The first claimant challenged the RRT's decision on the basis that, although it applied s 91R(3) in disregarding whether he had a well-founded fear based on the activities undertaken in Australia, the RRT in fact took these activities into account in drawing adverse inferences as to his credibility overall. The second claimant argued that the RRT's decision involved inherent contradictions. On the one hand, it proposed to disregard the man's Falun Gong contacts in Australia. On the other, the RRT referred to his motives for this conduct in concluding that he was unlikely to practise Falun Gong if he returned to China.[91]

---

85 (2001) 105 FCR 277 at [27].
86 Ibid at [20].
87 Germov and Motta, above n 67, at 191-2. See also UNHCR, above n 76, at [94]-[96] which also contains no such stipulation.
88 See *MIAC v SZJGV; MIAC v SZJXO* (2009) 238 CLR 642 (*SZJGV and SZJXO*).
89 See *NBKT v MIMA* (2006) 156 FCR 419; *SZKOZ v MIAC* [2007] FCA 1798; and *SZKHD v MIAC* [2008] FCA 112.
90 *SZJGV and SZJXO* (2009) 238 CLR 642.
91 *SZJGV and SZJXO* (2009) 238 CLR 642 at [28]-[35].

[13.43] In a majority ruling, the High Court held s 91R(3) does not require that evidence about a person's conduct in Australia, or the motive for that conduct, be disregarded for all purposes connected with an assessment of a claim. As a result, evidence of conduct in Australia found to be undertaken for the purpose of strengthening a refugee claim, and findings about the motivation for that conduct, may be used to discredit an applicant's claim.[92] The court confirmed that conduct in Australia engaged in solely to strengthen a refugee claim must be disregarded, even if it does strengthen the claim made. However, if the conduct reflects poorly on a claimant's credibility, it can be taken into account. Either way, it would seem, the applicant is disadvantaged.[93]

[13.44] Many of the cases in which the issue of *sur place* issues arise have involved refugee claims made on grounds of religious belief.[94] These matters are considered further below (at Part 13.6.3).

13.4 Persecution

[13.45] In spite of the prominence given to the 'real chance' test formulated by the High Court in *Chan*, one of the most radical aspects of the majority rulings in that case was the interpretation of the word 'persecution' in the Refugee Convention definition. McHugh J opted for the 'ordinary meaning of the word', favouring the United States Court of Appeal formulation in *Kovac v Immigration and Naturalization Service*.[95] That court spoke in terms of 'the infliction of suffering or harm ... in a way regarded as offensive'. The court described persecutory behaviour as any 'serious punishment or penalty', 'significant detriment or disadvantage', or 'selective harassment' directed against a person either as an individual or because of that person's membership of a group.[96]

[13.46] The point made by politicians and bureaucrats[97] in the wake of the High Court's ruling was that the standards expected by the developed world are dramatically different from those pertaining in most developing countries – and in most countries experiencing societal conflict. In determining what was 'offensive', whose standards should apply?

[13.47] The central problem is that the Convention definition does not contain any definition of the term 'persecution'. As many have noted, the jurisprudence on the subject from various courts of review around the globe is far from consistent.[98] For its part, UNHCR has declined invitations to delimit the concept, citing the infinite

---

92   Ibid at [49] and [65] (Crennan and Kiefel JJ (with whom French CJ and Bell J agreed)).
93   See *SZJGV* and *SZJXO* (2009) 238 CLR 642.
94   See, for example, *SZGYT v MIAC* [2007] FMCA 883; *SZJZN v MIAC* (2008) 169 FCR 1; and *SZKOZ v MIAC* [2007] FCA 1798. Cases involving religious conversions are particularly problematic in this regard.
95   407 F 2d 102 at 107 (9th Circuit) (1969).
96   See *Chan* (1989) 169 CLR 379 at 388 and 429-31.
97   See above Chapter 12 at [12.92]-[12.93].
98   See, for example, Volker Türk and Frances Nicholson, 'Refugee Protection in International Law: An Overall Perspective' in Erika Feller, Volker Türk and Frances Nicholson (eds), *Refugee Protection in*

variety of ways in which human beings can inflict cruelty on each other.[99] Some commentators have urged a restrictive or narrow interpretation, citing the dangers of undermining refugee protection through the encouragement of irregular migration of the multitudinous hordes seeking a better life abroad.[100]

[13.48] In October 2001, the Coalition government responded to the uncertainty surrounding the term by inserting a definition of persecution into the *Migration Act*.[101] Section 91R now stipulates that persecution must involve 'serious harm to the person' and 'systematic and discriminatory conduct'. The section then states in s 91R(2) that 'serious harm' includes (but is not limited to): threat to the person's life or liberty; significant physical harassment; significant physical mistreatment; and other actions which threaten the person's 'capacity to subsist'. What will constitute systematic and discriminatory conduct is not defined. It may be presumed that these amendments were proposed in part in response to decisions by single judges of the Federal Court in 2001 to the effect that persecution may be shown where harm is not trivial or insignificant, or where there is a denial to work in a chosen profession.[102] Whether these cases would have survived appeals to higher courts is a matter of conjecture. Whatever the motivation, it is clear that s 91R now refines or qualifies persecution for the purposes of Australian law, although it has been said not to 'replace' the Convention test for persecution.[103]

[13.49] The definition of persecution in s 91R seems broadly in line with jurisprudential trends since the ruling in *Chan*. Given that the definition is inclusive rather than exclusive in scope, one might argue also that the provision is not likely to restrict greatly the future development of this area of refugee law.[104] As the following brief review illustrates, there remain a number of contentious areas in the definition of persecution for refugee purposes. These are: the nature of the harms feared; the requirement (if any) that the harms be inflicted in a manner that discriminates against an individual or group; the relevance in this context of policies of general application; and state responsibility. The last of these raise issues relating to generalised violence and the identity of the person or authority engaging in persecutory behaviour.

13.4.1 The nature of the harm

[13.50] In his seminal text on international refugee law, James Hathaway argues that the norms of international human rights law should operate as a guide in the determination of what will constitute harm. He points out that the major human

---

International Law: UNHCR's Global Consultations on International Protection (Cambridge: Cambridge University Press, 2003) 3-46 at 38.
99   Hathaway, above n 18, at 102. See also *Applicant A v MIEA* (1997) 190 CLR 225 at 258 (McHugh J).
100 See John Vrachnas, Kim Boyd, Mirko Bagaric and Penny Dimopoulos, *Migration and Refugee Law: Principles and Practice in Australia* (Melbourne: Cambridge University Press, 2008) at 225-7.
101 *Migration Legislation Amendment Act (No 6) 2001* (Cth), Sch 1, Part 1, cl 5.
102 See *Ahmadi v MIMA* [2001] FCA 1070 and *Kord v MIMA* [2001] FCA 1163. See Sobet Haddad, 'Qualifying the Convention Definition of Refugee' (2002) 1 *Immigration Review* 20 at 20.
103 See *VBAS v MIMIA* (2005) 141 FCR 435 at [16]-[19] and *VBOA v MIMIA* (2006) 233 CLR 1 at [27].
104 This point is emphasised in the Revised Explanatory Memorandum to the *Migration Legislation Amendment Act (No 6) 2001* (Cth).

rights instruments create or recognise a hierarchy of rights from which one can derive a hierarchy of prohibited behaviours. At the top are the key civil and political infringements involving wrongful death, torture, arbitrary detention and other gross abuse of the person. Social and cultural rights fall towards the opposite end of the spectrum, the denial of which should only found a refugee claim where the rights are fundamental to the identity or human dignity of the person.[105]

[13.51] In rulings since *Chan*, the High Court has avoided an exhaustive or precise articulation of the harms that will constitute 'persecution', noting that such an approach would be inappropriate (if not impossible). Whether a particular act or threat will constitute persecution will depend on the circumstances of each case.[106] Without referring directly to Hathaway's hierarchy of harms, the Australian courts have adopted the language of human rights protection. In *Applicant A*,[107] the High Court made it plain that gross abuses of human rights in the form of 'the denial of fundamental human rights and freedoms' will always constitute 'persecution'. That case involved a couple from the PRC who had borne a child in contravention of that country's 'one-child policy'. The couple alleged that they would face forced sterilisation and forced abortion if returned to the PRC. The High Court held that the Full Federal Court had fallen into error in assuming that policies of general application cannot constitute persecution. It accepted without demur the contention that forced sterilisation and forced abortion can constitute persecution. McHugh J observed that persecution for a Convention reason may take an infinite variety of forms from death or torture to the deprivation of opportunities to compete on equal terms with other members of the relevant society.[108]

[13.52] This approach was taken also in *Chen Shi Hai*[109] where the High Court described as persecution any conduct that 'offends the standards of civil societies which seek to meet the calls of common humanity'. That case concerned an asylum claim made on behalf of a child born in contravention of China's one-child policy. The Court found that persecution could be constituted by the denial of access to basic services such as education, food and health care.

[13.53] McHugh J provided a more comprehensive analysis of persecution in *Ibrahim*.[110] His Honour stated that persecution will ordinarily be constituted by unjustifiable and discriminatory conduct directed at an individual or group for a Convention reason which:

- constitutes an interference with the basic human rights or dignity of that person or the persons in the group;
- the country of nationality authorises or does not stop; and

---

105 See Hathaway, above n 18, Ch 4.
106 See McHugh J in *MIMA v Ibrahim* (2000) 204 CLR 1 (*Ibrahim*) at [65]; *Gersten v MIMA* [2000] FCA 855 at [45]; and *MIMA v Kord* (2002) 67 ALD 28 at [35].
107 (1997) 190 CLR 225.
108 Ibid at 258-9.
109 (2000) 201 CLR 293 at [29].
110 (2000) 204 CLR 1 at [65].

- is so oppressive or likely to be repeated or maintained that the person threatened cannot be expected to tolerate it, so that flight from, or refusal to return to, that country is the understandable choice of the individual concerned.

[13.54] Although all of the examples listed in s 91R of the *Migration Act* involve physical harm, there appears to be little dispute that serious mental harm can also constitute persecution. Examples include mock executions or threats to harm close family members.[111] The treatment of threatened harm had led to a division of sorts in the Federal Court. In *Applicant M256/2003 v MIMIA*,[112] Gray J had no difficulty in finding a threat of imprisonment to be persecution. In *MIMIA v VBAO*,[113] Marshall J found that a 'declaration of intention' to harm could not automatically *of itself* constitute a serious harm.[114] While Marshall J's observation may be accurate, it is probably something of a distraction from the central issue facing decision-makers. Whether a person has been or will be *threatened* with harm is of less importance than an assessment of whether such threats will be translated into actual harm.

[13.55] In some cases, denial of work rights has been found to constitute persecution. In *Thalary v MIEA*,[115] for example, the RRT accepted that the applicant was unable to find work in the public sector of India due to her religious and political beliefs. However, the tribunal ruled that this discrimination did not constitute persecution because the claimant could obtain employment in the private sector. The Federal Court disagreed, holding that the denial of government work could amount to persecution if a state is sanctioning discrimination against some of its nationals for Convention reasons. Mansfield J found it difficult to envisage circumstances where such discrimination could be regarded as insignificant, and accepted 'the fundamental significance of the state positively excluding certain of its citizens for Convention reasons from employment by the state and its organs'.

[13.56] In other cases, denial of work rights has been interpreted as (mere) discriminatory conduct that does not amount to persecution.[116] In *Prahastono v MIMA*,[117] Hill J did not disagree directly with Mansfield J. However, he explained that the 'true position' is that one must consider carefully all the circumstances in a case. He opined that the denial of employment opportunities is most likely to amount to persecution in an economy where there is no private enterprise at all. Here, the discrimination would amount to an 'act of oppression'. His Honour noted that permanent employment in the Australian Public Service is still limited to those of Australian nationality. He commented that few would consider this rule as 'persecutory' of foreign nationals, although it is clearly discriminatory. What these cases underscore in fact is that the

---

111 See *NBCY v MIMIA* (2004) 83 ALD 518; and *SZKUV v MIAC* [2008] FMCA 326 at [56].
112 [2006] FCA 590.
113 (2004) 139 FCR 405.
114 Ibid at [37]-[40]. The High Court appears to have agreed with Marshall J, although the matter was not in issue on appeal. See *VBAO v MIMIA* (2006) 233 CLR 1.
115 [1997] FCA 201. See also *Ahmadi v MIMA* [2001] FCA 1070. Note that these decisions pre-dated the introduction of s 91R of the Act and may indeed have prompted the amendment.
116 *Ibrahim* (2000) 204 CLR 1 at [55] (McHugh J).
117 [1997] FCA 586.

nature of the discrimination suffered must compromise in some manner the ability of a person to subsist. Again, this reflects the language adopted in defining persecution in s 91R of the *Migration Act*.

[13.57] Clearly, not all forms of economic harm or interferences with civil rights will reach the standard of persecution. In *Ibrahim*, McHugh J observed that 'while persecution always involves the notion of selective harassment or pursuit, selective harassment or pursuit may not be so intensive, repetitive or prolonged that it can be described as persecution'.[118] At the same time, McHugh J held in *Chan*[119] that a series of acts are not needed; a single incident can suffice. His Honour reiterated this principle in *Ibrahim*.[120] McHugh J's observations on this point have been relied on in subsequent cases.[121] In *Trujillo v MIMA*,[122] Tamberlin J held that a death threat made by a police officer to parents in the presence of their children was capable of constituting persecution for the purposes of the Convention. That case concerned a couple from Colombia who were practising members of the Eklesia Church, an organisation known for its opposition to drug trafficking. In all of the circumstances, Tamberlin J found that the death threat was 'a serious matter'. The decision of the applicant parents to refuse to return to Colombia was an 'understandable choice'.[123]

[13.58] The requirement that persecutory behaviour *discriminate* against the refugee has been affirmed and applied in many subsequent cases.[124] This aspect of the definition is reflected in the s 91R definition where reference is made to systematic and discriminatory conduct. In *Ibrahim*,[125] McHugh J held that the term 'systematic' refers to non-random or intended acts, but does not require the applicant to show habitual, methodical or organised conduct.[126] In s 91R(1)(c), the courts have confirmed that the word 'systematic' does not imply a requirement that an applicant has to fear 'organised or methodical conduct, akin to the atrocities committed by the Nazis in the Second World War'.[127] Although there is a requirement that the conduct feared be directed at the claimant, it does not follow that the persecutor hold a particular animus or hatred for the claimant. 'Antipathy' is not a requirement for persecution.[128]

---

118 (2000) 204 CLR 1 at [55].
119 (1989) 169 CLR 379 at 430.
120 *Ibrahim* (2000) 204 CLR 1 at [94].
121 See *Roguinski v MIMA* [2001] FCA 1327 at [25]-[26]; and *Trujillo v MIMA* [2001] FCA 1452 at [11].
122 [2001] FCA 1452.
123 Ibid at [13].
124 See, for example, *Perampalam v MIMA* (1999) 84 FCR 274 at [13] (Burchett and Lee JJ); *Paramananthan v MIMA* (1998) 94 FCR 28 at 39-40 (Wilcox J), 42 (Lindgren J) and 68-9 (Merkel J); and *W250/01A v MIMA* [2002] FCA 400.
125 (2000) 204 CLR 1 at [5] (Gleeson CJ), [146]-[147] (Gummow J) and [205] (Hayne J).
126 Ibid at [99].
127 See *Ibrahim* (2000) 204 CLR 1 at [99] (McHugh J); and *VSAI v MIMIA* [2004] FCA 1602 at [52] (Crennan J); and *VQAD v MIMIA* [2003] FMCA 481 at [32].
128 See *Chen Shi Hai* (2000) 201 CLR 293 at [33] and *Applicant S v MIMA* (2004) 217 CLR 387 (*Applicant S*) at [38].

13.4.2 An 'eggshell skull' rule[129] for refugees?

[13.59] An issue that has gained increasing prominence in recent years is the extent to which the personal attributes of an asylum seeker can be taken into account in determining whether a feared harm – or indeed the past experience of harm – can be regarded as 'serious'. The Australian jurisprudence on this point is not particularly evolved. In *Prahastono v MIMA*,[130] the court held that an extreme *subjective* fear on the part of a claimant cannot convert non-persecutory actions into persecution. Raphael FM went further in *SZALZ v MIMIA*[131] to rule that 'serious harm' should be an absolute concept that is not affected by attributes such as personal frailty. With the greatest respect, this cannot be correct.

[13.60] In our view account should be taken of the fact that actions or conduct will have a different impact on different people. Age and frailty or youth and vulnerability will indeed transform harms that are trivial for able bodied persons into something much more serious. We would go so far as to say that most decision-makers understand this reality. It is reflected in the high acceptance of claims lodged by unaccompanied children or by persons who live with a disability of some kind.[132]

[13.61] Research conducted into unaccompanied and separated children has explored this differential understanding of persecution at some depth in the context of children. Bhabha and Crock[133] point out that persecution can manifest itself in at least three ways for children. Children can face persecution in exactly the same way as adults. They can also be persecuted in ways that are unique to their condition as children: only children can be subjected to under-age marriage, conscription as child soldiers or as members of street gangs. Finally, children can suffer persecution by being subjected to harms that might not constitute persecution if perpetrated on an adult but which becomes serious because of the vulnerability of the child. Children are more at risk of harm if they are detained, separated from a protective adult, forced to undertake hard physical labour, or subjected to other physical or psychological mistreatment. It is this last characterisation that is likely to present most problems in the present context. Although Australia's record in recognising children as refugees is generally good, the *Seeking Asylum Alone* research suggests that in the vast majority of cases there was no discernable difference between the way decision-makers treated the question of persecution in children as opposed to in cases involving adults.

---

129 This is the principle in tort and criminal law that a wrongdoer must take a victim as he or she is found, so that full account is taken of pre-existing frailties that might make the person more susceptible than would otherwise be the case. See *Smith v Leech Brain & Co* [1962] 2 QB 405.
130 (1997) 77 FCR 260 at 271.
131 [2004] FMCA 275.
132 In this context see, for example, the comments of Tamberlin J in *SZBQJ v MIMIA* [2005] FCA 143 at [21] where his Honour said that 'it is obvious that ... a national policy may impact differently on different persons' so that what is persecution for one person is not for another.
133 See Jacqueline Bhabha and Mary Crock, *Seeking Asylum Alone: Unaccompanied and Separated Children and Refugee Protection in Australia, the UK and the US – A Comparative Study* (Sydney: Themis Press, 2007) Ch 7. See also Mary Crock, *Seeking Asylum Alone*, above n 48, Ch 11; and Mary Crock, 'Re-thinking the Paradigms of Protection: Children as Convention Refugees in Australia' in Jane McAdam (ed), *Forced Migration, Human Rights and Security* (Oxford: Hart Publishing, 2008) Ch 6.

13.4.3 Policies of general application

[13.62] From its inception, the RRT has distinguished between persecutory conduct and policies of general application that may involve the deprivation of property or basic freedoms. For example, in *N93/00732*,[134] the RRT denied refugee status to a family whose bakery in Vietnam was seized in 1975 under a policy of nationalisation of business enterprises. As a general rule, the 'enforcement of a generally applicable criminal law does not constitute persecution'.[135]

[13.63] As noted earlier, however, where the policy involved results in gross abuse of human rights, the general impact of the policy will not remove its persecutory effect. In *Applicant A*,[136] the High Court held that the enforcement of the PRC 'one-child' policy through coerced abortion and mandatory sterilisation did constitute persecution. In *Chen Shi Hai*,[137] the High Court held that laws or policies of general application which target or impact adversely on a particular class or group may constitute persecution. A majority of the court noted that while China's one-child policy 'may be reflected in laws of general application ... that does not mean that the laws or practices applied to children born in contravention of that policy are laws or practices of general application'. The majority in *Chen Shi Hai* also recognised that general laws 'may impact differently on different people and, thus, operate discriminatorily' and that 'selective enforcement of a law of general application may result in discrimination'.[138] In line with this approach, the Federal Court has noted that the selective prosecution of criminal laws, or the imposition of greater punishments for certain groups, could amount to persecution if done for a Convention reason.[139]

[13.64] The High Court explored this issue further in *Applicant S v MIMA*,[140] which concerned a claim for protection made by a young Pashtun man from Afghanistan who feared forcible conscription into the Taliban military. The High Court reiterated the proposition that a law of general application is capable of being implemented or enforced in a discriminatory manner. Citing earlier High Court jurisprudence, Gleeson CJ, Gummow and Kirby JJ concluded that the question of whether the discriminatory treatment of persons on Convention grounds amounts to persecution depends on whether the treatment is 'appropriate and adapted to achieving some legitimate object of the country' and 'whether it offends the standards of civil

---

134 [1994] RRTA 1363.
135 *Applicant A* (1997) 190 CLR 225 at 258 (McHugh J). See also *MIMA v Yusuf* (2001) 206 CLR 323 at 354-5 (McHugh, Gummow and Hayne JJ) and at 342 (Gaudron J).
136 (1997) 190 CLR 225. On this issue, see Crock, above n 25; and Penelope Mathew, 'Applicant A v Minister for Immigration and Ethnic Affairs – The High Court and Particular Social Groups: Lessons for the Future' (1997) 21(1) *Melbourne University Law Review* 277.
137 (2000) 201 CLR 293 at [18] (Gleeson CJ, Gaudron, Gummow and Hayne JJ).
138 Ibid at [19]-[21] (Gleeson CJ, Gaudron, Gummow and Hayne JJ).
139 See *Applicant Z v MIMA* (1998) 90 FCR 51 at 58; *Wang v MIMA* (2001) 105 FCR 548 at [63]; *Weheliye v MIMA* [2001] FCA 1222. In *Weheliye*, the RRT concluded that the applicant's prosecution, conviction and sentencing for adultery in Somalia were the result of the enforcement of a law of general application, and thus did not amount to persecution. The Federal Court held that the tribunal erred by failing to consider whether the law against adultery was in fact applied and administered in a discriminatory manner.
140 (2004) 217 CLR 387.

societies which seek to meet the calls of common humanity'.[141] The majority reflected that the superficial objective of the Taliban's conscription policy was to protect the nation. However, the fact that the Taliban was considered a ruthless and despotic political body founded on extremist religious tenets must impugn the legitimacy of that objective.[142]

13.4.4 State responsibility for persecution

[13.65] Australian courts have traditionally emphasised the public face of the persecution which enlivens a protection obligation. It was thought not to include purely private, individual or sectional persecution that does not implicate the controlling authorities of the country in question.[143] What is clear is that persecution must have an official quality, in the sense that it originates from, is tolerated or cannot be controlled by the government of the country of nationality.

[13.66] While the Refugee Convention is designed first and foremost to protect persons fleeing persecution at the hands of their state of nationality, the instrument does not require persecution to be perpetrated by that state. It is sufficient that the state is *unable or unwilling* to offer to its nationals protection against persecution perpetrated by non-state actors for a Convention reason. That this must always have been the correct interpretation of the Convention is underscored by a hypothetical posited by Lord Hoffman in *Islam v Secretary of State for the Home Department*.[144] Lord Hoffman portrays a scenario in Nazi Germany where a Jewish shopkeeper is attacked by an Aryan competitor who knows that the authorities will allow him to act with impunity. Such an archetypal situation of persecution must have loomed large in the minds of the original Convention drafters.

[13.67] This reading of the Convention definition both expands and contracts the protections available to persons in need today. The fact that refugee status can inhere in persons who fear violence at the hands of non-state actors means that the Convention works in favour of persons who face discrimination within a particular society. On the other hand, the Convention does not extend to individuals fleeing violence in circumstances where society has broken down to the extent that it is no longer possible to speak in terms of 'state' and 'non-state' actors.

[13.68] In *MIMA v Khawar*,[145] the High Court affirmed the principle that the serious harm involved in persecution may be perpetrated by non-state agents where this

---

141 Ibid at [43], citing *Applicant A* (1997) 190 CLR 225 at 258 (McHugh J) and *Chen Shi Hai* (2000) 201 CLR 293 at [29] (Gleeson CJ, Gaudron, Gummow and Hayne JJ). See also *Nagaratnam v MIMA* (1999) 84 FCR 569 at 579; and *Paramananthan v MIMA* (1998) 94 FCR 28.
142 (2004) 217 CLR 387 at [47].
143 See *Magyari v MIMA* (1997) 50 ALD 341.
144 [1999] 2 AC 629 at 654. Kirby J referred to these dicta in *Chen Shi Hai* (2000) 201 CLR 293 at [79].
145 (2002) 210 CLR 1 (*Khawar*). For extended discussion of this case and its precedents in the UK and US, see Anna Dorevitch and Michelle Foster, 'Obstacles on the Road to Protection: Assessing the Treatment of Sex-Trafficking Victims Under Australia's Migration and Refugee Law' (2008) 9(1) *Melbourne Journal of International Law* 1; Alex de Costa, 'Assessing the Cause and Effect of Persecution in Australian Refugee Law: *Sarrazola*, *Khawar* and the *Migration Legislation Amendment Act (No 6) 2001* (Cth)' (2002) 30 *Federal Law Review* 535; Hélène Lambert, 'The Conceptualisation of "Persecution" by

is tolerated by the state. *Khawar* involved a female asylum seeker who had fled a situation of domestic violence in Pakistan, and claimed a well-founded fear of persecution on the basis of her membership of a particular social group. Before the RRT, Ms Khawar gave evidence of the serious and prolonged domestic violence she had suffered at the hands of her husband and his family. On four separate occasions she had unsuccessfully sought the assistance of the police. In order to show that the police neglect and indifference were characteristic of the attitude shown towards women by the Pakistani police and other state authorities, Ms Khawar tendered a number of reports concerning the status of women in Pakistani society and culture generally. While the RRT accepted that the abuse suffered by Ms Khawar was severe enough to constitute 'persecution', it found the abuse was inflicted for personal and private reasons relating to her marital situation (not to the Convention ground of particular social group). On appeal to the High Court, the central issue for determination was whether the failure of a country of nationality to provide protection against domestic violence to women, in circumstances where the motivation of the perpetrators is private, can result in persecution under the Convention.

[13.69] The High Court risked the disapprobation of the government of the day,[146] ruling that Ms Khawar did indeed meet the definition of refugee. Gleeson CJ noted that the definition of refugee 'does not refer to any particular kind of persecutor', but rather to conduct of a particular kind. Persecution can therefore encompass 'the combined effect of conduct of two or more agents' and 'in certain circumstances ... include inaction'.[147] For the Chief Justice, a legitimate form of inaction included 'tolerance or condonation of the inflicting of serious harm in circumstances where the state has a duty to provide protection against such harm'.[148] Kirby J expressed a similar view that persecution can be constituted by 'a risk of serious harm to the applicant from human sources and a failure on the part of the state to afford protection that is adequate to uphold the basic human rights and dignity of the person concerned'.[149] Or, in a simpler formulation, 'Persecution = Serious Harm + The Failure of State Protection'. McHugh and Gummow JJ, on the other hand, focused on the discriminatory inactivity of the state. Their Honours framed Ms Khawar's complaint as a 'denial of fundamental rights or freedoms otherwise enjoyed by nationals of the country concerned', brought about by the 'selective or discriminatory treatment' of the state.[150]

---

the House of Lords: *Horvath v Secretary of State for the Home Department*' (2001) 13 *International Journal of Refugee Law* 16; Deborah Anker, Lauren Gilbert and Nancy Kelly, 'Women Whose Governments are Unable or Unwilling to Provide Reasonable Protection from Domestic Violence May Qualify as Refugees under United States Asylum Law' (1997) 11 *Georgetown Immigration Law Journal* 709.

146   Then Immigration Minister Philip Ruddock was vociferous in his criticism of earlier attempts by the RRT and the Federal Court to grant refugee status to victims of domestic violence. Indeed, he threatened RRT members with non-renewal of their contracts should they attempt to 're-write the Convention' to cover refugee claimants fleeing domestic violence: see 'Ruddock Warns Tribunal', *The Canberra Times*, 27 December 1996, at 6; Editorial, 'Ruddock's Threats to Refugee Body', *The Canberra Times*, 27 December 1996, at 14. The Minister repeated his statements in a public forum, 'Immigrant Justice: Courts, Tribunals and the Rule of Law', held at the University of Sydney on 6 June 1997.

147   (2002) 210 CLR 1 at [27].

148   Ibid at [30].

149   Ibid at [115].

150   Ibid at [76], referring to the formulation of Mason CJ in *Chan* (1989) 169 CLR 379 at 388.

[13.70] The High Court has since affirmed that, in addition to such official toleration by a state of non-state actors' persecution of its nationals, protection obligations are owed to applicants whose states are simply unable to protect them from persecution.[151] In *MIMA v Respondents S152/2003*,[152] a majority of the High Court ruled that a state's obligation is 'to take reasonable measures to protect the lives and safety of its citizens, and those measures would include an appropriate criminal law, and the provision of a reasonably effective and impartial police force and justice system'. Commentators have criticised the standard of 'reasonable measures' on the basis that it has led adjudicators to resolve asylum applications by reference to a state's notional willingness to protect rather than by examining its present ability to do so, often without due attention to the actual measures in place for victim protection and assistance.[153] Nevertheless, it is now clear that a decision-maker's inquiries about state protection must no longer be confined to the narrow issue of whether or not the state actively condoned or tolerated the relevant harm, as opposed to passively failed to provide protection against it.[154]

13.4.5 Situations of generalised violence

[13.71] Decision-makers, in Australia and abroad, have long denied claims by individuals caught up in or affected by incidents of communal violence, especially where this cannot be characterised as either systematic or targeted at the claimant for one of the five Convention reasons.[155] For instance, the House of Lords, in *Adan v Secretary of State for the Home Department*,[156] held that 'a state of civil war whose incidents are widespread clan and sub-clan based killing and torture' does not give rise to a well-founded fear of persecution for the purposes of the Convention if the 'individual claimant is at no greater risk ... than others who are at risk ... for reasons of their clan and sub-clan membership'.

[13.72] However, as Goodwin-Gill and McAdam note[157] a civil conflict, or general instability, is not logically incompatible with an applicant's well-founded fear of persecution on a Convention ground. What is required is attention to the background to the conflict and the ways in which it is fought, to determine the existence of a link to the Convention. Indeed, Australian courts have accepted this approach, and rejected *Adan's* requirement of a showing of differential treatment to similarly situated individuals. The Full Court of the Federal Court has concluded that, where the civil war is based not on racial grounds but on generalised struggles for power, territory or wealth, 'it is necessary, of course, to establish the existence of selective

---

151 *MIMA v Respondents S152/2003* (2004) 222 CLR 1.
152 Ibid at [26] (Gleeson CJ, Hayne and Heydon JJ).
153 Dorevitch and Foster, above n 145, at 22.
154 *M93 of 2004 v MIMIA* [2006] FMCA 252 at [80].
155 In *Periannan (Murugasu) v MIEA* (unreported, FCA, 28 July 1987) at 13 where Wilcox J stated: 'The word "persecuted" suggests a course of systematic conduct aimed at an individual or a group of people. It is not enough that there be a fear of being involved in incidental violence as a result of civil or communal disturbances'. See also Walter Kälin, 'Refugees and Civil Wars: Only a Matter of Interpretation?' (1991) 3 *International Journal of Refugee Law* 435.
156 [1999] AC 293 at 308, 311 (*Adan*).
157 Goodwin-Gill and McAdam, above n 20, at 126.

harassment on a Convention ground' while where the civil war is itself based on a racial conflict such a ground is already present.[158]

[13.73] However, barriers to a successful claim are still posed by reading the Convention to require the existence of a government which is unable or unwilling to offer effective protection. The classic example of lack of state protection is the situation that has faced Somalis. In spite of the generosity of the High Court's statements about what will constitute persecution in *Ibrahim's* case, the applicant in that case failed ultimately in his attempt to gain recognition as a refugee. The High Court ruled that the protective constructs of the Refugee Convention operate only where a state of sorts can be identified to take direct or indirect responsibility for the violence in question.[159] Although the civil war had officially ended in Somalia by 2000, there was still no central recognised government to protect citizens from the harm arising from ongoing clan warfare and thus, apparently, no protection obligations were enlivened for Australia.

13.5 The nexus requirement – 'for reasons of'

[13.74] A critical determinant of a person's status as a refugee is the ability to show a nexus between the persecution feared and the five Convention grounds. The leading case on the linkage requirement of the definition of refugee is *Applicant A*.[160] The issue before the High Court in that case was whether the applicant's fear of forced sterilisation pursuant to the PRC one-child policy constituted persecution feared *for reasons of* membership of a particular social group or political opinion. In the majority, McHugh J emphasised the importance of the nexus requirement. He held that the concept of persecution in the Convention definition depends less on the nature of the conduct feared than on whether the persecutor discriminated among the people on the basis of one of the five Convention grounds. The High Court endorsed the approach taken by the Full Federal Court in *Ram v MIEA*.[161] In that case, Burchett J enjoined decision-makers to adopt the perspective of the persecutor to determine both the motivation of persecutory conduct and the claimant's membership or otherwise of a cognisable social group. He commented:[162]

> Persecution involves the infliction of harm, but it implies something more: an element of an attitude on the part of those who persecute which leads to the infliction of harm, or an element of motivation (however twisted) for the infliction of harm. People are persecuted for something perceived about them or attributed to them by their persecutors.

[13.75] While the requirement of motivation or intention on the part of the persecutor has been endorsed in subsequent cases, the High Court has repeatedly stressed

---

158   *MIMA v Abdi* (1999) 87 FCR 280 at [42].
159   *Ibrahim* (2000) 204 CLR 1; Susan Kneebone, 'Moving Beyond the State: Refugees, Accountability and Protection' in Susan Kneebone (ed), *The Refugee Convention: Fifty Years On* (Burlington: Ashgate Publishing, 2003) Ch 11.
160   (1997) 190 CLR 225.
161   (1995) 57 FCR 565.
162   Ibid at 568.

that it need not be based on enmity or malignity.¹⁶³ In short, the applicant must be persecuted for something perceived about or attributed to him or her.

[13.76] An enduring issue is the significance of situations where there are dual or multiple motivations for the feared persecution. For instance, an elderly Tamil woman was found to have been brutalised in police interrogation in Sri Lanka partly as a result of normal security procedures, partly as a random 'indiscriminate abuse of authority' and partly as a result of being initially targeted for police interest because of her ethnicity and political opinion.¹⁶⁴ In that case, it was held to be sufficient if one of the motivations was related to a Convention ground. The fact that this approach did not find favour with the government of the day is reflected in the terms of s 91R of the *Migration Act*. Although the Act allows for the possibility of dual or multiple motivations, the Convention reason must now be 'the essential and significant reason' for the persecution: s 91R. Having said that, the case law supports an holistic approach to the assessment of refugee claims, in that decision-makers have been enjoined to focus on behaviours that do engage the Refugee Convention. Where persecutory acts do have an underlying connection with (for example) a claimant's membership of a particular social group, there has been a tendency to regard this as transforming the acts into Convention-related harms.¹⁶⁵

[13.77] The nexus requirement is further complicated in cases where persecution involves the 'combined effect' of private harm and the state's toleration or condoning of that harm (failure to protect). In the first instance decision in *Khawar v MIMA*,¹⁶⁶ Branson J outlined a number of possible scenarios falling within Art 1A(2) that depart from the traditional fact pattern which arises when the state or its agents directly persecute a claimant for Convention-based reasons. The first is where the state either condones or ignores persecution by individuals for whom it is not responsible, but both the state and the individual share the discriminatory motive. The spectre of this scenario is raised by the example given by Lord Hoffman (mentioned earlier) where a Jewish shopkeeper in Nazi Germany is attacked by an Aryan competitor who knows that the authorities will allow him to act with impunity.¹⁶⁷ Another is where a non-state actor persecutes for a Convention reason and the state cannot protect the victim (although it does not share the persecutor's motivation). This scenario arose in *MIMA v Sarrazola (No 2)*¹⁶⁸ where the applicant claimed to fear persecution from her brother's debtors if returned to Colombia. The Full Federal Court found that the RRT erred in dismissing Ms Sarrazola's claim to persecution as a member of a particular social group (being her family association). Merkel J found that it was not open to the tribunal to conclude that the applicant's family relationship was not causally connected to the persecution.

---

163 See *Applicant S* (2004) 217 CLR 387; *Chen Shi Hai* (2000) 201 CLR 293 at [63]; and *Khawar* (2002) 210 CLR 1 at [115] (Kirby J).
164 *Perampalam v MIMA* (1999) 84 FCR 274.
165 See *Rajaratnam v MIMA* (2000) 62 ALD 73; and the later cases of *SHKB v MIMIA* [2004] FCA 545; and *SZFZN v MIAC* [2006] FMCA 1153 at [21].
166 (1999) 168 ALR 190 at [18]. See also *Okere v MIMA* (1998) 87 FCR 112.
167 [1999] 2 AC 629 at 654.
168 (2001) 107 FCR 184 (*Sarrazola (No 2)*).

[13.78] Another constellation occurs where a non-state agent persecutes a person for a reason that is not Convention related, but then the victim is denied redress or protection for a Convention reason. This pattern is exemplified in the facts as found by the tribunal in *Khawar* (discussed earlier). The High Court has held that the requisite nexus may be found in any of these scenarios; in other words the causal link may be satisfied by the motivation of either the private actors or the state.[169]

[13.79] One final point is worth noting in the context of this 'nexus' requirement. It is that care must be taken to align the motivation of the persecutor with that of a refugee so as to ensure that the persecution is not simply a response to an illegal action committed by the refugee. In this context, the motivation of the *refugee* in committing an illegal act will not of itself convert a law enforcement action into persecution.[170]

13.6 The Convention grounds

[13.80] In many respects the most passive of the five Convention grounds are those of race and nationality: claimants relying on these grounds do so because of who they are, rather than because of anything they may have done. 'Social group' has also been characterised as a passive ground, but debate has raged over whether it is always possible, or analytically useful, to distinguish a person's identity from their behaviour. As explored below, it is frequently the perception of the persecutor (and/or of the objective observer) that is critical, whatever the ground for the persecutory behaviour.

13.6.1 Race

[13.81] The leading Australian case on the interpretation of the word 'race' did not concern refugees at all, but arose in the context of a constitutional challenge to a Tasmanian government decision to dam a river subject to World Heritage protection. In *Commonwealth v Tasmania*,[171] Brennan J acknowledged that the word 'race' is neither a term of art nor a precise concept. He noted the 'immutable' nature of race as a description of the human characteristics with which a person is born but concluded that additional complexity is required:

> Though the biological element is, as Kerr LJ pointed out, an essential element of membership of a race, it does not ordinarily exhaust the characteristics of a racial group. Physical similarities, and a common history, a common religion or spiritual beliefs and a common culture are factors that tend to create a sense of identity among members of a race and to which others have regard in identifying people as members of a race.[172]

---

169 See *Khawar* (2002) 210 CLR 1 at [31] (Gleeson CJ) and [120] (Kirby J).
170 See, for example, *Mai Xin Lu v MIEA* (unreported, FCA, French J, 19 July 1996), a case where the claimant asserted that he feared persecution because he had left the PRC without authorisation.
171 (1983) 158 CLR 1.
172 Ibid at 244.

[13.82] This formulation was adopted in *Calado v MIMA*.[173] Tamberlin J said:

> There can be no single test for the meaning of the expression 'race' but the term connotes considerations such as whether the individuals or the group regard themselves and are regarded by others in the community as having a particular historical identity in terms of colour, and national or ethnic origins. Another consideration is whether the characteristics of members of the group are those with which a person is born and which he or she cannot change.

[13.83] That case involved an asylum seeker from Angola who claimed refugee status on the basis of his identity as a Bakongo man. Tamberlin J held that the RRT in that case had used the wrong understanding of 'race' by finding the applicant's fluency in Portuguese (the official language of Angola) as determinative evidence that he was not a Bakongo man. His Honour accepted expert evidence that a more accurate inquiry would have been to ask whether the man spoke Bakongo.

[13.84] In most cases, the identification of race is not in dispute: the key question concerns whether the claimant can show that she or he fears persecution because of her or his race. 'Mere' constitutional discrimination against racial minorities may not result in an applicant benefiting from the provisions of the Refugee Convention. For example, in *Uma Chand v MIEA*,[174] a Fijian-Indian failed in his claim that 'democratic deficiencies in the Constitution of Fiji' rendered him a refugee. Branson J upheld the RRT's decision to refuse refugee status. She expressed sympathy for the applicant, but ruled that limitations placed on the democratic powers of a particular race within a state did not amount to persecution for a Convention reason.

[13.85] Affirmative action or positive racial discrimination policies have been treated by the courts in a similar manner. In *Gunaseelan v MIMA*,[175] the applicant was a Malaysian citizen of Indian ethnicity who claimed that the adverse impact of the policy of preferring indigenous Malays in employment and education constituted persecution. The Federal Court was not persuaded. French J held that the question of whether an affirmative action policy can constitute persecution for a non-assisted group will depend on the nature and operation of the policy and on the impact that it has on the group to which the refugee claimant belongs. A state's exercise of police powers (such as arrest, detention and harassment) may constitute persecution when done in a manner that discriminates against people of a particular ethnicity, even if they are also underpinned by a legitimate security concern.[176] On the other hand, the Federal Court in *SZEGA v MIMIA*[177] ruled that cases based on the persecution of caste members should not be considered on grounds of race – but rather on grounds of a particular social group.

---

173 (1997) 81 FCR 450 at 455 (*Calado*).
174 [1997] FCA 1198.
175 [1997] FCA 434.
176 *Paramananthan v MIMA* (1998) 94 FCR 28.
177 [2006] FCA 1286 at [19].

13.6.2 Nationality

[13.86] As Goodwin-Gill and McAdam point out, the reference in the Convention definition to persecution for reasons of nationality is somewhat odd given that states are unlikely to persecute their own nationals because of their 'membership of the body politic'.[178] In practice, however, this ground of the definition has been interpreted to cover persons fearing persecution on account of their ethnicity or membership of a minority ethnic, religious or cultural sub-group within a state. In this context, the issues that arise are very similar to those encountered by persons making claims of persecution based on race. This point was made by Tamberlin J in *Calado*:[179]

> The references in the definition of 'refugee' to race, religion, nationality and social groups are not discrete, independent categories but rather they overlap. In some circumstances persons of the same race may also form an independent social community or have the same nationality. A common language may be a feature of such communities or groups. As Hathaway points out in *The Law of Refugee Status*, 1991 at pp 144-145: 'In addition to notions of formal nationality, it is generally suggested that nationality encompasses linguistic groups and other culturally defined collectivities, thus overlapping to a significant extent with the concept of race. Because many such groups share a sense of political community distinct from that of the nation state, their claims to refugee protection may reasonably be determined on the basis of nationality as well as on race.'

[13.87] These cases aside, the most significant arguments concerning the nationality of refugee claimants have arisen in instances where uncertainties exist as to the country responsible for receiving and protecting the individuals involved.[180] There has also been one instance where nationality was raised (unsuccessfully) by an asylum seeker who had left his country without authorisation and who faced sanctioning if returned. The court in that case held that the man faced a legal penalty (not persecution) that was based anyway on his unlawful conduct and not on his nationality.[181]

13.6.3 Religion

[13.88] Where applicants have been targeted for persecution because of their religious beliefs or practices, the courts and the RRT have had little difficulty in upholding refugee claims made on the 'religion' ground. The more controversial cases have been those in which the repression of religion has a generalised impact on believers, through the destruction of places of worship or the imposition of a curfew that prohibits religious observances outside of the home. From early days such generalised repressive measures have been held by the RRT not to amount to persecution of individuals.

[13.89] The Full Federal Court affirmed the tribunal's approach in *MIMA v Zheng*.[182] In that case, the court held that conduct that amounts to no more than governance of

---

178 Goodwin-Gill and McAdam, above n 20, at 72.
179 (1997) 81 FCR 450 at 454-5.
180 See, for example, *Husein Ali Haris v MIMA* [1998] FCA 78.
181 See *Su Wen Jian v MIEA* [1996] FCA 1422.
182 [2000] FCA 50.

a church, and involves no prohibition of the practice of the person's religion, does not of itself amount to persecution on the grounds of religion. In that case, the RRT found that there were no essential differences in religious practice between a registered and an unregistered church in China. It was found that the applicant had no significant belief which prevented him from practising at a registered Church.

[13.90] However, in subsequent cases with similar factual situations, *Zheng* has been distinguished. In *Wang v MIMA*,[183] for example, the applicant also claimed a fear of persecution on the ground that he could not practise as a Protestant Christian at an unregistered church in China. The RRT rejected his claim on the basis that he could practise as a Protestant Christian at an official church, and that any punishment for practising at an unregistered church was the result of enforcement of a law of general application. At first instance Lindgren J followed *Zheng* and upheld the RRT's decision.[184] Lindgren J's decision was set aside by the Full Federal Court. After discussing *Chen Shi Hai*, Merkel J (with whom Wilcox and Gray JJ agreed) held that 'a law regulating the practice of religion, requiring that it be practised or observed in a particular way or targeting or applying only to persons practicing religion, is not a law of "general application"'.[185] Consequently, a fear of punishment for breach of such laws can give rise to a well-founded fear of persecution for a Convention reason.

[13.91] Merkel J noted that the concept of 'religion' in Art 1A(2) has two elements: first, the manifestation or practice of a personal faith or doctrine and, secondly, the manifestation or practice of that faith or doctrine within a like-minded community.[186] The court held that the tribunal had erred by considering the possibility of persecution only with respect to the first element of the applicant's religious practice and not with respect to the second, 'congregational and community', element.[187]

[13.92] The *RRT Refugee Law Guide* provides some useful examples of how persecution on grounds of religion can be manifest.[188] These include the application of generally applicable religious-based laws, departing from orthodox religious beliefs or transgressing religious mores, conversion, apostasy and mixed marriage.[189] Another issue that has received differential treatment in the jurisprudence is that of the evangelising refugee claimant. Some RRT members have held that the lack of freedom to proselytise for fear of persecution is a basis for refugee status.[190] Others have taken the view that the Refugee Convention does not recognise an absolute right to freedom of religion, and measures which restrict proselytising may not amount

---

183 (2000) 105 FCR 548.
184 [2000] FCA 511. Note that his Honour did question the validity of the distinction made by the tribunal between governing 'religion' and governing 'religious institutions'.
185 (2000) 105 FCR 548 at [66].
186 Ibid at [81].
187 See also *MIMA v Darboy* (1998) 52 ALD 44 at 50; *W244/01A v MIMA* [2002] FCA 52; *Mandavi v MIMA* [2002] FCA 70; and *Liu v MIMA* [2001] FCA 257.
188 See above n 12, Ch 5 at 14-15.
189 Citing *VCAD v MIMIA* [2004] FCA 1005. It is noted also in this context that persecution can occur because a person does not have a religion. See *Prashar v MIMA* [2001] FCA 57; and *NAQJ v MIMIA* [2004] FCA 946.
190 See *N93/00044* [1994] RRTA 72.

to persecution but may, instead, simply be laws of general application designed to maintain public order.[191]

[13.93] The Federal Court considered the issue of whether the inability to proselytise amounts to Convention persecution in *Thalary v MIEA*.[192] Mansfield J held that there was some basis for the applicant's assertion that the RRT erred in finding that proselytising was not relevant to her right to practise her religion. Ultimately, however, the court found that it did not need to decide the question as the applicant was unable to show that the persecutory conduct feared was either initiated by the state or tolerated by it.

[13.94] Even so, where public worship is an essential tenet of an applicant's faith, a decision-maker cannot reject the applicant's well-founded fear of persecution on the basis that they could avoid the persecutory consequences of practising their religion by 'keeping a low profile'.[193] In such cases, the Federal Court has indicated that the need (or a perceived need) to conceal one's religion will usually support the existence of a well-founded fear of persecution.

[13.95] Although the distinction is a fine one, the High Court has confirmed that it is acceptable for decision-makers to distinguish between the practice of a person's religion (for which protection from persecution is available) and evangelistic behaviour that might attract adverse attention (which is unprotected). In *NABD/2002 v MIMA*,[194] the court held that the tribunal would fall into error if it imposed a metaphorical requirement on the (Iranian) claimant that he practise his religion discreetly. However, it was legitimate for the tribunal to find that Christians in Iran could live without persecution providing they did not engage in proselytising their faith. On this basis the court upheld the RRT's rejection of the applicant's claim for protection.

[13.96] This jurisprudence illuminates some assumptions which are embedded in refugee law and judicial interpretations of it. The first relates to the distinction between 'public' and 'private' behaviour. The second relates to the orthodox view that refugee law protects claimants who are targeted because of attributes that are immutable, as opposed to their voluntary conduct. If this view ever held sway, it seems now to have been definitively rejected by the High Court's ruling. Applicants should not be required to choose to be discrete in observing their religion to avoid state sanction. As the Full Court of the Federal Court concluded in *Wang*, the fact that an applicant engaged in unnecessary or unreasonable voluntary conduct (like attending a non-registered church) is not relevant to the well-foundedness of their fear (although it may be considered in assessing their credibility). As explored in the following section, similar issues have arisen in the context of applicants claiming persecution on the basis of their sexual orientation.

---

191   See *SZDTM v MIAC* [2008] FCA 1258.
192   [1997] FCA 20.
193   See *Woudneh v MILGEA* [1988] FCA 318; *Farajvand v MIMA* [2001] FCA 795.
194   (2005) 216 ALR 1.

13.6.4 'Particular social group'

[13.97] Of all the Refugee Convention grounds, the most contentious has been the ground of 'membership of a particular social group'.[195] In the Australian courts, the judges have agreed that this phrase was added to extend the protection afforded by the Refugee Convention and that it should be interpreted broadly.[196] The issue of determining 'social groupings' is a discrete task that should be undertaken before any inquiry into whether a person faced persecution *by reason of* membership of the social group.[197] Otherwise, there is little consensus about the extent to which this ground broadens the protections available to refugees.

[13.98] The Canadian Supreme Court has identified three approaches to the interpretation of 'particular social group':[198]

(1) a wide definition pursuant to which the class (group) serves as a safety net to prevent any possible gap in the other four categories;
(2) a narrower definition that confines its scope by means of some appropriate limiting mechanism, recognising that this class (group) is not meant to encompass all groups; and
(3) a yet more limited definition, that responds to concerns about morality and criminality by excluding terrorists, criminals and other persons who might represent a threat to public security.

[13.99] The move to limit the reach of the phrase 'particular social group' is founded in the understanding that the adjectives 'particular' and 'social' demand that a group be identifiable within a community and that the phrase does not encompass every broadly defined segment of a population.[199] The starting point in Australian jurisprudence on the interpretation of this phrase is *Applicant A*.[200] In that case the minority judges appear to have adopted the first of these approaches, and the majority judges, the second. No member of the court favoured the most restrictive option.

[13.100] In *Canada (Attorney General) v Ward*,[201] La Forest J identified three classes of groups that could be characterised as 'particular social groups':

(1) groups identified by an innate or unchangeable characteristic;
(2) groups whose members voluntarily associate for reasons so fundamental to their human dignity that they should not be forced to forsake the association; and

---

195 For a selection of literature on the subject of 'social group' generally, see Michelle Foster, *International Refugee Law and Socio-Economic Rights* (Cambridge: Cambridge University Press 2007) at 291ff; T Alexander Aleinikoff, 'Protected Characteristics and Social Perceptions: An Analysis of the Meaning of "Membership of a Particular Social Group"' in Feller et al, above n 98, at 263; Guy Goodwin-Gill, 'Judicial Reasoning and "Social Group" after *Islam* and *Shah*' (1999) 11 *International Journal of Refugee Law* 537; Crock, above n 25; Arthur Helton, 'Persecution on Account of Membership in a Social Group as a Basis for Refugee Status' (1983) 15 *Columbia Human Rights Law Review* 39.
196 See *Morato v MILGEA* (1992) 39 FCR 401 at 415-16; and *Kashayev v MIEA* (1994) 50 FCR 226 at 230.
197 See *Dranichnikov v MIMA* (2003) 214 CLR 496 at [26]; *SGBB v MIMIA* (2003) 199 ALR 364 at [24]-[25]; *NAPU v MIMIA* [2004] FCAFC 193; and *SXCB v MIMIA* [2005] FCA 102 at [16]-[17].
198 *Ward* (1993) 103 DLR (4th) 1 at 32.
199 See *Sanchez-Trujillo v INS* 801 F 2d 1571 at 1576 (1986).
200 (1997) 190 CLR 225.
201 (1993) 103 DLR (4th) 1 at 33-4.

(3) groups associated by a former voluntary status, unalterable due to its historical permanence.

[13.101] In *Applicant A*, the High Court confirmed that social groups can comprise people who identify themselves as a group through voluntary association or other 'immutable' characteristic. However, it went further to hold that a social group can also exist where a class of persons is *perceived* to exist, whether or not an individual recognises himself or herself as being a member of a group.[202] The views of American and Canadian courts have in some ways been narrower and in others broader.[203] For instance, the US Board of Immigration Appeals has held that a social group must be characterised by an immutable characteristic but that immutability should be defined broadly.[204] This has meant that matters such as gender, sexual orientation and many other characteristics 'fundamental to personal identity' have been allowed to define social groupings in the US, but others such as transsexuality may not.[205]

[13.102] Where the High Court divided in *Applicant A* was on the legitimacy of using the shared experience of persecution as a means of identifying a particular social group. Dawson, McHugh and Gummow JJ rejected this approach as self-serving or circuitous, holding that for a social group to be cognisable the group must share immutable characteristics, apart from any common fears.[206] McHugh J did note, however, that the acts of persecutors may 'serve to identify or even cause the creation of a particular social group in society' even though they could not alone define the group.[207] Dawson J warned against a tendency to argue that 'the more abhorrent the persecution is, the more likely it is that the targets of that persecution are members of a particular social group'.[208]

[13.103] The majority in *Applicant A* confirmed that members of a social group must have associative qualities that go to the members' identity. In other words, the association must relate to who a person *is* rather than to what she or he *does*. In the majority, Dawson J found that the applicants were simply one of any number of 'disparate couples from all walks of life who do not know each other and may have nothing in common save for the fact that they are parents of one child who do not wish to be forcibly prevented from having more'.[209]

[13.104] In dissent Kirby J expressly disagreed with the majority view that shared persecutory experiences cannot be used to identify a particular social group. His Honour held that the targeting of opponents to the PRC government's fertility control

---

202 (1997) 190 CLR 225 at 264-5 (McHugh J) and 285 (Gummow J). See also *Ram v MIEA* (1995) 57 FCR 565.
203 For a discussion of the conflicting interpretations, see *Applicant A* (1997) 190 CLR 225 at 260-3.
204 *Matter of Acosta* (US Board of Immigration Appeals (BIA), (1985) Interim Division 2986).
205 *Hernandez-Montiel v INS*, 225 F 3d 1084 (9th Cir 2000); *Reyes-Reyes v Ashcroft*, 284 F 3d 782 (9th Cir 2004).
206 (1997) 190 CLR 225 at 242 (Dawson J).
207 Ibid at 264. See also *Applicant S* (2004) 217 CLR 387 at [31] (Gleeson CJ, Gummow and Kirby JJ).
208 Ibid at 245-6.
209 (1997) 190 CLR 225 at 247. See also *Morato v MILGEA* (1992) 39 FCR 401 at 404; and *Ward* (1993) 103 DLR (4th) 1 at 33.

policies highlighted the fact that such people were identified (and punished) as dissentients within the community.[210]

[13.105] Agreeing with Kirby J, Brennan CJ concentrated on both the identification of the applicants as dissentients within PRC society and the denial to them of their fundamental rights and freedoms. He formulated the question of the applicants' refugee status in terms of protection of their basic human rights. The central issue for him was whether 'the feared persecution was practised or likely to be practised because of a characteristic of the victims that is not common to the members of the society at large'.[211] Unlike the majority, his Honour focused less on internal associational characteristics than on common objectives: in this case, common opposition to the PRC one-child policy. The sole concession to the 'is/does' distinction in the judgment of Brennan CJ is found in the stipulation that conduct be 'non-criminal'.[212] He accepted that the phrase 'particular social group' was intended as a safety net for people who could not demonstrate that the persecution they faced was for one of the other four enumerated reasons: race, religion, nationality or political opinion.

[13.106] The notion that the particular social group cannot be defined by the persecutory conduct was affirmed in *Chen Shi Hai v MIMA*[213] and in more recent cases.[214] However, the majority in *Chen Shi Hai* held that children born in contravention of China's one-child policy were 'defined other than by reference to the discriminatory treatment or persecution that they fear'.[215] In subsequent PRC cases involving 'hei zi' or 'black children', arguments have arisen over whether the detriment suffered by these children can be attributed to a Convention reason. Some tribunals (and some judges) have answered this question in the negative by focusing on the central issue of household registration (or lack thereof) as the cause of any detriment suffered by the child.[216] In *SZBXV v MIMA*,[217] it was held that penalties imposed on unregistered children did not amount to serious harm, although it was accepted that the applicant child could face 'social ostracism'.[218] A different result was reached by Merkel J in *VTAO v MIMIA*.[219] His Honour overturned a tribunal ruling that parents of a black child could not invoke their fear of being penalised under a law of general application as the basis for membership of a particular social group. Merkel J ruled that laws of general application may impact differently on different people and be enforced selectively such that they operate in a discriminatory manner.

---

210 (1997) 190 CLR 225 at 302-3.
211 Ibid at 237.
212 Ibid at 234.
213 (2000) 201 CLR 293.
214 See, for example, *SZMKY v MIAC* (2008) 105 ALD 493, a case where a PRC woman had been forced to have an abortion of a pregnancy at seven months. See also *SZJRU v MIAC* (2009) 108 ALD 515.
215 (2000) 201 CLR 293 at [23] (Gleeson CJ, Gaudron, Gummow and Hayne JJ).
216 See, for example, *SZBQJ v MIMIA* [2005] FCA 143. See also *SZBPQ v MIMIA* [2005] FCA 568 at [28]; *SZBQJ v MIMIA* [2005] FCA 143 at [16].
217 [2007] FCA 1286.
218 As Moore J noted at the end of the judgment in this case, the applicant child had been born in Australia. Never having lived in China, real issues arose over whether the child could meet the basic requirements of Art 1A(2) of the Convention of being outside his country of nationality or of habitual residence. See ibid at [58]. See also *SZJTQ v MIAC* (2008) 172 FCR 563.
219 (2004) 81 ALD 332.

[13.107] The approach adopted by the Chief Justice and Kirby J in *Applicant A* is similar to that adopted in the United States by the BIA in *Matter of Kasinga*.[220] In this case, the applicant's fear of female genital mutilation was found to constitute fear of persecution by reason of membership of a particular social group. The decision was based, in part, on an approach to the social group ground as a ground included deliberately as a 'catch-all' for individuals not falling into the other enumerated Convention grounds. This echoes the reading given by Arthur Helton that the phrase was designed to cover 'all bases for and types of persecution which an imaginative despot might conjure up'.[221] For Helton, the primary interpretative principle when considering the reach of the Refugee Convention should be the framers' intent to save individuals from future injustice. As our review of jurisprudence in this area makes clear, this attitude has not been uniformly held by decision-makers.[222]

The determination of a social group should involve an objective test

[13.108] The overarching principles used to determine the contours of a 'particular social group' continue to vex decision-makers. In *MIMA v Zamora*,[223] the Full Federal Court stated that, in order to conclude that a particular social group exists, three conditions must be satisfied:

> First, there must be some characteristic other than persecution or the fear of persecution that unites the collection of individuals; … Second, that characteristic must set the group apart, as a social group, from the rest of the community. Third, there must be recognition *within the society* that the collection of individuals is a group apart from the rest of the community'.

[13.109] This formulation was considered by the High Court in *Applicant S*.[224] The applicant, a young Afghan man of Pashtun ethnicity, claimed to be at risk of persecution on account of his membership of a particular social group. The Minister's delegate and the tribunal accepted that he left Afghanistan to avoid the Taliban who were recruiting for military service. The Taliban had tried twice forcibly to enlist him. On the first occasion, the young man avoided recruitment by paying off the recruiters. The second time he had told the recruiters that he needed to speak to his parents. He then immediately fled Afghanistan with the assistance of a people smuggler.[225] The particular social group within the meaning of the Convention was identified by the Federal Court as able-bodied young men (or possibly able-bodied young men without the financial means to bribe the conscriptors).[226] The sticking point was that, in Afghan society, young men were not necessarily seen as belonging to a cognisable group. Overruling *Zamora*, the High Court held that a social group

---

220 *In re Fauziya Kasinga* (1996) 21 Administrative Decisions under Immigration and Nationality Laws 357; 1996 Westlaw 379826 (BIA). See Karen Musalo and Stephen Knight, 'Steps Forward and Steps Back: Uneven Progress in the Law of Social Group and Gender Based Claims in the United States' (2001) 13 *International Journal of Refugee* Law 51.
221 Helton, above n 195, at 45.
222 For an Australian example of a case involving female genital mutilation, see *A234/2003 v MIMIA* [2003] FCA 1110.
223 (1998) 85 FCR 458 at 464 (emphasis added).
224 (2004) 217 CLR 387.
225 Ibid at [9].
226 See *Applicant S v MIMA* [2001] FCA 1411 at [48].

should be determined from the perspective of an objective observer. There should not be a requirement that a society itself recognise the group as such, although evidence of societal attitudes can assist in determining whether a group exists.[227]

Spousal violence, gender and the 'public-private' distinction

[13.110] Recent decades have seen the progressive deployment of the 'particular social group' ground in refugee claims made on the basis of gender-related violence, including spousal violence.[228] The application of the definition to domestic violence cases raises squarely the extent to which international laws governing refugee status extend into what has been regarded traditionally as the private domain of familial relationships. As international law is concerned primarily with the relations between nation states, the traditional view was that the Convention definition could be invoked only to protect individuals threatened by 'public' forms of harm either perpetrated by or permitted by the individual's state of usual residence. The changing perceptions of the scope of the Convention definition of refugee in Australia were given tangible expression in 1996 with the issue for the first time in this country of 'Gender Guidelines' for the determination of refugee status.[229]

[13.111] The most significant indication of the conceptual shift that has occurred in relation to these issues, however, is undoubtedly the High Court's decision in *Khawar*, discussed earlier (at Part 13.4.4). The case demonstrates just how sweeping the court is prepared to be in its characterisation of cognisable groups. In that case, a majority held that it was open to the RRT to find that 'women in Pakistan' constituted a particular social group for the purposes of the Convention. Although it was not contested in the Minister's submissions, the majority reiterated that the size of a group's membership was not a barrier to classification as a 'particular social group'.[230] Gleeson CJ observed: 'It is power, not number, that creates the conditions

---

227 (2004) 217 CLR 387 at [27].
228 Among the extensive literature in this area, see Musalo and Knight, above n 220; Andrea Binder, 'Gender and the "Membership in a Particular Social Group" Category of the 1951 Refugee Convention' (2001) 10 *Columbia Journal of Gender and the Law* 167; and, in Australia, Rachael Bacon and Kate Booth, 'The Intersection of Refugee Law and Gender: Private Harm and Public Responsibility' (2000) 23(3) *UNSW Law Journal* 135; Leanne McKay, 'Women Asylum Seekers in Australia: Discrimination and the Migration Legislation Amendment Act [No 6] 2001 (Cth)' (2003) 4 *Melbourne Journal of International Law* 439; and A Widney Brown and Laura Grenfell, 'The International Crime of Gender-Based Persecution and the Taliban' (2003) 4 *Melbourne Journal of International Law* 347.
229 See DIMA, *Guidelines on Gender Issues for Decision Makers*, July 1996, available at <http://cgrs.uchastings.edu/documents/legal/guidelines_aust.pdf>. See also the (5 June 2009) RRT guidelines on Vulnerable Persons at <http://www.mrt-rrt.gov.au/ArticleDocuments/118/GuidanceOnVulnerablePersons.pdf.aspx>. These have replaced the earlier guidelines specific to women, children and other vulnerable groups.
230 Kirby J acknowledged that the size and breadth of groups such as 'women in Pakistan' or even 'married women in Pakistan' have led some to express doubt that this is the kind of 'particular social group' to which the Convention was referring. However, his Honour went on to note that it was open to the tribunal to find that Ms Khawar was a member of a particular social group of a more specific character: (2002) 210 CLR 1 at [128]-[129]. See also *Ward* [1993] 2 SCR 689 at 716-17; *Applicant A* (1997) 190 CLR 225 at 232-3, 257; *Shah* [1999] 2 AC 629 at 639, 651, 656, 658; *Refugee Appeal No 71427/99* (unreported, New Zealand Refugee Status Appeals Authority, 16 August 2000); Hathaway, above n 18, at 163; and Deborah Anker, *Law of Asylum in the United States* (Washington: American Immigration Law Foundation, 3rd ed, 1999) at 377, [129].

in which persecution may occur'.[231] McHugh and Gummow JJ pointed out that 'the inclusion of race, religion and nationality in the Convention definition shows that that of itself can be no objection to the definition of such a class'.[232] Gleeson CJ added that cohesiveness is not an essential element in the category.

[13.112] Although the majority in *Khawar* endorsed McHugh J's statement in *Applicant A* that the persecutory conduct cannot define the 'particular social group', they regarded the criterion as having little bearing on the case. Gleeson CJ stated: 'Women in any society are a distinct and recognisable social group; and their distinctive attributes and characteristics exist independently of the manner in which they are treated, either by males or by governments'.[233] The reasoning of the majority on this issue generally reflects that of the House of Lords in *Islam v Secretary of State for the Home Department*,[234] which also held that women in Pakistan could constitute a particular social group for Convention purposes.

[13.113] Another particularly controversial aspect of spousal violence cases is the issue of state complicity in the persecution feared. In all of the cases in which victims of domestic violence have been granted refugee status the RRT has found that the claimant's home state has been 'unable or unwilling' to provide protection to the claimant. Indeed, the adequacy of state protection is frequently the deciding issue in such cases. The controversial nature of the finding in *Khawar* is soon apparent when one considers how prevalent the problem of domestic violence is throughout the world, including in Australia, and how generally inadequate is the protection afforded to victims by governments.

Homosexuality

[13.114] Another area of incremental development in refugee law has been the status of individuals who face persecution because of their sexual orientation. Although the Convention definition does not list gender or sexual orientation as one of the refugee grounds, in recent years the catch-all ground of 'particular social group' has been used to protect persecuted lesbians and gay men. Like cases involving religious persecution, claims related to sexual orientation and social group often challenge implicit biases in refugee jurisprudence about the appropriateness of distinguishing between public and private behaviours and requiring 'discretion' in claimants' behaviour.

[13.115] Until the High Court's ruling in *S395/2002 v MIMA*,[235] the recognition of lesbians and gay men as members of a particular social group did not necessarily lead to the recognition of their claims for protection.[236] Decision-makers typically required that if a gay man or a lesbian were able to have an affair or relationship discreetly,

---

231   (2002) 210 CLR 1 at [33].
232   Ibid at [82].
233   Ibid at [35]. See also McHugh and Gummow JJ at [82].
234   [1999] 2 AC 629 (Lords Steyn, Hoffman, Hope of Craighead, Hutton; Lord Millett dissenting).
235   (2003) 216 CLR 473 (*S395*).
236   See further Jenni Millbank, 'Imagining Otherness: Refugee Claims on the Basis of Sexuality in Canada and Australia' (2002) 26 *Melbourne University Law Review* 144.

they would not be seen to have a 'well-founded fear of persecution'.[237] For example, in *WABR v MIMA*, the Full Federal Court held that it was open to the RRT to conclude 'that there was no active program for the persecution of homosexuals in Iran, so long as they were discreet and concluded their affairs privately'.[238] The tribunal also found 'that it was reasonable to expect that the appellant would accept the constraints that were a consequence of the exercise of that discretion'.[239] As Dauvergne and Millbank have noted, the rationale for this requirement was expressed by the RRT as 'a reasonable expectation that persons should, to the extent that is possible, co-operate in their own protection'.[240]

[13.116] In *S395*, the High Court reversed this jurisprudence, bringing Australia into line with other refugee-receiving countries. The court acknowledged first that gay men and lesbians will form a particular social group in most societies. A majority of the High Court ruled that the RRT fell into error by ruling that the gay couple could avoid a well-founded fear of persecution by living 'discreetly', in other words by keeping their sexual orientation a secret. In so doing, the High Court considered that the RRT had failed to consider whether the applicants might suffer harm if people in their country of nationality discovered that they were gay. In addition, the RRT had erroneously failed to take into account whether the requirement of non-disclosure of their sexual identity to avoid harm was in fact itself persecutory.[241]

[13.117] In a comprehensive study of published tribunal and judicial decisions determining the refugee claims on the basis of sexuality, Jenni Millbank has discovered that, since the High Court's ruling in *S395*, the rate of acceptance of these claims has not significantly increased.[242] Instead, it seems that while before *S395* such claims were frequently rejected on the grounds that the applicant could avoid persecution by living a 'closeted' life in their country, since 2003 claims are typically rejected on the basis of the applicant's credibility with the decision-maker rejecting outright the claim that the applicant is in fact lesbian or gay. Further, her research uncovers a considerable number of decisions in which the RRT has used rigid, stereotyped and Westernised notions of a 'gay identity' or typical 'coming out story' as the standard against which to assess the applicant's narrative.[243]

---

237   See, for instance, *LSLS v MIMA* [2000] FCA 211. There Ryan J upheld the RRT decision that a gay man from Sri Lanka did not meet definition of refugee on the basis that he could 'avoid a real chance of serious harm simply by refraining from making his sexuality widely known'.
238   (2002) 121 FCR 196 at [27].
239   Ibid.
240   *V95/03527* [1996] RRTA 246, as quoted in Catherine Dauvergne and Jenni Millbank, 'Applicants S396/2002 and S395/2002, A Gay Refugee Couple From Bangladesh' (2003) 25(1) *Sydney Law Review* 97 at 104.
241   (2003) 216 CLR 473 at [55]-[57].
242   Jenni Millbank, 'From Discretion to Disbelief: Recent Trends in Refugee Determinations on the Basis of Sexual Orientation in Australia and the United Kingdom' (2009) 13(2/3) *International Journal of Human Rights* 391.
243   Jenni Millbank, 'The Ring of Truth: A Case Study of Credibility Assessment in Particular Social Group Refugee Determinations' (2009) 21(1) *International Journal of Refugee Law* 1; Laurie Berg and Jenni Millbank, 'Constructing the Personal Narratives of Lesbian, Gay and Bisexual Asylum Claimants' (2009) 22(2) *Journal of Refugee Studies* 195.

Families

[13.118] In recent years, there has been both judicial and academic support for the proposition that a family can constitute a 'particular social group' for the purposes of the Convention.[244] In *Sarrazola (No 2)*,[245] the Federal Court held that a person fearing harm by reason of a family connection could fear persecution for a Convention reason, even if the other family member could not claim to be a refugee. In that case, the applicant's brother was a criminal who had been murdered by his criminal associates, apparently for failure to pay his debts. The criminals had made threats and demands on the applicant to pay her brother's debts. The applicant claimed a well-founded fear of persecution on the ground of 'membership of a particular social group' (being her family). The Full Federal Court held that it was open for the RRT to accept her claim. It rejected the submission that a family can only constitute a 'particular social group' if it is either linked to a broader group identified by one of the Convention grounds or has some degree of celebrity or reputation (and is therefore perceived as unusual in the society of the country of nationality).[246]

[13.119] The government responded to this jurisprudence in 2001 by introducing s 91S of the *Migration Act*. In determining whether a person has a well-founded fear of persecution by reason of membership of a particular social group consisting of family, the decision-maker must now disregard any persecution or fear of persecution that the person or any family member (including deceased family members) has experienced if it is not based on Convention grounds. The effect of this provision is to require decision-makers to focus on the *family members* of an applicant for refugee status so as to ask why the family members might have been subjected to discriminatory behaviour. If the family member was or is being targeted for their criminal behaviour (or their *perceived* criminal behaviour), s 91S operates to disqualify the *applicant* from refugee protection in Australia.[247] The statutory amendment has led to the denial of refugee or other protection to fugitives from a series of countries – among them Colombia and Albania. In some circumstances return has resulted eventually in the assassination of the individual concerned.[248] The largest group of such cases has involved refugee claimants from Albania who have alleged that they are at risk of being killed in accordance with the Albanian Code of Leke Dukagjini, a system whereby wrongful death is avenged by an affected family seeking out and killing a member of the family of the person who killed their relative.[249] In *STCB v MIMIA*,[250] the High Court (with Kirby J in dissent) confirmed that s 91S operates to

---

244 See Dawson J in *Applicant A* (1997) 190 CLR 225 at 241; *Sarrazola (No 2)* (2001) 107 FCR 184; *C v MIEA* (1999) 94 FCR 366; Hathaway, above n 18, at 166; Goodwin-Gill and McAdam, above n 20, at 76.
245 (2001) 107 FCR 184.
246 For other examples of such reasoning, see *SCAL v MIMIA* [2003] FCA 548; *SCAL v MIMIA* [2003] FCAFC 301; and *STYB v MIMIA* [2004] FCA 705.
247 See, for example, *SZLGS v MIAC* [2008] FMCA 253.
248 See, for example, the case of Alvaro Morales, denied protection as a fugitive from paramilitary violence in Colombia. The man was indeed killed upon his return. See Edmund Rice Centre, *Deported to Danger II*, available at <http://www.ajustaustralia.com/resource.php?act=attache&id=290>, at 46.
249 See, for example, *STXB v MIMIA* (2004) 139 FCR 1; and *MIAC v SZCWF* (2007) 161 FCR 441 at [24]-[35].
250 (2006) 231 ALR 556.

deny protection to potential victims of Albania's blood feud code. It should be noted that, even without s 91S, these cases also raise *Applicant A* issues[251] about whether the social group claimed for these people is defined solely by virtue of a shared fear of persecution.[252]

13.6.5 Political opinion

[13.120] To establish a well-founded fear of persecution on the ground of political opinion, an applicant must hold (or be believed to hold) views which are antithetical to those of the government or instrumentalities to which the applicant is subject. This implies in turn that the applicant's views are both critical of those authorities and that the views are not tolerated by the authorities to the point where the applicant could face persecution because of the views.[253] In *V v MIMA*,[254] Wilcox J stated that it is not necessary 'that the person be a member of a political party or other public organisation or that the person's opposition to the instruments of government be a matter of public knowledge'. However, he acknowledged that a higher political profile will make it easier for the applicant to convince the tribunal of persecution on that ground. The Federal Court has recognised also that a claimant's resistance to government criminality or systemic corruption can have a political dimension, bringing the claimant within the category of 'political opinion'.[255] This accords with Hathaway's conclusion that '[e]ssentially any action which is perceived to be a challenge to governmental authority' can be appropriately considered to be the expression of political opinion.[256]

[13.121] The issue of imputed political opinion has been addressed by the RRT and by the courts in a number of cases. The claims range from cases of conscientious objectors to persons caught up in some way with the workings of politically dissident groups. The High Court has confirmed that, for the purposes of this Convention ground, the political opinion need not be actually held by the refugee. It is sufficient that such an opinion is imputed to him or her by the persecutor.[257] In *Chan*,[258] Gaudron J stated that 'persecution may as equally be constituted by the infliction of harm on the basis of perceived political belief as of actual belief'. As Gummow J noted in *Akyaa v MIMA*,[259] falsely imputed political opinion may lead to well-founded fear of persecution 'for reasons of political opinion', even though that opinion is in truth not held.

---

251   See, for example, the comments of McHugh J at *Applicant A* (1997) 190 CLR 225 at 257.
252   See, for example, *SCAL v MIMIA* [2003] FCAFC 301; and *STXB v MIMIA* (2004) 139 FCR 1 at [37].
253   See generally UNHCR, above n 76, at [80]-[86]. See also *MIMA v Y* [1998] FCA 515; and *Voitenko v MIMA* (1998) 92 FCR 355.
254   (1999) 92 FCR 355 at [16].
255   See Hathaway, above n 18, at 154. See also *Ramirez v MIMA* (2000) 176 ALR 514.
256   See Hathaway, above n 18, cited in *V v MIMA* (1999) 92 FCR 355 at [14] (Wilcox J) and at [33] (Hill J). See also *Rajanayake v MIMA* [2001] FCA 352.
257   See *Guo* (1997) 191 CLR 559; and *NACM of 2002 v MIMIA* (2003) 134 FCR 550.
258   (1989) 169 CLR 379 at 416.
259   *Akyaa v MIEA* [1987] FCA 137.

[13.122] An applicant for refugee status may succeed in her or his claim where the very act of seeking refugee status abroad may lead to their having a political opinion imputed to them by the authorities. One such example occurred in *V97/06531*,[260] where the applicant was a Shi'a Muslim who feared returning to Iraq. The RRT found that the applicant had such a profile that he would attract attention if he returned to Iraq. It accepted that persons leaving Iraq and applying for refugee status overseas had an anti-government political opinion imputed to them by the authorities. In *V97/06042*,[261] a decision which also concerned an Iraqi national, the RRT noted the extensive surveillance system operated by Iraqi intelligence. It accepted that the authorities would be aware of both the applicant's presence in Australia, and his application for refugee status. These two factors created a real chance that the applicant would be regarded as hostile to the regime in Iraq which would place him at risk of detention and torture. The tribunal concluded that the applicant had a well-founded fear of persecution due to the political opinion imputed to him by the Iraqi authorities.

[13.123] The requirement of public manifestation of the claimant's identity as a dissentient is a common theme in these decisions.[262] Dissidence in this context can include whistleblowing activities, where an applicant has exposed corruption in government. A tension arises here because the Convention definition refers to 'political opinion', not to 'political activities'. As Hathaway notes, this means that in principle an opinion need not be expressed at all.[263] In practice, however, analysis tends to focus on how the alleged persecutor came to form the view of the applicant's alleged political opinion. As a result, this ground has tended to favour the grant of protection to persons who engage in activities that are openly and publicly in defiance of the state or other persecutory authorities from whom the state is unable or unwilling to offer protection. Bibler Coutin has analysed a similar trend in American jurisprudence requiring applicants to explain how and why their actions had placed them at risk.[264] She has concluded that asylum seekers in the US were effectively required to prove that they were individually targeted because of being somehow 'different' from the population at large. This is so even when the persecution has obscured the motivations for targeting particular individuals. Others have shown the ways in which the requirement of a public expression of political opinion has a differential impact on women. Too often the model of agency relied on by decision-makers is highly gendered.[265]

[13.124] The treatment of the claims at the heart of *Applicant A* is an Australian example in point. In the High Court, Kirby J was the only judge to find that the couple's actions in opposition to the PRC one-child policy could constitute the

---

260 [1997] RRTA 2775. See also *MZXQS v MIAC* (2009) 107 ALD 33; *Htun v MIMA* (2001) 194 ALR 244.
261 [1997] RRTA 2528.
262 See *Guo* (1997) 191 CLR 559.
263 Hathaway, above n 18, at 149.
264 Susan Bibler Coutin, 'The Oppressed, the Suspect and the Citizen: Subjectivity in Competing Accounts of Political Violence' (2001) 26 *Law and Social Inquiry* 63.
265 See, for example, Ninette Kelley, 'The Convention Refugee Definition and Gender-Based Persecution: A Decade's Progress' (2001) 13 *International Journal of Refugee Law* 559; Heaven Crawley, 'Gender, Persecution and the Concept of Politics in the Asylum Determination Process' (2000) 9 *Forced Migration Review* 17; Crock, above n 25; UNHCR, above n 76.

expression of (imputed) political opinion.[266] McHugh J accepted that opposition to the PRC one-child policy could be a ground for refugee status, but only if the claimants participated in public demonstrations or in a political campaign agitating for the abolition of the policy.[267] His comments suggest that one of the reasons why the couple in *Applicant A* could not be considered refugees was that their opposition to the one-child policy was not given public expression. The couple merely conceived a child and then took (private) evasive action to avoid the enforcement of the policy that would have denied them further children.

---

266   *Applicant A* (1997) 190 CLR 225 at 310.
267   Ibid at 269.

14

The Extent of Australia's Protection Obligations

[14.01]   The most important obligation Australia has assumed as signatory to the UN Convention relating to Refugees and its attendant Protocol is the obligation not to refoule, or send back, a refugee (as defined) to a country where the refugee would face persecution on one of the five Convention grounds.[1] Although vigorous arguments have been made about the extent of a state's duty to admit refugees,[2] the non-refoulement requirement operates to some extent to override the niceties of state sovereignty in situations where the territorial options for Convention refugees are truly limited. Just as importantly, there are other human rights conventions that echo and extend the Convention prohibition on *refoulement* beyond refugees.

[14.02]   In this chapter we explore the nature and extent of obligations Australia has assumed to offer protection to non-citizens who find themselves on Australian territory and in situations of need. Touching upon an extensive body of law, policy and practice, the chapter looks first at qualifications that apply to the protection of Convention refugees. We begin in Part 14.1 with the rights of refugees who travel beyond the country in which they might have initially sought refuge. We examine in turn the notion of safe countries of origin and three aspects of 'protection elsewhere' doctrines: internal relocation within a persecutory state, safe third countries and effective nationality. Part 14.2 outlines the law governing the cessation of refugee status, an area of acute sensitivity for refugees granted Temporary Protection visas in the days of the conservative Coalition government (especially between 1999 and 2007). Part 14.3 examines the exclusion from refugee protection of non-citizens convicted of certain serious crimes. In Part 14.4 we outline a scheme slated for introduction in 2011 for the protection of persons to whom obligations are owed under international human rights conventions. The chapter concludes in Part 14.5 with a brief overview of measures introduced to protect victims of human trafficking.

---

1   See Art 33 of the Refugee Convention (adopted 28 July 1951, entered into force 22 April 1954) 189 UNTS 137.
2   On this point, see the discussion at Chapter 4.3.

14.1 The politics of protection elsewhere: Qualifications on the rights of refugees

[14.03] The Refugee Convention (as amended by the Protocol relating to the Status of Refugees) is primarily a human rights instrument. In spite of the efforts of eminent academics to articulate and promote the rights there enshrined,[3] however, there are features of the Convention that undermine its effectiveness in offering protection to the world's refugees. The first problem is that the Convention sits outside of the general human rights treaty framework. Devised by and for the states that are party to it, the administration of the Refugee Convention is funded by its members rather than by way of grant from the UN General Assembly. Where other human rights conventions establish independent committees to oversee their operation – which in turn are answerable to the General Assembly – the Refugee Convention has no independent or expert oversight body. Instead, the state parties meet every October in Geneva at a specially convened conference of the 'Executive Committee of UNHCR' which issues 'Conclusions' about how the Convention should be interpreted. While these conclusions have similar 'soft law' status as opinions issued by the treaty bodies established under the various human rights treaty bodies, it is relatively rare to see the conclusions cited as authoritative legal sources. If the Refugee Convention was born in an era of acute political tension, these arrangements mean that it has continued to this day to be among the most highly politicised of all of the UN human rights conventions.

[14.04] The second (related) problem with the Refugee Convention is that it was never designed to meet the protection needs of all persons displaced from their homes and in need of protection. The inherent limitations in the Convention's protective scheme have been acknowledged on many occasions by the Australian courts.[4] The combination of a scheme steeped in political compromise and the absence of any central authority governing its implementation has not always worked in the interests of the world's refugees. States like Australia have enjoyed considerable latitude in their interpretation of the Convention. Although privately critical of actions that have been taken, UNHCR has often found itself practically powerless to prevent countries from adopting increasingly restrictive measures which they assert to be consistent with the terms of the Convention.

[14.05] Two examples serve to illustrate this point, both involving the interpretation of Art 31 of the Refugee Convention. The first is the interdiction and deflection of so-called 'secondary movement' refugees; the second, the grant to Convention refugees of 'temporary protection' rather than permanent residence.

[14.06] Article 31 of the Refugee Convention provides that states shall not impose penalties on refugees 'coming directly from a territory where their life or freedom was threatened' for their 'illegal entry or presence', provided that the refugees 'present themselves without delay and show good cause for their illegal entry or

---

3   See James C Hathaway, *The Rights of Refugees under International Law* (Cambridge: Cambridge University Press, 2005); and Michelle Foster, *International Refugee Law and Socio-Economic Rights* (Cambridge: Cambridge University Press, 2007).
4   See Chapter 12 above; and, for example, Gummow J in *MIMA v Ibrahim* (2000) 204 CLR 1 at [137].

presence'. UNHCR and academic commentators have encouraged states to read this 'no penalty' provision generously so as to acknowledge the reality that refugees are often forced to flee in circumstances where they are unable to observe the technicalities of immigration regulations.[5] In spite of the reference to the refugee 'coming directly' from a situation of persecution, the drafters of the Convention were cognizant of the fact that refugees often transit through more than one country in their quest for safe haven.[6]

[14.07] In establishing its 'Pacific strategy' (which endured in a modified form after the change of government in 2007), Australia asserted that Art 31 did not apply to persons dubbed 'secondary movement' refugees. The basis for the claim was that many of those interdicted en route to the country were coming from out of the region – transiting through many countries before seeking asylum in Australia. The Refugee Convention, it was asserted, was never intended as an instrument that permits refugees to achieve an 'immigration outcome' by selecting the country in which they wish to be resettled. In the alternative, Australia argued that if Art 31 did apply, the mechanisms devised for assessing the refugee claims of asylum seekers offshore did not amount to a penalty under Art 31. Nor did the grant to asylum seekers of Temporary Protection visas in place of permanent residence (which was reserved for asylum seekers who entered Australia on valid visas) constitute a penalty.[7] However unhappy with the arrangements, UNHCR was effectively made complicit in the Australian model when it was called upon to first assist with the offshore processing on Nauru and Papua New Guinea and then to undertake status determinations in Indonesia.

14.1.1 The declaration of 'safe' countries of origin

[14.08] There are other ways too in which the protection afforded under international refugee law is regularly compromised. Depending on the choices made by the government of a refugee receiving country, status determination in practice can be a highly politicised process. At its most extreme, governments have declared certain countries to be 'safe', precluding anyone coming from that country from making an asylum claim. In Australia, one of the first examples of such a measure was a product of a Memorandum of Understanding (MOU) made with the Peoples' Republic of China (PRC) in 1993. The scheme covered persons who had fled Vietnam after the war in that country and sought refuge (or been resettled) in one of several countries in the region under what became known as the 'Comprehensive Plan of Action' (CPA).[8] The objective was to block refugee applications from persons who came to Australia from UNHCR-controlled camps in Indonesia and Malaysia who were included in the CPA. It also declared the PRC a 'safe third country' with respect to Sino-Vietnamese asylum seekers who had once been under the mandate of the

---

5 Guy Goodwin-Gill and Jane McAdam, *The Refugee in International Law* (New York: Oxford University Press, 3rd ed, 2007) at 264ff.
6 Ibid at 264-5 (notes 368-9).
7 DIMIA, *Australia's Contribution to the Interpretation of the Refugees Convention*, 2001, available at <http://www.immi.gov.au/media/publications/refugee/convention2002/>.
8 Done at Geneva by the International Conference on Indo-Chinese Refugees, 13-14 June 1989.

UNHCR.[9] The agreement with the PRC was justified on the basis that the asylum seekers in question had either been resettled in the PRC as refugees (and so in leaving that country were deemed to be seeking a better life rather than refugee protection) or they had had refugee claims denied under the CPA processes. The MOU was undertaken with the approval of UNHCR which had overseen both the CPA status determinations throughout South East Asia and the resettlement of the Sino-Vietnamese in the PRC after the Vietnam War. The MOU was highly effective in stopping the flow of boats carrying asylum seekers from the PRC to Australia in and after 1994.[10]

[14.09] Although less confronting than direct exclusionary devices such as this, the politics of refugee protection also intrudes in more subtle ways into status determination procedures. State officials hearing the claims both at first instance and on appeal often rely heavily on the assessments made by their government of conditions within the country from which an asylum seeker has fled. Inquiries into Australia's refugee and humanitarian programs have often seen refugee advocates complain about decision-makers relying on sanitised and often inaccurate 'country information' provided by Australian government sources.[11] Evidence before a Senate inquiry in 2000 described certain country information provided by the Australian government as views 'from the cocktail bar of the Teheran Hilton'.[12] The strength of political influences on decision-makers was apparent when Australian officials began rejecting asylum seekers from Afghanistan in late 2001 following early reports that the coalition bombing offensive had defeated the Taliban. In virtually no other asylum-receiving country was Afghanistan assessed so promptly as being 'safe' for returning refugees.

14.1.2 Internal relocation

[14.10] The Refugee Convention defines a refugee in Art 1(2) as one who is *unable* or, owing to her or his *well-founded fear of persecution*, is *unwilling* to avail herself or himself of the protection of her or his country of nationality. The protection offered

---

9   See ss 91F-91G of the *Migration Act 1958* (Cth) and *Migration Regulations 1994* (Cth), regs 2.12A-2.12B.
10 This is not to say, however, that it occurred without the *refoulement* of some genuine Convention refugees. The record of outcomes for status determinations before and after the statutory change is stark. A boat arriving on 4 June 1994 carrying 51 Sino-Vietnamese asylum seekers resulted in the grant of 51 Protection visas. Similar results were recorded in respect of 17 Vietnamese from the CPA camp at Galang in Indonesia who arrived on 17 July 1994: all were granted Protection visas as Convention refugees. In contrast, a boat arriving on 9 September 1994 with 31 Vietnamese asylum seekers saw one escape and the balance removed from the country. With the exception of the odd escapee, the vast majority of subsequent arrivals in 1994 and 1995 were recorded as having been removed. See DIMA, *Fact Sheet No 74a*, 31 July 2004, available at <http://sievx.com/articles/psdp/DIMIA74a_boatarrivals.pdf>.
11 See Savitri Taylor, 'Australia's Interpretation of Some Elements of Article 1A(2) of the Refugee Convention' (1994) 16 *Sydney Law Review* 32 at 70; Jenni Millbank, 'Imagining Otherness: Refugee Claims on the Basis of Sexuality in Canada and Australia' (2002) 26 *Melbourne University Law Review* 144; and Catherine Dauvergne and Jenni Millbank, 'Burdened by Proof: How the Australian Refugee Review Tribunal has Failed Lesbian and Gay Asylum Seekers' (2003) 31 *Federal Law Review* 299.
12 See Senate Legal and Constitutional References Committee, *A Sanctuary Under Review: An Examination of Australia's Refugee and Humanitarian Determination Processes* (Canberra: 2000) (*A Sanctuary Under Review*) at 132, n 100.

under the Refugee Convention, in this sense, is 'surrogate or substitute protection', activated only on failure of national protection.[13] Accordingly, one of the first tasks in determining an application for refugee status is to evaluate the extent of the 'protection' available from the country of nationality.[14] Connected to this is the principle that a grant of asylum may be denied to applicants who might find protection by relocating to a different part of their state of origin.

[14.11] The internal relocation principle allows a contracting state to reject a claim for refugee status if, in all of the circumstances of the case, it would be reasonable to expect the claimant to return to another part of their country of nationality.[15] The logic of the principle is explained by Hathaway[16] as flowing from the absence of a need for asylum abroad. He explains that the Refugee Convention should be restricted in its application to persons who can *genuinely access* domestic protection from persecution, and for whom the reality of protection is *meaningful*.

[14.12] There has been some debate as to the textual basis for this limitation. As the High Court has acknowledged, neither the Refugee Convention nor Australian domestic law refers specifically to any 'relocation principle'.[17] Nevertheless, the dominant view is that this principle is to be inferred from the 'more generally stated provisions of the definition' of refugee.[18] According to Black CJ in *Randhawa v MILGEA*:[19]

> The focus of the Convention definition is not upon the protection that the country of nationality might be able to provide in some particular region, but upon a more general notion of protection by that country. If it were otherwise, the anomalous situation would exist that the international community would be under an obligation to provide protection outside the borders of the country of nationality even though real protection could be found within those borders.

[14.13] The Australian jurisprudence on this principle parts company with the Hathaway formulation on which it is based, which stresses the importance of the refugee's non-access to *domestic* protection. In *MIMA v Khawar*,[20] McHugh and Gummow JJ set as the relevant test the ability of a refugee to avail himself or herself of the *external* protection of a country:

> The definition of 'refugee' is couched in the present tense and the text indicates that the position of the putative refugee is to be considered on the footing that that person is *outside* the country of nationality. The reference then made in the text to 'protection' is to 'external' protection by the country of nationality, for example

---

13   See James C Hathaway, *The Law of Refugee Status* (Toronto: Butterworths, 1991) at 135.
14   This was emphasised by the Supreme Court of Canada in *Attorney-General of Canada v Ward* (1993) 103 DLR (4th) 1 at 12.
15   *R v Secretary of State for the Home Office; Ex parte Gunes* [1991] Imm AR 278 at 282.
16   Hathaway, above n 13, at 134. See also James Hathaway and Michelle Foster, 'Internal Protection/Relocation/Flight Alternative as an Aspect of Refugee Status Determination' in Erika Feller, Volker Türk and Frances Nicholson (eds), *Refugee Protection in International Law: UNHCR's Global Consultations on International Protection* (Cambridge: Cambridge University Press, 2003) at 357-417.
17   *SZATV v MIAC* (2007) 233 CLR 18 (*SZATV*) at [11]-[12] and [48].
18   Ibid at [11].
19   (1994) 52 FCR 437 at 440-1.
20   (2002) 210 CLR 1 (*Khawar*) at [62].

by the provision of diplomatic or consular protection, and not to the provision of 'internal' protection provided inside the country of nationality from which the refugee has departed. (emphasis in original)

[14.14] The Australian jurisprudence takes a rather broad-brush approach to explaining the legal basis for the relocation principle, at the same time noting that the principle has been adopted in the United States,[21] in Europe[22] and in England.[23] The principle has also been recognised implicitly in the successive editions of the UNHCR Handbook,[24] as well as in guidelines issued by this authority.[25]

[14.15] Although the majority's interpretation in *Khawar* of 'protection' as implying 'external' protection could lead to a narrowing of the definition in practice, this is not how the jurisprudence has played out in the cases litigated. Instead, the issue of a refugee's ability to subsist within any part of the country from which the refugee has fled is central to the eventual ruling made.[26] Subsistence in this sense is predicated on the domestic protection available from the state.

[14.16] In deciding the fate of an asylum seeker, the High Court and Full Federal Court have confirmed that a decision-maker must ask not simply whether the applicant could relocate to another area of the country of nationality, but whether the refugee claimant could reasonably be expected to relocate to such an area.[27] The practical realities facing a person who claims to be a refugee must be considered carefully. This includes any physical or financial barriers preventing an applicant from reaching safety within the country of nationality and whether internal safety is otherwise illusory or unpredictable.[28] Questions of reasonableness will also involve consideration of the quality of internal protection and whether there has been a failure to meet basic norms of civil, political and socio-economic human rights.[29] In *SZATV v MIAC*,[30] Kirby J called for extreme caution in making this assessment:

> In the nature of things, country information available to refugee adjudicators is often expressed at a high level of generality. It may not extend in sufficient detail to establish, in a convincing way, the differential safety of other ... regions of the

---

21 See US Code of Federal Regulations, § 208.13, 'Establishing asylum eligibility', cited at *SZATV* (2007) 233 CLR 18 at [13].
22 See European Union Directive of 29 April 2004 at Art 8, cited at *SZATV* (2007) 233 CLR 18 at [14].
23 See *Januzi v Secretary of State for the Home Department* [2006] 2 AC 426 at 440.
24 Office of the UNHCR, *Handbook on Procedures and Criteria for Determining Refugee Status* (Geneva: 1979, reedited 1992) (UNHCR Handbook) at [91].
25 See UNHCR, 'Guidelines on International Protection No 4: "Internal Flight or Relocation Alternative" Within the Context of Article 1A(2) of the 1951 Convention and/or 1967 Protocol relating to the Status of Refugees', HCR/GIP/03/04, 23 July 2003 (UNHCR Relocation Guidelines).
26 *SZATV* (2007) 233 CLR 18; and *SZAJB v MIAC* (2008) 168 FCR 410.
27 *SZMCD v MIAC* (2009) 174 FCR 415. See also *SZATV* (2007) 233 CLR 18 at [32] (Gummow, Hayne and Crennan JJ, with whom Callinan J agreed) and at [95]-[104] (Kirby J).
28 See *Randhawa v MILGEA* (1994) 52 FCR 437 at 442-3; and *R v Immigration Appeal Tribunal; Ex parte Jonah* [1985] Imm AR 7.
29 On this point, see *SZATV* (2007) 233 CLR 18 at [28] (joint judgment) and [87]-[90] (Kirby J). See also *S395/2002 v MIMA* (2003) 216 CLR 473; and the modification of the principle in *NALZ v MIMIA* (2004) 140 FCR 270. The High Court's formulation in *SZATV* has been followed in subsequent cases. See, for example, *SZNIM v MIAC* [2009] FMCA 790.
30 (2007) 233 CLR 18 at [82] (Kirby J).

one country … [W]here otherwise a relevant 'fear' is shown, considerable care will need to be observed in concluding that the internal relocation option is a reasonable one when, by definition, the applicant has not taken advantage of its manifest convenience and arguable attractions.

[14.17] In deciding whether it is reasonable to require an asylum seeker to relocate within a country, consideration needs to be given to issues such as whether the persecutor is the state itself, in which case relocation is less likely to deliver effective protection and/or whether the source of the persecution feared was localised.[31] Where the persecutor is a non-state actor, care needs to be taken to consider the totality of the situation in the country, including the potential that a person be pursued into apparently 'safe' areas.[32] The Federal Court in some cases has made it clear that an asylum seeker's preference not to relocate where this is an option will not make that person a refugee[33] nor will a fear to relocate that is not well-founded. However, the High Court has fallen short of *requiring* an asylum seeker to act reasonably by relocating. The test rather is to ask whether a person, acting reasonably, would relocate, bearing in mind the person's identity and all the circumstances of the case including issues such as human rights standards.[34] Across the many cases in which relocation has been considered by the courts, the central question is always whether the applicant meets the definition of refugee within a given geographical area or areas.[35]

14.1.3 Safe third countries and effective nationality

[14.18] In practice, receiving states have moved to exclude refugees who have access to other protection on three bases. The first is where a claimant is a national of more than one state, at least one of whom is able to offer protection from persecution under Art 1A(2). Second, Art 1E of the Refugee Convention provides that:

> [T]he Convention shall not apply to a person who is recognised by the competent authorities of the country in which he has taken residence as having the rights and obligations which are attached to the possession of the nationality of that country.

In practice, the first two of these exclusionary principles often merge or become intertwined so that issues of multiple nationality involve also discussions of whether the nationality or protection offered by the third state is effective. Third, a broader principle appears to have developed at international law whereby a receiving state can avoid its protection obligations in a situation where the refugee can gain or has gained the protection of a third country.[36]

---

31 For a discussion of these issues see *MIMA v Jang* (2000) 175 ALR 752; and *NABM of 2001 v MIMIA* (2002) 124 FCR 375.
32 See *Perampalam v MIMA* (1999) 84 FCR 274.
33 See *Abdi v MIMA* (2000) 61 ALD 101; and *Singh v MIMA* [2000] FCA 1858.
34 See *S395/2002 v MIMA* (2003) 216 CLR 473; *Hehar v MIMA* (1997) 48 ALD 620; *Montes- Granados v MIMA* [2000] FCA 60; *NAIZ v MIMIA* [2005] FCAFC 37; and *SYLB v MIMIA* (2005) 87 ALD 498.
35 For a discussion of the 'chicken and egg' debates about whether relocation must be considered before or after determining an asylum claim, see Legal Services, Refugee Review Tribunal, *A Guide to Refugee Law in Australia* (Sydney: RRT, 2010) Ch 6 at 12-13, available at <http://www.mrt-rrt.gov.au/Conduct-of-reviews/Guide-to-Refugee-Law-in-Australia/default.aspx>.
36 For a discussion of this area of refugee law in Australia, see Savitri Taylor 'Protection Elsewhere/Nowhere' (2006) 18 *International Journal of Refugee Law* 283; Andrea Hadaway, 'Safe Third Countries

[14.19] In Australia, these principles are qualified by the terms of s 36 of the *Migration Act 1958* (Cth) as it was amended first in 1999.[37] Section 36(2)(a) establishes the concept of the person to whom Australia 'owes protection obligations' under the Refugee Convention and Protocol. Section 36(3)-(5) qualifies this statement by deeming Australia not to owe protection obligations to non-citizens who have 'not taken all possible steps' to avail themselves of a right to enter any country apart from Australia. The exclusion is said to apply where a person has any form of right to reside in the other country – whether on a temporary or permanent basis. Exceptions are where a person fears persecution for a Convention reason in that country (s 36(4)), or where that country may return the person to a country where persecution is feared for a Convention reason (s 36(5)). Before turning to the interpretation of s 36, we review briefly some of the cases in which the Australian courts have considered the notion of 'effective protection' for refugees.

Dual nationality

[14.20] The availability of alternative protection for people with multiple nationalities first arose in the context of asylum claims by East Timorese made during the final years of Indonesian rule in that country. While Australia traditionally regarded East Timorese as nationals of Indonesia, in the late 1990s the government asserted that East Timorese were also to be regarded as Portuguese nationals. Evidence was cited that Portugal (as the former administering power of East Timor) had offered protection in Portugal as an *option* for East Timorese. The Full Federal Court in *Jong Kim Koe v MIMA*[38] held that, while East Timorese may have been Portuguese nationals as a matter of Portuguese law, the Refugee Review Tribunal (RRT) was required to reconsider whether Portuguese nationality was in fact available to and effective for these people. The court noted the ambiguity of Portugal's offer which fell short in practice of assimilating the East Timorese into the Portuguese nation.

[14.21] An asylum seeker's entitlement to nationality is often critical in instances of civil war where a state literally disintegrates. For example, the break-up of the former Yugoslavia saw the dislocation of persons from a variety of ethnic backgrounds. Many faced persecution because of their ethnicity and/or religion. The inability to call on a state of nationality for protection was central to the success or failure of their refugee claims in Australia. In a case before the Full Federal Court, an ethnic Albanian from Serbia was found to be able to enter and reside in Albania and face no risk of *refoulement* to Serbia.[39]

[14.22] There is some debate in the literature about the nature and extent of 'effective nationality' in these situations. One line of argument has it that Art 1E requires that the asylum seeker should have the right of entry and freedom from removal in the alternative state, rather than an entitlement to the full range of rights incidental

---

in Australian Refugee Law: *NAGV v Minister for Immigration and Multicultural Affairs*' (2005) 27 *Sydney Law Review* 727.
37   See *Border Protection Legislation Amendment Act 1999* (Cth), s 3 and Sch 1, cl 65.
38   (1997) 74 FCR 508.
39   *Kola v MIMIA* (2002) 120 FCR 170. Compare *N93/01995* [1994] RRTA 1702.

to citizenship.⁴⁰ On the other hand, Federal Court jurisprudence has held that, in excluding an asylum seeker on the basis of their dual nationality, the country of second nationality must be found to provide 'all of the protection and rights to which a national is entitled', over and above mere protection from persecution.⁴¹ At the same time, it appears not to be necessary that the third state be party to the Refugee Convention.⁴² As noted earlier, this case law must now be read in the light of the amendments to s 36 of the *Migration Act*.

Safe third country

[14.23] Until 2005, judicial authority favoured an expansive reading of the safe third country principle, with less attention paid to the notion of effective nationality contained in Art 1E of the Refugee Convention. This jurisprudence supported the view that Australia was not obliged to protect applicants who had 'effective protection' in a foreign country. The jurisprudence began with *MIMA v Thiyagarajah*, which involved an application by a Sri Lankan Tamil.⁴³ The RRT found that the applicant was excluded from Convention protection in Australia because he had previously been granted refugee status in France. It found that the applicant did not have rights equivalent to nationals in France (for example, he was not entitled to enter the French public service, or enter certain professions). However, the tribunal ruled that such disabilities were not inconsistent with the status of a permanent resident or a status that generally included the rights and obligations of nationals.

[14.24] In setting aside the decision of the tribunal, Emmett J found that the applicant was not recognised by the authorities in France as having the rights and obligations attaching to French nationality. He held that Art 1E of the Refugee Convention was excluded in circumstances where the applicant was restricted from access to any of the rights held by nationals other than actual citizenship. His Honour held that some disabilities suffered by a non-citizen may be so slight as to be insufficient to exclude the operation of Art 1E. However, in the circumstances of the case before him, Emmett J was of the opinion that the disabilities suffered by the applicant in France were not minimal or insignificant.

[14.25] The Full Federal Court rejected both the approach taken by Emmett J and the conclusions reached by him on the facts. The court based its view on a reading of Art 33(1) of the Refugee Convention which prohibits the refoulement of a refugee to the 'territory or frontiers of the territory' of a country where a refugee has a well-founded fear of persecution for a Convention reason. The Full Court reasoned that, Art 1E aside, the term 'territories' in Art 33(1) refers not just to the applicant's country of nationality but to territories more broadly.⁴⁴ Where an applicant has been granted refugee status in a third country, refoulement to this territory will not be prohibited under Art 33(1) as long as protection in that country is determined to be effective. The

---

40   Goodwin-Gill and McAdam, above n 5, at 162. On this point, see also *Barzideh v MIEA* (1996) 69 FCR 417; and *Nagalingam v MILGEA* (1992) 38 FCR 191 at 200-1.
41   *Lay Kon Tji v MIEA* (1998) 158 ALR 681 at 691.
42   *Patto v MIMA* (2000) 106 FCR 119; *MIMA v Al-Sallal* (1999) 94 FCR 549.
43   (1997) 80 FCR 543.
44   Ibid at 557-8.

applicant must not have asserted a well-founded fear of persecution on Convention grounds in respect of that country.[45] Because the Full Court focused on the existence or otherwise of effective protection from the third country (France), there was no need to explore whether the applicant had rights equivalent to those of a French national.[46]

[14.26] One year later, the Full Federal Court broadened this interpretation of Art 33(1) to deny an applicant protection in Australia not only where the applicant is recognised as a refugee in a foreign country but also where the applicant is entitled to permanent residence elsewhere.[47] The principle of 'effective protection' was then expanded to encompass an applicant with a temporary right to re-enter a country of former residence, as long as the applicant could claim asylum there.[48] In *Tharmalingam v MIMA*,[49] the Federal Court confirmed that the doctrine requires an applicant to have a right to enter, reside in and re-enter the third country. In *Al-Zafiry v MIMA*,[50] the court ruled that this 'right' did not have to be 'legally enforceable'. Effective protection meant that 'as a matter of practical reality and fact, the applicant is likely to be given effective protection by being permitted to enter and to live in a third country'.

[14.27] In 2005, the High Court overturned this line of authority and held that Australia's protection obligations (under the law applicable in that case) extended to any person in Australia satisfying the definition of refugee. *NAGV and NAGW v MIMIA*[51] concerned a Jewish father and non-Jewish son from Russia who claimed that they faced persecution because of the father's political opinions and religion. The RRT relied on *MIMA v Thiyagarajah*[52] to hold that the applicants had a right of entry and protection in Israel under the Israeli Law of Return. This operates to empower any Jew and their non-Jewish spouse, child or grandchild, to enter, reside and seek citizenship in Israel. The RRT and Stone J on review found that this amounted to effective protection elsewhere. The finding precluded the applicants' claim for a Protection visa in Australia, notwithstanding that the applicant had had no prior contact with Israel.[53]

[14.28] On appeal, the High Court agreed with the Full Federal Court that the relevant issue was not Australia's international obligations under the Convention in general, but rather what protection obligations are owed to the applicants to engage s 36(2) of the *Migration Act*.[54] In other words, Australia might owe protection

---

45 Ibid at 562 (von Doussa J).
46 The High Court upheld an appeal on the basis that the matter should not be remitted to the RRT for reconsideration. The High Court did not, however, disturb any of the principles set down by the Full Federal Court on the question of effective nationality: *MIMA v Thiyagarajah* (2000) 199 CLR 343.
47 *Rajendran v MIMA* (1998) 86 FCR 526 at 529-30.
48 *MIMA v Gnanapiragasam* (1998) 88 FCR 1.
49 [1999] FCA 1180 at [12].
50 [1999] FCA 443 at [26]. See also *NAFG v MIMIA* (2003) 131 FCR 57.
51 (2005) 222 CLR 161 (*NAGV*).
52 (2000) 199 CLR 343 (*Thiyagarajah*).
53 *NAGV of 2002 v MIMIA* [2002] FCA 1456.
54 *NAGV* (2005) 222 CLR 161 at [26] (Gleeson CJ, McHugh, Gummow, Hayne, Callinan and Heydon JJ).

obligations to the applicants under the Refugee Convention sufficient to trigger the grant of a Protection visa under s 36(2), even if Australia would not be in breach of its *international* legal obligations by sending the applicants to Israel. Concurring with the majority view but in a separate judgment, Kirby J described the reasoning flowing from *Thiyagarajah* as a 'process of implication inimical to the Convention's objectives, terms and practical operation'.[55]

[14.29] In effect, *NAGV* decoupled the doctrine of 'effective protection' in a 'safe third country' from the decision-maker's task of determining whether Australia owes protection obligations to an asylum seeker under Art 1A(2) of the Refugee Convention. The High Court observed that it would be open to parliament to expressly qualify the operation of the Convention definition under the *Migration Act*. This is exactly what happened with the amendments to s 36 of that Act in 1999. The express purpose was to discourage 'forum shopping' by applicants 'choos[ing] Australia as a preferred place of asylum'.[56]

14.1.4 Protection obligations under s 36(3) of the *Migration Act* and the 'seven-day' rule

[14.30] Section 36(3)-(5) is in fact only one of a series of amendments made to the *Migration Act* in 1999 and 2001 with the purpose of ensuring that refugees seek asylum elsewhere whenever this is humanly possible. Clauses limiting Australia's obligations to protect anyone who had spent seven days in a country other than Australia where they could have sought protection were inserted into the regulatory scheme for all of the offshore and onshore refugee and humanitarian visa categories.[57] How these provisions were interpreted by the courts is interesting. Even before some of the more extreme of these measures were quietly removed in August 2008 there appears to have been some acknowledgment that the measures were more of a political gesture than a practical constraint on asylum seekers. Once on Australian territory the capacity of the Australian government to remove asylum seekers to any country other than the country in which they faced persecution is often negligible.

14.1.5 A right to enter and reside

[14.31] The starting point for all cases involving protection elsewhere is determining whether a person has a right to enter or reside in a 'third' country. Where a person has more than one nationality,[58] ss 91N-91Q operate to block applications for a Protection visa without the express permission of the Minister for Immigration. In all other cases, the exclusionary provisions will only operate where a person

---

55 Ibid at [93].
56 Supplementary Explanatory Memorandum to the *Border Protection Legislation Amendment Bill 1999* (Cth). See Michelle Foster, 'Protection Elsewhere: The Legal Implications of Requiring Refugees to Seek Protection in Another State' (2007) 28 *Michigan Journal of International Law* 223 at 226.
57 See, for example, *Migration Regulations*, Sch 2, cl 200.212 and cl 866.215, both repealed by SLI 168 of 2008, reg 3 and Sch 1 [18]. All of the changes were introduced by the *Migration Amendment (Excision from Migration Zone) (Consequential Provisions) Act 2001* (Cth).
58 Or has resided for more than seven days in a country in respect of which the Minister has made a declaration under s 91N(3).

has entitlements that extend beyond a right to *enter* another country. In *WAGH v MIMIA*,[59] Hill J noted that the word 'reside' must be given its ordinary meaning. The Full Federal Court in that case allowed an appeal by applicants who were citizens of Colombia but who also held business and tourist visas for the United States. Lee J found that s 36(3) is triggered by a right to receive protection equivalent to that under the Convention, rather than a mere capacity to enter a country and access refugee determination procedures there.[60] Lee and Carr JJ held that a tourist or business visa would not meet this description as the visa only operated to allow entry for business purposes.[61] Gummow J, in obiter dicta, has explained this requirement as a right with a correlative duty of the relevant country, owed under municipal law to the applicant personally, which must be shown to exist by acceptable evidence.[62]

'Right' means legally enforceable and presently existing right

[14.32] The Full Federal Court has rejected suggestions that s 36(3) codifies the principle of effective protection in *Thiyagarajah*.[63] While echoing the earlier common law jurisprudence, the operation of s 36(3) departs from the earlier jurisprudence in key respects. The word 'right' in s 36(3) has been interpreted as a legally enforceable right to enter and reside in a country (and not just a capacity to enter and reside 'as a matter of practical reality and fact').[64] The right must be one that allows a person to enter and reside in the future: past (or cancelled) entitlements do not count.[65]

[14.33] In one striking regard, however, s 36(3) has codified a situation which the High Court noted flowed from *Thiyagarajah* as the tribunal had applied it to the Jewish applicants in *NAGV*. If Israel's Law of Return amounted to effective protection in a safe third country (removing Australia's protection obligations under s 36), no Jewish asylum seeker would ever be eligible for protection in Australia. This is so, notwithstanding the fact that the Refugee Convention was founded in global outrage at the plight of Jewish refugees during and after the Holocaust.[66] Indeed, this has been held to be precisely the impact of s 36(3).[67] One Federal Magistrate has questioned this interpretation. Where the applicant has no voluntary desire to invoke the Law of Return, McInnis FM found that any right of residence in Israel must be regarded as conditional and not existing, such that s 36(3) is not engaged.[68] This construction of the provision accords more with the commentary of the Executive Committee of the UNHCR which has stated that 'asylum should not be refused solely on the ground that it could be sought from another State'. If an asylum seeker has 'close links with

---

59　(2003) 131 FCR 269 at [64]-[65].
60　Ibid at [41] (Lee J).
61　Ibid at [42]-[44] (Lee J), [64] (Hill J), [75] (Carr J).
62　*MIMIA v Al Khafaji* (2004) 219 CLR 664 (*Al-Khafaji*) at [19]-[20].
63　*MIMA v Applicant C* (2001) 116 FCR 154.
64　*MIMA v Applicant C* (2001) 116 FCR 154; *Kola v MIMA* (2002) 120 FCR 170.
65　See *Suntharajah v MIMA* [2001] FCA 1391; and *N1045/00A v MIMA* [2001] FCA 1546.
66　*NAGV* (2005) 222 CLR 161 at [30] (majority) and [95]-[97] (Kirby J).
67　See *NAEN v MIMIA* (2004) 135 FCR 410; *NAPI v MIMIA* [2004] FCA 57.
68　See *MZXLT v MIAC* (2007) 211 FLR 428.

another State, he may if it appears fair and reasonable be called upon first to request asylum from that State'.[69]

[14.34] An even more startling result occurred in the case of *MIMIA v Al Khafaji*[70] where an Iraqi asylum seeker was denied a Protection visa on the basis that he had not taken all possible steps to avail himself of a right to enter and reside in Syria under s 36(3). Some years later, the Federal Court found that there was no reasonable prospect in the foreseeable future of Mr Al Khafaji's removal to Syria or anywhere else.[71] The High Court ultimately upheld the legality of his indefinite detention although Gummow J, in a dissenting judgment, considered it 'odd, if not paradoxical' that Mr Al Khafaji was denied refugee status on the basis that he had a right to reside in Syria but he had been unable to exercise that right.[72] His Honour questioned whether, in the circumstances, it could be said that 'there exists a "right" of the nature identified in s 36(3) where it is insusceptible of exercise within a reasonable time'.[73]

'All possible steps'

[14.35] That s 36(3) can operate unfairly for some asylum seekers emerges forcefully in cases involving fugitives from North Korea. Although South Korea treats these people as citizens and offers them full entitlements, it is practically impossible for North Koreans to enter South Korea directly. Many undergo hugely perilous journeys through China and a range of South East Asian countries before finding a country in which they can safely make an asylum claim. For North Korean defectors, the requirement that they take 'all possible steps' to seek protection in South Korea can come at a high price. In practical terms, s 36(3) may represent an almost insurmountable barrier to North Koreans wishing to claim refugee status in Australia.[74]

[14.36] The suite of legislative changes augmenting the safe third country principle introduced a bar on Protection visa applications by any non-citizen who has a right to re-enter and reside in a third country where they had previously resided for at least seven days and which has been declared to be safe by the Minister.[75] To effect such a bar, the Minister must declare that a country does three things. It must provide protection to persons in respect of whom the country has protection obligations. It must maintain effective procedures for assessing protection needs; and it must meet relevant human rights standards.[76] This suggests that a country could be deemed 'safe' without being party to the Refugee Convention. The fact that the provision is triggered by a unilateral ministerial act means that individual asylum seekers would

---

69   UNHCR Executive Committee Conclusion No 15 (XXX), 'Refugees Without an Asylum Country' (1979) [(h)(iv)].
70   (2004) 219 CLR 664.
71   *Al Khafaji v MIMIA* [2002] FCA 1369.
72   (2004) 219 CLR 664 at [18] (Gummow J).
73   Ibid at [19] (Gummow J).
74   See *SZGKB v MIMIA* [2005] FMCA 1544; *NBCY v MIMIA* (2003) 83 ALD 518; *NBLC v MIMIA* (2005) 149 FCR 151; and *SZFIG v MIMIA* [2006] FCA 1218.
75   *Migration Act*, ss 91N, 91P, and *Migration Regulations*, reg 2.12A.
76   *Migration Act*, s 91N(3).

14.2 Cessation of refugee status

[14.37] A great many commentators have noted the temporal and circumstantial nature of refugee protection afforded by the Refugee Convention.[77] The Convention may prohibit the return of refugees to a country where they face persecution. However, there is no legal requirement to grant long-term or even short-term protection to such persons. This is underscored by Art 1C which stipulates that the Refugee Convention may cease to apply to a person who has been recognised as a refugee by a contracting state party in six circumstances. These are where a refugee:

(1) has voluntarily re-availed himself of the protection of his country of nationality;
(2) has voluntarily re-acquired (previously lost) nationality;
(3) has acquired a new nationality of a country that offers him protection;
(4) has voluntarily re-established himself in the country from which he fled;
(5) (absent compelling circumstances) can no longer refuse to avail himself of the protection of his former country of nationality because conditions have changed; and
(6) (absent compelling circumstances) can no longer refuse to avail himself of the protection of his former country of habitual residence because conditions have changed.

The significance of the cessation provision is that when a person ceases to be a refugee, the *non-refoulement* provisions (see Art 33) also cease to apply.[78]

[14.38] It will be noted that the first four paragraphs in Art 1C involve changes in the personal circumstances of a refugee brought about by actions taken by the refugee themselves. In Australia one of the rare occasions where Art 1C(1) was invoked involved an Iranian couple who returned to Iran (on Iranian passports to which Australian Protection visas were affixed) and took up residence for the purpose of adopting an Iranian baby. The action was held to constitute voluntary re-availment of the protection of Iran.[79]

[14.39] Because Art 1C only operates in relation to a person who has already been recognised as a refugee by state authorities, the provision has rarely been applied in

---

[77] Goodwin-Gill and McAdam, above n 5, at 139ff; Hathaway, above n 13, at 189-205; Joan Fitzpatrick and Rafael Bonoan, 'Cessation of Refugee Protection' in Feller et al, above n 16, at 491.
[78] See UNHCR, *Guidelines on International Protection: Cessation of Refugee Status under Article 1C(5) and (6) of the 1951 Convention relating to the Status of Refugees*, 10 February 2003, HCR/GIP/03/03; and Executive Committee of the High Commissioner's Program, Sub-Committee of the Whole on International Protection, *Discussion Note on the Application of the "Ceased Circumstances" Cessation Clauses in the 1951 Convention*, 20 December 1991, EC/SCP/1992/CRP.1 at [1].
[79] See *Rezaei v MIMA* [2001] FCA 1294. See also *A v MIMA* [1999] FCA 227, a case where a Vietnamese man returned to Vietnam (on an Australian-issued travel document) to visit his ailing mother (or to engage in illicit business activities).

courts throughout the world.⁸⁰ The jurisprudence that exists on cessation provisions has been concerned largely with Art 1C(5) and (6), which provide that a refugee may lose that status if circumstances in relation to their recognition as a refugee have ceased to exist. These usually involve changed circumstances in the refugee's (feared) country of origin. The provisions took on great significance after the introduction of Temporary Protection visas (TPVs) under the conservative Coalition government in 1999. Decision-makers were called upon to determine whether to grant further Protection visas to individuals who had previously been recognised as refugees. For a time, Art 1C(5) was used to deny refugee status to individuals who were re-applying for protection at the expiration of their TPV. The abolition of the temporary protection regime in August 2008⁸¹ made Art 1C less relevant to the regular course of Protection visa decision-making. More recent cases have tended to involve the cancellation of a permanent visa (typically where the holder has been convicted of a criminal offence).

[14.40] Australian jurisprudence on the operation of Art 1C(5) and (6) for many years manifested great confusion in assimilating the international framework with domestic law as applied to TPV holders. The tension between the approaches adopted is best illustrated by the case in which the High Court ultimately resolved this issue, *MIMIA v QAAH*.⁸² Applicant QAAH was a Hazara Shi'a from Afghanistan who had been granted a three year TPV in 2000. In 2003, he was refused a permanent Protection visa. At the time, the view of the Department was that Art 1C(5) was only 'one of a number of relevant considerations that will go to determining whether protection obligations continue to be owed and therefore whether the further protection visa is to be granted'.⁸³ The approach taken by the Department was to determine whether the applicant could make out a fresh claim to asylum under s 36(2) as it incorporated the definition of refugee under Art 1A(2) of the Refugee Convention.

[14.41] The RRT upheld the decision denying QAAH a permanent Protection visa. The tribunal took the view that Art 1C(5) should be considered first to determine whether there had been a change in circumstances since the grant of a Protection visa to the TPV holder. If the answer to this question was in the affirmative, the RRT would then consider whether the applicant could make out a fresh claim for a well-founded fear of persecution under Art 1A(2). The RRT tended to the view that any change in circumstance – the replacement of one dominant warlord by another, for example – would suffice to trigger a reversion to an Art 1A(2) inquiry. In *QAAH*, the RRT found that the applicant no longer had a well-founded fear of persecution, and was denied permanent protection.

[14.42] By the time *QAAH*'s case came to the High Court, the Federal Court jurisprudence on the effect of Art 1C(5) and (6) was split. The most popular view was that

---

80   Maria O'Sullivan, 'Withdrawing Protection Under Article 1C(5) of the 1951 Convention: Lessons from Australia' (2008) *International Journal of Refugee Law* 586 at 587.
81   Repealed by *Migration Legislation Amendment Regulations 2008 (No 5)* (Cth). Persons recognised as refugees by decision-makers are now granted permanent Protection visas: see *Migration Regulations*, Sch 2, subclasses 850 and 866.
82   (2006) 231 CLR 1 (*QAAH*). See also *NBGM v MIMA* (2006) 231 CLR 52.
83   DIMIA, 'Protecting Refugees: Cessation under Article 1C', UNHCR Discussion Paper No 1/2003, available at <www.unhcr.org.au/pdfs/dpaper012003.pdf>.

the grant of a TPV placed an onus of sorts on the Minister to show that an individual had lost the status of refugee (through change in circumstances) when the refugee came to seek a permanent visa.[84]

[14.43] While the Full Court acknowledged that administrative decisions traditionally involve no strict burden of proof by either party, the court considered that in this context the parties did indeed bear an onus in relation to particular matters. The applicant had the onus to make out his claim for refugee status at the initial application for protection (for, in this case, a TPV). On application for a permanent Protection visa, the onus shifted to the government to prove substantial changes in the applicant's country of origin, to engage Art 1C(5).[85]

[14.44] In applying the cessation clause in these cases, the Full Federal Court adopted a test which was widely supported by the UNHCR and expert commentators whereby cessation of refugee status would occur only where the changes in the refugee's country were 'substantial', 'effective' and 'durable'.[86] First, the change must be of substantial political significance, in the sense that the power structure under which persecution was deemed a real possibility no longer exists. Professor Hathaway stresses, however, that it would be premature to consider cessation simply because relative calm had been restored in a country still governed by an oppressive political structure. Second, there must be reason to believe that the substantial political change is truly effective. Third, the change of circumstances must be shown to be durable. Cessation is not a decision to be taken lightly on the basis of transitory shifts in the political landscape, but rather should be reserved for situations in which there is reason to believe that the positive conversion of the power structure is likely to last. Hathaway points out that the rationale for cessation due to a fundamental change in circumstances is the existence of a government in the refugee's state of origin that is able and willing to protect the refugee.[87] The UNHCR has taken a similar approach, recommending that for Art 1C(5) to be invoked the changed country conditions must be 'fundamental', 'enduring' and amount to a 'restoration of protection'.[88] Only after the application of the cessation clause would the issue arise of whether the applicant in the particular case still qualified for protection on account of a well-founded fear of persecution for a Convention reason. In *WAHK v MIMIA*,[89] for example, the Full Federal Court rejected a tribunal decision which determined that the applicant should lose his status as a refugee because his first application for temporary protection was based on persecution by the Taliban which had since been removed from government in Afghanistan. The Full Federal Court remitted the decision for reconsideration of the different issue of whether

---

84   See *NBGM v MIMIA* (2004) 84 ALD 40 at [65].
85   *QAAH v MIMIA* (2005) 145 FCR 363 at [58], [71]; *NBGM v MIMIA* (2006) 150 FCR 522 at [172]. See also Goodwin-Gill and McAdam, above n 5, at 143.
86   Hathaway, above n 13, at 200-3.
87   Hathaway, *The Rights of Refugees*, above n 3, at 921.
88   *Guidelines on International Protection: Cessation of Refugee Status under Article 1C(5) and (6) of the 1951 Convention relating to the Status of Refugees* (HCR/GIP/03/03), 10 February 2003; see also UNHCR Handbook, above n 24, at [135].
89   (2004) 81 ALD 322.

the interim government was able and willing to protect the applicant from acts of persecution in the area where the applicant had lived.

[14.45] In *QAAH*,[90] the High Court rejected this approach on the basis that the primary guide for Australian decision-makers had to be Australia's domestic legislation. It ruled that the cessation clause in the Refugee Convention did not provide any additional analytical framework for determining an applicant's claim for a further Protection visa. Instead, the correct approach was simply to apply the definition of refugee in Art 1A(2) as though the determination of refugee status was being made for the first time. The court adopted a strictly legalistic approach which focused on s 36(2) of the *Migration Act*. An applicant seeking a further Protection visa must convince the Minister, afresh, that he or she satisfies the definition of refugee under Art 1A(2) of the Refugee Convention as set out in s 36(2). On this view, the cessation clause has virtually no role to play.

[14.46] Having said this, the High Court did consider the meaning of the cessation clause to the extent that it may apply in Australian law. The majority found that, under international law, Art 1C(5) has the effect of automatically altering the 'status' of a refugee upon changing circumstances in their country of origin.[91] The majority disagreed with the Full Federal Court that any changes must be 'substantial, effective and durable' in order to trigger the cessation clause.[92] Instead, the court held that Art 1C(5) mirrors the effect of the Art 1A(2) definition of refugee, and does not afford a recognised refugee a different test in applying for further or permanent asylum.

[14.47] In the result, a TPV holder applying for permanent protection is required to re-prove their refugee status under Art 1A(2) and does not benefit from any shift in the burden of proof to the departmental decision-maker to show a relevant change in circumstances. The court, by majority, considered that such an approach was inconsistent with the nature of administrative decision-making and the tribunal as an inquisitorial body.

[14.48] Kirby J was the sole dissentient in *QAAH*.[93] His Honour criticised the majority for holding that provisions of the *Migration Act* override the international framework. He supported international commentators who see the cessation clause as incorporating a distinct test from the definition of refugee in Art 1A(2) and the *Migration Act* should be read in conformity with the Refugee Convention. UNHCR, which acted as an *amicus curiae* intervenor in the case, echoed this critique.[94]

---

90   (2006) 231 CLR 1. For commentary on this case, see Maria O'Sullivan, '*MIMIA v QAAH*: Cessation of Refugee Status' (2006) 28(2) *Sydney Law Review* 359.
91   (2006) 231 CLR 1 at [43] (Gummow ACJ, Callinan, Heydon and Crennan JJ). For criticism of this view, see Goodwin-Gill and McAdam, above n 5, at 140 n 28.
92   (2006) 231 CLR 1 at [39]ff.
93   Ibid at [65]ff.
94   UNHCR Regional Office for Australia, New Zealand, Papua New Guinea and the South Pacific, *Press Release*, 20 November 2006, available at <http://www.unhcr.org.au/pdfs/TPVHighCourt.pdf>, at 1.

14.3 Refugees who are undeserving of protection: The national security exception to the *non-refoulement* rule

[14.49] Qualifications are placed on the grant of refugee status and on the non-refoulement principle by Arts 1F and 33(2) of the Refugee Convention. These provisions mandate the exclusion of three classes of undesirable persons. The provisions apply if there are serious reasons for considering that a person has: (a) committed 'crimes against peace, a war crime, or a crime against humanity'; (b) committed 'a serious non-political crime outside the country of refuge'; or (c) acted in contravention of the principles and purposes of the United Nations.[95] Various rationales for the exclusion have been identified. One view is that the nature of the crimes committed renders these individuals undeserving of protection.[96] Another view emphasises the fact that criminals should not be able to use the Convention to evade prosecution for crimes committed.[97] A third view, often cited by Australian courts, emphasises the desire of states to deny admission to of criminals who may present a danger to security and public order.[98]

[14.50] The Refugee Convention distinguishes between persons seeking refugee status (Art 1F) and those whom a state seeks to expel, presumably after having been admitted and judged to be a refugee (Art 33(2)). In the first instance, a state need have only 'serious reasons for considering' that one of the three exclusion provisions in Art 1F applies. On the other hand, Art 33(2) requires a state of refuge to make a finding by way of final judgment that a person has committed a 'particularly serious crime' and constitutes a danger to the community.[99] In practice, the difference is stark. It underscores the central purpose of the exclusionary provisions which is to afford protection to the state being asked to take in the refugee.[100] The relatively low threshold for the exclusion of undesirable refugees recognises that states have a right to protect their integrity. Once a refugee is admitted and offered protection, however, the rights of the refugee become more defined relative to those of the receiving state.[101] In either case, the exclusion of a person from protection can literally be a matter of life and death.[102]

---

95 Hathaway, above n 13, at 214; Goodwin-Gill and McAdam, above n 5, at 163-97; Geoff Gilbert, 'Current Issues in the Application of the Exclusion Clauses' in Feller et al, above n 16, at 426; Peter J van Krieken (ed), *Refugee Law in Context: The Exclusion Clause* (The Hague: TMC Asser Press, 1999).
96 UNHCR Handbook, above n 24, at [148]; Gilbert, above n 95, at 428.
97 Hathaway, above n 13, at 221; cf McAdam and Goodwin-Gill, who state that this view is 'inconsistent with the ordinary meaning of the words [of the Convention]': above n 5, at 175.
98 UNHCR Handbook, above n 24, at [148], [151]; Goodwin-Gill and McAdam, above n 5, at 176; *Ovcharuk v MIMA* (1998) 88 FCR 173 at 179 (Whitlam J), and 185 (Branson J); *MIMA v Singh* (2002) 209 CLR 533 (*Singh*) at [95] (Kirby J) and [15] (Gleeson CJ).
99 Hathaway, above n 13, at 225-6.
100 See Matthew Zagor, 'Persecutor or Persecuted: Exclusion Under Article 1F(a) and (b) of the Refugees Convention' (2000) 23 *UNSW Law Journal* 164 at 188-9.
101 On this issue, see also UNHCR Handbook, above n 24, at [151]; and Goodwin-Gill and McAdam, above n 5, at 175; and Ben Saul, 'Exclusion of Suspected Terrorists from Refugee Status' in Jenny Hocking et al (eds), *Democracy at the Crossroads: Counterterrorism and the State* (London: Edward Elgar, 2006).
102 See *WAKN v MIMIA* (2004) 138 FCR 579 at [53].

[14.51] The evidentiary test in Art IF will be satisfied where there are *serious reasons* for considering a person has engaged in the conduct outlined in paras (a)-(c). In *Arquita v MIMA*,[103] the Federal Court adopted a plain language interpretation of this expression:

> The expression 'serious reasons for considering' means precisely what it says. There must be reason, or reasons, to believe that the applicant has committed an offence of the type specified. That reason or those reasons must be 'serious'.

Because positive proof that a crime was committed is not required, the question of whether a criminal or civil standard of proof should apply does not arise.[104] It is enough to adduce strong evidence that a crime has been committed.[105] Evidence that a person has been charged or convicted of an offence is not necessary.[106]

[14.52] Having said this, the courts have urged caution in the approach taken to these cases. In *SRYYY v MIMIA*,[107] the Full Federal Court held that, in considering whether a person has committed a particular offence, it is essential to address all the elements of the offence. This seems to depart from earlier dicta to the effect that Art 1F(a) can be engaged without every element of an offence being particularised.[108] In 2004, the Federal Court observed that:

> [T]he absence of a requirement for a positive finding of the commission of conduct of the kind contemplated by Art 1F is not inconsistent with the need for 'meticulous investigation and solid grounds' in order to meet the standard of 'serious reasons for considering that' the conduct has been engaged in.[109]

[14.53] In Australia, review of a departmental determination of whether an individual is to be excluded under Art 1F or removed under Art 33(2) is a matter for the Administrative Appeals Tribunal (AAT), not the RRT.[110] This arrangement is thought appropriate in view of the jurisdiction of this tribunal to review visa cancellations of criminal permanent residents: see further Chapter 17. This Part focuses on the judicial consideration of the matters which have arisen in relation to Art 1F before the AAT.

14.3.1 Article 1F(a) – Crimes again peace, war crimes and crimes against humanity

[14.54] The Full Federal Court considered the meaning of the phrase, 'crimes against peace, a war crime, or a crime against humanity' in *SRYYY v MIMIA*.[111] The case

---

103 (2000) 106 FCR 465 at [56].
104 *Arquita v MIMA* (2000) 106 FCR 465 at [52]-[54]; *SRYYY v MIMIA* (2005) 147 FCR 1 at [79]; *VWYJ v MIMIA* [2006] FCAFC 1 at [25]; *WAKN v MIMIA* (2004) 138 FCR 579 at [51]; *SZITR v MIMA* (2006) 44 AAR 382 at [8]. In the words of the former president of the AAT, Matthews J: 'To re-state the test in terms of standard of proof is unnecessary and may in some cases lead to confusion and error': *Re W97/164 and MIMA* (1998) 51 ALD 432 at [42].
105 *Arquita v MIMA* (2000) 106 FCR 465; *WAKN v MIMIA* (2004) 138 FCR 579.
106 See *Ovcharuk v MIMA* (1998) 88 FCR 173 at 179; and *SRYYY v MIMIA* (2005) 147 FCR 1 at [79].
107 (2005) 147 FCR 1 at [109].
108 *Ovcharuk v MIMA* (1998) 88 FCR 173 at 186 (Branson J, Sackville J agreeing).
109 *WAKN v MIMIA* (2004) 138 FCR 579 at [52]. See also Zagor, above n 100, at 168-70.
110 *Migration Act*, s 500(1).
111 (2005) 147 FCR 1.

concerned an application for a Protection visa by a Sri Lankan man who claimed that he had a well-founded fear of persecution because he had fought against the Tamil Tigers (LTTE) as a soldier in the Sri Lankan army and would be killed if returned to Sri Lanka. In describing his claim, the applicant explained that he had been involved in the interrogation of Tamil civilians detained on suspicion of having links with the LTTE. He had engaged in violent acts against the detainees including having made death threats to children in an effort to extract information. The AAT considered that there were serious reasons for believing that the applicant was involved in acts 'which could be characterised as lower level torture or cruel and inhuman treatment involving the intentional infliction of both physical and mental pain and suffering'. It accepted that the applicant had been following the orders of superior officers and had protested the interrogation techniques he was directed to use. However, the AAT found that he had not been subjected to pressure or compulsion which vitiated the element of intention in such an offence.

[14.55] On appeal, the Full Federal Court held that 'crimes against peace, a war crime, or a crime against humanity' under Art 1F(a) are defined in a range of international instruments. It is permissible to seek guidance on the elements of relevant crimes from any such instrument, whether or not the instrument was in force at the time the alleged crime was committed.[112] Since these instruments might contain varying definitions of different crimes, it is permissible for a decision-maker to use the most appropriate instrument in the circumstances of the case.[113]

14.3.2 Article 1F(b) – Serious non-political crimes committed outside the country of refuge

[14.56] There has been much discussion of what constitutes a 'serious' crime for the purposes of Art 1F(b). Many commentators have argued that the humanitarian objects of the Convention require a 'balancing test' to be used.[114] This would require the decision-maker to balance the seriousness of the crime committed against the seriousness of the persecution that the putative refugee is likely to face if returned to their country of origin. Such a balancing act was expressly rejected by the Full Federal Court in *Applicant ANBD of 2001 v MIMA*:[115]

> [T]he Article provides that the commission of such a crime, of itself, is sufficient to exclude the person in question from the protection of the Refugees Convention ... In determining whether the disqualifying crime is 'serious' it is appropriate to have regard to the fact that it must be of such a nature as to result in Australia not having protection obligations to persons who commit such crimes. However, there is no

---

112   Ibid at [63]-[67].
113   Ibid at [73].
114   See UNHCR, *Guidelines on International Protection No 5: Application of the Exclusion Clauses: Article 1F of the 1951 Convention relating to the Status of Refugees* (2003) at [24]; Akbar Rasulov, 'Criminals as Refugees: the "Balancing Exercise" and Article 1F(b) of the Refugee Convention' (2002) 16 *Georgetown Immigration Law Journal* 815 at 815-18; Jason Cabarrus, 'Exclusion of Serious Criminals from Protection as Refugees in Australia', Unpublished essay, LLM program, The University of Sydney, manuscript in possession of authors, at 6.
115   (2002) 126 FCR 453 at [41] (Merkel J, Madgwick and Conti JJ agreeing). See also *Dhayakpa v MIEA* (1995) 62 FCR 556 at 563; *Singh* (2002) 209 CLR 533 at [141] (Kirby J).

textual or contextual basis for reading into Art 1F(b) an additional requirement of a balancing test nor would such a requirement be justified on the basis that it is giving effect to a purpose or object of Art 1F(b) of the Refugees Convention.

[14.57] The question of the 'seriousness' of the 'non-political crime' was raised in a case involving a Sri Lankan fisherman applying for a Protection visa who had been found guilty in Australia of 'people smuggling'.[116] The tribunal noted dicta in *Ovcharuk v MIMA*[117] that the relevant standards for determining the seriousness of the applicant's criminality are those accepted within the receiving state.[118] It acknowledged that the 'people smuggling' conviction was unquestionably serious in the eyes of the Australian government (attracting as it does a prison sentence of up to 20 years). Nevertheless, the AAT accepted the counsel of French J who recommended that decision-makers exercise discretion in arriving at an evaluative judgment about the nature of the allegedly disqualifying crime.[119] The tribunal also noted the observation by Merkel J that the seriousness of the crime 'must be of such a nature as to result in Australia not having protection obligations to persons who commit such crimes'.[120] The AAT found that in light of the applicant's personal circumstances (his lack of education and opportunities in Sri Lanka), and the fact that initially he did not know the purpose of the trip, his crime was not of sufficient severity to warrant application of the exclusion clause.

[14.58] The Full Federal Court in *Ovcharuk v MIMA* considered the meaning of the term 'crime' in 'serious non-political crime'. The court held that there may be serious reasons for considering that an applicant has committed a crime whether or not there is evidence of a charge or conviction.[121] There may be serious reasons for finding that a person has committed a crime without being formally charged, and equally it may be clear that there is no basis to conclude that a person has committed a crime notwithstanding the fact that they have been charged or convicted. Accordingly, Art 1F(b) is not restricted to fugitives from foreign courts; a 'serious non-political crime' includes conduct that amounts to a crime in the country of refuge.[122] The criminal conduct at the centre of that case – conspiracy to import heroin into Australia – was sufficient to trigger the operation of the exclusion clause because the crime had been committed both inside and outside of the country of refuge.

[14.59] The requirement that the crime committed be 'non-political' recognises that those who commit political crimes may be engaged in a struggle for liberation, compelled by the political circumstances in their state of origin.[123] The 'non-political' nature of the criminal conduct which triggers Art 1F(b) was considered by the High

---

116 *Re SRCCCC and MIMIA* [2004] AATA 315. He had pleaded guilty to the charge under s 232A of the *Migration Act* of 'facilitat[ing] the bringing to Australia of a group of 24 people ... reckless as to whether the people had a lawful right to come to Australia'.
117 (1998) 88 FCR 173.
118 Ibid at 185 (Branson J, Sackville J agreeing).
119 *Dhayakpa v MIEA* (1995) 62 FCR 556 at 563.
120 *Applicant NADB of 2001 v MIMA* (2002) 126 FCR 453 at [41].
121 *Ovcharuk v MIMA* (1998) 88 FCR 173 at 179 (Whitlam J).
122 Ibid at 179 (Whitlam J) and 186 (Branson J, Sackville J agreeing).
123 Cabarrus, above n 114, at 10.

Court in *MIMA v Singh*.[124] Here, the High Court affirmed the principle that political crimes are not restricted to 'pure' political acts such as treason, sedition and spying, but can include 'common crimes' such as murder. In the context of a political struggle where government agents, including police, have a policy of torturing and killing opponents of the government, crimes directed at those agents may be regarded as political even though they may also be characterised as crimes of revenge.[125] The court overturned the tribunal decision excluding a former senior officer in the Khalistan Liberation Front who had murdered a police officer 'out of retribution'.

[14.60] Gleeson CJ stated that identifying murder as a political act 'ordinarily requires a close and direct connection between the act and the achievement of an objective such as a change of government, or change of government policy, which might include relief from government sponsored or condoned oppression'.[126] The political outcome must be the 'substantial purpose' of the crime in question. Kirby J added that, in order to be political, an act must 'in some appropriately close way, be linked with the purpose of changing the political environment, commonly the government, by the commission of the crime'.[127]

[14.61] The phrase 'serious non-political crime' must also be interpreted with reference to the *Migration Act*. Section 91T, which took effect on 1 October 2001, provides that a serious crime will be non-political 'where the person's motives for committing the crime were *wholly or mainly* non-political in nature' (emphasis added).[128] It also includes offences that are defined as non-political for the purposes of the *Extradition Act 1988* (Cth). The purpose of this legislative amendment was to override jurisprudence which 'had set too low a threshold when determining the degree of political motivation needed in order for a criminal act to fall outside the Art 1F exclusion clause'.[129]

[14.62] Obvious crimes caught by Art 1F(b) include those against 'physical integrity, life, and liberty' such as murder, rape, arson, armed robbery, child molesting, wounding and drug trafficking.[130] As Jason Cabarrus notes:[131]

> Decisions in which the AAT has found that Article 1F(b) was applicable generally accord with these categories and have included crimes such as murder,[132] supplying petrol to burn down a building,[133] bombing a building and committing assaults,[134]

---

124 (2002) 209 CLR 533.
125 *Singh v MIMA* (2000) 102 FCR 51.
126 *Singh* (2002) 209 CLR 533 at [22].
127 Ibid at [87].
128 Inserted by *Migration Legislation Amendment Act (No 6) 2001* (Cth).
129 Explanatory Memorandum to Migration Legislation Amendment Bill (No 6) 2001 (Cth), at [33].
130 See Goodwin-Gill and McAdam, above n 5, at 177-9. See also Martin Gottwald, 'Asylum Claims and Drug Offences: the Seriousness Threshold of Article 1F(b) of the 1951 Convention Relating to the Status of Refugees and the UN Drug Conventions' (2006) 18 *International Journal of Refugee Law* 81.
131 See Cabarrus, above n 114, at 9.
132 *Re Ballibay and MIMA* [2000] AATA 1147; *Re Arquita and MIMA* [1999] AATA 410; *Re SRLLL and MIMIA* (2002) 35 AAR 523 (SRLLL).
133 *Re WBA and MIMIA* [2003] AATA 1250.
134 *Re Shahidul and MIMA* [1998] AATA 331.

trafficking commercial quantities of hard drugs[135] and organising an attack that caused considerable damage to a police station and the death of three officers.[136]

14.3.3 Article 1F(c) – Acts contrary to the purposes and principles of the United Nations

[14.63] The purposes and principles of the United Nations (UN) are set out in the Preamble and Arts 1 and 2 of the UN Charter.[137] They include broad aspirations such as peace and security, friendly relations amongst states, self-determination and international cooperation. On the basis that the UN Charter applies only to states, the traditional view has been that only people high up in the hierarchy of a state can be guilty of acts contrary to these purposes and principles.[138] Recent decisions however, both in Australia and other jurisdictions, indicate an increasing willingness on the part of decision-makers to extend the applicability of Art 1F(c) exclusion to non-state actors.[139] In one matter before the AAT, the tribunal found that an Indian man associated with a Sikh terrorist organisation, who had been complicit in the murder of police officers, was excluded on all three prongs of the exclusion clause. Article 1F(c) was engaged on the basis that the applicant's conduct amounted to terrorist activity which is contrary to the purposes and principles of the UN, and contrary to Security Council resolutions.[140]

14.4 Complementary protection

[14.64] Since the drafting of the Refugee Convention, the causes of refugee movements have become more varied, leaving many who do not qualify as refugees unable or unwilling to return to their home country and in need of humanitarian assistance.[141] In 2009, a formal 'complementary protection' regime was introduced into the Australian Parliament.[142] The initiative follows a trend in Western states to implement protection systems to supplement the Refugee Convention. These cater for people whose protection needs lie outside of the scope of the Refugee Convention on the rationale that a 'refugee-like predicament should result in a refugee-like

---

135 *Re Ovcharuk and MIMA* [1997] AATA 329; *Re SRIII and MIMA* [2001] AATA 945; *Re WAT and MIMIA* [2002] AATA 1150; *Re WAR and MIMA* [2001] AATA 475.
136 *Re Hapugoda and MIMA* [1997] AATA 108.
137 Text in Bruno Simma (ed), *The Charter of the United Nations: A Commentary* (Oxford: Oxford University Press, 2nd ed, 2002) at 39-47, 63-171.
138 See UNHCR Handbook, above n 24, at [162]-[163]; Gilbert, above n 95, at 456; Saul, above n 101, at 17.
139 *Pushpanathan v Canada* [1998] 1 SCR 982; *Sivakumar v Canada (Minister for Employment and Immigration)* (CA) [1994] 1 FC 433; *SRLLL* (2002) 35 AAR 523.
140 *SRLLL* (2002) 35 AAR 523.
141 Mary Crock, 'The Refugees Convention at 50: Mid-life Crisis of Terminal Inadequacy? An Australian Perspective' in Susan Kneebone (ed), *The Refugees Convention 50 Years On: Globalisation and International Law* (Ashgate: Aldershot, 2003) at 47-91.
142 Migration Amendment (Complementary Protection) Bill 2009, which would introduce a new s 36(2)(aa). The Bill had not been debated by the new parliament in December 2010 but was expected to be considered in 2011 with some possible changes. The provisions discussed in this section are from the 2009 Bill.

status'.¹⁴³ In some regions, the international instrument governing refugees has itself been expanded to include persons falling outside the Convention definition.¹⁴⁴ Other states, such as the US, Canada, the European Union and New Zealand, have opted for a separate visa regime to cover persons in need of protection who fall outside the Refugee Convention.¹⁴⁵

[14.65] The need for a complementary protection system has arisen because since 1989 the only avenue for an individual who has failed to gain protection under the Refugee Convention has been to request the Minister to intervene under s 417. Section 417 grants the Minister discretionary powers to 'substitute a decision that is more favourable to the applicant' than the decision of the RRT on humanitarian grounds.¹⁴⁶ This mechanism has failed some applicants fearing serious human rights violations if removed from Australia. First, the exercise of ministerial power is non-compellable and non-reviewable, which, in the words of one Senate Committee review, places it 'beyond the reach of parliamentary scrutiny and leave[s] a significant accountability "black hole" in the administration of immigration policy'.¹⁴⁷ In addition, no reasons are given for a Minister's decision to exercise this power, so the decision-making is neither transparent nor consistent across like cases. While guidelines include reference to protection needs arising under international human rights treaties,¹⁴⁸ it is not mandatory for the Minister to take these into account. The Minister's discretion is close to absolute. Finally, the Minister's s 417 power is triggered only by an unsuccessful appeal to the RRT, meaning that applicants must spend time, energy and money pursuing a potentially fruitless claim through two levels of merits adjudication before even accruing the right to approach the Minister.

[14.66] For reasons of principle, it is inappropriate for Australia to use a Minister's discretion to discharge its international obligations to prevent refoulement of individuals fearing human rights violations. A discretionary mechanism, by its very nature, cannot ensure compliance with an obligation. Further, using s 417 to provide complementary protection confuses protection rights of individuals under international law with a residual (humanitarian) discretion to offer protection to individuals

---

143   Jane McAdam, *Complementary Protection in International Refugee Law* (Oxford: Oxford University Press, 2007) at 2, which provides the most comprehensive account of the scope of this principle. See also UNHCR, *Draft Complementary Protection Visa Model: Australia UNHCR Comments*, January 2009; Goodwin-Gill and McAdam, above n 5, Ch 6.

144   For example, the Organisation of the African Union Convention Governing the Specific Aspects of Refugee Problems in Africa 1969, adopted 10 September 1969 by the Assembly of Heads of State and Government, CAB/LEG/24.3, entered into force 20 June 1974, Art 1(2); and the Latin American Cartagena Declaration on Refugees 1984, Art 3, adopted by the Colloquium on the International Protection of Refugees in Central America, Mexico and Panama, Cartagena de Indias, Colombia, 22 November 1984.

145   Council Directive 2004/83/EC on minimum standards for the qualification and status of third country nationals or stateless persons as refugees or as persons who otherwise need international protection and the content of the protection granted, 29 April 2004; *Immigration and Refugee Protection Act 2001* (Canada), c 27, s 97; 8 CFR §§208.16, 208.17 (US); Immigration Bill 2007 (No 132-2) NZ; *Attorney-General v Zaoui* [2006] 1 NZLR 289 (SC).

146   See Chapter 5 and Chapter 19.4.

147   See Senate Select Committee on Ministerial Discretion in Migration Matters, *Inquiry into Ministerial Discretion in Migration Matters* (March 2004).

148   MSI 387 Guidelines.

on compassionate grounds. For reasons of both principle and pragmatism, successive Senate Committees over more than a decade have recommended that Australia's *non-refoulement* obligations under international human rights treaties be explicitly incorporated into domestic law.[149] Australia should no longer rely solely on the Minister's discretionary powers under s 417 to meet this purpose.

[14.67] In earlier times, Australia had a much broader onshore humanitarian visa system. Former s 6A(1)(e) of the *Migration Act*[150] conferred a general power on the Minister to grant visas (or 'entry permits') to individuals with 'strong compassionate or humanitarian' grounds for remaining in Australia. In July 1993, with one stroke of the legislative pen, the generic power to act with compassion and humanity was removed from mainstream decision-making – to be channelled ultimately into the hands of a single politician, the Minister for Immigration.

[14.68] The inadequacy of ministerial intervention to discharge Australia's protection obligations was illustrated by the case of Mr Sadiq Shek Elmi.[151] Elmi arrived in Australia in October 1997, having fled Somalia as a member of a persecuted minority. His application for refugee status was rejected by the Department and RRT on the basis that any persecution he feared in Somalia was due to the generalised situation of civil war rather than any Convention ground. The Minister declined to intervene to grant a visa under s 417. In November 1998, Elmi's lawyers lodged a complaint to the UN Committee against Torture arguing that, if he were removed to Somalia, Elmi would be at personal risk of torture, in breach of the Convention Against Torture and Other Cruel, Inhuman or Degrading Treatment or Punishment (CAT).[152] The Committee agreed, holding that Art 3 of the CAT prohibits Australia from forcibly returning Elmi to Somalia, where he had proved he was vulnerable to torture by the majority clan in Somalia acting as de facto public officials. Nevertheless, the Minister continued to refuse to exercise his s 417 discretion. Elmi was allowed to reapply for a Protection visa which was rejected by the Department and RRT on credibility grounds.

[14.69] Under the proposed scheme, complementary protection would be granted where the Minister has substantial grounds for believing that, as a necessary and foreseeable consequence of removal from Australia, a non-citizen faces a real risk of being irreparably harmed by way of arbitrary deprivation of life, imposition of the death penalty, torture, cruel or inhuman treatment or punishment, or degrading treatment or punishment.[153] The scheme is designed to give effect to Australia's

---

149   See Senate Legal and Constitutional References Committee, *A Sanctuary Under Review*, above n 12, Recommendation 2.2 at 60; Senate Select Committee on Ministerial Discretion in Migration Matters, above n 147, at [8.82]; Senate Legal and Constitutional References Committee, *Administration and Operation of the Migration Act 1958*, Commonwealth, March 2006, Recommendation 33; and Elizabeth Proust, *Report to the Minister for Immigration and Citizenship on the Appropriate Use of Ministerial Powers under the Migration and Citizenship Acts and Migration Regulations* (January 2008), Recommendation 19.
150   This provision was inserted into the *Migration Act* in 1981.
151   *Sadiq Shek Elmi v Australia*, Communication No 120/1998: Australia, 25/05/99, CAT/C/22/D/120/1998.
152   *Convention against Torture and Other Cruel, Inhuman or Degrading Treatment or Punishment*, opened for signature 10 December 1984, 1465 UNTS 85 (entered into force 26 June 1987).
153   See proposed s 36(2A)(a)-(e) of the *Migration Act*.

non-refoulement obligations under the CAT, the International Covenant on Civil and Political Rights (ICCPR), including its Second Optional Protocol, and the Convention on the Rights of the Child (CRC).[154] However, only the ICCPR is mentioned in the actual amending legislation.[155]

[14.70] The complementary protection regime first proposed in 2009 would provide beneficiaries with the same status and rights as refugees receive in Australia, unlike the US and EU where concessions result in a lesser status. Under the Australian scheme, a claimant's protection needs would be assessed, first, against the refugee definition, and only if that definition is not met would the complementary grounds be considered. Although this would still mean that some fruitless refugee claims would need to be pursued before an applicant's claims can be considered against more relevant standards, the benefit of this approach is that refugee jurisprudence would continue to be tested and developed through novel claims.[156] The arrangements also make it clear that the scheme would operate through the administrative structures established to determine refugee claims.

[14.71] The chief benefit of the scheme is that complementary protection would be considered in a transparent process, subject to merits and judicial review. In theory, the number of requests for (non-reviewable, non-compellable) Ministerial intervention should diminish. Providing both recognised refugees and complementary protection claimants with permanent residence status sits well with the principles underlying international protection and the rule of non-discrimination under international human rights law. If implemented, the scheme should provide a more efficient, effective and fairer mechanism for dealing with 'near miss' refugee cases. The chief disappointment is that there appears to be little will to include in the package broader issues of compassion that arise outside of humanitarian law.

14.5   Human trafficking

[14.72] Since 2001, the phenomenon of human trafficking has gained prominence in Australia, with particular focus on the traffic in women and children for sexual exploitation.[157] The issue received public attention when a Thai woman, Puongtong Simaplee, died in Villawood Detention Centre three days after being found in a

---

154   *Convention on the Rights of the Child*, opened for signature 20 November 1989, 1577 UNTS 3 (entered into force 2 September 1990); *International Covenant on Civil and Political Rights*, opened for signature 16 December 1966, 999 UNTS 172 (entered into force 23 March 1976); *Second Optional Protocol to the International Covenant on Civil and Political Rights, aiming at the abolition of the death penalty*, opened for signature 15 December 1989, 29 ILM 1464 (entered into force 11 July 1991).

155   See Commonwealth, *Parliamentary Debates*, House of Representatives, 9 September 2009, at 8988 (Laurie Ferguson). We have left the discussion of the proposed legislation brief because of the possibility that the provisions will be altered in 2011.

156   Indeed, it is also in keeping with the ExCom Conclusion on the Provision of International Protection Including Through Complementary Forms of Protections No 103 (LVI), 2005, which affirms that complementary forms of protection should only be resorted to after full use has been made of the 1951 Refugee Convention. See also UNHCR, *Agenda for Protection* (3rd ed, 2003), available at <http://www.unhcr.org/refworld/docid/4714a1bf2.html>.

157   Parliamentary Joint Committee on the Australian Crime Commission, Parliament of Australia, *Inquiry into the Trafficking of Women for Sexual Servitude* (2004).

brothel by immigration officials. The woman was suffering from serious drug addiction, malnutrition and pneumonia.[158] Victims of human trafficking do not automatically come within the UNHCR mandate to protect refugees. Trafficked persons are individuals who are coerced into moving across borders and working in conditions to which they do not consent. They will not qualify for refugee status unless they can demonstrate a well-founded fear of persecution in their country of nationality for a Convention-based reason. While the importance of international and domestic Australian refugee law as a remedy for many trafficking victims has been acknowledged,[159] the need for government action in this area has been patent.

[14.73] The perceived gap in international protection was met in 2000 with the first international instrument specifically targeting all aspects of trafficking in persons – the UN Convention Against Transnational Organised Crime and the Palermo Protocol.[160] The Protocol defines trafficking in persons as

> the recruitment, transportation, transfer, harbouring or receipt of persons, by means of the threat or use of force or other forms of coercion, of abduction, of fraud, of deception, of the abuse of power or of a position of vulnerability or of the giving or receiving payments or benefits to achieve the consent of a person having control over another person, for the purpose of exploitation. Exploitation shall include, at a minimum, the exploitation of the prostitution of others or other forms of sexual exploitation, forced labour or services, slavery or practices similar to slavery, servitude or the removal of organs … The recruitment, transportation, transfer, harbouring or receipt of a child for the purpose of exploitation shall be considered 'trafficking in persons' even if this does not involve any of the means [above].[161]

Australia ratified the Protocol on 14 September 2005, undertaking specific steps to prevent and combat trafficking in persons and to protect and assist victims 'with full respect for their human rights'.[162] A suite of criminal offences relating to trafficking and slavery were introduced into the *Criminal Code* (Cth) in 2005.[163]

[14.74] States parties to the Protocol are required to 'consider adopting legislative or other appropriate measures' to permit trafficking victims to 'remain in [the state's]

---

158 Jennifer Burn, Sam Blay and Frances Simmons, 'Combating Human Trafficking: Australia's Responses to Modern Day Slavery' (2005) 79 *Australia Law Journal* 543 at 544.
159 Anna Dorevitch and Michelle Foster, 'Obstacles on the Road to Protection: Assessing the Treatment of Sex-Trafficking Victims Under Australia's Migration and Refugee Law' (2008) 9 *Melbourne Journal of International Law* 1; Kaori Saito, 'International Protection for Trafficked Persons and Those Who Fear Being Trafficked' *New Issues in Refugee Research; Research Paper No 149* (Geneva: UNHCR, 2007); Office of the UNHCR, *Guidelines on International Protection No 7: The Application of Article 1A(2) of the 1951 Convention and/or Its 1967 Protocol relating to the Status of Refugees to Victims of Trafficking and Persons at Risk of Being Trafficked*, DocHCR/GIP/06/07 (7 April 2006).
160 Protocol to Prevent, Suppress and Punish Trafficking in Persons, Especially Women and Children, supplementing the United Nations Convention Against Transnational Organised Crime (Palermo Protocol) GA Res 55/25, UN GAOR, 55th sess, 62nd plen mtg, Annex II, Agenda Item 105, UN Doc A/RES/55/25 (8 January 2001) (opened for signature on 15 November 2000, entered into force on 25 December 2003).
161 Palermo Protocol, Art 3(a).
162 Ibid, Art 2(b).
163 See Bernadette McSherry, 'Trafficking in Persons: A Critical Analysis of the New Criminal Code Offences' (2007) 18 *Current Issues in Criminal Justice* 385. See also *R v Tang* (2008) 237 CLR 1.

territory, temporarily or permanently'.[164] In January 2004, Australia introduced a trafficking visa framework under the auspices of an Action Plan to Eradicate Trafficking in Persons.[165] When first introduced, the scheme involved four stages: a Bridging visa F (subclass 060), the (pre-existing) Criminal Justice Stay visa, the Witness Protection (Trafficking) (Temporary) visa (Class UM, subclass 787, under reg 2.07AJ), and the Witness Protection (Trafficking) (Permanent) visa (Class DH, subclass 852, under reg 2.07AK).

[14.75] The scheme was originally geared almost entirely towards criminal prosecution of alleged traffickers. Each visa was available to victims of trafficking so as to facilitate their participation in the criminal justice process. Migrants entered the scheme through the grant of a Bridging visa F, which conferred 30 days lawful presence in Australia to persons 'of interest' to law enforcement in relation to a crime of trafficking or slavery. If police officers decided to continue to investigate an alleged crime, the Department would issue a Criminal Justice Stay visa, which permitted the visa holder to remain in Australia for such time as they were 'required for law enforcement purposes'. The temporary Trafficking visa was not subject to an application process. Its grant was contingent on a decision of both the Attorney-General and the Minister for Immigration. The temporary Trafficking visa was granted only if the Attorney-General issued a certificate that the holder of a Criminal Justice visa had made a 'significant contribution' to the prosecution of a person by the Commonwealth Director of Public Prosecutions (CDPP) (or had cooperated closely with the CDPP). The Minister for Immigration had to be satisfied that the person would be in danger if returned to their country of nationality. The permanent visa was available after the trafficking victim had held a temporary Trafficking visa for two years, as long as the criteria that inhered at the time of the grant of the temporary visa continued to apply.

[14.76] While social support was available from the time of holding a Bridging visa F, the scheme as introduced was onerous for trafficking victims. The regime lacked a transparent application process, resting variously on prosecutorial, departmental and ministerial discretions. It promised no clear process or outcome at the conclusion of a psychologically arduous and physically dangerous ordeal of the victim.[166] More particularly, the Bridging visa (and attendant social support) was contingent on the trafficked person being identified by or approaching police as a potential witness, a step which many migrants who were vulnerable and in situations of exploitation were unwilling or unable to take. The duration of the Bridging visa meant that the visa holder had only 30 days to decide whether to participate in any potential criminal justice process and seek to remain in Australia to do so. Conversely, law enforcement had 30 days to investigate and decide whether to pursue prosecution. Operational policy dictated that temporary Trafficking visas should not be granted until the end of the criminal justice process,[167] leaving the trafficked person in great uncertainty, notwithstanding the fact that they may have contributed to a prosecution. The dual

---

164 Palermo Protocol, Art 7(1).
165 *Migration Amendment Regulations (No 11) 2003* (Cth), Sch 8.
166 Jennifer Burn and Frances Simmons, 'Trafficking and Slavery in Australia: An Evaluation of Victim Support Strategies' (2006) 15 *Asian and Pacific Migration Journal* 553 at 564-5.
167 Jennifer Burn, 'Australian Trafficking Visas: 15 Recommendations to Better Protect Victims of Human Trafficking' (2007) 35 *Immigration Review* 7 at 9.

requirement of decisions by both the Attorney-General and Minister for Immigration, as pre-conditions for the grants of both temporary and permanent Trafficking visas, was extremely cumbersome. The spouse and dependent children of a Trafficking visa holder could be granted a visa only where the family member was in Australia and had been identified on the letter from the Immigration Department setting out the offer of a visa.[168] Finally, and anomaly arose in the access afforded to the victims' support program, administered by the federal Department of Families, Housing, Communities and Indigenous Affairs and Community Services. This was available only to holders of the Bridging visa F or Criminal Justice visa. As a result, a trafficked person could have assisted in a police investigation or prosecution, but did not qualify for support because a substantive visa was held. Eligibility for support was contingent on the trafficking victim holding a visa which placed them in an uncertain and legally precarious position.

[14.77] In 2009, the scheme was modified substantially to provide better support for victims. The Bridging visa F was extended from 30 to 45 days and is now available to identified victims regardless of whether they are willing to assist police. This provides a short period in which a trafficked person may access support and evaluate their options. A further Bridging visa F may be granted to victims who are willing but not able to assist police because of trauma or other special circumstances, providing a total of 90 days' support. In a significant reform, the social support program was extended to any identified victim regardless of the visa they held. The temporary Trafficking visa was abolished and the government committed to move towards granting the permanent Trafficking visa before the prosecution had concluded. The threshold for Attorney-General certification was reduced from having made a 'significant contribution' to 'making a contribution'. Finally, immediate family members outside Australia may now be included in a Trafficking visa application.[169]

[14.78] While the 2009 reforms represent a significant step forwards in enhancing assistance for victims, these reforms do not correct some problematic aspects of Australia's anti-trafficking strategy. First, the focus remains centred on prosecutions with victim protection seen as an element of the criminal justice response rather than a human rights issue in its own right. The reasons for this are rooted in the transnational organised crime focus of the international regime which the domestic legislation seeks to implement, to the detriment of Australia's human rights obligations.[170] This is reflected in the low numbers of recognised 'trafficked persons' being reported. Between 1 July 2008 and 30 June 2009, 77 visas were granted under the people trafficking visa framework. Of these, only five people were granted Witness Protection (Trafficking) (Permanent) visas.[171]

---

168 *Migration Regulations*, reg 2.07AJ.
169 Jennifer Burn and Frances Simmons, 'Prioritising Protection – A New Visa Framework for Trafficked People' (2009) 41 *Immigration Review* 3.
170 Bernadette McSherry and Susan Kneebone, 'Trafficking in Women and Forced Migration: Moving Victims Across the Border of Crime into the Domain of Human Rights' (2008) 12 *International Journal of Human Rights* 67; Audrey Macklin, 'At the Border of Rights: Migration, Sex Work and Trafficking' in Neve Gordon (ed), *From the Margins of Globalization: Critical Perspectives on Human Rights* (Lanham: Lexington Books, 2004) at 161.
171 DIAC, *Annual Report 2008-09*, at 116.

[14.79] Second, the definitional thresholds of 'trafficked persons' tend to entrench certain artificial distinctions (such as consent/coercion, smuggling/trafficking, free labour/exploitation) which can fail to capture the complex reality of the lives of many migrant workers. For instance, social support and permanent visa status may be available to a migrant who has been coerced into exploitative work without consent, but denied a migrant who felt compelled to voluntarily accept exploitative work. Support and status may be given to a migrant transferred into Australia for the purpose of exploitation but denied a migrant who travelled to Australia independently and found herself working in abusive conditions.[172] In some ways the ascendancy of the trafficking discourse has shifted much needed public attention and resources to systemic human rights violations among many vulnerable migrants. However, in other ways, the dominance of this paradigm has meant that many marginalised migrants are relegated into categories that allow some to slip unfairly through the protection net. Seen first and foremost as 'victims', or witnesses assisting a prosecution, some will be eligible for social assistance. However, those characterised as consenting 'economic migrants' who have submitted to voluntarily exploitative working conditions find themselves ineligible for social or legal support. Often, the line between 'victim' and 'villain' can become blurred in the context of irregular migration. It is to the complexities of this area of law and practice that we now turn.

---

172 Laurie Berg and Anna Samson, 'Space for Economic Migrants? Poverty, Migrants and Australian Civil Society ' in Fiona Holland et al (eds), *Global Civil Society* (London: Sage, 2009) at 166; Ratna Kapur, 'The Tragedy of Victimization Rhetoric: Resurrecting the 'Native' Subject in International/Post-Colonial Feminist Legal Politics' (2002) 15 *Harvard Human Rights Journal* 1; Catherine Dauvergne, *Making People Illegal: What Globalization Means for Migration and Law* (Cambridge: Cambridge University Press, 2008) Ch 5.

PART VII Unlawful Status and Enforcement

15

Unlawful Status and Visa Cancellations

15.1 Becoming unlawful – An overview[1]

[15.01] Australia's experience of unlawful or irregular migration has been relatively limited in world terms, thanks in large measure to the geographical isolation of the country and the early adoption of screening measures such as pre-travel visas. The number of unlawful migrants is also small in comparison with the overall flow of human traffic into and out of Australia. For many years, estimations of the number of unlawful non-citizens living in the community have hovered around 50,000, with the number of such people located and removed representing a small proportion of these figures.[2] The consistency of the so-called 'overstay' statistics is remarkable given the various measures introduced to clamp down on irregular migration. The figures available as at 2005 placed the unlawful non-citizen population at 47,800.[3] In 2004-05, the Department located 18,341 unlawful non-citizens and people breaching their visa conditions and a total of 3870 illegal workers, predominantly working in the hospitality, agriculture and manufacturing industries.[4] By June 2009, the population of unlawful non-citizens was estimated at 48,700.[5] In 2008-09 the Department located 990 people working illegally, the top three industries being agriculture, hospitality and construction. In a climate where public concerns about national security and about any form of migration are high, the control of illegal migration remains a pre-eminent concern for the government.

[15.02] The evolution of the law in this area bears witness to both the progressive toughening of the government's approach to immigration outlaws and its preoccupation with controlling the quality and quantity of migrants entering the country. What have changed are the legal methods used to restrict unlawful entry and stay. The grounds on which non-citizens lose their right to remain in Australia have never been

---

1 Over the years, many different terms have been used to describe non-citizens who do not have a legal right to enter or remain in Australia. These have included 'prohibited non-citizen' and 'illegal entrant'. In the present legislation, the phrase used is 'unlawful non-citizen'. For ease of reference, this terminology is used throughout the book.
2 DIMA, *Review of Illegal Workers in Australia: Improving Immigration Compliance in the Workplace* (Canberra: 1999) at 18; DIAC, *Fact Sheet 86: Overstayers and Other Unlawful Non-Citizens*, 31 August 2009.
3 DIMIA, *Managing the Border: Immigration Compliance* (Canberra: 2005) at 37.
4 Ibid at 59-60.
5 DIAC, *Fact Sheet 87: Initiatives to Combat Illegal Work in Australia*, 24 November 2009.

clearer. The concept of deemed illegality, or unlawful status that devolves automatically by operation of law, has been abandoned in favour of a more transparent system involving the cancellation of visas on stated grounds. The only deeming provisions that remain are those relating to nominal visas held by persons recognised as having a special right to remain or visit the country. These include the Special Purpose visa and the Absorbed Person visa.[6] The most striking feature of the present regime is its conceptual simplicity. If the end stage of the enforcement process has become automated (see Chapter 16), the reverse is true of the system for determining the legal status of non-citizens. The result is to return the focus to the substantive entitlements of those seeking a temporary or permanent place in Australia.

[15.03] On 1 September 1994 the law governing unlawful migration status in Australia underwent a process of quite radical rationalisation. The plethora of terms and concepts that had dogged this area of law was replaced by a simple binomial system: persons with a valid visa authorising their stay in Australia became 'lawful non-citizens', while those without such a visa became 'unlawful non-citizens'.[7] It is now a universal requirement that non-citizens possess a visa, actual or deemed. Without a valid visa, non-citizens are liable to mandatory detention and removal from the country, as well as the costs of any enforcement action.[8] It is no longer an offence to become an unlawful non-citizen,[9] but breach of the law can still render a non-citizen liable to prosecution. It remains an offence to present forged or false documents in connection with entry or to work without authorisation.[10] As well as being a passport to physical freedom within the community, the visa held by a non-citizen determines her or his entitlements to reside, work and/or change migration status.

[15.04] Underlying this simplification in concepts and terminology, there remain two broad groups of unlawful non-citizens, each comprising two sub-groups. There are those who have no valid visa, either because they arrive without any authority to enter, or because they overstay the period permitted by their original visa. We discuss this cohort, who hold unlawful status by operation of law, in Part 15.2. The second group are those whose visas are cancelled. We discuss those whose visas are cancelled because of their conduct at or before entry into the country in Part 15.3. We consider those whose visas are cancelled because of their conduct after entering Australia in Part 15.4.

[15.05] Within the 'unlawful' population, the most numerous are the overstayers, visa holders who have become unlawful at the expiry of the date or period of time specified on their visa.[11] Those who arrive at point of entry either without a visa or without a valid visa hold unlawful status by virtue of having by-passed or been

---

6   See *Migration Act 1958* (Cth), ss 33 and 34.
7   See *Migration Act*, ss 13, 14, 15 and 82(7) (referring to the consequences of cancellation or expiry of a visa). The concepts of 'deemed illegal entrants', 'prohibited entrants', 'prohibited non-citizens' and deemed non-entry disappeared.
8   See *Migration Act*, ss 189 and 198, and Part 2, Divs 10 and 14.
9   Compare s 77 of the Act before 1 September 1994.
10 *Migration Act*, ss 234 and 235; and below, Part 15.8.
11 Ibid, s 82(7).

refused immigration clearance, or having entered Australia in a way not permitted by the Act.[12] Of those persons whose visas are cancelled as the result of things they have done or failed to do at or before entry into Australia, some have obtained their visas on the basis of a false statement or through the production of 'bogus' documentation. Others are found to be suffering from a 'prescribed disease' that operates normally as a bar to the issue of a visa. Visas can also be cancelled where the holder has failed to declare his or her criminal record at the time of applying for the visa.[13] The final sub-group of visa cancellations comprises people who have worked without permission, committed serious offences warranting removal, or acted otherwise in breach of conditions imposed on their visa.[14]

[15.06] After considering these categories of unlawful migration, the chapter will examine mechanisms for regularising unlawful status in Part 15.5. In Part 15.6 we review the substantive visas, permanent and temporary, which are available to unlawful non-citizens. Part 15.7 outlines some historical approaches taken to the regularisation of status: quasi-amnesties that have become very much unfashionable policies of the past. We conclude with a brief discussion of offences under the Act in Part 15.8.

15.2 Unlawful status by operation of law: Unauthorised arrivals and overstayers

[15.07] Visas issued to non-citizens confer a right to enter and remain for the period stated on the visa. In the case of non-citizens arriving in Australia without any form of authority to enter the country, the law is clear. These people become unlawful non-citizens at point of entry into the migration zone. In the same way, persons who overstay their visas become unlawful on the expiry of their visa unless they are issued with a replacement authority. The Regulations become more complex, however, in the provision made for the regularisation of unlawful status for these groups of immigration outlaws.

[15.08] Persons apprehended at point of entry into Australia who fail to gain immigration clearance are only eligible to apply for either a Border visa (temporary) (Class TA) or a Protection visa (Class XA). Applications for a subclass 773 Border visa are assessed at the airport and can be made by certain 'innocent' but careless non-citizens who have failed to obtain a visa before arriving in Australia. Typical examples are persons who have forgotten to obtain a permit for their dependent child, returning residents, spouses of Australians, returning temporary visa holders who had to leave Australia on short notice and were unable to obtain a visa before departure, and 'risk-free' tourists who wish to enter Australia for a visit.[15] The Border visa may be subject to the conditions applicable to the visa last held by the applicant,

---

12   Ibid, ss 172(4) and 173. Section 177 also accords unlawful status to 'designated persons' who are defined as those without visas who arrived on a boat between 1989 and 1994.
13   See *Migration Act*, s 15 (consequence of visa cancellation), read together with ss 97, 109, 128, 140 and 500A-501J. See further Chapter 17.
14   Ibid, s 116, discussed below at Part 15.4.
15   See *Migration Regulations 1994* (Cth), Sch 2, subclass 773.

or the visa for which they appear to be eligible, and the courts have upheld the wide discretion vested in immigration officials in this regard.[16] Eligibility for a subclass 866 Protection visa allows non-citizens to apply for refugee status.[17] Such applications take some time to process and generally applicants will be detained until they are granted a bridging visa.

[15.09] The options available to overstayers will vary according to the length of time the person has been unlawful, the type of visa held at first instance, the reasons for the breach and the type of visa being sought: see below, Part 15.6.

15.3 Loss of lawful status: Cancellation of visa on grounds of irregularity upon or before entry into Australia

[15.10] For many years, lawful residence has been denied to holders of visas obtained on the basis of fraud, misrepresentation, or factual information that is incorrect or misleading. In the case of persons granted permanent residence, the government's ability to cancel an improperly obtained visa represents a significant exception to the rule that permanent residence can be lost only where a non-citizen is convicted of certain serious crimes.[18] In this section we outline sequentially the cancellation powers as they operate in geographical terms: before and after entry into Australia.

15.3.1 Offshore cancellation under s 128

[15.11] Providing incorrect information or bogus documents is a ground for visa cancellation under the general cancellation power which may be exercised when the visa holder is either in immigration clearance or still physically outside Australia. Section 128 provides that the Minister may cancel a visa *without notice* if the person is outside Australia, if the Minister is satisfied that a ground for cancellation exists under the general cancellation provision (s 116) and that cancellation in accordance with Part 2 Subdiv 3F of the *Migration Act 1958* (Cth) would be appropriate. In *Doukmak v MIMA*,[19] the Full Federal Court held that s 128 empowers the Minister to cancel the visa of a non-citizen who is outside Australia at the time of cancellation whether or not the non-citizen has been present in Australia at some time in the past.[20] Section 129 provides that the visa may be cancelled without notice, but affords the person an opportunity to have the cancellation revoked. In *Doukmak*, Moore J held that while recourse to s 116 is necessary to ascertain whether a ground for

---

16 See *Weir v MIAC* (2008) 104 ALD 67.
17 However, under s 48A of the *Migration Act*, a person who has previously been refused a Protection visa will be prevented from lodging a further application for a Protection visa unless the Minister personally gives permission to lodge the application under s 48B. Other restrictions on Protection visa applications are found in ss 91A-91W of the Act.
18 The general power to cancel a visa in s 116 of the Act cannot be used to cancel a permanent visa if the holder is in the migration zone and was immigration cleared on last entering Australia: s 117.
19 (2001) 114 FCR 432 at [48].
20 *Cheaib v MIMA* (1997) 75 FCR 308, confirmed in amendment introduced by *Migration Legislation (Amendment) Act (No 1) 1998* (Cth).

cancellation exists, s 128 does not incorporate an equivalent of s 116(3) (a provision that mandates cancellation in certain circumstances). Hence, when the Department considers exercising the power to cancel without notice under s 128, the power to cancel is discretionary. Moore J held that the record of decision in *Doukmak*, which referred to a 'discretion not to cancel' rather than a discretion to cancel, indicated that the delegate was asking himself or herself the wrong question.[21]

15.3.2 The procedure for cancellation under s 109

[15.12] Specific provisions allowing for the cancellation of visas because of incorrect information or fraudulent documentation are contained in and around s 109 of the Act, which are applicable when the applicant is present in Australia. This cancellation regime includes a variety of procedural safeguards, including requirements for notice and a right of appeal to the Migration Review Tribunal (MRT). The power to cancel an improperly obtained visa in s 109 of the Act is the centrepiece of a legislative regime that places positive obligations on visa applicants to provide correct information, not to furnish 'bogus' documentation and to inform the Department of any relevant changes in circumstances.[22] The three broad types of irregularity covered are those involving the provision of irregular immigration documentation or information about the visa applicant,[23] the entry of a person suffering from a prescribed disease or medical condition,[24] and the failure to disclose prior criminal convictions.[25] Visas may be cancelled even where false or misleading information is provided through inadvertence or simple error.[26] Perhaps in recognition of the harsh and, in some instances, dramatically retrospective operation of s 109, the case law suggests that reviewing courts have scrutinised s 109 cancellations very closely over the years.

[15.13] The *Migration Act* stipulates, in ss 101-105, that all visa applications and passenger cards must be fully completed, with no 'incorrect answers', and that no 'bogus' document be presented to an immigration official. These positive obligations on visa applicants extend to informing the Department of any change in circumstances that may have rendered incorrect a previously correct answer. Any incorrect answer must also be notified and corrected as soon as an applicant becomes aware of the error. If the Minister considers that the visa holder has not complied with these requirements, the Act states that he or she 'may' give the holder a notice indicating the particulars of any possible non-compliance and the possibility of cancellation. The 'notice of intention to cancel' must state that the holder has an opportunity to show the Minister that there was compliance, or show cause why the visa should not be cancelled.[27]

---

21   Ibid at [50].
22   See *Migration Act*, ss 97-104.
23   See ibid, ss 99-103.
24   See the public interest requirements set out in Sch 4 to the *Migration Regulations* and the definitions of 'health criterion' and 'health concern non-citizen' in s 5 of the Act.
25   See the 'character' provisions in ss 500A-501J, read together with the definition of 'behaviour concern non-citizen' in s 5 of the Act. The substantive dictates of the health and character rules are discussed at Chapter 6.3.
26   See *Migration Act*, ss 99-100, 111.
27   See ibid, s 107.

15.3.3 The meaning of 'incorrect answer'

[15.14] The meaning of the phrase 'incorrect answer' in s 101(b) of the Act was considered by Gray J in *Sandoval v MIMA*.[28] In that case, a Venezuelan citizen's tourist visa was cancelled at the airport on the basis that he had given an incorrect answer in his application form, within the meaning of s 101(b). In answer to the question 'Why do you want to visit Australia?', Mr Sandoval had written that his Australian friends (Ms Fenner and Dr Fenck) were offering him an opportunity to improve his English and that he was going to help them translate their books (in return for food and accommodation at their home). On his arrival at the Australian airport, Mr Sandoval was interviewed about the genuineness of his visit and his luggage was searched. Correspondence was found revealing an intimate relationship between and Mr Sandoval and Ms Fenner, with mention of marriage and starting a new life in Australia. After further questioning, the immigration inspector cancelled the visa under, inter alia, s 116(1)(d).[29]

[15.15] This cancellation decision was set aside in the Federal Court. Gray J observed that a person may have various purposes for visiting a country, but that the 'purpose' with which the relevant visa application form was concerned was 'what the visa applicant proposes to do during the period for which the visa is to be granted'.[30] His Honour also recalled the legislative history of the Act, noting that the former provisions referred to the making of 'a statement which is false or misleading in a material particular', in contrast to the current provisions which refer simply to 'incorrect answers'. His Honour concluded:[31]

> [T]he question 'Why do you want to visit Australia?' requires an applicant to give a reason, disclosing a purpose, genuinely held by the applicant, falling within the criteria for the visa concerned. It does not require an applicant to set out all of the reasons that he or she may have for wishing to come to Australia. As long as the reason specified in the answer is a genuine one, the answer cannot be said to be incorrect for the purposes of s 101(b) of the Migration Act.

[15.16] Gray J held, therefore, that it was not open to the immigration officer, as a matter of law, to be satisfied that Mr Sandoval had given an incorrect answer on the basis that Mr Sandoval had omitted information which he considered relevant:[32]

> Unless he was satisfied that the answer itself, or the material supplied with it, contained incorrect information he could not lawfully have found that the ground specified in s 116(1)(d) was made out. In purporting so to find, [the immigration officer] made an error of law, being an error involving an incorrect interpretation of the applicable law.

---

28 (2001) 194 ALR 71.
29 This was on the basis that the visa would be liable to cancellation under Subdiv C: incorrect information given by the visa holder had the holder entered Australia or been immigration cleared. Gray J held that the reference to Subdiv C in s 116(1)(d) is intended to import all of the provisions in Subdiv C into the section, except those only applicable to someone who has entered Australia and been immigration cleared (that is, ss 107-109). Therefore the interpretation of the phrase 'incorrect answer' is relevant to cancellation under both ss 109 and 116(1)(d).
30 (2001) 194 ALR 71 at [48]ff. His Honour referred to *Saravanan v MIMA* [2001] FCA 938.
31 Ibid at [50].
32 Ibid at [51].

[15.17] This interpretation of the phrase 'incorrect answer' has been confirmed in subsequent decisions. In *Singh v MIMA*,[33] the Federal Magistrates Court considered delegates' decisions to cancel the permanent residence visas of twin sisters from Fiji. The delegate had cancelled the sisters' visas on the basis that they made a false declaration in a change of circumstances form two years earlier in failing to disclose that they had become engaged to be married. Granting the visas one month earlier, the MRT had found that the sisters were dependent single children although one of the sisters was contemplating marriage. After the sisters' boyfriends lodged prospective spouse applications, and after interviews with all the parties, the delegate concluded that the engagements had been formalised before the sisters' change in circumstances forms, in other words that the engagements had been longstanding and had not been disclosed, amounting to an 'incorrect answer'. The sisters' permanent residence visas were cancelled. On review, the Federal Magistrates Court overturned the cancellation decisions, finding that it was not open to the delegate on the evidence before her to conclude that the sisters had been formally engaged and failed to disclose this in the change of circumstances form. Evidence pointed to the fact that the boyfriends had proposed to the sisters, and that the sisters had accepted, but in the family's cultural context this did not amount to a formal betrothal since the sisters' parents had not yet given permission. With this final step not having been taken, there was no engagement and nothing to disclose on the change of circumstances form. There was no 'incorrect answer'.

[15.18] The judgment in *Singh* in some respects recalls an earlier line of authority where the ambiguity of the applicant's personal situation meant that their answers did not fit neatly into the simple true/false matrix envisaged in the Act. For example, in *Nolan v MIEA*[34] the applicant was alleged to have made a false statement when she marked 'never married' on her passenger card. The applicant argued that the statement was not false because she did not regard her live-in boyfriend as a de facto spouse. The Federal Court accepted her position, and held that the applicant could not be considered to have made a false statement for the purposes of the former incarnation of s 109 (former s 20). However, an applicant's intention to mislead is irrelevant to a decision to cancel a visa under either the former s 20 or the present s 109 of the Act,[35] and, in the present day legal setting where a de facto relationship is defined in the Act (see further Chapter 7.2), an applicant's subjective perception of their relationship status now seems far less relevant.

15.3.4 The cancellation decision

[15.19] The most distinctive feature of the present system is that visa cancellation is not automatic. In recognition of the harsh and, in some instances, retrospective operation of s 109, the visa holder is entitled to a hearing before cancellation (by interview). The Minister may only cancel a visa under s 109 after having decided that there was non-compliance; and having considered any submissions by the visa

---

33 [2006] FMCA 1163.
34 (1992) 27 ALD 755.
35 See *Migration Act*, ss 99-100, 111; and earlier *Re MILGEA v Dela Cruz* (1992) 34 FCR 348 at 352.

holder under s 107 and other matters enumerated in the *Migration Regulations 1994* (Cth).[36]

[15.20] In deciding that a breach of s 109 has occurred, the Minister bears the onus of proving the case against the applicant.[37] Given the gravity of the consequences flowing from an adverse finding, the standard of proof required has been said to be one of 'a high degree of satisfaction'.[38] The decision-maker must identify the 'correct' information and the content of the genuine document (if any). The Minister must consider the visa holder's submissions and the circumstances in which the non-compliance occurred; the likely effect of the correct information on the decision to grant the visa; the circumstances of the visa holder, including the time that has elapsed since the breach; and the contribution that the person has made to the community.[39] A purported cancellation will be unlawful unless a decision-maker considers fully the extent of an individual's integration into a community; the seriousness of the breach; and whether the visa holder has engaged in other dishonest conduct either before the breach or subsequent to it.[40]

[15.21] In general, failure to particularise the non-compliance in the s 107 notice will also render a purported cancellation unlawful.[41] However, the Federal Magistrates Court has cautioned that this should not be taken so far as 'to abandon in the analysis of this issue commonsense or the substance of the issue'.[42]

[15.22] A person whose visa is cancelled under s 109 may appeal the cancellation to the MRT. Strict time limits apply. Those whose visas are cancelled while in immigration clearance do not have this right of appeal.[43] This appeal right is similar to that which is held by a visa holder whose visa is cancelled on character grounds under s 501 or whose business visa is cancelled under s 134, who generally have a right of appeal to the Administrative Appeals Tribunal (AAT) (unless the Minister issues a conclusive certificate) (see further Part 15.4.2).

[15.23] These provisions stand in sharp contrast to the former regime in which visas or entry permits gained by irregular means were deemed to have been cancelled from the moment of a person's entry into the country. The provisions operated automatically and with retrospective effect. There was no right to appeal the merits of a determination that a visa had been obtained by irregular means. While the Secretary of the Department had the power to 'endorse' a person's visa so as to allow admission in spite of a former irregularity, this procedure was far from a formal review

---

36 As a result of amendments made by the *Migration Legislation Amendment (Procedural Fairness) Act 2002* (Cth), the Subdivision dealing with the cancellation of visas under s 109 is taken to be 'an exhaustive statement of the requirements of the natural justice hearing rule in the matters it deals with': see s 97A.
37 *NBDY v MIMA* [2006] FCAFC 145 at [31]; *Singh v MIEA* (1994) 127 ALR 383.
38 See *Tarasovski v MILGEA* (1993) 45 FCR 570 at 572-3.
39 See *Migration Regulations*, reg 2.41.
40 *Zhong v MIAC* (2008) 171 FCR 444; *von Kraft v MIAC* [2007] FCA 917.
41 See *Saleem v MRT* [2004] FCA 234.
42 *Gido-Christian v MIAC* [2007] FMCA 825 at [87]. In this case, the court denied an applicant's challenge to the general language in the notice of intention to cancel her visa following some years of investigation for 'marriage fraud'.
43 See *Migration Act*, s 338(3).

mechanism. Instead, persons who were deemed unlawful were forced to litigate their cases in the Federal Court, arguing that the Minister had either misconstrued the legislation or made an error of fact so fundamental that it rendered unlawful the deemed revocation of the visa.[44]

[15.24] The jurisprudence concerning the earlier deeming provisions provides interesting examples of how the migration legislation has been changed progressively in response to particular court rulings. A source of great controversy was determining the significance of any misstatement or provision of false information in the context of the original decision to grant a visa or entry permit. Throughout the 1980s, there were a number of cases in which the Federal Court took issue with the Department's interpretation of the phrase 'false and misleading in a material particular', importing into it an element of purpose. The court found that the requirement of materiality meant that there had to be some nexus between the false and misleading statement made and the issue of the entry permit. Where the connection between the misstatement and the issue of the visa could not be made, the court declined to deem unlawful the holder of the visa. For example, in *Naumovska v MIEA*,[45] Sheppard J used this line of reasoning to hold that the incorrectly completed passenger card tendered by the applicant on disembarkation was not produced for the purpose of gaining entry to Australia. His Honour held that the documents produced for this purpose were the woman's passport and visa. The Act was amended to address this element of Sheppard J's judgment.[46]

[15.25] Although issues of materiality and purpose continued to be the subject of argumentation in the early 1990s,[47] the trend in the courts seems to have been against questioning the significance ascribed by the immigration authorities to false or misleading information proffered by an applicant for a visa. In a similar vein, the courts accepted that an applicant's state of mind or intention to mislead is irrelevant to a decision to cancel a visa under either the former s 20 or the present s 109 of the Act.[48]

---

44 For its part, the Federal Court scrutinised closely both the legislation and its application to the facts of the cases presented before it, showing particular concern for the draconian impact of the law in cases involving the deemed revocation of permanent resident status. For example, it rejected the Minister's contention that where a determination was made under s 16 (later s 20) the onus lay on the applicant to disprove the fraud or irregularity alleged: *Naumovska v MIEA* (1982) 60 FLR 267, affirmed at (1983) 88 ALR 589. However, where no error of law could be identified, the courts had no option but to uphold the determination made. In the context of the struggle between the courts and the government over the control of immigration, it is interesting that some of the most prolonged and intimate exchanges between the two arms of authority occurred in the context of cases involving deemed unlawful status: see Mary Crock, *Administrative Law and Immigration Control in Australia: Actions and Reactions* (unpublished PhD Thesis, University of Melbourne, 1994) Ch 6.2.

45 (1982) 60 FLR 267.

46 See the former *Migration Act*, s 20(10), (11) and (12), read with the definition of 'bogus document' in s 20(15) of the Act. The issue of passenger cards and their significance is dealt with now in ss 102 and 105 of the Act and *Migration Regulations* reg 3.02.

47 See, for example, in *Re MILGEA v Dela Cruz* (1992) 34 FCR 348 and *Re Rubrico v MIEA* (1989) 23 FCR 208.

48 See *Re MILGEA v Dela Cruz* (1992) 34 FCR 348 at 352; *R v Governor of Metropolitan Gaol; Ex parte Di Nardo* (1962) 3 FLR 271 at 275; *Re Silva v MILGEA* [1989] FCA 212; and *Re Jovcevski v MILGEA* [1989] FCA 422.

In *Hsiao v MILGEA*,[49] the Federal Court held that s 20 operated to deem unlawful an applicant who did not understand the contents of a document tendered for the purpose of gaining entry into the country. It ruled that, in signing the document in question, the applicant had adopted its contents, even though it was prepared by a third party in a language that the applicant did not understand. The court held that the fact that the document contained material that was false and misleading in a material particular was sufficient to bring the applicant within s 20 of the Act.

[15.26] The cases in which both the Federal Court and the tribunals have taken issue with cancellation decisions are those where some ambiguity has surrounded the applicant's personal situation. For example, as noted above in [15.18], in *Nolan v MIEA*[50] the applicant was alleged to have made a false statement when she marked 'never married' on her passenger card. The applicant argued that the statement was not false because she did not regard her live-in boyfriend as a de facto spouse. The Federal Court accepted her position, and held that the applicant could not be considered to have made a false statement for the purposes of s 20 of the Act. In the context of this case, it is noteworthy that s 104 of the Act now imposes a positive obligation on applicants to notify changes in circumstances that would render any answers given in an application incorrect.

[15.27] The Federal Court and MRT have continued to approach cancellation decisions involving alleged marriage fraud with caution. As Wilcox J commented in *Tarasovski v MILGEA*,[51] it is well for decision-makers to be conscious of a tendency in former partners involved in a bitter break-up to re-write history. In cases where there are mitigating circumstances surrounding the misstatements or misrepresentations made, the Immigration Review Tribunal (IRT) did not hesitate to use its discretion to excuse the non-citizens involved. This is particularly so where the tribunal took the view that cancellation of a visa would constitute an unfair and disproportionately harsh penalty for the visa holder.[52] On the other hand, the Federal Court and the review authorities have endorsed the hard line taken by the immigration authorities in dealing with people who seek to benefit either directly or indirectly from immigration fraud.[53] Even where a person's dishonest conduct may not result directly in a visa cancellation, it can be invoked as evidence of general misconduct so as to exclude the person on character grounds.[54]

[15.28] Successive governments have been determined to maintain an uncompromising approach to persons who seek to benefit from immigration fraud. In December 1996, the *Australian Citizenship Act 1948* (Cth) was amended so as to confer on the Minister unprecedented power to revoke a grant of citizenship to a person who has gained the status of Australian citizen as a result of immigration fraud or

---

49 (1992) 36 FCR 330.
50 (1992) 27 ALD 755.
51 (1993) 45 FCR 570 at 584.
52 See *Re McQuade* [1996] IRTA 7840.
53 See *Re Slayman* [1996] IRTA 7927; and *Re Jason Kiat Chung Lo* [1996] IRTA 7986.
54 See *Re Naidu and MIEA* (1996) 42 ALD 137; *Re Lachmaiya and MIEA* (1994) 19 AAR 148; and *Re Prasad and MIEA* (1994) 35 ALD 780. See Chapter 6.3.2 and Chapter 17.

misrepresentation. The power to revoke is without limitation as to the time a person has spent as a naturalised Australian.[55]

15.4 Loss of lawful status: Cancellation of temporary visas after entry into Australia

15.4.1 The general cancellation power under s 116

[15.29] The other broad sub-group of visa cancellation decisions in respect of which there exists a right of appeal to the MRT is that of non-citizens who have breached the terms of their temporary visas. The history of the legislation governing this area of migration law is interesting, if somewhat conflicting. Over the years the relevant provisions of the Act have come almost full circle, from a situation where the Minister had an 'absolute discretion' to cancel a temporary permit,[56] to one where 'terminating conditions' made cancellation automatic,[57] to the present regime where breach of a visa condition once again triggers (in most cases) a discretion to cancel a visa.

[15.30] The general power to cancel a visa after entry is set out in s 116 of the Act. The power does not extend to the cancellation of a permanent visa if the holder of the visa is in the migration zone and has been immigration cleared: s 117. Unlike persons who have their visas cancelled under s 109, notice of a proposed cancellation under s 116 must be given in accordance with ss 119-127 of the Act. Decisions to cancel a temporary visa can be reviewed directly by the MRT.[58]

[15.31] In most cases the Minister has a discretion to cancel the visa if a ground for cancellation is established. However, there are certain grounds that, if established, trigger mandatory cancellation of the visa. Discretionary grounds include: where circumstances which permitted the grant of the visa no longer exist; breach of a visa condition; the visa holder has provided incorrect information or bogus documents; and the visa holder poses a risk to Australian health, safety or good order. Cancellation is mandatory if the visa holder's presence would prejudice Australia's relations with a foreign country or if the visa holder is a threat to national security.[59] In most cases the visa holder will be given notice that the Minister is considering cancellation of the visa.

[15.32] The statutory recognition that temporary visa holders have a right to be heard before cancellation of their visa is consistent with jurisprudence that has developed concerning the hearing rights of these people.[60] After 1989, the Minister retained

---

55 See *Australian Citizenship Act 2007* (Cth), s 34. See former s 21 of the *Australian Citizenship 1948* (Cth), as amended in 1997.
56 Former s 35(1).
57 See *Migration Regulations 1989* (Cth) (*1989 Regulations*), reg 27.
58 See *Migration Act*, s 338(3).
59 *Migration Regulations*, reg 2.43(2)(a).
60 In spite of the language of 'absolute' discretion used in the Act, and the contrary authority of the High Court in *Salemi v MacKellar (No 2)* (1977) 137 CLR 396, the push towards recognising the procedural rights of temporary permit holders was already strong in the early 1980s. See, for example: *Arslan v Durrell* (1983) 48 ALR 577 (overruled in (1984) 4 FCR 73). In *Sezdirmezoglu v MIEA* (1983) 51 ALR 561, Smithers J avoided the natural justice 'problem by' using the doctrine of

the power to cancel temporary entry permits at any time, at his or her 'absolute discretion', under what used to be s 35(1) of the Act. An attempt was made to remove or reduce the scope for the review of cancellation decisions through the imposition of 'terminating conditions' on visas. These provided for the automatic cancellation of a permit on the occurrence of certain events, or on the performance by the holder of certain actions.[61] Such provisions removed the need to make a decision to cancel a permit, because this occurred as a matter of law. It is doubtful that these precluded altogether the permit holder's right to be heard. Once a breach was established, however, temporary permits were deemed to have been cancelled. The elimination of any discretion in the cancellation of the permit also removed the holder's right to be heard on matters going to explain or excuse the breach.[62]

[15.33] The present regime has abandoned these attempts to restrict review, in recognition that the former system forced visa holders to litigate cancellation decisions in the Federal Court – a form of recourse that is both expensive and time consuming.

Procedure for cancellation under s 116

[15.34] The procedure for cancellation of visas under s 116 is set out in ss 118A-127 of the Act. Notice of the proposed cancellation must be given to the holder, together with any 'relevant information', and they must be given the opportunity to make submissions. Like the Subdivision dealing with cancellation pursuant to s 109, this code of procedure is taken to be 'an exhaustive statement of the requirements of natural justice'.[63]

[15.35] In *Walton v Ruddock*,[64] Merkel J considered the requirements under ss 120 and 121 of the Act and the rules of natural justice in relation to the cancellation of visas at immigration clearance under s 116. The applicant in that case had his tourist visa cancelled at the airport under s 116(g) of the Act and reg 2.43(1)(k) of the *Migration Regulations*, on the basis that the immigration officer was satisfied that the applicant did not have 'an intention to visit Australia only for tourism purposes'. On arrival, the applicant carried a return ticket to the USA dated three weeks later. However, documents in his possession showed that he had arranged for the shipment to Australia of his personal effects. Immigration officials also found a letter stating that he was moving to Australia and that he intended to lodge an application for

---

ultra vires. By the end of the decade, the right to a hearing before cancellation was no longer an issue for the courts. Under the Act as it stood before December 1989, this meant that the range of matters in respect of which a decision-maker could be required to grant a hearing was as broad as the discretion to grant a temporary permit under what was s 7(1) of the Act. See, for example, *Waniewska v MIEA* (1986) 70 ALR 284; *Taveli v MIEA* (1990) 23 FCR 162; *Akbas v MIEA* (1985) 7 FCR 363; *Daguio v MIEA* (1986) 71 ALR 173; *Broussard v MIEA* (1989) 21 FCR 472; and *Youssef v MIEA* (1987) 14 ALD 550.

61 See *1989 Regulations*, reg 27.
62 This result seemed almost to bring the law back to what it was thought to be before *Kioa v West* (1985) 159 CLR 550. See, for example, *MIEA v Gaillard* (1983) 49 ALR 277 where the Full Federal Court held that a temporary resident could have no right to be heard in respect of a visa cancellation.
63 See s 118A of the Act.
64 (2001) 115 FCR 342.

permanent residency. An interview was then conducted with the applicant's partner (Ms Hart), an Australian citizen, in which she stated that, if the applicant could not obtain permanent residency in Australia, his return air ticket would be a safeguard, and that she would like this to be the applicant's first Christmas in Australia, then months away.

[15.36] On appeal to the Federal Court, the applicant contended that by failing to disclose Ms Hart's statements to the applicant, the delegate had not given him particulars of information that 'would be the reason, or part of the reason, for cancelling [the] visa', or an opportunity to comment on that information (as required by ss 120 and 121). However, Merkel J dismissed this ground of appeal on the basis that the record of the cancellation decision did not state or imply that Ms Hart's statements were a reason, or part of the reason for the delegate's decision to cancel the visa. Merkel J also rejected the applicant's contention that the delegate had breached the rules of natural justice by failing to give him an opportunity to respond to Ms Hart's statements, which were adverse matters taken into account in the delegate's decision to cancel the visa. His Honour first stated that Ms Hart's statements were not necessarily inconsistent with the genuineness of the applicant's visit. His Honour went on to note that, even if an adverse interpretation of the statements were taken, he was satisfied that the 'gravamen or substance of the issue' raised by the statement was put to the applicant, and he was on notice as to its 'essential features'.[65]

[15.37] In *Zhaou v MIMIA*,[66] Kenny J also considered the requirements of a notice and opportunity to comment under ss 119 and 121 of the Act. In that case, the applicant's tourist visa was cancelled on the basis that the he did not have, or had ceased to have, an intention only to visit Australia temporarily for tourism purposes. An immigration official, Mr Tobin, signed a 'notice of intention to consider cancelling a visa', which identified the possible ground for cancellation and informed the applicant: 'You will need to provide your comments within 10 minutes of the start of the interview'. Mr Tobin explained the notice to the applicant twice and then left him alone in the interview room, returning for roughly 12 minutes. After the interview, the visa was cancelled. On appeal, the applicant argued that he had not been afforded time to consider his response to the notice as required,[67] and that the time specified in the invitation was not a reasonable period in the circumstances of the case. The Federal Court rejected both of the applicant's submissions. Kenny J held that what is a reasonable place and period for a visa holder's response under s 121(3)(b) of the Act must be determined in light of all the circumstances of the case. These circumstances may include:

> the nature of the cancellation grounds that the decision-maker is considering, the personal attributes of the visa holder (ie, age, facility in the English language, physical infirmity or well-being), the presence of an interpreter or lawyer, the visa holder's familiarity with the matters of concern to the decision-maker, the circumstances in which the decision falls to be made, and the availability of matters corroborative of the applicant.[68]

---

65 Ibid at [69]. See also *Li v MIAC (No 2)* [2007] FMCA 22.
66 [2002] FCA 748.
67 See *Migration Act*, s 119(1)(b), read together with s 121(3)(b).
68 [2002] FCA 748 at [78].

[15.38] Kenny J noted that, before giving Mr Zhaou the notice, Mr Tobin had made him aware that he was considering cancelling the visa. In particular, he had informed Mr Zhaou of his concern that Mr Zhaou intended to work as a service manager or cook in a friend's restaurant, and drew his attention to the evidence that tended to support this view. During the interview Mr Zhaou appeared to have understood Mr Tobin's questions and responded to them adequately. There was nothing to indicate that he could not physically cope with the interview. Mr Zhaou had not claimed that there was anything else he would or could have added had he had a longer opportunity to consider and make his response.[69]

[15.39] The powers of the MRT have been considered by the Full Federal Court in a series of cases where the original decision to cancel was flawed because of a failure to provide notice of the considered cancellation.[70] Affected visa holders have argued that a failure to give adequate notice under s 119 means that neither the original decision-maker nor the tribunal has power to cancel a visa. In such circumstances, the tribunal on review must exercise its power under s 349(2) to set aside the cancellation decision. This argument is based on the fact that the MRT stands in the shoes of the original decision-maker. If the original decision-maker had no jurisdiction to make a decision because of a procedural irregularity, the jurisdictional prerequisite for the tribunal to make a new decision did not exist. A stream cannot rise higher than its source. The Minister has argued in response that inadequate notice under s 119 does not preclude the tribunal from examining the cancellation on the merits.

[15.40] The Full Federal Court has endorsed the Minister's interpretation, ruling that the MRT does have jurisdiction to cancel the visa. This is so even where the original decision-maker failed to comply with the procedural requirements leading to the initial purported cancellation. In effect, compliance or non-compliance with the procedures set out in s 119 only affects the jurisdiction of the Minister's delegate to make a cancellation decision.[71] By the time the review process is enlivened, procedures under s 119 are relevant only as to whether the visa was cancelled or purportedly cancelled. The tribunal may re-make the cancellation decision in accordance with the procedures governing the conduct of its review.[72]

15.4.2 The cancellation of business visas

[15.41] A business visa may be cancelled under the general cancellation powers in the Act. However, business skills visas granted under the visa program existing before 2003 are subject to special cancellation provisions.[73] The Business Talent visa

---

69 This decision can be contrasted with *Zhang Jia Qing v MIMA* [1997] FCA 1177, in which Burchett J held that it was not reasonable to require the applicant to respond 'when and where he had been kept for so long without eating, and after he had indicated – that he was feeling unwell'.
70 See *MIMIA v Ahmed* (2005) 143 FCR 314; *Zubair v MIMIA* (2004) 139 FCR 344; and *Krummrey v MIMIA* (2005) 147 FCR 557.
71 See ibid. Note that these decisions are consistent with the reasoning of the High Court in *Shi v Migration Agents Registration Authority* (2008) 235 CLR 286.
72 *MIMIA v Ahmed* (2005) 143 FCR 314; *Zubair v MIMIA* (2004) 139 FCR 344; *Krummrey v MIMIA* (2005) 147 FCR 557.
73 See *Migration Act*, ss 134-137, and *Migration Regulations*, reg 2.50.

(subclass 132) is the only visa that remains susceptible to this special cancellation scheme. The reason for this is that most business visa applicants are now granted provisional visas. Eligibility for a permanent visa depends on fulfilment of expectations connected to the provisional visa.

[15.42] The special business visa cancellation provisions give the Minister power to cancel a visa if the holder:
- has not obtained a substantial ownership interest in an eligible Australian business; or
- is not or does not intend to continue using his or her skills in actively participating in the day-to-day management of the business at a senior level.

The visa must not be cancelled if the Minister is satisfied the holder has made a genuine effort to obtain a substantial ownership interest in an eligible business, or to use their senior management skills. The person must also intend to continue to make genuine efforts in the future. Section 134(3) sets out the matters which may be taken into account in assessing whether a genuine effort has been made. The visas are cancelled by giving the holder written notice. The holder can then respond by setting out reasons why the visa should not be cancelled. A decision to cancel a visa under these provisions is reviewable by the AAT.

15.4.3 The automatic cancellation of student visas

[15.43] As explored in Chapter 11.1.5, specific provision is made for the automatic cancellation of student visas under ss 137J-137P of the Act. A student visa will be cancelled automatically if the holder fails to comply, within 28 days, with a notice sent to the holder by an education provider under s 20 of the *Education Services for Overseas Students Act 2000* (Cth) (regarding non-compliance with course requirements), by attending in person at the Department's office. If the student does attend, the delegate has discretion not to cancel the student visa where there are exceptional circumstances beyond the visa holder's control.[74]

[15.44] A student can apply for revocation of a cancellation within 28 days of the cancellation if they are outside of Australia or within two working days if they are in Australia and in detention. The Minister may revoke the cancellation if satisfied that the student did not in fact breach the visa condition or the breach was due to exceptional circumstances beyond the student's control. These do not include that the student was unaware of the notice or the automatic cancellation mechanism.

15.4.4 The cancellation of visas on character grounds

[15.45] There is one further regime for the cancellation of visas after entry into the country: cancellation on grounds that an individual is of bad character. Raising unique issues, this area is considered separately, in Chapter 17.

---

74 See Condition 8202 and Ministerial Direction 38. For background to this scheme, see *Morsed v MIMIA* (2005) 88 ALD 90 discussed in detail at Chapter 11.1.5. See also *Hossain v MIAC* (2010) 183 FCR 157; and *Mo v MIAC* [2010] FCA 162.

15.5 General requirements for the regularisation of unlawful status

15.5.1 Time limits, Bridging visas and other 'threshold' requirements

[15.46] The flexibility given to decision-makers in respect of the cancellation of visas stands in contrast to the law governing the grant of a visa to a non-citizen in Australia who has lost her or his lawful status. The Act and the Regulations contain detailed specifications about who can apply for a permit within Australia and on what grounds. In essence, a person's entitlement to a visa will depend on where they are; the visa (if any) held previously; how lawful status was lost and the length of time that the person has been an unlawful non-citizen.

[15.47] The most immediate issue of concern when advising an unlawful non-citizen is whether the person has been arrested and placed in immigration detention. Quite apart from the inconvenience and indignity entailed, such enforcement action has an immediate impact on the options available for an unlawful non-citizen to regularise her or his status. An application for a substantive visa must be lodged within two working days (extendable to seven on application) of a non-citizen being detained. The only substantive visa available to a person detained for longer than these periods is a Protection visa.[75] The constraints placed on persons who are detained while still in immigration clearance have already been noted: see Part 15.2 above.

[15.48] The primary mechanism for avoiding the arrest and detention consequences of unlawful status is the acquisition of one of the seven classes of Bridging visa, discussed in more detail in Chapter 16.5.1. With the exception of the Return Pending Bridging visa, these visas do not affect a person's longer term right to remain in the country. As the name suggests, they are visas designed to place a hold on a person's immigration status for the purpose of ascertaining entitlement to a substantive visa. This is defined in s 5 as any visa other than a Bridging visa; a Criminal Justice visa; or an Enforcement visa.

[15.49] As with all applicants for a visa who are in the migration zone, unlawful non-citizens are restricted in the classes of visas for which they may apply both by Sch 1 and Sch 2 to the Regulations. The first schedule sets out the visa classes in respect of which an application must be lodged offshore. An unlawful non-citizen is not required to leave Australia to lodge applications for some of these 'overseas' visas. (Where an applicant must be situated at the time a visa is granted is set out in the visa subclasses in Sch 2 under the heading 'circumstances applicable to grant'.) However, the Regulations make it difficult for unlawful non-citizens in the country to gain permission to wait out in Australia the processing periods for applications made overseas. Since 1 October 1996 an applicant cannot get a Bridging visa on the basis of lodging an application overseas. For those who do leave the country and seek a visa overseas, some restrictions continue to be placed on the readmission of persons who left Australia as unlawful non-citizens: see Sch 5.

---

75 *Migration Act*, s 195.

Repeat applications and change in circumstances

[15.50] A person within Australia who has had a visa cancelled or has had an application for a visa refused is only permitted to apply for certain classes of visas prescribed by the Regulations.[76] Where an application is withdrawn before determination, it is not taken to be refused.[77] This means that while a person holds a substantive visa, in theory she or he can apply for as many other visas as desired until such time as one of the applications is determined. In practice, simultaneous visa applications are discouraged.

[15.51] The limited provision for 'second' visa applications does not extend to persons who have had their initial visa cancelled under ss 501, 501A or 501B of the Act (for bad character, misconduct or related grounds). Bars are placed also on repeat applications for refugee status where a refugee claim has been rejected, unless the Minister exercises a residual (non-compellable, non-reviewable) discretion to allow a second application under s 48B of the Act.[78]

15.5.2 The Schedule 3 criteria

[15.52] The final threshold or generic requirements that must be met by unlawful non-citizens are those set out in Sch 3 to the Regulations. The five parts of this schedule are identified by numbers which are used in turn as cross-referencing codes in the visa subclasses of Sch 2. The parts provide, in turn, for the times within which unlawful non-citizens must seek regularisation of their status (cll 3001 and 3002) and what might be referred to as the 'exculpatory' prerequisites for the grant of a substantive visa. The time limits must be read in conjunction with the time limits imposed by s 195 of the Act on persons who have been arrested and placed in immigration detention. These exculpatory requirements include specifications that an applicant demonstrate that she or he became unlawful due to 'factors beyond (his or her) control'; that there are compelling reasons for the grant of a visa; and that the applicant has complied 'substantially' with any conditions subject to which the last visa or entry permit was granted. Most of the onshore visas available to unlawful non-citizens include one or more of the Sch 3 criteria.

---

76   Ibid, s 48 and *Migration Regulations*, reg 2.12. At the time of writing, the visa subclasses prescribed by reg 2.12 are: Partner (Temporary) (Class UK); Partner (Residence) (Class BS); Protection (Class XA); Medical Treatment (Visitor) (Class UB); Territorial Asylum (Residence) (Class BE); Border (Temporary) (Class TA); Special Category (Temporary) (Class TY); the various classes of Bridging visas; Resolution of Status (Temporary) (Class UH); Resolution of Status (Residence) (Class CD); and Child (Residence) (Class BT).
77   *Migration Act*, s 49.
78   See *MIMA v Ozmanian* (1996) 141 ALR 322; *Bedlington v Chong* (1998) 87 FCR 75; *QAAB v MIMIA* [2004] FCAFC 309. Note that these cases must be read in conjunction with *Plaintiff M61/2010E v Commonwealth and Plaintiff M69 of 2010 v Commonwealth* (2010) 272 ALR 14. See Mary Crock and Daniel Ghezelbash, 'Due Process and Rule of Law as Human Rights: The High Court and the "Offshore" Processing of Asylum Seekers' (2011) 18(2) *Australian Journal of Administrative Law* 101.

Time limits

[15.53] The strictest of the Sch 3 criteria are those imposing time limits on the regularisation of status. Where a non-citizen in immigration detention fails to apply for a visa within the statutory two or seven day period specified in s 195 of the Act, he or she becomes ineligible for change of status except on refugee grounds (or where the Minister exercises his or her residual discretion). The MRT ceases to have jurisdiction to hear an appeal. Although questions have arisen in some cases about the point in time at which a non-citizen became unlawful, once this status (and the right to apply for a visa in the specified time period) is communicated to the applicant the matter becomes one of simple arithmetic.[79] The MRT has no scope to excuse an applicant who has failed to lodge an application within the stated time, even where the failure is inadvertent or the result of bad advice or the incompetence of a third party.[80] The MRT has determined that it has no discretion in determining whether an application was recorded as being received in time: the matter is simply a question of fact. The tribunal has no power to consider excuses for lateness.[81]

[15.54] An early example in point is the case of *Re Song Mao Li*.[82] There the applicant lodged his request for a subclass 820 Spouse visa one day late after a blood test taken for the purposes of the application had been mislaid by the medical authorities. The IRT had no power to grant a permit, even though the applicant's Australian wife gave birth to the couple's first child shortly before the tribunal hearing. The tribunal recommended that the applicant seek an exercise of the Minister's residual discretion to grant a permit under s 351 of the Act.

[15.55] Where more extensive jurisprudence has developed is in considering the 'exculpatory' criteria relating to why applicants became unlawful non-citizens in the first place. Interestingly, while the early tribunal cases focused on the identification of factors beyond an applicant's control, in more recent jurisprudence the emphasis has been on the notion of 'compelling reasons' for the grant of a visa.

Factors beyond the applicant's control

[15.56] On the question of whether legal status was lost due to 'factors beyond the control' of an applicant, the tribunals have accepted as excuses matters such as serious illness, physical injury and other events impeding or preventing the renewal of a visa that was due to expire. In *Ramos*,[83] the nominator lodged his wife's various applications for visas on her behalf because she was sick. Although she was lawful on that day, the nominator failed to lodge the correct visa application fee. This meant that the application could not be processed until the following Monday, by which

---

79 *Tan v MIAC* [2007] FCA 1427.
80 See, for example, *Liu v MIAC* [2008] FMCA 725; *McCarthy, Kevin* [2002] MRTA 339; and older cases such as *Chand v MILGEA* (1993) 30 ALD 777; and *Qalovi v MIEA* (1994) 50 FCR 301.
81 See, for example, *Re F W* [1996] IRTA 6790 and *Re MGC* [1996] IRTA 6788.
82 [1995] IRTA 5785.
83 [2002] MRTA 5201. The wife applied for an Extended Eligibility (Temporary) (Class UK) visa, subclass 820 (Spouse) and a General (Residence) (Class BS) visa, subclass 801 (Spouse) visa.

time the applicant's tourist visa had expired. The delegate of the Minister refused the application on the basis that the applicant had not met the Sch 3 criterion. This decision was set aside by the MRT. The tribunal was satisfied that the error made by the nominator, and his inability to remedy the error before the close of business, were factors beyond the control of the visa applicant.

[15.57] Both the tribunal and the courts have ruled that ignorance of the law and bad or no advice from a responsible migration agent do not constitute factors beyond the control of an applicant.[84] However, departmental policy advises that 'claims that an applicant was unaware they were an illegal entrant or a person in Australia without a substantive visa should be considered on a case by case basis'. It seems that incorrect advice given by the Department may constitute such a factor.[85] For example, the tribunal was prepared to excuse an elderly visa applicant who incorrectly formed the view that her visa was of 12 months' duration when in fact it expired after six months. The tribunal considered as factors 'beyond her control' her reliance on her son for guidance as well as circumstantial matters (such as a 12-month Medicare card in her name) which encouraged her mistaken belief.[86] The case law on fraudulent advisers is also of relevance in this context.[87]

[15.58] The early migration tribunals found the phrase to cover applicants who failed to observe temporal and other conditions on their first visa because of a fear of returning to their country of origin. In *Re Seneca-Pinchon v MIEA*,[88] for example, the applicant claimed that she was afraid of returning to a drug-addicted partner at whose hands she had suffered domestic violence. The tribunal considered that the cumulative effect of the emotional state of the applicant, the continued threats made against her person, and her genuine confusion as to the real period of stay to which she was entitled, amounted to factors beyond her control. In *Re Mr B*,[89] the applicant claimed that his fears were generated by memories of sexual abuse suffered as a child at the hands of his mother. The evidence before the tribunal included a psychiatric report indicating that the applicant was suffering from post-traumatic stress disorder, and that his condition would be aggravated if he were to return to his country of origin. There was also evidence of a suicide attempt: the applicant overdosed on tablets during a visit by his mother. The tribunal was prepared to acknowledge that these circumstances amounted to factors beyond the control of the applicant. Despite this finding, the applicant was ultimately unsuccessful. The applicant failed to satisfy the criterion in Sch 3, cl 3003(f), of the *Migration Regulations* due to his lack of entitlement to be granted an equivalent entry permit immediately before becoming an unlawful non-citizen.[90]

---

84 See *Su v MIAC* [2007] FMCA 318. See also *Susaki v MIMA* [1999] FCA 196.
85 *Mcbeth, John* [2003] MRTA 3546.
86 *Hayes, Audrey Joan* [2003] MRTA 4607.
87 See *SZFDE v MIAC* (2007) 232 CLR 189 at [48]-[52], discussed in Chapter 18.4.6.
88 [1996] IRTA 6473.
89 [1996] IRTA 6394.
90 See also *Re Marshall* [1996] IRTA 6397 (fear of discrimination on religious grounds accepted as an excuse).

Compelling reasons for the grant of a visa

[15.59] The phrase 'compelling reasons' for granting a visa has long been interpreted as a requirement that there be something to 'drive' the Minister to grant a visa. This may include matters of a compassionate nature, such as hardship and prejudice; matters 'touching on the public interest'; or a 'very strong or powerful reason' for the concession. Although enjoined from making decisions that are not 'authorised by the Act and the Regulations', the tribunals have taken the view that the Sch 3 criteria allow regard to compassionate considerations. The phrase requires an assessment of the hardships faced by both the applicant and the Australian parties involved. These approaches have been confirmed by the Federal Court.[91]

[15.60] In practice, this means that the courts have tended to regard the tribunal findings on these issues as findings of fact rather than of law. The courts have also supported tribunal interpretations of the phrase 'compelling circumstances' as something that requires compulsion of some kind. In *Babicci v MIMIA*,[92] the Full Federal Court said:

> In our opinion there is no error in construing 'compelling circumstances' to mean circumstances which force or drive the decision-maker, in a metaphorical rather than a physical sense, to decide whether or not the jurisdictional fact exists for the exercise of the discretion. We were told that no case has authoritatively construed the phrase and the whole of the debate depended upon dictionary definitions of the word 'compelling'.
>
> In our view nothing turns on the fact that the MRT's interpretation relied upon the present participle of the verb 'to compel' ... In our opinion the true issue for consideration is whether the MRT asked itself the correct question by proceeding on the basis that 'compelling circumstances' were those which 'forced or drove' or 'compelled' a particular result. There are, as was acknowledged in the debate, shades of differences between the various dictionary definitions of compelling. But on any view of the meaning of that word the circumstances must be so powerful that they lead the decision-maker to make a positive finding that the [relevant prohibition] should be waived. We do not consider that the definition of 'compelling circumstances' adopted by the MRT deflected it from deciding the question it had to decide. It is plain that the MRT addressed all of the circumstances put forward by the appellant as affecting him. It considered whether each of the circumstances alone or together 'compelled' the exercise of the discretion. We can see no error, let alone jurisdictional error.

[15.61] In *Ho v MIMIA*,[93] Pascoe CFM said:

> Whether reasons are or are not 'compelling' is a question of fact and degree (See *Patel v Minister for Immigration and Multicultural and Indigenous Affairs* [2003] FCA 115 at [10], per Hely J; *Khanfer v Minister for Immigration and Multicultural and Indigenous Affairs* [2003] FMCA 238 at [10]-[11], per Raphael FM), for the Tribunal, and its determination on that issue does not involve a question of law

---

91 See, for example, *Patel v MIMIA* [2003] FCA 115 at [10]; *Khanfer v MIMIA* [2003] FMCA 238 at [10]-[11].
92 (2005) 141 FCR 285 at [21]-[25]. See also *Jeong v MIMIA* [2005] FMCA 804 at [22]-[23]; and *McNamara v MIMIA* [2004] FCA 1096 at [10].
93 See [2005] FMCA 1104 at [25]. See also *Khan v MIMA* [2005] FMCA 1970.

as contended for the applicant. So long as the Tribunal asked itself the correct question, as it did, its characterisation of reasons as not being compelling was a finding of fact that does not and cannot disclose jurisdictional error unless it is a jurisdictional fact.

[15.62] In *Paduano v MIMIA*,[94] Crennan J explored the etymological bases for the words 'compel' and 'compelling' and concluded that the words should be interpreted to include forceful reasons which raise moral necessity or which are convincing.

[15.63] However, a more stringent approach to various aspects of the operation of cl 3003 has been taken in a number of cases. For instance, to be 'compelling' the reasons for applying a waiver of Sch 3 criteria must be relevant to the purpose of the criteria. In *Monakova v MIMA*,[95] in the context of an application for onshore Partner visas, the Federal Magistrates Court held that the reasons must be relevant to the purpose of permitting the person to make and application for the Partner visa in Australia. Indeed, to take into account a consideration that is not relevant to the purpose may be to take into account an irrelevant consideration. In *Bozanich v MIMA*,[96] the Federal Court concluded that a misunderstanding about the expiry date of a visa did not constitute 'compelling reasons'.

[15.64] In *MIMA v Dunne*,[97] Branson J considered the meaning of 'compelling reasons' in the context of another provision of the Act, and held that compelling reasons must involve something in addition to the basic prerequisite criteria for the grant of the visa. In *Boakye-Danquah v MIMIA*,[98] Wilcox J held that the MRT must consider whether there are compelling reasons for not applying the Sch 3 criteria based on circumstances that existed at the time of the application, not at the time of the decision.

[15.65] Just as the criteria for these visas give prominence to the needs and circumstances of the Australian parties involved, so too have the tribunals favoured applicants who can demonstrate that the compelling circumstances for the grant of a visa involve hardship to an Australian citizen or permanent resident. An example in point is the early case of *Re Norris*[99] where the IRT found compelling reasons for the grant of a permit in the devastating personal and financial effects refusal would have on the Australian citizen spouse. Hardship on the Australian party nominator was also considered in *Re Prestoza*.[100] In that case, the MRT was satisfied that the elderly nominator of a Spouse visa applicant suffered from both physical and psychological conditions that resulted in a need for strong ongoing support, which had been provided by the visa applicant. Therefore, despite the fact that the couple did not meet policy guidelines suggesting the need for a two-year relationship, the tribunal concluded there were compelling reasons to waive the Sch 3 requirements.

---

94   (2005) 143 FCR 204 at [37].
95   [2006] FMCA 849 at [28].
96   [2002] FCA 81.
97   (1999) 94 FCR 72. See also *Copland v MIMA* [2006] FMCA 39; *Re Mosfequr Rahman* [2005] MRTA 118.
98   (2002) 116 FCR 557. See also *Phan v MIAC* [2007] FMCA 88.
99   [1995] IRTA 6352.
100 [2002] MRTA 6067.

It considered it unreasonable to expect an elderly couple to be separated and to live apart whilst the visa application was processed overseas.

Substantial compliance with previous visa conditions

[15.66] The question of whether an applicant has complied substantially with any conditions subject to which the last visa was granted has proven a more difficult issue over the years. In *Myeong Il Kim v Witton*,[101] Sackville J detailed a non-exhaustive list of factors that the tribunal ought to take into account in determining whether an applicant had complied substantially with the conditions of the visa or entry permit. These included the nature of the breach of the condition; the significance of the breach, especially by reference to the purposes for which the visa or entry permit was granted; whether or not the applicant deliberately flouted the condition; and, if the applicant failed to appreciate that he or she was in breach of the condition, whether anything contributed to this failure and, in particular, whether the Department misled the applicant.

[15.67] These considerations were reiterated by Katz J in *Baidakova v MIMA*[102] and Ryan J in *Soegianto v MIMA*.[103] However, in *Shrestha v MIMA*,[104] Gray J emphasised that the factors outlined by Sackville J are not a test or 'compulsory checklist', and will not be relevant considerations in every case. Rather, the statutory duty of the decision-maker must be determined in light of all the circumstances of the case. This approach was endorsed by the Full Federal Court in *Modi v MIMA*.[105]

[15.68] *Baidakova, Modi,* and *Lam v MIMA*[106] each considered substantial compliance with the conditions of a student visa, namely that the holder 'satisfy course requirements'. In *Baidakova*,[107] the relevant course requirement was 90 per cent class attendance. In determining whether there was substantial compliance, Katz J held that it was appropriate to take into account qualitative factors (such as the health problems experienced by the visa holder) as well as quantitative factors (such as the amount of classes actually attended).

[15.69] Gray J endorsed this approach in *Lam*,[108] a case concerning a visa holder who had failed a considerable number of his subjects. His Honour stated that a quantitative approach is not to be disregarded, and that it was open to the tribunal to rely on the proportion of subjects failed by the applicant as a significant indication of whether he had complied substantially with course requirements. His Honour then went on to note that the tribunal had, in any event, taken into account qualitative factors such as the applicant's psychological state and his 'bona fides', or lack thereof.

---

101 (1995) 59 FCR 258.
102 [1998] FCA 1436.
103 [2001] FCA 1612.
104 [2001] FCA 1578.
105 [2001] FCA 529.
106 [2001] FCA 1866.
107 [1998] FCA 1436.
108 [2001] FCA 1866.

[15.70] The fact that every situation must be considered in context was underscored by the Full Federal Court in *Jayasekara v MIMIA*.[109] There the Full Court held that the relevant sub-condition in 8202 that required certification of satisfactory academic achievement is not a sub-condition to which the concept of substantial compliance has any logical application.[110] In such a situation, there was 'no scope for operation of the distinction between strict compliance and substantial compliance'.[111]

15.6 Substantive visas available to unlawful non-citizens

15.6.1 Permanent visas available to unlawful non-citizens

Persons who have been unlawful for any length of time

[15.71] One of the major determinants of the visas available to regularise the status of an unlawful non-citizen in Australia is the length of time that the person has been an unlawful non-citizen. The most generous concessions continue to be made for refugee claimants and unlawful non-citizens with long standing and close family ties to Australian citizens or permanent residents. The subclass 866 Protection visa is available to non-citizens irrespective of the length of time they may have spent in Australia unlawfully.

[15.72] Others permitted to change status without any limitation as to time are partners who can demonstrate 'compelling reasons' for not applying the Sch 3 criteria (Sch 2, cl 820.211(2)(d)(ii)) and dependent children (cl 802.211(a)). Compelling reasons for not applying Sch 3 include the existence of children of a relationship and evidence that the relationship relied on has endured for two years or longer.

[15.73] Until 2005, concessions were also made for persons known colloquially as 'innocent illegals': non-citizen minors who first entered Australia with their parents and who spent their 'formative years' in the country.[112] Provided that they were over 18 years of age, had not entered on a transit visa[113] and were no longer living with the family with whom they entered Australia, these people used to be eligible for a permanent visa.

'Absorbed persons'

[15.74] Concessions are made also for an increasingly small group of unlawful non-citizens who have lived in Australia for so long that they have become absorbed

---

109 (2006) 156 FCR 199. Special leave to appeal to the High Court from this decision was dismissed on 24 April 2007. See also *Jiang v MIAC* [2007] FCA 907; *Hasan v MIAC* [2007] FCA 697.
110 Indeed, in *Dai v MIAC* (2007) 165 FCR 458, the Full Federal Court held that condition 8202 was invalid because certification of satisfaction of the condition by the educational provider was not provided by a student and so there was no act that the student could do themselves that could satisfy the condition.
111 *Weerasinghe v MIMIA* [2004] FCA 261 at [10].
112 See former subclass 832.21 (Close Ties) visa.
113 Subclass 771 Transit visas are issued to non-citizens passing through Australia on their way to another country. They permit a stay of up to 72 hours in the country.

into the community. Section 34 of the Act operates to deem lawful persons who have been in Australia unlawfully since at least 2 April 1979 and who have lived in Australia continuously since 2 April 1984. Applicants are required to show that their initial entry was not irregular for the purposes of the former s 20 of the Act. The present s 34 echoes (but does not refer directly to) what used to be s 7(4) of the Act before 2 April 1984. This section provided that persons who remained in Australia unlawfully undetected for five years or more could regularise their status. In keeping with the spirit of these provisions, the Federal Court has confirmed that s 34 cannot be called in aid by persons who had not *already* been 'absorbed' for the purposes of the repealed s 7(4) of the Act on 2 April 1984. In other words, if an applicant was an unlawful non-citizen at this date, she or he could not thereafter become a full member of the community at law – 'ceasing to be an immigrant' – in the absence of an express legislative provision conferring lawful status.[114]

[15.75] This visa class is unusual as it is one that is deemed to apply to individuals: it is not a visa in respect of which formal application may be made. As discussed further in Chapter 17, it is a visa that was virtually unheard of until the approach to permanent residents convicted of serious crimes was altered dramatically with the election of the conservative Coalition government in 1996. The eventual move to exile even permanent residents of the longest standing led advocates to realise that, in spite of the cancellation of a permanent visa on character grounds, a non-citizen could still be regarded as an 'absorbed person' for the purposes of s 34.[115] Absent an order directed against the s 34 Absorbed Person visa, removal under s 501 could be unlawful. As the High Court confirmed in *MIMIA v Nystrom*,[116] however, nothing inherent in s 34 limits the ability of the Minister to cancel an Absorbed Person visa where the holder has been found to be of bad character.

Non-citizens who are unlawful for 12 months or less (Sch 3, cl 3002)

[15.76] For non-citizens who have been unlawful for 12 months or less, concessions are made for persons applying on partner grounds who have come to Australia as diplomats or in similar roles, or as serving members of certain visiting armed forces (Sch 2, cl 820.211(2)(d)(i) and (2A)). Permanent residence visas are available to aged parents who meet the balance of family test (see reg 1.05(2) and Chapter 8.3); and to persons who meet the criteria for the following visas: Remaining Relative (subclass 835); Carer (subclass 836); Orphan Relative (subclass 837); and Aged Dependent Relative (subclass 838).

---

114   On the early interpretation of s 34, see *Chee v MIMA* [1997] FCA 46; *Rooney v MIMA* [1996] FCA 656; *Yong Khim Teoh v MIMA* [1996] FCA 572; and *Tjandra v MIMA* (1996) 67 FCR 577. On the question of 'absorption into the community', see also *R v Forbes; Ex parte Kwok Kwan Lee* (1971) 124 CLR 168.

115   In addition to the leading case of *Nystrom* (below) see, for example, *Toia v MIAC* (2009) 177 FCR 125; *Gilbert v MIAC* [2008] FCA 16; *Pull v MIMIA* [2007] FCA 20; *Moore v MIAC* [2007] FCA 626; and *Moran v MIMIA* (2006) 151 FCR 1.

116   (2006) 228 CLR 566.

15.6.2 Temporary visas available to unlawful non-citizens

[15.77] Finally, in provisions reminiscent of s 13 of the Act after 1989 which used to confer a 'period of grace' on unlawful non-citizens,[117] a broad range of visas are available to persons who have been unlawful for 28 days or less. The Regulations permit non-citizens who have come to Australia on certain tourist and other temporary visas to seek permanent residency on the basis of their skills, provided that the Sch 3, cl 3004, criteria can be met (for instance through the employer nomination scheme or on the basis of distinguished talent). Until the Regulations were relaxed in 1996, unlawful non-citizens who wished to gain residence on spouse or interdependency grounds also had to make their application within 28 days of becoming unlawful.[118]

15.7 From compassion to control: Historical approaches to unlawful migration

[15.78] The desire to clamp down on illegal migration and to reduce the options for unlawful non-citizens was a prime motivation for the move in December 1989 from statute-based discretion to codified decision-making. One of the first measures taken was to introduce a general restriction on the grant of entry permits (as they were then) to persons who had been unlawful non-citizens for 12 months or more. More specific constraints were introduced for unlawful non-citizens who had been arrested and placed in detention. As a general rule – as is still the case – these people were allowed only two days, extendable to seven, in which to apply for regularisation of their status.[119]

[15.79] In recognition that there had to be a transition period to allow time for people to modify their conduct in accordance with the new rules and to accommodate other compelling cases, concessions were made almost immediately allowing various categories of immigration outlaws to regularise their status.[120] In the absence of any mechanism available to change status on humanitarian grounds,[121] special concessional permits were introduced for the expatriate nationals of certain troubled countries.[122] The requirement that applications be lodged within 12 months of a person becoming unlawful did not apply to refugee claimants or to 'prescribed' applicants.[123]

---

117 On this phrase as it was used in s 13 of the Act after 19 December 1989, see *Simonsz v MIEA* (1995) 56 FCR 492.
118 Clauses 820.211(2) and 826.212(2)(e) of Sch 2 to the *Migration Regulations* were amended by SR 211 of 1996, reg 130, and SR 75 of 1996, reg 13.2. As noted, this temporal restriction no longer applies to partner visas.
119 See *1989 Regulations*, reg 42(1A) and (1B).
120 See ibid, reg 35AA, introduced 15 January 1990 by SR 1 1990, reg 6.
121 Note that the 'humanitarian' provisions in reg 129 of the *1989 Regulations* were never made operative because of the requirement that the Minister 'gazette' the countries and conflicts in respect of which requests for permits could be made: see Chapter 5.3.3.
122 See *1989 Regulations*, regs 118 (citizens of the former Socialist Federal Republic of Yugoslavia), 119F (Lebanese); 119G (Sri Lankan); 119H (PRC).
123 That is, 'prescribed' in reg 42(1C) for the purposes of reg 42(1A) of the *1989 Regulations*: see regs 42(1D), 117A and 134. The classes of persons granted this exemption included long-term

[15.80] A series of concessions, quasi-'amnesties' and humanitarian provisions followed. These came to characterise the early 1990s as representing a period of moderation which stands in contrast to the contemporary attitude to unlawful non-citizens.

[15.81] A quasi-amnesty in early 1990[124] waived the visa requirements relating to lawful status for five main groups of applicants. The first were those who could show that they had developed close personal ties with Australia. Second were unlawful non-citizens who entered Australia before 19 December 1989 who applied before 31 October 1990 and who could demonstrate a 'compelling reason' for the grant of a permit. The third group were non-citizens who entered Australia on or after 1989 who applied for a substantive permit either no later than 16 February 1990, if they became unlawful before 20 January 1990, or within 28 days of losing their legal status. In addition, concessions were made for persons eligible to apply for a permit under the Regulation Second Application Scheme, a transitional arrangement that operated for a brief period in 1989.[125] Finally, persons served with a cancellation notice deeming them to be unlawful non-citizens were allowed seven days from the date of service in which to apply for a permit. Such applicants were then exempt from the requirement that they hold a valid temporary entry permit.

[15.82] A more general scheme to lure unlawful non-citizens out of the shadows was introduced later in 1990 following a parliamentary inquiry into illegal migration in Australia.[126] The scheme ran for three years and involved both incentives and punishments. Those who came forward in the first year and who were not successful in their application for a permit were allowed to leave Australia and apply for a visa from abroad without any penalty or exclusion period. Those who gave themselves up in the second and third years of the scheme and who were not eligible for a permit faced exclusion periods of two and five years respectively. At the same time, concessions were made for the grant of permanent residence to: spouses of Australian citizens or permanent residents; dependent children; aged parents; aged dependent relatives; orphan relatives; special need relatives and the remaining relatives of 'settled' Australian citizens and residents.[127] Most importantly, a permit could be granted where there was 'any other compassionate ground', where refusal of the permit would cause 'extreme hardship or irreparable prejudice' to an Australian citizen or permanent resident.[128] This general concession focused not on the circumstances of the applicants in question, but on the hardships that

---

unlawful non-citizens who had entered Australia before 1 January 1975; certain persons who had entered Australia as fiancés or on prospective marriage visas; certain New Zealand citizens and nationals of the Peoples' Republic of China; certain returning residents; and persons known as 'innocent illegals' (see [15.73] above).

124 See *1989 Regulations*, reg 35AA, introduced 15 January 1990.
125 See Chapter 18 at [18.12]. This aspect of reg 35AA was replaced on 31 May 1990 by reg 173A of the *1989 Regulations*.
126 Joint Standing Committee on Migration Regulations, *Illegal Entrants in Australia: Balancing Control and Compassion* (Canberra: AGPS, 1990).
127 *1989 Regulations*, reg 131A.
128 See ibid, reg 131A(i)(v).

might befall an Australian party, targeting the provisions squarely at the Australian electorate.[129]

[15.83] Two further schemes are worthy of mention. On 1 November 1993, the government announced a number of concessions, aimed primarily at resolving the position of the PRC nationals who had been granted four-year temporary entry permits following the events in China in 1989. Three categories of permanent visa were created. The subclass 815 visa accommodated PRC nationals in Australia at the time of the Tiananmen Square massacre. The subclass 816 visa was designed to cater for better qualified asylum seekers and nationals of Sri Lanka and the former Yugoslavia temporarily in Australia. This was subject to their ability to meet certain criteria. The final visa subclass, the subclass 818, covered highly qualified students undertaking postgraduate study in Australia. This visa subclass was also subject to the applicant meeting the prescribed criteria.

[15.84] Applicants of all visa subclasses were required to meet the public interest criteria. For the subclass 815 applicants, this was one of the few criteria they had to meet other than being in Australia on 20 June 1989, the date nominated following the Tiananmen Square uprising. The Department received a total of 12,898 applications under this visa subclass, covering a total of 27,373 people. Not surprisingly, the overwhelming majority of the applicants were granted the subclass 815 visa. After the processing of the applications, only 165 people were refused a grant of the visa.[130]

[15.85] If the subclass 815 visa was granted out of compassion, the subclass 816 visa was intended to temper compassion with self-interest by ensuring that these migrants would be a benefit to Australia. Applicants for the subclass 816 visa were subject to stricter requirements.[131] The critical date for the applicant of this visa class was 1 November 1993. As at that date, the applicant had to be younger than 45 years of age; possess employment qualifications, work experience or a business interest; have sought a determination of refugee status or have lodged an application for a subclass 435 or subclass 443 entry permit. They also had to have been granted a visa for travel to Australia before 12 March 1992, and had to have arrived in Australia before 1 November 1993. Failure to meet any of the criteria was fatal to the application. The principal applicant also had to demonstrate an ability to speak English. This criterion, as well as the health and character requirements, was to be satisfied at the date of the decision.

[15.86] One aggrieved subclass 816 applicant attempted to argue that the English language requirement was inconsistent with s 9 of the *Racial Discrimination Act 1975* (Cth). The argument was disposed of swiftly by the Federal Court in *Qiu v MIMA*.[132]

---

129   In *Ali v MIEA* (1992) 38 FCR 144 at 148, Heerey J confirmed the domestic orientation of the provisions. He ruled that the provisions required an examination of the effect that failure to grant a permit would have on the circumstances of the Australian nominator. This was endorsed by the Full Court in *Teo v MIEA* (1995) 57 FCR 194.
130   See former DIMA Fact Sheet 28.
131   In fact, the criteria were described as being without flexibility, latitude or discretion on the part of the decision-maker, characterised by rigid criteria that do not allow flexibility in interpretation and with the potential to produce harsh outcomes: *Re Gry* [1996] IRTA 8209 at 17-18.
132   (1994) 55 FCR 439 at 449-50: see also *Re Kaufman* (1997) 44 ALD 701 at 703.

Another applicant had more success in challenging the legality of some of the English tests themselves when the Department scheduled extra examinations, but failed to have the new tests approved by the Minister. The Federal Court held that the omission rendered the new tests *ultra vires* the Act.[133] The result rendered invalid all the results of tests done in January and May 1995 and acted as one of the impetus for the creation of the Resolution of Status for Chinese and Others (ROSCO) visa (see below).

[15.87] The subclass 818 visa was of a completely different nature in that it lacked the requirement that the applicant must have applied for refugee status. The purpose of the visa was to provide permanent residence to people who either held, or were undertaking study towards, higher education qualifications. The criteria of this visa subclass again were rigid. Failure to meet any of the specified criteria was fatal to the application.[134] The imposition of a high standard of educational qualifications meant that the number of applications received for the subclass 818 visa subclass was significantly less than the other 1 November categories.

[15.88] The last of the quasi-amnesties was announced on 13 June 1997 to resolve the status of certain groups of people who had been allowed to stay in Australia as long-term temporary residents for humanitarian reasons.[135] The decision included people not covered by earlier concessions and involved a two-stage process. The first stage led to the grant of a temporary visa, and the second stage, available to eligible persons 10 years after the date of their first arrival in Australia, yielded permanent residence. Onshore applications must have been made by 31 March 1998, and offshore applications by immediate family members must have been made by 30 June 1998.

[15.89] The ROSCO (temporary) visa was available to applicants who arrived lawfully in Australia from Kuwait or Iraq on or before 31 October 1991; from Lebanon on or before 30 November 1991; or from China, Sri Lanka, or the former Yugoslavia on or before 1 November 1993. The applicants must have been citizens of, or normally resident in, these countries; they must have travelled to Australia on documents issued by those countries; and must have arrived here lawfully. They must have continued to reside in Australia from the relevant dates; and had to meet public interest criteria. Unlike the 1 November 1993 concessions, the ROSCO decisions did not require an applicant to have applied for refugee status, although they were open to people who had applied for recognition as refugees.

[15.90] This last visa scheme appears to have been created to deal with the practical difficulties (and inequities) encountered in administering the quasi-amnesties

---

133 See *Din v MIMA* (1997) 147 ALR 673.
134 For example, in *Re W* [1995] IRTA 6159, the applicant failed despite being highly educated and qualified because he was over the age of 45 as at 1 November 1993. In *Re Chishti* [1997] IRTA 8671, the applicant had enrolled in a commercial programming course in order to aid him in his doctoral studies. The tribunal found that, while the skills learnt from that course were a distinct benefit to the completion of a PhD, they were not a requirement for its completion. On this basis, the tribunal found that the applicant did not meet the higher educational qualification requirements.
135 See MPS 56/97, 13 June 1997; and former DIMA Fact Sheet 29.

of 1 November 1993.¹³⁶ The visa subclass survived a class action challenge in the Federal Court that the concessions were discriminatory and in breach of the *Racial Discrimination Act 1975*.¹³⁷ The fact that it has not been followed by any further amnesties suggests that these 'soft' tactics have not been particularly helpful as management tools over all. It is to the more punitive measures that we now turn.

15.8   Immigration offences

[15.91]   Offences under the *Migration Act* fall into six broad categories: those relating to entry and stay in Australia; offences relating to migration fraud; offences relating to detention; offences relating to decisions made under the Act; offences arising out of the scheme governing the giving of migration advice (which we discuss in Chapter 5.6); and the miscellany of offences found in Part 9 of the Act.

15.8.1   Offences relating to entry and stay in Australia

[15.92]   The desire to preserve the integrity of the country's borders is fundamental to Australia's migration laws. Non-citizens found to breach that integrity are subject to penalties under the Act. Offences relating to entry and stay in Australia are concerned largely with the presence and activities of non-citizens and with the punishment of those responsible for bringing unlawful non-citizens into the country or for aiding and abetting contraventions of migration laws. In 2009-10, DIAC reported 164 formal investigations into possible breaches of immigration law. It lodged 35 briefs of evidence with the Commonwealth Director of Public Prosecutions and secured four convictions.¹³⁸

Carrier sanctions

[15.93]   The *Migration Act* places the responsibility on carriers to ensure that non-citizens travelling to Australia are able to lawfully enter Australia. Section 229 makes it an offence for a master, owner, agent, charterer and operator of a vessel to bring a non-citizen into Australia without a valid visa. This measure was introduced in 1979 as part of the first moves to formalise the requirement that non-citizens obtain a visa before travelling to Australia. Section 230 provides that carriers will also be responsible for the entry of stowaways unless the carrier upon arrival at an Australian port both notifies the immigration authorities that a non-citizen is on board and prevents the non-citizen from landing. These are offences of absolute liability, which means that there are no fault elements for any of the physical elements of the offence, and the defence of mistaken fact is not available.¹³⁹ The penalty for either offence is a fine of up to $10,000. In 1999-2000, more than 5000 infringement notices were

---

136   Problems arose in particular concerning the validity of the English language tests administered between January and May 1995 following the ruling in *Din v MIMA* (1997) 147 ALR 673.
137   See *Macabenta v MIMA* (1998) 154 ALR 591; upheld on appeal (1998) 90 FCR 202. Special leave to the High Court was also refused: *Macabenta v MIMA S5/1999* [1999] HCATrans 191.
138   DIAC, *Annual Report 2009-2010* (Canberra: 2010) at 156.
139   *Criminal Code* (Cth), s 6.2.

issued to airlines. A decade later, this had dropped by more than 91 per cent to 407 infringement notices.[140]

People smuggling offences

[15.94] Domestic anti-people smuggling measures aim to contain unauthorised asylum flows by criminalising the facilitation of such movements into Australia. These measures were first introduced in 1999.[141] This coincided with the United Nations' adoption of the Convention Against Transnational Organised Crime, with its attached Protocol Against the Smuggling of Migrants (the Smuggling Protocol), and the Protocol Against Trafficking in Persons.[142] Under Art 3 of the Smuggling Protocol, people smuggling is defined as 'the procurement, in order to obtain, directly or indirectly, a financial or other material benefit, of the illegal entry of a person into a state party of which the person is not a national or permanent resident'. States parties are required to criminalise people smuggling activities undertaken for profit (Art 6). According to the Protocol's preamble, this is motivated by a 'concern that the smuggling of migrants can endanger the lives or security of the migrants involved'. The legislative framework around people smuggling became more punitive under the Coalition government following the *Tampa* Affair.[143] More recently, the *Anti-People Smuggling and Other Measures Act 2010* (Cth), which commenced on 1 June 2010, cast the net of people smuggling offences so wide as to significantly depart from the Smuggling Protocol.

[15.95] The *Migration Act* now provides for a broad range of offences which criminalise a range of activities around the entry of unauthorised non-citizens.[144] Section 233 makes it is an offence to take part in bringing into Australia a non-citizen who intends to enter Australia illegally, or to conceal or harbour an unlawful non-citizen. These are strict liability offences and subject to a penalty of 10 years' imprisonment, a fine of up to $110,000, or both. Under s 232A, persons convicted of organising groups of five or more people to enter Australia illegally face 20-year gaol terms and fines of up to $220,000. Section 233A sets out an offence of people smuggling, defined as where a person organises or facilitates the bringing of an unlawful non-citizen to Australia. An aggravated offence of people smuggling, in s 233B, may occur in three circumstances: where a person commits an offence of people smuggling in circumstances where the victim will be exploited after entry; where their conduct gives rise to danger of death or serious harm to the victim and they are reckless to that danger; or where the offender subjects the victim to cruel, inhuman or degrading treatment. A further aggravated offence of people smuggling arises, in s 233C, where the people smuggling involves the entry of more than five people. The offence of

---

140 DIAC, above n 138, at 141.
141 *Migration Amendment Act (No 1) 1999* (Cth).
142 *United Nations Convention against Transnational Organized Crime; Protocol Against the Smuggling of Migrants by Land, Sea and Air; Protocol to Prevent, Suppress and Punish Trafficking in Persons, Especially Women and Children*, UN Doc A/RES/55/25, UN GAOR, 55th sess, 62nd plen mtg, (8 January 2001) (opened for signature on 15 November 2000, entered into force on 25 December 2003). For discussion of Australia's implementation of anti-trafficking measures, see Chapter 14.5.
143 *Border Protection (Validation and Enforcement) Powers Act 2001* (Cth).
144 See also *Criminal Code*, Div 73.

people smuggling is punishable by imprisonment for 10 years or up to $110,000 or both. The penalties for the aggravated offences are 20 years' gaol or up to $220,000 or both. Section 233E provides for the offences of concealing or harbouring unlawful non-citizens. Further offences relate to the presentation of false or forged papers, and the making of false and misleading statements, in connection with illegal entry.[145] In 2001, the Coalition government introduced mandatory penalties following conviction for certain of these offences.[146] Since that time, adults charged with these offences cannot be released on probation under s 19B of the *Crimes Act 1914* (Cth).[147]

[15.96] In 2010, the anti-people smuggling regime was made even more draconian. First, the 2010 Act removed the requirement that offenders act for a profit motive. This is a significant departure from the Smuggling Protocol which is expressly targeted at the commercial exploitation of vulnerable migrants. In dispensing with the profit motive, the offences in the *Migration Act* and *Criminal Code* have been transformed. There is now a general prohibition on assisting anyone to find safety in Australia if the person does not hold a valid visa. It makes no difference if the unlawful entrant is an asylum seeker or person rescued at sea.[148] Second, the smuggling offences require only that a person be reckless as to whether his or her conduct will result in the commission of a people smuggling offence.[149] This also departs from the Smuggling Protocol which requires that people smuggling activity shall be established as a criminal offence 'when committed intentionally'.[150] Finally, the 2010 Act introduced a new offence of providing material support to another person that aids them, or another person, to engage in people smuggling.[151] This is punishable by 10 years' gaol or up to $110,000 or both. This constitutes a startling example of overreach of criminal law, with the punitive aims of anti-people smuggling efforts directed at those who may provide assistance to vulnerable persons in need of protection. On the face of the legislation, the humanitarian actions of aid organisations and others could fall within the scope of people smuggling.[152]

Work offences for migrants and employers

[15.97] Non-citizens who enter Australia on a valid visa but then breach the conditions placed on their entry are also the subject of punitive measures. A non-citizen who works without authorisation can have their visa cancelled under s 116(1)(b) of the Act (see above Part 15.4.1) and may face prosecution under s 235. Working illegally includes more than only flagrant contraventions of the 'no work' condition

---

145   *Migration Act*, s 234. Section 234A provides for an aggravated offence of presenting false documents or information with the entry of at least five unlawful non-citizens: s 234A. This is punishable by 20 years' gaol.
146   See now ibid, s 236B, which applies to ss 233B, 233C and 234A.
147   See now ibid, s 236A, which applies to ss 233B, 233C and 234A.
148   Sydney Centre for International Law, Submission to the Inquiry into the Anti-People Smuggling and Other Measures Bill 2010 (15 April 2010), available at <http://www.aph.gov.au/Senate/committee/legcon_ctte/antipeoplesmuggling/submissions.htm>.
149   See *Criminal Code*, ss 5.4 and 5.6(2).
150   Smuggling Protocol, Art 6.
151   *Migration Act*, s 233D; see also *Criminal Code*, s 73.3A.
152   See, further, Hannah Quadrio, '*Anti-People Smuggling and Other Measures Act 2010* (Cth): A Comment' (2010) 21 *Public Law Review* 159.

of a visa. The Federal Court has interpreted prohibitions on work to include any work done in a voluntary or unpaid capacity.[153] For unlawful non-citizens, s 235(3) provides that '[a]n unlawful non-citizen who performs work in Australia *whether for reward or otherwise* commits an offence against this section' (emphasis added). In addition, some visas restrict the hours that a non-citizen can work or the type of work in which the person can engage. It is an offence to work for longer than the period authorised.

[15.98] There are far-reaching consequences for those who fall foul of this section. A migrant convicted under s 235 may be precluded from applying for a subsequent visa by virtue of the character test in s 501.[154] A visa holder challenging the cancellation of a visa may be precluded from engaging in employment (in accordance with the visa held) while an appeal is pending. The person will be at risk of committing an offence under s 235 if the visa is found to have been validly cancelled.[155] Section 235 has been found by various courts to have significance far beyond the regulation of migration. In *Australian Meat Holdings Pty Ltd v Kazi*,[156] the Queensland Court of Appeal held that workers compensation protections do not apply where a claimant is an unlawful non-citizen in Australia. The court reasoned that a migrant who was injured while committing an offence under s 235 was working under a contract of employment that was void for illegality. As a result, the injured person was not a worker within the meaning of s 12(1) of the *WorkCover Queensland Act 1996* (Qld) and could not claim compensation against his employer.

[15.99] Specific offences targeting the *employers* of illegal workers were not enacted until August 2007, earlier attempts having been defeated by the farming and business lobbies. This follows countries such as the United Kingdom and United States where 'employer sanctions' regimes have been in place for some time.[157] Section 245AB provides for a criminal offence where a person knowingly or recklessly allows an unlawful non-citizen to work. Section 245AC makes it is an offence for a person to allow someone to work contrary to their visa conditions, where the offender knows or is reckless as to that fact. Aggravated offences apply if the migrant worker is being exploited through slavery, forced labour or sexual servitude. Penalties for individuals are imprisonment for two years, or five years for aggravated offences. Companies may be subject to fines of up to $66,000 for each illegal worker, or up to $165,000 for each illegal worker who is exploited. In 2008-09, the Department located 990 people working illegally. The top three industries in which unlawful migrant workers were located were agriculture, hospitality and construction.[158] DIAC's success regarding these compliance activities does not appear to have yielded any prosecutions of the employers concerned.

---

153   See, for example, *Braun v MILGEA* (1991) 33 FCR 152.
154   See further Chapter 17.
155   See, for example, *Johnson v MIMIA* (2003) 130 FCR 394.
156   [2004] QCA 147. See also *WorkCover Corporation (San Remo Macaroni Co Pty Ltd) v Da Ping* (1994) 175 LSJS 469. But for a different result on this issue see *Nonferral (NSW) Pty Ltd v Taufia* (1998) 43 NSWLR 312.
157   In the UK since 1997 (introduced by the *Asylum and Immigration Act 1996* (UK)) and in the US since 1986 (introduced by the *Immigration Reform and Control Act*, Pub L 99-603, 100 Stat 3359).
158   DIAC, *Fact Sheet 87: Initiatives to Combat Illegal Work in Australia*, 29 September 2010.

15.8.2 Offences relating to migration fraud

[15.100] A person may be subject to criminal prosecution for engaging in a range of fraudulent activities in relation to the Immigration Department. Several offences arise in the context of illegal entry into Australia. Section 234 provides for 10 years' imprisonment for any person found guilty of presenting false papers or making false statements in an attempt to gain entry or immigration clearance in Australia. An aggravated offence is set out in s 235 for the presentation of false documents in relation to the entry of five or more people, punishable by 20 years' gaol. A non-citizen who attempts to use a visa that has not been granted to him or her is also liable for imprisonment for 10 years.[159] The significance of convictions has been heightened by the power that is now given to the Minister to revoke the citizenship of any person convicted of such an offence.[160]

[15.101] Subdivision 12B of Part 2 of the Act is directed to people who enter into contrived relationships for the purpose of gaining permanent residence in Australia (see further Chapter 7.2.4). Section 243 creates an offence of applying for a visa on the basis of a contrived marriage or de facto relationship, subject to imprisonment for two years. This offence applies equally to the non-citizen nominee as well as the Australian nominator, although the penalties may vary.[161] This is complemented by a provision making it an offence to make false or unsupported statements related to the nature of a relationship upon which an application for a visa is based: s 245. The harshest penalty, however, is reserved for those convicted of arranging sham relationships for migration purposes.[162] These offences are punishable by a $110,000 fine, or imprisonment for 10 years, or both. Those who contrive marriages for immigration purposes may also face charges under the *Crimes Act 1914* (Cth).[163]

15.8.3 Offences relating to detention

[15.102] Offences relating to the proper conduct of non-citizens in detention have been introduced in an effort to safeguard effective immigration administration. The criminal offence of escape from immigration detention is punishable by five years' imprisonment.[164] It is widely acknowledged that this penalty regime reflects parliament's conviction of the need for general deterrence in this area.[165] One might consider that the hopeless circumstances in which an unlawful non-citizen finds herself or himself upon escape in Australia might provide deterrence enough to discourage prospective escapees. As one sentencing magistrate commented:

> The facts of this case in which the three men, having escaped from the detention centre then just found themselves hanging around in the jungle, as it was described,

---

159 *Migration Act*, s 236.
160 See *Australian Citizenship Act 2007* (Cth), s 34.
161 See, for example, *Dhingra v R* [1999] NSWCCA 359.
162 *Migration Act*, ss 240 and 241. See, for example, *R v McLean* (2001) 121 A Crim R 484.
163 In *R v Hardy* [1996] NSWSC 524 and *R v Troutman* (unreported, NSWCCA, 23 April 1997) the appellants were convicted of conspiring to defeat the execution of the *Migration Act* under s 86 of the *Crimes Act 1914* (Cth).
164 *Migration Act*, s 197A.
165 See, for example, *Shillabeer v Hussain* (2005) 220 ALR 239.

until they became thirsty and hungry and gave themselves up, might of themselves present some sort of deterrence to other people who might think about escaping from the detention centre on Christmas Island.[166]

[15.103] In the sentencing process, issues such as deterrence may be balanced against considerations personal to the detainee or the circumstances of the crime, such as her or his poor psychological condition.[167] The fact that protestors encouraged and facilitated the escape can also be relevant,[168] as is the fact that a conviction may jeopardise the detainee's chances of obtaining a Protection visa for which he is otherwise eligible, by virtue of the character test in s 501.[169] Still, it remains clear that deterrence is seen as the principal policy and purpose behind s 197A.[170]

[15.104] In 2001, the Coalition government introduced a new offence where a detainee manufactures, possesses, uses or distributes a weapon, punishable by three years' imprisonment.[171] This followed a number of high profile incidents of escapes and riots in remote detention centres.[172] Other criminal offences may also be applicable to immigration detainees, for instance the offence of damaging Commonwealth property,[173] or causing harm to a Commonwealth public official.[174]

15.8.4 Offences relating to decisions made under the Act

[15.105] To preserve the integrity of the process of decision-making under the Act, various offences have been created for persons who obstruct or hinder a tribunal or tribunal member from performing the functions of the tribunal, or disrupt the taking of evidence by the tribunal.[175] Witnesses who fail to appear before a tribunal without reasonable excuse may face imprisonment for six months. It is also an offence for a person to knowingly or recklessly make a false or misleading statement about his or her ability to induce or influence the making of a decision.[176] Section 335 prohibits a person from entering into an arrangement whereby she or he undertakes, in return for payment, that a decision under the Act will be made in a particular way. This section could apply to tribunal members, who accept a bribe to make a decision in a particular way, or to migration agents who accept payments in return for an undertaking that a favourable decision will be made. A court may order a person convicted under ss 334 or 335 to pay reparation to any other person who has suffered loss as a result of the crime, in addition to any penalty imposed. Offences also arise where a

---

166 *Warnakulasuriya v R* [2009] WASC 257 at [23].
167 *Morrison v Behrooz* (2005) 155 A Crim R 110.
168 *Police v Kakar* [2005] SASC 222.
169 *Boonstoppel v Hamidi* (2005) 192 FLR 327. See Savitri Taylor, 'Exclusion from Protection of Persons of "Bad Character": Is Australia Fulfilling its Treaty-based Non-refoulement Obligations?' (2002) 8(1) *Australian Journal of Human Rights* 83.
170 *Bridle v Gomravi* [2005] SASC 295.
171 *Migration Act*, s 197B, introduced by *Migration Legislation Amendment (Immigration Detainees) Act 2001* (Cth).
172 M Saunders and M Spencer, 'Refugees Riot in Desert', *The Australian*, 29 August 2000, at 1.
173 *Crimes Act 1914* (Cth), s 29.
174 *Criminal Code*, ss 147.1(1) and 147.2(1).
175 See *Migration Act*, ss 370-372 (MRT) and ss 432-434 (RRT).
176 Ibid, s 334.

tribunal member or officer, or an interpreter, records or communicates confidential information.[177] Further offences relate to the provision of migration advice, as we explain in Chapter 5.6 above.

[15.106] Finally, it is an offence to tamper with the movement records of the Department. Section 488 makes it an offence for a person to read, examine, reproduce, use or disclose any part of the movement records without proper authorisation. It is also an offence under this section to delete, alter or in any way tamper with the movement records of the Department (punishable by up to 10 years' imprisonment).

---

177 See ibid, ss 377-378 (MRT) and ss 439-440 (RRT).

16

The Enforcement of Decisions

16.1 Introduction

[16.01] One of the key features of the migration legislation that has been in force since September 1994 is the relationship between the grant of visas and the enforcement of decisions. The law reflects the philosophy that disputes over status and rights to remain should be confined to the 'front' end of the immigration process, when entitlement to a visa is determined. Once a person is found to be an unlawful non-citizen (who is not entitled to a visa), the present Act is as simple as it is draconian: detention and removal are mandatory.[1] Of equal note is the almost complete absence of curial oversight of the arrest, detention and removal process. The omission is a reminder that the scheme was enacted at the same time as the changes made to the regime limiting the judicial review of migration decisions.[2]

[16.02] Beneath the surface of these baldly stated provisions, however, some of the complexity remains that characterised the *Migration Act 1958* (Cth) before the 1994 changes. Not all unlawful non-citizens are equal. Some can regularise their status and/or are eligible for release through the grant of a Bridging visa, while others are not. There continue to be different regimes for both arrest and detention that vary according to a non-citizen's immigration status before becoming unlawful. Permanent residents convicted of serious crimes are subject to special arrest, detention and deportation provisions, as explored in Chapter 17. In fact, the unwanted former permanent residents are now the only 'deportees': other non-citizens are simply 'removed'. The biggest losers in the system – or the persons with fewest rights – continue to be those who arrive in the country without any documentation, or without a valid visa. It is in this area that the drama is still being played out between governments bent on controlling Australia's borders and the judges and advocates concerned about the human rights of those seeking entry into the country.

---

1 See *Migration Act 1958* (Cth), ss 189 and 198-199.
2 See further Chapter 19. Note that the amending legislation that came into force on 1 September 1994 was passed in May 1992. It was the same enactment that inserted the first Part 8 into the *Migration Act*: see *Migration Reform Act 1992* (Cth). The passage of the legislation came hard on the heels of the controversy surrounding the Cambodian boat people which involved a legislated attempt to specifically restrict the judicial review of detention rulings. See *Migration Amendment Act 1992* (Cth), discussed in Chapters 3 and 4.

[16.03] This chapter examines in turn the enforcement laws as they apply at each stage of the migration process. Part 16.2 discusses the law that applies before and at point of entry while Part 16.3 looks at arrest and detention after formal admission (or 'immigration clearance') into the country. General issues relating to immigration detention are dealt with in Part 16.4, which is followed by a discussion of the rules governing release from custody and associated oversight processes. The final parts deal in turn with stay orders and matters relating to the removal process.

16.2 Border applicants, immigration clearance and detention

16.2.1 Control measures before entry: Interdiction of ships and aircraft

[16.04] As we have seen, the powers conferred on immigration and customs officers to protect Australia's borders were expanded considerably between 1999 and 2001.[3] The legislation now confers on officers of the Commonwealth powers to chase, board and search ships and aircraft suspected of carrying unauthorised arrivals. Following the *Tampa* Affair,[4] these powers were increased even further.[5] As they currently stand, the commander of a Commonwealth ship or Commonwealth aircraft can request to board, and chase, both Australian and foreign ships in virtually any part of the ocean –from Australia's territorial sea to the high seas. Similarly, Australian and foreign aircraft may be intercepted, identified and requested to land.[6] Once boarded, officers of the Commonwealth have quite extraordinary powers of search, examination, arrest and seizure.[7] These include the power to search, examine and seize any goods found on the ship or aircraft; to require all persons found on the ship or aircraft to answer questions and produce documents in their possession; and to arrest, without warrant, any person on board the vessel for suspected offences against the *Migration Act*. A ship or aircraft reasonably suspected of being involved in a contravention of the Act, and persons on board, may also be detained. The Act also permits persons detained under these provisions to be taken outside Australia.

---

3   See *Migration Act*, Part 2, Div 12A and the discussion in Chapter 6.1.
4   See above Chapter 4.3.
5   The stated purpose of the *Border Protection (Validation and Enforcement Powers) Act 2001* (Cth) was to provide increased powers to protect Australia's borders and for other related purposes. Part 1 of the amending Act contained provisions to validate the actions of the Commonwealth, Commonwealth officers and anyone acting on behalf of the Commonwealth in relation to the *Tampa* Affair. For the purposes of the amending Act, a 'Commonwealth officer' was defined to include a member of the Australian armed forces. It also created 'additional statutory authority for future action in relation to vessels carrying unauthorised arrivals and the unauthorised arrivals themselves': DIMIA, *Fact Sheet 71: New Measures to Strengthen Border Control*, 11 March 2004. At the same time, the provisions confirm the power of the executive to act outside of any legislative authority: see s 7A of the Act.
6   As these laws authorise Australian officers to operate outside of Australia's territorial jurisdiction, some commentators have suggested that they are in breach of Australia's international obligations: see, for example, Nathan Hancock, 'Border Protection (Validation and Enforcement Powers) Bill 2001 (Cth)' *Bills Digest*, No 62 2001-02, available at <http://www.aph.gov.au/library/pubs/bd/2001-02/02bd062.htm>.
7   See *Migration Act*, ss 245F and 245FA. The provisions do not apply to ships on the high seas unless an officer is satisfied the ship is an Australian ship: see s 245F(1).

[16.05] In exercising these powers, officers may use 'such force as is necessary and reasonable'.[8] In the context of arresting or detaining persons, this is defined as not doing anything likely to cause the person grievous bodily harm, unless the officer believes on reasonable grounds that doing the thing is necessary to protect the life of, or prevent serious injury to another person.[9] Searches of a person, their clothing, and any property under the person's immediate control are also permitted, for the purpose of finding out whether the person is carrying or hiding a weapon, or any other thing capable of being used to inflict bodily injury or help the person escape.[10] Full strip searches are forbidden, but s 245F(4) does authorise the removal of the person's outer garments (including, but not limited to, the person's overcoat, coat, jacket, shoes and head covering). Provided officers act in good faith, the Act generally prohibits the commencement or continuance of both civil and criminal proceedings in respect of actions taken pursuant to these provisions. Once a person is detained on board an 'Australian ship' (defined in s 245A), a different regime applies. In theory, the Act would appear to allow for strip searching of persons if they meet the description of 'detainee'.[11]

The Pacific Strategy

[16.06] In order to prevent the use of Christmas Island and nearby reefs as delivery points for asylum seekers, the *Tampa* amendments also conferred on the Minister for Immigration power to declare parts of Australia's territory to be outside the 'migration zone'. The effect is to limit the operation of the *Migration Act* in these areas, although this it not to say that the land is not part of Australia for the purposes of international law. Pursuant to these amendments, the Act now defines Christmas Island, Ashmore and Cartier Islands and the Cocos (Keeling) Islands as 'excised offshore places'. Any unlawful non-citizen who enters an excised offshore place is declared to be an 'offshore entry person', and cannot make a valid application for an Australian visa unless the Minister determines it is in the public interest to do so: s 46A(1). Under s 198A, these persons can be taken to 'declared countries' (such as Nauru and Papua New Guinea), where their claims for refugee status are considered. These people are deemed not to be in 'immigration detention', and therefore have no right to seek legal advice or assistance as would otherwise be an entitlement under the Act. Although the use of Nauru was discontinued with the election of the Rudd Labor government in November 2007, the legislative structures (such as they are)[12] remained unchanged at time of writing. There appears to be no immediate intention in the new government to abandon offshore processing – although processing is taking place on the Australian territory of Christmas Island rather than in a foreign country. Where change has occurred is in the provisions creating a special visa scheme for people who arrive at 'excised offshore places', which precluded access

---

8   Ibid, s 245F.
9   Ibid, s 245F(12) and (13).
10 Ibid, s 245FA.
11 See ibid, s 252, read with ss 252A-252B. Note that these provisions appear to have been introduced primarily to allow for the strip searching of persons being held in immigration detention centres.
12 It is worth noting that many aspects of the so called Pacific Strategy had no legislative underpinning, but were done in exercise of the executive power of government. See Chapter 3 above.

to permanent residence in Australia: the temporary visas created for these people were abolished in August 2008.[13]

[16.07] Persons who arrive on territory that has been 'excised' from the migration zone (defined in s 5 as an 'excised offshore place') become 'offshore entry persons'. Accordingly, under s 46A such a person is disabled from making a 'valid' visa application of any kind, without the express permission of the Minister (exercising one of the Minister's non-compellable, non-reviewable discretionary powers). When such a person travels to Australia – as occurs on occasion for medical treatment or for another reason – the individual becomes a 'transitory person'. Such persons are also legally barred from making a valid visa application of any kind unless permitted by the Minister. The seriousness of the Minister's discretionary power to 'lift the bar' in these cases is underscored by the requirement that the Minister table a statement in parliament within 15 sitting days, setting out in writing the Minister's reasons for permitting an application to be made in the public interest.[14] As noted earlier,[15] the regime is one that has not stood the test of time well.

16.2.2 Control measures at point of entry

[16.08] For persons who make landfall on the Australian mainland, a distinction continues to be drawn between people who arrive with a valid visa and then lose their legal status, and those who either arrive with no visa at all or otherwise fail to pass immigration clearance.[16] On the arrival of a non-citizen at a port of entry, the Act facilitates the detention of persons 'reasonably suspected' of being unlawful.

[16.09] As noted earlier, detention is mandatory for any person in the migration zone who is known or reasonably suspected to be an unlawful non-citizen: s 189(1). Section 189(2) provides further that an officer must detain any person who is in Australia (but outside the migration zone) who he or she reasonably suspects is seeking to enter the migration zone, and would, if in the migration zone, be an unlawful non-citizen.

[16.10] Again, the Act provides for the detention of persons on board a ship suspected of being involved in a contravention of the Act, and allows those persons to be brought into the migration zone.[17] The legal standing of people who seek to enter Australia either unlawfully, or in connection with the commission of an offence, is now spelt out very clearly. The reference in s 189 to persons suspected of irregular immigration status is echoed in s 250 which introduces a separate notion of immigration 'suspect'. 'Suspects', or suspected criminals, must be kept in custody until they

---

13   See former subclasses 447 (Secondary Movement (Offshore Entry)) and 451 (Relocation (Temporary)), read with reg 2.07AN of the *Migration Regulations 1994* (Cth) – repealed by the *Migration Amendment Regulations 2008 (No 5)* (Cth), in operation on 9 August 2008.
14   See *Migration Act*, ss 46A and 46. See *Plaintiff M61/2010E v Commonwealth* and *Plaintiff M69 of 2010 v Commonwealth* (2010) 272 ALR 14; and the discussion of the recent case law on these provisions at Chapter 12.4.3 and Chapter 19.6.4.
15   See Chapter 12 at [12.56]ff and 12.4.2. See also Chapter 3 at [3.65] and Chapter 19 at [19.102]-[19.104].
16   See above Chapter 6.2 and Chapter 15.2 and 15.3.
17   See *Migration Act*, s 245F(9).

are either granted a visa or removed. The section empowers the Minister to keep a suspect in custody for the purposes of determining whether to prosecute or so as to pursue a prosecution. What it does not do is place any temporal limitation on the detention of a person suspected of or charged with an offence. The provisions in Part 2, Div 4 of the Act, relating to Criminal Justice Stay Certificates and visas, may enable the release of persons wanted as witnesses in a criminal trial. However, the requirement that an individual or organisation meet the cost of keeping the detainee in Australia can preclude the release of many of those charged with offences.

[16.11]   For those detained in immigration clearance, provision is made for a special period of four hours 'questioning detention', as defined.[18] This enables departmental officers to investigate the entitlement or legal standing of those who present at immigration clearance with difficulties of some kind. If an applicant fails to obtain immigration clearance during this period, he or she is then taken into custody as an unlawful non-citizen, as a prelude to removal.

[16.12]   In the case of stowaways, ship-jumpers and persons who attempt to enter the country without going through immigration clearance, the arrest provisions of the Act have undergone some change since 1994. Individuals who are apprehended are liable to have their clothes and belongings searched, and may also be required to pass through a metal detector. In this context authorised officers do now have the power to conduct a strip search to find out whether a detainee has a weapon or any other thing capable of being used to inflict bodily injury, or to assist them in escaping from immigration detention.[19]

[16.13]   Border applicants detained after failing to be immigration cleared are disadvantaged in a range of ways. At the top of the unspoken hierarchy are those who have their visa cancelled at immigration clearance because they no longer meet the criteria for entry. An example in point is the case of *Li v MILGEA*,[20] where the applicant's husband withdrew his sponsorship just before she travelled to Australia. Unlike non-citizens who have their visas cancelled in Australia, these people have no right of appeal to the Migration Review Tribunal (MRT), which means that their only source of redress is to seek judicial review of the cancellation in the Federal Court under Part 8 of the Act.[21] Persons who arrive with no visa have no right of appeal and little prospect of continued stay in Australia unless they are either eligible for a Border visa[22] or claim to be refugees and apply for a Protection visa. All

---

18   Ibid, s 192. In determining the four-hour period, note the periods excluded under s 192(7). See Joint Standing Committee on Migration (JSCM), *Asylum, Border Control and Detention* (Canberra: 1994) at [3.140].

19   See *Migration Act*, s 252A. These provisions were introduced in response to unrest in the detention centres in and after 2001. The officer must suspect on reasonable grounds that the weapon or object is hidden on the detainee, and that a strip search is necessary to recover the object. Authorisation is also required (from the Secretary or a SES Band 3 officer in the Department if the detainee is over 18, and from a magistrate if the detainee is between 10 and 18).

20   (1992) 33 FCR 568.

21   Note that at one stage these people were granted a right of appeal for a brief period. However, if they wished to exercise this right while in Australia the Regulations required them to signal their intention to appeal within five minutes of cancellation of their visa: see reg 2.46(b)(i) of the *Migration Regulations 1993* (Cth).

22   Subclass 773. See above Chapter 6.2.

refugee decisions made on mainland Australia are reviewable by the Refugee Review Tribunal (RRT).

[16.14] Once in immigration detention, border applicants also have fewer rights than other detainees. All detainees must be afforded reasonable facilities for obtaining legal assistance if they request it.[23] However, departmental officers are not obliged to inform border applicants that they can apply for a visa, or that they must do so within two days (extendable to seven days on written request) of being detained.[24] In contrast, people detained after being lawfully admitted into the country are entitled to be informed of these rights and of the ramifications of their situation.[25]

[16.15] One of the big changes made on 1 September 1994 was the abolition of the concept of deemed non-entry for border applicants. Before that date persons who arrived without a valid visa were subject to turn around provisions that required them to be placed back on board the vessel on which they arrived within 72 hours.[26] Pending such return, the non-citizens were deemed not to have 'entered' Australia. This was so even where the wait stretched from days to weeks and even to years.[27] The purpose of the provisions was to distinguish border applicants from persons who became unlawful non-citizens after arrival. The latter group could only be detained for 48 hours and then for periods of up to seven days with the permission of a magistrate (see further below at Part 16.3.1).

[16.16] While the concept of non-entry has been abolished, border applicants in many cases are still subject to mandatory and potentially prolonged detention. In the case of most border detainees, the most significant discrimen continues to be the restrictions placed on eligibility for release pending determination of an application for a visa. The only group who is eligible for a Bridging visa – the mechanism for release on bail – is those who have applied as refugees for a Protection visa. Even in these cases, release is available only in limited circumstances for children; persons over 75 years of age; the spouses of Australian parties; and for former victims of trauma or torture. The Human Rights and Equal Opportunity Commission (HREOC) noted that these categories of eligible border applicants were 'very limited in practice'.[28] It took the development of almost unbearable conditions within the remote detention centres and the scandalous arrest and prolonged detention of over 240 citizens and permanent residents before significant changes were made (see Part 16.4 below).

---

23   See *Migration Act*, s 256.
24   Note that s 256 puts the onus on the detainee to request application forms and access to legal advice: 'Where a person is in immigration detention under this Act, the person responsible for his or her immigration detention shall, at the request of the person in immigration detention, give to him or her application forms for a visa or afford to him or her all reasonable facilities for making a statutory declaration for the purposes of this Act or for obtaining legal advice or taking legal proceedings in relation to his or her immigration detention.'
25   See *Migration Act*, ss 193-196 and 198.
26   See *Migration Act*, former ss 88-89A.
27   See, for example, *Gunaleela v MIEA* (1987) 15 FCR 543; *Park Oh Ho v MIEA* (1988) 20 FCR 104 (on appeal (1989) 167 CLR 637); and *Ahamed v MILGEA* (1991) 30 FCR 137. Compare *Chu Kheng Lim v MILGEA* (1992) 176 CLR 1 (*Chu Kheng Lim*).
28   See HREOC, *Those Who've Come Across the Seas: Detention of Unauthorised Arrivals* (Sydney: HREOC, 1998) at 20. Note that HREOC is now the Australian Human Rights Commission (AHRC).

[16.17] In December 2001, the government established a trial of alternative detention arrangements for women and children at the Woomera Detention Centre. This project enabled 25 volunteer women and children to live in 'family-style accommodation' while their immigration status was resolved. In early 2002 with the closure of Woomera Immigration Reception and Processing Centre (IRPC), the program was transferred to Whyalla, the town nearest to Baxter IRPC. These arrangements are now in place in most capital cities and on Christmas Island, reflecting in part the decision in June 2005 to make the detention of non-citizen children truly a measure of last resort.[29] Having said this, in January 2011 1065 children were still being held in 'alternative' accommodation that still effectively constituted immigration detention. The situation underscores how slow change has been in this area.[30]

[16.18] In most cases, persons seeking release must show that adequate arrangements have been made to care for them on release and that they will not abscond before the determination of their application.[31] For persons who do not meet the regulatory definition of 'eligible non-citizen' in s 72 of the Act and reg 2.20 of the Regulations, detention continues to be mandatory.

16.2.3 Special detention measures and *Chu Kheng Lim*

[16.19] As explored earlier,[32] the detention of border applicants for refugee status has been the source of extraordinary controversy, with public concern about these asylum seekers in marked disproportion to the extent of the 'control' problem facing the government. At the centre of the debate have been border applicants from various countries. We will begin the account here with the asylum seekers (predominantly from Cambodia) who were detained for up to four years in Sydney and at Port Hedland in North Western Australia between 1989 and 1994. The group included over 40 children born in detention.[33] Although small in number, these detainees were responsible, directly or indirectly, for many of the amendments made to the enforcement and review laws in the 1990s, creating the framework for a regime that became ever harsher in and after the turn of the Millennium.

---

29 See *Migration Act*, s 4AA and Part 2, Div 7(2),, encompassing ss 197AA-197AG, inserted by the *Migration Amendment (Detention Arrangements) Act 2005* (Cth), s 3 and Sch 1, in operation on 29 June 2005.
30 See <http://www.immi.gov.au/managing-australias-borders/detention/_pdf/immigration-detention-statistics-20110114.pdf>. See also AHRC, 'Immigration Detention in Darwin', available at <http://www.hreoc.gov.au/human_rights/immigration/idc2010_darwin.html>; and Louisa Rebgetz, 'Human Rights Body Blasts Detention Facilities' ABC News (Australia), 14 December, 2010, available at <http://www.abc.net.au/news/stories/2010/12/14/3092900.htm?section=justin>.
31 See *Migration Regulations*, reg 2.20, as amended by the *Migration Regulations (Amendment) 1994* (Cth) (No 280). Note that this regulation has been amended over the years to include a whole range of persons to whom Bridging visas are granted, including those involved in alleged human trafficking or otherwise required for the purposes of a criminal justice matter.
32 See Chapter 4 and Chapter 6.2.
33 For accounts of this period, see Andrew Hamilton 'Three Years Hard' (1993) 3(1) *Eureka Street* 24 and (1993) 3(2) *Eureka Street* 22; Frank T Brennan, 'Litigating the Rights of the Marginalised – A Revolution in the Rights of Asylum Seekers and Indigenous Peoples', *Revolution by Lawful Means: Law and Politics*, New Zealand Law Conference, Christchurch, 1993; and Mary Crock (ed), *Protection or Punishment: The Detention of Asylum Seekers in Australia* (Sydney: The Federation Press, 1993).

[16.20] The government's fight with the courts was enjoined in May 1992, just after the first set of decisions refusing refugee status were voluntarily remitted by the Department for reconsideration. Lawyers for the applicants moved to seek the release of their clients on the ground that their continued detention was not authorised at law. In essence, they argued that the 'deemed non-entry' or turn around provisions could not be used to authorise extended detention of individuals who were seeking Australia's protection as refugees. Two days before the case was due to be heard by the Federal Court, the government rushed through parliament what became Part 2 Div 4B (now Part 2, Div 6) of the Act.[34]

[16.21] Division 4B had the effect of preventing the release of the detainees who were given the new title of 'designated persons'. Under s 177 of the Act, this phrase includes border applicants who have been on a boat in the territorial sea of Australia between 19 November 1989 and 1 September 1994. The Act specified (and still specifies) that designated persons can be held in detention for 273 days of 'application custody' (extendable by a further 90 days) and that no court may order their release.[35] Lawyers for the detainees launched a challenge to Div 4B in the High Court. The action was premised on the notion that the legislation constituted an usurpation by the parliament of the judicial power conferred by Chapter III of the Constitution exclusively on the courts.[36]

[16.22] The effect of Div 4B was to render futile the Federal Court action pending in May 1992. The fact that the amending provisions were targeted at a particular court action was not enough to make them an abuse of the judicial power.[37] The plaintiffs in *Chu Kheng Lim v MILGEA*[38] argued that the amending Act was unconstitutional because it allowed for the administrative detention of 'designated persons' without giving the judiciary any role in the process.

[16.23] The plaintiffs failed in their argument that the detention of non-citizens necessarily involves an exercise of the judicial power that should have been reserved to the courts. The High Court held that custody without the sanction of a court can be lawful if its purpose is to safeguard the security of the country.[39] It found that the power to detain was incidental to parliament's power to legislate with respect to aliens contained in s 51(19) of the Constitution. In holding that the function of Div 4B was protective rather than punitive, the court was swayed by the fact that the detainees were free to leave Australia (and detention) at any time. Further, the court took notice of the fact that detention was nominally limited to 273 days in 'application' custody.[40] The majority of Brennan, Dawson, Deane and Gaudron JJ did find one aspect of Div 4B of the Act unconstitutional: the attempt in s 54R to exclude curial

---

34 See *Migration Amendment Act 1992* (Cth).
35 See *Migration Act*, ss 182 and 183.
36 See *Chu Kheng Lim* (1992) 176 CLR 1 and Chapter 3.3.2 and Chapter 4.2.
37 See *Australian Building Construction Employees and Builders' Labourers' Federation v Commonwealth* (1986) 161 CLR 88 at 96.
38 (1992) 176 CLR 1.
39 Ibid at 114-15.
40 See Mary Crock, 'Climbing Jacob's Ladder: The High Court and the Administrative Detention of Asylum Seekers in Australia' (1993) 15 *Sydney Law Review* 338.

scrutiny of detention. Their Honours found it a usurpation of the judicial power to prohibit any court from ordering the release of designated persons where a question could arise as to the legality of the detention.

16.2.4 Detention policy after *Chu Kheng Lim*

[16.24] The impact of the findings in *Chu Kheng Lim* was felt by the government on two fronts. Although Div 4B was upheld in most respects, the High Court found that the plaintiffs' detention before 5 May 1992 may have been unlawful. Within days of the judgment in *Chu Kheng Lim*, applications were made to the High Court seeking damages for wrongful detention. The government's response was to enact s 54RA, later s 184 of the Act, stipulating that any damages payable for wrongful detention be limited to one dollar per day. This provision was repealed in 1995,[41] and replaced by provisions that attempted to retrospectively remedy the illegality (if any) attaching to the detention of designated persons.[42]

[16.25] The other ramification of *Chu Kheng Lim* was the High Court's affirmation that the courts could not be excluded from the review of Div 4B detention. While the Cambodian detainees had been fighting their battles in the courts, another group of boat people had been waiting patiently for decisions in their cases. These were the Chinese nationals from the boat codenamed the 'Isabella'. They gained notoriety when they landed in Australia on Christmas Eve 1991 and embarked on a near-fatal trek through the Kimberley Ranges before being apprehended. In June 1993, supporters became aware that the Isabella Chinese had been in custody for more than the 273 days (as defined). The group sought and obtained their release and were eventually successful in their claim for damages for wrongful detention.[43] The terms of the settlement reached in 1996 were not made public.[44]

[16.26] Throughout the period of the many court actions brought on behalf of the Cambodian detainees, academic and media coverage became more and more extensive of the government's policies and of the plight of those in custody.[45] The then Labor government eschewed a direct back down, seeking instead a political solution to the problem of the prolonged detention. The Cambodian boat people were offered residency in Australia on condition that they return to their country of origin for one year before being sponsored back by community groups in Australia.[46] The problem of administrative delay in processing refugee claims was addressed by an overhaul

---

41 See *Migration Legislation Amendment Act (No 2) 1994* (Cth); and Senate Standing Committee on Legal and Constitutional Affairs, *Report on the Migration Amendment Act (No 2)* (Canberra: 1994). Section 184 was repealed quietly by the *Migration Legislation Amendment Act (No 6) 1995* (Cth), s 6.
42 See *Migration Legislation Amendment Act (No 6) 1995* (Cth), s 9.
43 See *Tang Jia Xin v Bolkus* [1996] FCA 1379. For the earlier actions, see *MIEA v Tang Jia Xin (No 1)* (1993) 116 ALR 329; *MIEA v Tang Jia Xin (No 2)* (1993) 116 ALR 349 (order for release); *Tang Jia Xin v MIEA* (1993) 47 FCR 176; and *Bolkus v Tang Jia Xin* (1994) 69 ALJR 8. Both appeals failed.
44 See Minister Ruddock's answer to a question from the Member for Oxley, Ms Pauline Hanson, *Weekly Hansard*, House of Representatives, 18 November 1996, at 6943.
45 See the articles cited at n 33 above. To these can be added numerous pieces published in daily newspapers and magazines, as well as programs on the television and on national and regional radio stations.
46 See *Migration Regulations*, Sch 2, former subclass 214.

of the refugee status determination system, culminating in the establishment of the RRT.

[16.27] The government's detention policy was considered by the Joint Standing Committee on Migration in 1993.[47] The Committee included a number of politicians who had been intimately involved in the events surrounding the passage of Div 4B of the Act. Although the vast majority of submissions made to the inquiry urged the abolition or substantial modification of the detention policy, the Committee recommended that the policy of mandatory detention continue for the majority of border claimants. The Regulations governing the grant of Bridging visas to border claimants that survive to this day reflect these recommendations, with some exceptions. Most notably, the government rejected the Committee's views that the Minister alone should have power to order release; and that release of the target group should be allowed only after six months and where further delay was the fault of the administration.[48] In some respects, at least, common sense prevailed.

[16.28] With the election of a conservative Coalition government in 1996, the resolve to make immigration detention both mandatory and immune from judicial oversight seems only to have strengthened. In fact, this objective was achieved when the final provisions of the *Migration Reform Act 1992* (Cth) came into force in September 1994. The detention mandated by s 198 of the Act is not subject to any temporal limitation. As explored in Chapters 3 and 4, a series of cases litigated before the High Court in 2004 confirmed the constitutional validity of the legislative scheme. A slim majority of that court held that detention is lawful even where non-citizens are held indefinitely in circumstances where they have requested removal from Australia but removal is not possible.[49] Under Labor governments in power after 2007, detention policy softened appreciably, but the fundamentals of mandatory detention for unauthorised arrivals remained unchanged.

16.3 The arrest and detention of actual and suspected unlawful non-citizens after entry into Australia

16.3.1 The legislative scheme governing arrest and detention

[16.29] Before 1 September 1994, different regimes were established for the arrest and detention of *suspected* unlawful non-citizens, deportees (now removees) and border claimants. In the case of suspected unlawful non-citizens, detainees were required to be brought before a 'prescribed authority' within 48 hours of arrest, and then could not be detained for more than seven days without being re-presented before that authority.[50] The prescribed authority, in turn, could only authorise the continued detention of a suspect if he or she was satisfied that the detention was reasonably required in order to enable the Minister to consider either the unlawful

---

47   See JSCM, above n 18.
48   Ibid, recommendation 3, at xiii, and Chapter 3.
49   *Al-Kateb v Godwin* (2004) 219 CLR 562 at [33] (McHugh J, agreeing with Hayne J (with whom Callinan and Heydon JJ concurred)). See Chapter 3 at [3.50]ff.
50   See former s 88 of the *Migration Act*.

status of the detainee or whether a deportation order should be made.[51] By way of contrast, the arrest and custody of a prospective deportee were not subject to the same temporal and procedural restraints. Officers were required only to furnish the detainee with details of why he or she was arrested and with particulars of the deportation order.[52] The only circumstances in which a deportee had to be brought before a prescribed authority (again, within 48 hours) was where he or she made a statutory declaration claiming that a mistake had been made in the identification of the person named in the deportation order.[53]

[16.30] Although not without problems,[54] this regime had a distinct advantage over the scheme that has been in force since 1 September 1994. Immigration officials since that date have not been required uniformly to obtain warrants before an arrest is made and have not been required to submit persons arrested to any form of external scrutiny. In the early years of the new Millennium, this regime produced some egregious examples of maladministration.

[16.31] As noted earlier, the migration legislation confers on migration officers sweeping powers of entry, search and seizure where there is 'reason to suspect' that a vessel, building, premises or vehicle may contain an unlawful non-citizen, or any documents or papers relevant to the apprehension of such a person.[55] The master of a vessel is required to facilitate the boarding and searching of his or her vessel, by an officer who is not bound to supply a search warrant. A warrant *is* required for land searches under s 251(6). However, an officer equipped with such a document may enter and search any building, vehicle or place at any time in the day or night with such assistance and using 'such reasonable force' as considered necessary. As noted earlier individuals who are apprehended are not only liable to have their clothes and belongings searched, but may also be required to pass through a metal detector; and may, in certain circumstances, be strip searched.[56]

[16.32] These powers are supplemented by provisions relating to the mandatory furnishing of information. Persons served with a notice under s 18 (formerly s 22A) of the Act can be required to disclose any information in their possession regarding the

---

51 *Grech v Heffey* (1991) 34 FCR 93.
52 See former s 89 of the *Migration Act*, now s 253(1)-(3).
53 See *Migration Act*, s 253(4)-(7).
54 While this detention regime worked well enough in the majority of cases, the legislative regime was at once too specific and yet not specific enough. Problems arose, for example, in determining the purpose for which non-citizens were being detained. The former s 92 of the Act permitted the apprehension of non-citizens for the purpose of determining their legal status, while the more liberal s 93 facilitated the detention of prospective deportees: see present s 253. The courts condoned the prolonged detention of persons whom the government was finding difficult to remove. However, they held that the detention of persons for purposes ulterior to their immediate removal was unlawful: see *Park Oh Ho v MIEA* (1989) 167 CLR 637. The courts became increasingly careful in their scrutiny of the legislation relied on by the Department to justify the custody of non-citizens: see *Grech v Heffey* (1991) 34 FCR 93 and *Chu Kheng Lim* (1992) 176 CLR 1.
55 See *Migration Act*, ss 249-252A.
56 See ibid, ss 252AA-252E and the discussion at [16.05]ff. Vessels may be also detained for the purposes of conducting a search, or pending recovery of a penalty for an offence under the Act. Division 13A, inserted in 1999, provides for the automatic forfeiture, to the Commonwealth, of vessels and equipment used or involved in bringing unlawful non-citizens to Australia in contravention of the Act: ss 261A-261K.

identity or whereabouts of an unlawful non-citizen. Detainees can also be compelled to answer questions; they can be moved from place to place and can be photographed and 'measured' for the purpose of recording or future identification.[57] The last of these provisions enables finger-printing.

[16.33] The central problem with this regime is that both arrest and detention turns on the formation by an officer of the Department of a 'reasonable suspicion' that an individual is an unlawful non-citizen. As noted earlier, detention is mandatory for any person in the migration zone who is *known or reasonably suspected* to be an unlawful non-citizen.[58] The only mechanism for challenging the 'suspicion' of an officer is for a detainee to seek judicial review of her or his detention. The system does not provide any regular mechanism for the oversight or checking of either initial decisions to detain or the continued detention of a person in immigration custody. As the high profile cases of Cornelia Rau and Vivian Solon-Alvarez illustrated, there are many reasons why detainees may be incapable of initiating their own challenge to the lawfulness of their detention. At best they may be unaware of their legal entitlement to advice relating to their detention and so may not make the request in writing that must trigger access to a lawyer. At worst, they may suffer from a mental or other disability that effectively prevents them from taking the appropriate action. As chronicled elsewhere,[59] Cornelia Rau had been an Australian permanent resident for 18 years before she was arrested on suspicion of being an unlawful non-citizen. She spent more than 10 months in detention, which included periods in solitary confinement at Baxter Immigration Reception and Processing Centre (IRPC) in South Australia. Her plight became public because of alarms raised not by her guards, but by other immigration detainees concerned by the extent of her (obvious) mental illness. Vivian Solon-Alvarez suffered from both mental illness and physical incapacity (having suffered spinal and other injuries in an accident shortly before her arrest). This Australian citizen of 20 years standing, mother to two Australian-born children, was both detained and removed in what can only be called deplorable circumstances to the Philippines.

[16.34] The then Coalition government responded quickly to these outrages with two government-sponsored inquiries.[60] Interestingly, however, no attempt was made to reinstate judicial oversight of the arrest and detention process – a system which rarely saw individuals detained inappropriately for any length of time. Instead, the Commonwealth Ombudsman was given a new role and designation as 'Immigration Ombudsman'. All persons who have been held in detention for two years or more were made subject to review by that authority. For those detained (originally for

---

57   See *Migration Act*, ss 257-258.
58   See ibid, s 189(1). Section 189(2) provides that an officer must also detain any person who is in Australia (but outside the migration zone) who he or she reasonably suspects is seeking to enter the migration zone, and would, if in the migration zone, be an unlawful non-citizen. As noted above, the Act also provides for the detention of persons on board a ship suspected of being involved in a contravention of the Act, and allows those persons to be brought into the migration zone: s 245F(9).
59   See Mary Crock, Ben Saul and Azadeh Dastyari, *Future Seekers II: Refugees and Irregular Migration in Australia* (Sydney: The Federation Press, 2006) at 154-62.
60   See Mick Palmer, *Inquiry into the Circumstances of the Immigration Detention of Cornelia Rau: Report* (July 2005), available at <http://www.immi.gov.au/media/publications/pdf/palmer-report.pdf>; and Neil Comrie, *Inquiry into the Circumstances of the Vivien Alvarez Matter Report No 3 of 2005*, available at <http://www.immi.gov.au/media/publications/pdf/alvarez_report03.pdf>.

two years – now six months), the Ombudsman must report on their situation at six-month intervals.[61] In the course of undertaking initial reviews in 2005 over 240 cases of wrongful detention were identified.[62] The government subsequently paid out millions of dollars in damages for wrongful detention.[63]

[16.35] In August 2008, then Labor Minister, Chris Evans, announced an overhaul of immigration detention that would see this aspect of enforcement governed by a new set of values.[64] The policy changes were supposed to ensure that children are never detained in detention centres; and that detention is used only in circumstances where an individual poses a threat of some kind. The processing of applications was to be expedited wherever possible to minimise detention. The Minister stated that the treatment of persons placed in detention must always be humane and cognisant of human rights and a person's basic dignity. Ombudsman oversight of detainees was directed to take place six months, rather than two years, after initial detention. The announcements made in 2008 were followed by a parliamentary inquiry and by the introduction of the Migration Amendment (Immigration Detention Reform) Bill 2009. The Bill had not been debated when parliament rose at the end of 2010. As we noted earlier, immigration detention remained a live issue.

[16.36] The proposed legislation would enshrine the general principle that immigration detention should be used as a last resort and for the shortest possible period of time, and that it be used as a device to manage risks to the Australian community (see proposed new s 4AAA of the Act). This is reflected in proposed changes to s 189 with a new qualifier on the arrest power. An officer could only arrest and detain a person if the officer 'knows or reasonably suspects' that the person is an unlawful non-citizen who meets one of five descriptors in proposed s 189(1)(b). The first of these is that the person 'presents an unacceptable risk to the Australian community'; the rest describe various ways in which a non-citizen might have become unlawful, starting with the by-passing of immigration clearance. The phrase 'unacceptable risk' would be defined in s 189(1A) to include cases with a criminal or national security element and other matters that will be defined by regulation.

---

61   See *Migration Act*, Part 8C, ss 486L-486Q.
62   Reports on the findings made by the Immigration Ombudsman are available at <http://www.ombudsman.gov.au/reports/immigration-detention-review/>.
63   It is difficult to ascertain the actual amounts paid out in damages as payouts are usually made in the context of confidentiality agreements. Ms Rau is reported as having accepted $2.4 million in damages for false imprisonment: see *Sydney Morning Herald*, 19 February 2008, at 2; while Ms Solon-Alvarez is reported to have sought compensation in the order of $10 million. Amnesty International has reported that an Iranian man detained at Woomera Detention Centre was awarded $800,000 in damages (see <http://www.amnesty.org.au/refugees/comments/8229/>), while an Iranian child, Shayan Badraie, received a payout of $400,000: see 'Badraie payout not "a backdown"', *The Age*, 5 March 2006; and Dan Box 'Visas follow payout', *The Australian*, 4 March 2006. His story is recounted in Jacqueline Everett, *Bitter Shore* (Sydney: Macmillan, 2008). See, generally, Mark Robinson, 'Damages in False Imprisonment Matters', address to NSW Legal Aid Commission, 22 February 2008, available at <http://www.wentworthchambers.com.au/marobinson/MAR%20Damages%20in%20False%20Imprisonment%20Matters-as%20Delivered%2022%20February%202008.pdf>.
64   See Chris Evans, 'New Directions in Detention: Restoring Integrity to Australia's Immigration System', 29 July 2008, available at <http://www.chrisevans.alp.org.au/news/0708/immispeeches29-01.php?mode=text>.

[16.37] The amending Bill would not alter Part 8C which deals with the reporting times for Ombudsman oversight of immigration detention. Indeed, although s 194A would confer new power on 'authorised officers' to grant temporary community access permission to persons in immigration detention, no attempt is being made to alter the basic legislative structure of the arrest and detention provisions. Arrest and detention would still be based on the 'reasonable' suspicion of immigration officials. The courts would continue to be denied any oversight role.[65]

'Reasonable suspicion'

[16.38] Neither Cornelia Rau nor Vivian Alvarez ever saw their detention litigated in court: settlements were reached in both instances. What is alarming is that their experiences were not isolated. Some of the wrongful detention cases did result in court challenges, from which a jurisprudence of sorts is emerging on the meaning of the phrase 'reasonable suspicion'.

[16.39] In *Goldie v Commonwealth*,[66] a majority of the Full Federal Court held that in forming a reasonable suspicion an officer is obliged to make due inquiry to obtain material likely to be relevant to the formation of that suspicion. In that case, the appellant had been arrested and detained on the basis of a computer record which showed that the last visa granted to the applicant had expired. The computer record was two years old, and was based on immigration cards filled out by the appellant on movements to and from Australia (it did not purport to be a record of visas granted after the appellant entered the country). The immigration officer did not make any search of the appellant's file to ascertain whether visas had been extended. In these circumstances, the court found the suspicion held by the immigration officer was not reasonable:

> [The immigration officer] chose to prefer to base his state of mind on the computer record, the information in which was incomplete and older than the other materials available to him. He chose to disregard the other facts, and rely on the information obtained from a partial search of the record. In choosing to form a suspicion on the basis of a computer record two years old, without making inquiries or checking more recent records, Mr Cain did not act reasonably.[67]

The court ruled that, while the word 'suspects' could be construed 'to include the formation of an imagined belief', notice had to be taken of the qualifying effect of the word 'reasonable'.[68]

[16.40] As the High Court seems to confirm in the later case of *Ruddock v Taylor*,[69] there must be an objective and rational basis for believing that a person is an unlawful non-citizen. In that instance, Mr Taylor failed in his attempt to challenge his lengthy detention. A British national with long standing as an Australian permanent resident,

---

65   See further the discussion of the circumstances in which the courts can order the release of a person in detention. See Part 16.5.
66   [2002] FCAFC 10.
67   Ibid at [19].
68   Ibid at [4].
69   (2005) 222 CLR 612.

Taylor won the constitutional battle that resulted in the High Court finding that he could not be deported from Australia.[70] However, a differently constituted High Court refused to find that this victory rendered the ongoing 'suspicion' of those holding him in custody 'unreasonable' for the purposes of the Act.[71]

16.3.2 The rights of detainees: Access to legal advice

[16.41] One of the major sources of conflict (generated first when the IRPC at Port Hedland was established) has been the right of detainees to seek independent legal advice about their detention and visa prospects, if any. Some commentators have suggested that isolated sites have been chosen so as to allow the government almost complete control over who is given access to detainees.[72] Most of the advocacy and migrant support groups are located in the big cities and in the eastern States. Without access to funding, the cost of flying to remote parts of Australia has been a powerful disincentive to the involvement of volunteer groups. More importantly, the policy of the immigration authorities has generally been to allow detainees access to advisers, but only where they request such access – there being no onus on departmental officials to inform detainees of their rights.[73] The limitations of the law in this regard have created ongoing problems for detainees.[74] With press and other interested parties denied access to detainees, the problem was that no-one could be sure how detainees were being treated and whether, indeed, they had requested and were being denied access to advisers.

[16.42] Although only the first of many allegations made subsequently of detainees being held incommunicado,[75] the issue of access to detainees first gained prominence in 1996 when HREOC became involved in the case of detainees from a boat code named the 'Teal'. HREOC acted on a request to investigate circumstances surrounding the detention of asylum seekers from that boat. The Commission took the matter to the Federal Court when the manager of the Detention Centre refused to pass the communication on to the detainees. Lindgren J did no more than insist on compliance with s 20(6)(b) of the *Human Rights and Equal Opportunity Commission Act 1986* (Cth) (*HREOC Act*)[76] which establishes a prisoner's right to receive communications from

---

70 See *Re Patterson; Ex parte Taylor* (2001) 207 CLR 391, discussed in Chapter 3.2.
71 The High Court reversed an earlier determination that the man should be awarded $116,000 in damages. See ABC News Online, 'Man awarded damages after wrongful detention', 18 December 2002, available at <http://www.abc.net.au/news/newsitems/200212/s750129.htm>. On this point, see also *VHAF v MIMIA* (2002) 122 FCR 270.
72 See, for example, Nicholas Poynder, 'Marooned in Port Hedland: The Case of the Boat People – The UN Human Rights Committee in Practice' (1993) 18(6) *Alternative Law Journal* 272.
73 See *Migration Act*, s 256, which places the onus on detainees to request assistance, but otherwise creates no obligation in officers to explain any rights a detainee might have. Compare the provisions governing the detention of deportees (permanent residents convicted of serious crimes) at s 253 of the Act. See also ss 193-195 of the Act that spell out further the relative rights of these people.
74 See, for example, the experience of the applicant in *Tan v MIAC* (2007) 211 FLR 118.
75 HREOC, above n 28; Mary Crock, *Seeking Asylum Alone: Unaccompanied and Separated Children and Refugee Protection in Australia* (Sydney: Themis Press, 2006).
76 Note that this legislation was renamed the *Australian Human Rights Commission Act 1986* (Cth) in 2009. To avoid confusion, the name for the commission contemporary with the case under discussion is used here.

the Commission.[77] In response, the government introduced Migration Legislation Amendment Bill (No 2) 1996. This was designed to ensure that neither the Minister nor the Department had any obligation to give a person in immigration detention an application form for a visa unless a direct request for such a form was made in accordance with s 256 of the Act. While initially defeated, the Bill was revived successfully in 1999.[78] Section 193(3) of the *Migration Act* was amended to provide that s 20(6)(b) of the *HREOC Act* and s 7(3)(b) of the *Ombudsman Act 1976* (Cth) do not apply to immigration detainees unless they have personally made a complaint to HREOC (in writing), or to the Ombudsman (orally or in writing).[79] In spite of these measures, the controversy surrounding the 'Teal' case does appear to have induced some concession for detainees.

[16.43] Although the practice of segregating new arrivals continues,[80] arrangements were made in 1996 to put the task of advising non-citizens held in immigration detention out to tender under what became known as the Immigration Advice and Assistance Scheme. Detainees are thereby assured of some assistance from non-government advisers.[81]

16.4 Issues surrounding immigration detention

16.4.1 The detention facilities

[16.44] Unlawful non-citizens are usually detained in one of several Immigration Detention Centres (IDCs) or IRPCs around Australia. By 2010 the country had seen more than a dozen prison-like detention facilities commissioned for the purpose of detaining asylum seekers arriving in Australia or attempting to do so. Two were established in foreign countries – on Nauru and on Manus Island in Papua New Guinea.[82] The 'Australian' facilities include (or have included): various facilities (including a high security prison) on Christmas Island;[83] Port Hedland IRPC, Willie Creek IDC, Curtin IRPC and Perth IDC in Western Australia; Woomera and Baxter IRPCs in South Australia; Villawood IDC in Sydney; Maribyrnong IDC in Melbourne; and facilities in Brisbane and Darwin. To these must be added the

---

77 See *Human Rights and Equal Opportunity Commission v Secretary* (1996) 67 FCR 83.
78 See *Border Protection Legislation Amendment Act 1999* (Cth), s 3, and Sch 1 Part 3.
79 Note that these provisions were not altered with the change of government in 2007.
80 See the discussion at Chapter 6.2. This practice continues to be a source of serious criticism of Australia's practices – especially as no concessions are made for children or vulnerable people who may be at particular risk if interviewed without legal assistance of some kind.
81 The scheme essentially replaces work that would otherwise be done by federal Legal Aid Commissions, although in some cases the Legal Aid Commissions have been awarded contracts under the tender process. On the early scheme, see Pene Mathew, 'Sovereignty and the Right to Seek Asylum: The Case of the Cambodian Asylum-Seekers in Australia' (1995) 15 *Australian Yearbook of International Law* 303. See also Senate Legal and Constitutional References Committee, *A Sanctuary Under Review: An Examination of Australia's Refugee and Humanitarian Determination Processes* (Canberra: 2000) (*A Sanctuary Under Review*) Ch 3. See also Crock, above n 75, Ch 15.7.
82 Michael Gordon, *Freeing Ali: The Human Face of the Pacific Solution* (Sydney: UNSW Press, 2005).
83 For an account of the arrangements on Christmas Island, see David Marr, 'The Indian Ocean Solution: Christmas Island' (2009) *The Monthly*, available at <http://www.themonthly.com.au/monthly-essays-david-marr-indian-ocean-solution-christmas-island-1940>.

'residential housing projects' at Woomera, Whyalla and the Adelaide Hills in South Australia; Leonora township in Western Australia; Christmas Island and Villawood and East Hills in New South Wales. These operate as gated communities where detainees are allowed freedom of movement during the day (if accompanied by a designated person). The high security facility constructed on Christmas Island which was commissioned in late 2008 reached capacity in 2010 with the rise in boat arrivals, leading to contingency plans for detention facilities in other parts of the country (notably in Darwin). The Act also provides for detention in police watch houses, prisons, remand centres, and other places approved by the Minister in writing.

[16.45] Since 1998, the Australian government has contracted private companies to manage these centres, reducing the involvement of the Immigration Department to something akin to an observing role.[84] The initial contract was with Australasian Correctional Services Pty Ltd, through its operational arm, Australasian Correctional Management – ACM. In December 2002, Group 4 Falck Global Solutions Pty Ltd won a tender to take over the role.[85] This group was replaced in June 2009 by Serco Pty Ltd.[86]

[16.46] The merits of privatising the detention centres are debateable. While it is not possible to explore in detail the conditions within the detention centres, it would seem fair to say that these places have been the site of quite egregious human rights abuses over the years. The situation, which had deteriorated during the years of the Keating Labor government, went from bad to worse under the conservative Coalition governments of 1996-2007.[87] By late 2010, overcrowding, suicides, disturbances and incidents of self-harm created an alarming sense of déjà vu.[88]

[16.47] A couple of cases serve to illustrate judicial responses to the conditions in the detention centres and the effect these had on the mental and physical health of the detainees. The cases also offer guidance on the legal duty of care owed by the government to immigration detainees. In *S v Secretary, DIMIA*,[89] Finn J offered a thinly veiled critique of the High Court in sanctioning the legality of indefinite detention, criticising the government for breaching a non-delegable duty of care to ensure adequate health care for detainees in immigration detention. Although the two applicants in this matter ('S' and 'M') had been transferred from Baxter detention centre to a mental health facility before the case was heard, Finn J held anyway that the applicants had made out a case for appropriate relief and so awarded them their costs in the action. His Honour said:

---

84   The Department certainly has a presence at all of the detention facilities but no longer has responsibility for their day-to-day operation.
85   See DIMA, *Fact Sheet 82: Immigration Detention*, 2003.
86   See <http://www.immi.gov.au/managing-australias-borders/detention/services/provider-contract.htm>.
87   See generally Crock et al, above n 58, Ch 11.
88   See Sean Parnell and Lanai Vasek, 'Self-harm in Detention Centres on Rise', *The Australian*, 9 December 2010, available at <http://www.theaustralian.com.au/news/nation/self-harm-in-detention-centres-on-rise/story-e6frg6nf-1225967906031>.
89   (2005) 143 FCR 217.

These two applications are a predictable consequence of the decisions of the High Court in *Al-Kateb v Godwin* (2004) 208 ALR 124 and *Behrooz v Secretary, Department of Immigration & Multicultural & Indigenous Affairs* (2004) 219 CLR 486. A majority of the Court in *Al-Kateb* held that the *Migration Act 1958* (Cth) ("Migration Act") on its proper construction authorised the indefinite detention of an unlawful non-citizen in circumstances where there is no reasonable prospect of removing that person from Australia. In *Behrooz* it was held that the conditions of immigration detention do not affect the legality of that detention. Nonetheless a clear majority of the Court accepted, to use the words of Gleeson CJ (at [21]), that:

> Harsh conditions of detention may violate the civil rights of an alien. An alien does not stand outside the protection of the civil and criminal law. If an officer in a detention centre assaults a detainee, the officer will be liable to prosecution, or damages. If those who manage a detention centre fail to comply with their duty of care, they may be liable in tort.

See also McHugh, Gummow and Heydon JJ at [51]-[53]; Kirby J at [82].[90]

[16.48] The same judge was asked to rule on an application for the removal from detention of an Iranian man, Mr Mastipour, who became a *cause célèbre* for activists when he was placed in solitary confinement at Baxter detention centre, during which time his young daughter was removed from the country and sent back to Iran to live with her mother, from whom the child had been separated as a baby. The man was described in the following terms by his two treating psychiatrists:

> Mastipour is one of the most distressed individuals that either assessor has encountered in our clinical careers. We are of the opinion that the severity of his depressive illness necessitates that Mr Mastipour receive treatment in an acute psychiatric setting. We are also of the opinion that Mr Mastipour's mental state is highly reactive to the detention environment and that he is unable to be cared for in the foreseeable future in such a setting without placing his mental health in serious jeopardy.[91]

[16.49] Finn J agreed with Selway and Lander JJ that the man's situation involved a variety of serious breaches of the duty of care owed by the Commonwealth by virtue of its special relationship with immigration detainees. The court had no trouble in both ordering the man's release from Baxter detention centre and injuncting the Minister from moving the man to Port Hedland detention centre. Selway J made this criticism of the legislation, offering as it does an insight into the management of the detention facilities. Although the *Migration Act* envisages the making of regulations addressing such matters, no such regulations were made. His Honour said:

> What is surprising is that there are virtually no provisions, either in the Act or in the *Migration Regulations* which purport to regulate the manner and conditions of that detention. As I mentioned in my reasons for judgment in *Alsalih v Manager Baxter Immigration Detention Facility* [2004] FCA 352 at [47]-[48] it is usual when powers of detention are conferred for the Parliament to make provision for the manner of the exercise of those powers. There are at least two reasons for this. The first is to curtail the possible abuse of the powers. The second is to protect those

---

90 Ibid at [1].
91 *Secretary, DIMIA v Mastipour* (2003) 207 ALR 83 at [81].

who have to exercise them by providing some guidance as to what the powers are ...

The pleadings identify a number of issues which directly concern what powers relevant persons have in relation to detainees at detention centres. For example, it would seem that the following issues may well need to be addressed: whether there was an 'administrative' power to detain Mr Mastipour in the Management unit; whether that power could be exercised without affording Mr Mastipour a right to be heard; whether there was an 'administrative' power to separate Mr Mastipour from his daughter; whether that power could be exercised without affording Mr Mastipour a right to be heard; whether there was a power to send Mr Mastipour's daughter back to Iran without some judicial determination that Mr Mastipour did not have lawful custody of his child and whether that power could be exercised without affording Mr Mastipour a right to be heard. There may well be others.

These issues concern the powers of those having the right to detain Mr Mastipour. The mere fact that those powers exist (if they do) does not mean that the Secretary cannot be liable in negligence for the performance of them: see *Council of the Shire of Sutherland v Heyman*(1985) 157 CLR 424 at 457-458. ...

In this case there is no detailed regulatory regime against which to consider the duty of care owed by the Secretary to Mr Mastipour. In the absence of such a detailed regulatory regime there is no obvious reason for limiting the common law duty of care by reason of some inferred power or duty of the Secretary. The power and the duty of the Secretary is a power and duty to detain. In determining the extent of the powers inherent in, or necessarily implied by, the power to detain there are at least two issues that need to be considered and balanced:

(a) The power of detention is conferred for the purpose of preventing an unlawful non-citizen entering the Australian community before their entitlement to do so is established and, if it is not established, for the purpose of their removal if possible; and

(b) A detainee retains all of his or her civil rights other than those that are only available to a citizen, and other then those taken away by law, either expressly or by necessary implication.[92]

At the very least this case illustrates the dehumanising effect the immigration detention centres appears to have had on those responsible for the care and control of the asylum seeker inmates.[93]

[16.50] While matters improved after the change of government in 2007, the continuation of the policy of detaining most unauthorised boat arrivals in remote locations continued to place considerable strains on the system. The logistics involved in transporting goods and people to Christmas Island creates inherent inefficiencies and pressures that can be expected to create problems as long as the maintenance of offshore processing continues. These became more acute as the

---

92 (2003) 207 ALR 83 at [8]-[14]. See also *MZUAZ v MIMIA* [2003] FCA 1390 – an unsuccessful application seeking interlocutory relief to prevent the removal into detention of the parents of a child applicant of tender years; and *Akpata v MIMIA* [2003] FCA 514, involving an action to restrain the respondent from detaining the applicant in a form of immigration detention that breached his duty of care to her as a minor or to the mother by separating her from her other child.

93 On this point, see 'The Guards' Story', 4 *Corners*, 15 September 2008, available at <http://www.abc.net.au/4corners/content/2008/s2362098.htm>.

centre became over-crowded.⁹⁴ The situation was exacerbated by the decision to suspend the processing of asylum claims lodged by Afghan and Sri Lankan claimants in 2010.

[16.51] Although a comprehensive history of immigration detention in Australia has yet to be written, it is difficult to think of another issue in recent years that has attracted as much attention from media (domestic and international), parliament, the courts, activists and human rights bodies. The many inquiries conducted over the years document the cost of Australia's immigration detention policies in human terms. The HREOC report, *Those Who've Come Across the Seas: Detention of Unauthorised Arrivals*,⁹⁵ published in 1998 set the standard. The following summary of that report is taken from the Commission website:

> The Commission found that the policy of mandatory detention violates international law which permits detention only where necessary to verify the detainee's identity, to determine the elements on which the claim to refugee status or asylum is based, to deal with people who have destroyed their documents to mislead the authorities or to protect national security or public order. The Commission recommended that those whose detention cannot be justified for one of these reasons should be released, subject to reporting requirements, until their status is determined. It proposed a range of community release options.
>
> The Commission found that the conditions, treatment and services for detainees vary considerably among the three detention centres which were the focus of the inquiry: Port Hedland, Perth and Villawood. The most serious findings of human rights violations related to
> - the use of Villawood Stage One and Perth for long-term detention due to the lack of privacy
> - inadequate recreation facilities, inadequate educational opportunities and restrictions on movement
> - the segregation of new arrivals at Port Hedland
> - the inappropriate management of detainees' behaviour including the misuse of observation rooms
> - physical and chemical restraints and transfers to police cells and prisons; and
> - the failure to inform new arrivals of their right to request the assistance of a lawyer.⁹⁶

The Commission has continued thereafter to conduct annual inspections of immigration detention facilities. Among the major issues of concern highlighted in the 1998 Report were prolonged and indeterminate detention; the limited opportunity for judicial review of detention; detainees' access to legal assistance, general information and contact with the outside world; the mental health of detainees; the needs of children in detention; and security and discipline in detention facilities.⁹⁷

---

94 See generally, Marr, above n 83.
95 See above n 28.
96 See <http://www.humanrights.gov.au/human_rights/immigration/seas.html>. See also the other four HREOC reports published over the years by the Commission, see <http://www.humanrights.gov.au/human_rights/asylum_seekers/index.html>.
97 See the reports at <http://www.humanrights.gov.au/human_rights/publications.html>.

[16.52] The involvement of the Commonwealth Ombudsman began in earnest in 2001 with a report in which evidence was found at every detention centre investigated of detainees engaging in self-harm; damage to property; and fights and assaults. The findings suggested that there were systemic deficiencies in the management of detainees.[98] Although an initial inquiry conducted by the parliamentarians responsible for the regime produced somewhat anodyne comments,[99] by 2001 deteriorating conditions resulted in a fairly damning report. The Joint Standing Committee on Foreign Affairs, Defence and Trade's Human Rights Sub-Committee expressed the view that medical treatment in detention centres was not always satisfactory; educational facilities were limited; and the range of activities provided for detainees was often inadequate. Particular concern was expressed over the impact of detention on families, women and children.[100]

[16.53] The plight of children in detention was the focus of two studies initiated over these years. The first and most influential was the mammoth inquiry conducted by HREOC into Children in Immigration Detention. The Commission visited all immigration detention centres across Australia; conducted a number of public hearings and confidential focus groups; and received over 340 submissions. The report was tabled in Federal Parliament in 2004.[101] As well as encouraging the development of policies across a range of areas involving asylum seeking children, this report can be credited with the eventual decision in June 2005 to release children from immigration detention.

[16.54] The second report that may have had some impact over this period involved a study of Australia's treatment of unaccompanied children and refugee protection. Published in August 2006 as part of a three nation inquiry, the *Seeking Asylum Alone* Report identified Australia as the country with the most regressive practices of the three countries studied.[102] Australia seemed to have cherry picked all of the most

---

98   Commonwealth Ombudsman, *Report of an Own Motion Investigation into The Department of Immigration and Multicultural Affairs' Immigration Detention Centres* (March 2001), available at <http://www.ombudsman.gov.au/files/investigation_2001_05.pdf>

99   See JSCM, *Not the Hilton* (Canberra: 2000). This Report was generally positive in its conclusions. The Committee was 'impressed with the operation of the temporary centres in the face of the demands on their resources and infrastructure' and believed that 'the facilities provided were adequate, and that the cultural sensitivities of detainees were being accommodated'. It did, however, express concern at the pressure that unauthorised arrivals place on the detention facilities and the Commonwealth's resources generally.

100 See *A Report on Visits to Australian Detention Centres* (Canberra: 2001). See also Philip Flood AO, *Report of Inquiry into Immigration Detention Procedures*, presented to parliament, 27 February 2001. This report made a number of recommendations to improve the processes in place for identifying, dealing with, reporting on, and following up of incidents and situations of sexual assault in detention centres.

101 See HREOC, *A Last Resort? – Report of the National Inquiry into Children in Immigration Detention*, tabled in Parliament on 13 May 2004, available at <http://www.humanrights.gov.au/human_rights/children_detention_report/index.html>.

102 See Crock, above n 75; and Jacqueline Bhabha and Mary Crock, *Seeking Asylum Alone: Unaccompanied and Separated Children and Refugee Protection in Australia, the UK and the US* (Sydney: Themis Press, 2007); Jacqueline Bhabha and Susan Schmidt, *Seeking Asylum Alone: Unaccompanied and Separated Children and Refugee Protection in the United States* (Cambridge, Mass: Harvard University, Committee on Human Rights Studies, 2006); and Jacqueline Bhabha and Nadine Finch, *Seeking Asylum Alone: Unaccompanied and Separated Children and Refugee Protection in the United Kingdom*

restrictive and punitive laws and policies devised in other refugee countries around the world.

[16.55] In June 2005, the Coalition government announced that children were no longer to be detained, except as a measure of 'last resort'. This initiative, together with the embarrassment caused by the Cornelia Rau and Vivian Solon-Alvarez debacles, led to a concerted effort within the bureaucracy to improve the 'culture' within the Department. In 2008-09, the percentage of unlawful non-citizens detained after being located by the Department decreased from around 17 per cent in 2007-08 to around 13 per cent. The Department also ensures that those who are found to have no right to remain in Australia and who do not want to depart voluntarily are removed expeditiously.[103]

[16.56] The disappointment following the change of government has been the failure to translate policy change into anything approximating real legislative reform. Although there are signs that the distrust of the judiciary that dominated the years of conservative governance is fading under the new administration, the structures that underpinned the cruelty of the 1990s and 2000s remained untouched.[104]

16.4.2 International oversight of immigration detention in Australia

[16.57] The geographical isolation of Australia's remote detention centres was only partially successful in keeping applicants out of the international eye. The extreme nature of the measures taken by the government during the late 1990s and 2000s served as a catalyst for human rights and other interested groups. After the failure of the challenge to the detention provisions in *Chu Kheng Lim*, a complaint was made by one of the detainees to the UN Human Rights Committee. The Committee ruled on the complaint in May 1997, upholding the allegation that Div 4B of the Act created a detention regime that breached Australia's international legal obligations as a signatory to the International Covenant on Civil and Political Rights (ICCPR).[105] It held that the mandatory nature of the provisions and the failure to provide for any mechanism for release where detention was either unnecessary or inappropriate rendered the detention 'arbitrary' for the purposes of Art 9(1) of the ICCPR. The Committee ruled also that the exclusion of curial review in s 54R (now s 183) of the Act ran counter to Art 9(4) of the Covenant. The government responded to the Committee's ruling

---

(Cambridge, Mass: Harvard University, Committee on Human Rights Studies, 2006). The reports can be accessed at <www.humanrights.harvard.edu>; and <http://www.law.usyd.edu.au/scil/publications/#reports>.

103 The number of people in immigration detention for more than two years decreased significantly in 2008-09 to 25 people by 30 June 2009 as compared to 72 in March 2008 and 74 in December 2007. In 2008-09, about 73 per cent of people were removed within two weeks of being detained, reflecting the Department's focus on more prompt resolution of cases. See DIAC, *Annual Report 2008-09* (Canberra: 2010) at 114-15.

104 See Mary Crock, 'First Term Blues: Labor, Refugees and Immigration Reform' (2010) 17 *Australian Journal of Administrative Law* 1; and Mary Crock, 'Alien Fears: Politics and Immigration Control' (2010) 2 *Dialogue* 20.

105 See A v Australia, Communication No 560/1993: Australia, CCPR/C/59/D/560/1993 (30 April 1997) and Nicholas Poynder, 'A (Name Deleted) v Australia: A Milestone for Asylum Seekers' (1997) 4(1) *Australian Journal of Human Rights* 155. The case is discussed in Chapter 3.3.2.

by stressing the changes that have occurred in the laws governing the detention of asylum seekers in Australia. Later cases brought before this Committee led to further adverse rulings from this body, putting the lie to government assertions that these changes were sufficient to remedy the breaches of the ICCPR identified by the Committee in its first ruling.[106]

16.5 Release from detention

16.5.1 Bridging visas A-E

[16.58] All unlawful non-citizens who have not been permanent residents are subject to the same mandatory detention provision, namely s 189 of the Act. Whether an individual is actually detained, however, depends on her or his eligibility for a Bridging visa. In effect, these visas are mechanisms for granting bail or parole. Their purpose is to regularise the status of a non-citizen for the period needed to determine entitlement to a 'substantive' visa, allowing temporary or permanent stay in the country. Bridging visas generally remain in effect until the non-citizen is granted a substantive visa, their substantive visa (if any) is cancelled or until 28 days after notification that the person's application for a substantive visa has been refused. If review rights are exercised, the Bridging visa continues to operate until 28 days after notification of the review decision. This regime makes it possible for decision-makers to inform non-citizens exactly when their Bridging visas will cease, so ensuring that a non-citizen does not become unlawful inadvertently and so become liable for detention.[107] It also grants the unlawful non-citizen a reasonable time in which to leave Australia.

[16.59] As the refusal of Bridging visas is reviewable by the MRT, this tribunal has taken on a new role akin to that of a bail magistrate in the district courts. This is demonstrated in early cases such as *Re Feng Guan Lin*.[108] There, the tribunal affirmed a decision to refuse a Bridging visa because of the applicant's inability to either demonstrate any connection with the community or provide any funds as surety against release. In an effort to maintain the integrity and efficiency of the system, the legislation requires the MRT to make a ruling on Bridging visa appeals within seven days of hearing the appeal.[109]

[16.60] The Regulations set out seven classes of Bridging visas. Entitlement to the different visas is determined by the applicant's status before applying for a substantive visa. At the top of the hierarchy are Bridging visas (BVs) classes A and B.[110] The first confers permission to work, the second permission to work and travel. Both are available only to persons who apply for a substantive visa during the life of their previous visa, and whose previous visa does not preclude either working rights or the grant of a further visa. The Department reports that in 2008-09, 316,730 BVAs

---

106 See the discussion of the case law on this point at Chapter 4.4 above.
107 See *Nguyen Van Chuong v MIEA* [1996] FCA 653.
108 [1995] IRTA 6107.
109 See *Migration Act*, s 367, and *Migration Regulations*, reg 4.27.
110 *Migration Regulations*, Sch 2, subclasses 010 and 020.

and 27,668 BVBs were granted. This compares with 253,744 BVAs and 18,593 BVBs granted in 2007-08.[111]

[16.61] Further down the scale, the BVC (Sch 2, subclass 030) is available to unlawful non-citizens who come forward voluntarily and who make a valid application for a substantive visa. In 2008-09, 7754 such visas were granted (compared with 5487 in 2007-08).[112] Holders of BVCs may be granted permission to work if the person can demonstrate compelling need. A non-citizen will have a compelling need to work only if he or she is suffering financial hardship.[113]

[16.62] The class D Bridging visas (Sch 2, subclasses 040 and 041) can be grouped together as true bail authorities that allow the release of persons whom the Department does not wish to keep in custody. The visas are issued to provide a person a short period of time in which to apply for a substantive visa or to voluntarily depart the country. The visa lasts for five working days from the date of grant. In 2008-09 743 such visas were granted, up from 487 in the preceding year.[114]

[16.63] The fifth and most contentious class of Bridging visa, the 'general' class, BVE,[115] is given to unlawful non-citizens who are either making acceptable arrangements to depart Australia or who have an unresolved application for a substantive visa. Department policy defines 'acceptable arrangements to depart' as including evidence of a ticket, proof of a reservation and possession of a travel document. The Federal Court has observed that, when deciding whether a person 'is making' acceptable arrangements to depart Australia, it is clearly not an error of law to consider what that person has done to date. The tribunal may properly have regard to what, if any, arrangements that person has already made and what further arrangements remain to be made.[116] In other cases it may be sufficient to have a genuine intention to make the arrangements to depart. However, the MRT decision which was the subject of review in *Smith v MIMIA*[117] found that an applicant's forwarding of a passport application to the Fijian High Commission, with no indication of how long the processing of this application would take, did not satisfy the tribunal that the applicant had acceptable arrangements to depart. Whether a decision-maker is satisfied that an applicant is making acceptable arrangements is clearly a question of fact that involves an exercise of discretion.[118]

[16.64] The BVE is designed primarily for unlawful non-citizens detected by the Department, rather than those who volunteer themselves to the Department. It allows the release of people who are waiting for the determination of an application for a

---

111 See DIAC, *Population Flows – Immigration Aspects 2008-2009* (Canberra: 2010) at 70.
112 Ibid.
113 See *Migration Regulations*, reg 1.08(a). See, for example, *Abcjkl* [2003] MRTA 5977, where the applicant failed to make out financial hardship when he adduced no documentary evidence of debt or outstanding bills. Certain non-citizens sponsored by employers are also accepted as having a compelling need to work for the purposes of the Regulations: see reg 1.08(b) and (c).
114 See DIAC, above n 111, at 62.
115 See *Migration Regulations*, Sch 2, subclasses 050 (general) and 051 (Protection visa applicant).
116 *Chen v MIMA* [2001] FCA 285; *Huang v MIMA* [2001] FCA 284.
117 [2002] FCA 306. See also *NABL v MIMA* [2002] FCA 102; *Masila v MIMA* [2001] FCA 1611.
118 *Ahmed v MIMA* [1999] FCA 430 at [7]; *Arkan v MIMA* [2000] FCA 1134 at [9].

substantive visa, who have sought judicial review of a refusal, or who wish to depart the country voluntarily within a specified period. The definition of 'eligible non-citizen' extends the grant of a visa to overstayers and non-citizens who by-passed immigration clearance and managed to evade the authorities for more than 45 days. Concessions are made also for applicants for refugee status detained within 45 days of arrival who meet certain hardship criteria.[119] In 2008-09, 42,569 BVEs were issued, compared with, 40,350 BVEs issued in 2007-08 and 42,383 in 2006-07.[120]

[16.65] Applicants granted a BVE are not generally granted authority to work. Permission to work requires a further application and is granted only where a person can demonstrate a 'compelling need to work' as defined by reg 1.08 of the Regulations. Persons holding a BVE because they are seeking judicial review, or have requested the Minister to exercise her or his personal discretion to grant a visa, are not eligible for permission to work.

[16.66] In *De Silva v MIMA*,[121] Merkel J drew attention to the injustices that can arise as a result of this mandatory no work condition. The applicant in that case had lived in Australia with his wife since 1996. During that time, they had also produced a son (aged 3 at the date of the hearing). He was issued a Bridging visa because his wife was a party to a class action in the High Court. As the applicant could not work, he and his family were forced to rely on assistance from his brother-in-law, food vouchers from charities such as the Red Cross, and to beg for food from fast food outlets. The applicant then resorted to working in order to provide for his family, and was apprehended by the Department on two occasions. On the first occasion, a $10,000 security bond was imposed on the applicant. On the second occasion, this bond was increased to $50,000. As the applicant was unable to pay the bond, he was placed in detention. Although the matter was resolved by consent of the parties involved, Merkel J expressed his concern 'that the current regulatory environment can operate to require that persons employing proper procedures to remain in Australia be required to live off such charity as may be available or to beg to make up the shortfall to enable their sustenance'.

[16.67] The tribunals and Federal Court have recognised that the underlying purpose of the legislation, as well as government policy, is to reduce the number of people held in detention (at the expense of the taxpayer). Thus, the object of parliament in providing a right to apply for a BVE is to bring detention to an end in appropriate circumstances and to have detainees 'regularise' their position to enable them to leave Australia with dignity, within an appropriate period and at their own cost.[122] This must be offset by the national interest in regulating the presence in Australia of non-citizens through the discretion to grant a Bridging visa, or to impose conditions on such a visa. In this regard, a serious view is taken of non-compliance by visitors to this country with the conditions they are required to meet to enter and remain in this country. Relevant to the decision to release is the question whether the detainee might escape into the community or perhaps become involved in activities that are

---

119 See *Migration Regulations*, reg 2.20(7)-(11).
120 See DIAC, above n 111, at 62.
121 (2001) 113 FCR 350 at [11].
122 *Tutugri v MIMA* (1999) 95 FCR 592 at [56] and [57].

illegal.[123] The likelihood of non-compliance may be assessed on the basis of previous immigration history.[124] However, whether the balance of these aims is achieved by the Act and Regulations is another question: Madgwick J has observed that '[t]he density of the delegated legislation would challenge anybody'.[125]

16.5.2 Security for compliance with conditions of a Bridging visa

[16.68] The MRT can review both a decision to refuse a Bridging visa, and any related bond or security decision.[126] The MRT may therefore review a decision to request, or not to request, a security as well as the amount of security requested.[127]

[16.69] The Federal Court has outlined the correct procedure to be followed in making a decision with respect to security as follows:

(1) The decision-maker must first decide what conditions (if any) ought to be imposed on the grant of a visa.
(2) If conditions are to be imposed, the decision-maker must then determine whether the applicant will comply with these conditions without any security being taken.
(3) If the answer is yes, no security should be imposed. If the answer is no, the decision-maker must proceed to the next question which is:
(4) Will the conditions be complied with if security is taken? If the answer is no, the visa ought not to be granted because the criterion set out in cl 050.223 will not be met. If the answer is yes, security should be required and the decision-maker must assess the appropriate amount and type of security to be imposed.
(5) If security has been required, the decision-maker must see whether or not it has been lodged. If it has not been lodged, the visa application should be rejected because cl 050.224 will not be satisfied. If it has been lodged (provided all other relevant criteria have been met), the visa must be granted.[128]

[16.70] The court has cautioned against fixing an excessive amount for security. In *Mitrevski v MIMA*,[129] Merkel J stated:

> The power to fix a security amount is a decision that affects the liberty of an individual. The fixing of an amount that is oppressive will necessarily result in the continued involuntary detention of an individual who has not been convicted of any offence. In such circumstances, caution should be exercised to ensure the amount fixed as security is reasonable in all the circumstances.

To ensure that the amount fixed is not excessive or unreasonable in all the circumstances, consideration must be given to the purpose of the power (which is to secure

---

123 *Foo v MIMIA* [2003] FCA 1277 at [26].
124 *Delatabua v MIMIA* [2004] FCA 884.
125 *Mouradian v MRT* [2001] FCA 1413 at [8].
126 See *Migration Regulations*, reg 4.02(4)(f)(i).
127 See, for example, *Anarwala* [2002] MRTA 1875; *Ahmed* [2002] MRTA 2520.
128 See *Tennakoon v MIMA* [2001] FCA 615 at [18]ff.
129 [2001] FCA 221 at [8]. See also *Applicant VAAN of 2001 v MIMA* (2002) 70 ALD 289 at [26] where Finkelstein J noted that '[i]f excessive security is requested, it would only be to punish, and not to secure compliance with the Migration Act, the regulations or any conditions'.

compliance with conditions attached to the grant of the visa).[130] This, in turn requires consideration of the nature of the conditions to be imposed, and the individual circumstances of the applicant, such as their financial position, and their previous record in dealing with the Department.[131]

16.5.3 The trafficking visas: Bridging visa F (BVF)

[16.71] The sixth class of Bridging visa is somewhat different from the others in so far as it is designed to grant temporary legal status to persons of interest in a prosecution or law enforcement matter involving people trafficking. (For more extended discussion, see Chapter 14.5.) First introduced in 2004, the visas are designed to allow the federal or State police authorities time to determine whether a non-citizen can assist in relation to a criminal prosecution for people trafficking, and also to give the visa holder time to evaluate their options. The trafficking visa framework has been criticised for its heavy focus on criminal justice outcomes to the neglect of the human rights of victims of trafficking.

[16.72] Initially, the BVF operated for a period of 30 days or as specified by the Minister. It was extended to 45 days in 2009. The BVF (and specific social support attendant upon it) was originally contingent on the trafficked person being able and willing to cooperate with police in relation to investigations and prosecutions.[132] This requirement placed Australia at odds with the UN Protocol on Trafficking to which Australia is party and in respect of which legislation was passed in 2005.[133] Since 2009, reforms to this framework have broken the nexus between initial victim support and the obligation to provide assistance to law enforcement. Social support is available now to any identified victim regardless of the visa they hold or held. Where a BVF has been granted, a second BVF may be granted for a further 45 days. The decision to grant a second BVF is made on a case-by-case basis, including, for example, where a person is willing to assist the police but is unable to do so, say, as a result of trauma.

[16.73] If a victim of trafficking decides to assist the police, a Criminal Justice Stay Certificate may be issued, and the non-citizen may be granted a Criminal Justice Stay visa. This permits the visa holder to remain in Australia for such the time as they are 'required for law enforcement purposes'. Between January 2004 and April 2009, 119 suspected victims of trafficking were given BVFs and 73 were granted Criminal Justice Stay visas (in relation to investigation of trafficking offences).[134]

---

130 *VWEX v MIMIA* [2004] FCA 460.
131 *VAZ v MIMA* [2001] FCA 1805.
132 Jennifer Burn and Frances Simmons, 'Trafficking and Slavery in Australia: An Evaluation of Victim Support Strategies' (2006) 15(4) *Asian and Pacific Migration Journal* 553.
133 See Protocol to Prevent, Suppress and Punish Trafficking in Persons, Especially Women and Children, supplementing the United Nations Convention Against Transnational Organised Crime (the Palermo Protocol) GA Res 55/25, UN GAOR, 55th sess, 62nd plen mtg, Annex II, Agenda Item 105, UN Doc A/RES/55/25 (8 January 2001), opened for signature on 15 November 2000, entered into force on 25 December 2003; and *Criminal Code Amendment (Trafficking in Persons Offences) Act 2005* (Cth); Burn and Simmons, ibid.
134 Australian Government, Inaugural Report of the Anti-People Trafficking Interdepartmental Committee, *Trafficking in Persons. The Australian Government Response January 2004-April 2009* (Canberra: Commonwealth of Australia, 2009) at 28.

[16.74] Divisions 270 and 271 of the Commonwealth *Criminal Code* deal with slavery and trafficking offences. The *Criminal Code Amendment (Trafficking in Persons Offences) Act 2005* inserted new offences of trafficking in persons into the *Criminal Code*. These offences include people trafficking, debt bondage and specific offences for trafficking in children. From the time the trafficking offences were introduced in 2005 until April 2009, 34 people were charged with trafficking offences and there were seven convictions for slavery and trafficking offences.[135]

16.5.4 Removal Pending visas

[16.75] The seventh and final class of Bridging visa is again an unusual creation that is closer to a more permanent visa. Following the High Court's ruling in *Al-Kateb v Godwin*,[136] the then Coalition government created the Removal Pending visa to enable the release of long-term detainees, the removal of whom is not reasonably practicable in the foreseeable future. The visas are granted in exercise of one of the Minister's non-compellable, non-reviewable discretions.[137] In 2007-08 five such visas were issued, in comparison with 34 two years earlier.[138]

16.5.5 Seizure of assets and costs of detention

[16.76] For many years, legislative provisions enabled the Department to seize assets of detainees and deportees for the purpose of repaying costs of detention and removal or deportation.[139] In 2009 legislative amendments abolished the detention debt regime imposed on immigration detainees.[140] This move accorded with the unanimous recommendation of the Joint Standing Committee on Migration in December 2008.[141] However, people convicted of people smuggling or illegal foreign fishing are still liable for their costs of detention and removal. Further, unlawful non-citizens remain liable for costs associated with their removal or deportation.[142]

16.6 The removal of unlawful non-citizens

16.6.1 Theories of removal and deportation

[16.77] The most serious consequence of breach of Australia's migration laws is removal or, in the case of criminal permanent residents, deportation. Unlike America,[143] Australian laws do not establish separate mechanisms for 'exclusion' and 'removal', although different substantive entitlements apply according to whether or

---

135   Ibid at 22.
136   (2004) 219 CLR 562.
137   *Migration Act*, s 195A.
138   DIAC, *Population Movements, 2006-2007* (Canberra: 2008) and DIAC, above n 111, at 62.
139   See former ss 208, 209 and 222 and ss 21A, 21B and 21C of the *Migration Act* before 1989.
140   *Migration Amendment (Abolishing Detention Debt) Act 2009* (Cth).
141   JSCM, *Immigration Detention in Australia: A New Beginning* (Canberra: 2008) at 126.
142   Section 210.
143   See Stephen Legomsky and Cristina Rodriguez, *Immigration and Refugee Law and Policy* (New York: Thomson Reuters/Foundation Press, 5th ed, 2009).

not a non-citizen has been immigration cleared. Removal is now a simple by-product of unlawful status. It is only in the case of criminal permanent residents that any discretion attaches to the end-stage process.

[16.78] In the case of persons who have been in Australia for any length of time, the impact of removal can be substantial. Families can be separated, livelihoods ruined. The consequences of a bad immigration 'record' can also hamper an individual's freedom to travel to other countries. Many states will refuse to admit non-citizens who have been deported from another country on the ground that the person is demonstrably of 'bad character'.[144] For criminal permanent residents, deportation now constitutes permanent exile from Australia because of a ban in perpetuity on re-admission.

[16.79] If the laws governing the removal and deportation of unlawful non-citizens have been toughened substantially over the years, there also appears to have been a subtle shift in the theoretical bases of the provisions in question. The accepted wisdom is that the purpose of deportation and/or removal is to safeguard the security and well being of the Australian community.[145] The ability to remove unlawful non-citizens has been regarded as central to immigration control and a key incident of national sovereignty. The converse of such a theoretical approach is that removal and deportation should not be directly punitive: that the powers should act as a shield rather than as a sanction directed at an individual.

[16.80] The rhetoric of successive governments has been to emphasise the issues of sovereignty, control and protection in the removal of immigration outlaws. However, the changes that have occurred in the law bring into question the extent to which these theoretical assumptions are correct. The practical impact of deportation or removal can be highly punitive on the individuals affected both directly and indirectly. As explored below, the theoretical underpinnings of the removal laws have not always been given the primary consideration they deserve, especially in cases where choices have arisen as to the destination to which a removee is to be sent.[146]

16.6.2 The evolution of legislative scheme

[16.81] In recent times the statutory law concerning unlawful non-citizens has become harsher but more even-handed. The distinction between immigrants and aliens (or non-British subjects) was abolished in 1983, and with it the provisions granting immunity from deportation to those unlawful non-citizens who had avoided detection for five years.[147] British subjects are now granted no special favours and are just as liable to removal as the nationals of other countries where they have fallen foul of the Act.[148] The greatest change in recent years, however, has been in

---

144　See Chapter 17 below.
145　This reasoning underpins the policies announced by Labor Minister Chris Evans in the July 2008 detention changes.
146　For a discussion on the theoretical bases of America's deportation laws, see Legomsky and Rodriguez, above n 143, at 515ff.
147　See Chapters 3 and 17, and ss 7(4), 12 and 13 of the *Migration Act* as of 1973.
148　On this point, see the discussion in Chapter 3.2 above.

the decision-making processes governing the removal of unlawful non-citizens and the power given to officers to make concessions in cases where they are minded to decide against removal.

[16.82] Before 1989, the removal of unlawful non-citizens was a matter of discretion for the Minister. Section 18 of the *Migration Act* then read simply: 'The Minister may order the deportation of a person who is a prohibited non-citizen under any provision of this Act'. The unfettered nature of this discretion left considerable scope for argument concerning which matters were or were not relevant to an exercise of the power to deport. The fact that a separate decision had to be made to deport a person after the refusal of an entry permit also encouraged the making of serial applications or submissions to the Minister.[149]

[16.83] The major change to the removal regime in 1989 was the attempt to reduce the extent to which a separate decision had to be made. The Act retained the old discretion to deport unlawful non-citizens (former s 60) but superimposed a provision making deportation mandatory in certain circumstances: former s 59. Unlike the old s 18 orders, s 59 orders were stated to be irrevocable. They were required where an unlawful non-citizen's period of grace had expired and where the prescribed procedures for the making of the order had been followed. The procedures set down by reg 178 of the *Migration Regulations 1989* (Cth) required the Minister to ascertain whether the person had applied for or been granted refugee status; whether the person had applied for another type of entry permit or had sought review of a decision; whether there was a court order in force affecting the power to deport; and whether the prescribed number of working days had elapsed since the arrest of the person under the Act.

[16.84] Since 1 September 1994, discretionary removal has become a thing of the past for all but former permanent residents convicted of serious crimes.[150] Section 198 now requires the removal of non-citizens who have failed in their attempt to gain a visa to enter or remain in the country. Section 198(2A) mandates the removal of persons who have had their visa cancelled on character and related grounds (under ss 501, 501A and 501B of the Act). The mandatory removal provisions operate as the (automatic) end stage of the immigration process. For the non-citizen, arguments about the right to remain must be made through the medium of an application for a substantive visa. In fact, the making of such an application, or the prosecution of an appeal, are the only mechanisms available to prevent removal – eligibility for a visa will not suffice (s 198(3)). The one discretion that remains is the officer's power to remove the dependants of a 'removee'.

16.6.3 Removal and the courts

[16.85] The abandonment of a discretionary mechanism for the removal of unlawful non-citizens reflected the government's discontent with the judiciary's treatment of deportation (removal) cases throughout the 1980s. What is interesting about the

---
149 See Commonwealth Parliamentary Debates, *Hansard*, Senate, Vol 134, 30 May 1989, at 3040.
150 See *Migration Act*, ss 200-203, and Chapter 17 below.

present regime is the extent to which it attempts to turn back the clock to a time when the Minister's power to remove was regarded as absolute and an inappropriate subject for judicial challenge.

[16.86] In *Salemi v MacKellar (No 2)*,[151] Gibbs J expressed the view that the old s 18 of the Act gave the Minister an 'unconditional right to order the deportation' of an unlawful non-citizen.[152] By the early 1980s, when the first orders were sought under the *Administrative Decisions (Judicial Review) Act 1977* (Cth) (*ADJR Act*), the courts had begun to qualify the ruling in *Salemi* by pointing out that the mere existence of a discretion to deport under s 18 implied that deportation was not the inevitable result of unlawful status. The Minister was bound to consider the merits of the case, including all relevant circumstances.[153] Because of the breadth of the discretion to deport, applicants initially found it difficult to show that a consideration was one the Minister was bound to take into account.[154] The courts confirmed that the onus was on the applicant to provide all relevant information.[155]

[16.87] As the 1980s progressed, the courts became more demanding of the Minister in both the procedures followed and in the matters they held relevant to the decision to deport. They intervened on occasions where reliance was placed on facts shown by the applicant to be erroneous. They also guarded jealously an applicant's right to pursue legal action initiated in Australia, holding that any prejudice to the action caused by removal must be considered by the decision-maker.[156]

[16.88] Towards the close of the decade, the change in judicial attitude to the sweeping powers conferred by the Act made s 18 of the Act particularly susceptible to judicial review. As in other instances of broadly expressed migration powers, the courts moved from seeing the Minister's discretion to deport as an instrument of autonomy to one that conferred a power but also imposed an obligation to exercise that power responsibly. The deportation (removal) cases decided by the Federal Court during the late 1980s illustrate the breakdown that occurred in the distinction between the judicial review of an exercise of discretion and the review of decisions on their merits. At a time when removal decisions were subjected to little outside scrutiny, it was virtually impossible to obtain relief from the courts on the grounds that the Minister had failed to take a relevant matter into account or had decided the case on the basis of an irrelevant consideration. Once the courts had moved to the point of saying that the Minister was legally obliged to exercise his or her discretion reasonably and responsibly, it was a short step to find removal decisions legally flawed because of matters improperly taken into account or disregarded.

---

151   (1977) 137 CLR 396.
152   See Mary Crock, 'Administrative Law and Immigration Control in Australia: Actions and Reactions' (unpublished PhD Thesis, University of Melbourne, 1994) Ch 4.2.2.
153   See, for example, *Turner v MIEA* (1981) 55 FLR 180; *Tagle v MIEA* (1983) 67 FLR 164; and *Kioa v West* (1985) 159 CLR 550.
154   See, for example, *Akpan v MIEA* (1982) 58 FLR 47; *Aygun v MIEA* (1983) 68 FLR 276; and *Alpaslan v MIEA* (1985) 9 ALN N78.
155   See *Ertan v Hurford* (1986) 11 FCR 382; and *Singh v MIEA* (1985) 9 ALN N13.
156   See *Ates v MIEA* (1983) 67 FLR 449; and *Ertan v Hurford* (1986) 11 FCR 382. Compare, however, *Singh-Dhillon v Mahoney* [1986] FCA 334 and *Singh-Dhillon v MIEA* (1987) 14 FCR 351.

[16.89] The breadth of the discretion to deport made it a matter of subjective judgment as to the range of matters considered relevant or irrelevant at law. It became increasingly common in removal cases to see the courts advert to the legal concept of unreasonableness in decision-making. Most of these were extreme cases, where the decision under review posed a direct threat to the life, liberty or health of either the applicant or that of an unborn child.[157] In cases such as these, the human predicament facing the applicants and the lack of any alternative avenue through which to seek redress may have further encouraged the courts to take an activist approach to judicial review.

[16.90] It is difficult to 'blame' the judiciary for its use of the curial review process in removal cases over this period.[158] In essence, the courts were doing no more than calling the Minister and parliament to account for the operation of a legislative scheme (governing the removal of unlawful non-citizens) that was otherwise not subject to oversight or supervision. Where the power conferred by the Act was expressed in absolute terms, the courts found it unacceptable that the device of policy be used in an attempt to limit or structure the exercise of discretion. The change in judicial approach made it clear to the executive that discretions expressed in unfettered terms were not a viable administrative option in an age of open government.[159]

[16.91] If the grounds on which a non-citizen's legal status can be lost are now more defined, so too are the remedies available to illegal migrants. As noted in the previous chapter, the Regulations provide few opportunities for the regularisation of unlawful status. The Minister's discretion to depart from the terms of the legislation is also very limited. The effect of the detention provisions discussed earlier is to push the focus of the discretionary powers away from the enforcement process so that where a non-citizen is unable to meet the substantive criteria for the grant of a visa the consequences become almost automatic.

[16.92] Several attempts have been made since December 1989 to address suggestions that the Act's enforcement provisions are too harsh. Concessions were made for certain unlawful non-citizens seeking to regularise their status after the expiry of what used to be a 28-day 'period of grace'.[160] The ramifications of mandatory removal in refugee cases were addressed by amending the Act so as to require certain procedures to be followed before making an order under what was s 59. Under the present regime, removal is stayed automatically upon the lodging of an application for a Protection visa. However, the safeguards are few for persons who have a credible fear of death or abuse of human rights who do not meet the narrow definition of refugee.

[16.93] In so far as they could impact on refugees and persons fearing torture, the removal provisions are far from satisfactory. Under international law, Australia is

---

157 See, for example, *Latu v MIEA* (1985) 8 ALN N293a; *Videto v MIEA* (1985) 8 FCR 167; and *Chan Yee Kin v MIEA* (1989) 169 CLR 379.
158 For an alternative view on this point, see John McMillan, 'Recent Themes in Judicial Review of Federal Executive Action' (1996) 24 *Federal Law Review* 347 at 381.
159 On this point, see the comments of Robyn Bickett, 'Controlling Immigration Litigation: The Commonwealth Perspective' (2010) 63 *AIAL Forum* 40.
160 See former s 13 of the *Migration Act*.

obliged not to refoule or return refugees who are in fear of persecution on certain grounds in their country of origin. That obligation sits uneasily with a scheme that requires removal where no valid application is on foot, yet creates no duty in officers to inform people of their right to seek protection as refugees. The obligation to remove an unlawful non-citizen exists irrespective of the merit of any claim for refugee status or for clemency on other grounds. It is no defence of the scheme to argue that the administration can overcome its defects by selectively breaching the law in cases where its application would be harsh or unconscionable.

[16.94] A by-product of the mandatory regime is that exceptions to the general rule must be legislated. One example of how the early provisions worked against the government's (and the public's) interest was *Attorney-General (NSW) v Ray*.[161] There, the Minister moved to deport an unlawful non-citizen wanted as a witness in a murder trial. The case involved a discretionary deportation order made under what was s 18 of the Act. The Federal Court held that, were the Minister to execute his order, he could be in contempt of the criminal court which required the presence of the witness in question. The conflict arose because of the uncertainty generated by the High Court's decision in *Park Oh Ho v MIEA*.[162] That case questioned the legality of detaining a deportee where there is no immediate intention to deport. These difficulties were addressed by the insertion of special provisions for 'criminal justice visitors'. The Act now provides for both federal and State Criminal Justice Stay Certificates and spells out that removal in the absence of such a certificate will not be a contempt of court.[163]

16.7 The execution of deportation orders and determinations to remove

[16.95] This part of the chapter deals with a miscellany of issues that arise in the course of removing an unlawful non-citizen. It begins with an examination of the mechanisms available to stay or suspend removal pending the hearing of applications for judicial review. The chapter concludes by discussing two issues that have arisen at the final point of removal. These are: (1) determining who has the power to choose the place to which a removee is sent; and (2) the limitations placed on the choice of destination. These last classes of migration decisions are chosen for their interest for migration lawyers, rather than for their pure legal content. They are areas where the controversy between the government and the courts has arisen not because of a clash over the roles assumed by each body, but because of the intrinsic difficulties posed by the problems under consideration.

16.7.1 Stay orders and injunctive relief

[16.96] One bi-product of the move to 'automate' the removal process is that, once a determination (for the refusal of a visa or for the cancellation of a visa) is made, there

---

161 (1989) 90 ALR 263.
162 (1989) 167 CLR 637.
163 See *Migration Act*, Part 2, Div 4, ss 147-148 and 153.

is technically no process in respect of which to seek injunctive relief: the 'decision' is fully implemented.[164] In practice, an application for a stay must be attached to an application alleging serious error of law in the substantive decision such that the determination to remove under s 198 of the Act is impugned. While removal under s 198 may not involve a decision in a strict sense, it is a precondition to the application of the section that determinations on substantive entitlements to a visa are made correctly. Issues going to the validity of an application for a visa and powers to grant or cancel visas are decisions made under the Act, therefore coming within the definition of 'judicially reviewable decision' in s 475.

[16.97] In the vast majority of cases involving applications for the judicial review of a refusal to grant a substantive visa, the stay provisions are not brought into play because applicants are granted a BVE for the duration of the period leading up to and including a court challenge. Once a non-citizen is in possession of a Bridging visa, the mandatory removal provisions have no operation. It is only in cases where the Minister declines to grant a Bridging visa that applicants must obtain a stay order from the Federal Court or an injunction from the High Court. This was dealt with originally in s 482 of the *Migration Act*, although this was amended in October 2001 with the insertion of a new Part 8 of the Act.[165] Section 481 now provides that the making of an application for judicial review will no longer result automatically in the stay of any order that has been made. In practice, applicants have had to rely on the stay procedure enshrined in ss 20 and 23 of the *Federal Court of Australia Act 1976* (Cth).

[16.98] The use of the Bridging visa device as a *de facto* stay order mechanism reflects a government policy that judicial review applications should be a one-step process, involving one rather than two 'bites' into the court's time. Even in those cases in which a stay order is sought, the practice is to proceed almost directly to the hearing of the application for review of the main issues to be tried. The minimal use of stay proceedings contrasts with the approaches taken in countries such as Canada where preliminary hearings are used as a filter to the judicial review process.

[16.99] Much of the jurisprudence that developed over the 1980s in relation to the grant of injunctive relief in removal cases remains apposite to the determination of interlocutory remedies. The real change has been in the application of the established principles. By tightening control of the enforcement process, and at the same time narrowing the scope for judicial review, the current system inevitably presents more obstacles for unlawful non-citizens seeking a stay of removal or deportation.

[16.100] Until October 2001 there were two sources of the Federal Court's power to suspend removal. The first was then s 482(2) of the *Migration Act* which gave the court express power to stay the operation of a decision or of proceedings taken pursuant to the decision. The second was (and remains) s 23 of the *Federal Court of Australia*

---

164   See, for example, the comments of Nicholson J in *Long v MIMIA* (2002) 122 FCR 159, confirmed in *Long v MIMIA* [2002] FCAFC 438.
165   See *Jurisdiction of the Federal Magistrates Service Legislation Amendment Act 2001* (Cth), s 3 and Sch 3, in operation on October 2001. These provisions were amended again by *Migration Litigation Reform Act 2005* (Cth), s 3 and Sch 1, in operation on 1 December 2005.

[16.101] Stay orders made before the repeal of the 'first' Part 8 were limited in the sense that a court could not suspend an order where an application for judicial review was lodged outside the strict 28-day time limit.[166] This stands in direct contrast to orders made formerly under s 15 of the *ADJR Act*.[167] In spite of the changes made to the regime governing the curial review of migration decisions, the jurisprudence that has grown up around s 23 (and s 15 of the *ADJR Act*) continues to be relevant to a large extent.

[16.102] The original interpretation made of s 15 of the *ADJR Act* was that the factors giving rise to an exercise of power are the same as those required in relation to an interlocutory injunction under s 23 of the *Federal Court of Australia Act*. The leading authorities on interlocutory injunctions initially required applicants to make out a prima facie case showing an entitlement to relief.[168] The test was restated by Gibbs CJ in *Australian Coarse Grain Pool Pty Ltd v Barley Marketing Board of Queensland*.[169] There, his Honour held that an interlocutory order will only be made where the applicant can show that there is a serious question to be tried and that the balance of convenience favours the making of a stay order.[170]

[16.103] Most of the immigration cases from the early 1980s in which stay orders were sought refer to the dual requirements of the seriousness of the issue to be tried and the balance of convenience.[171] In practice, this test required applicants to show special reasons for the grant of either a stay order or an injunction.[172]

[16.104] The change in judicial attitude during the 1980s was manifest in the courts' recognition that the criteria devised in commercial contexts to determine eligibility for injunctive relief were not necessarily helpful in judging whether a stay of removal should be granted. In *Perkins v Cuthill*,[173] Keely J pointed out that the legality of an order to deport, or the seriousness of the issue to be tried, will not always be readily apparent before the full review of a case.[174] Neither will it be appropriate in most removal cases to speak in terms of a 'balance of convenience'. Keely J proposed a more relaxed test for s 15 stays, requiring no more than an 'arguable case', or evidence that reasons or circumstances exist which make it just to grant the order sought.

---

166   See Chapter 19.5 below.
167   See, for example, *Collins (No 2) v MIEA* (1982) 5 ALD 32; *Barrett v MIEA* (1989) 18 ALD 129; and *Manoher v MILGEA* (1991) 24 ALD 405. For the principles involved in granting an extension of time, see *Hunter Valley Developments Pty Ltd v Cohen* (1984) 3 FCR 344.
168   See *Beecham Group Ltd v Bristol Laboratories Pty Ltd* (1968) 118 CLR 618.
169   (1982) 46 ALR 398.
170   See also *Epitoma Pty Ltd v Australasian Meat Industry Employees Union (No 2)* (1984) 3 FCR 55; *Bullock v Federated Furnishing Trades Society of Australasia (No 1)* (1985) 5 FCR 464; and *Dage v Baptist Union of Victoria* [1985] VR 270.
171   See, for example, *Collins (No 2) v MIEA* (1982) 5 ALD 32; *Gaillard v MIEA* (1983) 5 ALN N25; *Rifki v MIEA* (1983) 5 ALD 117; and *Kioa v West* (1984) 6 ALN N21.
172   See *Kioa v West* (1984) 6 ALN N21. A similar approach was taken by Toohey J in *Dean v Woodward* (1984) 6 ALN N288; and *Aqbal v Hurford* (1984) 7 ALN N79.
173   (1981) 34 ALR 669.
174   See also *Capello v MIEA* (1980) 2 ALD 1014.

[16.105] Towards the late 1980s most judges accepted that a stay of removal should only be granted where an applicant can demonstrate an 'arguable' case for relief.[175] Nevertheless, the trend was plainly towards a more flexible application of the test governing the grant of stay orders – however expressed. This is borne out by the tendency for judges to mix the language of the tests applied, referring to both the 'justice' of the case and to the seriousness of the issue to be tried.[176]

[16.106] The amendments to the Act in 1989 addressed the matter of interlocutory orders at several levels. By introducing the concept of a period of grace for unlawful non-citizens, the former s 13 of the Act provided for an automatic stay of removal that could be extended by lodging an application for an entry permit or by seeking review of a decision refusing such a permit. Although this statutory concession ensured the immediate security of those eligible to apply for a permit, persons wishing to regularise their status had and still have very few options available to them. In recognition of the futility of s 13, the concept of a period of grace was formally abandoned in September 1994.

16.7.2 Stay orders and release from detention

[16.107] In *MIMIA v VFAD of 2002*,[177] the Full Federal Court confirmed that the power to make interlocutory orders under s 23 can be used to order the temporary release of persons in immigration detention. On the appeal, the Minister argued that this power had been withdrawn with the introduction of s 196(3) of the *Migration Act*. The Full Court disagreed, finding nothing in this provision that affects the general power to grant interlocutory relief conferred by s 23.[178] More specifically, it held that there is nothing in s 196(3) to prevent the court from 'ordering the release, on an interlocutory basis, of a person who establishes that there is a serious question to be tried regarding the lawfulness of that person's detention'.[179]

[16.108] The applicant in *VFAD of 2002* was an Afghani asylum seeker who applied for and was accepted as being eligible for a Protection visa. In the chaos that reigned in the detention centres in 2001 around the time of the *Tampa* Affair, the positive decision on his application was not communicated to him and so he remained in detention. Following changes in Afghanistan, a second decision was made on his application – this time to refuse a Protection visa. This time the decision was 'delivered' to the applicant. An appeal to the RRT failed. Presumably, it was in the course of obtaining his file for the purposes of seeking review that the original decision was discovered. The applicant sought a declaration in the Federal Court that he was

---

175 See, for example, *Huang v Owen* (1989) 17 ALD 695; *Rizki v MILGEA* (1989) 18 ALD 643.
176 See, for example, *Manoher v MILGEA* (1991) 24 ALD 405; and *MILGEA v Msilanga* (1992) 34 FCR 169.
177 (2002) 125 FCR 249 (*VFAD of 2002*).
178 The High Court has ruled that the power in s 23 may be exercised in any proceeding in which the Federal Court has jurisdiction, unless the jurisdiction is conferred in terms which expressly or impliedly deny the power to the court in that class of proceeding: *Patrick Stevedores Operations No 2 Pty Ltd v Maritime Union of Australia (No 3)* (1998) 195 CLR 1 at 29 (Brennan CJ, McHugh, Gummow, Kirby and Hayne JJ); *Cardile v LED Builders Pty Ltd* (1999) 198 CLR 380 at 40 in the joint judgment of Gaudron, McHugh, Gummow and Callinan JJ.
179 (2002) 125 FCR 249 at [159].

granted a Protection visa by the first decision-maker. He also sought an interlocutory order that he be released from detention pending the determination of his substantive application. The Full Federal Court agreed with Merkel J at first instance[180] that the Federal Court has power under s 23 to order an applicant's release from detention pending the hearing and determination of a substantive application.

[16.109] The Full Court emphasised that personal liberty is 'the most elementary and important of all common law rights',[181] and that, accordingly, an intention to curtail, or interfere with, the right must be clearly manifested in unmistakeable and unambiguous language.[182] It concluded that parliament had not made 'unmistakably clear' its intention to abrogate the power of the Federal Court to protect a 'fundamental freedom' 'by ordering the release, in appropriate circumstances, on an interlocutory basis, of persons in detention who have seriously arguable claims to be lawful non-citizens and thus to have their liberty'. This construction of s 196 was reinforced by the principle that the domestic legislation should, so far as the language permits, be interpreted and applied in a manner consistent with established rules of international law and Australia's treaty obligations (noting the relevance of Arts 2(3), 9(1) and 9(4) of the ICCPR to the case). The court was also guided by the fact that the two members of the High Court who addressed the issue of interlocutory relief in *Chu Kheng Lim* (Mason CJ and Toohey J) considered that the legislative precursor to s 196(3) did not deny the s 23 power.

[16.110] The Full Court also rejected the Minister's submission that the provisions in the *Migration Act* constitute an 'exhaustive code' of the remedies available to protect the rights of persons aggrieved by decisions under the Act. By way of example, the court noted that s 475A of the Act preserves the remedies available under s 39B of the *Judiciary Act 1903* (Cth).[183]

[16.111] After the decision of the High Court in *Al-Kateb v Godwin* and the related litigation on the lawfulness of immigration detention,[184] the circumstances in which release from detention may be sought have been narrowed considerably. In essence the challenge needs to be to the basis on which a person is being detained in the first place. Although the substantive finding on the law in *Al Masri v MIMIA*[185] was overturned in the later detention cases, Merkel J's statement of the law on the principles to apply in an application for release pending an appeal stand as correct: 'a stay will not usually be granted save in exceptional circumstances, such as where the appeal rights will be rendered nugatory'.[186]

---

180   See *Applicant VFAD of 2002 v MIMA* (2002) 194 ALR 304.
181   Citing Fullagar J in *Trobridge v Hardy* (1955) 94 CLR 147 at 152.
182   See *Coco v The Queen* (1994) 179 CLR 427 at 437-8 (Mason CJ, Brennan, Gaudron and McHugh JJ); *Re Bolton; Ex parte Beane* (1987) 162 CLR 514 at 523.
183   See (2002) 125 FCR 249 at [116]ff.
184   See *Al-Kateb v Godwin* (2004) 219 CLR 562; *MIMA v Al Khafaji* (2004) 219 CLR 664; and *Re Woolley; Ex parte Applicants M276/2003* (2004) 225 CLR 1. These cases are discussed above, Chapter 3.3.2 and Chapter 4.
185   (2002) 192 ALR 609, affd *MIMIA v Al Masri* (2003) 126 FCR 54.
186   (2002) 192 ALR 609 at [62].

16.7.3 Delay in removal

[16.112] The present scheme for the removal of unlawful non-citizens avoids a number of problems for the government at the end stage of the enforcement process. There is no order made; removal is merely the end result of a failure to obtain a valid visa. While removal was the subject of a decision, evidenced by a deportation order, issues could arise about both the making and execution of the order. Under the former s 63 (now s 206) of the Act, deportation orders could be revoked, which meant that the Minister had power to vacate a deportation order once made. Before 1989, this power was regarded as co-extensive with the discretion to deport: it was thought that the discretion to deport would be undermined if the Minister had no power to change his or her mind once an order had been made.[187] This, in turn, made the exercise of the revocation power a prime target for judicial review.

[16.113] The more enduring issues, however, relate to the problems that arise where deportation or removal cannot be effected as planned. Where every effort is made to carry out a deportation order, without success, the courts have held that the validity of a deportation order will not be impugned by delay in execution.[188] The judiciary has taken a more critical approach, however, where the delay in execution is deliberate. In *Park Oh Ho v MIEA*,[189] the applicants were detained with deportation orders pending so that they could be called as witnesses in relation to criminal proceedings brought against a third party. The response of the High Court was to rule unlawful both the applicants' detention and the deportation orders made against them. The court held that a deportation order could only be made for the purpose of securing the removal from Australia of a non-citizen who had somehow contravened the terms of the Act. Once an order was made, the Minister was obliged by the Act to give effect to the order at the earliest possible opportunity.

[16.114] The earlier case of *Singh-Dhillon v MIEA*[190] established that the Minister's power to enforce a decision did not extend to the suspension of a deportation order once made. Accordingly, the High Court's ruling in *Park Oh Ho* left the Minister with three legal courses of action. He could either grant the applicants temporary entry permits, allow them to remain at large or deport them. The invidious position in which this placed the Minister became apparent when he was faced again with the conflict of an unlawful non-citizen wanted as a witness in criminal proceedings in *Attorney-General (NSW) v Ray*.[191]

[16.115] The courts' scrutiny of the purposes for which deportation orders were signed also affected orders made in respect of unlawful non-citizens who had not been located by the Department. The Federal Court struck down an order made in

---

187   See *Dallikavak v MIEA* (1985) 9 FCR 98 at 100-4 (Northrop and Pincus JJ) and at 108-9 (Jenkinson J); and *Singh-Dhillon v MIEA* (1987) 14 FCR 351 at 357.
188   See *Srokowski v MIEA* (1988) 15 ALD 775; and *Vazquez v MIEA* (unreported, FCA, Davies J, 18 December 1990). These old authorities are confirmed by the more recent rulings of the High Court in *Al-Kateb v Godwin* (2004) 219 CLR 562; *MIMA v Al Khafaji* (2004) 219 CLR 664; and *Re Woolley; Ex parte Applicants M276/2003* (2004) 225 CLR 1 (cf *MIMIA v Al Masri* (2003) 126 FCR 54).
189   (1989) 167 CLR 637.
190   (1987) 14 FCR 351.
191   (1989) 90 ALR 263.

advance of the subject's apprehension. It found that the purpose of the order was not to facilitate removal, but to confirm the person's unlawful status and so preserve the Department's ability to remove at a later date.[192]

[16.116] The difficulties posed by the old deportation orders were addressed by tightening the Minister's control of the removal process. The issues of suspending and revoking orders no longer arise. All the problems associated with the execution of deportation orders, however, have not been capable of solution through legislation. The difficulty in removing unlawful non-citizens where there is no country willing to receive them is one instance where neither the courts nor the bureaucracy have been able to find a ready answer.[193] As a matter of international law, states are bound to admit their own nationals.[194] Nonetheless, problems have arisen in instances where countries act in contravention of this principle, or where the person involved is stateless. The limitations placed on the Minister's powers are apparent also in the final stage of the removal process: the choice of destination to which a removee is sent.

16.7.4 Choosing the destination of a removee and removal as disguised extradition

[16.117] The two related issues at the point of removal are whether the removal document must specify the destination to which the deportee is to be sent and whether there are legal constraints placed on the choice of destination. The details included on the face of the old deportation orders became important in the 1980s when the practice developed of the Minister signing general orders that did not specify the place to which the removee was to be sent. In most cases, the omission was not significant as the question of destination was determined according to the deportee's country of origin or citizenship. However, destination was and is of vital importance for a person concerned to avoid removal to a certain country or city.

[16.118] During the 1980s, judicial opinion was divided on the issue of whether the Minister is required at law to specify a destination on the face of a deportation order. In *Sheng v MIEA*,[195] Gray J granted a stay of deportation on the basis that it was 'seriously arguable' that an order that failed to spell out the place to which the deportee was to be taken was wholly invalid for want of certainty. Northrop J reached the opposite conclusion in *Chua v MIEA*,[196] holding that a deportation order may be expressed in general terms, without reference to a destination. Northrop J's ruling was followed by Ryan J in *Daguio v MIEA*.[197]

---

192   See *Ang v MIEA* (1994) 48 FCR 437; and *Seiler v MIEA* (1994) 48 FCR 83.
193   See, for example, *Srokowski v MIEA* (1988) 15 ALD 775; *Vazquez v MIEA* (unreported, FCA, Davies J, 18 December 1990); *MIMIA v Al Masri* (2003) 126 FCR 54; *Al-Kateb v Godwin* (2004) 219 CLR 562; and *MIMA v Al Khafaji* (2004) 219 CLR 664.
194   See Art 12(4) of the ICCPR; and Mary Crock and Penelope Mathew, 'Immigration Law and Human Rights' in David Kinley (ed), *Human Rights in Australian Law* (Sydney: The Federation Press, 1998).
195   [1986] FCA 27.
196   (1986) 13 FCR 158.
197   (1986) 71 ALR 173.

[16.119] The two views are interesting in so far as each reflects a different approach to the question of how the removal process should operate. By requiring the specification in the deportation order of the destination to which the deportee is to be sent, Gray J's reasoning underscores the responsibility of the Minister for the totality of the removal process. The alternative view presupposes a separation between determining the preconditions for removal and removal itself, permitting the involvement of different parties at each stage of a two-part process.

[16.120] In *Chua v MIEA*,[198] Northrop J examined the various provisions in the pre-1989 Act governing the execution of the various types of deportation and removal orders that could be made under the Act. His Honour pointed out that, in each instance, different parties were responsible for determining the destination of the person to be expelled from the country. He found that the reference to the function performed by the authorised officer in s 22 of the Act was sufficient to imply that the discretion to choose destination lay with that officer and not with the Minister. According to his Honour, the only power or duty on the Minister concerned the making of the deportation order authorising the expulsion in question. His Honour justified this view by looking at a dictionary definition of the word 'deportation' which emphasised its removal or exiling function over the question of destination. He saw as quite separate the two functions of ordering deportation and determining where the deportee is to be sent.

[16.121] Although he only considered the issue in the context of interlocutory proceedings, in *Sheng* Gray J appears to have been more concerned with both the source of the power to decide the deportee's destination and with the accountability of the Minister for the totality of the enforcement process. His Honour found it

> unthinkable that the Parliament intended that a deportee should simply be removed from Australia and nothing more. Such an intention would permit the dropping of a deportee into the ocean outside the territorial limits of Australia. Section 22 of the Act appears to be based on the assumption that the deportee will be bound for a specific destination; it allows for a requirement to be addressed in writing to the Master [etc] ... of a vessel, requiring the deportee to be conveyed to a specified place. It would be odd if such a provision were held impliedly to give rise to a power in some officer of the Department ... or some other person, to choose the specified place.[199]

Like Northrop J, Gray J noted that counsel had produced no authority for the proposition that a deportation order must specify a destination. However, he doubted whether the cases cited before him necessarily supported the opposite contention.[200]

[16.122] The changes to the Act in and after September 1994 have not addressed directly the issue of specifying destination to the person to be removed. However, they make it clear that the power to choose is vested in the Secretary of the Department. Sections 217 and 218 of the Act are the loose equivalent of the former s 70 which

---

198 (1986) 13 FCR 158 at 161.
199 [1986] FCA 27 at [21]. See also *R v Secretary of State for Foreign Affairs; Ex parte Greenberg* [1947] 2 All ER 550 at 555.
200 [1986] FCA 27 at [21]ff.

replaced s 22. They empower the Secretary to require the controller of a specified vessel or vessels to remove a non-citizen. The first of the two sections deals with 'turn around' cases, directing carriers to take back non-citizens with no right to enter the country whom the carriers have transported to Australia. The inference in these cases is that the carriers will return their passenger to his or her country of embarkation. 'Turn arounds' are generally removed within 72 hours of their arrival. While the Department has asserted that these persons have had the opportunity of being assessed under the Refugee Convention, officials do not always know their removal destination. Bodies such as Amnesty International have therefore highlighted the danger of refoulement in such processes.[201]

[16.123] Section 218 covers cases where the carrier may not have been responsible for bringing the non-citizen to Australia. It allows the Secretary to direct a carrier to remove a non-citizen 'to a destination of the vessel or one of the vessels specified in the notice'. The Secretary's ability to specify vessels for the transportation of a removee seems to indicate a legislative intent that the Secretary is free to choose the destination of a removee.

[16.124] This interpretation of the legislation finds support in cases like *Mayer v MIEA*.[202] That case concerned the legislative source of the Minister's power to grant refugee status. The High Court held that the reference in the Act to the Minister making a determination about a person claiming to be a refugee was sufficient to imply a grant of power to grant or refuse refugee status. By way of analogy, reference to the function performed by the Secretary in s 218 could be seen as an implied grant of power to that person to determine issues going to destination.

[16.125] Although the Secretary must make a decision before issuing directions to a carrier, it is not so clear that he or she has a duty to inform the removee of the choice made. Removal happens by operation of law. The Act requires notice to be given to an applicant of a decision to refuse a visa under s 66. However, it is silent as to the requirements for informing an unsuccessful applicant about the details of removal. This omission in the legislation underscores the power relationship between the non-citizen on the one hand and the Minister and the Department on the other. Although the Secretary must make a decision before issuing a notice to a carrier, that decision is not 'judicially reviewable' by the Federal Court (s 475). The question that will arise for determination is whether the removee has any common law right to be told of the Secretary's choice, and to be heard in relation thereto. If access to the Federal Court is denied, this issue will have to be determined by the High Court. The structure of the legislation and the absence of rights to obtain reasons provide fairly strong evidence of a legislative intent to restrict the rules of procedural fairness.

[16.126] Leaving aside the question of who should control the removal process, the issue of the destination chosen for a removee can be important in its own right. Persons who meet the international legal definition of refugee may have very strong reasons for wishing to avoid deportation to their country of origin. So too, may

---

201 See *A Sanctuary under Review*, above n 81, at 302-3.
202 (1985) 157 CLR 290.

removees wanted by a foreign government in respect of alleged criminal or other offences. In *Schlieske v MIEA*,[203] the applicant sought judicial review of a decision to remove him to Germany where he was wanted by the West German police for the alleged commission of certain crimes. Extradition proceedings against him having failed on two occasions, Schlieske challenged the removal arrangements on the basis that they amounted to a disguised extradition and were an exercise of power for an improper purpose. His claim was upheld at first instance when it emerged that arrangements had been made for German police to travel to Australia to 'accompany' Schlieske back to West Germany. However, Beaumont J declined to order that the Minister had no power at all to remove Schlieske to Germany if no direct arrangements were made with the authorities in that country.[204]

[16.127] On appeal, the Full Court upheld Beaumont J's ruling. Wilcox and French JJ pointed out that any power to deport or remove must be exercised in accordance with the scope and purposes of the enactment which is its source.[205] It is not enough to examine the validity of a deportation order on its face: one must also consider the manner in which the order was executed and the purpose served by the method of execution chosen.

[16.128] In an era when national sovereignty and ministerial power were regarded as absolute concepts, the courts showed a marked reluctance to rule against deportation orders.[206] This was so, even where an order was executed in a manner that ensured the delivery of the deportee to a foreign government at the hands of which the alien could suffer persecution or prosecution.[207] A deportation order had only to be good on its face. This reasoning was followed by the Australian High Court in *Ferrando v Pearce*,[208] a case involving the deportation of an Italian alien to Italy during the First World War in accordance with an agreement with the Italian government. The legislation in that case did not authorise deportation to a particular destination. Nevertheless, the High Court held that this did not prevent the execution of a deportation order in a manner that would ensure that a certain destination was reached.[209] In *Schlieske*, Wilcox and French JJ pointed out that the modern cases[210] are notable for their implicit shift away from the view that ministerial purpose is irrelevant to the propriety of an exercise of power.[211]

---

203 (1988) 84 ALR 719.
204 *Schlieske v MIEA* (1987) 79 ALR 554.
205 (1988) 84 ALR 719 at 724-5. See *Shrimpton v Commonwealth* (1945) 69 CLR 613 at 620; *Water Conservation and Irrigation Commission (NSW) v Browning* (1947) 74 CLR 492 at 505; *Murphyores Inc Pty Ltd v Commonwealth* (1976) 136 CLR 1 at 23; and *R v Australian Broadcasting Tribunal; Ex parte 2HD Pty Ltd* (1979) 144 CLR 45 at 49.
206 See, for example, *Robtelmes v Brenan* (1906) 4 CLR 395 at 403.
207 Early examples include the English cases of *R v Secretary of State for Home Affairs; Ex parte Duke of Château Thierry* [1917] 1 KB 922 at 930 (Swinfen Eady LJ), 932-3 (Pickford LJ) and 935 (Bankes LJ); and *R v Superintendent of Chiswick Police Station; Ex parte Sacksteder* [1918] 1 KB 578. See, generally, Paul O'Higgins, 'Disguised Extradition: The *Soblen* Case' (1964) *Modern Law Review* 521 at 522-5.
208 (1918) 25 CLR 241.
209 Ibid at 249 and 263.
210 See *R v Governor of Brixton Prison; Ex parte Soblen* [1963] 2 QB 243; *Znaty v MIEA* (1972) 126 CLR 1; *Barton v Commonwealth* (1974) 131 CLR 477; and *Utter v Cameron* [1974] 2 NSWLR 50.
211 *Schlieske v MIEA* (1988) 84 ALR 719 at 727.

[16.129] Lord Denning MR noted in *R v Governor of Brixton Prison; Ex parte Soblen*[212] that removal cases require the resolution of two conflicting principles. On the one hand, the government is bound to respect the difference between removal and extradition. Officers of the Crown must not surrender a fugitive criminal to another country at its request except in accordance with the legislation passed for this purpose. On the other hand, the Minister (in England, the Home Secretary) clearly has power to remove an alien to a certain country, if that course of action is in the public interest. In deciding which principle should apply in a particular case, Lord Denning MR concluded that it depends on the purpose for which an act is done. This, in turn, can only be determined by looking at all the circumstances of the case. In *Soblen*, the applicant failed in his bid to challenge the deportation order in question. The English Court of Appeal held that the deportation would only be unlawful if carried out for the sole purpose of returning the deportee to a country where he or she faced legal sanctions. The court held that this was not established on the facts of the case, notwithstanding the fact that the Home Secretary refused to supply reasons for his choice of destination.[213]

[16.130] The 'purpose' test propounded in *Soblen* was accepted by the High Court in *Znaty v MIEA*[214] and in the later case of *Barton v Commonwealth*.[215] As in *Soblen*, the High Court in both cases rejected the argument that the deportations were a sham or being carried out for a purpose other than the public good.[216]

[16.131] Although they follow these earlier cases, Wilcox and French JJ in *Schlieske* appeared to be more critical in their examination of the purpose behind the deportation order in that case. Their Honours held that it is 'plainly extraneous to the decision to deport a person, and to deport that person to a particular country, that the person is wanted by the government of that country upon criminal charges'.[217] Their Honours followed *Znaty* and *Barton* by holding that the deportation of a person to a country will not necessarily be invalid where the Minister is aware that the deportee is wanted in another country on criminal charges. This will be most obviously so where the proposed deportee is a national of the country in question, and that country is the only one willing to receive the deportee. However, if the Minister chooses that country where another is prepared to accept the deportee, there may be an inference drawn of improper purpose. In drawing that inference, their Honours continued, the court is entitled to take into account official conduct outside that authorised by statute, such as the communication to foreign authorities of flight details.[218] While it was permissible for the applicant Schlieske to be escorted outside of Australia (to Germany) by an authorised officer, the officer could not arrange for the deportee to be

---

212 [1963] 2 QB 243 at 302.
213 For critiques of this finding, see O'Higgins, above n 207; and Legomsky and Rodriguez, above n 143, at 39-40, 97-9. Soblen wished to be deported to Czechoslovakia rather than to America where he was wanted on espionage charges. The disturbing postscript to the case is that when the Court of Appeal rejected his case, he committed suicide.
214 (1972) 126 CLR 1 at 15-16.
215 (1974) 131 CLR 477 at 483-4 and 503-4.
216 See also *Utter v Cameron* [1974] 2 NSWLR 50.
217 (1988) 84 ALR 719 at 729.
218 Ibid at 730.

surrendered to the German authorities on arrival in the country. Wilcox and French JJ summarised the law as follows:

> The golden rule is that the Australian authorities are entitled, notwithstanding their knowledge that a particular deportee is wanted in the country of destination, to do everything which is necessary for the enforcement of the Migration Act and the proper implementation of the deportation order. But they are not entitled to go beyond that, and in purported exercise of powers under that Act, to take steps whose only purpose is the bringing to justice of the deportee in a foreign country. At that stage the Australian authorities would not be exercising deportation powers; they would be involved in an unlawful extradition.[219]

[16.132] *Schlieske* illustrates the limitations inherent in the statutory power to remove unlawful non-citizens or other undesirable aliens. It also highlights the administrative problems that can be encountered in attempting to remove known or suspected criminals. The Minister's power to remove cannot be considered in isolation from Australia's international legal obligations with respect to refugees: see Chapter 12.5 and Chapter 14.3. Where the government is minded to deport a person to a country contrary to the removee's wishes, it should at the very least provide reasons for the choice made, so as to permit the courts to review the decision for abuse of discretion.

[16.133] In the final analysis, however, Australia has a basic right to remove a non-citizen who is not wanted. As the more recent case of *Applicant M 117 of 2007 v MIAC*[220] illustrates, cases will continue to arise where an individual is wanted in their home country in respect of crimes committed before their arrival in Australia. In this instant, the applicant was wanted on charges of kidnapping, ransom and murder in the Peoples' Republic of China. Although it would appear that the Australian government sought an assurance from the PRC government that the man would not be executed for crimes committed before entry into Australia, it was not prepared to otherwise withhold removal. The Federal Court agreed that there was nothing improper in the course of action adopted, nor was there a failure to take into account any relevant considerations.

[16.134] The execution of removal presupposes that there is another country that is willing or obliged to accept the deportee. Deportees who literally have nowhere to go have always represented one of the more intractable problems facing the Minister in the enforcement of the Act. If the deportation of these people is not a matter capable of statutory solution, neither have the courts given much direction on their eventual immigration status. In *Srokowski v MIEA*,[221] *Vazquez v MIEA*[222] and the 2004 cases of *Al-Kateb v Godwin*[223] and *MIMIA v Al Khafaji*,[224] the courts confined themselves to questions concerning the legality of the applicants' continued detention. The issue of the continued legality of removal orders that were incapable of execution was not addressed at any length. In each instance, it was assumed simply that the validity of

---

219 Ibid at 731.
220 [2008] FCA 1838.
221 (1988) 15 ALD 775.
222 Unreported, FCA, Davies J, 18 December 1990.
223 (2004) 219 CLR 562.
224 (2004) 219 CLR 664.

the orders was not affected by delay in execution. For the government, these cases will always be unpopular with electors, but difficult to handle in practice.[225]

16.7.5 Timing and methods of deportation or removal

[16.135] The final issues relating to the ultimate enforcement of immigration law relate to the timing and manner in which deportation or removal is effected. There have been a number of high profile cases over the years that underscore the sometimes inadequate safeguards that have been put in place to guard against gross abuse of human rights. One example is the removal from Australia of an individual identified only as 'The Chinese Woman' who was removed from Australia in 1997 into the hands of the PRC government. Eight and a half months' pregnant, she was forced to undergo an abortion on her arrival – just as she claimed would be the case. One of two cases reviewed at great length by the Senate Legal and Constitutional References Committee in 1999,[226] its tragic outcome does not appear to have encouraged any real reform of the Department's removal processes in the years that followed. The removal of Vivian Solon-Alvarez – an Australian citizen mistaken for an unvisaed Filipina sex worker – was equally striking in its inhumanity. Ms Solon-Alvarez was removed in spite of obvious physical (she was effectively a paraplegic as the result of a car accident) and mental health problems.[227]

[16.136] A central issue in these cases has been the tendency for governments to out-source the removal process, using private contractors to provide escort services for persons being removed. Parties contracted for this purpose in the past include Australasian Correctional Services Pty Ltd (subcontracted to ACM); Correction Enterprise (CORE) staff; Protection and Indemnity (a private South African firm); as well as off-duty police officers. After examining the issue of private contracting in the removal process in 2000, the Senate Legal and Constitutional References Committee expressed concerns over the transparency of the contractual relation-ship between the Commonwealth and the contractors; the accountability of the contractors to parliament and the public; and the relative responsibilities of the various parties involved. The Committee noted with concern allegations that sedation and other means of restraint are used in the removal process and criticised the lack of an external and independent body to audit contract removal service providers.[228] There is no immediate evidence that any of these concerns have been addressed.

---

225 Following the rulings in 2004, the government recognised that keeping a person in detention for the term of his natural life was not an option. The response was to create the subclass 695 Return Pending visa, which allowed for the release of detainees on strict reporting conditions. Recipients of this visa were given no right to work or access to benefits of any kind. The visa class was abolished under Labor by the *Migration Amendment Regulations 2008 (No 5)*, reg 3 and Sch 1[18], in operation on 9 August 2008.
226 See *A Sanctuary under Review*, above n 81.
227 See Inquiry into the Circumstances of the Vivian Alvarez Matter Report under the *Ombudsman Act 1976* by the Commonwealth Ombudsman, Prof John McMillan; Comrie, above n 60; David Marr, 'Guilty Secrets', *Sydney Morning Herald*, 20 August 2005; and follow up article, Monday 22 August 2005, available at <http://www.calcutta.com.au/calcutta-articles/2005/8/20/guilty-secrets/>.
228 *A Sanctuary under Review*, above n 81, at 306.

[16.137] For its part, the judiciary has shown a willingness to respond where injunctive relief has been sought to prevent the removal of persons alleged to be in no fit state to travel. In *Beyazkilinc v Manager, Baxter Immigration Reception and Processing Centre*,[229] Besanko J refused to strike out an application to restrain the commission of a tort and the abuse of statutory authority. Injunctions were being sought to prevent the respondents from removing the applicant until he was medically fit to travel. The applicant made a claim in tort for a breach of a duty of care, and claimed that his proposed removal from Australia was beyond power (ultra vires and unlawful). Besanko J held that the interlocutory injunction should only be discharged if the claim for relief and the allegations the subject of substantive challenge could not possibly succeed.[230] As we will see in the following chapter, however, it has become increasingly difficult to fight removal when a government becomes truly determined to remove a non-citizen whose criminal behaviour has made them *persona non grata*.

---

229   (2006) 155 FCR 465.
230   See also *M38/2002 v MIMIA* (2003) 131 FCR 146: the removal of a non-citizen may be practicable in the sense of feasible, but not 'reasonably practicable' as required by s 198(6).

17

The Deportation of Permanent Residents: Character, Conduct and Criminality

17.1 Introduction

[17.01] From the time of Federation, Australia's immigration legislation has always provided for the removal of unwanted persons, most particularly those convicted of criminal offences.[1] As is the case for all countries of immigration, moral and political difficulties have arisen in the treatment of criminal migrants who have permanent resident status. These people may have resided in Australia for many years, producing children who are citizens, putting down deep cultural and social roots, making them 'aliens by the barest of threads'.[2] In Chapter 3 we examined the constitutional arguments that have raged over the tenure and status of long-term permanent residents convicted of serious crimes – a bi-product of the failure to provide in the Australian Constitution for an Australian citizenship. We revisit here only tangentially the complex and sometimes troubling jurisprudence that has developed around the question of 'constitutional aliens', 'absorbed persons' and the question of who is and is not to be considered a constituent member of the Australian community. The focus of this chapter is on the legal and policy frameworks governing the removal or 'deportation' of immigrants convicted of serious crimes under s 200 of the *Migration Act 1958* (Cth) or found to be of 'bad character' under s 501. This area has seen sweeping changes in the first decade of the Millennium, largely because of the abandonment of the understanding that long-term permanent residents should be immune from deportation or removal.

[17.02] The deportation of non-citizens convicted of criminal offences will almost inevitably incite political controversy. On the one hand, non-citizens convicted of criminal offences threaten what may be fragile societal acceptance of persons who, in simple legal terms, are strangers to the polity. Politicians who are perceived to be soft

---

1   See *Immigration Restriction Act 1901* (Cth), s 3, definition of 'prohibited immigrant', read with s 8; and the *Pacific Islanders Labourers Act 1901* (Cth). For a discussion of the early deportation laws, see Glenn Nicholls, *Deported: A History of Forced Departures from Australia* (Sydney: UNSW Press, 2007) Chs 1 and 2. We are grateful for the assistance of Matt Costa in the background research conducted for this chapter.
2   See *Nystrom v MIMIA* (2005) 143 FCR 420 at [1] (Moore and Giles JJ). For the best account of the law in this complex area, see Michelle Foster, '"An Alien by the Barest of Threads": The Legality of the Deportation of Long-Term Residents from Australia' (2009) 33 *Melbourne University Law Review* 483.

on migrants convicted of criminal activities will often suffer electorally; conversely tough policies can be vote winners. On the other hand, migrants who spend extended periods in a country will just as inevitably found families and make connections in the community such that deportation can cause great hardships – both for those forced into exile and those left behind. Sadly, the development of law and policy in this fraught area of social control has seen the raw politics of populism prevail over the human rights of both deportees and their families. While there have been select instances throughout Australian history of very long-term residents being sent into permanent exile, during the early years of the new Millennium, the incidence of such cases became almost the norm. As Michelle Foster writes:

> While it is difficult to obtain precise figures concerning the use of s 501 in the context of long-term residents,[3] in June 2008 the Minister for Immigration informed the Senate that as of 7th May 2008 there were 25 people in immigration detention following the cancellation of their visas pursuant to s 501.[4] Of those 25 persons, only 1 had been in Australia for less than 5 years, with the remaining 24 having been in Australia for 11-45 years prior to visa cancellation. Indeed 2 of those persons had been in Australia for between 41-45 years prior to visa cancellation. Further, by far the majority of those persons had first entered Australia when they were children, with 19 of the 25 having arrived in Australia before the age of 21.[5]

[17.03] If the removal of criminal non-citizens who have effectively spent their entire lives in Australia is not inherently offensive on basic grounds of human rights and even international comity, what is additionally troubling is that many of the offenders sent into exile have suffered from intellectual disabilities or mental illnesses.[6] As Foster notes,[7] the application of s 501 to long-term residents has been widely criticised, including by the Senate Legal and Constitutional References Committee,[8] the Commonwealth Ombudsman,[9] the Australian Human Rights Commission,[10] and by various members of the Federal Court of Australia.[11]

---

3   The DIAC annual reports record only the total number of cancellations under s 501 without a breakdown as to other factors: see, for example, DIAC, *Annual Report 2007-08*, at 31. In the Senate Legal and Constitutional References Committee Report, *Administration and Operation of the Migration Act 1958* (Canberra: 2006), the Committee published figures provided by the Department as to the numbers of permanent residents deported in 2002-03 (115), 2003-04 (44) and 2004-05 (74) but again these do not indicate length of residence: see [9.76].
4   See Commonwealth Parliamentary Debates, *Hansard*, Senate, Tuesday 17 June 2008, at 138.
5   See Foster, above n 2, at 486.
6   See, for example, the cases of Stefan Nystrom and Robert Jovicic: see Nicholls, above n 1, at 7-10 and Ch 10; and Foster, above n 2.
7   Foster, above n 2, at 486.
8   See Senate Legal and Constitutional References Committee Report, above n 3, at [9.85].
9   See Commonwealth Ombudsman, *Administration of s 501 of the Migration Act 1958 as it Applies to Long Term Residents* (February 2006).
10   See Submission of the Human Rights and Equal Opportunity Commission (HREOC) to the Joint Standing Committee on Migration, *Inquiry into Immigration Detention in Australia*, 4 August 2008, at [60]-[68]; and 'Background Paper: Immigration Detention and Visa Cancellation under Section 501 of the Migration Act', January 2009, available at <http://www.hreoc.gov.au/human_rights/immigration/501_migration_2009.html>.
11   See *Nystrom v MIMIA* (2005) 143 FCR 420 at [1], referring also to previous criticisms in other Federal Court decisions. See also the comments by the Administrative Appeals Tribunal (AAT) in *Say v MIMA* (2006) 91 ALD 212 at [59].

[17.04] The chapter begins in Parts 17.2 and 17.3 with a brief historical account of the law governing the two regimes for the expulsion of 'undesirable' non-citizens. First are the traditional criminal deportation provisions in the *Migration Act* and, second, the 'character and conduct' provisions in ss 501-506 of that Act. This is followed by an examination in Part 17.4 of the evolution of policy under the two regimes and how this has been affected by individual cases and by the politicians' relationships with or attitudes towards the review authorities. The chapter concludes in Part 17.5 with some reflections on the justice and propriety of Australian law and practice.

17.2 A brief history of criminal deportation law

[17.05] Given its colonial origins as a penal outpost of Great Britain, there is much in Australia's criminal deportation history that speaks directly of its development as an independent nation. The very first deportation provisions are an example in point. Section 8 of the *Immigration Restriction Act 1901* (Cth) provided for the deportation of any person who was not a British subject either 'natural born or naturalised' under UK, Commonwealth or state law; who was convicted of 'any crime of violence against the person'; and who failed the dictation test 'of 50 words in length in an European language'.

[17.06] The provision is interesting at a number of levels. First, it underscores Australia's deference to Britain that continued well after Federation in its reluctance to send criminal elements back to the motherland. Second, only those convicted of *crimes of violence* against the person were deportable: presumably crimes of other kinds were acceptable. Finally, the link between deportation and the dictation test suggests elements of class and race[12] discrimination and underscores the discretionary nature of the deportation sanction.[13]

[17.07] As we explain in Chapters 2 and 3, the regime for the removal or exclusion of undesirable people was complicated from the start by the uncertain status of the persons who came to call themselves 'Australians'. Without the benefit of a constitutionally enshrined Australian citizenship, the primary division was between those categorised rather randomly as 'immigrants' and those deemed to have been absorbed into the community.[14] What has made the deportation issue so contentious is that the criminals targeted for removal have often been resident in Australia for protracted periods – for some, most of their lifetime. Deportation in such cases almost always carries grave implications for family members, some of whom may be Australian citizens, as well as for the deportee.

[17.08] In the decades following Federation in 1901, there appears to have been a positive reluctance to foist criminals on 'some other country', a socially responsible

---

12   See above Chapter 2.3.1-2.3.3.
13   As noted in Chapter 2, immigration officers were given great latitude in their choice of language and passages for the dictation test. Where an officer was determined to mark a person for removal, it was not uncommon for the person to be required to sit a series of tests until he or she made an error. See Chapter 2 at [2.43]ff (discussing the case of Egon Kisch); and Nicholls above n 1, at 30-1.
14   See above Chapters 2 and 3.

policy not without some irony given Australia's original *raison d'être*.[15] Although this early history is littered with incidents suggestive of a harsh approach being taken to people labelled as outsiders – particularly during and between the two World Wars[16] – the number of people deported on criminal grounds has never been huge in absolute terms. Nicholls records an increase in the mid 1920s following improved coordination between State and federal law enforcement agencies. However, he describes a claim in 1927 by Minister for Home and Territories, Charles Marr, that 'two immigrants per week were being deported following criminal convictions' as fanciful.[17] In the previous year Prime Minister Bruce reported 34 deportations on criminal grounds, 30 of them to Britain.[18] Under the conservative government of Lyons, 140 criminal deportations were recorded between 1931 and 1934.[19] From that time onwards the records suggest that criminality has been a factor in the deportation or removal of between 23 and 216 permanent resident non-citizens every year. Overall, the statistics collected by Nicholls suggest that conservative Coalition governments have tended generally to take a more draconian approach than their Labor party counterparts.[20]

[17.09] In the immediate aftermath of the Second World War, legislation was passed to strengthen the government's powers to remove or deport unwanted non-citizens from Australia. Although greatest historical attention has focused on measures to remove persons evacuated to Australia during the war,[21] these years also saw the introduction of the *Aliens Deportation Act 1948* (Cth). While never invoked in the actual deportation of anyone, this legislation is noteworthy for two reasons. In the legislation one sees for the first time broad powers conferred on the Minister for Immigration to deport a non-citizen on the ill-defined grounds of 'bad character and conduct'. Second, the legislation established (or formalised) the office of a 'Commissioner' to advise the Minister on the deportation of criminal permanent residents.[22] Both of these features have characterised criminal deportations under the *Migration Act*, into which the *Aliens Deportation Act* was subsumed.

---

15   See comments of MP Michael Considine, quoted in Nicholls, above n 1, at 31.
16   See, for example, the cases of *Lloyd v Wallach* (1915) 20 CLR 299; *Jerger v Pearce (No 1)* (1920) 28 CLR 526 and *Jerger v Pearce (No 2)* (1920) 28 CLR 588; and Karl Schulz, the latter recounted by Nicholls, above n 1 at 52-7.
17   Nicholls, above n 1, at 63.
18   Ibid.
19   Ibid at 65.
20   Nicholls presents the statistics derived from parliamentary debates and from Department of Immigration annual reports from 1950-2006. See ibid at 103 (1950-65); 114 (1966-1981/82); 131 (1982/83-1994/95); and 155 (1995/96-2005/06). The ascension of the Howard Coalition government in 1996 led to an almost immediate doubling of deportations in 1996-97 (jumping from 34 to 60). On the other hand, the Whitlam government effected more deportations in a single year (216 in 1972-73) than in any other period in Australian history. How this related to the abolition of the White Australia policy in 1972 is unclear, although public sensitivity to immigration issues at this time was at an unprecedented high.
21   See *Wartime Refugees Removal Act 1948* (Cth); and the litigation in *Koon Wong Law v Caldwell* (1949) 80 CLR 533.
22   On earlier Commissioners appointed to oversee the treatment (and removal) of 'enemy aliens', see Nicholls, above n 1, Ch 5.

17.2.1 The special status of British subjects and 'absorbed persons'

[17.10] When Australian citizenship was given a statutory basis in 1948, 'British subjects', 'Irish nationals' and 'protected persons' retained special privileges that gave these people parity in most respects with Australian citizens. All other non-citizens were 'aliens'. While the term 'immigrant' was used for all permanent or long-term arrivals in the country, it was easier for British subjects, Irish citizens and 'protected persons' to pass beyond the reach of immigration regulation than it was for 'aliens'.[23] The former group could become immune from deportation upon absorption into the community: ceasing to be 'immigrants', these people were also effectively defined by statute as 'non-aliens'. In contradistinction, aliens could never acquire this immunity, even if by their absorption they passed beyond the reach of the immigration power.[24] In the 1958 Act, 'absorption' was marked initially at five years.[25] This was also the period of time that had to elapse before a person who entered Australia without authorisation (and remained undetected) would be deemed to be a lawful permanent resident.[26] The Minister was empowered to deport both 'immigrants' (under s 12) and 'aliens' (under s 13) on the basis of criminal and other conduct. Deportation could be ordered on several grounds, the principal one being conviction of an offence attracting a prison sentence of one year or longer.[27] While 'aliens' remained susceptible to deportation at any time, 'immigrants' could only be deported on the basis of offences or conduct which occurred within the first five years of entry into Australia.

[17.11] Section 14 of the Act in 1958 included another deportation power, enlivened by what can be broadly referred to as 'character issues'.[28] Section 14 made an immigrant liable to deportation (again during their first five years in Australia), on the basis that their 'conduct (whether in Australia or elsewhere) had been such that he [or she] should not be allowed to remain in Australia'.[29] The Minister could activate the provision by serving a notice on the person stating grounds for the proposed deportation. The affected person had a right to a hearing before an appointed Commissioner. If the Commissioner considered the grounds to be established, or if the affected person did not request or appear at the hearing, the Minister could order the person be deported.[30] This arrangement appeared to create appeal rights in persons threatened with deportation. However, Nicholls points out that the system was crippled when the Minister argued successfully that the Commissioner had no

---

23 See s 5(1) of the *Migration Act* in 1973. A protected person was defined by reference to ss 5-9 of the *Australian Citizenship Act 1948* (Cth) as a person granted protection by Australia. The distinction created two classes of permanent settlers in Australia. See Kim Rubenstein, *Australian Citizenship Law in Context* (Sydney: Law Book Co, 2002) at 82-6.
24 See the discussion in Chapter 3 above. See, for example, *Pochi v Macphee* (1982) 151 CLR 101; *Chu Kheng Lim v MILGEA* (1992) 176 CLR 1; and *Al-Kateb v Godwin* (2004) 219 CLR 562.
25 Note that in the *Immigration Act 1901* immunity from deportation was achieved after three years.
26 See *Migration Act*, s 7(4) (repealed 2 April 1984).
27 The power in s 13 could also be exercised in respect of persons who had committed an offence involving prostitution or had been an inmate of a mental hospital or public charitable institution. The power in s 12 additionally extended to persons who had committed (or attempted to commit) crimes of violence, extortion by force or threat.
28 See *MIMIA v Nystrom* (2006) 228 CLR 566 at [136] (Heydon and Crennan JJ).
29 Section 14 could also be activated on the stricter basis that an immigrant 'advocates the overthrow of a government or is a member of an organisation which does so'.
30 As noted earlier, this mechanism echoed the repealed *Aliens Deportation Act 1948* (Cth).

discretion to examine anything other than whether an individual had in fact been convicted and sentenced in respect of a deportable crime.[31]

[17.12] Since 1958 the story has been one of increasingly harsh treatment of criminal permanent residents, with diminishing consideration given to the length of a person's tenure in Australia and of criteria such as family and other relationships within the community.

17.2.2 Shifting constitutional powers: The move from 'immigration' to 'alien'

[17.13] As noted in Chapter 3, the late 1970s and early 1980s saw a series of cases litigated on the nature and extent of the Minister's powers to deport long-term permanent residents convicted of drug offences.[32] The High Court's rulings in the *Pochi* cases drew attention to the unfettered nature of parliament's power to legislate with respect to 'aliens' under s 51(19) of the Constitution. The court accepted that 'immigrants' could escape the reach of the legislature by being absorbed into the Australian community – thereby passing beyond the scope of the 'immigration power' in s 51(27) of the Constitution. In contrast, the 'aliens' power was held to apply to all persons who did not have the status of Australian citizen. With the election of a Labor government in 1983, the criminal deportation provisions were amended to reflect this new understanding. The special concessions in the *Migration Act* for British subjects, Irish nationals and protected persons were abolished – and temporal immunity from deportation was extended to virtually all permanent residents regardless of national origin.[33] The period required to gain immunity from deportation was extended from five to 10 years' *lawful permanent residence*.[34]

[17.14] Amendments to the *Migration Act* in 1983 replaced what were ss 12 and 13[35] with a new s 12 covering 'Deportation of non-citizens present in Australia for less than 10 years who are convicted of crimes'. The new section provided that deportation could only be ordered by the Minister when a person had been sentenced to 'death or to imprisonment for life or for a period of not less than one year' (s 12(c)) if that person had been present in Australia as a 'permanent resident' for a period of less than 10 years (s 12(b)(ii)).[36] This provision was the forerunner of the present

---

31   See Nicholls, above n 1, at 106-7, discussing the case of Antonio Panozzo.
32   See the discussion of *Pochi v Macphee* (1982) 151 CLR 101 and *Nolan v MIEA* (1988) 165 CLR 178 in Chapter 3 at [3.12]ff.
33   The exclusions were persons convicted of certain crimes. Note that s 203(1) does apply to certain offenders regardless of the length of their stay in Australia. However, the specified crimes are exotic ones such as treason, sabotage, inciting mutiny and assisting prisoners of war to escape. They are rarely, if ever, relied on. For a fuller account of the 1983 amendments, see Foster, above n 2, at n 123ff.
34   The concessions made for these people in the *Australian Citizenship Act 1948* were not removed until 1987. See *Australian Citizenship Amendment Act 1984* (Cth), which commenced 1 May 1987. See Rubenstein, above n 23, at 86.
35   *Migration Amendment Act 1983* (Cth), s 10.
36   In addition, s 14 was amended at this time to allow for deportation within 10 years for conduct constituting a threat to security, or at any time for conviction of certain serious offences. A new s 14A was also inserted, which provided a definition of 'permanent resident' for the purpose of calculating the period of 10 years, excluding terms of imprisonment.

s 201,[37] and s 12(b)(ii) was the forerunner of s 201(b)(i). The 10-year rule was crafted such that immunity from deportation applied thereafter only to those who spend 10 years as lawful permanent residents, discounting any time spent in any form of correctional institution.[38]

[17.15] The *Migration Act* as it has operated since that time allows for the deportation[39] of permanent residents in three circumstances. The general power to deport is conferred on the Minister by s 200 of the Act. This provision applies to certain non-citizens convicted of serious criminal offences (s 201); non-citizens who pose a threat to the security of the nation (s 202); and non-citizens convicted of certain other serious offences such as treason, treachery, sabotage, sedition, incitement to mutiny and assisting prisoners of war to escape (s 203). In addition, permanent residents can lose their legal status as a result of irregularities relating to their entry or grant of visa.[40] Having lost their legal status, these people are removed in the same way as other unlawful non-citizens.[41]

[17.16] With the repeal of the former s 15 of the *Migration Act* in 1983, a less lenient approach was taken also to persons who were ambivalent about their decision to reside in Australia permanently. Under that section immigrants had been allowed virtual freedom of movement in and out of the country after two years' residence, provided that they did not remain away for more than five years at a time. Since 1983, all permanent residents have had to acquire a visa before leaving the country to ensure their re-admission.[42]

[17.17] Having said that, the next watershed event affecting the tenure of permanent residents convicted of serious crimes was the passage of the *Migration (Offences and Undesirable Persons) Amendment Act 1992* (Cth) which came into force on 1 September 1994. This legislation laid the groundwork for the regime that has since come to cause such heartache for long-term permanent residents in Australia who are convicted of serious crimes or otherwise deemed to be of bad character.

17.2.3 Migration (Offences and Undesirable Persons) Amendment Act 1992

[17.18] This legislation amended the *Migration Act* by inserting s 180A, which for the first time conflated the power to *exclude* undesirable (and contentious) non-citizens

---

37 Section 35 of the *Migration Legislation Amendment Act 1989* (Cth) came into effect on 20 December 1989 and it renumbered all the provisions of the Act, resulting in s 12 becoming s 55. Section 14 of the *Migration Reform Act 1992* (Cth) enacted s 55A, which provided that '[t]he Minister may order the deportation of a non-citizen to whom this Division applies'. This section was the predecessor to s 200 of the Act. The 1994 Amendment Act, which came into effect at the same time as the 1992 Reform Act on 1 September 1994, renumbered ss 55A and 55, so that they became ss 200 and 201 in the Act.
38 The result of this change was to render liable to deportation some individuals who came to Australia as children and spent much of their formative years in corrective institutions: see, for example, *Re Haoucher and MIEA* (1987) 12 ALD 217.
39 Where the word 'deportation' was used formerly to describe the forced removal of all types of immigration outlaws, its use is confined now to the process for removing criminal permanent residents.
40 See *Migration Act*, Part 2, Subdiv 3C.
41 See above, Chapters 15 and 16.
42 See *Migration Regulations 1994* (Cth), Sch 2, subclass 155.

with the power to *expel* non-citizens on grounds of criminality, character and conduct. The passage of this legislation presaged the eventual abandonment of the restrained and measured regime for deporting criminal permanent residents in favour of an unfettered power to cancel visas on grounds of character and conduct.

[17.19] Section 180A read as follows (emphasis added):

> (1) The Minister may refuse to grant a visa or an entry permit to a person, *or may cancel a valid visa or a valid entry permit* that has been granted to a person, if:
>
>   (a) subsection (2) applies to the person; or
>   (b) the Minister is satisfied that, if the person were allowed to enter or to remain in Australia, the person would:
>   (i) be likely to engage in criminal conduct in Australia; or
>   (ii) vilify a segment of the Australian community; or
>   (iii) incite discord in the Australian community or in a segment of that community; or
>   (iv) represent a danger to the Australian community or to a segment of that community, whether by way of being liable to become involved in activities that are disruptive to, or violence threatening harm to, that community or segment, or in any other way.
>
> (2) This subsection applies to a person if the Minister:
>   (a) having regard to:
>   (i) the person's past criminal conduct; or
>   (ii) the person's general conduct;
>   is satisfied that the person is not of good character; or
>   (b) is satisfied that the person is not of good character because of the person's association with another person, or with a group or organisation, who or that the Minister has reasonable grounds to believe has been or is involved in criminal conduct.[43]
>
> (3) The power under this section to refuse to grant a visa or an entry permit to a person, or to cancel a valid visa or a valid entry permit that has been granted to a person, is in addition to any other power under this Act, as in force from time to time, to refuse to grant a visa or an entry permit to a person, or to cancel a valid visa or a valid entry permit that has been granted to a person.

[17.20] The electoral significance of deporting permanent residents convicted of serious crimes is evident in arrangements that have been made for reviewing the merits of deportation decisions. In addition to the Commission system established during and after the Second World War, the Administrative Appeals Tribunal (AAT) has had power to review criminal deportation decisions since its inception in 1975.[44] Yet criminal permanent residents were initially in a very unusual position before the AAT. Until the 1992 legislation came into force the AAT could recommend that a deportation order be affirmed or revoked, but in the final analysis the Minister was free to accept or reject the tribunal's recommendation.[45] In a sense, it was a system

---

43   Note that this provision was introduced in response to the case of *Hand v Hell's Angels Motor Cycle Club Inc* (1991) 25 ALD 667, discussed in Chapter 6 at [6.65]ff.

44   See cl 22 of the Schedule to the *AAT Act*, later s 66E of the Act. Where a permanent resident is the subject of an adverse security assessment, there is a further right to review by the Security Appeals Division of the AAT: ss 202 and 500. However, such appeals are rare.

45   See former s 180 of the Act, read with *AAT Act*, s 43(1)(c)(ii); and *Pochi v McPhee* (1981) 149 CLR 139 at 143. In few other jurisdictions was the AAT's function so circumscribed.

that allowed the government to lay its bets a little each way. By deferring to the AAT's judgment of cases, it was able to depoliticise decisions by giving them the appearance of independence from the Minister and the Department. At the same time, the Minister sought to maintain ultimate control by reducing the role of the tribunal to that of a recommendatory body.

[17.21] The *Migration (Offences and Undesirable Persons) Amendment Act 1992* provided as a counterbalance to the new cancellation powers in s 180A that the AAT should have *determinative* powers to review the merits of both criminal deportations and s 180A cancellations. However, the amending Act also enabled the Minister to issue conclusive ministerial certificates in respect of the deportation of criminals and undesirable persons, termed 'excluded persons'.[46] This regime maintained some sense of control and (as we explore further below) reduced but did not eliminate the potential for confrontation with the tribunal and other review authorities.

17.3 Broadening the scope for removal: The Migration Legislation Amendment (Strengthening of Provisions relating to Character and Conduct) Act 1998 (Cth)

[17.22] The terminology used in the 1992 legislation – undesirable persons – marked something of a turning point in the modern history of criminal deportations. The amendments flagged criminality and bad character in migrants as significant political issues, underscoring the status of non-citizens as outsiders to be tolerated only so long as they did not transgress societal norms. Once initiated, such a discourse is difficult to reverse and easy to escalate. The Labor party went to its electoral defeat with a legislative agenda targeting criminal 'migrants' which the in-coming conservatives were quick to adopt in even stronger form.[47]

[17.23] The *Migration Legislation Amendment (Strengthening of Provisions relating to Character and Conduct) Act 1998* (Cth) (the *Character and Conduct Act*) had as its primary aim the strengthening of powers vested in the Immigration Minister to cancel or refuse visas and to remove non-citizens on grounds of criminality or bad conduct. Demonstrating a commitment to keeping the migration program 'clean' by moving to change the law governing the exclusion or expulsion of 'bad aliens', the legislation cemented s 180A (re-numbered as s 501) as a parallel mechanism for expelling non-citizens (including permanent residents) deemed to be of bad character or whose 'conduct' is unacceptable. Unlike s 200, the provisions do not involve a removal order. Rather, by creating grounds for the cancellation of visas, they enliven the automatic removal provisions discussed in the previous chapter.[48] The amendments altered dramatically the ability of individuals to access independent merits review. They also reduced the role of the AAT where it retained jurisdiction to review cancellation

---

46 See then s 502 of the Act.
47 The *Character and Conduct Act* was put to the previous Parliament as the Migration Legislation Amendment (Strengthening of Provisions relating to Character and Conduct) Bill 1997 (Cth). The Bill had not been passed when Parliament was prorogued for the election.
48 See ss 189 and 198 of the *Migration Act*.

decisions. Most importantly, by creating a system where the ultimate power to admit or expel is restored to the Minister, the legislation resulted in the re-politicisation of character and conduct cases.

[17.24]   The changes were made in response to a number of cases in the late 1990s where the AAT and the courts intervened to overrule deportation orders, prompting the intervention of the Minister in an attempt to ensure the expulsions went ahead. In *Gunner v MIMA*,[49] controversy arose over the relationship between the power to deport criminal permanent residents under s 200 of the Act and the power in s 501 to cancel or refuse a visa on grounds that an individual is not of good character. The Full Federal Court ruled that s 501 could be used to override a decision by the AAT to cancel a s 200 deportation order. In *Jia Le Geng v MIMA*,[50] the decision of the Minister to countermand the AAT by making a second decision under s 501 was challenged on the ground that the Minister's cancellation ruling evinced actual or perceived bias. Although ultimately unsuccessful before the High Court[51] this case appears to have strengthened the resolve of then Minister Ruddock to consolidate his power to remove unwanted non-citizens. He railed against rulings made by both the AAT and the lower courts as going against the intention of parliament and therefore 'against the will of the people'.[52]

[17.25]   The 1998 legislation altered the balance of power so as to confirm the ability of the Minister to overrule the AAT or to remove from AAT review cases that are of concern to the government. It strengthened the power of the Minister to issue conclusive certificates where he or she 'believes that it is contrary to the national interest' that a decision be changed or made subject to review. The relationship between the character and the deportation powers is clarified by a new provision empowering the Minister to give written Directions to a person or body concerning the performance of relevant functions or the exercise of relevant powers.[53] The person or body is compelled to comply with those Directions.[54] Perhaps most significantly, however, it created a test that places the onus on the non-citizen to prove that he or she is of good character. Under s 180A as originally drafted the onus was placed on the Minister to show that an individual was of bad character.

17.3.1   The character test

[17.26]   The *Character and Conduct Act* raised the barrier for 'unworthy' migrants several notches by introducing deeming provisions that reversed the onus of proving bad character. Under the amended s 501(1), the Minister (or his or her delegate[55]) now has discretion to refuse to grant a visa to a person if the person 'does not satisfy the Minister' that the person passes the character test.[56] The character test set out in

---

49   See *Gunner v MIMA* (1997) 50 ALD 507; and *MIMA v Gunner* (1998) 84 FCR 400.
50   [1998] FCA 768.
51   See *MIMA v Jia* (2001) 205 CLR 507. See the discussion of this case in Chapter 19 at [19.39].
52   See the address by Philip Ruddock MP to the National Press Club, Canberra, 18 March 1998, discussed in Chapter 19 below at [19.04].
53   See *Migration Act*, s 499(1) and (1A).
54   See ibid, s 499(2A).
55   *Migration Act*, s 496.
56   See *MIMIA v Godley* (2005) 141 FCR 552.

s 501(6) *deems* individuals to be of bad character if they fit any of the criteria listed. A person does not pass the character test if he or she has a 'substantial criminal record'. This is defined in s 501(7)-(10) as a conviction for one or more offences resulting in a death sentence, or sentence of imprisonment ranging from life, to periodic detention or involvement in drug or mental health rehabilitation programs for periods totalling two years. A person is also of bad character if he or she has an association with someone else, or with a group or association, whom the Minister reasonably suspects has been or is involved in criminal conduct: s 501(6)(b).[57] A person's character can also be impugned by 'having regard to' the person's past and present criminal or *general* conduct: s 501(6)(c). The final paragraph of s 501(6) replicates previous character provisions by listing the types of unacceptable risks posed by non-citizens wishing to enter or remain in the country. These include risks that the person will engage in criminal conduct in Australia;[58] harass, molest or stalk another person in Australia; or vilify, incite discord or otherwise represent a danger to a segment of the Australian community.[59]

[17.27] In *Irving v MILGEA*,[60] Davies J held that the phrase 'good character' should be given its ordinary meaning – as a reference to a person's 'enduring moral qualities' rather than to 'the good standing, fame or repute of that person in the community'. Assessments must be made on objective factual criteria – and not on the subjective basis of opinions held about a person.[61]

17.3.2 General and criminal conduct

[17.28] In *MIEA v Baker*,[62] the Full Federal Court considered the reference in s 501(2)(c) (as it then was) to 'general' and 'criminal' conduct.[63] In interpreting the provisions, the court held that past criminal conduct cannot be read down to refer only to past conduct the subject of criminal convictions.[64] The court held:

> We do not think there is any warrant for extracting, from the broad word 'general', a meaning that would eliminate conduct other than conduct so frequently indulged in as to be described as prevalent or usual. Just as a person's criminal conduct on a few occasions may be very revealing of character, so also some instances of general conduct, as we understand the term, displayed but once or twice, may lay character bare very tellingly ... [The terms 'general' and 'criminal' do not denote limited categories of 'conduct'.] We do not think Parliament intended anything of the kind, but simply to comprehend all forms of conduct that could be relevant to a determination about character within two easily stated categories.[65]

57　See further the discussion at Part 17.3.4.
58　On this issue, see *Hand v Hell's Angels Motorcycle Club Inc* (1991) 25 ALD 667, discussed in Mary Crock, *Immigration and Refugee Law in Australia* (Sydney, Federation Press, 1998) at 63, 166 and above Chapter 6 at [6.65]ff.
59　On these issues, see the series of cases involving the erstwhile historian, David Irving, discussed in Crock, ibid, at 65, 166.
60　(1996) 68 FCR 422 at 422.
61　On this point, see also *MIEA v Baker* (1997) 73 FCR 187 at 197; and *Goldie v MIMA* (1999) 56 ALD 321.
62　(1997) 73 FCR 187.
63　This provision was worded similarly to the present s 501(6)(c) of the Act.
64　(1997) 73 FCR 187 at 194.
65　Ibid at 195-6.

[17.29] Decided shortly before the passage of the 1998 amendments, the court in *Baker* attracted the ire of Minister Ruddock by ruling that policy guidelines on what should be considered to be 'a substantial criminal record' were 'inhumane and irrational' and 'could not lawfully be implemented'.[66] It was no mere coincidence that the 1998 amendments moved to enshrine the 'inhumane and irrational' guidelines into s 501 of the *Migration Act*. Even in the context of the more recent amendments, the Federal Court has cautioned against an approach which unduly focuses on the past conduct:

> Before past and present general conduct may be taken to reveal indicia that a visa applicant is not of good character continuing conduct must be demonstrated that shows a lack of enduring moral quality. Although in some circumstances isolated elements of conduct may be significant and display lack of moral worth they will be rare, and as with consideration of criminal conduct there must be due regard given to recent good conduct.[67]

[17.30] This perspective was endorsed by the Full Federal Court in setting aside the AAT's ruling that s 501(6)(c) of the *Migration Act* required the refusal of a visa to an applicant who had entered into a sham marriage in order to stay in Australia 15 years earlier.[68] The court found that the tribunal in that case had applied the wrong test by asking whether the applicant had enduring (good) moral qualities rather than by asking whether it was satisfied that he did *not* have enduring moral qualities. The court found that the tribunal had improperly limited its focus to the applicant's past criminal and general conduct, dismissing evidence as to his recent character. The court ruled that the tribunal should have taken the lack of continuing criminal conduct as evidence of rehabilitation and lawful behaviour. In response, the AAT appears to be adopting the practice of treating recent periods of non-offending as a neutral factor rather than as a consideration favourable to the review applicant, at least where these periods are relatively short.[69]

[17.31] In this context it is worth noting that bad general conduct has been read to include migration misconduct in the form of the provision of false and misleading information leading to the grant of a visa. Interesting overlaps occur in these cases between s 109 visa cancellations which do not result in permanent exile from Australia – and s 501 which does have this effect. In recent cases even the existence of an Australian-born child has been insufficient to move either the primary decision-maker or the review authorities.[70]

17.3.3 'Substantial criminal record'

[17.32] The phrase 'substantial criminal record' is defined to include having been sentenced to: death or life imprisonment; a term of imprisonment of 12 months or

---

66 Ibid at 195.
67 *Godley v MIMIA* (2004) 83 ALD 411 at [26], approved on appeal by the Full Court in *MIMIA v Godley* (2005) 141 FCR 552 at [34].
68 *Mujedenovski v MIAC* (2009) 112 ALD 10 at [49].
69 *Puafisi and MIAC* [2009] AATA 689; *Obele and MIAC* [2010] AATA 58.
70 See *Re Ren and MIAC* [2007] AATA 1805; and *Ren v MIAC* (2008) 100 ALD 567. Compare *Re Xia and MIAC* [2007] AATA 1803; *Re Williams and MIMA* [2007] AATA 1012; and *Re Fanchon and MIAC* [2008] AATA 20 where the cancellations under s 501 were set aside.

more; two or more terms of imprisonment totalling 2 or more years; or having been institutionalised after being acquitted on grounds of unsoundness of mind or insanity. The Act defines a 'term of imprisonment' broadly. It includes time that a court has ordered a person to spend in drug rehabilitation or a residential program for the mentally ill. For sentences of periodic detention, the 'term of imprisonment' is calculated as the total number of days for which a person is required to be detained.[71]

[17.33] Sentences served concurrently cannot be totalled for the purposes of s 501(7), rather decision-makers should look at the actual length of the person's sentences for imprisonment. Section 501(7) deems a person to have a substantial criminal record where they have been 'sentenced to 2 or more terms of imprisonment (whether on one or more occasions), where the total of those terms is 2 years or more'. In *MIMIA v Ball*,[72] Ms Ball, a New Zealand citizen, was convicted of 49 criminal offences. She was sentenced to imprisonment for two months each for 24 of the offences, and sentenced to 11 months' imprisonment for each of the remaining 25 offences. The sentences were served concurrently, such that Ms Ball spent a total of 11 months in prison. The Minister decided that Ms Ball had a substantial criminal record on the basis that the 49 terms of imprisonment totalled over 26 years in prison. Jacobson and Bennett JJ found that s 501(7) was ambiguous with respect to the treatment of concurrent sentences,[73] and the preferred construction should not derogate from the person's rights.[74] However, the Full Court has since clarified that s 501(7) is concerned with the sentence imposed on the person rather than the term of imprisonment actually served.[75]

17.3.4 'Criminal association'

[17.34] Individuals are also deemed to fail the character test if they have or have had 'an association with someone else, or with a group or organisation whom the Minister reasonably suspects has been or is involved in criminal conduct'.[76] Ministerial policy states that s 501 may only be used to cancel a visa on the basis of an association that has 'some negative bearing upon the person's character'.[77] In this respect the policy reflects the controversy that prompted the inclusion of this 'association' provision – namely an attempt by the Hell's Angels Motorcycle Club to convene a meeting in Alice Springs in 1991.[78] Section 503 of the Act provides that information concerning associations can be protected from disclosure. Decision-makers (other than the Minister) are directed to take great care not to disclose information that might put the life or safety of informants or other persons at risk;[79] and are enjoined to consider the nature, degree and frequency, and duration of the association.[80] Mere knowledge of an associate's criminality is not enough by itself to constitute an 'association'.

---

71 *Migration Act*, s 501(8).
72 (2004) 138 FCR 450.
73 Ibid at 463-5.
74 Ibid at 467. See also *MIMIA v Hicks* (2004) 138 FCR 475.
75 *Seyfarth v MIMIA* (2005) 142 FCR 508 at [27].
76 *Migration Act*, s 501(6)(b).
77 See *Direction No 41 Visa Refusal and Cancellation under s 501* (2009) (Cth) (Direction 41) at [7.2(3)].
78 See *Hand v Hell's Angels Motorcycle Club Inc* (1991) 25 ALD 667, discussed in Chapter 6 at [6.65ff.
79 See Direction 41.
80 Ibid at [7.2(2)].

[17.35] The interpretation of the provisions relating to character attainted by 'association' were considered in a highly controversial case involving an Indian doctor, Dr Mohamed Haneef,[81] employed on a 457 visa at Southport Hospital in Queensland. In June 2007, there were attempted terrorist bombings in London and a vehicle loaded with explosives was driven into the front doors of Terminal One at Glasgow airport. Two of the suspects arrested for offences under the *Terrorism Act 2000* (UK) were second cousins of Dr Haneef.

[17.36] On 2 July 2007, Dr Haneef was arrested and detained by the Australian Federal Police (AFP) and members of the Queensland Police under s 23C of the *Crimes Act 1914* (Cth). The AFP sought several extensions of Dr Haneef's detention in the Brisbane Magistrate's Court, until it withdrew its application on 13 July 2007. The following day Dr Haneef was charged with intentionally providing resources to a terrorist organisation, and being reckless as to whether the organisation was a terrorist organisation.[82]

[17.37] On 16 July 2007 the Minister decided to cancel Dr Haneef's visa under s 501 of the *Migration Act*. It was claimed that Dr Haneef was not of good character because he had an 'association' with a person, persons or organisation, who the Minister reasonably suspected had been involved in criminal conduct in accordance with s 501(6)(b) of the Act. Dr Haneef decided not to seek bail, ensuring that he remained in the custody of the Queensland Department of Corrective Services and could not be taken into immigration detention. The following day the Attorney-General issued a Commonwealth Criminal Justice Stay Certificate under s 147 of the Act, stating that, although Dr Haneef was an unlawful non-citizen, he should remain in Australia temporarily for the purposes of the administration of criminal justice. Dr Haneef sought an order in the nature of certiorari to quash the Minister's decision to cancel his visa, and an injunction to prevent the Minister from acting on the purported cancellation.

[17.38] On 27 July 2007, the charge against Dr Haneef was dismissed when the Commonwealth Director of Public Prosecutions announced that he could offer no evidence that would be likely to lead to a conviction. The Queensland Department of Corrective Services released Dr Haneef, whereupon he was taken into immigration detention. Although Dr Haneef then voluntarily returned to Bangalore, he pursued his application to have his visa cancellation set aside, as the decision had affected his reputation and would affect his ability to travel to other countries in the future. He also wished to return to his job in Australia.

[17.39] At first instance, Spender J held that the Minister's cancellation decision was affected by a jurisdictional error in the interpretation of the word 'association'. Haneef argued that an 'association' capable of enlivening the Minister discretion to

---

81   See *MIAC v Haneef* (2007) 163 FCR 414 at 416-20.
82   Because of the secrecy surrounding the English anti-terrorist investigations, the basis for Dr Haneef's arrest and detention was not clear, with different allegations being made and then refuted in the media at various stages. In laying the charges the police appear to have relied on the fact that a mobile phone SIM card purchased by Dr Haneef was found in the possession of one of the accused. See generally Susan Harris Rimmer, The Dangers of Character Tests: Dr Haneef and other Cautionary Tales', The Australia Institute, *Discussion Paper Number 101* (October 2008), available at <http://www.apo.org.au/research/dangers-character-tests-dr-haneef-and-other-cautionary-tales>.

cancel a visa under s 501(6)(b) must be one that 'reflects adversely on the character' of a visa holder, and that an 'innocent association' was insufficient.[83] The Minister maintained that any form of 'association' was enough to render someone of bad character.[84] Spender J expressed concern that the Minister's interpretation would mean that (by way of example) a victim of domestic violence would fail the character test by reason of her 'association' with her abuser. He said:

> In my opinion 501(6)(b) is a composite phrase and has to be construed as such. In my opinion it has the connotation that there is an alliance or link or combination between the visa holder with the persons engaged in criminal activity. That alliance, link, or combination reflects adversely on the character of the visa holder. Such a meaning would exclude the victim of domestic violence.[85]

[17.40] Spender J's decision was upheld on appeal. The Full Federal Court ruled:

> Having regard to its ordinary meaning, the context in which it appears and the legislative purpose, we conclude that the association to which s 501(6)(b) refers is an association involving some sympathy with, or support for, or involvement in, the criminal conduct of the person, group or organisation. The association must be such as to have *some* bearing upon the person's character. It is, of course, not necessary, to enliven the Minister's discretion to cancel the visa, that the Minister be satisfied that such an association actually exists. It is enough for the purposes of s 501(6) that the Minister reasonably suspects that the visa holder has *such* an association with someone else or a group or organisation which the Minister reasonably suspects has been or is involved in criminal conduct.[86]

For once, the views of the judiciary – founded as they are on basic common sense – appear to have been quietly accepted by the politicians.[87]

17.3.5 'Significant risk' of engaging in certain conduct

[17.41] Persons do not pass the character test if there is a 'significant risk' that, if they were allowed to enter or remain in Australia, they would engage in criminal conduct; harass, molest, intimidate or stalk another person; vilify a segment of the Australian community; or incite discord or represent a danger to the Australian community (or a segment of the community). 'Harassment' or 'molestation' need not involve violence or threatened violence. Damaging or threatening to damage a person's property may, on its own, constitute harassment or molestation.[88]

17.3.6 Constraints on the right to 'natural justice' and AAT review

[17.42] If the range of people caught by the character provisions is broader than ever before, other amendments to the *Migration Act* also make it much more difficult for non-citizens to challenge an adverse ruling. Applications for review by the AAT (where this is available) must be lodged within seven days after notification

---

83   *Haneef v MIAC* (2007) 161 FCR 40 at 67-8.
84   Ibid. The Minister relied on the ruling of Emmett J in *MIMA v Chan* (2001) 34 AAR 94.
85   (2007) 161 FCR 40 at 81.
86   *MIAC v Haneef* (2007) 163 FCR 414 at 447-8.
87   See 'Haneef Lesson Learnt As Rules Quietly Reformed', *The Age*, 23 June 2009, available at <http://www.theage.com.au/national/haneef-lesson-learnt-as-rules-quietly-reformed-20090622-ctzj.html>.
88   *Migration Act*, s 501(11).

of decision.[89] This compares with the standard 28 days allowed in respect of most other AAT appeals. There are also significant temporal constraints imposed on the hearing process and on the matters that the AAT can disclose to an applicant in the course of a hearing. First, an applicant is not entitled to reasons for a decision as is the normal course under s 28 of the *Administrative Appeals Tribunal Act 1975* (Cth) (*AAT Act*). Rather, s 500(6A) provides that an applicant must be provided with details of the decision, less any 'non-disclosable material'. Although the latter phrase is not defined, s 503A provides for the protection from disclosure of information provided by law enforcement agencies or intelligence agencies. Under s 500(6F), the Minister must lodge with the AAT duplicate copies of all documents in his or her possession or control – including non-disclosable material – within 14 days of notification of an appeal. The AAT must have regard to all the material but is prevented from revealing any non-disclosable material to the applicant. It is then precluded from making a decision within 14 days, but must do so within 70 days of the appeal being lodged. Where no decision is made within the stated time, the original decision to exclude or remove is deemed to be affirmed.[90] The AAT can compel the Minister to produce relevant documents.[91] However, where an application is made for review under s 501, and the decision relates to a person in the migration zone, the tribunal must not have regard to any information presented orally unless the information was set out in a written statement given to the Minister at least two business days before the tribunal holds a hearing.[92] Similar provisions apply to the submission of written material to the AAT by an applicant under s 500(6J).

[17.43] Perhaps the most controversial aspects of the regime, however, are those empowering the Minister to decree whether or not the rules of natural justice apply in individual cases. The legislation creates two powers exercisable by the Minister. The first power is subject to the rules of 'natural justice'.[93] The second power – available only to the Minister acting personally – is not.[94] Decisions of this second type are also stated to be outside of the code of procedure set out in Part 2, Subdiv 3AB, of the Act.[95] This discretion has been described by the Full Court as a 'broad' one.[96] In *M238/2002 v MIMIA*,[97] Kenny J observed that:

> [T]he power is conferred in order that the Minister can act in the public interest to protect the Australian community. Under this provision, the legislature has entrusted to the Minister the responsibility for deciding whether the public interest should prevail over the private interest of a visa holder.

[17.44] In summary, where either the Minister's delegate or the AAT makes a non-adverse decision on character or conduct, the Act now empowers the Minister, acting personally, to intervene so as to refuse or cancel a visa. The Minister must

---

89   See ibid, s 500(6B). Section 37 of the *AAT Act* does not apply.
90   See ibid, s 500(6L).
91   See ibid, s 500(6K).
92   See ibid, s 500(6I).
93   See ibid, s 501(1) and (2).
94   See ibid, s 501(3) and (4).
95   These procedures were introduced by the *Migration Legislation Amendment Act (No 4) 1997* (Cth).
96   *MIMIA v Huynh* (2004) 211 ALR 126.
97   [2003] FCA 936 at [41].

'reasonably suspect' that a person does not pass the character test. Where the Minister forms this view, she or he may choose between two powers – either a power to which the rules of natural justice do apply or one to which they do not. These powers are expressed (as in other parts of the Act) to be non-compellable and non-reviewable.[98] The Minister's power extends to cases where an original decision remains subject to an application for review by the AAT.[99]

[17.45] Section 501 thus establishes two separate regimes for reviewing decisions. If the cancellation power is exercised by a ministerial delegate, a person who loses his or her visa under s 501 has access to natural justice and full merits review by the AAT. If, however, the Minister exercises the s 501 power personally, the person whose visa is cancelled has access neither to natural justice nor AAT review. In these cases, the individuals affected can also be provided with very little about the reasons why they were considered liable for visa cancellation.[100] As the Ombudsman noted in 2006, information can be deemed to be protected under s 503(A) even where the information – for instance the person's criminal history – is on the public record.[101]

[17.46] There is evidence that the bifurcated structure of s 501 has meant that persons have tended to have different review options depending on the personal style of the Minister of the day. In 2002-03, for instance, Immigration Minister Philip Ruddock made 80 per cent of a total of 236 visa cancellations personally.[102] The Minister also had an explicit policy of personally considering the cases of long-term permanent residents, which effectively ensured such persons had limited options for seeking review. By contrast, the next Minister, Amanda Vanstone, preferred only to review exceptional cases, making only 12 per cent of the 105 cancellation decisions in 2003-04.

[17.47] If a visa is refused or cancelled on character grounds a person cannot make an application for another visa unless permitted by regulation.[103] In practical terms, this will mean that cancellation is forever. In this respect the provisions mirror the criminal deportation provisions which also result in irreversible exile.[104]

---

98   See *Migration Act*, s 501B.
99   See ibid, s 501B(5). Under s 501C, where the Minister chooses to exercise the powers conferred by either s 501(3) or s 501A(3), as soon as practicable after the making of the original decision, the Minister must give the person, in the way the Minister considers appropriate in the circumstances, written notice of the decision and particulars of 'relevant information'. This is defined as information that is personal to the applicant and not just about a class of persons of which the applicant is a member. Except in cases where the applicant is not entitled to make representations, the Minister must invite the person to make representations. Regulations are to set out who is not entitled to make representations and the period that will be allowed for the making of submissions (s 501D). Decisions revoking an original decision must be notified to parliament in writing.
100 See, for example, *Evans v MIMIA* (2003) 135 FCR 306.
101 See Commonwealth Ombudsman, above n 9, at 23.
102 Ibid.
103 *Migration Act*, s 501E.
104 Where a person is deported on security grounds or after being convicted of a criminal offence, the Regulations now impose a permanent ban on re-admission. This is achieved by requiring that offshore visa applicants who had previously been in Australia did not leave Australia while the subject of a deportation order under s 200: see Sch 5, cl 5001. The practical effect of this requirement is a lifetime re-entry ban which cannot be avoided by leaving the country voluntarily before the deportation order is executed. The criteria do not specify that the deportation order was executed, but merely require that the applicant left Australia while subject to such an order.

17.3.7 Closing the last loopholes: Responding to the decisions in *Sales*[105] and *Nystrom*[106]

[17.48] The assumption that s 501 could be relied on to effect the removal of even the most entrenched of permanent residents was shaken briefly in 2008 with the Full Federal Court's decision in *Sales v MIAC*.[107] That case concerned a very long-term permanent resident who migrated to Australia as a child in 1954, before the passage of the *Migration Act*. The court held that the appellant was the holder of a 'Transitional Permanent (Class BF) visa'. Because he was deemed to hold this visa – it had not been 'granted' within the meaning of s 501(2) – the court ruled that the visa could not be cancelled under that section.[108] This ruling was overturned by the High Court in *Nystrom*.[109] As Foster writes:

> The High Court affirmed the position that while a person who has been lawfully in Australia for more than 10 years is protected from deportation pursuant to the deportation power in ss 200 and 201, he or she always remains liable to visa cancellation and removal under s 501 of the Migration Act, regardless of length of residence or connection to the Australian community. There is thus apparently no domestic legal barrier to the government's continuing reliance on this section for those considered 'undesirable'.[110]

[17.49] Although the Labor government generally softened the approach being taken to s 501 deportations after 2007 (see below), it did not hesitate in moving to amend s 501 so as to rectify the 'technical error' uncovered by the decision in *Sales*.[111]

17.4 Immigration politics, and 'bad aliens': The evolution of policies governing deportation and removal

17.4.1 Introduction

[17.50] However draconian the legislative changes may have appeared on their face, the real impact of the character and conduct provisions has been felt in the *policies* issued to guide decision-makers in the exercise of discretionary powers. In this part we explore the relationship between the matters taken into account for the purpose of the criminal deportation regime, on the one hand, and the s 180A/501 character and conduct visa cancellation regime, on the other. The plain intention in

---

105 *Sales v MIAC* (2008) 171 FCR 56.
106 *Nystrom v MIMIA* (2005) 143 FCR 420.
107 (2008) 171 FCR 56.
108 See ibid at [18]-[19] (Gyles and Graham JJ) and at [85] (Buchanan J). Foster notes: 'In the wake of this judgment 23 people were released into the community from immigration detention, many of whom were long-term residents who came to Australia as children (see Sarah Smiles, 'Labor reverses detainee freedom', *The Age*, 10th October 2008 at 3)'. See Foster, above n 2, at n 24.
109 *MIMIA v Nystrom* (2006) 228 CLR 566, overturning the decision of the Full Federal Court in *Nystrom v MIMIA* (2005) 143 FCR 420 which had relied on the same ruling as the court in *Sales*.
110 Foster, above n 2, at 484.
111 *Migration Legislation Amendment Act (No 1) 2008* (Cth) inserted s 501HA into the Act which reversed *Sales* by providing that the holder of a relevant visa is taken to have been granted a visa. A number of challenges to this move have failed: *Martinez v MIAC* (2009) 177 FCR 337; *Bainbridge v MIAC* (2010) 181 FCR 569.

1998 (if not in 1994) was that the character and conduct provisions should capture a broader range of permanent resident non-citizens than did the s 200 deportation scheme.[112] The exculpatory criteria that may be considered are also narrower in range than the matters decision-makers have been able to take into account historically in deciding to deport under s 200.

[17.51] In these circumstances, it is hardly surprising that the strengthening of the 180A/501 regime in 1998 marked the virtual abandonment of the s 200 deportation regime. The Ombudsman noted in 2006 that s 501 has been used increasingly to cancel visas of long-term permanent residents of more than 10 years' standing. This is so even though such use of s 501 was not made explicit in the Explanatory Memorandum or Second Reading Speech when the provision was introduced into parliament. As we have seen, provisions already existed in ss 200 and 201 for the deportation of permanent residents on the grounds of their criminal conduct.[113]

[17.52] The following table shows the decline in the use of the deportation power after the introduction of s 501:

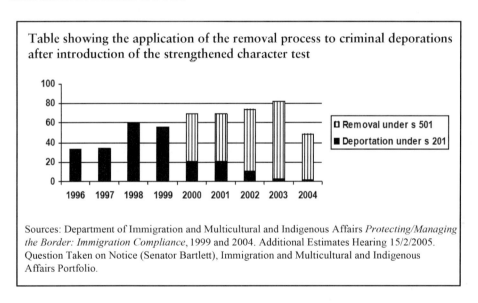

Sources: Department of Immigration and Multicultural and Indigenous Affairs *Protecting/Managing the Border: Immigration Compliance*, 1999 and 2004. Additional Estimates Hearing 15/2/2005. Question Taken on Notice (Senator Bartlett), Immigration and Multicultural and Indigenous Affairs Portfolio.

Policy guidelines governing s 200 deportations and s 501 visa cancellations

[17.53] The Minister's criminal deportation policy has always had one key function – the protection of the Australian community. This is also identified as Primary Consideration 1 in the Ministerial Directions issued under s 499 of the *Migration Act* in respect of s 501 visa cancellations. Against this, however, the Minister must balance the rights of the individual and of his or her family and friends. Issues arise also about obligations Australia has assumed under international law.

---

112   That scheme excluding from deportation persons who have been lawful permanent residents for 10 years or more.
113   See Commonwealth Ombudsman, above n 9, at 13. This point is made also by the Senate Legal and Constitutional References Committee, above n 3, at [9.30] and [9.34].

[17.54] Over the years, the guidelines promulgated under both schemes have become increasingly explicit and dogmatic about the various factors that must be taken into account when deciding to both deport and cancel visas. The evolutionary process is one that has owed much to the AAT's and the Federal Court's scrutiny of deportation decisions. One of the very first cases to go to the AAT, *Re Becker and MIEA*,[114] is in many respects the starting point for modern criminal deportation policies. It was Brennan J's insistence in that case on a written policy, rather than oral assurances from the Minister's counsel,[115] that led to the promulgation of the first (formal) policy guidelines for the exercise of the deportation power in 1978.[116] Since that time a number of policy guidelines (now referred to as Ministerial Directions) have been issued in respect of s 200 deportations.[117] The enactment of s 501 has also seen a series of Ministerial Directions issued in accordance with s 499 of the *Migration Act*. These have prescribed specific 'primary considerations' which decision-makers (other than the Minister)[118] must take into account in every case, as well as 'other considerations' which must be taken into account 'where relevant'.[119]

Policies guide – they cannot 'bind' completely

[17.55] In emphasising the primary function of protecting the community, the latest policies downplay notions of choice in favour of more explicit directives. Section 499 empowers the Minister to issue 'Directions' that statutory decision-makers 'must comply with'. Directions are said to 'bind' delegated decision-makers and merits review bodies, including the AAT, to the extent to which they are consistent with the Act or its Regulations.[120] In contrast, Ministerial Directions do not bind the Minister, and the Minister will be in error if he or she treats a Direction as binding. However, the Minister can use a Ministerial Direction as a guide.[121]

[17.56] Having said this, the fact that neither deportation nor visa cancellations under s 501 are automatic for criminal permanent residents means that decision-making processes in both instances are based inevitably on a balancing of factors and interests. The jurisprudence on policy-making generally also limits the directive force of the various guidelines that have been issued over the years. Brennan J's comments

---

114 (1977) 1 ALD 158.
115 Ibid at 163-5.
116 See the covering letter to Brennan J from the then Minister Mackellar dated 28 March 1978, reproduced in Jennifer M Sharpe, *The Administrative Appeals Tribunal and Policy Review* (Melbourne: Law Book Co, 1986) at 200-1.
117 Policy Statements relating to the Deportation of Criminals (and related matters) were made in 1978, 1980, 1983, 1988, 1992, 1994, 1997, 1998, 1999 and 2000. The most significant recent Direction appears to be *Direction – Deportation under section 201 No 9 1998*, issued 21 December 1998.
118 The Direction does not bind the Minister: *Halmi v MIMA* [2000] FCA 113 at [20]; *Damanik v MIMA* [2000] FCA 771 at [6]. Indeed, in cases where the Minister voluntarily but rigidly applies the provisions of the Ministerial Direction to her or his decision-making, she or he may unlawfully fetter the exercise discretion under s 501: *Ruhl v MIMA* (2001) 184 ALR 401.
119 Since 1998 different Directions have been issued: *Direction No 17 Visa Refusal and Cancellation under s 501* (Cth) (Direction 17), in 1998; *Direction – Visa refusal and cancellation under section 501 – No 21 2001* (Cth) (Direction 21), issued 23 August 2001; and *Direction No 41 Visa Refusal and Cancellation under s 501* (2009) (Cth) (Direction 41), issued in June 2009. See [9] of the last of these Directions.
120 *Migration Act*, s 499(2).
121 See *Black v MIAC* [2007] FCA 1249 at [19]; *Howells v MIMIA* (2004) 139 FCR 580 at [31].

regarding the deportation powers then in ss 12 and 13 are a classic statement of the law in this area. He said:

> [T]he Minister must decide each of the cases … on its merits. His discretion cannot be so truncated by a policy as to preclude consideration of the merits … A fetter of that kind would be objectionable, even though it were adopted by the Minister on his own initiative.[122]

[17.57] In *Howells v MIMIA*,[123] the Full Federal Court considered the extent to which Directions issued under s 499 confine the decision-making functions of the AAT in respect of s 501 decisions. In that case, Direction 17 purported to ascribe weightings to the factors considered by decision-makers exercising their discretion under s 501, regardless of the circumstances of the particular case. Affirming several first instance authorities, the court held that s 501 created an 'unfettered discretion' in decision-makers. It ruled that Direction 17 was inconsistent with the s 501 discretion to the extent that it purported to ascribe *a priori* weights to certain s 501 considerations.[124] While the Minister was 'entitled to have regard' to a Ministerial Direction as a reminder of relevant matters, the Minister could not adhere to the Direction 'slavishly'.[125] The court concluded that if the Minister's discretion could not be fettered by a Direction, 'then so must also the *Minister's delegate* have an unfettered discretion when exercising the powers under s 501(1) and (2)'.[126]

[17.58] Ministerial Directions issued after the 2004 decision in *Howells* have not attempted to ascribe specific weight to particular considerations with respect to the s 501 cancellation discretion. The preamble to Ministerial Direction 21 (issued in 2001, succeeding Direction 17) attests to the government's desire to use Ministerial Directions to 'give precise written directions on what weight is to be given to each factor' considered in the exercise of s 501 and to bind 'all decision makers … to ensure a consistency of approach'.[127] The body of the Direction, however, does not attribute particular weight to prescribed considerations. Rather, it states that decision-makers should have 'due regard to the importance placed by the Government' on prescribed primary considerations, while adopting 'a balancing process which takes into account all relevant considerations'.[128] Direction 41, which replaced Direction 21 in 2009, is completely silent on the weight to be attributed to various considerations under s 501, reflecting a further acceptance of the unfettered discretion of s 501 decision-makers.

Inherent limitations in any balancing process – the inability to 'go behind' convictions

[17.59] From the earliest days of AAT review of criminal deportation cases, the Federal Court has underscored the limitations inherent in the tribunal's power to inquire into the facts on which a deportation order is based. In *MIEA v Daniele*,[129]

---

122 See *Re Drake and MIEA (No 2)* (1979) 2 ALD 634 at 640.
123 (2004) 139 FCR 580 (*Howells*).
124 Ibid at [120]-[128]; see also *Shaw v MIMIA* (2005) 142 FCR 402 at 422.
125 *Howells* (2004) 139 FCR 580.
126 Ibid at [104] (emphasis added).
127 Direction 21, preamble.
128 Ibid at [2.2].
129 (1981) 39 ALR 649.

for example, the court held that the AAT must accept as correct the facts leading to the conviction of the permanent resident. Fisher and Lockhart JJ clarified that it is no part of the tribunal's task to go behind a conviction by hearing evidence calling into question the findings of a judge or jury.[130] The tribunal has respected this approach even where evidence has become available to bring the result of a criminal trial into doubt. An example in point was the applicant in *Re Wiggan and MIEA*.[131] There, the prospective deportee was convicted of murder arising out of a pub brawl. The man's claim of innocence was given credence by evidence that someone else may have struck the fatal blow. However, the police were unable to secure the new suspect's extradition to test the issue. The tribunal held that it would be making an error of law if it determined the application on facts inconsistent with the conviction.[132]

[17.60] This limitation on the tribunal's power works to positively disadvantage those applicants who remain adamant that they are innocent of the crime of which they were convicted. In the face of protestations of innocence, it is difficult for the tribunal to assess the risk of recidivism or to give credit for any willingness on the part of the applicant to reform or make restitution for the criminal act.[133] The inability to go behind the findings of a jury or sentencing judge, however, does not prevent the tribunal from hearing the applicant in relation to the interpretations to be placed on remarks made by a sentencing judge, particularly where these relate to the issue of likely re-offending.[134]

[17.61] In *MIMA v SRT*,[135] the AAT was roundly rebuked by the Federal Court for attempting to 'go behind' a conviction in a case involving a man who had been found responsible for stabbing and strangling a drug dealer to death. Initially convicted of manslaughter, SRT was re-tried after an appeal to the Court of Criminal Appeal, but again convicted of manslaughter. The Minister ordered his deportation under s 200 on the basis of that conviction. The AAT found that the man should not be deported, reasoning that it was not bound to accept the judge's finding in the re-trial. The Full Federal Court held that the tribunal committed a jurisdictional error by asserting that it was not open to the judge or jury in the re-trial to find that the respondent had inflicted the stabbing. The tribunal accepted the respondent's assertion that he had handed a knife to an accomplice who committed the actual offence.[136] The Full Federal Court found that, while the conviction stands, 'it must be accepted that the jury convicted on the basis of the charge that was in fact given to it'.[137] The tribunal (like the primary decision-maker) is not permitted to enter into its own factual inquiries such as might impugn a sentence: 'Accordingly, at least the

---

130 See also *Gungor v MIEA* (1982) 42 ALR 209 at 215-16 and 233; and *Re Cain and MILGEA* (1990) 20 ALD 418.
131 (1987) 12 ALD 226.
132 Compare, however, *Re Bakri and DIEA* (1987) 12 ALD 517.
133 See, for example, *Renata v MIEA* [1986] FCA 361.
134 See *Re Beckner v MIEA* (1991) 30 FCR 49 and *Wing-Yuen Sui v MIEA* (1996) 47 ALD 528.
135 (1999) 91 FCR 234 at [25], citing *MIEA v Gungor* (1982) 39 ALR 649; and *MIEA v Gungor* (1982) 42 ALR 209.
136 (1999) 91 FCR 234 at [17].
137 Ibid at [34].

essential facts found by a sentencing judge in the course of his or her deliberations concerning sentence and upon which the sentence is based must be accepted by the Tribunal'.¹³⁸

Policy conflicts

[17.62] Without challenging the government's pre-eminent concern to safeguard the community from criminal permanent migrants, the jurisprudence emanating from the AAT over the years underscores the tribunal's desire to balance public protection against the rights of those affected by a decision. For example, the AAT quickly made it clear that the onus was on the Minister to justify the removal of persons who had been admitted into the community as permanent residents.¹³⁹ Where the prospective deportee had been resident in Australia for a long time and had become absorbed into the community, the tribunal held that 'a strong, clear case will be required to persuade the decision-maker that it is in the best interests of Australia to banish [that person] from our shores'.¹⁴⁰ The early policy statements did not distinguish between 'immigrants' who gained immunity from deportation after only five years' residence in the country and 'aliens' who never gained such immunity, even when they had become absorbed into the community.¹⁴¹ However, the tribunal regarded the distinction as significant in view of the fact that short-term 'immigrants' were less likely to have formed strong ties within the community than longer term resident non-citizens.¹⁴² As we will see, many of the approaches adopted by the AAT have been met with equal and opposite responses from the government.

[17.63] In the following sections we track the changes that have occurred in the broad areas that now constitute or have constituted the 'primary' considerations in both criminal deportation and visa cancellation policy. Although the framework adopted is that used in relation to s 501 visa cancellations, there are substantial overlaps with the policy guidelines governing deportations under s 200.¹⁴³ For this reason, judicial and other consideration of both sets of policies are discussed together. The number one constant (featuring in all of the policies) has been the protection of the community.¹⁴⁴ Under the Coalition government's Directions 17 and 21, the second priority was 'expectations of the Australian community', while the third 'primary consideration' was the 'best interests of the children'. In contrast, the Labor

---

138 Ibid at [40]. See also *MIMA v Ali* (2000) 106 FCR 313.
139 See, for example, *Re Sergi and MIEA* (1979) 2 ALD 224 at 226-7 and *Re Pochi and MIEA* (1979) 2 ALD 33 (*Re Pochi*) at 39-40.
140 See *Re Pochi* (1979) 2 ALD 33 at 40.
141 Sections 13 and 12 respectively.
142 See *Re Beets* (1979) 2 ALD 417 at 421.
143 The most important difference between the s 200 *Deportation policy – General Direction No 9* (Direction 9) issued 21 December 1998 – and subsequent Directions made under s 501 (Directions 17, 21 and 41, above n 119) is that the Minister bears the onus of proof under s 200 while s 501 requires the non-citizen to prove good character under s 501. Direction 9 also places a much greater emphasis on considerations personal to a prospective deportee in terms of hardship suffered by the deportee and his or her family than do the Directions issued with respect to s 501 visa cancellations.
144 See Direction 9 (Criminal Deportation Policy, issued 21 December 1998) at [4]; Direction 21.

government's Direction 41, issued June 2009, lists 'Australian ties' as the second priority followed by 'international obligations'.[145]

17.4.2 Protecting the Australian community

The seriousness of the offence committed

[17.64] The acknowledgment that deportation involves an element of choice and the balancing of interests is apparent both in the early deportation policies and in the tribunal rulings in which they were applied.[146] In some respects, the government's view of how this balancing of interests should be performed coincided closely with that of the tribunal. As Sharpe demonstrates,[147] the guidelines developed by the tribunal concerning the weight to be given to such matters as the seriousness of the offence committed were picked up in the 1983 policy. An example is found in the rules of thumb formulated by the tribunal for dealing with drug-related offences. To supply the deficiencies of the early policies[148] the tribunal drew distinctions between different types of drugs.[149] It considered the degree of involvement of the offender in the criminal enterprise; the scale of the operation in question; as well as other factors relevant to assessing the degree of guilt of the prospective deportee.[150] In an apparent response to such cases, the 1983 policy made particular reference to offences related to the production, importation, distribution or trafficking of illicit drugs. It also acknowledged that a deportation order may be made more readily in the case of a large-scale dealer than in that of a small-time pusher or addict.[151] The tribunal's approach to the deportation of persons convicted of serious crimes of violence was echoed also in the 1983 policy.[152]

[17.65] As the 1980s progressed, however, conflict between the Minister and the tribunal became more marked as ministerial attitudes to persons convicted of serious crimes became increasingly harsh. The 1980 policy directed decision-makers to deport serious offenders in all but exceptional cases.[153] The deportation policies of

---

145 See Direction 41 at [9]. In this respect the policy has been brought more closely into line with the policy on criminal deportations (Direction 9).
146 See statement by Minister West, Commonwealth Parliamentary Debates, *Hansard*, House of Representatives, 4 May 1983, at 166-9. The policy is reproduced in Sharpe, above n 116, at Appendix D, 207. For a sample of tribunal rulings, see *Re Chan and MIEA* (1977) 17 ALR 432 at 433; *Re Sajatovic and MIEA* (1979) 2 ALN 549; and *Re Tenenboim and MIEA* (1980) 2 ALN 1036.
147 See Sharpe, above n 116, at 179-80.
148 For example, the 1980 policy merely directed decision-makers to have regard to the nature and quantity of illicit drugs involved and to consider whether the offence was part of a pattern of similar crimes: see Sharpe, above n 116, at 206, [13].
149 See, for example, *Re Salazar-Arbelaez and MIEA* (1977) 18 ALR 36 at 39 and *Re Gungor and MIEA* (1980) 3 ALD 225 at 228-9. Compare *Re Hilton and MIEA* (1980) 2 ALD 1035 at 1036, where McGregor J questioned whether it was proper for the tribunal to distinguish between 'hard' and 'soft' drugs if the Minister's policy did not do so.
150 See, for example, *Re Gallo and MIEA* (1980) 3 ALN N12; *Re Pochi* (1979) 2 ALD 33; and *Re Sergi and MIEA* (1979) 2 ALD 224.
151 See Sharpe, above n 116, at 208.
152 For example, the comments made in *Re Tcherchian and MIEA* (1978) 1 ALN N20 can be compared with the discussion of what constitutes a 'serious crime' in the 1983 policy.
153 See [8] to [13], in Sharpe, above n 116, at 203-6.

1983 and 1988 were more moderate in their language, but continued the trend by making more explicit the crimes that constituted a serious offence, and the weight that should be given to mitigating factors.[154] The general tendency for the tribunal to affirm deportation orders in cases involving violence and 'hard' drugs continued in the 1990s,[155] although the AAT resisted the pressure to regard deportation as inevitable in such cases.[156] Other questions of fact and emphasis which have been the source of disagreement between the Minister and the tribunal are the likelihood of the prospective deportee re-offending;[157] the impact of the deportation on persons associated with the offender;[158] and the hardship the deportee would face in the country of exile.[159] It is these cases that have raised the ire of successive Ministers.

[17.66] In spite of the severity of the approach taken by the Ministers between 1987 and 1990, the tribunal maintained a certain stoic independence in its review of deportation decisions. While it was prepared to defer to the harshness of the Minister's policy in some cases,[160] it retained a willingness to give offenders a second chance, especially where family relationships were involved.[161] The tribunal also continued to take views different from those of the Minister's delegate on matters such as the seriousness of the applicant's conduct;[162] the likelihood of recidivism;[163] and even the interpretation of the Act.[164]

[17.67] The tendency of the Minister to meet the tribunal head on became a feature of the Ministries of Mr Young, Senator Ray and Mr Hand between 1987 and 1992. Those years saw an almost complete reversal of the earlier practice of accepting tribunal recommendations to revoke a deportation order. Between 1987 and 1989 no less than 10 recommendations against deportation were rejected by the Minister.[165]

---

154 See Sharpe, above n 116, at 208, and Commonwealth Parliamentary Debates, *Hansard*, Senate, Vol 130, 8 December 1988, at 3770-1.
155 See, for example, *Re Vazquez and MILGEA* (1989) 20 ALD 33; *Re Campbell and DILGEA* [1993] AATA 344; *Bengescue v MIEA* (1994) 35 ALD 429; and *Re Hordila and MIMA* [1997] AATA 82.
156 See, for example, *Re Gogebakan and MIEA* (1987) 6 AAR 544; *Re Wiggan and MIEA* (1987) 12 ALD 226; *Re Epiha and MILGEA* (1988) 18 ALD 114; *Re Batey v MILGEA* [1992] FCA 494; and *Re Sharpe and MILGEA* [1994] AATA 87.
157 See, for example, *Re Bardek and MIEA* (1987) 8 ALD 382; *Re Epiha and MILGEA* (1988) 18 ALD 114; and *Re Batey v MILGEA* [1992] FCA 494.
158 See, for example, *Re Weir and MIEA* (1988) 33 AALB [1226]; and *Re Tamani and DILGEA* [1993] AATA 60.
159 See, for example, *Re Wiggan and MIEA* (1987) 17 ALD 226; *Re Abbott and MILGEA* (1991) AALD [2781-2]; and *Re Gilbert and MILGEA* [1993] AATA 510.
160 See, for example, *Re Uyanik and MILGEA* (1989) 10 AAR 38.
161 See, for example, *Re Bong and MILGEA* (1990) 20 ALD 143; *Re Ameri and MILGEA* (1989) 16 ALD 640; *Re Percerep and MILGEA* (1990) 20 ALD 669 (*Re Percerep*); *Re Thain and MILGEA* (1989) 21 ALD 215; and *Re Mulugeta and MILGEA* (1989) 19 ALD 639.
162 See *Re Leaupepe and MILGEA* (1990) 21 ALD 382.
163 See *Re Paki-Titi and MILGEA* (1990) 21 ALD 359.
164 In *Re Thain and MILGEA* (1989) 21 ALD 215 the tribunal held that a sentence requiring an offender to attend a youth training centre did not amount to a term of imprisonment for the purpose of determining liability to deportation under what is now s 200 of the Act. Again, in *Re Loh and MILGEA* (1990) 52 AALB [1869], the tribunal was at pains to stress that the Minister's policy was one factor to be taken into account, and not something that it was bound to follow slavishly.
165 See Commonwealth Parliamentary Debates, *Hansard*, House of Representatives, Vol 126, 24 February 1982, at 519; and ibid, Senate, Vol 130, 8 December 1988, at 3770ff.

Senator Ray's attitude to the tribunal was demonstrated by both the policy statement he made on 8 December 1988 and by his private correspondence with the tribunal president. The ministerial statement of 1988 chided the tribunal for its wayward interpretation of policy.[166] Minister Ray identified six 'areas of difference', all of which were reflected in the series of cases summarised at the end of his report in which he or the previous Minister had declined to accept a tribunal recommendation. The first and second of these related to the AAT's treatment of prospective deportees convicted of crimes involving the trafficking of illicit drugs; and the failure by the tribunal to have regard to the total criminal history of applicants.

[17.68] The later deportation policies avoid the rather emotive language of Senator Ray but nevertheless continue the trend established by that Minister towards zero tolerance of wayward non-citizens. The policy of 1992 emphasised the role of the AAT as risk assessor. The 1998 policy issued by (Coalition) Minister Ruddock listed as primary factors the seriousness of the crime committed by the permanent resident; whom it affected; and the 'abhorrence' of the offence to the community.[167]

[17.69] In cases involving crimes perceived to be abhorrent – particularly those involving child abuse – the AAT has had little trouble affirming orders to deport.[168] It has also accepted that the deportation should follow on conviction for a very serious offence, absent mitigating factors of equal gravamen.[169] Conversely, where the offences in question were not in the top order of seriousness, the AAT has shown a more lenient approach.[170]

'Serious offences' and visa cancellations under s 501

[17.70] The deportation policy issued in 1998 was reflected in due course in the Directions issued in respect of s 501, with the protection of the Australian community from 'serious criminal and other harmful conduct, particularly crimes involving violence' being the first priority for decision-makers.[171] Decision-makers are required to give due consideration to the government objectives, including protection of the Australian community from 'unacceptable risks of harm' as a result of criminal or other conduct by non-citizens.[172] Thus, in each case, decision-makers are required to assess the level of risk of harm posed by a person's entry into or presence in the community. In doing this, decision-makers are required to consider relevant factors including the seriousness and nature of the person's conduct, and the risk that the conduct may be repeated.[173] Decision-makers are also required to consider the government's objective 'to protect the safety of the community's more vulnerable members'.[174]

---

166   See ibid at 3771-81.
167   See Direction 9 at [8(a)] and [8(b)].
168   See, for example, *Re Velasco and MIMA* (1997) 44 ALD 655 and *Re Arias and DIMA* (1996) 44 ALD 679.
169   See, for example, *Re McIvor and DIMA* (1997) 45 ALD 731; *Re Birceru and MIMA* [1997] AATA 434; and *Re Percerep and MIMA* [1997] AATA 527.
170   See, for example, *Re Rose and DIMA* [1997] AATA 567.
171   Direction 41 at [10(a)].
172   Ibid at [10.1(1)] and [5.1(2)].
173   Ibid at [10.1(2)].
174   Ibid at [5.1(3)].

[17.71] When assessing the seriousness of a person's conduct to determine the risk of harm they pose to the Australian community, decision-makers must consider several factors. Crimes of violence or threatened violence, especially against vulnerable persons (like children, the elderly or the disabled), remain matters of 'special concern'.[175] Conduct that will be considered 'serious' includes any unlawful killing, certain violent crimes, all sexually based offences, any offence against a child, robbery (armed or otherwise), serious theft, certain drug trafficking offences, terrorist activity, people smuggling, kidnapping, abduction, organised crime, arson, blackmail, extortion, and certain offences ancillary to offences that are considered serious.[176] With respect to the seriousness of criminal offences, decision-makers must consider the extent of a person's criminal record, including the number and nature of offences, the period between offences, and the time elapsed since the most recent offence.

[17.72] Decision-makers are directed to look at the sentence(s) imposed for any crimes as an indicator of seriousness of the offender's conduct against the community.[177] In determining the seriousness of a person's crimes or conduct, there is a wide requirement for decision-makers to consider 'any relevant information',[178] including evidence from independent authorities like judges, psychologists, and information such as pre-sentence reports, parole assessments, and victim impact statements. Decision-makers must consider any relevant mitigating factors the person raises, and must also take exonerative pardons into account.[179]

[17.73] The 2009 Direction, like its predecessor, seeks to ensure that s 501 does not exacerbate persecution committed by other states. While s 501 deems anyone with a 'substantial criminal record' to fail the character test, the policy concedes that 'it may be appropriate' to allow persons to enter or remain in Australia despite having a substantial criminal record, if the record was acquired 'as a result of political, religious or ethnic persecution'.[180]

[17.74] In 2006, the Ombudsman expressed concern about the Department's assessment of the seriousness of a person's crimes or conduct. It found evidence that 'issues papers' provided to the Minister (which form the basis of decisions to cancel visas and deport) sometimes mischaracterised a person's crimes and their seriousness (for instance, mischaracterising a charge of 'possession of drugs' as a charge for 'trafficking, supply or possession of commercial quantity of drugs'). In other cases the Ombudsman pointed to circumstances that evidenced that issues papers included 'cherry picked' information. For instance, one issues paper relied on a police report to conclude that certain offences were 'serious', while making no examination of judges'

---

175   Ibid at [5.2] and [10.1.1(1)].
176   Ibid at [10.1.1(1)].
177   Ibid at [10.1.1(3)].
178   Ibid at [10.1.1(4)].
179   Ministerial Directions also provide for the consideration of offences committed overseas. Decision-makers must consider whether offences or conduct that occurred in another country are classified as an offence in Australia. For conduct that would be an offence in Australia, decision-makers must consider whether a lighter sentence would have been incurred if the offence had occurred in Australia.
180   Direction 41 at [10.1.1].

pre-sentencing and sentencing comments.[181] Another mentioned charges related to stealing, but not that the theft involved property worth only $25.[182] The Full Federal Court has made it clear that a failure to accurately consider the individual's criminal record may amount to jurisdictional error.[183] The Ombudsman's findings, therefore, have uncovered numerous instances of decisions which may have been liable to be set aside for jurisdictional error and which have been left unchallenged.

Mental health considerations

[17.75] If a non-citizen does not pass the character test in circumstances where he or she has been acquitted on the basis of unsound mind or insanity, then, in assessing the risk of harm to the Australian community, the decision-maker must take into account the person's 'degree of recovery'.[184] A mental health report must be obtained through a qualified professional, outlining the nature and extent of any mental impairment. Decision-makers must consider any hardship that would be faced by the person, or the danger they would pose to others, if they were to be removed to a country where they would not have access to treatment. Decision-makers are required to consider the person's reliance on any medication, and the danger of their deliberately or accidentally not taking it.

Assessing the risk of recidivism

[17.76] In the list of factors to be taken into account in deciding whether or not to deport a criminal non-citizen, the 1992 policy at [19] listed first the risk of further offences. The willingness of the AAT to give an offender one more chance has been an enduring source of conflict between the tribunal and the Minister. There is evidence that the tribunal has sometimes been mistaken or too lenient in placing its trust in the reformation of a non-citizen's character.[185] The cases which have caused most conflict are those in which offenders have claimed to have undergone a radical transformation, or those where there has been some mitigating factor, suggesting that the offences in questions were out of character.

[17.77] A prominent case in the early 1990s was that of Batey, a permanent resident who was sentenced to 13 years in prison for a sex offence. He claimed to have undergone a cathartic change in outlook while in prison. The AAT found that there was 'quite minimal risk' that he would reoffend and recommended that the order to deport him be revoked.[186] The Minister stated that he agreed with the tribunal's assessment of Mr Batey, but moved to affirm the deportation order on the ground that there was 'a real risk, however minimal', that Batey would re-offend. Batey's application for judicial review succeeded at first instance – prompting the Minister to

---

181   See Commonwealth Ombudsman, above n 9, at 22.
182   Ibid at 24.
183   *Lu v MIMIA* (2004) 141 FCR 346 at [7] and [8] (Black CJ) and at [56] (Sackville J).
184   Direction 41 at [10.1.1(5)(a)].
185   Compare *Re Thain and MILGEA* (1989) 21 ALD 215 with *Re Thain* (unreported, AAT, DP Forgie, 1988); and *Re Percerep and MILGEA* (1990) 20 ALD 669 with *Re Percerep and MIMA* [1997] AATA 527.
186   See *Re Batey* (1991) 25 ALD 369.

issue new guidelines and to introduce the *Migration (Offences and Undesirable Persons) Amendment Act 1992* (Cth).[187]

[17.78] The issue of a person's recidivist tendencies has remained a matter of primary importance under the s 501 Directives. The 2009 policy states that a person's 'previous general conduct and total criminal history' are highly relevant to a decision-maker's assessment of a person's risk of re-offending. A recent history of convictions is regarded as a 'highly relevant' indicator of an increased risk of re-offending. Any breach of judicial orders is also relevant. Decision-makers are also required to consider evidence of the extent of the person's rehabilitation, with greater weight placed on evidence from 'independent and authoritative sources'.[188] Thus, the Federal Court has set aside a decision of the tribunal affirming a s 501 cancellation, on the basis that the tribunal assessed recidivism solely by reference to the applicant's results from a psychological risk assessment test known as 'Static-99'. Recidivism must be measured by a range of individual factors rather than one psychological test alone.[189]

Deterrence as a factor in s 501 cancellation decisions

[17.79] One significant difference between the 2009 Direction 41 and earlier policies issued with respect to both s 200 deportations and s 501 visa cancellations is the abandonment of any reference to deterrence as a factor in decision-making.[190] In *Djalic v MIMIA*,[191] the applicant argued that the cancellation of his visa was motivated in part by the desire to make an example of him – in other words that deterrence was a factor in the decision made under s 501. Djalic had arrived in Australia in 1970 at the age of five, and lived in Australia for 32 years before being convicted of several offences, including breaking and entering a building with intent to steal. He was sentenced to 12 months in prison. Djalic argued that, to the extent that s 501 permits the consideration of deterrence, it is punitive and, hence, invalid in the face of the Commonwealth judiciary's monopoly on punishment powers under Chapter III of the Constitution. The Full Court disagreed, holding:

> [D]eterrence is a matter that is squarely concerned with the protection of the Australian community. Different views may be held about how far a cancellation decision is likely to have a deterrent effect on other potential (non-citizen) offenders. But the very point of taking account of general deterrence as a factor in making a cancellation decision is to enhance the safety and well-being of the Australian community by discouraging non-citizens from engaging in criminal conduct. It is treated in exactly this way in the Ministerial Direction. The mere fact that deterrence also happens to be an element that courts take into account in

---

187 The Full Federal Court later reversed the ruling of Beaumont J: see *Re MILGEA v Batey* (1993) 40 FCR 493. The effect of the legislation was to empower the Minister to remove from the jurisdiction of the AAT cases that are of particular concern on public interest grounds: s 502. As noted earlier, as an apparent counter-balance to this measure, the AAT was given determinative review of deportation decisions.
188 Direction 41 at [10.1.2].
189 *Tirtabudi v MIAC* (2008) 101 ALD 103 at [25].
190 See Direction 9 at [14]; and Direction 21 at [2.5(c)].
191 (2004) 139 FCR 292.

sentencing offenders does not convert a cancellation decision under s 501(2) from a protective to a punitive measure.[192]

[17.80] One reason why consideration of 'general deterrence' may have been removed from the decision-making process is borne out in *Lafu v MIAC*.[193] Here the Full Federal Court set aside the tribunal's decision to affirm a cancellation decision because the tribunal had not explained the relevance of general deterrence to its decision. With Direction 41, the AAT is now relieved of reaching a conclusion as to whether and to what extent the broad societal considerations of general deterrence are relevant to the personal circumstances of the review applicant.

17.4.3 'Community expectations' versus the significance of an offender's ties with Australia

[17.81] The Minister's approach to the balancing process appears to have differed most from that of the AAT and of the Federal Court over the years in assessing the importance of matters personal to the prospective deportee and how these might clash with inchoate notions of community expectations. Two early examples are the cases of *Re Pochi and MIEA*[194] and *Re Barbaro and MIEA*.[195] There, the offenders' long-standing connections with the community were regarded by the tribunal as outweighing the seriousness of the crimes of which they were convicted. Minister McPhee strongly disagreed with this approach. However, he was reluctant to go against the AAT without exhausting the available appeal procedures. In *Pochi*, the Minister appealed unsuccessfully against the tribunal's decision under s 44 of the AAT Act.[196] Only after the High Court declined to rule on the appeal from the Full Federal Court did the Minister finally refuse to accept the tribunal's recommendations in February 1982.[197] Minister McPhee issued new deportation orders against Vincenzo Barbaro, Luigi Pochi and one other criminal resident.[198]

[17.82] The later conflict between Senator Ray and the tribunal was most noted in the series of cases after 1988 where the tribunal was asked to review deportation orders made in respect of offenders who had spent most or all of their formative years in Australia. For example, in *Re Ameri and MILGEA*[199] and *Re Percerep and MILGEA*,[200] the tribunal recommended against deportation on the ground that it ill-became the

---

192   Ibid at [45]. This contributes to ample authority that, in cancelling the applicant's visa, the Minister is not imposing any further punishment for the applicant's crimes or exercising judicial power: *Tuncok v MIMIA* [2004] FCAFC 172 at [44]; *Tapel v MIAC* [2008] FCA 857 at [20].
193   (2009) 112 ALD 1.
194   (1979) 2 ALD 33.
195   (1981) 3 ALN N21. See also *Re Nolan* (1986) 9 ALD 407; *Re Haoucher* (1987) 12 ALD 217; *Re Wiggan* (1987) 12 ALD 226; and *Re Baias v MILGEA* (1996) 43 ALD 284.
196   See *Pochi v Macphee* (1982) 151 CLR 101, discussed above, Chapter 3.2.
197   Ibid.
198   See Commonwealth Parliamentary Debates, *Hansard*, House of Representatives, Vol 126, 24 February 1982, at 518-20. In the last of these cases, the deportee was killed in a car accident before the order could be brought into effect. In the cases of *Barbaro* and *Pochi*, the deportation orders were revoked by Minister West after the change of government in 1983.
199   (1989) 16 ALD 640.
200   (1990) 20 ALD 669.

country to export trouble-makers whose character and behaviour were attributable entirely to influences within Australia.[201] As the tribunal recorded in the later case of *Re Malincevski and MILGEA*,[202] the Minister responded to *Re Ameri* by writing to the former president of the tribunal, Hartigan J, criticising the decision as involving a fundamental misinterpretation of government policy. Although the tribunal accepted this letter in evidence in *Re Malincevski*, it took much the same view of the communication as Brennan J took of the document produced to him in *Re Becker and MIEA*.[203] The tribunal held that the Minister's letter did not amount to a statement of government policy that could be taken into account on a formal level. It said, further, that the letter revealed a misunderstanding of the relationship between the tribunal president and its members in so far as it assumed that the decisions of tribunal members could be controlled by presidential or ministerial Direction. The tribunal observed that the interpretation and application of policy was a matter for individual tribunal members in the course of reviewing all the circumstances affecting the case before them. It was not something that could be the subject of control by either the tribunal president or even the Minister.[204]

[17.83] In his 1988 policy, Senator Ray complained that the AAT was placing too much emphasis on the difficulties the prospective deportee might encounter in his or her country of exile. The deportee's lack of job opportunities, he said, was not a persuasive argument against deportation. These issues arose in at least two of the cases summarised in the policy statement.[205] The Minister also complained that the tribunal was too lenient towards multiple offenders who had come to Australia as minors and who, because of their criminal record, had never acquired immunity from deportation.[206] The applicants failed to gain immunity from deportation because of the operation of the then s 14A of the Act (now s 204). In this, he specifically repudiated the view taken by some tribunal members that such offenders should be regarded as Australia's problem because their formative years had been spent in this country.[207]

[17.84] Senator Ray's lack of sympathy for long-term permanent residents appears to have been shared by most of his successors in title. The first Directions made in respect of visa cancellations under s 501 made no mention whatsoever of the length of time a person may have spent in Australia – and whether indeed the behaviour of the person may properly be regarded as Australia's responsibility. Rather, the second 'primary consideration' was expressed as 'expectations of the Australian community'.[208]

---

201 See also *Re Koloamatangi and DILGEA* (1990) 60 AALB [2152].
202 (1991) 24 ALD 331.
203 (1977) 1 ALD 158, discussed above at [17.54]ff.
204 *Re Malincevski and MILGEA* (1991) 24 ALD 331 at 336.
205 See Commonwealth Parliamentary Debates, *Hansard*, Senate, vol 130, 8 December 1988, at 3770ff; Case 'D' (*Haoucher*) and Case 'F' (*Wiggan*), discussed at 3771-3 and 3779-80 respectively.
206 See, ibid, Case 'C' (*Gogebakan*) and Case 'F' (*Wiggan*), discussed at 3774-6 and 3779-80 respectively.
207 See, for example, *Re Gogebakan and MIEA* (1987) 12 ALD 572; *Re Gogebakan v MILGEA* (1988) 92 ALR 167; and *Re Ameri and MILGEA* (1989) 16 ALD 640.
208 See Direction 17 and Direction 21 at [2.12].

[17.85] This did not prevent some members of the AAT from resisting an overly harsh interpretation of the directive.[209] In *Re Jupp and MIMIA*,[210] DP Block pointed out that the Direction is incorrect if it assumed that the 'Australian community' thinks 'as one':

> The supporters of One Nation would have one view as regards immigration, and there is of course a very large diametrically opposed body of opinion in Australia. I construe (the reference in direction 17) as being correctly made to middle-of-the-road reasonable members of the Australian community who do not hold extreme views one way or the other. And I think that there is a further limiting factor and that is that one must import into that Australian community, knowledge of the evidence before me. If told only and concisely that a person incarcerated for armed robbery was seeking to come to live in Australia, there might well be a general view that this should not be allowed. On one facile view, these are the facts in this case. They entirely ignore the fact that the event happened nearly 20 years ago, since which time there has been a complete rehabilitation transforming a young drug-addicted person into a responsible family man. I believe that the Australian community, so informed, would expect me to interpret the Direction in a humane fashion.[211]

[17.86] In *M238 of 2002 v MIMIA*,[212] the Full Federal Court described the reference to the 'expectations of the Australian community' as fundamentally a 'political notion'. It involves the Minister, as an elected member responsible to parliament, assessing a case based upon evidence placed before him or her together with the views of others. Still, in 2004, French J (as he then was) observed that the phrase 'expectations of the Australian community' 'invites a judgment akin to judgments about the "public interest" which is necessarily evaluative and conclusionary in character and not amenable to challenge or judicial review on its merits'.[213]

[17.87] The jurisprudence from the courts after the 1998 amendments is littered with expressions of dissent from a judiciary plainly ill at ease with the removal from Australia of persons like Stefan Nystrom who were truly 'aliens by the barest of threads'. As the Full Federal Court observed in that case:

> The appellant has indeed behaved badly, but no worse than many of his age who have also lived as members of the Australian community all their lives but who happen to be citizens. The difference is the barest of technicalities. It is the chance result of an accident of birth, the inaction of the appellant's parents and some contestable High Court decisions. Apart from the dire punishment of the individual involved, it presumes that Australia can export its problems elsewhere.[214]

---

209 See, for example, *Re Leha v MIMA* [2000] AATA 1054. See also the comments made by the Commonwealth Ombudsman, above n 9, at 24.
210 [2002] AATA 458.
211 Ibid at [7(m)]. See also *Re Gonzales and MIMIA* [2002] AATA 895 at [62]; and Kerry Murphy, 'AAT Review of Character Cases: Section 501' (2004) 18 *Immigration Review* 7.
212 [2003] FCAFC 260 at [59].
213 *Preston v MIMIA (No 2)* [2004] FCA 107 at [23]. See also *Pull v MIMIA* [2007] FCA 20; *Morrison v MIAC* [2008] FCA 54.
214 *Nystrom v MIMIA* (2005) 143 FCR 420 at [29] (Moore and Gyles JJ).

[17.88] The distinction between the policy governing criminal deportations and that governing removal under s 501 before 2009 is particularly stark in this regard. As the AAT explained in *Re Glusheski v MIMA*:[215]

> [T]he resort to section 501 when the delegate is precluded from relying on section 201 has serious consequences for the person affected. Ministerial Directions under both sections have been given under section 499. Direction Number 9, dealing with deportations, directs the decision maker specifically to take into account hardship expected to be suffered by the potential deportee. Direction Number 17, relating to section 501, makes no specific reference to hardship to be suffered by the person primarily affected. The only reference to hardship is in paragraph 2.17(c) and that is restricted to hardship caused to immediate family members. Thus, a person who has been in this country for less than ten years is entitled to be heard as to his own hardship before he is deported. A person who has been in this country for twenty years before committing a deportable offence is not entitled to be heard specifically as to his own hardship before being virtually deported.[216]

[17.89] The judicial criticisms of this policy are set out by Foster who adds her own critique:[217]

> Given that many long-term residents could be said to be products of their life in Australia, particularly in the case of persons who immigrated to Australia under the age of criminal responsibility and have therefore spent their formative years in Australia, the better view is that they are 'members[] of society who ha[ve] committed offences',[218] and as such, their banishment is best understood as an attempt to 'export [our] problems elsewhere'.[219] Indeed so much appears to have been later conceded by at least Callinan J in *Shaw* where his Honour held that the applicant's residence for more than ten years prior to 'the commission by him of serious crime' produced the result that he had become an absorbed member of the Australian community at least for the purpose of the immigration power.[220]

---

215   [2000] AATA 717 at [15].
216   See also *Cockrell v MIAC* (2007) 100 ALD 52 at [53].
217   See Foster, above n 2, at 500.
218   See *Hollis v MIMA* (2003) 202 ALR 483 at [40].
219   *Nystrom v MIMIA* (2005) 143 FCR 420 at [29]. Similar sentiments have been expressed in decisions of the Federal Court. See *Watson v MIMIA* [2004] FCA 1654 at [6] where Spender J remarked that 'it seems extraordinarily unfair to Scotland to send Mr Watson there'; and in *Shaw v MIMIA* (2005) 142 FCR 402 at [18] where Spender J stated: 'He is now thirty-two years of age. I note that it seems thoroughly unfair to the United Kingdom to send Mr Shaw there for no good reason other than that he is now a person of poor character who happens to have spent the first eighteen months of his life there'. The AAT has made similar comments. For example, in *Re Glusheski v MIMA* [2000] AATA 717, the AAT commented in relation to a Macedonian citizen who had arrived in Australia aged 25 and had lived in Australia for 37 years that 'it seems fairer to believe that if Mr Glusheski is now a problem, he should be regarded as Australia's problem'. See also Nicholls, above n 1, at 10, 160. On this point, see a very interesting discussion of whether other states are indeed required to take back such persons as a matter of international law by Gregor Noll, 'Return of Persons to States of Origin and Third States' in TA Aleinikoff and V Chetail (eds), *Migration and International Legal Norms* (The Hague: Asser Press, 2003) at 61-74. For an account of the impact of deportation in countries of deportation, see Daniel Kanstrom, 'Post-Deportation Human Rights Law: Aspiration, Oxymoron, or Necessity?' (2007) 3 *Stanford Journal of Civil Rights and Civil Liberties* 195 at 218-21.
220   *Shaw v MIMA* (2003) 218 CLR 28 at [154]. Callinan J also noted that he 'would not regard that first conviction, occurring as it did when he was so young [at age 14] as putting him beyond the community of ordinary Australians': at [183]. This was so despite the fact that Callinan J described Shaw as 'this criminal who would, in consequence of my decision if it were to prevail, continue to

[17.90] It was not until June 2009 that the directives made in respect of s 501 visa cancellations instructed decision-makers to consider issues such as 'whether the person was a minor when they began living in Australia';[221] and 'the length of time that the person has been ordinarily resident in Australia prior to engaging in criminal activity or other relevant conduct'.[222] Direction 41 states that 'it may be appropriate for the Australian community to accept more risk where the person concerned has, in effect, become part of the Australian community owing to their having spent their formative years, or a major portion of their life, in Australia'.[223]

[17.91] Ministerial Direction 41 requires certain 'other considerations' to be taken into account as 'non-primary considerations' where they are relevant to the circumstances of the case, though with less weight to be given to them in general.[224] Decision-makers are required to consider: the person's family ties and relationships; the person's age; the person's links or lack of links to the country to which they will probably be removed; the hardship likely to be experienced by the person or their immediate family members lawfully resident in Australia; the person's level of education; and whether the person had been formally advised that they were within the deportation or character and conduct provisions.

[17.92] A person's health status may also be a relevant non-primary consideration.[225] Health conditions suffered by a person are given favourable consideration. Information assessing a person's health should be obtained from an 'appropriately qualified professional'. For persons onshore, decision-makers must consider whether the person would have appropriate access to necessary treatment if he or she were removed from Australia, and any hardship he or she would suffer as a result. Health issues also have other potential impacts on decision-making under s 501. The Ombudsman has pointed out that health matters may be relevant to matters such as why the visa holder committed a crime, the seriousness of the offence, and the likelihood of recidivism.[226]

[17.93] Again, although these matters are expressed to be relevant considerations, a number of cases have emerged in recent years that throw doubt on the extent to which weight is given to these matters. A great many of the very long-term residents deported or removed from Australia in recent years appear to have been suffering

---

be a charge upon the Australian people': at [188] and 'an immigrant from the United Kingdom of persistent criminal inclination': at [129]. See also Kirby J at [73]. It was not necessary for the majority members of the court to discuss the immigration power since they upheld the legislation on the basis of the aliens power.

221   Direction 41 at [10(1)(d)(i)].
222   Ibid at [10 (1)(d)(ii)].
223   Ibid at [5.2]. Favourable consideration must be given to a person who 'was a minor when they began living in Australia and spent their formative years in Australia', though less weight is given if the person was close to adulthood when they arrived. More favourable consideration must also be given 'the longer the person has been ordinarily resident in Australia prior to engaging in criminal activity or activity that bears negatively on their character'.
224   Direction 41 at [11(1)], [11(2)].
225   See Direction 41 at [11(3)(c)].
226   See Commonwealth Ombudsman, above n 9, at 27.

from mental illnesses.[227] In December 2009, 43-year-old Andrew Moore, who came to Australia at the age of 11, was removed to Britain following cancellation of his visa under s 501. Described as a recovering alcoholic – 'his body racked by a failing liver, hepatitis C, fibromyalgia and bowel problems' – Moore died of unexplained causes within three days of his arrival in London.[228] If the policy directives have changed, this is not immediately apparent in the decisional outcomes.

17.4.4 International obligations

[17.94] The third 'primary consideration' in Direction 41 requires decision-makers to have regard to obligations Australia has assumed under international law. In fact, this has been a feature of policy since the mid 1990s, although not always expressed as directly as in Direction 41. The first policies made in respect of s 501 referred instead to the 'best interests of the child', this being seen perhaps as the area in which Australia would be most vulnerable to international criticism given the popularity of the UN Convention on the Rights of the Child (UNCRC).[229]

[17.95] Long-term permanent residents aside, the most problematic deportation cases for the AAT are those involving offenders who are parents of Australian citizen children. The landmark High Court ruling in *MIEA v Teoh*[230] is of very direct relevance to decision-makers in the criminal deportation field as it concerned the grant of residence to an individual who had been convicted of serious drug offences. Teoh gained notoriety because he was the father or stepfather of no less than seven Australian children born to a dysfunctional, drug-dependent mother. The case has been a source of enduring controversy because of the High Court's ruling that Australia's accession to the UNCRC created certain procedural entitlements in Teoh. This Convention states in Art 3 that, in all matters affecting children, the rights of the child should be a primary consideration. The majority held that, in the absence of executive indications to the contrary, Teoh had a legitimate expectation that he would be granted a hearing about the impact his removal would have on his children.[231]

[17.96] Direction 41 instructs decision-makers to regard as a primary consideration the best interests of any child in Australia who is potentially affected by a visa refusal or cancellation.[232] The Full Court has been prepared to assume that if the Minister fails to regard the interests of the individual's children as a primary consideration, the cancellation decision would be affected by jurisdictional error.[233] In *Long v MIMIA*,[234] the Full Court inferred from a briefing paper presented to the Minister that he had not balanced the best interests of Long's children against other relevant considerations

---

227 See, for example, the cases of Stefan Nystrom, Robert Jovicic and others discussed by Nicholls, above n 1, Ch 10 (at 150ff).
228 See Joel Gibson, 'Deported, ill … and dead days later', *Sydney Morning Herald*, 7 December 2009, at 1.
229 Opened for signature 20 November 1989, 1577 UNTS 3 (entered into force 2 September 1990).
230 (1995) 183 CLR 273.
231 See further Chapter 4.2.1.
232 Direction 41 at [10] and [10.4.1].
233 *MIMIA v Lorenzo* [2005] FCAFC 13. See also *Wan v MIMA* (2001) 107 FCR 133.
234 (2003) 76 ALD 610 at [55].

and set the cancellation decision aside on this basis. The Full Court in *Vaitaiki v MIEA*[235] set aside a deportation order on the basis that the AAT had simply assumed that the deportation would be carried out and had not sought 'to identify what would ... be the result that would overall be conducive to the best interests of the children'. However, cases since these have shown that a finding as to what decision would be in the child's best interests may be inferred in a variety of circumstances.[236] In *MIMA v W157/00A*,[237] for example, the respondent was advised of the cancellation of his visa in a letter which stated that a copy of the decision record was attached. The decision record was a departmental briefing paper which the court ruled did not constitute the Minister's actual reasons for decision. The document did set out various matters concerning the respondent's children and was before the Minister at the time the decision was made. Branson J concluded that, 'as the content of the issue document reflects, everything pointed towards the best interests of the children favouring a decision not to cancel the respondent's visa. It would, in my view, be unrealistic to conclude that this was not appreciated by the Minister'.[238]

[17.97] Decision-makers must examine the interests of each affected child individually. The Direction provides that decision-makers are to presume that the best interests of a child are to remain with its parents, but are to consider factors in favour of separation, such as child abuse, neglect, or trauma resulting from the visa holder's conduct. A range of factors must be considered in determining the best interests of a child. These include: the nature and duration of the relationship between the child and the visa holder; the extent to which the visa holder is likely to play a full parental role while the child is a minor; the child's age; whether the child is an Australian citizen or permanent resident, or New Zealand citizen;[239] the likely effect of separation on the child; the existence of other parental figures; the visa holder's impact on the child; the time the child has spent in Australia; any court orders relating to parental access and care; any wishes the child has expressed; whether the child is likely to accompany the person overseas if their visa is cancelled or refused; the circumstances of the probable country of future residence (including health and education standards); and any language or cultural barriers for the child in their probable future country of residence. It is unclear whether the welfare of an unborn child falls within the meaning of 'best interests of the child' in the policy applied pursuant to the character and conduct cancellation provisions. The tribunal has concluded that it does not, based on a reading of the UNCRC.[240] However, the Federal Magistrates Court in *Griffiths v MIMA*[241] appeared more open to a wider interpretation of the UN Convention, concluding that it is within the power of the decision-maker to have regard to the best interests of a child whose birth is anticipated, and this should be considered

---

235   (1998) 150 ALR 608 at 631.
236   *Van Son v MIMIA* [2003] FCA 875; *Chai v MIMIA* [2005] FCA 1460.
237   (2002) 125 FCR 433.
238   Ibid at [77].
239   Indeed the Federal Court has concluded that, while Direction 41 does not specifically refer to children in Australia, this is clearly what is intended and a tribunal's failure to consider the best interests of a child outside of Australia does not amount to jurisdictional error: *Brown v MIAC* [2010] FCA 52 at [41].
240   *Re Ly and MIMA* [2000] AATA 339.
241   (2003) 176 FLR 272 at [108].

as a primary consideration. An appeal from this decision was allowed by the Full Federal Court, although on other grounds.[242] This has led the tribunal to take the approach, contrary to the Federal Magistrate's dicta, that the interests of an unborn child are properly had regard to as a relevant consideration, other than a 'primary consideration'.[243]

[17.98] The ruling in *MIEA v Teoh*[244] in 1995 heightened consciousness within the AAT of the rights of the innocent parties who are affected by the decision to deport.[245] The case also increased awareness of international legal obligations assumed by Australia and how these affect the exercise of statutory discretions in the domestic sphere. The reviewers have had to consider the interface between the power to deport criminal permanent residents and the obligation not to 'refoule' a recognised refugee to a country where he or she faces persecution. The lapse into criminality may be an easy one – and in some cases understandable – for people accustomed to living on the fringes of society, or who are bereft of friends and family networks. In the controversial case of *Re Jia Le Geng*,[246] the AAT showed that it was prepared to take a compassionate approach to one such individual. Le was a fugitive from China who had been involved in demonstrations in Tiananmen Square in 1989. He was convicted of serious sex offences against his former lover who had stolen his savings to feed her gambling addiction and who had left him for another man. In other cases, however, both the AAT and the Federal Court have taken a strict approach to refugee offenders, invoking the public interest/national security exception to the non-refoulement obligation contained in the Convention and Protocol Relating to the Status of Refugees (the Refugee Convention).[247]

[17.99] Direction 41 instructs decision-makers under s 501 to consider all relevant international obligations.[248] These include the non-refoulement obligations in the Refugee Convention. In relation to the International Covenant on Civil and Political Rights (ICCPR), decision-makers must consider whether, 'as a necessary or foreseeable consequence of their removal from Australia, the person would face a real risk of violation of their rights under Article 6 (right to life), or Article 7 (freedom from torture and cruel, inhuman or degrading treatment or punishment), or face the death penalty, no matter whether lawfully imposed (Second Optional Protocol)'.[249] Decision-makers are also required to specifically consider Australia's obligations under the Convention Against Torture and other Cruel, Inhuman or Degrading

---

242 *MIMIA v Griffiths* [2004] FCAFC 22.
243 *Romero and MIAC* [2010] AATA 196.
244 (1995) 183 CLR 273, discussed in Chapter 4.2.1.
245 See, for example, *Re Francis and DIEA* (1996) 42 ALD 555. See also *Re 'WAG' and MIMA* (1996) 44 ALD 663 – cases involving issues of character (s 501) exclusions.
246 *Jia Le Geng and MIMA* (1996) 42 ALD 700. This case went ultimately to the High Court where the Minister's ruling that the man be removed was upheld. See the discussion above at [17.24].
247 *Convention Relating to the Status of Refugees* 189 UNTS 137 (adopted 28 July 1951, entered into force 22 April 1954). See, for example, *Re Todea* (1994) 2 AAR 470; *Bengescue v MIEA* (1994) 35 ALD 429; *Dhayakpa v MIEA* (1995) 62 FCR 556; and *Vabaza v MIMA* [1997] FCA 148. This issue is discussed at Chapter 14.3.
248 Direction 41 at [10(d)].
249 Ibid at [10.4.3(1)(a)]. See *International Covenant on Civil and Political Rights*, opened for signature 16 December 1966, 999 UNTS 172 (entered into force 23 March 1976).

Treatment or Punishment (CAT).[250] The Minister has directed that if removal from Australia 'would amount to refoulement under the ICCPR or the CAT', the person is not to be removed, regardless of any other factors.[251]

[17.100] Again, it is unclear whether this occurs in practice. In 2006, the Ombudsman found that decision-makers often fail to identify what weight was given to a consideration, and that visas were often cancelled without explanation, when primary considerations, like the best interests of the child, suggested that the visa should not be cancelled.[252] As Savitri Taylor[253] and Michelle Foster[254] document, Australia's policies and practices in deporting or removing very long-term permanent residents raise many questions about its compliance with a raft of obligations it has assumed under international law. Cases where deportees have died or suffered grievously upon removal raise issues about the right to life and the right not to be subjected to cruel, humiliating or degrading treatment. If arguments on these points have generally failed,[255] so too have attempts to assert that removal constitutes double punishment, contrary to the *ne bis in idem* principle enshrined in Art 14(7) of the ICCPR.[256] Perhaps the area where Australian practice has departed most sharply from that of other developed countries is in the acknowledgement of the right to family life.[257] As Foster documents, the factors that must be considered in s 501 visa cancellations and removals are considerably narrower than those prescribed by the European Court of Human Rights in respect of Art 8 of the European Convention on Human Rights.[258]

[17.101] By way of postscript to Foster's excellent analysis, one further comment could be made about the operation of Australia's character and conduct policies. Having signed and ratified the UN's newest human rights treaty – the Convention on the Rights of Persons with Disabilities[259] – consideration needs to be given to the implications this instrument may have for Australia. As noted earlier, many of the long-term permanent residents convicted of serious crimes and removed in recent years are persons suffering from mental (and sometimes physical) disabilities. Their removal from Australia could well be seen to be in breach of both the

---

250 *Convention against Torture and Other Cruel, Inhuman or Degrading Treatment or Punishment*, opened for signature 10 December 1984, 1465 UNTS 85 (entered into force 26 June 1987).
251 Ibid at [10.4.3(1)(c)].
252 See Commonwealth Ombudsman, above n 9, at 26.
253 Savitri Taylor, 'Exclusion From Protection of Persons of Bad Character: Is Australia Fulfilling its Treaty Based Non-refoulement Obligations?' (2002) 8(1) *Australian Journal of Human Rights* 83.
254 Foster, above n 2, at Part III, 503ff.
255 See Arts 6 and 7 of the ICCPR. See *AB v MIAC* (2007) 96 ALD 53 and *Cockrell v MIAC* (2007) 100 ALD 52 on the Federal Court's view of (the immateriality of) arguments to this effect.
256 See the discussion in Foster, above n 2, at Part III B, 507ff.
257 See the right not to suffer arbitrary interference with his or her family (Art 17) and the right to protection of the family by the state (Art 23 of the ICCPR). See also Art 9 of UNCRC.
258 Opened for signature 4 November 1950, 213 UNTS 221 (entered into force 3 September 1953). See Foster, above n 2, at Part III C, 511ff. See also the author's discussion of the individual's right to 'one's own country' and to other rights enshrined under international human rights law in Part IV A, 514ff.
259 See *Convention on the Rights of Persons with Disabilities* (New York, 30 March 2007) [2008] ATS 12 (entered into force for Australia 16 August 2008).

17.5 A free and confident nation?

> The expression 'the best interests of Australia' leaves much open to judgment. It is my view that in the application of policy as stated that expression is to be understood not in a narrow and restricted sense, but as extending to such interests broadly regarded, and embracing, on occasion and according to circumstances, the taking of decisions by reference to a liberal outlook appropriate to a free and confident nation.[261]

> Over the last 24 years I have watched this area of immigration law slide into something light-years away from '…a liberal outlook appropriate to a free and confident nation'. Successive Immigration Ministers from both sides of politics have pandered to populist radio shock-jocks and have refused to leave the review of character decisions to an impartial tribunal. They have vied to be seen as the toughest on crime and have pursued ever stronger legislation to expel what they regard as the 'criminal' alien from our midst.[262]

[17.102] The anonymous and undignified death of long-term permanent resident Andrew Moore on a London street in December 2009 marked a particular low point in Australian immigration history. Mr Moore was deported in spite of the policy issued in June 2009 that now directs decision-makers to consider the length of a person's tenure in Australia, their family and other ties, as well as matters such as a person's health and wellbeing. He was removed in spite of his evident ill-health and mental and physical frailty. The decision was defended as an 'operational matter'; the death marked with outrage by one journalist but otherwise invoking little comment.[263]

[17.103] The jurisprudence concerning long-term permanent residents convicted of serious crimes is extensive, complex and quite divided. On one side are those determined to assert or affirm ministerial control over non-citizens and to underscore the privilege and contingent status of these people. On the other are those who have attempted to confront the exclusionary rhetoric of the right wing media commentators. They have done so in the name of human rights, basic dignity and responsible behaviour befitting a free and confident nation. The battle has been won

---

260 Articles 10 to 23 and Art 29 of this Convention guarantee the right to life; to protection in situations of risk and humanitarian emergencies; to equal protection before the law including legal capacity and access to justice; to liberty and security of the person; to freedom from torture or degrading treatment; to freedom from exploitation, violence or abuse; to protection of personal integrity; to liberty of movement and nationality; to freedom of expression and opinion, including access to information; to respect for privacy; to the rights to marry, to parent children and to participate in family life.
261 *Re Chan and MIEA* (1977) 17 ALR 432 at 434.
262 Michael Clothier, 'Character Provisions', address to Leo Cussen Institute, 20 February 2002, paper on file with authors.
263 See Joel Gibson, 'Deported, ill … and dead days later', *Sydney Morning Herald*, 7 December 2009, at 1. Gibson followed this article with a second on 8 December, *Sydney Morning Herald*, at 3. See also Michael Grewcock, 'The Detention and Removal of "Non-citizen" Prisoners: Some Recent Cases' (2010) 44 *Immigration Review* [622] at 9.

most resoundingly by the politicians whose power to determine who enters and remains in Australia has been confirmed and re-confirmed by the High Court. While it is now clear that parliament *can* make laws to remove from Australia even the most 'absorbed' of non-citizens, the time has surely come to ask whether it *should* make such laws.

[**17.104**] In the face of confronting crimes, it is easy for politicians to follow the lynch mob, throwing the rule book after pitch fork and scythe to ensure the exile of criminal non-citizens. Australia is not the only country to develop a disproportionately harsh response to 'bad aliens'.[264] As we acknowledged at the outset, returning to a more balanced and humane approach in this complex and fraught area presents difficult political challenges. In opposition, Coalition politicians are both keen to defend their legacy and alive to the electoral potential of denouncing the government for being soft on criminal migrants. The publication of Direction 41 in June 2009 did mark a change in direction. The experience of Andrew Moore suggests, however, that *policy* changes alone will not affect real transformation of decisional outcomes and culture within a bureaucracy. As long as the law permits the removal of very long-term permanent residents and throws the onus on prospective deportees to show why they should be allowed to remain in the country, one can expect the deportation of vulnerable individuals like Andrew Moore to continue.

[**17.105**] It is well to note that for most of Australia's history politicians have taken the view that individuals who spend their formative years in this country should rightly be the responsibility of Australia.[265] However challenging, it is our view that statutory change is required to reinstate the 10-year rule so as to render immune from removal permanent residents who have become truly absorbed into the Australian community – diverse and imperfect as that community is.

---

264 See Stephen Legomsky, 'The New Path of Immigration Law: Asymmetric Incorporation of Criminal Justice Norms' (2007) 64(2) *Washington and Lee Law Review* 469; and Juliet Stumpf, 'The Crimmigration Crisis: Immigrants, Crime and Sovereign Power' (2006) 56 *American University Law Review* 367. For a literature review of this issue in America, see note 1 in the Legomsky article.

265 See the discussion in Part 17.2 above.

PART VIII Appeals and Judicial Review

18

Immigration Appeals – Merits Review

18.1 Introduction

[18.01] Merits review is a process that involves the establishment of a body or bodies empowered to look at the whole of an administrative process, from the collection of evidence through to the reasoning process used in reaching a decision. Review bodies can be endowed with different powers that range from making recommendations to the making of a substitute decision. A common feature of this form of review or appeal is that the reviewer is said to 'stand in the shoes' of the original decision-maker, often with co-extensive powers to assemble evidence and to consider the application of the law to the factual findings made.[1] Although empowered to make rulings on questions of both fact and law, another characteristic of merits review bodies is that they cannot make final determinations on points of law – this being the province of the courts in judicial review.[2]

[18.02] This chapter begins with a brief account of the development of the system for the merits review of decisions involving immigration, refugees and Australian citizenship. The chapter continues with a discussion of the role played by the federal Ombudsman and the Australian Human Rights Commission as avenues for redress in cases of maladministration or breach of human rights. This is followed in Part 18.4 by an extended examination of the jurisprudence that has developed around the operation of the two most significant tribunals in this area: the Migration Review Tribunal (MRT) and the Refugee Review Tribunal (RRT). This part draws on principles of procedural fairness or natural justice developed through the judicial review of migration decisions and for this reason should be read in conjunction with Chapter 19.

18.2 A brief history of the merits review of migration, refugee and citizenship decisions

[18.03] The idea that government departments should be subject to a range of external supervision mechanisms took root in the 1960s and 1970s.[3] Although legislation

---

1 See *Drake v MIEA* (1979) 24 ALR 577 at 589 and the discussion in Chapter 19.1, below.
2 See, for example, *Craig v South Australia* (1995) 184 CLR 163 at 176, 179. See also *Shi v Migration Agents Registration Authority* (2008) 235 CLR 286.
3 Commonwealth Administrative Review Committee, *Report*, Parliamentary Paper No 144 of 1971 (Kerr Committee Report); Committee on Administrative Discretions, *Final Report*, Parliamentary Paper No 316

establishing the federal Administrative Appeals Tribunal (AAT) in 1977[4] allowed for a limited form of review of a narrow range of migration decisions,[5] immigration seems to have been one of the last areas of administrative law to experience the revolution that took place in those years. It was not until 1989 that the first (quasi-) independent tribunal specialising in immigration was created. The Immigration Review Tribunal (IRT) began operation almost 15 years after the Social Security Appeals Tribunal heard its first case. In light of the controversies that surrounded this area of public administration at the turn of the Millennium, one might be forgiven for surmising that Australians have always regarded the control of immigration as one of the last bastions of the executive branch of government. As we explore below, the history of administrative review in this area is one characterised by a persistent reluctance to allow for truly independent decision-making. Interestingly, the delay in extending the scope of administrative review into immigration may well have had something to do with the AAT's vigorous assertion of independence from government policy in the earliest deportation cases.[6]

18.2.1 Review of decisions by the AAT and the 'Section 203' Commissioner

[18.04] The political sensitivity of decisions made to deport or remove permanent residents convicted of serious crime was reflected in the fact that such quasi 'tenured' migrants were the first to benefit from the establishment of a formal merits review system. To a certain extent, migrants considered by the government as having most entitlement or as most desirable continue to enjoy the most expansive access to administrative review.

[18.05] Review by the AAT was available from the inception of that body for decisions made to deport certain permanent residents convicted of serious crimes under s 12 (now s 200) of the *Migration Act 1958* (Cth). In more recent years the migration jurisdiction of the tribunal has been increased to include decisions relating to citizenship; registration as a migration agent; certain business visas; and the cancellation of visas on grounds of bad character or conduct.

[18.06] As noted in the previous chapter, the limitation in the range of the AAT's powers in the migration field was reinforced by the fact that, until 1992, it could do no more than affirm a deportation order or recommend the revocation of a decision. The AAT's function is to review a deportation decision so as to determine on the material before it the correct or preferable decision.[7] This enables applicants to present their case in person and to hear and answer the arguments raised by the Department.

---

of 1973 (Canberra: AGPS, 1973) (Bland Committee Report); *Prerogative Writ Procedures: Report of Committee of Review*, Parliamentary Paper No 56 of 1973 (Canberra: AGPS, 1973) (Ellicott Committee Report).

4   The *Administrative Appeals Tribunal Act 1975* (Cth) (*AAT Act*) was passed in 1975 but the tribunal did not begin operations until two years later.
5   See *AAT Act*, s 44; and Jennifer M Sharpe, *Administrative Appeals Tribunal* (Sydney: Law Book Company, 1986).
6   See *Re Becker and MIEA* (1977) 1 ALD 158 and *Re Drake and MIEA (No 2)* (1979) 2 ALD 634, discussed below at [18.07].
7   See *Drake v MIEA* (1979) 24 ALR 577; and Geoff Warburton, 'The Rights of Non-Citizens in Australia' (1986) 9 *UNSW Law Journal* 90.

[18.07] Although each case is reviewed on its merits, the requirement that the tribunal supply written reasons for its decisions has allowed a considerable body of jurisprudence to develop around s 200 of the Act.[8] Early tribunal decisions had a significant impact on both the articulation of government policy and on the quality and consistency of departmental decision-making.[9] It is regrettable that successive governments have chosen not to extend the tribunal's jurisdiction to other migration decisions as recommended by the Administrative Review Council (ARC) and others in the 1980s.[10]

[18.08] The AAT's early effectiveness as a reviewing body was reflected in the general acceptance by successive Ministers of its rulings.[11] Before 1986, only two AAT rulings had not been followed by the Minister, and in both cases supervening events led to the cancellation of the deportation orders. This was in spite of the fact that, in some years, the AAT recommended the revocation of more deportation orders than it affirmed.[12] Over the years, the statistics reveal a much more conservative tribunal evolving. For example, between 1993 and 1997, the AAT overturned only 15 deportation orders out of a total of 157 made by the Minister. These figures reflect the controversy surrounding criminal deportations in the early 1990s and the seriousness with which the tribunal has performed its task after being given determinative powers in 1992. The adoption of a more conservative approach was not enough to save the tribunal from a wholesale assault on its powers after the change of government in 1996. As detailed in Chapter 17, by the turn of the Millennium the old criminal deportation jurisdiction of the AAT had been rendered virtually obsolete by a regime that restored to the Minister sweeping powers to cancel visas – both permanent and temporary – on grounds of general conduct and bad character.

[18.09] Permanent residents under threat of deportation on security grounds, who receive an adverse security assessment under s 202 of the Act, have a right to apply to the Security Appeals Division of the AAT.[13] Under s 203 of the Act, the specially appointed Commissioner is given power to investigate the merits of a decision to deport a permanent resident who has committed certain offences under the *Crimes Act 1914* (Cth). The Minister may not deport a permanent resident under ss 200 and 203 unless the accused fails to make a request for a Commissioner to review the case, or does not attend the appointed hearing; or unless the Commissioner upholds the decision to deport.[14] Although less attractive than AAT review, the Commissioner system offers some procedural advantages. There is discretion to conduct a formal

---

8   See *AAT Act*, ss 28 and 37 and Chapter 17 above.
9   See *Re Becker and MIEA* (1977) 1 ALD 158 and *Re Drake and MIEA (No 2)* (1979) 2 ALD 634. These cases led to the articulation of policy which was virtually non-existent at the time the first of these cases was decided.
10 See Administrative Review Council (ARC), *Report No 25: Review of Migration Decisions* (Canberra: AGPS, 1985) (ARC, *Report No 25*) at [246]-[250], recommendation 20; and Committee to Advise on Australia's Immigration Policies, *Final Report* (Vol 1) (Canberra: AGPS, 1985) (CAAIP Report) at 115.
11 ARC, *Report No 25*, ibid, at [79].
12 In 1986, the AAT affirmed 10 orders and recommended the revocation of 15: see DIEA, *Review '88* (Canberra: DIEA, 1989) at 116.
13 *Migration Act 1958* (Cth), ss 200 and 500.
14 Ibid, s 203(8).

hearing, 'without regard to legal forms'.[15] Provision is made for legal representation and for the examination and cross-examination of witnesses. The Commissioner is bound also to make a written report to the Minister, although deportees may find it difficult to obtain a statement of reasons for the Commissioner's decision.[16]

18.2.2 The introduction of generalist review of migration decision-making

[18.10] Formal review of the merits of certain general migration decisions[17] was instituted in January 1982 with the creation of the quasi-independent Immigration Review Panels (IRPs), which also operated as a recommendatory body for the Minister. There was no statutory basis for any of these non-statutory review bodies or the work they performed. Cases were reviewed on paper and applicants could neither correspond with the bodies nor adduce oral evidence, although the IRPs, at their discretion, could take evidence if they regarded such steps as essential for their deliberations. The IRPs were criticised for their inappropriate membership, their inadequate procedures, as well as for their perceived bias in favour of the Department. When the ARC conducted its review of the migration jurisdiction in 1985, it was estimated that some 88 per cent of the recommendations made by the panels favoured the Department.[18]

[18.11] The absence of a comprehensive system for the review of cases on their merits was responsible (at least in part) for the long-standing perception of the Immigration Department as a law unto itself.[19] The frustration experienced by disgruntled applicants before the 1989 legislative changes was reflected in the reliance placed on the most traditional avenue of redress: petition to the Minister or to the Department. As the ultimate repository of power, the Minister was seen as the last hope of having a decision overturned. Throughout the 1980s, Ministers received, on average, over 12,000 representations each year concerning individual cases.[20] Immigration petitions constituted (and still constitute) a large part of the workload of many politicians, even though they have a poor success rate in interceding with the Minister or the Department.[21] In the past, cases were brought before parliament itself in an attempt to sway the Minister through a motion by one or other House.

15　Ibid, s 203(6).
16　See Warburton, above n 7, at 106 and above, Chapter 17 at [17.09].
17　The panels sat with three members and reviewed a narrow range of decisions dealing with migrant entry to Australia from within the country and from abroad. The range of reviewable decisions was reduced from 13 to five over the course of the decade. In 1989 the five classes were: refusal of sponsorship or entry of a sponsored relative (other than refugee and Special Humanitarian Program cases); refusal of permanent residence to persons lawfully in Australia; 'return endorsement' decisions; grant of temporary rather than permanent residence to the holder of a visa; and refusal of a further temporary entry permit to persons lawfully in Australia or cancellation of a temporary entry permit.
18　See ARC, *Report No 25*, above n 10, at [64]ff.
19　See the discussion above, Chapter 5.2.
20　See ARC, *Twelfth Annual Report 1987-88* (Canberra: AGPS, 1989) at 50; and ARC, *Report No 25*, above n 10, at [120].
21　See ARC, *Report No 25*, above n 10, at [81]-[82], [120]-[121].

Few met with any success, given the reality of voting patterns determined on party lines.[22]

[18.12] Pressure to replace the panels with a more serious review authority came from a number of sources. Apart from the dissatisfaction of the users, the system coped badly with the rise in the number of review actions that followed the tightening of immigration policies in the late 1980s. An attempt was made in September 1987 to improve the situation by increasing the number of panel members from 32 to 159 and by introducing a $240 impost on appeals.[23] However, the appeal fee proved to be an embarrassment to the government because legislation was never passed to sanction the measure.[24] After a complaint was made to the Ombudsman in 1988, the then Minister was forced to concede that 'the better view' was that the fee was being collected illegally.[25] To remedy the situation, the government announced a scheme whereby persons wishing to challenge an adverse decision were required to make a second application for the visa or permit sought. The arrangements were known as the Regulation Second Application Scheme. The resultant 'Second Applications' continued to be reviewed by the panels as if they were appeals on the merits of the original decision. It was clear, however, that the measure could be only a temporary one. The solution lay in the creation of the IRT.

18.2.3 Migration Internal Review Office and the Immigration Review Tribunal

[18.13] The jurisdiction of the Migration Internal Review Office (MIRO) and Immigration Review Tribunal (IRT) was much broader than that of the old panels.[26] In reviewing a decision, both stood in the same position as the original decision-maker, with powers to affirm, vary or set aside the decision or to remit the matter for re-determination by the Department. Where an appellant was unsuccessful, both the MIRO and the IRT were required to give reasons for their decisions. The MIRO retained the old panels' function of reviewing cases on the basis of written submissions only, although it could interview applicants. It was subject to strict time limits, which could not be either waived or extended. Periods were specified also for the time allowed an applicant to respond to requests for further information. The detail

---

22 See Stephen Churches, 'Justice and the Executive Discretion in Australia' [1980] *Public Law* 397 at 416-17; and Peter W Hogg, 'Judicial Review of Action by the Crown Representative' (1969) 43 *Australian Law Journal* 215 at 218-19.
23 See DIEA, *Review '88*, above n 12, at 67-9.
24 The Crown – or the government – may only levy money for its own use if this is done with the express authority of parliament: see *Attorney-General v Wilts United Dairies* (1921) 37 TLR 884 at 886; affirmed (1922) 38 TLR 781 (HL).
25 See Senator Ray, Commonwealth Parliamentary Debates, *Hansard*, Senate, Vol 133, 3 March 1989, at 412; Senator Jenkins, ibid, 7 March 1989, at 532-3; Commonwealth and Defence Force Ombudsman, *Annual Report 1988-89* (Canberra: AGPS, 1989) at 87-9; Mary Crock, 'Fees For Immigration Appeals: Coming Legal or Not' (1988) 13 *Legal Service Bulletin* 83; and Mary Crock, 'Running a Test Case: A Taxing Problem for Migrants' (1988) 62 *Law Institute Journal* 515.
26 However, there are some decisions that are not covered that were reviewable by these authorities: most notably, decisions concerning applications made on humanitarian grounds. As the first level of review, the MIRO had jurisdiction to consider most visa decisions made in Australia, together with decisions made overseas that involved an Australian sponsor: *Migration Act*, ss 337-338.

and rigidity of these requirements reflected the malaise that developed in the early 1990s about the unconscionable delays experienced in the processing of refugee appeals.

[18.14] The IRT was the second tier review authority for persons wishing to appeal against a general migration decision. For the first time applicants were given the right to appear in person to argue their case. However, as we explain below, the quasi-inquisitorial procedures of the tribunal have limited the ability of applicants to be represented or to examine or cross-examine witnesses.

[18.15] In turn, the IRT's jurisdiction and powers were broader than those of the MIRO. Where internal review was not available, the IRT could review directly: decisions affecting persons in immigration detention; certain change of status decisions; decisions made by a delegate of the Minister at the level of Secretary or person holding or acting in a Senior Executive Service position; decisions to cancel visas; and decisions to keep non-citizens in custody.[27] Once again, the Regulations set strict time limits for the lodging of review applications and for the submission of evidence.[28]

[18.16] The legislation governing IRT review was unusual in the curious mix of procedural discretion and the substantive constraints of the law governing the grant of visas. In spite of broad powers given to the tribunal to determine its own procedures, its ability to decide appeals 'according to the substantial justice and merits of a case' was subject always to the legislation governing its decision-making.[29] Neither the MIRO nor IRT could go outside the terms of the Act and Regulations.[30] Under what was s 118(3), the tribunal was forbidden from 'purporting to grant an entry permit on humanitarian grounds'. Section 116 ensured that the tribunal had no discretion to extend the time for lodging appeals and could not consider appeals lodged out of time. The apparent obligation to grant applicants a hearing where a 'favourable' decision could not be made on the papers under s 129 could also be illusory as the phrase 'decision favourable to the applicant' was defined to include decisions mandated by the terms of the legislation.

[18.17] By the mid to late 1990s, the operational statistics for the MIRO reveal an organisation that seemed to have declined in its productivity and effectiveness, even where quite dramatic staff cuts are taken into consideration. By the time it was abolished in 1999, determinations by the internal departmental body were costing on average $591 per case, with average processing times of around four months. While

---

27   *Migration Act*, ss 346 and 349, read with former reg 4.09 of the *Migration Regulations 1994* (Cth).
28   The limits on applications for review replicated those for the MIRO, varying between 21 and 70 days according to the location of the applicant for review. In the case of persons in immigration detention, persons appealing a decision to refuse a Bridging visa and persons whose visas were cancelled, applications for IRT review had to be lodged within two days of notification of the decision in question. Those appealing against the cancellation of a visa could be granted an extension of five days in which to appeal: see former reg 4.10. The Regulations provided for the expedited review of certain decisions involving family members (reg 4.23); visa cancellations (reg 4.24); and decisions relating to certain applicants in immigration detention: reg 4.25. For its part, the IRT was required to make decisions involving Bridging visas within seven days: see reg 4.26. Many of these time limits still apply to review by the MRT.
29   *Migration Act*, s 123(2).
30   Ibid, s 349.

the IRT was overturning, on average, 39 per cent of the decisions on appeal, the overturn rate of the MIRO was running at 19.97 per cent.[31] In view of the cost of the second stage review, a preferable situation was to see these statistics reversed, with the majority of decisions reversed at first instance. In the result, the MIRO and IRT were replaced in 1999 with a single review authority – the Migration Review Tribunal.

18.2.4 The Migration Review Tribunal

[18.18] The Migration Review Tribunal (MRT) is an independent statutory body with jurisdiction co-extensive to that of the former IRT. That is, it reviews the merits of a range of migration decisions relating to the grant and cancellation of visas, with the significant exceptions of refugee applications (which are reviewable by the RRT), decisions to refuse or cancel a visa based on character grounds, and decisions to deport a permanent resident (which are both reviewable by the AAT). The layer of internal review previously performed by the MIRO was abolished, with pre-screening processes now undertaken by the MRT. Changes to the powers and procedures of the review bodies (both the MRT and RRT) were also made in 1999, discussed in more detail in Part 18.3 below. These reforms were implemented largely with the objectives of cost saving and increased efficiency.[32] However, taking the first stage of review outside the Department was also seen to increase the real and perceived independence of the merits review process.[33] Whether this has been sustained in the longer term, however, is debateable.

[18.19] The powers and procedures of the MRT generally reflect those of its predecessor, the IRT. It has the power to affirm a decision under review; remit the matter for reconsideration; vary a decision; or set it set aside and substitute a new decision.[34] Like the RRT, the MRT's statutory objective is to provide a mechanism of review that is 'fair, just, economical, informal and quick'.[35] In doing so, the MRT is not bound by technicalities, legal forms or rules of evidence, but must act 'according to substantial justice and the merits of the case'.[36] At the same time, however, the MRT's discretionary powers are constrained by the legislation governing its decision-making. Strict time limits still apply for the lodging of review applications and for the submission of evidence. These limits for applications vary between two and 70 days, depending on the location and circumstances of the applicant. In the case of persons in immigration detention, persons appealing a decision to refuse a Bridging visa and persons whose visas are cancelled, applications for MRT review must be lodged within two

---

31 Statistics for the period of 1 July 1997 to 31 December 1997 supplied by Mr John Eastwood, Director, Program and Performance Reporting, DIMA. See IRT, *Annual Report* (Canberra: IRT, 1997) at 12. The IRT figure was down from an average of 52 per cent in 1995-96.
32 See Michael Chaaya, 'Proposed Changes to the Review of Migration Decisions: Sensible Reform Agenda or Political Expediency?' (1997) 19 *Sydney Law Review* 547. Note that the fees for the new appeal body were raised to $1400: see *Migration Regulations*, reg 4.13.
33 See Committee for the Review of the System for Review of Migration Decisions, *Non Adversarial Review of Migration Decisions: The Way Forward* (Canberra: AGPS, 1992) at 47-52.
34 *Migration Act*, s 348.
35 Ibid, s 353(1).
36 Ibid, s 353(2).

days of notification of the decision in question.[37] The Regulations provide for the expedited review of certain decisions involving family members,[38] visa cancellations[39] and decisions relating to certain applicants in immigration detention.[40] The tribunal again has no discretion to extend the time for lodging appeals and cannot consider appeals lodged out of time.[41]

18.2.5 Refugee status appeals

[18.20] As explained in Chapter 12, a regime both for making formal determinations of refugee status and for review of the merits of such decisions was instituted in March 1978 in response to the arrival of boats carrying refugees from the conflict in Vietnam. The Determination of Refugee Status (DORS) Committee was a system established by ministerial fiat that operated outside of the auspices of the migration legislation for more than a decade after its inception.[42]

[18.21] It was not until 1993 that the system for determining refugee appeals was brought into line with the processes governing general migration appeals. The decision not to touch this area of the law when the major reforms were made to the Act in 1989 was a remarkable one, if only because the prevailing decisional mechanisms were so inefficient. The DORS Committee not only heard applications for refugee status – it functioned also as a review authority, ruling on cases sent back to it for reconsideration. It was perhaps the least satisfactory of all the review arrangements as the committee did no more than reconsider, on the papers, its own decision. No provision was made for appellants to present oral arguments at a formal hearing of the case or otherwise to correspond with the committee.[43]

[18.22] In 1991, the two tasks of hearing applications and determining appeals were separated. The structure of primary decision-making remained substantially the same, except that the secretariat of the old DORS Committee made its recommendations to the Minister directly, instead of advising the committee. Where refugee status was denied, applicants had a right to appeal to the re-named Refugee Status Review Committee. This committee was comprised of representatives from the Department as well as from the Departments of Foreign Affairs and Trade and Attorney General. It also included a nominee representing the Refugee Council of Australia and an observer appointed by the United Nations Human Rights Commissioner (UNHCR). The committee's function was to review, on the papers, cases rejected by the DORS officers at first instance. Its task was to recommend to the Minister the grant or refusal of refugee status and the results that should flow from such decision.[44]

---

37 *Migration Regulations*, reg 4.10.
38 Ibid, reg 4.23.
39 Ibid, reg 4.24.
40 Ibid, reg 4.25
41 *Migration Act*, s 347.
42 See the discussion above at Chapter 12.3.1.
43 See ARC, *Report No 25*, above n 10, at [74]-[75], where the review function of the Committee was criticised.
44 For refugees, there was a choice in recommending the grant of a domestic protection entry permit or visa which allowed temporary residence for four years (see *Migration Regulations 1989* (Cth) (*1989*

[18.23] The committee also had a recommendatory function in respect of applicants who did not meet the requirements for the grant of refugee status. Providing the applicants were not prohibited entrants[45] or, after 1 July 1991, unlawful non-citizens, the committee could advise the Minister to grant or refuse a permit (now visa) on humanitarian grounds. The guidelines for the exercise of the Minister's residual discretion under what was s 115 of the Act in these cases suggested that humanitarian entry would be granted in exceptional cases only. Applicants had to show that they faced a 'significant threat to personal security on return as a result of targeted actions by persons in the country of return'.[46]

[18.24] This system for the review of refugee status decisions had many drawbacks. Delays in processing were caused by the cumbersome requirements generated by the need to give applicants the opportunity to respond in writing to matters raised, or decisions proposed to be made, by the Refugee Status Review Committee. As explored in earlier chapters, the inadequacies of the system were exacerbated by events outside Australia which led to a quite dramatic increase in the number of people seeking asylum in Australia between 1989 and 1992. At a time when the courts were becoming increasingly vigilant to ensure the fairness of procedures used in administrative decision-making, the old 'paper' system proved slow and cumbersome to administer and was highly susceptible to judicial review.[47]

[18.25] With hindsight it seems almost self-evident that the oral hearing of refugee appeals would be faster and more efficient than the paper warfare that developed in some of the cases of the early 1990s. In practice, however, the government was reluctant to instigate oral appeals for refugee claimants. Ironically, while it won many of the court battles where the litigants tried to force such oral hearings[48] it lost the procedural 'war'. The curial prerequisites for procedural fairness in refugee cases, where all exchanges had to be reduced to writing, proved ultimately to be too costly and onerous for the administration.

[18.26] The RRT was established in July 1993. Like the MRT, it is a quasi-inquisitorial body with considerable powers to set the parameters of any appeal. However, this discretion has also been affected by the introduction of codes of procedure for the conduct of reviews. Under s 425 of the *Migration Act*, the RRT must grant an oral hearing where a favourable determination of a case cannot be made on the papers. Applicants have no right to be represented, although they may obtain the assistance

---

Regulations), regs 117A and 117B); or a refugee (temporary) entry permit, which gave the holder immediate access to permanent residence (see *1989 Regulations*, regs 118I and 142A). Between 1991 and November 1993, this choice was removed, so that all refugees were granted four-year temporary permits: reg 119I was repealed by SR 285 of 1991, reg 56.

45 That is, persons detained before 'entry' in to Australia under ss 88 or 89 of the Act, and held in custody under ss 54A-54H of the Act: see above, Chapter 4.1.
46 See MPS 15/91 and Attachments A and B, dated 15 March 1991, and *1989 Regulations 1989*, reg 8E.
47 See Mary Crock, 'Judicial Review and Part 8 of the *Migration Act*: Necessary Reform or Overkill?' (1996) 18 *Sydney Law Review* 267; and Kathryn Cronin, 'A Culture of Control: An Overview of Immigration Policy-making' in James Jupp and Maria Kabala (eds), *The Politics of Australian Immigration* (Canberra: AGPS, 1993).
48 See, for example, *Zhang de Yong v MILGEA* (1993) 45 FCR 384; *Chen v MILGEA* (1994) 48 FCR 591; and *Li Shi Ping v MILGEA* (1994) 35 ALD 395.

of an interpreter.[49] The RRT has power to affirm a departmental decision; vary the decision; remit a case for reconsideration; or set the ruling aside.[50] It is distinguished from its fellow migration tribunal by the directions that it conduct all hearings 'in private'[51] and that none of its published statements contain material that could be used to identify an applicant or any relative or dependant of an applicant before it: s 431. In carrying out its functions under the Act, the tribunal is enjoined 'to pursue the objective of providing a mechanism for review that is fair, just, economical, informal and quick'. Like the MRT, the RRT is not bound by 'technicalities, legal forms or rules of evidence' and 'must act according to substantial justice and the merits of the case'. Applications for the review of a refusal of a Protection visa are nominally without charge. However, changes to the *Migration Regulations 1994* (Cth) on 1 July 1997 saw the introduction of a $1000 'post-application' fee for persons who fail before the tribunal.[52] The measure is intended to provide a disincentive to frivolous refugee appeals and was initially subject to a two-year sunset clause. It has since become a permanent feature of the refugee appeals regime.

[18.27] A comparison of the operational statistics for the RRT and the IRT in 1997 suggested that the system for determining refugee appeals was both more expensive and less efficient than that of the generalist appeals body.[53] The total budget for the RRT was double that of the IRT, while members processed on average about 75 cases compared with the IRT's per capita rate of 99 cases per annum. Of greater concern to the government, however, was the rate at which unsuccessful applicants before the RRT took their cases on judicial review before the Federal Court and High Court. The litigation statistics at the end of 1997 revealed that refugee claimants accounted for 307 of the 644 active cases before the courts.[54] A dozen years later, this picture had not altered greatly in terms of the ratios between the tribunals, although the volume of cases processed had increased exponentially. By this stage the two tribunals were being treated as one entity.

[18.28] The Annual Report for 2009-10 records that the MRT was funded to decide 7700 cases and made rulings on 7580 matters (an increase of 31% over the previous year). The RRT was funded to decide 3050 cases and made rulings on 2157 (a decrease of 12% over the previous year). The combined appropriation for the two tribunals was $41,172,000.[55] Appeals to the MRT were much more likely to succeed than appeals against adverse asylum rulings. The MRT set aside or remitted the primary (DIAC) decision in 45 per cent of cases decided. The RRT set aside or remitted the primary (DIAC) decision in 24 per cent of cases decided.[56] The RRT statistics represent a decline in the set aside rate, compared with 30 per cent in 2005-06. It is, however, an increase over the previous years of Labor rule where set asides dropped as low as

---

49 *Migration Act*, s 427(6) and (7).
50 Ibid, s 415(2).
51 Ibid, s 429. On the interpretation of this section, see *SZAYW v MIMIA* (2006) 230 CLR 486: the RRT is empowered to hear together cases involving refugee claimants who present with a 'common cause'.
52 See *Migration Regulations*, reg 4.31B, introduced by SR 109 and 185 of 1997.
53 See Chaaya, above n 32, at Table 1.
54 DIMA, *Litigation Report*, December 1997 (Canberra: DIMA, 1998).
55 See MRT/RRT, *Annual Report 2009-2010* (Canberra: MRT/RRT, 2011) at 25-6.
56 Ibid at 33-4.

18%. The data on applications for judicial review continue to show a huge discrepancy between the appeal rates of the two tribunals. The Annual Report provides applications for judicial review as a percentage of total tribunal decisions. When the data on rates for the affirmation of decisions is aggregated against the applications for judicial review, however, the story is different. In 2009-10 the MRT affirmed 2700 cases and had 242 cases go on judicial review. The RRT rejected the appeals of 1540 asylum seekers and had 508 cases go on judicial review (down from 1044 in 2007-08). This would represent a 8.9 per cent appeal rate for the MRT and 32.9 per cent for the RRT.[57] The appeal rate for the RRT is out of all proportion to the rate at which the decisions of any other tribunal in Australia are taken on judicial review. In purely financial terms, appeals from the RRT account for a large part of the government's litigation bill. The statistics provide an important impetus for a more radical overhaul of the merits review system than had yet been proposed at time of writing.

[18.29] The government's problems with the judicial review of refugee status appeals were heightened in late 2010 when the High Court delivered its ruling in *Plaintiff M61/2010E v Commonwealth and Plaintiff M69 of 2010 v Commonwealth*.[58] As explained earlier,[59] the decision to process refugee claims by unauthorised boat arrivals on Christmas Island was predicated originally on the notion that judicial review would not be available to these people. In practice, the Labor government established procedures outside of the *Migration Act* to allow for both 'Refugee Status Assessment' (RSA) and for the 'Independent Merits Review' (IMR) of negative rulings. The IMR is conducted by reviewers employed by the private company, 'Wizard People Pty Ltd'. As we consider further in Chapter 19, the High Court all but abolished the distinction between RRT appeals and the 'offshore' appellate process by ruling that both RSA and IMR decision-makers are bound by common law rules of procedural fairness as well as by other aspects of substantive refugee law.[60]

18.3   Other avenues of redress

[18.30] There are two further bodies outside the Department that can assist in challenging an adverse migration decision. The first of these is the Commonwealth Ombudsman, who receives and acts on complaints made about any matter of maladministration by Commonwealth departments and prescribed authorities.[61] The second is the Australian Human Rights Commission (formerly the Human Rights and Equal Opportunity Commission) which can inquire into administrative acts alleged to be in breach of human rights and mediate in disputes between an individual and a government department or agency.[62] Together with the many investigations undertaken by committees of the Commonwealth Parliament, the numerous investigations and

---

57   Ibid.
58   (2010) 272 ALR 14 (*Plaintiffs M61/ M69*).
59   See Chapter 12.4.2.
60   For a discussion of this case, see Mary Crock and Daniel Ghezelbash, 'Due Process and Rule of Law as Human Rights: The High Court and the "Offshore" Processing of Asylum Seekers' (2011) 18(2) *Australian Journal of Administrative Law* 101.
61   See *Ombudsman Act 1976* (Cth), s 5. See Commonwealth Ombudsman, 'Defective Administration – What is Unreasonable or Unjust?' *Third Annual Report 1979-80*, at 18.
62   *Australian Human Rights Commission Act 1986* (Cth), s 5.

18.3.1 The Commonwealth Ombudsman

[18.31] The homepage of the Commonwealth Ombudsman website provides the following summary of the functions of this office:

> Under the *Ombudsman Act 1976* (Cth), the Commonwealth Ombudsman investigates the administrative actions of Australian Government agencies and officers. An investigation can be conducted as a result of a complaint or on the initiative (or own motion) of the Ombudsman.
>
> The *Ombudsman Act 1976* confers five other roles on the Commonwealth Ombudsman — [These include] the role of Defence Force Ombudsman, to investigate action arising from the service of a member of the Australian Defence Force; the role of Immigration Ombudsman, to investigate action taken in relation to immigration (including immigration detention); and the role of Law Enforcement Ombudsman, to investigate conduct and practices of the Australian Federal Police (AFP) and its members. There are special procedures applying to complaints about AFP officers contained in the *Australian Federal Police Act 1979*. Complaints about the conduct of AFP officers prior to 2007 are dealt with under the *Complaints (Australian Federal Police) Act 1981* (Cth).[63]

[18.32] The Immigration Ombudsman (the Ombudsman) is precluded from investigating actions taken by a Minister personally, by courts or by bodies empowered to take evidence on oath and/or that include a judge as a member.[64] This precludes the investigation of decisions made by a s 14 Commissioner, by the AAT, or by the IRT. Decisions taken by the delegate of the Minister may be scrutinised,[65] as may both the advice tendered to the Minister for the purpose of reaching a decision and the actions taken by the Department in implementing the Minister's orders.[66] While it has its shortcomings, this avenue can be a useful political tool for disgruntled applicants. Interestingly, as the battle royal between the government and the courts has raged on, the government has turned increasingly to the Ombudsman to mediate solutions in difficult cases. In the result, the role and importance of this body has increased considerably over the years.[67]

[18.33] Where an administrative malpractice is identified, the Ombudsman is bound to afford the department in question an opportunity to explain its behaviour before making a critical report to the departmental secretary. In compiling the report, the Ombudsman is empowered to conduct investigations in private;[68] to require answers to questions and the production of specified documents;[69] and to examine witnesses

---

63   See <http://www.ombudsman.gov.au/>.
64   *Ombudsman Act 1976* (Cth), s 5(2).
65   Ibid, s 5(3).
66   Ibid, s 3(3A).
67   See Katrine del Villar, 'Who Guards the Guardians? Recent Developments Concerning the Jurisdiction and Accountability of Ombudsmen' (2003) 36 *AIAL Forum* 25.
68   *Ombudsman Act*, s 8(2). On the operation of investigations, see *Chairperson, Aboriginal and Torres Strait Islander Commission v Commonwealth Ombudsman* (1995) 134 ALR 238.
69   *Ombudsman Act*, s 9.

on oath.⁷⁰ If the recommendations of the report are not followed, the Ombudsman may then report to the Prime Minister and to parliament.⁷¹ Such reports appear to have been taken very seriously by the government and by the Department from the very inception of the office of Ombudsman.

[18.34] The usefulness of the Ombudsman as a review alternative is borne out where other avenues are either not available or are inaccessible. An early example in point is the case of Manjit Kaur, where the applicant sought to challenge the legality of the appeal fee introduced in 1987 (before the establishment of the IRT). In that instance, the Ombudsman's intervention acted as a powerful disincentive to the Department repeating its experiment with non-legislated 'fees for service'.⁷²

[18.35] The parliament's intention that the Ombudsman operate as a supplement to other avenues of review is underscored by the discretion given to decline to investigate a complaint where alternative review is available by a court or tribunal. On this basis, the Ombudsman declined to investigate departmental decisions that were reviewable by the IRPs. The same arrangements apply to the current review bodies, as they do with Federal Court litigation.⁷³ The Ombudsman also declines to handle complaints that can be dealt with more appropriately by other authorities. These cases are identified as matters in which the merits of the decision are in issue, rather than the propriety of the administrative procedures taken.⁷⁴

[18.36] The limitations placed on the Ombudsman's power restrict the usefulness of the office in cases where specific action is required.⁷⁵ The inability to order a stay in the implementation of a deportation order, for example, can render an investigation all but worthless from the point of view of a deportee. This has not prevented the Ombudsman from being used extensively in the migration jurisdiction. The attraction of the office appears to lie in the ability of the Ombudsman to negotiate the settlement of complaints between individuals and the government without the government being embarrassed or burdened by directives or normative rulings. However egregious the maladministration uncovered by the Ombudsman, it is a review system that leaves the government in charge.

[18.37] This is not to say that the office has not caused annoyance over the years. The decision to conduct two 'own-motion' inquiries in 2001 into immigration detention centres⁷⁶ and into the use of State correctional facilities for immigration detainees⁷⁷ are examples.

---

70 Ibid, s 13.
71 Ibid, ss 15-17.
72 Crock, above n 25 (both references).
73 *Ombudsman Act*, s 6(2).
74 See ARC, *Report No 32: Review of the Administrative Decisions (Judicial Review) Act 1977: The Ambit of the Act* (Canberra: AGPS, 1989) at 34-5.
75 See ARC, *Report No 25*, above n 10, at [87]-[89].
76 See *Report of an Own Motion Investigation into DIMA's Detention Centres*, Report No 5 2001, available at <http://www.ombudsman.gov.au/files/investigation_2001_05.pdf>.
77 See *Own Motion Investigation into Immigration Detainees Held in State Correctional Facilities*, March 2001, Report No 06 2001, available at <http://www.ombudsman.gov.au/files/investigation_2001_06.pdf>.

[18.38] From the perspective of immigration, the greatest changes occurred after the scandals that erupted over the discovery in 2005 that the immigration authorities had been detaining and even removing from Australia both permanent residents and citizens. Although the inquiry into the wrongful arrest and detention of Cornelia Rau was conducted by a private individual, Mick Palmer,[78] subsequent inquiries became the responsibility of the office of Ombudsman.[79] The Office's Neil Comrie prepared a report into the wrongful detention and removal from Australia of Australian citizen Vivian Solon-Alvarez.[80] When it was discovered that as many as 240 lawful residents and citizens may have been detained by immigration officials, it was clear that broader measures were required.

[18.39] In June 2005, the government responded by creating the office of Immigration Ombudsman, inserting Part 8C into the *Migration Act*. The amendments provide for the referral to the Ombudsman for review of all persons who have been held in immigration detention for two years or more and for cases to be reviewed thereafter every six months.[81] The Ombudsman is enjoined to give the Minister for Immigration an assessment of the detention arrangements and to make recommendations about appropriate forms of detention for the detainee. The Minister is not bound by any recommendation made.[82] Since 2005, the Ombudsman has published no less than 25 reports relating to immigration detention practices – a veritable collection of shame files in many instances.[83]

[18.40] The creation of a special Immigration Ombudsman was interesting at a number of levels. Most significantly, the office has provided a politically palatable device for the oversight of the most contentious aspect of immigration law and policy. While successive governments have resented judicial review of all and any aspects of migration decision-making, the Ombudsman appears to have been accepted because of the non-normative, negotiable nature of the review function. Even when the Ombudsman's jurisdiction was limited to persons who had been in detention for over two years,[84] the office appears to have played an important role in pushing for more humane and accountable practices in the immigration detention facilities.

18.3.2 The Australian Human Rights Commission

[18.41] The other government agency that has taken a very active role in reviewing both individual migration decisions and the administration of immigration law is the Australian Human Rights Commission (AHRC). The Commission is empowered to

---

78 See Mick Palmer, *Inquiry into the Circumstances of the Immigration Detention of Cornelia Rau*, available at <http://www.immi.gov.au/media/publications/pdf/palmer-report.pdf>.
79 See ARC, *Report No 25*, above n 10.
80 See Inquiry into the Circumstances of the Vivian Alvarez Matter Report under the *Ombudsman Act 1976* by the Commonwealth Ombudsman, Prof John McMillan, of an inquiry undertaken by Mr Neil Comrie AO APM Report No.03 2005 available at <http://www.ombudsman.gov.au/files/investigation_2005_03.pdf>.
81 *Migration Act*, ss 486L and 486M.
82 Ibid, s 486O.
83 See <http://www.ombudsman.gov.au/reports/immigration-detention-review/>.
84 The jurisdiction was extended after the change in government in 2007 to cover persons detained for six months or longer.

inquire into any act or practice that may be inconsistent with or contrary to human rights.[85] Human rights within the Commission's jurisdiction are those defined in eight international instruments that include the International Covenant on Civil and Political Rights; the UN Convention on the Rights of Persons with Disabilities; the Convention on the Rights of the Child; the Declaration on the Rights of Mentally Retarded Persons; and the UN Convention on the Elimination of All Forms of Racial Discrimination.[86] The Commission's functions include the settlement or attempted settlement of disputes through conciliation and, where this is not achieved, the preparation of a report to the minister involved and, ultimately, to parliament.[87] Like the Ombudsman, the Commission has the power to obtain information and documents and to examine witnesses.[88] Failure to comply can result in substantial fines (although this aspect of the Commission's functions involves an application to and an order from the Federal Court). The Commission is bound to assist complainants if they require help in lodging a complaint.[89] Where a department and/or a minister chooses to ignore an attempt at conciliation, however, the Commission has no power to enforce its views on an issue. Like the Ombudsman, it must rely on its credibility in the political arena.

[18.42] In 1999, both the *Human Rights and Equal Opportunity Commission Act 1986* (Cth) (*HREOC Act*, as it then was) and the *Ombudsman Act 1976* (Cth) were amended to ensure that there was no obligation on the Minister or any other officer to provide legal advice to persons in immigration detention, if that advice had not been requested. These amendments were a response to the decision in *Human Rights and Equal Opportunity Commission v Secretary, DIMA*.[90] The Federal Court held that, notwithstanding s 256 of the *Migration Act*, s 20(6)(b) of the *HREOC Act* provided detainees with the right to receive a 'sealed envelope' containing information on legal rights, without a complaint having been made to HREOC. The court also ruled that s 7(3)(b) of the *Ombudsman Act* provided detainees with a similar right to information, regardless of whether the information was requested. Section 193(3) of the *Migration Act* now states that these provisions do not apply to immigration detainees unless they have personally made a complaint to the AHRC (in writing), or to the Ombudsman (orally or in writing).

[18.43] The AHRC, in its various incarnations, has played an active role in the migration field over many years. In as early as 1985, it published a lengthy report on the administration of the Act and found the legislation deficient in a number of areas. It criticised the treatment of unlawful non-citizens and the lack of a proper system for the review of migration cases on their merits.[91] Other reports during the 1980s included an examination of departmental practices in detaining the children

---

85 *Australian Human Rights Commission Act 1986* (Cth), s 11(1)(f).
86 See also the *Racial Discrimination Act 1984* (Cth); and the *Sex Discrimination Act 1984* (Cth).
87 *Australian Human Rights Commission Act 1986*, ss 20(1) and 51(1)(f).
88 Ibid, ss 21-23.
89 Ibid, s 20(5).
90 [1996] FCA 444.
91 Human Rights Commission (HRC), *Report No 13: Human Rights and the Migration Act* (Canberra: AGPS, 1985).

of unlawful non-citizens,[92] and the conditions at the Villawood Detention Centre in Sydney,[93] as well as the policy of excluding disabled family members from the family reunion program.[94] The Commission became a major source of annoyance for the Howard Coalition government with its serial investigations into the detention of asylum seekers. The decision by the Commission to use a line from the national anthem as the title of a major report into the treatment of asylum seekers was not well received.[95] The Commission's report into children in immigration detention[96] played an important role in building pressure for law reform in this area where Australia was most clearly in breach of obligations it had assumed under international human rights law. Like the Ombudsman, the Commission has become a permanent and significant feature of the oversight processes for the immigration bureaucracy.

18.4 The quasi-inquisitorial experiment: The tribunals' manner of operating

[18.44] The specialist migration tribunals represented something of a departure from the norm of administrative review in Australia in the early 1990s in that they were modelled on a quasi-inquisitive process that involves a single tribunal member asking questions of an applicant. The Department of Immigration is not represented at the hearing – an arrangement that has been promoted on many occasions as a model that obviates the need for an applicant to have legal representation.[97] Conversely, the legislation vests almost complete control in the tribunals in the conduct of hearings: applicants have no absolute right to an oral hearing.[98] They have no right to dictate the issues or the evidence that will be discussed; and they have no right to examine or cross-examine witnesses where these are selected by the tribunal.[99] Applicants have no right to be represented by any person, although they do have a right to an interpreter[100] and the tribunal has discretion to permit a representative to attend and speak at a hearing.[101] The legislation creates strict liability offences punishable by substantial terms of imprisonment where a person (other than the applicant) fails to attend a tribunal hearing without excuse or who otherwise acts in contempt of the tribunal.[102]

---

92 HRC, *Report No 8: Deportation and the Family: A Report on the Complaints of Mrs M Roth and Mr CJ Booker* (Canberra: AGPS, 1984); and HRC, *Report No 10: The Human Rights of Australian-Born Children – A Report on the Complaints of Mr and Mrs RC Yeung* (Canberra: AGPS, 1985).

93 HRC, *Report No 6: The Observance of Human Rights at the Villawood Immigration Detention Centre* (Canberra: AGPS, 1983).

94 HRC, *Report No 22: Human Rights, Family Migration and Disabled Family Members* (Canberra: AGPS, 1986).

95 HREOC, *Those Who Come Across the Seas: Detention of Unauthorised Arrivals* (1998), available at <http://www.humanrights.gov.au/human_rights/publications.html>.

96 HREOC, *A Last Resort: The National Inquiry into Children in Immigration Detention* (2004), available at <http://www.humanrights.gov.au/human_rights/publications.html>.

97 See, for example, Senate Legal and Constitutional References Committee, *A Sanctuary Under Review: An Examination of Australia's Refugee and Humanitarian Processes* (Canberra: AGPS, 2000) at 149 (and Ch 5 generally).

98 *Migration Act*, s 360 and Part 5 Div 5 (MRT) and s 425; and Part 7 Div 4 (RRT).

99 Ibid, s 427 (RRT).

100 Ibid, ss 366B and 366C (MRT); and s 427(7) (RRT).

101 Ibid, s 366A (MRT); and s 427 (RRT).

102 Ibid, Part 5 Div 7(MRT); and Part 7 Div 6 (RRT).

[18.45] Paradoxically, the High Court frequently makes reference to the 'inquisitorial' character of the migration tribunals, noting that this differs from the courts' way of operating. However, this court has never actually defined the term 'inquisitorial' with any precision.[103] In *MIAC v SZIAI*,[104] the court noted:

> The relevant ordinary meaning of 'inquisitorial' is 'having or exercising the function of an "inquisitor"', that is to say 'one whose official duty it is to inquire, examine or investigate'. As applied to the Tribunal 'inquisitorial' does not carry that full ordinary meaning. It merely delimits the nature of the Tribunal's functions. They are to be found in the provisions of the *Migration Act*. The core function, in the words of s 414 of the Act, is to 'review the decision' which is the subject of a valid application made to the Tribunal under s 412 of the Act.

[18.46] As we explore in this chapter, there are many aspects of the judiciary's interpretation of the code of procedures governing the migration tribunals that verge on the counter-intuitive. Not the least of these are the lengths taken by the courts to affirm that these 'inquisitorial' tribunals are not burdened with any over-arching duty to inquire into the cases before them.[105]

[18.47] The central problems with the regime, in our view, are the assumptions made that tribunal members are independent of government and that they are neutral arbiters of the cases brought before them. In practice, tribunal members have been affected by what might be termed loosely 'politics' both in the manner of appointment/reappointment[106] and (on occasion) in their decision-making.[107] Where members have been appointed from within the bureaucracy and/or have been placed on relatively short-term contracts the pressure to toe the government line can be considerable. The performance goals set for the tribunals, while ostensibly directed towards efficiency in decision-making, also have the effect of making it more difficult for members to fully consider cases. In the result, users of the tribunals have sometimes emerged deeply dissatisfied with their experience. The litigation phenomenon in the immigration field has really been an explosion in applications for the judicial review of tribunal decisions – most particularly review of RRT rulings on asylum claims. This tribunal stands out from its generalist sister, the MRT, in two respects. The first, and most obvious, is in the nature of the cases considered: refugee decisions by definition tend to imply more serious consequences for a person seeking to avoid removal from the country; and asylum seekers as a group are much more likely to be indigent. The second, significant, difference is that RRT hearings are conducted 'in private'.[108] Although designed as a measure to protect the interests of the refugee and asylum seeker, the closed hearings create quite a different atmosphere in hearings and in the ethos of secrecy that surrounds this tribunal.

---

103   See, for example, *SZBEL v MIMIA* (2006) 228 CLR 152 (*SZBEL*) at [40]; *MIAC v SZKTI* (2009) 238 CLR 489 at [27].
104   (2009) 259 ALR 429 at [18].
105   See below Part 18.6.3.
106   Joint Standing Committee on Migration, *The Immigration Review Tribunal Appointment Process* (Canberra: AGPS, 1994).
107   See also the comments made in Chapter 19 at [19.37].
108   *Migration Act*, s 429. In this context see *SZAYW v MIMIA* (2006) 230 CLR 486 where the High Court remarked that the concept of 'in private', at least as it is used in the *Migration Act*, is not easy to define.

[18.48] This part provides an overview of some of the jurisprudence on the operation of the tribunals. It begins with a discussion of the tribunals' basic powers and the controversy that has arisen over their ability to re-make decisions that are obviously affected by fundamental legal error. There follows consideration of the complex case law that has developed on the threshold requirements for *notification* of various decisions. The balance of this part deals in turn with the emergent jurisprudence on the various provisions that dictate how the tribunals are to behave in both conducting hearings and crafting the decisions that decide the fate of the migrant and the refugee. As we explore in this series of studies, the case law provides a fascinating insight into the struggles that have developed between a government bent on controlling every aspect of the appeal process and courts that have used statutory procedures to try to secure substantive fairness for applicants. The end result is a statutory scheme that has increased in complexity over the years as successive governments have sought to provide legislative antidotes to each new court ruling. Nowhere is this more apparent than in the dazzling complexity of the provisions governing notification and disclosure in the various contexts in which these concepts appear in the review process.

18.4.1 Threshold issues: The tribunals' power to review

[18.49] A threshold issue that has arisen in at least one case is the ability of both primary decision-makers and tribunals to re-make decisions where they are persuaded that they have made a mistake or committed a fundamental error. In *MIMA v Bhardwaj*,[109] the decision-maker was the MRT, charged with making a ruling in a case involving a foreign student who was alleged to have been in breach of his visa requirements. Unable to attend the hearing set down for his case, the student sent a facsimile to the tribunal requesting another hearing date. The communication was filed correctly but placed behind the letter to the applicant. It did not come to the attention of the member who, in the absence of the student, proceeded to affirm the visa cancellation. The student complained loudly when notified of the decision, with the result that the tribunal retrieved the applicant's file from the registry, conducted a (fresh) hearing and reversed the decision made previously. The Minister sought judicial review of the ruling on the basis that, in the absence of any relevant statutory provision, the tribunal had no power to vacate and re-make the decision in this way. The Minister argued that once the tribunal member exercised the power vested by the migration legislation, the tribunal was *functus officio*, and the member's power was exhausted. Only a court of law, it was argued, could declare a decision to be affected by fundamental legal error sufficient to vacate the decision. The case made its way all the way to the High Court where a majority held 6:1 (with Kirby J in dissent) that the tribunal did indeed have power to re-make the decision in question.

[18.50] The majority ruled that the first decision made by the tribunal was affected by jurisdictional error, was void and therefore was no decision at all.[110] Gleeson CJ offered two explanations for his ruling. The first was that the tribunal's duty to grant

---
109 (2002) 209 CLR 597 (*Bhardwaj*).
110 Ibid at [51] (Gaudron and Gummow JJ).

a hearing under s 360 of the Act is a condition precedent to the tribunal's exercise of jurisdiction. Until it reopened the case, his Honour reasoned, the tribunal had failed to perform its statutory duties. The Chief Justice also referred to s 353 which provides that the tribunal is not bound by legal technicalities and should act according to 'substantive justice and the merits of the case'.[111] The other members of the majority differed in their reasoning, although all focused on the fact that the tribunal's initial decision was void by reason of jurisdictional error.[112]

[18.51] In dissent, Kirby J held that the statutory regime governing merits review represented a complete statement of the powers conferred on the migration tribunals. As the Act did not include provisions allowing the tribunals to reopen cases that had been decided, his Honour ruled that the tribunal had no power to rectify any error it might have made.

[18.52] The practical significance of *Bhardwaj* is that the High Court opened the way for what could amount to informal appeals against tribunal rulings, allowing applicants to petition tribunal members in an effort to induce a change of mind. For Kirby J, the uncertainty and confusion generated by this possibility offered a practical rationale for his approach.[113]

[18.53] In spite of the decision in *Bhardwaj*, the burgeoning discourse on 'void' decisions seems to have encouraged arguments in some cases that primary decisions affected by jurisdictional error are *not* reviewable by the tribunals. In other words, arguments have been made to the effect that such decisions should be reviewed immediately by the courts, it being the province of the courts to make final determinations on points of law.[114] The jurisprudence on this issue appears to be divided. Some judges have affirmed that primary decisions affected by serious legal error should go straight to the courts by virtue of the fact that there is no 'decision' for the tribunals to review.[115] The alternative view seen in the more recent decisions of *Zubair v MIMIA*[116] and *MIMIA v Ahmed*[117] is that the tribunals may proceed with the review of a flawed decision. The rationale in these cases seems to be that the tribunals are endowed with powers that are co-extensive with those of the primary decision-makers but they are not bound by the same rules of procedure. Accordingly, as long as there is a matter brought into being at departmental level, the tribunals should be able to go ahead and make a basic (non-binding) ruling on their own jurisdiction. Where the legal failure has been one of process, it will be open to the tribunals to remedy the procedural error, if this can be done in the exercise of the procedural powers conferred on the tribunals.

---

111 Ibid at [14].
112 For a discussion of the meaning of this phrase, see below Chapter 19.6.2. For a fuller description of *Bhardwaj* and of its significance, see Benjamin O'Donnell, 'Jurisdictional Error, Invalidity and the Role of Injunction in s 75(v) of the Constitution' (2007) 28 *Australian Bar Review* 291, notes 100ff; Mark Aronson, 'Nullity' (2004) 40 *AIAL Forum* 19.
113 (2002) 209 CLR 597 at [122].
114 *Zubair v MIMIA* (2004) 139 FCR 344.
115 See, for example, *Wang v MIMIA* [2002] FCA 167 and *MIMA v Li* (2000) 103 FCR 486.
116 (2004) 139 FCR 344.
117 (2005) 143 FCR 314.

[18.54] If *Bhardwaj* stands as an affirmation of the tribunal's powers (and duties) to review decisions within its jurisdiction, in other respects the Act is very definite about the circumstances in which the various tribunals can entertain appeals. Even though the administration of the MRT and the RRT has been merged and members of both tribunals have cross-appointments, neither tribunal can hear cases defined as 'reviewable' by the other.[118] The jurisdiction of the tribunals is also circumscribed by provisions dictating criteria that must be met by either applicants or the sponsors of applicants for visas granted either offshore[119] or within Australia.[120]

[18.55] The legislative scheme also confers special powers on the Minister to block access to review by all or any of the tribunals through the issue of conclusive certificates.[121] Such certificates can also be issued to suppress disclosure of documents to an applicant in the course of a hearing,[122] although the tribunal is given discretion to determine for itself whether non-disclosure is in the public interest. The sparse case law on such certificates in the migration tribunals suggests that the courts have tended to regard these provisions with suspicion. Hence, applicants should either be given a hearing before the issue of a conclusive certificate[123] or the public interest test should be applied so as to favour disclosure in all but very serious cases.[124] Whether this jurisprudence remains sound is less certain following the rulings of the High Court in *MIAC v Kumar*[125] and *K-Generation Pty Limited v Liquor Licensing Court*.[126] In *Kumar*, a case discussed in greater detail below, the High Court found no difficulty in ruling that the statutory scheme operated to exclude common law notions of procedural fairness. In the *K-Generation* case, the court ruled to similar effect in respect of statutory provisions requiring the South Australian Licensing Court to maintain the confidentiality of certain information classified by the Commissioner of Police as 'criminal intelligence'. The court ruled that the legislation did not operate to deny the Licensing Court the character of an independent and impartial tribunal. *K-Generation* involved a very different statutory scheme from that of the *Migration Act*, involving, among other things, the interaction between State courts and federal judicial power. Nevertheless, this case and *Kumar* may suggest that the mood in the High Court has shifted in favour of deference to statutory schemes that run counter to basic precepts of natural justice and open decision-making.[127]

---

118   *Migration Act*, s 338. Note that under s 134 decisions involving certain business visas are reviewable by the AAT. This tribunal also has exclusive jurisdiction to hear criminal deportation appeals under ss 200ff; and character and conduct appeals under ss 500ff.
119   See *Migration Act*, s 338.
120   Ibid, s 338.
121   Ibid, s 339 (MRT); ss 375 and 375A (RRT); and ss 503A-503D.
122   Ibid, s 376.
123   See *Nguyen Thanh Trong v MILGEA* (1996) 68 FCR 463.
124   Se, for example, *Kokcinar v MIAC* [2008] FMCA 1307.
125   (2009) 238 CLR 448 (*Kumar*).
126   (2009) 237 CLR 501 (*K-Generation*).
127   Note that in the absence of any statute excluding the rules of procedural fairness, the High Court has responded with some very different decisions. See, for example, *Saeed v MIAC* (2010) 267 ALR 204; and *Plaintiffs M61/ M69* (2010) 272 ALR 14. These cases are discussed below, Chapter 19.6.4.

18.4.2 Notice of appeal and time limits

[18.56] One of the most striking characteristics of immigration decision-making and review since 1989 has been in the imposition of strict time limits on applications of all kinds. An early and persistent point of conflict because of the potential for injustice to migrant applicants, the High Court is the only body that has been able to resist the temporal dictates of parliament.[128] Access to merits review is dependent on applicants lodging their appeals to the MRT within 21 days in respect of decisions made in Australia and 70 days where the applicant is overseas. Appeals to the RRT must be lodged within 28 days. Between 1994 and 2001, failure to lodge an application for merits review within the statutory period would operate also as a block on judicial review by the courts, the time limits for both being coterminous.[129]

[18.57] Where the legislative scheme has allowed some wriggle room is in determining the date from which the time limits should run: namely the date of *notification* of the decision. The result is a long series of cases on the meaning of the various provisions outlining how applicants are to be told of the decisions made on their applications, cases that underscore just how peculiar Australian law and practice is in this critical area of administrative justice.[130] Although some of the cases relate to the notification of decisions for the purpose of judicial review rather than tribunal appeals, they raise similar issues and will be considered here. 'Notification' is also relevant to the conduct of hearings before the tribunals in so far as appellants have rights to be notified of certain material and issues: the concept will reappear in this context later in the chapter.

[18.58] The notification cases provide an interesting case study of the sometimes overt battles that have raged between an increasingly restrictive government and a judiciary concerned about the human impact of the measures taken. On more than one occasion the rulings by the courts have resulted in changes to the legislation – designed always to tighten the rules so as to make life easier for the bureaucracy. Within the courts it is also possible to see an interesting trend develop whereby judges have moved away from invoking common law rules of procedural fairness or natural justice in favour of using techniques of strict literalism in the interpretation of the migration legislation. The game is well described as one of cat and mouse. Sadly, it is the traditions of the common law that appear to have suffered most grievously.

[18.59] The most important overriding provision governing the notification of any decision is s 66 which sets out a list of criteria that must be met for a notification to be valid. In accordance with s 66(2) and (3), notice of a refusal of a visa must specify:

(a) the criterion that the applicant was required to meet;

---

128 See *Bodruddaza v MIMA* (2007) 228 CLR 651; and *MZXOT v MIAC* (2008) 233 CLR 601, discussed at Chapter 19.6.3.

129 That is, the time limits for both appeals and judicial review began from the date of the primary decision. Lodging an application for merits review was the only way to have the clock re-set for the purpose of seeking judicial review. See the discussion in Chapter 19.6.3 below.

130 Compare, for example, the British House of Lords' decision in *R (on the application of Anufrijeva) v Secretary of State for the Home Dept* [2004] 1 AC 604. There, the Lords ruled that an administrative decision does not take effect at law until the person affected receives actual notice of it.

(b) the provision (if any) in the migration legislation that prevented the grant of the visa;
(c) the reasons for the decision made; and
(d) whether and how the decision can be appealed.

[18.60] In addition to this general provision, special regimes for the notification of decisions are contained in ss 501C and 501G of the Act (governing decisions made concerning character and conduct). Notification of decisions of the MRT and the RRT are dealt with in Part 5, Divs 6 and 8A, and Part 7, Divs 5 and 7A, respectively, with corresponding regulations at regs 4.39, 4.40 and 5.02 of the *Migration Regulations* (the latter relating to persons in immigration detention). Other notification provisions are sprinkled throughout the Act, for example in those parts of the legislation dealing with the cancellation of visas. Where the tribunal complies with the relevant provisions governing modes of 'giving' documents to a person, the person is deemed to have been notified of the contents of the document. These provisions echo s 53(3), repealed in August 2001, which provided that notifications sent to the address given by an applicant in an application were 'taken' to be received (even if it was not received in fact). Interestingly, in Part 8 of the Act, the time limits placed on applications to the Federal Court are expressed to run from the time of actual (as opposed to deemed) notification of a decision: see s 477A.

[18.61] Although a failure to comply with the notification provisions does not affect the validity of the primary decision (s 66(4)), lack of compliance with the basic criteria of s 66(2) and (3) will mean that notification has not occurred and so time will not run against an applicant who wishes to appeal the decision to one of the tribunals. An early example of how this can operate is seen in *Chun Wang v MIMA*.[131] That case involved a Chinese student whose application was rejected for one of the visas available during a quasi-amnesty in the mid 1990s. The IRT generated a refusal letter that complied with s 66 in all respects except (crucially) that Mr Wang's name was misspelled. In the result, he did not open the letter sent to him. When Mr Wang made inquiries of his own, he was informed orally of the refusal but told that he no longer had a right of appeal. He was given a second letter and advised to try his luck in the Federal Court. Opening his judgment with a quotation from Frantz Kafka,[132] Merkel J ruled that the man had not been notified properly for the purposes of s 66 until given both the details of the rejection of his application and the correct advice about his entitlement to lodge an appeal. This case can be contrasted with a number in which the courts have confirmed that, where the Minister and the tribunals *have*

---

131 (1997) 71 FCR 386.
132 His Honour said: 'In *The Trial*, Frantz Kafka tells the story of a man who comes from the country to gain admittance to *the Law*. Before *the Law* stands a door-keeper who says that he cannot admit the man at the moment. The man had not expected to meet this difficulty as he thought that *the Law* should be accessible to every man and at all times. But he decides that he had better wait until he gets permission to enter. He waits for days and years. Finally the man asks how does it come about that in all these years no one has come seeking admittance but me? The door keeper perceives that the man is at the end of his strength and his hearing is failing, so he bellows in his ear: "No one but you could gain admittance through this door, since this door was intended only for you. I am now going to shut it". Occasionally a case arises which makes the word *Kafkaesque* appear to be a description of fact rather than fiction. The present is such a case.' See ibid at 386 ([1]-[2]).

complied with the letter of the notification requirements, notification will be deemed even where it has not occurred as a matter of fact.[133]

[18.62] There have been some Federal Court judges who have taken a hard line, ruling that a failure to comply with statutory requirements for notification need not 'stop the clock' for the purpose of determining time limits on appeal. In *Yu v MIMIA*,[134] Emmett J drew a distinction between the contents of a notice of cancellation (under s 127 of the Act) and the provisions governing receipt of the notice. The applicant's notice was properly delivered. The contents of the notice referred to the wrong date by which an appeal could be lodged. Emmett J ruled that the statutory appeal limit prevailed such that the applicant relied on the erroneous date in the letter at his peril.[135] In contrast, other judges have ruled invalid regulations deeming notification to have occurred where this is plainly a fiction.[136]

[18.63] A case that provides an interesting comparator to *Yu* is that of *WACB v MIMIA*.[137] In that instance issues of notification arose for a 15-year-old Afghan asylum seeker who arrived in Australia as an unaccompanied minor. Held at Curtin Detention Centre in the Kimberly region of Western Australia, the young boy was refused protection as a refugee at both first instance and on appeal to the RRT. He sought judicial review of the RRT decision but was initially excluded from the Federal Court on the basis that his application had been lodged outside the 28-day time limit. As detailed elsewhere,[138] the central argument was that the young man had not been properly notified of the RRT's adverse ruling because he had been given neither a copy of the tribunal's reasons nor a briefing on why he had been rejected. The Minister argued that there had been substantial compliance with the notification provisions. The evidence suggested that the young man had been called into a designated office in the detention centre where he was told that his case had been rejected. He had responded by breaking down in tears, whereupon he was taken aside and comforted by an interpreter. He was not handed a copy of the decision until some time later and no effort was made to translate it for him.

[18.64] At first instance,[139] French J found it more likely that the DIMIA official did advise the young man about applying for review and that he did explain the 28-day time limit. His Honour commented: 'It is quite possible that the applicant was so distressed at hearing that he was not to receive a visa, that he did not register

---

133   On the operation of former s 53(3), see *Tabet v MIMA* [1997] FCA 547. In that case Mansfield J ruled that the Post Office's failure to redirect mail pursuant to a redirection notice provided no excuse for an applicant who sought to lodge a notice of appeal to the IRT out of time. See also *Susiatin v MIMA* [1998] FCA 825, a case that concerned the interaction between *Migration Act*, s 478(1)(b) and *Migration Regulations*, reg 5.03.
134   [2002] FCA 912 (*Yu*).
135   The authors agree with MPE-KGA Lawyers that this case should not be regarded as good law. See MPE-KGA Lawyers, 'Challenging Decisions – A Review Case Study', October 2008 at 15 (document in possession of authors).
136   *Guo Heng Li v MIMA* [1999] FCA 1147.
137   (2004) 210 ALR 190 (*WACB*).
138   Mary Crock, 'Lonely Refuge: Judicial Responses to Separated Children Seeking Refugee Protection in Australia' (2005) 22 *Law in Context* 120 at Part 3.5.
139   *Jaffari v MIMA* (2001) 113 FCR 10.

the other things he was told'.¹⁴⁰ This observation did not prevent the judge from ruling that the boy had been properly notified. French J concluded with the following broadside:

> The question of unaccompanied minors seeking asylum is a pressing, current issue. ... While this case has been decided adversely to the applicant on the facts, that is the result of applying the statute, properly construed, to the evidence before the Court. The Act provides little in the way of the kinds of protections contemplated by the UNHCR guidelines. At the very least, there is a case for considering the provision of legal advice and assistance to unaccompanied minors up to and including the point of judicial review. It is of concern that the application for judicial review in this case was lodged by a 15 year old non-citizen and lodged out of time thus depriving him of such limited rights of review as he would otherwise have enjoyed.¹⁴¹

[18.65] Although rejected also by the Full Federal Court,¹⁴² on appeal to the High Court counsel for WACB argued successfully that the statutory provisions governing notification had not been complied with to the letter. It was argued that the terms of then s 478 had to be read together with the comprehensive provisions in ss 430-430B governing the preparation and delivery by the RRT of the reasons for decision. The High Court found for the appellant on the basis that he should have been handed physically a copy of the RRT's judgment. As this did not occur he was not properly notified.¹⁴³ Interestingly, it was this rather mechanical argument that prevailed: submissions that the legislation should be read down so as to acknowledge the particular vulnerabilities of the applicant were rejected. The young man won on a strict and literal meaning of the relevant legislation which required the young man to be *given* a copy of the RRT's decision.

[18.66] The litigation in this case induced a response from the government even before the first judgment in the case was handed down. This is seen in the provisions relating to the circumstances in which notification is to be presumed or deemed, inserted by amending legislation that was passed shortly before French J delivered his ruling in *Jaffari v MIMA* on 26 July 2001.¹⁴⁴ These provisions include s 495D whereby an applicant is deemed to have received a communication if it has been sent to the applicant's representative in circumstances where that person is registered as an authorised recipient.¹⁴⁵ The changes made in 2001 did not stop the Full Federal Court from ruling in 2007 that the retention of the provisions relating to 'giving' an applicant reasons for a decision means that the physical delivery of the documentation is still required.¹⁴⁶ This litigation again induced a legislative response, bundled this time with a raft of amendments giving the tribunals more flexibility in their mode

---

140   Ibid at [34].
141   Ibid at [44].
142   *WACB* (2002) 122 FCR 469 at [7]-[8].
143   For the record, the young man eventually gained recognition as a refugee. Information provided by Dr John L Cameron, counsel for Mr Syed Mehdi Jaffari.
144   *Migration Legislation Amendment Act (Electronic Transactions and Methods of Notification) Act 2001* (Cth).
145   *Durrani v MIMIA* [2005] FCA 629.
146   *MIAC v SZKKC* (2007) 159 FCR 565. The case remained on appeal to the Federal Court in early 2011, leave to appeal having been granted in *MIAC v SZKKA* [2008] HCATrans 86.

of operation.¹⁴⁷ Applicant SZKKC was one of a great many asylum seekers who joined a class action in 2001 when their claims were rejected.¹⁴⁸ When this case was remitted for re-hearing in the Federal Court, the Department conceded that the failure to properly notify the applicant when his visa was refused did constitute a serious legal error. However, Siopsis J found that the seven-year delay by the applicant in seeking judicial review warranted the dismissal of this error as a ground for invalidating the visa refusal.¹⁴⁹

[18.67] The tendency for the courts to read strictly the notification obligations contained in the migration legislation is seen also in other cases. In instances where notice is a pre-condition or trigger for the automatic cancellation of a visa, it has been accepted that the giving of notice is a jurisdictional fact.¹⁵⁰ As such, it is a matter in respect of which the courts will require evidence to be adduced as to the steps taken by a decision-maker to effect notice.¹⁵¹ This has led in turn to a series of cases in which applicants have attempted to take notification issues to rather extreme levels. One example is *Zhang v MIAC*¹⁵² where the Full Federal Court ruled that the reference to a 'post box' address in reg 2.55(3)(c) should be read not as a *post office box* as usually understood but as a postal address given for the purpose of receiving correspondence. On this occasion notification was ruled to have been effective because the information had been sent to the postal address provided by the applicant. It was deemed irrelevant that an email sent contemporaneously with the hard copy of the document did not reach its intended recipient. The applicant was denied leave to appeal the decision to the High Court.¹⁵³

[18.68] More extreme examples of 'points of order' involving notification are cases like *SZOFE v MIAC*,¹⁵⁴ *Maroun v MIAC*¹⁵⁵ and *SZOBI v MIAC (No 2)*.¹⁵⁶ In the first of these cases, the applicant argued that a failure to give proper notification meant that the RRT had no jurisdiction to hear the applicant's appeal. The mischief alleged was that DIAC's rejection letter had failed to identify *all* of the places where an appeal could be lodged. The case followed a line of decisions in which issues had arisen about the implications of decision-makers failing to include brochures on appeals with the refusal letters.¹⁵⁷ The Full Federal Court found no difficulty in rejecting the applicant's argument in a situation where it was clear that notification had been effected in practice. The second and third of the cases are more concerning, in that both appear to have involved instances where the applicants may not

---

147 *Migration Legislation Amendment Act (No 2) 2008* (Cth).
148 See *Muin v RRT; Lie v RRT* (2002) 190 ALR 601, discussed at Chapter 19 at [19. 75] and [19.108].
149 See *SZKKC v MIAC* [2009] FCA 362.
150 See *Hossain v MIAC (No 2)* (2010) 114 ALD 523.
151 See *Uddin v MIMIA* [2005] FMCA 841; *Morsed v MIMIA* (2005) 88 ALD 90; and *Shao v MIMIA* (2007) 157 FCR 300; *Zhan v MIMIA* (2003) 128 FCR 469; and *Maroun v MIAC* (2009) 112 ALD 424 at [21].
152 (2007) 161 FCR 419.
153 *Zhang v MIAC* [2008] HCATrans 79.
154 (2010) 185 FCR 129.
155 (2009) 112 ALD 424.
156 [2010] FCAFC 151.
157 See *Hasan v MIAC* (2010) 184 FCR 523; *Zhan v MIMIA* (2003) 128 FCR 469; and *Maroun v MIAC* (2009) 112 ALD 424.

have been notified in fact of the time-critical visa refusals. In both, the refusal letters were returned to the Department, raising issues about the circumstances in which an applicant will be deemed to have been notified of an adverse decision. In *Maroun*, the court accepted a factual finding by the Federal Magistrate that the decision-maker had complied with the statutory requirements for notification. The departmental file contained the envelope of the returned correspondence, but not the contents. The applicant argued that the refusal letter was rendered unlawful by the failure to include a brochure notifying where an appeal could be lodged. Evidence was provided as to the decision-maker's usual practice in issuing refusal letters. The court held that this was sufficient to justify the Magistrate's factual finding that the officer had fulfilled the requisite statutory requirements.

[18.69] In *SZOBI*, the facts were more disturbing.[158] Although the applicant received a letter from the Department sent by ordinary post, two attempts by the Department to send letters by registered post to the same address failed. The first of the registered letters contained an invitation to attend an interview. The second contained notification of the refusal of the applicant's refugee claim which followed the applicant's failure to attend the interview. By the time the applicant contacted the Department to find out how his application was progressing, the statutory period allowed for appeals from the DIAC decision to the RRT had expired. Although the applicant lodged an application for review by the RRT on the same day that he became aware of the mix up, the Full Federal Court confirmed that the RRT had no jurisdiction to hear an appeal lodged out of time. The court rejected the applicant's rather complicated submission that an endorsement on the envelope containing the notices constituted a breach of s 494B of the *Migration Act*. The impugned endorsement was a statement directing the return of the letter to the Department in the event that delivery was not effected. The majority ruled that:

> Section 494B(4)(a) requires the Minister to date the document and then dispatch it within 3 working days of the date of that date. This requirement ensures that the related provisions, ss 494C(4)and 412, can operate effectively. Section 494C(4)(a) deems receipt to have occurred 7 working days after the date of the document (not the date of dispatch). The prescribed period of 28 days in s 412(1)(b) runs from the date of notification of the decision. Given that the statutory provisions contain their own detailed temporal sequence there is no basis for construing 'dispatch' in s 494B(4) as meaning anything other than 'send' ... [Section] 494B(4) has nothing to do with receipt. Section 494B(4) is concerned solely with dispatch. The consequence of dispatch as required under s 494B(4) is deemed receipt under s 494C(4).[159]

Bromberg J concurred with the majority's finding that the Department had complied with the procedural requirements for notification of the applicant on the facts. However, he ruled that the requirement 'to dispatch' does have implications for the receipt of a document. He said:

> I agree that to dispatch means to send. But the requirement of s 494B(4) is not simply to send off the document. It is a requirement to send the document to a

---

158 [2010] FCAFC 151 at [3].
159 Ibid at [19] and [17].

particular address and by a specified means. As McHugh J said in *Re Minister for Immigration and Multicultural Affairs; ex parte Radojicic* (unreported, High Court of Australia, 21 January 2000):

> 'To send something is to cause it to be conveyed or transmitted to a person at a destination'

The obligation to send or dispatch is to be looked at, as McHugh J suggested, in terms of what the Minister did at the time that the document left his or her custody.[160]

[18.70] The issue of notice was considered by the High Court in *MIAC v SZIZO*.[161] In this instance the central question was whether the notification of a hearing sent to a person other than the authorised recipient constituted a jurisdictional error. This was another case where the invitation was communicated to the applicant in fact, so that the applicant did attend and was heard by the RRT. In a unanimous decision, the High Court ruled that ss 441A and 441G of the *Migration Act* constitute procedural steps. Failure to comply exactly with each step will not necessarily constitute a jurisdictional error. The court overruled the Full Federal Court to hold:

> Notwithstanding the detailed prescription of the regime under Divs 4 and 7A and the use of imperative language it was an error to conclude that the provisions of ss 441G and 441A are inviolable restraints conditioning the Tribunal's jurisdiction to conduct and decide a review. They are procedural steps that are designed to ensure that an applicant for review is enabled to properly advance his or her case at the hearing; a failure to comply with them will require consideration of whether in the events that occurred the applicant was denied natural justice. There was no denial of natural justice in this case.[162]

18.4.3 The applicant's right to appear and give evidence

[18.71] The most distinctive feature of the migration tribunals established in and after 1989 is that they were constructed around the idea that applicants should have a right to appear in person and to give oral evidence in their appeals. For the best part of a decade, ss 360(1)(a) and 425(1)(a) of the Act required the MRT and RRT to 'give the applicant an opportunity to appear before it to give evidence' if a decision in the applicant's favour could not be made on the papers.[163] In the years of the Coalition government, however, the nature and quality of the right to an oral hearing was altered progressively in response to various court rulings. In the result, the right is now qualified by three circumstances in which a tribunal member can proceed to a decision without taking oral evidence from an applicant. The first is where the tribunal is able to make a decision favourable to the applicant on the papers; and the second where an applicant consents to the decision being made without an oral hearing. The third exception occurs where an applicant has been invited to provide further information within either a prescribed period or within a 'reasonable' period

---

160 Ibid at [29].
161 (2009) 238 CLR 627.
162 Ibid at [37].
163 In *Liu v MIMA* (2001) 113 FCR 541, Black CJ, Hill and Weinberg JJ reviewed the statutory context and legislative history of s 425, and said that 'the right to a hearing is clearly an important and central right in the merits review system established by Part 7 of the Act' (at [44]).

(whichever is applicable) and fails to do so. Although designed to deal with applicants who fail to appear at scheduled hearings, this third exception has produced a great deal of controversy around what will constitute the giving of a 'reasonable' opportunity to appear.[164]

[18.72] In the leading case of *MIMA v Capitly*,[165] the Full Federal Court held that a refusal to grant an adjournment to an applicant who could not attend a hearing because of illness denied the applicant a reasonable opportunity to appear to give evidence. Similar rulings were made in cases where the courts considered that applicants had been given unreasonably short periods of time in which to respond to an invitation to appear and give evidence. In *Sook Rye Son v MIMA*,[166] the applicant was sent a letter while in immigration detention. Leaving aside the fact that the letter never reached the applicant until the day before the scheduled hearing, the dates specified in the letter did allow the applicant sufficient time to comply with s 426(2) of the Act.[167] Where these cases stand out is that in some no issues arose about the validity of the notifications given to the applicants. In other words, although notified in accordance with the Act, the courts ruled that there existed an overriding requirement that the opportunity given to the applicant to appear and to give evidence should be reasonable.[168]

[18.73] The concept of 'reasonable opportunity' for a hearing was extended further by the High Court in *SZBEL v MIMIA*.[169] In that case an Iranian seaman jumped ship at Port Kembla and claimed asylum on the basis that he faced persecution on religious grounds following his conversion to Christianity. The High Court ruled that the failure by the RRT to communicate any misgivings about the applicant's evidence, which was described in the reasons for decision as 'implausible', constituted a failure to provide a sufficient opportunity to present his case. In granting the applicant relief, the High Court noted that, while a decision-maker cannot be expected to give the applicant a 'running commentary on the evidence that is given', the applicant must be informed about the matters on which a decision is likely to turn:

> [Where], as here, there are specific aspects of an applicant's account, that the Tribunal considers *may* be important to the decision and may be open to doubt, the Tribunal must at least ask the applicant to expand upon those aspects of the account and ask the applicant to explain why the account should be accepted.[170]

[18.74] In this statement the court comes close to ruling that s 425 of the Act mandates compliance with the essential elements of the common law rules of procedural fairness – notwithstanding the very particular provisions governing the

---

164 *Migration Act*, ss 360 and 425.
165 (1999) 55 ALD 365 (*Capitly*).
166 (1999) 161 ALR 612 (*Sook Rye Son*).
167 Even if the applicant were deemed to have received the letter under reg 5.03, the date set for the hearing was only six days later. Under s 426(2), a period of seven days is prescribed. See also *Budiyal v MIMA* (1998) 82 FCR 166, where it was held that the giving of an unreasonably short notice of a hearing date could contravene s 425(1); and *Sun Zhan Qui v MIEA* (1997) 81 FCR 71.
168 *Rahman v MIMA* [1999] FCA 846.
169 (2006) 228 CLR 152.
170 Ibid at [47].

conduct of review that we consider in the following section. The passage is consistent with the wider habit of the courts to impose minimal obligations on the migration tribunals – but in very vague terms.

[18.75] In cases interpreting the original s 425(1)(a), the Federal Court often explicitly rejected submissions put forward on behalf of the Minister that the provision was concerned only with the acts of the tribunal and not with anything that might happen thereafter to an applicant. In *Capitly*,[171] for instance, the Federal Court stated that:

> [A]n opportunity to give evidence is not given once and for all by the notification to an applicant of a hearing date in the future. The opportunity must be a continuing opportunity and take account of the circumstances which from time to time exist, up until the opportunity is either availed of or not.

[18.76] Over the years there have been interesting variations in the way the courts have interpreted the tribunal's obligation to give applicants the right to appear and give evidence. In *De Silva v MIMA*,[172] for instance, the Full Federal Court rejected the contention that s 425(1) obliges the tribunal to identify issues and draw them to the applicant's attention for his or her response. The court ruled that:

> The governing word in s 425(1) is 'invite'. The purpose of the invitation is to enable an applicant to attend the hearing so that he or she can give evidence and present arguments relating to the issues in the case.[173]

Following the High Court ruling in *SZBEL*, however, the Federal Court has made it plain that the provision of a meaningful opportunity to give evidence does require the articulation of what the tribunal considers to be the main issues to be determined. The obligation is not limited to a duty to advise an applicant 'of any adverse conclusion which has been arrived at'.[174] This does not mean that the tribunal has to disclose every aspect of his or her thought processes.[175] However, as Flick J explains in *SZDFZ v MIAC*,[176] an applicant must be informed of the case they have to answer. In *AZAAD v MIAC*,[177] the Full Federal Court made it clear that the issuance of an invitation to appear before the RRT will not fulfil the terms of s 425. The appellants had a right to be 'put on notice' of those elements of the (applicant wife's) history that were in issue. In that case the failure to identify the point at which the tribunal switched from considering the couple's asylum claim to doubting the woman's credibility meant that the applicants were denied procedural fairness.[178] Sending a letter to

---

171   (1999) 55 ALD 365 at [34].
172   (2000) 98 FCR 364 (*De Silva*) at 367.
173   Ibid. See also *SZDTM v MIAC* [2008] FCA 1258 (hearing invitations do not have to specify the issues in question). Note, however, that in cases such as *Mazhar v MIMA* (2000) 183 ALR 188; *W284 v MIMA* [2001] FCA 1788; *Tobasi v MIMA* (2002) 122 FCR 322 (*Tobasi*); and *Arif v MIMA* [2002] FCA 1053, the Federal Court held (at least with regards to interpretation) that it is appropriate to proceed on the basis that the obligation imposed by s 425(1) of the current Act is in effect of the same nature as that which existed under s 425(1)(a) as it previously stood.
174   See *Commissioner for ACT Revenue v Alphaone Pty Ltd* (1994) 49 FCR 576 at 591-2.
175   See *SZBEL* (2006) 228 CLR 152 at 162 [31].
176   (2008) 168 FCR 1 at [17]ff.
177   [2010] FCAFC 156.
178   On this point, see also the judgment of Rares J in *SZJYA v MIAC (No 2)* (2008) 102 ALD 598 and the discussion below at Part 18.5.

an appellant after an initial hearing pursuant to s 424A will not excuse a failure to accord procedural fairness at the hearing.[179] The RRT's duty to inform the applicant of adverse issues is one that must be performed in a manner that is fair and free from bias.[180]

18.4.4 The use of interpreters

[18.77] The jurisprudence on the requirement that applicants be given a (reasonable) opportunity to appear and to give evidence has implications for the use of interpreters in the tribunals. On the one hand, the courts have made clear that an interpreter cannot be expected to provide perfect translations.[181] On the other, gross inadequacies in interpretation have been found to frequently render a hearing unlawful. In *Perera v MIMA*,[182] Kenny J held that s 425(1)(a) requires the tribunal to afford an effective opportunity to a non-English speaking applicant to give evidence through a competent interpreter. Her Honour also discussed factors that may indicate such incompetence in interpretation that the applicant can be said to have been effectively prevented from giving his or her evidence. These factors include:

> the responsiveness of the interpreted questions to the questions asked, the coherence of those answers, the consistency of one answer with another and the rest of the case sought to be made and, more generally, any evident confusion in exchanges between the Tribunal and the interpreter.[183]

[18.78] The courts have also been quick to admonish tribunals who depart from the rule that interpreters should be used to interpret and no more. In *Sook Rye Son*,[184] the Federal Court held that the RRT's misuse of the interpreter constituted a failure to act in accordance with substantial justice and the merits of the case, and denied the applicant a reasonable opportunity to give evidence. In that case the RRT had directed questions to the refugee applicant's interpreter about whether the applicant's accent was from North Korea or Seoul. The interpreter's answers contradicted the applicant's claims and were treated as probative material in the RRT's decision to reject the visa application.

[18.79] In *W284 v MIMA*,[185] French J rejected the respondent's contention that s 425(1) is complied with once an invitation in appropriate terms has been given. His Honour quoted with approval the following passage of Goldberg J in *Mazhar v MIMA*:[186]

> The invitation must not be a hollow shell or an empty gesture. If an invitation to appear is extended to an applicant, where the Tribunal knows that an interpreter is

---

179 *SZIOZ v MIAC* [2007] FCA 1870 at [59]; *SZJYA v MIAC (No 2)* (2008) 102 ALD 598 at 611 [56].
180 See *SZITH v MIAC* (2008) 105 ALD 541. See also cases such as *SZEJF v MIMIA* [2006] FCA 724; *SZILQ v MIAC* (2007) 163 FCR 304; and *SZIOZ v MIAC* [2007] FCA 1870.
181 See *Tobasi* (2002) 122 FCR 322; *NAUV v MIMIA* (2003) 79 ALD 149 at [42] (affirmed (2004) 82 ALD 784); and *SZJZE v MIAC* [2007] FCA 1653 at [22].
182 (1999) 92 FCR 6.
183 Ibid at [37]. See also *Phan v MIMA* (2000) 171 ALR 323 and *Sook Rye Son* (1999) 161 ALR 612.
184 (1999) 161 ALR 612.
185 [2001] FCA 1788 at [31]. See also *De Silva* (2000) 98 FCR 364.
186 (2000) 183 ALR 188 at [31].

required, the obligation to extend the invitation will not be satisfied if the Tribunal provides an interpreter whose interpretation is such that the applicant is unable adequately to give evidence and present argument to the Tribunal. If that situation arises the Tribunal will not have fulfilled its obligation under s 425(1).

[18.80] In *Tobasi v MIMA*,[187] Mansfield J referred to both *De Silva* and *W284*, as well as to comments of the Full Federal Court in *Liu v MIMA*.[188] On the bases of these decisions, Mansfield J held that 'the provision contemplates attendance at the hearing to give evidence and present arguments in a meaningful way', and that erroneous interpretation may prevent this from occurring.

[18.81] Having said that, it is worth noting that the appeals in *Mazhar*, *Tobasi* and *Arif v MIMA*[189] were all dismissed. In each case, the court held that any departures from the requisite standard of interpretation were not significant to the applicant's case or to the tribunal's decision, including the tribunal's assessment of the applicant's reliability as a witness.[190] It is thus clear that the errors in interpretation must be material, resulting in 'a miscarriage in the decision-making process'.[191] This line of reasoning has been confirmed in more recent cases. Interpretation deficiencies must relate to matters that were material to the decision made.[192]

[18.82] Even if there have been problems at one stage in the process, leading to an invalid decision, it does not follow that evidence collected during the process cannot be used subsequently to make a valid decision. In *SZIBW v MIAC*,[193] McKerracher J, sitting as the Full Federal Court, ruled that the RRT was under no obligation to grant a second oral hearing to an applicant upon a matter being remitted by the Federal Court. In that case the applicant alleged that errors had occurred in the translation of his evidence at the first RRT hearing. At both first instance[194] and on appeal, the court accepted that the second tribunal had had the applicant's evidence reviewed by a fresh interpreter, thereby correcting any errors that might have occurred in the initial interpretation process.[195] Granted leave to appeal to the High Court, the matter was eventually settled with an agreement that the decision of the RRT be quashed and the appeal be heard afresh.[196]

---

187 (2002) 122 FCR 322.
188 (2001) 113 FCR 541.
189 [2002] FCA 1053.
190 See also *Phan v MIMA* (2000) 171 ALR 323 at [22]-[23], in which Kiefel J conceded that errors in interpretation had occurred during the hearing in question, but held that 'it could not be concluded that they resulted in a breakdown of communication, significant and unresolved misunderstandings, or that they could have created a wrong impression of the witnesses such as might affect their credibility'.
191 *Soltanyzand v MIMA* [2001] FCA 1168 at [18]. See generally Kira Raif, 'The Role of Interpreters in the Refugee Determination Process' (2003) 11 *Immigration Review* [182] and Michael Barnett, 'Mind Your Language – Interpreters in Australian Immigration Proceedings' [2006] UWSLawRw 5; and (2004) 10(1) *UWS Law Review* 109.
192 See, for example, *WACO v MIMIA* (2003) 131 FCR 511; *M175 of 2002 v MIAC* [2007] FCA 1212; *SZKLX v MIAC* [2007] FCA 1414 at [12]; and *SZJBD v MIAC* (2009) 179 FCR 109.
193 [2008] FCA 160.
194 *SZIBW v MIAC and RRT* [2007] FMCA 1660.
195 See also *SZEPZ v MIMA* (2006) 159 FCR 291 at [37] and [38].
196 See *SZIBW v MIAC* [2009] HCATrans 73.

[18.83] In *SZJBD v MIAC*,[197] the Full Federal Court confirmed that the adequacy of interpretation is a question of fact that must be decided by a reviewing court through the taking of evidence. Indeed, the applicant, the Minister or the court itself may adduce evidence in this respect.[198] In that particular case, the applicant's complaints about the interpretation before the RRT evaporated when the transcript of the hearing was played in court. Claims that the interpreter was aggressive and that the tribunal member was angry were not substantiated. Although the applicant's case failed in this respect, Perram J found in a separate judgment that the Federal Magistrate in the court below had erred in failing to comply with a Federal Court direction that he listen to the impugned recording of the RRT hearing.[199]

18.4.5 The right to be represented

[18.84] Another matter that has been relevant to the rights of persons appearing before the migration tribunals is the right of applicants to be assisted by an adviser or representative. As noted earlier, the legislation seems to exclude entitlement to representation at hearings[200] in the RRT. Section 427(6)(a) of the *Migration Act* provides that:

> A person appearing before Tribunal is not entitled to be represented before the Tribunal by any other person.

[18.85] The sections governing representation in the MRT are significantly different, stipulating that applicants are entitled to have an *assistant* in attendance. However, that person has no entitlement to 'present arguments' to the tribunal unless the tribunal is satisfied that, because of exceptional circumstances, the assistant should be allowed to do so.[201]

[18.86] The provisions governing representation before the RRT were considered by the Full Federal Court in *WABZ v MIMIA*.[202] In that case the tribunal had prevented a legal aid solicitor from making any statement in the applicant's hearing, although the solicitor was permitted to stay as an observer. The Full Federal Court ruled that, although the applicant had no statutory entitlement to be represented, the applicant did have a right to be properly heard before the tribunal. French and Lee JJ ruled that the discretion given to the tribunal to allow representation meant that in some circumstances failure to permit representation can amount to a denial of

---

197   (2009) 179 FCR 109.
198   On this point, see also *NAPS v MIMIA* [2003] FCA 1091 and *NAPS v MIMIA* [2004] FCA 159, two cases referred to by Buchanan J in the leading judgment in *SZJBD v MIAC* (2009) 179 FCR 109.
199   (2009) 179 FCR 109 at [108]-[109] where His Honour said: 'It is not open to a court lower in the judicial hierarchy to disobey a determination of an appellate court in that manner. ... The federal magistrate took this course because he believed that two decisions of Allsop J ... required this result. I agree with Buchanan J that that conclusion was incorrect. However, even if it had been correct it would not possibly have justified the federal magistrate in disobeying the outcome of the very appeal from his own decision.'
200   A distinction is drawn here between a right to representation and a right to be provided with representation. *Dietrich v The Queen* (1992) 177 CLR 292 has been applied narrowly and clearly does not apply to administrative proceedings. See, for example, *Nguyen v MIMA* (2000) 101 FCR 20 at 26.
201   See s 366A(3) of the Act.
202   (2004) 134 FCR 271.

the applicant's right to be heard. Their Honours identified a series of circumstances where applicants might have a right to be represented. As Kira Raif notes, factors to consider include:

1. The applicant's capacity to understand the nature of the proceedings and the issues for determination.
2. The applicant's ability to understand and communicate effectively in the language used by the Tribunal [but note the discretion provided by s 427(7) to offer an interpreter if the applicant is not fluent in English].
3. The legal and factual complexity of the case.
4. The importance of the decision to the applicant's liberty or welfare.[203]

In the result, the whole court found that the failure to allow the solicitor to speak meant that applicant WABZ was not afforded the hearing required under s 425 of the Act. This case has been cited with approval on many occasions.[204] As Crennan J noted in *Plaintiff M90/2009 v MIAC*,[205] however, the issue is essentially one of fact. It is also one that really requires either the applicant or their representative to make a complaint during or immediately after a hearing.

18.4.6   Representatives and fraud on the tribunal

[18.87]   The issue of representatives advising applicants before the migration tribunals has seen questions arise as to the consequences that can flow for persons given bad advice.[206] The general rule seems to be that people rely on the advice given to them at their own risk.[207] One exception to the rule is instances where applicants are prevented from attending a tribunal hearing because of the fraudulent behaviour of an adviser. In *SZFDE v MIAC*,[208] the High Court said:

> The fraud of [the migration agent] Mr Hussain had the immediate consequence of stultifying the operation of the legislative scheme to afford natural justice to the appellants …
>
> In short, while the tribunal undoubtedly acted on an assumption of regularity, in truth, by reason of the fraud of Mr Hussain, it was disabled from the due discharge of its imperative statutory functions with respect to the conduct of the review. That state of affairs merits the description of the practice of fraud 'on' the tribunal.
>
> The consequence is that the decision made by the Tribunal is properly regarded, in law, as no decision at all. This is because, in the sense of the authorities, the jurisdiction remains constructively unexercised.

[18.88]   In acknowledging the court's decision in *SZFDE*, it should be noted that their Honours make it clear that a distinction must be drawn between negligent or

---

203   Ibid at [69]. See note on this case by Kira Raif, above n 191, at [336].
204   See for example *Appellant P119/2002 v MIMIA* [2003] FCAFC 230; and *SYSB v MIMIA* [2005] FCA 1259.
205   [2009] HCATrans 279.
206   On this issue, see Matthew Groves, 'Third Party Fraud and Fault in Public Law' (2009) 125 *Law Quarterly Review* 48.
207   This is consistent with the High Court's endorsement of agency (and the liability that can flow from it) in other circumstances. See, for example, *Smits v Roach* (2006) 227 CLR 423.
208   (2007) 232 CLR 189 at [48]-[52].

bad advice (which gives rise to no rights in an applicant) and fraud (which *can* vitiate a decision). The line between these two is not clear, although the facts in *SZFDE* are instructive. In that case the adviser had been struck off as both a solicitor and as a migration agent. The example was particularly clear cut.

18.5 The conduct of the hearing

[18.89] The jurisprudence surrounding the conduct of hearings by the migration tribunals is significant for two reasons. First, the emergent body of law is the most sophisticated development in Australia of jurisprudence on the conduct of quasi-inquisitorial tribunals, or processes where the adjudicator acts as inquisitor and exerts considerable control over the manner and nature of the hearing given. Second, the case law represents a particular illustration of the battle that has raged between the courts and the legislature over the determination of what is just, fair and efficient in administrative decision-making. Sections 353 and 420 of the Act provide that in the case of both the MRT and the RRT:

> (1) The Tribunal shall, in carrying out its functions under this Act, pursue the objective of providing a mechanism for review that is fair, just, economical, informal and quick.
> (2) The Tribunal, in reviewing a decision:
>   (a) is not bound by technicalities, legal forms or rules of evidence; and
>   (b) shall act according to substantial justice and the merits of the case.

[18.90] Over the years the migration legislation has been made increasingly explicit in the directions given as to how tribunal members are to conduct review. The fact that the statutory provisions do not always mirror the rules of procedural fairness developed by the courts under the common law is underscored by amendments made in 2002. Placed at strategic intervals throughout the Act, these spell out that the statutory directions concerning process are 'to be taken as an exhaustive statement of the requirements of the natural justice hearing rule' in relation to the matters with which the directions deal.[209]

[18.91] Under the common law, 'natural justice' or procedural fairness is addressed in three broad rules which are anything but simple in their application. The first and most complex is the hearing rule expressed in the Latin adage, *audi alteram partem* – to make a lawful decision, an adjudicator must consider (and listen to or *hear*) both sides of a dispute. The second is the rule against bias – *non sua judex in sua propria causa*. A lawful process is one that is not affected by bias or pre-judging on the part of the decision-maker. The third and final common law rule is related to the other two. A decision must be based on evidence that is *probative* in the sense that it has been tested and shown to have substance.[210] This chapter considers only the first of these three rules of procedural fairness.[211]

---

209 *Migration Act*, ss 357A and 422B.
210 This is sometimes described as the 'no-evidence' rule.
211 The bias and no evidence rules are discussed below, Chapter 19.3.2 and 19.3.3.

18.5.1 Hearing both sides

[18.92] Over the years, the hearing rules have become more general in their application as the democratisation of Western societies has led to a broadening in the circumstances in which people expect to be treated fairly. If this is reflected in fewer controversies over the basic issue of when people should be afforded a hearing in administrative processes,[212] the focus of dissent has moved to the content of the rules. In other words, the concern in modern times has been over what is required in order to effect a fair hearing where it can be assumed that the hearing rules apply.

[18.93] Under the common law, the case law on fair hearings has been concentrated around two key principles. These are that persons who are likely to be affected adversely by a decision should be informed of the case they have to answer and that they should be given the opportunity to respond to adverse information before a decision is made. The complexity of these principles in practice has arisen in the articulation of what constitutes adverse information; from what source the information has to come; and the nature of the opportunity that has to be given to respond. As the Full Federal Court said in *Commissioner for ACT Revenue v Alphaone Pty Ltd*:[213]

> It is a fundamental principle that where the rules of procedural fairness apply to a decision-making process, the party liable to be directly affected by the decision is to be given the opportunity of being heard. That would ordinarily require the party affected to be given the opportunity of ascertaining the relevant issues and to be informed of the nature and content of adverse material.

[18.94] The hearing regime established by the *Migration Act* is both more generous and more restrictive than the common law. It is more generous in that the common law has never insisted that all applicants be afforded an *oral* hearing of their claims.[214] It is less generous in so far as the common law is inherently more flexible, being informed by both relevant legislation and by the circumstances of individual cases.[215] The most obvious constraints in the divisions governing the conduct of review in the tribunals[216] are the provisions specifying the range and nature of the material that must be disclosed to applicants.

[18.95] The most important provisions are ss 57, 359ff and 424ff of the *Migration Act*, read together with ss 368 and 430. Sections 359A and 424A require tribunal members to set out in writing certain information that would be 'the reason or part of the reason' to make a relevant decision (on a visa or on the grant of protection). The tribunal must also 'ensure, as far as is reasonably practical, that the applicant

---

212   *Kioa v West* (1985) 159 CLR 550. See the discussion in Chapter 19.3.1.
213   (1994) 49 FCR 576 at [27].
214   The classic common law authority confirming that there is no such right is *Local Government Board v Arlidge* [1915] AC 120 at 134. For migration cases that have reached a similar conclusion, see *Zhang de Yong v MILGEA* (1993) 45 FCR 384; and on appeal (1994) 121 ALR 83; *NAHF v MIMA* (2003) 128 FCR 359 at [33]; and *SZCRP v MIMA* (2005) 149 FCR 36 at [21]-[22].
215   See, for example, *Plaintiff S157/2002 v Commonwealth* (2003) 211 CLR 426; and *Saeed v MIAC* (2010) 267 ALR 204.
216   *Migration Act*, Part 5 Div 5 and Part 7 Div 5.

understands why it is relevant to the review; and invite the applicant to comment on it'.[217] The catch is that not all adverse information is disclosable in writing. Exceptions are made for:

- information provided to an applicant orally during a hearing;[218]
- information that is not specific to an applicant (such as country information in refugee cases);[219]
- information provided by an applicant (other than orally during the course of a hearing);[220] and
- non-disclosable information, defined as information that the Minister has certified as exempt from disclosure on grounds of public interest; and other information that has not been certified by the Minister but that was given to the tribunal in confidence.[221]

Susan Kneebone has noted that these provisions are significantly narrower than the RRT's first Practice Direction 5b, which required that the tribunal give applicants 'an opportunity to respond to any relevant or significant material which is or may be adverse to his or her case'.[222] It also marks a considerable departure from the common law requirement to disclose *any* adverse information that is 'credible, relevant and significant to the decision to be made'.[223]

[18.96] Before the passage of the *Immigration Legislation Amendment (Procedural Fairness) Act 2002* (Cth), the courts used the common law hearing rules to supplement the procedures required by the Act. In cases such as Re MIMA; Ex parte Miah[224] and Plaintiff S157 v MIMA,[225] for example, the High Court not only invoked the common law principles but also found that a breach of the rules constituted a *jurisdictional error* of sufficient gravity to render the original decisions nullities in the eyes of the law.[226] The Full Federal Court has ruled that s 422B excludes the common law rules of procedural fairness in relation to reviews by the RRT.[227] Nevertheless, the spirit of the old law has resonated on occasion in the interpretations placed on the statutory procedures. The courts have responded to the exclusion of the common law by viewing even minute departures from the prescribed procedures as fundamental legal errors.[228]

---

217   Ibid, s 359A(1)(b) and (c) and s 424A(1)(b) and (c).
218   Ibid, ss 359AA and 359A(3) in the MRT; and ss 424AA and 424A(2A) in the RRT. Note that these provisions were inserted in response to judicial rulings on earlier disclosure provisions.
219   Ibid, ss 359A(4)(a) and 424A(3)(a).
220   Ibid, ss 359A(4)(b) and 424A(3)(b).
221   Ibid, s 359A(4)(c), read with ss 375, 375A and 376 (for the MRT); and s 424A(3)(c), read with ss 437 and 438 (for the RRT). This issue is discussed further below.
222   Susan Kneebone, 'The Refugee Review Tribunal and the Assessment of Credibility: An Inquisitorial Role?' (1998) 5 *Australian Journal of Administrative Law* 78 at 85.
223   *Kioa v West* (1985) 159 CLR 550 at 628 (Brennan J).
224   (2001) 206 CLR 57.
225   (2003) 211 CLR 426.
226   See further below, Chapter 19.6.
227   *SZCIJ v MIMA* [2006] FCAFC 62.
228   For an account of the jurisprudence here, see Grace Ma, 'Effect of the Migration Legislation Amendment (Procedural Fairness) Act 2002' (2007) 34 *Immigration Review* [520].

[18.97] For example, it has been established that s 424A (and, by analogy, s 359A) operate not simply before but also in the course of the hearing. This means that a legal error will be committed if at any stage the tribunal identifies but does not disclose a matter that is both adverse to the applicant and likely to be a reason or part of the reason for the decision that is ultimately made.[229] Again, as noted earlier, this is not to say that the tribunal is required to disclose as 'information' the tribunal's subjective thought processes engaged in for the purposes of making a decision.[230] However, the task of determining whether information falls within s 424A is determined by reference to the written reasons produced by the tribunal.[231] The critical question is whether comment has been sought in relation to information that formed part of those reasons.[232]

18.5.2 Disclosable information

[18.98] The hardening of the courts' attitude to non-compliance with the statutory rules is apparent in *SAAP v MIMIA*,[233] which became something of a landmark case when it reached the High Court. There, a failed refugee claimant alleged that the RRT had breached s 424A by taking evidence from her daughter while she was not in the room. The tribunal had used this evidence to make adverse findings as to her credibility and claims of persecution, without giving her particulars of that information, or an opportunity to respond. At first instance,[234] Mansfield J accepted the applicant's claim that the tribunal had failed to comply with s 424A on the basis that it had not given the applicant particulars of the relevant information in writing as required by ss 424A(2)(a) and 441A of the Act. Nor had it invited the applicant in writing to comment on that information. However, his Honour noted that the applicant had learned of her daughter's evidence through her migration agent (who had been present throughout the whole hearing). The tribunal member had asked the applicant about significant features of her daughter's evidence, and given her an opportunity to comment upon that material. In light of these circumstances, it was held that the breach had not deprived the applicant of the practical opportunity that s 424A is intended to provide (to learn of material adverse to the claim and to comment on it), and was not one that might have affected the outcome of the tribunal's decision.

[18.99] A majority of the High Court disagreed, ruling that the failure of the RRT to comply with the written notification requirements in s 424A in respect of adverse information taken from the daughter's evidence was fatal to the decision made. While

---

229 See *MIMA v Al Shamry* (2001) 110 FCR 27 at [20] (Ryan and Conti JJ) and at [38] (Merkel J); *Paul v MIMA* (2001) 113 FCR 396; *SAAP v MIMIA* [2002] FCA 577, upheld *SAAP v MIMIA* (2005) 215 ALR 162.
230 See [18.73] above.
231 *Paul v MIMA* (2001) 113 FCR 396 at [42]-[43] (Emmett J) and at [94] (Allsop J, with whom Heerey J agreed).
232 *SZEEU v MIMA* (2006) 150 FCR 214 at 262 (Allsop J) (special leave to appeal to the High Court refused: [2008] HCASL 351). See also *SZBYR v MIAC* (2007) 235 ALR 609 (*SZBYR*) at [17].
233 (2005) 215 ALR 162.
234 *SAAP v MIMIA* [2002] FCA 577.

the tribunal did not have to follow the statutory procedures in a particular sequence,[235] the procedures did have to be complied with strictly. The majority rebuked Mansfield J's attempts to gauge whether there had been substantial compliance with the legislative procedures, ruling that it did not matter that the breach had caused no unfairness to the applicant – the terms of the legislation were clear.[236]

[18.100] The effect of the High Court's ruling in *SAAP* was to force the introduction of a new and distinct step in the tribunal's hearing process whereby the tribunal would write to applicants after conducting an initial hearing. The letter would set out the matters identified by the tribunal as both adverse to the applicant and likely to form part of the ultimate decision. Further judicial rulings stressed that the legislative scheme governing the obtaining of 'further information' required all invitations to be made in writing.[237] The Federal Court has also confirmed that in cases involving more than one applicant, adverse information concerning one applicant that might affect others should be given to all affected parties.[238] As day follows night, this led people to examine the reasons for decisions to ascertain whether the tribunal had sought appropriate comment in respect of information relied on in making the decision.[239] Where it is not obvious that a matter is material and significant, the courts have held that the tribunals are required to explain why the information is relevant.[240] The jurisprudence prompted a legislative response that now allows the tribunals to both furnish information orally and to invite submissions orally, either by telephone or in person during the course of a hearing.[241]

18.5.3 Where a hearing is not required

[18.101] The Federal Court has confirmed that in most cases ss 359A and 424A will have no application where the basis of the tribunal's decision is the absence of information or other material.[242] In *Tran v MIMA*,[243] Kenny J noted that it is generally for

---

235 *SAAP v MIMIA* (2005) 215 ALR 162 at [60]-[63], [154]-[170] and [202].
236 (2005) 215 ALR 162 at [71], [208], [209].
237 *SZKTI v MIAC* (2008) 168 FCR 256 (rev'd *MIAC v SZKTI* (2009) 238 CLR 489); and *SZKCQ v MIAC* (2008) 170 FCR 236.
238 See Marshall J in *SZGSI v MIAC* (2007) 160 FCR 506 at [51]. His Honour in that case took the unusual step of declaring incorrect his own ruling in *MZWMQ v MIMIA* [2005] FCA 1263. See also *SZBYR v MIAC* (2007) 235 ALR 609.
239 See *SZEEU v MIMIA* (2006) 150 FCR 214 at 262; see also *SZBYR v MIAC* (2007) 235 ALR 609 at [17].
240 See, for example, *MIMA v SZGMF* [2006] FCAFC 138 at [40]-[41].
241 *Migration Act*, ss 359AA and 424AA, introduced by *Migration Amendment (Review Provisions) Act 2007* (Cth). On these changes, see Denis O'Brien, 'The Pursuit of Quality Decision Making in the Australian Refugee Review Tribunal' Conference paper, *Best Practice for Refugee Status Determination: Principles and Standards for State Responsibility*, Monash University, Prato, Italy, 29-30 May 2008, available at <www.cerium.ca/IMG/doc/Denis_O_Brien.doc>. See generally the discussion at Part 18.4.3 above.
242 See *V346 of 2000 v MIMA* (2001) 111 FCR 536 at [55]; *Paul v MIMA* (2001) 113 FCR 396 at [95] (Allsop J, with whom Heerey J agreed); *Tin v MIMA* [2000] FCA 1109 at [54]; *Malik v MIMA* (2000) 98 FCR 291 at 294-5; and *Tran v MIMA* [2002] FCA 1522 at [26]. See also *VAF v MIMIA* (2004) 206 ALR 471 at [24] (Finn and Stone JJ); affirmed by the High Court in *SZBYR* (2007) 235 ALR 609 at [18].
243 [2002] FCA 1522 at [25]. Her Honour's statement here is consistent with the common law which holds that it is no part of a decision-maker's function to make out a case for an applicant. See *Kioa v West* (1985) 159 CLR 550.

the applicant to provide the decision-maker with whatever information or material he or she may have that tends to support his or her case, and that 'the law imposes no obligation on the Tribunal to request the review applicant to meet a deficiency in the case that the applicant chooses to advance to the Tribunal'. The one qualification to this is the observation of the Full Federal Court in *NBKS v MIMIA*[244] that the 'positive use' of information omitted from an application can amount to a 'positive assertion that is detrimental to the applicant's case'. In these cases information not included in an application can become information that must be provided to the applicant.[245]

[18.102] A hearing will not be required when the information provided goes to essential criteria to be satisfied in relation to which any comment from the applicant can have no bearing. In *Pomenti v MIMA*,[246] Lindgren J ruled that the MRT did not have to give the applicant a hearing where the applicant's estranged wife withdrew her sponsorship for his application for a Spouse visa. His Honour also rejected the contention that the MRT could be required to hold a preliminary hearing of some kind.

18.5.4   Information supplied by the applicant

[18.103] It will be recalled that one of the exceptions to the statutory hearing rules in ss 359A and 424A respectively is where information is provided by an applicant (other than orally during the course of a hearing).[247] Here again, the courts have taken a rather hard line. For example, information provided by one family member cannot be used in deciding the case of another family member without soliciting comment from that family member – even where the appeals are heard together.[248]

[18.104] Before amendments to the Act in June 2007, information given by the applicant to the Immigration Department in the course of making an application was not counted as 'information' given to the tribunals. This means that where a tribunal member proposed to rely on such information for the purpose of making a decision, it had to be disclosed to the applicant and the applicant's comment had to be sought.[249] The information was not transformed into non-disclosable information by general affirmations by an applicant, or by the applicant providing the written reasons of a departmental officer referring to the information in question.[250] The same was not true if the applicant affirmed a specific fact before the tribunal.[251]

[18.105] As noted earlier, the *Migration Amendment (Review Provisions) Act 2007* introduced ss 359AA and 424AA into the Act. These provisions enable tribunals to

---

244 (2006) 156 FCR 205.
245 Ibid at [32]-[41] (Weinberg J) and [74] (Allsop J).
246 [1998] FCA 1400.
247 *Migration Act*, ss 359A(4)(b) and 424A(3)(b).
248 *SZGSI v MIAC* (2007) 160 FCR 506 at [45]-[58].
249 *MIMIA v Al Shamry* (2001) 110 FCR 27; affirmed by the High Court in *SZBYR* (2007) 235 ALR 609 at [16].
250 See *NBKT v MIMA* (2006) 156 FCR 419 at [59]; and *SZGGT v MIMIA* [2006] FCA 435 at [30]-[51].
251 The specific information will be covered by the exclusion in s 424A(3)(b). See *SZDPY v MIMA* [2006] FCA 627 at [35].

give to an applicant during a hearing 'clear particulars' of information that might be used in making a decision. The tribunal is required to ensure that the applicant understands why the information is relevant and important; the applicant must be invited to comment on or respond to the information; and the applicant must be allowed additional time to comment or respond (including by way of adjournment of the hearing) if the applicant requests this and the tribunal considers the request to be reasonable. The issue of material provided by an applicant to the Department *'during the process that led to the decision that is under review'* is dealt with specifically in ss 359A(4)(ba) (MRT) and 424A(3)(ba) (RRT). This information is no longer disclosable unless provided *orally* by the applicant to the Department. The changes allow for a faster but potentially harsher hearing process. For example, an oral consent during a hearing now suffices to waive privacy rights where permission is sought to check claims made by an applicant with third parties.[252] On the other hand, unreasonable behaviour on the part of a tribunal in refusing a request for extra time can constitute a jurisdictional error if the ultimate decision is flawed.[253] Whether a tribunal decides to seek comment on adverse information in writing or during a hearing, it must specify clearly the nature of the adverse information or evidence. Failure to do this will constitute a jurisdictional error.[254]

18.5.5 Non-disclosable information

[18.106] The final category of information in respect of which the tribunals are not required to seek comment is that categorised expressly as non-disclosable.[255] The scheme in the migration legislation is similar to that used in other enactments that provide for the giving of reasons in administrative decision-making.[256] The regime confers on the Minister the ability to certify information the release of which might compromise national security or otherwise be against the public interest. In addition, the tribunals are given discretion not to disclose material given to them in confidence (other than material certified as not disclosable under ss 375A or 437) that might found an action in equity for breach of confidence.[257] Before the passage of the *Migration Legislation Amendment (Procedural Fairness) Act 2002*, the High Court found no difficulty implying into these statutory provisions an obligation to observe the common law hearing rules.

---

252   *SZLIQ v MIAC* [2008] FCA 1405.
253   *Khergamwala v MIAC* [2007] FMCA 690 at [56].
254   *SZLIQ v MIAC* [2008] FCA 1405.
255   *Migration Act*, s 359A(4)(c), read with ss 375, 375A and 376 (for the MRT); and s 424A(3)(c), read with ss 437 and 438 (for the RRT).
256   See, for example, ss 13, 13A and 14 of the *Administrative Decisions (Judicial Review) Act 1977* (Cth).
257   *Migration Act*, s 376 (MRT) and s 438 (RRT), read with s 5, definition of 'non-disclosable information'. As the High Court noted in *MIAC v Kumar* (2010) 238 CLR 448 (*Kumar*) at [16]: 'The term "non-disclosable information" appears not only in s 359A. It appears also in s 57 (exclusion from "relevant information" to be given to non-citizen visa applicants); s 66 (exclusion from written reasons for visa refusals); ss 119, 120 and 129 (exclusion from relevant information to be given by the Minister in visa cancellation procedure); s 424A (to which reference has been made); and ss 501C, 501G and 500(6F) (respectively refusals and cancellations of visas by the Minister, and review thereof)'.

[18.107] The change affected by this legislation emerges starkly when the case of *VEAL v MIMIA*[258] is compared with the later High Court ruling in *MIAC v Kumar*.[259] Both cases involved situations where the tribunal received adverse material from sources who wished to remain anonymous. In both instances the central questions for the court were whether the tribunal was required by law to reveal either or both the existence and content of the confidential information.

[18.108] In *VEAL*, the tribunal received a letter alleging that the applicant worked for the government of Eritrea and that he had admitted to being accused of the murder of a prominent political figure in that country. In rejecting the applicant's asylum claim, the RRT asserted that it had given no weight to the adverse information. The tribunal went on to provide a variety of bases for rejecting the protection claim. The High Court quashed the decision made on the basis that procedural fairness required the tribunal to inform the applicant of the nature of the assertions made against him. Because the tribunal had not done this and so had not afforded the applicant the opportunity to make submissions on the allegations, its decision was affected by serious legal error. The court found that the tribunal was not obliged to reveal the identity of the informant or to supply a copy of the communication it had received. However, the appellant was entitled to be told of the essence of the allegations made against him. The court said:

> The Tribunal was not an independent arbiter charged with deciding an issue joined between adversaries. The Tribunal was required to review a decision of the Executive made under the Act and for that purpose was bound to make its own inquiries and form its own views upon the claim which the appellant made. And the Tribunal had to decide whether the appellant was entitled to the visa he claimed. ... The information which was contained in the letter was relevant to the inquiry and could not be ignored by the Tribunal.[260]

[18.109] The ruling in *Kumar* was markedly different. In that case the applicant was the foreign party in a failed immigration marriage. When the matter went on appeal to the MRT, that tribunal received a classic dob-in letter from a party who expressed a wish to remain anonymous. The MRT informed the applicant that it had received a letter, stating simply that it had received allegations to the effect that the applicant's marriage to his Australian citizen wife was contrived for immigration purposes. The applicant argued that procedural fairness required that without further and better particulars of the allegations he was not able to make appropriate submissions to support his case. Unlike in *VEAL*'s case, the tribunal did give weight to the confidential communication in its decision to affirm the Department's (negative) decision. In its reasons dated 3 February 2006, the tribunal stated:

> The Tribunal is not satisfied that there is sufficient evidence before it of the financial aspects of the relationship to indicate that the relationship is a genuine relationship. The Tribunal is not satisfied as to the nature of the household of the visa applicant and the nominator. The visa applicant has not been able to satisfactorily explain to the Tribunal why he is not residing with the nominator.

---

258   (2005) 225 CLR 88 (*VEAL*).
259   (2010) 238 CLR 448.
260   (2005) 225 CLR 88 at [26]-[27].

There is insufficient evidence before the Tribunal to satisfy it that at the time of decision the visa applicant and the nominator hold themselves out to the world as being in a genuine spousal relationship. Most importantly, the credible and significant adverse information before the Tribunal leads the Tribunal to find that the visa applicant and the nominator are not in a genuine and continuing spousal relationship.[261]

[18.110] In a relative short and unanimous judgment, the High Court ruled that the tribunal had complied with its statutory obligations by informing Mr Kumar of the existence of the adverse letter and of its essential contents – namely that the informant had evidence to the effect that the marriage was contrived solely for immigration purposes. The court acknowledged by implication that disclosure of the 'dob-in' letter would probably not found an action for breach of confidence under the general law. The information received was both highly damaging and could have been used as the basis for laying criminal charges. However, the court ruled that the matter should not be confused by the rules of equity on disclosure, because the proper operation of the migration legislation was advanced by the maintenance of confidentiality. The court said:

> The consideration which impressed the Full Court was that the general law does not protect confidences about such matters as the commission of crimes and frauds. In *A v Hayden*, when giving their reasons for answering the questions in the case stated and questions reserved by Dawson J to the Full Court, Mason, Wilson, Deane and Dawson JJ concluded that a court will not lend its aid to the enforcement of a contractual obligation of confidentiality undertaken by the Commonwealth, the effect of which would be to obstruct the administration of the criminal law. That situation may be contrasted with that on the present appeal. The preservation of the confidence of the informant's disclosures respecting the position of Mr Kumar tends to advance not obstruct the operation of the spousal visa provisions of the Act.
>
> It may be accepted that similar considerations to those which underpinned the result in *A v Hayden* apply also in the general law regarding non-contractual and purely equitable obligations of confidence. It has been said both in the courts of Australia and the United Kingdom that the disclosure of an 'iniquity' will not be restrained as the subject matter of an obligation of confidence. ...
>
> However, the second point is that these remarks are not directed to the situation in which the Tribunal is placed. ...
>
> Upon the proper construction of the Act, the circumstance that the information supplied in confidence to the Tribunal may have disclosed or related to the commission of offences by Mr Kumar or others did not deny to the information and the identity of the informer the character of non-disclosable information within the meaning of s 359A(4).[262]

[18.111] The High Court acknowledged that any argument for disclosure did not give any weight to the public interest in maintaining the confidence of the person who supplied the information. However, the court pointedly refused to lay down general rules about disclosure of protected information, instead saying that the balancing of

---

261 Cited in *Kumar* (2010) 238 CLR 448 at [10].
262 (2010) 238 CLR 448 at [25], [26], [28] and [33] (footnotes omitted).

competing considerations would be context dependent.²⁶³ The failure to require the tribunal to communicate the full details of the allegations made against him is at odds with both common law rules of procedural fairness and with the disclosure rules under the general law in equity. The ruling sits awkwardly with the warning given by Brennan J (as he then was) about the probative force of evidence that has not been tested through a process of hearing both sides in a case.²⁶⁴ It may be that the court saw Mr Kumar as a man with a lot of evidence stacked against him.²⁶⁵ It provides few safeguards against evidence adduced by mendacious or vindictive persons. Given the normative impact of High Court rulings, the potential for this case to encourage the migration tribunals towards greater secrecy in their procedures is regrettable. The case is unlikely to lead to decision-making that is either fairer or more likely to induce confidence in either applicants or observers of the system.

18.6 The investigative and reasoning process

[18.112] The harsh impact of the procedural rules governing the tribunals' review of migration and refugee decisions is most apparent in the jurisprudence that has developed around the tribunals' reasoning process. It is in this context that the 'quasi' nature of the tribunals becomes most apparent in so far as the law stops short of requiring a truly inquisitorial function. As noted earlier, the migration legislation provides considerable flexibility to the tribunals in the manner in which they can require applicants to provide information or further information.²⁶⁶ However, there is no express provision *requiring* either the MRT or the RRT to investigate or inquire about any matter. The passage of time has seen the gulf between the statutory procedures and the requirements of common law procedural fairness broaden considerably. For some judges, this state of affairs has been accepted grudgingly: every effort has been made to find other grounds of judicial review to make up the deficits in procedural fairness.

18.6.1 Onus and standard of proof

[18.113] It is often said that it is not appropriate to speak of a burden of proof in refugee status determinations in particular and administrative processes in general. In *MIMA v Hughes*,²⁶⁷ Merkel J stated:

> It is well established that in determining whether the requisite state of satisfaction is met for the purpose of s 65(1), concepts such as onus and burden of proof have no role to play before the IRT ... The question is not one of onus but one of satisfaction.

---

263 *VEAL* (2005) 225 CLR 88 at [25].
264 See *Re Pochi and MIEA* (1978) 2 ALD 33 at 56-7.
265 See the comments of the court at [35].
266 *Migration Act*, ss 359, 359AA and 359A and ss 424, 424AA and 424B.
267 (1999) 86 FCR 567 at [35] (Carr J agreeing). While taking a different construction to the legislative provisions in question, Nicholson J (at [4]) also expressed the view that there is no place for the importation of the concept of an onus or burden of proof before the IRT. The Full Court thus rejected the Minister's contention that reg 1.15 (relating to the grant of Remaining Relative visas) requires the applicant to prove they do *not* usually reside in the same foreign country as the overseas near relative.

[18.114] In *Huang v MIMA*,[268] Drummond J affirmed that common law concepts of onus of proof have no role in proceedings before the MRT.[269] However, in some circumstances it may be appropriate for the tribunal to have regard to common law standards of proof 'to reach conclusions of fact on some matters only if satisfied as to the existence of those facts "on the balance of probabilities arising from the available information before the decision-maker"'.[270]

[18.115] In the case of refugee applicants, however, the comments of the High Court in decisions such as *MIEA v Wu Shan Liang*[271] and *MIEA v Guo Wei Rong*[272] indicate that the 'real chance' test is concerned with 'degrees of probability', rather than balance of probabilities (which would place too high an onus or standard of proof on the applicant).

[18.116] Having said that, the reality is that both refugee claimants and migration applicants are expected to make out a case for the visa class sought.[273] The standard that applies may not be strictly that expected in civil cases – the balance of probabilities. Nevertheless, inability to persuade a decision-maker will most often be fatal to a person's claim.

18.6.2 The duty to hear and consider all substantive issues raised

[18.117] In considering the reasoning process, the starting point must be the notion that the MRT and RRT (like the primary decision-maker) have an obligation to consider all the evidence and material before the tribunal.[274] Over the years, however, the number and sheer variety of challenges to tribunal decisions (especially by the RRT) make it difficult to assert any principles without qualification. The difficulty is that some of the most problematic rulings – if their normative effect is considered – come from cases that involved highly controversial claims. The results are an object lesson in the old adage that hard cases make bad law.

[18.118] Generally speaking, the tribunals' obligation to consider evidence does not mean that a tribunal is bound to consider mountains of inaccessible information dumped on it by an applicant. For example, in *Cabal v MIMA*,[275] the tribunal was presented with a large number of untranslated documents in Spanish, including 19 textbooks, with no attempt made to explain the relevance of the material. The court ruled that in the first instance the onus is on the applicant to explain why material should be considered. However, the court noted that there may be circumstances in

---

268 [2001] FCA 901.
269 His Honour referred to *McDonald v Director-General of Social Security* (1984) 1 FCR 354 at 356-7, 366 and 369; *Cam v MIMA* (1998) 84 FCR 14. Compare *MIEA v Wu Shan Liang* (1996) 185 CLR 259 at 282-3.
270 See *MIMA v Epeabaka* (1999) 84 FCR 411 (*Epeabaka*) at [18].
271 (1996) 185 CLR 259 at 282-3.
272 (1997) 191 CLR 559 at note 25ff.
273 *Epeabaka* (1999) 84 FCR 411 at [10]ff.
274 See *Addo v MIMA* [1999] FCA 940 at [19]; *Khan v MIEA* (1987) 14 ALD 291 at 292; *Hindi v MIEA* (1988) 20 FCR 1 at 12-15; *Broussard v MIEA* (1989) 21 FCR 472 at 482-3; *Surinakova v MILGEA* (1991) 33 FCR 87 at 96; and *Mocan v RRT* (1996) 42 ALD 241 at 245.
275 [2001] FCA 546 at [25].

which the tribunal *is* obliged to obtain a translation of a foreign document whose relevance has been explained to the tribunal. This reasoning was echoed in *X v MIMA*.[276] There, the Full Federal Court held that s 424B (which allows the tribunal to direct the way in which information is to be given) did not allow the RRT to disregard material submitted by the applicant (notes in a personal diary) simply because the notes were not translated into English. The court pointed out that the tribunal 'could have asked the appellant to nominate particular passages in the diary that he regarded as relevant, and to have provided a translation of them into English'. The court also noted that the tribunal 'has ready access to interpreters, who, without great difficulty, could also function as translators of documents'.[277]

[18.119] Similar reasoning was employed in *Dertli v MIMA*.[278] That case concerned an application for refugee status by an illiterate Kurdish woman from Turkey, who claimed she would suffer persecution on the grounds of her Kurdish ethnicity, political opinion and membership of a particular social group (being Kurdish, Alevi and the parent of children involved in political activities). The RRT affirmed the decision of the Minister not to grant her a Protection visa, finding that she had suffered mistreatment before 1982, but none thereafter. It made no findings on detailed documentary evidence, some of which was left untranslated; and no finding on evidence submitted that she had used bribery to obtain her passport, nor on evidence tending to show that her family had been harassed since she had left Turkey. The Federal Court held that it was 'not sufficient to merely discuss relevant issues without coming to stated conclusions supported by evidence', nor was it sufficient to 'hear documentary evidence discussed in evidence, but not have it translated when it was made available ... or reach a conclusion about it'.[279]

18.6.3 Paradoxical functions: 'Inquisitorial' tribunals with no duty to make further inquiries

[18.120] The duty to consider all the material and evidence also raises the issue of whether the tribunals must consider jurisprudence not specifically raised by an applicant. Here a real divide appears to have opened between judges mindful of the inquisitorial role of the tribunals and others more concerned that the onus of making out a case should lie with the applicant. The courts traditionally have been reluctant to impose an obligation to consider all relevant matters, particularly where an applicant has been represented before the tribunal.[280] However, where applicants are not represented, some judges have required the tribunal to consider issues not

---

276 (2002) 67 ALD 355.
277 Ibid at [31]. See also *Abedi v MIMA* (2001) 114 FCR 186; and *S14/2002 v MIMA* [2003] FCA 1153 at [49] (affirmed *S14/2002 v RRT* [2004] FCAFC 171).
278 (1999) 56 ALD 409.
279 Note, however, that the court found the RRT to have a positive statutory obligation to make findings on material questions of fact. See ibid at [30] and [35]. This may not be good law following the High Court's ruling in *MIMA v Yusuf* (2001) 206 CLR 323, discussed below.
280 See *Perampalam v MIMA* (1999) 84 FCR 274; *Z v MIMA* (1998) 90 FCR 51; and *Emiantor v MIMA* [1998] FCA 1186. For a review of the case law in this area, see Mark Smyth, 'Inquisitorial Adjudication: The Duty to Inquire in Merits Review Tribunals' (2010) 34 *Melbourne University Law Review* 230.

specifically articulated by the applicant.[281] In *Paramanathan v MIMA*,[282] Merkel J went further, holding that the RRT has an obligation to consider all cases raised by the evidence and material placed before it, and must not limit its determination to the 'case' articulated by the applicant. His Honour stated that this obligation 'arises by reason of the nature of the inquisitorial process and is not dependent upon whether the applicant is or is not represented'.[283] Merkel J's conclusion (if not his specific reasoning) was accepted by a majority of the Full Federal Court in *Sellamuthu v MIMA*.[284]

[18.121] This is the point where the jurisprudence on the inquisitorial function of the tribunals (in particular of the RRT) begins to fracture.[285] The fault line begins with the ruling of the High Court in *Re MIMIA; Ex parte Applicants S134/2002*.[286] That case concerned a family of asylum seekers from Afghanistan who had gained considerable notoriety by the time this matter came to be heard in the High Court. The father, Mr Ali Bakhtiyari, arrived in Australia in 2000 and was granted a Temporary Protection visa on the basis that he was a refugee on 3 August of that year. Applicants S134 were Mrs Bakhtiyari and the couple's five children who arrived by boat (without documentation) on 1 January 2001. Taken into custody at South Australia's Woomera Detention Centre, Mrs Bakhtiyari lodged asylum claims for herself and her children without reference to her husband who she reported had been 'missing' for the previous two years. The claims were rejected both at first instance and by the RRT on the basis that Mrs Bakhtiyari and her family were from Quetta in Pakistan rather from Afghanistan as claimed. Although the Department and the tribunal appeared to have become aware of the existence and status of the husband (who had been accepted as an Afghan), this was not communicated to the applicant and was not listed as a matter taken into account in making the adverse decisions against Mrs Bakhtiyari. In the face of a very vigorous dissent from Gaudron and Kirby JJ, a majority of the High Court ruled that no error of law had been committed by the RRT. Their Honours found that the RRT had no obligation to inform Mrs Bakhtiyari of her husband's whereabouts and status. Nor did the inquisitorial nature of the tribunal oblige it to take into consideration the details of her husband's claim which would have been readily available to it.

[18.122] What is not apparent from the text of the judgments in *Applicants S134 of 2002* is that by 2003 the Bakhtiyari family had become the face of resistance to the harsh regime of mandatory detention under the Howard government. The separation of the wife and children from their father had made the case a *cause célèbre* for refugee activists, while the family came to embody dodgy 'queue jumpers' for the government. In early 2002, Mrs Bakhtiyari and her two sons had gone on hunger strike, sewing

---

281   See *Bouianov v MIMA* [1998] FCA 1348; *Saliba v MIMA* (1998) 89 FCR 38; *SZFEH v MIMIA* [2005] FMCA 963. Compare, however, *SZAOG v MIMIA* (2004) 86 ALD 15.
282   (1999) 94 FCR 28.
283   Ibid at 63.
284   (1999) 90 FCR 287 at [23] (Wilcox and Madgwick JJ).
285   On the dissonance in the Australian jurisprudence with that of the United Kingdom, see Matthew Groves, 'Judicial Review and the Concept on Unfairness in English Public Law' (2007) 18 *Public Law Review* 244.
286   (2003) 211 CLR 441.

shut their lips. In February, her brother threw himself from the rooftops at Woomera Detention Centre into the razor wire to draw attention to the family's plight.[287] At Easter in the same year, the two oldest Bakhtiyari boys gained international attention when they joined hundreds who broke out of Woomera detention centre when the centre was stormed by rioting protesters. The boys were hidden by activists who took them to Melbourne where an attempt was made to seek political asylum for the children in the British embassy.

[18.123] In August, a freelance New Zealand journalist in Afghanistan took it upon himself to investigate the family's claims. He visited the village of Charkh where it was alleged the family claimed to have lived, filing a dramatic story to the effect that he could find nobody in the village who had ever heard of Mr Bakhtiyari or who could recognise his photograph.[288] The allegations became 'truth' under a banner headline[289] which was unable to be questioned after the journalist was killed in a car accident a short time later.[290] Mr Bakhtiyari gave a series of press interviews through interpreters, fuelling both curiosity about and confusion surrounding the family. Later assertions that the journalist had visited the wrong village and that the investigation was otherwise flawed failed to persuade successive Immigration Ministers who became fixed in their determination to have the family removed from Australia. It was against this fraught and highly political background that the High Court came to hear Mrs Bakhtiyari's case in 2003. In all of the circumstances, it may not be surprising that the court declined to intervene in her case given the large amounts of very adverse publicity the family had received. By 2003 many Australians had made up their minds that the Bakhtiyari family lacked credit. What is highly regrettable is that the majority should rule as they did, given the process that had been followed in Mrs Bakhtiyari's case. It is our view that an investigative tribunal so-called should not be able to avoid censure when the tribunal failed either to reveal or consider evidence that was *actually* (not even constructively) before it and that was relevant and critical to the decision at hand.

[18.124] There are some aspects of *Applicants S134 of 2002* that are difficult to reconcile with roughly contemporary rulings by the High Court if the case is approached on a purely doctrinal basis. The most obvious example is the case of *MIMA v Bhardwaj*,[291] in which the High Court had little difficulty in finding that a decision-maker who failed to have regard to a facsimile transmission on an applicant's file did result in a decision rendered void by virtue of jurisdictional error. In other respects, however, the case set the approach that has been taken in later attempts to read a duty to inquire into the statutory scheme.

---

287   See Andrew West, 'Innocents in centre of a storm', *Sun Herald*, 10 February 2002, at 10-11.
288   See Alistair McLeod, 'In Bakhtiyari's "home", no hint of recognition', *The Australian*, 14 August 2002, at 1 (see also Editorial).
289   See Russell Skelton, 'The truth behind Bakhtiyari', *The Age*, 23 August 2002 at 1, available at <http://www.theage.com.au/articles/2002/08/22/1029114163552.html>.
290   See 'Correspondent killed in car crash', *The Australian*, 26 August 2002, at 1. See also International Federation of Journalists, Report on Media Casualties in the field of journalism and newsgathering, 2002, available at <http://www.ifj.org/assets/docs/164/101/d8640a4-aa6db65.pdf>.
291   (2002) 209 CLR 597. See the discussion at Part 18.4.1 above.

[18.125] Another low point in the jurisprudence on the tribunal's (lack of) duty to inquire was the decision of the High Court in *MIMIA v SGLB*.[292] Decided at the height of the troubles at Woomera Detention centre, the case involved an Iranian man whose refugee claim was rejected on grounds of credibility and inconsistencies.[293] The man's appeal was heard by the RRT via video link between the detention centre and Sydney, and proceeded in the face of evidence that the man was in no fit state to give evidence in any form. Before the hearing the RRT member had written to the Detention Centre manager about the applicant's mental state. Callinan J records the response by the centre's psychologist as follows:[294]

> [The respondent] presents as extremely tense, and shows signs of being both emotionally and physically volatile. In general he presents as a very angry self-focused person. [The respondent] has had a lot of contact with the medical staff due to his self-harming behaviour, and continues to behave in a threatening fashion towards staff. After physically violent acts either to himself or property, [the respondent] shows no sign of remorse or reflection on his behaviour. I have discussed with [the respondent] managing his anger through physical activities available at the centre such as use of the gym, etc but [the respondent] is not receptive to these suggestions.
>
> *[The respondent's] Powers of Recall*:
> [The respondent] has not been interested in discussing his past with me however I don't believe that he cannot recall his past. He says it makes him too angry to discuss his past. He holds very strong views on a variety of situations but expresses his views in few words. [The respondent] has sworn on the Koran that if he gets a negative RRT he will kill himself. [The respondent] has referred to conversations we have had previously. He does not seem to have blurred or confused recall. Although [the respondent] is tense and angry I believe he has the ability and the resources to present information if he felt he would benefit from that process. [The respondent] claims to suffer from headaches, poor concentration, and insomnia through anxiety however it seems that many of his actions are still clearly thought through and premeditated so I believe he has the capacity to think through events if required.

The tribunal held two hearings with the man. In spite of assurances that the applicant wished the hearings to proceed, it quickly became apparent that the man was in something approximating a psychotic state. Callinan J continues:[295]

> A further hearing by video link was conducted by the Tribunal on 26 June 2002. At the hearing, an incident occurred which the Tribunal subsequently described in this way:
>> 'I asked [the respondent] what problems he thought he might have if he went back to Iran now, and what might motivate them. He responded that he would take his life rather than return to Iran. At this point in the hearing [the respondent] became highly agitated. As it was apparent that he was not in a condition to answer any further questions, I agreed to send my final questions to his new

---

292   (2004) 207 ALR 12.
293   A detailed account of the factual basis for the man's claims and of the inconsistencies in his claims dating from the time of his arrival in Australia are set out in the judgment of Callinan J at [98]-[103].
294   Ibid at [107].
295   Ibid at [109].

adviser (who was present via telephone link) in the hope that she could obtain his responses to them.'

[18.126] With Kirby J in vigorous dissent, a majority of the High Court held that the tribunal was under no duty to ascertain whether the applicant was able to properly participate in the hearing. Gummow and Hayne JJ rejected any suggestion that proceedings before the RRT were subject to a requirement of competency akin to the requirement of fitness to plead in criminal trials.[296] Callinan J accepted that a tribunal should satisfy itself that parties can understand the proceedings in which they are seeking to participate,[297] but clearly felt the evidence on its face allowed the RRT to be satisfied of the applicant's competency. His Honour's account of the factual history of the man's claim creates a linear account of inconsistencies that (although not expressly acknowledged) seem to underpin his Honour's reluctance to find fault with the procedures followed.[298] The High Court's acceptance of procedures which on any view were weighted against a very vulnerable person came close to a statement that, in immigration, anything goes. The case certainly adds a new thread to jurisprudence on the duty to inquire if only because previous cases focused on the evidence that was or could be in issue about substantive matters. If there is no duty on the tribunals to seek information about a person's competency or ability to participate in a hearing, what chance is there that the court will demand of the tribunals a more general duty to inquire?[299]

[18.127] The jurisprudence on the duty to inquire was summarised neatly by Flick J, sitting as the Full Federal Court in *SZIAI v MIAC*.[300] That case involved an asylum seeker from Bangladesh who submitted two certificates in support of his claim that he had converted to Christianity and as a consequence feared persecution on religious grounds. The RRT's rejection of his claim was explained in part on the basis that the certificates were forgeries. The central issue on appeal was whether the tribunal could be required by law to make some simple inquiries into the genuineness of the certificates. Flick J said:

> [B]y reason of s 422B of the 1958 Act *'there is no scope for the operation of general requirements of procedural fairness outside the specific provisions of Div 4 of Pt 7 of the Act'*: *NBKT v MIMA* [2006] FCAFC 195 at [85]; 93 ALD 333 at 353 per Young J (Gyles and Stone JJ agreeing).
>
> ... No submission was advanced on behalf of the Appellant, nor could it have been advanced, that the power of the Tribunal to make further inquiries imposed upon it *'any duty or obligation to do so'*: *MIMIA v SGLB* [2004] HCA 32 at [43]; 207 ALR 12 at 21-2 per Gummow and Hayne JJ. See also: *SZJBA v MIAC* [2007] FCA 1592 at [46]; 164 FCR 14 at 25 per Allsop J; *WAGJ v MIMIA* [2002] FCAFC 277 at [24]. Nor was any submission advanced on behalf of the Respondent Minister that there was not a line of inquiry which was readily available to the Tribunal and centrally relevant to the task being undertaken: eg, *Li v MIAC* [2007] FCA 1098 at [28]; 96 ALD 361 at 367 per Kenny J. The simple submission advanced on behalf

---

296   Ibid at [45].
297   Ibid at [123].
298   Gleeson CJ seems to have taken a similar view: ibid at [19].
299   On this point, we agree with Mark Aronson, Bruce Dyer and Matthew Groves, *Judicial Review of Administrative Action* (Sydney: 4th ed, Law Book Co, 2009) at [5.90]-[5.100] that the odds are slim.
300   (2008) 104 ALD 22. For an older case that raised similar issues, see *Singh v MIMA* [1999] FCA 416.

of the Respondent Minister was that there was material upon which the Tribunal could justifiably have based its decision and there was, in those circumstances, no duty to inquire further. The response of the Association was disclosed to the now Appellant and he provided his response.[301]

[18.128] In the result, Flick J relied not on procedural fairness but on the question of whether the failure to inquire constituted *behaviour* on the part of the tribunal that was manifestly unreasonable. His Honour invoked a line of authorities going back to the English Court of Appeal decision in *Associated Provincial Picture Houses v Wednesbury Corporation*.[302] In that case Lord Greene MR articulated what is now regarded as a classic principle that a decision will be regarded as *ultra vires* or invalid if it is 'so unreasonable that no competent authority could ever have come to it'.[303] Flick J acknowledged that claims of unreasonableness succeed before the courts in very rare cases.[304] The failure to make inquiries will only constitute an error of law in narrow circumstances where material is readily available but is ignored. His Honour invoked the finding of Wilcox J in *Prasad v MIEA*[305] where that judge said:

> The circumstances under which a decision will be invalid for failure to inquire are, I think, strictly limited. It is no part of the duty of the decision-maker to make the applicant's case for him. It is not enough that the court find that the sounder course would have been to make inquiries. But, in a case where it is obvious that material is readily available which is centrally relevant to the decision to be made, it seems to me that to proceed to a decision without making any attempt to obtain that information may properly be described as an exercise of the decision-making power in a manner so unreasonable that no reasonable person would have so exercised it.

[18.129] Flick J refers to the aberrant behaviour that will lead a court to intervene as 'vitiating unreasonableness', ruling that the principle does not conflict with the general rule that decision-makers (in normal circumstances) are not obliged to make inquiries.[306] His Honour cites, by way of example, circumstances where a facsimile transmission arrives with pages that are obviously missing. The tribunal's failure to inquire about the missing pages has been held to be unreasonable.[307] Flick J acknowledged that academics have expressed different views about the 'merits' of unreasonableness as a ground of review.[308] However, in the result he ruled in

---

301 Ibid at [17]-[18].
302 [1948] 1 KB 223.
303 Ibid at 230.
304 See *Applicant M17 of 2002 v MIMIA* [2003] FCA 1364 at [29].
305 (1985) 6 FCR 155 at 169-70. The quotation is taken from *SZIAI v MIAC* (2008) 104 ALD 22 at [25]. Flick J notes that the ruling in *Prasad* was endorsed by the Full Federal Court in *Tickner v Bropho* (1993) 40 FCR 183 at 197-8 (Black CJ).
306 This principle was applied in *Bunnag v MIAC* [2008] FCA 357 at [36].
307 *SZJBA v MIAC* (2007) 164 FCR 14.
308 *SZIAI v MIAC* (2008) 104 ALD 22 at [28]. John McMillan argues that 'the risk [is] that an inquiry could never be satisfactorily concluded in the knowledge that another unturned stone may be hiding additional relevant information'. See 'Recent Themes in Judicial Review of Federal Executive Action' (1996) 24 *Federal Law Review* 347 at 381. The contrasting view is put by Savitri Taylor who notes 'the comparative difficulty in some circumstances confronted by an applicant seeking refugee status and the comparative ability of decision-makers to elicit further information'. See 'Informational Deficiencies Affecting Refugee Status Determination: Sources and Solutions' (1994) 13 *University of Tasmania Law Review* 43, cited by Flick J at [26].

SZIAI that the RRT's failure to make inquiries that could easily have been made did constitute unreasonable behaviour of sufficient gravity to constitute a legal error.[309]

[18.130] On appeal, the High Court disagreed with this final ruling on the facts of the case. It did not disturb Flick J's characterising of the law governing the (limited circumstances) where principles of reasonableness may require a tribunal to engage in further inquiries. Coming as the ruling did after a series of decisions rebuffing attempts to fault the procedures followed by the migration tribunals,[310] the case underscores once again that the High Court has shown no enthusiasm to develop even the smallest requirement that the tribunals should be duty bound to institute their own inquiries.[311]

18.6.4 Credibility findings and challenges to the methodology adopted by the tribunals

[18.131] The breadth of the statutory power given to the tribunals to determine the procedures adopted within the hearing room has generally left little scope for challenging the tribunals' reasoning in individual cases. It is particularly difficult to ascribe legal invalidity to a decision founded on the applicant's lack of credibility. This fact appears to have lead the RRT in many cases to use credibility as a ground for refusing Protection visa applications.[312] Susan Kneebone has noted also that official country information obtained by the RRT is often preferred to the applicant's evidence and that some members of the tribunal 'tend to rely too heavily on the reasons of the primary decision-maker in assessing the credibility of the applicant'.[313]

[18.132] The task of challenging adverse findings of the RRT in relation to credibility has been termed 'formidable'.[314] The difficulty in challenging such findings lies largely in the courts' ruling that credibility is an issue of fact not law.[315] In rejecting appeals, the courts have emphasised the specialist role of the tribunals in making findings on credibility, and warned that those findings should not be 'dissected'.[316] As Merkel J found in *Emiantor v MIMA*,[317] an error of law will not be found if the RRT's approach to credibility issues 'was open to it on the material, was based on rational grounds and was arrived at after consideration of matters that were logically probative of the issue of credibility'.

---

309   (2008) 104 ALD 22 at [27]. See also *MIAC v Le* (2007) 164 FCR 151 at [63].
310   See, for example, *MIMIA v SCAR* (2003) 128 FCR 553; *NAMJ v MIMIA* (2003) 76 ALD 56; *MIAC v SZNVW* (2010) 183 FCR 575.
311   *MIAC v SZIAI* (2009) 259 ALR 429 at [26]-[27]. See also *Khant v MIAC* (2009) 112 ALD 241; and *MIAC v SZGUR* [2011] HCA 1.
312   See comments by Einfeld J in *Meadows v MIMA* [1998] FCA 1706.
313   See Susan Kneebone, 'The RRT and Assessment of Credibility: An Inquisitorial Role' (1998) 5 *Australian Journal of Administrative Law* 78 at 82 and 83-4.
314   *Thevendram v MIMA* [1999] FCA 182.
315   *Chemaly v MIMA* [1998] FCA 1403.
316   *Pandari v MIEA* [1998] FCA 1698; *Sivalingam v MIMA* [1998] FCA 1167; *Kharroubi v MIMA* [1998] FCA 178; *Applicant NADL of 2001 v MIMA* [2002] FCA 274; and *Ibrahim v MIMA* (2000) 63 ALD 37.
317   (1997) 48 ALD 635 at 649. This approach was endorsed as correct by the Full Federal Court in *Kopalapillai v MIMA* (1998) 86 FCR 547. See also *Re MIMA; Ex parte Durairajasingham* (2000) 168 ALR 407 at [67]; and *SZKJU v MIAC* [2008] FCA 802; and *SZKSU v MIAC* [2008] FCA 610.

[18.133] However there are cases that illustrate that the tribunal's findings and reasoning in relation to credibility are not completely immune from review. In *Meadows*, for instance, the RRT had formed an adverse opinion of the applicants' credibility on the basis that two letters submitted in support of their claim had been fabricated. The tribunal concluded that the applicants were themselves implicated in the fabrication, despite the tribunal member having said during the hearing, 'I am not accusing you of anything' (when questioning the applicants in relation to the letters and their authenticity). The Full Court held that in accordance with the tribunal's duty to act according to substantial justice and the merits of the case, it was incumbent on the tribunal to make it known to the applicants that it was considering making such a serious finding against them. The Full Court in *Sellamuthu v MIMA* also set aside the decision of the RRT on the grounds that the tribunal had found the applicant lacked credibility without considering 'the more or less objective circumstantial evidence' that he had nevertheless been mistreated in Sri Lanka and was likely to suffer similar mistreatment if he returned.[318]

[18.134] Another practice adopted by the RRT (and by the Department of Immigration) at the height of the influx of boat people from Afghanistan and the Middle East in the early 2000s is worthy of mention in this context. This is the use of experts to analyse the language and speaking patterns of asylum seekers whose voices were recorded during interviews. The practice involved analysts with tertiary qualifications 'preferably in linguistics' listening to relevant tapes of the applicant in order to determine their country of origin. A favoured service provider was Skandinavisk Sprakanalys AB, a company that operated out of Sweden.[319] Both the tribunals and courts drew attention to the problems associated with this process, and the dangers of relying too heavily on such material. In *Alamdar v MIMA*,[320] for instance, Tamberlin J accepted the practice as lawful but noted that 'the methodology, the identity of the person expressing the opinion and the experience, training and expertise of that person were not specified'. In *SBAQ v MIMIA*,[321] Mansfield J was also reluctant to rely on evidence provided by analysts who were neither identified nor available for cross-examination. His Honour also noted that the two language analysts in that case had come to differing conclusions as to the applicant's origin. At the same time, if a linguistic analysis is undertaken, the results will be treated as probative material which the tribunal is obliged to consider.[322] Therefore, while the appropriate weight to be given to the analysis is a matter for the decision-maker, a complete failure to address the evidence in rare cases may amount to jurisdictional error.[323] Linguistic analysis was used in many of the cases involving unaccompanied and separated children from Afghanistan. It was a feature in all of those whose asylum claims were rejected. However unreliable as an identification tool, the linguistic tests were taken frequently as conclusive evidence – representing daunting hurdles for the children involved.[324]

---

318 (1999) 90 FCR 287.
319 See Raif, above n 191.
320 [2001] FCA 1698 at [3].
321 [2002] FCA 985.
322 *SCAS v MIMA* [2002] FCA 598.
323 *MIMA v SBAA* [2002] FCAFC 195.
324 For a critique of the practice, see Mary Crock, *Seeking Asylum Alone: Unaccompanied and Separated Children and Refugee Protection in Australia* (Sydney: Themis Press, 2006) Ch 11.2 at 157ff.

18.6.5 Findings on material questions of fact and the duty to provide reasons for decisions

[18.135] The final obligations for tribunal members in any administrative proceeding are to make a decision and to articulate the reasons for the decision made. Sections 368(1) and 430(1) of the Act require the MRT and the RRT respectively to prepare a written statement that:

(a) sets out the decision of the tribunal on the review;
(b) sets out the reasons for the decision;
(c) sets out the findings on any material questions of fact; and
(d) refers to the evidence or any other material on which the findings of fact were based.

[18.136] In *MIMA v Yusuf*,[325] the High Court addressed the central issue of what this statutory scheme requires of the tribunals. Does s 430(1)(c) require the RRT to simply state its findings on what the tribunal considers to be material questions of fact? In the alternative, should the tribunal's written statement conform to some objective standard to be ascertained by reference to the particular application and the material available to the tribunal in respect of that application? A majority of the court upheld the first, subjective, interpretation of s 430(1)(c). As McHugh, Gummow and Hayne JJ stated:

> All that s 430(1)(c) obliges the Tribunal to do is set out its findings on those questions of fact which it considered to be material to the decision which it made and to the reasons it had for reaching that decision.[326]

[18.137] In taking this approach the court rejected the interpretation placed on the provision by the majority of the Full Federal Court in *MIMA v Singh*,[327] to the effect that 'material' in the expression 'material questions of fact' means 'objectively material'.[328] McHugh, Gummow and Hayne JJ (with whom Gleeson CJ agreed) also explicitly dismissed the contention that s 430(1)(c) imposes on the tribunal a positive duty to make findings on material questions of fact.[329] The court held that, if the tribunal does not set out a finding on a question of fact, it can be inferred that the tribunal did not consider the matter to be material. This may or may not disclose a reviewable error under s 476(1), or jurisdictional error which will ground relief under s 75(v) of the Constitution, depending on the matter in issue and the context in which it arises.

[18.138] In *Yusuf*, Ms Yusuf had recounted a number of events in which she claimed that she and her family had been the subject of attacks by the Hawiye clan in Somalia,

---

325   (2001) 206 CLR 323.
326   Ibid at [68]. See also Gleeson CJ at [9], Gaudron J at [33]-[34] and Callinan J at [215]-[217].
327   (2000) 98 FCR 469.
328   Note that Kirby J dissented, adopting the objective test of materiality described by the majority in *Singh*: '[I]f a decision, one way or the other, turns upon whether a particular fact does or does not exist, having regard to the process of reasoning the Tribunal has employed as the basis for its decision, then the fact is a material one ... A fact is material if the decision in the practical circumstances of the particular case turns upon whether that fact exists': (2001) 206 CLR 323 at [136]-[137].
329   The court relied on the reasoning in *MIEA v Guo Wei Rong* (1997) 191 CLR 559, discussed earlier.

to support her claim of persecution on the grounds of race or membership of a particular social group. In confirming the Minister's decision to reject her application, the RRT stated that it accepted Ms Yusuf had twice been attacked by members of the Hawiye, but found that her clan membership was not the motive for those attacks. It rejected other claims with respect to attacks on her sister and her sister's children, but made no finding with respect to a third incident in which Ms Yusuf claimed her home had been attacked and her husband forced to flee. The High Court held that the RRT's failure to make a finding in relation to this third incident did not amount to a breach of s 430. Relying on the subjective interpretation of s 430(1)(c) outlined above, the court held that even if the invasion and its consequences were said to be a material question of fact, it must be inferred that they were not material to the decision the tribunal actually made. The court was divided on the issue of whether this disclosed reviewable error.

[18.139] The majority of appeals lodged on the basis that the tribunal's reasons are inadequate appear to have failed.[330] However, in *Huang v MIMA*,[331] Drummond J stated that, in his view, the *Wu Shan Liang* principle[332] (that courts should not be overly zealous in scrutinising the reasons of administrative decisions) does not apply equally to all decisions. He noted that the MRT is a specialist decision-maker which performs a significantly different role from most public servants, and is capable of providing a coherent and informative explanation for how it reaches its ultimate conclusion. In the case at hand, the MRT had stated that the applicant for a student visa 'appears not to have complied with condition 8202 of [her expired] visa regarding satisfying course requirements', but did not make clear how it had reached this finding, and whether it had relied on information disputed by the applicant.

[18.140] In the past, the Federal Court has also set aside decisions of the RRT on the grounds that it failed to give reasons for rejecting key matters going to the credibility of the applicant, in breach of s 430(1)(b).[333] However, this ground for challenging a tribunal decision will most often come back to *Yusuf*-related questions about what the tribunal is and is not obliged to articulate in its reasons.[334] In *Re MIMA; Ex parte Durairajasingham*,[335] the RRT had found the applicant's claim that members of a rebel group had tried to recruit him 'utterly implausible'. McHugh J dismissed the prosecutor's contention that the RRT had breached s 430(1) by failing to set out reasons for this finding, stating:

> [T]his was essentially a finding as to whether the prosecutor should be believed in his claim – a finding on credibility which is the function of the primary decision-maker par excellence. If the primary decision-maker has stated that he or she does not believe a particular witness, no detailed reasons need to be given as to why that particular witness was not believed. The Tribunal must give the reasons for

---

330 See, for example, *Shumilov v MIMA* (2001) 65 ALD 487; *Dissanayake v MIMA* [2001] FCA 491; *Kyi v MIMA* [2001] FCA 580; *Zan v MIMA* [2001] FCA 473; and *Phan v MIMA* (2000) 171 ALR 323.
331 [2001] FCA 901.
332 *MIEA v Wu Shan Liang* (1996) 185 CLR 259.
333 See, for example, *Thevendram v MIMA* [1999] FCA 182; and *Kandiah v MIMA* [1998] FCA 1145. Compare *MIMA v SBAN* [2002] FCAFC 431.
334 See, for example, *MIAC v MZYCE* (2010) 116 ALD 156.
335 (2000) 168 ALR 407.

its decision, not the sub-set of reasons why it accepted or rejected individual pieces of evidence.[336]

[18.141] The change of government in 2007 did not bring with it great changes in the manner of the two migration tribunals' ways of operating. In many respects, indeed, it seems to have been business as usual. Having said that, the tribunals do appear to have been affected – as the rest of the immigration bureaucracy was affected – by the change in ethos within the administration. Gentler policies seem to have resulted in an increase in acceptances at primary level, especially in onshore protection[337] and in fewer applications for review at both tribunal and court levels. It is to the oft times fraught issue of judicial review that we now turn.

---

336 Ibid at [67].
337 See the statistics discussed in Chapter 12.6 above.

19

Judicial Review of Migration Decisions

19.1 Introduction

[19.01] The final legal avenue for seeking the redress of an adverse migration decision is the courts. The Federal Court, the Federal Magistrates Court and the High Court have power to review the lawfulness of such decisions by virtue of Part 8 of the *Migration Act 1958* (Cth) and (in the case of the High Court) s 75(v) of the Australian Constitution. In some circumstances, the Federal Court continues to have jurisdiction to review migration decisions under the *Administrative Decisions (Judicial Review) Act 1977* (Cth) (*ADJR Act*),[1] the *Federal Court of Australia Act 1976* (Cth) and the *Judiciary Act 1903* (Cth). The High Court is also the final arbiter of the constitutionality of legislation.

[19.02] Judicial review is a mechanism designed to allow oversight by the courts of the legality of administrative decisions, in contradistinction to the merits of a ruling. Unlike members of the various administrative tribunals – the Migration Review Tribunal (MRT), the Refugee Review Tribunal (RRT) and the Administrative Appeals Tribunal (AAT) – the courts do not stand in the shoes of the decision-maker so as to determine the correct or most preferable decision to make in all the circumstances.[2] Their role is to oversee the application and interpretation of the law. This means that the focus of the court is on the facts and the law applicable at the time a tribunal or departmental decision is made. It is not open to the court of its own motion to consider fresh evidence or other material that would draw the judges into reviewing the merits of the decision that should be made.

[19.03] Judicial review embodies the notion that in a democracy every exercise of power should be qualified or made subject to a system of checks and balances.[3] In *Council of Civil Service Unions v Minister for Civil Service*,[4] Lord Diplock noted that judicial review has three key functions. The role of the courts is to:

---

1 This Act began operation on 1 October 1980. See Mark Aronson, Bruce Dyer and Matthew Groves, *Judicial Review of Administrative Action* (Sydney: 4th ed, Law Book Co, 2009) at 93-101.
2 See *Drake v MIEA* (1979) 24 ALR 577 at 589; cited in *Shi v Migration Agents Registration Authority* (2008) 235 CLR 286 at [35].
3 On this issue, see Aronson, Dyer and Groves, above n 1, at 93ff.
4 [1985] 1 AC 374 at 407.

(i) oversee the application of the law by ensuring that all and only relevant matters are taken into account in making a decision;
(ii) ensure that fair procedures are followed; and
(iii) ensure that the decision made is rational and reasonable in all the circumstances.

If this formulation should be unremarkable, the sad truth is that the practice of judicial review is rarely free from controversy.

[19.04] In immigration, the central problem is that parliament and the executive have come to see the courts as political subversives which preference the human rights of individuals over the policy objectives of those elected to govern. Nowhere was this stated more clearly than by former Minister Philip Ruddock. Well before the *Tampa* hove into the limelight of Australia's political consciousness, Mr Ruddock was saying:

> It is the government, not some sectional interests, or loud intolerant individual voices, or ill-defined international interests, or, might I say, the courts that determines who shall and shall not enter this country, and on what terms. ...
>
> Only two weeks ago a decision to deport a man was overturned by the Federal Court although he had been convicted and served a gaol sentence for possessing Heroin with an estimated street value of $3 million. Again, *the courts have reinterpreted and re-written Australian law – ignoring the sovereignty of Parliament and the will of the Australian people. Again, this is simply not on.*[5]

[19.05] Although expressed most vehemently during the years of Coalition government between 1998 and 2007, such hostile attitudes towards the courts and judicial review have been a bi-partisan affair that had their provenance in the Labor governments of Prime Ministers Hawke and Keating.[6] In this chapter we attempt to capture the essence of the battle royal that has been fought over the role that the courts should play in the review of migration decisions. We begin in Part 19.2 with a discussion of what might be described as the irreducible minimum entitlements to judicial review in Australia. Thereafter we decided that the best way to both explain the judicial review process and to capture what has happened in the immigration area is to present the material historically.

[19.06] The story begins with the revolution of the 1960s and 1970s that saw the creation of the Federal Court of Australia and the passage of a raft of statutes that changed forever the nature of the relationships between individuals and officialdom in Australia. As explained in Part 19.3, immigration was one of the last areas of public administration to be affected by these changes. However, when the changes took hold in the mid to late 1980s, the reaction from government was probably more dramatic

---

5   Address to the National Press Club, Canberra, 18 March 1998 (emphasis added). The same theme was repeated in the Minister's address to the Victorian Press Club, 26 March 1998: '[I]t is the role of the Government, not other marginal voices, or ill-defined international interests, or might I say, the courts, that make decisions about who shall and who shall not enter this country and on what terms. This has been an axiomatic principle of successive Australian governments and I take that claim as of right. I believe that the Government has a moral obligation to make those decisions on behalf of all Australians.'

6   See Denis C Pearce, 'Executive Versus Judiciary' (1991) 2 *Public Law Review* 179.

than in any other field. In Parts 19.4 to 19.6 we explore in sequence the attempts made to rein in the perceived power of the courts. This began with the codification of the criteria governing the making of migration decisions. It was followed by more and more explicit measures designed to define and constrain the power of the courts to judicially review migration decisions.

[19.07] Two themes emerge in this discussion that have recurred throughout this book. One relates to the notion of discretion – or the range of choice that should be left to a decision-maker. The other relates to the locus of power – or who should be vested with the ability to decide between decisional referents. The end of the chapter brings us back to where we began – with the High Court reminding us that the Constitution guarantees that judicial review cannot be excluded completely from the immigration process.

19.2   Constitutional guarantees

[19.08] Although Australia's Constitution does not contain a Bill of Rights, it does include some limited guarantees. One such is the right of *all persons* to seek judicial review of decisions made by federal officials. Section 75(v) of the Constitution provides that the High Court has original jurisdiction to hear cases relating to 'all matters in which ... a writ of mandamus or prohibition or an injunction is sought against an officer of the Commonwealth'. The phrase 'officer of the Commonwealth' is a term of art that has been interpreted to include ministers of the Crown[7] and judges of federal courts.[8] Accordingly, migration decisions are reviewable in the High Court whether they are made by the Minister, public servants, or by any of the various administrative tribunals: the determining factor is the person exercising federal power.[9] Section 75(v) specifies that judicial review must be sought in one of two ways. The first is through the prerogative writ procedure, while the second is via the equitable remedies of declaration and injunction.

[19.09] The prerogative writs go back over 500 years to the time when the English kings were endeavouring to subjugate England and Wales.[10] A prerogative writ is a command by the Sovereign to persons or bodies to appear in the King's court to justify their administrative actions. The three primary prerogative writs are mandamus, prohibition and certiorari. Other writs that can be obtained are the writs of habeas corpus, seeking the release of a person; and quo warranto, or challenge to the authority

---

7   Usually ministers will only be amenable to a writ of mandamus or to a declaration. For general comment, see HE Renfree, *The Federal Judicial System of Australia* (Sydney: Legal Books, 1984) at 211-12.
8   See, for example, *R v Commonwealth Industrial Court Judges; Ex parte Cocks* (1968) 121 CLR 313; and *R v Gray; Ex parte Marsh* (1985) 157 CLR 351.
9   The linkage between judicial review and the exercise of federal power in Australia is interesting to contrast with the situation in the United States where much more emphasis is placed on territory or the place in which the federal power is exercised.
10 For an account of the history of judicial review in England and the development of the prerogative writs, see Stanley A De Smith, Harry Woolf and Jeffrey Jowell, *Judicial Review of Administrative Action* (London: Sweet and Maxwell, 5th ed, 1995) Ch 13.

of an official to make a decision.[11] Habeas corpus is unusual because it can be issued both by the Federal Courts[12] and by State Supreme Courts[13] and because it is a remedy that can be sought by *any* person (whether affected by the decision to detain or not).[14]

[19.10] Mandamus commands officials to justify to the courts the manner in which they have exercised a discretionary power that has been reposed in them. If the courts find that this power has not been exercised in accordance with the law, then mandamus will issue to command the official to re-exercise the discretion, but this time to do so according to law.

[19.11] Prohibition and certiorari command officials making decisions that may affect the rights or expectations of persons to justify their manner of adjudication. Prohibition is sought generally where a challenge is made to the process or procedures that have been followed by a body in its deliberations. The writ will issue if the authority has been acting improperly – outside of its powers. On the other hand, certiorari may be granted if a decision has been made contrary to law. Its effect is to order that the determination be nullified or quashed. Although s 75(v) mentions mandamus and prohibition, no mention is made of certiorari. This constitutional oversight has been remedied by the High Court either allowing the writ of prohibition to issue in place of certiorari, or by simply issuing certiorari in conjunction with another remedy.[15] In more recent times the omission has been explained by some as an indication that the constitutional writs only guarantee the ability of the High Court to correct errors of law so serious that they meet the description of 'jurisdictional errors'. The meaning of this somewhat elusive phrase is considered in detail in Part 19.6.2 below. Certiorari, on the other hand, is a remedy that is used to correct all types of legal errors, serious or otherwise.[16]

[19.12] Prohibition and certiorari will only issue against persons or bodies that make adjudicated decisions having an effect in law. They are not available where proceedings do not result in determinative decisions.[17] In these cases, the appropriate remedy will be to seek an injunction and declaration. These are known as the 'equitable remedies'.

---

11   See *High Court Rules 2004* (Cth), r 25.14. For a recent discussion of the writs available in the High Court in the immigration context, see *MZXOT v MIAC* (2008) 233 CLR 601.

12   See generally David Clark and Gerard McCoy, *Habeas Corpus: Australia, New Zealand and the South Pacific* (Sydney: The Federation Press, 2000).

13   It is in this context that most of the Supreme Court immigration cases have been brought: see, for example, *R v Governor of Metropolitan Gaol; Ex parte Tripodi* (1961) 3 FLR 134; *R v Liveris; Ex parte da Costa* (1962) 3 FLR 249; *R v Governor of Metropolitan Gaol; Ex parte Di Nardo* [1963] VR 61. Other cases that have been brought in the Supreme Courts include an action against a minister for contempt of a Supreme Court: see *Attorney-General (NSW) v Ray* (1989) 90 ALR 263.

14   See, for example, *Victorian Council for Civil Liberties v MIMA* (2001) 110 FCR 452, discussed in Chapter 4.3.4 above.

15   See Lee JW Aitken, 'The High Court's Power to Grant Certiorari – The Unresolved Question' (1986) 16 *Federal Law Review* 370.

16   See the comments of McHugh and Gummow JJ in *Re MIMA; Ex parte Applicant S20/2002* (2003) 198 ALR 59 (*Applicant S20/2002*) at [27]. See also *Craig v South Australia* (1995) 184 CLR 163 at 179 (Brennan, Deane, Toohey, Gaudron and McHugh JJ); and *MIMA v Yusuf* (2001) 206 CLR 323 (*Yusuf*) at [82] (McHugh, Gummow and Hayne JJ, with whom Gleeson CJ agreed at [1]).

17   See *Ainsworth v Criminal Justice Commission* (1992) 175 CLR 564 (*Ainsworth*).

[19.13] Ever since the middle of the 19th century, the courts of equity have not simply issued injunctions that are enforceable commands; they have also handed down declarations of right. After the fusion of the common law and equitable courts, the judges began to develop the declaration of right as a special remedy against governmental maladministration. Although a declaration is merely a statement by a court, governments usually obey these rulings and correct any errors or omissions that have been made. The modern remedy of the declaration is not surrounded by the technicalities of the prerogative writs. For example, it is not necessary to show that an adjudicative body is affecting rights in law before a declaration can be granted.[18] In *Plaintiff M61/2010E v Commonwealth and Plaintiff M69 of 2010 v Commonwealth*,[19] the High Court said:

> The power to grant declaratory relief is a power which '[i]t is neither possible nor desirable to fetter … by laying down rules as to the manner of its exercise'.[20]

As pointed out in *Ainsworth v Criminal Justice Commission*,[21] it is a form of relief that is confined by considerations which mark out the boundaries of judicial power.

[19.14] Before any of the prerogative writs can even be served on the government, applicants must show a judge or a master that they have an arguable case in law. In practical terms, this means that the applicants must obtain an order nisi.[22] Both the prerogative writs and the remedy of declaration are discretionary. The High Court is not required to grant the remedies, even where the applicants have established some wrong-doing, if the High Court considers that their granting would not be appropriate or where the order would be futile.[23] Where the High Court is the only avenue left open to litigants, however, the court often has little option but to grant the appropriate remedy where there has been a transgression and where the applicants have complied with the necessary procedures. This became a real issue in immigration when various restrictions were placed on access to judicial review in courts other than the High Court.[24]

[19.15] Although judicial review using what have been termed the constitutional writs[25] has been available since Australia became a nation, in fact only a tiny number of cases were brought in the immigration field in the first 80 or so years after Federation. As seen in earlier chapters, these largely concerned challenges to the constitutionality of laws or actions in particular cases or applications for habeas corpus based on other illegalities. There were both practical and legal impediments for disgruntled migrant

---

18 For example, in *Ainsworth* (1992) 175 CLR 564, although certiorari would not issue against a recommendatory body, the High Court was prepared to issue a declaration to the effect that there had been a denial of natural justice.
19 (2010) 272 ALR 14 at [102] (*Plaintiffs M61/M69*).
20 *Forster v Jododex Aust Pty Ltd* (1972) 127 CLR 421 at 437; *Ainsworth* (1992) 175 CLR 564 at 581-2.
21 (1992) 175 CLR 564 at 582. See also *Pape v Federal Commissioner of Taxation* (2009) 238 CLR 1 at 68.
22 See *High Court Rules 2004* (Cth), Part 25, rr [25.01] and [25.02].
23 See *Re RRT; Ex parte Aala* (2000) 204 CLR 82 (*Aala*) at [42]-[57] (Gaudron and Gummow JJ, Gleeson CJ agreeing). For examples where relief has been denied, see *Hao Jiang v MIAC* [2007] FCA 907; and *SZJSP v MIAC* [2007] FCA 1925.
24 See, for example, *Re MIMA; Ex parte Miah* (2001) 206 CLR 57 (*Miah*).
25 See generally Stephen Gageler, 'The Legitimate Scope of Judicial Review' (2001) 21 *Australian Bar Review* 279.

applicants. Access to the High Court was both expensive and rendered difficult by the technicalities of the writ system. The judiciary's interpretation of the grounds on which intervention should occur also limited the relief available. Migrants fared badly because of the deference shown by the courts to Ministers of the Crown[26] and to the exercise of prerogative powers.[27] Persons who could not point to legal entitlements were also at a disadvantage.[28] All this began to change with the social and cultural upheaval that occurred in the 1960s and 1970s.

19.3 The first revolution: Immigration and the new administrative law

[19.16] For disgruntled migration applicants, the most significant developments from this period were the creation of avenues for review of the merits of some decisions;[29] the creation of the Federal Court of Australia[30] and the passage of the *ADJR Act* in 1977. For the first time, applicants were able to obtain reasons for adverse decisions[31] and they had a series of avenues available through which to challenge the rulings made. The High Court was at pains to stress that the *ADJR Act* did no more than codify the common law grounds for the review of decisions 'of an administrative character' made under federal enactments.[32] The revolution was in the ease of access to the courts. The new legislation cut through the technicalities of the writ system and provided a neat list of the circumstances in which either decisions[33] or conduct engaged in for the purpose of making a decision[34] would be rendered unlawful.

[19.17] The new mood of openness and accountability appears to have created more friction and resentment in immigration than in other areas of public administration. The problem was that the migration legislation was characterised by broad discretions and powers vested somewhat misleadingly in 'the Minister'. The practical effect was that the immigration bureaucracy operated in something of a world of its own, with officers described as 'angels or arrogant gods'.[35] The so-called 'new administrative law' forced the Department to write and publish guidelines on how decisions were to be made.[36] The inadequacies of the procedures followed or the reasoning employed were laid bare before tribunals and courts. Faced with the human impact

---

26   *Lloyd v Wallach* (1915) 20 CLR 299; *Jerger v Pearce* (1920) 28 CLR 588.
27   See *Musgrove v Toy* [1891] AC 272 and the discussion above in Chapter 2 at [2.24]–[2.25].
28   See, for example, *Koon Wing Lau v Calwell* (1949) 80 CLR 533; and *Salemi v Mackellar (No 2)* (1997) 137 CLR 396 (*Salemi (No 2)*).
29   See the discussion in Chapter 18.2 above.
30   See *Federal Court of Australia Act 1976* (Cth). See Aronson, Dyer and Groves, above n 1, at 29-31, 40-4.
31   Compare the situation at common law in *Public Service Board (NSW) v Osmond* (1986) 159 CLR 656. See Aronson, Dyer and Groves, above n 1, at 833, 835.
32   See, for example, *Kioa v West* (1985) 159 CLR 550 at [14] (Mason J); *Minister for Aboriginal Affairs v Peko-Wallsend* (1985) 162 CLR 24 at 39-42. See also Aronson, Dyer and Groves, above n 1, at 53.
33   *ADJR Act*, s 5.
34   Ibid, s 6.
35   See Helen Martin, *Angels and Arrogant Gods: Migration Officers and Migrants Reminisce 1945-1985* (Canberra: AGPS, 1988).
36   See Denis C Pearce, 'The Fading of the Vision Splendid: Administrative Law Retrospect and Prospect' (1989) 58 *Canberra Bulletin of Public Administration* at 15-24.

of the decisions being made, the newly appointed Federal Court judges made rulings that rocked the administration to the core: preventing deportations and in one case even ordering officials to return an individual who it was claimed had been removed from the country illegally.[37] Where the existence of broad discretions had hitherto been regarded as a signal for judicial deference, the list of grounds enumerated in the *ADJR Act* was read by some judges as an open invitation to engage in review. Unlike decisions made by the tribunals, court rulings were normative in their effect, requiring sustained, systemic changes in procedures and substantive decision-making.[38]

[19.18] In this section we present case studies of two areas in which developments in federal judicial review appear to have set off major concerns for the immigration bureaucracy and ultimately for governments concerned about decisional control. Both concern the adjudicative process: the first goes to the procedures followed and the second to the matters taken into account and the reasoning process itself. They are at the heart of what might be regarded as 'broad' judicial review. This is review undertaken by the courts based on principles that have been developed through the evolutionary processes of the common law. They stand in contrast to the narrower functions that the courts perform when reviewing the lawfulness of administrative decisions made in the context of an explicit statutory scheme. Here the decisional referents and the procedures to be followed are spelt out in legislation. The case studies are significant as they help to explain the subsequent attempts that have been made to stop the courts from engaging in the 'broad' judicial review of migration decisions.

19.3.1 Natural justice or procedural fairness

[19.19] The most significant factor in the change that occurred in the judicial review of migration decisions during the 1980s was the High Court's development of the rules of natural justice or procedural fairness.[39] Until their right to a hearing was recognised, people affected by migration decisions found it very difficult to prove that particular rulings were flawed, either because of the matters taken into account or because of the procedures followed. With the benefit of hindsight, the change in the approach taken by the courts had profound consequences. In a sense, what the courts did was to forge links between the hearing rights and the human rights of migration applicants. The significance of this association of rights may explain why the courts have resisted so forcefully the ouster of their jurisdiction. We will examine here the two principal common law rules of natural justice: those going to the procedures followed in reaching a decision and the rule against bias. Mention will be made also to a third principle, known as the 'no evidence' rule which posits that a decision will only be lawful if supported by legally probative evidence.[40]

---

37   See, for example, *Azemoudeh v MIEA* (1985) 8 ALD 281.
38   On this history, see Mary Crock, 'The Impact of the New Administrative Law on Migrants' (1989) 58 *Canberra Bulletin of Public Administration* 150.
39   The literature on the rules of procedural fairness is considerable. A good starting point, however, is Aronson, Dyer and Groves, above n 1, Chs 7, 8 and 9.
40   See also the discussion in Chapter 18.5.1.

The hearing rules

[19.20] The basic hearing rule requires a decision-maker to invite and accept submissions from a person whose interests may be adversely affected by a decision before deciding the matter in dispute. The content of the rule is described best as the procedures that must be followed to effect a fair hearing. These required procedures may vary according to the circumstances of the case, although there is some dispute as to whether or not there is an 'irreducible minimum' content of the hearing obligation.[41] Before a disgruntled applicant can call natural justice in aid, however, she or he must show first that the decision-maker is bound by law to grant an opportunity of being heard. This duty may be expressly imposed by the legislation or otherwise implied by the circumstances of a case. The existence of a right to be accorded procedural fairness and what has to be done in respect to that right are separate issues. However, the two matters are intermingled and so are liable to be confused with one another.

[19.21] Although the language used has differed over the years, the essential question facing both jurists and legal commentators concerned with the issue of natural justice has been this: if not every decision affecting an individual attracts the duty to grant a hearing, what kinds of rights and interests deserve procedural protection? The courts have addressed this question in two different ways. The first approach has been to regard the application and content of the rules of procedural fairness as matters determined by the common law and by the terms of any statute governing the making of the decision in question. The alternative approach has been to regard natural justice as a matter determined solely by the terms of particular statutes. This requires the rules of procedural fairness to be written into the legislation, either expressly, or by implication. Although these divergent methodologies add considerable complexity to the discussion of natural justice, it is well to remember that they are no more than different approaches to the same problem. The approach chosen does not necessarily determine the conclusions reached. In a sense, neither answers the question of which criteria to use in drawing the line between interests worthy of procedural protection and those that are not. These criteria have evolved in a piecemeal fashion, reflecting developments in social and cultural mores and attitude as much as any judicial or legislative revolution.[42]

[19.22] The migration cases are a quintessential example of this process. The major change in judicial thinking that occurred between 1977, when *Salemi v Mackellar (No 2)*[43] was decided, and 1985, when the decision in *Kioa v West*[44] was handed down, cannot be explained solely in terms of the intervening amendments to the Act. The

---

41 This issue is discussed by Graham Johnson, 'Natural Justice and Legitimate Expectation in Australia' (1985) 15 *Federal Law Review* 39 at 71. See also Vivienne Bath, '*Heatley v Tasmania Racing & Gaming Commission*, Case Note' (1978) 9 *Federal Law Review* 504 at 509; *Kioa v West* (1985) 159 CLR 550 at 615 (Brennan J); and *FAI Insurances Ltd v Winneke* (1982) 151 CLR 342 at 379-80 (Aickin J).
42 See Pamela Tate, 'The Coherence of "Legitimate Expectations" and the Foundations of Natural Justice' (1988) 14 *Monash University Law Review* 15 at 21-54.
43 (1977) 137 CLR 396. There, a statutory majority of the High Court held that an unlawful non-citizen who came forward in response to an offer of amnesty had no right to be heard before being deported.
44 (1985) 159 CLR 550.

two decisions are distinguished by a subtle, but important, modification in judicial attitude. It is this new attitude that appears to have placed the migration cases at the cutting edge of the natural justice debate.[45]

[19.23] In *Kioa v West*, the High Court put an end to the notion that the terms of the migration legislation left the Minister free to make decisions without granting hearings of any kind.[46] Crucially, the majority held that the open-ended discretion to deport in what was s 18 of the Act did not evince an inherent intention in the legislature to exclude the rules of natural justice.[47]

[19.24] In many ways, *Kioa v West* was a conservative decision. The majority found that there were few specific matters in respect of which the family in question had not been heard. It is also a difficult decision from which to extract a clear statement of legal principle as no two majority judges took exactly the same approach. For example, Mason, Wilson and Deane JJ spoke of the crucial importance of the notion of the applicant's 'legitimate expectation'. However, the unlawful status of the Kioa family made it difficult to identify such an expectation in that case.[48] Unlike Mr Salemi, the Kioa family had not come forward in response to an offer of amnesty, nor was there in place any regular practice from which they might have expected to benefit. The finding in favour of the Kioas is only consistent with this analysis of the law if one regards the very nature of the decision to deport – or the severity of the sanction it represents – as creating an expectation of fair treatment. For Mason and Wilson JJ, this conclusion was strengthened by the terms of the Act and mechanisms established for the review of decisions under the *ADJR Act*. Their Honours pointed to the structuring of the powers to admit aliens and the criminal sanctions attaching to illegal status as indicators that the Minister's discretions were no longer unfettered.[49] Mason J also stressed the significance of the obligation under s 13 of the *ADJR Act* to provide reasons for adverse migration decisions.[50] Deane J took a more straightforward (and radical) approach, holding that the power to deport always should have been regarded as being qualified by the rules of procedural fairness. He was the only member of the bench to overrule – rather than distinguish – the earlier ruling in *Salemi (No 2)*.[51]

[19.25] Brennan J, on the other hand, insisted that the implication of the rules of natural justice in cases involving a legislative power is purely a matter of statutory

---

45   Some commentators have preferred to classify the immigration cases in a separate category illustrating a new doctrine of 'good administration': see Margaret Allars, 'Natural Justice – Writ Large or Small?' (1987) 11 *Sydney Law Review* 306; and Tate, above n 42. More recent cases suggest that the High Court will not embrace any specific or legally enforceable doctrine of good administration in judicial review on the ground that it breaches the merits/legality divide that underpins much of Australian administrative law: Matthew Groves, 'Substantive Legitimate Expectations in Australian Administrative Law' (2008) 32 *Melbourne University Law Review* 470 at 506-11.
46   (1985) 159 CLR 550 at 582, 593, 612 and 632.
47   Gibbs CJ dissented on grounds similar to those relied on in *Salemi (No 2)*. See (1985) 159 CLR 550 at 563.
48   See Tate, above n 42.
49   (1985) 159 CLR 550 at 578ff and 599ff. See also Brennan J at 623-6.
50   Ibid at 557-8.
51   Ibid at 632.

interpretation.[52] He took the phrase 'legitimate expectation' to require some form of assessment of the state of mind of the individual[53] and found this to be quite at odds with the notion of the 'universal' interpretation of a statute.[54] He also regarded the phrase as patently inadequate for the task of describing the 'almost infinite variety of interests which are protected by the principles of natural justice'.[55] Instead, Brennan J preferred to use as a test the impact on the individual of a statutory power.

[19.26] In *Kioa*, all four majority judges included in their test a consideration of the impact on the individual of the statutory power in question. The real difference, however, was the vantage point from which the individual's interests were considered. By regarding the issue of procedural fairness as a matter of statutory construction alone, Brennan J's test leaves no room for the consideration of expectations raised by matters extraneous to the legislation governing the making of a decision.

[19.27] The difference between the approach taken by Brennan J and those of his fellow judges in *Kioa* is borne out in later cases such as *Annetts v McCann*,[56] where Brennan J found himself in dissent. That case involved the procedures to be followed by a coroner who refused to hear submissions from the parents of two young men who had perished in the West Australian desert while working as jackeroos. The majority held, inter alia, that the coroner's own behaviour in allowing the parents to be represented created in them an expectation that they would be heard. For Brennan J, this was irrelevant as it did not affect the interpretation of the statute in question.[57]

[19.28] The distinction is significant in the context of the present migration legislation. If the implication of the rules of procedural fairness is determined solely by the statute, there will be some strength in the argument that the present Act effectively excludes the common law rules of procedural fairness.[58] Where the extraneous circumstances of a case play a central role in determining the application of the rules, however, the terms of the Act may not have this effect. Brennan J's statute-based approach is not one that gained immediate favour with other members of the High Court. However, with the relentless pressure placed on the courts over the years, the role played by legislation in cases involving procedural challenges has grown in importance.[59]

[19.29] Perhaps the most striking feature of the majority ruling in *Kioa*, however, is the move away from the hard-edge legalism of earlier cases like *Salemi (No 2)* towards a more humanist approach to procedural fairness. With the exception of Brennan J,

---

52 Ibid at 611.
53 This interpretation of the phrase is criticised by Tate, above n 42, at 67-8, who points out that the word 'legitimate' transforms the 'expectation' from state of mind or personal hope into an objectively justifiable expectation. It is the latter and not the former with which the law is concerned. See also Allars, above n 45, at 316, who makes a similar criticism of this aspect of Brennan J's judgment.
54 (1985) 159 CLR 550 at 617-20.
55 Ibid at 617.
56 (1991) 170 CLR 596.
57 See also *Ainsworth* (1992) 175 CLR 564.
58 See the discussion of the effect of the amendments made to the Act in 2002 in Chapter 18.5.1 above.
59 See the discussion in Chapter 18 at [18.94]ff and Grace Ma, 'Effect of the Migration Legislation (Procedural Fairness) Act 2002' (2007) 34 *Immigration Review* [520]. See further the discussion of the procedural rules of the migration tribunals in Chapter 18 above.

the whole court found that the right to be accorded natural justice is a matter determined by operation of the common law in consideration of all the aspects of a case. Although Brennan J considered that the issue was a matter of statutory interpretation alone, he, too, examined the human impact of the legislation in question.

[19.30] This change in approach proved to be truly revolutionary – and enduring. By the end of the 1980s, there was no class of migration decision that was found to be unqualified by the rules of procedural fairness. Even the pariahs of immigration law, people arriving at the border without a visa and seeking admission, were found to have some procedural rights.[60] Although there were instances where the court held that unlawful non-citizens had no expectation that warranted a hearing,[61] most judges after 1985 accepted that the rules of natural justice did apply.

[19.31] As to the matters in respect of which a hearing was required, the impact of *Kioa v West* was just as great. In that case, the majority focused on the notion that people are entitled to a hearing in respect of matters that are crucial or critical to the decision-making process. The significance of the case lay in the identification of the factors crucial to the decision made. Under the Act as it stood before December 1989, the wide discretionary powers meant that the factors that could exercise a decision-maker's mind were not defined. The end result was that the range of 'crucial' matters in respect of which a decision-maker could be required to grant a hearing became as broad as the discretion to grant or refuse a permit.

[19.32] The debate over the content of procedural fairness related to both the nature of the hearing required and the matters in respect of which a hearing had to be given. The courts held that immigration officials were obliged to give applicants an adequate opportunity to present all matters relevant to their case. Although they never went so far as to require a formal hearing, the judges' formulation of the rules of procedural fairness came to place considerable burdens on administrators.

[19.33] The courts held that the rules of procedural fairness did not require a decision-maker to either assist applicants in presenting their case, or embark on independent inquiries into matters not raised directly by the applicant.[62] However, they pronounced it unlawful for decision-makers to close their mind to relevant matters by refusing to inquire into matters reasonably available to them.[63] The courts also found it improper to prevent applicants from presenting evidence by misleading them as to their prospects of success.[64]

[19.34] The lack of finality of the 'hearing' game was illustrated most graphically in the late 1980s in the two cases of *Somaghi v MILGEA*[65] and *Heshmati v MILGEA*.[66]

---

60 See, for example, *Sinnathamby v MIEA* (1986) 66 ALR 502; *Singthong v MIEA* (1989) 18 FCR 486; and *Pesava v MILGEA* (1989) 18 ALD 95.
61 See, for example, *Koh Ah Soo v MIEA* (1986) 10 ALN N46.
62 See, for example, *Prasad v MIEA* (1985) 6 FCR 155; *Barrett v MILGEA* (1989) 18 ALD 129; and *Broussard v MIEA* (1989) 21 FCR 472.
63 See, for example, *Prasad v MIEA* (1985) 6 FCR 155.
64 See, for example, *Videto v MIEA* (1985) 8 FCR 167.
65 (1991) 31 FCR 100.
66 (1991) 31 FCR 123.

The applicants were asylum seekers who, it was said, tried to improve their chances of gaining refugee status by sending an inflammatory letter to the Canberra-based embassy of their native country. The two argued that they had been denied procedural fairness because the decision-maker had disregarded the actions taken by the pair as a 'bootstrap' device designed to improve their chances of gaining refugee status. The Full Federal Court agreed that the applicants had suffered from a breach of the rules of natural justice. It found that the decision-maker could not lawfully put a negative interpretation on material submitted by the applicants without first hearing them on the issue.

[19.35] The effect of these two cases, the government argued, was to require an extra step in the decision-making process in each case to allow applicants to respond to interpretations made of the applicant's own material.[67] The courts were accused of being insensitive to the administrative (and financial) ramifications of their rulings. As the extended case study of the operation of the migration tribunals in Chapter 18 demonstrates, these cases set the parameters for a discussion that continues to this day. The central issues about how hearings should be conducted have not really changed over time. Absent legislation excluding the rules of procedural fairness, it would appear that the principles laid down by the High Court in *Kioa v West* remain something of a gold standard.[68]

The rule against bias

[19.36] The second of the rules of natural justice or procedural fairness is the principle that decision-makers must neither act with (actual) bias in making a decision, nor decide matters in a manner that gives the appearance or apprehension of bias. Over the years, migration cases have pushed the boundaries of the law in this area, in part because of the special efforts made in 1992 to exclude the Federal Court from reviewing migration decisions on grounds of apprehended bias, leaving 'actual bias' as the only option in that Court.[69] As Aronson, Dyer and Groves explain, the rule against bias can be stated simply, but is fraught with complication because of the many exceptions that have been created over the years.[70] First, the rules only apply to persons exercising determinative powers: they cannot be used to impugn participants in a process who do not have a duty to act with impartiality. Second, as with the hearing rules, the content of the bias rules is flexible and will vary according to context, temporal mores and who is making a decision.[71] Although developed first as a vehicle for controlling judicial misbehaviour, bias has become an increasingly important weapon used in challenging decisions by tribunals, even where these operate using inquisitorial rather than adversarial techniques.[72] The standard

---

67 A more recent parallel – which had a similar effect of requiring an extra stage in the review process – is the ruling of the High Court in *SAAP v MIMIA* (2005) 215 ALR 162 (*SAAP*). See the discussion in Chapter 18.5.2 above.
68 See, for example, *Saeed v MIAC* (2010) 267 ALR 204 at 208 [11].
69 See the discussion at Part 19.5.
70 See Aronson, Dyer and Groves, above n 1, Ch 9.
71 See *Ebner v Official Trustee* (2000) 205 CLR 337 at 350.
72 See Aronson, Dyer and Groves, above n 1, at 639; and Margaret Allars, 'Neutrality, the Judicial Paradigm and Tribunal Procedure' (1991) 13 *Sydney Law Review* 377.

expected of non-judicial officers has traditionally been lower than that applicable to judges, although the approach taken by the High Court in recent cases suggests a growing uniformity in approach.[73] In *Ebner v Official Trustee*,[74] the court adopted a two-step approach articulated by Gleeson CJ, McHugh, Gummow and Hayne JJ in the following terms:

> First (bias) requires the identification of what is said might lead a judge (or juror) to decide a case other than on its legal and factual merits. The second step is no less important. There must be an articulation of the logical connection between the matter and the feared deviation from the course of deciding the case on its merits.

[19.37] The bias cases in the migration arena have raised an interesting variety of issues. One of the earliest and most politically fraught examples was a test case brought on behalf of one of three women from Cambodia who had arrived by boat without authorisation in 1989.[75] The three had gone on hunger strike after languishing in detention for over three years. Mok Guek Buoy alleged that the decision to deny her refugee status was affected by an institutional bias that prevented the decision-makers from deciding her case on the merits. She alleged that there was a policy to reject asylum seekers from Cambodia and that this created an apprehension of bias on the part of the official who denied her claim. An important focus of the case was interviews given by then Prime Minister Hawke and Foreign Minister Evans in which assertions were made that the Cambodians were mere 'economic' refugees who could not be considered genuine (Convention) refugees.[76] At first instance, Keely J rejected attempts by successive Ministers (Hand and Bolkus) to disown the statements made by the Prime Minister and Foreign Minister. His Honour upheld the applicant's claim on bases that included a finding that the decision was affected by apprehended bias. In essence the judge accepted the allegations of institutional or systemic bias, a brave ruling that few litigants have been able to achieve even though the problems identified were not unique.[77]

[19.38] In subsequent cases allegations of bias have been made more usually in the context of allegations personal to the decision-maker. The allegations have rarely been upheld.[78] An example in point is the decision in *Re MIMA; Ex parte Epeabaka*.[79] In that case the RRT member who had rejected the refugee claim brought by a Congolese

---

73   Note that in *Ebner v Official Trustee* (2000) 205 CLR 337 a majority of the High Court rejected the notion that judges faced automatic disqualification in cases where judges hold a direct pecuniary interest in the outcome of proceedings. See (2000) 205 CLR 337 at 356.
74   Ibid at 345. See Aronson, Dyer and Groves, above n 1, at 650, note 66.
75   See *Mok Gek Bouy v MILGEA and Paterson* (1993) 47 FCR 1. Although not decided until 1993, this case helps to explain the exclusion of apprehended bias from the review grounds left to the Federal Court in the first Part 8 of the *Migration Act 1958* (Cth). See *Migration Reform Act 1992* (Cth) which came into force in September 1994 and the discussion below at Part 19.5.
76   Ibid at [19].
77   For an interesting empirical study of institutional and other biases in refugee decision making in the United States, see Jaya Ramji-Nogales, Andrew Ian Schoenholtz, Philip G Schrag, *Refugee Roulette: Disparities in Asylum Adjudication and Proposals for Reform* (New York: New York University Press, 2009).
78   See *Sun v MIEA* (1997) 151 ALR 505 at 555; and *Gamaethige v MIMA* (2001) 109 FCR 424 at 443.
79   (2001) 206 CLR 128.

man posted the following blog on a personal website reflecting on his job as a tribunal member:

> When I was first appointed, a colleague who shall remain nameless said to me, 'Let 'em all in, Rory!'. But while I would like to let in to Australia at least 95% of the applicants who come to us, who are usually deserving cases and decent human beings even if they lie through their teeth (as they often do) in their desperation to find a better life, it's not as simple as that. … We work with dishonesty and corruption on all sides: foreign governments who practise the most abhorrent forms of cruelty against their citizens, immigration officials bent on keeping out as many people as they can irrespective of need, other parties who in my present position I had better not mention, applicants who weave webs of lies, lawyers and migration agents who prey on them to rip off what little money they have. In these sordid surroundings, it is, I firmly believe, only the RRT and the courts (and, to be fair, a small minority of honest lawyers and migration agents) who stand up for decent values and who honestly seek to do what is right.[80]

The High Court described the remarks as 'regrettable' but did not find the material exhibited an apprehension of bias.[81] The High Court has been less forgiving, however, of tribunal members exhibiting bias in their behaviour during the course of a hearing. In *Re Refugee Review Tribunal; Ex parte H*,[82] the High Court found that the tribunal exhibited an appearance of bias by constantly interrupting the claimant couple, preventing them from getting their story out. The court quashed the tribunal's ruling on the ground that it could not be assumed that the applicants' claims would have failed had they been given a proper hearing.[83]

[19.39] A more extreme example of the High Court's reluctance to uphold claims of bias in migration cases is the decision in *MIMA v Jia*.[84] In that instance Minister Ruddock gave radio and television interviews in which he upbraided the AAT for going soft on migrants convicted of serious crimes. The interviews were conducted in the context of a complex case involving a former refugee convicted of serious sex and other offences against another (unlawful) migrant who was under threat of removal from the country. The Minister subsequently overrode the AAT's decision by ordering the man removed under s 501 of the *Migration Act*. The High Court overruled the Full Federal Court's finding that the Minister's decision was affected by actual bias.[85] The majority (with Kirby J in dissent) found that politicians should not be expected to act with the same impartiality expected of judges because their role requires them to engage with public opinion.[86]

---

80   Ibid at [13]. Note that a challenge to a refugee ruling by this member was successful in the Federal Court. See *Ferati v MIMA* [1998] FCA 1709.
81   See (2001) 206 CLR 128 at 133 and 138. Kirby J wrote a separate judgment but also dismissed the application.
82   (2001) 179 ALR 425.
83   Compare the ruling by the High Court in *MIAC v SZJSS* [2010] HCA 48 where a similar allegation of apprehended bias was rejected.
84   (2001) 205 CLR 507.
85   See *Jia v MIMA* (1999) 93 FCR 556.
86   See *Re MIMA; Ex parte Jia* (2001) 205 CLR 507 at 539 (Gleeson CJ and Gummow J) and 565 (Hayne J). See also Callinan J at 583. Compare Kirby J at 556.

Procedural fairness and the 'no evidence' rule

[19.40] The final principle worthy of mention as we chart the impact of the migration cases on the development of the rules of procedural fairness in Australia is the rule that findings of fact (or law) will be unlawful if there is no factual basis to support them. The common law has traditionally taken a very tough approach, with courts ruling that evidence of any kind will suffice to legitimise a finding of fact.[87] The link between the 'no evidence' rule and procedural fairness was forged by Brennan and Deane JJ in one of the earliest cases involving the deportation of a permanent resident convicted of serious crimes. In that case the Minister sought to adduce evidence from an undercover police informer *in camera* (excluding the applicant from the hearing). Having agreed to hear the evidence in question, Brennan J in the AAT was disappointed at its quality. He opined that evidence that was not tested by hearing both sides of a story lacked 'rational probative force'.[88] Deane J made the link with procedural fairness explicit, ruling that acting on mere suspicion could breach the rules of natural justice.[89]

[19.41] The willingness of the courts to restrict use of this ground for review may explain why it was left untouched when the regime for the judicial review of migration cases was overhauled in and after 1992.[90]

19.3.2 Merits review by another name: Relevancy and reasonableness as grounds of review

[19.42] The other broad grounds of judicial review that were a source of concern related to the relevancy of material taken into account in the exercise of a discretion; and the ground of legal 'unreasonableness'. The 'relevancy' heads are best described as the failure to take into account relevant considerations and the taking into account of irrelevant considerations. Legal unreasonableness is sometimes referred to as *Wednesbury* unreasonableness, after the comments of Lord Greene MR in *Associated Provincial Picture Houses Ltd v Wednesbury Corporation*.[91] It is used in relation to decisions that are found to be so unreasonable that they could not have been made by a reasonable person: see also *Bromley London Borough Council v Greater London Council*;[92]

---

87 See, for example, *SZAPC v MIMIA* [2005] FCA 995 at [47] where the court ruled that the fact in respect of which no evidence is given must be a 'jurisdictional' fact. See *VAS v MIMA* [2002] FCAFC 350 at [18]-[19]; and *WAJS v MIMA* [2004] FCAFC 139 at [11]-[12]. In other cases the Federal Court has distinguished between findings of fact and the expression of an opinion. See *SZFWB v MIAC* [2007] FCA 167 at [37]. This is reinforced by the jurisprudence on credibility findings. See *Re MIMA; Ex parte Durairajasingham* (2000) 168 ALR 407 at [67].
88 See *Re Pochi and MIEA* (1979) 2 ALD 33 at 41.
89 See *MIEA v Pochi* (1980) 31 ALR 666 at 688-90. As Aronson, Dyer and Groves point out (above n 1, at [4.380]), Deane J's approach was rejected by the High Court. See *Attorney-General (NSW) v Quin* (1990) 170 CLR 1; and *Re MIMA; Ex parte Lam* (2003) 214 CLR 1 at 9-10.
90 For a discussion of the case law in this area, see Aronson, Dyer and Groves, above n 1, at 259-65. For a typically lucid explanation of the law on this review ground, see Kenny J in *SZNKV v MIAC* [2010] FCA 56 at [37]-[38]. See also *MIAC v SZLSP* (2010) 187 FCR 362.
91 [1948] 1 KB 223 at 229-30.
92 [1983] 1 AC 768 at 821.

Parramatta City Council v Pestell;[93] and *Chan Yee Kin v MIEA*.[94] These heads of review continue to be apposite in actions brought before the High Court. Depending on the Federal Court's interpretation of the concept of 'substantial justice', they can also be linked to procedural challenges brought under Part 8 of the Act.

[19.43] In *Minister for Aboriginal Affairs v Peko-Wallsend Ltd*,[95] Mason J identified five 'propositions' governing the court's use of these heads of review. The first is that a matter will only be legally relevant to a decision if a decision-maker is bound to take it into account. Second, his Honour posited that matters of legal relevance must be determined by looking at the subject-matter, scope and purpose of any enactment. Third, he noted[96] that the court's task is not to engage in merits review by ruling on the proper weight to be given to different considerations. While mere preference for a different result should not suffice, Mason J added that the weight given to different factors could properly be reviewed where the decision made is 'manifestly unreasonable'. Finally, his Honour pointed out the special position of Ministers of the Crown and the allowance that must be made for broader policy considerations that might be relevant in the exercise of ministerial discretions.[97]

[19.44] The major breakthrough that occurred during the 1980s in the review of migration decisions was the court's interpretation of the subject-matter, scope and purpose of the migration legislation. Although the 'public' function of the Act in protecting and controlling the composition of Australian society was recognised, the case law reveals a heightened concern for the individuals affected by the exercise of ministerial powers.

[19.45] Before December 1989, the 'relevancy' heads of judicial review presented particular problems for the government in the migration area because of the potentially infinite range of matters that could be considered significant to the decision-making process. The Federal Court's use of these heads of review went hand in hand with its evolving interpretation of the rules of procedural fairness. In the result, the demands made by the courts of decision-makers brought the courts very close on occasion to reviewing the merits of decisions.

[19.46] By the end of the 1980s, the courts had become both more expansive in their interpretation of the migration legislation, and more critical in reviewing the exercise of open-ended discretions. Nowhere was this more evident than in the judicial review of decisions made under the old s 6A(1)(e) of the Act. This provision empowered the Minister to grant permanent residence to non-citizens lawfully in Australia on 'strong humanitarian or compassionate' grounds.

[19.47] In a series of cases, the Federal Court made s 6A(1)(e) into a major safety net for unlawful non-citizens, refugee claimants and a vast array of unusual cases involving less fortunate individuals. It overrode the notion that the provision be

---

93 (1972) 128 CLR 305 at 327.
94 (1989) 169 CLR 379.
95 (1986) 162 CLR 24 at 39.
96 Ibid at 41.
97 Ibid at 42.

accessible only to persons in Australia legally. In *McPhee v MILGEA*,[98] for example, Lee J held that decision-makers who entertained an application for entry on compassionate or humanitarian grounds could not exclude illegal applicants. He made this finding on the basis that illegal status could be cured through the grant of a temporary permit.

[19.48] The breadth of s 6A(1)(e) was manifest most forcefully, however, in the range of matters the courts found to be covered by the terms 'humanitarian' and 'compassionate'.[99] The two cases of *Dahlan v MILGEA*[100] and *Damouni v MILGEA*[101] have been discussed already. The effect of these and other rulings was to strike down the policy regime that treated 'humanitarian' cases as those involving people in refugee-like situations, while 'compassion' was reserved for cases involving family and personal misfortune.

[19.49] The distance between merits and judicial review became even smaller with the courts' growing willingness to rule against the legality of decisions on grounds that they were manifestly unreasonable. The courts linked the notion of legal unreasonableness with both misconstruction of the law and failure to make decisions having regard to all (and only) relevant material.

[19.50] The trend towards a more critical interpretation of the migration legislation, together with a greater willingness to criticise the matters taken into account became apparent across the whole range of migration decisions. The courts were accused of being insensitive to the administrative impact of the rulings in the burden they were placing on decision-makers.[102] Just as importantly, they were charged with overstepping the bounds of judicial review. The courts' use of the doctrine of legal unreasonableness appears to have been particularly offensive to the Minister and to the higher echelons of the immigration bureaucracy. In test cases like *Chan Yee Kin v MIEA*,[103] that were fought through to the High Court, the decisions under review were ones in which the Minister and the Secretary of the Department became involved at a very personal level. For those rulings to be held 'manifestly unreasonable' – that is, so unreasonable that they could not have been made by a reasonable person – must have been directly affronting to the Minister and his administrators. Statements from other members of parliament involved in the formulation of policy throughout the late 1980s suggest that the sense of injury and outrage extended beyond the Minister into at least one of the Parliamentary Standing Committees. Then Shadow Minister for Immigration, Philip Ruddock, complained that in creating the *ADJR Act* the government had made a 'rod for its own back'.[104]

---

98 (1988) 16 ALD 77.
99 See the discussion in Chapter 12.5.
100 [1989] FCA 507.
101 (1989) 87 ALR 97.
102 See Evan Arthur, 'The Impact of Administrative Law on Humanitarian Decision-Making' (1990) 66 *Canberra Bulletin of Public Administration* 90.
103 (1989) 169 CLR 379.
104 See Commonwealth Parliamentary Debates, *Hansard*, House of Representatives, 16 December 1992, 3935; and Joint Standing Committee on Migration Regulations, *Australia's Refugee and Humanitarian System: Achieving a Balance between Refuge and Control* (Canberra: 1992) at 59ff.

19.4 The codification of migration decision-making and the introduction of 'non-reviewable' discretions

[19.51] Whether the courts were at fault in overstepping the line between merits review and judicial review or whether the fault lay with the legislation itself is debatable. In any event, the 'problem' was addressed in December 1989 with the codification of decision-making criteria in the *Migration Regulations 1989* (Cth).[105] The fact that this regulatory regime was created with a view to wresting control back from the courts finds support in the fact that most of the significant cases emerging from the courts around this period met with a legislative response of some kind.[106] As we have detailed elsewhere, controversy surrounding the first boat people in the same year set the scene for a battle royal between the executive and the judiciary that seems to have raged ever since.[107]

[19.52] In the late 1980s and early 1990s, much of the rhetoric surrounding the legislative changes spoke of the need for certainty and of the desirability of removing the potential for corrupt and arbitrary practices inherent in a system based on discretionary decision-making. It is ironic that there was no recognition by parliament that intervention by the courts had in fact provided a useful check on such problems. In an era where computers were beginning to come into their own, the idea of policy generating binomial (black or white) outcomes became high fashion. As we have detailed earlier, attempts to turn back the clock to a putative era where the government had almost complete control of immigration were not directed solely at the courts. To render the process impervious to review the decisional powers of individual decision-makers had to be either curtailed or reinforced in some way. Hence the removal of discretion from many areas and/or the transformation of decision-making from objective to subjective processes. One of the most striking examples of such changes was in the area of refugee status decision-making. Simple references to the UN Convention definition of refugee were replaced after 1989 with provisions referring to the Minister being 'satisfied' that an individual met this definition. This meant that, instead of the courts adjudicating directly on the standard set by the UN Convention, decisions could only be reviewed using the standard of whether there were any grounds on which the Minister (or official) could have formed an opinion on the person's status as a refugee.[108]

[19.53] The most extreme protections from review were reserved for a new, special class of decision reserved to the Minister acting personally that was said to be non-compellable and non-reviewable.[109] The non-compellable nature of the power contained in s 417 of the Act (the power to override adverse refugee status rulings

---

105 For a discussion of these changes, see above Chapter 5.3.
106 See Mary Crock, *Administrative Law and Immigration Control in Australia: Actions and Reactions* (unpublished PhD Thesis, University of Melbourne, 1994).
107 See Pearce, above n 6.
108 The two cases that bear out the changes made are *Chan Yee Kin v MIEA* (1989) 169 CLR 379 (objective test) and *MIEA v Wu Shan Liang* (1996) 185 CLR 259 (subjective test). Both cases are discussed above, Chapter 12.3.
109 See above Chapter 5.1.

by the RRT) was articulated in *Ozmanian v MILGEA*.[110] On appeal, the Full Federal Court stated that:

> [Section] 417(7) makes it clear that the Minister is not under a duty to consider whether to exercise the power under s 417(1) in respect of any decision, whether or not the Minister is requested to do so by the applicant or any other person, or in any other circumstances.[111]

[19.54] In *Bedlington v Chong*,[112] the Full Court found that the 'no duty to consider' provision[113] contained in the Minister's related discretion under s 48B[114] was intended to excuse the Minister from any obligation of considering whether to exercise the s 48B power. The court ruled further that there was no duty under s 48B which required any matter to be drawn to the attention of the Minister.[115] The net effect of such principles was to make the Minister virtually immune from the prerogative writ of mandamus or any equivalent statutory remedy that could compel the performance of this power.

[19.55] The various provisions allowing for ministerial intervention have been considered over the years in the context of the various regimes governing judicial review. While the predominant view appears to have been that the ministerial process has been and remains immune from curial oversight,[116] the decision by the High Court in 2010 to allow review of offshore processing has the potential to disrupt the jurisprudence in this area.[117] While the Minister's decision might remain immune from review, the process engaged in at the Departmental level may now be open to challenge. Having said this, the real focus over the years has been on the substantive rulings made in the individual cases. This is where the real battle lines have been drawn.[118] As we explore in the concluding section of this chapter, the codification of

---

110   (1996) 137 ALR 103.
111   *MIMA v Ozmanian* (1996) 141 ALR 322 at 336. See also *Morato v MILGEA* (1992) 39 FCR 401.
112   (1998) 87 FCR 75.
113   *Migration Act*, s 48B(6), and correspondingly s 417(7).
114   Section 48B still operates to enable the Minister to allow applicants to make a second or further application for a Protection visa where it is in the public interest to do so, and comprises one of the courses of action the Minister may take when exercising the discretion under s 417.
115   Section 417(3) provides that the power under s 417(1) may only be exercised by the Minister personally. In effect, the act of exercising his other discretion cannot be delegated by the Minister. However, the ministerial decision to decide not to consider whether to consider exercising the discretion can be delegated to Department staff. This decision can be delegated because it has been held by the Federal Court as not within the scope of s 417(3), and s 496 allows the Minister to delegate his power to refuse a visa. In practice, Departmental officials assess cases against the Guidelines and need not draw to the Minister's attention cases that fall outside those Guidelines. See Senate Legal and Constitutional References Committee, *A Sanctuary Under Review: Inquiry into Australia's Refugee and Humanitarian Program* (Canberra: 1999) at [8.108].
116   For example, in *Kolotau v MIMIA* [2002] FCA 1145 at [8], Tamberlin J stated: 'Relief cannot be available under s 39B of the *Judiciary Act 1903* (Cth) by reason of the Minister's failure to consider a matter which the Migration Act specifically says that he is not obliged to consider'. This view was confirmed but qualified by the High Court in *Plaintiffs M61/M69* (2010) 272 ALR 14. See the discussion at Part 19.6.4 below.
117   See the discussion at Part 19.6.4 below.
118   In this context, much attention has been focused on the residual discretion vested in the Minister to intervene in cases where strict compliance with the rules results in unduly harsh outcomes. See Senate Select Committee on Ministerial Discretion in Migration Matters, *Report* (Canberra: 2004), discussed at Chapter 5.5.

migration law did nothing to curb the number of applications for judicial review. On the contrary, the changes represented a field day for the lawyers as people scrambled to contest the meaning and application of regulations that grew over time in both volume and complexity.

19.5 Declaration of hostilities: The first Part 8 of the Migration Act

[19.56] The first significant generic assault on the power of the courts to engage in the judicial review of migration decisions occurred with the passage of the *Migration Reform Act 1992* (Cth) which came into force on 1 September 1994. This legislation introduced the first Part 8 of the Act, creating a regime for the judicial review of migration decisions that was different from that applying to any other federal administrative portfolio. The system then introduced had no precedent and has not since been replicated – and for good reason. Its effect was to bar the Federal Court from exercising its broad (or common law) judicial review function. What was left was the less controversial function of checking that decisions were made in accordance with relevant legislation.

[19.57] First, the amendments removed most classes of migration decisions from both the *ADJR Act* and the *Judiciary Act*. Access to the High Court remained because of the guarantees of s 75(v) of the Constitution. However, the legislators were careful to preclude backdoor use of the Federal Court through the High Court's power to remit cases to the lower courts. The Federal Court's jurisdiction on remittal was limited by the terms of the migration legislation.[119]

[19.58] Second, the migration decisions 'judicially reviewable' by the Federal Court were restricted to final decisions of the administrative review bodies and other decisions made under the Act or the regulations relating to visas.[120] Access to the Federal Court was also confined through the imposition of strict time limits. In determining whether a decision was reviewable by the Federal Court, regard had to be had also to the time between the making of a decision and any application for merits review. As is still the case, time limits on the lodging of appeals to the administrative tribunals could not be extended under any circumstances.[121] There was also a non-extendable time limit of 28 days after notification of a decision placed on applications for judicial review.[122] The scheme forced people to exercise their rights to seek administrative review of adverse decisions. While a right of appeal lay on the merits of a decision,

---

119 *Migration Act*, s 485.
120 Ibid, s 475. The section excluded from review a variety of matters that were justiciable previously. Section 475(2) expressly excluded a variety of decisions from judicial review. These included any decisions made before a final determination, that is, rulings from which an appeal lay to the Migration Internal Review Office (MIRO), the Immigration Review Tribunal (IRT) or the RRT. Section 475(2)(e) of the Act also expressly excluded the judicial review of a decision by the Minister not to exercise or consider the exercise of the various 'non-compellable' discretions conferred by the Act: see Part 19.4. Decisions relating to the reference of an appeal to the AAT from the IRT or the RRT were also not reviewable.
121 See former ss 339 and 347 of the *Migration Act*.
122 See s 478(2) and *Mahboob v MIEA* [1996] FCA 1319.

applicants were barred from seeking judicial review. If, on the other hand, they did not exercise their right to appeal at first instance within the time specified, they also lost their right to seek judicial review. This was because there was no second decision to restart the clock for the judicial review application. In practice, the effect of the provisions was to require people who missed out on tribunal review to seek judicial review in the High Court.[123]

[19.59] Finally, and most importantly, the first Part 8 of the Act set out the grounds on which a 'judicially reviewable' decision could be reviewed by the Federal Court. The traditional grounds for review that survived for migration cases were: failure to follow prescribed procedures; lack of jurisdiction in the decision-maker; decision not authorised by the Act or the Regulations; improper exercise of power; error of law, being an incorrect interpretation or application of the law; fraud or actual bias (but not apparent bias); and no evidence.[124]

[19.60] The grounds on which decisions could *not* be reviewed were: denial of natural justice; unreasonableness; taking an irrelevant consideration into account; failure to take into account a relevant consideration; bad faith; and any other abuse of power. The omissions were significant because of the body of common law that attaches to phrases such as 'natural justice' and 'unreasonableness'.[125]

[19.61] Standing to apply for review was limited to people who were either the subject of the decision or, in cases where tribunal review was available, the applicants for review.[126] Examples of people who no longer had standing in migration cases were the dependants of people directly affected by a visa decision.

[19.62] Under s 13 of the *ADJR Act*, most persons with standing to seek review also have a right to obtain reasons for the decision in question. After the introduction of Part 8 of the *Migration Act*, this generalised right to reasons no longer applied for many migration applicants. Decisions excluded from the s 13 requirements are set out in Sch 2 to the *ADJR Act*. The schedule includes decisions made in respect of 'visas'. Hence, even if migration applicants had standing under the Act, they could not use s 13 to obtain reasons for a decision. The migration legislation as amended contained no provision equivalent to s 13. Neither does the common law provide any solace in this regard as the prevailing jurisprudence is that the rules of procedural fairness

---

123   See, for example, *Miah* (2001) 206 CLR 57.
124   See former s 476. Improper exercise of power under s 476(1)(d) was defined as:
    (a)   exercise of power for purpose other than that for which it was conferred;
    (b)   acting under dictation; and
    (c)   exercise of a discretionary power without regards to the merits of a case.
The scope of the 'no evidence' head in s 476(1)(g) was restricted in a way that replicated s 5(3) of the *ADJR Act*: s 475(4). In addition, review could be sought where there was a failure to make a decision: former s 477. See the discussion at Part 19.3.1 at [19.36]–[19.41] above.
125   See former ss 476(2) and (3)(d)-(g).
126   See former s 479. This provision was narrower than the parallel definition of 'person aggrieved by [an administrative] decision' in s 3(4) of the *ADJR Act*. This extends standing to seek judicial review under the *ADJR Act* to all persons whose interests are adversely affected by a decision and has been interpreted broadly by the courts. See, for example, *Tooheys Ltd v Minister for Business and Consumer Affairs* (1981) 36 ALR 64. On the interpretation of the standing provisions of the *ADJR Act* and at common law, see Margaret Allars, *Introduction to Australian Administrative Law* (Sydney: Butterworths, 1990) at 308ff; Aronson, Dyer and Groves, above n 1, Ch 11.

do not imply a right to be given reasons for a decision.[127] In some cases applicants would be informed of the grounds for refusing a visa because access to judicial review was linked to merits review by one or other of the immigration tribunals. Those who sought review of a decision where tribunal review was not available had no legislative right to reasons under the Act. This fact underscored the inferior legal status of such applicants. The uncertainty surrounding entitlement to reasons is reflected in a number of cases in which arguments have been raised about what will constitute 'reasons' for the purpose of a decision. The High Court split on this issue in *Re MIMIA; Ex parte Palme*.[128] In that case the Department released to the applicant a detailed brief that had been prepared for the Minister and argued that this was sufficient to meet the statutory requirement to supply 'reasons' for the decision made. Gleeson CJ, Gummow and Heydon JJ sidestepped the central issue by accepting that the brief *contained* enough information to demonstrate a reasoned factual basis for the decision made. Kirby and McHugh JJ, on the other hand, ruled that the brief did not constitute 'reasons' because it did not explain why particular conclusions were reached. This case followed a series of lower court decisions in which the reasons prepared by the Minister were attacked for their failure to align properly with the central issues in a case.[129]

[19.63] Once a matter was before the Federal Court, the court's powers under the first Part 8 were much the same as those conferred on the court by the *ADJR Act*.[130] Similar powers were given to the court where there was a failure to make a decision.[131] The one exception was the absence of any power in the migration legislation to make orders in respect of conduct engaged in for the purpose of reaching a decision. Such conduct was no longer reviewable by the Federal Court in migration cases.[132]

[19.64] The differences between the first Part 8 of the Act and the provisions of the *ADJR Act* were significant. The excluded grounds went to the very heart of the *ADJR Act* and of the common law judicial review that this Act essentially codifies.

[19.65] The judicial politics generated by the first Part 8 were pernicious in two respects. First, the measure exacerbated the divide within the judiciary between judges who were or were not prepared to take a stand against the restrictive measures

---

127 *Public Service Board (NSW) v Osmond* (1986) 159 CLR 656.
128 (2003) 216 CLR 212.
129 See, for example, *Ayan v MIMIA* (2003) 126 FCR 152 at 164; and *Long v MIMIA* [2003] FCAFC 218 at [32]-[52].
130 Section 481 empowered the Federal Court to: (a) affirm, quash, set aside a decision or part thereof, with effect from the date of the order or earlier as specified; (b) refer the matter back for further consideration, with directions; (c) declare the rights of the parties in respect of any matter; and (d) order any of the parties to do or refrain from doing anything as the court thinks necessary in order to do justice between the parties.
131 See former s 481(2). The leading case on failure to make a decision and/or inordinate delay is *NAIS v MIMIA* (2005) 228 CLR 470 at [8] (Gleeson CJ). See also *SZIIF v MIAC* (2008) 102 ALD 366 at [83].
132 Note, however, that stay orders are dealt with in s 482 of the Act. These empower the Federal Court to stay the operation or effect of a decision so as to ensure the effectiveness of the hearing and determination of the appeal. Without an order under s 482(3), however, an application for judicial review will not affect the operation of a decision: see above, Chapter 16.7.1. The Federal Court also has power to correct errors of law through the issue of writs by virtue of s 23 of the *Federal Court of Australia Act 1976*.

in the interests of justice for individual migrants. Second, as government pressure against judicial review mounted, the High Court responded by adopting an increasingly deferential approach in its interpretation of the law. It also turned on the Federal Court so as to slap down any perceived activist tendencies. Two cases decided in 1999 illustrate these trends. Both involved challenges to the first Part 8 of the Act.

[19.66] In *Abebe v Commonwealth*,[133] a young Ethiopian woman refused protection as a refugee argued that Part 8 amounted to an unconstitutional constraint on the powers of the Federal Court. Ms Abebe also sought prerogative relief under s 75(v) of the Constitution, on the ground that the tribunal's decision in her case was unreasonable. In a narrow 4:3 decision,[134] she failed on both counts. The constitutional argument was based on the claim that the judicial power exercised by the Federal Court pursuant to Chapter III of the Constitution could not be divided. By allowing the Federal Court to adjudicate only some aspects of the legality of migration decisions, it was alleged that Part 8 diminished the court to the extent that it could not be said to be exercising judicial power. The majority ruled that the repeated use of the word 'matter' in Chapter III of the Constitution could validly imply part of a matter. Thus some grounds (or some 'matters' of a legal dispute) could be excluded from judicial review.[135] The majority held that it was within parliament's ability to narrow the exercise of judicial power by the Federal Court, and to restrict the available grounds of judicial review. As the vigorous dissents of the minority pointed out, the ruling confirmed that the only court in which parliament could not constrain the judicial review function was their own court – the High Court of Australia, staffed by a mere seven judges who struggle each year to produce written judgments in more than between 70 and 80 cases.

[19.67] A second important case to come before the High Court in 1999 was *MIMA v Eshetu*.[136] This case was handed down shortly after *Abebe*, and in some senses is a companion to that judgment. The issue at stake in *Eshetu* was whether some scope remained (in spite of Part 8) for the Federal Court to review migration decisions using the standards set by common law rules of procedural fairness, relevancy and reasonableness.

[19.68] The argument was based on a reading of s 420 of the Act which provided for the RRT's manner of operation. That section (and the equivalent for the MRT) requires the RRT to 'pursue the objective of providing a mechanism for review that is fair, just, economical, informal and quick' and to make decisions in accordance with 'substantial justice' and the merits of a case. The issues for determination were twofold. The first question concerned whether s 420 required decision-makers to comply with the broad common law rules governing procedural and substantive justice. The second issue was the scope of the power to review decisions for procedural illegalities under s 476(1)(a) of the Act. The specific question was whether s 420 created mandatory procedures that had to be followed by decision-makers.

---

133   (1999) 197 CLR 510 (*Abebe*).
134   The majority consisted of Gleeson CJ, McHugh, Callinan and Kirby JJ.
135   *Abebe* (1999) 197 CLR 510 at [28] (Gleeson CJ and McHugh J).
136   (1999) 197 CLR 611 (*Eshetu*).

[19.69] The High Court sided with those Federal Court judges who had rejected the use of s 420 as a back door to reinstate common law judicial review.[137] The court ruled that s 420 does not establish procedures that must be followed. It and similar provisions do no more than exhort the tribunals to act with justice and expedition.[138] Therefore, the tribunal could not be compelled to follow any putative procedure set out under s 420; neither could the Federal Court review a decision on that basis. The effect of *Eshetu* was to uphold Part 8's ability to prevent review by the Federal Court of tribunal decisions on the broad grounds of natural justice: procedural fairness, relevance and reasonableness.

[19.70] It was in this case that Gummow J began to develop the notion of a universal divide in administrative law between what Taggart[139] and Aronson[140] describe as 'process' and 'quality' in administrative decision-making and review.[141] The first is said to be readily susceptible to review, while the second will permit of interference from the judiciary in rare and exceptional cases. Matters of process are best described as those describing quantifiable attributes such as considerations that have to be taken into account and procedures that must be followed under the terms of a statute. Gummow J groups review of the 'objective existence of facts' with review of some aspects of more subjective decision-making where a decision-maker is conferred with a power to decide on matters to his or her 'satisfaction'. Here, the court may rule on the criteria on which a decision-maker is required to be satisfied to the extent to which these operate as jurisdictional facts. He contrasts this with fully 'discretionary' power which Aronson suggests would allow the decision-maker free range to take into account public interest, policy and values. These are issues which in themselves go to the 'quality' (and/or the 'merits') of a decision. So, in *Eshetu*, Gummow J said:

> [W]here the question is whether the Minister was obliged by s 65 [of the Act] to grant a protection visa upon satisfaction that the applicant met the criterion under s 36(2) for a protection visa, '*Wednesbury* unreasonableness' does not enter the picture.[142]

[19.71] *Eshetu* was the first case after *Abebe* in which the High Court was faced with demonstrating the superior reach of the judicial review function guaranteed by s 75(v) of the Constitution relative to the limited 'process' review permitted by the first Part 8 of the *Migration Act*. Yet in this and later decisions, Gummow J would come close to asserting that the dominant judicial review function conferred by the Constitution is one that goes to the oversight of process only.[143] It is not designed

---

137 See, for example, *Sun Zhan Qui v MIEA* (1997) 81 FCR 71. For a discussion of the controversies surrounding s 420 and the first Part 8, see Mary Crock, *Immigration and Refugee Law in Australia* (Sydney: The Federation Press, 1998) at 284-8.
138 (1999) 197 CLR 611 at 628-9 (Gleeson CJ and McHugh J).
139 See Michael Taggart, '"Australian Exceptionalism" in Judicial Review' (2008) 36 *Federal Law Review* 1; and Michael Taggart, 'Proportionality, Deference, *Wednesbury*' [2008] *New Zealand Law Review* 423; and the discussion at Chapter 20.3.
140 See Mark Aronson, 'Process, Quality and Variable Standard: Responding to an *Agent Provocateur*' in David Dyzenhaus, Murray Hunt and Grant Huscroft (eds), *A Simple Common Lawyer: Essays in Honour of Michael Taggart* (Oxford and Portland, Oregon: Hart Publishing, 2009) Ch 2.
141 (1999) 197 CLR 611 at 658.
142 Ibid at 658.
143 See also *Applicant S20/2002* (2003) 198 ALR 59; and *MIMIA v SGLB* (2004) 207 ALR 12.

to contest the 'quality' of the decisions being made using anything approximating general values or standards of fairness or justice.[144]

[19.72] The deference shown by the majority of the High Court in headline cases like *Abebe* and *Eshetu* did not mean that the High Court turned its back completely on migrant applicants. When presented with cases involving obvious injustice, the High Court was prepared to issue constitutional writs so as to order decisions to be re-made in accordance with the law. It was in this context that the High Court invoked again the common law rules of procedural fairness. An example in point is its ruling in *Re RRT; Ex parte Aala*.[145] This was one of a number of cases in which failed refugee claimants have gone back and forth between the RRT, the Federal Court and the High Court. On each occasion the courts have found procedural error, only to have the reconstituted tribunal reject the refugee claim when the matter was remitted for re-hearing.[146] What *Aala* confirmed in 2000 was that the common law rules of procedural fairness continued to apply in migration cases. If the Federal Court was powerless to correct breaches of the common law rules, the High Court was ready, willing and able to do so.

[19.73] In *Aala*, Gummow J confirmed that a breach of the common law rules of procedural fairness could amount to jurisdictional error[147] sufficient to render a decision voidable by the High Court. He took the opportunity to continue his discourse on the limitations placed by the Constitution on the court's judicial review function. He noted the omission from s 75(v) of any reference to the writ of certiorari – a remedy that is used by the courts to quash or vacate a decision affected by (any manner of) error of law. His Honour took the view that the omission indicated that the High Court's (constitutionally guaranteed) powers of judicial review were limited to the correction of serious, *jurisdictional* errors of law. They did not extend to the correction of non-jurisdictional errors that might be characterised by some as errors going to the merits or preferred outcome of an administrative decision.

[19.74] The procedural fairness cases illustrate what appears to be a systemic problem in the manner in which the migration tribunals operate. It can be extremely difficult for the applicant in a remitted case to get a fair hearing *and* extremely difficult for the tribunal to devise a process that is fair.[148] This is because of the volume of

---

144   The consequence of this line of reasoning is that the High Court has made clear that the weight of Australian authority stands against new principles of judicial review adopted in other jurisdictions that enable wider consideration of fairness and justice than is currently possible in Australian law. The most obvious example is the English principle of substantive unfairness, which appears to have no future in Australia in spite of Kirby J's attempts to recognise a remedy of 'serious administrative injustice'. On this point, see Matthew Groves, 'Substantive Legitimate Expectations in Australian Administrative Law' (2008) 32 *Melbourne University Law Review* 470.
145   (2000) 204 CLR 82.
146   In *Aala* the applicant had his case remitted to the RRT on no less than four occasions. He was eventually granted a Protection visa.
147   See the discussion of this legal term of art below in Part 19.6.2.
148   The difficulty in establishing fairness is made harder by the fact that the High Court and Full Federal Court have no problem with defective cases being sent back to the same RRT member. This often creates problems, both of perception (for the applicant) and in fact where members seem intent on achieving the same outcome, where they can do so while avoiding carefully the problems nominated by the review court.

material that builds up in each applicant's file over time.[149] Tribunal members can find it an almost impossible task to articulate the range of adverse material that is contained on the file in a manner that allows the applicant to address all the adverse inferences. For their part, the courts have been resolute that the failure to do this constitutes a breach of the common law rules of procedural fairness.[150] As seen below, the issue of fair process became something of an intractable problem from the government's perspective, even where moves were made to codify the procedures to be followed by the tribunals.

[19.75] If the first Part 8 was designed specifically to limit what was perceived to be undue judicial activism on the part of the courts,[151] the measure was an abject failure. As Crock predicted in 1996 would be the case,[152] the number of migration appeals continued to mount – in fact at an exponential rate. Cases brought before the High Court in its original jurisdiction increased as plaintiffs sought alternative avenues of redress to compensate for the reduced grounds of review available in the Federal Court. The High Court found itself granting relief in cases involving rulings by primary decision-makers that would not have survived even cursory review by a merits review body.[153] Huge class actions brought in this jurisdiction were won by the test plaintiffs,[154] with the result that literally thousands of individual actions came to be lined up in the High Court for individual hearings.[155] Australia's most senior court of constitutional review was brought to its knees.

19.6 Battlelines

19.6.1 The privative clause

[19.76] With the change of government in 1996, attempts were made almost immediately to replace the first Part 8 of the Act so as to bring an end to the burgeoning industry in judicial review. Interestingly, the first two attempts to introduce a

---

149   See, for example, cases such as *Aala* (2000) 204 CLR 82 in which files have gone back and forth between the Federal Court and the RRT and, in the process, material crucial to the applicant has gone missing and therefore not been put to the tribunal and the applicant was not informed about this.
150   *Aala* (2000) 204 CLR 82. Many cases may be cited as examples here. See *Chey v MIAC* [2007] FCA 871; *Herft v MIAC* [2007] FMCA 756; and *SZJLE v MIMA* [2007] FMCA 970.
151   The Joint Standing Committee on Migration, which addressed concerns arising from the Part 8 legislative reforms, stated: 'The tightly defined framework for judicial review … is intended to provide a guard against de facto merits review by the courts, and to remove the fluidity or uncertainty which has characterised the grounds for review under the common law and AD(JR)': Joint Standing Committee on Migration, *Asylum, Border Control and Detention* (Canberra: 1994) at 95.
152   Mary Crock, 'Judicial Review and Part 8 of the Migration Act: Necessary Reform or Overkill?' (1996) 18 *Sydney Law Review* 267.
153   See *Miah* (2001) 206 CLR 57.
154   *Muin v RRT* (2002) 190 ALR 601; and *Herijanto v RRT* (2000) 170 ALR 379. Another class action that did not make it to the High Court was *Fazal Din v MIMA* [1998] FCA 961.
155   Eventually in the Federal Court and later in the newly created Federal Magistrates Court. Federal Magistrate Matthew Smith estimates that 'about 6,700 on-shore refugee applicants joined "representative" actions, for several years (gaining) the benefit of bridging visas without being called upon to show any merits. For an example of how Emmett J dealt with 707 of them, see: *Applicant S1174 of 2002 v Refugee Review Tribunal* [2004] FCA 289': Matthew Smith, 'The Constitutional Right to Judicial Review of Administrative Action: Reflections on *Boddrudazza*' (2008) 84 *Precedent* 39.

comprehensive privative clause[156] failed to gain the bi-partisan support needed to pass through the Senate (where Labor and the minor parties held the balance of power).[157] It took the dramas surrounding the *Tampa* Affair and the US terrorist attacks on 11 September 2001 for parliament to acquiesce in the passage of the ultimate restrictive measure.[158] Amendments banning class actions in migration cases were passed at the same time.[159]

[19.77] The second Part 8 of the *Migration Act* is built around a comprehensive privative clause in s 474. This provision states:

> A privative clause decision:
> (a) is final and conclusive, and
> (b) shall not be challenged, appealed against, reviewed, quashed or called into question in any court; and
> (c) is not subject to prohibition, mandamus, injunction, declaration or certiorari in any court on any account.

[19.78] A 'privative clause decision' is defined in s 474(2) as a decision of an administrative character made under the Act or the Regulations. Most migration-related decisions were intended to be privative clause decisions. The intent of the legislation was to exclude review not only by the Federal Court, but also by the High Court, notwithstanding its constitutionally protected review powers. Although the government cannot entirely oust the jurisdiction of the High Court,[160] it can signal its preference that the court not intervene in certain cases. Privative clauses have been used, successfully, to this effect since the case of *R v Hickman; Ex parte Fox and Clinton*[161] was decided in 1945. In fact the wording of the clause used in s 474 is identical to that used in the statute giving rise to the challenge in *Hickman*.

[19.79] It is clear from the construction of s 474 and the secondary material submitted with the *Migration Legislation Amendment (Judicial Review) Act 2001* (Cth)[162] that the government intended it to be interpreted in light of the 'classical' principle enunciated by Dixon J in *Hickman*. His Honour ruled in that case that:

> [A privative clause] is interpreted as meaning that no decision shall be invalidated on the ground that it has not conformed to the requirements governing its proceedings or the exercise of its authority or has not confined its acts within the limits laid down by the instrument giving it authority provided always that its decision

---

156   This is the term used to describe provisions which on their face appear to ban all forms of judicial review.
157   See Migration Legislation Amendment Bill (No 4) 1997; and Migration Legislation Amendment (Judicial Review) Bill 1998. See Senate Legal and Constitutional Legislation Committee, *Report on Migration Legislation (Judicial Review) Bill 1998* (Canberra: 1999).
158   See *Migration Legislation Amendment (Judicial Review) Act 2001* (Cth).
159   See *Migration Legislation Amendment Act (No 1) 2001* (Cth), inserting s 486B into the Act.
160   On the face of things, it is beyond the power of the Parliament to withdraw any matter from the grant of jurisdiction or to abrogate or qualify the grant: see *Waterside Workers' Federation of Australia v Gilchrist, Watt and Sanderson Ltd* (1924) 34 CLR 482; *Australian Coal and Shale Employees' Federation v Aberfield Coal Mining Co Ltd* (1942) 66 CLR 161; and *Deputy Commissioner of Taxation v Richard Walter Pty Ltd* (1995) 183 CLR 168.
161   (1945) 70 CLR 598 (*Hickman*).
162   See Second Reading Speech, Minister Philip Ruddock, Australian Parliamentary Debates, *Hansard*, House of Representatives, 26 September 2001, at 31559-62.

is a bona fide attempt to exercise its power, that it relates to the subject matter of the legislation, and that it is reasonably capable of reference to the power given to the body.[163]

[19.80] In other words, a decision made under a privative clause will be legal so long as the decision was a bona fide attempt to exercise the tribunal's power; it relates to the subject-matter of the legislation; it is capable of reasonable reference to the tribunal's power; the decision does not display jurisdictional error on its face; and it does not breach a statutory constraint so important as to be regarded as unprotected by the operation of the privative clause.[164] Where the government broke new ground, however, was in its interpretation of this principle relative to the guarantees contained in ss 73 and 75(v) of the Constitution.

[19.81] The government's argument went something like this. The *Hickman* principle, in application, expands the relevant tribunal's jurisdiction, rather than acting as an ouster of remedies designed to enforce constitutional and statutory jurisdictional constraints. Therefore, it does not exclude judicial review (an effect that would make such clauses unconstitutional), but brings certain decisions that would otherwise be outside the law within its purview, *deeming* them to be lawful. It was an interpretation that conveniently omitted reference to earlier statements by the High Court to the effect that privative clauses could not override 'inviolable' aspects of a statute.[165]

[19.82] As day follows night, a constitutional challenge was mounted to the new Part 8 in two cases that were argued together before the High Court in 2003.[166] Interestingly, the first (and successful) applicant, code named Plaintiff S157, was a refugee claimant who had been caught up in the class action litigation, with the result that they had been 'in the system' for many years. As in previous test cases,[167] a two-pronged approach was taken, with both a challenge to the constitutionality of s 474 and a claim that the substantive decision in the case was affected by fundamental legal error. Plaintiff S157[168] challenged the privative clause scheme as an unconstitutional Act of Parliament that deprived him of lawful relief. He claimed further that ss 476 and 486(a), which would act to bar his application for review of the tribunal decision to the High Court, were invalid. The alternative argument going to issues of substantive illegality was raised by counsel in the second case of *Applicants S134*[169] and represented a direct assault on the government's interpretation of the *Hickman* principle. There it was argued that no privative clause could operate to expand the powers of the executive so as to put them beyond curial intervention.

---

163 (1945) 70 CLR 598 at 615 (Dixon J).
164 Aronson, Dyer and Groves, above n 1, at 968ff
165 See, for example, *R v Coldham; Ex parte Australian Workers Union* (1983) 153 CLR 415 at 418.
166 *Plaintiff S157/2002 v Commonwealth* and *Re MIMA; Ex parte Applicants S134/2002* were heard together, both for special leave application (on 23 July 2002) and in Canberra (on 3-4 September 2002).
167 See, for example, the cases of *Abebe* (1999) 197 CLR 510 and *Eshetu* (1999) 197 CLR 611 discussed earlier.
168 *Plaintiff S157/2002 v Commonwealth* (2003) 211 CLR 426 (*Plaintiff S157*) at [46].
169 See *Re MIMA; Ex parte Applicants S134/2002* (2003) 211 CLR 441 (*Applicants S134/2002*). John Basten SC, counsel for the Bakhtiyari family (Applicants S134), put the arguments described at paras [59]-[61] of the decision in *Plaintiff S157/2002* (2003) 211 CLR 426.

[19.83] Then Solicitor General, David Bennett QC, presented the Minister's interpretation of the privative clause to the High Court on 4 September 2002. By way of example, he argued that the effect of the new provisions was to render immune from challenge any interpretation placed on the Refugee Convention, provided that the Minister acted in 'good faith'. Gleeson CJ saw that the Minister's reading of the clause in question would have removed the power of the court to review the executive's understanding of substantive refugee law. His Honour brought out this fact by invoking as an example the High Court's ruling in *MIMA v Khawar*.[170] The exchange between the two is worth reciting:

> GLEESON CJ: What if, instead of granting a visa to a person who is an alien, he [the Minister] refuses to grant a visa to a person who is a refugee within the meaning of the Refugees Convention?
>
> MR BENNETT: The question then would be whether it was a bona fide exercise of the power.
>
> GLEESON CJ: Suppose the reason he refuses to grant the visa is that he has an erroneous understanding of the meaning of the language of the Refugees Convention?
>
> MR BENNETT: Then, your Honour, it is not challengeable. He is given that power. That is not within the Hickman exception rule.
>
> GLEESON CJ: Is another way of saying that that he is given power to make a conclusive decision as to the question of law involved in the true construction of the Refugees Convention?
>
> MR BENNETT: No, your Honour. That, we would submit, is not a correct characterisation of what he is doing. The effect of that clause, read with the Hickman clause, is that so long as the Minister bona fide attempts to apply what the section requires and so long as one is within the other limitations, then he may make the decision either way and he is empowered to do so.
>
> GLEESON CJ: Take the case that we had recently involving a question of whether women could be a particular social group. Suppose the Minister decides that it is impossible for women to be regarded as a particular social group within the meaning of the Refugees Convention. Does that not amount to the Minister making a conclusive and incontestable decision about a matter of law?
>
> MR BENNETT: No, your Honour, because the Minister is not ultimately deciding a question of law; the Minister is deciding whether to grant a visa and he is making a bona fide effort to apply a criterion which he may apply wrongly.[171]

[19.84] In so far as the Solicitor General was suggesting that the High Court would not be at liberty to make the ruling that it did in *Khawar* under the privative clause regime, one can sense the affront to the Chief Justice. In the result, the High Court was unanimous in its rejection of the Minister's arguments on the effect of the privative clause. Although it upheld the provisions as constitutional, the court accepted an argument that had been put by counsel in *Applicants S134/2002* that the clauses simply had no application in cases where decisions were affected by fundamental

---

170 (2002) 210 CLR 1, discussed above in Chapter 13 at [13.68].
171 See *Plaintiff S157 of 2002 v Commonwealth* [2002] HCATrans 423.

legal errors that infringed against 'inviolable limitations' or other matters that defined the jurisdiction of a decision-maker.[172]

[19.85] In this respect, the High Court's ruling in *Plaintiff S157 v Commonwealth*[173] was a curious mix of deference and assertion. While holding that the privative clause regime was indeed constitutional, the court nonetheless stated that *any* tribunal decision evidencing jurisdictional error would fall outside the privative clause scheme and therefore be open to review by either the Federal or High Courts.[174] The crucial statement by the High Court, asserting its intention to continue to review migration decisions, was the following:

> This Court has clearly held that an administrative decision which involves jurisdictional error is 'regarded, in law, as no decision at all'. Thus, if there has been jurisdictional error because, for example, of a failure to discharge 'imperative duties' or to observe 'inviolable limitations or restraints', the decision in question cannot properly be described in the terms used in s 474(2) as 'a decision ... made under this Act' and is, thus, not a 'privative clause decision' as defined in ss 474(2) and (3) of the Act.[175]

[19.86] The deferential strain in the judgment is illustrated by the fact that the privative clause scheme was held to be constitutional. Although hardly a surprising outcome given the frequent use of such clauses in both State and federal laws,[176] it was enough to encourage then Attorney General Philip Ruddock to claim that the result constituted a victory for the government.[177] The costs order made by the High Court raises some doubts about this claim.[178] Where the ruling represented a comprehensive loss for the government was that it operated to ensure the continued – intimate – involvement of the courts in determining the correct interpretation of both domestic and international law affecting migration decision-making.

---

172   (2003) 211 CLR 476 at [37] (Gleeson J), at [76] (Gaudron, McHugh, Gummow, Kirby and Hayne JJ), at [160] (Callinan J). For a discussion of the reasoning in the case, see Aronson, Dyer and Groves, above n 1, at 968-75; and Enid Campbell and Matthew Groves, 'Privative Clauses and the Australian Constitution' (2004) 4 *Oxford University Commonwealth Law Journal* 51.
173   (2003) 211 CLR 476.
174   Further, the High Court took pains to make clear that the construction of s 474 has implications for remitter of actions by it to both the Federal Court and the Federal Magistrates Court. In short, '[t]he limitation, ... of the jurisdiction otherwise enjoyed by the Federal Court and the Federal Magistrates Court ... will be controlled by the construction given to s 474. Decisions which are not protected by s 474 such as that in this case, ... will not be within the terms of the jurisdictional limitations just described; jurisdiction otherwise conferred upon federal courts ... will remain, to be given full effect in accordance with the terms of that conferral': *Plaintiff S157* (2003) 211 CLR 426 at [95]-[96].
175   Ibid at [76] (Gaudron, McHugh, Gummow, Kirby and Hayne JJ) (footnotes omitted).
176   For a general account of the use of privative clauses, see Aronson, Dyer and Groves, above n 1, Ch 17; and Mary Crock and Edward Santow, 'Privative Clause and the Limits of the Law' in Matthew Groves and HP Lee (eds), *Australian Administrative Law: Fundamentals, Principles and Doctrines* (Melbourne: Cambridge University Press, 2007) Ch 22.
177   See, for example, Max Blenkin and Sharon Mathieson, 'High Court upholds tough stance on asylum seekers' *AAP General News (Australia)*, 4 February 2003, available at <http://www.highbeam.com/doc/1P1-71498256.html>.
178   The costs order was that the costs be borne 25 per cent by the plaintiff and 75 per cent by the defendant (the government). See *Plaintiff S157* (2003) 211 CLR 426 at [179].

[19.87] On a practical level, it is important to note that, while the High Court's decision in *Plaintiff S157* has been hailed as a victory for the institution of judicial review, it is not necessarily a victory for all litigants. Applicants still have to persuade the court that a decision is affected by a 'jurisdictional error'. It is noteworthy (if ironic) that the applicants in the companion case to *Plaintiff S157* did not result in success, despite the expanded grounds of review once again available.[179]

19.6.2 Slippery concepts:[180] Defining the 'jurisdictional error'

[19.88] One of the most difficult tasks for any administrative lawyer is to articulate a clear and logical explanation of the concept of 'jurisdictional error'. In *Plaintiff S157*, as it has in other cases, the High Court resisted the temptation to provide an exhaustive definition. Despite the many thousands of words written on the subject, the central problem seems to be that fundamental legal errors can be manifest in an almost infinite variety of ways.[181] For this reason the courts have been reluctant to make statements that might limit their ability to intervene in future cases.

[19.89] Compounding the natural complexity of defining legal error is the fact that judicial rulings are affected inevitably by the personal leanings, politics or proclivities of individual judges, much as the courts fight to deny this. Lord Denning MR summed up the cynics' view of the jurisprudence on jurisdictional error in *Pearlman v Keepers and Governors of Harrow School*.[182] He said:

> The distinction between an error which entails absence of jurisdiction – and an error made within jurisdiction – is very fine ... So fine is the distinction that in truth the High Court has a choice before it whether to interfere with an inferior court on a point of law. If it chooses to interfere, it can formulate its decision in the words: 'The court below had no jurisdiction to decide this point wrongly as it did.' If it does not choose to interfere, it can say: 'The court had the jurisdiction to decide it wrongly and it did so.'[183]

[19.90] Aronson, Dyer and Groves note that Kirby J is the only Australian judge to agree wholeheartedly with Lord Denning's call for the abolition of distinctions between jurisdictional errors and errors of law within jurisdiction.[184] Making sense of this area of law is made more difficult by the fact that the courts frequently confirm the importance of jurisdictional error while also refusing to clarify the doctrine. A recent example is the majority's comment in *Kirk v Industrial Relations Commission*[185] that 'it is neither necessary, nor possible, to mark the metes and bounds of jurisdictional error'!

---

179   See *Applicants S134/2002* (2003) 211 CLR 441.
180   See the comments of Finkelstein J in *Bray v F Hoffman-La Roche Ltd* (2003) 130 FCR 317 at [235].
181   This point is made by McHugh, Gummow and Hayne JJ in *MIMA v Yusuf* (2001) 206 CLR 323 at [82].
182   [1979] QB 56.
183   Ibid at 69-70. On this point, see Allars, above n 126, at [5.123]; and Aronson, Dyer and Groves, above n 1, at 207-27.
184   See, for example, his Honour's comments in *Miah* (2001) 206 CLR 57 at 211. See Aronson, Dyer and Groves, above n 1, at 211-12 (and the cases there cited).
185   (2010) 239 CLR 531 at [71].

[19.91] However indeterminate the concept has become, it is possible to make some general comments about circumstances in which judges have identified legal errors so serious that the errors literally or figuratively take a decision-maker beyond her or his jurisdiction. For example, one fact that has emerged from the growing body of jurisprudence is that in circumstances where a court is reviewing decisions made by tribunals – typically staffed in part by non-lawyers – no fine distinctions are to be made between what some have identified as 'broad' and 'narrow' jurisdictional errors. Put another way, whereas some deference might be shown to decisions made by inferior courts, no such courtesy will be shown to a tribunal.[186] These bodies will not be at liberty to make errors in their interpretation of the law. In practice, testing for jurisdictional error in tribunal decisions seems to have brought the courts back (almost) full circle to a situation where all of the traditional grounds for broad and narrow judicial review are invoked, although some with more likelihood of success than others.

[19.92] Other general principles can also be extracted from the collected case law. In *Craig v South Australia*[187] and again in *MIMA v Yusuf*[188] the High Court ruled that:

> Identifying a wrong issue, asking a wrong question, ignoring relevant material or relying on irrelevant material in a way that affects the exercise of the power is to make an error of law. Further, doing so results in the decision maker exceeding the authority or powers given by the relevant statute. In other words, if an error of those types was made; he or she did not have the jurisdiction to make it.[189]

[19.93] As noted earlier, the most frequent grounds for intervention seem to be where a decision-maker misconstrued the terms of a statute.[190] There have been many cases in which the courts have found jurisdictional error where the decision-maker failed to consider significant information submitted or claims made by an applicant,[191] or misinterpreted or misapplied an established legal principle.[192] As explored in some detail in Chapter 18, the High Court has been resolute in regarding serious breaches of procedural fairness as jurisdictional errors.[193] Such rulings include cases where the courts have found rulings to be affected by actual[194] or apprehended bias[195] on the part of the decision-maker. Although the cases are rare, there are even some

---

186   See *Craig v South Australia* (1995) 184 CLR 163, discussed in Aronson, Dyer and Groves, above n 1, at 212-14.
187   (1995) 184 CLR 163 at [50].
188   (2001) 206 CLR 323.
189   Ibid at [82] (McHugh, Gummow and Hayne JJ).
190   See, for example, *MIMIA v Nystrom* (2006) 228 CLR 566; *NBGM v MIMA* (2006) 231 CLR 52. In the Federal Court, see *NAAA v MIMA* (2002) 117 FCR 287.
191   See, for example, *MIMA v Yusuf* (2001) 206 CLR 323 at [82]; *MIMIA v SGLB* (2004) 207 ALR 12; *S395/2002 v MIMA* (2003) 216 CLR 473.
192   See, for example, *S395/2002 v MIMA* (2003) 216 CLR 473; and *SZATV v MIAC* (2007) 233 CLR 18.
193   See *Plaintiff S157* (2003) 211 CLR 426; *VEAL v MIMIA* (2005) 225 CLR 88; *NAIS v MIMIA* (2005) 228 CLR 470; *SAAP* (2005) 215 ALR 162; *SZAYW v MIMIA* (2006) 230 ALR 486; *SZBYR v MIAC* (2007) 235 ALR 609; *Saeed v MIAC* (2010) 267 ALR 204 at 208; and *Plaintiffs M61/M69* (2010) 272 ALR 14.
194   See *Jia v MIMA* (1999) 93 FCR 556, overruled in *MIMA v Jia* (2001) 205 CLR 507.
195   *Re RRT; Ex parte H* (2001) 179 ALR 425 at 434-5.

rulings now in which the courts have found jurisdictional error on the basis of legal unreasonableness.[196]

[19.94] Where the courts have declined to intervene in cases, the usual reason given is that the decision-maker has either committed no legal error at all or the error alleged is characterised as one of fact rather than of law.[197] It is not proposed in this context to attempt to summarise the ever changing jurisprudence on jurisdictional error in the migration cases.[198] To some extent, the courts' rulings have been covered already in so far as their statements on what does and does not constitute legal error shape the substantive law in this area.

19.6.3 Further attempts to constrain the judicial review of migration decisions

[19.95] In *Plaintiff S157*, the High Court drew a figurative line in the sand, announcing in effect that it could not and would not accede to any further incursions into its power to adjudicate on the lawfulness of migration decisions. This stance may have frustrated the government. What it did not do was discourage further attempts to confine judicial review by other means.

[19.96] As noted earlier,[199] one of the first changes made after the introduction of the privative clause regime was to amend the Act so as to expressly exclude the common law rules of procedural fairness from migration decision-making. The *Migration Legislation (Procedural Fairness) Act 2002* (Cth) came into force on 4 July 2002 and applies to all applications made after that date. A series of provisions inserted into the Act[200] specify that the codes of procedure contained in the Act are to be taken as an exhaustive statement of the procedural rules that are to apply in migration cases. This legislation has generated quite a sophisticated jurisprudence on the procedures that must be followed by the migration tribunals.[201] If it is possible to make any general comments on this case law, our view is that the old common law of procedural fairness has continued to inform the judiciary's interpretation of the statutory procedures prescribed in the Act. This is seen in particular in the tendency to require strict adherence to the terms of the legislation. Again, as noted earlier, this has generated a series of tit for tat amendments to the Act. For example, the High

---

196 See, for example, *Yusuf* (2000) 206 CLR 323 at [69]; *Applicant S20/2002* (2003) 198 ALR 59 at [34]-[37]; *NADH v MIMIA* (2004) 214 ALR 264 at [12], [130] and [135]-[136]; *MIAC v Le* (2007) 164 FCR 151; and *QAAA of 2004 v MIMIA* (2007) 98 ALD 695.
197 See, for example, *Re MIMA; Ex parte Cohen* (2001) 177 ALR 473 at [36] (McHugh J); and *Re MIMA; Ex parte Cassim* (2000) 175 ALR 209 at [25], [31] (McHugh J).
198 For a useful summary of the emergent jurisprudence, see Caron Beaton-Wells, 'Judicial Review of Migration Decisions: Life after S157' (2005) 33 *Federal Law Review* 141; Caron Beaton-Wells, 'Australian Administrative Law: The Asylum Seeker Legacy' [2005] *Public Law* 267; Enzo Belperio, 'What Procedural Fairness Duties do the MRT and RRT Owe to Visa Applicants?' (2007) 54 *AIAL Forum* 81; and Alice Ashbolt, 'Taming the Beast: Why a Return to Common Law Procedural Fairness Would Help Curb Migration Litigation' (2009) 20 *Public Law Review* 264.
199 See Chapter 18 at [18.94]ff.
200 See, for example, *Migration Act*, s 51A (regarding primary decisions), s 357A (MRT decisions) and s 422B (RRT decisions).
201 For an account of this jurisprudence, see Grace Ma, above n 59, and Chapter 18 above.

Court's insistence that review applicants be given written notification of material in respect of which comments are required[202] has been countered with provisions allowing the tribunals to give oral notice of such matters.[203]

[19.97] A more serious assault on the judicial review 'problem' was made in 2005 with the passage of the *Migration Litigation Reform Act 2005* (Cth), which commenced operation on 15 November 2005. Perhaps the most striking aspect of the changes was the referral to the new Federal Magistrates Court of the vast bulk of judicial review applications,[204] with provision made for appeals to single judges of the Federal Court.[205] These provisions are complicated slightly by the fact that, while the Act appears to confer jurisdiction on the Federal Magistrates Court across the board, the *Administrative Appeals Tribunal Act 1975* (Cth) refers only to the Federal Court as the authority to which appeals may be lodged under s 44 of that Act.[206]

[19.98] A rearguard attempt to stifle applications was made with the institution of uniform time limits of 28 days from the time that the applicant receives actual notice of the decision.[207] One extension of up to 56 days is permitted if requested within 84 days of actual notification of the decision, and if the court is satisfied that it is in the interests of the administration of justice to extend the time limit.[208] For its part, the High Court wasted no time in declaring time limits in its jurisdiction to be unconstitutional.[209] This has re-created the unfortunate position whereby applicants can be excluded arbitrarily from judicial review in the lesser federal court system such that the High Court is the only option.[210] One can only hope that the more generous time periods specified for review mean that few litigants are disadvantaged in practice.

[19.99] There are some aspects of the *Migration Litigation Reform Act 2005* that have operated to make the judicial review of migration cases more efficient. Procedures in the Federal Magistrates Court have been streamlined; the High Court can remit matters to lower courts without the need for an oral hearing.[211] Litigants are also required to disclose all of their dealings with the courts (preventing serial

---

202 See, for example, s 57 (primary decisions), s 359A (MRT decisions) and s 424A (RRT decisions) and the ruling of the High Court in *SAAP* (2005) 215 ALR 162 at 183 (McHugh J), 203 (Kirby J), 211 (Hayne J). See also *SZEEU v MIAC* (2006) 150 FCR 214 at 253 (Weinberg J).
203 See *Migration Amendment (Review Provisions) Act 2007* (Cth) which commenced on 29 June 2007, with effect on all applications made after that date (s 33). See discussion in Chapter 18 at [18.93].
204 *Migration Act*, s 476A.
205 *Federal Court of Australia Act 1976*, s 25(1AA). (The provision does not apply if a judge considers it appropriate to refer the case to a Full Bench. See, for example, *Zhang v MIAC* 161 FCR 419.)
206 *Migration Act*, s 483A. On this point see *Blanco v MIMA* [2005] FMCA 136. Similar issues arise in relation to decisions made on grounds of character and conduct. See *Chhun v MIMIA* [2006] FMCA 203.
207 This is an improvement on earlier provisions in which notification could be *deemed*. On these provisions, see *MIAC v SZKKC* [2007] 159 FCR 565.
208 *Migration Act*, amended ss 477 (Federal Magistrates Court), 477A (Federal Court) and 486A(1A) (High Court). For an example of how these provisions work in practice, see *SZJQP v MIAC* (2007) 98 ALD 575.
209 *Bodruddaza v MIMIA* (2007) 228 CLR 651.
210 Neither the Federal Magistrates Court nor the Federal Court has any discretion to permit the making of applications outside of the stated time limits.
211 *Judiciary Act*, s 44(4).

applications for judicial review).²¹² However, the more regressive aspect of the changes are those which we are told are designed expressly to 'deter unmeritorious applications'.²¹³ Part 8B of the Act now provides for a series of penalties for any person who 'encourages' another to commence or continue migration litigation in a court if the litigation has no reasonable prospects of success, and the person does not give proper consideration to the prospects of success or a purpose of commencing or continuing the litigation is unrelated to the objectives of the court process.²¹⁴ Any 'person' found to have encouraged unmeritorious litigation is liable to have a costs order made against them personally.²¹⁵ Legal practitioners can be required to certify that an application has merit before filing any migration proceedings.²¹⁶ It remains to be seen whether the provisions make a real difference to the conduct of reviews. The courts were already able to make costs orders against lawyers and migration agents²¹⁷ who assist in bringing an action that is vexatious or without merit of any kind.²¹⁸

19.6.4 The judicial review of decisions made extra-territorially

[19.100] The final device trialled as a mechanism for excluding or discouraging judicial review is the regime described variously as 'offshore processing', the 'Pacific Solution' or strategies named after various 'offshore' locations selected for processing the asylum claims of unauthorised boat arrivals.²¹⁹ The regime was modelled most obviously on America's use of Guantanamo Bay as a centre for detaining and processing first unauthorised boat arrivals from Cuba and Haiti and later 'enemy combatants' from the wars in Iraq and Afghanistan. The centres at Guantanamo and on Nauru and Christmas Island were established to deny detainees access to territory and to the protections of US/Australian law respectively.²²⁰ Both have historical antecedents in attempts by Charles II to decree detention centres on Jersey and the Isle of Man exempt from the writ of *habeas corpus* which allowed oversight by the English courts.²²¹

---

212 *Migration Act*, amended s 486D.
213 *Migration Litigation Reform Act 2005*, Explanatory Memorandum.
214 *Migration Act*, s 486E. For a discussion of what is meant by 'proper consideration', see *SZFDZ v MIMA* (2006) 155 FCR 482.
215 *Migration Act*, s 486F.
216 Ibid, s 486I.
217 See, for example, *MIMA v Shen* (2002) 70 ALD 636.
218 For a useful discussion of the court's power, see *Ex Christmas Islanders Association Inc v Attorney-General (Cth) (No 2)* (2006) 91 ALD 313. For a more general discussion regarding the circumstances in which liability for costs should be imposed on a legal practitioner, see *Baik v MIAC* (2008) 217 FLR 386.
219 These include the Pacific, the Indian Ocean, Christmas Island and East Timor. See Mary Crock and Daniel Ghezelbash, 'Do Loose Lips Bring Ships?: The Role of Policy, Politics and Human Rights in Managing Unauthorised Boat Arrivals' (2010) 19 *Griffith Law Review* 239 at 255-7.
220 See Gerald Neuman, 'Anomalous Zones' (1996) 48 *Stanford Law Review* 1197 at 1128-33; Azadeh Dastyari, 'Refugees on Guantanamo Bay: A Blueprint for Australia's "Pacific Solution"?' (2007) 78 *Australian Quarterly* 1.
221 See Geoffrey Robertson, *The Tyrannicide Brief* (London: Vintage, 2006) at 349; and Geoffrey Robertson, 'Freedom, Soldier', *New Statesmen*, 21 May 2007, at 55; and David Dyzenhaus, *The Constitution of Law – Legality in a Time of Emergency* (Cambridge: Cambridge University Press, 2006).

[19.101] It is a reflection of the centrality of judicial oversight to the notion of the rule of law in the systems of government in these three countries that the various initiatives to exclude the courts have failed in each. The detention regimes on Jersey and the Isle of Man were addressed by the British Parliament in 1679 with the *Habeas Corpus Act 1679*.[222] While the US Supreme Court initially quarantined detention and refugee status determination processes from the protections of international law,[223] that Court later affirmed the capacity of Guantanamo Bay detainees to invoke the jurisdiction of US federal courts.[224]

[19.102] The challenge to Australia's offshore processing regime was heard by Australia's High Court in 2010, almost a decade after the first interdicted asylum seekers were shipped off to Nauru for processing.[225] Plaintiffs M61 and M69 were Tamil asylum seekers who claimed refugee protection on the basis that they faced persecution from the Sri Lankan Army and paramilitary groups. Their protection claims were rejected by both the (departmental) refugee status assessment (RSA) officer and the independent merits reviewer (IMR).[226] Both plaintiffs instituted proceedings in the original jurisdiction of the High Court, alleging that they were not afforded procedural fairness during either the original RSA assessment or the subsequent IMR process. They also alleged errors of law had been made because the decision-makers proceeded on the basis that they were not bound to apply relevant provisions of the *Migration Act* and case law. Plaintiff M69 alleged further that s 46A of the *Migration Act* is unconstitutional if it has the effect of precluding judicial oversight of the status determination process. The Commonwealth conceded that the High Court had jurisdiction to hear the case under s 75(iii) of the Constitution.[227] Orders of mandamus and injunction were sought against 'officers of the Commonwealth', namely the Minister (and the Secretary of DIAC in proceeding M69), which enlivened s 75(v) of the Constitution. In a unanimous but sparsely reasoned judgment, the court upheld the plaintiffs' claims. The court found that mandamus could not issue because the decision-makers were not exercising a 'compellable' power. However,

---

222   See the *Habeas Corpus Act 1679* (Imp): An Act for the better securing the Liberty of the Subject, and for Prevention of Imprisonment beyond the Seas, available at <http://www.british-history.ac.uk/report.asp?compid=47484>.

223   See *Sale v Haitian Centers Council Inc* 113 S Ct 2549 (1993). See James R Zink, 'Race and Foreign Policy in Refugee Law: A Historical Perspective of the Haitian Refugee Crises' (1998) 48 *De Paul Law Review* 559; Bill Frelick, 'US Policy in the Caribbean: No Bridge Over Troubled Waters' (1996) 20(2) *The Fletcher Forum of World Affairs* 67; Hiroshi Motomura, 'Haitian Asylum Seekers: Interdiction and Immigrants' Rights' (1993) 26 *Georgetown Immigration Law Review* 695; and Stephen Legomsky, 'The USA and the Caribbean Interdiction Program' (2006) 18 *International Journal of Refugee Law* 677.

224   See *Hamdi v Rumsfeld* 124 S Ct 2633 (2004); and *Rasul v Bush* 123 S Ct 2686 (2004).

225   See *Plaintiffs M61/ M69* (2010) 272 ALR 14. See generally Mary Crock and Daniel Ghezelbash, 'Due Process and Rule of Law as Human Rights: The High Court and the "Offshore" Processing of Asylum Seekers' (2011) 18(2) *Australian Journal of Administrative Law* 101. Note that this was not the first case in which the regime was challenged. See, for example, *Sadiqi v Commonwealth (No 2)* (2009) 260 ALR 294; and *Plaintiff P1/2003 v MIMIA* [2003] HCATrans 787 (remittal of the case to the Federal Court); and *P1/2003 v MIMIA* [2003] FCA 1029.

226   For a description of the regime in place on Christmas Island, see above Chapter 12.4.2 and Chapter 18 at [18.29].

227   The action was a matter in which the Commonwealth, and persons being sued on behalf of the Commonwealth, were parties. See submissions of the first and second defendant in the matter of *Plaintiffs M61/M69* (2010) 272 ALR 14 at [6].

it did suggest that an injunction might have been ordered if there was a threat to remove the plaintiffs before the lawful completion of the refugee determination process.[228] More importantly, it issued a declaration to the effect that the decisions in question were unlawful.

[19.103] The significance of the High Court's ruling was twofold. First, the court rejected the Minister's argument that the offshore RSA and IMR regimes were undertaken in a statutory vacuum as an exercise of the executive power conferred by s 61 of the Constitution. The court found that the Minister had linked his decision to 'lift the bar' on refugee applications under s 46A of the *Migration Act* to the decisions made by the officials offshore. Second, the court found that the decision-makers on Christmas Island were bound to follow the common law rules of procedural fairness and to comply with the tenets of substantive refugee law laid down by the Australian courts. The fact that the legislation requires the detention of asylum seekers for the duration of status determination processes offshore[229] pointed to an obligation to act fairly. The court reasoned that a statutory power to detain should not be interpreted readily to permit detention at the unconstrained discretion of the executive.[230] Because the Minister's decision directly affected the plaintiffs, both were entitled have their cases decided fairly and in accordance with Australian law.[231] Just as it had done earlier in 2010 in respect of decisions made in respect of foreign visa applicants,[232] the court based its reasoning on that in *Kioa v West*.[233] The focus was on the impact of the process on the plaintiffs' *interests* – even if they could assert no right to enter Australia. The court had no difficulty in finding that the pair had not been treated fairly. Neither had been allowed to comment on adverse country information on conditions in Sri Lanka and about the treatment of returnees. Plaintiff M61 had claimed further that he risked harm on account of 'his profile as a shop owner' and on account of his membership of particular social groups – 'Tamil business owners' or 'Tamils who are perceived to be wealthy'.[234] The reviewer's reasons (which were to be the basis for the Minister's decision) made no reference to these claims. In the result, the court found that the decision impacted on the Minister's central task which was to assess whether Australia owed the plaintiff protection obligations.[235] In addition to

---

228   See *Plaintiffs M61/M69* (2010) 272 ALR 14 at [51] and [99]. Section 75(v) jurisdiction therefore seems to be best based on the injunction and ancillary declaration powers. The court held that jurisdiction could also be found in s 75(i) of the Constitution as the matters could be said to be arising under a treaty, in the form of the Refugee Convention and Protocol. One issue that the court pointedly refused to consider was whether the IMR officials were 'officers of the Commonwealth' for the purposes of s 75(v) of the Constitution. In so doing the Court left for another day the reviewability of decisions made by these 'private' actors. See *NEAT Domestic Trading Pty Ltd v AWB Ltd* (2003) 216 CLR 277; *General Newspapers Pty v Telstra Corporation* (1993) 45 FCR 164; and *Griffith University v Tang* (2005) 221 CLR 99.
229   *Migration Act*, s 189.
230   *Plaintiffs M61/M69* (2010) 272 ALR 14 at [63]-[64].
231   Ibid at [77].
232   See *Saeed v MIAC* (2010) 267 ALR 204.
233   (1985) 159 CLR 550.
234   *Plaintiffs M61/M69* (2010) 272 ALR 14 at [83].
235   Ibid at [90]. It is arguable that such a finding would have been made also in respect of onshore applicants, given the constraints of the *Migration Act*. See *NABE v MIMIA (No 2)* (2004) 144 FCR 1 at [63].

affirming a duty to act fairly, the court found that the reviewer had erred by treating the *Migration Act* and decided cases as no more than guides to decision-making. Having ruled that the offshore process was tied to this legislation and that the whole matter was reviewable, the court went on to dismiss the claims that the legislative scheme was unconstitutional.[236]

[19.104] The burning question for the government following the judgment in *Plaintiffs M61/ M69*, was whether the creation of an offshore processing centre on East Timor[237] or on Nauru[238] would take the process outside the jurisdiction of the Australian courts. As long as the foreign status determination process is tied to the issue of a visa to enter Australia, the court leaves open the possibility that the process may be reviewable. The 'private' status of decision-makers would not necessarily break the nexus with the exercise of the Minister's power. Asylum seekers would continue to have interests worthy of protection if they were held in detention at the behest of the Australian authorities and in all events by virtue of the dangers faced if returned to their countries of origin. There can be no certainty that a return to this regime would see the High Court demur from the review of relevant decisions. The central problem, Crock and Ghezelbash argue, is that any regime established and funded by Australia would relate to asylum seekers who are ultimately Australia's responsibility. They write:

> The schema that the current government appears to be seeking to replicate is that which operates within the major refugee camps managed by UNHCR around the world. In these cases, UNHCR determines claims made by asylum seekers. Sometimes this is done for the purpose of identifying worthy candidates for resettlement in third countries. The primary purpose, however, is to identify persons whose claims not to be returned to the country from which they have fled should be respected. The problem with establishing a regime of this kind on East Timor, or for that matter on Nauru, is that the system would depend on breaking the nexus between the relevant asylum seekers and Australia's obligation not to *refoule* or send back a genuine refugee to a place of persecution.[239] This obligation extends to indirect as well as direct return.[240] Unlike the asylum seekers processed by UNHCR in its many field operations, the boat people interdicted by Australia are first and foremost Australia's responsibility. If Australia is the only country involved in the creation of the offshore centre, this responsibility – and the connection with Australia – will be hard to shake. Whichever country is chosen to house such a centre, it is difficult to imagine that the arrangements would not involve a guar-

---

236 For a discussion of this aspect of the case, see Crock and Ghezelbash, above n 225, at Part 4.2.
237 See Chris Bowen MP, Interview with Kerry O'Brien, 7:30 Report, ABC TV, 11 November 2010, transcript available at <http://mia.org.au/media/File/Bowen__HCA__730_report.pdf>; Interview with Samantha Hawley, ABC AM, 12 November 2010, transcript available at <http://mia.org.au/media/File/Bowen__HCA.pdf>; Interview with Marius Benson, ABC Newsradio, 12 November 2010, transcript available at <http://mia.org.au/media/File/Bowen__ABC_newsradio.pdf>.
238 Scott Morrison, 'High Court Sinks Labor's Asylum Policy Credibility', *Media Release*, 11 November 2010.
239 Articles 32 and 33 of Refugee Convention create basic obligations that refugees should neither be *refouled* nor returned to 'the frontiers of territories where his [or her] life or freedom would be threatened'.
240 See James Hathaway, *The Rights of Refugees under International Law* (Cambridge: Cambridge University Press, 2005) at 326.

antee of some kind that Australia will bear the ultimate responsibility of ensuring that recognised refugees are resettled in a third country.²⁴¹

19.6.5 Judicial review as dysfunction: Australian 'exceptionalism' and the burden of legal formalism

Senator Bartlett: You have given a number of examples of various changes that have been made, back to 1992 or so ,... aimed at reducing access to the courts, which basically have not been successful. Most of these reforms have been aimed at curtailing rights of appeal ... Out of all the others that you have been continually putting in place, why is this one going to succeed, also taking into account that the number of appeals continues to increase?

Mr Metcalfe: I think that is a good question. I suppose what you are asking is: have we identified the last loophole?

Senator Bartlett: I could be asking whether we are going in the right direction.²⁴²

[19.105] In many respects the regime governing the judicial review of migration decisions is one that, ultimately, has left no-one happy. Predictably, the drafting of tighter and tighter rules governing migration decision-making has simply magnified the trend towards formalism in the courts that was set in train by the 'process' focus of the first Part 8 of the *Migration Act* in 1994. The introduction of a full blown privative clause did not put a stop to applications for judicial review. On the contrary, this and most subsequent attempts to block access to the courts have been abject failures. Although the rate of applications has slowed since the change of government in 2007,²⁴³ even the Department's Chief Lawyer concedes that the trend probably has more to do with broad policy changes and revised management techniques than with the legislation put in place.²⁴⁴ At the same forum in 2009, the Principal Member of the migration tribunals, Denis O'Brien, went so far as to call for the repeal of Part 8 of the *Migration Act* and for the return of immigration to mainstream systems for both merits and judicial review.²⁴⁵

[19.106] On the other side of the equation, applicants have found little joy in the judicial review process. The ability to draw out the fight to remain in Australia is rarely beneficial to an applicant's psycho-social wellbeing. The Minister's 90 per cent plus success rate²⁴⁶ also means that the outcome for litigants is rarely favourable in the long term.

---

241   See above n 225, at Part 5.2.
242   Transcript of evidence given to Joint Standing Committee on Migration inquiry into the Migration Legislation Amendment Bill (No 2) 2000, evidence of Mr Andrew Metcalfe, Deputy Secretary of the Department of Immigration and Multicultural Affairs, cited by Susan Harris, 'Another Salvo Across the Bow: Migration Legislation Amendment Bill (No 2) 2000 (Cth)' (2000) 23 *UNSW Law Journal* 208 at 208.
243   See DIAC, *Fact Sheet No 9*, 13 September 2010.
244   See Robyn Bickett, 'Controlling Immigration Litigation: The Commonwealth Perspective' (2010) 63 *AIAL Forum* 40.
245   See Denis O'Brien, 'Controlling Migration Litigation' (2010) 63 *AIAL Forum* 29.
246   See Bickett, above n 244, at 46. What the author does not acknowledge, however, is that the 10 per cent included some spectacular losses – most notably in test cases for the major class actions. See, for example, *Muin v RRT* (2002) 190 ALR 601; *Herijanto v RRT* (2000) 170 ALR 379; and *Fazal Din v MIMA* [1998] FCA 961.

[19.107] A brief return to two strands in the jurisprudence on judicial review in immigration serves to illustrate these universal and significant frustrations. The first relates to the codification of the procedures that must be followed by decision-makers. The second concerns the judiciary's general tendency to eschew issues of 'quality' in favour of 'process' in exercising the judicial review function. The peculiar jurisprudence that has emerged on the issue of 'reasonableness' as a ground of review will be used as an example in point.

[19.108] As noted earlier, judicial rulings based on the common law rules of procedural fairness have met with legislative resistance in the immigration portfolio that probably dates back as far as 1989 when the *Migration Act* underwent its first great transformation into a regime of codified decision-making. The most marked attacks on the common law rules, however, postdate the introduction of a full blown privative clause in 2001. The 2003 legislative amendments, once and for all, ousted the common law in favour of codes of procedure that represent an 'exhaustive' statement of the procedures that must be followed. As Alice Ashbolt argues eloquently – and with whom O'Brien and Bickett would seem to agree – the codification of procedures has done nothing to improve either efficiency or fairness within the migration tribunals.[247] Rather, the increasingly precise and directed rules have stultified interactions between the review bodies and their 'clients'. Whichever way you look at it, the pressure on the courts has not made for healthy and wholesome outcomes. Judges looking to find a just result in the face of perceived injustice have sometimes pushed the boundaries of sound interpretative method.[248] More generally, however, tit for tat legislation (whereby every significant court ruling over many years has been met with 'corrective' amendments to the *Migration Act*) has encouraged courts to be both conservative and increasingly literal or formalist in their interpretation of statutory codes. On more than one occasion, court rulings have been made with judges acknowledging that no substantive unfairness or miscarriage of justice had occurred in the particular case.[249] O'Brien cites the observation of Weinberg J in *SZEEU v MIMIA*:[250]

> With great respect, I doubt that the legislature ever contemplated that s 424A would give rise to the difficulties that it has, or lead to the results that it does. The problems that have arisen stem directly from the attempt to codify, and prescribe exhaustively, the requirements of natural justice, without having given adequate attention to the need to maintain some flexibility in this area. This desire to set out by way of a highly prescriptive code those requirements was no doubt well-intentioned, and perhaps motivated by a concern to promote consistency. However, the achievement of consistency (assuming that this goal can be attained) comes

---

247 See Ashbolt, above n 198.
248 An example in point may be the decision in *Miah* (2001) 206 CLR 57 where a majority of the High Court ruled that what parliament described as the 'replacement' of common law rules of procedural fairness with a code of procedures was not enough to displace the common law, see at [128] (McHugh J) and [181] (Kirby J). See also Lyria Bennett, 'Re Minister for Immigration and Multicultural and Indigenous Affairs; Ex Parte Miah: A Statute in the Eye of its Beholder' (2001) 29 *Federal Law Review* 437. For an example of this in an area of substantive immigration law, see the discussion of the courts' treatment of the exceptions made for victims of domestic violence, above Chapter 7.3.
249 See *SZEEU v MIMIA* (2006) 150 FCR 214 at [18] (Weinberg J); and *SZEWL v MIMIA* [2006] FCA 968 at [11]-[12].
250 (2006) 150 FCR 214 at [183]. See O'Brien, above n 245, at 40.

at a price. As is demonstrated by the outcome of at least some of these appeals, codification in this area can lead to complexity, and a degree of confusion, resulting in unnecessary and unwarranted delay and expense. To put the matter colloquially, and to paraphrase, 'the cake may not be worth the candle'.

[19.109] The second example of the calcifying impact of excessive legislative intrusion into administrative decision-making is the direction taken by the Australian courts in identifying 'jurisdictional error' generally and (more particularly) in reviewing decisions on grounds of 'reasonableness'. We tend to agree with Taggart[251] and Aronson[252] that the High Court's characterisation of jurisdictional error as a 'conclusory' term is an invitation to complexity and confusion in judicial review.[253] It is a conceptualisation that is built inevitably on opaque and formalistic interpretations of statutory provisions and what Aronson describes as a multiplicity of labels, the boundaries of which are manipulable or porous. At the very least, bland assertions that distinctions can be made between jurisdictional errors and lesser (non-jurisdictional) errors of law fail to explain why courts intervene in some cases and not in others. It is a trend that has sent the Australian jurisprudence off at right angles to that of comparator common law nations.

[19.110] The case of *Re MIMA; Ex parte Applicant S20/2002*[254] is a fine example in point. As noted earlier, this was one of the three cases in which Gummow J argued that, in reviewing a decision on grounds of unreasonableness, a distinction must be drawn between the review of objective decision-making (or 'matters of judgment') and 'pure' discretions.[255] Gummow J ruled that the decision by the RRT in that case did not involve the exercise of a pure discretion and that, accordingly, the court could only intervene on evidence that the tribunal's decision involved serious irrationality or illogicality – something that was not apparent on the face of the decision made.

[19.111] As Aronson explains, the essence of this approach is that the rationality standard is applied as a monolithic concept, with no variation occurring to take account of the human rights implications of the decision at hand. This approach (which permits of no notion of an underlying value system in judicial review) is greatly at odds with judicial review trends in other parts of the common law world.[256] In dissent, Kirby J offers a blistering criticism of the majority's ruling and of Gummow J's approach in particular. He takes issue with the assumption that the various grounds of judicial review can be compartmentalised in the way suggested by his colleague.[257] Typically, Kirby J provides a strong impression of the facts at issue and of the impact that the RRT's decision is having on the asylum seeker at the centre

---

251 See Taggart, above n 139.
252 See Aronson, above n 140. See also Aronson, Dyer and Groves, above n 1, at [1.85]-[1.90] and [10.5]-[10.10].
253 See also to like effect *SDAV v MIMIA* (2003) 199 ALR 43 at [27].
254 (2003) 198 ALR 59.
255 See also *Eshetu* (1999) 197 CLR 611; and *MIMIA v SGLB* (2004) 207 ALR 12.
256 See the cases summarised by Aronson, above n 140, at 6-7.
257 See (2003) 198 ALR 59 at [143], where Kirby J said: 'The statutory restriction upon the Federal Court's review jurisdiction in s 476(2) was somewhat curious. It proceeded on what is arguably a misconceived assumption that the grounds of judicial review can be neatly compartmentalised into completely separate kinds of error. This cannot always be done.'

of the appeal. Judicial review, for this judge, is not some intellectual exercise that bears no relationship to real life and events with real consequences. Having decided the applicant lacked credibility, the RRT refused to have regard to either the man's physical injuries or the testimonies of the man's treating dentist, surgeon and of an independent witness. Kirby J is worth quoting at some length:

> [As far as the first two of these sources of evidence] are concerned, there is at least a superficial logic to the way the Tribunal reasoned. Thus, where the opinion of a medical specialist is dependent upon factual assumptions provided in a patient's history, such an opinion will only be as acceptable as the history on which it is based. However, as Finkelstein J pointed out in the Full Court, the injuries and complaints recorded by the dentist and the surgeon (whose honesty was not impugned) were confirmatory of the history given by the appellant to the Tribunal concerning torture and gross assaults whilst he was in official custody at Colombo Fort.
>
> The dentist, for example, had seen the appellant in December 1994, immediately after his release. He described fractures of the front six teeth requiring their extraction, complete rest and further dental treatment. The dentist also noted 'wounded and swollen hands', 'swelling in lips', 'depression' and 'post-traumatic stress disorder'. The Tribunal rejected the last-mentioned diagnoses as outside the specialty of a dentist. The record of the dentist's observations of the extensive dental injuries could not be so easily dismissed.
>
> It is possible that, walking down the hill to the city from Colombo Fort, the appellant might have fallen over, suffered a random assault, bitten on a very large object or been struck in the face by a cricket ball hit for six. However, the peremptory dismissal of such significant injuries, recorded at a point in time so close to the events of assault and torture alleged by the appellant, happening in a country in which so many citizens have been killed or injured in communal conflict, appears unsatisfactory. With all respect to the contrary view, it amounts to a failure in the process of fact-finding by the repository of the power. It cannot be explained on the footing that the appellant's credibility had otherwise been so weakened that the corroborative evidence deserved no weight at all. ...
>
> To similar effect is the Tribunal's treatment of the surgery which the appellant underwent in 1999 in Australia to repair a right inguinal hernia.
>
> Again, it is possible that such an injury might have occurred in some extraneous way: straining in the Bentota surf or in some unidentified work effort in Australia. But, at the very least, the fact of his age suggested the need for some explanation as to why the condition found on operation was given no weight but dismissed because of the earlier recorded lack of confidence in the appellant's credibility.
>
> In this field, as in others, tribunals and courts need to be guarded in their reliance upon their ability to assess the truthfulness of a witness from that witness' appearance alone. Yet here the Tribunal seems to have felt able to do just that. In essence, it reached a conclusion, adverse to the appellant, on the basis of its estimate of his untruthfulness and the 'plausibility' of his story. Because that estimate was adverse to the appellant the Tribunal felt entitled to reject out of hand reports about his condition given by the dentist and surgeon. A moment's thought should have convinced the Tribunal that this was a highly illogical, if not an irrational and perverse, way of going about the process of decision-making. A proper approach to that process, as mandated by the Act, would have required weighing any impressions, and perceived defects, in the appellant's testimony,

together with any supporting evidence before coming to a final conclusion. That is not the way this Tribunal went about reaching the decision entrusted to it.[258]

[19.112] With the retirement of Justice Kirby, the High Court appears to have lost its principal advocate for a variable standard approach to unreasonableness and to judicial review generally. In our view, jurisprudence like that of *Applicant S20/2002* underscores the need in Australia for a human rights regime that might force the judiciary (and tribunal members) to reconsider the harshness of their approach.

19.7 Towards the future

[19.113] From the perspective of the judges charged with hearing applications for the judicial review of migration cases, the litigation explosion in the area of migration decision-making has been a matter of great concern. Neither the phenomenon nor the mechanisms put in place to address the problem are unique to Australia. In spite of every attempt to restrict access to the courts, the number of applications for judicial review has remained stubbornly high.

[19.114] For those studying the jurisprudence emanating from the various courts – and indeed for those involved in litigating migration cases – it is not so clear that this area of administrative law is overwhelmingly comprised of vexatious litigants or persons whose claims lack any merit. The wealth of authority on immigration law that now informs works such as this text suggests that many of the cases brought before the courts have a great deal of merit, if only for the contributions they have made to an increasingly complex area of public law. It is our view that there are many problems inherent in the rhetoric that has developed over the years around purported abusive or unmeritorious judicial review applications in immigration. The most significant in our view is that the discourse undermines the central role that the courts play in upholding the rule of law. As John Basten QC (as he then was) wrote in 2004:

> [A]n applicant for a visa entitling him or her to enter and remain in Australia has a procedural right to have the application determined according to law. If that course has not been properly undertaken, relief will flow to ensure that it is, and that the Commonwealth, through its officers, does not take steps on the basis that an adverse decision has been made, when that is not the case.[259]

[19.115] For our part, we will end with some reflections on the worth of judicial review that Crock penned in 1998 in a submission made on behalf of the Law Council of Australia in its (then successful) fight against the introduction of a privative clause into the *Migration Act*:

> In his play 'A Man for All Seasons', Robert Bolt has Sir Thomas More make an eloquent defence of the English legal system and of the Rule of Law. More's son-in-law, Will Roper, reprimands him for allowing an unsavoury character to go free because he had not broken the law. To Roper's suggestion that the end should

---

258   (2003) 198 ALR 59 at [88]-[93] (footnotes omitted).
259   John Basten QC, 'Judicial Review under Section 75(v)' (unpublished paper prepared for the 2004 Constitutional Law Conference, 20 February 2004), <http://www.gtcentre.unsw.edu.au/Basten-Paper.doc>, at 12.

justify the means: that he would 'cut down every law in England' (to get after the Devil), More replies:
> Oh? And when the last law was down, and the Devil turned around on you – where would you hide, Roper, the laws being flat? This country's planted thick with laws from coast to coast – Man's Laws, not God's – and if you cut them flat ... d'you really think you could stand upright in the winds that would blow then?[260]

Australia's system of law and government is predicated on a Constitution; the Common Law and the distribution of power between three authorities: the Parliament, the Executive or Administration and the Courts. The judiciary has none of the primary powers of the parliament, but it stands as a vital check on the powers being exercised by both the Legislative and the Executive arms of government. For their part the Courts operate subject to the Constitution and subject to the laws made by Parliament. [Privative clauses] do nothing to recognise the significance of this tripartite arrangement.

In the final analysis the [privative clause] is all about power and the removal of obstacles to its exercise. It is very much about cutting down the structures of administrative law. In considering their vote on this measure, Members of Parliament should consider the ramifications of the measure and where it leads this country. At risk is the notion of accountable government and the notion that decision makers should be answerable for their actions. At risk is the Rule of Law as we know it.[261]

[19.116] The change of government in 2007 did not signal an immediate change in the judicial review of migration decisions, although the softening of attitudes within the bureaucracy does appear to have engendered a new willingness to examine the totality of the appeal and review structures. The extent of the cultural change that has occurred is apparent in the fact that both the Department's (then) Chief Lawyer and the Principal Member of the review authorities have called for a cessation of hostilities with the courts. Both even seem prepared to sanction a return to the common law in the form of abandoning codified procedures and the privative clause regime.[262] The next step should be for the government to take the rational step of replacing what, in our view, was always a suspect legislative regime. The need for this to occur was only strengthened in 2010 by decisions such as *Saeed v MIAC*[263] and *Plaintiffs M61/M69*[264] which signalled a new willingness in the High Court to scrutinise decisions made outside Australia.

[19.117] Whether the government is willing to brave the political posturing that would likely accompany proposals for reform is another (considerably vexed) question. What should be clear is that the rigid codification of migration decision-making and attempts to stifle judicial review have done little for the health of administrative decision-making in the immigration portfolio. The infective influence of the jurisprudence and of the reasoning processes adopted in the migration cases mean that these developments have also damaged the fabric of public law in Australia more generally. It is indeed time to change direction.

---

260 See Robert Bolt, *A Man for All Seasons* (London: Heinemann Educational Books, 1960) at 39.
261 See Submission 5, Senate Legal and Constitutional Legislation Committee, Consideration of *Migration Legislation Amendment (Judicial Review) Bill 1998* (Canberra: April 1999).
262 See Bickett, above n 244, and O'Brien, above n 245.
263 (2010) 267 ALR 204 at [11].
264 (2010) 272 ALR 14.

PART IX Conclusion

20

Facing the Future: Immigration and Global Citizenship

20.1　Introduction

[20.01]　Determining which non-citizens should enter and remain in Australia and on what terms almost inevitably involves controversy. As guardians of the national interest, politicians face the difficult task of managing the selection and admission of migrants needed to foster growth and development whose presence may nevertheless be resented. The phenomenon of irregular migration, both in the forms of persons who remain in breach of their visa conditions and asylum seekers and refugees who are able to assert rights to protection under international law, poses even greater challenges. Australia's experiences in managing immigration are not unique. As a country, we monitor closely the strategies adopted by comparator countries. Our laws and practices are scrutinised in turn by other nations. At the same time, academic interest in comparative immigration law and policy is in its infancy, with the result that understandings of what other countries are doing or have done in the past are often based more on assertion and assumption than on deep research. It is our hope that the approach taken in this book will both provide a longitudinal perspective on immigration law and policy in Australia and encourage an interest in comparative research in this area.

[20.02]　We have argued that certain features of Australia's history – including the choices that were made in drafting the nation's Constitution – have heightened electoral sensitivity surrounding immigration control in this country. The failure to entrench any form of citizenship in the Australian Constitution means that basic concepts of membership of, and participation in, Australian society have been uncertain and subject to the vagaries of politics, almost from Australia's inception as a nation. Citizenship in Australia is a somewhat fragile status determined by statutory fiat rather than by birthright or de facto membership or absorption into the community.[1] Crock has argued further that the conferral on parliament of the power to legislate with respect to immigration and naturalisation and aliens may

---

[1]　As we explore in Chapter 2 the criteria for the recognition or grant of Australian citizenship have changed over the years. See Chapter 2.2.

also have affected basic notions of power balances in this country.[2] Silences in the Constitution were informed by shared understandings at Federation about the British common law tradition. Nevertheless, the text of this document is invoked by modern politicians to denounce the role that the judiciary might play in interpreting immigration legislation or in reviewing its application in particular cases. In the battle royal that has raged between the courts and the judiciary over the administration of immigration, parliament has emerged as the dominant force at virtually every turn, trumping both common law traditions and norms of international law.[3] The question that remains is whether the victory has been truly in Australia's national interest.

[20.03] In this final chapter we review aspects of the immigration program in respect of which we have identified unresolved problems. We begin in Part 20.2 by reflecting on the impact of immigration on the development of public law in Australia and the implications this may have for administrative justice in this country. Part 20.3 addresses what we see as the most significant problem areas relating to who has power in immigration matters: namely the balance (or lack thereof) between prescriptive regulation and the exercise of choice or discretion on the part of decision-makers. There follows in Part 20.4 a series of case studies through which we explore the *exercise* of power in immigration and the relationship between a migrant's obligations and Australia's responsibility as receiving state. We conclude with a brief consideration of the role of human rights in immigration policy viewed through the prism of debates about the respective roles of parliament and the judiciary.

20.2 The impact of immigration on the development of public law in Australia

[20.04] As we explore in the early chapters in this book, many of the leading cases in constitutional and administrative law since 1901 have involved migrants and non-citizens. Because the Constitution did not enshrine an Australian citizenship, the early cases determining who was and was not an 'immigrant' substituted for jurisprudence on citizenship in both the formal and substantive senses of that word.[4] The special place occupied by British subjects, Irish nationals and protected persons until as late as 1987 complicated attempts by government to define membership of the Australian polity – and to assert its power to exclude or expel criminal non-citizens found ultimately to be aliens by the 'barest of threads'.[5] For most of Australia's history as a nation, the law governing concepts of immigration has quite literally defined who is and is not Australian. The migration cases have gone much further than this, however, in shaping the development of law and policy in each of the three 'branches' of public law – constitutional, administrative and international.

---

2   See Mary Crock, 'Defining Strangers: Human Rights, Immigrants and the Foundations of a Just Society' (2008) 31 *Melbourne University Law Review* 1053.
3   See the discussion in Chapters 3 and 4; and Hilary Charlesworth, Madelaine Chiam, Devika Hovell and George Williams, 'Deep Anxieties: Australia and the International Legal Order' (2003) 25 *Sydney Law Review* 423. See also Hilary Charlesworth, Madelaine Chiam, Devika Hovell and George Williams, *No Country is an Island: Australia and International Law* (Sydney: UNSW Press, 2006).
4   See Chapter 2.3.2ff.
5   See the discussions in Chapter 3.2 and Chapter 17. The reference is to *Nystrom v MIMIA* (2005) 143 FCR 420 at [1] (Moore and Giles JJ).

[20.05] In constitutional law, immigration cases have helped to define the power of the executive and the nature of prerogative power. In *Ruddock v Vadarlis*,[6] French J advanced the view that the executive power of government to determine who enters Australian territory cannot be fettered by either statute or common law precedent: it is truly a plenary power. Although tested in recent cases challenging decisions made offshore,[7] this concept was given statutory expression in s 7A of the *Migration Act 1958* (Cth) which asserts that:

> The existence of a statutory power under this Act does not prevent the exercise of any executive power of the Commonwealth to protect Australia's borders, including, where necessary, by ejecting persons who have crossed those borders.

[20.06] Immigration cases have played a seminal role in shaping the nature and limits of the judicial power of government. The case law on the mandatory detention of non-citizens is one example in point.[8] The immigration jurisprudence on the effect of 'privative clauses' (which on their face appear to prohibit judicial review) is another.[9]

[20.07] In Chapters 3 and 4 we canvassed briefly the many migration cases relating to the interpretation of grants of legislative power under s 51 of the Constitution. Adopting a broad perspective, these cases could be attributed with starting a trend in modern times towards a more literal and 'subject-based' reading of the Constitution. Witness in this regard the significance of the rulings from *Pochi v Macphee*,[10] *Chu Kheng Lim v MILGEA*,[11] and *Shaw v MIMA*[12] to *Al-Kateb v Godwin*[13] on the constitutional meaning of alienage. These cases are notable for their gradual elimination of the complex communal understandings that existed previously about membership in Australia. In their place is the now binomial concept of the citizen and the alien. If the *subject-matter* of legislation concerns non-citizens, the courts in these cases have confirmed that few constraints apply to parliament's power to make laws. The methodological legacy of the reasoning in these cases finds resonance in cases in fields as diverse as race relations;[14] industrial relations and labour law;[15] defence;[16] and external affairs.[17] As

---

6 (2001) 110 FCR 491 at 543-4. See the discussion in Chapter 3.4.
7 See the discussion in Chapter 19.6.4.
8 See *Chu Kheng Lim v MILGEA* (1992) 176 CLR 1; *Al-Kateb v Godwin* (2004) 219 CLR 562 (*Al-Kateb*); *MIMIA v Al Khafaji* (2004) 219 CLR 664 (*Al Khafaji*); *Behrooz v Secretary, DIMIA* (2004) 219 CLR 486; *Re Woolley; Ex parte Applicants M276/2003* (2004) 225 CLR 1, discussed in Chapter 3.3.
9 See *Plaintiff S157 v Commonwealth* (2003) 211 CLR 426; *Bodruddaza v MIMA* (2007) 228 CLR 651, discussed at Chapter 3.3 and Chapter 19.6.
10 (1982) 151 CLR 101.
11 (1992) 176 CLR 1.
12 (2003) 218 CLR 28.
13 (2004) 219 CLR 562. The cases are discussed at Chapter 3.2 and 3.3.2.
14 See, for example, the interpretation of the 'race' power in s 51(26) of the Constitution in *Kartinyeri v Commonwealth* (1998) 195 CLR 337.
15 See the reliance placed on the corporations power in s 51(20) of the Constitution in the passage of the *Workplace Relations Amendment (Work Choices) Act 1995* (Cth): see *New South Wales v Commonwealth* (2006) 229 CLR 1, discussed in Ronald C McCallum, 'The Work Choices Case: Some Reflections' (2007) 19(4) *Judicial Officers' Bulletin* 29 at 29, 33.
16 See the discussion of *Koon Wing Lau v Caldwell* (1949) 80 CLR 533 at Chapter 2.3 at [2.46].
17 See in particular the use of s 51(29) of the Constitution in cases like *MIEA v Teoh* (1995) 183 CLR 273 at 316-17, discussed at Chapter 4.2 and Chapter 17.4.4.

noted earlier, the cases relating to the placita in s 51 most relevant to immigration and emigration have quite literally defined notions of citizenship and belonging in Australia.[18]

[20.08] Within administrative law it would seem fair to describe the impact of the migration cases as having a distorting effect. In the early days of the Federal Court, when the potential of the *Administrative Decisions (Judicial Review) Act 1977* (Cth) was being discovered, migration cases helped to blow open the citadels of closed government. Cases like *Kioa v West*[19] redefined understandings of natural justice or procedural fairness, ushering in an era where decision-makers would start from a presumption that all applicants should be granted a hearing before an adverse decision is made. As we noted in Chapter 19, the federal judiciary's use of the relevancy grounds of review turned the whole notion of discretionary decision-making on its head. *Chan Yee Kin v MIEA*[20] did not only signal the beginnings of refugee law in Australia: it also represented a radical departure in the use of 'unreasonableness' as a ground of judicial review.

[20.09] The distortion of federal administrative law through the migration jurisprudence began in earnest after the codification of migration related decision-making in 1989. The tit for tat changes to the law following seminal cases seem to have fostered a broader distrust of the courts and of common law notions of procedural fairness. Within the immigration field, regulation and codes of procedure came to replace common law standards of fairness in decision-making, starting a trend that has done very little to foster either open or efficient governance.[21] Within the general grounds of judicial review, the migration cases have also produced jurisprudence that has constrained previous understandings of review grounds used to challenge seriously irrational or illogical fact finding.[22] In many cases the contorted reasoning seems to stem from judicial reluctance to allow failed refugee claimants a remedy in the courts.[23] Over the years the jurisprudence has created an increasing divide between Australian administrative law and that of other common law countries like the United Kingdom and Canada, leading two academics to write of Australian 'exceptionalism' in this area.[24]

[20.10] The final area where immigration cases has shaped public law in Australia is at the intersection of international law and domestic constitutional and administrative

---

18 See Chapter 2.
19 (1985) 159 CLR 550.
20 (1989) 169 CLR 379.
21 See Alice Ashbolt, 'Taming the Beast: Why a Return to Common Law Procedural Fairness Would Help Curb Migration Litigation' (2009) 20 *Public Law Review* 264; and the discussion in Chapters 18 and 19.
22 See *Re MIMA; Ex parte Applicant S20/2002* (2003) 198 ALR 59 (*Applicant 20/2002*); and *MIMIA v SGLB* (2004) 207 ALR 12 and the discussion at Chapter 19.6.5.
23 For a discussion of the evolution of the law in this area, see Mark Aronson, Bruce Dyer and Matthew Groves, *Judicial Review of Administrative Action* (Sydney: Thomson, 4th ed, 2009) at 265-73. Note that the authors in this edition modify their assessment of the lasting effects of the decision in *Applicant S20/2002*. See also 3rd ed, 2004, at 263-7.
24 See Peter Cane, 'The Making of Australian Administrative Law' (2003) 24 *Australian Bar Review* 114; and Michael Taggart, '"Australian Exceptionalism" in Judicial Review' (2008) 36 *Federal Law Review* 1; and the discussion at Chapter 19.6.5.

laws. As we document, under the auspice of migration case determination, the Australian courts have at times incorporated international legal standards into domestic law and (more recently) have underscored the irrelevance of international standards that have not been adopted through parliamentary enactments. In *MIEA v Teoh*,[25] the High Court ruled that the signature and ratification of international legal instruments could create a legitimate expectation sufficient to attract the rules of procedural fairness. In *Al-Kateb*,[26] a differently constituted bench ruled (albeit by a narrow majority) that unincorporated treaties could not be used to influence the interpretation of legislation that on its face was egregiously in breach of obligations assumed by Australia under international law. Whatever their merits, migration cases have been at the very cutting edge of public law jurisprudence in Australia and have shaped the approach taken to norms of international law in this country.

20.3 The focus of power and the discretion question: Regulation versus leeways of choice

[20.11] There are other respects also where immigration has been at the cutting edge of public law and administration in Australia. In Chapter 5 we identified three revolutions in the management of immigration in Australia. The first was in 1958 with the replacement of the opaque dictation test with simple legislation vesting sweeping discretionary powers in 'the Minister' for immigration. The second occurred in 1989 with the implementation of the codified regulatory scheme that has operated since that time. The third is represented by the move to split up the decision-making process, outsourcing many of the key elements in the selection process to private bodies. The combined effect of the last two reforms has been to create something of a legislative funnel, focusing ultimate power on one person – the incumbent Minister for Immigration. The Minister's control of decision-making has been increased at two levels: by the parameters set by legislation and by the terms of the contracts made with the service providers. As Crock wrote in 2004:[27]

> Failure to follow the rules carries the economic sanction of cancellation or non-renewal of the contract. In matters such as health and employability as much as in the determination of an individual's status as a refugee, control is also achieved through the segmentation of the process. The private contractors (and increasingly, the public servants) are given a narrow function to perform. In quite literal terms the decision makers are reduced to the level of functionaries. Performing only a narrow part of the process, they cannot be 'blamed' – or held to account – for the emotional or human impact of the decisions that they make … The only person exercising real 'power' in this context is the Minister for Immigration. In most of the key areas of decision making in the *Migration Act 1958* the Minister is quite literally given the final say through what are known as 'non-compellable, non-reviewable' discretions.

---

25 (1995) 183 CLR 273. See Chapter 4.2.1.
26 (2004) 219 CLR 562, discussed at Chapter 4.2.2.
27 See Mary Crock, 'Immigration Mindsets – How our Thinking has Shaped Migration Law in Australia' (2004) 27 *International Journal of Law and Psychiatry* 571 at 582.

[20.12] In 2005, Commissioner Mick Palmer explained some of the failures that resulted in the wrongful arrest and prolonged detention of Cornelia Rau as being the result of the 'siloing' of functions within the Department.[28] By this he meant the isolation and dividing up of decision-making functions and the lack of connectivity between people charged with the different aspects of decision-making. This is a creature of legislative and administrative structures, not just the result of 'culture' within the Department. While much has been said about reforming the DIAC culture, little change to the structures has occurred. Accountability continues to be hampered by segmented decision-making, with important aspects devolved into the hands of private bodies.[29]

[20.13] The 'cash for visas' scandal in 2003 demonstrated that the concentration of non-reviewable power in one Minister leaves the system vulnerable to a perception of corruption, if not to the actual abuse of power.[30] Of equal concern, however, is the potential that the regime holds for delivery of unjust outcomes in individual cases.[31] Where only one person is vested with true power in the sense of authority conditioned only by vague principles of reasonableness and fairness, the potential for bad decision-making should be obvious. Codified rules cannot anticipate all of the permutations and combinations of human experience. Neither can one person be expected to respond to the diverse vulnerabilities that often accompany the migrant experience.[32]

[20.14] In 2009, (then) Minister Evans sought to address concerns in the area of refugee and humanitarian cases with the introduction of legislation to expand protection to persons with *non-refoulement* claims outside of the confines of the UN Convention relating to the Status of Refugees.[33] The Bill had not been debated by the new parliament in December 2010 but was expected to be considered in 2011. While we welcome this initiative, we argue that discretionary powers need to be restored to decision-makers in a much broader range of cases. The proposed complementary protection regime would cover only a narrow band of claims involving *non-refoulement* obligations assumed under international human rights law. There remains almost no provision for the consideration of individual claims involving the

---

28 See *Inquiry into the Circumstances of the Immigration Detention of Cornelia Rau* (July 2005), available at <www.minister.immi.gov.au/media_releases/media05/palmer-report.pdf> (the Palmer Report), discussed at Chapter 5.5.1.
29 See Chapter 5.4.
30 See Senate Select Committee on Ministerial Discretion in Migration Matters, *Report* (Canberra: March 2004) discussed in Jessie Hohmann, 'Report of the Senate Select Committee on Ministerial Discretion in Migration Matters: Inconclusive Witch Hunt or Valuable Contribution to the Immigration Debate?' (2004) 19 *Immigration Review* [321].
31 On his appointment in 2007 Minister Chris Evans expressed his disquiet about the nature and extent of the discretions vested in him under the *Migration Act 1958* (Cth). See, for example, Jewel Topsfield, 'Bigger Say for Courts on Migrants: Ministerial Rulings to be Scaled Back', *The Age*, 29 February 2008, available at <http://www.theage.com.au/news/national/bigger-say-for-courts-on-migrants/2008/02/29/1204226991494.html>.
32 See Jerry Mashaw, 'Prodelegation: Why Administrators Should Make Political Decisions' [1985] *Journal of Law, Economics and Organization* 81 at 86. Mashaw writes: '[T]he demand for justice seems inextricably linked to the flexibility and generality of legal norms, that is, to the use of vague principles (reasonableness, fairness, fault and the like), rather than precise rules'.
33 See Migration Amendment (Complementary Protection) Bill 2009 (Cth), discussed at Chapter 14.4.

more unique family, health, professional or other personal circumstances of the visa applicant, other than by the Minister personally. It is difficult to see this other than as a continuing distrust of the notion that administrators and review authorities can exercise discretion in hard cases responsibly.

[20.15] Putting to one side the lack of discretion to deal equitably with hard cases, there are a number of areas where the rigid codification of rules have run the government into trouble, to the point where it would be timely to re-consider the whole *modus operandi*. Two are worthy of brief mention here.

[20.16] In 2010, the regime governing the allocation of points to skilled migrants, along with the gazetted occupations lists, was significantly overhauled. The codification of requirements for skilled visas – down to the gazettal of specified occupations – had created rigidities in the program that were seen as not sufficiently responsive to labour market conditions. This approach led to chaotic backlogs as migrants scrambled to reorganise their lives and their curriculum vitae to meet the advertised requirements.[34] In these instances, the removal of discretion from decision-makers has not delivered 'certainty' to migrants.

[20.17] The second example of excessive and counter-productive attempts to use rules to control process – allegedly in an attempt to wrest control away from the courts – is of course the codes of procedure governing decision-making at departmental and review levels. In Chapters 18 and 19 we joined our voices to what seems to be a growing chorus of calls to restore immigration to mainstream administrative and judicial review methodologies forged over time under the common law.

20.4 The exercise of power: Responsibility and good international citizenship

[20.18] One of the ironies of much of the academic legal and political literature on immigration around the world is its predominantly domestic focus.[35] While it may be natural to see the control of immigration through the prism of national sovereignty, immigration as a phenomenon has quite the opposite effect. Migrants are the quintessential crusaders of globalisation, bringing into the country their diverse cultures and experiences, exposing residents to the troubles and triumphs of the lands from which they have come.[36] The transnational movement of people also involves, inevitably, aspects of international law and international comity. Immigration proves, indeed, that no country is an island, in a legal or conceptual sense.

[20.19] Yet Australia has repeatedly and obviously resisted compliance with basic tenets of international human rights law. In this section we focus on four areas

---

34 See the discussion in Chapter 9.2.5 and Chapter 11.1.6.
35 There are, however, initiatives that are being undertaken to improve comparative understanding of immigration law. See, for example, the International Encyclopedia of Laws project, which will eventually include monographs on domestic immigration laws. See <http://www.ielaws.com/>.
36 This point is made by Jacqueline Bhabha, 'Rights Spillovers: The Impact of Migration on the Legal System of Western States' in Elspeth Guild and Joanne van Selm (eds), *International Migration and Security: Immigration as an Asset or a Threat?* (London: Routledge, 2005) Ch 2.

of concern: the treatment of long-term residents convicted of crimes; the offshore processing of asylum seekers; the arrest and detention of unlawful non-citizens; and the oversight of temporary worker and student visa programs. Each threatens harm to either or both Australia's image as a liberal democracy and its economic interests as a country reliant on immigration to meet skills shortages and to generate revenue.

20.4.1 The tenure of permanent residents

[20.20] The deportation or removal of permanent residents convicted of serious crimes was one of the first areas where populism on both sides of the political divide led to increasingly punitive policies. As documented in Chapter 17, the bitter legal struggle to define the nature and extent of federal constitutional powers seems to have marginalised the simple question of whether it is right and just to exile persons who are 'aliens by the barest of threads'. The most cursory perusal of the historical record shows that politicians in earlier times readily accepted responsibility for the behaviour of long-term residents on the basis that these people should be regarded as Australia's problem. However, in recent years, the admixture of law and order politics with xenophobia has created a toxic cocktail for migrant families with children who are non-citizens in name only, having spent virtually all of their lives in this country. As Foster and others have documented,[37] the operation of the 'character and conduct' provisions places Australia in breach of the 'right to family life' provisions in the International Covenant on Civil and Political Rights (ICCPR).[38] Sharply at odds with practices in the United Kingdom and Europe, cases like that of Stefan Nystrom and Andrew Moore underscore Australia's juridical and ideological distance from the human rights regimes that now operate there.

20.4.2 Human rights and asylum seekers

[20.21] A turning point of sorts in the discourse on immigration and human rights appears to have been reached in 2004. The defeat of legal challenges to the mandatory immigration detention regime[39] placed responsibility for the human rights abuses associated with this and other restrictive measures squarely with the government. Pressure from both civil society and government backbenchers led to a softening of policy on a number of fronts. Mr Al-Kateb and other unlawful non-citizens who could not be removed from Australia were released from detention and (eventually) granted permanent resident visas.[40] In 2005, the government committed to

---

37 See Michelle Foster, '"An Alien by the Barest of Threads": The Legality of the Deportation of Long-Term Residents from Australia' (2009) 33(2) *Melbourne University Law Review* 483; and Glenn Nicholls, *Deported: A History of Forced Departures from Australia* (Sydney: UNSW Press, 2007).
38 *International Covenant on Civil and Political Rights*, opened for signature 16 December 1966, 999 UNTS 172 (entered into force 23 March 1976). See the right not to suffer arbitrary interference with one's family (Art 17) and the right to protection of the family by the state (Art 23). See also *United Nations Convention on the Rights of the Child* (UNCRC) opened for signature 20 November 1989, 1577 UNTS 3 (entered into force 2 September 1990), Art 9. These matters are discussed in Chapter 17.4.4.
39 See *Al-Kateb* (2004) 219 CLR 562; *Al Khafaji* (2004) 219 CLR 664 and the discussions at Chapter 4.2.2 and Chapter 16.2.
40 Al-Kateb was granted a subclass 695 'Return Pending' visa which allowed him to leave detention but with no right to work or to medical or other benefits. He was eventually granted permanent residence after the change of government in 2007.

detain children only as a measure of 'last resort'.[41] In July of that year, then Minister Vanstone announced that all families with children in detention had been moved into 'residence determination arrangements' within the community.

[20.22] The change of government in 2007 did remove some of the most abusive and inefficient aspects of the 'Pacific Strategy'. The closure of the facilities on Nauru saw the last refugees held there finally gaining residence in Australia. However, few of the changes made after that time represented a radical departure from the approaches of the previous government. Indeed, the quiet acceptance of some of the policy changes suggest that these, too, were predicated more on practicalities than on a revolutionary shift in thinking. For example, the decision to abolish Temporary Protection visas (TPVs) masked the fact that the vast majority of persons recognised as refugees during the years of Coalition governance were ultimately granted permanent residence. By 2007, the TPV scheme had outlived any political purpose it might once have had. As explored further below, the decision to close the detention centres on Nauru was also inevitable given the fiscal and human costs of the scheme – and was achieved with barely a murmur of opposition at the time.

[20.23] The real disappointment is that the Labor government did not act more decisively to rationalise and humanise both its refugee and enforcement policies more generally. In 2008 the government announced new guidelines for the detention of unlawful non-citizens. These favour the release on reconnaissance of children and families in all but 'last resort' cases and the use of detention only in cases where non-citizens pose a security or flight risk, and then only for the shortest possible time.[42] Sadly, perhaps because the changes were made at the level of policy rather than law, the positive effects were short-lived. In January 2011 over 1000 children were being held in various facilities around Australia.

[20.24] While the centres on Nauru were closed, the commitment to 'offshore' processing remains – and with it the 'excision' from the migration zone of Australia's offshore territories continues. If the refugee determination procedures set up in places like Nauru and Manus Island were qualitatively inferior to those established within Australia, the High Court confirmed in late 2010 that the same is true of the processes on Christmas Island.[43] Both advocates and decision-makers are constrained in the time they can spend with refugee claimants. Efficiencies are hampered severely by the twin tyrannies of a remote location and inferior access to resources of all kinds. As we explain in Chapter 19, the High Court confirmed that the creation of an offshore processing regime did not oust judicial oversight of the decisions made. Because the offshore procedures are tied to the process of granting an Australian visa, individuals making decisions offshore will be required to act in accordance with both the common law rules of procedural fairness and with domestic refugee law. The government responded to this ruling in January 2011 by promising to fast track asylum seekers found to have credible protection claims. Less straightforward cases

---

41   *Migration Act*, s 4AA.
42   See Andrew Metcalfe, Secretary, DIAC, speech, 'New Directions in Detention – Restoring Integrity to Australia's Immigration System', Australian National University, Canberra, 29 July 2008.
43   See *Plaintiff M61/2010E v Commonwealth and Plaintiff M69 of 2010 v Commonwealth* (2010) 272 ALR 14, discussed in Chapter 19.6.4.

would be referred straight to the Independent Merits Review (IMR) officials. Those refused protection have a right to seek judicial review in the Federal Magistrates Court.[44] It remains to be seen whether these safeguards are sufficient to prevent genuine refugees from being 'refouled'. The Minister also announced that a Memorandum of Understanding had been concluded with Afghanistan for both the voluntary and involuntary return of asylum seekers whose claims are rejected.[45]

[20.25] Instead of retreating from offshore processing, Prime Minister Gillard went to the federal election in 2010 committed to establishing a regional processing centre in East Timor.[46] The rationale for offshore processing (whether on Christmas Island or foreign soil) appears to be founded in a belief that the measure acts as a deterrent to would-be asylum seekers. In spite of repeated and strident Opposition claims to the contrary, there is no solid evidence that offshore processing has ever had this effect – with or without the accompaniments of TPVs and other punitive measures. While it is true that the programs instituted in the wake of the *Tampa* Affair in 2001 did stop the flow of boats to Australia in that and the following year, a number of factors appear to have contributed to achieve this result. The nastiest and most immediate reason for the cessation in boat departures from Indonesia may have been the disaster of the 'unknown' Suspected Illegal Entry Vessel, or 'SIEV X', on 19 October 2001. No less than 353 asylum seekers drowned at sea following the sinking of an overcrowded boat of dubious structural integrity onto which (it is alleged) people had been forced at gunpoint. If the Indonesian and Australian governments were perceived by people smugglers to be complicit in this catastrophe,[47] this single event could have acted as a major deterrent. The combined effects of the Coalition policies – interdiction, offshore processing and the harsh conditions in the detention centres – certainly worked together to stop the flow of asylum seekers coming by boat. The numbers arriving by plane continued to be significant, however.[48] In broader terms, however, asylum flows all around the world slowed with the disruptions caused by the terrorist attacks of 11 September 2001 and the 'War Against Terror' that followed. Australia was not the only country to experience a fall in irregular migration movements in 2002.[49]

[20.26] What is lost in claims about the efficacy of the Pacific Strategy is that by 2004 it was clear that the strategy was never going to be a sustainable solution to the intractable (global) problem of irregular migration.[50] The boats had begun arriving again well before the change of government in 2007. As was the case with earlier waves of arrivals, the causes of the upsurge have not been difficult to identify,

---

44 The Hon Chris Bowen MP, MIAC, 'Government Announces Faster, Fairer Refugee Assessment Process', *Media Release*, 7 January 2011.
45 See MIAC, 'Migration and Humanitarian MoU Signed with Afghanistan and UNHCR', *Press Release*, 17 January 2011.
46 Prime Minister Julia Gillard, 'Moving Australia Forward' speech given at Lowy Institute, Sydney, 6 July 2010, at <http://www.pm.gov.au/node/6876>.
47 See Tony Kevin, *A Certain Maritime Incident the sinking of SIEV X* (Sydney: Scribe Publications, 2004); and <www.sievx.com>.
48 See Mary Crock and Daniel Ghezelbash, 'Do Loose Lips Bring Ships? The Role of Policy, Politics and Human Rights in Managing Unauthorised Boat Arrivals' (2010) 19 *Griffith Law Review* 238.
49 See UNHCR, *2003 Global Refugee Trends*, available at <http://www.unhcr.org/40d015fb4.pdf>.
50 On this issue, see Crock and Ghezelbash, above n 48.

with major upheavals in Sri Lanka and ongoing problems in Afghanistan and the Middle East. Permanent 'outsourcing' of refugee status determinations and/or the 'warehousing' of refugees within the region were not an option. Finding countries to resettle the 'offshore' asylum seekers found to be refugees became harder and harder as years wore on: by 2006 the last of those processed on Nauru were being taken in by Australia. The un-sustainability of strategies that require heavy commitments by foreign nations was underscored in late 2009 with the failed attempt to force Indonesia to accept two boatloads of asylum seekers interdicted en route to Australia.[51]

20.4.3 Mandatory detention

[20.27] The second, related area where reform was slow after Labor's return to office was in the law governing the arrest and detention of non-citizens suspected of being in Australia without authorisation. While some prominence was given to the government's change in policy, no attempt has been made to alter the legal structures that underpin enforcement in immigration. There has been no reinstatement of judicial oversight of the arrest and detention process: both remain dependent on an immigration official's 'reasonable suspicion' of unlawful status. Just as importantly, the placement of detention facilities in remote locations perpetuates the notion that detainees need to be isolated from the critical support structures that underpin the protection of human rights: lawyers, social services and human rights advocates. By early 2010, the detention facilities on Christmas Island were full to breaking point. Moves were made to re-commission centres in Darwin,[52] and Curtin Detention Centre in remote north western Australia was reopened.[53] No consideration appears to have been given to the whole notion of isolating asylum seekers from the centres of decisional business – Sydney and Melbourne.

[20.28] The prolonged detention of people who are either in the immigration process or whose removal from the country cannot be effected remains an ongoing problem. The harm caused to the mental health of detainees has been very well documented. As we argue in Chapter 15, it is our view that Australia should revert to the arrest and detention regime that applied before September 1994. All persons arrested on suspicion of unlawful status should be brought before a magistrate within 48 hours and thereafter every seven days until the person's identity and immigration status is determined. Where a person poses no risk to the community, there should be a presumptive limit of six weeks on the length of time that person is held in immigration detention. This is the model used in many countries of asylum. The criteria used to permit release from detention should include an assessment of the risks posed by the individual of flight or of any threat the individual might pose to the Australian community. Consideration should be given also to the time likely to be involved in assessing a case and/or the likely ability to secure the removal of the

---

51 See Ben Doherty, 'Oceanic Viking Stalemate Ends', *Sydney Morning Herald*, 17 November 2009 (and related articles, available at <http://www.smh.com.au/national/oceanic-viking-stalemate-ends-20091117-ijml.html>).
52 Local News, ABC Radio 105.7 (Darwin), 8 March 2010.
53 Chris Evans, 'Curtin to Hold Suspended Asylum Seekers', *Media Release*, 18 April 2010.

applicant to another country. While the office of Ombudsman can play an important role in the oversight of detention facilities, the unenforceable nature of that oversight means it can be no substitute for merits or judicial review.

20.4.4 The human rights of temporary workers and students

[20.29] For those involved in the broader administration of the immigration program there is some irony in the publicity that typically surrounds either the arrival of boats carrying asylum seekers or the removal of controversial non-citizens. However justified in individual instances, the heavy media coverage distracts attention from what are undoubtedly the biggest (under reported) immigration news stories. These concern the many thousands of non-citizens who enter Australia each year as temporary workers and as students. Like many Western developed countries, Australia is experiencing shortages of professionals and skilled tradespeople to cater for a naturally aging population and ever-changing economy. Skilled immigration is seen as a part of a complex policy response to these economic and demographic phenomena. Indeed, significant industries in Australia cater to the short-term entry of tourists and international students. Around the country, universities and other training institutions are relying ever more heavily on foreign students who pay for the privilege of their tuition.

[20.30] The assumption that migrants to Australia should come fully formed, job ready and in perfect health inevitably raises questions about the treatment and reception of these people on and after their arrival. The volume of temporary workers and students entering the country each year has placed great pressures on immigration authorities to monitor both the behaviour of these migrants and their treatment at the hands of local employers and institutions of learning. Investigative reports in 2007 suggested that the deregulation of employment laws under the 'Work Choices' regime created a toxic environment for 457 visa holders – and for their dependants. It is no coincidence that these years saw a sharp rise in the number of cases involving the death, serious injury or abuse of non-citizens in Australia on temporary visas. Although the many remedial measures we discuss in Chapters 10 and 11 are to be welcomed, few would suggest that the battle has been won to establish a regime that is truly respectful of the human rights of migrant workers. The abuses of subclass 457 visa holders have been addressed only in part by initiatives aimed at imposing sanctions on employers and at reducing the incidence of trafficking in Australia. Serious concerns persist about the adequacy of detection and policing measures within the immigration admission and enforcement regimes.

20.5 Recognising and enforcing human rights: Of Bills of Rights and judicial review

[20.31] For some time now Australia has been one of only two countries in the developed world not to have any kind of Bill of Rights or a Charter of Rights and Freedoms (the other is Israel). Although most Australians would see their society as one that is respectful of human rights, the experiences of non-citizens in their interaction with Australian immigration laws and policies belie the universality of such claims. The strength of opinion within the community that Australia has set its human rights bench-mark too low is reflected in the response generated by the establishment in 2009 of a Committee to inquire into how best to improve the protection of human rights in Australia. Over 40,000 people participated in the Consultation chaired by Fr Frank Brennan, making this the largest public inquiry in Australian history. To address concerns that the inquiry had been polarised by campaigns led by different interest groups, the Committee commissioned its own market research to gauge opinions within the Australian community more generally. A clear majority of the submissions made to the inquiry and of those canvassed by the pollsters supported the introduction of an Australian Human Rights Act.[54]

[20.32] The recommendations made in the National Human Rights Consultation Committee Report (the Report) included a number of measures aimed at improving the protection of human rights in Australia. Putting to one side the suggestions for improving civics education on human rights and improved parliamentary consideration of human rights issues, the Report made two sets of recommendations that we believe would make a critical difference to immigration law and policy in Australia. The first is the recommendation that a Human Rights Act be enacted, using a 'dialogue model' similar to that adopted in the Australian Capital Territory, Victoria, New Zealand and the United Kingdom. An ordinary Act of Parliament, the Human Rights Act, would embed in domestic law an agreed range of basic human rights, using as a starting point obligations assumed by Australia as party to the major international human rights instruments.[55] The Act would then require other laws to be interpreted consistently with protected rights, unless excluded by express words of statutory intendment. The High Court would be empowered to issue a 'declaration of incompatibility' in cases where a law was found to be inconsistent with the Human Rights Act. However, no court would be able to invalidate the law in question. The finding would operate to notify government of the incompatibility, leaving parliament with the ultimate decision on amending the law.[56] The Committee's recommendations

---

54 Edward Santow writes: '27,888 submissions (ie, 87% of those who considered this issue) favoured a Human Rights Act [HRA] … [T]he Committee commissioned independent opinion polling, which showed 57% of respondents supported a HRA, 14% were opposed, and 30% were neutral' in Edward Santow, 'The Brennan Committee Report: Reform of Discrimination Law' (2009) 17(1) *Australian Journal of Administrative Law* 21 at 22.

55 See Frank Brennan et al, *National Human Rights Consultation Report* (Canberra: Commonwealth of Australia, 2009) Recs 24-25. The Committee recommended that further consultations be undertaken to settle the content of the rights to be protected. However, it recommended strongly that the Act protect key civil and political rights in accordance with the ICCPR, the Convention Against Torture; and the Refugee Convention and Protocol, as well as the rights of children under UNCRC. It acknowledged that reference should be made also to economic, social and cultural rights enshrined in the UN Convention on Economic, Cultural and Social Rights – such as the right to adequate food, healthcare and housing. However, it suggested that these rights not be judicially enforceable. See, for example, Edward Santow, 'The Impact of an Australian Human Rights Act on Refugee Law' (2009) 16(4) *Australian Journal of Administrative Law* 183.

56 See Brennan, ibid, Rec 29 and accompanying text. Note that the Committee sought an opinion from Solicitor General Stephen Gageler on the constitutionality of this recommendation in response to suggestions from some conservative groups that the measure would amount to requiring the High Court to issue advisory opinions, contrary to Chapter III of the Constitution. The Committee also received advice from a panel of constitutional experts, who unanimously agreed that a dialogue model *Human Rights Act* could be drafted in a way that was constitutionally valid. See Australian

also included suggestions for new measures in the federal parliamentary system to ensure consideration of the human rights implications of new legislation upon introduction into parliament.[57]

[20.33] The second set of recommendations of particular relevance to immigration concerns changes to legislation governing the interpretation of statutes generally and the judicial review of federal administrative action. These reforms would be targeted at decision-makers and review authorities (including the courts). The Committee recommended that the *Acts Interpretation Act 1901* (Cth) be amended to require that:

> [A]s far as it is possible to do so consistently with the legislation's purpose, all federal legislation is to be interpreted consistently with [listed human rights].

The *Administrative Decisions (Judicial Review) Act 1977* (Cth) would be amended to require government decision-makers to take into account listed human rights as 'relevant considerations' whenever making a decision.

[20.34] Former High Court Justice Michael McHugh has denied that a statutory Bill of Rights would have altered his decision in *Al-Kateb* – in his view the legislative intention mandating the indefinite detention of unlawful non-citizens would have trumped any such instrument.[58] However, given the judge's own description of his ruling as 'tragic', it is difficult to accept that no effort be made to prevent or at least impede future governments from engaging in the blatantly abusive treatment experienced by Mr Al-Kateb. The practical impossibility of securing agreement for constitutional reform to entrench human rights in Australian law means that the measures suggested by the Brennan Committee represent at least a tentative move towards creating a new human rights culture in Australia. Opinion on the worth of human rights legislation will continue to be divided.[59] It is our view that we should welcome any measure that increases the recognition and protection of basic human rights. Migrants may be 'strangers' to the Australian polity, but they are not thereby denuded of all rights to decent treatment. The experiences of Cornelia Rau and of Vivian Solon-Alvarez teach us that the line between the citizen and the alien in a multicultural society like Australia is often invisible to the naked eye. Exclusionary

---

Human Rights Commission, *Constitutional Validity of an Australian Human Rights Act* (Sydney: 2009), <www.humanrights.gov.au/letstalkaboutrights/roundtable.html>. The members of the panel were the Hon Catherine Branson QC, President, Australian Human Rights Commission; Pamela Tate SC, Solicitor-General of Victoria; Simeon Beckett, New South Wales Bar Association; the Hon Sir Anthony Mason AC, KBE; the Hon Michael McHugh AC QC; Sarah Moulds, Law Council of Australia; Edward Santow, University of New South Wales; Associate Professor James Stellios, Australian National University; Associate Professor Anne Twomey, University of Sydney; Bret Walker SC, New South Wales Bar Association; Associate Professor Kristen Walker, University of Melbourne; Professor George Williams, University of New South Wales; Professor Spencer Zifcak, Australian Catholic University.

57 See Brennan, above n 55, Recs 6-7. When new Bills are introduced to parliament, ministers would have to issue a Statement of Compatibility, triggering a process to consider their compatibility with human rights by a special joint committee of both Houses of Parliament. This recommendation is designed to operate whether or not the government introduces a *Human Rights Act*.

58 See 'Human Rights dialogue develops a stutter', *Sydney Morning Herald*, 13 March 2009, available at <http://www.smh.com.au/opinion/human-rights-dialogue-develops-a-stutter-20090312-8wcd.html?page=-1>.

59 See Julian Leeser and Ryan Haddrick (eds), *Don't Leave Us with the Bill: The Case Against an Australian Bill of Rights* (Melbourne: Menzies Research Centre, 2009).

and punitive practices done in the name of border control and national security can ultimately destroy the fabric that unites the very society that we are seeking to protect and nurture.

[20.35] The initial response of the Labor government to the Brennan Committee recommendations was somewhat disappointing. Then Prime Minister Rudd made it clear that a Human Rights Act was not a priority for his government, even if elected for a second term. Moves were made, however, to introduce legislation to improve parliamentary oversight of the human rights implications of enactments.[60] This legislation could have far reaching implications because as it would involve a parliamentary sub-committee certifying the compatibility of enactments with international human rights standards. Such certification would become extrinsic evidence of parliamentary intent and would plainly be relevant to any subsequent judicial consideration of statutory meaning. The Bill was not passed before parliament was prorogued in 2010.

20.6 Towards the future

[20.36] Amidst the maze of laws and policies that govern or have governed immigration in Australia, many areas remain in a state of flux and/or in need of serious reform. A central theme in our critique, where one is offered, is that immigration law in Australia has been regarded too often as 'exceptional'. The creation of zones 'excised' from Australian immigration law is perhaps the most physical manifestation of this trend. More generally, however, administrators have been quarantined from judicial or other oversight of decisions involving basic civil liberties. They have been exempted from common law duties to act in accordance with natural justice beyond legislated codes of procedure. The migration legislation contains many instances where applicants bear a reverse onus of proof[61] – the obligation to prove one's 'good character' being perhaps the most prominent. Offences of strict and absolute liability underscore the supplicant status of the migrant and the privilege that attaches still to the grant of a visa.

[20.37] Justice North has described refugee law in this country as a 'billabong' – a stagnant pool of water cut off from the mainstream of trends in international law and comparative domestic jurisprudence.[62] Renowned academic, Michael Taggart, lamented the distorting effect of jurisprudence in immigration as generating 'Australian exceptionalism' in administrative law,[63] a critique made also by the Immigration Department's then Chief Lawyer, Robyn Bickett,[64] among others.[65] It is

---

60 Human Rights (Parliamentary Scrutiny) Bill 2010 (Cth).
61 See Chapter 15.8.
62 See Anthony North and Peace Decle, 'The Courts and Immigration Detention: Once a Jolly Swagman Camped by a Billabong' (2003) 10 *Australian Journal of Administrative Law* 5.
63 See Taggart, above n 24, and the discussion above at Chapter 19.6.5.
64 See Robyn Bickett, 'Controlling Immigration Litigation: The Commonwealth Perspective' (2010) 63 *AIAL Forum* 40 and the discussion in Chapter 19.6.5.
65 See Ashbolt, above n 21; and Denis O'Brien, 'Controlling Migration Litigation' (2010) 63 *AIAL Forum* 29.

our view that the treatment of immigration as an administrative 'world apart' has not been healthy for either administrators or their clients.

[20.38] A primary focus for any reform of this area of the administration should be to remove the anomalies and exceptions. The system for determining refugee status should be uniform and should not vary according to how a person enters or seeks to enter the country. Returning the jurisdiction to a more wholesome oversight regime would involve the repeal of the privative clause regime and the restoration of judicial oversight of arrest and detention. It would also favour the opening up of merits review, with less exclusionary hearing processes.

[20.39] Whatever the direction taken, immigration control will always involve difficult political decisions. Perhaps the most disappointing feature of the jurisdiction in recent years has been the bare-faced use of immigration issues as a vehicle for electoral game playing. Wedge politics have been used to push through a raft of cruelly restrictive 'popular' measures that have had pernicious effects on both migrants to Australia and on social cohesion in this country. The *Tampa* Affair and the 'children overboard' incident are perhaps the most striking examples in point. The *Haneef* affair, increasingly punitive conditions of immigration detention, and the treatment of permanent residents convicted of serious crimes or who are otherwise regarded as being of bad character are others. As outlined in this chapter, too many aspects of these populist measures remain. People continue to die as a result. A commitment to abandon the politicisation of immigration would be an important step in the right direction. Only then will it be possible to formulate laws and policy that truly operate in the national interest.

Index

A v Australia, [4.71]–[4.74]
Abebe v Commonwealth, [13.21], [19.66], [19.67], [19.71]–[19.72]
Aboriginal Australians *see* Indigenous Australians
Absorbed persons, [15.74]–[15.75], [17.01], [17.10], [17.13], [17.105]
Acheng, The [4.36]
Administration of immigration law
    changing face of decision-making, [1.28], [5.01]–[5.03]
    contracting out, privatising and outsourcing [5.61]–[5.69], [5.81]–[5.90], [20.11]
        Competitive Contracting Out Report, [5.91]
        health assessments, [5.70]
        immigration detention, [5.74]–[5.76]
        judicial response to, [5.91]–[5.98]
        problems with, [5.81]–[5.90]
        removals, [5.77]–[5.80]
        skills assessments, [5.71]–[5.73]
    Department of Immigration, [5.07], [5.09]
        changes to, [5.10]–[5.16]
        Joint Management Review, [5.13]–[5.15], [5.20]
        review section, creation of, [5.16]
    inquiries *see* Inquiries and reviews
    judicial review, [5.25]–[5.29], *see also* Judicial review of migration decisions
    migration decision-making, external review of, [5.17]–[5.24]
    Minister of Immigration, discretionary powers of, [5.86], [20.11]–[20.17]
    post-war policy, [5.04]–[5.16]
    regulation versus discretion, [20.11]–[20.17]
    responsibility and good international citizenship, [20.18]–[20.30]
    system failures, [5.81]–[5.90]
Administrative Appeals Tribunal (AAT) [2.80], [5.16], [5.20], [5.21], [6.58], [14.54], [14.57], [14.63], [17.42], [18.32], [19.02], [19.39], [19.97]
    acceptance of decisions by Minister, [18.08]
    cancellation or refusal of visa, review of, [18.05]
        character grounds, [6.60], [17.42]–[17.47], [18.05]
    citizenship, decisions relating to, [18.05]
    criminal deportation appeals, [6.57], [6.77], [17.20]–[17.21], [18.05]
        inability to 'go behind' convictions, [17.59]–[17.61]
    establishment, [5.14], [18.03]
    independence of, [18.03], [18.47]
    migration jurisdiction, [18.05]
        alteration of powers, [6.56]
        limitations, [17.59]–[17.61], [18.06]
    Ministerial power to override decisions by, [8.04], [18.08]
    reviewable decisions, [5.103], [6.61], [6.68], [14.53], [15.22], [15.42], [18.08], [18.09], [18.18]
    rights of applicant at hearing, [18.44]
    written reasons for decisions, [18.06]
Administrative Decisions (Judicial Review) Act 1977 (ADJR Act) (Cth), [3.32], [5.19], [5.25], [5.73], [5.91], [9.44], [12.30], [16.86], [19.01], [19.16], [19.24], [19.57], [20.08]
    amendments to, recommended, [20.33]
    first Part 8 of Migration Act 1958 (Cth), differences with, [19.64]
Administrative Review Council (ARC), [5.20], [5.21], [18.07]
Administrative tribunals *see* Administrative Appeals Tribunal (AAT); Immigration Review Tribunal (IRT); Migration Review Tribunal (MRT); Refugee Review Tribunal (RRT)
Adopted children, [8.12]
    adoption agreements, [8.19]
    Adoption Convention, [8.19], [8.20], [8.23]
    best interests of child, considering, [8.20], [8.24]
    definition, [8.13]
    People's Republic of China, bilateral agreement, [8.19]
Adoption visa
    criteria, [8.16], [8.19]
    eligibility, [8.26]
    physical location of parents, [8.18]
Afghan asylum seekers, [12.55], [12.97], [14.09], [20.24]
    language testing and, [13.35], [18.134]
    suspension of refugee status determinations, [12.56]
'Afghan', The, [2.24]
Aged Dependent Relative visas
    eligibility criteria, [8.43]–[8.46], [15.76]
    quota for number of visas issued, [8.03]
Aged Parent visa, [8.36], [8.39], [15.76]
Al-Kateb v Godwin, [3.48], [3.50], [3.52], [4.01], [4.14], [4.26]–[4.30], [4.77], [16.75], [16.111], [16.134], [20.07], [20.10], [20.21], [20.34]
Aliens
    constitutional status of, [2.11], [3.67], [17.01], [17.10]

INDEX

definition, [3.11]
Aliens Deportation Act 1948 (Cth), [17.09]
Ame, Amos, [2.68], [2.69]
American Civil War, [2.23]
Amnesty International, [13.33], [16.122]
Anti-People Smuggling and Other Measures Act 2010 (Cth), [15.94]
Applicant A v MIEA, [13.51], [13.63], [13.74], [13.99], [13.101], [13.102], [13.103], [13.107], [13.119], [13.124]
Aronson, Mark, [19.109], [19.111]
Arrest *see* Enforcement
Ashmore Reef
  'excised offshore place', as, [6.04]
Asian immigrants *see also* White Australia Policy; *Wartime Refugees Removal Act*
  Asiatic Restriction Bill 1861 (NZ), [2.26]
  'Asiatics', exclusion of [2.20], [2.33], [2.41], [2.42], [2.78]
  Chinese Act 1881 (Vic), [2.29]
  limits on number of, [2.22]
  Potter v Minahan, [2.37]–[2.42]
  removal after World War II, [2.46]
  residence tax for, [2.22]
  vote, right to, [2.53]
Assurances of support, [6.23]
Asylum seekers
  Afghan, [12.55]
    child, [8.41], [13.07], [13.13], [13.22], [13.35], [13.51], [13.60], [13.61], [13.63], [13.101]–[13.106], [13.124], [18.63]–[18.65] *see also* Seeking Asylum Alone Study
  class actions by, [18.66]
  failed, indefinite detention of, [1.25], [3.48], [3.50], [3.52], [4.01], [4.14], [4.26]–[4.30], [4.77], [16.75], [16.111], [16.134], [20.07], [20.10], [20.21], [20.34]
  human rights and, [20.21]–[20.26]
  language testing and, [13.35], [18.134]
  legal and policy responses to, [12.18]–[12.22], [12.95]–[12.99]
  Ministerial discretion, [12.77]–[12.83]
    compassionate and humanitarian grounds, [12.77], [12.78]
  'offshore entry persons', as, [6.04]
  prevention of entry to Australia, [6.05] *see also* Tampa Affair
  processing claims of, [3.64], [3.65], [3.66], [12.41], [12.42], [12.67], [12.75], [18.24], [18.28], [18.47] [18.63], [18.76], [18.121], [18.134]
    UNHCR, by, [4.36], [4.40], [4.43], [4.60], [4.66], [12.49]
  Sri Lankan, [12.55]–[12.56]
Australia
  'culture of control', [1.02]
  development as a nation, [2.01]–[2.11], [4.03]
  excision of outlying island territories, [1.25]
  geographical and cultural isolation, [4.03]
  human rights record, [4.10]
  international instruments, signatory to, [4.09]
  international legal obligations, [1.26], [4.01]–[4.06], [12.18]
  national insecurity, predisposition to, [4.03], [4.04]
  off-shore island territories
    migration zone, outside, [12.48]
  penal colony, as, [1.02]
  protection obligations to non-citizens *see* Protection obligations to non-citizens
  settlement of, [1.02]
Australian and New Zealand Standard Classification of Occupations (ANZSCO) Dictionary, [9.34], [9.42]
Australian Citizenship Act 1948 (Cth), [2.56], [2.57], [2.59], [2.60], [2.65], [2.66], [2.71], [3.16], [15.28]
Australian Citizenship Act 2007 (Cth), [2.65], [2.70], [2.80], [8.41]
Australian Constitution, [1.21], [1.23], [2.04], [2.09], [2.10], [2.12]–[2.20], [2.23], [20.02]
  citizenship omitted from, [1.21], [1.23], [2.04], [2.05], [2.09], [2.12]–[2.20], [20.02]
  constitutional frameworks, [3.01]–[3.06]
  Federal Constitutional Conventions, [2.12], [2.13]
  judicial power of, reaction to usurpation of, [3.30]–[3.52]
  limited guarantees in, [19.08]
  s 41, [2.51]
  s 51(19) and (27), [2.35], [2.75], [2.81], [2.82], [3.08]–[3.10], [3.12], [3.13], [3.19], [3.42]
  s 61, [3.03], [3.55], [3.56], [3.66]
  s 71, [3.03]
  s 75(v), [19.08], [19.71], [19.80]
Australian Human Rights Commission (AHRC), [4.27], [5.19], [16.16], [17.03], [18.02], [18.42]
  functions, [18.41]
  immigration law, administration of, [18.41]
  jurisdiction, [18.40]
  migration decisions, review of, [18.30], [18.41]
  reports published by, [5.20], [5.76], [16.51], [16.53], [16.54] [16.75], [18.43]
Australian Naturalisation Act 1897, [2.19]
Australian Security and Intelligence Organisation (ASIO), [6.75]
Baird, The Honourable Bruce, [11.65]
Bakhtiyari family removal, [4.74], [18.121]–[18.124]
Barton, Edmund, [2.4]
Barton v Commonwealth, [16.130], [16.131]
Baxter Detention Centre, [16.17], [16.33], [16.44], [16.47], [16.48]
Bennett QC, Solicitor General David, [19.83]

Bill of Rights
  failure to provide for, [3.04], [3.46], [4.04], [20.31], [20.34]
Bland committee, [5.18]
'Boat people' *see* Unauthorised boat arrivals
Bona fides
  immigration clearance, persons lacking in, [6.11], [6.16]
  partner visas
    'bona fides units'(BFUs), [7.19]
Border control, [1.06], [1.25], [1.37], [4.30], [4.65], [4.75], [6.69], [7.01], [20.34]
  'hot pursuits', [6.02]
  measures and strategies, [3.44], [4.05], [4.68], [12.56], [12.97], [16.04]
  non-citizens, entry of, [6.01]
  permission to board ships and aircraft, [6.02]
  political sensitivity surrounding, [6.02]
  powers of officials, increase of, [6.03]
  Tampa Affair *see* Tampa Affair
Border Protection Act 1999 (Cth), [6.02]
Border Protection (Validation and Enforcement Powers) Act 2001 (Cth), [6.03], [12.48]
Border (Temporary) visa, [6.13]
Bosniak, Linda, [1.15], [1.16], [1.18]
Brennan Committee, [20.31], [20.34], [20.35]
Brennan SJ, Father Frank, [4.59], [20.31]
Bridging visas
  A–E, [16.58]–[16.67]
  classes of, [15.48]
  eligibility, [6.17], [15.49]
  refusal to grant, [16.97]
    stay orders *see* Stay orders
  removal pending visa, [16.75]
  security for compliance with, [16.68]–[16.70]
  trafficking visas, [16.71]–[16.74]
Britain
  migration policies of, [1.05], [9.17]
British nationals
  criminal deportation and, [17.05]–[17.06], [17.10], [17.13]
  rights of, [2.58]–[2.62], [9.12], [9.14]
Bruce, Prime Minister Stanley, [17.08]
Business (Long Stay) visa *see* Temporary business visas
Business Owner visa, [9.87]–[9.94]
Business skills migration [9.77]–[9.103]
  business, meaning, [9.88]
  business owners, requirements, [9.87]–[9.89]
  Business Skills Assessment Panel, [9.80]–[9.82], [9.95]
  classes of, [9.83]–[9.103]
  history, [9.80]–[9.82]
  investment-based, [9.95]–[9.97]
  number of visas issued, [9.79]
  points testing, abolition, [9.84]
  senior executives, requirements, [9.87], [9.90]–[9.94]

temporary visas *see* Temporary business visas
two-stage process, [9.78], [9.84]
Business Talent visa, [9.103], [15.41]
Cambodian refugees, [3.40]–[3.52], [12.34], [12.37]
Campbell, Enid, [5.04]
Canada
  Canada's Seasonal Agricultural Workers' Program (CSWAP), [10.56], [10.57], [10.58], [10.63], [10.82]
  Points test [9.06], [9.17]
Cancellation of visa *see also* Unlawful status
  appeal of decision, right of, [6.17]
  'best interests of the child' consideration, [17.94]–[17.97]
  character grounds, on, [6.57]–[6.60], [6.77], [17.42]–[17.47] *see also* Character test
    application for another visa, prohibition on, [17.47]
    discretion of decision-makers, [17.57]–[17.58]
    intervention by Minister, [17.44]
    review of decision *see* Migration Review Tribunal (MRT)
  criminal deportation *see* Deportation of permanent residents
  deterrence as factor in decisions, [17.79]–[17.80]
  false or misleading information, providing, [6.09], [6.10], [6.19], [6.60], [17.31]
  hearing rights, [6.17]
  injunctive relief against decision, [16.96]
  notification of decisions, [18.67]
  primary considerations for, [17.63]
    non-primary considerations, [17.91]–[17.93]
  procedural fairness and, [6.14]–[6.16]
  reasons, right to, [19.62]
  Regulation Second Application Scheme, [18.12]
  repeat or sequential applications, restriction on, [12.40]
  review of decision, [17.42]–[17.47]
    exercise of s 501 powers by Minister, [17.45]–[17.47]
    Migration Review Tribunal, by *see* Migration Review Tribunal (MRT)
  temporary visa, cancellation of
    business visas, cancellation of, [15.41]–[15.42]
    character grounds, on, [15.45]
    general power, [15.29]–[15.33]
    procedure, [15.34]–[15.40]
    student visas, automatic cancellation of, [11.30]–[11.49], [15.43]–[15.44]
  unlawful decisions, [6.15]–[6.16]
  upon or before entry
    cancellation decision, [15.19]–[15.28]

'incorrect answer', meaning of, [15.14]–[15.18]
    offshore cancellation, [15.11]
    procedure for, [15.12]–[15.13]
Carens, Joseph, [1.11], [1.13]
Carer visas
    care, provision of, [8.65]
        availability of Australian family members, [8.66]
    carer, definition, [8.56]
    criteria, [8.38], [8.56]–[8.57], [15.76]
        impairment requisite, [8.58]–[8.59]
        Medibank Health Solutions (MHS) certificate, [8.58]
    quota for number of visas issued, [8.03]
    Special Need Relative visa, replacement, [8.56]
'Cash for visas' scandal, [5.86], [20.13]
'Certificates of Exemption', [2.50]
Chain migration, [1.29]
Chan Yee Kin v MIEA, [4.14], [12.92], [12.93], [12.94], [13.10]–[13.15], [13.16], [13.19], [13.25], [13.26], [13.29], [13.45], [13.49], [13.51], [13.57], [13.121], [19.42], [19.50], [20.08]
Character test, [6.24]
    association, negative, grounds of, [17.34]–[17.40]
    'bad aliens', [6.56], [6.57]
    cancellation of visa, [6.57]–[6.60], [6.77], [17.42]–[17.47]
        review by AAT, [6.60], [17.42]
    Character and Conduct Act, [6.56]–[6.57], [6.69], [17.22]–[17.27]
    character test, [17.25]–[17.27]
    civil liberties and, [6.69]–[6.78]
    Communist Party members, [6.72]
    controversial individuals or groups, [6.69]–[6.75]
    criminal deportation *see* Deportation of permanent residents
    criminal record, failure to disclose, [6.60]
    family reunion applications, in, [6.63]
    'good character', assessing, [6.68]
    Ministerial intervention in cases, [6.58]
    review of decisions, [6.60]–[6.61]
    waiver of, [6.70]
Charles II, [19.100]
Chen Shi Hai v MIMA, [13.52], [13.63], [13.106]
Chesterman, John, [2.17], [2.50], [2.51], [2.52], [2.53], [2.55]
Child
    adopted children *see* Adopted children
    asylum claims, [12.62]–[12.66]
        unaccompanied minors, [18.63]–[18.65]
    best interests of, considering, [8.20], [8.21], [8.24], [8.25], [8.29]–[8.31]
        criminal deportation cases, in, [17.94]–[17.97]
    Close Ties visa, [8.40]–[8.42]
    custody criteria, [8.27]–[8.31]
        permission for removal of child, [8.28]
    definition, [8.07]
    dependent, [7.05], [8.07], [8.12], [8.15]
        definition, [8.08]–[8.09]
        resuming dependency after independence, [8.15]
        secondary applicants, as, [8.17]
    detention of, [3.48], [4.29], [6.14], [12.52], [12.66], [12.98], [16.35], [16.53]–[16.56], [18.43], [20.23]
    immigration law, treatment through, [8.07]
    'innocent illegals', [8.02], [8.40]–[8.42]
    interests of, [4.15]–[4.17]
    refugee or humanitarian visa application, in, [8.09]
    relationship, of a, definition, [7.20]
    unaccompanied minors seeking asylum, [18.63]–[18.65]
    vulnerable, [8.40]–[8.42]
Child visas
    adopted children, for, [8.16] *see also* Adoption visa
    categories of, [8.12]
    criteria for sponsorship, [8.08]–[8.11]
    dependent children *see* Dependent child visa
    eligibility, [8.12]
    orphaned relatives *see* Orphan Relative visas
China *see* Peoples' Republic of China
Chinese Act 1881 (Vic), [2.22]
Christmas Island
    detention and offshore processing centre, [1.36], [3.64], [4.57], [4.66], [4.67], [4.76], [12.53], [12.67], [12.68], [15.102], [16.17], [19.100], [19.103]
    'excised offshore place', as, [6.04], [12.53]
    migration zone, outside, [12.48]
    Tampa Affair *see* Tampa Affair
Chu Kheng Lim v MIEA, [3.42]–[3.44], [3.46], [4.21], [4.47], [4.71], [16.19]–[16.28], [16.109], [20.07]
Citizenship
    acquisition, [6.01]
    attributes of, [2.06]
    belonging and, [1.15]–[1.17]
    birthright, as, [2.63]–[2.80]
    definition of, attempts at, [2.12]–[2.20], [2.61]
    'equal citizenship', [1.15], [1.17]
    historical legacies, [2.58]–[2.80]
    inherent birthright, whether, [1.22]
    jus sanguinis, [2.66]
    jus soli, [2.63], [2.66], [2.76], [2.77], [2.78]
    merits review of decisions *see* Merits review
    race factor in development of, [2.49]–[2.57]
    status, [20.02]
    unqualified right to enter Australia, [6.01]
    vulnerable children, for, [8.41]

Close Ties visa, [8.40]–[8.42]
  abolition, [8.41]
Coco Islands
  'excised offshore place', as, [6.04]
Cole Enquiry, [5.95]
Colombo Plan, [11.06], [11.07]
Colonial naturalisation, [2.18]
Coloured migration
  restrictions on, [2.23], [9.12]
Coloured Races Restriction Bills, [2.26]
Committee for Economic Development, [9.18]
Committee of Inquiry into the Temporary Entry of Business People and Highly Skilled Specialists *see* Roach Committee
Committee of Review of the Employer Nomination Scheme and Labour Agreements (Lin Report), [5.24]
Committee to Advise on Australia's Immigration Policies (CAAIP), [5.21]
Common entry requirements *see* Entry to Australia; Public interest criteria
Commonwealth Administrative Review Committee *see* Kerr Committee
Commonwealth Franchise Act 1902 (Cth), [2.51]
Commonwealth Ombudsman *see* Ombudsman
Compassionate or humanitarian grounds
  meaning, [8.05], [8.06]
  ministerial discretion *see* Ministerial discretion
  restrictions on permits granted, [8.05]
Conclusive certificates, [18.55]
Constitution *see* Australian Constitution
Contract Immigrants Act 1905 (Cth), [9.12], [9.13]
Contributory Aged Parent visas, [8.34], [8.36]
  see also Parent visa
Costs
  'user pays' migration process, [6.23], [7.07]
Crimes Act 1914 (Cth), [15.95], [15.101], [17.36], [18.09]
Criminal Code Amendment (Trafficking in Persons Offences) Act 2005 (Cth), [16.74]
Criminal conduct *see also* Character test
  cancellation of visa, ground for, [6.56]–[6.60], [17.23]–[17.25]
    intervention by Minister, [6.58], [17.44]
    serious offences, [17.70]–[17.74]
  criminal record, failure to disclose, [6.60]
  deportation of grounds of *see* Deportation of permanent residents
  'significant risk' of, [17.41]
Criminal deportation *see* Deportation of permanent residents
Critical Skills List (CSL), [9.29], [9.56]–[9.57], [11.54]
  abolition, [9.57]
Curtin Detention Centre, [12.56], [18.63], [20.27]

De facto relationship, [7.05] *see also* Partner migration
  child of the partnership, [7.35]
  genuineness of relationship, [7.23], [7.33]
    considerations, [7.39]–[7.40]
    mutual commitment test, [7.36]
    proving, [7.36]–[7.47]
  married partner, where, [7.34]
  meaning, [7.33]
  partner visa eligibility, [7.11], [7.27]
  recognition of, [7.11]
  valid relationship, [7.33]–[7.35]
    cohabitation requirement, [7.23], [7.35]
    12 month existing relationship requirement, [7.16], [7.35], [7.48]
Deakin, Alfred, [2.4]
Deegan, Barbara (Deegan Report), [10.46], [10.48]
Definition of refugee, [12.02]
  Convention grounds, [13.80]
    nationality, [13.86], [13.87]
    'particular social group', [13.97]–[13.117]
      family, based on, [13.118]–[13.119]
      homosexuality, based on, [13.114]–[13.117]
    political opinion, [13.120]–[13.124]
    race, [13.81]–[13.85]
    religion, [13.88]–[13.96]
  countries of nationality or habitual residence, [13.06]–[13.09]
  frameworks for protection, [13.01]–[13.05]
  nexus requirement – 'for reasons of', [13.74]–[13.79]
  persecution, [13.45]–[13.49]
    'eggshell skull' rule, [13.59]–[13.61]
    generalised violence, situations of, [13.71]–[13.73]
    nature of harm, [13.50]–[13.58]
    policies of general application, [13.62]–[13.64]
    State responsibility for, [13.65]–[13.70]
  refugees *sur place*, [13.36]–[13.44]
  'well-founded fear', [13.10]–[13.18]
    country information, use of, [13.33]–[13.35]
    past events, relevance of, [13.25]–[13.32]
    'real chance' test, [13.19]–[13.24]
    standard of proof, [13.19]–[13.24]
Dependent child visa *see also* Child
  circumstances, [8.14], [8.16], [8.17]
  dependent child, [7.05], [8.07], [8.12], [8.15]
    definition, [8.08]–[8.09]
    resuming dependency after interdependence, [8.15]
  secondary applicants, as, [8.17]
Deportation *see also* Removal
  accepting country, failure to find, [16.134]
  alleged foreign criminals, of, [16.126], [16.129], [16.131], [16.133]

INDEX

criminal *see* Deportation of permanent residents
deportation cases, [3.12]-[3.29]
destination, specification of, [16.118]
fitness to travel, [16.137]
human rights abuses and, [16.135]
methods of, [16.135]-[16.137]
out-sourcing of process, [16.136]
permanent residents, of *see* Deportation of permanent residents
timing of, [16.135]
zero tolerance policy, [1.38]
Deportation of permanent residents
absorbed persons, [17.10], [17.13]
Administrative Appeals Tribunal, appeals to, [6.57], [6.77], [17.20], [17.23]-[17.25]
conflicts with Minister, [17.65]-[17.67]
drug-related offences, [17.64]
inability to 'go behind' convictions, [17.59]-[17.61]
review of decisions, [17.21], [17.23], [17.42]-[17.47], [17.66]
aliens, of, [17.10]
association, grounds of, [17.34]-[17.40]
character test, [17.25]-[17.27]
'best interests of the child' consideration, [17.94]-[17.97]
British subjects, special status of, [17.10], [17.13]
character test, [17.25]-[17.27]
children who are citizens, cases involving, [17.95]-[17.97]
circumstances for, [17.15]
Commissioner, office of, [17.09]
appeal rights, [17.11]
community expectations, [17.81], [17.85], [17.86]
offender's ties to Australia, conflict, [17.81]-[17.93]
conduct, grounds of, [17.11], [17.18]-[17.19], [17.22]-[17.23]
criminal 'aliens', of, [3.11], [17.10], [17.13]
criminal association, [17.34]-[17.40]
criminal conduct, grounds of, [6.57], [6.77], [17.01]-[17.02]
criminal deportation law, history, [17.05]-[17.09]
deterrence as factor in decision, [17.79]-[17.80]
discretion of decision-makers, [17.57]-[17.58]
drug-related offences, [17.13], [17.64]
exclusion, power of, [17.18]
expulsion, power of, [17.18]
general and criminal conduct provisions, [17.28]-[17.31]
government powers, [17.08]-[17.09]
human rights of deportees, [17.02]-[17.03], [17.98]-[17.100]
immunity from, [17.10], [17.13], [17.83]
innocent parties, effect on, [17.98]
intellectual disabilities, [17.03], [17.101]
international obligations, [17.94]-[17.101]
long-term residents, [17.01]-[17.04], [17.07], [17.87]-[17.90], [17.101]-[17.105]
reasons for deportation, [17.15]
loss of legal status, [17.15]
mental illness, [17.03], [17.75], [17.101]
Migration Legislation Amendment (Strengthening of Provisions relating to Character and Conduct) Act 1998 (Cth), [6.56]-[6.57], [6.69], [17.22]-[17.27]
Migration (Offences and Undesirable Persons) Amendment Act 1992 (Cth), [17.17]-[17.21], [17.77]
Ministerial powers, [17.23]-[17.25]
'national interest', in the, [17.25]
natural justice, constraints on right to, [17.42]-[17.47]
onus on Minister to justify removal, [17.62]
policy guidelines
binding nature of, [17.55]
changes in, [17.50]-[17.54]
s 200 deportations, [17.53]-[17.54]
s 501 visa cancellations, [17.53]-[17.54]
primary considerations for, [17.63]
non-primary considerations, [17.91]-[17.93]
protected persons, [17.10], [17.13]
protection of Australian Community, policy of, [17.53], [17.64]-[17.80]
considerations, [17.71]-[17.72]
racial discrimination, [17.06]
recidivism, risk of, [17.76]-[17.78]
review of decision by Migration Review Tribunal *see* Migration Review Tribunal (MRT)
security grounds, [18.09]
seriousness of offence committed, [17.64]-[17.69]
Departmental assessment of, [17.74]
visa cancellations under s 501, [17.70]-[17.74]
'significant risk', [17.41]
'substantial criminal record', meaning, [17.29], [17.32]-[17.33]
undesirable persons, [17.18], [17.22]
zero-tolerance policy, move towards, [17.68]
Deportation orders, [16.95]
destination
discretion to choose, [16.120]
duty to inform removee of choice, [16.125]
specification of, [16.118]-[16.119], [16.122], [16.126]
execution of, [16.127]-[16.128], [16.134]
Ministerial discretion regarding, [16.112]
purpose of an order, [16.115], [16.129]-[16.131]
reluctance of courts to rule against, [16.128]

Deportation orders (*cont*)
  revocation of, [16.112], [16.116]
  right to obtain reasons for, [16.125]
  suspension of, [16.114], [16.116]
  'turn around' cases, [16.122]
  validity, [16.113], [16.127], [16.131]
Detention
  Australian Human Rights Commission, reports published by, [18.43]
  border detainees, [16.08]–[16.18]
  children, of, [3.48], [4.29], [6.14], [12.52], [12.98], [16.17], [16.53]–[16.56], [18.43], [20.23]
  community, [12.56]
  detainees, rights of, [16.41]–[16.43]
  detention facilities
    Christmas Island *see* Christmas Island
    Commonwealth Ombudsman, involvement of, [16.34], [16.52]
    establishment of, [12.41], [16.44]
    inspection of, [16.51]
    judicial response to conditions, [16.47]–[16.49]
    Nauru *see* Nauru
    Papua New Guinea *see* Papua New Guinea
    privatisation and outsourcing of, [5.74]–[5.76], [16.45]–[16.46]
    problems with, [5.81]–[5.90], [16.46]–[16.56]
  detention measures, special, [16.19]–[16.28]
    Chu Kheng Lim v MIEA, [16.22], [16.23]
    policy after Chu Kheng Lim, [16.24]–[16.28]
  HREOC Report on, [16.51]
  human rights implications of, [4.28]
  inquiry by Ombudsman, [18.38], [18.39]
  international oversight, [16.57]
  lawful residents, of, [18.38]
  lawfulness of, [16.111]
  legal advice
    access to, [6.17]
    obligations, [18.42]
  legislative scheme governing, [16.29]–[16.40]
  mandatory detention, [1.37], [3.47], [3.48], [4.26], [4.29]
  new Labor guidelines concerning, [12.52], [20.23]
  offences relating to *see* Immigration offences
  Pacific strategy *see* Pacific strategy
  questioning, procedures for, [6.12]
  release from, [16.58]–[16.76], [16.109]
    bridging visas A-E, [16.58]–[16.67]
    bridging visa F, [16.74]
    compliance with conditions of bridging visa, [16.68]–[16.70]
    stay orders and, [16.107]–[16.111]
  review of decisions affecting persons in, [18.15]
  seizure of assets, [16.76]
  women, of, [16.17]
  wrongful
    claims for, [6.10]
    inquiry by Ombudsman, [18.38], [18.39]
Detention centres, [4.65], [4.75] , [5.23], [5.63], [5.65], [5.74]–[5.76], [12.52], [12.70], [15.104], [16.16], [16.46]–[16.53], [16.57], [16.108], [20.25]
  Baxter, [16.17], [16.33], [16.44], [16.47], [16.48]
  children *see* Child, detention of
  Christmas Island *see* Christmas Island
  Curtin, [12.56], [18.63], [20.27]
  Nauru *see* Nauru
  ombudsman, inquiry by, [18.37]
  Papua New Guinea *see* Papua New Guinea
  Perth, [16.44], [16.51]
  Port Hedland, [6.14], [12.41], [16.41], [16.44], [16.49], [16.51]
  Villawood, [6.16], [11.35], [14.72], [16.44], [16.51], [18.43]
  Woomera, [16.17], [16.44], [18.121]–[18.122], [18.125]
  workers, [5.85], [5.92]
Determination of Refugee Status Committee (DORS) 1978–90, [5.17], [5.67], [12.22]–[12.38]
  establishment, [18.20]
  functions, [18.21]
  reconstitution of, [12.39], [12.42]
'Dictation test' *see* 'White Australia Policy'
Disability
  disability support pension, criteria for grant, [6.50]
  exclusion of disabled family members from family reunion program, [18.43]
  health requirement, part of, [6.26]
Discretion *see* Ministerial discretion
Disease *see* Health criteria
Distinguished Talent visas, [9.73]–[9.76]
  criteria, [9.74]–[9.76]
  nomination by Australian person or organisation [9.74]
Dworkin, Ronald, [2.09]
East Timor
  mooted 'regional' processing solution, [4.66], [12.56], [19.104], [20.25]
  turmoil in, [12.44]
Education institutions
  accreditation and registration of, [11.56]
Education Services for Overseas Students Act 2000 (Cth) (ESOS Act), [11.47], [11.49], [11.57], [11.58]
Education Services for Overseas Students (Registration of Providers and Financial Regulation) Act 1991 (Cth), [11.11]
Electronic Travel Authority visa, [6.20], [11.71], [11.73]
Ellicott committee, [5.18]

Elmi, Sadiq, [4.74], [14.68]
Employer Nomination Scheme (ENS), [9.07], [9.63], [10.11]
　employee eligibility, [9.68]–[9.72]
　　English language requirements, [9.50], [9.70]–[9.72]
　　exemptions [9.68]–[9.69], [9.71]
　employer requirements, [9.64]–[9.65]
　expansion of, [9.24]
　nominated position requirements, [9.66]–[9.67]
　stages of, [9.63]
Employer Nomination Skilled Occupations List (ENSOL), [9.66], [10.11], [10.30] *see also* Skilled Occupation List (SOL)
Enforcement
　arrest and detention
　　legislative scheme governing, [16.29]–[16.37]
　　reasonable suspicion, [16.38]–[16.40]
　control measures at point of entry, [16.08]–[16.18]
　control measures before entry, [16.04]–[16.07]
　deportation *see* Deportation; Deportation orders
　detention *see* Detention
　injunctive relief, [16.96]–[16.106]
　　eligibility, [16.104]
　interdiction of ships and aircraft, [16.04]–[16.07]
　legal advice, access to, [16.41]–[16.43]
　overview, [16.01]–[16.03]
　removal of unlawful non-citizens
　　alleged foreign criminals, [16.126]–[16.127], [16.129], [16.131], [16.133]
　　controls, tightening of, [16.116]
　　delay in, [16.112]–[16.116]
　　destination where removee is sent, [16.116]–[16.134]
　　disguised extradition, as, [16.126], [16.129]
　　fitness to travel, [16.137]
　　grace period for, [16.106]
　　human rights abuses and, [16.135]
　　legislative scheme, evolution of, [16.81]–[16.84]
　　methods of, [16.135]–[16.137]
　　out-sourcing of process, [16.136]
　　removal and the courts, [16.85]–[16.94]
　　Senate Legal and Constitutional References Committee, [5.78], [16.135], [16.136], [17.03]
　　statutory powers, limitations of, [16.132]
　　theories concerning, [16.77]–[16.80]
　　timing of, [16.135]
　stay orders, [16.96]–[16.06]
　　application, [16.96]
　　balance of convenience, [16.103], [16.104]
　　bridging visa, refusal of, [16.97]–[16.98]
　　Federal Court, power to make, [16.100]
　　release from detention, and, [16.107]–[16.111]
　　special reasons for grant, [16.103]
　'turn around' cases, [16.122]
Engledow, LWB, [5.13], [5.16]
English language proficiency, [9.28], [9.29], [9.48]–[9.54], [9.70]–[9.72]
　International English Language Test System (IELTS), [9.28], [9.51]–[9.52]
　levels of, [9.52]
　'Occupational English Test' (OET), [9.51]–[9.52]
　pre-migration testing, mandatory, [9.48]
　waiver, [9.49], [9.53]
　threshold criterion, as, [9.50]
Entry permit
　exemptions from requirement, [6.06]
Entry to Australia *see also* Public interest criteria
　common criteria for, [6.22]–[6.25]
　non-citizens, controlled entry of, [6.01], [6.03]
　people smuggling *see* Immigration offences
　permit for *see* Entry permit
　powers to control, increase in, [6.03]
　public interest tests, [6.22]
　right to enter, [6.01]
　'user pays' migration process, [6.23], [7.07]
Established Business visa, [9.98]–[9.101]
European Convention on Human Rights, [17.100]
European Court of Human Rights, [17.100]
Evans, Minister Chris, [4.22], [4.64], [4.75], [9.02], [9.24], [9.36], [12.52], [16.35], [19.37], [20.14]
Excision of territory, [1.25], [4.34], [4.65], [6.04], [12.13], [12.48], [12.53], [12.55], [20.24]
Executive power, plenary nature of, [3.53]–[3.67]
Family Law Act 1975 (Cth), [7.68], [8.27]
Family migration
　aged dependent relatives *see* Aged Dependent Relative visas
　'balance of family' test, [7.05]
　carers *see* Carer visas
　changes in intake programs, [7.02]–[7.06]
　children *see* Child visas
　compassionate grounds, on, [8.05]–[8.06]
　constraints on, [8.03]
　disabled family members, exclusion of, [18.43]
　economic costs associated with, [7.07]
　family violence provisions *see* Family violence provisions
　history, [7.03]
　limit on visa numbers, [8.03]
　parents *see* Parent visas
　partner relationships *see* Partner migration
　permanent residence, concessions for, [7.06], [8.02]

Family migration (*cont*)
  preferential family cases, [7.05]
  priority given to, [1.29], [1.30], [7.01]–[7.09]
  reduction in, [7.04], [8.01]
  relatives *see* Remaining Relative visas
  skilled migrant intake, ratio to, [7.03]–[7.04]
  Special Need Relative visa, [8.38]
Family violence provisions, [7.20], [7.54], [7.58]–[7.60]
  acceptable evidence requirements, [7.62]–[7.63], [7.69]–[7.76]
    statutory declaration requirements, [7.70]–[7.76]
  access to, [7.87]
  application of, [7.61], [7.64]
  education programs, [7.89]–[7.90]
  'family violence', meaning, [7.66]–[7.68]
  Family Violence Monitoring Committee, [7.62]
  introduction, [7.58]
  men, claims by, [7.65]–[7.66], [7.69], [7.77]
  misuse of, [7.58]–[7.59]
  psychological violence, [7.66]
  referral of cases to independent expert, [7.77]–[7.82]
  serial sponsors and, [7.88]
Federal Council of Australasia, [2.19]
Federal Court
  creation of, [3.32], [19.06]
  migration decisions before *see* Judicial review of migration decisions
Federal parliament
  powers of, [2.11], [3.53]–[3.67]
  unauthorised boat arrivals, response to, [6.02]
Federation, [1.21], [2.02], [2.04], [2.05], [2.06], [2.23]
Fees
  visa application charge, [6.23]
Fiancée (Prospective Marriage) visa, [8.03]
  annual quota for, [8.03]
Foreign students
  assaults on, [11.03]
  complaints, [11.56]–[11.66]
  course requirements, failure to meet, [11.36]–[11.49]
  education institutions
    accreditation and registration of, [11.56]
  financial benefits of, [11.01]
  human rights of, [20.29]–[20.30]
  International Student Strategy, [11.65]
  international student visa program, [1.33], [11.02], [11.12]–[11.15]
    early years, [11.06]–[11.11]
    integrity risks associated with, [11.09]
    interaction with general skilled migration program, [11.50]–[11.55]
  Job Ready Program, [11.55]
  safety, [11.03], [11.56]–[11.66]
  short-term migration of, [1.33]
skilled migration visas
  removal of incentives, [9.25]
  student protections, [11.56]–[11.66]
student visas
  assessment levels, [11.10]
  cancellations, [11.30]–[11.49], [15.43]–[15.44]
  Commonwealth register of institutions and courses for overseas students (CRICOS), [11.11], [11.16], [11.28], [11.57], [11.66]
  conditions, [11.21]–[11.29]
  requirements, [11.16]–[11.20]
'45 day rule', [1.17]
Fraser, Prime Minister Malcolm, [12.27], [12.28]
Freedom of Information Act 1982 (Cth), [5.19]
Freedom of speech, [3.45], [6.69]–[6.78]
Galligan, Brian, [2.17], [2.50], [2.51], [2.52], [2.53], [2.55]
Garran, Robert, [2.16]
Gay men, [13.114]–[13.117] *see also* Same-sex relationships
General Agreement on Trade in Services (GATS), [4.09], [10.04]
General skilled migration *see* Skilled migration
Genuine relationship, [7.23], [7.33]
  considerations, [7.39]–[7.40]
  mutual commitment test, [7.36]
  proving, [7.36]–[7.47]
Gillard Labor government, [3.64], [10.47], [12.56], [20.25]
Global financial crisis, [1.32], [9.24], [10.35], [10.41], [10.53], [11.13], [11.53]
Global Special Humanitarian visa, [6.55]
Gold rush, [2.22]
Goodwin-Gill, Guy, [4.42], [13.72], [13.86]
Grassby, Minister Al, [5.10]
Guantanamo Bay, [19.100]–[19.101]
Habeas corpus, [3.61], [3.62], [4.44], [4.47], [19.100]
Habeas Corpus Act 1679, [19.101]
Hand, Minister Gerry, [17.67], [19.37]
Haneef, Dr Mohammed, [17.35]–[17.40], [20.39]
Hanson, Pauline, [6.74]
Hathaway, James C, [4.33], [4.43], [13.01], [13.50], [13.51], [13.120], [13.123], [14.11]
Hawke, Prime Minister Bob, [13.36], [19.05], [19.37]
Health assessments
  medical officer's opinion, [6.39]–[6.40]
  outsourcing of, [5.70], [6.25], [6.32]
  process of, [6.32]
  review, power of, [6.34]
Health criteria, [6.24]
  assessments *see* Health assessments
  burden on the community, considering, [6.42]
  'community service', access to, [6.49]–[6.50]

disability
    disease, distinction, [6.26]
        support pension, criteria for grant, [6.50]
    disease or condition, identifying, [6.35]–[6.46]
    Downs Syndrome, [6.40], [6.41]
    family group assessments, [6.31]
    fast track screening, [6.30]
    health care, access to, [6.47]–[6.48]
    Health Rules report, [6.42]
    HIV-AIDS, [6.48]
    mental disability, [6.38]
    non-citizens, screening of, [6.26]
    permanent visa applicants, [6.30]
    provisional visa applicants, [6.30]
    'significant cost', issues of, [6.31], [6.44], [6.47]–[6.48]
        monetary estimate, [6.47]
    temporary visa applicants, [6.28]–[6.30]
    tests imposed on applicants, [6.27], [6.29]
    tuberculosis, [6.31]
    undue cost and undue prejudice provisions, [6.51]–[6.55]
    waiver of, circumstances for, [6.30], [6.51]–[6.53]
Hell's Angels motorcyclists, [6.65]–[6.67], [11.78], [17.34]
Helton, Arthur, [13.107]
'Hickman' test *see R v Hickman; Ex parte Fox and Clinton*
High Court of Australia
    migration decisions, [19.57] *see also* Judicial review of migration decisions
        Federal Court restrictions, effect of, [19.58], [19.66]–[19.69], [19.72], [19.75]
        increase in migration appeals, [19.75]
    powers and jurisdiction, [1.39], [3.03], [3.30]–[3.52]
    time limits, [19.98]
Homosexuality [13.114]–[13.117] *see also* Same-sex relationships
Howard, Prime Minister John, [1.14], [4.36], [4.38], [4.63], [5.01], [5.74], [10.44], [10.69], [11.02] *see also* Howard Coalition government of 1996–2007
Howard Coalition government of 1996-2007, [1.06], [1.14], [1.17], [1.37] [10.13], [10.44], [10.68], [10.69], [11.02], [11.04], [11.14], [11.50], [12.15], [12.17], [12.19], [12.41], [13.35], [16.46], [18.43], [18.122], [19.05]
Hughes, Prime Minister WM, [2.28]
Human rights
    asylum seekers, [20.21]–[20.26]
    Australia and , [4.02], [4.10], [4.28], [20.31]
    deportees, of, [17.02]–[17.03], [17.98]–[17.100]
    detention, implications in, [4.28]
    Human Rights Act, recommendation for enactment of, [20.32], [20.35]
    Human Rights Watch, [13.33]
    National Human Rights Consultation Committee Report, [20.32]
    protection of, [4.11]–[4.30]
    recognising and enforcing, [20.31]–[20.35]
    removal of unlawful non-citizens, implications in, [16.135]
    temporary workers and students, of, [20.29]–[20.30]
    treaty bodies, complaints to, [4.69]–[4.74]
Human Rights and Equal Opportunity Commission (HREOC) *see* Australian Human Rights Commission (AHRC)
Human Rights Commission *see* Australian Human Rights Commission (AHRC)
Human Rights Commission Act 1981 (Cth), [4.16]
Human trafficking, [14.72]–[14.79]
    Action Plan to Eradicate Trafficking in Persons, [14.74]–[14.77]
    children, of, [8.20]
    international protection, gap in, [14.73]
    offences, [7.56], [14.73], [16.74]
    partner migration, through, [7.55]–[7.57]
    Simaplee, Puongtong, [14.72]
    Trafficking Protocol *see* UN Protocol to Prevent, Suppress and Punish Trafficking in Persons, Especially Women and Children (Palermo Protocol)
    victims, immigration concessions for, [7.57]
    visa framework, [14.74]–[14.78], [16.71]–[16.74]
Ibrahim v MIMIA, [8.14], [13.53], [13.57], [13.58], [13.73]
Immigration
    attitudes to, [1.01]–[1.06]
    comparative policies, [1.05], [20.01]
    control of, [1.03]
    global citizenship and, [20.01]–[20.39]
    history of, [1.01]–[1.06], [2.01]–[2.11]
    justice in, evolving approaches to, [1.07]–[1.09]
    law
        administration of *see* Administration of immigration law
        evolution of, [2.21]–[2.30], [20.01], [20.01]–[20.39]
    management of, [20.01]
    responsibility and good international citizenship, [20.18]–[20.30]
    themes and theories, [1.18]–[1.20]
Immigration and Naturalization Service v Cardoza-Fonseca, [13.15]
Immigration assistance
    Code of Conduct, [5.103], [5.106]
    Immigration Advice and Application Assistance Scheme (IAAAS), [12.70]
    see also Migration Agents Registration Authority (MARA)

Immigration advice (cont)
   regulation of advice, [5.99]–[5.111], [15.105]
Immigration clearance, [6.07]–[6.11]
   bona fides, persons lacking, [6.11], [6.16]
   cancellation of visa in see Cancellation of visa
   evidence requirements, [6.08]
   procedures, [6.08], [6.14]
      procedural fairness, [6.14]–[6.16]
   unaccompanied children in, [6.14]
   visas granted in, classes, [6.13]
Immigration Legislation Amendment (Procedural Fairness) Act 2002 (Cth), [18.96], [18.106], [19.96]
Immigration offences, [15.91]
   decisions made under Act, relating to, [15.105]–[15.106]
   detention, relating to, [15.102]–[15.104]
   entry and stay in Australia, relating to, [15.92]–[15.99]
      carrier sanctions, [15.93]
      employer sanctions, [15.99]
      people smuggling, [6.03], [15.94]–[15.96]
      work offences, [15.97]–[15.99]
   migration fraud, relating to, [7.50], [15.100]–[15.101]
Immigration Ombudsman, [18.39]–[18.40] *see also* Ombudsman
Immigration Restriction Act 1901 (Cth), [2.26]–[2.29], [2.38]–[2.42], [2.45], [2.50], [5.30], [17.05]
Immigration Review Panels (IRPs), [5.17], [5.20], [18.10]
Immigration Review Tribunal (IRT) *see also* Migration Review Tribunal (MRT)
   establishment, [18.03]
   immigration detention, decisions affecting persons in, [18.15]
   jurisdiction, [18.13]
   legislation, [18.16]
   medical assessments, [6.35]
   Migration Review Tribunal (MRT), replacement by, [18.17]
   overturned decisions, rate of, [18.17]
   powers, [6.34], [18.13], [18.16]
   reasons for decision, [18.13]
   right to appear in person, [18.14]
   time limits, [18.13], [18.15]
Independent Merits Review (IMR), [18.29], [20.24]
Independent skilled migrants *see* Skilled – Independent visa
Indian students
   attacks on, [11.03], [11.65]
Indigenous Australians
   exclusion and deprivation, [2.08]
   political participation, [1.15]
   treatment of, [2.50], [2.51], [2.55], [2.83]
      parallels between treatment of migrants and, [2.10]

Indonesia
   'regional cooperation arrangement', [12.47]
   unauthorised boat arrivals, role in, [12.44]
Inquiries and reviews, [1.32], [5.23], [5.81], [10.47], [10.48], [10.71], [12.81], [16.35], [18.03]
   Asylum, Border Control and Detention Inquiry, [16.11], [16.27]
   Bland Committee Report (Committee on Administrative Discretions), [5.18], [18.03]
   Ellicott Committee Report, [5.18], [18.03]
   Future Skills: Targeting High Value Skills Through the General Skilled Migration Program; Review of the Migration Occupations in Demand List, [9.57]
   Illegal Entrants in Australia: Balancing Control and Compassion, [15.82]
   Immigration Functions Related to Control and Entry, [5.13], [5.15], [5.20]
   Inquiry into certain Australian companies in relation to the UN Oil-For-Food Programme (Cole Enquiry), [5.95]
   Inquiry into Coastwatch, [12.51]
   Inquiry into Immigration Detention Procedures, [16.52], [17.03]
   Inquiry into Ministerial Discretion in Migration Matters, [5.86], [5.88], [12.80], [14.65]
   Inquiry into Skilled Migration, [10.02]
   Inquiry into Temporary Business Visas, [10.46], [10.48]
   Inquiry into the Anti-People Smuggling and Other Measures Bill 2010, [15.96]
   Inquiry into the Circumstances of the Immigration Detention of Cornelia Rau (Palmer Report), [5.24], [5.81], [16.34], [18.38], [20.12]
   Inquiry into the Circumstances of the Vivian Alvarez Matter (Comrie Report), [5.24], [5.81], [16.34], [16.135], [18.38]
   Inquiry into the Migration Legislation Amendment Bill (No 2) 2000, [19.104]
   Inquiry into the Migration Treatment of Disability, [4.69], [5.23]
   Inquiry into the provisions of the Migration Amendment (Designated Unauthorised Arrivals) Bill 2006, [6.04]
   Inquiry into the Temporary Entry of Business People and Highly Skilled Specialists (Roach Report), [5.24], [5.76], [5.81], [6.26], [10.06]–[10.09]
   Inquiry into the Trafficking of Women for Sexual Servitude, [14.72]
   International Students Strategy for Australia, [11.03]
   Kerr Committee Report (Commonwealth Administrative Review Committee), [5.18], [18.03]

National Inquiry into Children in
    Immigration Detention, [12.63], [12.66],
    [16.53], [18.43]
National Population Council's Refugee
    Review, [5.24]
New Faces, New Places, Review of State
    Specific Migration Mechanisms, [9.58]
A Pacific Engaged Inquiry, [10.69]
Review of Illegal Workers in Australia:
    Improving Immigration Compliance in
    the Workplace, [15.01]
Review of Migration Assessment, [5.16]
Review of Skilled Migration, [5.23], [9.36]
Review of the Education Services for
    Overseas Students (ESOS) Act 2000,
    [11.03], [11.61], [11.65]
Review of the Employer Nomination Scheme
    and Labour Agreements (Lin Report),
    [5.24]
Review of the General Skilled Migration
    Points Test, [9.37]
Review of the Independent and Skilled
    Australian Linked Categories (Hodges
    Report), [9.22], [9.23], [9.25], [9.60]
Review of the System for Review of
    Migration Decisions, [5.24], [18.18]
A Sanctuary Under Review, [4.74], [5.76]
    [12.63], [12.66], [12.71], [12.81], [13.33],
    [14.09], [14.66], [16.43], [16.122],
    [16.135], [16.136], [19.54]
Select Skills: Principles for a New Migration
    Occupation in Demand List; Review of
    the Migration Occupations in Demand
    List, [9.57]
Inquiry into A Certain Maritime Incident,
    [4.50], [12.51]
Seeking Asylum Alone Inquiry, [12.62]-
    [12.66], [12.68], [12.70], [13.61], [16.54],
    [18.63]-[18.65]
Those Who've Come Across the Seas:
    Detention of Unauthorised Arrivals,
    [16.16], [16.51], [18.43]
To Make a Contribution: Review of Skilled
    Labour Migration Programs, [9.04]
Visa Subclass 457 Integrity Review, [10.46],
    [10.48]
Welfare of International Students Inquiry,
    [11.03]
Interdependency visa, [7.24], [7.26]
International Convention for the Safety of Life
    at Sea (SOLAS), [4.52]
International Convention on Maritime Search
    and Rescue (SAR), [4.37], [4.52]
International Covenant on Civil and Political
    Rights (ICCPR) *see* UN International
    Covenant on Civil and Political Rights
International English Language Test System
    (IELTS), [9.28], [9.51]-[9.52], [10.34]
International human rights *see* Human rights

International law *see also treaties and conventions
    by name*
    ambiguity in, identification of, [4.12], [4.31]
    Australia signatory to international instru-
        ments, [4.09]
    Australia's approach to
        how viewed in time, [4.75]-[4.77]
    domestic legislation and policy, conflict
        with, [4.13], [4.27], [4.29], [4.30],
        [12.18]-[12.21]
    ineffectiveness of, [4.06]
    influence of, [1.24]-[1.26], [4.01]-[4.77]
    international refugee law, [4.39]-[4.43],
        [12.18]-[12.21]
    limitations and uncertainties in, [1.26]
    sea, of the, [4.37], [4.38]
    significance of, [4.07]-[4.10]
    treaty commitments, [4.15]-[4.25]
    United States defiance of, [4.75]
International Organisation for Migration
    (IOM), [4.36], [4.60], [4.62]
International students *see* Foreign students
Interpreters
    translation of documents, [18.118]
    tribunal hearings, use in, [18.77]-[18.83]
Investor visa, [9.95]-[9.97]
Irving, David, [6.70]-[6.73], [11.78]
Isaacs, Sir Isaac, [2.15]
Job Ready Program, [11.55]
Joint Standing Committee on Migration
    (JSCM), [5.23], [10.46], [16.27], [16.76]
Judicial review, [1.39], [3.06], [3.62], [5.25]-
    [5.29], [19.01]-[19.07]
    applications, rate of, [19.105], [19.113]
    class actions, [19.75], [19.76]
    codification of procedures, [19.107], [20.11]
    compassionate or humanitarian grounds, on,
        [19.46]-[19.48]
    contracting out, effect of, on, [5.91]-[5.98]
    costs orders against lawyers and migration
        agents, [19.99]
    decision-making criteria, codification,
        [19.51]-[19.55]
        non-compellable decisions by Minister,
            [19.53]-[19.54]
    declarations, [19.08], [19.12]-[19.14]
        discretionary nature of, [19.14]
    developments in, [19.16]-[19.18]
    discretionary decision-making, [19.42]-
        [19.43], [19.52], [19.70]
        removal of, [19.52]
    encouragement to commence or continue
        action, penalties for, [19.99]
    equitable remedies, [19.08]
    Federal Court, by
        applicants, limitations on, [19.61]
        bar on exercise of functions,
            [19.56]-[19.58]

Judicial review (cont)
  Federal Court, by (cont)
    grounds on which a decision may be reviewed, [19.59]–[19.60]
      High Court, effect of restrictions on, [19.58], [19.66]–[19.69], [19.72], [19.75]
      scope to review decisions, [19.67]–[19.69]
      strict time limits, introduction, [19.58]
    Federal Magistrates Court, referral to, [19.97]
  First Part 8 of *Migration Act,* [19.56]–[19.75], [19.77], [19.105]
    ADJR Act, differences to, [19.64]
    challenges to, [19.65]–[19.67], [19.82]
    changes to Federal Court functions, [19.56]–[19.61], [19.63]
    failure of, [19.75]
    replacement, [19.76]
    right to reasons, [19.62]
  formalism in the courts, trend towards, [19.105]
  functions, [19.03]
  future, towards, [19.113]–[19.117]
  government criticism of, [19.04], [19.65]
  grounds
    bias, [19.19], [19.36]–[19.39], [19.93]
    jurisdictional error, [19.87]
      meaning, [19.88]–[19.90]
      tribunal decisions, in, [19.91]–[19.94]
    no evidence, [19.19], [19.40]–[19.41]
    natural justice *see* Natural Justice
    procedural fairness *see* Natural Justice
    relevant considerations, [19.42]–[19.50], [19.93]
    unreasonableness, [19.42]–[19.50], [19.93], [20.08]
  hearing, entitlement to, [19.30]–[19.32]
  human rights implications, [19.111]
  immigration bureaucracy and, [19.17]
  injunctions, [19.08], [19.12]–[19.13]
  legislative intrusion, [19.105]–[19.112]
  merits review, similarity with, [19.49]
  migration legislation, court's interpretation of, [19.44]–[19.46], [19.50]
  natural justice, rules of *see* Natural Justice
  offshore processing, [19.100]–[19.104]
  prerogative writ, [19.08]–[19.12]
    discretionary nature of, [19.14]
    service on government, [19.14]
  privative clause decision, [19.77]–[19.87], [19.105], [19.115]
    constitutional challenge to, [19.82]–[19.87]
    exclusion of review, [19.78]
  process, matters of, [19.70]
  reasons, entitlement to, [19.62]
  restricting, [3.31]–[3.40]
  review, exclusion of, [19.78]
  right of all persons, as, [19.08]
  role of the courts, [19.02]
  success rate of Minister, [19.106]
  time limits, [3.40], [5.33], [15.22], [16.101], [18.13], [18.15], [18.19], [18.56], [18.57], [18.60]–[18.64], [19.58], [19.98]
  voidable decisions, [19.73]
  worth of, [19.115]–[19.117]
Judiciary Act 1903 (Cth), [19.01], [19.57]
Judiciary
  immigrant status, role in determining, [1.23], [2.34]–[2.42], [3.04]–[3.06], [3.07]
  internationalisation of law, effect of, [4.11]–[4.14]
  points of law, final determinations, [18.01]
  power of, nature and extent of, [3.41]–[3.52]
Jumbunna, [4.27]
Kagan, Michael, [12.59]
Keating Labor government, [10.06], [16.46], [19.05]
Keeling Islands
  'excised offshore place', as, [6.04]
Kerr Committee, [5.18]
Kershaw, Bruce, [2.21]
Khmer Rouge regime, [3.40]
Kiane, Shahraz, [6.55]
Kioa v West, [2.66], [4.15], [4.16], [12.86], [19.22]–[19.35], [20.08]
Kisch, Egon, [2.43], [6.72]
Labor government policies, [4.65]–[4.68], [12.67], [12.96], [20.23], [20.25] *see also* Gillard Labor government; Rudd Labor government
Labour migration *see also* Business skills migration; Skilled migration; Temporary business visas
  history of, [1.31]
  migration program
    changes to, [9.01]–[9.02]
    focus of, [9.02], [9.04]
  temporary, [1.32]
Lake, Marilyn, [2.22], [2.23]
Lavarch, Attorney General, [4.22], [4.25]
Legislative power, [3.07]–[3.29]
Legislative regime
  discretion to codification, [5.30]–[5.37], [20.11]
Legitimate expectation, doctrine of, [4.17]–[4.22]
Lesbians [13.114]–[13.117] *see also* Same-sex relationships
Lin Report, [5.24]
McAdam, Jane, [13.72], [13.86], [14.64]
Mandatory detention, [1.37], [3.47], [3.48], [4.26], [4.29], [20.27]–[20.28]
Manus Island *see* Papua New Guinea
Mares, Peter, [9.45]
Marriage *see also* Partner migration; Family violence provisions
  violence within
    refugee claim based on, [13.110]–[13.113]

Marriage Act 1961 (Cth), [7.29]
Medibank Health Solutions (MHS)
   carer visa, certificate for, [8.58]
Medicare, [8.34]
Merits review, [1.39]
   access to, [18.56], [19.16]
   history of system, [18.03], [18.10]–[18.12]
   judicial review, similarity with, [19.49]
   migration decisions
      introduction, [18.10]
      Migration Review Tribunal *see* Migration Review Tribunal (MRT)
   migration tribunals, powers of, [18.51]
   points of law, final determinations, [18.01]
   process, [18.01]
   refugee status appeals, [18.20]–[18.29]
      Independent Merits Review (IMR), [18.29], [20.24]
      Regulation Second Application Scheme, [18.12]
   temporary business visa decisions, [10.37]
MIEA v Teoh, [4.14], [4.15]–[4.25], [4.26], [17.95], [17.98], [20.10]
MIEA v Wu Shan Liang, [18.115], [18.139]
Migration agents, [5.99]
Migration Agents Registration Authority (MARA), [5.100], [5.101], [5.103]
Migration Amendment (Excision from Migration Zone) Act 2001 (Cth), [6.04], [12.48]
Migration Institute of Australia Ltd (MIA), [5.101]
Migration Internal Review Office (MIRO),
   abolition, [18.17]
   jurisdiction, [18.13]
   legislation, [18.16]
      Migration Review Tribunal (MRT), replacement by, [18.17]
   overturned decisions, rate of, [18.17]
   powers, [18.13]
   reasons for decision, [18.13]
Migration Legislation Amendment (Worker Protection) Act 2008 (Cth), [10.40]
Migration Legislation (Strengthening of Character and Conduct Provisions) Act 1998 (Cth), [6.56]–[6.57], [6.69], [17.22]–[17.25]
Migration Litigation Reform Act 2005 (Cth), [19.97]–[19.99]
Migration Occupations in Demand List (MODL), [9.29], [9.56]–[9.57]
   abolition, [9.57]
Migration (Offences and Undesirable Persons) Amendment Act 1992 (Cth), [17.17]–[17.21], [17.77]
Migration Reform Act 1992 (Cth), [16.28], [19.56]–[19.77], [19.105]
Migration Reform (Judicial Review) Act 2001 (Cth), [16.79]
Migration Regulations, [5.38]–[5.50], [9.52], [15.19], [15.35], [16.83], [19.51]

   judicial response to, [5.51]–[5.60]
   Schedule 5A, [11.18]
Migration Review Tribunal (MRT), [5.70], [5.72], [6.31], [6.40]–[6.62], [8.58]–[8.60], [8.65], [9.93], [9.99], [11.26], [11.72], [15.12], [15.27], [15.29], [15.30], [16.13], [16.59], [18.02]
   advice given to applicants, [18.87]–[18.88]
   appointment of members, politics of, [18.47]
   conclusive certificates, issue of, [18.55]
   deportation of permanent resident, [18.18]
   fraudulent behaviour of advisor, [18.87]–[18.88]
   government influence over, [18.47]
   health assessment review, [6.35]–[6.37], [6.51]
   hearings
      breach of rules, [18.96]
      conduct of, [18.89]–[18.91]
      interpreters, use of, [18.77]–[18.83], [18.118]
      not required, when, [18.101]–[18.102]
      obligation to consider all issues, [18.117]–[18.119]
      oral hearing, [18.94]
      procedural fairness, [18.90]–[18.97]
      representation, right of, [18.84]–[18.86]
      right to appear in person and give evidence, [18.71]–[18.76]
      rights of applicant at, [18.44]
   Immigration Review Tribunal (IRT), replacement of, [18.17]
   information
      disclosable, [18.95], [18.98]–[18.100]
      non-disclosable, [18.106]–[18.111]
      supplied by applicant, [18.103]–[18.105]
   inquisitorial nature of, [18.44]–[18.46], [18.112], [18.120]–[18.130]
   jurisdiction, [18.18], [18.54]
   jurisdictional error, decisions affected by, [18.49]–[18.54], [19.91]
   jurisprudence on the duty to inquire, [18.120]–[18.130]
   material questions of fact, consideration, [18.135]–[18.141]
   Migration Internal Review Office (MIRO), replacement of, [18.17]
   Ministerial power to override decisions by, [8.04]
   notification of decisions, [18.48], [18.57]–[18.70]
      compliance with provisions, [18.61]–[18.65]
      criteria, [18.59]
   onus and standard of proof, [18.113]–[18.116]
   operational statistics, [18.27]–[18.28]
   powers, [6.34], [6.51], [6.60], [8.58], [15.39]–[15.40], [16.68], [18.18]–[18.19], [18.54]
      re-make decisions, [18.49]
   pre-screening processes, [18.18]

Migration Review Tribunal (*cont*)
  procedures, [18.18]–[18.19]
  reasons for decisions, [18.95], [18.131], [18.135]–[18.141]
    challenges to, [18.131]
    written statement, [18.135]
  skills assessments, [10.36]
  special need relative applications, consideration of, [8.58]–[8.60]
  systemic problems with, [19.74]
  time limits for applications, [15.22], [15.53], [18.19], [18.56]–[18.57]
  visa, refusal or cancellation, [6.34], [10.37], [11.26]
    character grounds, on, [18.18]
Migration zone, [6.04]
Millbank, Jenni, [13.30], [13.115], [13.117]
Minahan, James Francis Kitchen, [2.38], [2.63]
Minister for Immigration
  conclusive certificates, issue of, [18.55]
  criminal or bad conduct cases, [6.57]–[6.60]
    intervention, [6.58]
  intervention by, [6.58], [12.82], [19.55]
  limits on visa numbers, powers, [8.03], [9.27]
  migration decisions, [18.11]
    natural justice, application of, and, [17.43]
    non-reviewable discretion, [19.53]–[19.55]
    s 501 power, personal exercise of, [17.45]
  power of, [20.11]
  public interest criteria
    powers to regulate entry, [6.69]–[6.78]
  review bodies, power to override decisions by, [8.04], [18.08]
  Ministerial discretion, [5.23], [5.36], [5.86], [6.25], [6.45], [6.52], [6.68], [7.21], [7.22], [8.04], [12.23], [12.77]–[12.83], [14.65]–[14.68], [14.76], [15.54], [19.17], [19.43], [19.51]–[19.55], [20.13]
    intervention rates, [12.82]
Minor *see* Child
Moore, Andrew, [17.93], [17.102], [17.105], [20.20]
National Code of Practice for Registration Authorities and Providers of Education and Training to Overseas Students 2007 (the National Code), [11.58], [11.59], [11.61], [11.63]
National security, [6.24]
  ground of exclusion from refugee status, [14.49]–[14.63]
Nationality Act 1920 (Cth), [2.53]
Nationality and Citizenship Act 1948 (Cth), [2.05], [2.54], [2.57], [2.59], [2.60], [3.11]
Natural Justice, [2.45], [3.34], [3.65], [5.49], [5.93], [6.16], [6.74], [9.44], [12.75], [12.76], [15.34], [18.02], [18.25], [18.29], [18.55], [18.70], [18.112], [20.08]–[20.10], [20.24], [20.36]
  breach of, as jurisdictional error, [19.73]

  constraint on decision-making, as, [19.19]–[19.39], [19.60], [19.69], [19.72]–[19.74], [19.108]
  criminal deportation, in, [17.42]–[17.47]
  exclusion of from decision-making, [18.55], [19.96], [19.108]
  hearing rules, [18.71]–[18.76], [18.89]–[18.111], [19.20]–[19.35]
  notice of appeal and time limits, [18.56]–[18.70]
  principles, [5.27], [6.21], [6.58], [12.92], [15.35], [15.36], [16.125], [18.90], [18.91]
  Rule against bias, [19.36]–[19.39]
  statutory exclusion of, [18.55]
Naturalization Act 1903 (Cth), [2.52]
Nauru *see also* Offshore processing
  detention and offshore processing centre, [1.25], [4.36], [4.57], [4.59], [4.60], [4.61], [4.62], [4.63], [4.64], [4.66], [12.49], [12.67], [12.68], [16.44], [19.100], [19.102]
  closure of, [12.53], [20.22], [20.24]
  domestic laws of, [4.63]
NEAT Domestic Trading Pty Ltd v AWB Ltd, [5.95]–[5.98]
New Zealand
  detention centre in, [4.36]
  Recognised Seasonal Employer (RSE) scheme, [10.54]–[10.58], [10.63], [10.75], [10.78], [10.82], [10.83], [10.87]
New Zealand citizens
  exemptions from visa and entry permit requirements, [6.06]
  Maoris, [2.51]
  Special Category (Temporary) (Class TY) visa, [6.13]
  temporary visas, [5.35]
Nolan v MIEA, [3.14]–[3.18], [3.20], [3.21], [15.18], [15.26]
Non-refoulement obligation, [4.54], [12.81], [14.01], [14.10], [14.25], [14.37], [14.66], [14.69], [17.98], [17.99], [20.14]
  national security exception, [14.49]–[14.63]
Norfolk Island Permanent Resident (Residence) visa, [6.13]
North Korean defectors, [14.35]
Notification
  cancellation of visa, [18.67]
  migration decisions, of, [18.48], [18.57]–[18.70]
Nystrom, Stephan, [3.29], [17.48], [17.87], [20.20]
Occupational English Test (OET), [9.51]–[9.52]
Oceanic Viking, [4.41]
Offences *see* Immigration offences
Office of the Migration Agents Registration Authority (OMARA) *see* Migration Agents Registration Authority (MARA)
'Offshore entry persons', [6.04]

Offshore processing, [4.05], [4.57]–[4.65], [12.31], [12.53], [12.56], [12.60], [12.68], [12.65], [14.07], [16.06], [16.50], [19.100]–[19.104], [20.19], [20.24], [20.25] *see also* Detention centres; Pacific Strategy
Ombudsman, [5.19], [6.55], [17.03]
  functions of office, [18.31]
  Immigration Ombudsman, creation of, [18.39]–[18.40]
  investigation by
    actions precluded from, [18.32]
    administrative malpractice, [18.33]
    discretion to decline complaint, [18.35]
    immigration detention centres, into, [18.37]
    wrongful detention and removal, [18.38]
  limitations, [18.36]
  migration decisions, appeal of, [18.30]
Ombudsman Act 1976 (Cth), [18.42]
One Nation Party, [9.21], [17.85] *see also* Hanson, Pauline
'Operation Relex', [4.50], [4.51], [4.54], [12.50]
Opperman, Minister Hubert, [5.04]
Organisation for Economic Co-operation and Development (OECD), [9.06]
Orphan Relative visas, [8.12]
  best interests of child, considering, [8.21], [8.25]
  criteria, [8.21], [8.22]–[8.23], [8.26], [15.76]
  definition, [8.21]
  relevant evidence for, [8.22]
Overstayers *see also* Unlawful status
  demographic profile of, [11.80]–[11.87], [15.01]
Pacific Island labourers
  Pacific Island Labourers Act 1901 (Cth), [10.70]
  removal of, [2.23]
Pacific Strategy, [1.25], [4.10], [12.53], [20.22], [20.26]
  'migration zone', declaration of areas outside, [6.04], [12.48], [16.06], [16.07]
  offshore processing under, [4.57]–[4.64], [20.24]
  UNHCR and IOM, involvement of, [4.60], [12.49]
Palapa I, [4.39]
Palapa II, [6.02]
Palmer, Mick, [5.82], [18.38], [20.12]
Papua New Guinea
  detention and offshore processing centre, [1.25], [4.36], [4.57], [4.59], [4.60], [4.66], [12.31], [12.49], [12.53], [12.67], [16.44]
  domestic laws of, [4.63]
Papuans
  asylum seekers, [12.29], [12.31]
  Australian citizenship of, [2.67]–[2.70], [3.28]
  uprising by, [12.29]

Parent visas
  applications, backlog on, [8.32]
  'balance of family test', [8.35]
  cap on number of visas issued, [8.03], [8.32]
  eligibility, [8.35]
  health charges, payment of, [8.33]–[8.34]
  Minister's discretionary powers in cases, [8.39]
  minor children as sponsors, [8.36]–[8.39]
  parent visa, [8.36], [8.38]
  restrictions, [8.32]
  sponsorship requirements of children, [8.37]
  support bond, payment of, [8.34]
  two streams of, creation, [8.34]
Parliamentary reviews *see* Inquiries and reviews
Partner migration *see also* Family migration
  abuses of program, [7.08], [7.12], [7.18]–[7.19], [7.49]–[7.57]
    exploitation of foreign party, [7.55]–[7.57]
    penalties, [7.50]
    serial sponsorship, [7.52]–[7.53], [7.88]
    sham marriages, [7.08], [7.19], [7.50]–[7.51]
  abusive relationships, [7.22]
  'bona fides units' (BFUs), [7.19]
  breakdown of partnership, [7.37]–[7.38]
    family violence, grounds of *see* Family violence provisions
  children of a relationship, [7.20]
  family violence provisions *see* Family violence provisions
  foreign marriages, recognition, [7.29]
  genuineness of partnership, [7.16]–[7.17], [7.23], [7.28], [7.33]
    considerations, [7.39]–[7.40]
    mutual commitment test, [7.36]
    proving, [7.36]–[7.47]
  overview, [7.10]–[7.12]
  partner visa *see* Partner visa
  permanent residency
    applications, increase in, [7.49]–[7.50]
    grant, [7.15]
    requisites, [7.22]
  polygamous marriages, [7.31]–[7.32]
  provisional period, [7.13], [7.15], [7.20], [9.78]
    exemptions, [7.15], [7.20]
    introduction, [7.18]
    restrictions on, [7.10], [7.15]
  sham marriages, [7.08], [7.19], [7.50]–[7.51]
  sponsored migration of foreign partner, [7.12]
    exploitation of foreign party, [7.55]–[7.57]
    offshore non-citizens, [7.13]
    onshore applicants, [7.14]
    serial sponsorship, [7.52]–[7.53], [7.88]
  unlawful non-citizens, [7.14]

Partner migration (*cont*)
  valid partnership, [7.28] *see also* genuineness of partnership above
    age limits, [7.30]
    foreign marriages, recognition, [7.29]
    polygamous marriages, [7.31]–[7.32]
Partner visas
  applications, [7.13]–[7.14]
  dependent children and, [8.17]
  eligibility, [7.11], [7.16], [7.27]–[7.32]
Patterson, Re; Ex parte Taylor, [3.10], [3.14], [3.15], [3.17], [3.18], [3.19], [3.20], [3.21], [3.30]
People smuggling offences *see* Immigration offences
Peoples' Republic of China
  adopted children bilateral agreement, [8.19]
  Falun Gong practitioners, [13.42]
  Memorandum of Understanding (MOU) with, [12.96], [14.08]
  one-child policy, [13.51], [13.52], [13.63], [13.74], [13.101]–[13.106], [13.124]
  pro-democracy demonstrators, protection sought by, [12.33], [12.35]–[12.38], [12.40], [12.83], [13.36]
  subclass 815 visa, creation of, [15.83]–[15.87]
  Tiananmen Square massacre *see* Tiananmen Square massacre
Perth Detention Centre, [16.44], [16.51]
Plaintiff M61/2010E v Commonwealth; Plaintiff M69 of 2010 v Commonwealth, [12.56], [12.75], [12.82], [18.29], [19.13], [19.102]–[19.104], [19.116]
Plaintiff M90/2009 v MIAC, [18.86]
Plaintiff S157 v Commonwealth, [3.37]–[3.40], [18.96], [19.82], [19.85]–[19.87], [19.88], [19.95]
Platters case, The, [5.27], [5.29], [11.78]
Pochi and MIEA, Re, [17.81]
Pochi v Macphee, [3.13], [17.13], [20.07]
Points test
  bonus points, [9.29]
  business visas, for, [9.100]–[9.101]
  Critical Skills List (CSL), [9.29], [9.56]–[9.57]
  English language proficiency, [9.28], [9.29], [9.48]–[9.54]
  formulation of, [9.17]
  local qualifications, [9.55]
  Migration Occupations in Demand List (MODL), [9.29], [9.56]–[9.57]
  1999 revisions to, [9.22]
  priority processing, [9.29]
  regional migrants, for *see* Regional migration
  requirements, [9.28]
  restrictions, [9.26]
  Skilled Occupation List *see* Skilled Occupation List (SOL)
  skills shortages lists, [9.56]–[9.57]
  work experience, [9.46]–[9.47]

Port Hedland Detention Centre, [6.14], [12.41], [16.41], [16.44], [16.49], [16.51]
Potter v Minahan, [2.37]–[2.42], [2.50], [2.63], [2.78]
Pre-application skills assessment (PASA), [9.39], [9.41], [9.44]
  English language proficiency requirement, [9.50]
  outsourcing of, [9.40]–[9.45]
  review of decisions, [9.44]
  Trades Recognition Australia (TRA), [9.41], [9.45]
  Vocational Education and Training Assessment Services (VETASSESS), [9.41]
Prerogative powers, [3.55]–[3.57]
Prerogative writs, [19.08]–[19.12]
  certiorari, [19.09], [19.11]–[19.12], [19.73]
  mandamus, [19.09], [19.10]
  prohibition, [19.09], [19.11]–[19.12]
Privatisation of administrative functions, [5.61]–[5.69]
  health assessments, [5.70]
  immigration detention, [5.74]–[5.76]
  judicial response to, [5.91]–[5.98]
  problems with, [5.81]–[5.90]
  removals, [5.77]–[5.80]
  skills assessments, [5.71]–[5.73]
Privative clauses, [3.36]–[3.40], [5.50], [19.76]–[19.87]
Procedural fairness *see* Natural justice
Prospective Marriage visa
  application, [7.13]
  family violence provisions, access to, [7.87]
  requirements, [7.29]
Protection obligations to non-citizens
  'complementary protection' regime, [14.64]–[14.71]
  human trafficking, victims of, [14.72]–[14.79]
  non-refoulement *see* Non-refoulement obligation
  refugee processing, [14.08], [14.37]–[14.48]
  rights of refugees, qualifications on, [14.03]–[14.07]
    cessation, [14.40]–[14.48]
    effective nationality, [14.18]–[14.22]
    exclusion [14.49]–[14.53]
      acts contrary to United Nations principles and purposes, [14.63]
      crimes against peace, war crimes and crimes against humanity, [14.54]–[14.55]
      national security, [14.49]–[14.63]
      serious non-political crimes committed outside country of refuge, [14.56]–[14.62]
    internal relocation, [14.10]–[14.17]
    Migration Act 1958 s 36(3), under, [14.30]–[14.36]

right to enter and reside, [14.31]–[14.36]
   'safe' countries of origin, declaration of,
      [14.08]–[14.09]
   safe third countries, [14.18]–[14.19],
      [14.23]–[14.29]
   'seven-day' rule, [14.30]
Protection visa, [3.64], [6.13], [10.63], [12.40],
   [13.02], [14.28], [14.31], [14.36], [14.39]–
   [14.45], [15.08], [15.47], [15.71], [16.13],
   [16.16], [16.92], [18.26], [18.131] *see also*
   Asylum seekers; Refugees
   Ministerial discretion, [12.13], [12.20], [12.67],
      [12.79], [19.70]
   temporary visas, [12.13], [12.45], [12.52],
      [14.02], [14.07], [14.39], [14.42], [20.22]
Public interest criteria, [6.22]–[6.25]
   character *see* Character test
   codification, [6.25]
   community impacts of an individual,
      assessing, [6.54]
   definition, [6.67]
   health *see* Health criteria
   Ministerial powers to regulate entry,
      [6.69]–[6.78]
   national security, [6.24]
   public interest tests, [6.22]
   public order, [6.24], [6.56] *see also* Character
      criteria
   undue cost and undue prejudice provisions,
      [6.51]–[6.55]
   'user pays' migration process, [6.23], [7.07]
   waiver of, [6.30], [6.51]–[6.53], [6.70]
Public law
   development of, [1.39]
      role of immigration in, [20.04]–[20.10],
         [20.11]–[20.17]
   strands of, [1.19]
Public Service Act 1922 (Cth), [5.17]
Queen, allegiance to, [2.59], [2.72], [3.18]
Quick, John, [2.04], [2.14], [2.16]
Racial Discrimination Act 1975 (Cth), [15.86],
   [15.90]
Rau, Cornelia, [5.81], [5.82], [5.88], [5.90],
   [16.33], [16.38], [16.55], [18.38], [20.12],
   [20.34]
Ray, Senator, [17.67], [17.68], [17.82]–[17.84]
Refugee Review Tribunal (RRT), [1.35], [12.69]–
   [12.74], [18.02], [18.18]
   advice given to applicants, [18.87]–[18.88]
   appointment of members, [18.47]
   closed hearings, [18.47]
   conclusive certificates, issue of, [18.55]
   credibility findings, [18.131]–[18.134],
      [18.140]
   duty to inquire, [18.120]–[18.130]
   establishment, [18.26]
   fraudulent behaviour of advisor,
      [18.87]–[18.88]
   government influence over, [18.47]
   hearings
      breach of rules, [18.96]
      conduct of, [18.89]–[18.91]
      interpreters, use of, [18.77]–[18.83],
         [18.118]
      not required, when, [18.101]–[18.102]
      obligation to consider all issues,
         [18.117]–[18.119]
      oral hearing, [18.94]
      procedural fairness, [18.90]–[18.97]
      representation, right of, [18.84]–[18.86]
      right to appear in person and give
         evidence, [18.71]–[18.76]
      rights of applicant at, [18.44]
   information
      disclosable, [18.95], [18.98]–[18.100]
      non-disclosable, [18.106]–[18.111]
      supplied by applicant, [18.103]–[18.105]
   inquisitorial nature of, [18.44]–[18.46],
      [18.112], [18.120]–[18.130]
   jurisdiction, [18.54]
   jurisdictional error, decisions affected by,
      [18.49]–[18.54], [19.91]
   material questions of fact, consideration,
      [18.135]–[18.141]
   Ministerial power to override decisions by,
      [8.04]
   notification of decisions, [18.48],
      [18.57]–[18.70]
      compliance with provisions,
         [18.61]–[18.65]
      criteria, [18.59]
   onus and standard of proof, [18.113]–[18.116]
   operational statistics, [18.27]–[18.28]
   oral hearings, [18.26]
   'post-application' fee, [18.27]
   powers, [18.18], [18.26], [18.54]
      re-make decisions, [18.49]
   procedures, [18.18]
   reasons for decisions, [18.95], [18.131],
      [18.135]–[18.141]
      challenges to, [18.131]
      written statement, [18.135]
   systemic problems with, [19.74]
   time limits for applications, [18.56]–[18.57],
      [18.69]
Refugee Review Tribunal, Re; Ex parte Aala,
   [19.72]–[19.73]
Refugee Status Review Committee (RSRC)
   establishment, [12.39], [18.22]
   functions, [18.23]
Refugees
   African, [12.16], [12.17]
   child, [8.09]
   claims
      rise in, [12.22]–[12.38]
      statistical data on, [12.99]
   Comprehensive Plan of Action (CPA),
      [12.28], [12.35], [14.08]

Refugees (cont)
  concept of, [12.01]–[12.08]
  definition see Definition of refugee
  Determination of Refugee Status Committee (DORS) 1978-90, [5.17], [5.67], [12.22]–[12.38], [18.20]–[18.21]
    reconstitution of, [12.39], [12.42]
  entry permits, grant of, [12.40]
  exclusion from protection, where, [14.49]–[14.53]
    acts contrary to United Nations principles and purposes, [14.63]
    crimes against peace, war crimes and crimes against humanity, [14.54]–[14.55]
    serious non-political crimes committed outside country of refuge, [14.56]–[14.62]
  Global Special Humanitarian visa, [6.55]
  Independent Merits Review (IMR) see Offshore processing
  international refugee law, [4.39]–[4.43], [4.49]–[4.77], [16.132]
  jurisprudence on, development of, [12.84]–[12.94]
  non-refoulement see Non-refoulement obligation
  offshore refugee/humanitarian program, [12.09]–[12.17]
    change in character of, [12.15], [12.16]
    visa categories, [12.09]–[12.14]
  'Orderly Departure Program', [12.28]
  politics of refugee protection, [12.95]–[12.99]
  protection obligations to see Protection obligations to non-citizens
  protection regime, access to, [6.04]
  protection visa eligibility, [6.13] see also Protection visa
  Refugee Convention and Protocol see UN Convention relating to Status of Refugees
  Refugee Status Assessment (RSA), [3.64]–[3.66], [12.67], [12.75], [18.29], [19.102], [19.103]
  resettlement of
    Australia's involvement in, [12.01]
  review authorities see Refugee Review Tribunal (RRT); Refugee Status Review Committee (RSRC)
  rights of, qualifications on, [14.03]–[14.07]
    effective nationality, [14.18]–[14.22]
    internal relocation, [14.10]–[14.17]
    Migration Act 1958 s 36(3), under, [14.30]–[14.36]
    right to enter and reside, [14.31]–[14.36]
    'safe' countries of origin, declaration of, [14.08]–[14.09]
    safe third countries, [14.18]–[14.19], [14.23]–[14.29]
    'seven-day' rule, [14.30]
  status determinations, [12.18], [12.41], [12.42]
    administrative appeals, [12.69]–[12.76], [18.21]
    cessation of, [14.37]–[14.48]
    ministerial discretion, [12.77]–[12.83], [16.124]
    offshore, [12.67]–[12.68]
    onshore, [12.63]–[12.66]
    politicised process, [14.08], [14.09]
    procedures for, [12.57]–[12.66]
    regime, introduction of, [18.20]
    regulatory system, use of, [12.83]
    suspension of, [12.56]
  Tamil, [12.54]
  temporary protection see Temporary protection visa
  treatment of
    Coalition years, [12.43]–[12.51]
    post 2007, [12.52]–[12.56], [12.67]
  UN Convention relating to see UN Convention relating to Status of Refugees
Regional migration
  allocation of places for, [9.58]
  business visas and regional development, [9.102]–[9.103]
  Established Business visa, [9.100]
  incentives, [9.58]–[9.62]
  points test, additional points for, [9.59]
  settlement, visa classes for, [9.30]
  Skilled – Regional Sponsored visa, [9.60]
  Skilled State/Territory Nominated Independent visa, [9.62]
  'Skills Matching' visa, [9.61]
  State Migration Plans, [9.60]
Relationships
  family see Family migration
  partnerships see Partner migration
Relative see also Aged Dependent Relative visas; Family migration; Orphan Relative visas; Remaining Relative visas; Special Need Relative visa
  definition, [8.43]
Remaining Relative visas
  eligibility, [8.49]–[8.50], [8.55], [15.76]
  'near' relatives, [8.49]–[8.52]
  quota for number of visas issued, [8.03]
  remaining relatives, definition, [8.48]
  'usually resident', meaning, [8.53]–[8.54]
Removal of non-citizen see Deportation; Enforcement
Removal of unwanted persons see Deportation of permanent residents
Resolution of status visa, [15.89]
Review of migration decisions see Judicial review of migration decisions; Migration Review Tribunal (MRT); Refugee Review Tribunal (RRT)

Reynolds, Henry, [2.23]
Rinnan, Captain, [4.33], [4.36], [4.37], [4.38]
Roach Committee, [10.06]–[10.09]
Roach Report, [5.24, [6.26], [10.06]–[10.09]
Rothwell, Don, [4.33], [4.37]
Rubenstein, Kim, [2.09], [2.12], [2.15], [2.19], [2.61], [2.67], [2.80], [3.45]
Rudd Labor government, [1.17], [1.25], [3.64], [4.41], [4.65]–[4.68], [4.74], [10.13], [10.40], [10.72], [11.81], [12.52], [12.80], [12.82]
   Coalition's criticism of, [4.68]
   replacement of, [10.47]
Ruddock, Minister Phillip, [4.55], [5.86], [9.21], [10.09], [12.96], [17.24], [17.29], [17.68], [19.04], [19.39], [19.50], [19.86]
   person cancellation of visas, [17.46]
Ruddock v Taylor, [16.40]
Ruddock v Vadarlis, [3.63], [20.05]
Salemi v MacKellar (No 2), [16.86], [19.22], [19.24], [19.29]
Sales v MIAC, [17.48]–[17.49]
Same-sex relationships, [7.09] *see also* Partner migration
   interdependency visas, [7.24], [7.26]
   Partner visa eligibility, [7.11], [7.24]–[7.27]
   persecution due to, [13.114]–[13.117]
   recognition of, [7.11], [7.21], [7.24]–[7.27]
Sanctuary Under Review Inquiry, [4.74], [5.76] [12.63], [12.66], [12.71], [12.81], [13.33], [14.09], [14.66], [16.43], [16.122], [16.135], [16.136], [19.54]
Sandoval v MIMA, [6.19], [15.14]–[15.16]
Seasonal migration program
   administration of, [10.80]
   benefits of, [10.73]–[10.79]
   failings, [10.87], [10.88]
   international trends, [10.54]–[10.56]
   labour market issues, [10.64]–[10.67]
   migration as development, [10.73]–[10.79]
   opposition to, [10.63], [10.67], [10.68]–[10.72]
   permanent settlement, eschewing, [10.68]–[10.72]
   structure, [10.57]–[10.63]
   worker exploitation, potential for, [10.80]–[10.86]
Seeking Asylum Alone Study, [12.62]–[12.66], [12.68], [12.70], [13.61], [16.54], [18.63]–[18.65]
Senate Legal and Constitutional References Committee, [5.78], [16.135], [16.136], [17.03]
Senate Select Committee Inquiry into a Certain Maritime Incident, [4.50], [4.59], [12.51]
September 11 terrorist attacks, [4.36], [4.44], [6.03], [12.46], [12.97], [19.76], [20.25]
Shachar, Ayelet, [9.06], [11.04]
Shaw v MIMA, [3.19]–[3.22], [20.07]
Silveira v Australian Institute of Management, [5.73], [5.93], [5.94], [9.44]

Simaplee, Puongtong, [14.72]
Singh, Tania, [2.71]–[2.79]
Skilled – Independent visa, [9.16]–[9.57]
   points test for *see* Points test
   threshold criteria for, [9.28], [9.31]–[9.54]
Skilled – Regional Sponsored visa, [9.60]
Skilled migration
   applicants
      average age, [9.05]
      English language proficiency, [9.25], [9.28], [9.29], [9.48]–[9.54]
      'job-readiness' of, [9.39]
      racial profile, [9.05]
   British migrants, [9.12], [9.14]
   business *see* Business skills migration
   controls, [9.04], [9.08], [9.10], [9.16]–[9.18]
   Distinguished Talent visas, [9.73]–[9.76]
   dovetailing with overseas student program, [11.50]–[11.55]
   economic growth, boost to, [9.18]
   employer nomination *see* Employer Nomination Scheme (ENS)
   history of, [9.12]–[9.15]
   independent skilled migrants *see* Skilled – Independent visa
   intake, [1.31], [9.01]
      family migrant intake, ratio to, [7.03]–[7.04], [9.01]
      increase, [9.01]–[9.02]
   limits on visa numbers, powers, [8.03], [9.27]
   local workers, impact on, [9.09]
   1989 reforms, [9.19]–[9.20]
   1999 reforms, [9.21]–[9.23]
   overview of program, [9.08]–[9.11]
   points based system, *see* Points test
   pre-application skills assessment (PASA), [9.39], [9.44]
      outsourcing of, [9.40]–[9.45]
      review of decisions, [9.44]
      Trades Recognition Australia (TRA), [9.41], [9.45]
      Vocational Education and Training Assessment Services (VETASSESS), [9.41]
   processing backlog, [9.27]
   recent trends, [9.24]–[9.27]
   recruitment tactics of Western countries, [9.06]
   reduction, [9.24]
   reforms of program, [9.23], [9.25], [9.104]–[9.106]
   regional settlement *see* Regional migration
   skills shortages
      incentives to settle in regions of, [9.04]
      lists, [9.56]–[9.57]
   temporary *see* Temporary skilled migration
   two-stage process of, [9.03], [9.78]
   work experience, [9.46]–[9.47]

Skilled Occupation List (SOL), [9.22], [9.28], [9.31]–[9.45] *see also* ENS Skilled Occupation List
   Australian and New Zealand Standard Classification of Occupations (ANZSCO) Dictionary, [9.34], [9.42]
   gazettal of occupations, [9.33]
   introduction, [9.22], [9.31]–[9.32]
   removal of occupations from, [9.33]
   review of, [9.36] [9.38]
   selection criteria, [9.34]–[9.38]
Skilled State/Territory Nominated Independent visa (STNI), [9.62]
Skills Matching visas, [9.61]
Social group
   definition of refugee based on, [13.97]–[13.119]
Social Security Act 1991 (Cth), [6.50]
Social Security Appeals Tribunal, [18.03]
Social security benefits
   access to, [6.49]
   'Impairment tables' and, [6.50]
Solon-Alvarez, Vivian, [5.81], [5.82], [5.88], [5.90], [16.33], [16.38], [16.55], [18.38], [20.34]
Somaghi v MILGEA, [12.42], [13.38], [19.34]
Special Category (Temporary) visa, [6.13]
Special Need Relative visa, [8.38]
   abuse of provisions, [8.64]
   criteria, [8.56]
   replacement by Carer visa, [8.56]
Sponsorship
   applicants for permanent entry, of, [6.23]
   child, of, [8.08]–[8.11]
   employers, by *see* Employer Nomination Scheme (ENS); Temporary business visas
   parents, of, [8.37]
      minor children, by, [8.36]–[8.39]
   partners, of, [7.12]
      exploitation of foreign party, [7.55]–[7.57]
      offshore non-citizens, [7.13]
      onshore applicants, [7.14]
      serial sponsorship, [7.52]–[7.53], [7.88]
   State or Territory authority, by, [9.102]–[9.103]
   support offered by sponsor, [8.46]
Spouses *see* Partner migration
Sri Lankan asylum seekers, [12.55]
   suspension of refugee status determinations, [12.56]
State Migration Plans, [9.60]
Stay orders, [16.96]–[16.111]
   application, [16.96]
   balance of convenience, [16.103], [16.104]
   bridging visa, refusal of, [16.97]–[16.98]
   Federal Court, power to make, [16.100]
   release from detention, and, [16.107]–[16.111]
   special reasons for grant, [16.103]

S395/2002 v MIMA, [13.115]–[13.117]
Structured Selection Assessment System, [5.12], [5.16]
Students *see* Foreign students
Support, assurances of *see* Assurances of Support
'Suspected illegal entry vessels' (SIEVs) *see* Unauthorised boat arrivals
Sydney and Surrounding Areas Skills Shortages List (SSASSL), [9.56]
Taggart, Michael, [19.109], [20.37]
Tampa Affair, [1.25], [3.36], [3.54], [3.57], [3.60], [4.10], [4.31]–[4.56], [4.61], [6.02], [6.03], [12.06], [12.16], [12.27], [12.47], [12.48], [12.49], [15.94], [16.04], [16.06], [16.108], [19.04], [19.76], [20.25], [20.39]
   background to, [4.33]–[4.36]
   international refugee law, [4.39]–[4.43]
   judicial responses to, [4.44]–[4.48]
Temporary business visas, [9.84]–[9.85], [10.04]–[10.50] [10.71], [10.81], [10.87], [20.30]
   cancellation, [10.38], [15.41], [15.42]
   condition 8112, [10.16]
   controversies over, [10.41]–[10.46]
   Deegan report, [10.46], [10.48]
   deficiencies in structure, [10.43]
   employer abuse of, [1.32], [10.02], [10.13], [10.42], [10.45], [10.81]
   employer sanctions, [10.39]–[10.40]
   historical development of, [10.04]–[10.09]
   merits review, [10.37]
   nominated employee, [10.32]
      English language requirements, [10.34]–[10.35]
      non-portability in labour market, [10.33]
      skills assessments, [10.36]
   nominated position, [10.29]–[10.31]
      Temporary Skilled Migration Income Threshold, [10.30]
   reform of, [10.47]–[10.50]
   sponsorship requirements, [10.19]–[10.28]
      benefit to Australia test, [10.21]–[10.22]
      commitment to training local workers, [10.23]
      'direct employer', meaning of, [10.24]
      employer obligations, [10.25]–[10.28]
Temporary entrants, [11.01]–[11.05]
   students *see* Foreign students
   tourists *see* Visitors
   visitors *see* Visitors
Temporary protection visa (TPV)
   reinstitution of, [12.45]
   termination of, [12.52], [20.22]
   trial of, [12.40]
Temporary skilled migration
   deregulation, [10.12]
   growth in numbers of, [1.32], [10.01]
   skills transfers, [10.01]

INDEX

union advocacy, role of, [1.32], [10.02]
Terrorism Act 2000 (UK), [17.35]
Terrorist attack, [4.36], [4.44], [17.35]
Tiananmen Square massacre, [12.83], [13.36]
Tourist *see* Visitors
Toy v Musgrove, [2.24], [2.25]
Trade unions, [6.72], [9.11], [9.12], [9.14], [9.66], [10.02], [10.05], [10.47], [10.49], [10.67]
Trades Recognition Australia (TRA), [9.41]
   Job Ready Program, [9.45]
Trafficking *see* Human trafficking
Transitional Permanent visa, [17.48]
UN Convention Against Torture and All Forms of Cruel, Inhumane and Degrading Treatment or Punishment 1984 (CAT), [4.53], [4.54], [4.58], [4.69]-[4.74], [14.69]
   UN Committee Against Torture, [4.06]
UN Convention Against Transnational Organised Crime, [14.73], [15.94]
UN Convention on the Elimination of all Forms of Discrimination against Women (CEDAW), [4.09]
UN Convention on the Law of the Sea (UNCLOS), [4.37], [4.52]
UN Convention on the Rights of Persons with Disabilities (CRPD), [4.69], [17.101], [18.41]
   UN Committee on the Rights of Persons with Disabilities, [4.06], [18.41]
UN Convention on the Rights of the Child, [8.20], [18.41]
   UN Committee on the Rights of the Child, [4.06], [4.09], [4.16]-[4.18], [4.27], [4.58], [4.69], [14.69], [17.94]
UN Convention relating to Status of Refugees, [1.34], [1.35], [4.02], [4.10], [4.36], [4.40], [4.43], [4.45], [4.54], [4.55], [4.56], [4.57], [4.60], [4.62], [4.66], [6.05], [12.01]-[12.04], [12.15], [12.18], [12.19], [12.49], [12.57]-[12.59], [12.60], [13.01], [16.122], [17.98], [18.22]
   administration of, [14.03]
   Art 1C, [14.37]-[14.48]
   Art 1F and 33(2), [14.49]-[14.63]
   Art 31, interpretation of, [14.05]-[14.07]
   Australia's accession to, [4.02], [4.10]
   Australia's obligations to, [6.05], [14.01]
   cessation of refugee status, [14.37]-[14.48]
   'complementary protection' regime, [14.64]-[14.71]
   politics of protection, [14.03]-[14.07]
   problems with, [14.03]-[14.07]
   processing of asylum seekers, involvement in, [4.60], [12.49], [14.07]
   prohibition on refoulement, [14.01], [14.10]
      national security exception to, [14.49]-[14.63]
   rights of refugees, qualifications on, [14.03]-[14.07]
      effective nationality, [14.18]-[14.22]
      internal relocation, [14.10]-[14.17]
   Migration Act 1958 s 36(3), under, [14.30]-[14.36]
      right to enter and reside, [14.31]-[14.36]
      'safe' countries of origin, declaration of, [14.08]-[14.09]
      safe third countries, [14.18]-[14.19], [14.23]-[14.29]
      'seven-day' rule, [14.30]
UN Declaration on the Rights of Mentally Retarded Persons, [18.41]
UN Declaration on the Rights of the Child, [8.62]
UN Human Rights Committee, [4.06]
   complaints to, [4.69]-[4.74]
UN International Convention on the Elimination of all forms of Racial Discrimination (CERD), [4.09], [4.69], [18.41]
UN International Covenant on Civil and Political Rights (ICCPR), [4.09], [4.27], [4.53], [4.54], [4.58], [4.66], [4.69], [7.10], [14.69], [17.99], [18.41], [20.20]
UN Protocol to Prevent, Suppress and Punish Trafficking in Persons, Especially Women and Children (Palermo Protocol), [7.56], [14.73], [14.74], [16.72]
Unauthorised boat arrivals, [3.32], [3.40], [3.41]-[3.52]
   children on, [12.45]
   children overboard incident, [4.50], [5.23], [12.51], [20.39]
   Coalition years, in, [12.43]-[12.51]
   first arrival, [12.22]
   increase in number of, Parliament response to, [6.02]
   interdiction program, [4.50]-[4.56], [12.55]
   'Operation Relex', [4.49]-[4.51], [4.54], [6.02]
   Pacific Strategy, offshore processing under, [4.57]-[4.64], [12.31], [20.24]
   phenomenon of, [1.03], [4.03]
   processing asylum claims of, [3.64]
   second arrival, [12.29]
   'secondary movement' refugees, [4.55]
   'suspected illegal entry vessels'(SIEVs), [4.50], [4.51], [12.51]
      SIEV 4, [4.50], [12.51]
      SIEV X tragedy, [4.50], [4.51], [4.54], [5.23], [12.50], [20.25]
   Tampa Affair *see* Tampa Affair
   third wave, [12.32]-[12.38]
   2008 and 2009, in, [12.54]
   visas available to, [6.12]-[6.13]
United States
   Constitution, [2.13]
   liberal immigration policy, [1.04]
   Mexico, relationship with, [1.05]
   State Department, [13.33]

Unlawful status, [1.37], [1.38], [6.08]
  becoming unlawful, [15.01]–[15.06]
  cancellation of temporary visa after entry
    business visas, cancellation of,
      [15.41]–[15.42]
    character grounds, on, [15.45]
    general power, [15.29]–[15.33]
    procedure, [15.34]–[15.40]
    student visas, automatic cancellation of,
      [11.30]–[11.49], [15.43]–[15.44]
  cancellation of visa upon or before entry
    cancellation decision, [15.19]–[15.28]
    'incorrect answer', meaning of,
      [15.14]–[15.18]
    offshore cancellation, [15.11]
    procedure for, [15.12]–[15.13]
  child, as a, [8.40]
  concessions for permanent residency, [8.02]
  enforcement of decisions *see* Enforcement
  historical approaches to, [15.78]–[15.90]
  immigration offences *see* Immigration
    offences
  'innocent illegals', [8.02], [8.40]–[8.42]
  overstayers, [15.05], [15.07]–[15.09]
  permanent visas available
    'absorbed persons', [15.74]–[15.75], [17.01]
    non-citizens unlawful for 12 months or
      less, [15.76]
    persons unlawful for any length of time,
      [15.71]–[15.73]
  regularisation of, general requirements for
    Schedule 3 criteria, [15.52]–[15.70]
    time limits, bridging visas and other
      'threshold' requirements,
      [15.46]–[15.51]
  removal of unlawful non-citizens *see*
    Enforcement
  temporary visas available, [15.77]
  unauthorised arrivals, [15.07]–[15.09]
Vanstone, Minister Amanda, [17.46], [20.21]
VEAL v MIMIA, [18.107]–[18.108]
Victorian Council for Civil Liberties, [4.44]
Vietnamese boat people, [12.22], [12.23],
  [12.27], [12.28], [12.29], [12.35]
Villawood Detention Centre, [6.16], [11.35],
  [14.72], [16.44], [16.51], [18.43]

Visitors
  admission of
    evolution of law governing, [1.33]
      [11.67]–[11.72]
    advanced processing of, [11.70]
    Electronic Travel Authority (Visitor) visa
      (ETA visa), [11.71], [11.73]
    genuine, [11.73]–[11.79]
    overstayers, breakdown of, [11.80]–[11.87]
    (pre-entry) visa requirement, introduction
      of, [11.67]
    risk factor profiles, [11.80]–[11.87]
    Sponsored Family Visitor visa, [11.87]
    Tourist (Short Stay) visa, [6.19], [11.71],
      [11.88]
    work, restrictions on, [11.88]–[11.89]
Vocational Education and Training Assessment
  Services (VETASSESS), [9.41]
Walzer, Michael, [1.12], [1.13], [1.14]
War-Time Refugees Removal Act 1949 (Cth),
  [2.46]
Welfare of International Students Inquiry,
  [11.03]
West Papua, uprising in, [12.29]
White Australia Policy, [2.20]–[2.26], [5.02],
  [5.04], [5.06], [7.03], [9.10]
  abolition of, [5.05], [5.07], [5.09], [5.10], [5.13],
    [9.15], [20.11]
  dictation test, [2.10], [2.29]–[2.33],
    [2.43]–[2.48]
Whitlam, Prime Minister Gough, [5.05], [5.09],
  [5.10], [5.13]
Winterton, George, [3.03], [3.55]–[3.59]
Wizard People Pty Ltd, [12.67]
Woomera Detention Centre, [16.17], [16.44],
  [18.121]–[18.122], [18.125]
Work experience, [9.46]–[9.47]
  'employed', definition, [9.47]
Working Holiday visa, [10.03], [10.51]–[10.53]
*Workplace Relations Amendment (Work Choices)
  Act 2005* (Cth), [10.44], [20.30]
World War II, [2.43], [2.46], [5.02], [5.04],
  [10.01], [12.01], [12.09], [13.58]
Young, Minister Mick, [17.67]
Yugoslavia conflicts, [12.83]